Guide to TCP/IP

Fourth Edition

Jeffrey L. Carrell

Laura A. Chappell

Ed Tittel

with James Pyles

COURSE TECHNOLOGY
CENGAGE Learning®

Australia • Brazil • Japan • Korea • Mexico • Singapore • Spain • United Kingdom • United States

COURSE TECHNOLOGY
CENGAGE Learning

Guide to TCP/IP, Fourth Edition

Jeffrey L. Carrell, Laura A. Chappell, Ed Tittel, with James Pyles

Vice President, Careers & Computing: Dave Garza

Director of Learning Solutions: Matthew Kane

Executive Editor: Steve Helba

Acquisitions Editor: Nick Lombardi

Managing Editor: Marah Bellegarde

Product Manager: Natalie Pashoukos

Development Editor: Kent Williams

Editorial Assistant: Sarah Pickering

Vice President, Marketing: Jennifer Ann Baker

Marketing Director: Deborah Yarnell

Associate Marketing Manager: Erica Glisson

Production Director: Wendy A. Troeger

Production Manager: Andrew Crouth

Content Project Manager: Brooke Greenhouse

Art Director: GEX

Technology Project Manager: Joe Pliss

Media Editor: William Overocker

Cover photo: ©Shebeko/Shutterstock

For product information and technology assistance, contact us at **Cengage Learning Customer & Sales Support, 1-800-354-9706**

For permission to use material from this text or product, submit all requests online at **cengage.com/permissions** Further permissions questions can be emailed to **permissionrequest@cengage.com**

Library of Congress Control Number: 2012944726

ISBN-13: 978-1-133-01986-2

ISBN-10: 1-133-01986-2

Course Technology
20 Channel Center Street
Boston, MA 02210
USA

Cengage Learning is a leading provider of customized learning solutions with office locations around the globe, including Singapore, the United Kingdom, Australia, Mexico, Brazil, and Japan. Locate your local office at: **international.cengage.com/region**

Cengage Learning products are represented in Canada by Nelson Education, Ltd.

For your lifelong learning solutions, visit **www.cengage.com/coursetechnology**

Purchase any of our products at your local college store or at our preferred online store **www.cengagebrain.com**

Visit our corporate website at **cengage.com**.

Printed in the United States of America
1 2 3 4 5 6 7 16 15 14 13 12

Brief Table of Contents

PREFACE xv

CHAPTER 1
Introducing TCP/IP 1

CHAPTER 2
IP Addressing and Related Topics 57

CHAPTER 3
Basic IP Packet Structures: Headers and Payloads 109

CHAPTER 4
Data Link and Network Layer Protocols in TCP/IP 155

CHAPTER 5
Internet Control Message Protocol 253

CHAPTER 6
Neighbor Discovery in IPv6 321

CHAPTER 7
IP Address Autoconfiguration 371

CHAPTER 8
Name Resolution on IP Networks 441

CHAPTER 9
TCP/IP Transport Layer Protocols 513

CHAPTER 10
Transitioning from IPv4 to IPv6: Interoperation 563

CHAPTER 11
Deploying IPv6 615

CHAPTER 12
Securing TCP/IP Environments 659

APPENDIX A
Student and Instructor Online Resources 697

GLOSSARY 699

INDEX 723

Table of Contents

PREFACE. XV

CHAPTER 1
Introducing TCP/IP 1

What Is TCP/IP? 2

The Origins and History of TCP/IP. 2
   TCP/IP's Design Goals 3
   TCP/IP Chronology 3
   Who "Owns" TCP/IP? 5
   Standards Groups That Oversee TCP/IP 6
   IPv4 and IPv6 6

TCP/IP Standards and RFCs. 7

OSI Network Reference Model Overview. 8
   Breaking Networking into Layers 8
   The ISO/OSI Network Reference Model Layers 10
   How Protocol Layers Behave. 10

TCP/IP Networking Model. 15
   TCP/IP Network Access Layer. 16
   TCP/IP Network Access Layer Protocols 17
   TCP/IP Internet Layer Functions 18
   TCP/IP Internet Layer Protocols 18
   TCP/IP Transport Layer Functions. 19
   TCP/IP Transport Layer Protocols 19
   TCP/IP Application Layer 20

TCP/IP Protocols, Services, Sockets, and Ports 21
   TCP/IP Protocol Numbers. 22
   TCP/IP Port Numbers. 23
   TCP/IP Sockets. 23

Data Encapsulation in TCP/IP. 23

Protocol Analysis 24
   Useful Roles for Protocol Analysis. 24
   Protocol Analyzer Elements. 25
   Placing a Protocol Analyzer on a Network 28

Chapter Summary 30

Key Terms 31

Review Questions 39

Hands-On Projects. 43

Case Projects 54

CHAPTER 2
IP Addressing and Related Topics. 57

IP Addressing Basics. 58

IPv4 Addressing 60
   IPv4 Address Classes 60
   Network, Broadcast, Multicast, and Other Special IPv4 Addresses 61
   Broadcast Packet Structures. 62

IPv4 Networks and Subnet Masks 65
IPv4 Subnets and Supernets 66
Classless Inter-Domain Routing in IPv4 68
Public versus Private IPv4 Addresses 70
Managing Access to IPv4 Address Information 72

Obtaining Public IP Addresses 72

IPv4 Addressing Schemes 73
The Network Space 73
The Host Space 74

The End of the IPv4 Address Space 76

Introducing IPv6 77
Request for Comments Pages and Depreciation 78

IPv6 Addressing 78
Address Format and Notation 79
Network and Host Address Portions 79
Scope Identifier 80
Interface Identifiers 80
Native IPv6 Addresses in URLs 82
Address Types 82
Address Allocations 87

IPv6 Addressing and Subnetting Considerations 88

The IPv4 to IPv6 Transition 89

Chapter Summary 91

Key Terms 93

Review Questions 97

Hands-On Projects 101

Case Projects 107

CHAPTER 3
Basic IP Packet Structures: Headers and Payloads. **109**

IP Packets and Packet Structures 110

IPv4 Header Fields and Functions 110
Version Field 111
Header Length Field 111
Type of Service Field 111
TOS Field Function: Differentiated Services and Congestion Control 113
Total Length Field 117
Identification Field 117
Flags Field 117
Fragment Offset Field 118
Time to Live Field 118
Protocol Field 118
Header Checksum Field 119
Source Address Field 120
Destination Address Field 120
Options Fields 120
Padding 121

IPv6 Header Fields and Functions 121
Version 122
Traffic Class 122

Flow Label Field 123
Payload Length Field 123
The Role of the Next Header Field 123
Hop Limit Field 125
Source Address Field 125
Destination Address Field 125

IPv6 Extension Headers 125
Extension Header Ordering... 126
Hop-by-Hop Options Extension Header................................. 127
Destination Options Extension Header................................ 127
Routing Extension Header 128
Fragment Extension Header 129
Authentication Extension Header..................................... 130
Encapsulating Security Payload Extension Header and Trailer 131
Jumbograms 132
Quality of Service.. 133
Router Alerts and Hop-by-Hop Options 134

IPv6 MTU and Packet Handling 135

Upper-Layer Checksums in IPv6 137

A Rationale for IPv6 Header Structures vis-à-vis IPv4 139
Comparing IPv4 and IPv6 Headers 140
A Summary of the IPv4 to IPv6 Transition........................... 141

Chapter Summary 142

Key Terms 143

Review Questions 144

Hands-On Projects 149

Case Projects 153

CHAPTER 4
Data Link and Network Layer Protocols in TCP/IP **155**

Data Link Protocols 156

Point-to-Point Protocol 158

Frame Types and Sizes 159
Ethernet Frame Types... 159
Ethernet II Frame Structure.. 160

Hardware Addresses in the IP Environment 163
Address Resolution Protocol and Network Discovery Protocol......... 164
ARP Protocol Characteristics and Handling 164
NDP Protocol Characteristics and Handling 172

Understanding the Internet Protocol 175
Sending IP Datagrams... 175
The Route Resolution Processes..................................... 176
How IPv4 and IPv6 Differ 179

Lifetime of an IP Datagram 180

Fragmentation and Reassembly 181

Service Delivery Options 183

Precedence 184

Type of Service 184

Understanding IP Routing. 186
   How Entries Are Placed in the Routing Table. 188
   Routing Protocols and Routed Protocols 188
   Grouping Routing Protocols 189

Routing Characteristics. 193
   Route Convergence 193
   IPv4 Routing Mechanisms. 193

IPv6 Routing Considerations. 197
   IPv6 Routing Mechanisms. 198
   Multicast Listener Discovery in IPv6 204

Routing Protocols. 210
   IPv4 210
   IPv6 219

Managing Routing on an In-House Internetwork 227

Routing on and off a Wide Area Network 228
   Several Small Offices 228
   Hub and Spoke 228
   Multiprotocol 228
   Mobile Users 229
   Mobile IP 229
   Local Area Mobility 229

Routing to and from the Internet. 230

Securing Routers and Routing Behavior 231

Troubleshooting IP Routing 231

Chapter Summary 232

Key Terms 235

Review Questions 241

Hands-On Projects 245

Case Projects 251

CHAPTER 5
Internet Control Message Protocol. **253**

ICMP Basics 254
   Roles That ICMP Plays on IP Networks. 254

ICMPv4 255
   Overview of RFC 792 256
   ICMPv4 Header. 256
   Types of ICMPv4 Messages 260
   The Variable ICMP Structures and Functions 264

ICMPv6 276
   Overview of ICMPv6 276
   Types of ICMPv6 Messages 276
   ICMPv6 Header. 278

ICMPv6 Error Messages. 278
   Destination Unreachable Messages. 279
   Packet Too Big Messages 280
   Time Exceeded Messages 280
   Parameter Problem Messages. 281

ICMPv6 Informational Messages. 282
   Echo Request and Echo Reply Messages 282

Router Advertisement and Router Solicitation Messages 283
Neighbor Solicitation and Neighbor Advertisement Messages. 286
Redirect Messages 287
Router Renumbering Messages 288
A Short Comparison of ICMPv4 and ICMPv6 Messages. 290

Path MTU Discovery 290
Changes to PMTU 291

Testing and Troubleshooting Sequences for ICMP 291
Connectivity Testing with Ping 291
Path Discovery with Traceroute. 293
Path Discovery with Pathping 294
Path MTU Discovery with ICMP. 294
Routing Sequences for ICMP. 298
Security Issues for ICMPv4 302
Security Issues for ICMPv6 304

Decoding ICMP Packets 304
ICMPv4 305
ICMPv6 306

Chapter Summary 307

Key Terms 308

Review Questions 311

Hands-On Projects 315

Case Projects 319

CHAPTER 6
Neighbor Discovery in IPv6 . . . . **321**

Understanding Neighbor Discovery 322

Comparing IPv6 Neighbor Discovery Protocols to IPv4 Protocols. 323

Neighbor Discovery Message Formats 324
Router Solicitation 324
Router Advertisement. 326
Neighbor Solicitation 329
Neighbor Advertisement 331
Redirect. 333

Neighbor Discovery Option Formats 335
Source and Target Link-Layer Address Options 336
Prefix Information Option. 338
Redirected Header Option 340
MTU Option 341
Advertisement Interval Option. 343
Home Agent Information Option. 344
Route Information Option 345

Conceptual Host Model 345
Storing Neighbor Data on a Host 346
Conceptual Sending Algorithm 346

Neighbor Discovery Process 347
Address Resolution. 348
Neighbor Unreachability Detection 350
Duplicate Address Detection 351
Router Discovery 352
Redirect Messages 354

Chapter Summary 358

Key Terms 358

Review Questions 359

Hands-On Projects 364

Case Projects 369

CHAPTER 7
IP Address Autoconfiguration **371**

Understanding Autoaddressing 372

Introducing Dynamic Host Configuration Protocol 373
   How DHCP Works 374
   Role of Leases 375
   DHCP Software Elements 376
   DHCP Lease Types 376
   More about DHCP Leases 377

IPv4 Autoconfiguration 378
   Automatic Private IP Addressing (APIPA) 378
   DHCPv4 379

IPv6 Autoconfiguration 395
   Types of IPv6 Autoconfiguration 395
   Functional States of an IPv6 Autoconfigured Address 400
   Node Interface Identifiers 401
   DHCPv6 404
   IPv6 Autoconfiguration Process 415

Autoconfiguration in Microsoft Windows Operating Systems 417

Microsoft Windows Server 2008 DHCP Scopes 419

Setting Up A Simple DHCP Server 420

Troubleshooting DHCP 425

Chapter Summary 428

Key Terms 429

Review Questions 430

Hands-On Projects 435

Case Projects 438

CHAPTER 8
Name Resolution on IP Networks **441**

Understanding Name Resolution Fundamentals 442

Network Name Resolution Protocols 443
   NetBIOS over TCP/IP 443
   WINS 444
   DNS 447
   LLMNR 447

Name Resolution in IPv4 Networks 449
   DNS Database Structure 450
   The DNS Namespace 452
   DNS Database Records 452
   Delegating DNS Authority 453
   Types of DNS Servers 453

How Domain Name Servers Work 455
    Recursive Query. 456
    Iterative or Nonrecursive Queries 457
Importance of DNS Caching 457
DNS Configuration Files and Resource Record Formats 458
    Start of Authority Record 459
    Address and Canonical Name Records 460
    Mapping Addresses to Names 462
Name Resolution in IPv6 Networks 463
    DNS in IPv6 464
    Source and Destination Address Selection 466
    Source Address Selection Algorithm 467
    Destination Address Selection Algorithm 469
    Using Address Selection 472
Name Resolution Support in Windows Operating Systems 474
    Hosts File 474
    DNS Resolver 476
    DNS Server Service 477
    DNS Dynamic Update 479
    Source and Destination Address Selection 481
    LLMNR Support 482
    Working with ipv6-literal.net Names 484
    Peer Name Resolution Protocol 484
Troubleshooting Name Resolution Problems and Failures 486
    Common Sources of Failure 487
    Tools for Troubleshooting NetBIOS and WINS Problems 488
    Tools for Troubleshooting DNS Problems 488
    Nbtstat 489
    Netstat 490
    Nslookup 491
Chapter Summary 494
Key Terms 496
Review Questions 500
Hands-On Projects 504
Case Projects 511

CHAPTER 9
TCP/IP Transport Layer Protocols **513**
Understanding UDP and TCP 514
    UDP with IPv4 and IPv6 514
    TCP with IPv4 and IPv6 516
User Datagram Protocol 519
    UDP Header Fields and Functions 520
    UDP Port Numbers and Processes 523
    UDP and IPv6 525
Transmission Control Protocol 526
    TCP and IPv4 527
    TCP and IPv6 545
UDP, TCP, and IPv6 Extension Headers 547
Choosing between TCP and UDP 548

Chapter Summary 549

Key Terms 550

Review Questions 553

Hands-On Projects 557

Case Projects 561

CHAPTER 10
Transitioning from IPv4 to IPv6: Interoperation **563**

How Can IPv4 and IPv6 Interact? 564
   Dual-Stack Approach 564
   Tunneling through the IPv4 Cloud 565
   IPv6 Rate of Adoption 565
   Transitioning to IPV6: The Reality 566
   Interoperability 566
   Network Elements 567
   Software 567
   Transitioning to IPv6 from the Windows Perspective 568
   Availability 568
   What's Next? 569

Hybrid IPv4/IPv6 Networks and Node Types 569
   Basic Hybrid Network Model 570
   Nested Hybrid Network Model 571
   True Hybrid Network Model 572

IPv6 Transition Addresses 573

Transition Mechanisms 574
   Dual Protocol Stacks for IPv4 and IPv6 574
   Dual-IP-Layer Architecture 575
   Dual-stack Architecture 576
   Dual Architecture and Tunneling 577
   IPv6-over-IPv4 Tunneling 578
   DNS Infrastructure 579

Tunneling Configurations for Mingling IPv4 and IPv6 580
   Router-to-Router 580
   Host-to-Router and Router-to-Host 581
   Host-to-Host 582
   Types of Tunnels 582

ISATAP 583
   Overview 583
   ISATAP Components 584
   Router Discovery for ISATAP Nodes 585
   ISATAP Addressing and Routing 586
   ISATAP Communications 588
   Configuring an ISATAP Router 589

6to4 591
   Overview 592
   6to4 Components 592
   6to4 Addressing and Routing 594
   6to4 Communication 595
   Using ISATAP and 6to4 Together 596

Teredo 596
   Overview 596
   Teredo Components 597

Teredo Addressing and Routing 597
Teredo Processes 599

Chapter Summary 601

Key Terms 603

Review Questions 605

Hands-On Projects 609

Case Projects 613

CHAPTER 11
Deploying IPv6 . . . . **615**

Understanding IPv6 Deployment 616

Planning an IPv6 Deployment 617
Success Criteria 618
Architectural Decisions 618
Migration and Transitioning Techniques 625
Tasks 631

Deploying and Using IPv6 637
Establish an IPv6 Test/Pilot Network 637
Start Migrating Applications 639
Upgrade IPv4-Only Hosts to IPv4/IPv6 639
Create a Tunneled IPv6 Environment Using 6to4 643
Create a Tunneled Environment Using ISATAP 643

Exploring Some Network Administration Tasks 645

Chapter Summary 647

Key Terms 648

Review Questions 649

Hands-On Projects 653

Case Projects 656

CHAPTER 12
Securing TCP/IP Environments **659**

Understanding Network Security Basics 660

Principles of IP Security 661

Typical TCP/IP Attacks, Exploits, and Break-Ins 662
Key Terminology 663
Key Weaknesses in TCP/IP 663
Flexibility versus Security 664

Common Types of IP-Related Attacks 664

Which IP Services are Most Vulnerable? 665
Holes, Back Doors, and Other Illicit Points of Entry 667

Phases of IP Attacks 667
Reconnaissance and Discovery Phases 668
Attack 669
Cover-Up 669

Common Attacks and Entry Points in More Detail 670
Viruses, Worms, and Trojan Horse Programs 670
Adware and Spyware 670
Denial of Service Attacks 670

Distributed Denial of Service Attacks 670
Buffer Overflows/Overruns 672
Spoofing 672
TCP Session Hijacking 672
Network Sniffing 673

Maintaining IP Security **674**
Applying Security Patches and Fixes 674
Knowing Which Ports to Block 676
Using IP Security (IPSec) 676
Protecting the Perimeter of the Network 678
Implementing Firewalls 680
Roles of IDS and IPS in IP Security 683

Honeypots and Honeynets **684**

Chapter Summary **684**

Key Terms **685**

Review Questions **689**

Hands-On Projects **693**

Case Projects **696**

APPENDIX A
Student and Instructor Online Resources **697**

GLOSSARY **699**

INDEX **723**

Preface

Welcome to *Guide to TCP/IP, Fourth Edition*! TCP/IP stands for Transmission Control Protocol/Internet Protocol and defines the broad family of protocols and services that make the Internet able to function as we know it today. In covering TCP/IP, this book offers you real-world examples, interactive examples, and many Hands-On Projects that reinforce key concepts and teach the use of important monitoring and management tools. This book also includes voluminous protocol traces, or decodes, that will help you understand what TCP/IP looks like, and how it behaves, on your networks.

This book offers in-depth coverage of all the salient models, protocols, services, and standards that govern TCP/IP and that guide its behavior on modern networks. Throughout the book, we provide pointed questions to reinforce the concepts introduced in each chapter and to help prepare you to interact with TCP/IP in its native habitat—that is, on the vast majority of networks in use in the world today. In addition to the review questions, we provide detailed Hands-On Projects that provide you with firsthand experience in installing, configuring, using, and managing TCP/IP on a working network. Finally, to put a real-world slant on the concepts introduced in each chapter, we also include Case Projects that pose problems and require creative solutions that should prepare you for the kinds of situations and needs you'll face on a real, live network.

Intended Audience

This book is intended to serve the needs of individuals and information systems professionals who are interested in learning more about working with and on TCP/IP-based networks. These materials have been specifically designed to prepare individuals to take an active role in administering a network infrastructure that uses TCP/IP, either as its only protocol suite or in concert with other protocol suites. Those students who work their way through this entire book should be well equipped to recognize, analyze, and troubleshoot a broad range of TCP/IP-related networking problems or phenomena.

Chapter Summaries

Chapter 1, "Introducing TCP/IP," presents the broad outlines of TCP/IP's capabilities and identifies its most important constituent elements—namely, the protocols and services that TCP/IP provides. In addition, it explores the Open Systems Interconnection (OSI) reference model for networking, as standardized by the International Organization for Standardization (ISO), and compares and contrasts this standard model to the model around which TCP/IP is built. This chapter then covers the structure and origins of the standards documents known as Requests for Comments (RFCs), which describe and govern TCP/IP protocols, services, and practices. The chapter concludes with an overview of the key tool that will play a significant role throughout the remainder of the book—a special software utility called a protocol analyzer that captures, unpacks, and displays the contents of traffic on a network, including TCP/IP. In this book, we use a protocol analyzer named Wireshark.

Chapter 2, "IP Addressing and Related Topics," covers the intricacies involved in managing unique IP addresses for both 32-bit IPv4 addresses and 128-bit IPv6 addresses. Beginning with the anatomy of a numeric IPv4 address, the chapter explores IPv4 address classes, special cases such as broadcast and multicast addresses, subnets and supernets, and reviews the reasons for classless IPv4 addressing, public versus private IPv4 addresses, and IPv4 addressing schemes. The rest of the chapter repeats this coverage for IPv6, including a review of address formats and notation, address layouts and types, and address allocations. You'll also find addressing schemes and subnetting considerations covered, along with some discussion about how to manage the transition from IPv4 to IPv6 addresses.

Chapter 3, "Basic IP Packet Structures: Headers and Payloads," covers the key components of any IP packet (both for IPv4 and IPv6): the header that describes the packet for routing, forwarding, and filtering, and the payload that contains the data that the packet is meant to convey. IPv4 and IPv6 headers are laid out and dissected in detail, including IPv6 Extension Headers, and the use of transport and packet handling controls are described and explored. The chapter concludes with a comparison of header structures in IPv4 versus IPv6, with a rationale to explain redesign and changes involved.

Chapter 4, "Data Link and Network Layer Protocols in TCP/IP," explores and explains the TCP/IP protocols that operate at the Data Link and Network layers in the OSI reference model. In that context, it discusses data link protocols in general, examines IP frame types, and talks about hardware addresses in the IP environment and the various protocols—particularly ARP and RARP, for IPv4, and the Neighbor Discovery Protocol, or NDP, for IPv6—that support their use. The chapter also covers TCP/IP's most important protocol at the Network layer, the Internet Protocol, along with routing protocols, mechanisms, and characteristics for IPv4 and IPv6, including RIPv1 and v2, OSPF, EIGRP, and BGP, with considerations for both IPv4 and IPv6 protocols and behaviors.

Chapter 5, "Internet Control Message Protocol," covers a key Network layer protocol for TCP/IP whose job is to ferry status and error messages about IP traffic back to its senders and to other "interested devices," such as routers or switches. Starting with a review of ICMPv4 and ICMPv6 structures and functions, this chapter examines ICMP testing and troubleshooting methods, security issues, and ICMP message types and codes, and concludes with a thorough review of testing and troubleshooting sequences for ICMP and decoding ICMP packets.

Chapter 6, "Neighbor Discovery in IPv6," digs into NDP to explain how neighbor discovery works on IPv6 networks. Topics covered include comparing NDP to related IPv4 protocols, various NDP message formats and options, and the overall neighbor discovery process on IPv6 networks.

Chapter 7, "IP Address Autoconfiguration," describes various auto-addressing schemes and mechanisms used on IPv4 and IPv6 networks, including the Dynamic Host Configuration Protocol, or DHCP, as well as autoconfiguration mechanisms used for IPv4 (APIPA and DHCP) and IPv6 (host/interface address determination, stateless and stateful address autoconfiguration, and DHCPv6).

Chapter 8, "Name Resolution on IP Networks," deals with key services used to resolve symbolic, human-readable network names and addresses into machine-intelligible network addresses. Topics covered include name resolution fundamentals and various network name resolution protocols. IPv4 and IPv6 name resolution via the Domain Name Service, or DNS, is described in detail, as is name resolution support for Windows operating systems, including issues related to setup, configuration, troubleshooting, and relevant utilities.

Chapter 9, "TCP/IP Transport Layer Protocols," covers two key protocols that operate at the Transport layer of the OSI reference model: the heavy-duty, robust, reliable Transmission Control Protocol (TCP) and the lighter-weight but faster User Datagram Protocol (UDP). TCP is examined in great detail, with particular attention on its packet structures and functions (including IPv6 extension headers for TCP), whereas UDP gets the brief coverage it deserves. The chapter concludes with a discussion of common and appropriate uses for these two protocols.

Chapter 10, "Transitioning from IPv4 to IPv6: Interoperation," deals with issues and techniques that apply when IPv4 and IPv6 must coexist on the same networks, as will surely be the case for many networks for the foreseeable future. It explains the means whereby IPv4 and IPv6 can interact, explains hybrid IPv4/IPv6 networks and node types, and explores transition addresses and switchover mechanisms to make the change from IPv4 to IPv6 as straightforward as possible. Tunneling mechanisms and protocols, including ISATAP, 6to4, and Teredo, are described in detail.

Chapter 11, "Deploying IPv6," jumps into an area of great interest to Internet professionals—namely, what's involved in understanding, planning, deploying, and using IPv6 on modern TCP/IP networks. Topics covered include evaluating potential software and hardware changes, addressing schemes and autoaddressing, and priority schemes for various classes or types of network services.

Chapter 12, "Securing TCP/IP Environments," covers general network security basics, with a particular emphasis on IP security topics. It also addresses key topics that include perimeter security, infrastructure security, and host device security.

The book also includes **Appendix A,** which explains the required software and trace files available on the book's online resources Web site. In addition, this site includes the following, plus much more:

- A list of the important RFCs mentioned throughout the text and the available IPv6-specific RFCs

RFCs are a dynamic collection of documents, so anything collected in static form represents a snapshot of what was current at the time the snapshot was taken. Always consult online RFCs for information **NOTE** about the most current documents and standards.

- A reference to TCP/IP-related command-line utilities for Windows desktop and Windows Server
- A list of the Windows desktop and Windows Server Registry settings found in numerous tables in this book

Features

To ensure a successful learning experience, this book includes the following pedagogical features:

- **Chapter Objectives:** Each chapter in this book begins with a detailed list of the concepts to be mastered within that chapter. This list provides you with a quick reference to the contents of that chapter as well as a useful study aid.

- **Illustrations and Tables:** Numerous illustrations of server screens and components aid you in the visualization of common setup steps, theories, and concepts. In addition, many tables provide details and comparisons of both practical and theoretical information and can be used for a quick review of topics. This book also includes a great number of protocol traces from both IPv4 and IPv6 protocols. Because of formatting differences between the two protocol families, these traces differ slightly, but they present more or less the same information, subject only to minor differences.

- **End-of-Chapter Material:** The end of each chapter includes the following features to reinforce the material covered in the chapter:

  - **Summary:** A bulleted list providing a brief but complete summary of the chapter

  - **Key Terms List:** A list of all new terms and their definitions

  - **Review Questions:** A list of review questions that test your knowledge of the most important concepts covered in the chapter

  - **Hands-On Projects:** Projects that help you to apply the knowledge gained in the chapter

  - **Case Study Projects:** Projects that take you through real-world scenarios

- **Student and Instructor Online Resources:** The book's online resources Web site provides self-extracting files that contain the trace (data) files and the software required to work through the Hands-On Projects in this book—Wireshark for Windows and the Bitcricket IP Subnet Calculator. In addition, you will find documents containing descriptions of other handy networking tools and utilities. Student and instructor resources for this book are available at *www.cengage.com*. To locate the resources, search for **Guide to TCP/IP** in the Higher Education catalog.

Text and Graphic Conventions

Wherever appropriate, additional information and exercises have been added to this book to help you better understand what is being discussed in the chapter. Icons throughout the text alert you to additional materials. The icons used in this textbook are as follows:

The Caution icon warns you about potential mistakes or problems and explains how to avoid them.

The Note icon is used to present additional helpful material related to the subject being described.

Tips based on the authors' experience provide extra information about how to attack a problem or what to do in real-world situations.

Each Hands-On Project in this book is preceded by the Hands-On icon and a description of the exercise that follows.

Case Project icons mark the case projects. These are more involved, scenario-based assignments. In this extensive case example, you are asked to implement independently what you have learned.

Instructor Resources

The following supplemental materials are available when this book is used in a classroom setting. All the supplements available with this book are provided to the instructor on a single CD-ROM (ISBN: 978-1-1330-1987-9) and online at www.cengage.com.

Electronic Instructor's Manual. The Instructor's Manual that accompanies this textbook includes additional instructional material to assist in class preparation, including suggestions for classroom activities, discussion topics, and additional projects.

Solutions. The answers to all end-of-chapter material, including the Review Questions and, where applicable, Hands-On Projects and Case Projects, are provided.

ExamView®. This textbook is accompanied by ExamView, a powerful testing software package that allows instructors to create and administer printed, computer (LAN-based), and Internet exams. ExamView includes hundreds of questions that correspond to the topics covered in this text, enabling students to generate detailed study guides that include page references for further review. The computer-based and Internet testing components allow students to take exams at their computers and also save the instructor time by grading each exam automatically.

PowerPoint presentations. This book comes with Microsoft® PowerPoint® slides for each chapter. These are included as a teaching aid for classroom presentation, to make available to students on the network for chapter review, or to be printed for classroom distribution. Instructors, please feel to add your own slides for additional topics you introduce to the class.

Figure Files. All the figures in the book are reproduced on the Instructor Resources CD, in bitmap format. Similar to the PowerPoint presentations, these are included as a teaching aid for classroom presentation, to make available to students for review, or to be printed for classroom distribution.

Acknowledgments

The authors would like to thank Course Technology for this opportunity to revise *Guide to TCP/IP* to include detailed coverage of IPv6. We deeply appreciate their patience and indulgence, especially that of Nick Lombardi, our acquisitions editor; Natalie Pashoukos, our product manager; Brooke Baker, our content project manager and Susan Pedicini, our technical editor in charge of manuscript quality assurance. Thanks also to Kent Williams, our wonderful developmental editor, whose in-depth and detailed work turned these materials into the finely polished form they now take.

The authors would also like to thank the behind-the-scenes author team who helped to bring this book to fruition, such as Tom Lancaster, who provided Chapter 11, and especially James Pyles, who revised several chapters and added plenty of new information about IPv6. His diligence and hard work earned him a spot on the cover. Thanks also to Kim Lindros and Mary Kyle, who jumped in to help manage the project on behalf of the authors.

Jeff Carrell: With God's help, all things are possible. Thank you to my wife and best friend Cynthia for all your love, encouragement, and patience; I am truly blessed to have you in my life. Thank you to my friends and colleagues who provided input and encouragement along the way. Thanks to Ed Tittel for the opportunity, inspiration, and mentoring. The project was huge, exciting, and awesome to be a part of. Thanks to Kim Lindros and Mary Kyle who not only kept us moving but made sure we stayed on task. I could not imagine working on this project without y'all. Finally, thanks to James Pyles and Tom Lancaster, who provided updates and much new content; we could not have completed this project without you guys.

Ed Tittel: My profound thanks to Jeff Carrell for taking over as lead author and architect for the fourth edition of this book, and to James Pyles and Tom Lancaster for helping us provide new content and exercises. Also, thanks again to Kim Lindros and Mary Kyle for making this book so much easier to finish than it was to start without their able and competent presence. Finally, thank you to my lovely wife Dina and son Gregory, who have brought me much joy and happiness.

Laura Chappell: Special thanks to Ed Tittel and Jeff Carrell for their enthusiasm and wonderful writing efforts on this book. Thanks also to James Pyles and Tom Lancaster for their tremendous technical contributions to this title—this book could not have been completed in such a timely manner without your assistance. Also, very special and sincere thanks to Kent Williams and Kim Lindros for keeping all the loose ends tied on this project. Finally, my deepest thanks to my children, Scott and Ginny, who make me laugh and enjoy life way beyond the packet-level.

James Pyles: I appreciate the opportunity to contribute to updating this fine book for its fourth edition. I especially want to thank Ed Tittel and Kim Lindros for inviting me along for the ride. I also am extremely grateful to Jeff Carrell, at whose feet I would gladly sit at any time in order to learn the arcane mysteries of IPv6. I also want to thank Mary Kyle for her excellent management skills and her infinite patience, as well as Tom Lancaster for his invaluable contributions.

No acknowledgement would be complete without my recognition of my lovely wife Lin and the invaluable support she has provided me in all of my endeavors. Given the rapidly evolving nature of the Internet as we proceed into the twenty-first century, I can't help but think of my three-year old grandson Landon, who will inherit the future from us. May we leave him and his generation a worthy legacy.

Readers are encouraged to e-mail comments, questions, and suggestions regarding *Guide to TCP/IP, Fourth Edition* and the accompanying student and instructor resources Web site to *tcpip4e@networkconversions.com.*

Read This Before You Begin

To the User

This book is intended to be read in sequence, from beginning to end. Each chapter builds upon those that precede it to provide a solid understanding of TCP/IP concepts, protocols, services, and deployment practices. Readers are also encouraged to investigate the many pointers to online and printed sources of additional information that are cited throughout this book.

Some of the chapters in this book require additional materials to complete the end-of-chapter projects. The student and instructor resources Web site for this book contains the necessary supplemental files. To download the resources, go to *www.cengage.com* and search for **Guide to TCP/IP** in the Higher Education catalog.

This Web site includes:

- Software required to complete the Hands-On Projects, which includes Bitcricket IP Calculator and the Wireshark for Windows protocol analyzer
- A link to the Student Data Files (referred to as "trace" or "packet" files in this book) required to complete the Hands-On Projects
- Additional resources for topics in select chapters

 This book was written using the popular Wireshark protocol analyzer. The Wireshark version used in the Hands-On Projects is available for download from the companion Web site for this book. You may also download the latest version of the software from the Wireshark Web site at *www.wireshark.org*.

To the Instructor

When setting up a classroom lab, make sure each workstation has Windows Vista or Windows 7 Professional, Internet Explorer 9 or later, and a network interface controller (NIC) capable of working in promiscuous mode. Students will install Wireshark and the Bitcricket IP Subnet Calculator on these computers in the course of working through the book. In addition, students will need administrative rights on their workstations to perform many of the operations covered in the Hands-On Projects throughout the book. Students will also need access to Windows Server 2008 R2 for a small number of projects.

Coping with Change on the Web

Sooner or later, at least a few of the Web links in the book will go stale or be replaced by newer information. In that case, there's always a way to find what you want on the Web, if you're willing to invest some time and energy. To begin with, most large or complex Web sites—and Microsoft's qualifies on both counts—offer a search engine. As long as you can get to the site itself, you can use this tool to help you find what you need.

Finally, feel free to use general search tools such as *www.google.com*, *www.bing.com*, or *www.yahoo. com* to find information related to topics in this book. For example, although certain standards bodies may offer the most precise and specific information about their standards online, there are plenty of third-party sources of information, training, and assistance in this area that do not have to follow the party line like a standards group typically does. The bottom line: If you can't find something where this book says it's supposed to be, start looking around. It's got to be around there somewhere! If you find it on your own, send an e-mail to *tcpip4e@networkconversions.com* and we will do our best to update this book's companion Web site in short order. Plus, you will have the satisfaction of knowing you helped all the instructors and students who are using this book.

Lab Requirements

Following are the recommended hardware and software requirements to perform the end-of-chapter projects:

- 1 GHz CPU or higher, 2 GB of RAM, 80 GB hard disk with at least 2 GB of storage available
- CD-ROM drive
- NIC in promiscuous mode connected to a LAN
- Windows Vista or Windows 7 Professional (Service Pack 1 or later) and Internet Explorer 9 or later
- Access to a Windows Server 2008 R2 system with TCP/IP installed and configured; an IP address must be defined either statically or via DHCP
- Internet access

Ideally, you should have two computers with the same hardware specifications listed above—one running Windows 7 and one running Windows Server 2008 R2, as well as a Layer 3 switch or router that supports both IPv4 and IPv6.

Introducing TCP/IP

After reading this chapter and completing the exercises, you will be able to:

- Describe TCP/IP's origins and history
- Explain the process by which TCP/IP standards and other documents, called Requests for Comments (RFCs), are created, debated, and formalized (where appropriate)
- Describe the "huge difference" between IPv4 and IPv6 and explain why a switch to IPv6 is both necessary and inevitable
- Describe the Open Systems Interconnection network reference model, often used to characterize network protocols and services, and how it relates to TCP/IP's own internal networking model
- Define the terms involved and explain how TCP/IP protocols, sockets, and ports are identified
- Describe data encapsulation and how it relates to the four layers of the TCP/IP protocol stack
- Describe and apply the basic practices and principles that underlie network protocol analysis

This chapter introduces the background and history of the collection of networking **protocols** known as **TCP/IP**, which is an abbreviation for **Transmission Control Protocol/Internet Protocol**. Two of the most important protocols in the overall collection known as TCP/IP give their names to this protocol collection—namely, the **Transmission Control Protocol (TCP)**, which handles reliable delivery for messages of arbitrary size, and the **Internet Protocol (IP)**, which manages the **routing** of network transmissions from sender to receiver, among other capabilities.

In addition, this chapter covers TCP/IP's networking model, its various ways of identifying specific protocols and services, how TCP/IP standards are defined and managed, and which elements of the TCP/IP collection are most noteworthy. It also includes coverage of the original version of TCP/IP, sometimes called IPv4, and the newer versions, known as IPv6. The chapter concludes with an overview of the art and science of protocol analysis, which uses special tools to gather data directly from a network itself, characterize a network's traffic and behavior, and examine the details inside the data that's moving across a network at any given point in time.

What Is TCP/IP?

The large collection of networking protocols and services called TCP/IP comprises far more than the combination of those two key protocols that gives this collection its name. Nevertheless, these two protocols deserve an introduction. Transmission Control Protocol, or TCP, offers reliable delivery for messages of arbitrary size, and it defines a robust delivery mechanism for all kinds of data across a network. Internet Protocol, or IP, manages the routing of network transmissions from sender to receiver, along with issues related to network and computer addresses, and much more. Together, these two protocols ferry the vast bulk of data that moves across the Internet, even though they represent only a tiny fraction of the total TCP/IP protocol collection.

To gain a better appreciation for the importance of TCP/IP, keep in mind that anyone who uses the Internet must also use TCP/IP because the Internet runs on TCP/IP. Its roots run deep and long, as computing technologies go—all the way back to 1969. Knowing where TCP/IP comes from and what motivated its original design can enhance one's understanding of this essential collection of protocols (often called a **protocol suite**). For that reason, we will explore this protocol suite's roots and design goals in the following section.

The Origins and History of TCP/IP

In 1969, an obscure arm of the United States Department of Defense (DoD), known as the **Advanced Research Projects Agency (ARPA)**, funded an academic research project involving a special type of long-haul (long-distance) network, called a **packet-switched network**. In a packet-switched network environment, individual chunks of data (called **packets**) can take any usable path between the sender and receiver. The sender and receiver are identified by unique network addresses, but the packets are not required to follow the same path in transit (although they often do). The network built as a result of this project was known as the **ARPANET**.

TCP/IP's Design Goals

The design of the ARPANET and protocols that evolved to support it were based on the following government needs:

- *A desire for a communications network with the ability to withstand a potential nuclear strike*—This explains the need for packet switching, in which the routes from sender to receiver can vary as needed, as long as a valid route exists. It also explains why, in a world that could blow up at any time, robust and reliable delivery was a concern.

- *A desire to permit different kinds of computer systems to communicate easily with one another*—Because proprietary networking was the order of the day, and because the government owned many different kinds of incompatible networks and systems, it was necessary that this technology permit dissimilar systems to exchange data.

- *A need to interconnect systems across long distances*—The late-1960s was an era of "big iron," in which large, expensive individual systems with terminals dominated the computer landscape. At that time, interconnecting multiple systems meant interconnecting far-flung locations. Thus, the original ARPANET linked systems at the Stanford Research Institute (SRI), the University of Utah in Salt Lake City, and campuses in the University of California system at Los Angeles and Santa Barbara.

These design goals may not seem terribly important in the early twenty-first century. That's because the concern about a global nuclear holocaust has largely subsided and networking is now taken for granted. Likewise, high-bandwidth, long-distance data communication is a big business. However, some would argue that the Internet is responsible for the prevalence of high-bandwidth, long-distance data communication in today's modern world!

TCP/IP Chronology

TCP/IP appeared on the scene in the 1970s. By that time, early networking researchers realized that data had to be moved across different kinds of networks as well as among multiple locations. This was especially necessary to permit **local area networks (LANs)**, such as those using **Ethernet,** to use long-haul networks, such as the ARPANET, to move data from one local network to another. Although work on TCP/IP began in 1973, it wasn't until 1978 that **Internet Protocol version 4** (also known as **IPv4**—the very same version used today on most TCP/IP networks) was developed.

The original Internet (notice the initial capital letter) helped establish a model for a network composed of other networks. Thus, the term **internetwork** (notice the lack of an initial capital letter) refers to a single logical network composed of multiple physical networks, which may all be at a single physical location or may be spread around multiple physical locations. We distinguish the "Internet," a proper name for the worldwide collection of publicly accessible networks that use TCP/IP, from an "internetwork," which can appear anywhere in the world and may or may not be part of the Internet (and may not use TCP/IP, even though the majority do).

In 1983, the Defense Communications Agency (DCA, now known as the **Defense Information Systems Agency,** or **DISA**) took over operation of the ARPANET from DARPA (Defense Advanced Research Projects Agency). This allowed more widespread use of the Internet, as more colleges and universities, government agencies, defense facilities, and government contractors began to rely on it to exchange data, e-mail, and other kinds of information. In the same year, the DoD instituted its requirement that all computers on the Internet switch to TCP/IP from a hodgepodge of earlier, mostly experimental protocols that had been used on the ARPANET since its inception. In fact, some people argue that the Internet and TCP/IP were born at more or less the same time.

By no coincidence whatsoever, 1983 also was the year that the Berkeley Software Distribution version of UNIX known as 4.2BSD incorporated support for TCP/IP in the operating system. There are those who argue that this step, which exposed computer professionals at colleges and universities around the world to TCP/IP, helps explain the birth and proliferation of Internet protocols and how they became the behemoths they are today.

At roughly the same time—we're still in 1983—the all-military MILNET was split off from the ARPANET. This divided the infrastructure of the Internet into a military-only side and a more public, freewheeling side that included all nonmilitary participants. Also in 1983, the development at the University of Wisconsin of name server technology, which allowed users to locate and identify network addresses anywhere on the Internet (this remains a hallmark of its operation to this day), capped off a banner year in the Internet's history.

After that, the Internet and TCP/IP experienced a series of landmarks that led to the global Internet we know today. Here are some additional highlights:

- 1986—The **National Science Foundation (NSF)** launches a long-haul, high-speed network known as **NSFNET**, with a network backbone running at 56 Kbps. NSF also imposes a set of policies known as **Acceptable Use Policies (AUPs)**, which governs Internet use and sets the tone for how users interact on the Internet.
- 1987—The number of hosts on the Internet breaks 10,000.
- 1989—The number of hosts on the Internet breaks 100,000.
  - The NSFNET backbone is upgraded to T1 speeds, at 1.544 megabits per second (Mbps).
- 1990—ARPANET ceases doing business under that name, and commercial enterprises, academic institutions, and government organizations begin supporting the Internet.
  - Work begins on the **Hypertext Transfer Protocol (HTTP)**; the notion of the World Wide Web is born at the **Centre Europeen de Researche Nucleaire (CERN)** in Switzerland.
- 1991—The **Commercial Internet Exchange (CIX)**, a consortium of Internet operators, system providers, and other commercial operations with Internet interests, is formed.
- 1992—The Internet Society (ISOC) is chartered.
  - The number of hosts on the Internet breaks one million.
  - The NSFNET backbone is upgraded to T3 speeds, at 44.736 Mbps.
  - CERN releases HTTP and Web server technology to the public ("birth of the Web").

- 1993—The **Internet Network Information Center (InterNIC)** is chartered to manage **domain** names.
  - The first-ever, high-powered graphical browser, Mosaic, emerges from the **National Center for Supercomputing Applications (NCSA)**. This starts the Web revolution.
  - The U.S. White House goes online at *www.whitehouse.gov*.
- 1994—The U.S. Senate and House of Representatives establish Internet Web servers.
  - Online junk mail and shopping malls begin to proliferate.
- 1995—Netscape launches Netscape Navigator and begins the commercialization of the Web.
  - The number of hosts on the Internet breaks five million.
- 1996—Microsoft launches its Internet Explorer Web browser, even though Netscape dominates the Web browser marketplace.
- 1997—The number of registered domain names breaks 31 million.
- 2000—The Love Letter worm infects over one million personal computers.
- 2001—The number of hosts on the Internet breaks 150 million.
  - Sircam virus and Code Red worm infect thousands of Web servers and e-mail accounts.
- 2002—The number of hosts on the Internet breaks 204 million.
  - The Internet2 backbone utilizes native IP version 6.
- 2003—Public Interest Registry (PIR) assumes responsibility as the .org registry operator.
- 2005—The number of hosts on the Internet breaks 250 million.
- 2008—The number of hosts on the Internet breaks 600 million.
- 2009—The number of hosts on the Internet breaks one billion, and the number of Chinese users surpasses the number of U.S. users.

Today, there are few aspects of commerce, communications, and information access that do not involve the Internet in one way or another. Living without e-mail, the Web, and online e-commerce has become unthinkable. As we progress through the twenty-first century, new Internet services and protocols continue to appear, but TCP/IP keeps going strong.

For more information about the fascinating history of the Internet, visit the ISOC's "A Brief History of the Internet" Web page at *www.isoc.org/internet/history/brief.shtml*.

Who "Owns" TCP/IP?

Given that its roots are everywhere and its reach is unlimited, who owns and controls TCP/IP can seem puzzling. Even though TCP/IP and related protocols are under the purview of specific standards-making bodies, which we'll discuss later, TCP/IP also falls into the public domain because it's been publically funded since its inception. In other words, both everybody and nobody owns TCP/IP.

Standards Groups That Oversee TCP/IP

The standards groups involved with TCP/IP are:

- **Internet Society (ISOC)**—This is the parent organization for all Internet boards and task forces. It is a nonprofit, nongovernmental, international, professional membership organization funded through membership dues, corporate contributions, and occasional support from governments. For more information, visit *www.isoc.org*.

- **Internet Architecture Board (IAB)**—Also known as the Internet Activities Board, this arm of the ISOC is the parent organization for standards-making and research groups that handle current and future Internet technologies, protocols, and research. The IAB's most important tasks are to provide oversight for the architecture of all Internet protocols and procedures and to supply editorial oversight regarding the documents known as Requests for Comments (RFCs), in which Internet Standards are stated. For more information, visit *www.iab.org*.

- **Internet Engineering Task Force (IETF)**—This is the group responsible for drafting, testing, proposing, and maintaining official Internet Standards (in the form of RFCs) through the participation of multiple working groups under its purview. The IETF and the IAB use a process accurately described as "rough consensus" to create Internet Standards. This means that all participants in the standards-making process, a type of peer review process, must more or less agree before a standard can be proposed, drafted, or approved. Sometimes, that consensus can be pretty rough indeed! For more information, visit *www.ietf.org*.

- **Internet Research Task Force (IRTF)**—This group handles the more forward-looking activities of the ISOC, including research and development work for topics too far out or impractical for immediate implementation but that may play a role on the Internet some day. For more information, visit *http://irtf.org/*.

- **Internet Corporation for Assigned Names and Numbers (ICANN)**—This group has the ultimate responsibility for managing Internet domain names, network addresses, and protocol parameters and behaviors. However, it delegates the management of customer interaction, money collection, database maintenance, and so forth to commercial authorities. For more information, visit *www.icann.org*. Also, there's a list of accredited and accreditation-qualified name registrars on the ICANN site at *www.icann.org/registrars/accredited-list.html*.

Of all these organizations, the most important one for TCP/IP is the IETF because it is responsible for creating and managing RFCs, in which the rules and formats for all related protocols and services are described.

IPv4 and IPv6

By the time TCP/IP had established itself, in the mid- to late-1980s, IPv4 was the only Internet protocol around. It uses 32-bit addresses, which means it supports around four billion distinct network addresses, of which over three billion are usable on the public Internet. At the time, this address space seemed inexhaustible. However, by the early 1990s, when the public Internet became a global phenomenon, it became obvious that IPv4 addresses would run out someday.

By February 2011, ICANN had dispensed its last few unallocated Class C address blocks. (These are explained in Chapter 2.) By June 2011, all those addresses had been assigned to specific organizations. Thus, the entire IPv4 address space is now occupied, and the only way to obtain a public IPv4 address these days is to buy or otherwise acquire an address from some other organization or user.

IPv6, on the other hand, supports 128-bit addresses, which means that its address space is roughly $3.4 * 10^{38}$, whereas IPv4's is roughly $4.3 * 10^9$; that means the IPv6 address space is roughly $8 * 10^{28}$ larger than the IPv4 space. This difference is almost too large to comprehend, but here's a way to put it in perspective: these days, Internet service providers who supply IPv6 addresses to customers routinely supply them with what's called a /64 (pronounced "slash 64") public IPv6 address. That means that each individual user gets a 64-bit address. Each individual address space is 4.3 billion times larger than the entire IPv4 address space.

There's no question that the future of TCP/IP networking involves a switchover to IPv6. That's why this fourth edition of our book covers IPv6 topics in detail. Because IPv4 won't disappear in the foreseeable future, however, this edition provides information you will need to work with IPv4-only networks, IPv6-only networks, or the increasingly likely IPv4/IPv6 hybrids.

TCP/IP Standards and RFCs

Although "**Request for Comments**" sounds like a pretty tentative name for a document, the impact of RFCs on TCP/IP is nothing less than overwhelming. After going through a multistep process of proposals, drafts, test implementations, and so forth, they become official standards, providing the documentation necessary to implement and use TCP/IP protocols and services on the Internet.

Older versions of RFCs are often replaced by newer, more up-to-date versions. Each RFC is identified by a number, the most recent of which are in the 6300 range. (Visit *www.rfc-editor.org/new_rfcs.html* to see the latest ones.) When two or more RFCs cover the same topic, they usually share the same title; the RFC with the highest number is considered the current version, and all the older, lower-numbered versions are considered obsolete.

One special RFC is titled Internet Official Protocol Standards. It provides a snapshot of current prevailing standards and best practices documents. If you visit your favorite Internet search engine (e.g., Yahoo! or Google), you can find many online locations for Internet RFCs. We recommend using, say, the search string "RFC 5000" to find RFC 5000, or "RFC 2026" to find RFC 2026. (Depending on which search engine you use, you may need to put the entire string in quotation marks.) We recommend the Internet RFC/STD/FYI/BCP Archives site, where an index for all RFCs is available at *www.faqs.org/rfcs/*.

RFC 2026 is another important document. It describes how an RFC is created and what processes it must go through to become an official standard adopted by the IETF. It also describes how to participate in that process.

A potential Standard RFC begins its life when a process or protocol is developed, defined, and reviewed, and it is then tested and reviewed further by the Internet community. After it is revised, tested further, proven to work, and shown to be compatible with other Internet Standards, it may be adopted as an official Standard RFC by the IETF. It is then published as a Standard RFC and assigned a number.

Actually, an RFC passes through several specific phases while becoming a standard and acquires specific status designations during the process. These are fully defined in RFC 2026. For example, a potential Standard RFC goes through three phases on its way to becoming a standard. It starts as a **Proposed Standard**, moves up to a **Draft Standard**, and, if formally adopted, becomes an **Internet Standard**, or a Standard RFC. Eventually, when replaced by a newer RFC, it can be designated an **Historic Standard**.

Best Current Practice (BCP) is another important category of RFCs. A BCP does not define a protocol or technical specifications; rather, it defines a philosophy, or a particular approach, to a network design or implementation that is recommended as tried and true, or that enjoys certain desirable characteristics worthy of consideration when building or maintaining a TCP/IP network. BCPs are not standards per se, but because they present highly recommended design, implementation, and maintenance practices, they are well worth reading and applying where appropriate.

OSI Network Reference Model Overview

Before discussing TCP/IP protocols and services in further detail, let's explore a model of how networks operate in general. This will help you better understand what protocols are for and what roles they play on contemporary networks. This kind of model is often called a **network reference model**, but it is formally known as the **International Organization for Standardization Open Systems Interconnection** network reference model and may sometimes be called the **ISO/OSI network reference model**. No matter what you call it, its job is to describe how networks operate from the hardware or device level (signals and bits) all the way to the software or program level (application interfaces).

Governed by ISO Standard 7498, the ISO/OSI network reference model, also known as the reference model or the seven-layer model, was developed as part of an international standards initiative in the 1980s that was intended to usher in a new and improved suite of protocols to replace TCP/IP. Although the OSI protocols were never widely adopted outside Europe, the network reference model provides a standard way to talk about networking and explain how networks operate. Despite the 10-year, multibillion-dollar effort to complete the OSI protocols and services, TCP/IP remained the open standard protocol suite of choice and remains so to this day.

Breaking Networking into Layers

The network reference model's value lies in its ability to break a big technical problem into a series of interrelated subproblems and then solve each subproblem individually. Computer scientists call this approach **divide and conquer**.

The network reference model handles networking all the way from hardware to the high-level software involved in making networks work. The divide-and-conquer approach keeps concerns related to networking hardware completely separated from those related to networking software. It even further divides networking software into multiple **layers,** each of which represents a separate kind or class of networking activity. (You will read more about this in the section titled "The ISO/OSI Network Reference Model.") Thus, the whole series of independent but interconnected layers of hardware and software work together to enable one computer to communicate with another across a network.

In fact, a layered approach to networking is a good thing. That's because the kind of expertise that makes it possible for an electrical engineer to specify how a network medium must behave, as well as specify what kinds of physical interfaces are necessary to attach to such a networking medium, is quite different from the kinds of expertise that software engineers need. In fact, software engineers must not only write drivers for network interfaces, they must implement the networking protocols that operate at various layers in the network reference model (or in another layered model for whatever networking protocols may be in use).

Before we dive into the details of the network reference model and describe its layers, you should understand and appreciate these key points about networking:

- The challenges of networking are easier to overcome when big tasks are broken into a series of smaller tasks.

- Layers operate more or less independently of one another, enabling modular design and implementation of specific hardware and software components that perform individual network functions.

- Because individual layers encapsulate specific, largely independent functions, changes to one layer need not affect other layers.

- Individual layers work together on pairs of computers. The sending computer performs operations on one layer that are in some sense "reversed" or "undone" by the operations performed at the same layer on the receiving computer. Because such layers work in concert across the network, they are called **peer layers**.

- Different expertise is needed to implement the solutions necessary for the networking functions or tasks handled at each layer.

- The layers in a network implementation work together to create a general solution to the general problem known as networking.

- Network protocols usually map to one or more layers of the network reference model.

- TCP/IP itself is designed around a layered model for networking.

In fact, breaking down networking into an interconnected series of layers defines a general abstract reference model that explains what networks do and how they work. The same kind of model is expressed in somewhat different terms as part of TCP/IP's very definition. The key insight that makes divide and conquer such a powerful tool for implementing networks has been part of TCP/IP's design from its earliest days. This abstraction into layers explains why TCP/IP is so good at allowing different computers, operating systems, and even types of networking hardware to communicate with one another.

The ISO/OSI Network Reference Model Layers

The network reference model described in ISO Standard 7498 breaks network communication into these seven layers (see Figure 1-1):

- Application layer
- Presentation layer
- Session layer
- Transport layer
- Network layer
- Data Link layer
- Physical layer

The roles that each of these layers plays are explained later in this chapter. In the next section, you learn how layers in the network reference model behave, in a more general way.

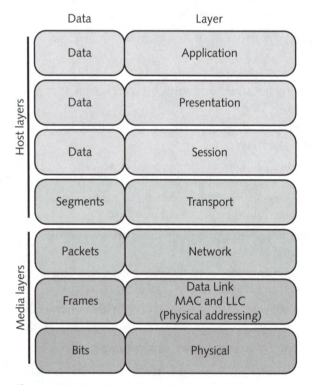

Figure 1-1 ISO/OSI network reference model layers

Source: Figure adapted from illustration at ccnaGuru.com

How Protocol Layers Behave

Within the context of the network reference model, layers exist to encapsulate or isolate specific types of functionality, which allows the divide-and-conquer approach to be applied to networking.

In general, layers in the network reference model exist to provide services to the layer above and to deliver data for outbound traffic or accept data for inbound traffic to or from the layer below.

For each network reference model layer, the software handles packages of data, which are called **protocol data units** (**PDUs**). These are often generically described as packets (for packages of data), irrespective of which model layer is being addressed.

PDUs typically include "envelope information" in the form of specific headers and trailers. In this context, a header represents a layer-specific label for whatever PDU it precedes. Likewise, a trailer (which may be optional for some layers and some specific protocols) may include error-detection and error-correction information, explicit "end of data" flags, or other data designed to clearly indicate the end of a PDU.

The network reference model, as shown in Figure 1-1, looks something like a layer cake, given that it presents a stack of named layers from which the model is built. Because this stacklike structure so accurately depicts how many networking protocol suites are implemented— including TCP/IP—it is common to talk about the components of hardware and software that map in this model as a **protocol stack** when implemented on a specific computer. Thus, on a Windows computer, the **network interface controller** (**NIC**), the driver that permits the operating system to "talk" to the NIC, and the various software components that make up TCP/IP's other layers may be called a protocol stack or, more accurately, the TCP/IP protocol stack for that machine.

 A network interface controller goes by several other names, such as Ethernet card, network adapter, network interface, and network interface card.

In the following sections, we examine the network reference model layers in more detail, starting at the bottom of the stack.

Physical Layer
The **Physical layer** includes the physical transmission medium (cables or wireless media) that any network must use to send and receive the signals that constitute the physical expression of networked communications. The details of such signaling, along with the physical and electrical characteristics of the interfaces to the network medium, are specified in the Physical layer. Its job is to activate, maintain, and deactivate network connections. Senders attempt to establish a connection to transmit data across the network medium; receivers respond to these attempts, either by accepting or rejecting the connection attempt.

A simplified view of the Physical layer is that it concerns itself with the networking hardware and the connections that permit that hardware to access some networking medium. In addition, this layer coordinates the sending and receiving of signals across the networking medium and determines what kinds of cables, connectors, and network interfaces must be used to access a specific area on a network.

The Physical layer manages communications with the network medium going down the protocol stack and handles the conversion of outgoing data from bits that computers use into the signals that networks use. For incoming messages, the Physical layer reverses this process and converts incoming signals from the networking medium into the bit patterns that must be sent to the computer through the network interface.

PDUs at the Physical layer consist of specific serial patterns of signals that correspond to bit patterns for frames at the Data Link layer.

Data Link Layer The **Data Link layer** sits between the Physical layer and the Network layer in the network reference model. It enables reliable transmission of data through the Physical layer at the sending end and checks the reliability at the receiving end. The Data Link layer also manages **point-to-point transmission** across the networking medium, from one computer to another on a single logical or physical **cable segment**. It recognizes individual devices on the local medium through a special address that uniquely identifies each individual interface. Because the Data Link layer manages point-to-point communications between interfaces, it also handles LAN connections between the machines to which those interfaces are attached.

In the course of managing connections between machines, the Data Link layer handles the sequencing of data from sender to receiver. Patterns of bits must be mapped into corresponding patterns of signals for transmission from sender to receiver, and the process is reversed on the receiving end. To that end, the Data Link layer can also control the pace at which data is transmitted from sender to receiver—a process called **media flow control** that responds to local congestion and helps keep the network medium from becoming swamped by local traffic. Finally, the Data Link layer requests data transfers to occur when outgoing PDUs are ready to be transmitted and handles the accepting and constructing of incoming PDUs for incoming data.

PDUs at the Data Link layer must fit into specific bit patterns that map to the carrying capacity of the network medium in terms of format, structure, and maximum data size. Data Link layer PDUs are called **frames** or **data frames**.

The Data Link layer is also responsible for brokering certain connection types when they apply to networked communications. A prime example of this is when a particular connection uses a communications technology called circuit switching. Best known for its use in the telephone system, circuit switching (also known as line switching, electronic switching, or analog or digital circuit switching) establishes a dedicated channel for the duration of a transmission between two end points. TCP/IP can use such communications links, but treats them no differently than other point-to-point links that it uses for data transmissions.

Network Layer The **Network layer** is where notions of network location are addressed and where the intricacies involved in directing a PDU from sender to receiver are handled. Thus, the Network layer handles the logical addresses associated with individual machines on a network, which permit the Domain Name System (DNS) to correlate human-readable names for such machines with unique, machine-readable numeric addresses. The Network layer also uses that **addressing** information to determine how to send a PDU from a sender to a receiver when the source and destination for traffic do not reside on the same physical segment of a network. The primary function of the Network layer is to provide a globally unique address to every host on the Internet and paths to and from hosts.

The Network layer also embodies the notion of multiple simultaneous connections between different IP addresses, so that numerous applications can maintain network connections at the same time. The Network layer is able to identify which network connection belongs to an individual process or application on a computer and not only direct traffic to the proper receiver from its sender but also deliver the incoming data to a specific process or application on the receiving machine. This explains how you can have a Web browser open on your machine at the same time you're reading e-mail, and it is what permits incoming e-mail messages to be delivered to your e-mail client and incoming Web pages to be delivered to your Web browser without mixing up the two data streams.

In fact, the Network layer is even flexible enough to recognize and use multiple routes between a sender and a receiver while ongoing communications are underway. The technique that's used to forward or relay individual PDUs from a sender to a receiver using one or multiple routes is called packet switching, and that's why the Network layer handles forwarding and relaying on a per-PDU basis. In fact, the Network layer is also sensitive to delays associated with routes and can manage how much traffic is sent across them while it is forwarding data from a sender to a receiver. This process is called **congestion control**, and it helps networks avoid being overrun when high levels of activity occur.

Remember, the PDU associated with the Network layer is called a packet. It may be helpful to refer back to Figure 1-1 occasionally while learning about the various layers in this section.

Transport Layer The **Transport layer**'s name is highly evocative of its function: this layer's job is to ensure reliable end-to-end transmission of PDUs from sender to receiver. To enable this function to occur, the Transport layer often includes end-to-end error-detection and error-recovery data. Such data is usually packaged as a part of the trailers for Transport layer PDUs, where special values called **checksums** are calculated before and after data delivery, then compared to check whether error-free delivery occurred. If the checksum as sent agrees with the checksum as calculated locally, it is assumed that error-free delivery occurred; if not, some protocols at the Transport layer request retransmission of PDUs when errors are detected.

Finally, the amount of data that may be sent from sender to receiver varies. However, the containers that transport the data from end to end have a fixed maximum size (called the **MTU**, for **maximum transmission unit**), thus the Transport layer also handles the activities known as segmentation and reassembly. Simply put, **segmentation** involves cutting up a big message into a numbered sequence of chunks, called segments, whereby each chunk represents the maximum data payload that the network media can carry between sender and receiver. In equally simple terms, **reassembly** is the process whereby the chunks are put into their original order and used to re-create the data as it was before it was segmented for transmission.

Normally, segmentation occurs at the sender's end as the data payload for TCP is broken into a sequence of fixed size TCP packet payloads formally called segments. These are reassembled by TCP at the receiving end. The only exception to this occurs when a TCP segment must travel across a link for which the MTU is smaller than the current packet size for the TCP segment generated by the sender. This is called *fragmentation*, and it occurs at the IP layer (and gets

> a special IP header flag) at whatever host connects across a link with a smaller MTU before those now-fragmented packets can be forwarded to the next host in the routing sequence. However, these will not be reassembled until they arrive at the receiving host, where that host handles reassembly of fragments as well as original segments as incoming packet structures require.

The Transport layer is equipped to request retransmission of all erroneous or missing PDUs when reassembly is underway, so that it can guarantee reliable delivery of data from sender to receiver. The PDUs used at the Transport layer are called **segments** or **data segments**.

Session Layer The **Session layer** is where ongoing communications between a sender and a receiver (somewhat like in a telephone conversation) are set up, maintained, and then terminated or torn down, as needed. Thus, the Session layer provides mechanisms to permit senders and receivers to request that a conversation start or stop, as well as mechanisms to keep a conversation going even when traffic may not be flowing between the two parties.

In addition, the Session layer provides mechanisms called **checkpoints** to maintain reliable ongoing conversations. Checkpoints define the last point up to which successful communications have occurred, and they define the point to which a conversation must be rolled back to recover missing or damaged elements to recover from the effects of missing or damaged data. Likewise, the Session layer defines a variety of mechanisms whereby conversations that fall out of synchronization are resynchronized.

The Session layer's primary job is to handle communications between two networked parties, in which a sequence of messages or PDUs is exchanged. A good example of this type of interaction occurs when a user logs on to a database (the setup phase), enters a bunch of queries (the data exchange phase), and then logs off when finished (the teardown phase).

At this layer, PDUs come in a variety of types (the OSI protocol suite recognizes more than 30); they are known as Session PDUs or SPDUs.

Presentation Layer The **Presentation layer** manages the way data is presented to the network on its way down the protocol stack and the way it is presented to a specific machine/application combination on its way up the protocol stack. Thus, the Presentation layer handles transforming data from generic, network-oriented forms of expression to more specific, platform-oriented forms, and vice versa. This transformation is what permits such radically different types of computers (that may represent numbers and characters quite differently) to communicate with each other across a network.

By convention, a special type of operating system driver is said to reside at the Presentation layer. This driver is sometimes called a redirector (in Microsoft terms) or a network shell (in Linux and UNIX terms). Either way, this driver's job is to distinguish requests for network resources from requests for local resources and to redirect such requests to the appropriate remote or local subsystem. This permits computers to use a single subsystem to access resources, whether those resources reside on the local machine or on a remote machine, without having to discriminate by the type of resource involved. This makes it much easier for developers to build applications that can access local or remote resources at will. Likewise, it makes it easier for users to access such resources because they can simply request the resources they need and let the redirector worry about how to satisfy their requests.

The Presentation layer can also supply special data-handling functions for applications, including protocol conversions (when applications use protocols distinct from those used for networked communications, as may be the case for e-commerce, database, or other transaction-oriented services), data encryption (for outgoing messages), decryption (for incoming messages), data compression (for outgoing messages), or expansion (for incoming messages). For this kind of service, whatever the Presentation layer does on the sending side, the Presentation layer must undo on the receiving side, so that both sides of the connection share similar views of the data at some point.

At this layer, PDUs come in a variety of types and are called Presentation PDUs.

Application Layer Although the temptation is always strong to equate the **Application layer** with whatever application is requesting network services (and there's always an application involved when network access is requested), the Application layer defines an interface that applications can use to request network services rather than referring directly to applications themselves. Thus, the Application layer basically defines the kinds of services that applications can request from the network and stipulates the forms that data must take when accepting messages from, or delivering messages to, such applications.

In the most direct way, the Application layer defines a set of access controls over the network, in the sense that it determines what kinds of things applications can ask the network to carry or deliver and what kind of activities the network can support. For example, permission to access specific files and services is granted at the Application layer, as well which users are allowed to perform what kinds of actions on specific data elements.

At this layer, PDUs are called Application PDUs.

TCP/IP Networking Model

Because TCP/IP's architecture was designed long before the OSI reference model was finalized in the 1980s, it should come as no surprise that the design model that describes TCP/IP differs somewhat from the OSI reference model. Figure 1-2 shows the layers identified for the native TCP/IP model and maps its layers to those of the reference model. These layers are quite similar, but not identical, to the layers in the OSI reference model. That's because some functions associated with the Session layer and the Presentation layer in the OSI reference model appear in the TCP/IP Application layer, whereas some aspects of the Session layer in the OSI reference model appear in the TCP/IP Transport layer.

By and large, the Transport layers for both models map together quite well, as does the Network layer from the OSI reference model and the Internet layer from the TCP/IP model. Just as the TCP/IP Application layer more or less maps to the Application, Presentation, and Session layers in the OSI reference model, the TCP/IP Network Access layer maps to the Data Link and the Physical layers in the OSI reference model.

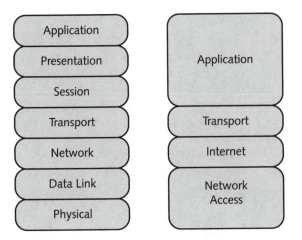

Figure 1-2 OSI reference model and TCP/IP networking model layers
© Cengage Learning 2013

TCP/IP Network Access Layer

The TCP/IP Network Access layer is sometimes called the Network Interface layer. Either way, it's the layer where LAN technologies, such as Ethernet, token ring, and wireless media and devices come into play. It's also the layer in which WAN and connection-management protocols, such as **Point-to-Point Protocol (PPP)** and **X.25**, come into play. Diverging somewhat from the terminology for the OSI reference model, PDUs at this layer are called datagrams, although they are also referred to as packets.

At the Network Access layer, the **Institute of Electrical and Electronic Engineers (IEEE)** standards for networking apply. These include the **IEEE 802** family of standards:

- *802.1 Internetworking*—A general description of how internetworking (exchanging data from one physical network to another) works for the entire 802 family.

- *802.2 Logical Link Control*—A general description of how logical links between two devices on the same physical network may be established and managed.

- *802.2 Media Access Control*—A general description of how media interfaces are identified and accessed on a network, including a scheme to create unique MAC layer addresses for all media interfaces.

- *802.3 CSMA/CD*—A general description of how the networking technology more commonly called Ethernet operates and behaves. Ethernet is a shared medium that supports multiple access; it uses a special signal called carrier sense to detect when the medium is in use, and likewise uses special circuitry to detect when two transmissions run into each other (collision detection). In fact, "**CSMA/CD**" stands for "**Carrier Sense Multiple Access with Collision Detection**." The Ethernet family includes Gigabit Ethernet (802.3z), as well as 10-Mbps and 100-Mbps varieties, despite the name for 802.12 being "High-Speed Networking."

- *802.5 Token Ring*—A general description of how the networking technology developed at IBM, known as token ring, operates and behaves.

- *802.11 Wi-Fi*—A family of wireless packet radio networking standards that supports networking speeds from 1 Mbps to as high as 540 Mbps (theoretical maximum). The most common members of this family are the 11 Mbps 802.11a and 802.11b standards, the 54 Mbps 802.11g standard, and the 802.11n multi-channel technology, which claims a theoretical maximum bandwidth of 540 Mbps.

For more information about the IEEE 802 family of standards, visit IEEE's Web site at *www.ieee.org* and search on "802."

TCP/IP Network Access Layer Protocols

PPP is the most important TCP/IP Network Access layer protocol; it is used to establish a direct connection between a pair of networked devices. PPP can provide connection authentication to establish the identities of both parties, apply encryption to transmissions to ensure privacy, and apply compression to reduce transmission data volume (both encryption and compression must be "undone" at the receiving end). One common variety of PPP is known as PPPoE which stands for "PPP over Ethernet." PPPoE is widely used on Ethernet networks or networks with Ethernet-like characteristics (such as Ethernet channels on CATV networks for use with cable modem networking technology).

Though not part of the TCP/IP protocol suite, the following Network Access (OSI Layer 2) protocols are most likely to be encountered today:

- *High-level Data Link Control (HDLC) protocol*—Based on IBM's SNA Data Link Control (SDLC) protocol, HDLC uses data frames to manage network links and data transmission.
- *Frame relay*—A telecommunications service designed to support intermittent data transmission between local area networks and wide area network end points. Frame relay uses data frames to manage network links and data transmission.
- *Asynchronous Transfer Mode (ATM)*—A high-speed, cell-oriented connection-switching technology used for digital voice and data communications. ATM is widely used for telecommunications and data networking backbones and infrastructure.

For more information on these and other protocols you'll encounter in this book, visit *whatis.techtarget.com*.

PPP is widely used for Internet and private TCP/IP network connections. PPP is protocol neutral and used for point-to-point serial links over a single connection, such as for a modem, a T-carrier connection like a T1 or T3 line, or similar connections. The Windows implementation of PPP supports other Windows protocols—namely TCP/IP, Internetwork Packet Exchange/ Sequenced Packet Exchange (IPX/SPX), and NetBIOS Enhanced User Interface (NetBEUI), along with tunneling protocols, such as **Point-to-Point Tunneling Protocol (PPTP)**, and other **Virtual Private Network (VPN)** protocols—across a single connection. Other implementations add support for numerous other protocols—including AppleTalk and **Systems Network Architecture (SNA)**—to this mix. PPP is the serial line protocol of choice for end users, but most routers and network-level connections use HDLC because of its lower overhead. PPP works well for end users because it supports a variety of security options that includes encryption of login information or encryption of all traffic across the serial link as well as a rich mix of protocols and services. PPP is described in RFC 1661.

TCP/IP Internet Layer Functions

The TCP/IP Internet layer protocols handle routing between machines across multiple networks and also manage network names and addresses to facilitate the routing. More specifically, the Internet layer handles three primary tasks:

- *MTU fragmentation*—When a router carries data from one type of network to another, the largest chunk of data that the network can carry, an MTU, varies. When data moves from a medium that supports a larger MTU to a medium that supports a smaller MTU, that data must be reduced to smaller pieces to match the smaller of the two MTUs. This only needs to be a one-way transformation, given that smaller packets don't have to be combined into bigger ones in the opposite direction, but it must be performed while the data is in transit.

- *Addressing*—This is the mechanism whereby all network interfaces on a TCP/IP network are associated with unique bit patterns that identify each interface individually and also identify the network (or even the network locale) to which that interface belongs.

- *Routing*—This is the mechanism that forwards packets from sender to receiver, in which numerous intermediate relays may be involved in achieving delivery from sender to receiver. This function includes not only the processes involved in successful delivery but the methods to track delivery performance and report on errors when delivery fails or is otherwise hampered.

Overall, the Internet layer handles moving data from sender to receiver. It also repackages data into smaller containers when required, handles issues of identifying where sender and receiver are located, and defines how to get from "here" to "there" on a network.

TCP/IP Internet Layer Protocols

The primary protocols that function at the TCP/IP Internet layer are:

- *Internet Protocol (IP)*—This protocol routes packets from sender to receiver.

- *Internet Control Message Protocol (ICMP)*—This protocol handles information about IP-based routing and network behavior, especially as it relates to "traffic conditions" and errors.

- *Packet Internetwork Groper (PING)*—This protocol checks accessibility and round-trip time between a specific sender-and-receiver pair of IP addresses.

- *Address Resolution Protocol (ARP)*—This protocol converts between numeric IP network addresses and Media Access Control (MAC) addresses on a specific cable segment (always used for the final step of packet delivery).

- *Reverse Address Resolution Protocol (RARP)*—This protocol converts a MAC layer address into a numeric IP address. Although ARP and RARP have to bridge the Layer 2–Layer 3 divide because they work with both MAC and IP addresses, by convention they are considered Layer 2 protocols. Perhaps that's because most protocol stack implementations include these functions within Data Link layer code modules.

- *Bootstrap Protocol (BOOTP)*—This protocol is the precursor to the Dynamic Host Configuration Protocol (DHCP), which manages network allocation of IP addresses and other IP configuration data. BOOTP permits network devices to obtain boot and configuration data across the network instead of from a local drive. Most protocol analyzers report DHCP packets as being of type BOOTP because they share most of their header data, as you'll learn in Chapter 7.

- *Routing Information Protocol (RIP)*—This protocol defines the original distance-vector and most basic routing protocol for local routing regions within local internetworks. (A distance vector is basically an integer count of the number of router links, called hops, that a packet must traverse between sender and receiver; RIPv1 has a 4-bit hop count field, which makes 15 the maximum number of hops allowed. There are also RIPv2 and a RIPv6 versions for this protocol.)

- *Open Shortest Path First (OSPF)*—This protocol defines a widely used link-state routing protocol for local or interior routing regions within local internetworks.

- *Border Gateway Protocol (BGP)*—This protocol defines a widely used routing protocol that connects to common Internet backbones, or other routing domains within the Internet where multiple parties jointly share responsibility for managing traffic.

By the time you finish this book, you will know quite a bit more about all these protocols and a fair amount more about several other related protocols. For now, you need to know their names, acronyms, and basic functions as well as understand that these are all networking protocols that function at Layer 2 or Layer of the OSI reference model.

TCP/IP Transport Layer Functions

Devices that operate on the Internet are generically identified as **hosts**, thus the TCP/IP Transport layer is sometimes called the host-to-host layer because it helps move data from one host to another. Transport layer protocols provide reliable delivery of data from sender to receiver. They also provide the necessary segmentation of outgoing messages prior to transmission and the reassembling of the messages prior to delivery to the Application layer for further processing. Thus, the OSI reference model and the TCP/IP model more or less map to one another.

TCP/IP Transport Layer Protocols

There are two TCP/IP Transport layer protocols: the Transmission Control Protocol (TCP) and the User Datagram Protocol (UDP). They come in two flavors: connection-oriented and connectionless; TCP is **connection-oriented**, and UDP is **connectionless**. The distinction rests on the fact that TCP negotiates and maintains a connection between sender and receiver prior to sending data (obtaining a positive acknowledgment for data successfully transmitted and obtaining a request for retransmission of missing or erroneous data), whereas UDP simply transmits data in what's called a "best-effort delivery" and does no follow-up checking on its receipt. This makes TCP much more reliable but also slower and more cumbersome than UDP, but it also allows TCP to provide guaranteed delivery services at the protocol level, which UDP does not offer.

TCP/IP Application Layer

The TCP/IP Application layer is also known as the **Process layer** because this is where the protocol stack interfaces with applications or processes on a host machine. The user interfaces to a process or application are defined here. The common overlap between TCP/IP protocols and services occurs here as well. For example, File Transfer Protocol (FTP) and Telnet represent specific TCP/IP-based protocols and also define services for file transfer, terminal emulation, and so forth. Most of the higher-level TCP/IP-based services we discuss later in this book operate at the TCP/IP Application layer.

The best-known TCP/IP-based services use TCP as transports rather than UDP. However, some services, such as **Network File System (NFS)**, Voice over IP (VoIP), and various forms of streaming media, including those supported by the H.323 protocol, often use UDP. No matter what transport is used, higher-level services all depend on IP for their networking protocol (that's why there are separate protocols at the Network or Internet layer to provide special-purpose network services, such as ICMP, ARP, and RARP).

TCP/IP services depend on two elements to operate:

- *Daemons*—In UNIX terminology, a special "listener process," called a **daemon**, operates on a server to handle incoming user requests for specific services. On Windows Server 2008, a process called INETINFO.EXE appears in the Task Manager's Processes tab whenever the Web server, IIS, or FTP server is running. (On a UNIX host, the FTP service is associated with a process named ftpd, and Internet services run under a process named inetd.)

- *Port addresses*—TCP/IP service has an associated port address (also called a port number, which you'll learn about shortly) that uses a 16-bit number to identify a specific process or service. Addresses in the range from 0 to 1024 are often called **well-known port numbers** and associate a specific port address with a specific service. For example, FTP's well-known port address is port 21. We cover this topic in more detail later in this chapter.

Any daemon or listener process essentially hangs around, listening for attempts to connect on the well-known port address (or addresses) associated with its services. A well-known port address can often be changed as a configuration option, which is why you sometimes see Web **Uniform Resource Locators (URLs)** that specify a different port address at the end of the domain name portion of the string. Thus, a URL might appear as *www.gendex. com:8080* to indicate that an alternate port address of 8080 should be used to establish the connection, rather than the default standard port address of 80.

When a connection request arrives, the listener process checks to see if the request should be allowed to proceed. If so, it creates another temporary process (on UNIX) or spawns a separate execution thread (on Windows Server 2008) to handle that particular request. This temporary process or thread lasts only long enough to service that user request and uses temporary port addresses in the range from 1025 through 65535 to handle it. (Sometimes, services use four port addresses so that both parties can manage separate connections at the same time. These may be used to separate data transfer and control information, for example.) As soon as a process or thread is created to handle some specific request, the listener process or daemon returns to its job of listening for additional requests for service.

TCP/IP Protocols, Services, Sockets, and Ports

Think back for a moment to the TCP/IP chronology that appears earlier in this chapter. You may recall that TCP/IP's inclusion in the version of UNIX known as **4.2BSD** was a milestone in its history and was the point at which the worldwide research and academic communities began working with TCP/IP.

Actually, there's more to the relationship between UNIX and TCP/IP than its successful introduction may suggest. For a good while after this relationship formed, the connection between UNIX and TCP/IP was strong and useful. Thus, not only did the introduction of TCP/IP into UNIX greatly enhance that operating system's networking abilities, the techniques that were used to describe and configure TCP/IP protocols and services within the UNIX environment have also become customary for TCP/IP at large, even when UNIX isn't the operating system. In fact, the terminology describes how data conveyed by TCP/IP to a specific network host is handled once it is delivered to its destination.

On any given computer running TCP/IP, numerous applications may be running at the same time. On many desktops, for example, it's typical for users to have an e-mail program, a Web browser, and an instant messaging client all open and running at the same time. Within the TCP/IP environment, a mechanism is required to permit multiple applications to be distinguished from one another. This allows the transport protocols (TCP or UDP) to handle multiple outgoing streams of data separately (from distinct applications) before they are passed to IP for addressing and delivery instructions. Incoming data requires reversing this process. The incoming stream of Transport layer PDUs must be inspected and separated, and the resulting messages must be delivered to the appropriate requesting application.

Combining the various sources of outgoing data into a single output data stream is called **multiplexing**; breaking up an incoming data stream so that separate portions may be delivered to the correct applications is called **demultiplexing**. This activity is typically handled at the Transport layer, where outgoing messages are also broken into chunks sized for the networks over which they'll travel, and where incoming messages are reassembled in correct order from a stream of incoming chunks.

To help make this job easier, TCP/IP uses **protocol numbers** to identify distinct protocols, and those protocols use **port numbers** to identify specific Application layer protocols and services. The fact that this technique originated in the UNIX environment through a series of configuration files, explains how the techniques used in all TCP/IP implementations came to exist.

Numerous port numbers are reserved to identify well-known protocols. **Well-known protocols** (also called **well-known services** in some contexts) assign a series of numbers to represent a sizable collection of TCP/IP-based network services, such as file transfer (FTP), terminal emulation (Telnet), and e-mail (SMTP, short for Simple Mail Transfer Protocol; IMAP, short for Internet Message Access Protocol; and POP3, short for Post Office Protocol, version 3). Well-known and preassigned protocol numbers and port numbers are documented in the Assigned Numbers RFC. UNIX machines define these values in two text files: protocol numbers are defined in /etc/protocols, and port numbers are defined in /etc/services.

TCP/IP Protocol Numbers

In an IP **datagram** header, the protocol number appears in the 10th byte. (Chapter 3 discusses IP datagrams in detail.) This 8-bit value indicates which Transport layer protocol should accept delivery of incoming data. A complete list of protocol numbers for TCP/IP can be found at *http://www.iana.org/assignments/protocol-numbers/protocol-numbers.xml*. Table 1-1 shows the first 21 entries.

Number	Acronym	Protocol name
0	HOPOPT	IPv6 Hop-by-Hop Option
1	ICMP	Internet Control Message Protocol
2	IGMP	Internet Group Management Protocol
3	GGP	Gateway-to-Gateway Protocol
4	IPv4	Internet Protocol v4 (encapsulation)
5	ST	Internet Stream Protocol
6	TCP	Transmission Control Protocol
7	CBT	Core Based Trees
8	EGP	Exterior Gateway Protocol
9	IGP	Interior Gateway Protocol, any private interior gateway (used by Cisco for their IGRP)
10	BBN-RCC-MON	BBN RCC Monitoring
11	NVP-II	Network Voice Protocol
12	PUP	PARC Universal Packet
13	ARGUS	ARGUS Protocol
14	EMCON	Emission Control Protocol
15	XNET	Cross Net Debugger Protocol
16	CHAOS	CHAOS Protocol
17	UDP	User Datagram Protocol
18	MUX	Multiplexing
19	DCN-MEAS	DCN Measurement Subsystems
20	HMP	Host Monitoring Protocol

Table 1-1 TCP/IP protocol numbers
Source: Table adapted from www.iana.org

On a UNIX system, the contents of the text file /etc/protocols need not contain every entry in the Assigned Numbers RFC. To work properly, /etc/protocols must identify which protocols are installed and used on a particular UNIX machine. For that reason, we do not include the entire list in this chapter. To look up numbers associated with protocols you're using on your system, visit *www.iana.org* and look for information about protocol numbers. (Hint: You can use the Find command in your Web browser to look up protocols by acronym or full name.)

TCP/IP Port Numbers

After IP passes incoming data to TCP or UDP at the Transport layer, the protocol must perform its duties, then pass that data to its intended **application process** (whatever program is running that should accept that data on the user's behalf). TCP/IP application processes are sometimes called **network services** and are identified by port numbers. The **source port number** identifies the process that sent the data, and the **destination port number** identifies the process to receive that data. Both these values are represented by two-byte (16-bit) values in the first header word of every TCP segment or UDP packet. Because port numbers are 16-bit values, they fall anywhere in the range from 0 to 65535 when expressed in decimal form.

Traditionally, port numbers below 256 were reserved for well-known services, such as Telnet and FTP, and numbers from 256 to 1024 were reserved for UNIX-specific services. Today, all port addresses below 1024 represent well-known services, and there are many so-called **registered ports** associated with specific application services in the range from 1024 to 65535. Here again, perusal of *www.iana.org* is the quickest way to understand what's what in this sizable address space.

TCP/IP Sockets

Well-known or registered ports represent preassigned port numbers with specific associations to particular network services. This simplifies the client/server connection process because both sender and receiver agree by convention that particular services are associated with particular port addresses. In addition to such agreed-upon port numbers, there is another type of port number, known as a dynamically allocated port number. This number is not preassigned; rather, it is used, as needed, to provide a temporary connection between a sender and a receiver for a limited exchange of data. This permits each system to maintain numerous open connections and to assign each connection its own unique, dynamically allocated port address. These port addresses fall in the range of addresses over 1024, in which any port number not currently in use represents fair game for such temporary use.

After a client or server uses a well-known port address to establish communications, the connection established (called a **session**) is invariably handed to a temporary pair of socket addresses that provides the sending and receiving port addresses for further communications between sender and receiver. The combination of a particular IP address (for the host machine on which the process is running) and a **dynamically assigned port address** (where the connection is maintained) is called a **socket address** (or **socket**). Because both IP addresses and dynamically assigned port numbers are guaranteed to be unique, each socket address is also guaranteed to be unique across the entire Internet.

Data Encapsulation in TCP/IP

At each layer in the TCP/IP protocol stack, outgoing data is packaged and identified for delivery to the layer underneath. Incoming data, on the other hand, has its encapsulating information from the underlying layer stripped before it's delivered to its upper-layer partner.

Thus, each PDU has its own particular opening component called a **header** (or **packet header**) that identifies the protocol in use, the sender and intended recipient, and other information.

Likewise, many PDUs include a closing component called a **trailer** (or **packet trailer**) that provides data integrity checks for the data portion of the PDU, known as the **payload**. The enclosure of a payload between a header and (optional) trailer is what defines the mechanism known as **encapsulation**, wherein data from an upper layer gets manipulated and then enclosed with a header (and possibly a trailer) before being passed to the layer below or across the networking medium for delivery elsewhere.

Studying the actual contents of any communications on the network medium—"across the wire," as it's sometimes called—requires that you understand typical header and trailer structures and can reassemble data moving across the network up the protocol stack into something that approximates its original form. That work represents the task known as protocol analysis, which is discussed in the remainder of this chapter.

Protocol Analysis

Protocol analysis (also referred to as **network analysis**) is the process of tapping into the network communications system, capturing packets that cross the network, gathering network statistics, and **decoding** the packets into readable form. In essence, a protocol analyzer "eavesdrops" on network communications. (Because these tools can reveal many kinds of valuable or even damaging information, many organizations have rules forbidding their unsupervised use on production networks). Many protocol analyzers can also transmit packets—a useful task for testing a network or device. You perform protocol analysis using a software or hardware/software product loaded on a desktop or portable computer.

Useful Roles for Protocol Analysis

Protocol analyzers are often used to troubleshoot network communications. Typically, they're placed on the network and configured to capture any problematic communication sequence. By reading the packets that cross the cabling system, you can identify faults and errors in the process.

For example, if a Web client cannot connect to a specific Web server, a protocol analyzer can be used to capture the communication. Reviewing it then reveals the processes used by the client to resolve the IP address of the Web server, locate the hardware address of a local router, and submit the connection request to the Web server.

Protocol analyzers are also used to test networks. This can be performed in a passive manner by listening to unusual communications or in an active manner by transmitting packets onto the network. For example, if a firewall is configured to block a specific type of traffic from entering the local network, a protocol analyzer can listen to the traffic from the firewall to determine if unacceptable traffic is forwarded. Alternately, an analyzer can be configured to transmit test packets to the firewall in order to determine if certain unacceptable traffic will be forwarded by that firewall.

Protocol analyzers can also be used to gather trends on network performance. Most analyzers have the ability to track short- and long-term trends in network traffic. These may include network utilization, packets-per-second rate, packet size distribution, and protocols in use. The administrator can use this information to track subtle changes on the network over time. For example, a network reconfigured to support DHCP-based addressing experiences greater broadcasts due to the DHCP Discovery process. For more information on DHCP, refer to Chapter 7, "IP Address Autoconfiguration."

In this book, we use the Wireshark protocol analyzer as a teaching tool. We examine various packet structures and communication sequences used in TCP/IP networking. Analyzers are available for a variety of platforms, including Windows 7, Windows Server 2008, Windows Vista, Windows XP, UNIX, Linux, and Macintosh OS X versions. For a list of popular protocol analyzer solutions, refer to the document "Protocol Analyzer Vendors" on the same Web page where you find protocol trace files that accompany this book.

 Wireshark is a very popular protocol analyzer for Windows, UNIX, Linux, and Apple OS X systems. We use the Windows version in the examples in this book. Wireshark software is available as a free download from *www.wireshark.org*.

Protocol Analyzer Elements

Figure 1-3 depicts the basic elements of a protocol analyzer. Different analyzers offer different features and functions, but these are found on most:

- Promiscuous mode card and driver
- Packet filters
- Trace buffer
- Decodes
- Alarms
- Statistics

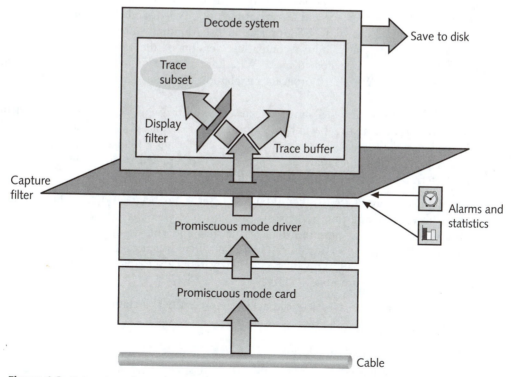

Figure 1-3 Network analyzer elements

Promiscuous Mode Card and Driver As shown in Figure 1-3, packets enter the analyzer system from the network where the analyzer is connected using a network interface card. The network interface card and driver used on the analyzer must support **promiscuous mode operation**. A card that runs in promiscuous mode can capture **broadcast packets, anycast packets, multicast packets,** and **unicast packets** sent to other devices, as well as error packets. For example, an analyzer running with a promiscuous mode card and driver can see **Ethernet collision fragments, oversized packets, undersized packets** (a.k.a. **runts**), and packets that end on an illegal boundary.

Ethernet collision fragments plus oversized and undersized packets reflect transmission errors and are normally ignored by network interface cards when they're not operating in promiscuous mode. An Ethernet collision fragment represents garbled traffic that appears on a network when two packets transmitted at about the same time run into one another, producing a random hash of signals. Collisions increase in frequency as traffic volumes go up, and it's important to be able to gather statistics about them. Oversized packets exceed the MTU for the type of network in use and generally indicate some kind of problem with a network interface card or its driver software. Undersized packets do not meet requirements for minimum packet sizes and also indicate potential hardware or driver problems. Packets that end on an illegal boundary do not close properly and may have been truncated or affected by hardware or driver problems. (For more information, see the IEEE 802.3 specifications at *www.ieee.org*.)

Most over-the-counter network cards or built-in network interfaces and drivers run in promiscuous mode and work with a protocol analyzer. In the case of the Wireshark software, the program can show errors only when it is used with the special WinPcap packet capture driver, also known as **pcap,** and a compatible NIC. Pcap stands for "packet capture" and is based on the well-known UNIX application programming interface (API), also known as libpcap. Winpcap is a Windows-compatible version of the same code, and it is thus an important component needed to make Wireshark work. For user convenience, WinPcap is now built into the Wireshark program installation process.

Packet Filters Figure 1-3 shows packets flowing through a **packet filter** that defines the type of packets the analyzer wants to capture. For example, if you are interested in the type of **broadcasts** that are crossing a network, you can set up a filter that allows only broadcast packets to flow into the analyzer. When filters are applied to incoming packets, they are often referred to as **capture filters,** or **pre-filters**.

You can also apply filters to a set of packets after it has been captured. This enables you to create subsets of interesting packets that are easier to view than the entire set. For example, if you set up a filter to capture broadcast packets and you do indeed capture 1,000 broadcasts, you can apply a second filter (a **display filter**) based on a specific source address to create a subset of broadcast packets. This may reduce the amount of packets you need to view to a reasonable amount.

Filters can be based on a variety of packet characteristics, including:

- Source data link address
- Destination data link address
- Source IP address

- Destination IP address
- Application or process

Trace Buffer The packets flow into the analyzer's **trace buffer**, a holding area for packets copied off the network. Typically, this is an area of memory set aside on the analyzer, although some analyzers allow you to configure a "direct to disk" save option. The packets in the trace buffer can be viewed immediately after they are captured or saved for viewing at a later time.

Many analyzers have a default trace buffer size of 4 MB. This is typically an adequate size for most analysis tasks. Consider how many 64-byte packets can fit into a 4-MB trace buffer. (Hint: the answer is 65,536, or 2^{16}.)

Decodes Decodes are applied to the packets that are captured in the trace buffer. They enable you to see the packets in a readable format, with the packet fields and values interpreted for you. Decodes are packet-translation tools.

For example, decodes can separate all the fields of a header within a packet, defining the source and destination IP addresses and the purpose of the packet. The Wireshark interface offers numerous display options for captured trace files. Figure 1-4 shows a decoded view on top (the packet list pane), a packet details pane in the middle, and an encoded view or byte-level data (in the packet bytes pane) on the bottom.

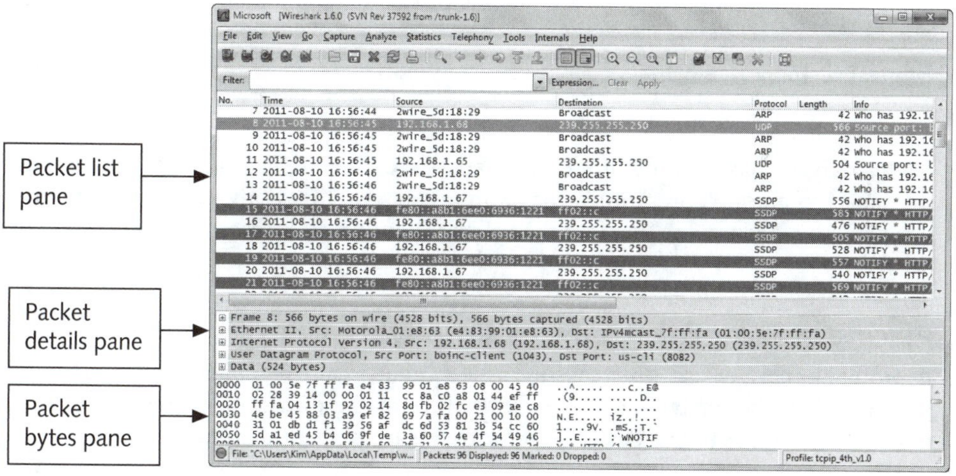

Figure 1-4 Difference between packet trace views
Source: Wireshark

Alarms Many analyzers have configurable **alarms** that indicate unusual network events or errors. Here are some alarms typically included with an analyzer product:

- Excessive broadcasts
- Utilization threshold exceeded
- Request denied
- Server down

Statistics Many analyzers also display **statistics** on network performance, such as the current packet-per-second rate or network utilization rates. Network administrators use these statistics to identify gradual changes in network operations or sudden spikes in network patterns. The Wireshark interface can provide many statistical displays. Figure 1-5 shows network traffic over time in packets per second. It is only one example of the many network statistics available from most protocol analyzers. Wireshark also offers a summary page, a protocol hierarchy listing, and all kinds of protocol-specific information that it gathers while capturing network traffic.

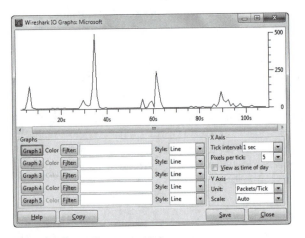

Figure 1-5 Traffic rate statistics
Source: Wireshark

Each analyzer has a different set of statistics capabilities. The ones mentioned here are the most common. For more information, refer to the analyzer manufacturer Web sites listed in the document "Protocol Analyzer Vendors," located with the student files for this book.

Placing a Protocol Analyzer on a Network

A protocol analyzer can only capture packets that it can see on the network. In some cases, you can place the analyzer on a network close to the device of interest. In other cases, you must reconfigure network devices to ensure the analyzer can capture packets.

On a network connected with hubs, you can place the analyzer anywhere on the network. All traffic is forwarded out of all ports on a hubbed network.

On a network connected with switches, an analyzer only sees multicast packets, broadcast packets, packets specifically directed to the analyzer device, and the initial packets sent to addresses that do not have ports identified yet (typically during the network's startup time). There are three methods for analyzing switched networks (see Figure 1-6):

- Hubbing out/tap device
- Port redirection
- Remote Monitoring (RMON)

Hubbing Out By placing a hub between a device of interest (such as a server) and the switch, and by connecting the analyzer to the hub, you can view all traffic to and from the server. In the same vein, a tap device splits the signal from a single switch port so that all traffic gets copied into two ports (one for the target device, one for the protocol analyzer).

A tap is required to analyze full-duplex communication. A tap effectively duplicates all RX (receive) and TX (transmit) communications down a single RX channel into the analyzer.

NOTE

Port Redirection Many switches can be configured to redirect (actually, to copy) the packets traveling through one port to another port. By placing your analyzer on the destination port, you can listen in on all the conversations that cross the network through the port of interest. Switch manufacturers refer to this process as port spanning or port mirroring.

Remote Monitoring (RMON) Remote Monitoring (RMON) uses Simple Network Management Protocol (SNMP) to collect traffic data at a remote switch and send the data to another device. The management device, in turn, decodes the traffic data and can even display entire packet decodes.

In Figure 1-6, method 1 depicts an analyzer capturing packets from a redirected port, method 2 depicts an RMON Agent loaded on the switch, and method 3 depicts an analyzer hubbed out.

For more information on switching technology, refer to *The All-New Switch Book: The Complete Guide to LAN Switching Technology* by Rich Seifert and James Edwards (John Wiley & Sons, 2nd Edition, 2008, ISBN: 0470287152).

NOTE

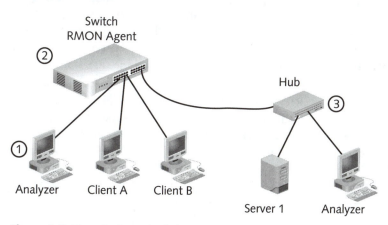

Figure 1-6 Three basic methods for analyzing a switched network
© Cengage Learning 2013

Chapter Summary

- TCP/IP was designed with the following goals in mind: (1) to support multiple, packet-switched pathways through the network so transmissions could survive all conceivable failures; (2) to permit dissimilar computer systems to easily exchange data; (3) to offer robust, reliable delivery services for both short- and long-haul communications; and (4) to provide comprehensive network access with global scope. Although TCP/IP has been revised and changed since its initial implementation, its ongoing success derives in no small part from meeting these goals.

- Initial implementations of TCP/IP were funded under the auspices of the Advanced Research Projects Agency (ARPA), a research and development arm of the U.S. Department of Defense (DoD). Until the late 1980s, the ARPANET—which evolved into what we know today as the Internet—remained largely in government hands, supported by government funding. However, the DoD's requirement that all communications on ARPANET use TCP/IP, as well as the more or less simultaneous inclusion of TCP/IP in 4.2BSD UNIX in 1983, helped makeTCP/IP and the Internet as nearly synonymous as we think of them today.

- Even though the U.S. government no longer has much involvement in the TCP/IP community (other than as an interested party), TCP/IP remains in the public domain as an open and collaborative set of standards and best practices. The documents that govern TCP/IP standards and practices are called RFCs, and the process of their creation, development, and approval involves representatives from government, industry, research, and academia. The standards creation and management processes fall within the purview of the IETF, and final approval of Internet Standards rests in its parent organization, the IAB. Although the process of creating such standards is rightfully called "rough consensus," it works well enough to define literally hundreds of protocols and services used every day on the Internet.

- In the approval process, Standard RFCs begin life as Proposed Standard documents. After discussion and debate, as well as demonstration that two or more separate reference implementations can successfully interoperate, RFCs become Draft Standards. After further discussion and revisions as well as approval from the parent working group within the IETF, the Draft Standard is turned over to the IAB for final approval. When the Draft Standard is approved, it becomes a Standard RFC (sometimes called an "Internet Standard").

- Another popular type of RFC is an informational (non-standard) RFC called a Best Current Practice, or BCP. Although a BCP does not have the force of a Standard RFC, it does provide useful information that represents best approaches to designing, configuring, implementing, or maintaining TCP/IP-based networks and related services. For that reason, BCPs are highly regarded and can be useful tools for network administrators seeking to make the most out of their TCP/IP networks.

- IPv6 supports an enormous number of network addresses and is taking root on the global Internet because the supply of IPv4 network addresses has been completely exhausted. Whereas IPv4 supports a 32-bit address space (for a total of just over four billion network addresses), IPv6 supports a 128-bit address space (for a staggering 3.4 * 10^{38} network addresses—roughly 8 * 10^{28} times as many addresses as for IPv4).

- In general, networking is a big, complex problem most easily solved if divided into a series of smaller, less complex, and interrelated problems. The ISO/OSI network reference model breaks networking into seven distinct layers that allow issues related to hardware, media, and signaling to be separated from issues related to software and services. Likewise, this model permits activities in software to be distinguished on the basis of machine-to-machine communications. Such communication involves handling information delivery from any sender to any receiver, moving large amounts of data across the network, and handling various issues related to ongoing communication, data formats, and application interfaces for network access. TCP/IP uses an older, simpler, four-layer model that lumps the latter three issues into a single layer, but it is otherwise very much like the ISO/OSI reference model.

- TCP/IP uses a variety of encapsulation techniques at its various layers to label the type of data contained in the contents, or payloads, of its PDUs. TCP/IP also uses numbering techniques to identify well-known protocols at the lower layers (protocol numbers) and to support ready access to well-known applications and services at upper layers (well-known ports). When a client makes a request to a server that requires an ongoing exchange of information, a listening process on the server creates a temporary connection that combines a computer's numeric IP address with a specific port address (called a socket address) for the process involved. This ensures that the right process on the right computer may be accessed when both sending and receiving machines.

- Protocol analysis is a process whereby a network interface is used to inspect all traffic moving across a segment of network medium. Protocol analyzers are software programs that can manage this task and can capture not only "healthy" (properly formed) traffic but erroneous (ill-formed) traffic. This lets protocol analyzers characterize network traffic on a descriptive basis (the protocols used, the active station addresses, the conversations, and the parties involved) and on a statistical basis (percentage of errors, percentage of traffic per protocol, peak loads, low loads, average loads, and so forth). Much of the remaining text depends on putting the topical and theoretical discussions about TCP/IP protocols together with the traces and decodes (formatted contents of packets) to see how theory and practice fit together.

Key Terms

4.2BSD   The version of the Berkeley Software Distribution (BSD) of UNIX that was the first to include a TCP/IP implementation.

Acceptable Use Policy (AUP)   A formal policy document that dictates what kinds of online behavior or system use are acceptable to the overall user community.

addressing   A method of assigning a unique symbolic name or numerical identifier to an individual network interface on a network segment to make every such interface uniquely identifiable (and addressable).

Advanced Research Projects Agency (ARPA)   An agency within the U.S. Department of Defense that funded forward-thinking research in computing technology.

alarm   Notification of events or errors on the network.

anycast packet   An IPv6 multicast method that permits multiple recipients to be designated for a single message, usually for a single cable segment or broadcast domain.

Application layer   The uppermost layer of the ISO/OSI network reference model (and the TCP/IP model) where the interface between the protocol suite and actual applications resides.

application process   A system process that represents a specific type of network application or service.

ARPANET   An experimental network, funded by ARPA, designed to test the feasibility of a platform-neutral, long-distance, robust, and reliable internetwork that provided the foundation for what we know today as the Internet.

Best Current Practice (BCP)   A specific type of Internet RFC document that outlines the best ways to design, implement, and maintain TCP/IP-based networks.

broadcast   A specific type of network transmission (and address) meant to be noticed and read by all recipients on any cable segment where that transmission appears; a way of reaching all addresses on any network.

broadcast packet   A type of network transmission intended for delivery to all devices on the network. The Ethernet broadcast address is 0xFF-FF-FF-FF-FF-FF for IPv6 and 255.255.255.255 for IPv4.

cable segment   Any single collection of network media and attached devices that fits on a single piece of network cable or within a single network device, such as a hub or, in a virtual equivalent, a local area network emulation environment on a switch.

capture filter   A method used to identify specific packets that should be captured into a trace buffer based on some packet characteristic, such as source or destination address.

Carrier Sense Multiple Access with Collision Detection (CSMA/CD)   A formal name for Ethernet's contention management approach. CSMA means "listen before attempting to send" (to make sure no later message tramples on an earlier one) and "listen while sending" (to make sure messages sent at roughly the same time don't collide with one another).

Centre Europeen de Researche Nucleaire (CERN)   The European Organization for Nuclear Research, where Tim Berners-Lee invented protocols and services for the World Wide Web between 1989 and 1991.

checkpoint   A point in time at which all system state and information is captured and saved so that, after a subsequent failure in systems or communications, operations can resume at that point in time, with no further loss of data or information.

checksum   A special mathematical value that represents the contents of a message so precisely that any change in the contents will cause a change in the checksum—calculated before and after network transmission of data and then compared. If transmitted and calculated checksums agree, the assumption is that the data arrived unaltered.

Commercial Internet Exchange (CIX)   An early consortium of commercial Internet users that pioneered the extension of Internet use to e-commerce and business communications.

congestion control   A TCP mechanism, also available from other protocols, that permits network hosts to exchange information about their ability to handle traffic volumes and thereby causes senders to decrease or increase the frequency and size of their upcoming communications.

connectionless A networking protocol that does not require network senders and receivers to exchange information about their availability or ability to communicate; also known as "best-effort delivery."

connection-oriented A type of networking protocol that relies on explicit communications and negotiations between sender and receiver to manage delivery of data between the two parties.

daemon Taken from James Clerk Maxwell's famous physics idea, a daemon is a computer process whose job is to "listen" in on connection attempts for one or more specific network services and hand off all valid attempts to temporary connections known as sockets.

data frame The basic PDU at the Data Link layer, which represents what is transmitted or received as a pattern of bits on a network interface.

datagram The basic protocol data unit at the TCP/IP Network Access layer. Used by connectionless protocols at the Transport layer, a datagram simply adds a header to the PDU, supplied from whichever Application layer protocol or service uses a connectionless protocol, such as UDP; hence, UDP is also known as a datagram service.

Data Link layer Layer 2 of the ISO/OSI network reference model. The Data Link layer is responsible for enabling reliable transmission of data through the Physical layer at the sending end and for checking such reliability upon reception at the receiving end.

data segment The basic PDU for TCP at the Transport layer. *See also* segment.

decode The interpreted value of a PDU, or a field within a PDU, performed by a protocol analyzer or similar software package.

decoding The process of interpreting the fields and contents of a packet and presenting the packet in a readable format.

Defense Information Systems Agency (DISA) The DoD agency that took over operation of the Internet when ARPA surrendered its control in 1983.

demultiplexing The process of breaking up a single stream of incoming packets on a computer and directing its components to the various active TCP/IP processes based on socket addresses in the TCP or UDP headers.

destination port number A port address for incoming TCP/IP communication that identifies a target application or service process.

display filters Filters that are applied to the packets that reside in a trace buffer, for the purpose of viewing only the packets of interest.

divide and conquer A computer design approach that consists of decomposing a big, complex problem into a series of smaller, less complex, and interrelated problems, each of which can be solved more or less independently of the others.

domain The name of a first-level entry in the domain name hierarchy, such as *cengage.com* or *whitehouse.gov*.

Draft Standard A Standard RFC that has gone through the draft process, been approved, and for which two reference implementations must be shown to work together before it can move on to Internet Standard status.

dynamically assigned port address A temporary TCP or UDP port number allocated to permit a client and server to exchange data with each other only as long as their connection remains active.

encapsulation Enclosure of data from an upper-layer protocol between a header and a trailer (the trailer is optional) for the current layer to identify sender and receiver and, possibly, include data integrity check information.

Ethernet A network access protocol based on carrier sense, multiple access, and collision detection.

Ethernet collision fragments The garbled traffic on a network produced when two packets transmitted at about the same time collide, resulting in a hodgepodge of signals.

fragmentation The process of dividing a packet into multiple smaller packets to cross a link that supports an MTU than the link where the packet originated.

frame The basic Data Link layer PDU for the ISO/OSI reference model.

header That portion of a PDU that precedes the actual content for the PDU and usually identifies sender and receiver, protocols in use, and other information necessary to establish context for senders and receivers.

Historic Standard An Internet RFC that was superseded by a newer, more current version.

host TCP/IP terminology for any computer with one or more valid TCP/IP addresses (hence, reachable on a TCP/IP-based network). A host also can be a computer that offers TCP/IP services to clients.

Hypertext Transfer Protocol (HTTP) The TCP/IP Application layer protocol and service that supports access to the World Wide Web.

IEEE 802 A project undertaken by the IEEE in 1980 that covers Physical and Data Link layers for networking technologies in general (802.1 and 802.2), plus specific networking technologies, such as Ethernet (802.3).

Institute of Electrical and Electronic Engineers (IEEE) An international organization that sets standards for electrical and electronic equipment, including network interfaces and communications technologies.

International Organization for Standardization (ISO) An international standards organization based in Geneva, Switzerland, that sets standards for information technology and networking equipment, protocols, and communications technologies.

International Organization for Standardization Open Systems Interconnection *See* International Organization for Standardization, and Open Systems Interconnection.

Internet Architecture Board (IAB) The organization within the Internet Society that governs the actions of both the IETF and the IRTF and has final approval authority for Internet Standards.

Internet Corporation for Assigned Names and Numbers (ICANN) The organization within the Internet Society responsible for proper assignment of all domain names and numeric IP addresses for the global Internet. ICANN works with private companies called name registrars to manage domain names and with ISPs to manage assignment of numeric IP addresses.

Internet Engineering Task Force (IETF) The organization within the Internet Society that's responsible for all currently used Internet Standards, protocols, and services as well as for managing the development and maintenance of Internet Requests for Comments (RFCs).

Internet Network Information Center (InterNIC) A quasi-governmental agency that was responsible for assigned names and numbers on the Internet (this responsibility now falls on ICANN).

Internet Protocol (IP) The primary Network layer protocol in the TCP/IP suite. IP manages routing and delivery for traffic on TCP/IP-based networks.

Internet Protocol version 4 (IPv4)   The original version of IP that's still in widespread public use, although IPv6 is currently fully specified and moving into global deployment and use.

Internet Protocol version 6 (IPv6)   The latest version of IP that's moving into global deployment and use (IPv4 remains the predominant TCP/IP version in use but will slowly be supplanted by IPv6).

Internet Research Task Force (IRTF)   The forward-looking research and development arm of the Internet Society. The IRTF reports to the IAB for direction and governance.

Internet Society (ISOC)   The parent organization under which the rest of the Internet governing bodies fall. ISOC is a user-oriented, public-access organization that solicits end-user participation and input to help set future Internet policy and direction.

Internet Standard   An RFC document that specifies the rules, structure, and behavior of a current Internet protocol or service. Also called a Standard RFC.

internetwork   Literally, a "network of networks," an internetwork is better understood as a collection of multiple interconnected physical networks that together behave as a single logical network (of which the Internet is the prime example).

ISO/OSI network reference model   The official name for the seven-layer network reference model used to describe how networks operate and behave.

layer   A single component or facet in a networking model that handles one particular aspect of network access or communications.

local area network (LAN)   A single network cable segment, subnet, or logical network community that represents a collection of machines that can communicate with one another more or less directly (using MAC addresses).

maximum transmission unit (MTU)   The biggest single chunk of data that can be transferred across any particular type of network medium—for example, 1518 bytes is the MTU for conventional Ethernet.

media flow control   The management of data transmission rates between two devices across a local network medium that guarantees the receiver can accept and process input before it arrives from the sender.

multicast packet   A packet sent to a group of devices, often multiple routers.

multiplexing   The process whereby multiple individual data streams from Application layer processes are joined together for transmission by a specific TCP/IP transport protocol through the IP protocol.

National Center for Supercomputing Applications (NCSA)   An arm of the University of Illinois at Urbana-Champaign, where supercomputer research is undertaken and where the first graphical Web browser, Mosaic, was developed and released in 1993.

National Science Foundation (NSF)   A U.S. government agency charged with oversight and support for government-funded scientific research and development. *See also* NSFNET.

network analysis   Another term for protocol analysis.

Network File System (NFS)   A TCP/IP-based, network-distributed file system that permits users to treat files and directories on machines elsewhere on a network as an extension of their local desktop file systems.

network interface controller (NIC)   A hardware device used to permit a computer to attach to and communicate with a local area network.

Network layer Layer 3 of the ISO/OSI network reference model. The Network layer handles logical addresses associated with individual machines on a network by correlating human-readable names for such machines with unique, machine-readable numeric addresses. It uses addressing information to route a PDU from a sender to a receiver when the source and destination do not reside on the same physical network segment.

network reference model *See* ISO/OSI network reference model.

network services A TCP/IP term for a protocol/service combination that operates at the Application layer in the TCP/IP network model.

NSFNET A public network operated by the National Science Foundation in the 1980s to support the Internet backbone.

Open Systems Interconnection (OSI) The name of an open-standard internetworking initiative undertaken in the 1980s, primarily in Europe, and originally intended to supersede TCP/IP. Technical and political problems prevented this anticipated outcome from materializing, but the ISO/OSI reference model is a legacy of this effort.

oversized packets Packets that exceed the MTU for the network and usually point to a problem with a NIC or its driver software.

packet A generic term for a PDU at any layer in a networking model. The term is properly applied to PDUs at Layer 3, or the TCP/IP Internet layer.

packet filter A specific collection of inclusion or exclusion rules that is applied to a stream of network packets and determines what is captured (and what is ignored) from the original input stream.

packet header *See* header.

packet-switched network A network in which data packets may take any usable path between sender and receiver, where sender and receiver are identified by unique network addresses and there's no requirement that all packets follow the same path in transit (although they often do).

packet trailer *See* trailer.

payload That portion of a PDU that contains information intended for delivery to an application or to a higher-layer protocol (depending on where in the stack the PDU is situated).

pcap A generic term (short for "protocol capture") for a special network interface driver designed to permit capture of all network traffic in promiscuous mode while running. Though originally associated with the tcpdump open source command-line protocol analyzer, pcap is widely used in protocol analyzers today, including the one chosen as a teaching tool for this book, the Wireshark protocol analyzer.

peer layers Analogous layers in the protocol stacks on a sender and a receiver; the receiving layer usually reverses whatever operations the sending layer performs (which is what makes those layers peers).

Physical layer Layer 1 in the ISO/OSI network reference model. The Physical layer is where connections, communications, and interfaces—hardware and signaling requirements—are handled.

Point-to-Point Protocol (PPP) A Layer 2 or TCP/IP Network Interface layer protocol that permits a client and a server to establish a communications link that can accommodate a variety of higher-layer protocols, including IP, AppleTalk, SNA, IPX/SPX, NetBEUI, and many others. Today's most widely used serial line protocol for making Internet connections.

point-to-point transmission A type of network communication in which pairs of devices establish a communications link to exchange data with one another; the most common type of connection used when communicating with an Internet service provider.

Point-to-Point Tunneling Protocol (PPTP) A Layer 2 or TCP/IP Network Interface layer protocol that allows a client and a server to establish a secure, encrypted communications link for just about any kind of PPP traffic.

port number A 16-bit number that identifies either a well-known application service or a dynamically assigned port number for a transitory sender-receiver exchange of data through TCP or UDP. Also referred to as a port address.

pre-filter A type of data filter applied to a raw input stream in a protocol analyzer that selects only packets that meet its criteria for capture and retention. Because it is applied before data is captured, it's called a pre-filter.

Presentation layer Layer 6 of the ISO/OSI reference model. The Presentation layer is where generic network data formats are translated into platform-specific data formats for incoming data and vice versa for outgoing data. This is also the layer where optional encryption or compression services may be applied (or reversed).

Process layer A synonym for the TCP/IP Application layer, where high-level protocols and services, such as FTP and Telnet, operate.

promiscuous mode operation Network interface card and driver operation used to capture broadcast packets, multicast packets, packets sent to other devices, and error packets.

Proposed Standard An intermediate step for standards-level RFCs in which a Draft Standard goes through initial review, with two or more reference implementations to demonstrate interoperability between those implementations.

protocol A precise set of standards that governs communications between computers on a network. Many protocols function in one or more layers of the OSI reference model.

protocol analysis The process of capturing packets off the network for the purpose of gathering communication statistics, observing trends, and examining communication sequences.

protocol data unit (PDU) At any layer in a networking model, a PDU represents the package for data at that layer, including a header, a payload, and in some cases, a trailer.

protocol number An 8-bit numeric identifier associated with some specific TCP/IP protocol.

protocol stack A specific implementation of a protocol suite on a computer, including a network interface, necessary drivers, and whatever protocol and service implementations are necessary to enable the computer to use a specific protocol suite to communicate across the network.

protocol suite A named family of networking protocols, such as TCP/IP, IPX/SPX, or NetBEUI, where each such family enables computers to communicate across a network.

reassembly The process applied at the Transport layer in which messages segmented into multiple chunks for transmission across the network are put back together in the proper order for delivery to an application on the receiving end. The IP Fragment Offset field (discussed in Chapter 3) is used to identify the order of the fragments for reassembly.

registered port A TCP or UDP port number in the range from 1024 to 65535 and associated with a specific Application layer protocol or service. IANA maintains a registered port number list at *www.iana.org.*

Remote Monitoring (RMON) A TCP/IP Application layer protocol designed to support remote monitoring and management of networking devices, such as hubs, servers, and routers.

Request for Comments (RFCs) IETF standards documents that specify or describe best practices, provide information about the Internet, or specify an Internet protocol or service.

routing The process whereby a packet makes its way from a sender to a receiver based on known paths (or routes) from the sending network to the receiving network.

runts *See* undersized packets.

segment The name of the PDU for the TCP protocol in a TCP/IP environment.

segmentation The process whereby TCP takes a message larger than an underlying network medium's MTU and breaks it up into a numbered sequence of chunks less than or equal to the MTU in size.

session A temporary, but ongoing, exchange of messages between a sender and a receiver on a network.

Session layer Layer 5 in the ISO/OSI reference model. The Session layer handles setup, maintenance, and teardown of ongoing exchanges of messages between pairs of hosts on a network.

socket *See* socket address.

socket address A numeric TCP/IP address that concatenates a network host's numeric IP address (first 4 bytes) with the port address for some specific process or service on that host (last two bytes) to uniquely identify that process across the entire Internet.

source port number The sender's port address for a TCP or UDP PDU.

statistics Short- or long-term historical information regarding network communications and performance, captured by a protocol analyzer or other similar software.

Systems Network Architecture (SNA) The name of a protocol suite developed by IBM for use in its proprietary mainframe- and minicomputer-based networking environments.

TCP/IP *See* Transmission Control Protocol/Internet Protocol.

trace buffer An area of memory or hard disk space set aside for the storage of packets captured off the network by a protocol analyzer.

trailer An optional, concluding portion of a PDU that usually contains data integrity check information for the preceding content in that PDU.

Transmission Control Protocol (TCP) A robust, reliable, connection-oriented protocol that operates at the Transport layer in both the TCP/IP and ISO/OSI reference models and that gives TCP/IP part of its name.

Transmission Control Protocol/Internet Protocol (TCP/IP) The name of the standard protocols and services in use on the Internet, denoted by the names of the two key constituent protocols: theTransmission Control Protocol, or TCP, and the Internet Protocol, or IP.

Transport layer Layer 4 of the ISO/OSI network reference model and the third layer of the TCP/IP network model. The Transport layer handles delivery of data from sender to receiver.

undersized packets Packets that are below minimum packet size requirements and point to potential hardware or driver problems.

unicast packet A packet sent to a single device on the network.

Uniform Resource Locator (URL) Web terminology for an address that specifies the protocol (http://), location (domain name), directory (/directory-name/), and filename (example.html) so that a browser can access a resource.

Virtual Private Network (VPN) A network connection (containing one or more packaged protocols) between a specific sender and receiver in which information sent is often encrypted. A VPN uses public networks—like the Internet—to deliver secure, private information from sender to receiver.

well-known port number A 16-bit number that identifies a preassigned value associated with some well-known Internet protocol or service that operates at the TCP/IP Application layer. Most well-known port numbers fall in the range from 0 to 1024, but IANA (see *www.iana.org*) also documents registered port numbers above that range that behave likewise. Also called a well-known port address.

well-known protocol An 8-bit number in the header of an IP packet that identifies the protocol in use, as per IANA (at *www.iana.org*).

well-known service A synonym for a recognizable TCP/IP protocol or service; these assignments are documented at the IANA site (*www.iana.org*).

X.25 A popular standard for packet-switched data networks, originally defined by the InternationalTelephony Union (ITU), that's widely used for data communications networks outside North America.

Review Questions

1. Which of the following items represent design goals that motivated the development of TCP/IP? (Choose all that apply.)
   a. robust network architecture
   b. reliable delivery mechanisms
   c. ability of dissimilar systems to exchange data
   d. support for long-haul connections
   e. high performance

2. What version of IP supports 128-bit addresses?
   a. IPv1
   b. IPv2
   c. IPv4
   d. IPv6

3. Which of the following milestone events for TCP/IP occurred in 1983? (Choose all that apply.)
   a. NSF launches the NSFNET.
   b. The Department of Defense mandates TCP/IP as the "official ARPANET protocol."
   c. TCP/IP appears in the 4.2BSD UNIX distribution.
   d. Initial development of name server technology occurs.

4. Which of the following organizations develops and maintains RFCs?

    a. ISOC

    b. IAB

    c. IRTF

    d. IETF

5. Which of the following organizations manages Internet domain names and network addresses?

    a. ICANN

    b. IETF

    c. IRTF

    d. ISOC

6. What is the title of RFC 5000?

    a. Index of Official Protocols

    b. Index of Internet Official Protocols

    c. Internet Official Protocol Standards

    d. The Internet Standards Process

7. Which of the following steps must a Standard RFC go through to become an official standard? (Choose all that apply and list them in the correct order of occurrence.)

    a. Draft Standard

    b. Historic Standard

    c. Proposed Standard

    d. Standard (sometimes called "Internet Standard")

8. A Best Current Practice (BCP) RFC is a special form of Standard RFC. True or false?

9. List the seven layers of the ISO/OSI network reference model in ascending order, starting with Layer 1.

    a. Application

    b. Data Link

    c. Network

    d. Physical

    e. Presentation

    f. Session

    g. Transport

10. Which of the following statements represent benefits of a layered approach to networking? (Choose all that apply.)

    a. takes a big problem and breaks it into a series of smaller interrelated problems

    b. allows individual layers to be insulated from one another

    c. permits expertise to be applied from different disciplines for different layers

    d. permits hardware issues to be kept separate from software issues

11. Which of the following terms represent parts of a PDU that are always present in any PDU? (Choose all that apply.)

    a. header

    b. payload

    c. checksum

    d. trailer

12. Which of the following components operate at the Physical layer? (Choose all that apply.)

    a. network interface controllers (NICs)

    b. segmentation and reassembly

    c. connectors

    d. cables

13. What is the common name for PDUs at the Data Link layer?

    a. frames

    b. packets

    c. segments

    d. Data Link PDUs

14. What functions does the Session layer provide?

    a. segmentation and reassembly

    b. session setup, maintenance, and teardown

    c. checkpoint controls

    d. data format conversions

15. Which of the following TCP/IP network model layers maps most nearly to single layers in the ISO/OSI network reference model?

    a. TCP/IP Network Access layer

    b. TCP/IP Internet layer

    c. TCP/IP Transport layer

    d. TCP/IP Application layer

16. Which of the following two TCP/IP protocols operate at the TCP/IP Transport layer?

    a. ARP

    b. PPP

    c. TCP

    d. UDP

    e. XNET

17. In UNIX terminology, a listener process that operates on a server to handle incoming requests for services is called a _____ .

    a. listener

    b. monitor

    c. daemon

    d. service

18. The process of combining multiple outgoing protocol streams at the Transport and Network layers in TCP/IP is called _____ .

    a. folding

    b. multiplexing

    c. unfolding

    d. demultiplexing

19. On any system, only those protocol numbers for protocols that are actually in use must be defined on that system. True or false?

20. The purpose of a TCP/IP port number is to identify which aspect of a system's operation for incoming and outgoing protocol data?

    a. Network layer protocol in use

    b. Transport layer protocol in use

    c. sending or receiving application process

    d. none of the above

21. Which of the following terms is a synonym for a dynamically assigned port address, used to service a temporary TCP/IP connection for data exchange?

    a. protocol number

    b. well-known port address

    c. registered port address

    d. socket address

22. Which of the following activities may occur during the protocol analysis process? (Choose all that apply.)

    a. tapping into network communications

    b. capturing packets "off the wire"

    c. gathering statistics

    d. decoding packets into readable form

    e. retransmitting captured packets for testing

23. Why is promiscuous mode important for protocol analysis?

    a. It isn't.

    b. It allows the protocol analyzer to capture and inspect all traffic on the network medium, including errors and malformed packets.

    c. It bypasses normal packet-level security on a network.

    d. It enables the protocol analyzer to gather statistics.

24. A packet filter that's applied to incoming data in a protocol analyzer may be called a _____ . (Choose all that apply.)

    a. capture filter

    b. data filter

    c. pre-filter

    d. post-filter

25. Which of the following features are typical for most protocol analyzers? (Choose all that apply.)

    a. Packet filters may be applied to incoming data before capture or to store data after capture.

    b. Decodes may be applied to packets in the trace buffer.

    c. Alarms may be set to flag unusual network events or conditions.

    d. Packet filters display various statistical reports and graphs based on traffic analysis.

    e. Packet filters include built-in trend analysis and capacity-planning tools.

Hands-On Projects

The following Hands-On Projects assume you are working in a Windows 7 or Windows Vista environment. See the Preface in this book for details about system requirements.

Hands-On Project 1-1: Install Wireshark

Time Required: 15 minutes

Objective: Install Wireshark for use in the course.

Description: This project shows you how to install the Wireshark protocol analyzer software on your computer. Wireshark automatically installs WinPcap, a Windows driver for capturing network traffic.

1. Download the Wireshark installation file from the *Guide to TCP/IP* companion Web site or download the latest version of Wireshark from *www.wireshark.org*. If you use a newer version than Wireshark 1.6.0, you may need to modify the steps in this Hands-On Project to match your version of the software. Save the Wireshark installation file to a local directory. This may take a while, even on a broadband connection, because the executable version of version 1.6.0 is 22 MB.

2. When the download is complete, open the target directory and double-click the installation file.

3. If the Windows User Account Control window appears, click **Yes** or **Continue**.

4. Click **Next** on the Wireshark Welcome screen.

5. Click **I Agree** to the licensing agreement.

6. In the Choose Components screen, you may leave the default options selected, as shown in Figure 1-7. Click **Next**.

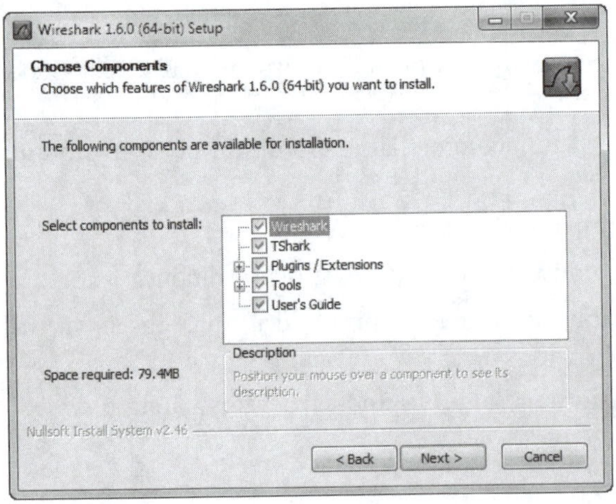

Figure 1-7 Choose Components screen
Source: Wireshark

7. In the Select Additional Tasks screen, you may leave the default options selected, as shown in Figure 1-8. Click **Next**.

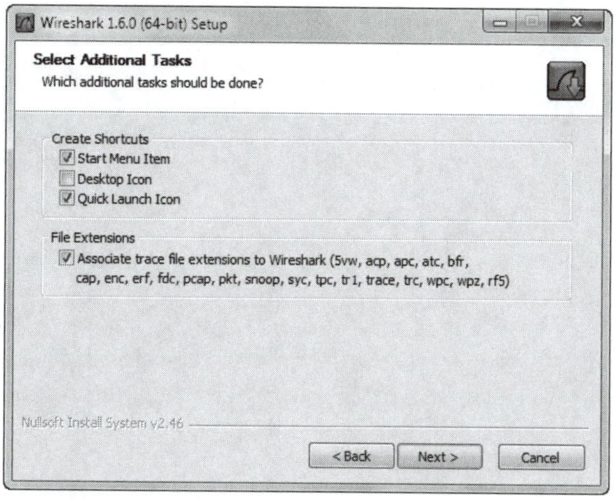

Figure 1-8 Select Additional Tasks screen
Source: Wireshark

8. In the Install Location Screen, leave the default location or click **Browse** and navigate to a new location in which to install Wireshark. Click **Next**.

9. Wireshark prompts you to install WinPcap if it's not already installed (see Figure 1-9). Click **Install** or follow the instructions to uninstall an existing version if it's older than the version Wireshark wants to install.

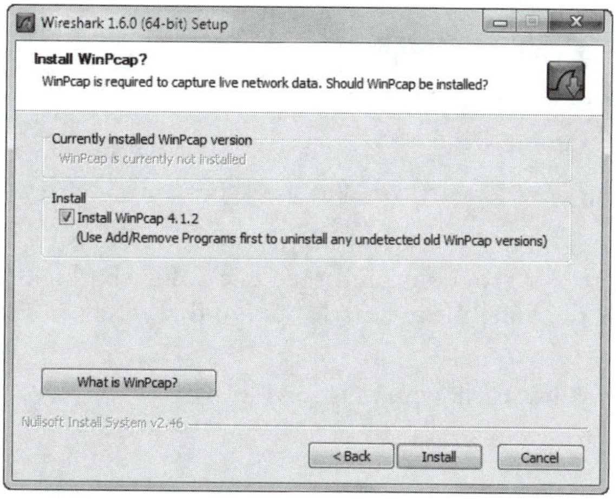

Figure 1-9 Install WinPcap? screen
Source: Wireshark

10. The WinPcap Installer screen appears. Click **Next**.

11. In the WinPcap Welcome screen, click **Next**.

12. Click **I Agree** to the WinPcap licensing agreement.

13. In the Installation Options screen (see Figure 1-10), leave the default option(s) and click **Install**.

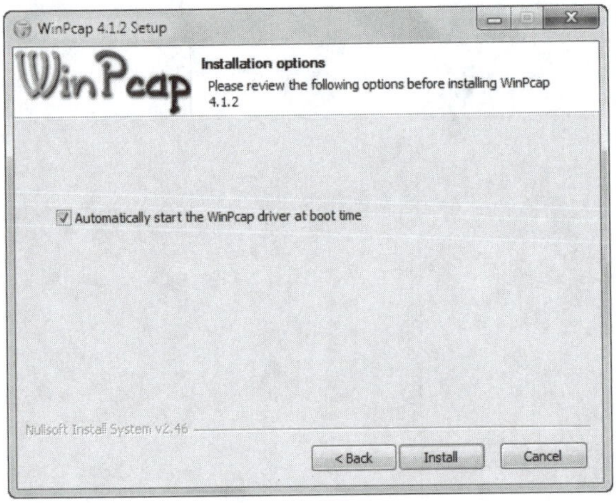

Figure 1-10 Installation options screen
Source: Wireshark

14. In the final WinPcap installation screen, click **Finish**. The Wireshark installation proceeds.

15. When the Wireshark Installation Complete screen appears, click **Next**.

16. The final screen gives an option to run Wireshark. Click **Finish** to close this window.

Hands-On Project 1-2: Start Wireshark

Time Required: 1 minute

Objective: Start the Wireshark program in Windows.

Description: This project shows you how to start the Wireshark program in a few different ways.

1. Click the **Start** button, point to **All Programs**, and then click **Wireshark**. Alternately, click **Start**, type **Wireshark** in the Start menu search box, and then click **Wireshark** in the resulting list.

2. The main Wireshark window opens, as shown in Figure 1-11.

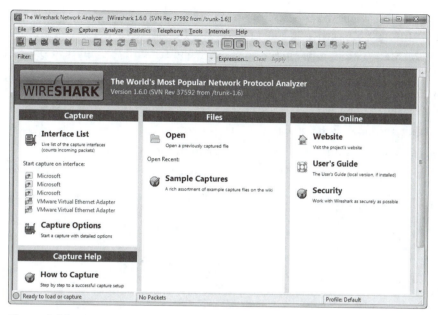

Figure 1-11 Main Wireshark window
Source: Wireshark

3. Leave the Wireshark window open if you are continuing to Hands-On Project 1-3.

Hands-On Project 1-3: Capture Basic Packets

Time Required: 10 minutes

Objective: Learn how to capture packets in Wireshark.

Description: This project shows you how to capture basic packets using Wireshark.

1. Follow the steps in Hands-On Project 1-2 to launch the Wireshark program if it is not already open.

2. Click **Capture** on the menu bar, and then click **Interfaces**.

3. The Capture Interfaces window appears, as shown in Figure 1-12. Several network interfaces may also appear. Locate the first one showing real-time packet counts under the Packets column, and then click **Start**.

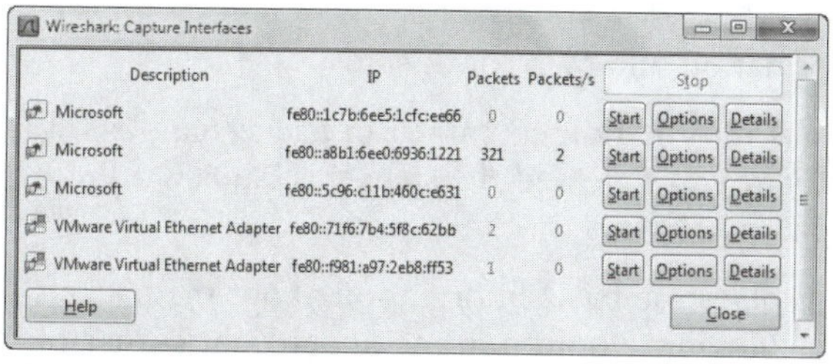

Figure 1-12 Wireshark Capture Interfaces window
Source: Wireshark

4. The Capturing window appears. If no traffic shows up in the Capturing window, follow Steps 5 through 8 to generate some packets from your workstation.

5. Click the **Start** button, type **cmd** in the Start menu search box, and then press **Enter**. A command prompt window opens.

6. Type **ftp server1** and then press **Enter**. Assuming you do not have an FTP server named server1, your request fails.

7. Type **quit** and press **Enter** to exit the FTP program.

8. Type **exit** and press **Enter** to close the command prompt window.

9. Click the **Stop** icon in the Capturing window when finished, as shown in Figure 1-13.

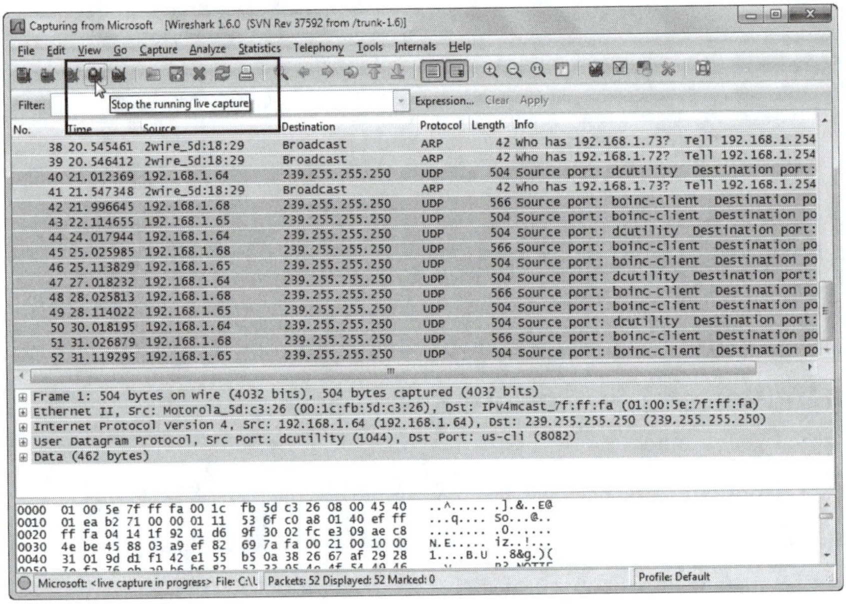

Figure 1-13 Stopping a Wireshark live capture
Source: Wireshark

10. Leave Wireshark open and proceed immediately to the next project.

Hands-On Project 1-4: Explore Basic Packets and Statistics

Time Required: 30–45 minutes

Objective: Learn about packet information and Wireshark statistics.

Description: This project explains the information contained in packets and shows you how to read Wireshark statistics. It assumes you followed the steps in Hands-On Project 1-3 and that the Wireshark program is open.

1. The Wireshark window now displays the basic information about the packets you captured. If necessary, click the **Maximize** button in the upper-right corner of the window to maximize the window. Click the down scroll arrow to view the entire list of packets (if they scroll out of view).

2. Scroll through the Source column in the packet list pane (the uppermost Wireshark window) to view the list of devices for which the Wireshark analyzer captured packets. Your screen may resemble Figure 1-14. Do you recognize your IP addresses? Do you see any broadcast addresses?

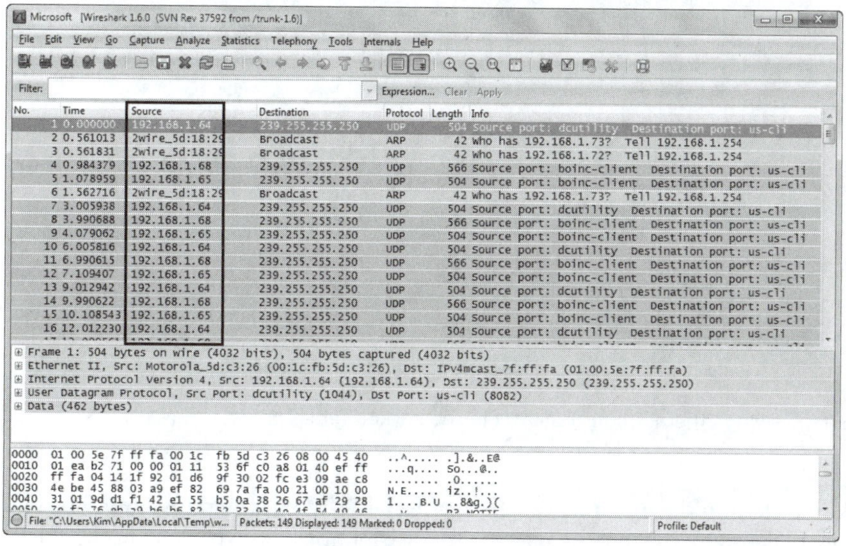

Figure 1-14 Viewing information in the Source column of the packet list pane
Source: Wireshark

3. Scroll through the Protocol column to view the protocols identified by Wireshark.

4. Click **Statistics** on the menu bar at the top of the Wireshark window, then click **Conversations** to view the conversations identified by Wireshark. An example of a Conversations window is shown in Figure 1-15. Click **Close** to close the Conversations window.

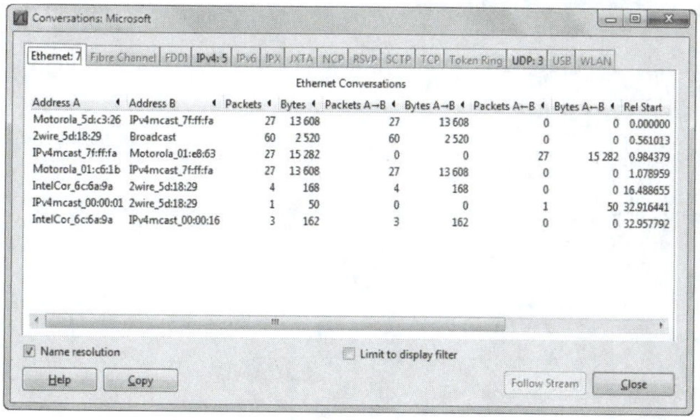

Figure 1-15 Viewing information in the Conversations window
Source: Wireshark

5. View the associated values in the Ethernet II field of the packet details pane (middle Wireshark window, as shown in Figure 1-16) to identify the MAC address of the workstation that sent the packet to the network. (Click the plus sign to expand the Ethernet II field.)

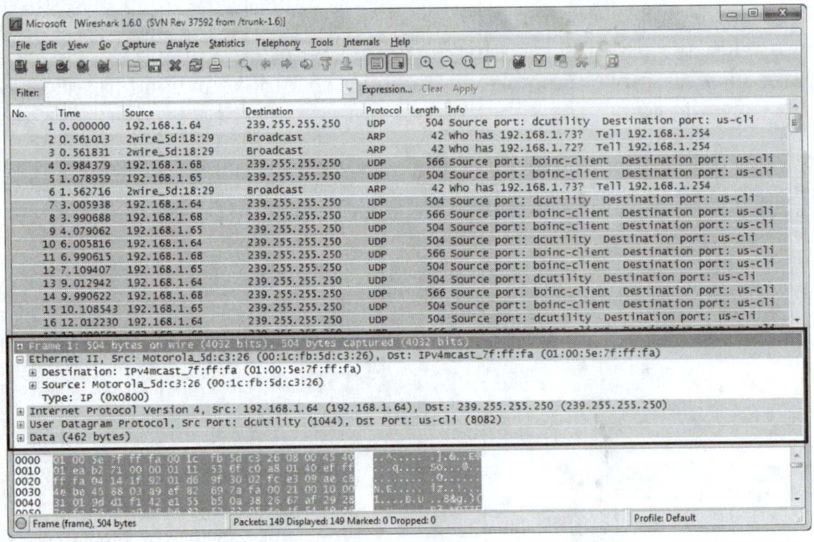

Figure 1-16 Viewing Ethernet II information in the packet details pane
Source: Wireshark

6. Click **Statistics** on the menu bar at the top of the Wireshark window and then click **Protocol Hierarchy** to view the packet size distribution of the packets in the trace buffer, as shown in Figure 1-17. Packet sizes are listed in bytes. Which packet size is most common in your trace buffer? Click **Close** to close the Protocol Hierarchy Statistics window.

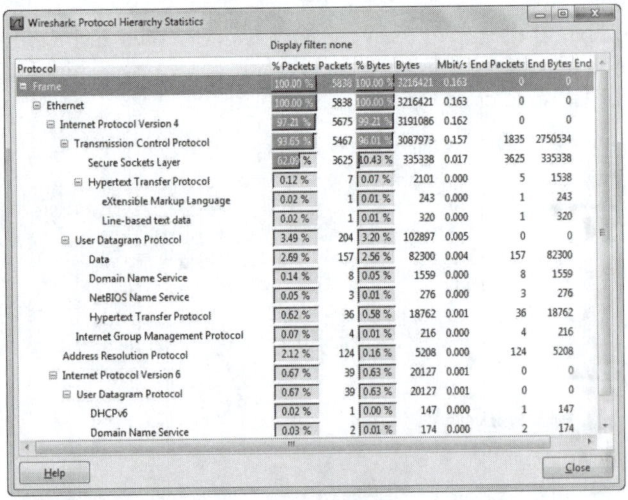

Figure 1-17 Viewing protocol hierarchy information
Source: Wireshark

7. Browse the packet bytes pane at the bottom of the Wireshark window, as shown in Figure 1-18. It contains a summary of information about the trace buffer contents. Can you identify the type of communications seen in the trace buffer?

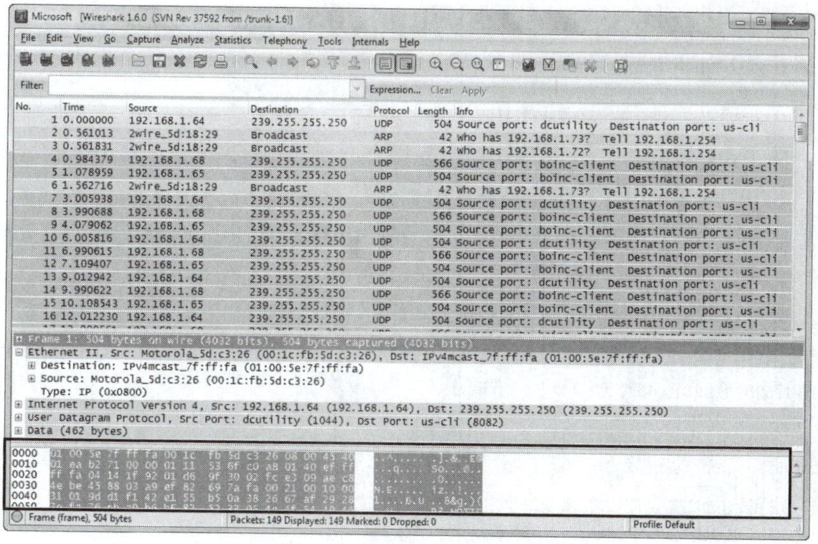

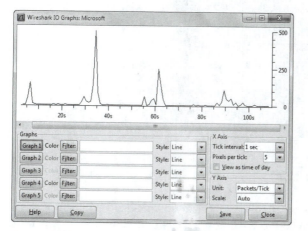

Figure 1-18 Viewing information in the packet bytes pane
Source: Wireshark

8. Click **Statistics** on the menu bar at the top of the Wireshark window and then click **IO Graphs** to view a graph that illustrates the number of packets captured per second by Wireshark, as shown in Figure 1-19. (To see a graph of the number of bytes captured per second, in the Y Axis section of the IO Graphs window, click the **Unit** list arrow, and then choose **Bytes/Tick**.) Click **Close** to close the IO Graphs window.

Figure 1-19 Viewing IO Graph statistics
Source: Wireshark

9. Close the Wireshark window by clicking **File, Quit,** and **Continue without Saving.** You'll focus on the Filter functionality in the next project.

Hands-On Project 1-5: Select a Filter and Capture Packets

Time Required: 10 minutes

Objective: Learn how to select a filter in Wireshark.

Description: This project helps you learn how to select a filter in Wireshark to narrow the types of packets being captured.

1. Follow the steps in Hands-On Project 1-2 to start the Wireshark program if it is not already open.

2. Click **Capture** on the menu bar and then click **Options**.

3. The Capture Options window appears. Choose your active interface from the Interface pull-down menu (shown in Figure 1-20).

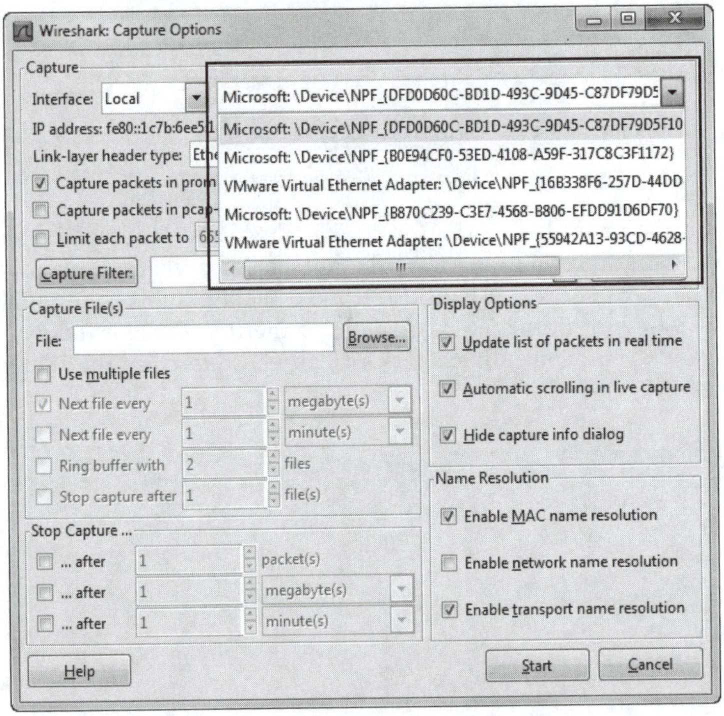

Figure 1-20 Selecting an interface
Source: Wireshark

4. Click **Capture Filter** to view available pre-built filters included with the Wireshark product. Click the filter named **No ARP and no DNS**, as shown in Figure 1-21. This sets a filter to ignore ARP and DNS traffic. Click **OK**.

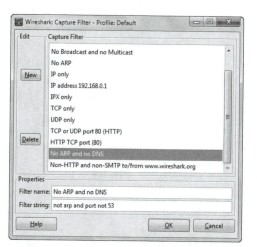

Figure 1-21 Selecting a pre-built filter
Source: Wireshark

5. In the Capture Options window, click **Start** to begin capturing broadcast packets.

6. Once data has accumulated, click **Stop** in the Capturing window to view the packets captured in this process. Examine the types of broadcasts identified in the Protocol column.

If no packets appear in the Capturing window, follow Steps 7 through 10 to generate traffic from the command prompt window.

7. Click **Start,** type **cmd** in the Start menu search box, and then select **cmd.exe** from the resulting list. A command prompt window opens.

8. Type **ftp server1** and then press **Enter**. Assuming you do not have an FTP server named server1, your request fails.

9. Type **quit** and press **Enter** to exit the FTP program.

10. Type **exit** and then press **Enter** to close the command prompt window.

Hands-On Project 1-6: Create a Display Filter

Time Required: 15 minutes

Objective: Learn how to create a display filter in Wireshark. A display filter reduces the amount of information that Wireshark displays from a trace file.

Description: This project shows you how to create a filter in Wireshark that displays only IPv6-related traffic.

1. Follow the steps in Hands-On Project 1-2 to start the Wireshark program if it is not already open.

2. Click **Analyze** on the menu bar, and then click **Display Filters**. The Display Filter dialog box appears.

3. Click the **New** button.

4. Highlight any text in the Filter name field and type **IPv6 only**. Press the **Tab** key.

5. Enter **ipv6 or icmpv6 or dhcpv6** in the Filter string field.

6. Click **OK**.

The filter should appear in the Filter field in the main window. Wireshark checks the syntax of your filter. If the Filter field has a green background, the check of your filter was successful. If the check fails, the background will be red which means you must correct your filter's syntax.

7. Close Wireshark.

Hands-On Project 1-7: Examine a Complete Packet Decode

Time Required: 15 minutes

Objective: Learn about decoded packet information in Wireshark.

Description: This project shows you how to read decoded information in a packet.

1. Follow the steps in Hands-On Project 1-2 to start the Wireshark program if it is not already open.

2. Follow the steps in Hands-On Project 1-3 or Hands-On Project 1-5 to capture some packets using the Wireshark for Windows program.

3. Click the packet list pane (the top pane) in the Wireshark window, if necessary, to view the list of packets captured by Wireshark.

4. Click any packet in the Wireshark window to open the packet details pane (middle pane), if it is not already displayed. Resize the packet list and packet details panes (referred to as the full decode portion) as necessary.

5. Click the **Ethernet II** header label in the packet details pane. Note that the corresponding area in the undecoded packet is highlighted in the packet bytes pane (bottom pane).

6. Scroll through the full decode portion (the packet list and packet details panes) to examine the entire contents of the packet fully decoded.

7. When finished, close the Wireshark program without saving.

Case Projects

CASE PROJECTS

Case Project 1-1: Troubleshooting Network Connectivity on a Small Network

You are asked to visit a small law firm to help troubleshoot some network connectivity problems. The law firm's network consists of 11 workstations connected by a single 24-port hub. A senior partner describes the problem as "consistent" and explains that every morning there is a five-minute delay to connect to the main server on the network. The senior partner indicates that every user on the network has the same problems. Of course, you brought your protocol analyzer. Where should you tap into this network?

Case Project 1-2: Arguing the Case for Upgrading to IPv6

Your company just bought a new subsidiary based in Des Moines, Iowa. Although your local operation already uses IPv6 for local networking and Internet access, the new subsidiary still uses IPv4 only, internally and to access the Internet. What kinds of arguments might you use to persuade your colleagues in Des Moines to switch their network to IPv6 or to enable dual use of IPv4 and IPv6 protocols?

Case Project 1-3: Determining Which IP Protocols Are in Use

Describe a method you can use to determine which IP protocols are in use on your network, so you can define the minimally possible protocol list for your Windows machines.

Case Project 1-4: Explaining Consequences of Protocol Errors and Broadcast Traffic

Explain why excessive protocol errors can be bad for a network. Likewise, explain why excessive broadcast traffic may have negative consequences.

chapter 2

IP Addressing and Related Topics

After reading this chapter and completing the exercises, you will be able to:

- Describe IP addressing, anatomy and structures, and addresses from a computer's point of view
- Recognize and describe IPv4 addressing and address classes, describe the nature of IPv4 address limitations, and define the terms *subnet*, *supernet*, *subnetting*, and *supernetting*
- Describe how to obtain public and private Internet addresses
- Explore IPv4 addressing schemes
- Describe the nature of IPv4 address limitations and why IPv6 is needed
- Discuss new and enhanced IPv6 features
- Recognize and describe IPv6 addressing schemes, features, and capacities
- Describe the impediments involved in transitioning from IPv4 to IPv6

This chapter covers the structure and function of IPv4 (Internet Protocol version 4) addresses—those arcane four-number sequences, such as 24.29.72.3, which uniquely identify all the public network interfaces that use TCP/IP on the Internet. IPv6 (Internet Protocol version 6) and its addressing scheme are also discussed in this chapter, as are the differences between IPv4 and IPv6 and the latest updates of and features included with version 6.

As you come to understand and appreciate IP addresses, you will learn how they are constructed, the classes into which they may (or may not) be relegated, and what roles these addresses play as traffic finds its way around a network. In fact, you will learn to identify how many devices can be attached to a network based on the structure of its IP address, and how to manage this structure to subdivide or aggregate addresses to meet specific connectivity needs.

IP Addressing Basics

Although human beings prefer symbolic names—for instance, we think it's easier to remember a string, such as *www.course.com*, than a **numeric address**, such as 192.168.0.1 (IPv4) or 2001:0db8:1234::c0a8:0001 (IPv6)—computers are the opposite. They deal with **network addresses** in the form of bit patterns that translate into decimal or hexadecimal numbers. Thus, what we express as 192.168.0.1 or 2001:0db8:1234::c0a8:0001 a computer "sees" as 11000000101010000000000000000001.

IP uses a three-part addressing scheme: symbolic name, logical numeric address, and physical numeric address.

The **symbolic name** is a human-recognizable name that takes a particular form, such as *www.support* or *dell.com*. These are called **domain names**. To be valid, a domain name must correspond to at least one unique **numeric IP address**. Domain names only point to numeric addresses; they are not the same as those addresses. Nevertheless, they are very important because they are what most people use to identify specific hosts on the Internet (and on their own networks). You'll learn a lot more about domain names in Chapter 8, where we discuss the **Domain Name System** (DNS) and the protocols and services that make it possible to translate symbolic domain names and numeric IP addresses.

For IPv4, the logical numeric address consists of a set of four numbers separated by periods—for example, 172.16.1.10. Each of these four numbers must be smaller than 256 in order to be represented by eight binary digits, or bits. This puts the range for each number between 0 and 255—the lowest and highest values that can be represented by an 8-bit string. You're probably used to referring to such 8-bit numbers as bytes, but the TCP/IP community likes to call them octets, which means the same thing. Most of what we talk about in this chapter concentrates on how to read, understand, classify, use, and manipulate logical numeric addresses.

For IPv6, an address consists of 128 bits, as opposed to the 32 bits for an IPv4 address, and it is expressed as a series of hexadecimal (base-16) values. The address is divided into eight blocks (called "**words**") of four characters each, with each word separated by a colon. This represents the IPv4 addressing in decimal numbers from 0 to 255. For words that contain only zeros, a group of contiguous zeros can be "compressed" by leaving separators to indicate where they occur. Using this approach, the address 21da:00d3:0000:2f3b:02aa:00ff:fe28:9c5a becomes 21da:d3:0:2f3b:2aa:ff:fe28:9c5a.

It's also important to understand that IPv4 decimal addresses and IPv6 hexadecimal addresses are logical network addresses. Each IP address functions at the Network layer of the ISO/OSI network reference model (the Internet layer of the TCP/IP network model), assigning a unique set of numbers to each network interface on a network (and each machine on the Internet that is visible on that network). The IP protocol operates at the Network layer of the OSI model as well.

The physical numeric address is a 6-byte numeric address burned into firmware (on a chip) by network interface manufacturers. The first 3 bytes (known as the **organizationally unique identifier, or OUI**) identify the manufacturer of whatever interface is in use. The final 3 bytes, another unique numeric identifier, are assigned by the manufacturer and give any interface on a network a unique physical numeric address.

In the OSI network reference model, the **physical numeric address** functions at a sublayer of the Data Link layer called the **Media Access Control (MAC) layer.** For that reason, the physical numeric address is also known as a **Media Access Control (MAC) layer address** (or MAC address). Although there's more to it than this explanation suggests, it is the job of the Logical Link Control (LLC) sublayer in the Data Link layer software (usually at the driver level) to enable the network interface to establish a point-to-point connection with another network interface on the same physical cable or network segment. ARP (Address Resolution Protocol) is used to permit computers to translate numeric IP addresses to MAC layer addresses, and RARP (Reverse ARP) is used to translate MAC layer addresses into IP addresses.

For the remainder of this chapter, you'll concentrate on both IPv4 and IPv6 addresses. It's important to remember that IP addresses can be represented by domain names to make it possible for users to identify and access resources on a network, particularly the Internet. It's also important to recognize that when actual network communication occurs, IP addresses are translated into MAC layer addresses using ARP so that a specific network interface is identified as the sender and another specific network interface is identified as the receiver.

In keeping with the layered nature of network models, it makes sense to associate the MAC layer address with the Data Link layer (or the TCP/IP Network Access layer) and to associate IP addresses with the Network layer (or the TCP/IP Internet layer). At the Data Link layer, one network interface arranges a transfer of frames from itself to another network interface, thus all communications occur on the same physical or local network.

As data moves through intermediate hosts between the original sender and the ultimate receiver, it moves between pairs of network interfaces, where each source and destination pair resides on the same physical network. Obviously, most of the machines between the sender and receiver must be attached to multiple physical networks so that what enters a machine on one interface can leave it on another interface, thereby moving from one physical network to another. This basically represents a series of interface-to-interface connections that move the data from MAC address to MAC address at the Data Link layer.

At the Network layer, the original sender's address is represented in the IP source address field in the IP packet header, and the ultimate recipient's address is represented in the IP destination address field in the same IP packet header. Even though MAC layer addresses change all the time, as a frame moves from interface to interface, the IP source and destination address information is preserved. In fact, the IP destination address value is what drives the sometimes long series of intermediate transfers, or **hops** (the data frame crossing a router), which occurs as data makes its way across a network, from sender to receiver.

IPv4 Addressing

Numeric IPv4 addresses use **dotted decimal notation** when expressed in decimal numbers and take the form *n.n.n.n*, where *n* is guaranteed to be between 0 and 255 for each and every value. Remember, each number is an 8-bit number called an **octet** in standard IPv4 terminology. For any domain name to resolve to a network address, whether on the public Internet or a private intranet, it must correspond to at least one numeric IP address.

In dotted decimal representations of numeric IPv4 addresses, the numeric values are usually decimal values, but they occasionally appear in hexadecimal (base 16) or binary (base 2) notation. When working with dotted decimal IPv4 addresses, you must know what form of notation is in use. Binary representations are easy to recognize because each element in the string is represented by eight binary digits (including leading 0s, for consistency's sake). However, it's possible to confuse decimal and hexadecimal, so be sure you know which one you're working with before you perform any calculations.

Duplication of numeric IP addresses is not allowed because that would lead to confusion. In fact, which network interface "owns" an IP address when duplication occurs is such a troublesome issue that the convention is to drop all interfaces that share an address from the network. Thus, if you configure a machine with an IPv4 address and it isn't able to access the network, you might reasonably speculate that IPv4 address duplication has occurred. The most common IPv4 configuration error is an incorrect subnet mask, which can lead to "partial" transmission failures. (This topic will be discussed in more depth later in the text.) More to the point, if you notice that another machine becomes unavailable at around the same time, or someone else complains about that phenomenon, you can be sure that address duplication has occurred.

There is a notion of "neighborhood" when it comes to interpreting numeric IP addresses. Proximity between two numeric IPv4 addresses (especially if the difference is only in the one or two octets farthest to the right) sometimes indicates that the machines to which those addresses correspond reside close enough together to be on the same general network, if not on the same physical cable segment. (This will be discussed further in the section titled "IP Networks, Subnets, and Masks.")

IPv4 Address Classes

You already know that IPv4 addresses take the form *n.n.n.n*. Initially, these addresses were further subdivided into five classes, from Class A to Class E. For the first three classes, the octets are divided as follows to represent how each class operates:

Class A: n h.h.h

Class B: n.n h.h

Class C: n.n.n h

In this nomenclature, *n* refers to a portion of the network address used to identify networks by number and *h* refers to a portion of the network address used to identify hosts by number. If more than one octet is part of the **network portion** or the **host portion** of the address, the bits are simply concatenated to determine the numeric address (subject to some limitations, which we explain shortly). For example, 10.12.120.2 is a valid Class A address. The network portion of that address is 10, whereas the host portion is 12.120.2, treated as a three-octet number. When seeking evidence of proximity in IPv4 addresses, please consider that "neighborliness" is inherently a networking phenomenon, so it's related to proximity within the network portion of an IP address, not within the host portion of the network address. In this example, the neighbor is said to be on the same network or subnet, meaning it has the same network address, IPv4-wise. Class B and C addresses work the same way; Class A, B, and C addresses are explained in more detail in the sections that follow.

Class D and Class E are for special uses. Class D addresses are used for multicast communications, in which a single address may be associated with more than one network host machine. This is useful only when information is broadcast to a selected group of recipients, so it should come as no surprise that videoconferencing and teleconferencing applications, for example, use multicast addresses.

Multicast addresses also come in handy when a class of devices, such as routers, must be updated with the same information on a regular basis. (That's why some routing protocols use a multicast address to propagate routing table updates, as you'll learn in Chapter 4.) Although you may see Class D addresses on your networks from time to time, you will only see Class E addresses if your network is conducting IPv4-related development work or experiments. That's because Class E addresses are reserved for experimental use.

For more information about IPv4 address classes, see Appendix B or search for *Guide to TCP/IP*, Fourth Edition in the higher education catalog at *www.cengage.com*.

Network, Broadcast, Multicast, and Other Special IPv4 Addresses

Normally, when an IP packet moves from its sender to its receiver, the network portion of the address directs that traffic from the sender's network to the receiver's network. The only time the host portion of the address comes into play is when the sender and receiver both reside on the same physical network or subnet. Although frames may be traveling from network to network for the majority of machine-to-machine transfers, most of these transfers occur only to move the packet ever closer to the destination network. On a local network, although all kinds of traffic may be whizzing by, individual hosts normally read only incoming traffic that is addressed to them, or traffic that must be read for other reasons (such as a multicast addressed to a service active on that host).

In explaining how to calculate the number of available addresses in a range of IPv4 numeric values, you must deduct two addresses from the total number that may be calculated by the number of bits in the address. That's because any IPv4 address that contains all 0s in the host portion, such as 10.0.0.0 for the private IPv4 Class A address, denotes the address for the network itself. The important thing to recognize is that a network address cannot identify a particular host on a network simply because it identifies the entire network itself. So any IPv4 address in which all host bits are "0" is said to be the network address or to identify "this network."

You'll recall that we said *two* addresses are reserved from each numeric IPv4 address range. In addition to the network address, the "other address" that cannot normally be used to identify a particular host on any network is the address that contains all 1s in the host portion, such as 10.255.255.255 or 00001010.11111111.11111111.11111111 (in binary), in which you can see that the last three octets—the host portion of this network address—consist entirely of 1s for the Class A 10.0.0.0 network.

This special address is called the **broadcast address** because it represents a network address that all hosts on a network must read. Although broadcasts still have some valid uses on modern networks, they originated in an era when networks were small and of limited scope, in which a sort of "all hands on deck" message represented a convenient way to ask for services when a specific server could not be explicitly identified. Under some circumstances—as when a Dynamic Host Configuration Protocol (DHCP) client issues a DHCP Offer message (discussed in Chapter 7)—broadcasts still occur on modern TCP/IP networks. However, broadcast traffic is seldom forwarded from one physical network to another these days. The routers separating the networks filter broadcasts as a way of managing network traffic and bandwidth consumption, so broadcasts remain a purely local form of network traffic in most cases.

Broadcast Packet Structures

IPv4 broadcast packets have two destination address fields—one Data Link layer destination address field and one destination network address field. Figure 2-1 depicts an Ethernet packet that contains the destination data link address 0xFF-FF-FF-FF-FF-FF (the broadcast address) and the decimal destination IP address 255.255.255.255. This packet is a DHCP broadcast packet. Chapter 7 covers DHCP in detail.

Addresses are often represented with "0x"—a hexidecimal value flag —at the beginning of the string.

Multicast Packet and Address Structures When a host uses a service that employs a multicast address (such as the 224.0.0.9 address used for RIPv2 router updates), it registers itself to "listen" on that address, as well as on its own unique host address (and the broadcast address). That host must also inform its **IP gateway** (the router or other device that will forward traffic to the host's physical network) that it is registering for this service so that that device will forward such multicast traffic to that network. Otherwise, it will never appear there.

The following URLs provide more information about multicasts and how they are facilitated by IGMP: *http://en.wikipedia.org/wiki/ Internet_Group_Management_Protocol, http://www.inetdaemon.com/ tutorials/internet/igmp/index.shtml, http://www.eetimes.com/design/ communications-design/4009334/Designing-for-Multicast-Operation- with-IGMP-A-Tutorial.*

Registration informs the network interface card to pass packets sent to that address to the IP stack so that their contents can be read, and it tells the IP gateway to forward such traffic

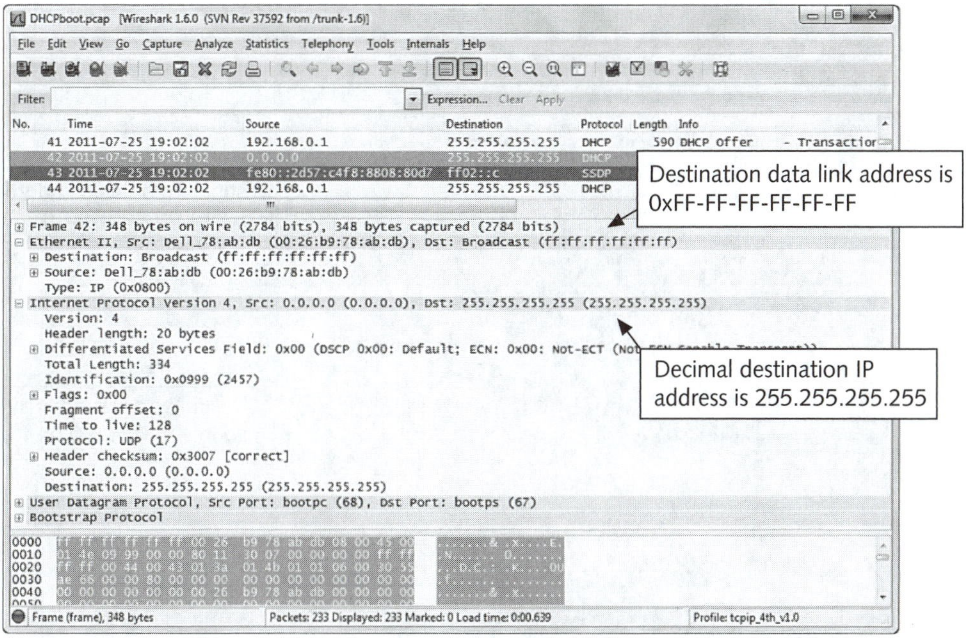

Figure 2-1 DHCP bootp packet containing the broadcast address

Source: Wireshark

on to the physical network, where the listening network interface resides. Without such explicit registration (part and parcel of subscribing to the related service), this traffic will be ignored or unavailable. The Internet Corporation for Assigned Names and Numbers (ICANN) allocates multicast addresses on a controlled basis. Formerly, addresses were under the auspices of IANA, the **Internet Assigned Numbers Authority**.

Multicast packets are quite interesting because the Data Link layer destination address is based on the Network layer multicast address. Figure 2-2 depicts a multicast Open Shortest Path First (OSPF) packet. The destination data link address is 0x01-00-5E-00-00-05. The destination Network layer address is 224.0.0.5.

As mentioned earlier in this section, multicast addresses are assigned by ICANN. In Figure 2-2, the destination network address 224.0.0.5 is assigned to multicast all OSPF routers.

The Data Link layer address 0x01-00-5E-00-00-05 is obtained with the following calculation:

1. Replace the first byte with the corresponding 3-byte OUI. In this case, 224 is replaced with 0x00-00-5E (assigned by IANA).

2. Change the first byte to an odd value (from 0x00 to 0x01).

3. Replace the second through fourth bytes with their decimal equivalents.

Figure 2-3 depicts these steps.

A mathematical formula is used to convert the last 3 bytes of the IPv4 address (e.g., 0.0.5) into the last 3 bytes of the MAC address (e.g., 0x00-00-05). No mathematical equation is used to convert the first byte of the IPv4 address (224) to the first 3 bytes of the MAC

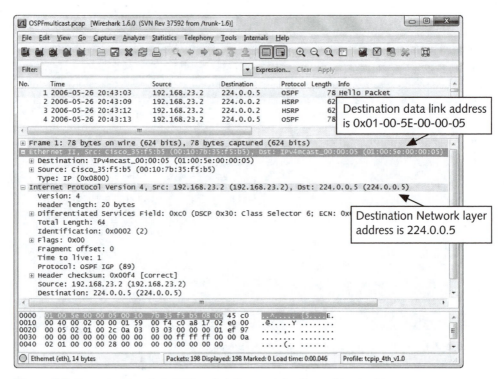

Figure 2-2 Example of an IPv4 OSPF packet that contains the multicast address
Source: Wireshark

address. Rather, it's done through a table lookup, based on unique 3-byte numbers assigned to specific network interface manufacturers for devices (managed by ICANN under the auspices of IANA) and to special broadcast and multicast addresses reserved for such use under IANA's control. The value 00005E is assigned to IANA, and then the first byte is changed to make it odd, with a resulting value of 01005E. RFC 1112 covers this and specifically discusses this example. (The address 224.0.0.5 is an OSPF multicast address, reserved to permit router updates and communications in an efficient way.)

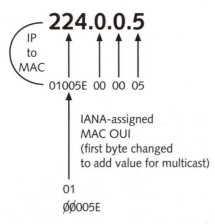

Figure 2-3 Data Link layer address conversion from IP to MAC
© Cengage Learning 2013

Understanding Basic Binary Arithmetic

Working with IP addresses is much simpler if you understand the basics of binary arithmetic.

Consider the following question: How many numbers are there between 0 and 3 (or, in binary, between 00 to 11)? To calculate the answer, subtract the lower number from the higher number, then add 1. Thus, 3 − 0 = 3 and 3 + 1 = 4. To check this fomula, let's enumerate the binary digits from 0 to 3: 00, 01, 10, and 11. Notice that there are four numbers in that list. Also notice that a number raised to the zero power is always equal to 1. (You'll use that fact when converting exponential notation to binary numbers.)

More information can be found about working with binary arithmetic in Appendix B and online by searching for *Guide to TCP/IP*, Fourth Edition in the higher education catalog at *www.cengage.com*.

You may hear about an anycast address, another special IP address. This is specific to IPv6, which is covered later in this chapter. For now, suffice it to say that packets sent to an anycast address go to the nearest interface with that address. Anycast is not used in IPv4.

IPv4 Networks and Subnet Masks

If two network interfaces are on the same physical network, they can communicate directly with one another at the MAC layer. How does the software "know" this is the case when communications begin between two machines? The key to this puzzle lies in a special bit pattern called a subnet mask (which must be defined for any network interface that uses TCP/IP).

In fact, each of the three primary IPv4 address classes—namely, Class A, Class B, and Class C—also has an associated default subnet mask. A **subnet mask** is a special bit pattern that "blocks off" the network portion of an IPv4 address with an all-ones pattern. Thus, the default masks for Classes A, B, and C are fairly obvious, as shown in Table 2-1.

Address type	Layout	Default subnet mask
Class A *n*	*h.h.h*	255.0.0.0
Class B *n n*	*h.h*	255.255.0.0
Class C *n.n.n h*		255.255.255.0

Table 2-1 Default subnet masks for IPv4

© Cengage Learning 2013

(Note: n *signifies network;* h *signifies the host portion of the address.)*

Simply put, every time an *n* occurs in the address layout, symbolizing the entire network portion of that address, a 255 replaces that value in the default subnet mask. The mathematics that explains this process (keeping in mind that a subnet mask replaces the network portion of the address with the all-ones bit pattern) comes from recognizing that the value 255 corresponds to the bit pattern 11111111. Thus, each 255 masks off one of the octets that makes up the network portion of the address. In other words, the subnet mask identifies the network portion of the IP address. Table 2.2 shows how the number of subnets that can be made available changes when different numbers of bits in the Class C subnet mask are masked. Notice this also changes the number of hosts per subnet.

Network bits	Subnet mask	Number of subnets	Number of hosts
/24	255.255.255.0	0	254
/25	255.255.255.128	2 (0)	126
/26	255.255.255.192	4 (2)	62
/27	255.255.255.224	8 (6)	30
/28	255.255.255.240	16 (14)	14
/29	255.255.255.248	32 (30)	6
/30	255.255.255.252	64 (62)	2

Table 2-2 A Class C subnet
© Cengage Learning 2013

IPv4 Subnets and Supernets

The reason concepts like subnets and supernets are important for TCP/IP networks is that each of these ideas refers to a single "local neighborhood" on such a network, seen from a routing perspective. When network addresses are further subdivided beyond their defaults for whatever class to which an address belongs, such **subnetting** represents "stealing bits" (borrowing bits) from the host portion of the address and using those stolen (borrowed) bits to create multiple routing regions within the context of a single network address.

Thus, a subnet mask that is larger than the default mask for the address in use divides a single network IPv4 address into multiple subnetworks. For a Class B address, in which the default subnet mask is 255.255.0.0, a subnet mask of 255.255.192.0 indicates that it's stealing two bits from the host portion to use for subnet identification (because 192 decimal is 11000000 in binary notation and shows that the upper two bits are used for the network portion). One way to describe this kind of network address layout is that there are 8 bits of the network prefix and two additional bits of subnetting. Here, the **network prefix** identifies the number of bits in the IP address, counting from the left, that represent the actual network address itself, and the additional 2 bits of subnetting represent the bits that were borrowed from the host portion of that IP address to extend the network portion. The entire network address, including the network prefix and the subnetting bits, is called the **extended network prefix**.

With a 2-bit subnet mask, you can identify a total of four possible subnets because each of the possible patterns that the two subnet bits can form—00, 01, 10, and 11—can identify a potential subnetwork. As with network and host addresses, however, the total number of usable subnet addresses is reduced by two because all 0s (00 in this case) and all 1s (11 in this case) are reserved for other purposes. This activity of stealing (borrowing) bits from the host portion to further subdivide the network portion of an address is called subnetting a network address, or subnetting.

From a routing perspective, subnetting allows network administrators to match subnetworks to actual routing regions on their networks so that machines on the same physical network can communicate using MAC layer addresses. Other pairs of machines that wish to communicate but do not reside on the same physical network belong to different subnetworks. (Their numeric IP addresses differ somewhere in the subnetwork portion of those addresses.) This is where the real sense of numerical neighborhoods, which we talked about earlier in this chapter, comes into play.

When a computer on one subnet wishes to communicate with a computer on another subnet, traffic must be forwarded from the sender to a nearby IP gateway to send the message on its way from one subnet to another. An IP gateway is a device that interconnects multiple IP networks or subnets. It is often called an interface on a "router" because it usually stores, in a routing table, "reachability" information about many networks, chooses the best (shortest, fastest, or least expensive) path (or "route") for each packet it receives, and then sends the packet on its way.

Here again, subnetting means stealing bits from the host portion of the address and using those bits to divide a single network address into multiple subdivisions called subnets. **Supernetting**, on the other hand, takes the opposite approach: by combining contiguous network addresses, it steals bits from the network portion and uses them to create a single, larger contiguous address space for host addresses. In the sections that follow, you will have the opportunity to investigate some examples that help cement these concepts. For more information on subnetting, please consult RFC 1878, "Variable Length Subnet Table for IPv4." (Among many other places, you can access it at *www.rfc-archive.org/getrfc.php?rfc=1878*.)

Calculating Subnet Masks There are several varieties of subnet masks that you can design for a network, depending on how you want to implement an address segmentation scheme. The simplest form of subnet masking uses a technique called **constant-length subnet masking** (CLSM), in which each subnet includes the same number of stations and represents a simple division of the address space made available by subnetting into multiple equal segments. Another form of subnet masking uses a technique called **variable-length subnet masking** (VLSM) and permits a single address to be subdivided into multiple subnets, in which subnets need not all be the same size.

When it comes to designing a subnet masking scheme, if all segments must support roughly the same number of devices, give or take 20 percent, CLSM makes the most sense. However, if one or two segments require larger numbers of users, whereas other segments require a lesser number, VLSM will let you make more effective use of your address space. (The only way to use CLSM in such a case would be to design for the biggest segments, which would waste lots of addresses on those segments with smaller populations.) In a VLSM addressing scheme, different subnets may have different extended network prefixes, reflecting their varied layouts and capacities. Of course, the binary nature of subnetting means that all subnets must still fit into the same kinds of structures described for CLSM. It's just that in VLSM, some of the individual higher-level subnet address spaces can be further subdivided into smaller sub-spaces, if that's desirable. For an extended discussion of subnetting schemes and design approaches, please read an older but excellent white paper titled "Understanding IP Addressing: Everything You Ever Wanted to Know," by Chuck Semeria, at *http://fens.sabanciuniv.edu/kcenter/tr/dokuman/documents/Understanding_IP_addressing.pdf*.

If the Web address for the white paper results in an error, search online for the article's title. It's been preserved on a number of Web sites. You can find more subnet mask information in Appendix B and online by searching for *Guide to TCP/IP*, Fourth Edition in the higher education catalog at *www.cengage.com*.

There are a number of utilities that make it easy to calculate subnets without having to "do the math." These tools are typically free to download and use and reduce the "administrative effort" associated with calculating and managing subnets.

Bitcricket IP Calculator Bitcricket IP Calculator (*www.wildpackets.com/resources/free_utilities/ipsubnetcalc*) is a free subnet mask calculator from WildPackets that is the first to support IPv6. IPv6 has no subnets to calculate, but it does have a number of different address types, and Bitcricket can display these types, their address patterns, and other useful information.

After installation, when you open Bitcricket, it automatically displays the IPv4 dotted decimal address of the host computer as well as dotted binary and binary. The computer's IPv6 address is also autocalculated. The IP address class for the host computer is also automatically calculated, including the class address range. You can also enter any IP address and select the number of subnet bits or the maximum number of subnets you want and the calculations are quickly performed. Classless Inter-Domain Routing (CIDR) routes can also be calculated using this utility. (You'll learn about CIDR in the next section.)

Bitcricket is available for both Windows and Mac OS X. Though slightly complicated to use for the beginner, Bitcricket's IPv6 support makes it the best choice for forward-looking network technicians and administrators.

SolarWinds IP Subnet Calculator SolarWinds IP Subnet Calculator (*www.solarwinds.com/products/freetools/free_subnet_calculator.aspx*) is available as a free download, although the company requires that you provide your company name and phone number.

This product's primary features include providing address details such as reverse DNS resolution and response time. It offers a classful subnet creator, calculating subnets based on subnet mask, mask bits, host bits, and other information. It also possesses a CIDR calculator and has the ability to generate a list of IP addresses for any subnet you input. Though not explicitly stated on the SolarWinds site, it appears that this tool is only available for Windows.

Classless Inter-Domain Routing in IPv4

Classless Inter-Domain Routing (CIDR), pronounced "cider" or "sidder," gets its name from the notion that it ignores the traditional A, B, and C class designations for IPv4 addresses and sets the network-host ID boundary wherever it wants to, in a way that simplifies routing across the resulting IP address spaces. One way to think of this is to imagine that a CIDR address sets the boundaries between the network and host portions of an IP address more or less arbitrarily, constrained only by the IP address space that an **Internet service provider** (**ISP**), organization, or company might need to manage. When multiple IP addresses are available, the best use of CIDR results if those addresses are contiguous (so that they can be managed in one or more logical blocks that operate at specific bit boundaries between the host and network portions of the address). Using CIDR also requires that routers be informed that they're dealing with CIDR addresses.

The CIDR specification is documented in RFCs 1517, 1518, and 1519. Basically, CIDR allows IPv4 addresses from Class A, B, or C to be combined and treated as a larger address space, or subdivided arbitrarily, as needed. Although CIDR can sometimes be used to combine multiple Class C addresses, it can also be used to subdivide Class A, B, or C addresses (especially when VLSM techniques are applied) to make the most efficient use of whatever address space is available. Most experts agree that CIDR's most positive impact on the Internet is the reduction in the number of individual Class C addresses that must be recognized (many are now aggregated and function with smaller subnet masks, thereby requiring fewer entries in top-level routing tables).

When configuring a router to handle a CIDR address, the routing table entry takes the form *address*, *count*, in which *address* is the starting address for a range of IPv4 addresses and *count* is the number of high-order bits in the mask.

Creating a CIDR address is subject to the following limitations:

- All the addresses in the CIDR address must be contiguous. However, use of the standard network prefix notation for addresses makes it tidy and efficient to carve up any kind of address, as needed. When multiple addresses are aggregated, this requires that all such addresses be in numerical order so that the boundary between the network and the host portion of the address can move to reflect such aggregation.

- When address aggregation occurs, CIDR address blocks work best when they come in sets that are greater than 1 and equal to some lower-order bit pattern that corresponds to all 1s—namely, in groups of 3, 7, 15, 31, and so on. That's because this makes it possible to borrow the corresponding number of bits (two, three, four, five, and so on) from the network portion of the CIDR address block and use them to extend the host portion instead.

- To use a CIDR address on any network, all routers in the routing domain must "understand" CIDR notation. This is not a problem for most routers that were built after September 1993, when RFCs 1517, 1518, and 1519 were approved, because most router vendors began to support CIDR addresses at that time.

The prefix notation, as it relates to Class A (/8), Class B (/16), and Class C (/24) addresses, really comes into its own when you see CIDR addresses that use this notation. Thus, if you see a network address of 192.168.5.0/27, you immediately know two things: that you're dealing with a Class C address and that this address was subnetted with three additional bits worth of network space, so that the corresponding subnet mask must be 255.255.255.224. This notation is both compact and efficient, and it explicitly denotes whatever subnet or supernet scheme may be in use for the IP network(s) in use.

CIDR addresses are commonly applied to Class C addresses (which are small and relatively plentiful). However, CIDR also works very well for organizations that wish to subdivide existing Class A or Class B addresses.

Public versus Private IPv4 Addresses

You have learned that RFC 1918 designates specific addresses, or address ranges, within the Class A, B, and C address space for use as private IPv4 addresses. This means that any organization can use these private IP addresses within its own networking domains without obtaining prior permission or incurring any expense.

The private IPv4 address ranges may be expressed in the form of IP network addresses, as shown in Table 2-3.

Class	Address Range	Networks	Total private hosts
Class A	10.0.0.0–10.255.255.255	1	16,777,214
Class B	172.16.0.0–172.31. 255.255	16	1,048,544
Class C	192.168.0.0–192.168.255. 255	256	65,024

Table 2-3 **Private IPv4 address information**
© Cengage Learning 2013

When selecting the kinds of private IPv4 addresses to use, you want to balance your needs for the number of hosts per network with your willingness to subnet larger address classes (usually Class B) or your willingness to supernet smaller address classes (usually Class C). One method is to use the Class B addresses and subnet them in the third octet, leaving the fourth octet for host addresses. (For our small networks, a maximum of 254 hosts per subnet hasn't proved problematic.) If you decide to use private IP addresses on your networks, you must review your networking requirements for the number of subnets and the number of hosts per subnet, and choose accordingly.

You already know one of the disadvantages of using private IP addresses—such addresses may not be routed across the public Internet. Thus, it's important to recognize that if you want to connect your computers to the Internet and use private IP addresses within your own local networks, you must add some extra software to whatever device sits at the boundary between the private side of your networks and the public side of the Internet, to make that connection workable. This sometimes depends on translating one or more private IP addresses into a **public IP address** for outgoing traffic and reversing that translation for incoming traffic. Another technique, known as **address masquerading**, or address substitution, may be performed by boundary devices that include proxy server capabilities to replace private IP addresses with one or more public IP addresses as outbound traffic exits the server, and to replace such public addresses with their proper private equivalents as incoming traffic passes through the server.

Private IP addresses have one other noteworthy limitation. Some IP services require what's called a secure **end-to-end connection**—IP traffic must be able to move in encrypted form between the sender and receiver without intermediate translation. Thus, if either party to such a connection uses a public IP address, it's easiest to configure if both parties use a public IP address because the address for the "private end" of the connection cannot be routed directly across the Internet. Secure protocols such as IP Security (IPSec) may require additional configuration at a firewall or proxy server when private IP addresses are in use at one or both ends of such a connection, as is the case with some virtual private networking technologies. So, if you want to use such services on your network, you may face extra work—and learning—if you want to use private IP addresses.

Ultimately though, private IP addresses have great value for many organizations simply because the vast majority of machines on TCP/IP networks are client workstations. Because these client machines seldom, if ever, advertise services accessible to a broad audience (or to the Internet at large), there is no real downside to using private IP addresses for such machines. Most clients simply want to read e-mail, access the Web and other Internet services, and use local networked resources. None of these requirements mandates using a public IP address nor forbids the use of a private IP address. Thus, the introduction of private IP addresses has greatly eased most organizations' needs for public IP addresses.

That said, public IP addresses remain important for identifying all servers or services that must be accessible to the Internet. This is, in part, a reflection of the behavior of the DNS that manages translations between symbolic domain names like *www.course.com* and numeric IP addresses like 198.89.146.30. Because human beings prefer to think in terms of such symbolic names and computers can use only the equivalent numeric IP addresses to access such public hosts, the way changes to the mapping between names and addresses are handled is important to the stability and usability of the Internet itself.

You will learn much more about this in Chapter 8. For now, be aware that it takes a relatively long time—up to 72 hours in some cases—for name-to-address changes to DNS to take complete effect across the Internet. It's very important not only that publicly accessible servers use public IP addresses (how else would they be publicly accessible?) but that those addresses change as infrequently as possible in order to keep the many copies of the translation information that are scattered widely across the Internet as correct and current as possible.

In more practical terms, this means that most organizations need public IP addresses only for two classes of equipment:

- Devices that permit organizations to attach networks to the Internet—These include the external interfaces on boundary devices of all kinds (such as routers, proxy servers, and firewalls) that help maintain the network perimeter between the "outside" and "inside."

- Servers that are designed to be accessible to the Internet—These include public Web servers, e-mail servers, FTP servers, news servers, and whatever other kind of TCP/IP Application layer services an organization may want to expose on the public Internet.

It is interesting that even though the number of such devices (more accurately, the number of network interfaces, because each network interface on a boundary device or server must have its own unique IP address) is not small, it pales when compared to the number of clients or purely internal devices and servers on most organization networks.

Exact estimates are hard to find, but it's not unreasonable to place the number somewhere in the hundreds to thousands in one neighborhood. (For every public IP address that's required, there can be as many as 100 to 1,000 private IP addresses in use as well.)

Managing Access to IPv4 Address Information

Although use of private IPv4 addresses mandates NAT or a similar address substitution or masquerade capability, some organizations elect to use address substitution or masquerade even when they use perfectly valid public IPv4 addresses on their internal networks. That's because allowing clients inside the network boundary to interact with the network without some form of address "hiding" could reveal the address structure of that internal network to knowledgeable outsiders who may try to use that information to break through organizational boundaries—from the public Internet into an organizational networking environment—and attack that network for a variety of reasons (none of them good).

 Because of the limited availability of IPv4 addresses, NAT was implemented to allow computers on LANs that do not directly connect to the Internet to use nonpublic IP addresses. IPv6 does not require the use of NAT.

That's why it's considered good IP security to use a proxy server or some similar kind of service, which interposes itself between traffic inside the boundary and traffic outside the boundary. When outbound traffic passes through the proxy from the internal network, the proxy service replaces internal network addresses with one or more different addresses so the traffic that actually travels over the public Internet does not reveal the address structure of the internal network to outsiders.

Likewise, proxy servers can provide what is sometimes called **reverse proxying**. This permits the proxy server to front for servers inside the boundary by advertising only the proxy server's address to the outside world and then forwarding only legitimate requests for service to internal servers for further processing. Here again, outsiders see only the address that the proxy server advertises on the internal server's behalf and remain unaware of the invisible middleman, in most cases.

Thus, one of the most important services that a proxy server provides is to manage what source addresses appear in outbound packets that pass through it. This prevents details about the internal network's actual addresses from leaking to outsiders, who might otherwise use address-scanning utilities to see exactly which addresses in any given address range are in use. This information, in turn, could allow outsiders to determine what kinds of subnet masks are in use and how an internal network is laid out. By blocking this information, savvy IP network administrators limit potential opportunities for break-ins or other attacks.

Obtaining Public IP Addresses

Unless you work for an organization that has possessed its own public IP addresses since the 1980s (or acquired such addresses through merger or acquisition), it's highly likely that whatever public IP addresses your organization uses were issued by the very same ISP that provides your organization with Internet access. This is one of the details that makes the decision to change from one ISP to another so challenging. Because all devices accessible to the Internet must have public IP addresses, changing providers often means going through a tedious exercise called **IP renumbering**. When this happens, you must switch the addresses on every machine that uses an address from the old ISP to another unique address you obtain from the new ISP.

Historically, IANA managed all IP-related addresses, protocol numbers, and well-known port addresses, and it also assigned MAC layer addresses for use in network interfaces. Today, ICANN manages this task, and you must contact it to apply for an IP address range from the few remaining public Class C addresses. Although IANA is no longer operating as the governing body for this activity, you can still find a lot of useful information about IP addresses and numbers at *www.iana.org*; likewise, you can find such information at *www. icann.org*.

IPv4 Addressing Schemes

To the uninitiated, it may appear that all these IPv4 addresses are assigned randomly or perhaps generated automatically by some computer somewhere. However, a great deal of thought has gone into the strategy for allocating IP addresses around the world. In this section, we discuss the need for IP addressing schemes and how to create and document one. You will be introduced to two key groupings for evaluating IP address range assignment: network space (physical allocation) and host space (logical allocation).

The Network Space

There are a number of critical factors that typically constrain IP addressing schemes, and we look at these in two groups. The first group of constraints determines the number and size of networks. These are:

- Number of physical locations
- Number of network devices at each location
- Amount of broadcast traffic at each location
- Availability of IP addresses
- Delay caused by routing from one network to another

Although it's possible to bridge from one physical location to another across a WAN connection, in practice it is only done with protocols that aren't capable of routing at all, such as SNA or NetBEUI. Routing (instead of bridging) is primarily done to prevent unnecessary broadcasts from clogging expensive WAN circuits. Because at least one IP network address is required for every physical location and physical link, the minimum number of IP networks needed is one for each such location in a company or organization, plus one for each WAN link.

Next, because IPv4 addresses are scarce, we want our networks to be as small as possible, but they should have at least enough usable addresses (remember, usable addresses = [total number of addresses in the network] – 2) to give one address to each device and allow adequate room for growth.

Last, recall that any IP network is also a broadcast domain. This means that when one host on the network sends a broadcast, every other host on that network must receive and process it. So the speed of your network links and your hosts' processors as well as the number and nature of protocols in use together constrain the practical size of your network.

Generally speaking, the more broadcasts that occur on any given network, the fewer hosts you should have per network. Likewise, the more protocols you have on any given network, the fewer hosts you should have per network.

In most routers, the Layer 3 routing decisions are typically made by software, so it's relatively slow when compared to similar decisions made at Layer 2 by switches. This is because switches make their decisions with specialized hardware known as **application-specific integrated circuits (ASICs)**. A **Layer 3 switch** simply implements the logic from the software into its own ASICs. The result is much faster routing. In practice, Layer 3 switching allows you to partition a large network into many smaller subnets, with almost no loss of performance.

The second group of constraints that helps us determine how to choose which IP addresses go where consists of these design objectives:

- Minimize the size of the routing tables.
- Minimize the time required for the network to "converge."
- Maximize flexibility and facilitate management and troubleshooting.

The time it takes to route from one network to another is affected by the size of the routing table; the larger the table, the more time it takes to search through it. In addition, router memory is often scarce, and minimizing the size of the routing tables uses memory more efficiently. At this point, however, we already defined the number of needed networks, so how do we reduce the number of routes in the routing table? The answer is called **route aggregation,** or **summary addresses**.

A critical concept to understand here is that there is no one-to-one relationship between networks and routes to networks. If a router receives a route to 10.1.1.0/25 and 10.1.1. 128/25, it can advertise a route to 10.1.1.0/24 to its upstream neighbors instead of the two /25 routes.

One advantage of summarization is that if the 10.1.1.128/25 network gets disconnected, routers that have a routing table entry for 10.1.1.128/25 will have to remove it but routers that have only summary routes will not know that a change has occurred.

The point of all this is simply to number your networks so that they can be easily summarized, which will minimize the number of routes in your routing tables and allow your routing tables to be more stable. This, in turn, allows processor time to be spent passing packets instead of fiddling with the routing table.

The Host Space

Now that you understand some of the factors involved in numbering the networks, let's take a brief look at assigning IPv4 addresses to hosts.

The advantages of a well-thought-out host-naming strategy are a more flexible environment and one that is easier to support. For example, imagine you have 500 branch offices around the world, each with a /24 network that uses a numbering convention such as in Table 2-4.

IP Address	Description
10.x.x.0	Network address
10.x.x.1–10.x.x.14	Switches and managed hubs
10.x.x.17	DHCP and DNS server
10.x.x.18	File and print server
10.x.x.19–10.x.x.30	Application servers
10.x.x.33–10.x.x.62	Printers
10.x.x.65–10.x.x.246	DHCP clients
10.x.x.247–10.x.x.253	Miscellaneous and static clients
10.x.x.254	Default gateway address
10.x.x.255	Broadcast address

Table 2-4 **Host address space example**
© Cengage Learning 2013

You can easily identify devices by their IP addresses, regardless of which office they're in. Even more important, and less obvious, is that these address groups should be done in binary, not decimal notation. This means that you want to keep your groups inside binary boundaries. The reason is that, in the future, you may want to implement Layer 3 switching to reduce the broadcast traffic, and if the devices fit in a binary boundary, you won't have to re-address them. In this example, servers can be identified by 10.x.x.16/28, even though the servers themselves are configured with a 255.255.255.0 subnet mask. If you started them at .10 and went to .20, it might make more sense in decimal notation, but in reality, it will only lead to confusion.

Another good reason to use binary boundaries is that one day you will want to classify your traffic to apply **quality of service** (QoS) or similar policies. You could apply a rule that says traffic to and from 10.x.x.32/27 (printers) gets a lower priority than other traffic. If the printers weren't in a binary boundary, some of them would be excluded from the rule or some other devices could be mistakenly included.

Another very common application of binary boundaries occurs in firewall rules. You might want to say that all traffic from 10.x.x.0/26 (network equipment, servers, and printers) to the Internet is denied. This could prevent the servers from becoming launchpads for hackers to attack other networks, while still allowing your DHCP clients access through the firewall.

As you can see, a well-planned IP addressing scheme not only dramatically improves the performance of your network but also makes maintenance and support tasks much simpler and allows a lot of flexibility.

The End of the IPv4 Address Space

IPv4 is clearly one of the most successful network protocols ever designed. Because IP packet-switched networking was robust, scalable, and relatively simple, it rapidly became the global standard for computer networking. In terms of connected devices, only the largest national telephone networks and the global telephone network combined are larger than the Internet.

However, you could say that IPv4 has fallen victim to its own success. At 32 bits, the IPv4 address space recognizes only four billion unique IP addresses in round numbers. At the time IPv4 was created, that amounted to nearly two addresses for every human being on the planet. However, the proliferation of networks (not to mention population growth) turned IPv4 address space into a valuable commodity, indeed.

Originally, when IP addresses were assigned for public use, they were assigned on a per-network basis. This helps explain why there are no unassigned Class A or Class B network addresses left. Likewise, the available number of Class C addresses is almost nonexistent; less than 5 percent of all Class Cs remain unassigned at present, and all have been allocated to regional address authorities. With the ever-increasing demand for public IP addresses for Internet access, it should come as no surprise that, as early as the mid-1990s, experts began to predict that the Internet would "run out" of available IPv4 addresses.

Historically, causes for concern about IPv4 address exhaustion have abated somewhat. Here's why:

- The IETF introduced a new way to carve up the IPv4 address space: CIDR.

- As available IPv4 addresses became increasingly depleted, owners of such addresses have occasionally found it advantageous to sell them to third parties. In the past decade, the "going rate" for a Class C network address has climbed to as high as $10,000, although lower offers are on record as well. Microsoft paid $7.5 million for just over 666,000 IPv4 addresses in March 2011 (for a net price of $11.25 per address) as part of the Nortel bankruptcy asset sale. In the past, a handful of private companies that owned Class A addresses were acquired or publicly traded on the strength of this asset alone, which, at the Microsoft-Nortel price, would be worth over $183 million! That said, most companies and individuals rent IP addresses from their ISPs today rather than own them outright. Given that a single typical IPv6 network address allocation is 64 bits in length (for a total of more than $1.84 * 10^{18}$ addresses), this high valuation for IPv4 addresses is bound to decline as the use of IPv6 addresses becomes more widespread.

- RFC 1918 reserves three ranges of IPv4 addresses for private use—a single Class A (10.0.0.0–10.255.255.255), 16 Class Bs (172.16.0.0–172.31.255.255), and 256 Class Cs (192.168.0.0–192.168.255.255). By definition, these addresses are not routed across the Internet because they may be freely used by anyone. No single organization can "own" these addresses; therefore, these addresses may not be used on the public Internet either, because they are not guaranteed to be unique.

- When used in tandem with a technology called **Network Address Translation (NAT)**, **private IP addresses** can help lift the "cap" on public IP addresses. That's because a single public IP address on the "Internet side" of a **firewall** or **proxy server** can "front" for an arbitrary number of private IPv4 addresses on the "private side" of the same firewall or proxy server. In other words, NAT lets networks use multiple private

IPv4 addresses internally and maps them to one or more public IPv4 addresses externally. This gives companies lots of addressing flexibility (they can even use a Class A address internally) and reduces the number of public IP addresses they must own or use.

Because of all the tactics and technologies described in this list, the current IPv4 address space was stretched a good deal further than many experts thought possible. However, the 32-bit IPv4 address space was not designed for a world of proliferating computing devices—notably, mobile devices—that all require their own IP addresses. Today, smartphones, Web appliances, even automobiles connect to the Internet.

The Internet engineering community recognized the vanishing IP address space as far back as the early-1990s and began developing solutions. The result of their combined efforts is IPv6. The 128-bit IPv6 address space promises to provide more than enough unique IP addresses for the foreseeable future. How many addresses is that? The answer depends on exactly how IPv6 is implemented, but it is roughly 2^{128}, which is a staggering 340,282,366,920,938,000,000,000,000,000,000,000,000 unique IP addresses. If you consider that there are about 6.5 billion people on earth today, that would be 5×10^{28} addresses for each human being alive right now.

Although the address shortage is and always has been the driving consideration in the upgrade from IPv4 to IPv6, many other problems and opportunities were considered at the same time. IPv6 includes important changes in the way IP handles security, autoconfiguration, and QoS, and it improves the efficiency of routing, name resolution, automatic address allocation, and the handling of mobile users.

Introducing IPv6

Although providing a much larger address space is one of the primary design goals for IPv6, it is hardly the only reason for implementing IPv6, nor is this the only change made in the latest version of the IP protocol. IP has required a number of other important updates besides the lack of available unique addresses.

IPv6 not only provides a vast abundance of IP addresses and better management of its address space, it eliminates the need for NAT and other technologies to be put in place to shore up the inadequate number of IPv4 addresses. IPv6 also makes it easier to administer and configure IP addresses. Although DHCP seems to be an effortless solution to IP address assignment, it does not eliminate address configuration efforts.

IPv4 was created before what we think of as the "modern Internet," thus routing wasn't a consideration in its design. IPv6 has modernized routing support and natively allows for expansion along with the growing Internet. The same could be said about IPv4 versus IPv6 regarding mobile computing. IPv6 builds on Mobile IP and natively supports mobility for the IP protocol.

Network security wasn't a particular concern when IPv4 was implemented, but the need for network security is now critical. IPv6 supports network security by using authentication and encryption extension headers, among other methods.

With all the updates made to IP for version 6, it's tempting to see it as an entirely new and revolutionary protocol implementation, but IPv6 is meant to be the next stage of evolution for IP, not an entirely new thing. The IP protocol has been stable and robust for decades, and with the introduction and application of the sixth version of IP, you can expect to see the same reliability of service experienced in IPv4, along with many new features and performance improvements.

IPv6 solves the address shortage problem by creating an address space that's more than 20 orders of magnitude larger than IPv4's address space. Routing in such a large space is impossible without also including some notion of hierarchy. Fortunately, the IPv6 address space provides hierarchy in a flexible and well-articulated fashion, with plenty of room for future growth. We discuss the IPv6 address format and allocations as well as address types in the following sections.

Request for Comments Pages and Depreciation

An invaluable resource to help you understand the intricacies of IPv6 are the Request for Comments (RFC) pages at the Internet Engineering Task Force (IETF) Web site: *www.ietf.org*. These papers describe the methods, innovations, and standards that are applied to every aspect of the Internet, including IPv6. For instance, RFC 5156 contains a summary of various other RFCs regarding special usage of IPv6 addresses, including IPv6 "subnetting" and interface identifiers (see *http://tools.ietf.org/html/rfc5156* for details).

RFCs are dynamic documents that describe changing methods and standards. Some or all of the methods described in any given RFC can be deprecated or superseded by newer information in subsequent RFC pages. The deprecated features may still exist in the software, but attempting to use these features is not supported in newer versions of networking hardware or software. Before implementing IPv6 within your network, please consult the most recent RFCs and verify that the information is current.

The worldwide internetworking infrastructure is rapidly accelerating toward IPv6 adoption, and all organizations that utilize internal networks and access the Internet will need to update their hardware and software network components to IPv6. However, the IETF standards defining IPv6 are continually evolving, and unless you stay current on the latest standards, you may end up developing your network based on solutions that are no longer supported. When you review RFCs, make special note of information that has been depreciated and RFCs that have been obsoleted by more recent documents.

For instance, you may currently use routers and router software in your network that are consistent with older IPv6 standards, and you can construct an IPv6 network that functions based on those standards. Your internal IPv6 network will work because your hardware and software was based on some of the older (but now deprecated) standards. However, the vendor who produced your routers will eventually release updated software based on the most current IPv6 standards. Once you update your router software to the latest version, you may find that your once fully functioning network no longer operates.

IPv6 Addressing

IPv6 addresses are 128 bits long. An IPv6 address may be viewed as a string that uniquely identifies one single network interface on the global Internet. Alternately, that string of 128 bits can be understood as an address with a network portion and a host portion. How much of the address belongs to either portion depends on who's looking at it and where they are located in relation to the host with that address. If an entity is on the same subnet as the host, both of them share a large part of that address, and only the last portion of the address must be evaluated to uniquely identify some particular host. If the entity doing the evaluation is near a backbone and the address is for a host near the edge of the Internet, only a small part at the beginning of the address is needed to send a packet on its way toward the host. In the following sections, we discuss address format and notation, network and host addresses, identifiers, IPv6 addresses that contain IPv4 addresses, and a proposal for expressing IPv6 addresses like the one used for Uniform Resource Locators (URLs) on the World Wide Web.

Address Format and Notation

Addresses in both versions of IP are actually binary numbers. That is, they are strings of ones and zeroes representing bits turned on or off. IPv6 addresses are 128 bits long, and IPv4 addresses are 32 bits long. When they are written down, IPv6 addresses are expressed using hexadecimal notation (00–FF), unlike IPv4 addresses, which are usually expressed using decimal notation (0–255). Because each hexadecimal digit represents 16 unique values (0–15 in decimal, or 0–9 plus A, B, C, D, E, and F in hexadecimal), 32 hexadecimal digits completely identify an IPv6 address ($16^{32} = (2^4)^{32} = 2^{128}$).

Because IPv6 addresses are much longer than IPv4 addresses, they are broken up differently. Instead of four 8-bit decimal numbers separated by dots or periods, IPv6 uses groups of four 16-bit numbers called "words," separated by a colon character (:). Both of the following strings represent valid IPv6 network addresses:

FEDC:BA45:1234:3245:E54E:A101:1234:ABCD

1018:FD0C:0:9:90:900:10BB:A

Because of the way IPv6 addresses are structured and allocated, there are often many zeroes in such an address; however, just as in IPv4, there is no need to show leading zeroes when expressed in binary. IPv6 allows a special notation that means "fill out this portion of the address with enough 16-bit sets of zeroes to make the whole address 128 bits long." You would use this notation whenever contiguous 16-bit sections of an address are all zeroes. For example, you could express the following IPv6 address:

    1090:0000:0000:0000:0009:0900:210D:325F

as

    1090::9:900:210D:325F

The adjacent pair of colon characters (::) stands for one or more groups of contiguous 16-bit groups of zeroes needed to make this address a proper 128-bit IPv6 address. Note that you can use this kind of notation only once in any address. Otherwise, it would be impossible to determine how many sets of ":0000:" you should add for any single instance of its use.

Network and Host Address Portions

To represent a network prefix in IPv6, you may use a type of "shorthand" notation familiar from CIDR, as used with IPv4. You can use "/ *decimal number*" after an address, in which the decimal number after the slash shows how many of the leftmost contiguous bits of the address are a part of the network prefix. Here are two examples:

1090::9:900:210D:325F / 60

1018:FD0C:0:9:90:900:10BB:A / 24

The following examples describe just the subnet portion of the above addresses:

1090:: / 60

1018:FD0C / 24

Zeroes trailing from the representation of a single 16-bit group cannot be omitted. If there are less than four (hexadecimal) digits in a 16-bit group, the missing digits are assumed to be leading zeroes. For example, in IPv6 address notation, the field ":A:" always expands to ":000A:"; it never expands to something like ":00A0:" or ":A000:."

Scope Identifier

Multicast addresses in IPv6 use a **scope identifier,** a 4-bit field that limits the valid range for a multicast address to define the portion of the Internet to which the multicast group pertains. More detail about this appears in the section titled "Multicast Addresses" later in this chapter.

Interface Identifiers

With one important exception, IPv6 requires that every network interface have its own unique identifier. Thus, whether the node itself is a workstation, a laptop, a cell phone, or a car, each single interface within each device must have its own unique **interface identifier**. The caveat is that in the restricted case, where a host with multiple interfaces can perform dynamic load balancing across all those interfaces, all the interfaces may share a single identifier.

Previously, IPv6 specified that these interface identifiers followed the modified **EUI-64 format,** which specifies a unique 64-bit interface identifier for each interface. For Ethernet networks, the IPv6 interface identifier is based directly on the MAC address of the NIC. The MAC address of an Ethernet NIC is a 48-bit number expressly designed to be globally unique. This is not entirely valid anymore, however. Hardware vendors tend to use the modified EUI-64 format, but software makers, including Microsoft, use the privacy format defined in RFC 4941.

For the EUI-64 format, the first 24 bits represent the name of the card's manufacturer and, within that name, perhaps the individual production run. The second 24 bits are chosen by the manufacturer to ensure uniqueness among its own cards. All that is required to create a unique interface identifier in this case is padding the number. The EUI-64 format adds the fixed, specific 16-bit pattern 0xFFFE (:FFFE:) between the two halves of the MAC address to create a unique 64-bit number.

Having the right-hand portion of your IPv6 address based on the computer's MAC or hardware address presents a security concern. It can allow an intruder to use your computer's public facing or global scope address to acquire your PC's hardware address. Privacy extensions can be used to create a IPv6 interface identifier that is unrelated to the computer's

MAC address. The privacy extension generates the interface identifier using methods such as random number generation. The extension also allows the interface identifier to change over time, making it more difficult for external "hackers" to determine which global scope address is connected to a particular network host.

Interfaces for serial connections—or the ends of IP tunnels—must also be identified uniquely within their contexts. These interfaces may have their identifiers configured by random number generation, may be configured by hand, or may use some other method.

To prepare for a day when globally unique identifiers (as opposed to locally unique ones) may have special importance, IPv6 requires that bits six and seven of the first octet of the EUI-64 format interface identifier be set, as outlined in Table 2-5.

Bit 6	Bit 7	Meaning
0	0	Locally unique, individual
0	1	Locally unique, group
1	0	Globally unique, individual
1	1	Globally unique, group

Table 2-5 Global/local and individual/group bits in the IPv6 interface ID
© Cengage Learning 2013

Not coincidentally, this allows administrators to create locally unique individual interface identifiers in the following form:

: :3

: :D4

The precise techniques used to create unique interface identifiers are specified for each type of network, such as Ethernet.

In the past several years, manufacturers such as Sony, Matsushita, Hitachi, Ariston Digital, Lantronix, and Axis Communications have announced products that are either Internet ready or Internet enabled, many with built-in interfaces to permit Web-based remote access for monitoring, programming, or operating instructions. Presumably, this means such manufacturers embed a serial number that can be used to generate a unique interface identifier for every individual device they manufacture. With some 18 billion billion (i.e., 10^{18}) possible combinations, the 64-bit identifier used for IPv6 addresses allows plenty of room for all kinds of interesting and innovative uses of networking access and technology.

To meet concerns about privacy and long-term security, RFC 3041 proposes methods for changing an interface's unique identifier over time, particularly when it is derived from the MAC address of the interface card. This is proposed as an optional approach to generating a unique interface identifier for those concerned with the security implications involved in defining one's identity with certainty, presumably through unauthorized traffic analysis.

Native IPv6 Addresses in URLs

RFC 2732 (originally proposed in 1999) describes a method to express IPv6 addresses in a form compatible with HTTP URLs. Because the colon character (:) is used by most browsers to set off a port number from an IPv4 address, native IPv6 addresses in their ordinary notation would cause problems. This RFC uses another pair of reserved characters, the square brackets ([and]), to enclose a literal IPv6 address. The RFC indicates that these square bracket characters are reserved in URLs exclusively for expressing IPv6 addresses. This RFC is now a standard, which means that this syntax represents the official format for expressing IPv6 addresses inside URLs.

Thus, an HTTP service available at port 70 of IPv6 address FEDC:BA98:7654:3210:FEDC:BA98:7654:3210 should be denoted as http://[FEDC:BA98:7654:3210:FEDC:BA98:7654:3210]:70/ (in literal form). (Chapter 8 covers literal addresses.)

Address Types

IPv6 allows only a few address types, and it sets up those types to allow maximum throughput of ordinary traffic on the now much larger Internet. In a sense, the old IPv4 classful address structure was designed as much for ease of human understanding as it was for machine usability. The new IPv6 address types take advantage of years of experience with routing across large hierarchical domains to streamline the whole operation. The IPv6 address space is optimized for routing.

The following sections discuss several types of addresses, including special use (unspecified and loopback), multicast, anycast, unicast, aggregatable global unicast, and link-local and site-local.

Special Addresses Two individual addresses are reserved for special use: the unspecified address and the loopback address. The **unspecified address** is all zeroes and can be represented as two colon characters (::) in normal notation. This is essentially an address that is no address. It cannot be used as a destination address. Thus far, the only proposed use for the unspecified address is for nodes that do not yet know their own addresses but must send a message upon machine start-up. Such a node might, for example, send a message asking attached routers on the local link to announce their addresses, thereby allowing the new node to understand where it is.

Loopback is the name of a special IP address that allows a host on a network to check the operation of its own local TCP/IP protocol stack. For IPv6, the loopback address is all zeroes except for the very last bit, which is set to 1. Thus, this address may be represented as two colon characters followed by a 1 (::1) in compact notation. The loopback address is a diagnostic tool for local use only and cannot be routed or used as either a source or destination address for packets actually sent onto a network. When a packet is sent with the loopback address as its destination, it means that the IPv6 stack on the sending host simply sends the message to itself—down through the stack and then back up without ever accessing an actual network interface. Such behavior is needed to make sure that a device's IP stack is properly installed and configured. (Think of it this way: A device that can't "talk to itself" surely can't talk to other devices.)

In IPv4, an entire Class A network, 127.x.x.x, was dedicated to the loopback function, removing millions of addresses from the available pool. This is a small but clear example of the way in which actual use guided the design improvements built into IPv6.

Multicast Addresses In IPv6, **multicast addresses** are used to send an identical message to multiple hosts. On a local Ethernet, hosts can listen for traffic addressed to multicasts to which they subscribe. On other types of networks, multicast traffic must be handled in a different way, sometimes by a dedicated server that forwards multicasts to each individual subscriber.

The whole point of multicast is that it is subscription based. Nodes must announce that they wish to receive multicast traffic bound for a particular multicast address. For multicast traffic originating off the local link, the connecting router(s) must subscribe to the same multicast traffic on behalf of connected nodes.

Multicast addresses follow the format shown in Figure 2-4. The first byte (8 bits) is set to all ones (0xFF), indicating a multicast address. The second byte is divided into two fields. The Flags field is 4 bits long and is followed by a Scope field, which is also 4 bits long. The remaining 112 bits define the identifier for the multicast group.

8	4	4	112 bits
11111111	FLAGS	SCOPE	GROUP ID

Figure 2-4 IPv6 multicast address format
© Cengage Learning 2013

The Flags field is treated as a set of four individual 1-bit flags. No meaning has yet been assigned to the first three flags. They are reserved for future use and must all be set to 0. The fourth flag is set to 1 when the multicast address is a temporary or transient address. If the address is a well-known multicast address, this flag is set to 0.

As you can imagine, the performance of the entire Internet could be severely inhibited without some way of limiting the range over which multicast traffic is forwarded. The Scope field of the multicast address limits the range of addresses over which the multicast subscriber group is valid. Possible values for the Scope field are shown in Table 2-6.

Transient or temporary multicast addresses are established for some particular temporary purpose and then abandoned. This is analogous to the way in which TCP might use an unassigned port for a temporary session. The Group ID of a temporary multicast address is meaningless outside its own scope. That is, two groups with identical Group IDs but different scopes are completely unrelated when the "T" flag is set to 1. In contrast, well-known Group IDs (where the T bit is set to 0) are assigned to such entities as all routers or all DHCP servers. In combination with the Scope field, this allows a multicast address to define all routers on the local link or all DHCP servers on the global Internet.

Although the last 112 bits of the multicast address are assigned to the Group ID, the first 80 bits are set to all zeroes for all multicast addresses currently defined or planned for the future. The remaining 32 bits of address space must contain the whole non-zero part of the Group ID. With over four billion possible Group IDs, this should be sufficient for all foreseeable purposes.

A special type of multicast address called the solicited node address is used to support Neighbor Solicitation (NS). The structure of this address and the method used to create it are described in the "Neighbor Discovery and Router Advertisement" section later in this chapter.

No More Broadcasts

Another result of usage experience is the abandonment, in IPv6, of the broadcast address. Broadcasts are extremely expensive in terms of bandwidth and routing resources. In IPv6, any functions once handled by a broadcast in IPv4 can be replicated with a multicast. The key distinction between the two versions is that nodes must subscribe to multicasts. In addition, multicasts are easier to control and route effectively in IPv6, in part because of the new Scope field and other address and routing features, as described in the following section.

Hexadecimal	Decimal	Scope assignment
0	0	Reserved
1	1	Interface-local scope
2	2	Link-local scope
3	3	Draft reserves for subnet-local
4	4	Draft proposes admin-local
5	5	Site-local scope
6	6	Unassigned
7	7	Unassigned
8	8	Organization-local scope
9	9	Unassigned
A	10	Unassigned
B	11	Unassigned
C	12	Unassigned
D	13	Unassigned
E	14	Global scope
F	15	Reserved

Table 2-6 **IPv6 multicast address scope field values**
© Cengage Learning 2013

Anycast Addresses IPv6 introduces a new type of address called an **anycast address**. Packets addressed to an anycast address go to the nearest single instance of that address. "Near" in this case is defined in terms of a router's view of network distance. The anycast address is used to address functions that are commonly deployed on the Internet at multiple network locations. Examples include routers, DHCP servers, and the like. Rather than using a multicast address to send a packet to all Network Time Protocol (NTP) servers on the local link, a node can send a packet to the anycast address for all NTP servers and be assured that the packet will be delivered to the nearest server with that anycast address.

An anycast address takes the same format as a unicast address and is indistinguishable from a unicast address. Each server or node wishing to receive anycast traffic must be configured to listen for traffic sent to that address.

RFC 3513 requires all subnets to support the subnet router anycast address. Likewise, all routers on a given subnet must support the subnet router anycast address. The format of the subnet router anycast address is the subnet prefix followed by all zeroes. In other words, the subnet prefix takes as many bytes or bits as are required to precisely identify the subnet that those routers serve. Their anycast addressses are the subnet's prefix padded to the right with enough zeroes to make up 128 bits. As an example, the subnet router anycast address is intended for use by mobile users seeking to communicate with any router on their home networks.

RFC 2526 proposes that the highest 128 interface ID values in each subnet be reserved for assignment to subnet anycast addresses. This means that the 64-bit interface ID portion of these addresses would be all ones except for the global/local bit, which must be set to 0 (local), and the last seven binary digits, which form the anycast ID. The only particular anycast assignment suggested in this RFC is for the Mobile IPv6 home agent servers, which are to be assigned an anycast ID of 126 (decimal) or 0xFE. All other anycast IDs are reserved.

Unicast Addresses The unicast address, as its name implies, is sent to one network interface. It can be thought of as the basic or ordinary address in the IPv6 address space. The format is a 64-bit interface ID in the least significant bits and a 64-bit network portion of the address in the most significant bits. (If n is a symbol for a 16-bit number in the networking portion, and h is a symbol for a 16-bit number in the host portion, such an IPv6 address takes the general form $n:n:n:n:h:h:h:h$.)

Aggregatable Global Unicast Addresses To aid in routing and the administration of addresses, IPv6 creates a particular kind of unicast address called the **aggregatable global unicast address**, which is an address that can be combined with other addresses into a single entry in the router table. The layout of such addresses breaks the leftmost 64 bits of the address (which includes fields FP through SLA ID—the network portion) into explicit fields to allow for easier routing. Specifically, it allows routes to these addresses to be "aggregated"—that is, combined into a single entry in the router table. The format of an aggregatable global unicast address is shown in Figure 2-5.

The FP, or Format Prefix, field is a 3-bit identifier used to show to which part of the IPv6 address space this address belongs. At this writing, all aggregatable addresses must have 001 (binary) in this field.

3	13	8	24	16	64 bits
FP	TLA ID	RES	NLA ID	SLA ID	INTERFACE ID

Figure 2-5 Aggregatable global unicast address format
© Cengage Learning 2013

The TLA ID, or Top-Level Aggregation ID, field is 13 bits long and allows 2^{13} top-level routes, or some 8,000 highest-level groups of addresses.

The next field, marked "RES," is 8 bits long and is reserved for future use.

The NLA ID, or Next-Level Aggregation ID, field is 24 bits long. This field allows the entities controlling any one of the TLAs to divide their address blocks into whatever size blocks they wish. These entities are likely to be large ISPs or other very large Internet entities. They can share some of this address space with others. For example, they might reserve only half of these bits for themselves, which allows smaller ISPs to allocate very large blocks of addresses. The smaller ISPs can then subdivide these blocks further, if there is enough space in the NLA field to permit them to do so.

The SLA ID, or Site-Level Aggregation ID, field is 16 bits long and permits the creation of 65,535 addresses as a flat address space. Alternatively, users can set it up hierarchically and use this portion of the address to create 255 subnets with 255 addresses each. As the name implies, individual sites are expected to be allocated an address block of this size.

The Interface ID field is the same EUI-64 format interface identifier described earlier.

Link-Local and Site-Local Addresses Another example of the ways in which IPv6 builds on the experience of IPv4 is the creation of link-local and site-local addresses. Similar to the 10.x.x.x or 192.68.x.x addresses of IPv4, these private addresses are not to be routed outside their own areas, but they use the same general 128-bit address length and the same interface ID format as any other unicast address. The formats for each of these address types are shown in Figure 2-6.

IPv6 Link-Local Address Format

10 bits	54 bits	64 bits
1111111010	0	INTERFACE ID

IPv6 Site-Local Address Format

10 bits	38 bits	16 bits	64 bits
1111111011	0	SUBNET ID	INTERFACE ID

Figure 2-6 IPv6 link-local and site-local address formats
© Cengage Learning 2013

The **link-local address** has its first 10 (leftmost) bits set to 1111111010 (all ones except for the last three digits, which are set to 010 [binary]). The next 54 bits are set to all zeroes. The final (rightmost) 64 bits of the link-local address represent a normal interface ID. When a router sees a link-local address prefix in a packet, it knows it can safely ignore it, as that packet is intended only for the local network segment.

The **site-local address** has its first 10 (leftmost) bits set to 1111111011 (all ones except for the last three digits, which are set to 011 [binary]). The next 38 bits are set to all zeroes, and the next 16 bits contain the subnet ID that defines the "site" to which this address is local. As in other unicast type addresses, the final (rightmost) 64 bits represent a standard interface ID. Site-local addresses allow packets to be forwarded internally within a site but prevent such packets from being visible on the public Internet.

Site-local and link-local addresses are each assigned a 1/1024 portion of the IPv6 address space (according to RFC 3513), as shown in Table 2-7.

Allocation	Prefix (binary)	Fraction of address space
Unassigned	0000 0000	1/256
Unassigned	0000 0001	1/256
Reserved for NSAP	0000 001	1/128
Unassigned	0000 01	1/64
Unassigned	0000 1	1/32
Unassigned	0001	1/16
Global unicast	001	1/8
Unassigned	010	1/8
Unassigned	011	1/8
Unassigned	100	1/8
Unassigned	101	1/8
Unassigned	110	1/8
Unassigned	1110	1/16
Unassigned	1111 0	1/32
Unassigned	1111 10	1/64
Unassigned	1111 110	1/128
Unassigned	1111 1110 0	1/512
Link-local unicast addresses	1111 1110 10	1/1024
Site-local unicast addresses	1111 1110 11	1/1024
Multicast addresses	1111 1111	1/256

Table 2-7 IPv6 address space allocations
© Cengage Learning 2013

Address Allocations

The raw address space available in a 128-bit numbering scheme is truly vast, on the order of $3.4 * 10^{38}$ unique values. Even with careful adherence to hierarchical addressing, reservations for special-purpose addresses, and additional reservations mentioned later in this section,

IPv6 pre-allocates only about 15 percent of its available addresses. That leaves at least $2.89 * 10^{38}$ addresses available for other uses.

Special addresses, such as the loopback address, the unspecified address, and IPv6 addresses that contain IPv4 addresses, are all taken from the Unassigned category shown in Table 2-4, as part of the group of addresses that begins with "0000 0000" (binary).

NSAP Allocation As shown in Table 2-4, 1/128 of all the IPv6 address space was set aside for addresses using **Network Service Access Point (NSAP)** addressing. These networks (ATM, X.25, and so forth) typically set up point-to-point links between hosts. This is a different paradigm from the one built into IP. The approach most customers take is to map their different IP addresses into IPv6.

Unicast and Anycast Allocations As the name implies, the routes to addresses taken from the aggregatable global unicast address blocks can be aggregated easily. Various schemes have been advanced for allocating IPv6 addresses. The current scheme is to assign address blocks to "exchanges," which then make further distributions. This sidesteps the issue rather than actually resolving objections raised against earlier proposals for separate blocks to be assigned by "providers" and geographically (by physical location of the hosts involved).

RFC 3513 notes that all addresses beginning with 001 through 111 (except the multicast addresses, which begin with 1111 1111 [binary]) must include a 64-bit interface identifier as their least significant (rightmost) portions. This entire section of addresses, though mostly still unallocated, is clearly intended to serve individual devices.

Multicast Allocations Multicast is allocated for all the IPv6 addresses beginning with 0xFF, as shown in Table 2-4. This constitutes 1/256 of the available address space. The maximum number of multicast addresses is further constrained by the requirement that the Group ID be contained in the last (rightmost) 112 bits of the address. This still leaves room for over four billion well-known multicast addresses and a far larger number of usable transient multicast addresses.

IPv6 Addressing and Subnetting Considerations

IPv6 is generally understood to not require subnetting, but that doesn't mean you can't allocate different portions of your address space to support multiple network segments or virtual LANs (VLANs). The extent to which you can "subnet" an IPv6 address depends on the length of the prefix, which is the network identifier portion of the address. The prefix for an address is expressed as a forward slash followed by the number of bits. The following example is an address with a 64-bit prefix: 2001:0db8:1234::c0a8:0001/64.

NOTE An address such as 2001:0db8:1234:c0a8:0001/64 is technically "subnetted," the first 64 bits being the network address and the second 64 bits being the host address. The number of bits following the forward slash represents the netmask of the address.

How you apportion the host addressing depends on the prefix length. Currently, many ISPs only issue public address space with a /64 mask, although some may provide other prefix lengths. A 64-bit prefix length provides about four billion times the addresses that are available in IPv4, which seems like a terrible waste of address space for one organization, but you may have no other option when requesting a block of IPv6 addresses from your ISP. However, you will need an address space with a /32 prefix length or greater to be able to effectively apportion the address space into "subnets."

A significant issue regarding how you will be able to apportion your address space into different host segments or VLANs is how well your networked devices support IPv6 address configuration. Some manufacturers may allow customers to change the network portion but not the host portion of their devices, whereas others support changing the address but not the gateway. Currently, there is no industry-wide consensus on how to manage hardware/firmware support of IPv6 addressing on networked devices, and this limits your ability to "subdivide" your company's IPv6 addresses.

To briefly illustrate the concept of apportioning an IPv6 address space into different network segments, let's look at 2001:db8:1xx:y::z/64, which takes a /64 address space and creates different "subnets" as VLANs: 2001:db8:1xx:y::z/64. In this example:

xx = group number (01–24)

y = VLAN-ID

z = host address

Using this scheme, here are some examples of how to apportion the address space for different VLANs. These use zero compression in the addresses, when applicable:

VLAN: group 1, vlan 0, host 1

  2001:db8:101::1

VLAN: group 3, vlan 101, host 101

  2001:db8:103:101::101

VLAN: group 15, vlan 101, host 101

  2001:db8:115:101::101

"Subnetting" an IPv6 address space isn't technically necessary—not for the reasons you subnetted IPv4 networks, anyway. IPv4 subnetting was implemented largely to make more efficient use of limited IPv4 address space. This is not a consideration with IPv6. However, you may want to subdivide your network space based on various factors, such as geographic locations, organizational divisions, and so forth.

The IPv4 to IPv6 Transition

As you can see, there are outstanding advantages to using IPv6 instead of IPv4. Given that RFC 2460, which introduced the IPv6 specification, was published in December of 1998, you might ask why haven't we changed to IPv6?

Unfortunately, IPv4 and IPv6 networks don't communicate well with each other. IPv6 is backward compatible with IPv4, but only in a limited sense that groups of IPv6 devices can communicate over IPv4 networks using tunneling. Also, IPv4 addresses can be embedded in the IPv6 address structure and allow those addresses to be recognized by (at least some) IPv6 devices as IPv4 addresses, but that approach has been deprecated and isn't used anymore.

The address embedding solution isn't viable to allow communication on mixed IPv4/IPv6 networks attempting to support a wide variety of IPv4 and IPv6 devices.

On June 8, 2011, the Internet Society held an event called World IPv6 Day (*www.worldipv6day. org/*). Over 1,000 companies participated, including Google, Facebook, Yahoo!, and Akamai. Each company offered dual versions of its Web site, one for IPv4 and one for IPv6. This was a way for everyone to test their IPv6 readiness, and it served as a wake-up call to everyone with a Web presence regarding how far away we are from an IPv6 Internet.

The worldwide implementation of IPv6 is an absolute necessity but will require the cooperation of many industries in producing the hardware, software, and infrastructure necessary to experience IPv6's benefits.

Several methods can be used to ease the transition between IPv4 and IPv6. Both network infrastructure types will be cohabitating for quite some time as the move from IPv4 to IPv6 progresses, and that move has barely begun. Here are some technologies that will allow IPv4 and IPv6 hosts and networks to exist together:

- *Teredo tunneling*—This is a tunneling technology specifically designed to allow full IPv6 connectivity between hosts on an IPv4 Internet. Teredo allows IPv6 datagrams to be encapsulated in IPv4 UDP packets. These IPv4 packets can then be forwarded, even through NAT devices, and routed on IPv4 networks. Once the packets have been received by the destination Teredo node, the IPv4 encapsulation is stripped away and the IPv6 packet can run on native IPv6 networks and be received by an IPv6 network host. Windows Vista and Windows 7 natively support Teredo; however, if only a link-local and Teredo address are available, Windows will not resolve IPv6 DNS AAAA records unless a DNS A record is already present.

- *ISATAP or Intra-Site Automatic Tunnel Addressing Protocol*—This protocol is specified in RFC 4214 and is another method of connecting IPv6 computers and routers to each other over IPv4 networks. ISATAP generates a link-local IPv6 address from a computer's IPv4 address and can perform IPv6 neighbor discovery on top of the IPv4 protocol. ISATAP uses IPv4 as a virtual nonbroadcast multiple-access network (NBMA) Data Link layer. This allows the use of multicast packets without IPv4 needing to support multicast messaging. ISATAP is supported on Windows XP and subsequent versions of Windows as well as Linux and some versions of the Cisco IOS.

- *6to4 tunneling*—This is a method used to facilitate IPv4 to IPv6 migration by allowing IPv6 packets to be sent over IPv4 networks, including the Internet, without the need to explicitly configure tunneling. It can be used by an individual IPv6 network node or by an IPv6 network. When used by a host, the computer must have a global IPv4 address connected, and the host must provide encapsulation of any IPv6 packets being transmitted and decapsulation of any IPv6 packets it receives. 6to4 assigns a collection of IPv6 addresses to a netwrok node possessing a global IPv4 address. It then can encapsulate IPv6 datagrams inside IPv4 packets and send them out over an IPv4 network.

This is an older "tunneling" technology and is meant to be a transitional method and not a permanent solution.

- *NAT-PT (Network Address Translation-Protocol Translation)*—Originally specified by RFC 2766, this is also meant to be used for IPv4-to-IPv6 transition, allowing IPv6 packets to be sent back and forth across IPv4 networks. RFC 4966 depreciated this technology because of numerous problems, and it now is considered to have "historic" status. NAPT-PT (Network Address Port Translation-Protocol Translation) is very similar to NAT-PT and was specified with NAT-PT in RFC 2766. It is also a depreciated method. (For more details about transitioning from IPv4 to IPv6, see Chapter 10.)

Chapter Summary

- IP addresses provide the foundation for identifying individual network interfaces (and, therefore, computers or other devices) on TCP/IP networks. Understanding address structures, restrictions, and behavior is essential to designing TCP/IP networks and appreciating how existing TCP/IP networks are organized.

- IPv4 addresses come in five classes named A through E. Classes A through C use the IPv4 32-bit address to establish different breakpoints between the network and host portions of such network addresses. Class A uses a single octet for the network address and three octets for the host address; Class B uses two octets each for network and host portions; and Class C uses three octets for the network portion and one octet for the host portion. Thus, only a few (124) Class A networks exist, but each can support more than 16,000,000 hosts; numerous (over 16,000) Class B networks exist, and each can support around 65,000 hosts, and approximately 2,000,000 Class C networks exist, each with only 254 hosts per network.

- To help ease the burden of address scarcity, the IETF created a form of classless addressing called Classless Inter-Domain Routing (CIDR) that permits the network-host boundary to fall away from octet boundaries. CIDR is best used in aggregating multiple Class C addresses to decrease the number of networks while increasing the number of addressable hosts. This technique is called supernetting.

- To make best use of IP network addresses, a technique called subnetting permits additional bits to be taken from the host portion of a network. Recognizing the fol-lowing bit patterns (decimal values appear in parentheses) helps when calculating or examining subnet masks: 11000000 (192), 11100000 (224), 11110000 (240), 11111000 (248), and 11111100 (252).

- There are several techniques for hiding internal network IP addresses from outside view, including address masquerading and address substitution. These techniques replace the actual internal network address from the source field in the IP header with a different value that reveals nothing about the actual address structure of the origi-nating network. Either Network Address Translation (NAT) software or a proxy server usually handles this kind of task.

- Within the Class A, B, and C IPv4 address ranges, the IETF has reserved private IP addresses or address ranges. Any organization may use these private IPv4 addresses without charge and without obtaining prior permission, but private IPv4 addresses may not be routed across the public Internet. In fact, another important job for NAT is software mapping a range of private IPv4 addresses to a single public IPv4 address, which permits computers that use private IP addresses to obtain Internet access.

■ The Internet Corporation for Assigned Names and Numbers (ICANN) is the ultimate authority in assigning public IP addresses. (Previously, the Internet Assigned Numbers Authority, or IANA, handled this task.) Today, unassigned public IPv4 addresses are extremely scarce and, therefore, unlikely to be allocated to most ordinary organizations. In fact, most IPv4 address assignments come from ISPs that subdivide already assigned Class A, B, or C addresses and then assign these public IPv4 addresses to their customers.

■ The world has all but run out of IPv4 addresses, the maximum being about four billion unique IP addresses. Although address classes, CIDR, and NAT have extended the lifetime of IPv4, there are currently too many types of devices that require their own IP addresses. Although IPv4 uses a 32-bit address space, IPv6 uses a 128-bit address space, producing 2^{128} (or approximately 340,282,366,920,938,000,000, 000,000,000,000,000,000) unique IP addresses.

■ IPv6 introduces a number of improvements and updates to the IP protocol, the chief among those being a vastly larger IP address space. Other improvements include eliminating the need for NAT and other technologies that were used to extend the lifetime of IPv4, easier IP address configuration administration, better routing support, better support for mobile IP devices, and support for IP security by using authentication and encryption extension headers.

■ IPv6 supports three address types: unicast, multicast, and anycast. Unicast addresses are standard IP addresses assigned to a single network interface on an individual host. Multicast addresses represent particular groups of network devices so that a message sent to a single multicast address is received by all the members of the multicast group. Although multicast was considered optional under IPv4, it is required in IPv6. Anycast addresses are used to communicate with only one member of a group, which is usually the member that is easiest to reach. This is typically used for load balancing among a group of network devices such as routers.

■ IPv6 employs two private or local-use address schemes that are implemented on the local or LAN network but not on global networks such as the Internet: site-local and link-local. Site-local addresses have a scope of the entire site of an organization and can be used to communicate with any device within the company's internal network infrastructure, but not with the Internet. Site-local communications transverses internal routers but not the Internet gateway. Link-local addresses have a more limited scope than site-local and can communicate only within a single network segment. This traffic will not transverse internal routers and can only be sent to other devices on the same physical network segment.

■ IPv6 prefix lengths define the number of bits apportioned to the network address and to the host address by using a forward slash followed by the number of bits. This can be expressed, for example, as 2001:0db8:1234::c0a8:0001/64. Although IPv6 addresses do not technically need to be subnetted for the reasons that IPv4 address space was subnetted, it is possible to divide the address space into different network segments or VLANs in order to organize networked devices by type, geographic location, or organizational division.

Key Terms

:: In IPv6 addresses, a pair of colon characters stands for several contiguous 16-bit groups, each of which is all zeroes. This notation can be used only once in any address.

address masquerading A method of mapping many internal (i.e., private), nonroutable addresses to a single external (i.e., public) IP address for the purpose of sharing a single Internet connection—also referred to as "address hiding."

aggregatable global unicast address The layout of these IPv6 addresses breaks the leftmost 64 bits of the address into explicit fields to allow for easier routing. Specifically, it allows routes to these addresses to be "aggregated"—that is, combined into a single entry in the router table.

anycast address A type of ordinary address in IPv6 that can be assigned to more than one host or interface. Packets pointed to an anycast address are delivered to the holder of that address nearest to the sender in terms of routing distance. An anycast address does not apply to IPv4.

application-specific integrated circuit (ASIC) A special-purpose form of integrated circuit that provides a way to implement specific programming logic directly into chip form, thereby providing the fastest possible execution of such programming logic when processing data. ASICs are what make it possible for high-speed, high-volume routers to perform complex address recognition and management functions that can keep up with data volumes and time-sensitive processing needs.

Bitcricket IP Calculator A downloadable subnet mask calculator produced by WildPackets that provides both IPv4 and IPv6 support.

broadcast address The all-ones address for a network or subnet, which provides a way to send the same information to all interfaces on a network.

Classless Inter-Domain Routing (CIDR) A form of subnet masking that does away with placing network and host address portions precisely on octet boundaries and instead uses the /*n* prefix notation, in which *n* indicates the number of bits in the network portion of whatever address is presented.

constant-length subnet masking (CLSM) An IP subnetting scheme in which all subnets use the same size subnet mask, which therefore divides the subnetted address space into a fixed number of equal-size subnets.

domain name A symbolic name for a TCP/IP network resource; the Domain Name System (DNS) translates such names into numeric IP addresses so outbound traffic may be addressed properly.

Domain Name System (DNS) The TCP/IP Application layer protocol and service that manages an Internet-wide distributed database of symbolic domain names and numeric IP addresses so that users can ask for resources by name and get those names translated into the correct numeric IP addresses.

dot quad *See* dotted decimal notation.

dotted decimal notation The name for the format used to denote numeric IP addresses, such as 172.16.1.7, wherein four numbers are separated by periods (dots).

end-to-end connection A network connection in which the original sending and receiving IP addresses may not be altered and where a communications connection extends all the way from sender to receiver while that connection remains active.

EUI-64 format An IEEE transformation permitting the burned-in MAC addresses of NICs to be padded in particular ways to create globally unique 64-bit interface identifiers for each interface.

extended network prefix The portion of an IP address that represents the sum of the network portion of the address plus the number of bits used for subnetting that network address; a Class B address with a 3-bit subnetting scheme would have an extended network prefix of /19—16 bits for the default network portion, plus three bits for the subnetting portion of that address, with a corresponding subnet mask of 255.255.224.0.

firewall A network boundary device that sits between the public and private sides of a network and provides a variety of screening and inspection services to ensure that only safe, authorized traffic flows from outside to inside.

hop A single transfer of data from one network to another through some kind of networking device. Router-to-router transfers are often called hops. The number of hops often provides a rough measure of the distance between a sender's network and a receiver's network. The number of routers that a packet must cross, or the number of routers that a packet crosses, represents the hop count from the source network to the target network.

host portion The rightmost bits in an IP address, allocated to identify hosts on a supernetwork, network, or subnetwork.

interface identifier In IPv6 addressing, unicast and anycast addresses have the lower-order bits of their addresses reserved for a bit string that uniquely identifies a particular interface, either globally or (at a minimum) locally.

Internet Assigned Numbers Authority (IANA) The arm of the ISOC originally responsible for registering domain names and allocating public IP addresses. This job is now the responsibility of ICANN.

Internet service provider (ISP) An organization that, as a primary line of business, provides Internet access to individuals or organizations. Currently, ISPs are the source of public IP addresses for most organizations seeking Internet access.

IP gateway TCP/IP terminology for a router that provides access to resources outside the local subnet network address. (A default gateway is the name given to the TCP/IP configuration entry for clients that identifies the router they must use to send data outside their local subnet areas.)

IP renumbering The process of replacing one set of numeric IP addresses with another set of numeric IP addresses, either because of a change in ISPs or an address reassignment.

Layer 3 switch A type of networking device that combines hub, router, and network management functions within a single box. Layer 3 switches make it possible to create and manage multiple virtual subnets in a single device while offering extremely high bandwidth to individual connections between pairs of devices attached to that device.

link layer This is the lowest level of the Internet Protocol suite and represents the elements and protocols found in the OSI layer's Data Link and Physical layers.

link-local address An addressing scheme that is designed to be used only on a single segment of a local network.

loopback address An address that points directly back to the sender. In IPv4, the Class A domain 127.0.0.0 (or 127.0.0.1 for a specific machine address) is reserved for loopback. In IPv6, there is a single loopback address, written "::1" (all 0s, except for that last bit, which is 1). By passing traffic down through the TCP/IP stack, then back up again, the loopback address can be used to test a computer's TCP/IP software.

Media Access Control (MAC) layer   A sublayer of the Data Link layer. This layer is part of the Media Access Control definition, in which network access methods, such as Ethernet and token ring, apply.

Media Access Control (MAC) layer address   A special type of network address, handled by a sublayer of the Data Link layer, normally pre-assigned on a per-interface basis to uniquely identify each such interface on any network cable segment (or virtual facsimile).

multicast address   One of a block of addresses reserved for use in sending the same message to multiple interfaces or nodes. Members of a community of interest subscribe to a multicast address in order to receive router updates, streaming data (video, audio, teleconferencing), and so on. In IPv4, the Class D block of addresses is reserved for multicast. In IPv6, all multicast addresses begin with 0xFF. ICANN, with the help of IANA, manages all such address adjustments.

network address   That portion of an IP address that consists of the network prefix for that address; an extended network prefix also includes any subnetting bits. All bits that belong to the extended network prefix show up as 1s in the corresponding subnet mask for that network.

Network Address Translation (NAT)   A method of address translation that modifies IP address information in a router, changing the public address used on the Internet to private addresses used on internal networks.

network portion   The leftmost octets or bits in a numeric IP address, which identifies the network and subnet portions of that address. The value assigned to the prefix number identifies the number of bits in the network portion of a IP address. (For example, 10.0.0.0/8 indicates that the first 8 bits of the address are the network portion for the public Class A IP address.)

network prefix   That portion of an IP address that corresponds to the network portion of the address; for example, the network prefix for a Class B address is /16, meaning that the first 16 bits represent the network portion of the address and 255.255.0.0 is the corresponding default subnet mask.

Network Service Access Point (NSAP)   A type of hierarchical address scheme used to implement Open System Interconnection (OSI) network layer addressing and a logical point between the network and transport layers in the OSI model.

numeric address   *See* numeric IP address.

numeric IP address   An IP address expressed in dotted decimal or binary notation.

octet   TCP/IP terminology for an 8-bit number; numeric IPv4 addresses consist of four octets.

organizationally unique identifier (OUI)   A unique identifier assigned by IANA or ICANN that's used as the first three bytes of a NIC's MAC layer address to identify its maker or manufacturer.

physical numeric address   Another term for MAC layer address (or MAC address).

private IP address   Any of a series of Class A, B, and C IP addresses reserved by IANA for private use (documented in RFC 1918) and intended for uncontrolled private use in organizations. Private IP addresses may not be routed across the Internet because there is no guarantee that any such address is unique.

proxy server   A special type of network boundary service that interposes itself between internal network addresses and external network addresses. For internal clients, a proxy server makes a connection to external resources on the client's behalf and provides address masquerading. For external clients, a proxy server presents internal resources to the public Internet as if they are present on the proxy server itself.

public IP address   Any TCP/IP address allocated by IANA or ICANN (or by an ISP to one of its clients) for the exclusive use of some particular organization.

quality of service (QoS)   A specific level of service guarantee associated with Application layer protocols in which time-sensitivity requirements for data (such as voice or video) require that delays be controlled within definite guidelines to deliver viewable or audible data streams.

reverse proxying   The technique whereby a proxy server presents an internal network resource (e.g., a Web, e-mail, or FTP server) as if it were present on the proxy server itself so that external clients can access internal network resources without seeing internal network IP address structures.

route aggregation   A form of IP address analysis that permits routers to indicate general interest in a particular network prefix that represents the "common portion" of a series of IP network addresses as a way of reducing the number of individual routing table entries that routers must manage.

scope identifier   In IPv6, a 4-bit field limiting the valid range for a multicast address. In IPv6 multicast addresses, not all values are defined, but among those defined are the site-local and the link-local scope. Multicast addresses are not valid outside their configured scope and will not be forwarded beyond it.

site-local address   An addressing scheme limited to use in private networks within a specific site.

subnet mask   A special bit pattern that masks off the network portion of an IP address with all 1s.

subnetting   The operation of using bits borrowed from the host portion of an IP address to extend and subdivide the address space that falls beneath the network portion of a range of IP addresses.

summary address   A form of specialized IP network address that identifies the "common portion" of a series of IP network addresses used when route aggregation is in effect. This approach speeds routing behavior and decreases the number of entries necessary for routing tables.

supernetting   The technique of borrowing bits from the network portion of an IP address and lending those bits to the host part, creating a larger address space for host addresses.

symbolic name   A human-readable name for an Internet resource, such as *www.course.com* or *www.microsoft.com*; also a name used to represent a device instead of an address.

unspecified address   In IPv6, the unspecified address is all zeroes and can be represented as "::" in normal notation. This is essentially the address that is no address. It cannot be used as a destination address.

variable-length subnet masking (VLSM)   A subnetting scheme for IP addresses that permits containers of various sizes to be defined for a network prefix. The largest subnet defines the maximum container size, and any individual container in that address space may be further subdivided into multiple, smaller sub-containers (sometimes called sub-subnets).

words Blocks of four, 16-bit values in an IPv6 address; each word is separated by a colon, and there are eight words in every IPv6 address. If a word is made up of contiguous zeros, it can be compressed so that the zeros do not appear in the address but the colon separators remain.

Review Questions

1. Which address is used to identify the sender and receiver in an IP packet header?

    a. domain name

    b. symbolic name

    c. numeric IP

    d. return

2. Which of the following is an 8-bit number that denotes various portions of an IPv4 address?

    a. byte

    b. dotted decimal

    c. octet

    d. bit string

3. Which of the following terms is a synonym for a physical numeric address?

    a. hardware address

    b. MAC layer address

    c. PROM address

    d. RIPL address

4. Which of the following protocols translates a numeric IP address to a physical numeric address?

    a. ICMP

    b. IP

    c. ARP

    d. RARP

5. Which of the following types of IPv4 addresses includes the most host addresses?

    a. Class A

    b. Class B

    c. Class C

    d. Class D

    e. Class E

6. Which of the following address types are supported by IPv6? (Choose all that apply.)

    a. anycast

    b. broadcast

    c. multicast

    d. unicast

7. How large is the IPv6 address space?

    a. 32 bits

    b. 64 bits

    c. 128 bits

    d. 256 bits

8. A Class A network address of 12.0.0.0 is written as 12.0.0.0/8 in prefix notation. True or false?

9. Zero compression is a method that allows a a word containing contiguous zeros in an IPv6 address to be replaced by double colons. True or false?

10. Which of the following address types are used for local network communications in IPv6? (Choose all that apply.)

    a. link-layer

    b. link-local

    c. local-use

    d. site-local

11. Which of the following IPv6 addresses are the same based on the correct use of zero compression? (Choose all that apply.)

    a. FE80::2D57:C4F8::80D7

    b. FE80:0000:2D57:C4F8:0000:80D7

    c. FE8::2D57:C4F8::8D7

    d. FE80:0:2D57:C4F8:0:80D7

12. Which of the following represents an improvement of IPv6 over IPv4? (Choose all that apply.)

    a. larger address space

    b. better security

    c. improved broadcast support

    d. better support for mobile IP

13. A default gateway is _____ .

    a. any IP router

    b. an IP router attached to the Internet

    c. an IP configuration element that names the router/gateway for a particular subnet

    d. an IP configuration element that names the boundary router to the Internet

14. IPv6 requires each device on the network to have its own unique address or identifier, with one exception:

    a. Mobile devices may use multiple identifiers because they frequently move from one network zone to the next.

    b. A host with multiple interfaces providing dynamic load balancing can use a single identifier for all interfaces.

    c. Network devices in a multicast group all use a single, unique identifier for their interfaces.

    d. Multiple devices on a local network may share the same anycast identifier.

15. Native IPv6 addresses in a URL use which of the following characters to enclose the literal IPv6 address, according to RFC 2732?

    a. two colons

    b. two braces

    c. two brackets

    d. two forward slashes

16. Which RFC covers Classless Inter-Domain Routing (CIDR)?

    a. 1519

    b. 1878

    c. 1918

    d. 2700

17. The loopback address for a network interface using IPv4 is 127.0.0.1 and lets the computer user test the interface. What is the loopback address using IPv6?

    a. 1

    b. ::1

    c. ::1::

    d. :1:

18. The first byte or 8 bits of an IPv6 multicast address must be set to which of the following values?

    a. 0000

    b. 1111

    c. 1010

    d. FFFF

19. An IPv6 unicast address is made up of which of the following?

    a. a 32-bit interface ID and a 96-bit network portion

    b. a 64-bit interface ID and a 64-bit network portion

    c. a 96-bit interface ID and a 32-bit network portion

    d. a 64-bit interface ID, a 32-bit network portion, and a 32-bit broadcast address

20. For an IPv6 aggregatable global unicast address, the FP or Format Prefix field contains how many bits in the identifier?

    a. 3

    b. 8

    c. 13

    d. 24

21. For an IPv6 multicast address, how many bits are assigned to the group ID?

    a. 32

    b. 64

    c. 96

    d. 112

22. To which of the following limitations are private IP addresses subject to? (Choose all that apply.)

    a. may not be routed on the Internet

    b. may not be used without permission from ICANN or an ISP

    c. will not work with NAT software

    d. may not work with protocols that require secure end-to-end connections

23. Which kinds of devices require public IP addresses? (Choose all that apply.)

    a. any device attached directly to the Internet

    b. any server whose services should be available to the Internet

    c. every client on an internal network

    d. every server on an internal network

24. Which of the following services perform address hiding? (Choose all that apply.)

    a. e-mail

    b. FTP

    c. NAT

    d. proxy

25. What does IPv4 renumbering involve?
    a. assigning new IP addresses to all boundary devices
    b. assigning new IP addresses to all routers
    c. assigning new IP addresses to all servers and routers
    d. assigning new IP addresses to all network interfaces

Hands-On Projects

Hands-On Project 2-1: Install an IP Subnet Calculator Program

Time Required: 10 minutes

Objective: Install the Bitcricket IP Calculator software on your computer.

Description: In this project, you download and install the Bitcricket IP Calculator software, which you'll use to complete other projects. You need a computer with Internet access and a Web browser to complete this project.

1. Download the **IPCalculator.msi** file from the the *Guide to TCP/IP* companion Web site, or download the latest version from *www.wildpackets.com/resources/free_utilities/ipsubnetcalc* and save the file to your hard drive. If you download a newer version than Bitcricket 1.02, the steps in this Hands-On Project might differ slightly.
2. Double-click the **IPCalculator.msi** file to begin the installation.
3. When the Security Warning dialog box appears, click **Run**.
4. On the Welcome to the IP Calculator Setup Wizard screen, click **Next**.
5. Click the **I Agree** button on the License Agreement screen, and then click **Next**.
6. On the Select Installation Folder screen, click **Next** to accept the default installation path (unless your instructor gives you an alternate path).
7. Click **Next** on the Confirm Installation screen to begin installing the IP calculator.
8. For Windows Vista and Windows 7, if the User Account Control dialog box appears, click **Yes** or **Continue**.
9. Click **Close** to complete the installation.
10. Close any open windows.

Hands-On Project 2-2: Become Familiar with an IP Subnet Calculator

Time Required: 10 minutes

Objective: Become familiar with the Bitcricket IP Calculator software interface and learn where to find important IPv6-related addresses of your computer.

Description: In this project, you explore the Bitcricket IP Calculator interface to find your computer's IPv6, link-local, and global addresses.

1. Open the IP Calculator. (Click **Start**, point to **All Programs**, and then click **Bitcricket IP Calculator**.)

2. On the Conversions tab, in the Dotted Decimal field, verify that the IP address of your computer is populated in that field.

3. Click the **IPv6** tab.

4. Confirm the IPv6 address of your computer in the Address field.

5. In the Address Type field, look under Unicast, expanding it, if necessary, to determine the link-local address of the computer, as shown in Figure 2-7.

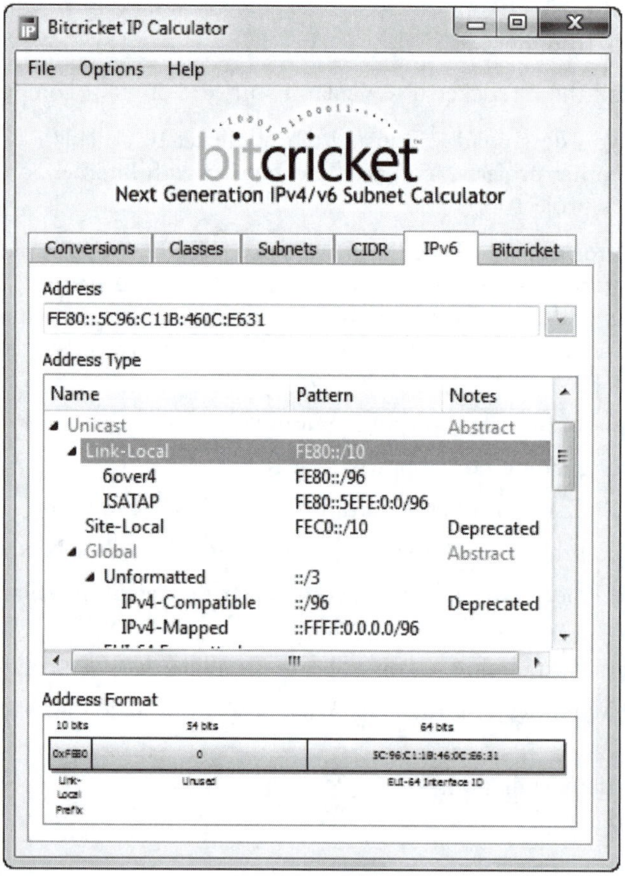

Figure 2-7 Address Type fields displayed in Bitcricket
Source: Bitcricket

6. Scroll to the bottom of the Address Type field and determine the global address of the computer.

7. Close Bitcricket.

Hands-On Project 2-3: Calculate the Subnet Mask for a Required Number of IPv4 Subnets

Time Required: 10 minutes

Objective: Learn how to determine the subnet mask required to support a specific number of subnets on an IPv4 network using the Bitcricket IP Calculator software.

Description: In this project, you use the Bitcricket IP Calculator software to define a range of network and host addresses that can be used on a subnetted Class C network. The network number assigned to you is 192.168.0.0. Define a network addressing system that supports 32 networks by subnetting the given address.

1. Open the Bitcricket IP Calculator. (Click **Start,** point to **All Programs,** and then click **Bitcricket IP Calculator.**)

2. On the Conversions tab, in the Dotted Decimal field, verify that the IP address of your computer is populated in that field.

3. Click the **Subnets** tab.

4. Notice that the Subnets tab displays information on the subnet mask, subnet bits, maximum subnets, and other data for your subnet, as shown in Figure 2-8.

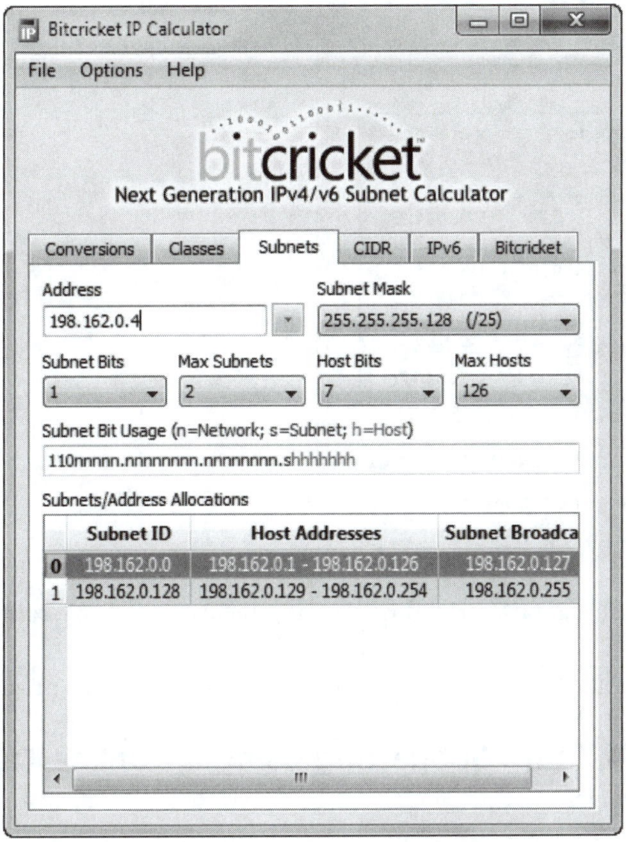

Figure 2-8 Subnets tab information displayed in Bitcricket

Source: Bitcricket

5. Your network must support 32 subnets. Open the **Max Subnets** drop-down menu and choose **32** from the list. Note that all the menus and fields automatically change to identify the network mask and other information consistent with supporting 32 subnets, as shown in Figure 2-9. Notice also to which subnet your computer now belongs (the host computer used for this exercise, which has an IP address of 192.168.0.4, belongs to the first subnet in the list).

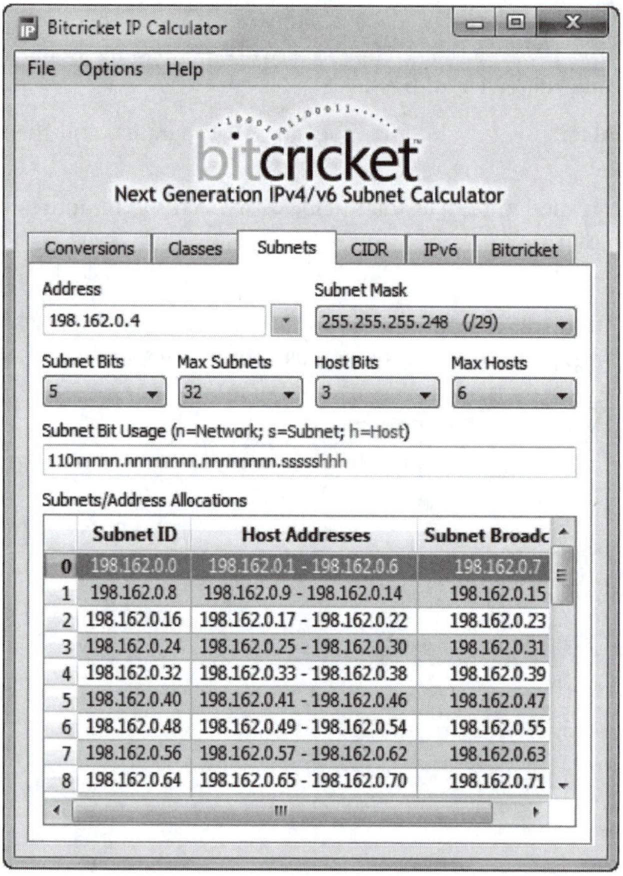

Figure 2-9 The result of changing the subnet mask to 32
Source: Bitcricket

6. Under Subnets/Address Allocations, scroll down to view the list of possible subnetworks and the host ID range.

7. When you are finished with this project, close the Bitcricket IP Calculator program.

Hands-On Project 2-4: Learn Subnetting Using an Online Tutorial

Time Required: 15 to 20 minutes

Objective: Master the basics of subnetting.

Description: In this project, you visit the Ralph Becker "IP Address Subnetting Tutorial" Web site and step through the tutorial. You need a computer with Internet access and a Web browser to complete this project.

1. Open your Web browser. (Click **Start,** point to **All Programs,** and then click **Internet Explorer,** or see your instructor if you use a different browser.)

2. Enter *www.ralphb.net/IPSubnet/index.html* in the Address text box and press **Enter.**

3. Step through the IP Address Subnetting Tutorial, which provides information about and examples of IP subnetting.

4. Close the Web browser, unless you plan to proceed immediately to the next project.

Hands-On Project 2-5: Review RFCs Related to IPv6 Addressing

Time Required: 20 minutes

Objective: Learn about IPv6 addressing and IPv4-to-IPv6 translators by reading IETF RFCs.

Description: In this project, you access the IETF Web site to look for information about RFCs related to IPv6 addressing. You need a computer with Internet access and a Web browser to complete this project. Feel free to spend some time browsing this Web site after you complete the steps.

To examine RFC 4291:

1. Open your Web browser. (Click **Start,** point to **All Programs,** and then click **Internet Explorer,** or see your instructor if you use a different browser.)

2. Enter *www.ietf.org* in the Address text box and press **Enter.**

3. Click the **RFC Pages** link.

4. Enter **4291** in the IETF repository retrieval RFC number field, and then press **Enter.**

5. Read the paper "IP Version 6 Addressing Architecture" and click the **include full document text** link at the bottom of the page to access the entire contents.

6. Close the Web browser when you are finished.

To examine RFC 6052:

1. Open your Web browser.

2. Enter *www.ietf.org* in the Address text box, and press **Enter.**

3. Click the **RFC Pages** link.

4. Enter **6052** in the IETF repository retrieval RFC number field, and then press **Enter.**

5. Read the paper "IPv6 Addressing of IPv4/IPv6 Translators" and click the **include full document text** link at the bottom of the page to access the entire contents.

6. Close the Web browser when you are finished.

Hands-On Project 2-6: Discover the IPv6 Address of a Computer

Time Required: 5 minutes

Objective: Use Ipconfig and Ping to discover your computer's IPv6 address and ping the loopback address.

Description: You need to access the command-prompt window on your Windows computer. The computer should be running Windows Vista or Windows 7.

1. Open a command-prompt window. (Click **Start**, type **cmd** in the Start menu search Search box, and then click **cmd.exe** in the resulting list.)

2. At the command prompt, type **ipconfig/all** and press **Enter**.

3. Look for the **Link-local IPv6 Address** entry in the output that appears, as shown in Figure 2-10. You may have to scroll up to find it.

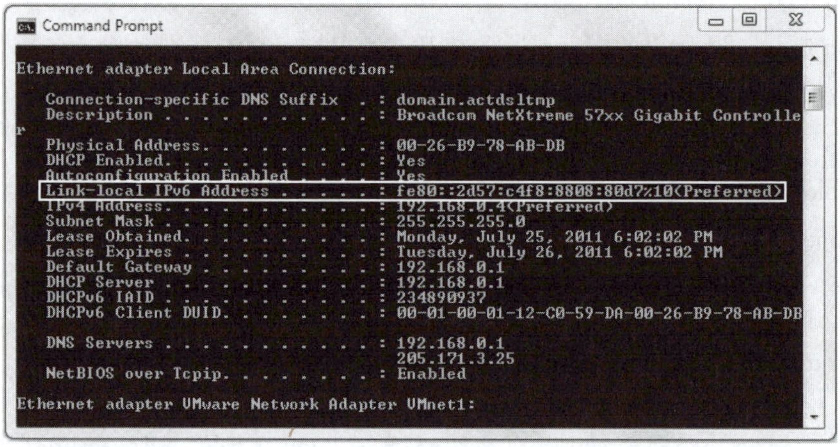

Figure 2-10 Link-local IPv6 address in IPconfig output
Source: Microsoft

4. Note the IPv6 address of your computer.

5. At the prompt, type **ping ::1** and then press **Enter**.

6. Note that you successfully ping the IPv6 loopback address of your computer.

7. Close the command-prompt window.

Hands-On Project 2-7: Access and Work with a Computer's ARP Table

Time Required: 10 minutes

Objective: Use the ARP utility on the command-line interface to examine and manipulate your computer's ARP table.

Description: The Address Resolution Protocol (ARP) is used to map Data Link layer addresses to a hardware address recognized on the local network. You need to access your computer's command-line interface; and, ideally, your computer should have previously communicated with one or more computers on the network. The computer should be Windows Vista or Windows 7.

1. Open a command-prompt window. (Click **Start,** type **cmd** in the Start menu search Search box, and then click **cmd.exe** in the resulting list.)

2. At the command prompt, type **arp -a** and press **Enter.**

3. Review the ARP table for the interface of your computer, noting the Internet address, physical address, and connection type for each entry, as shown in Figure 2-11.

```
Command Prompt                                          _  □  ⌗
C:\Users\G2TCPIP>arp -a

Interface: 192.168.0.4 --- 0xa
  Internet Address      Physical Address      Type
  192.168.0.1           00-0f-b3-56-1e-9a     dynamic
  192.168.0.5           00-0b-db-bd-49-48     dynamic
  192.168.0.255         ff-ff-ff-ff-ff-ff     static
  224.0.0.22            01-00-5e-00-00-16     static
  224.0.0.251           01-00-5e-00-00-fb     static
  224.0.0.252           01-00-5e-00-00-fc     static
  239.255.255.250       01-00-5e-7f-ff-fa     static
  255.255.255.255       ff-ff-ff-ff-ff-ff     static

Interface: 192.168.137.1 --- 0xd
  Internet Address      Physical Address      Type
  192.168.137.255       ff-ff-ff-ff-ff-ff     static
  224.0.0.22            01-00-5e-00-00-16     static
  224.0.0.251           01-00-5e-00-00-fb     static
  224.0.0.252           01-00-5e-00-00-fc     static
  239.255.255.250       01-00-5e-7f-ff-fa     static

Interface: 192.168.117.1 --- 0xf
  Internet Address      Physical Address      Type
  192.168.117.255       ff-ff-ff-ff-ff-ff     static
  224.0.0.22            01-00-5e-00-00-16     static
```

Figure 2-11 Data in the ARP table
Source: Microsoft

4. Type **arp -d** to delete the entries in the ARP table. (If this operation fails, you may need to run **cmd.exe** as an administrator. To do so, close the command-prompt window, enter **cmd** in the Start menu search box, and in the search results, right-click **cmd.exe**, then select **Run as administrator.**)

5. Type **arp -a** again and notice that the table is empty or greatly reduced.

6. Ping a host on the Internet such as *www.google.com*

7. Type **arp -a** again and notice the addresses added to the ARP table.

8. Close the command-prompt window.

Case Projects

Case Project 2-1: Designing a Corporate Network

You are asked to design a network for a medium-size company. The company decides to use the 10.0.0.0 private IP address. The network will span six buildings, with a router in each building to join the networks.

Currently, the company has approximately 1,000 workstations in the following locations:

- Building 1: 200 workstations
- Building 2: 125 workstations
- Building 3: 135 workstations
- Building 4: 122 workstations
- Building 5: 312 workstations
- Building 6: 105 workstations

Design a simple addressing solution that leaves ample room for growth and is easy to administer. Explain what happens to your design if the number of hosts per network jumps to over 1,024 per building.

Case Project 2-2: Implementing a Network for a Single Site

ABC Incorporated wants to implement a TCP/IP network for its only site. It has 180 employees and two buildings and requires Internet access for an e-mail server, a single Web server, a single FTP server, and two routers, each with a single high-speed Internet interface. If the company wants to hold ISP costs to a minimum, what kinds of IP addresses should it primarily use? What is the smallest block of public IP addresses that the company can purchase to cover its needs? (Hint: IP address blocks come in groups equal to 2b – 1, in which b is the number of bits in the total address block.)

Case Project 2-3: Designing an IPv6 Address Space

You have been asked by one of your corporate customers to design an IPv6 address space for its global network and then present the customer's board with a high-level proposal. Factors you must consider in preparing your presentation include IP address management, scalablity, the eventual obsolesence of IPv4, and IPv6 address security filtering. Remember, the board is expecting a brief, high-level proposal, so you shouldn't develop a detailed design at this stage of the plan.

chapter 3

Basic IP Packet Structures: Headers and Payloads

After reading this chapter and completing the exercises, you will be able to:

- Identify the various fields and features that make up an IPv4 header
- Identify the various fields and features that make up an IPv6 header
- Explain the purpose of IPv6 extension headers, as well as the function of each header
- Describe how MTU Discovery works in IPv6 and how it replaces fragmentation of IPv4 packets by routers
- Describe how upper-layer checksums work in IPv6 packets, including the use of pseudo-headers
- Explain the primary differences between IPv4 and IPv6 packet structures and why the differences are significant

This chapter covers IPv4 and IPv6 packet structures, including various header fields and how they allow IP packets to perform the complex functions that permit information to transverse different network environments, including the Internet. IPv4 and IPv6 headers are compared, and you learn how the packet structures in each version of IP operate, including the differing capacities of each.

IP Packets and Packet Structures

The Internet Protocol (IP) primarily works to transmit and deliver data between devices on inter-networks. In order to perform this task, information is encapsulated into "units" called packets or datagrams. Each packet contains a portion of the information being transmitted, and packets can take many different routes in traveling from the source to the destination address.

To allow a packet to perform the functions necessary to ensure the correct routing and safe delivery to its destination, each packet, in addition to the actual data, contains a header structure comprising a number of specialized fields. IPv4 and IPv6 packets differ significantly in how they are structured, but they both must perform the same basic duties of making sure data sent by the originating network node is reliably delivered to the receiving node. In the following sections of this chapter, you will learn about IPv4 packet structures that have been confidently used for decades; you will also learn about the details of IPv6 packet headers, the next generation in IP datagrams.

IPv4 Header Fields and Functions

All IPv4 headers have an identical structure, as shown in Figure 3-1. Each packet contains a header followed by a data field. The header can be between 20 and 60 bytes in length, with total packet size up to 65,535 bytes in length. However, most networks cannot handle packets at that maximum size, so the size of many packets is a modest 576 bytes.

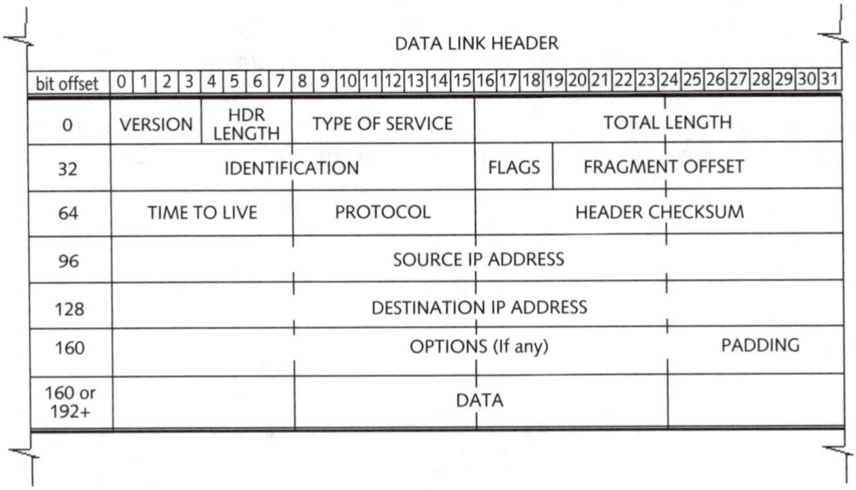

Figure 3-1 IPv4 header structure

Source: figure adapted from illustration at http://en.wikipedia.org/wiki/IPv4_Header#Header

There are 14 fields possible in the IPv4 header. Thirteen of them are required, and the 14th field is not only optional but also named "Options." Each field value is provided in multiples of 4 bytes. Because IPv4 headers can contain a variable number of options, each with its own bit length, the size of the header can also vary. In the IPv4 header, byte order is what is called "big endian," which means the most significant byte precedes the least significant ones. Likewise, the most significant bits (MSBs) come first within individual bytes. (This is called "most significant bit" or MSB 0 bit numbering, because the most significant bit is numbered 0.) Thus, the Version field, for example, occurs in the four most significant (leftmost) bits of the first byte in the header.

The following sections detail the header fields and their functions. For more details on each field, refer to the following sections and to RFC 791.

Version Field

The first field in the IP header is the Version field. In Figure 3-1, this field has a value of 4, which indicates IP version 4 or IPv4.

Header Length Field

The Header Length field, also referred to as the Internet Header Length (IHL) field, denotes the length of the IP header only. This is necessary because, as mentioned previously, the IP header can support options and, therefore, may vary in length.

IHL includes an offset to the data to make it fall on a 32-bit boundary value. The minimum value for IHL is 5, as defined in RFC 791; this produces a length of 5 * 32 = 160 bits, which equals 20 bytes. The IHL is a 4-bit field, so the maximum value it can represent is 16 − 1 = 15. The maximum length for the IHL is 15 * 32 = 480 bits, or 60 bytes.

Because the options are rarely used, the size of the IP header is typically 20 bytes.

Type of Service Field

The Type of Service field actually has two components: Precedence and Type of Service. **Precedence** is defined in the first 3 bits and may be used by routers to prioritize traffic that goes through router queues. A **router queue** is a router buffering system used to hold packets when the router is congested. **Type of Service (TOS)** is defined in the next 4 bits and should be used by routers to follow a specified path type. The last bit of the entire TOS field is reserved and set at 0, as specified by RFC 1349. The sections within the Type of Service field are shown in Figure 3-2.

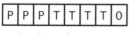

P = Precedence
T = Type of Service

Figure 3-2 TOS field includes Precedence and TOS bits
© Cengage Learning 2013

Table 3-1 lists the possible settings in the Precedence bits.

Binary	Decimal	Purpose
111	7	Network Control
110	6	Internetwork Control
101	5	CRITIC/ECP
100	4	Flash Override
011	3	Flash
010	2	Immediate
001	1	Priority
000	0	Routine

Table 3-1 Precedence bits settings
© Cengage Learning 2013

When you convert these binary values to decimal, the bits have the decimal values listed in Table 3-2.

Bit	Decimal Value
Bit 2	4
Bit 1	2
Bit 0	1

Table 3-2 Decimal values based on bit position
© Cengage Learning 2013

Table 3-3 lists the possible settings in the Type of Service bits.

Binary	Purpose
0000	Default (no specific route defined)
0001	Minimize Monetary Cost
0010	Maximize Reliability
0100	Maximize Throughput
1000	Minimize Delay
1111	Maximize Security

Table 3-3 Type of Service bits settings
© Cengage Learning 2013

Some analyzers only show the four basic service types: Default, Delay, Throughput, and Reliability.

TOS Field Function: Differentiated Services and Congestion Control

RFC 2474 recommends a complete redefinition of the TOS field values and functions. Most likely, you will find this field set at the default 00000000. In addition, RFCs 2474, 2475, and 3168 split the eight TOS field bits into two distinct functions: differentiating services (prioritization of traffic) and congestion notification.

Differentiated Services RFC 2474 defines a method for differentiating services for network traffic using the six high-order bits of the byte that was formerly the 3-bit Precedence field and the first bit of the TOS field, as shown in Figure 3-3.

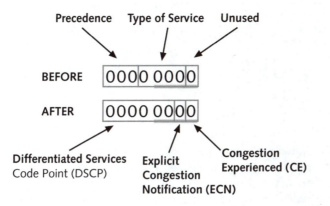

Figure 3-3 DSCP uses bits from the former Precedence and TOS fields
© Cengage Learning 2013

Using a special marker—the differentiated service code point (DSCP) identifier—traffic can be prioritized by an end device (node) or boundary device (router) and queued and forwarded according to this value. Routers that support DS technology would handle traffic according to the DSCP identifier.

The DSCP value may be assigned based on the flow of data witnessed by a router or on a specific set of values contained within the data packets (e.g., VoIP traffic versus e-mail traffic).

Some DSCP values have been specified in RFC 2597 ("Assured Forwarding PHB [Per-Hop Behavior] Group") and RFC 3246 ("An Expedited Forwarding PHB"). Table 3-4 characterizes the basic set of DSCP values defined by these two RFCs. In the RFCs, these values are referred to as Assured Forwarding (AF) classes and are assigned a drop probability classification, which groups DSCP traffic types based on the likelihood that this traffic type may be dropped by a router during highly congested times on the network when higher-priority traffic requires handling. AF number assignments indicate that the packet is assured of being handled in a specific method, with a specific prioritization. The prioritization decision is handled at each hop (router) along a path. The term *Per-Hop-Behavior* (PHB), as discussed in RFC 2597 and RFC 3246 (which obsoletes 2598), indicates that the routers (hops) make individual decisions on the handling of each packet.

Precedence Type	Class 1	Class 2	Class 3	Class 4	No Class
	DSCP 10	DSCP 18	DSCP 26	DSCP 34	
	AF11	AF21	AF31	AF41	
Low Drop Precedence	001010	010010	011010	100010	
	DSCP 12	DSCP 20	DSCP 28	DSCP 36	
	AF12	AF22	AF32	AF42	
Medium Drop Precedence	001100	010100	011100	100100	
	DSCP 14	DSCP 22	DSCP 30	DSCP 38	
	AF13	AF23	AF33	AF43	
High Drop Precedence	001110	010110	011110	100110	
					DSCP 46
Expedited Forwarding					101110

Table 3-4 DSCP values
© Cengage Learning 2013

Because PHB is dependent on how individual routers are configured, the end-to-end behavior of traffic is unpredictable, and it gets even worse when traffic crosses DS domains prior to reaching the destination. This makes it difficult to guarantee a particular quality of service (QoS) or service level agreement (SLA). Marking a packet for a specific SLA becomes a bit of wishful thinking rather than a completed act, because the level of service provided depends on the providers and routers along the path.

RFC 3248 provides a Delay Bound alternative revision for RFC 2598. The Expedited Forwarding (EF) per-hop-behavior (PHB) design team proposed a reexpression of this standard: Delay Bound per-hop-behavior (DB PHB). Delay Bound forwarding provides a strict bound on the delay variation for packets proceeding through a hop, assuming the traffic stream isn't exceeding the configured rate. Traffic absolutely must be managed or policed at the source edge, such as when it enters the Differentiated Services (DS) domain, for the traffic to become bound.

When the traffic is marked for DB, the hop device provides the DB behavior, but if more traffic arrives than the device can manage, this requirement is dropped. This means that as the traffic goes through subsequent hops, although it was originally bound or "shaped" upon entering the DB domain, it is not guarenteed to remain bound. The DB PHB definition provides no specific recommendation on how a hop device is to achieve DB behavior. It only provides a set of parameters identifying an operating range within which DB behavior can be delivered.

The process of a router dropping packet that exceeds the negotiated rate has a security application. The edge of a DS domain is required to police its boundaries in order to prevent denial of service (DoS) attacks. If two connecting DS domains do not have a negotiated DB traffic rate, all traffic from a domain will be marked as 0 and dropped. However, this would be a somewhat rare occurrence, given that traffic between domains must be negotiated and upstream domains must police and shape DB packets as per the negotiated rate. An overflow incident could be indicative of a service attack.

RFC 3248 was published as an informational document and is not intended to be implemented as an Internet standard. For the complete details on DB PHB, go to *www.ietf.org* and search for "RFC 3248."

Expedited forwarding (EF), which corresponds to DSCP 46, is considered a premium service connection, offering a service that appears as a "virtual lease line" between end points. If a source sends out a packet with the value 101110 in the DSCP field, routers that support DS functionality must expedite the packet forwarding and not change the DSCP field value to lower its priority.

Real-time applications (RTAs), in the current context, are any applications that must function within an immediate time frame on a continual basis, with little or no latency (delay). Whether a service can be defined as RTA depends on the maximum amount of time an application task requires to be executed on a particular hardware platform. This is referred to as worst-case execution time (WCET).

Voice over IP (VoIP), which uses IP to support voice communication, is one type of RTA that can benefit greatly from DSCP EF handling. VoIP is intolerant of any sort of delay (which causes echo and talker overlap). In fact, any time-sensitive traffic is intolerant of delay and is appropriate for special handling using DSCP.

Other RTA traffic types include:

- Chat
- Community storage solutions
- Instant messaging (IM)
- Online gaming
- Streaming media
- Videoconferencing
- Some e-commerce transactions

E-mail and Web-browsing traffic, on the other hand, can still function adequately with some delays.

For differentiated service functionality to be supported fully and properly, vendors must support the service and the end point and intervening points (routers), and network administrators must configure end points and intervening routers to assign and handle the DSCP values appropriately.

Explicit Congestion Notification Explicit Congestion Notification (ECN) was designed to provide devices with a method for notifying each other that a link is experiencing congestion before the routers start to drop packets. Both sides of a congested link (the sending node or router and the receiving node or router) must support ECN in order to take advantage of this technology.

A single dropped packet can drastically affect network throughput. ECN is an attempt to mitigate the negative effects of a dropped packet by alerting a receiver that there is congestion on a link in hopes that the receiver will decrease its traffic rate to accommodate the congested link. Ideally, ECN will reduce the number of dropped packets over a congested network and lead to better overall performance.

When a packet is sent between two ECN-capable routers, the packet is usually marked ECT(0) or ECT(1) for ECN Capable Transport. If the packet crosses a queue between the two routers and experiences congestion, the receiving router may change the code to Congestion Encountered or EC rather than dropping the packet. ECN/CE requires the use of 2 bits within the IP header, as shown in Figure 3-3. The combination of these 2 bits provides for several possible interpretations, as shown in Figure 3-4.

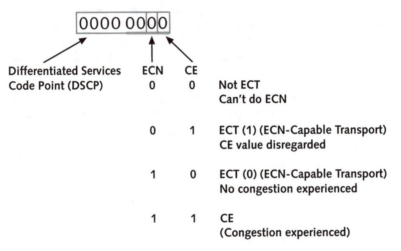

Figure 3-4 Interpretations of the ECN and CE bits
© Cengage Learning 2013

Unlike with many fields in TCP/IP headers, we must look at the values combined in both bits to interpret the ECN value. For example, if the ECN/CE bits are set to 01 or 10, the sending router is indicating that it supports ECN—it is an ECN-Capable Transport (ECT). If the value in the ECN/CE bits is set to 00, the sender is not an ECT. If the value in the ECN/CE bits is 11, the sender is an ECT and there is congestion on the link.

It is anticipated that there will be some differentiation between the ECN/CE values 01 and 10, but at this time, both are handled the same. ECN is defined in RFC 3168.

Wireshark decodes only the ECT(0) codepoint as "ECN-Capable Transport" and incorrectly decodes both ECT(1) and CE codepoints as "ECN-CE set."

Total Length Field

This field defines the length of the IP header and any valid data (although it does not include any data link padding). In the example shown in Figure 3-5, the total length is 60 bytes. The IP header is the first 20 bytes, indicating that the remaining packet length is 40 bytes.

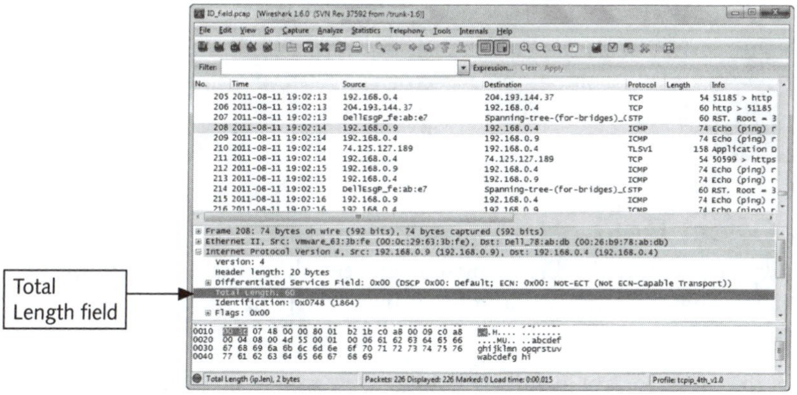

Total Length field

Figure 3-5 Total length of field is 60 bytes
Source: Wireshark

Identification Field

Each individual packet is given a unique ID value when it is sent. If the packet must be fragmented to fit on a network that supports a smaller packet size, the same ID number is placed in each fragment. This helps identify fragments that are part of the same set of data.

Flags Field

The Flags field is 3 bits long; the bit value assignments are shown in Table 3-5.

Location	Field Definition	Value/Interpretations
Bit 0	Reserved	Set to 0
Bit 1	Don't Fragment bit	0=may fragment; 1=don't fragment
Bit 2	More Fragments bit	0=last fragment; 1=more to come

Table 3-5 Flags field values
© Cengage Learning 2013

Typically, fragmentation is allowed. However, an application may, for some reason, decide not to allow fragmentation. If so, it sets the Don't Fragment bit to 1.

If fragmentation is allowed and a packet must be fragmented to cross a network that supports a smaller maximum transmission unit (MTU), the Don't Fragment bit is set to 0. When the packet is split into multiple fragments (e.g., three fragments), the first and second fragments have the More Fragments bit set to 1. The last fragment has the More Fragments bit set to 0 to indicate that it is the final fragment in the set.

Is fragmentation a good thing? Sometimes. A packet can only successfully arrive at its destination if the MTU is supported by the smallest link MTU in the path. IPv4 routers continually fragment traffic from one hop to the next depending on the MTU size tolerated by the next link, and in IPv6, source nodes use PMTU Discovery to determine the smallest link MTU in a path and then set the MTU of its packets to accommodate that link.

PMTU Discovery procedures are similar in IPv6 and IPv4. For more information on PMTU Discovery, refer to the "IPv6 MTU and Packet Handling" section later in this chapter.

Fragment Offset Field

If the packet is a fragment, the **Fragment Offset field** shows where to place this packet's data when the fragments are reassembled into a single packet (at the destination IP host).

This field gives the offset in 8-byte values. For example, the first fragment may have an offset of 0 and contain 1,400 bytes of data (not including any headers). The second fragment would have an offset value of 175 (175 x 8 = 1,400).

This field is only used if the packet is a fragment.

Time to Live Field

In networking terms, a packet's **time to live** (TTL) is the remaining distance that the packet can travel. Though defined in terms of seconds, the TTL value is implemented as a number of hops that a packet can travel before being discarded by a router. Therefore, the Time to Live field denotes the number of hops a packet takes through routers on its way to its destination. Typical starting TTL values are 32, 64, and 128. The maximum TTL value is 255. It's possible for the actual TTL duration to be greater or less than the starting values, as measured on the clock.

The duration of a network hop depends on a variety of factors, including the length of any given link and the speed of the network technology available for the network traffic in question. For instance, a hop through a high-speed fiber optic link, even one that is fairly long, will almost always be a lot less than 1 second. On the other hand, a hop through a geosynchronous satellite link will never be less than 4 seconds.

Protocol Field

Headers should have some field that defines what is coming up next. For example, in a TCP/IP packet, an Ethernet header should have a protocol Identification field (the Type or Ether Type field) to indicate what IP is coming up next. The IP header, likewise, has a Protocol field to indicate what is coming up next. Some of the common values in the Protocol field are listed in Table 3-6.

The values 253 and 254 are for experimentation, 143–252 are unassigned, and 255 is reserved by IANA. To obtain the most current list of Protocol field values, visit *www.iana.org/assignments/protocol-numbers*.

Number	Description
1	Internet Control Message Protocol (ICMP)
2	Internet Group Management Protocol (IGMP)
6	Transmission Control Protocol (TCP)
8	Exterior Gateway Protocol (EGP)
9	Any private interior gateway, such as Cisco's IGRP
17	User Datagram Protocol (UDP)
45	Inter-Domain Routing Protocol (IDRP)
58	Internet Control Message Protocol version 6 (ICMPv6)
88	Cisco EIGRP
89	Open Shortest Path First (OSPF)
92	Multicast Transport Protocol (MTP)
115	Layer Two Tunneling Protocol (L2TP)

Table 3-6   Common Protocol field values
© Cengage Learning 2013

Header Checksum Field

The Header Checksum field provides error detection on the contents of the IP header only—it does not cover other contents of the packet, nor does it include the Header Checksum field itself in its calculation.

This is an **error-detection mechanism** in addition to the data link error-detection mechanism (such as the Ethernet CRC). This additional checking mechanism is required for packets that pass through routers. For example, when an Ethernet packet arrives at a router, the router performs the data link cyclic redundancy check (CRC) to ensure that the packet was not corrupted along the way. After the packet passes the CRC check and is considered good, the router strips off the data link header, leaving behind an unencapsulated Network layer packet. If the packet does not have any error-detection process in place, a faulty router can alter the data and then apply a new data link header (with a new CRC on the invalid packet) and send the packet on. This Network layer error-checking mechanism is required to detect and defeat router packet corruption.

NOTE Wireshark sometimes captures packets before the checksum has been calculated. Checksum calcuations can be performed by the network driver, protocol driver, or even by network hardware. Current network hardware can perform advanced IP checksum calculations when the network driver hands the "responsibility" over to the hardware. This is known as "checksum offloading" and results in checksums being captured by Wireshark that are essentially "empty" and shows up as incorrect or invalid. The packets actually contain valid checksums when they leave the network hardware.

Source Address Field

This is the IP address of the IP host that sent the packet. In some cases, such as during the Dynamic Host Configuration Protocol (DHCP) boot process, the IP host may not know its IP address, so it may use 0.0.0.0 in this field. This field cannot contain a multicast or broadcast address because the source address must originate from a specific network interface with a specific IP address assigned to the interface.

Destination Address Field

This field can include a unicast, multicast, or broadcast address. This is the final destination of the packet.

Options Fields

The IP header can be extended by several options (although these options are not often used). If the header is extended with options, those options must end on a 4-byte boundary because the Internet Header Length (IHL) field defines the header length in 4-byte boundaries.

Table 3-7 lists the available set of options.

Number	Name
0	End of Options List
1	No Operations
2	Security
3	Loose Source Route
4	Time Stamp
5	Extended Security
6	Commercial Security
7	Record Route
8	Stream ID
9	Strict Source Route
10	Experimental Measurement
11	MTU Probe
12	MTU Reply
13	Experimental Flow Control
14	Experimental Access Control
15	ENCODE
16	IMI Traffic Descriptor

Table 3-7 Options field values

Number	Name
17	Extended Internet Protocol
18	Traceroute
19	Address Extension
20	Router Alert
21	Selective Directed Broadcast
22	Unassigned (Released 18 October 2005)
23	Dynamic Packet State
24	Upstream Multicast Packet
25	Quick-Start

Table 3-7 **Options field values** (*continued*)
© Cengage Learning 2013

As you might guess, the IP header options exist primarily to provide additional IP routing controls (or to record the route that individual packets take between sender and receiver). Thus, they can be useful when testing or debugging code or specific connections but are seldom used otherwise. The fact that the Options field can contain zero, one, or more options makes its length variable.

Padding

The padding is used to make sure the header ends at the 32-bit boundary and consists of whatever number of 0-filled bytes is required to make the IPv4 header end on a 32-bit boundary. This is to make sure that the IPv4 header length is always a multiple of 32 bits.

IPv6 Header Fields and Functions

The purpose of the IPv6 packet is essentially the same as the IPv4 packet's: to ensure that data or application information is successfully transported from a source to a destination node on a network. The packet contains the addressing and routing fields to make this possible. The IPv6 header also adds improvements over IPv4, such as enhanced support for extensions and options. Other enhancements allow more efficient packet forwarding and packet labeling for specific traffic flows. Of particular interest is that IPv6 headers are designed to make it easier to introduce new options in the future, allowing IPv6 headers to become more advanced as networking technology improves.

The specifications for IPv6, including the header format, were established in RFC 1883, which was subsequently obsoleted by RFC 2460. The fixed IPv6 header makes up the first 40 octets or 320 bits of the IPv6 packet. Figure 3-6 shows the IPv6 header structure.

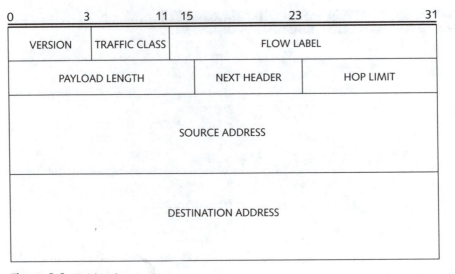

Figure 3-6 IPv6 header structure
© Cengage Learning 2013

Version

This is the 4-bit IP version number, which will always be 6 (bit sequence 0110).

Traffic Class

The 8-bit Traffic Class field is used by source network hosts and forwarding routers to distinguished classes or priorities in IPv6 packets. The general requirements for the Traffic Class field are that the network node's IPv6 service interface must provide a method for an upper-layer protocol to offer a value for the Traffic Class bits in any packets from the protocol, with the default value being 0. Any upper-level protocol "understands" that the value of the bits in this field may not be the same when they are sent by the source node as when they are received by the destination node.

Nodes that support specific Traffic Class bits are allowed to change the bit values if they are the source or destination node or if they are forwarding the IPv6 packet; otherwise, nodes should ignore the Traffic Class field bits that they do not support. The structure of this field is depicted in Figure 3-7.

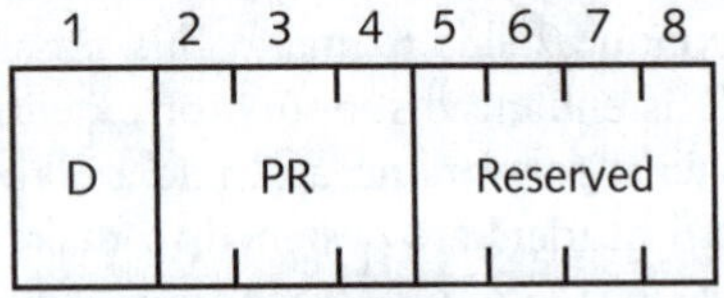

D = Delay Sensitive
PR = Precedence
Reserved = Set to 0000

Figure 3-7 Traffic Class field structure
© Cengage Learning 2013

The first bit of the Traffic Class field indicates whether this traffic is delay sensitive. If this bit is set to 1, the traffic is considered time sensitive. For example, interactive data exchanges, as well as voice and video communications, require low-delay connections. Thus, packets carrying those types of payloads will normally set the first bit of the Traffic Class field to 1.

The Precedence field is similar to the IPv4 header Precedence field and allows an application to differentiate traffic types based on their priorities. Accordingly, routers can reference the Precedence bits to determine how to prioritize traffic through the router processing and queuing system.

The last 4 bits of the Traffic Class field are reserved at this time. For more information on the definition of Traffic Class values, refer to the Differentiated Services (diffserv) working group information at *http://datatracker.ietf.org/wg/diffserv/charter/*.

Flow Label Field

A **flow** is a set of packets for which a source requires special handling by the intervening routers. The 20-bit Flow Label field is used by the source node to request special handling of the packet by IPv6 routers, such as for real-time applications or nondefault QoS. At the time RFC 2460 was being written, this specification was still experimental. RFC 3697 is the proposed standard for the Flow Label specification and defines the minimum requirements for this field.

The proposed Flow Label specification states that the value of the Flow Label is 0 for packets not part of any flow. Packet classifiers use the Flow Label, Source Address, and Destination Address fields to identify a packet's flow if it is part of a flow. The value of the Flow Label must not change between source and destination. Network nodes not supporting the Flow Label must ignore this field when forwarding or receiving the packet.

Payload Length Field

The 16-bit Payload Length field describes the size of the payload in octets, including any extension headers. The length is 0 when the Hop-by-Hop Options extension header possesses the jumbogram options. (Extension headers are explored in detail in the "IPv6 Extension Headers" section of this chapter. IPv6 jumbograms are specified in RFC 2675 as a proposed standard and are described in the "Jumbograms" section of this chapter.)

The Role of the Next Header Field

The 8-bit Next Header field specifies the header type of the header immediately following the IPv6 header—specifically, extension headers—and uses the same values as the IPv4 Protocol field (see RFC 3232, which made RFC 1700 obsolete).

The Next Header field is a significant addition to the IPv6 header format. When an IPv6 packet uses extension headers, this field points to the first extension header. That extension header contains within its own Next Header field the identifier for the following extension header, and so on to the final extension header, which then contains a reference to the encapsulated higher-level protocol. Figure 3-8 illustrates this process; and Figure 3-9, later in this chapter, shows the specific ordering for extension headers.

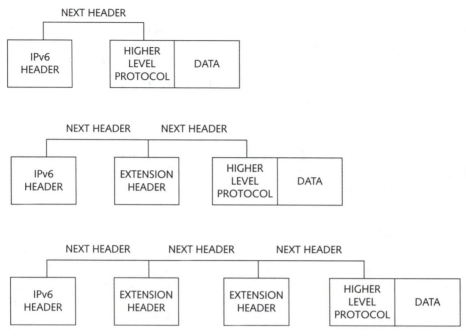

Figure 3-8 Next Header field progression
© Cengage Learning 2013

Table 3-8 contains the most common values for the Next Header field. Please keep in mind that this table is not comprehensive.

Decimal Value	Hexadecimal Value	Extension Header or Protocol Name
0	00	Hop-by-Hop Options extension header
1	01	ICMPv4
2	02	IGMPv4
4	04	IP-in-IP Encapsulation
6	06	TCP
8	08	EGP
17	11	UDP
41	29	IPv6
43	2B	Routing extension header
44	2C	Fragmentation extension header
50	32	Encapsulating Security Protocol extension header
51	33	Authentication extension header
60	3C	Destination Options extension header

Table 3-8 Next Header field values
© Cengage Learning 2013

In IPv6, any extension header must be inserted between the IP header and any higher-layer protocol headers. Currently, the IPv6 specification supports six extension headers (see the "Extension Header Ordering" section later in this chapter).

IPv6 also supports chaining headers together after the basic IPv6 header, which you'll learn about in the "IPv6 Extension Headers" section.

Hop Limit Field

The value in the 8-bit Hop Limit field decrements by one each time it is forwarded by a network node, and the IPv6 packet is discarded if the value in this field reaches 0. The Hop Limit field can accommodate a maximum value of 255, which also makes this the maximum possible number of hops.

Source Address Field

The Source Address field contains the 128-bit address of the source of the packet. The IPv6 addressing architecture is described in the ADDR-ARCH RFC draft version 4.4. (You can read this draft at *http://tools.ietf.org/html/draft-ietf-ipv6-addr-arch-v4-04.*) Also see RFC 5952, which is the recommendation for IPv6 address text representation, and RFC 6052, which is the proposed standard for IPv6 addressing of IPv4/IPv6 translators.

Destination Address Field

The Destination Address field contains the 128-bit address of the recipient of the packet. This may not be the final recipient of the packet if a Routing extension header is available (see ADDRARCH RFC version 4.4).

IPv6 Extension Headers

Extension headers allow additional functionality to be implemented in an IPv6 packet. These fields are used only for specific purposes. This permits the IPv6 packet to remain small and streamlined and possess only the fields that are required for its particular purpose.

Each extension header is identified by a specific Next Header value, and the most common values were shown in Table 3-8. An IPv6 packet can carry zero or more extension headers, as necessary.

Once an IPv6 packet is sent, any extension headers present are not examined by any node on the network path until the packet reaches the destination address (or destination addresses if this is a multicast). This is the address found in the packet header's Destination Address field. Once at the destination node, the Next Header field is processed and the first extension header is examined. If the first extension header points to a second, then that extension header will be processed next, and so on until the upper-layer protocol is reached. If no extension headers exist, when the Next Header field is processed, the upper-layer protocol will be immediately examined.

The extension headers are strictly processed in the required order, which you will read about in the next section of this chapter. This prevents the destination node from scanning the packet, looking for a particular type of extension header so that header can be processed ahead of the others.

Extension Header Ordering

In RFC 2460, the IPv6 specification recommends an order for the extension headers:

1. Hop-by-Hop Options

2. Destination Options

3. Routing

4. Fragment

5. Authentication

6. Encapsulating Security Payload (ESP)

The packet can then contain an upper-layer header, such as User Datagram Protocol (UDP), Transmission Control Protocol (TCP), or Internet Control Message Protocol (ICMP). The currently defined extension headers are "chained" after the basic IPv6 header through the use of the Next Header field in the basic IPv6 header and the extension headers themselves. The set of extension headers is shown in Figure 3-9.

```
+ - - - - - - - - + - - - - - - - - - - - - - -
|   IPv6 HEADER   |  TCP HEADER + DATA
|                 |
|  Next Header =  |
|      TCP        |
T - - - - - - - - T - - - - - - - - - - - - - -


+ - - - - - - - - + - - - - - - - - - - + - - - - - - - - - - - - -
|   IPv6 HEADER   |  ROUTING HEADER     |  TCP HEADER + DATA
|                 |                     |
|  NEXT HEADER =  |   NEXT HEADER =     |
|    ROUTING      |       TCP           |
T - - - - - - - - T - - - - - - - - - - T - - - - - - - - - - - - -


+ - - - - - - - - + - - - - - - - - - - + - - - - - - - - - - - - + - - - - - - - - - -
|   IPv6 HEADER   |  ROUTING HEADER     |  FRAGMENT HEADER        |  FRAGMENT OF TCP
|                 |                     |                         |   HEADER + DATA
|  NEXT HEADER =  |   NEXT HEADER =     |   NEXT HEADER =         |
|    ROUTING      |     FRAGMENT        |       TCP               |
T - - - - - - - - T - - - - - - - - - - T - - - - - - - - - - - - T - - - - - - - - - -
```

Figure 3-9 Chained headers on an Ethernet network
Source: http://tools.ietf.org/html/rfc2460

In any given packet, each extension header should only occur once, except for the Destination Options extension header, which may occur twice—once right before the Routing extension header and then before the upper-layer header. Although it's unlikely you'd ever encounter a single packet that included all the various header extension types in the order listed, note that those types that occur in the figure do follow the order prescribed in the preceding list (so the Data Link header precedes the IPv6 header, which precedes the Routing extension header, which in turn precedes the Authentication extension header, and so forth).

The following sections examine the various extension headers defined by the IPv6 specification.

Hop-by-Hop Options Extension Header

As shown in Figure 3-10, the Hop-by-Hop Options extension header structure allows maximum flexibility in header definition and functionality. The only two fields defined for this header are the Next Header field and the Extended Header Length field. The Next Header field references the Next Header value. The Extended Header Length field indicates the length of the Hop-by-Hop Options extension header, excluding the minimum 8 bytes required of all extension and options headers. Apart from this requirement, the header is not a set length.

The Hop-by-Hop Options extension header is designed to carry information that affects routers along a path. For example, if a multicast transmission is required to provide some special routing instructions on an internetwork, the instructions can be carried in the Hop-by-Hop Options extension header. Intervening routers along a path can examine this header as defined. Proposed uses of the Hop-by-Hop Options extension header include the router alert and the Jumbo Payload options, described in the "Router Alerts and Hop-by-Hop Options" and "Jumbograms" sections later in this chapter.

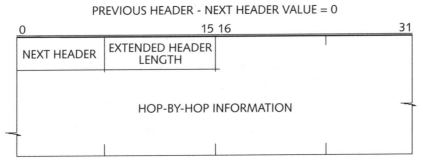

Figure 3-10 Hop-by-Hop Options extension header
© Cengage Learning 2013

Destination Options Extension Header

The Destination Options extension header provides a method for extending the IPv6 header to support options for packet handling and preferences. If the Destination Options extension header appears earlier in the packet, it is not encrypted; however, if it appears after the ESP extension header, it was sent through an **encryption** process. This extension header also makes room for future proprietary or standards-based communications. Option Type numbers must be registered with IANA and documented in a specific RFC.

The Destination Options extension header is the only header that may appear in more than one location. It may appear either immediately before the Routing extension header and/or as the last header before the actual higher-layer protocol data (i.e., after any ESP or Authentication headers). When it appears earlier in the packet, it is intended for use at an intermediate destination. The only such use defined so far is in conjunction with the Routing extension header. When it appears after the ESP extension header, it can only be examined at the final destination.

As shown in Figure 3-11, the Destination Options extension header uses the same format as the Hop-by-Hop Options extension header.

PREVIOUS HEADER - NEXT HEADER VALUE = 60

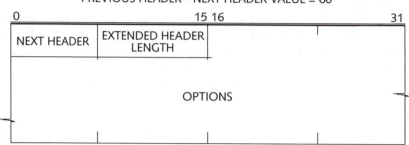

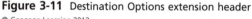

Figure 3-11 Destination Options extension header
© Cengage Learning 2013

Routing Extension Header

The Routing extension header supports strict or loose source routing for IPv6. This header includes fields for the intermediary addresses through which the IPv6 packet should be forwarded. The format of the Routing extension header is shown in Figure 3-12.

PREVIOUS HEADER - NEXT HEADER VALUE = 43

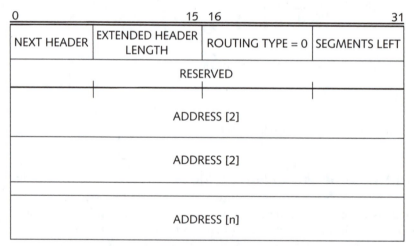

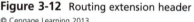

Figure 3-12 Routing extension header
© Cengage Learning 2013

The first 1-byte field of this header indicates the next header that follows the Routing extension header. The Extended Header Length field defines the length of this header, excluding the minimum 8 bytes required of all extension and options headers. Apart from this requirement, the header is not a set length.

Though designed to make it useful in a range of situations, only one option has been defined for the Routing extension header: the Routing Type = 0 routing option. This option uses the Routing extension header like a routing slip in an office. The sender calculates the path among all the routers it wishes this packet to visit. It places their addresses in an ordered list in the Hop-by-Hop Options extension header, with the final destination router at the end of the list.

The sender then places the address of the first router to be visited in the Destination Address field of the IPv6 header. Intervening routers forward the packet normally without having to examine the contents of any headers. When the packet arrives at the first destination (the first router), the router examines the packet and finds this header. If all is correct, the router places the address of the next router in the list in the Destination Address field and places its own address at the bottom of the list. This process continues until the packet reaches its final destination. Up to 255 routers may be included in such a list. The Segments Left field defines the number of remaining route segments that the packet must visit before reaching the final destination.

Due to security concerns, the use of type 0 routing headers has been deprecated. Any IPv6 node that receives a packet with a destination address assigned to it that contains a routing header type 0 will not run, as specified in RFC 2460, but instead will be processed as a packet with an unrecognized routing header type value. See RFC 5095 for details.

Fragment Extension Header

As mentioned earlier in this chapter, IPv6 does not support fragmentation at forwarding routers. All packets are treated as if an implicit Do Not Fragment bit was set. The PMTU Discovery process is used to provide source stations with the maximum fragment size supported by a path.

For more information on PMTU Discovery, refer to the "IPv6 MTU and Packet Handling" section later in this chapter.

If a transmitting device needs to send packets that are larger than the PMTU, the IPv6 Fragment extension header is used. The Fragment extension header format is shown in Figure 3-13.

PREVIOUS HEADER - NEXT HEADER VALUE = 44

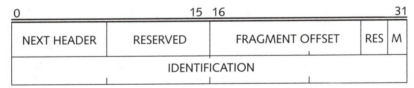

Figure 3-13 Fragment extension header
© Cengage Learning 2013

The fields of the Fragment extension header are almost identical to the IPv4 fragment fields except for the use of the Flags field. IPv6 has one Flags field: More Fragments (the M field in Figure 3-13). The Flags field is set to 1 in all fragment packets except the last one, which is set to 0.

The source node may fragment a packet in order to meet the requirements of the smallest link MTU in the network path to the destination as established by PMTU Discovery. The packet, before it is fragmented by the source node, is known as the "original packet" and is made up of two segments: the Unfragmentable Part and the Fragmentable Part. The Unfragmentable Part is made up of the IPv6 packet header and any extension headers that may exist up to and including the Routing extension header if it is present, or the Hop-by-Hop Options extension header if it is present. The Fragmentable Part is the rest of the packet, which includes any extension headers that must only be processed by the destination node as well as the upper-layer header and data.

The Fragmentable Part of the original packet is split into segments, each being eight octets in length. The possible exception is the last fragment, which doesn't have to follow this specification. Each individual fragment is made up of three parts: the Unfragmentable Part, the Fragment Header, and the fragment, as shown in Figure 3-14.

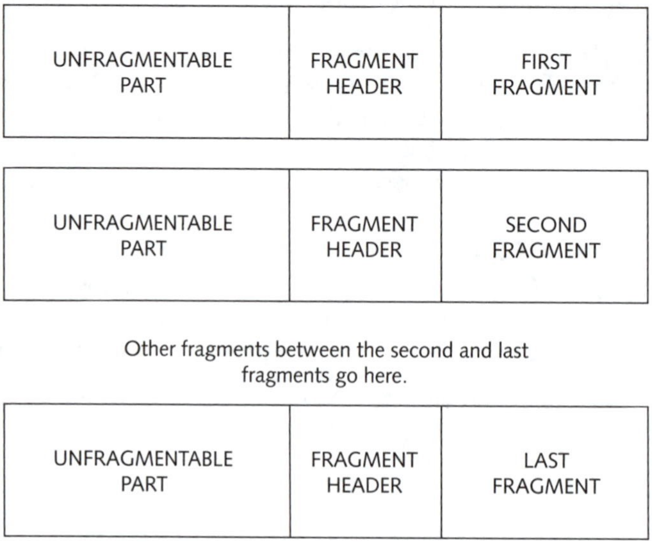

UNFRAGMENTABLE PART	FRAGMENT HEADER	FIRST FRAGMENT

UNFRAGMENTABLE PART	FRAGMENT HEADER	SECOND FRAGMENT

Other fragments between the second and last fragments go here.

UNFRAGMENTABLE PART	FRAGMENT HEADER	LAST FRAGMENT

Figure 3-14 Fragment packets
© Cengage Learning 2013

The Payload Length of the Unfragmentable Part in each fragment is changed from the size of the original packet to the length of the fragment packet, minus the length of the IPv6 header. The value of the Next Header field of the last header is changed to 44.

The Fragment Header contains the Next Header value, which identifies the first header of the Fragmentable Part of the original header. It also contains a Fragment Offset, with the offset of the fragment expressed in 8-bit units. This value is in relation to the start of the Fragmentable Part of the original packet. The Fragment Offset of the first fragment is set to a value of 0. The M flag is also set to a value of 0 for the very last fragment; otherwise, the M flag value is set to 1. The last element in the Fragment Header is the Identification value, which was generated for the original packet.

The fragment length is established to accommodate the smallest link MTU size in the Path MTU, ensuring that it will arrive at the destination node.

Authentication Extension Header

The Authentication extension header is designed to specify the true origin of a packet by preventing address spoofing and connection theft. This header also provides an integrity check on those parts of the packet that do not change in transit. (Authentication would not be calculated over the Routing extension header, for example.) In addition, the Authentication extension header can provide a limited defense against replay attacks. End devices may, if configured to do so, reject packets that are not properly authenticated.

The Authentication extension header format is shown in Figure 3-15.

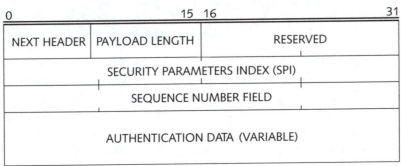

Figure 3-15 Authentication extension header
© Cengage Learning 2013

The Authentication extension header starts with a 1-byte Next Header field that indicates the next header in the chain.

The 1-byte Payload Length field indicates the number of 4-byte words following the Security Parameters Index (SPI) field. The bits in the Reserved field should be set to all 0s. The SPI field contains values that may point to an index or table of security parameters, or a Security Association (SA), at the receiver. The SPI is always a pointer to security details on its partner.

The Sequence Number field is used to ensure that receivers recognize old packets on the network.

The Authentication Data field contents are based on a computation of a cryptographic checksum on the payload data, some fields in the basic IPv6 and extension headers, and a secret shared by the authenticated devices.

Encapsulating Security Payload Extension Header and Trailer

The authentication process defined by the Authentication extension header does not encrypt or protect data from sniffing attacks. Data is still in its native transmission format. The Encapsulating Security Payload extension header should be used to encrypt data. This header must always be the last header of the IP header chain, and it indicates the start of encrypted data.

The format of the Encapsulating Security Payload extension header is shown in Figure 3-16.

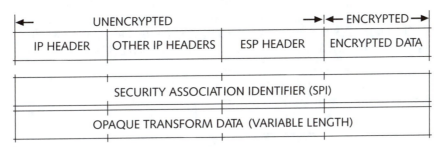

Figure 3-16 Encapsulating Security Payload extension header
© Cengage Learning 2013

AH, ESP, and IPSec

IP Security (IPSec), a suite of add-in security protocols for IP-based networks, provides access control, connectionless integrity, data origin authentication, protection against replay attacks, and more. The Authentication Header (AH) and Encapsulating Security Protocol (ESP) are part of the IPSec suite. AH specifies the true origin of a packet by preventing address spoofing and connection theft, and it provides integrity checking and a limited defense against replay attacks. ESP provides encryption services under IPSec.

In IPv4, AH protects the IP payload and all header fields of an IP datagram, with the exception of those that are unauthenticated—for example, fields that might be altered during transmission. These fields are DSCP/TOS, ECN, Flags, Fragment Offset, Header Checksum, and Time to Live.

In IPv6, AH protects the Authentication extension header itself, the Destination Options extension header after the AH, the IP payload, and the fixed IPv6 header. AH also protects the extension headers before the AH, with the exception of DSCP, ECN, Flow Label, and Hop Limit. (You will learn more about network security in Chapter 12.)

The Encapsulating Security Payload extension header is followed by an authentication checksum to protect against attackers that corrupt or truncate encrypted data. The exact format of the encrypted parameters is based on the particular encryption algorithm in use.

Jumbograms

RFC 2675 proposes one other type of special service for IPv6 packets: a very large packet called a **jumbogram**. The standard IPv6 packet header Payload Length field, at 2 bytes long, allows packets to carry up to 64 kilobytes of data. Jumbograms use the Hop-by-Hop Options extension header to add an alternate Packet Length field of 32 bytes. This allows the packet to carry a single chunk of data larger than 64 kilobytes, up to over four billion bytes. For an ordinary Internet link, this packet size is absurd. On the backbone and high-capacity network with link MTUs from 65,575 to 4,294,967,295 octets, there are significant operational advantages to carrying fewer very large packets as opposed to many smaller packets. The jumbogram allows these links to carry such large packets without straining the IPv6 fabric. This option does not need to be implemented or even understood by IPv6 network nodes not attached to such large capacity MTU links. The Jumbo Payload option is carried by the Hop-by-Hop Options extension header that follows the IPv6 header. The option has the format displayed in Figure 3-17.

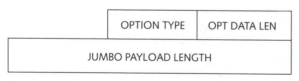

Figure 3-17 Jumbo Payload option format
© Cengage Learning 2013

Both the Option Type and the Opt Data Len fields have 8-bit values. The Jumbo Payload Length field has a 32-bit value, which is the length of the IPv6 packet in octets minus the header but with the Hop-by-Hop Options extension header and all other extension headers present. The length must be greater than 65,535.

To use the Jumbo Payload option, the value of the Payload Length field in the IPv6 header must be 0. A network node that understands the Jumbo Payload option will process a packet as a jumbogram if:

1. The packet header's Payload Length field is set to 0.

2. The Next Header field is set to 0, which means the Hop-by-Hop Options extension header comes next.

3. The Link-Layer framing indicates that additional octets exist beyond the IPv6 header.

The node will then process the Hop-by-Hop Options extension header to determine the actual length of the jumbogram payload.

The Jumbo Payload option is not consistent with the Fragment extension header, so they must not be used in the same packet.

Normally, upper-layer protocols use the Payload Length field to calculate the value of the Upper-Layer Packet Length field in the checksum pseudo-header. When the Jumbo Payload option is used, the upper-layer protocols must use the Jumbo Payload Length field for the calculation.

Quality of Service

Quality of service (QoS) is the ability of a network to provide better service to specific types of network traffic; it is handled by the diffserv working group at the IETF. Differentiated Services are what QoS is all about. The concept is quite simple: it should be possible to choose (and pay for) something other than the default level of service. This might be assured delivery, expedited delivery, temporary assignment of unusually large bandwidth, low latency, lowest delivered cost (perhaps at the expense of quick delivery), or any of several parameters of particular value to certain users at certain times and places. The **Resource Reservation Protocol (RSVP)** was one early attempt to promote a more formal approach to dynamic resource allocation on the Internet.

The latest drafts from the diffserv working group propose two basic approaches to QoS: **per-hop behaviors (PHBs)** and **per-domain behaviors (PDBs)**. Per-hop behaviors, as their name implies, are applicable along any path traced through routers supporting the required level of service, and they are able to understand the signaling of packets requesting it. Per-domain behaviors are available across all hops within a given domain. Decisions about QoS are made at the edge of such domains. Traffic traversing the domain is handled with a certain QoS. The "domains" referred to in "PDB" may not be actual IP subnets but rather a group of routers offering a certain unified approach to QoS.

QoS was implemented in one form or another in IPv4 for many years; however, it was never widely used. There may be many reasons for this, not the least of which is the explosive growth in demand for plain old "default-quality" Internet service. However, QoS is gaining momentum in many large Internet carriers' backbones, and this push requires IPv6 to reach maturity in terms of QoS before it can be deployed on production networks.

Router Alerts and Hop-by-Hop Options

IPv6 recognizes and responds to the current low demand for differentiated QoS, yet it still makes provisions for its gradual adoption in a smooth way. The IPv6 header eliminates all the fields relating to QoS, which were carried in the IPv4 header. Instead, IPv6 allows options headers—such as the Hop-by-Hop Options extension header, the Routing extension header, and the Destination Options extension header—to be used in flexible ways to implement current and future QoS schemes. By eliminating fields in the basic IPv6 header, which would have to be examined by every router, IPv6 speeds up the processing of default-quality service on the Internet. By creating headers that can be examined by all or by selected hops on a path through the Internet, IPv6 creates tools that can be used by QoS protocols to gain precise control of both per-hop and per-domain behaviors.

RFC 2711 defines the router alert option in the Hop-by-Hop Options extension header. The router alert option tells intervening routers to examine the packet more closely for important information. If this option is not present, routers can assume that any packet not addressed directly to them contains nothing of interest and should be forwarded normally. IPv6 packets containing RSVP instructions must use the router alert option in the Hop-by-Hop Options extension header. The router alert option is shown in Figure 3-18.

0 0 0	0 0 1 0 1	0 0 0 0 0 0 1 0	VALUE (2 octets)

Length = 2

Figure 3-18 Router alert option in Hop-by-Hop Options extension header
© Cengage Learning 2013

The first byte of the option is the Option Type field. Note that the first 3 bits of the Option Type field are set to all 0s. The first two zeroes mean, "If you don't understand this option, ignore it and continue processing the rest of the header." The last of these three zeroes means, "The data in this option cannot change en route." The remaining 5 bytes of the Option Type field equal 5 (i.e., the binary value 00101, which represents $1 * 2^2 + 1 * 2^0$, or 4 + 1, and is indeed the binary representation for the number 5), identifying the option as the Hop-by-Hop Option.

The second byte of the option is the Option Data Length field. The "payload" of the router alert option is only 2 bytes long, so this field is set to 2 (expressed as an 8-bit binary number, this becomes 00000010, as shown in Figure 13-18).

Only three possible values for the router alert option are defined in RFC 2711. They are shown in Table 3-9.

Value	Meaning
0	Datagram contains a Multicast Listener Discovery message
1	Datagram contains an RSVP message
2	Datagram contains an Active Networks message

Table 3-9 IPv6 router alert option values
© Cengage Learning 2013

All the rest are reserved for assignment by the Internet Assigned Numbers Authority (IANA).

IPv6 MTU and Packet Handling

As you might recall from Chapter 1, an MTU is the largest packet that can be transmitted across a network path. The larger the packet, the fewer the packets required to send a given amount of information. The MTU can be no larger than can be successfully transmitted through all the nodes on the network. In other words, the maximum size of the MTU must not exceed the minimum size of the network link.

Although you will learn all about packet assembly, routing, fragmentation, and reassembly in Chapter 4, this section helps you understand some essentials that will prepare you for that chapter.

RFC 1981 defines the mechanism used by IPv6 to discover the MTU of an arbitrary network path that is called **Path MTU (PMTU) Discovery**. IPv6 nodes execute PMTU Discovery to learn which network paths have a greater than minimum **link MTU** value. Once a path is discovered and the MTU packet size is set, packets can still be routed across different paths and packets can encounter network nodes that cannot manage the MTU size. When a node encounters a packet that is too large to be forwarded, it discards the packet and sends an ICMPv6 Packet Too Big message back to the source node. When the source node receives this message it adjusts the MTU size and retransmits the data. The node may receive numerous Packet Too Big messages until all packets successfully transverse the path. The minimum MTU size is 1,280 bytes. Figure 3-19 shows the basic PMTU Discovery process. The source node discovers the smallest link MTU in the path and then sets the size of the packet MTU size for the PMTU before transmission.

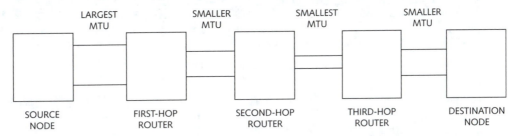

Figure 3-19 Source node uses PMTU Discovery to determine the smallest link MTU in a path
© Cengage Learning 2013

PMTU Discovery establishes the PMTU for an arbitrary path in the network from source to destination at any given point in time. Changing conditions on networks result in changes in the routing topology, which can make a source node's understanding of the desired PMTU path obsolete. Packet Too Big messages sent to a source node inform the node that the PMTU has been reduced, and the source node changes the MTU size accordingly.

PMTU Discovery can also attempt to determine if the PMTU has increased or can accommodate a larger PMTU size. A source node does this by periodically increasing the MTU size. If these packets are successfully received, then the discovery process is successful. If not, then the node will receive Packet Too Big messages and will reduce the MTU size. Ideally, all IPv6 nodes should initiate PMTU Discovery. However, minimal IPv6 implementations may choose to bypass this procedure. In this case, PMTU Discovery will use the minimum MTU size (as defined in RFC 1981) to send the data. This results in more packets being transmitted than probably is necessary because the smallest size packets are being used, wasting network resources and reducing throughput.

It's important to distinguish between link MTU and PMTU. Link MTU is the maximum size of a packet in octets that can be transmitted as a single unit over a link. PMTU is the minimum link MTU of all the links in a path between a source and destination address. In other words, the PMTU is the smallest pipeline in the chain of pipelines that form a network path.

PMTU Discovery supports multicast as well as unicast transmissions, which presents something of a problem. Discovery sets copies of a packet to be delivered to all the different multicast destinations, even though each destination has a different PMTU. This will likely result in the source node receiving multiple Packet Too Big messages, with each message reporting a different next-hop MTU. The size of the MTU, under this circumstance, isn't random and is usually the minimum PMTU for all paths through which the packet is to be transmitted.

An interesting characteristic of MTU Discovery is that it will be performed even when the source node believes it is directly connected to the destination node. This is actually an advantage because sometimes a router is used as a proxy for the destination and will be more than one hop away, even when, from the source node's point of view, the source and destination are on the same link.

Besides Packet Too Big messages, ICMPv6 provides the following informational and error messages as shown in Table 3-10.

ICMPv6 Message	Meaning
Destination Unreachable	When a packet is unable to reach the destination address for reasons other than network congestion
Parameter Problem	Can come from any node on the packet's path that has difficulty processing a field in the IPv6 packet header
Time Exceeded	Can come from any router in the path and is sent when the packet's Hop Limit field decrement to 0 or the packet does not reach its destination within the alloted fragment reassembly time

Table 3-10 ICMPv6 message types
© Cengage Learning 2013

ICMPv6 messages are transported in an IPv6 datagram containing a value of 58 in the Next Header field. Echo Request and Echo Reply messages are used for diagnostic purposes, and information about multicast group membership is sent from network nodes to neighboring routers using Group Membership Query, Group Membership Reduction, and Group Membership Report messages.

Upper-Layer Checksums in IPv6

Any upper-layer protocol containing addresses from the header in the checksum computation must include the 128-bit IPv6 address. When running UDP over IPv6, the checksum is mandatory and a pseudo-header is used to imitate the actual IPv6 header. Figure 3-20 shows the IPv6 pseudo-header.

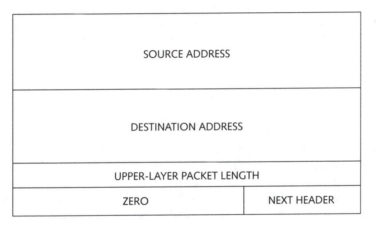

Figure 3-20 IPv6 pseudo-header
© Cengage Learning 2013

The Source Address field contains the originating address in the IPv6 packet. If the IPv6 packet contains a Routing extension header, the Destination Address is the final destination for the packet. If the Routing extension header is absent, the Destination Address will be the one in the IPv6 packet. The next header contains the value of the upper-layer protocol, such as 6 for TCP or 17 for UDP. This value will be different from the Next Header field in the IPv6 packet if there is one or more extension headers between the IPv6 header and the upper-layer header.

The Upper-Layer Packet Length field contains the length of the upper-layer header plus the associated data. UDP carries its own length information, but TCP does not. For TCP, the value in this field is the payload length obtained from the IPv6 header without the length of any of the extension headers that may exist between the IPv6 header and the upper-layer header.

 The UDP upper-layer protocol can be used to carry a wide variety of information across a network, including DHCPv6 address assignment requests and responses.

Because the UDP checksum is not optional, as it was in IPv4, the source network node must calculate the checksum for the packet and the pseudo-header. If the result is 0, the value is changed to a hexadecimal value of FFFF and inserted into the UDP header. The receiving nodes will discard UDP packets with a 0 checksum and record an error in a log.

When the upper-layer protocol is calculating the maximum payload size for the upper-layer data, it "considers" how much larger size the IPv6 header is (due to the IPv6 address space) than the IPv4 header. Also, there are differences between IPv4 and IPv6 in terms of the maximum lifetime of a packet. For instance, IPv6 nodes do not have the requirement to enforce a maximum packet lifetime, as is done for IPv4 (this is one of the differences between the Hop Limit and TTL fields). However, this IPv4 "limitation" has rarely been enforced, so the packet lifetime behavior between IPv4 and IPv6 won't yield many observable distinctions.

ICMPv6 includes the pseudo-header in its checksum calculation, which is another difference between IPv6 and IPv4, because ICMPv4 does not perform this computation on the pseudo-header. The action taken by ICMPv6 prevents it from being misdelivered or from corruption of the fields in the IPv6 header that depends on the checksum. These fields are not covered by the Internet-layer checksum calculation as are their IPv4 counterparts.

Because much of the discussion of checksums centers on upper-layer protocols and particularly UDP, it will be helpful to have a brief discussion of UDP and TCP as the two major protocols operating at the Transport layer of the OSI model.

UDP is a connectionless protocol that runs on top of IP networks and offers few, if any, error-checking, flow control, and recovery services. For this reason, UDP is considered "unreliable"; but it is also quick and is used when data must be sent immediately and cannot tolerate delay, such as with streaming audio and video. This means that if any packets using UDP for transport are lost, there is no way to recover them and their data. When UDP is used for transport, the primary concern is that the data must be transmitted quickly.

TCP is the de facto transport protocol on the Internet; it is a connection-oriented protocol. This means that TCP is considered "reliable" and guarantees data delivery. To do this, before the information is transmitted, a connection is negotiated and established between the source and destination. TCP employs flow control in order to determine when packets have been lost and need to be sent again. Flow control restricts the rate the source node sends data as the means of guaranteeing reliable delivery. The destination node communicates to the source the rate of data reception it can tolerate on a continual basis. The sender will stop data transfer if the destination's buffer fills and the destination node sends a "0" for its "window size" during the subsequent acknowledgement message. Information sent using TCP as the transport cannot tolerate loss, and the sender and receiver are willing to sacrifice speed in exchange for safe delivery. Protocols commonly using TCP for transport include File Transfer Protocol (FTP), Post Office Protocol version 3 (POP3), and Simple Mail Transfer Protocol (SMTP).

You will learn about TCP and UDP in detail in Chapter 9.

A Rationale for IPv6 Header Structures vis-à-vis IPv4

As you are aware of by now, the IPv6 protocol is a much-needed upgrade to IPv4 across the board, including the packet header structure; but what makes the IPv6 header an improvement? After all, the IPv6 header is much larger—24 bytes larger than an IPv4 packet, mainly to accommodate the larger address space. That said, the basic IPv6 packet seems much less "cluttered" than the basic IPv4 packet. Figure 3-21 shows what the two different packets look like side by side.

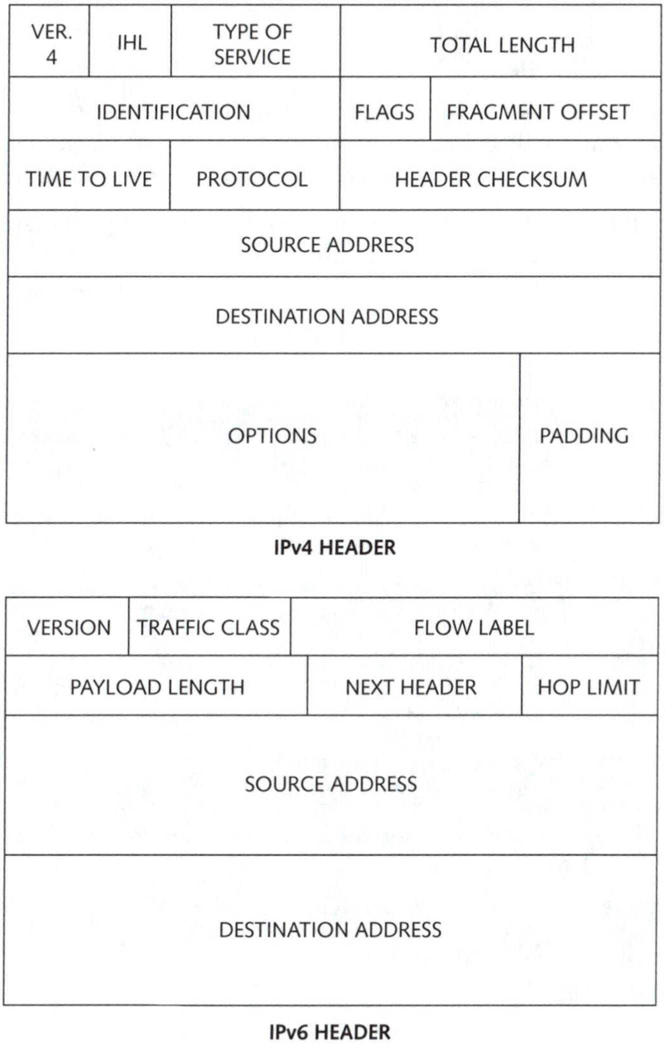

VER. 4	IHL	TYPE OF SERVICE	TOTAL LENGTH	
IDENTIFICATION			FLAGS	FRAGMENT OFFSET
TIME TO LIVE		PROTOCOL	HEADER CHECKSUM	
SOURCE ADDRESS				
DESTINATION ADDRESS				
OPTIONS				PADDING

IPv4 HEADER

VERSION	TRAFFIC CLASS	FLOW LABEL	
PAYLOAD LENGTH		NEXT HEADER	HOP LIMIT
SOURCE ADDRESS			
DESTINATION ADDRESS			

IPv6 HEADER

Figure 3-21 Side-by-side comparision of IPv4 and IPv6 packet structures
© Cengage Learning 2013

Now that you can see the differences, let's make a comparision of the two versions of the IP packet.

Comparing IPv4 and IPv6 Headers

As previously mentioned, although the IPv6 packet is much larger, it also has a less complicated structure, allowing it to be more efficiently processed. A significant difference is that there is no required checksum calculation for an IPv6 packet. Because this is already managed at Layer 2 of the OSI model, having the checksum calculated at Layer 3 was considered redundant, and the requirement was removed for the IPv6 header. The only downside is that if a router error occurs, the packet is lost, assuming invalid values are contained in the packet.

The IPv6 Header's Hop Limit field generally replaces the IPv4 Header's TTL field and with good reason. The TTL field measured time rather than hops, so each hop was considered one second. The calculation had to be made from seconds to hops and then back again. The Hop Limit manages hops, thereby simplifying the process.

The length of an IPv4 header can be variable, depending on the options it contains, and requires a Header Length field; an IPv6 header, because of the use of extension headers, remains a constant 40 bytes in length. IPv6 header length is indicated in the Data field.

In IPv6, packet fragmentation is only managed at the source and destination points, and routers never fragment an IPv6 packet, as they do IPv4 packets. IPv6 packet size is determined by the source network node using Path MTU Discovery, so packets are fragmented prior to transmission.

Table 3-11 summarizes the overall differences between IPv4 and IPv6 headers:

IPv4	IPv6
The IPv4 header includes a checksum.	The IPv6 header does not include a checksum.
The IPv4 header does not identify packet flows for QoS management by routers.	The IPv6 header uses a Flow Label field to identify packet flows for QoS management by routers.
The IPv4 header includes an Options field.	The IPv6 header does not manage options; any optional data is managed by extension headers.
ICMPv4 Router Discovery is used to determine the best default gateway to the destination address; however, this action is optional.	ICMPv6 Router Solicitation and Router Advertisement messages are used to discover the best default gateway to the destination address; this action is mandatory.
IPv4 must support a 576-byte packet size, which can be fragmented.	IPv6 must support a 1,280-byte packet size, which is not fragmented.
Packets are fragmented by the source network node and by routers.	Packets are fragmented only by the source network node.
TTL decrements packet hops as a function of time (1 second = 1 hop).	Hop Limit decrements packet hops as a function of distance.

Table 3-11   Comparison of IPv4 and IPv6 headers
© Cengage Learning 2013

IPv4 and IPv6 packets are generally incompatible. Network hardware and software that operates well with IPv4 will not manage IPv6 traffic at all. This has been one of the major stumbling blocks in the transition of local and global networks to IPv6. It is impossible to switch an entire network environment (particularly the Internet) from an IPv4 to IPv6 hardware and software platform in a single action. At some point in the transition, both IP versions must coexist in the same infrastructure.

A Summary of the IPv4 to IPv6 Transition

A full discussion of the transition from IPv4 to IPv6 is beyond the scope of this chapter, but how IPv4 and IPv6 "interoperate" has been briefly addressed. For instance, RFC 3056, "Connection of IPv6 Domains via IPv4 Clouds," specifies an optional method for IPv6 sites to communicate with one another over IPv4 networks without setting up tunneling. This mechanism treats IPv4 wide area networks (WANs) as a unicast point-to-point link. Please keep in mind that this is suggested as an interim solution only, whereas IPv4 and IPv6 are required to work together. Once the final transition to IPv6 is complete, IPv4 "clouds" will no longer need to exist.

The common name used to refer to this method is "**6to4**," sometimes referred to as "6to4 tunneling." (This is somewhat misnamed, because an explicit tunneling setup is not required.) 6to4 can be used at the level of the individual IPv6 node or by a local IPv6 network. Individual nodes using 6to4 must have a global IPv4 address connected to the node, and the node is required to provide IPv4 encapsulation of all the IPv6 packets it sends as well as decapsulation services for all packets it receives, stripping IPv4 encapsulation off the IPv6 packets. Addresses for these nodes can be provided through autoconfiguration rather than requiring a manual configuration. The first 16 bits of the node's address tells any 6to4 router that it can receive encapsulated packets over the IPv4 network.

The 6to4 system is prone to misconfigured network nodes, which results in poor performance, such as long retry delays or complete connection failures. For this reason, RFC 6343 was issued as an advisory statement on 6to4 deployment best practices. One of the common problems in encouraging early adoption of IPv6 using the 6to4 solution is that 6to4 use is transparent to the user and sometimes to first-line help desk support. Customers using PCs with IPv6 enabled when they call their local help desk are sometimes told to simply disable their IPv6 implementation, frustrating any efforts to use IPv6 nodes over IPv4 networks. The 6to4 advisory paper will hopefully correct this trend.

The **Transport Relay Translator** (**TRT**) allows IPv6 network nodes to send and receive TCP and UDP traffic with IPv4 network nodes. The advantage of using TRT is that it doesn't require any special configuration of either IPv6 or IPv4 nodes to allow them to exchange upper-layer protocol data. However, there are some disadvantages. TRT can be used for bidirectional traffic only. It also needs to be stateful between communicating nodes. TRT works somewhat like NAT in this respect, because the transport layer connection must go through a single TRT system, representing a single point of failure. RFC 3142, "An IPv6-to-IPv4 Transport Relay Translator," is an informational document that describes TRT and how to implement it using currently existing technologies. The document does not, however, indicate specific protocols to be used. Although the ideal is that traffic should go both ways, RFC 3142 describes only IPv6-source-to-IPv4-destination communication.

The problems and potential solutions discussed here illustrate not only the difficulty in the IPv4-to-IPv6 transition but the extent of IPv4-IPv6 incompatibility. This chapter has described in detail the differences between IPv4 and IPv6 packet headers, and although the advancements in IPv6 are extensive and greatly needed, the commitment to IPv6—from internetworking industry leaders to network administrators and engineers for business solutions around the globe—must be extremely high.

Chapter 10 covers transitioning from IPv4 to IPv6 in detail.

Chapter Summary

- IPv4 header fields have been the method for providing reliable sending and receiving of data on networks for decades. Version and header length are defined, and type of service (TOS) describes the parameters of the desired quality of service. The total length of the packet, measured in octets, is defined because IPv4 packet lengths are variable. The packet header contains a Flags field for control data, and the Time to Live field measures hops as a matter of time rather than distance. The Header Checksum field provides for error checking and is recalculated each time the packet is forwarded. The Source Address and Destination Address fields are 32 bits, and the Options field contains any special handling options for the packet as well as padding.

- The IPv6 header structure is much simpler than the one for IPv4, but it performs the same basic function of reliably getting data from a source to a destination node. The Traffic Class field is used to tell routers if the packet possesses a special class or priority. The Flow Label field is used to request special handling by routers for real-time applications or non-default QoS. Payload length identifies the overall length of the packet, including extension headers, and the Next Header field is used to identify the header immediately following the IPv6 header, pointing to the first extension header. The Hop Limit field takes the place of the TTL field in the IPv4 header and measures hops as distance rather than time. Source and Destination Address fields are 128 bits in length.

- IPv6 extension headers are used to add any special functionality to an IPv6 Packet, and their use is optional. They replace the Options field in the IPv4 header and allow the IPv6 header to remain more lightweight and to possess a fixed length. IPv6 extension headers must appear in a specific order: Hop-by-Hop Options, Destination Options, Routing, Fragment, Authentication, and Encapsulation Security Payload (ESP).

- The Hop-by-Hop Options extension header carries data that affects routers along the network path, such as special routing instructions. The Destination Options extension header extends the IPv6 header to support packet handling and preferences. It is also the only extension header that can appear twice in the extension header, once immediately before the Routing extension header and/or just before the upper-layer header. The Routing extension header supports strict or loose source routing and includes fields for intermediary addresses. The Fragment extension header is only used if the source node needs to send packets larger than the PMTU established by PMTU Discovery. The Authentication extension header prevents spoofing and connection theft by specifying the true source of the packet. The Encapsulating Security Payload (ESP) extension header and trailer are used to encrypt data because this is not done by the Autentication extension header.

- Jumbograms are a special type of service for IPv6 packets that can use the Hop-by-Hop Options extension header to add an alternate packet length field for the packet. By default, the Payload Length field is 2 bytes long and allows a packet to carry up to 64 kilobytes bytes of data. Jumbograms can carry between 64 kilobytes and over four billion bytes, which would be insane over a typical network link but can offer significant operational advantages over a backbone or other high-capacity path.

- IPv6 MTU Discovery (technically, PMTU Discovery) is the ability of a source node to discover the maximum MTU size a path to a destination can support and then set the size of IPv6 packets accordingly. This does away with the necessity of fragmentation, particularly by routers between the source and the destination. If any packets encounter a path that cannot support the PMTU size, the packet is dropped and an ICMPv6 Packet Too Big message is sent to the sending node. The node adjusts the size of the packet accordingly and retransmits. Some minimal IPv6 environments will not use MTU Discovery and instead send the smallest supported packet size. This wastes network resources by using more packets than are likely required by the path.

- Upper-layer checksums are manditory when running UDP over IPv6 (they were optional for IPv4), and a pseudo-header is used to imitate the actual IPv6 header. The pseudo-header contains a Source and Destination Address field. The Destination Address field is the final destination of the packet if the IPv6 header contains routing information. The Upper-Layer Packet Length field contains the length of the upper-layer header plus any associated data. The Zeros field contains the value for the upper-layer protocol, such as 6 for TCP or 17 for UDP, and the Next Header field's value changes depending on whether or not extension headers are being used.

- Although the IPv6 header is much larger than the IPv4 header, that's mainly because of the much larger address space for IPv6. IPv6 headers have fewer fields and a constant size of 40 octets, making them more streamlined than IPv4 headers. Whereas the IPv4 header has an Options field, where all customizations are added, causing the header size to be variable, options for the IPv6 header are all managed by optional extension headers. Also, there is no Checksum field in the IPv6 header because this is managed by upper-layer protocols. This makes UDP checksum calculation manditory rather than optional, as it is for IPv4 headers, and it is performed using a pseudo-header. IPv4 uses a TTL field to calculate hops but does so by counting hops as seconds rather than as units of movement between one node and the next. IPv6 uses a Hop Limit field to treat hops as distance rather than time. IPv6 packets are not fragmented, as IPv4 packets are. Instead, MTU Discovery is used to set the size of the IPv6 packets at the source node and then send them across a path that can support the MTU size.

- The significant differences between IPv4 and IPv6 packet headers illustrate these protocols' incompatibility and punctuate the difficulty in transistioning a worldwide internetwork infrastructure to the latest version of IP. Several interim solutions have been suggested, principally the "6to4" solution, which would allow IPv6 nodes to communicate with each other over IPv4 networks by encapsulating IPv6 packets within IPv4. Transport Relay Translators (TRTs) can also be used to send upper-layer protocol data, such as TCP or UDP from IPv6 source nodes to IPv4 destination nodes as well as from IPv4 source nodes to IPv6 destination nodes.

Key Terms

6to4   A method of allowing IPv6 network nodes to communicate with each other over an IPv4 network by special encapsulation of IPv6 packets.

error-detection mechanism   A method for detecting corrupted packets. The CRC process is an example of an error-detection mechanism.

extension headers   For IPv6 packets, these are optional headers or containers, placed between the IPv6 header and the upper-layer header, that allow more features to be added to the packet as required.

flow   A set of packets for which a source requires special handling by intervening routers.

Fragment Offset field   The field that defines where a fragment should be placed when the entire data set is reassembled.

jumbogram   A specification for allowing very large (beyond 4-gigabyte) packets to be transported using IPv6. Used only in special circumstances, such as on large backbone routes.

link MTU   This is the MTU capacity of a specific link within a Path MTU. The smallest link MTU determines the MTU size of IPv6 packets for the path.

path MTU (PMTU) Discovery   A technique used by IPv6 nodes to determine the size of packets that can be transmitted along a proposed network path from a source to a network address.

per-domain behavior (PDB)   In differentiated service, this is a class of descriptors of available service levels or a way of describing the entities offering such differentiated service levels—in this case, a "domain." Services are provided as specified throughout the domain and change at the edge of the domain. PDBs are available across all hops within a given domain.

per-hop behavior (PHB)   In differentiated service, this is a class of descriptors of available service levels or a way of describing protocols and priorities applied to a packet on traversing a router "hop."

precedence   A definition of priority for an IP packet. Routers may process higher-priority packets before lower-priority packets when a router queue is congested.

Resource Reservation Protocol (RSVP)   A protocol aimed at regularizing and formalizing the practice of securing particular levels of service for traffic flows over the Internet.

router queue   A router buffering system used to hold packets when the router is congested.

time to live (TTL)   An indication of the remaining distance that a packet can travel. Though defined in terms of seconds, the TTL value is implemented as a number of hops that a packet can travel before being discarded by a router. The Time to Live field is also often abbreviated as TTL.

Transport Relay Translator (TRT)   This is a method that allows an IPv6 network node to send upper-layer protocol data such as TCP or UDP to an IPv4 network node.

Type of Service (TOS)   A process used to define a type of path that a packet should take through the network. TOS options include the greatest throughput, lowest delay, and most reliability.

Voice over IP (VoIP)   A communications technology that allows voice and multimedia communication sessions over IP networks (e.g., the Internet or an intranet).

Review Questions

1. In an IPv4 packet header, what does the value in the Internet Header Length signify?

   a. the length of the IPv4 packet

   b. the length of the IPv4 header

   c. the length of the IPv4 header minus options

   d. the length of the IPv4 packet minus options

2. What is the purpose of the Precedence bits in the IPv4 header's Type of Service field?

   a. Precedence is used by routers to prioritize traffic through router queues.

   b. Precedence is used by MTU Discovery to adjust packet size for link MTUs.

   c. Precedence is used by routers to follow a specified path type.

   d. Precedence is used by upper-layer protocols for error checking.

3. Using the differentiated service code point (DSCP) identifier, IPv4 traffic can be prioritized by an end node or boundary device, such as a router, and queued and forwarded according to this value. DSCP expedited forwarding (EF) ensures that routers expedite the packet forwarding and don't lower the priority value. Of the following, which service most requires DSCP EF?

   a. E-mail

   b. instant messaging

   c. VoIP

   d. Web browsing

4. In an IPv4 Packet header, the Identification field contains a unique identifier for each packet; however, packets are sometimes fragmented further by routers to transverse a network that supports a smaller packet size. What happens to the value of the Identification field in a packet header if the packet is further fragmented?

   a. The unique ID for the packet is maintained, but for each fragment, a suffix is added to the original value.

   b. The unique ID for the packet is maintained, but for each fragment, a prefix is added to the original value.

   c. The unique ID is discarded, and completely new IDs are inserted in the Identification field for each of the fragments of the original packet.

   d. Each fragment of the original packet maintains the original ID value in the header Identification field.

5. The Flags field in an IPv4 header can be set to different values, depending on fragmentation requirements. Of the following, which is correct about the options that can be set in this field?

   a. The values can be set to allow more fragmentation but not to prohibit fragmentation.

   b. The values can be set to prohibit more fragmentation but not to allow further fragmentation.

   c. The values can be set to allow more fragmentation or prohibit more fragmentation, depending on the network's requirements.

   d. The value can only be set to Reserved (Bit 0), with no other available options.

6. The IPv4 header's Fragment Offset field is used, if the packet is a fragment, to show where to place the packet's data when the fragments are reconstructed. True or False?

7. The IPv4's Time to Live (TTL) field indicates the remaining lifetime of the packet defined as distance or as in hops through routers. True or False?

8. The IPv4 Protocol field contains the value of the protocol that is coming next. Of the following, which are valid protocols for this field? (Choose all that apply.)

   a. EGP

   b. ICMP

   c. NAND

   d. OSPF

9. What basic function does the IPv4 Header Checksum field perform?

   a. It provides error detection on the contents of the IP header, minus the Checksum field.

   b. It provides error detection on the contents of the entire IP packet, including the header.

   c. It provides error detection on the contents of the IP header, including the Checksum field itself.

   d. It provides error detection on the contents of the entire IP packet, minus the Checksum field.

10. Which address type can the Source Address field of an IPv4 packet header contain?

    a. anycast

    b. broadcast

    c. multicast

    d. unicast

11. The IPv4 header's Options field provides additional IP routing controls. What is the boundary where the options must end?

    a. 2-byte boundary

    b. 4-byte boundary

    c. 8-byte boundary

    d. 16-byte boundary

12. For the IPv6 header Traffic Class field, what function does the Precedence field serve?

    a. It allows an application to differentiate traffic types based on priorities.

    b. It allows forwarding routers to distinguish different flows of packets.

    c. It allows upper-layer protocols to insert a value in the Traffic Class field.

    d. It reserves the last 4 bits of the Traffic Class field for Differentiated Services.

13. Which fields in an IPv6 header do packet classifiers use to identify a packet's flow if it is part of a flow? (Choose all that apply.)

    a. Destination Address

    b. Flow Label

    c. Hop Limit

    d. Source Address

14. The Next Header field in the IPv6 header points to the first extension header for the packet if the packet possesses one or more extension headers. If more than one extension header exists, how is this extension header identified?

    a. The Next Header field points to the first extension header and then, if others exist, points to the subsequent extension headers.

    b. The Next Header field points to the first extension header and, if others exist, the first extension header uses its own Next Header field to point to the next extension header.

    c. The Next Header field points to the first extension header and, if others exist, they announce themselves using values in their own Next Header fields.

    d. The Next Header field points to the first extension header and, if others exist, the encapsulated higher-level protocol contains a reference to all subsequent extension headers.

15. RFC 2460 defines the recommended order in which extension headers should appear. Which extension header should appear first if it is present?

    a. Authentication

    b. Destination Options

    c. Hop-by-Hop Options

    d. Routing

16. Of the following, which extension header can appear more than once for an IPv6 packet?

    a. Authentication

    b. Destination Options

    c. Hop-by-Hop Options

    d. Routing

17. What is a valid proposed option for the IPv6 Hop-by-Hop Options extension header?

    a. jumbogram large payload options

    b. intermediary addresses options

    c. hop limit options

    d. minimum fragment size options

18. When is the Destination Options extension header encrypted?

    a. when it appears earlier in the packet

    b. when it appears later in the packet

    c. when its value is more than 0

    d. when it appears before the Hop-by-Hop Options field

19. Currently, the Routing extension header is designed to use only one option. Which option can it use?

    a. Routing Address = 0

    b. Routing Next Hop = 0

    c. Routing Preference = 0

    d. Routing Type = 0

20. When is the Fragment extension header used?

    a. when the transmitting device needs to send packets smaller than the PMTU

    b. when the transmitting device needs to send packets larger than the PMTU

    c. when the transmitting device needs to send packets consistent with the PMTU

    d. when the transmitting device needs to send a "Do Not Fragment" message to forwarding routers

21. How does the Authentication extension header specify the true origin of an IPv6 packet?

    a. by containing an encrypted copy of the sending host's username and password

    b. by preventing address spoofing and connection theft

    c. by possessing a true copy of the IPv6 host address in binary format

    d. by inhibiting data corruption of the ESP extension header

22. A network node that understands the Jumbo Payload option will process a packet as a jumbogram under what condition?

    a. The packet's header Payload Length field is set to greater than 0.

    b. The Next Header field is set to greater than 0.

    c. The Link-Layer framing indicates that additional octets exist beyond the IPv6 header.

    d. The Fragment extension header is present.

23. Once PMTU Discovery sets the MTU size for IPv6 packets and begins sending, how do forwarding nodes manage packets if a link MTU in the path reduces or becomes too small for the packet MTU size?

    a. The forwarding node drops the packet and sends an ICMPv6 Packet Too Big message to the sending node.

    b. The forwarding node drops the packet and sends an ICMPv6 Resend Packet message to the sending node.

c. The forwarding node performs PMTU Discovery to locate a path that will accommodate the current MTU size, and then forwards the packet along that path.

d. The forwarding node changes the value in the Fragment extension header from "Do Not Fragment" to "Fragment Type = 0" and then changes the MTU size to fit the reduced link MTU.

24. When running UDP over IPv6, the checksum is mandatory and a pseudo-header is used to imitate the actual IPv6 header. If the Routing extension header is present, what is the result in the pseudo-header?

a. The address in the Destination Address field is the final destination address.

b. The address in the Destination Address field is the one in the IPv6 packet.

c. The Next Header field contains the value of the upper-layer protocol.

d. The Upper-Layer Packet Length field contains the length of the upper-layer header plus the associated data.

25. IPv6 packet headers are much larger in size than IPv4 packet headers, even though the IPv6 header structure is less complex. What is the main cause of the size increase?

a. the larger IPv6 address space

b. the addition of extension headers

c. mandatory checksum calculations for IPv6 packet headers using the UDP upper-layer protocol

d. the Hop Limit field's measurement of hops as distance rather than time

Hands-On Projects

The following Hands-On Projects assume you are working in a Windows 7 or Windows Vista environment. You must have Wireshark installed.

Hands-On Project 3-1: Examining an IPv4 Packet Header with Wireshark

Time Required: 20 minutes

Objective: Learn to use Wireshark to examine the fields in an IPv4 header.

Description: This project shows you how to capture packets on a network, select a specific packet, and examine the IPv4 header data for the packet. You may capture your own data to analyze, or you may start Wireshark, open the **IPv4Fields.pcap** file available from the Student Companion Web site, and skip to Step 8.

1. Start Wireshark. (Click **Start**, point to **All Programs**, and then click **Wireshark**. Alternatively, click **Start**, type **Wireshark** in the Start menu search box, and then click **Wireshark** in the resulting list.)

2. Click the **Capture** menu, and then click **Interfaces**. The Capture Interfaces window appears.

3. Several network interfaces may appear. Locate the first one showing real-time packet counts under the Packets column, and then click **Start**. The Capturing window appears.

4. Open a command prompt window. (Click the **Start** button, type **cmd** in the Start menu search box, and then click **OK**.)

5. Ping the IPv4 address of a computer on your local network.

If you don't know the IPv4 address of a host on your network, ask your instructor.

6. Type **exit** and press **Enter** in the command prompt window to close it.

7. In Wireshark, click **Capture** on the menu bar and then click **Stop** (or click the **Stop** icon on the tool bar).

8. Select a TCP packet in the packet list pane (the upper pane).

9. In the packet details pane (the middle pane), expand **Internet Protocol Version 4**, as shown in Figure 3-22.

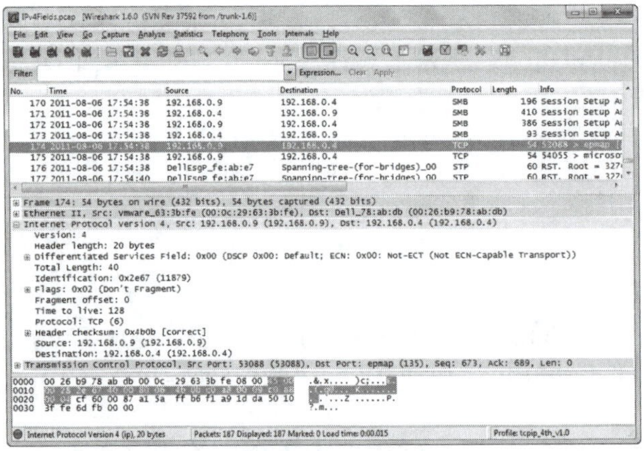

Figure 3-22 Selecting the IPv4 protocol to examine the IPv4 packet header
Source: Wireshark

10. Examine the values for the **Version** and **Header length** fields.

11. Expand **Differentiated Services Field,** examine the contents, and then collapse the selection.

12. Examine the values of the **Total Length** and **Identification** fields.

13. Expand **Flags**, examine the contents of this field, and then collapse the selection.

14. Examine the **Fragment offset, Time to Live,** and **Protocol** fields.

15. Expand the **Header checksum** field, examine the contents, and then collapse the selection.

16. Examine the **Source** and **Destination** fields.

17. If told to do so by your instructor, save the capture file and then close Wireshark.

Hands-On Project 3-2: Examining an IPv6 Packet Header with Wireshark

Time Required: 20 minutes

Objective: Learn to use Wireshark to examine the fields in an IPv6 header.

Description: This project shows you how to capture packets on a network, select a specific packet, and examine the IPv6 header data for the packet. You may alternately open the **IPv6Fields.pcap** file, available from the Student Companion Web site, in Wireshark rather than capturing data. You will use the IPv6-only display filter that you created using Wireshark in Hands-On Project 1-6.

1. Start Wireshark.

2. Click **Capture** on the menu bar, and then click **Interfaces**.

3. Select the network interface for your computer and click **Start**.

4. Open a command prompt window. (Click the **Start** button, type **cmd** in the Start menu search box, and then click **OK**.)

5. Ping the IPv6 address of a computer on your local network.

> If you don't know the IPv6 address of a host on your network, ask your instructor.

6. To use the Wireshark IPv6-only display filter, open the **Filter** drop-down menu on the Filter toolbar, select **ipv6 or icmpv6 or dhcpv6**, and then click **Apply**. The example in Figure 3-23 shows only IPv6, ICMPv6, and DHCPv6 traffic.

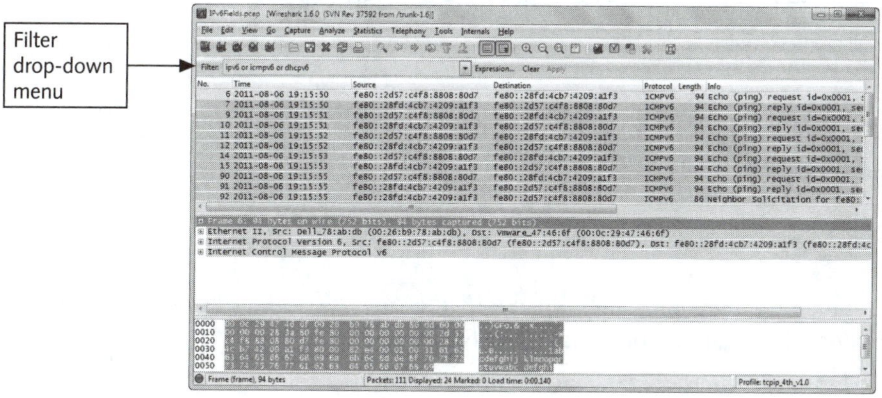

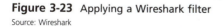

Figure 3-23 Applying a Wireshark filter
Source: Wireshark

7. Click on any IPv6 address in the packet list pane (the upper pane).

8. In the packet details pane (the middle pane), expand **Internet Protocol Version 6** as shown in Figure 3-24.

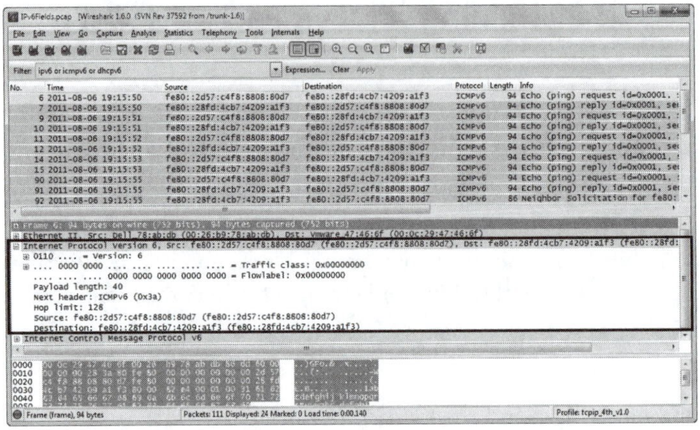

Figure 3-24 Examining an IPv6 packet header in Wireshark
Source: Wireshark

9. Expand **0110 = Version 6**, examine the Version field, and then collapse the selection.

10. Expand the **Traffic Class** field and examine the contents, as shown in Figure 3-25. Collapse the selection when you're finished.

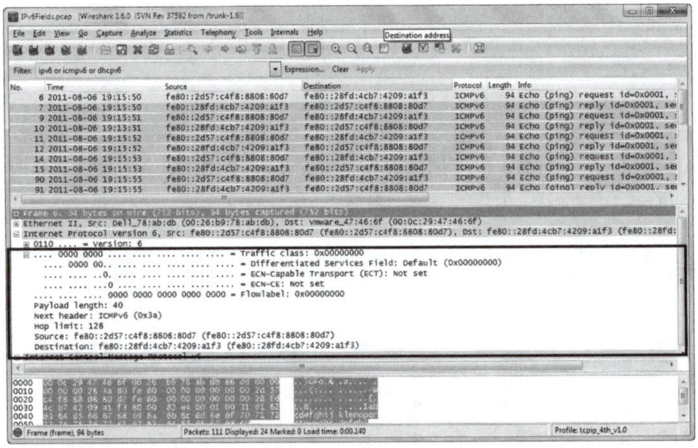

Figure 3-25 Examining the Traffic Class field in an IPv6 header
Source: Wireshark

11. Examine the remaining fields in the IPv6 header, including **Payload Length, Next Header, Hop Limit, Source**, and **Destination**.

12. Collapse the **Internet Protocol Version 6** section.

13. Leave Wireshark open for the next Hands-On Project without making any changes.

Hands-On Project 3-3: Examining an IPv6 Upper-Layer Protocol in Wireshark

Time Required: 15 minutes

Objective: Learn to use Wireshark to examine the upper-layer protocol in an IPv6 header.

Description: This project shows you how to examine the IPv6 header data and its upper-layer protocol.

1. Continue with Wireshark from the previous Hands-On Project.

2. Because the IPv6 packet capture used the UDP upper-layer protocol, click a **DHCPv6** entry in the packet list pane and expand **User Datagram Protocol** in the packet details pane, as shown in Figure 3-26.

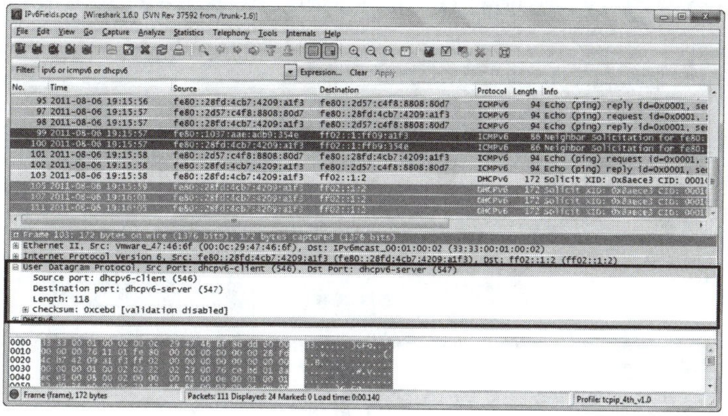

Figure 3-26 Examining the UDP upper-layer protocol in an IPv6 packet header in Wireshark
Source: Wireshark

3. Examine the **Source Port, Destination Port,** and **Length** fields.

4. Expand the **Checksum** field, examine its contents, and then collapse the selection.

5. Collapse **User Datagram Protocol.**

6. If told to by your instructor, save the capture log, and then close Wireshark.

Saving the capture log will include the data for Hands-On Projects 2 and 3.

Case Projects

Case Project 3-1: Wireshark versus NetMon

Throughout this book, you will make extensive use of the Wireshark packet capture tool; however, there are other utilities that provide a similar function. Microsoft uses NetMon (also known as Microsoft Network Monitor) to perform protocol and structural analysis on IPv4 and IPv6 traffic. First, go to *www.wireshark.org/faq.html* in a Web browser and, on a separate tab or window, go to *http://social.technet.microsoft.com/wiki/contents/articles/network-monitor-3-frequently-asked-questions.aspx*. Review the information for Wireshark and NetMon on their respective FAQ pages. Can you tell if the products are substantially similar just from their FAQ pages? From what you can read on the FAQ pages, is it possible to determine which one would be best for your needs?

Case Project 3-2: Interpreting a Checksum Error

You are a network technician, and you are using Wireshark to monitor IPv4 traffic between two nodes on the local network. You select a packet in the capture and then expand Internet Protocol Version 4. You notice that the header checksum is incorrect, as shown in Figure 3-27. What could be the cause of this error, based on your knowledge of modern network hardware and Wireshark?

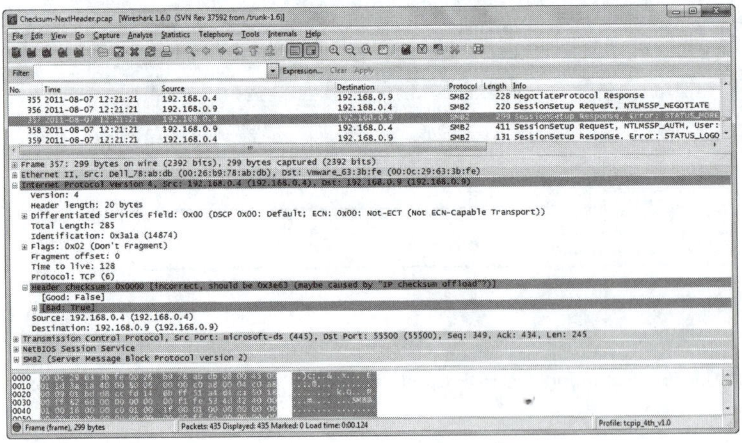

Figure 3-27 Examining a checksum error
Source: Wireshark

Case Project 3-3: Examining the IPv6 Next Header Field

You are a network technician, and you are monitoring IPv6 traffic on your local network using Wireshark. You select a packet using the DHCPv6 protocol and check the packet header. You notice in the Next Header field that the upper-layer protocol UDP is being used as shown in Figure 3-28. You know that UDP is used to transport DHCPv4 address requests and responses, but is this normal for DHCPv6?

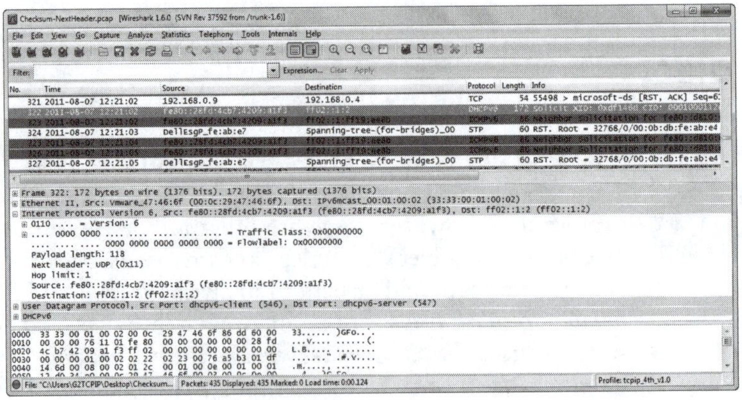

Figure 3-28 Examining the IPv6 packet header Next Header field
Source: Wireshark

chapter 4

Data Link and Network Layer Protocols in TCP/IP

After reading this chapter and completing the exercises, you will be able to:

- Explain the fundamental concepts associated with Data Link layer protocols that operate over different network link types
- Distinguish among the different types of frames used on IP networks
- Describe how hardware address resolution occurs for IPv4 and IPv6 with ARP and NDP protocols
- Explain the essentials of the Internet Protocol, both for IPv4 and IPv6, including route resolution processes, IP datagrams, fragmentation, and the differences between IPv4 and IPv6
- Explain the mechanics of IP routing, such as how entries are placed in a routing table and how the basics of routing operate on an internetwork
- Describe the intricacies of IPv4 and IPv6 routing characteristics, including methods of preventing routing loops, general behaviors of routers in an internetwork, and routing determination
- Provide detailed information about IPv4 and IPv6 routing protocols, including the structure of routing packets and the behavior of each routing protocol
- Describe the various factors involved in choosing how to route between different network environments and infrastructures
- Describe the fundamentals of routing to and from the Internet
- Explain the basics of securing routers.
- Describe the tools used to troubleshoot IP routing

This chapter covers key TCP/IP protocols that correspond to the Data Link and Network layers of the OSI reference model. Here, you learn about the various kinds of data link protocols that make it possible to connect to the Internet using an analog telephone line and a modem, X.25, or an always-on digital technology, such as T1, a cable modem, or a Digital Subscriber Line (DSL). You also learn how Internet Protocol (IP) frames may be identified, and how special protocols make it possible to translate between MAC layer hardware addresses and numeric IP addresses. Finally, you explore the capabilities of the IP, upon which so much of TCP/IP's networking capabilities depend. In particular, you learn how IP packets are organized internally and how they're handled as they move across a TCP/IP-based network from sender to receiver.

When a computer wants to send a packet to a destination that is not on its local subnetwork, it sends that packet to its **default gateway** (which is usually a router or a server configured to act like a router). Then, that default gateway forwards the packet to its true destination, to another router that knows how to reach that destination, or to another router, and so forth.

This process, known as packet forwarding, certainly sounds simple enough, but you should ask, "How does any router know where to send a packet?" In this chapter, we explain in detail the processes and protocols that routers use to make forwarding decisions and speed packets on their way to their intended destinations, whenever possible, and how they handle routing and delivery problems or failures.

Data Link Protocols

The Data Link layer performs several key jobs, the two most important being:

- Managing access to whatever networking medium is in use, called Media Access Control (MAC)
- Creating temporary point-to-point links between a pair of MAC layer addresses to enable data transfer, called **Logical Link Control (LLC)**

The existence of these two important functions and subprotocols is why the IEEE subdivided the Data Link layer into a MAC sublayer and an LLC sublayer when it designed the 802 family of network specifications. It is also why data link protocols play an important role in enabling the transfer of data from a particular sender to a particular receiver. This is called a **point-to-point** data transfer because it involves shipping data from a specific MAC layer address that represents the point of transmission to another specific MAC layer address that represents the point of reception on a distinct physical network segment, or TCP/IP subnet.

It is interesting that this same point-to-point technique also works for data transfer across wide area network (WAN) links—such as analog telephone lines, digital connections, or X.25—which is why certain TCP/IP data link protocols sometimes may be called WAN protocols.

The **data encapsulation** techniques used to enclose packet payloads for transmission across WAN links differ from those used for LAN connections and involve specialized protocols and methods that operate at the Data Link layer, such as:

- Point-to-Point Protocol (PPP)
- Special handling for X.25, frame relay, and Asynchronous Transfer Mode (ATM) connections also is typically required, primarily to ensure that relevant communication interfaces are assigned IP addresses and configured to carry TCP/IP traffic (once established, however, these connections invariably use PPP)

The rest of this section covers these protocols. The key to understanding the material is to recognize that PPP supports a straightforward point-to-point connection between two parties, or nodes, on a link. These kinds of two-party connections include analog phone lines, Digital Subscriber Line (DSL) connections, **T-carriers**, such as **T1, T3, E1,** or **E3** (E1 and E3 are the European counterparts of the American T1 and T3 and operate at different speeds), and Optical Carrier (OC) for high-speed SONET links, such as OC-1, OC-3, and OC-96. Because all parties on this kind of link are known to each other (and identities are established as the link is negotiated), point-to-point links do not include or require explicit Data Link layer addresses. Other kinds of WAN links support IP network segments, in which there may be more than two nodes active, which therefore require explicit addresses at the Data Link layer. That's why special handling is necessary for X.25, frame relay, and ATM WAN links, which use packet-switching or **circuit-switching** technologies and must explicitly address sender and receiver at the Data Link layer.

NOTE Cable modems are another popular Internet access technology that permits cable television companies to use existing broadband cable infrastructures to provide two-way Internet access to customers. Although they operate at WAN distances (over 2 miles for some cable segments), such systems use standard Ethernet II frames and behave more or less like Ethernet LANs. In fact, the protocol usually used in this situation is called **Point-to-Point Protocol over Ethernet (PPPoE).**

Generally speaking, WAN encapsulation of frames at the Data Link layer involves one or more of the following services (they vary according to the requirements of the type of link used):

- *Addressing*—For WAN links in which more than two nodes are involved in possible connections, a unique destination address is required.
- *Bit-level integrity check*—With a **bit-level integrity check,** checksums calculated before and after transmission, when compared, indicate if the message changed between when it was sent and when it was received. Such checks occur at each step in the transmission path (for each sender and receiver) when packet-switching networks are used and forwarding occurs.
- *Delimitation*—Data link frames require specific end-of-frame markers, and each frame's header and trailer must be distinct from its payload. With the **delimitation** service, **delimiters** mark these information boundaries.
- *Protocol identification (PID)*—When WAN links support multiple protocols, some method to identify individual protocols in the payload is required. A **protocol identification (PID)** in the header (discussed in the section titled "Point-to-Point Protocol" later in this chapter) supplies this information.

Point-to-Point Protocol

Point-to-Point Protocol (PPP) is a general-purpose protocol that provides WAN data link encapsulation services similar to those available for LAN encapsulations. Thus, PPP provides not only frame delimitation but also protocol identification and bit-level integrity check services. (Remember that addressing is not necessary on a point-to-point link, in which only two parties are involved in communications.)

RFC 1661 provides the detailed specifications for PPP and includes the following characteristics:

- Encapsulation methods that support simultaneous use of multiple protocols across the same link. (In fact, PPP supports a broad range of protocols, including TCP/IP, NetBEUI, IPX/SPX, AppleTalk, SNA, DECNet, and many others.)

- A special **Link Control Protocol (LCP)** used to negotiate the characteristics of any point-to-point link established using PPP.

- A collection of negotiation protocols used to establish the Network layer properties of protocols carried over the point-to-point link, called **Network Control Protocols (NCPs)**. RFCs 1332 and 1877 describe an NCP for IP, known as the **Internet Protocol Control Protocol (IPCP)**, used to negotiate an IP address for the sending party, addresses for DNS servers, and (optional) use of the Van Jacobsen TCP compression protocol, where possible.

PPP encapsulation and framing techniques are based on the ISO **High-Level Data Link Control (HDLC)** protocol, which is in turn based on IBM's work on the **Synchronous Data Link Control (SDLC)** protocol used as part of its Systems Network Architecture (SNA) protocols. It's not necessary to fully understand HDLC or SDLC in order to understand PPP; you should merely note that PPP's predecessors are well-known, well-understood, and widely implemented protocols (which allows it to leverage those stable and longstanding implementations). HDLC-like framing for PPP frames is described fully in RFC 1662.

Although PPP framing supports addressing and link control information derived from HDLC, most PPP implementations use an abbreviated form that skips this unnecessary information. Instead, LCP handles address and control field information during PPP link setup and otherwise dispenses with this information. Thus, the fields in the PPP header and trailer include the following values:

- *Flag*—The Flag is a single-byte delimiter field set to 0x7E (binary value: 01111110) to indicate the boundary between the end of one PPP frame and the beginning of another PPP frame. Only a single Flag value appears between frames.

- *Protocol identifier*—The protocol identifier is a 2-byte field that identifies the upper-layer protocol ferried by the PPP frame.

- *Frame Check Sequence (FCS)*—The **Frame Check Sequence (FCS)** field is a 2-byte field that provides bit-level integrity checks for data as sent. (It's recomputed upon receipt, then compared to the sent value; if the two values agree, the assumption is that the data was transmitted successfully; if they disagree, the payload is discarded.)

PPP must supply a method to replace Flag values should they occur in a frame's payload. Replacement methods differ, however, depending on what kind of connection is in use. For synchronous links, such as analog phone lines, in which characters are sent in as individual bytes, a character replacement approach is used for PPP. These substitution methods are covered in RFCs 1661 and 1662.

When PPP is used with synchronous technologies, such as T1, Integrated Services Digital Network (ISDN), DSL, or **Synchronous Optical Network (SONET)** links, a faster, more efficient technique of bit substitution is used rather than the wholesale character replacement used with asynchronous links. Here, any sequences of six 1 bits in a row (remember, the binary value of the Flag character is 01111110) can be escaped by inserting an extra 0 after the fifth 1 bit in a row (and stripped out upon receipt). This supports much more efficient (and faster) encoding of potentially illegal values for such link types, and it helps explain why PPP is the most popular of all point-to-point protocols used with TCP/IP. PPP also supports a multi-link implementation to enable multiple data channels of the same bandwidth to be aggregated to handle a single data stream between a single sender and a single receiver. (Two or more modem lines or two ISDN channels can be combined to increase the bandwidth between pairs of devices for a relatively low cost, which appeals in regions where broadband isn't available or where ISDN may be quite expensive.)

PPP supports a default maximum transmission unit (MTU) of 1,500 bytes, which makes it ideal for interconnecting Ethernet-based networks (or peers). However, LCP can negotiate higher or lower MTUs between PPP peers, depending on what kinds of networks they're attached to. (Many Gigabit Ethernet networks support so-called Jumbo Frames that have MTUs of 9,216 bytes; thus, as long as the PPP connections between them can also handle such large frames, PPP can carry them.)

Frame Types and Sizes

At the Data Link layer, protocol data units are called frames. A frame represents the same data that appears in digital form at the Network layer in an IP datagram in the form of whatever sequence of electrical signals maps to that data. Thus, the information from an IP datagram may be encapsulated in a variety of frame types. In this section, we examine TCP/IP communications on some common types of local area networks.

Ethernet Frame Types

The **Ethernet II frame type** is the de facto standard frame type used for IP datagram transmissions over Ethernet networks. Thus, Ethernet II frames receive the most coverage in this chapter and in this book. The Ethernet II frame has a **protocol identification field** (the Type field) that contains the value 0x0800 to identify the encapsulated protocol as IP. The value 0x86dd identifies the encapsulated protocol as IPv6.

Before an IP datagram is transmitted onto the cable, the data link driver puts the leading frame onto the datagram. The driver also ensures that the frame meets the minimum frame size specification. The minimum Ethernet frame size is 64 bytes. The maximum Ethernet frame size is 1,518 bytes. If a frame does not meet the minimum frame size of 64 bytes, the driver must **pad** the Data field.

The source or transmitting Ethernet network interface controller (NIC) performs a **cyclical redundancy check (CRC)** procedure on the contents of the frame and places a value at the end of the frame in the Frame Check Sequence field. Finally, the NIC sends the frame, led by a **preamble**, which is a leading bit pattern used by the receiver to correctly interpret the bits as 1s and 0s.

For more information on Ethernet technology, visit Charles Spurgeon's Web site at *www.ethermanage.com/ethernet/ethernet.html*. To order the IEEE 802.3 CSMA/CS specification, visit *http://www.techstreet.com/ieeegate.html* (type **802.3 CSMA/CS** in the Search text box, and then click **GO**). To view common questions regarding the IEEE 802.3 standard, visit the IEEE Standards Association Web site at *http://standards.ieee.org/index.html* and search for 802.3 standard.

There are two Ethernet frame types that TCP/IP can use:

- Ethernet II
- Ethernet 802.2 Logical Link Control

 Technically, there are two more Ethernet II frame types: Ethernet II Sub Network Access Protocol (SNAP) and Ethernet 802.3 (RAW). However, these are older technologies not commonly used in current WAN infrastructures. For more information, see *http://www.dataip.co.uk/Network/FrameTypes.php*.

Ethernet II Frame Structure

In this section, we concentrate on the Ethernet II frame structure, which is the most popular frame structure used on Ethernet TCP/IP networks. The Ethernet II frame type is the default frame type for TCP/IP on Windows 2000 and later versions of Windows on Ethernet networks. The IEEE 802.2 specification also defines a method for TCP/IP to run over the **IEEE 802.3** frame structure.

Figure 4-1 depicts the format of an Ethernet II frame.

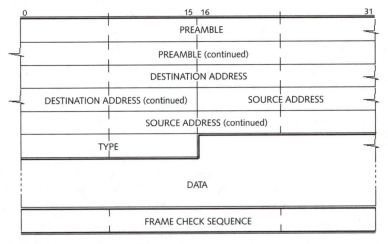

Figure 4-1 Format of an Ethernet II frame

The Ethernet II frame type consists of the following fields and structure:

- *Preamble*—The preamble is 8 bytes long and consists of alternating 1s and 0s. As its name indicates, this special string of bits precedes the actual Ethernet frame and is not counted as part of the overall frame length. The final byte ends in a pattern—the start frame delimiter (SFD)—of 10101011, indicating the start of the Destination Address field. This field provides the necessary timing used by the receiver to interpret the 1s and 0s in a frame, and it builds in the time necessary for Ethernet circuitry to recognize and begin to read incoming data.

- *Destination Address field*—The Destination Address field is 6 bytes long and indicates the **data link address** (also referred to as the **hardware address** or MAC address) of the destination IP host. The destination address may be broadcast, multicast, or unicast. The Address Resolution Protocol (ARP) is used to obtain the hardware address of the destination IP host (if the destination is local) or the next-hop router (if the destination is remote). ARP is covered in the "Hardware Addresses in the IP Environment" section later in this chapter.

- *Source Address field*—The Source Address field is 6 bytes long and indicates the sender's hardware address. This field can only contain a unicast address; it cannot contain a broadcast or multicast address.

- *Type field*—The Type field is 2 bytes long and identifies the protocol that is using this frame type. Table 4-1 illustrates some of the assigned type numbers maintained by IANA, available online at *www.iana.org*.

- *Data field*—The Data field can be between 46 and 1,500 bytes.

- *Frame Check Sequence field*—The Frame Check Sequence field is 4 bytes long and includes the result of the CRC calculation.

Type	Protocol
0x0800	IPv4
0x86dd	IPv6
0x0806	Address Resolution Protocol
0x809B	AppleTalk
0x8137	Novell Internetwork Packet Exchange (IPX)

Table 4-1 Assigned protocol types (by number)
© Cengage Learning 2013

For additional information on TCP/IP networking over the Ethernet medium, download and review RFC 894, "A Standard for the Transmission of IP Datagrams over Ethernet Networks."

Upon receipt of an Ethernet II frame, an IP host verifies the validity of the contents by performing a CRC check and comparing the result to the value contained in the Frame Check Sequence field.

After confirming that the destination address is intended for the recipient (or the broadcast address or an accepted multicast address), the receiving NIC strips off the Frame Check Sequence field and hands the frame to the Data Link layer.

At the Data Link layer, the frame is examined to determine the actual destination address (broadcast, multicast, or unicast). At this point, the protocol identification field (the Type field in the Ethernet II frame structure, for example) is examined. The remaining data link frame structure is then stripped off so the frame can be handed up to the appropriate Network layer (IP in this case).

In the following section, we cover the IEEE 802.2 LLC frame structure, even though IP is not typically seen over this frame type.

Ethernet 802.2 LLC Frame Structure Figure 4-2 depicts the format of an Ethernet 802.2 **Logical Link Control (LLC)** frame. Though similar to the Ethernet II frame structure, the Ethernet 802.2 LLC frame type uses a SAP field instead of a Type field to identify the protocol that is using the frame. The value 0x06 is assigned to IP.

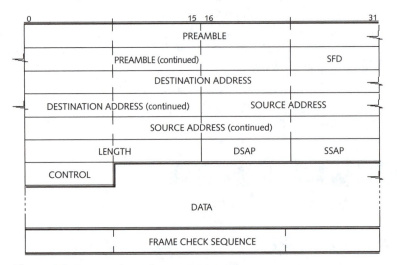

Figure 4-2 Format of an Ethernet 802.2 LLC frame
© Cengage Learning 2013

The Ethernet 802.2 LLC frame type consists of the following fields, but only the fields that are unique to the 802.2 LLC frame structure are discussed:

- *Preamble*—The preamble is seven bytes long and consists of alternating 1s and 0s. Unlike the Ethernet II frame structure, this preamble does not end in consecutive 1s. The Start Frame Delimiter field is used to mark the beginning of the Destination Address field.

- *Start Frame Delimiter field*—The 1-byte Start Frame Delimiter (SFD) field consists of the pattern 10101011 and indicates the start of the Destination Address field. As you may notice, the 802.2 preamble and Start Frame Delimiter field are equivalent to the Ethernet II frame's preamble.

- *Length field*—The 2-byte Length field indicates the number of bytes in the data portion of the frame. The possible values are between 0x002E (46 decimal) and 0x05DC (1,500 decimal). This frame does not use a Type field in this location; it uses a **Service Access Point (SAP)** field to indicate the upcoming protocol.

- *Destination Service Access Point (DSAP) field*—The 1-byte Destination Service Access Point (DSAP) field indicates the destination protocol. Table 4-2 lists some of the assigned SAP numbers (defined by the IEEE).

- *Source Service Access Point (SSAP) field*—The 1-byte Source Service Access Point (SSAP) field indicates the source protocol (typically the same as the destination protocol).

- *Control field*—The 1-byte Control field indicates whether this frame is **unnumbered format** (connectionless) or **informational/supervisory format** (for connection-oriented and management purposes).

- *Destination Address*

- *Source Address*

- *Data*

- *Frame Check Sequence*

Number	Destination Protocol
0	Null LSAP
2	Indiv LLC Sublayer Mgt
3	Group LLC Sublayer Mgt
4	SNA Path Control
6	DOD IP
14	PROWAY-LAN
78	EIA-RS 511
94	ISI IP
142	PROWAY-LAN
254	ISO CLNS IS 8473
255	Global DSAP

Table 4-2 **Assigned SAP numbers**
© Cengage Learning 2013

Hardware Addresses in the IP Environment

IP addresses are used to identify individual IP hosts on a TCP/IP internetwork. A hardware address is required to get the packet from one IP host to another IP host on a single network. For example, to get from one IP host to another IP host that is located on the other side of a router, the source needs to know the IP address of the destination IP host. The source must perform some manner of hardware address resolution to learn the hardware address of the router so that it can build a data link header (such as an Ethernet header) to get the packet to the local router or its "default gateway" in Windows parlance. When the packet is received at the router, the router must go through the same hardware address resolution process to determine the next local hardware address for the packet.

Address Resolution Protocol and Network Discovery Protocol

The **Address Resolution Protocol (ARP)** is the protocol used by IPv4 nodes to resolve Network layer, or IP, addresses into Data Link layer, or physical, addresses. Any IPv4 node on a network that needs to know another node's physical or hardware address can send an ARP request to that node's IP address and receive back the hardware address. IPv6 does not use ARP for this activity but instead uses Neighbor Discovery Protocol (NDP). NDP is very similar to ARP in that an IPv6 node that wants to know another node's physical address sends a Neighbor Solicitation request, and the desired node replies with a Neighbor Advertisement containing its Data Link layer address.

A major difference between ARP and NDP is that NDP runs over ICMPv6 and uses multicast packets rather than broadcast packets. This is an improvement over the IPv4 ARP solicitation method. Each IPv6 network node listens on a solicited-node multicast address, which is made up of the last three words of the node's unicast address. A node sending a Neighbor Solicitation request sends it to the other node's solicited-node multicast address. This prevents other nodes, even those with very similar IPv6 addresses, from being interrupted by neighbor solicitations.

Details about both ARP and NDP are covered in the following sections of this chapter. To learn more about ARP, go to *www.ietf.org* and search for RFC 826. Also see RFCs 5227 and 5494. To learn more about NDP, go to the IETF Web site and look up RFC 4861 (which obsoletes RFC 2461).

For complete details on NDP, see Chapter 6.

ARP Protocol Characteristics and Handling

TCP/IP networking uses ARP to determine the hardware address of the local target for the packet. IP hosts maintain an **ARP cache**—a table of hardware addresses learned through the ARP process—in memory. An IP host refers to the ARP cache first, before issuing an ARP request, broadcast-based, on to the network. If the desired hardware address is not found in cache, the IP host broadcasts an ARP request.

Figure 4-3 depicts the basic functionality of ARP. In this graphic, you can see that the source IP host, 10.1.0.1, uses ARP to obtain the hardware address of the local target.

ARP is used only to find the hardware address of local IP hosts. If the IP destination is remote (on another network), the IP host must refer to its **routing tables** to determine the proper router for the packet. This is referred to as the **route resolution process**.

ARP is not routable; it has no Network layer component in the packet structure, as shown in Figure 4-4.

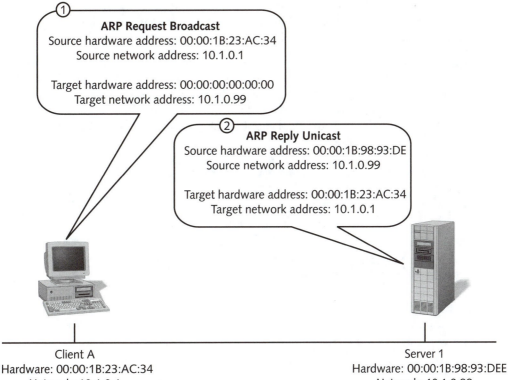

① **ARP Request Broadcast**
Source hardware address: 00:00:1B:23:AC:34
Source network address: 10.1.0.1

Target hardware address: 00:00:00:00:00:00
Target network address: 10.1.0.99

② **ARP Reply Unicast**
Source hardware address: 00:00:1B:98:93:DE
Source network address: 10.1.0.99

Target hardware address: 00:00:1B:23:AC:34
Target network address: 10.1.0.1

Client A
Hardware: 00:00:1B:23:AC:34
Network: 10.1.0.1

Server 1
Hardware: 00:00:1B:98:93:DEE
Network: 10.1.0.99

Figure 4-3 ARP broadcasts identifying the source and desired IP address
© Cengage Learning 2013

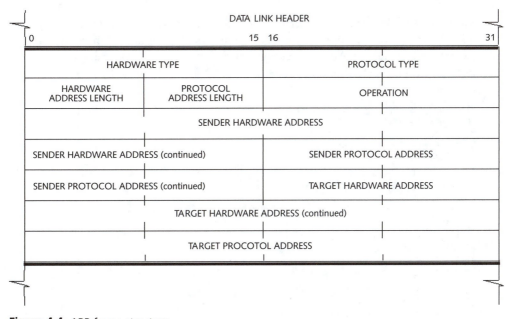

DATA LINK HEADER

0	15	16	31
HARDWARE TYPE		PROTOCOL TYPE	
HARDWARE ADDRESS LENGTH	PROTOCOL ADDRESS LENGTH	OPERATION	
SENDER HARDWARE ADDRESS			
SENDER HARDWARE ADDRESS (continued)		SENDER PROTOCOL ADDRESS	
SENDER PROTOCOL ADDRESS (continued)		TARGET HARDWARE ADDRESS	
TARGET HARDWARE ADDRESS (continued)			
TARGET PROCOTOL ADDRESS			

Figure 4-4 ARP frame structure
© Cengage Learning 2013

As straightforward as ARP is, as shown in its frame structure, it is often the protocol that signals problems with network addressing or configuration, as you will learn in the "If Remote, Which Router?" section later in this chapter.

ARP can also be used to test for a duplicate IP address on the network. Before an IP host begins to communicate on an IP network, it should perform a duplicate IP address test. During the duplicate address test process, an IP host sends an ARP request for its own IP address (called a gratuitous ARP), as shown in Figure 4-5. The host cannot initialize its TCP/IP stack if another host replies to the duplicate IP address test; a reply indicates that its intended IP address is already in use.

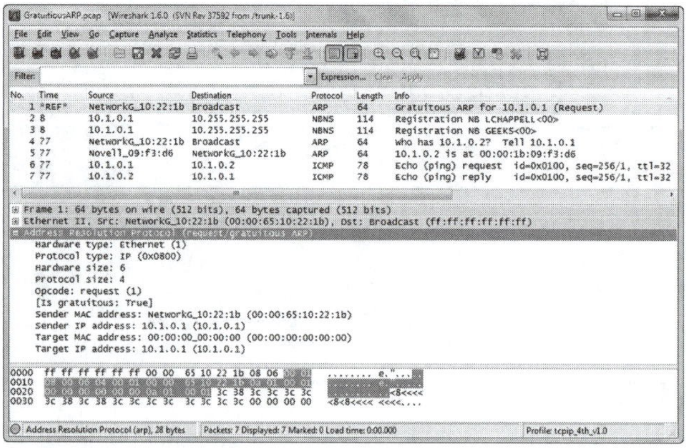

Figure 4-5 ARP duplicate IP address test
Source: Wireshark

Viewing the packets in a simple ARP transaction should further clarify ARP usage.

ARP Packet Fields and Functions By default, the Ethernet II frame type is used for all ARP traffic on Windows Vista and Windows 7 computers. There are two basic ARP packets: the broadcast ARP request packet and the directed, or unicast, ARP reply packet. Both packets use the same format, as shown in Figures 4-6 and 4-7.

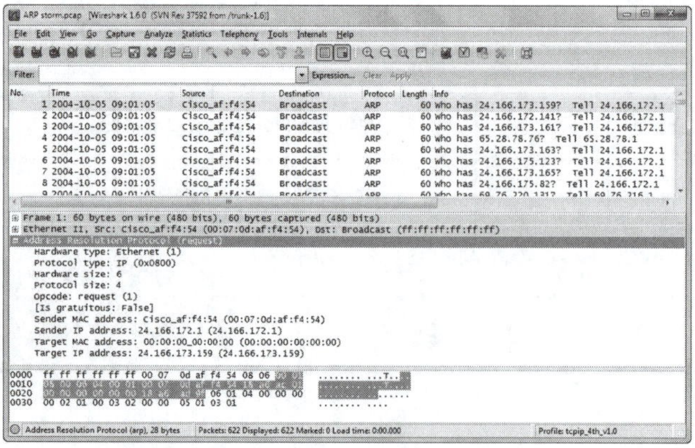

Figure 4-6 ARP broadcast packet
Source: Wireshark

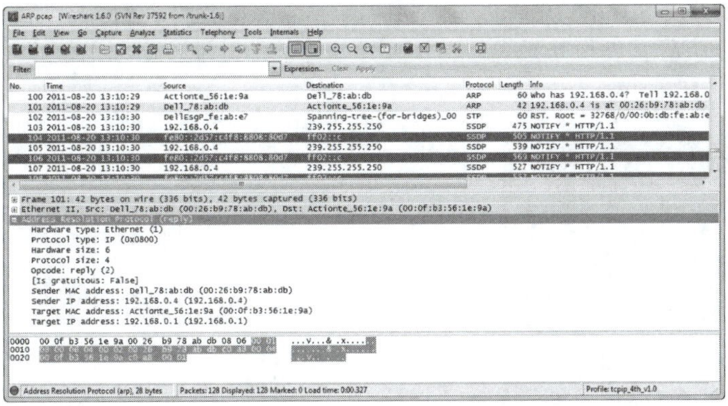

Figure 4-7 ARP unicast packet
Source: Wireshark

The most confusing part of ARP is the interpretation of the sender and target address information. When an ARP broadcast is being sent from a host, the sending host—Host A—puts the hardware and IP address in the Sender Address fields.

The Target Internet Address field includes the IP address of the desired IP host. The Target Hardware Address field is set to all 0s to indicate that the information is not known, as shown in Figure 4-6.

NOTE The ARP specification dictates that the Target Hardware Address field can be set to a value other than all 0s. In some implementations of ARP, the source sets the destination address to all 1s, which may confuse some routers, causing them to broadcast the ARP packet onto all connected networks. This type of problem is easy to spot with a network analyzer and is documented in Microsoft TechNet. (Look for the "Duplicate IP Address Detection" subsection of the "Core Protocol Stack Components and the TDI Interface" section at *http://technet.microsoft.com/en-us/library/cc780776(WS.10).aspx* or search for "Core Protocol Stack Components and the TDI Interface" with a search engine to find the Microsoft Technet page.)

Figure 4-7 shows the ARP reply packet. In this reply, the target information and sender information are reversed to show that the ARP responder is now the sender. The original station performing the lookup is now the destination.

It is interesting that the responding IP host updates its own ARP cache to include the IP address and hardware address of the IP host that was looking for it. Avoiding a responding ARP broadcast is a logical step and a more efficient use of network bandwidth. Most likely, there will be a two-way conversation between the IP hosts, so the responding IP host eventually needs the requesting IP host's address.

Hardware Type Field This field defines the hardware or data link type in use and also is used to determine the hardware address length, which makes the Length of Hardware Address field redundant.

Table 4-3 is a partial list of assigned hardware type numbers derived from the online list at *www.iana.org/assignments/arp-parameters*.

Number	Hardware Type
1	Ethernet
6	IEEE 802 Networks
7	ARCNET
11	LocalTalk
14	SMDS
15	Frame relay
17	HDLC
19	ATM
20	Serial line
21	ATM

Table 4-3 **Hardware type numbers**
© Cengage Learning 2013

Protocol Type Field This field defines the protocol address type in use, and it uses the standard protocol ID values that also are used in the Ethernet II frame structures. These protocol types are defined at *www.iana.org/assignments/ethernet-numbers*.

This field uses the same values assigned to the Ethernet Type field. At this time, IP is the only protocol that uses ARP for address resolution. This field also determines the length of the protocol address, making the Length of Protocol Address field redundant.

Length of Hardware Address Field This field defines the length (in bytes) of the hardware addresses used in this packet. This field is redundant because the Hardware Type field also determines the length value.

Length of Protocol Address Field This field indicates the length (in bytes) of the protocol (network) addresses used in this packet. This field is redundant because the Protocol Type field also determines this value.

Opcode Field This field defines whether this ARP packet is a request or reply packet and defines the type of address resolution taking place. Table 4-4 lists the ARP and Reverse ARP (RARP) operation codes.

RARP is a process that enables an IP host to learn a network address from a data link address. RARP is defined in RFC 903 and covered in the "Reverse ARP" section later in this chapter.

Code Value	Packet Type
1	ARP request
2	ARP reply
3	RARP request
4	RARP reply

Table 4-4 ARP and RARP operation codes
© Cengage Learning 2013

Sender's Hardware Address Field This field indicates the hardware address of the IP host that sends this request or reply.

Sender's Protocol Address Field This field indicates the protocol, or network, address of the IP host that sends this request or reply.

Target Hardware Address Field This field indicates the desired target's hardware address, if known. In ARP requests, this field is typically filled with all 0s. In ARP replies, this field should contain one of the following:

- The hardware address of the desired IP host if the sender and destination share a data link.
- The hardware address of the next router in the path to the destination if they don't share a data link. This is known as the **next-hop router** to that IP host, in which that device will be the first of one or more routers that will convey the data from sender to receiver. Each network, or router-to-router transition, is counted as a hop.

Target Protocol Address Field This field indicates the desired target's protocol, or network, address.

ARP Cache ARP information (hardware addresses and their associated IP addresses) is kept in an ARP cache in memory on most operating systems, including Linux, BSD UNIX, Windows Server 2003, Windows Server 2008, Windows XP, Windows Vista, and Windows 7. These operating systems also have tools for viewing ARP cache entries, manually adding or deleting entries in the ARP cache, and loading table entries from a configuration file. On Windows-based systems, the command arp -a is used to view the table contents, as shown in Figure 4-8.

Windows-based systems also have a utility you can use to view your IP and You can use the command-line utility **Ipconfig** on Windows Server 2003, Windows Server 2008, Windows XP, Windows Vista, and Windows 7 systems. Figure 4-9 shows the result of running the Ipconfig utility on a Windows 7 device.

As you can see in Figure 4-9, the Ipconfig utility, using the /all option to modify the output of the command, displays the adapter address (physical address) in hexadecimal such as 00-26-B9-78-AB-DB, the IPv4 address 192.168.0.4, and the subnet mask 255.255.255.0.

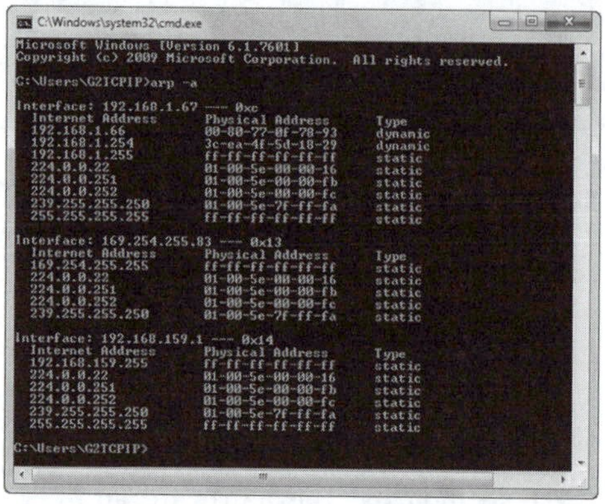

Figure 4-8 Output of the `arp -a` command
Source: Microsoft

Figure 4-9 Output of the `ipconfig/all` command
Source: Microsoft

The Ipconfig utility also indicates that the IPv6 link-local address is fe80::2d57: c4f8:8808:80d7%10.

On Windows systems, ARP cache entries are kept in memory for 120 seconds (2 minutes); this varies from a more common default of 300 seconds (5 minutes) on most other kinds of networking equipment. IP hosts must consult these tables before transmitting ARP broadcasts. If an entry exists in the ARP cache entries, the IP host uses the existing entry instead of transmitting an ARP request on the network.

You can change the entry lifetime in the ARP cache using the ArpCacheLife **Registry setting**, as listed in Table 4-5. (For systems that use Dynamic Host Control Protocol [DHCP] to obtain addresses, administrators can manage this setting via options provided when defining the terms of a DHCP lease.)

Windows Server 2008, Windows Vista, and Windows 7 retain ARP cache entries longer than 120 seconds if they were referenced while in the cache. The ArpCacheMinReferencedLife Registry entry is used to extend the referenced ARP entry past the default 600 seconds (10 minutes).

Registry Information	Details
Location	HKEY_LOCAL_MACHINE\SYSTEM\CurrentControlSet\ Services\Tcpip\Parameters
Data type	REG_DWORD
Valid range	0–0xFFFFFFFF
Default value	120
Present by default	No

Table 4-5 **ArpCacheLife Registry setting**
© Cengage Learning 2013

Proxy ARP Proxy ARP is a method that allows an IP host to use a simplified subnetting design. Proxy ARP also enables a router to "ARP" in response to an IP host's ARP broadcasts. Figure 4-10 shows a proxy ARP configuration that consists of one network that is divided by a router but maintains a single network address on both sides. The IP host 10.1.0.1 was configured with a subnet mask of 255.0.0.0. This IP host believes that the destination 10.2.77.33 is on the same network—network 10.0.0.0. The IP host believes the destination host has the same subnet mask because it has no way of determining that information. Because the source host believes that the destination host is on the same network, the source host knows that it can ARP for its hardware address.

But the destination is not on the same network. The destination host, 10.2.77.33, is on a separate network, but a connecting router was configured to support proxy ARP. When 10.1.0.1 sends an ARP looking for the hardware address 10.2.77.33, the proxy ARP router does not forward the broadcast; instead, it replies to the ARP request and supplies the router's hardware address on Interface 1 (the interface that is on the same network as the requesting IP host).

NOTE You should be aware that most network configurations may never need to use proxy ARP. It is, however, common for router manufacturers to turn it on by default in case of network misconfigurations. For example, if a network host has a subnet mask that is too short, it may think destination hosts are located on the same network. In that case, the host would ARP and the proxy ARP router would reply on behalf of the remote device—in other words, by "proxy."

Reverse ARP Reverse Address Resolution Protocol (RARP) is, as its name implies, the reverse of ARP. RARP is used to obtain an IP address for an associated data link address. RARP was initially defined to enable diskless workstations to find their own IP addresses upon booting or startup. RARP hosts would broadcast a RARP request and include their own hardware addresses but leave the source IP addresses blank (all 0s). A RARP server on the local network would answer the request, supplying the RARP host with its IP address by filling in the target IP address in the reply packet.

Bootstrap Protocol (BOOTP), and eventually DHCP, replaced RARP. Both BOOTP and DHCP offer a more robust, flexible method of assigning IP addresses.

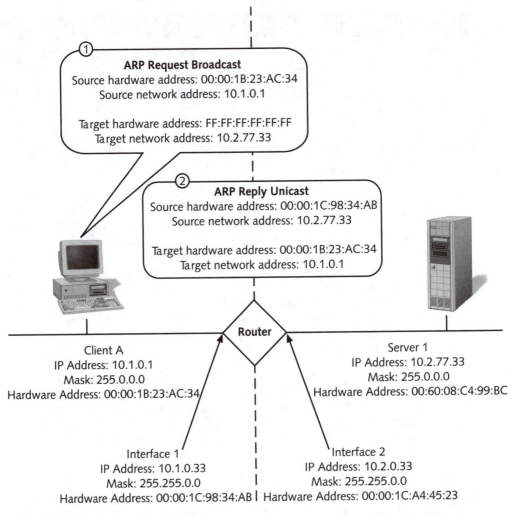

Figure 4-10 ARP proxy network design
© Cengage Learning 2013

RARP is documented in RFC 903.

NDP Protocol Characteristics and Handling

The NDP protocol specified by RFC 4861 describes how nodes on the same network link use this protocol to determine the presence of other nodes, to discover the link-layer addresses of another node, to find routers, and to discover network paths to network neighbors. IPv6 NDP covers several different IPv4 technologies, including ARP, ICMPv4 Router Discovery, and ICMPv4 Redirect. This section focuses on using NDP for link-layer address discovery on an IPv6 network link.

NDP messages are used to map a network node's link-layer address and its IP-layer address. A node sends out a Neighbor Solicitation message and requests a neighbor node's link-layer address by providing its own link-layer address. As previously mentioned, the message is sent out over ICMPv6 as a multicast. Figure 4-11 provides the basic format of a Neighbor Solicitation message.

Neighbor Solicitations are sent out as a unicast when a node needs to verify that another node is reachable across a network path.

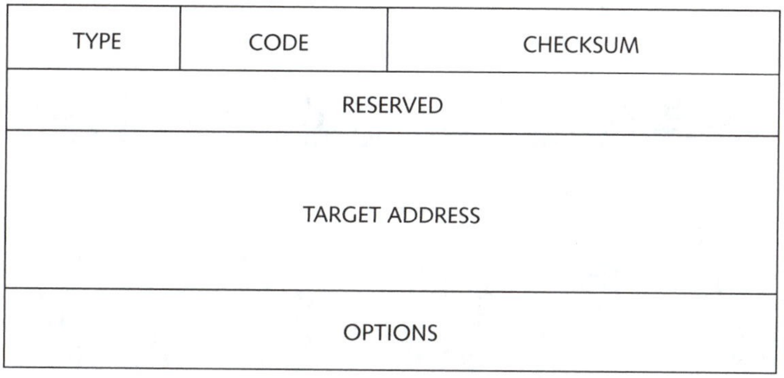

TYPE	CODE	CHECKSUM
RESERVED		
TARGET ADDRESS		
OPTIONS		

Figure 4-11 Neighbor Solicitation message format
© Cengage Learning 2013

The Neighbor Solicitation message is formatted in an ICMPv6 packet. Table 4-6 defines the fields in this message packet.

Fields	Details
Type	135
Code	0
Checksum	This is the ICMPv6 checksum (see RFC 4443).
Reserved	This field is unused and must be set with a value of 0 by the source node. The destination node must ignore this field.
Target Address	This is the IPv6 address of the destination or the target node for the Solicitation message.
Options	At the time RFC 4861 was written, the only option was the Source node's link-layer address. Future versions of this protocol may define additional option types. Any option types the target node does not recognize must be ignored.

Table 4-6 Neighbor Solicitation message ICMPv6 fields description
© Cengage Learning 2013

The IPv6 fields include the IPv6 source address of the node sending the Neighbor Solicitation and the destination address, which is the solicited-node multicast address of the target device. The Hop Limit field value is set to 255, which is the maximum legal limit.

The hop limit is also set to this value as a security measure to ensure that the message will not transverse routers.

Once the target node receives the Neighbor Solicitation, it responds with a Neighbor Advertisement message and, to propogate the new data as quickly as possible, sends unsolicited Neighbor Advertisement messages. The format of the Neighbor Advertisement message is virtually identical to the Neighbor Solitication message; however, the values of the ICMPv6 fields differ, as shown in Table 4-7.

Fields	Details
Type	136
Code	0
Checksum	This is the ICMPv6 checksum (see RFC 4443). There are three flags that can be set in this field: the R or Router Flag, the S or Solicitation Flag, and the O or Override Flag. In the case of a response to a Neighbor Solicitation message, the S-flag is set, indicating that this Advertisement message is being transmitted in response to a Neighbor Solicitation message from the target node.
Reserved	This field is unused and must be set with a value of 0 by the target node. The node receiving the Adverstisement message must ignore this field.
Target Address	This is the address of the node that sent the Neighbor Solicitation message.
Options	The only possible option is the target's link-layer address and must be included in response to mulitcast solicitations. Future versions of this protocol may define additional option types.

Table 4-7 Neighbor Advertisement message ICMPv6 fields description
© Cengage Learning 2013

The IPv6 fields also included source, destination, and hop limit fields. The source is the IPv6 address of the node sending the advertisement, the destination is the IPv6 address of the node that sent the solicitation, and the Hop Limit field is set to 255.

If a node's link-layer address changes, the Neighbor Advertisement can be used to send an unsolicited message advertising its new address.

Understanding the Internet Protocol

The primary function of Network layer protocols is to move datagrams through an internetwork connected by routers. Network layer communications are end-to-end communications that define the originator as the source Network layer address and the target as the destination Network layer address. When packets are sent to network routers, these routers examine the destination network address, based on the routable protocol being used, to determine which direction to forward the packets, if possible.

Internet Protocol is the Network layer protocol used in the TCP/IP suite. Currently, IP version 4 (IPv4) is widely implemented. Internet Protocol version 6 (IPv6) continues to be most often used in pilot or experimental implementations; however, there has recently been an impetus to prepare the worldwide internetwork structure for IPv6. World IPv6 Day, held on June 8, 2011, was only the start of this effort. Although most major ISPs do not offer IPv6 addresses yet, it is anticipated that there will be a significant, large-scale transition to IPv6 within the next serveral years.

The functionality and fields of IPv4 communications are documented in RFC 791, "Internet Protocol," which is updated by RFC 1349, "Type of Service in the Internet Protocol Suite." This section focuses only on IPv4. We examine how an IP datagram is formed, how an IP host learns whether the destination is local or remote, how packets are fragmented and reassembled, as well as the details of IP packet structures. This section also defines basic IP routing processes used to get an IP datagram through an internetwork.

Sending IP Datagrams

IP offers connectionless service with end-to-end Network layer addressing. The best way to illustrate how an IP datagram is formed and sent is by example. In Figure 4-12, we have one host (10.1.0.1) communicating with another IP host (10.2.0.2) that is located on the other side of a router.

Building an IP datagram packet to transmit on the wire has certain requirements. You must know the:

- IP addresses of the source and destination
- Hardware address of the source and next-hop router

An IP host can use either a manually entered destination IP address or the DNS to obtain a destination's IP address. For example, if you type `telnet 10.2.0.2`, your system knows the destination IP address. If you use the command `telnet fred`; however, your system needs to resolve the name "fred" to an IP address. This is called the **name resolution process**. Chapter 7 covers DNS in detail.

Telnet is not enabled by default in Windows 7 and Windows Server 2008. To find out how to enable telnet, go to *http://social.technet. microsoft.com/wiki/contents/articles/enabling-telnet-client-in-windows-7. aspx*.

As mentioned earlier in this chapter, before launching the ARP process, the IP host must know whether the destination is local or remote. Should the IP host be sending the packet directly to the desired destination, or should it send the packet to a local router? This is called the route resolution process.

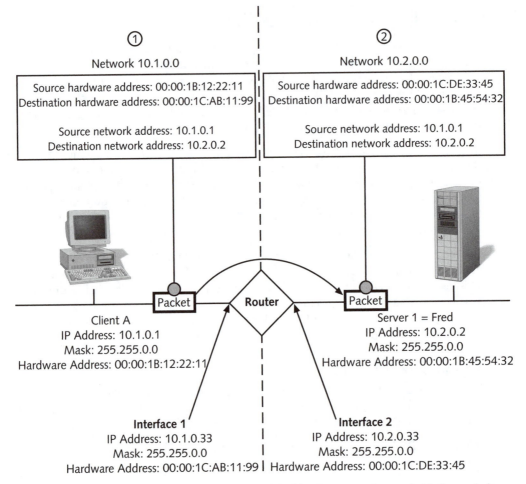

Figure 4-12 Data link header stripped off and reapplied by IP routers when packet is forwarded
© Cengage Learning 2013

Once the route resolution process is completed, the IP host can begin the ARP process to locate the desired destination hardware address.

The Route Resolution Processes

The route resolution process enables an IP host to determine if the desired destination is local or remote. If the destination is remote, this process enables the IP host to determine the next-hop router.

Local or Remote Destination? Upon determination of the IP address of the desired destination, the IP host compares the network portion of the destination address to its own local network address.

In our example, Fred's IP address is 10.2.0.2. The local IP host (Client A) has the IP address 10.1.0.1, with the subnet mask 255.255.0.0. Consider the following:

1. The source IP address is 10.1.0.1.
2. The source IP mask is 255.255.0.0.

3. The local network number is 10.1.0.0.

4. Fred's IP address is 10.2.0.2.

5. Fred's network address does not have matching network bits with the source IP network.

6. Because Fred's network address differs from the local network address, Fred is remote from the source.

7. The source must go through a router to reach Fred.

8. The source needs the hardware address of the router.

9. The source examines its routing tables.

10. The source transmits an ARP for the interface of the router's hardware address.

If Remote, Which Router? Now that the local IP host knows that the destination is remote, the IP host must determine the hardware address of the appropriate router for the packet. Remember that hardware addresses are used only to get packets from one IP host on a network to another IP host on the same network. The router receives a packet addressed to its hardware address, strips off the data link header, examines the Network layer header to determine how to route the packet, and then reapplies a data link header to move the packet along on the next network.

The IP host looks in its local routing tables to determine if it has a route entry for the target. There are two types of route table entries: a **host route entry** and a **network route entry**. A host entry matches the entire 4 bytes of the destination address and indicates the local router that can forward packets to the desired destination. A network entry indicates that a route to the destination network is known but that a route to the individual host is not known. This is typically sufficient because the router closest to the destination is responsible for getting the packet to the destination host.

It is common to refer to all the routing entries as equal in preference; however, the sending host will select the entry that has the longest matching bits. For example, an entry that matches 32 bits of the desired destination with a 32-bit mask will be preferred to an entry that matches only 24 bits of the desired destination with a 24-bit mask.

If neither a host entry nor a network entry is listed, the IP host checks for a default gateway entry. To summarize, the local host examines its own routing table for a host-specific route, then a network-specific route, then (if both of those fail) a default gateway route.

The default gateway offers a default route—a path of blind faith. Because the IP host does not have a route to the destination, it sends the packet to the default gateway and just hopes the default gateway can figure out what to do with the packet.

Regardless of whether a packet is sent to the default route (default gateway) or to a specific route located in the host's routing tables, the receiving gateway typically does one of the following:

- Forwards the packet (if there is a route to the destination)

- Sends an ICMP reply, called an ICMP redirect, that points to another local router that has the best route to the destination

- Sends an ICMP reply indicating that it's unclear where to send the packet—that is, the destination is unreachable

If the destination is remote and a source or interface handling the datagram knows a next-hop router or default gateway that can forward the packet, the source must use ARP to resolve the hardware address of the next-hop router or default gateway. Naturally, the source checks its ARP cache first. If the information does not exist in cache, the source sends an ARP broadcast to get the hardware address of the next-hop router.

If IP hosts cannot communicate with each other, you can use a protocol analyzer to determine what went wrong. Perhaps one of the following faults occurred:

- The IP host can ARP only for IP hosts that are local but the destination is remote. (Check the source subnet mask and the destination's IP address.)
- The destination is local but not replying to the ARP because it is not completely functional. (A duplicate IP address was detected, or the destination is simply down.)
- The IP address the source received from a name resolution process, such as DNS, is incorrect. (No IP host is using the desired IP address.)

It is not uncommon for problems to occur in the route resolution process. In Figure 4-13, we see that the subnet mask placed on the source host is 255.0.0.0. When we place this mask on the destination IP address 10.2.12.4, it implies that the destination is local to the source (on the same network: 10.0.0.0). The source begins to ARP for the hardware address that is associated with 10.2.12.4.

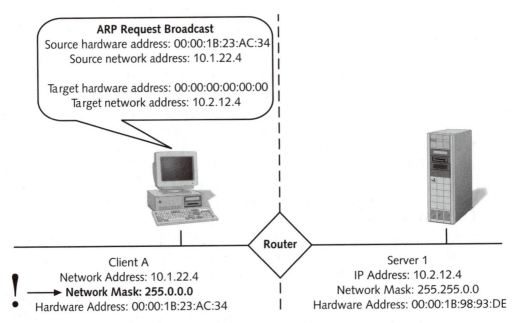

Figure 4-13 Sample of an ARP failure resulting from a misconfigured network mask
© Cengage Learning 2013

Will 10.2.12.4 answer? No. Routers do not forward ARP broadcasts, and no one else on the source's network is set up to reply on behalf of that IP host.

When you look at communications at the packet level, you can find the definitive answers to these questions—unlike blind troubleshooting, where you simply guess at the solution until one works out.

How IPv4 and IPv6 Differ

The basic function of IPv6 is the same as IPv4: to reliably send information from one network node to another across a path, with the information being forwarded by routers. In order to build an IPv6 packet, the source node needs to know the same information: the destination's address and the link-layer address of the next-hop router. Rather than ARP, the IPv6 node uses NDP to discover the link-layer address of the next-hop router by sending a Router Solicitation message as a multicast message. The source node essentially asks what IPv6 address prefix or prefixes are used on the network segment and asks for the addresses of the default routers servicing the segment. The next-hop router responds with a Router Advertisement message containing its link-layer address. Figure 4-14 shows the basics of a Router Solicitation and Router Advertisement exchange.

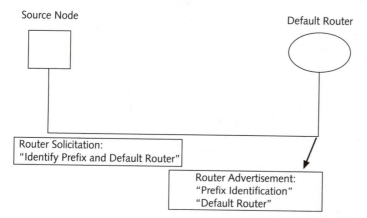

Figure 4-14 Router Solicitation and Router Advertisement exchange
© Cengage Learning 2013

In addition, the source node needs to know the largest size or MTU of packets that can be supported on the proposed path between the source and destination, because IPv6 packets cannot be fragmented by routers, as IPv4 packets can. The NDP protocol is used by the source node for PMTU Discovery to establish a proposed network path between the source and destination. This process discovers the Link MTU along the path with the most restricted or smallest MTU value. The source node then sets the MTU of its packets to that size prior to transmission. Should the Link MTU become smaller anywhere along the path, the forwarding node at that point will send a "Packet Too Big" ICMPv6 message. The source node responds by reducing the MTU value of its packets and resending the message. This process will be repeated until the entire message is successfully received by the destination node.

For IPv4, the source node must determine if the route to the destination node is local or if it must be routed. For IPv6, the source node uses PMTU Discovery, even if it believes it is directly connected to the destination node across a local link. For IPv6, it is all but irrelevant if the message is being sent locally or across a router, because the same discovery process is employed.

IPv6 uses multicasts rather than broadcasts. When IPv4 nodes send a broadcast message, all nodes on the local link must listen to the message to determine if it is meant for them, interrupting their network activities. IPv6 multicast messages use different addresses based on different functions, so most of the computers on the link will ignore the multicast rather than interrupt their network activities to attend to the message. In the case of a Router Solicitation, only routers need to listen for this particular multicast message, based on the IPv6 address prefix reserved for routers.

Both IPv4 and IPv6 network nodes can also discover the default router on the local link through a static configuration set on the node or via dynamic assignment. However, in the case of the IPv6 nodes, the NDP Router Solicitation/Advertisement exchange makes either a static or dynamic configuration of the default router's address on the node unnecessary, because NDP discovery exchanges occur by default. IPv6 routers also routinely send Router Advertisements on links that are local to the router using an IPv6 prefix in the multicast that is reserved only for IPv6 network nodes (as opposed to routers or other devices on the network). The IPv6 node can wait for the next advertisement but will send a Router Solicitation to speed up the process.

IPv4 and IPv6 nodes both need to know the IP address of one or more DNS servers for name resolution. Like an IPv4 node, an IPv6 computer can be configured with the addresses of the local DNS servers either through static or dynamic (DHCPv6) configuration. DHCPv6 can also provide the network node with the DNS domain name. Either Stateful or Stateless DHCPv6 can be used; however, stateless DHCP is more useful with stateless autoconfiguration.

Lifetime of an IP Datagram

Each IP packet has a predefined lifetime indicated in its Time to Live (TTL) field (for IPv4) or its Hop Limit field (for IPv6). This ensures that packets cannot indefinitely circle a looped internetwork. Although routing protocols attempt to prevent loops and the best routes are chosen when forwarding packets, there may be times when a link is reconfigured or temporarily shut down. In this case, the network may have a temporary loop.

The recommended starting TTL value is 64. The default TTL in Windows Server 2008, Windows Vista, and Windows 7 is 128, which is unusually high for a TTL. The TTL value is formally defined as a number of seconds. In actual practice, however, the TTL value is implemented as a hop count. Each time a packet is forwarded by a router, the router must decrement the TTL field by 1. Switches and hubs do not decrement the TTL value; they do not look at the Network layer of the packet.

If a packet with TTL=1 arrives at a router, the router must discard the packet because it cannot decrement the TTL to 0 and forward the packet.

If a packet with TTL=1 arrives at a host, what should the host do? Process the packet, of course. The hosts do not need to decrement the TTL value upon receipt.

Chapter 5 explains how one troubleshooting utility, Traceroute, uses the TTL value and the timeout process to trace the end-to-end path through an internetwork.

In Windows Server 2008, Windows Vista, and Windows 7, you can set the default TTL for a host using the Default TTL Registry setting, as shown in Table 4-8. Another common method for handling this setting is when configuring DHCP lease terms on such a server; as with other settings accessible through DHCP, this offers a centralized way to manage this kind of protocol behavior.

Registry Information	Details
Location	HKEY_LOCAL_MACHINE\SYSTEM\CurrentControlSet\ Services\Tcpip\Parameters
Data type	REG_DWORD
Valid range	1–255
Default value	128
Present by default	No

Table 4-8 **Default TTL Registry setting**
© Cengage Learning 2013

The location of the registry information for IPv6 is HKEY_LOCAL_MACHINE\SYSTEM\CurrentControlSet\Services\TCPIP6\Parameters.

Fragmentation and Reassembly

IP fragmentation enables a larger packet to be automatically fragmented by a router into smaller packets to cross a link that supports a smaller MTU, such as an Ethernet link. Once fragmented, however, no reassembly occurs until those fragments arrive at the destination, where they will be reassembled at the Network or Internet layer. The fragments will be recomposed into a complete TCP segment or UDP packet before being passed to the Transport layer; alternatively, an error message will be sent if reassembly isn't successful. Thus, it's safe to say that IP handles fragmentation and defragmentation but hands off reassembly of TCP segments to TCP at the Transport layer.

When a packet is fragmented, all fragments are given the same TTL value. If they take different paths through a network, they may end up at the destination with varying TTL values. However, when the first **fragment** arrives at the destination, the destination host begins counting down from the TTL value of that packet. All fragments must arrive before that timer expires, or the fragment set is considered incomplete and unusable. The destination sends an ICMP reply to the source stating that the packet's lifetime has expired.

Fragments are reassembled at the destination host. For example, if a router must fragment a 4,096-byte packet to forward the packet onto an Ethernet network that only supports a 1,500-byte MTU, the router must perform the following tasks to properly fragment the packet:

1. The router places the original packet's IP header Identification field value in all three fragments.

2. The router decrements the TTL value by 1 and places the new TTL value in each fragment.

3. The router calculates the relative location of the fragmented data and includes that value in the **Fragment Offset field** of each fragment.

4. The router sends each fragment off as a separate packet with a separate data link header and checksum calculation.

Figures 4-15 through 4-17 show the first, middle, and last fragments of a fragment set. In Figure 4-16, the Fragment Offset value of 1480 indicates that it is not the first fragment of the set. It's not the last fragment in the set either, as denoted by the More Fragments bit setting.

This trace was obtained by forcing an IP host to fragment a large ICMP echo packet by using the following command: `ping -l 5000 www.cisco.com`.

When the fragments arrive at the destination IP host, they are put back in order based on the Fragment Offset value contained in the IP header.

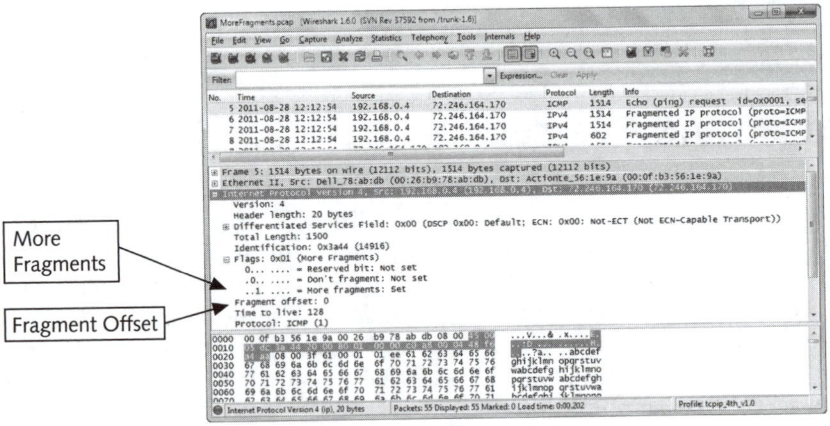

Figure 4-15 First packet of fragment (More Fragments bit set to 1 and Fragment Offset set to 0)
Source: Wireshark

Fragmentation has some ugly characteristics that make it undesirable traffic on a network. First, the fragmentation procedure takes processing time at the router or IP host that is

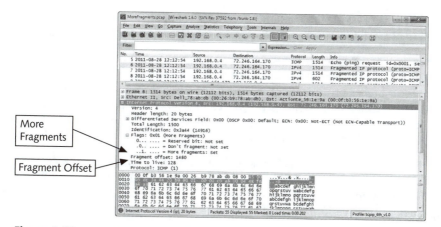

Figure 4-16 Second packet of fragment (More Fragments bit set to 1 and Fragment Offset set to 1480 [1,480 bytes])
Source: Wireshark

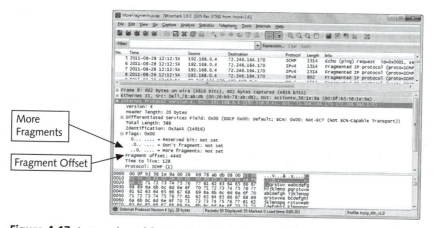

Figure 4-17 Last packet of fragment (More Fragments bit set to 0 and Fragment Offset set to 4440)
Source: Wireshark

fragmenting the packet. Second, all fragments must arrive before the expiration of the first-received fragment's TTL timer. If one of the fragments does not arrive in time, the receiver sends an ICMP message type 11 (Time Exceeded) with a code 1 (Fragmentation Reassembly Time Exceeded). In this case, the IP host that sent the packet sends another single packet (fragmented again). On a network that is low on available bandwidth, the fragment retransmission process causes more traffic on the wire.

Service Delivery Options

In the early IP development days, the IP header was built to support two fields that would support a method for defining **packet priority** and **route priority**: the Precedence field and

the Type of Service (TOS) field. These fields enabled an application or source TCP/IP stack to define its desired treatment as their packets were forwarded through a network.

Over time, it became obvious to network administrators that allowing vendors to define the importance of their traffic was not the best idea. Neither was the idea of individually configuring systems for a higher priority. Through time, the Precedence and TOS fields have been set aside for more centralized, router-based QoS configurations. Network administrators could configure priorities at a router based on source or destination IP address, the application contained in the packets, and many other factors.

As the Internet (and the TCP/IP stack) takes on more responsibility for commerce and corporate communications, people are always looking for ways to improve performance. Most recently, **Differentiated Services (Diffserv)** and **Explicit Congestion Notification (ECN)** have been suggested to improve IP-based traffic flows.

Precedence

A router uses precedence to determine what packet to send when several packets are queued for transmission from a single-output interface. Some applications can be configured to support a higher precedence to receive high-priority treatment.

There are eight levels of precedence. Level 0 is set for routine traffic that has no priority. Levels 1 through 5 are for prioritized traffic with a higher value, indicating a higher priority. Precedence Levels 6 and 7 are reserved for network and internetwork control packets.

One example of precedence use is Voice over IP (VoIP). The precedence for VoIP traffic may be set to Level 5 to support VoIP real-time delivery needs and to ensure minimum delay and best possible voice/sound quality.

Type of Service

Routers use Type of Service (TOS) to select a routing path when there are multiple paths available.

TOS functionality requires that the routing protocol being deployed understand and maintain varying views of the network based on the type of service possible. For example, a router must recognize that a satellite link is high delay because of the distance to the satellite. OSPF and **Border Gateway Protocol (BGP)** are two examples of routing protocols that support multiple types of services.

There are six possible types of services, as listed in Table 4-9.

In versions of Windows prior to Windows 2000, you can set the default TOS for a host using the DefaultTOS Registry setting, as shown in Table 4-10. Only one of the TOS bits can be set at a time. Windows 2000 and later operating systems do not allow you to specify a default TOS setting.

Binary	Decimal	Type of Service
0000	0	Default (no specific route defined)
0001	1	Minimize Monetary Cost
0010	2	Maximize Reliability
0100	4	Maximize Throughput
1000	8	Minimize Delay
1111	15	Maximize Security

Table 4-9 Type of Service values
© Cengage Learning 2013

Registry Information	Details
Location	HKEY_LOCAL_MACHINE\SYSTEM\CurrentControlSet\ Services\Tcpip\Parameters
Data type	REG_DWORD
Valid range	0–255
Default value	0
Present by default	No

Table 4-10 DefaultTOS Registry setting
© Cengage Learning 2013

The Registry entry is set in decimal for the entire TOS field. For example, to configure a host to use routine precedence and maximum reliability, you would set the DefaultTOS to 4 (00000100).

RFC 1349 defines the use of IP TOS and suggests uses of the TOS functionality, as shown in Table 4-11.

RFC 2474 ("Definition of the Differentiated Services Field [DS Field] in the IPv4 and IPv6 Header"), RFC 2475 ("An Architecture for Differentiated Services"), and RFC 3168 ("The Addition of Explicit Congestion Notification [ECN] to IP") offer a new use of the TOS field bits.

These three RFCs, and a number of supplemental RFCs, suggest that the TOS and Precedence field bytes be replaced by a Differentiated Services Code Point (DSCP) field.

Diffserv uses the DSCP value to enable routers to offer varying levels of service to traffic based on a marker placed in the DSCP field. The marker can be based on the source IP address or payload in the packet, or any other criteria, as desired by the network administrator. Diffserv offers more options and more flexibility through definition of a DSCP marker for traffic flow optimization than the old TOS and Precedence fields (which were limited to specific values, as defined earlier in this chapter).

In addition, these RFCs suggest that 2 bits be reserved to indicate that source IP devices can identify and notify other IP devices of congestion along a link.

Protocol	TOS Value	Functionality
TELNET	1000	Minimize Delay
FTP Control	1000	Minimize Delay
FTP Data	0100	Maximize Throughput
TFTP	1000	Minimize Delay
SMTP Command phase	1000	Minimize Delay
SMTP Data phase	0100	Maximize Throughput
DNS UDP Query	1000	Minimize Delay
DNS TCP Query	0000	Routine
DNS Zone Transfer	0100	Maximize Throughput
NNTP	0001	Minimize Monetary Cost
ICMP Errors	0000	Routine
ICMP Requests	0000	Routine
ICMP Responses	0000	Routine
Any IGP	0010	Maximize Reliability
EGP	0000	Routine
SNMP	0010	Maximize Reliability
BOOTP	0000	Routine

Table 4-11 **Type of service functionality**
© Cengage Learning 2013

Because of the increased interest in Diffserv and congestion notification technology, some vendors now refer to the TOS/Precedence bit use as the "legacy precedence" bits.

Many analyzer vendors do not recognize or decode the 6-bit DSCP field as such; they still decode it as a Precedence field.

Understanding IP Routing

We start our discussion by explaining the routing table. This table is a database that lives in the memory of the router. Entries in this database are known as "routes" and consist of a network address, a "next hop" (routing jargon for the IP address of the next router in the path to the destination), various metrics, and vendor-specific information.

A routing table is a compilation of information about all the networks that the router can reach. On small networks, this might be only a few entries. Most large enterprise networks, on the other hand, have several hundred entries in their routing tables. The biggest, of course, is the Internet. As of this writing, the routing tables of the Internet's backbone routers contain well over 100,000 entries.

Figure 4-18 shows an example of a small routing table from a Cisco router. In it, you can see that the network destinations are shown as IP addresses followed by a slash (/), for clarity, and a number that denotes the length of the subnet mask. For example, in the 10th entry, 137.20.30.0/24 means the mask is 24 bits long, or 255.255.255.0. This entry has a next hop out of its Serial0 Interface of 137.20.25.2. Also notice the "O IA" in front of the route entry. This indicates that the route was learned via Open Shortest Path First (OSPF), discussed in more detail later in this chapter.

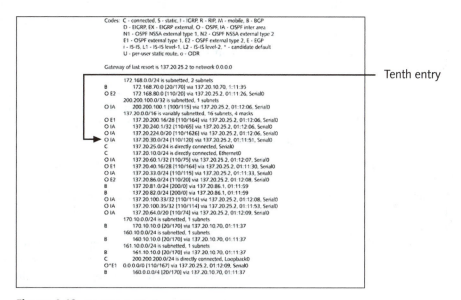

Tenth entry

Figure 4-18 Routing table from Cisco router
Source: Cisco

The routing table is used as follows: When a packet is received on a network interface, the router first must find out where the packet wants to go. To do so, the router reads the Destination Address field in the IP header and then looks in the Network field of its routing table for a match. If it finds a match, it sends the packet to the corresponding next hop, which is usually another router on a directly connected network.

It is important to understand that the methods used inside a router to forward packets may vary by manufacturer and are not standardized for any protocol.

NOTE

Now that you have a basic understanding of the routing table, we can begin to answer the question "How does the router know where to send packets?"

How Entries Are Placed in the Routing Table

A route entry can be placed in a routing table in three basic ways.

The first way is through direct connection. For example, a router that is connected to networks 10.1.0.0/16 and 10.2.0.0/16 knows about both networks because its physical network interfaces reside on those subnets.

The second way is through manual configuration. To do this, you log on to the router and use the menus or command line to define a network that it can reach, the next hop, and any metrics. You repeat this process for every network you want to reach.

The manual configuration method has several advantages and disadvantages. The primary advantage is control. With static routes, you specify the exact configuration and it doesn't change. Manual configuration is also very simple and secure, and the router immediately knows how to get to a network. The disadvantages are that on a large network you must type several hundred entries into each router; worse, any time a network changes, you must remember to go back to every single router on your network and make the appropriate change. As you can see in Figure 4-18, these tables can sometimes be confusing; it is easy to make mistakes and often extremely difficult to find them.

The third way that an entry can be placed in a routing table is dynamically, by using a **routing protocol**. Routers use routing protocols to share information about the various networks on an internetwork. Thus, you simply configure the protocol on each router, and the routers will convey **Network Layer Reachability Information (NLRI)** to each other.

The advantages and disadvantages of routing protocols are the opposite of the manual ones. They're much easier to maintain in a large environment, but they represent a point of failure that attackers can easily exploit. It can take a long time for a router on one side of an internetwork to learn about a network on the other side of an internetwork. More advanced routing protocols can be incredibly complex. Also, there is an inherent lack of control. For instance, if there are multiple paths to get to a network, the routing protocol will decide which one to take. You can, of course, tweak the metrics to make one path preferred, but you should completely understand the consequences of changes before you make them.

Routing Protocols and Routed Protocols

There are two types of protocols that cross an internetwork: routing protocols and routed protocols. Routing protocols are used to exchange routing information. Routing Information Protocol (RIP) and OSPF are routing protocols. (Recall that in our discussion of the route entry in Figure 4-18, the route was learned via OSPF.)

Routed protocols are Layer 3 protocols that are used to get packets through an internetwork. IP is the routed protocol for the TCP/IP protocol suite. Upon receipt of a TCP/IP packet, routers strip off the data link header and examine the IP header to determine how to route the packet.

Layer 3 switches are devices that can perform switching based on the MAC address and, when necessary, examine the Network layer header to make routing decisions. In essence, Layer 3 switches are a cross between a switch and a router.

Grouping Routing Protocols

There are two primary ways to group routing protocols, which help achieve routing efficiencies and minimize external needs for internal networking details.

The first grouping is an administrative one. When organizations began to connect to the Internet, they quickly realized that because the designs and philosophies of one company were often incompatible with another company's, they needed a way to extract this information. The solution was to create routing domains, or autonomous systems, which we'll define later. Thus, each organization can have complete control over its own routing domain, allowing it to set appropriate security and performance-tuning policies without affecting other organizations. The routing protocols used inside a routing domain are called **interior gateway protocols (IGPs)**, and the routing protocols used to connect these routing domains are known as **exterior gateway protocols (EGPs)**.

The second way to group routing protocols is by the method they use to communicate. The two primary "flavors" employed by routing protocols are **distance vector** and **link-state**. We discuss them next.

Distance Vector Routing Protocols There are several **distance vector routing protocols** in use today. The most popular by a wide margin is RIP, followed by a Cisco proprietary protocol called Interior Gateway Routing Protocol (IGRP). Border Gateway Protocol (BGP) also is a distance vector routing protocol. These protocols have several characteristics in common that distinguish them from link-state protocols.

The primary distinction is that they periodically broadcast their entire routing tables to all neighbors. This is done in conjunction with timers so that, when a router receives a list of networks from a neighbor, it installs them in its routing table and sets a timer. If the timer expires before the router receives another broadcast update, it removes the routes from its routing table. This means that the time it takes for a network to **converge**—to reach the point where all routers on the network have an accurate, stable routing table—is a function of this timer. For instance, if a router advertises a network to a neighbor and then a change occurs that results in the network no longer being available, the neighbor still forwards packets to this defunct network until the timer expires. If there are several routers between these two, the convergence time can quickly turn into several minutes.

The second major distinction of distance vector routing protocols is that they "route by rumor." If you have three routers, where Router A is connected to Router B and Router B is connected to Router C, Router A will send a message to Router B that says, "I have a route to Network 1." When Router B receives that message, it sends a message to Router C that says, "I have a route to Network 1" instead of "Router A has a route to Network 1, and I have a route to Router A." This sounds harmless enough until you realize that Router C doesn't know that Router A exists. It only knows that Router B can get to Network 1. This lack of complete information can cause several problems, which we'll discuss in detail later.

Also, a distance vector routing protocol shares information about how far away all networks are to the destination. Routing decisions are based on how far away networks are in distance—not the amount of time it takes to get to the destination, and they are considered quite "chatty" (which means they send more data than is necessary over the network) and inefficient.

In Figure 4-19, the following steps are taken to set up the routing tables on the three routers (A, B, and C).

1. Each router boots up and defines its own distance vector as 0.

2. Each router calculates a cost for its distance to each connected link. In this example, we assume that the cost is calculated as 1 for each hop.

3. Each router announces its distance vector information, which defines network reachability on all directly connected links. For example, Router A states that it is 0 hops to Networks 1 and 2, Router B states that it is 0 hops from Networks 2 and 3, and Router C states that it is 0 hops from Networks 3 and 4.

4. Upon receipt of this information from other routers, each router updates its routing table to reflect the new distance vector information. For example, in Figure 4-19 Router B learns of Network 1 from Router A's broadcast, Router B realizes it is 1 hop away from Network 1, and Router C realizes that it is 2 hops away from Network 1. If a device on Network 4 wants to communicate with a device on Network 1, it must cross three routers; the device itself is 3 hops away from Network 1.

5. Upon receipt of new route information, the routers send routing update information to other directly connected networks. This is called a triggered update. For example, Router B sends new route information to Network 2 after it receives new route information from Router C. After receiving information from Router A, Router B sends new route information to Network 3.

6. Distance vector routers periodically broadcast or multicast their route information on directly connected links. This is called a periodic update.

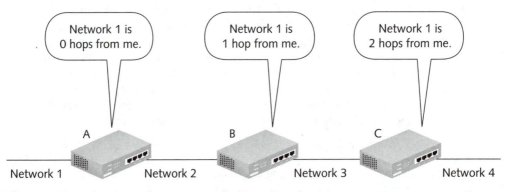

Figure 4-19 Routers on distance vector networks tracking distances
© Cengage Learning 2013

Routing Loops One of the most difficult challenges in automating the routing process is preventing **routing loops**. There are many different kinds of routing loops, but the simplest example of a routing loop occurs when one router believes the best path to a network is through a second router and, at the same time, the second router believes the best path to that network is through the first router. These two routers will pass a packet destined for the network in question back and forth until the Time to Live (TTL) on the packet expires.

For example, on the network depicted in Figure 4-19, consider what happens when Router C goes down—the route to Network 4 is gone. Router B (which is 1 hop away from Network 4) does not assume that the only path to Network 4 is gone. It thinks that Router A still has a path to Network 4 (although it is 2 hops away). Router B recalculates its distance vector information and adds a metric of 1 to the distance to Network 4. Router B now believes that Network 4 is 3 hops away going through Router A. Upon receipt of this information, Router A recalculates its distance to Network 4. Router A now believes it is 4 hops away from Network 4. Upon hearing this new calculation, Router B recalculates its routing table again. This process continues to infinity—well, not really, but you get the point.

Loop-Avoidance Schemes The method that distance vector protocols use to prevent packets from endlessly circulating around a routing loop is called **counting to infinity**. By defining "infinity" as a certain number of hops away (e.g., 16 for RIP), the protocol is essentially saying "Any route with a hop count of 16 is unreachable," so packets to that network will be dropped instead of forwarded. Although this doesn't prevent routing loops, it does limit damage when they occur. The downside is that an artificial limit is placed on the size of your network. The network **diameter** cannot be more than 15 hops.

Routers examine the IP header TTL field to determine if the packet can be processed for forwarding or if it should be discarded because it is too old. Whereas one technology (counting to infinity) defines the distance away for routes, the TTL field is used to define the remaining lifetime of a packet.

Another loop-avoidance scheme in distance vector routing protocols is **split horizon**. Split horizon simply prevents a router from advertising a network on the same interface from which it learned that network. Another feature often coupled with split horizon is called **poison reverse**. Poison reverse is a method of "poisoning a route" to indicate that you cannot get there. We cover split horizon and poison reverse in more detail in the "Routing Characteristics" section later in this chapter.

Link-State Routing Protocols Link-state routing protocols differ from distance vector routing protocols in two primary ways. The first is that they do not route by rumor. Each router generates information about only its directly connected links, and these are passed around the entire network so every router in the area has an identical view of the network topology. The routers then individually run an algorithm known as the **Dijkstra algorithm** to determine the optimal path through the internetwork.

The second major difference is that they do not periodically broadcast their entire tables. Link-state protocols build adjacencies with neighboring routers, and after an initial full exchange of information, they send only an update when a link state changes (e.g., goes "up" or "down"). This update occurs almost immediately after the change occurs, so unlike a distance vector protocol, the link-state protocol does not have to wait until a timer expires. Thus, the convergence time for link-state protocols is relatively short. This saves not only significant time but bandwidth as well because neighbors send only tiny Hello packets at short intervals to make sure the neighbor remains reachable. Only Hello packets are sent instead of complete routing tables.

Link-state routing uses the following process:

1. Link-state routers meet their **neighbor routers** through a process called the **Hello process**.

2. Each router builds and transmits a **link-state advertisement (LSA)** that contains the list of its neighbors and the cost to cross the network to each of those neighbors. Costs are typically based on fixed values that are calculated based on link bandwidth.

3. As these LSAs are propagated through the network and received by other routers, each router builds a picture of the network.

4. Link-state routers convert that picture into a **forwarding table**. They sort this table according to the lowest cost route. This table is used to determine how packets should be forwarded through the router.

5. Link-state routers periodically multicast summaries of their link-state databases on directly connected links.

6. If a receiving router does not have certain route information or detects that its information is out of date, that router can request updated information.

Figure 4-20 shows a link-state network. In this configuration, Routers A, B, and C discover each other by sending and receiving Hello packets on Network 1. The information received in these Hello packets is used to build an **adjacencies database**. Next, the routers create LSAs that describe their directly connected networks. The routers "flood" these LSAs to their neighbors by sending all the LSAs that each has to all neighbor routers. Those neighbor routers continue passing the LSAs along to their neighbors until every router on Network 1 has a copy of all LSAs.

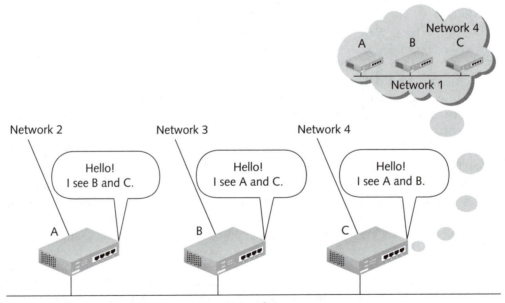

Figure 4-20 Adjacent databases on a link-state network
© Cengage Learning 2013

After this process is complete, each router knows exactly what Network 1 looks like, and each router independently runs a link-state algorithm to determine the correct path to each network. Because all routers use the same algorithm and have the same information, they all reach the same conclusions about what path is best, eliminating routing loops.

The process described previously is particular to the most popular link-state protocol, OSPF. Other link-state protocols, such as Intermediate System-Intermediate System (IS-IS), which is popular in Europe, and AppleTalk Update-based Routing Protocol (AURP), which is used for routing AppleTalk, behave in roughly the same manner, although their terminology is often quite different.

Routing Characteristics

When designing or operating a routing hierarchy, it's important to understand the characteristics of the networks involved and how they are interconnected. It's also important to understand the requirements and limitations of the various routing protocols that may be in use on an internetwork. You will learn more about these issues throughout this chapter, but those topics receive particular emphasis in the sections that follow.

Route Convergence

As mentioned earlier in this chapter, convergence is the process in which all the routers on the network recalculate the optimal paths after a change in the network. A network is usually said to be converged when all the routers know a loop-free path to get to all other networks. Ideally, a network should be in a converged state, in which all routers know the current networks available and their associated costs. This is true for both IPv4 and IPv6 networks.

In each of the routing designs shown earlier, if Network 3 suddenly becomes unavailable, each router must learn about this so that it stops forwarding any packets destined to Network 3. (Note that the distance vector network converges more slowly than the link-state network.)

IPv4 Routing Mechanisms

Routing mechanisms are used to help routers learn about paths to destinations. Usually, routers use multiple mechanisms to discover routes and build a routing table. Methods used by routers to discover routes include directly connected interfaces, default routes, dynamic routing methods, and static routing.

Directly connected interfaces lead to paths that are local to the router, such as a gateway router being connected to a subnet of the internal network. Static routes are usually entered manually into the routing table and define a route to a specific IP address such as a next-hop router or an interface to be used when forwarding traffic to a particular destination. Default routing is typically used with network nodes and defines the route by which node traffic can leave the local subnet, usually via a gateway router. Dynamic routing involves the router learning about routes to different destinations both through directly connected interfaces and from other routers that are advertising their routes. Dynamic routing protocols in IPv4 include RIP, RIP2, EIGRP, OSPF, IS-IS, and BGP.

 IPv4 routing protocols will be covered in the "Routing Protocols" section later in this chapter.

Routing loops are a specific network problem that occurs when a packet is routing through the same routers over and over again without resolution, until the packet's TTL value reaches zero and it is dropped. In a worst-case scenario, routing loops can bring a network to a virtual standstill, inhibiting all network activity. Routing loops are typically observed in large internetworks when a change occurs in a network before the routers can arrive at convergence from a previous change. If not all routers can agree on the optimal routes to destinations, then routers will forward packets based on routing table information that does not agree with information in the tables of other routers. This is sort of like Hansel and Gretel trying to find their way out of the forest by following multiple, conflicting bread crumb trails.

There are a number of routing mechanisms that can be put in place to avoid routing loops. These methods usually address speeding up convergence or preventing routers from advertising paths back to their source.

Split Horizon Split horizon is one of the methods devised to speed up the process of convergence and (in most cases) resolve the counting-to-infinity problem. Using the rule of split horizon, a router never advertises a path back out the same way the router learned about it. Figure 4-21 provides an example. In this figure, Router A learned about Network 3 from Router B, which advertised it as 1 hop away if you must go through Router B to get there. Router A adds its own cost of 1 hop and now updates its routing table to reflect that Network 3 is 2 hops away. Router A advertises this information to Network 1. According to the rules of split horizon, Router A is not permitted to advertise a path to Network 3 back the same way it learned about it.

Poison Reverse Poison reverse is a technique for assigning costs to routes designed to prevent routing loops. When one router learns about a route or a set of routes from another router, it assigns those routes an infinite cost value so it will never end up advertising routes back to their sources.

The routes B-A and B-C-B-C-A both define ways to get from B to A. C has no business advertising a route to B that goes through B. So, when C learns the route to A from B, it advertises back to B the route to A with an infinite metric. In other words, C tells B, "I can't get to A, so don't come this way." The poison reverse technique prevents this kind of looping from happening (and also prevents further recursion of such loops because repeating already-visited links only makes the loop longer, yet still topologically equivalent).

Time to Live To ensure that packets cannot loop endlessly through a network, each packet has a Time to Live (TTL) value—defined in the Network layer header. As packets travel through an internetwork, routers examine the TTL value to determine whether the packet has enough life remaining to be forwarded. For example, when a packet arrives at a router with a TTL value of 8, the router decrements this TTL value to 7 before forwarding

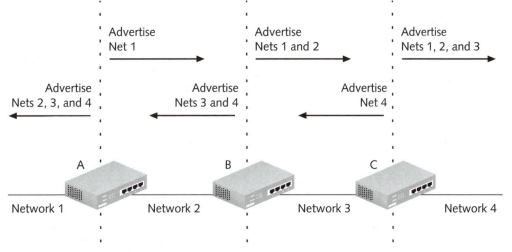

Figure 4-21 The rule of split horizon in operation
© Cengage Learning 2013

it. If, however, a packet arrives with a TTL value of 1, the router cannot forward it because the Time to Live field cannot be decremented to 0 and forwarded.

As you will learn in Chapter 5, routers transmit Internet Control Message Protocol (ICMP) Time Exceeded messages in response to expired packets. This permits information about reachability to be inferred in routers that receive such messages and provides a mechanism to manage routing information or compile hop counts.

Multicast versus Broadcast Update Behavior Some routing protocols can use only broadcasts to distribute their routing updates. Others can use either broadcasts or multicasts for their periodic updates. Broadcasts, of course, cannot traverse routers. Routers can be configured to forward multicasts, however.

There are two versions of RIP. Version 1 sends broadcast updates. Version 2, which supports nondefault subnet masks (see Chapter 2 for variable-length subnet mask [VLSM] information), can send multicast updates. OSPF also can send multicasts.

ICMP Router Advertisements Some routers can be configured to send periodic ICMP Router Advertisement packets. These periodic ICMP Router Advertisements do not mean that ICMP is a routing protocol. They simply allow hosts to learn passively about available routes.

These unsolicited ICMP Router Advertisements are sent periodically to the all-hosts multicast address 224.0.0.1. The advertisements typically include the IP address of the router that sent the ICMP Router Advertisement packet. The router also includes a **lifetime value** to indicate how long the receiving host should keep the route entry.

For more information on ICMP Router Advertisements, refer to RFC 1256, "ICMP Router Discovery Messages."

Black Holes A black hole occurs on a network when ICMP is turned off and a router discards packets without sending any notification about its actions. Because the sender doesn't receive notification indicating its packets were discarded, it continues to retransmit until it times out—that action depends on the behaviors and timeouts associated with upper-layer protocols, in fact. As an example of such behavior, if the communication is TCP based, the TCP layer retransmits the packet and awaits an ACK response.

There are many types of routers that create black holes. A specific example of a black hole router is shown in Figure 4-22. In this example, Router B is a Path Maximum Transmission Unit black hole router (referred to as a PMTU black hole router). The 4352 PMTU packet, which is oversized, arrives at the router, but this router does not support PMTU discovery; it also does not send an ICMP reply to the sending node indicating the PMTU value supported for the next hop. It just discards the packets.

Areas, Autonomous Systems, and Border Routers To reduce the number of entries in the link-state database, OSPF utilizes **areas**, which are groups of contiguous networks. The OSPF specification defines the need for a **backbone area**, Area 0 (also written in IP address format as Area 0.0.0.0). All other areas must be connected directly to this area (although there is some allowance for special tunneled connections). The routers that connect these areas are called **area border routers** (**ABRs**). These ABRs can summarize routing information before sending link-state packets to other networks. Figure 4-23 depicts a network that uses multiple areas.

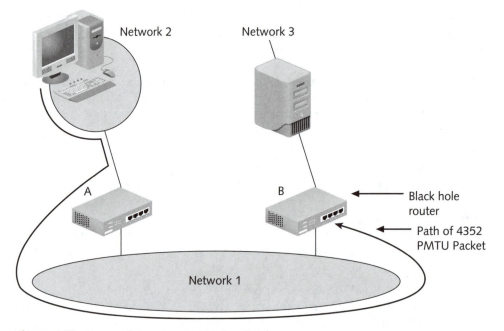

Figure 4-22 Process of dropping oversized packets
© Cengage Learning 2013

In this example, Area 1 consists of three variable-length subnets, based on CIDR addressing. Instead of advertising all three subnets, Router A summarizes these three networks into a single entry—10.1.0.0/16. Router B needs only a single route entry that summarizes all three networks. Likewise, Area 2 consists of three networks that can be summarized as 10.2.0.0/16.

Extremely large networks can be broken down into regions called **autonomous systems (ASs)**, which are groups of routers under a single administrative authority. Although individual autonomous systems were designed to operate independently of other ASs, sometimes it's helpful to break a network into multiple ASs, where they're all under the same control. An example of multiple ASs under centralized control is when one company acquires another and the networks may be owned by the same company and controlled by the same team, but it could take many months to merge them. In the meantime, they can be connected as separate ASs using an exterior gateway protocol.

All routers inside an AS use one or more interior gateway protocols to support internal routing. RIP and OSPF are examples of interior gateway protocols.

To connect ASs, routers use exterior gateway protocols (EGPs). The Border Gateway Protocol is an example of an EGP.

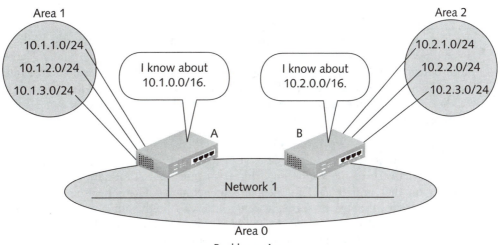

Figure 4-23 Areas connected to backbone area 0
© Cengage Learning 2013

The routers that connect autonomous systems are called **autonomous system border routers (ASBRs)**.

IPv6 Routing Considerations

How will routers change under IPv6? The short answer is, not much. This seems surprising until you realize that IPv6 was designed in very large part to solve routing problems encountered during the most explosive growth of the IPv4 Internet. IPv6 was designed from the ground up with routing efficiency and throughput in mind.

The structure of aggregatable global unicast addresses virtually builds the advantages of CIDR into the IPv6 protocol's native address space. The IPv6 header, the option headers, and the way in which they all fit together to form an IPv6 packet are all designed to optimize router performance.

Many of the same routing approaches familiar to IPv4, such as RIP, BGP-4, and OSPF, can make the transition to IPv6 with only minor changes. In many ways, the most important upgrades to these protocols are new provisions for 128-bit IPv6 addresses.

From top to bottom and side to side, IPv6 is designed to reduce the workload of Internet routers. Experience with IPv4 has shown that there are significant routing advantages to be gained when the address space matches the actual network topology. The allocation schemes for IPv6 addresses attempt to build in as much aggregatability as possible without unduly "tyrannizing" users. As the debate stands today, it seems that occasional network renumbering may be the price to pay for efficient routing, particularly when using the vast new address space that IPv6 provides. IPv6 support for autoconfiguration takes some of the sting out of this requirement. Another effort to reduce network administration costs is the way in which nodes "discover" their own environments, as covered in the following section.

IPv6 Routing Mechanisms

Routing in IPv6 networks performs the same function as in IPv4 networks: faciliating traffic from different network nodes across different network segments using routers. Network hosts and routers are responsibile for determining routes from source to destination. Routes can be general routes that potentially lead to all destinations on and off the local network segment, or they can be default routes to local nodes and to the default gateway that leads off of the local segment.

Routing mechanisms are those processes by which a router learns about network paths that lead to destinations. In the case of IPv6 network routing, network nodes must use PMTU Discovery to determine an arbitrary route to its destination prior to sending its packets on the local link. This mechanism includes determining the default router that leads off the local network segment, but routes can be dynamic and change after the network node completes its initial discovery process. Router Advertisement messages assist network nodes in determining default routes, but router configuration requires more complex methods.

Routing mechanisms are used by routers to help them build and update routing tables, and no one mechanism is used exclusively. The following sections describe IPv6 routing mechanisms. Dynamic routing protocols in IPv6 include RIPng, EIGRPv6, OSPFv3, IS-IS for IPv6, and BGP for IPv6.

IPv6 Routing Table Entry Types Both network nodes and routers maintain routing tables. A routing table is a collection of routes stored in the machine that contain data IPv6 network prefixes. The network prefixes are only attained if those networks can be reached directly or indirectly. On Windows Server 2008, Windows Vista, and Windows 7 computers, these routing tables are generated automatically when IPv6 is initiated on the system. The `netsh interface ipv6 show route` command can be used to view these tables on a Windows machine. This command does not have to be run as an administrator at the command prompt. See Figure 4-24 for an example.

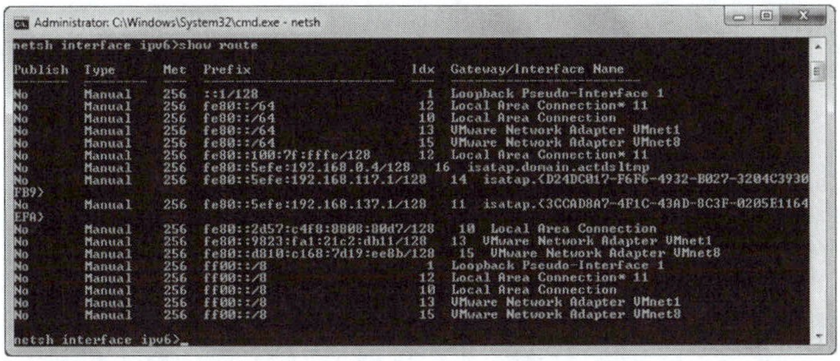

Figure 4-24 Routing table on a Windows 7 computer
Source: Microsoft

When a node, whether a computer or a router, receives a packet, it examines the destination address in the packet's header, but before checking the routing table, it checks its destination cache to see if there is a match to the address for the packet's destination. If no match exists, the node checks its routing table and attempts to determine the next-hop interface, which is the interface the router will use to forward the packet, and the next-hop IPv6 address. The next-hop IPv6 address can be the address of a node on the same network link that is directly connected to the router (direct delivery), or it can be the address of the next-hop router when the destination is not on the local link (indirect delivery). Once the next-hop interface and next-hop destination are arrived at, the router updates its destination cache and then forwards the packet. Subsequent packets arriving at the router will be forwarded by consulting the routing cache rather than the routing table.

IPv6 routing tables can store the routing table types shown in Table 4-12.

Routing Table Type	Details
Directly attached routes	These are routes with subnet prefixes that are directly attached to the router and that usually have a 64-bit length.
Remote routes	These are routes with prefixes that are either subnet prefixes 64 bits in length or prefixes summarizing an address space that are less than 64 bits in length.
Host routes	This is a route prefix to a specific IPv6 address that is 128 bits in length.
Default route	The IPv6 default route prefix is ::/0.

Table 4-12 IPv6 routing table types
© Cengage Learning 2013

Each IPv6 routing table contains specific fields, as shown in Table 4-13.

IPv6 Route Determination Process In order to determine which entry in its routing table the device should select as its forwarding decision, the IPv6 router performs a specific set of steps. The router compares the bits in the address prefix for each entry in its routing table to the identical bits in the destination address of the packet, looking for the number of bits in the prefix length of the route. If all the bits match between the destination address and a particular

Routing Table Fields	Details
Destination prefix	This is an IPv6 address prefix that can be between 0 and 128 in length.
Next-hop address	This is the IPv6 address to which the packet will next be forwarded.
Interface	This is the network interface on the node used to forward the packet to the next-hop node.
Metric	This is the value indicating the cost of the route allowing the best route, among multiple routes, to be selected.

Table 4-13 IPv6 routing table fields
© Cengage Learning 2013

route entry, that route is the correct destination for the packet. There may be multiple matches because more than one route can lead to the destination address for the packet.

Assuming there are multiple routes that lead to the correct destination address, the router creates a list of all matching routes and then chooses the route with the largest prefix length. This is the route that matches the greatest number of high-order bits in the destination address, which means it's the most direct route to the destination. It's possible for more than one route to have the same prefix address. In this case, the route selects the lowest metric value to select the best route. If more than one route matches the same prefix address and the lowest metric value, the IPv6 routing determination algorithm chooses the specific routing table entry to use to forward the packet.

For any specific destination, a IPv6 router using the procedure just described finds routes that match a packet's destination address in this order:

1. The host route that matches the entire destination address
2. The network route that has the longest address prefix length matching the destination address
3. The default route, which has the network prefix ::/0

Once the route determination process is complete, the router selects the path from the routing table and determines the next-hop interface and address and forwards the packet. If no route can be determined by the sending network node, IPv6 assumes the destination is on the local link. If the router can find no route, it sends an ICMPv6 "Destination Unreachable-No Route to Destination" message back to the sending host and then drops the packet.

How Strong and Weak Hosts Behave Although it is typical for routers to have multiple network interfaces, PCs on the network can also be multihomed (have more than one network interface). This allows the node to be physically connected to more than one network segment or network type, such as an intranet and the Internet. This also represents a security issue because multihomed nodes are more vulnerable to external attack and can allow an Internet intruder access to the nodes internal network.

RFC 1122 is the original specification describing the Weak and Strong Host models for multihomed network nodes, but this RFC has since been updated by several others, including

RFC 1349, RFC 4379, RFC 5884, RFC 6093, and RFC 6298. This specification describes a node that is multihomed, that is not acting as a router, and that is only unicast IP traffic. Although the original RFC 1122 specification was written for IPv4, the Weak and Strong Host models apply to multihomed IPv6 nodes as well. During the process of IPv6 adoption, there will be a significant period of time when IPv4 and IPv6 will coexist in a single network infrastructure. It won't be uncommon for a node to have two network interfaces: one for IPv4 and the other for IPv6.

Weak and Strong Hosts use different behaviors to determine when and how unicast traffic is sent and received and whether it must be associated with the network interface on which the traffic traverses. They also behave differently in how securely or insecurely services are maintained on computer hosts.

Weak Host send behavior is when an IP node, either IPv4 or IPv6, can send packets on an interface that is not set as the source IP address for those packets. Weak Host receive behavior is when the host can also receive packets on an interface not set as the destination IP address for the received packet. Weak Host behaviors can make the network node vulnerable to attack, particularly if the computer has two network interfaces, with one interface connected to the Internet and the other attached to the internal or local network. With Weak Host behaviors enabled on both interfaces, the host can send packets from the externally facing interface on the internally facing interface, assuming its firewall rules permit this behavior.

From the internal network's point of view, network traffic originating from the Internet will appear as if it is coming from the internal network. An external intruder can use this condition to send traffic to the node's externally facing interface to attack services on the node's internal network. Setting appropriate firewall rules on the node's Internet-facing interface will help, but a continued vulnerability of internal services accessible by the node still exists. Weak Host behavior makes network connectivity easier but compromises security.

Strong Host sending and receiving behavior dictates that an interface with a specific address can only send and receive packets with the interface's address as the source or destination. That is, in the Weak Host example, the Internet-facing interface could not receive a packet addressed to the internally facing interface. It also couldn't send a packet from the Internet-facing interface with the internally facing interface as the source IP address. This improves network security because an external intruder cannot send a malicious packet to the node's external interface addressed to the internally facing interface in order to attack network services. Any packets being received on one interface that are addressed to another interface on a multihomed strong host are dropped, without the need to configure firewall rules on those interfaces (although setting up appropriate firewall rules is still a good idea).

Strong Host model behavior may not be the best choice for some network connectivity types. For instance, some load-balancing activities work better with Weak Host behaviors. They can send and receive traffic on any interface, so the traffic can be sent to any other interface for faster connections.

Windows Server 2008, Windows Vista, and Windows 7 support strong host sending and receiving behavior on all network interfaces in both IPv4 and IPv6 by default. The exception is Teredo tunneling interfaces for a Teredo host-specific relay, which uses weak host sending and receiving.

RFC 3484 defines two algorithms that offer a standard method of choosing IPv4 and IPv6 source and destination addresses with which to attempt network connections. The first algorithm is used to choose the best source address for the destination address, and the second algorithm sorts the list of possible destination addresses in order of preference. Strong Host algorithms result in a list of possible source addresses made up of unicast addresses assigned to the sending interface for the destination address. Weak Host send behaviors compile a list of addresses that can include addresses assigned to any interface that has weak Weak Host sending enabled. For more information, go to *www.ietf.org* and look up RFC 3484, "Default Address Selection for Internet Protocol version 6 (IPv6)," and RFC 5220, "Problem Statement for Default Address Selection in Multi-Prefix Environments: Operational Issues of RFC 3484 Default Rules."

The IPv6 Delivery Process, End to End With some understanding of how the various IPv6 routing considerations are managed, the following section describes the process of sending and receiving a packet on an IPv6 network, from source to destination. In summary, the source node sends a packet to either a router or to the final destination if the destination is on the same local link. If sent to a router, the packet is forwarded to either another router or to its final destination if the node is on a link directly attached to the first-hop router. When received by the destination node, the packet transfers its data to the desired application on the computer. The details about the end-to-end delivery process being described provides a simple example where the IPv6 packet does not possess extension headers.

IPv6 Source Node In general, the host uses the following set of steps to send a packet to an arbitrary destination. The following steps illustrate the NDP discovery process as a computer creates a message for a destination network node.

1. Specify the value in the Hop Limit field.

2. Check the destination cache for an entry matching the destination address.

3. If a match is found between the cache and the destination address, the node gets the next-hop address and interface index and then proceeds to check the neighbor cache.

4. If a match isn't found in the destination cache, check the IPv6 routing table.

5. If no route is found, then the location of the destination node is on the same local link. The source node sets the next-address field value to the destination address, chooses the sending network interface, and then updates the destination cache.

6. Use PMTU discovery to check the path for the smallest link MTU size, and then set the packet size to match the smallest link.

7. Check the neighbor cache, which contains neighboring IPv6 addresses and the host's MAC addresses, to see if it contains an entry matching the destination address; if it does, send the packet using the link-layer address found in the neighbor cache.

8. If the neighbor cache doesn't contain a matching entry, send a Router Solicitation message to request the link-layer address of the next-hop router, and upon receiving the Router Advertisement message from the next-hop router, use that address to send the packet.

In the event that address resolution using Router Solicitation fails, an error will be logged.

IPv6 Router   Once the IPv6 router receives the packet sent by the source node, it will go through this series of steps to forward the packet to an arbitrary unicast or anycast destination address:

1. Upon receiving the packet, the router performs error checks to verify that the packet header fields contain the expected values, including verifying that the packet's destination address matches a router interface.

2. The router decrements the value in the Hop Limit field by 1 and, if the value is less than 0, drops the packet and sends an ICMPv6 "Time Exceeded-Hop Limit Exceeded in Transit" message to the source node.

3. The router checks its destination cache to see if an entry exists matching the packet header's destination address, and if a match is found, it gets the address of the next-hop router or node and the interface, then verifies that the MTU size of the next link is equal to or greater than the MTU size of the packet. (An ICMPv6 "Packet Too Big" error message is sent to the source node if the packet's MTU value is too large, and the packet is dropped.)

4. If no match is found in the destination cache, the router checks its routing table for the longest matching route to the destination address, and if one is found, gets the address index and interface for forwarding the packet. (If no entry is found, an ICMPv6 "Destination Unreachable-No Route to Destination" message is sent to the source node, and the packet is dropped.)

5. When a match is found, the router updates its destination cache and then checks the MTU size of the next link against the packet's MTU size, dropping the packet if its MTU is larger than the link and sending the appropriate message to the source node.

6. The router then checks its neighbor cache for the next-hop address, and if one exists, it will acquire the next-hop node's link-layer address; otherwise, it uses address resolution to get the next-hop node's link-layer address, uses it to send the packet out the appropriate interface, and then updates its neighbor cache.

IPv6 Destination Node   Once the packet is received by the destination host, this series of steps is followed:

1. When the destination node receives the IPv6 packet, it conducts a series of optional error checks to verify that the packet header fields contain the expected values, including verifying that the value in the destination address field matches the local host interface of the node. (If it doesn't, the packet is dropped.)

2. The destination node checks the packet header's next header field to make sure it matches an application being used on the node. (If it doesn't, the packet is dropped and an ICMPv6 "Parameter Problem-Unrecognized Next Header Type Encountered" message is sent to the source node.)

3. If the upper-layer protocol is either UDP or TCP, the node checks the destination port, and if an application exists for the port, the node processes the contents.

4. If the upper-layer protocol is not UDP or TCP, the node passes the data to the appropriate protocol running on the node.

5. If no application exists for the upper-layer protocol, the node sends an ICMPv6 "Destination Unreachable - Port Unreachable" message to the source node and drops the packet.

Multicast Listener Discovery in IPv6

Multicast Listener Discovery (MLD) is used by IPv6 routers to discover multicast listeners on any directly attached network link. It is similar to how Internet Group Management Protcol (IGMP) works in IPv6 except that it is embedded in ICMPv6 rather than requiring a separate protocol. MLD was initially described in RFC 2710 (MLD) and then updated in RFC 3810 (MLDv2). The specification for using IGMPv3 and MLDv2 is described in RFC 4064.

Understanding MLD and MLDv2 MLD enables each IPv6 router to discover nodes that want to receive multicast messages on links directly connected to the router. MLD allows the router to discover which of these addresses are of interest to neighboring network nodes, and this information is offered to any multicast routing protocol being used on the router. In this manner, multicast packets are reliably delivered to any links where receivers exist that want multicast packets.

MLD specifies different behaviors for multicast nodes and routers because routers can also be multicast listeners. A router, if a multicast listener, will perform both the sending and listening parts of the protocol, which includes listening to and responding to its own MLD messages. If the router has more than one interface to the same link, MLD messages only need to be sent out to one of the interfaces; however, nodes that are MLD listeners must listen on all their interfaces, assuming they possess more than one, and if an application or upper-layer protocol has used those interfaces to request mulicast information.

MLDv2 updates the protocol to support source filtering or the ability of a node to request multicast packets from only one or more specific source addresses. This supports Source-Specific Multicast, described in RFC 3569. MLDv2 also allows a node to request multicast packets from an "all but" list, so that multicasts are received from all sending nodes except for a specific group of source IPv6 addresses.

IPv6 Multicast Behaviors An IPv6 multicast is a method of sending a "one-to-many" message in real time, usually using ICMPv6 as the transport mechanism. IPv6 routers use MLD or MLDv2 to discover multicast listeners on links directly connected to the routers and to discover which multicast addresses are of interest to neighboring network nodes.

For each of the router interfaces using MLD, the router must configure the interface to listen to all link-layer multicast addresses that are created by IPv6 multicasts, such as a router attached to an Ethernet link configuring the interface to accept all multicast addresses starting with the value 3333 in hexadecimal. If the interface is unable to provide filtering services, it is set to accept all Ethernet multicast addresses.

Routers can be Querier or Non-Querier routes, with only one Querier on any given local link. The link's Querier periodically sends a query on the link, soliciting reports of all multi-cast addresses on the link in order to discover which nodes are members of a multicast group. Nodes, which can include routers, are receivers of queries that send report messages to the Querier informing it of their multicast group membership. Any set of Queriers and nodes that receives multicast data streams from the same source is defined as a multicast group. The MLD reports are used by nodes to join and exit from a multicast group.

Once the router starts receiving MLD reports from interested nodes, it builds a routing topology using either link-state or distance vector routing mechanisms. Network nodes use the IGMP protocol to manage their multicast group memberships and to "talk" to the local multicast routers.

Multicast messages can be sent by a node to a specific multicast group address and then delivered across one or more routers, so multicast group membership isn't limited to a single local link. Multicast group members can exist anywhere, so membership is virtual rather than geographic, as shown in the logical diagram in Figure 4-25.

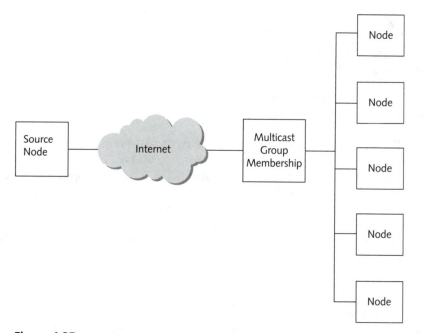

Figure 4-25 Logical diagram of a multicast message being sent to a multicast group
© Cengage Learning 2013

Although IPv6 uses a solicited-node address to query network nodes, this type of message would be picked up by all nodes on the local link. For multicast-related messages, a solicited-node multicast message is used, and only nodes listening for multicast traffic will receive notices sent to this address. Defined by RFC 4291, the IPv6 multicast address format prefix contains a scope field that describes the scope or range for which the multicast traffic is intended. Depending on the scope of the multicast address, multicast traffic is sent to certain portions of the internetwork, from just the local link to organization-wide or even globally. Table 4-14 defines the relevant scopes.

Value	Scope	Details
1	Interface-Local	Spans only one interface on the node and uses only loopback and multicast transmission
2	Link-Local	Spans the same network topology as the analogous unicast scope
4	Admin-Local	The smallest scope requiring administrative configuration as opposed to automatic or dynamic configuration
5	Site-Local	Spans the same network topology as the analogous unicast scope
8	Organization-Local	Spans multiple sites within a single organization
E	Global	Spans multiple sites and multiple organizations

Table 4-14 IPv6 Multicast address format prefix scopes
© Cengage Learning 2013

The site-local scope was deprecated in RFC 3879. If it is available on an interface, it should not be used by an application. The site-local scope is included in Table 4-14 because it is still used by Microsoft Windows operating systems.

The Scope field contains several unassigned values that can be used by administrators to define more multicast scope regions.

MLD and MLDv2 Packet Structures and Messages MLD and MLDv2 packet structures do not differ radically from each other; in fact, MLDv2 builds on the basic MLD packet. As previously mentioned, MLD is integrated as an ICMPv6 subprotocol, and MLD messages in IPv6 packets are recognized with a Next Header value of 58. MLD packets are all sent with a link-local source address and with a Hop Limit of 1. They are also sent with a router alert in the Hop-by-Hop options field to notify routers to review all MLD messages sent to multicast addresses to which the routers normally don't attend. Figure 4-26 illustrates the format of the MLD packet.

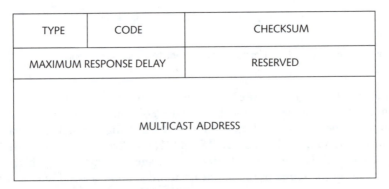

Figure 4-26 MLDv1 packet structure
© Cengage Learning 2013

The contents of the MLD packet fields should be somewhat familiar if you have any knowledge of ICMPv6 packets. Table 4-15 describes the specifics of these fields.

MLDv1 Packet Fields	Details
Type	There are three types of MLD messages, the values for which are found in the packet's Type field: Multicast Listener Query (130) Multicast Listener Report (131) Multicast Listener Done (132)
Code	This is set to 0 by the source node and ignored by the receiving nodes.
Checksum	This is the standard ICMPv6 checksum for the entire MLD message, including the pseudo-header of the IPv6 header fields.
Maximum Response Delay	This field contains a value in milliseconds specifying the maximum allowed delay before sending a responding Report, and the field is only relevant in query messages.
Reserved	This is set to 0 by the source node and ignored by the receiving nodes.
Multicast Address	For a query message, this field is set to 0 when a General Query is sent and set to a specific IPv6 multicast address when sending a Multicast-Address-Specfic Query. For a Report message, this field contains the specific IPv6 multicast address for message senders listening for reports.

Table 4-15 **MLDv1 packet fields**
© Cengage Learning 2013

In the Type field, the Multicast Listener Query has two subtypes: General Query, which is used to discover which multicast addresses have listeners on the attached link, and Multicast-Address-Specific Query, which is used to discover if any particular multicast address has listeners on an attached link.

The length of a received MLD message is calculated by subtracting the length of any IPv6 extension headers present between the IPv6 header and MLD message from the value of the IPv6 Payload Length. Any MLD message larger than 24 octets means that there are other fields present besides those already mentioned, indicating the possible presence of a future backward-compatible version of MLD, such as MLDv2. MLDv1 must not send a message longer than 24 octets, and any node expecting to receive an MLDv1 message will ignore any fields in an MLD message beyond the first 24 octets. Regardless of this, the checksum must be calculated for the entire MLD message rather than for just the first 24 octets.

The packet structure for a MLDv2 Multicast Listener Query message is shown in Figure 4-27. The structure for an MLDV2 Multicast Listener Report message will be described later in this section. The explanation for each field in this message is provided in Table 4-16.

The Type field can accept two additional message types for backward compatibility with MLDv1: Version 1 Multicast Listener Report (131) and Version 1 Multicast Listener Done (132). Any unrecognized message types are ignored. The format for MLDv2 Multicast Listener Report messages is illustrated in Figure 4-28.

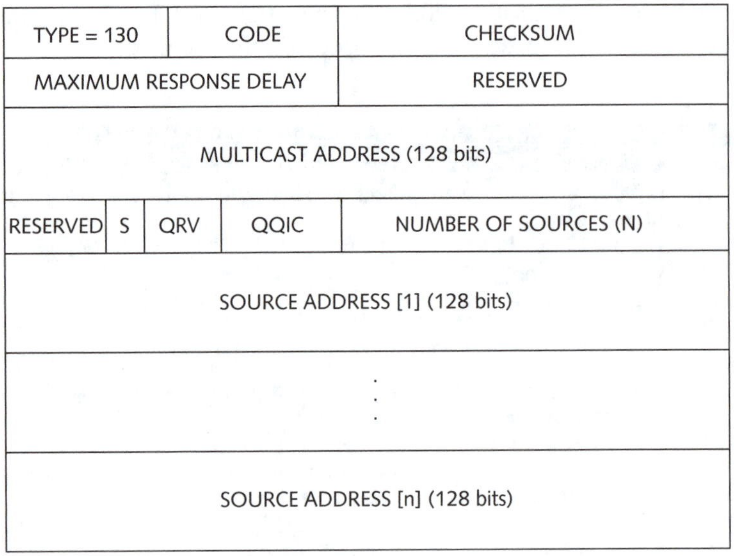

TYPE = 130	CODE	CHECKSUM
MAXIMUM RESPONSE DELAY		RESERVED

MULTICAST ADDRESS (128 bits)

RESERVED	S	QRV	QQIC	NUMBER OF SOURCES (N)

SOURCE ADDRESS [1] (128 bits)
. . .
SOURCE ADDRESS [n] (128 bits)

Figure 4-27 MLDv2 packet structure for Multicast Listener Query message
© Cengage Learning 2013

MLDv2 Packet Fields	Details
Type	There are two types of MLDv2 messages, the values for which are found in the packet's Type field: Multicast Listener Query (130) Version 2 Multicast Listener Report (143)
Code	This is set to 0 by the source node and ignored by the receiving nodes.
Checksum	This is the standard ICMPv6 checksum for the entire MLD message, including the pseudo-header of the IPv6 header fields. The field is set to 0 for computing the checksum, and the receiving node must verify the checksum before processing the message.
Maximum Response Code	This field specifies the maximum allowed time before sending a response Report. The actual time, measured in millliseconds, is referred to as the Maximum Response Delay and is derived from the Maximum Response Code.
Reserved	This is set to 0 by the source node and ignored by the receiving nodes.
Multicast Address	For a query message, this field is set to 0 when a General Query is sent and set to the specific IPv6 multicast address being queried when sending a Multicast-Address-Specfic Query or a Multicast Address and Source Specific Query. For a Report message, this field contains the specific IPv6 multicast address for message senders listening for reports.
S Flag	This is used to suppress router-side processing. When the flag is set to one, receiving multicast routers are directed to suppress the normal timer updates they usually perform when hearing a query. This does not suppress the Querier election or normal node-side processing of a query that routers are required to perform if the routers are also multicast listeners.

Table 4-16 MLDv2 Multicast Listener Query message packet fields

MLDv2 Packet Fields	Details
QRV (Querier's Robustness Variable)	This field contains the Robustness Variable value used by the Querier if the value is not 0. If the value is greater than 7, which is the maximum allowed value for this field, the field is set to 0.
QQIC (Querier's Query Interval Code)	This field specifies the Query Interval used by the Querier. The actual interval is called the Querier's Query Interval (QQI) and is measured in seconds. The QQI is derived from the QQIC.
Number of Sources (N)	This field specifies the number of source addresses present in the query. This value is set to 0 for a General Query or a Multicast Address Specific Query and is not 0 for a Multicast Address and Source Specific Query.
Source Address [i]	The source address fields are a vector of n unicast addresses where n is the value in the Number of Sources (N) field.

Table 4-16 MLDv2 Multicast Listener Query message packet fields (*continued*)
© Cengage Learning 2013

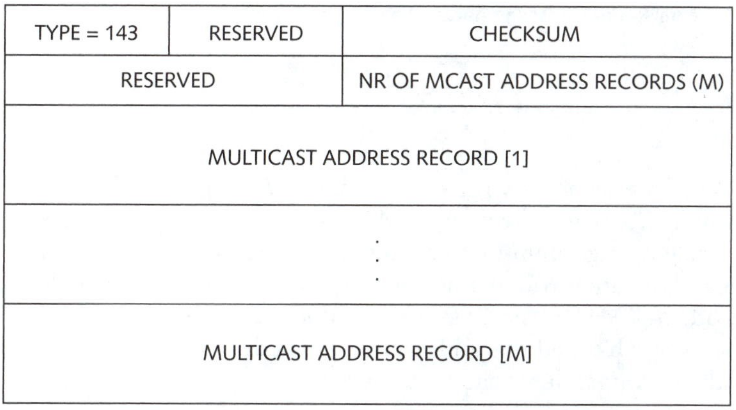

Figure 4-28 MLDv2 Multicast Listener Report message format
© Cengage Learning 2013

Table 4-17 describes the fields for the Multicast Listener Report messages.

MLD uses three types of messages:

- *Query messages*—These can be general, group-specific, and multicast-address-specific. The query messages being sent to learn which multicast addresses have listeners for a specific attached link. Group-specific and multicast-address-specific queries are the same, with the group address being the multicast address.

- *Report messages*—These are sent by nodes replying to queries declaring their multicast state to the device sending the queries.

- *Done messages*—These are sent indicating that a formerly listening node is no longer listening.

MLDv2 Packet Fields	Details
Type	There are two types of MLDv2 messages, the values for which are found in the packet's Type field: Multicast Listener Query (130) Version 2 Multicast Listener Report (143)
Reserved	This is set to 0 by the source node and ignored by the receiving nodes.
Checksum	This is the standard ICMPv6 checksum for the entire MLD message, including the pseudo-header of the IPv6 header fields. The field is set to 0 for computing the checksum, and the receiving node must verify the checksum before processing the message.
Nr of Mcast Address Records (M)	This field specifies the number of Multicast Address Records that exist in the Report.
Multicast Address Record	This field contains a block of fields representing the Multicast Address Record. The fields contain data on the source node, which is listening to a single multicast address on the interface from which the Report was transmitted. Each Multicast Address Record has an internal format, as described in RFC 3810, Section 5.2.

Table 4-17   **MLDv2 Multicast Listener Report message packet fields**
© Cengage Learning 2013

Routing Protocols

In general, routing protocols define how routers communicate with each other for the purpose of sharing and updating routing information. More specifically, a routing protocol is an implementation of a routing algorithm that uses metrics to discover a path or paths that can be used to a particular destination within a network. The metrics used can include bandwidth, delay, hop count, load, and MTU. Once discovered, information about each path to destinations is stored in a routing table, and this table can be updated manually by a network administrator or dynamically as routing information changes.

IPv4

IPv4 has long used a series of routing protocols that fall into three basic types: interior gateway routing using link-state routing, interior gateway routing using path vector or distance vector, and exterior gateway routing. IPv4 routing protocols are defined by multiple RFCs, including RFC 791, RFC 922, RFC 1716, RFC 1812, and RFC 1930.

RIP Routing Information Protocol (RIP) is a basic distance vector routing protocol. There are two versions of RIP. The first is version 1 (defined in RFC 1058), which is written as RIPv1. The second is version 2 (defined in RFC 2453), which is written as RIPv2. Among other features, RIPv2 adds support for variable-length subnets.

RIP communications are UDP based. RIP-based routers send and receive datagrams on UDP port number 520.

In the next sections, we examine the packet structures and functionality of RIPv1 and RIPv2. Figure 4-29 depicts the relationship between ASs, IGPs, and EGPs.

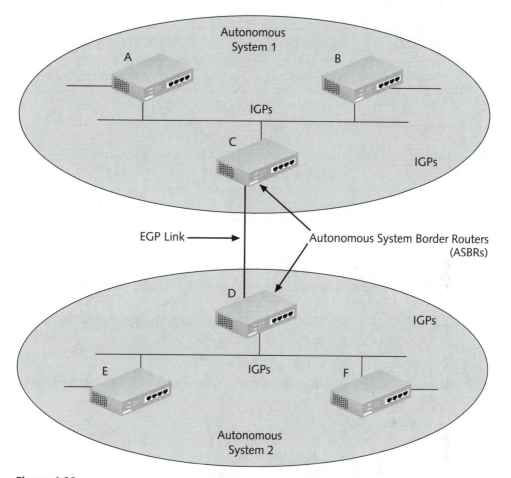

Figure 4-29 Exterior gateway protocol connecting two autonomous systems
© Cengage Learning 2013

RIPv1 When RIPv1 routers first come up, they send a RIP announcement about their directly connected links. Next, the router sends a RIP request to identify other networks. These two steps are used to build the routing table.

RIPv1 routers broadcast RIP network announcements every 30 seconds. Each RIP packet can contain information for up to 25 networks. Because RIPv1 does not support variable-length subnet masks (it uses only constant-length subnet masks), the routers make assumptions about the network portion of the addresses based on whether the address is a Class A, B, or C.

Figure 4-30 shows the format of a RIPv1 packet.

The fields of the RIP packet are defined in the following list:

- *Command*—This 1-byte field indicates whether this packet is a RIP request (1) or a response (2).

- *Version*—This 1-byte field indicates whether this is a RIPv1 (1) packet or a RIPv2 (2) packet.

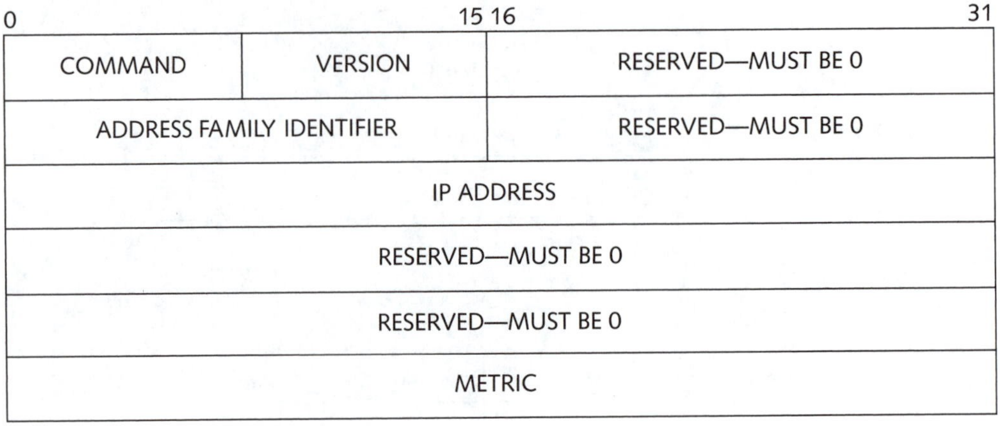

0	15 16	31
COMMAND	VERSION	RESERVED—MUST BE 0
ADDRESS FAMILY IDENTIFIER		RESERVED—MUST BE 0
IP ADDRESS		
RESERVED—MUST BE 0		
RESERVED—MUST BE 0		
METRIC		

Figure 4-30 RIPv1 packet format
© Cengage Learning 2013

- *Reserved (or Zero)*—These 2-byte fields are reserved and set to all 0s. (Note: Some protocol analyzers do not display the Reserved field.)
- *Address Family Identifier*—This 2-byte field is used to define the protocol that is using RIP. The value 2 indicates that IP is using RIP.
- *IP Address*—This 4-byte field contains the IP address.
- *Metric*—This 4-byte field contains the distance metric for the address listed in the IP Address field.

Figure 4-31 depicts a RIPv1 packet.

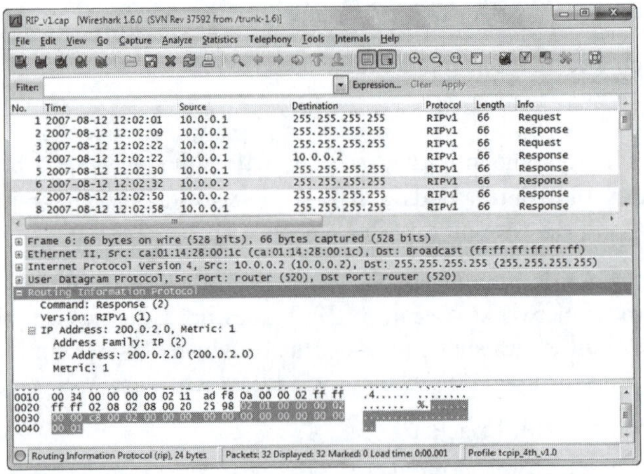

Figure 4-31 RIP exchange between two routers
Source: Wireshark

RIPv1 does an adequate job of providing routing information. It has two major faults, however: It does not support variable-length subnet masks, and it takes too long to converge.

Updating to RIPv2 solves the first problem. Replacing RIP-based routing with OSPF solves the second problem.

RIPv2 This version of RIP adds support for variable-length subnet masks, very basic authentication, and multicast routing updates. The RIPv2 IP multicast address is 224.0.0.9.

Figure 4-32 shows the format of a RIPv2 packet.

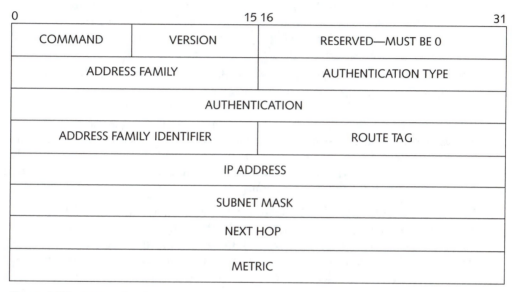

Figure 4-32 RIPv2 packet format
© Cengage Learning 2013

Some fields of note in a RIPv2 packet are:

- *Command*—This 1-byte field indicates whether this packet is a RIP request (1) or a response (2).

- *Version*—The value 2 in this 1-byte field is used to indicate that this packet is a RIPv2 packet.

- *Reserved*—This 2-byte field is reserved and set to all 0s.

- *Address Family*—This 2-byte field is used to define the protocol that is using RIP. The value 2 indicates that IP is using RIP. The value 0xFFFF indicates that the remainder of the message contains authentication. That leaves space for only 24 entries in the rest of the RIP packet.

- *AuthenticationType*—There is only one authentication type currently defined: type 2.

- *Authentication*—This 16-byte field contains a **plain text password**. If the password is shorter than 16 bytes, it is left-justified and padded with 0x00s on the right.

- *Address Family Identifier*—When this field contains the value 0x02, the next 20 bytes contain a route entry.

- *Route Tag*—This 2-byte field can be used to indicate whether the route information that follows is an **internal route entry** (received from within this routing area) or an **external route entry** (learned through another IGP or EGP outside this routing area).

- *IP Address*—This 4-byte field contains the IP address being advertised.

- *Subnet Mask*—This 4-byte field contains the subnet mask associated with the IP address being advertised.

- *Next Hop*–Typically, in RIP, routers only advertise for networks to which they can route packets. In RIPv2, however, the 4-byte Next Hop field can be used to associate another router with a route entry. It's a way to redirect traffic to a specific router without considering intervening hops. The value 0.0.0.0 in this field indicates that this router is advertising networks to which it can route packets.

- *Metric*—This 4-byte field indicates the distance, in hops, to the advertised network. This field is not used in request packets.

RIPv2 takes advantage of numerous improvements over its predecessor, RIPv1, and is still widely used on smaller, less complex networks to this day. Because RIPv2 is relatively easy to set up, configure, and manage, it should remain widespread for the foreseeable future. For more complex enterprise-level networks; however, the OSPF protocol fits much better, as you will learn in the following section.

Open Shortest Path First Open Shortest Path First, defined in RFC 2328, is the premier link-state routing protocol used on TCP/IP networks. (The word "Open" refers to the nonproprietary nature of this protocol.) OSPF routing is based on configurable values (metrics) that may be based on network bandwidth, delay, or monetary cost. By default, the metric used for route determination is based on network bandwidth.

The basic architectural definition of OSPF is shown in Figure 4-33. First, OSPF routers send multicast Hello packets to directly connected links to learn about their neighbors. As OSPF routers hear each other's Hello packets, they begin to include their neighbors' addresses in subsequent Hello packets. Depending on the configuration and type of media in use, OSPF routers establish adjacencies with some of these neighbors. Once an adjacency is established, they share copies of all LSAs (assuming they're in the same area). After the LSAs are shared, they continue sending Hello packets every 10 seconds (by default) as a keep-alive mechanism to ensure that the other router is still present and responding, thus building a small picture of their local worlds. The routers then run the Dijkstra algorithm to determine the optimal path through the internetwork, and the results are entered into the forwarding table (or database). The OSPF router checks this table before forwarding packets.

On a broadcast-based network, on which there can be more than two routers connected to a given segment, a full mesh is required for each router to establish an adjacency with every other router. Because of the processing and memory demands, this is not a scalable architecture. To alleviate some of this overhead, OSPF uses the concept of a **designated router (DR)**. Each broadcast segment has one DR, which is elected based on the router's priority (a number from 0 to 255, where higher numbers are preferred and 0 indicates that the router is incapable of becoming the DR). The router with the second-highest priority becomes the **backup designated router (BDR)**. Both of these routers establish adjacencies with all other OSPF-speaking routers on the subnet, but all other routers will establish only two

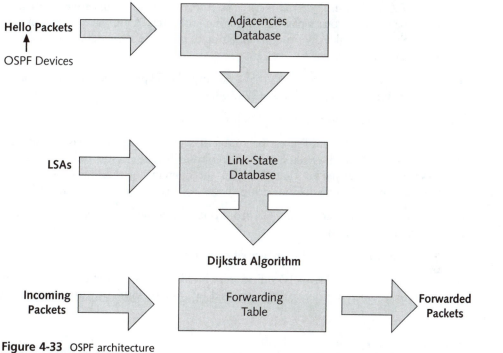

Figure 4-33 OSPF architecture
© Cengage Learning 2013

adjacencies: one to the DR and one to the BDR. The DR's responsibility is to inform all other routers of LSAs. The aptly named BDR's purpose is to allow service to be restored very quickly in the event of an outage affecting the DR.

All other routers multicast an LSA to the DR multicast address (224.0.0.6). This LSA represents the router and the costs associated with accessing the network.

There are six basic types of LSAs:

- *Type 1 (Router Links Advertisement)*—This advertisement is flooded within an area and contains information about the router's neighbors. All routers send this type of LSA.

- *Type 2 (Network Links Advertisement)*—This advertisement is generated by the DR on behalf of the LAN. It lists all the routers on the LAN. Only DRs send this type of LSA.

- *Type 3 (Network Summary Link Advertisement)*—This advertisement is generated by an ABR to define the networks that are reachable outside an area. ABRs send this type of LSA.

- *Type 4 (AS Boundary Router Summary Link Advertisement)*—This advertisement describes the cost of the path from the sending router to an AS boundary router. ABRs send this type of LSA.

- *Type 5 (AS External Link Advertisement)*—This advertisement is flooded to all the routers throughout an entire AS to describe the cost from the sending AS boundary router to destinations outside the AS. ASBRs send this type of LSA.

- *Type 7 (Not So Stubby Area Networks Advertisement)*—This advertisement is used to describe external routes passing through a stub area. A stub area does not accept Type 5 AS External Link Advertisements. Routers must use their default route to access networks outside their AS.

When routers advertise themselves, they transmit the Type 1 packets to the Shortest Path First (SPF) router's multicast address (224.0.0.5).

The DR transmits a Type 2 LSA on behalf of the network.

On each local network, OSPF uses the router IDs to establish one **master router**. All other OSPF routers are defined as **slave routers**. Periodically, the master router transmits a Database Description (DD) packet that describes the contents of the link-state database. Other routers send acknowledgments indicating successful receipt of the DD packets.

If the master does not receive an ACK from one of the slave routers, it sends a copy of the LSA directly to that SPF router.

Figure 4-34 shows the general sequence of communications used in OSPF.

Upon receipt of these LSAs, the OSPF routers build a link-state database or a picture of the entire network, which are networks connected by routers with costs associated for all links.

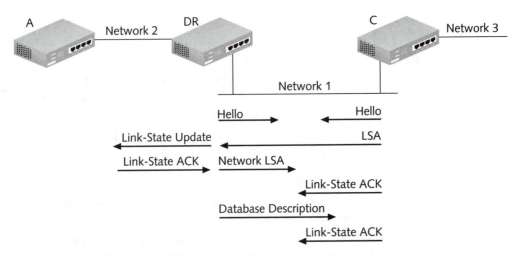

Figure 4-34 OSPF Hello, LSA, and link-state update process
© Cengage Learning 2013

This database cannot be used to route packets efficiently, however. The Dijkstra algorithm is run on the contents of the database to prioritize paths when there are multiple paths to a network. The result is the forwarding database. This table is referenced when the OSPF router wants to forward packets.

OSPF supports variable-length subnet masks and route summarization to reduce the number of routing entries maintained in the OSPF table.

Figure 4-35 shows the format of an OSPF packet header.

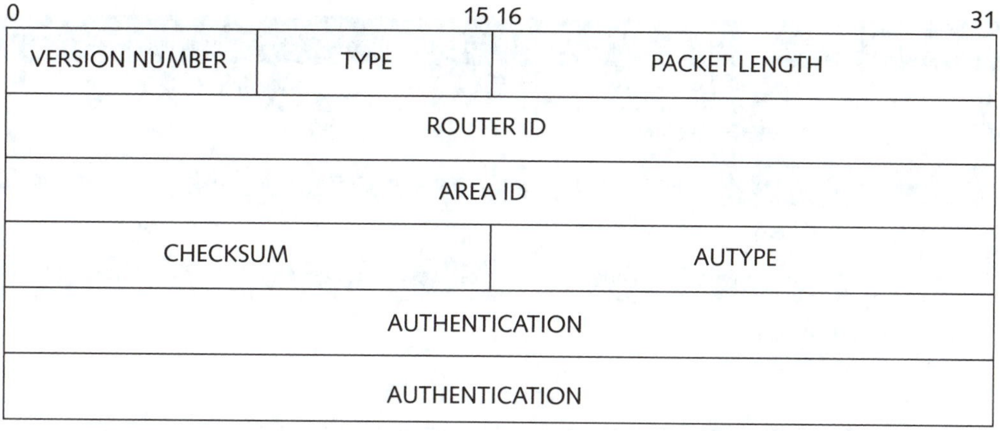

```
0                          15 16                              31
┌──────────────────┬──────────────┬──────────────────────────┐
│ VERSION NUMBER   │    TYPE      │      PACKET LENGTH        │
├──────────────────┴──────────────┴──────────────────────────┤
│                      ROUTER ID                              │
├─────────────────────────────────────────────────────────────┤
│                      AREA ID                                │
├────────────────────────────┬────────────────────────────────┤
│        CHECKSUM            │           AUTYPE               │
├────────────────────────────┴────────────────────────────────┤
│                   AUTHENTICATION                            │
├─────────────────────────────────────────────────────────────┤
│                   AUTHENTICATION                            │
└─────────────────────────────────────────────────────────────┘
```

Figure 4-35 Standard OSPF header structure
© Cengage Learning 2013

The following list details these header fields:

- *Version Number*—This 1-byte field contains the OSPF version number. The current widely implemented version of OSPF is version 2.

- *Type*—This 1-byte field defines the purpose of the OSPF packet. The Type field values are described in Table 4-18.

- *Packet Length*—This 2-byte field indicates the length of this OSPF packet. The Length field includes the OSPF header and any valid data that follows. It does not include any packet padding, if used.

- *Router ID*—This 4-byte field contains the ID of the transmitting router.

- *Area ID*—This 4-byte field contains the number of the area to which the transmitting router belongs. The field value can be expressed in decimal or dotted decimal notation. Often, as a way of managing large networks, designers assign the Area ID the same value as a network that resides inside it and display the Area ID in dotted decimal notation (e.g., Area 10.32.0.0). Other times, it is simpler to use nontechnical numbers to represent areas, such as a business unit, customer code, or zip code. These can be written as decimal numbers (e.g., Area 95129).

- *Checksum*—This 2-byte field contains the result of a checksum calculation run on the contents of the OSPF packet. The Authentication field is not included in this calculation.

- *AuType*—This 2-byte field defines the authentication type that is used in this packet. Refer to Appendix D of RFC 2328 for more details on authentication types.

- *Authentication*—The authentication process uses this 8-byte field.

After the OSPF header, the format of the packet varies, depending on the type of LSA packet.

Figure 4-36 depicts an OSPF Hello packet. As you can see, this router indicates that 10.3.99.99 is the DR.

Type Number	Type	Description
1	Hello packet	Used to locate neighboring routers
2	Database description	Used to transmit database summary information
3	Link-State request	Used to request link-state database information
4	Link-State update	Used to flood LSAs to other networks
5	Link-State acknowledgment	Used to acknowledge receipt of link-state information

Table 4-18 Type field values
© Cengage Learning 2013

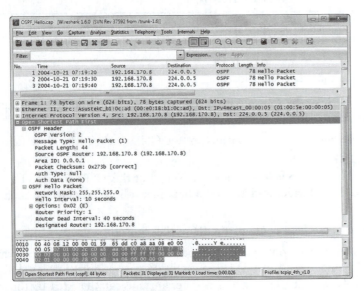

Figure 4-36 OSPF Hello packet
Source: Wireshark

Enhanced Interior Gateway Routing Protocol

Interior Gateway Routing Protocol (IGRP) was developed in the 1980s by Cisco Systems in an effort to provide a more efficient interior gateway protocol. IGRP was updated in the early 1990s; the updated version is called Enhanced Interior Gateway Routing Protocol (EIGRP).

EIGRP offers a strange mixture of routing technologies. It integrates the capabilities of link-state routing with a distance vector routing protocol. For more information on EIGRP, refer to *www.cisco.com*.

Border Gateway Protocol

Exterior gateway protocols (EGPs) are used to exchange routing information between separate autonomous systems. These protocols are also referred to as **interdomain routing protocols**. It is interesting that the name Exterior Gateway Protocol was assigned to the first implementation of this type of routing. EGP is defined in RFC 904. Currently, the Border Gateway Protocol (BGP) has replaced EGP routing.

BGP is a distance vector protocol and the replacement for EGP. The current version of BGP is version 4, which is defined in RFC 1771. BGP offers three types of routing operations:

- Inter-autonomous system routing
- Intra-autonomous system routing
- Pass-through autonomous system routing

Figure 4-37 illustrates how BGP is used for **inter-autonomous system routing**. In this configuration, BGP routers that reside in different ASs are configured as peers and exchange information about the internetwork topology of each AS.

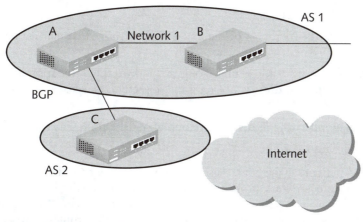

Figure 4-37 Typical BGP design
© Cengage Learning 2013

When BGP is configured for **intra-autonomous system routing**, the BGP routers are located within the same AS. **Pass-through autonomous system routing** enables BGP peer routers to exchange routing information across an AS that does not support BGP. See the section titled "Routing To and From the Internet" later in this chapter for additional information about BGP.

IPv6

The IPv6 routing protocols are largely extensions of their IPv4 counterparts. In general, IPv6 routing protocols can be organized into Interior Gateway Protocols (IGPs), Exterior Gateway Protocols (EGPs), distance vector based, link-state based, and so forth. The Autonomous system and the Autonomous System Number (ASN), a set of networks that are controlled by a single administrative entity, will still route both IPv4 and IPv6 traffic. The details of the similarities and differences between IPv4 and IPv6 routing protocols are presented in the following section.

RIPng for IPv6 RIPng for IPv6 is based on the protocols and algorithm currently being used by RIP IPv4; and RFC 2080, which is the proposed standard for RIPng for IPv6, represents a minimum change in the RIPv2 protocol. Distance vector has been used since the early days of ARPANET. RIPng was designed to work as an IGP within a medium-sized AS but not in larger, more complex environments.

Areas where RIPng and RIPv2 are the same include the use of a 15-hop radius, distance-vector, poison reverse, and split horizon. Features that have been specifically updated in RIPng are using IPv6 for transport and using IPv6 prefixes and an IPv6 next-hop address. RIPng also uses multicast group FF02::9 for all RIP updates, and these updates are sent on UDP port 521.

Routers implementing RIPng possess a routing table listing routes to destinations that can be reached via the RIPng system. Each entry in the routing table contains the following information at a minimum:

- The destination's IPv6 prefix
- A metric representing the total cost of sending a packet from the router to the destination address
- The IPv6 address of the next-hop router along the path to the destination address (assuming the destination address is not on a link directly connected to one of the router's interfaces)
- A route change flag indicating if any information about the route has recently changed
- Timers associated with the route

For directly connected networks, the router uses a simple hop count rather than the more complex metric indicating cost. Static routes can also be input manually by an administrator, which would likely be routes outside the scope of the routing system. Routers using the RIPng protocol would have to operate within an AS where all other routers participated in using RIPng protocol.

RIPng uses UDP as its upper-layer transport protocol using port 521. All router communications that include updates are transmitted and received using this port. RIPng uses the packet format shown in Figure 4-38.

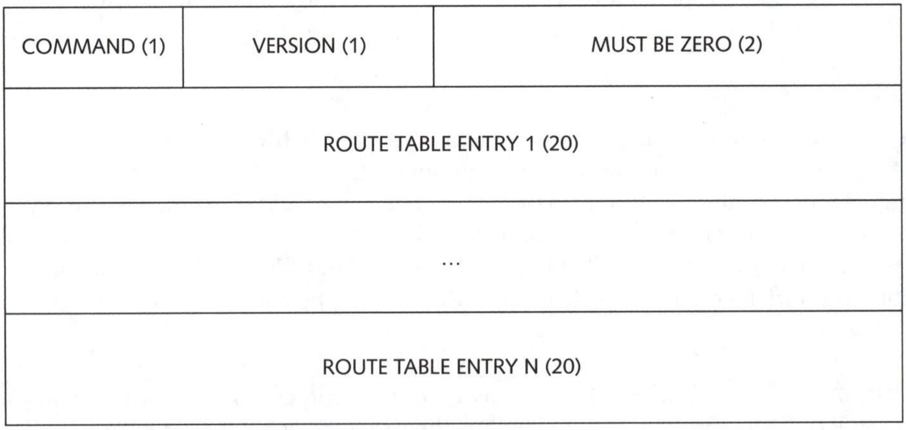

COMMAND (1)	VERSION (1)	MUST BE ZERO (2)
ROUTE TABLE ENTRY 1 (20)		
...		
ROUTE TABLE ENTRY N (20)		

Figure 4-38 RIPng packet format

The RIPng packet format has the following basic fields:

- *Command*—This is the type of message, with a request having the value 0x01 and a response having the value 0x02.
- *Version*—This is the version number of RIPng, and currently only the value 0x01 (version 1) exists.
- *Must be zero*—This field must always be set to zero.
- *RTC*—This is the routing table entry, which contains 20 bytes for each entry.

A Request message in an RIPng packet is sent to request that the responding router send all or part of its routing table. A Response message is sent by the responding router containing all or part of its routing table. A Response message can be sent unsolicited as well as in response to a Request message.

RIPng uses two types of RTEs:

- *Next Hop RTE*—This contains the IPv6 address of the next hop.
- *IPv6 Prefix RTE*—This describes the IPv6 destination address, the route tag, the prefix length, and the metric for the routing table. All the RTEs contained in the RIPng packet contain a destination prefix, the number of significant bits in the prefix, and the metric or cost to reach the destination. The destination prefix is 128 bits, and the IPv6 address prefix is stored as 16 octets in the network byte order.

The route tag field in the RTE is a value assigned to a specific route and used to differentiate internal RIPng routes from external RIPng routes, which may be imported from an EGP or another IGP.

OSPFv3 for IPv6   OSPF for IPv6 is specified by RFC 5340 (which obsoletes RFC 2740), which describes not only how OSPF has been updated for IPv6 but the modifications of OPSF from version 2 to version 3. For that reason, this protocol is commonly referred to as OSPFv3.

In a nutshell, OSPFv3 is based on OSPFv2, with various enhancements added, and it runs directly on IPv6 and distributes IPv6 prefixes. Specific IPv6 attributes added to OSPFv3 are 128-bit addresses, link-local addresses, and the ability to manage multiple addresses and instances per interface. OSPFv3 is now able to run over a link as opposed to a subnet and uses IPsec for authentication.

The significant differences between OSPFv2 for IPv4 and OSPFv3 for IPv6 include removing addressing semantics from OSPF packets and basic Link State Advertisements (LSAs), running OSPF on a per-link basis as opposed to a per-IP-subnet basis, generalizing the LSA flooding scope, and removing authentication from the protocol and instead allowing the IPv6 packet's Authentication Header and Encapsulating Security Payload (ESP) to manage authentication. With all of these enhancements, including the larger IPv6 addressing, OSPFv3 packets are nearly as compact as their OSPFv2 counterparts.

There have been a number of changes in the OSPF packet format for IPv6. As previously mentioned, OSPFv3 runs directly over IPv6; however, all addressing semantics have been eliminated from OSPF packet headers. This makes the OSPF packet dependent on the network protocol, and all addressing information is now stored in various types of LSAs.

Specifically, changes in the OSPFv3 packet header include:

- For Hello and Database Description packets, the Options field has been increased to 24 bits.

- Both the Authentication and AuType fields have been eliminated from the OSPF packet header.

- The Hello packet no longer contains any address information. Instead, it contains an Interface ID value that has been assigned to the originating router's interface to uniquely identify the interface. If the router becomes the link's Designated Router, the Interface ID will be used as the network-LSA's Link State ID.

- In the Options field, two new option bits have been added: the R-bit and the V6-bit. The R-bit can be used for multihomed nodes that want to participate in the routing protocol. In this case, the R-bit must be clear, allowing an OSPF speaker to participate in OSPF topology distribution without being required to forward transit traffic. The V6-bit is used to specialize the R-bit. If the V6-bit is clear, an OSPF speaker can participate in OSPF topology distribution without being required to forward IPv6 datagrams. If the R-bit is set but the V6-bit is clear, IPv6 datagrams will not be forwarded, but datagrams using another routing protocol can be forwarded.

An Instance ID has been added to the OSPF packet header that allows multiple OSPF protocol instances to run on a single link. Figure 4-39 shows the format of an OSPFv3 header format for reference.

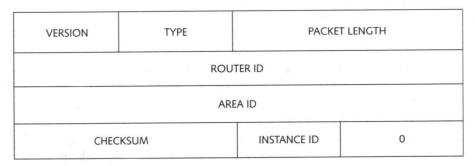

Figure 4-39 OSPFv3 header format
© Cengage Learning 2013

There have been a number of changes to the LSA format as well. The LSA header, router-LSAs, and network-LSAs no longer contain addressing semantics. The router-LSA and the network-LSA are now used to describe the routing domain topology in a network-protocol-independent way. There are now additional LSAs that distribute IPv6 address data and information required for the next-hop resolution.

Additional LSA formatting changes include:

- The Options field was eliminated from the LSA header and placed into the body of router-LSAs, network-LSAs, link-LSAs, and inter-area-router-LSAs. The Options field in those LSAs has been increased to 24 bits.

- The LSA Type field has been increased to 16 bits, with the upper 3 bits encoding flooding scope and handling unknown LSA types.

- The format for expressing addresses in LSAs is now [prefix, prefix length] rather than [address, mask].

- Router-LSAs and network-LSAs now contain no addressing information, making them network-protocol dependent.

- Router interface information is allowed to be spread across multiple router-LSAs; however, receivers must concatenate all the router-LSAs that originated at any specific router when calculating the SPF.

- The link-LSA is new and uses a link-local flooding scope, meaning the packets are never flooded beyond the link with which they are associated. They also provide the router's link-local address to other routers attached to the link, tell other routers on the link which IPv6 prefixes they can use to associate with the link, and let a router advertise a group of Options bits to associate with the network-LSA that will originate with the link.

- The network-LSA's Options field is either set to logical or is set to whatever options routers are advertising on the link.

OSPFv2 and OSPFv3 are not compatible with each other. The two protocols can be run simultaneously on the same link if they are needed to support the coexistence of IPv4 and IPv6 network infrastructures during the transfer from IPv4 to IPv6; however, each IP routing protocol domain is totally separate.

EIGRP for IPv6 EIGRP has changed little for IPv6. It's essentially the same protocol and still uses the best of distance vector and link-state. Multiprotocol EIGRP uses a protocol-dependent module for AppleTalk, IPX, IPv4, and IPv6 and is well known for ease of configuration and fast convergence. For more information on this protocol, go to *www.cisco.com.*

IS-IS for IPv6 IS-IS stands for Intermediate System-to-Intermediate System, which is an intradomain routing information exchange protocol. RFC 5308 is the most recent IETF document describing routing IPv6 using IS-IS. The IS-IS protocol was originally designed to route intradomain traffic for the Connectionless Network Service (CLNS). Its major features are largely the same as those for its IPv4 counterpart. Each IS device still transmits LSP packets, the neighborship process is the same as for IPv4, and it still has Cisco IOS software support for multitopology IS-IS (MT-IS-IS).

IS-IS is an extendible **intradomain routing protocol** (first specified in RFC 1195), in which each router within the routing domain sends a Link State Protocol (LSP) data unit containing information about the router. This information includes typed variable-length data called type-length-values (TLVs). For IPv6, IS-IS is extended with two new TLVs used to carry information about the router for IPv6 routing. IS-IS was originally designed to route in dual OSI/IPv4 environments or in "pure" OSI or IPv4 networks. This is also accomplished for IPv6 networks with the addition of the IPv6 Reachability TLV, the IPv6 Interface Address TLV, and the IPv6 protocol identifier.

The IPv6 Reachability TLV is directly related to the IPv4 IS-IS implementation. Figure 4-40 shows the format for this TLV.

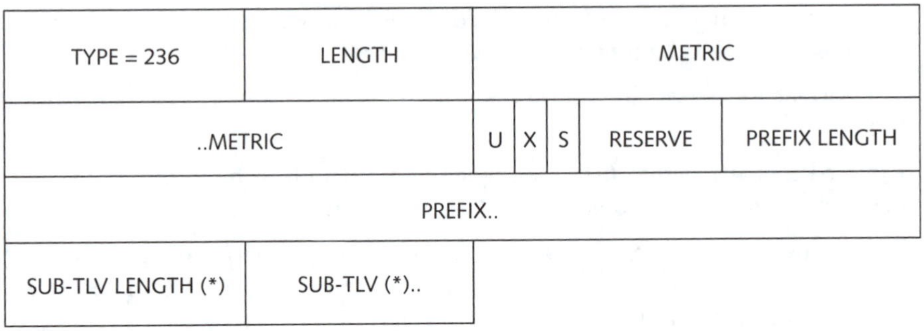

TYPE = 236	LENGTH	METRIC					
..METRIC		U	X	S	RESERVE	PREFIX LENGTH	
PREFIX..							
SUB-TLV LENGTH (*)	SUB-TLV (*)..						

Figure 4-40 IS-IS IPv6 Reachability TLV format
© Cengage Learning 2013

Table 4-19 defines the values for each field in this TLV.

IPvt Reachability TLV Field	Details
Type	236
Length	This is the length of the TLV.
Metric	This is the extended metric, with a range of values between 0 and 4261412864. If the metric value is greater than 4261412864, the IPv6 reachability information is ignored.
U Flag	This is the Up/Down bit and is used to prevent routing loops. This field is set to 1 when a route is advertised from a level-2 to a level-1 router to prevent the route from looping back.
X Flag	This is the route redistribution bit, and the value is set to 1 when the route is redistributed from another protocol.
S Flag	If this TLV contains no sub-TLVs, this field is set to 0; otherwise, it is set to 1, which means that the IPv6 prefix is followed by sub-TLV information.
Reserve	Reserved field
Prefix Length	IPv6 route prefix length
Prefix	IPv6 route prefix
Sub-TLV	Optional
Sub-TLV Length	Optional

Table 4-19 IS-IS IPv6 Reachability TLV fields
© Cengage Learning 2013

The IPv6 Reachability TLV describes a network's reachability using different factors, such as the specification of a routing prefix, metrics, a bit to indicate if the prefix is being advertised from a higher level, and a bit to indicate if the prefix is being distributed from another protocol.

The IP6 Interface Address TLV is analogous to the IS-IS IPv4 version. Figure 4-41 illustrates the format of this TLV.

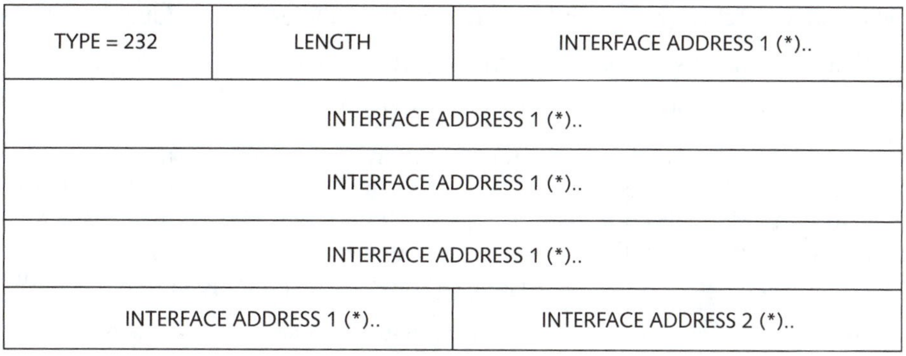

TYPE = 232	LENGTH	INTERFACE ADDRESS 1 (*)..
INTERFACE ADDRESS 1 (*)..		
INTERFACE ADDRESS 1 (*)..		
INTERFACE ADDRESS 1 (*)..		
INTERFACE ADDRESS 1 (*)..	INTERFACE ADDRESS 2 (*)..	

Figure 4-41 IS-IS IPv6 Interface Address TLV format
© Cengage Learning 2013

The type value is 232 for this TLV, and the Length field specifies the TLV length. The Interface Address fields identify the IPv6 address of the router interface. Hello PDUs for the TLV contain the link-local IPv6 address for the interface. LSPs for the TLV contain the non-link-local IPv6 address assigned to the IS, which is usually the IPv6 global unicat address for the interface. The asterisk displayed in the diagram for each Interface Address field indicates that it is an optional value.

The actual operation of IS-IS for IPv6 is the same as originally specified for IS-IS in RFC 1195, "Use of OSI IS-IS for Routing in TCP/IP and Dual Environments." For more information, go to *www.ietf.org*.

MP-BGP RFC 4760 (which obsoletes RFC 2858) defines the multiprotocol extensions that make BGP-4 available to other network layer protocols. MP-BGP allows MGP-4 to contain information about other protocols, such as MPLS, IPX, L3VPN, and of course, IPv6. The most recent standards paper for BGP-4 is RFC 4271, which is updated by RFC 6286, "Autonomous-System-Wide Unique BGP Identifier for BGP-4."

The only thing that allows this implementation of BGP-4 to run on IPv6 networks is the addition of extensions that enable this protocol to carry certain routing information, as already outlined. These extensions are backward compatible so that a router that supports these extensions can interoperate with a router that doesn't. In fact, there are only three information elements transported by BGP-4 that are specific to IPv4:

- The NEXT_HOP attribute when it's expressed as an IPv4 address
- AGGREGATOR, which contains an IPv4 address
- NLRI, which is expressed as IPv4 address prefixes

For BGP-4 to be able to be supported on IPv6 networks (or to support routing on other Network layer protocols), it needs to have only two additions:

- The ability to associate the IPv6 protocol with the next-hop information
- The ability to associate the IPv6 protocol with NLRI

For the sake of backward compatibility, two new attributes are introduced to BGP-4:

- Multiprotocol Reachable NLRI (MP_REACH_NLRI)
- Multiprotocol Unreachable NLRI (MP_UNREACH_NLRI)

MP_REACH_NLRI is used to carry the collection of reachable destinations with the next-hop information that is used for forwarding to these destinations. MP_UNREACH_NLRI is used to carry the collection of unreachable destinations. Both attributes are considered optional and nontransitive, thus a BGP speaker that doesn't support multiprotocol capacities can ignore the data carried by the attributes rather than pass it along to other BGP speakers.

The Multiprotocol Reachable NLRI attribute is used to advertise a feasible route to a peer device and to allow a router to advertise a Network Layer (in this case, IPv6) address of the next-hop router to the destinations listed in the NLRI field for the MP_NLRI attribute. The attribute has the following fields:

- *Address Family Identifier (AFI)*—This two-octet field, when used with the Subsequent Address Family Identifier (SAFI), identifies the Network layer protocols the address in the Next Hop field must belong to, the encoding for the address, and the semantics of the NLRI that follows.

- *Subsequent Address Family Identifier (SAFI)*—This one-octet field is used as described in the AFI description.

- *Length of Next Hop Network address*—This one-octet field contains the length of the Network Address of the Next Hop field.

- *Network Address of Next Hop*—This variable-length field contains the network address (again, IPv6 in this case) of the next-hop router to the destination address. The protocol associated with the address is identified by AFI and SAFI working in combination.

- *Reserved*—This one-octet field must be set to 0 and will be ignored by the destination node.

- *Network Layer Reachability Information (NLRI)*—This variable-length field lists NLRI or the feasible routes being advertised in this attribute. AFI and SAFI working together identify the semantics of NLRI.

The next-hop information contained in the MP_REACH_NLRI path attribute identifies the Network Layer address of the router that should be used as the next-hop router for destinations listed in the MP_NLRI attribute in the UPDATE Message.

The Multiprotocol Unreachable NLRI—MP_UNREACH_NLRI attribute is used to remove or withdraw multiple unfeasible routes from service and possesses the following fields:

- *Address Family Identifier (AFI)*—This was described earlier.

- *Subsequent Address Family Identifier (SAFI)*—This was described earlier.

- *Withdrawn Routes*—This is a variable-length field that lists NLRI for routers being withdrawn from service. AFI and SAFI working together identify the NLRI semantics carrried by the attribute. An UPDATE message containing the MP_UNREACH_NLRI attribute is not required to carry any other path attributes.

Beyond the information presented here, the extensions for IPv6 support the same features that BGP-4 possesses under IPv4.

Managing Routing on an In-House Internetwork

Simply configuring an IGP on an in-house network will likely establish connectivity between each subnet; however, there is much more to managing routing than simply establishing connectivity.

An administrator must consider policy first. IP routing protocols have a shortcoming in that they don't discriminate between users, types of traffic, and so on. They only know how to get to a network. Policy-based routing addresses this shortcoming.

Let's suppose you have a network with two paths between point A and point B. One path is a 1.544 Mbps T1 link that directly connects the two networks, and the other is a T3 (approximately 45 Mbps) that passes through three other networks between A and B. If you're running RIP, it will attempt to send all traffic over the T1 link because of the shorter hop count. If you are running OSPF, which has a metric based on bandwidth, it may prefer the much higher-speed T3. The point is that neither of these reflects what you really want to do. For instance, you might want to configure your network so a certain type of traffic, such as VoIP, prefers to use the first connection with a low latency, whereas other traffic, such as HTTP and FTP, is sent via a second link that is larger but has more latency. This configuration is called "policy-based routing."

Policies can be based on anything, from the type of protocol, as in the preceding example, to the source or destination address, where your policy could say, "I want all traffic from Host xyz to use Link 1 and other traffic to use Link 2."

Configuring policies makes your network more efficient, but it also makes it harder to troubleshoot.

Another item for consideration is that most IGPs allow load-balancing across multiple paths to the same network. These paths are typically managed on a "flow" basis as opposed to a per-packet load-balancing. This means that all traffic between Hosts A and X will take one link, whereas traffic between B and Y will take another. Per-packet load-balancing means the first packet takes Link 1, the second packet takes Link 2, the third packet takes Link 1, and so on. Per-packet load-balancing breaks a lot of protocols because packets often arrive out of sequence.

The routing services on your network also require routine maintenance, especially on large networks. You should monitor memory utilization (each type of route takes a certain amount of memory) to make sure that your routers are capable of handling any additions, and you should employ a management tool that sends alerts when routing problems occur. Also, most routing tables show the age of a route. In a link-state routing protocol, a young age is a sign of an unstable route. It changed recently, and you should find out why. For instance, if you observe a route in your table that has an age of 23 minutes, but you haven't made any changes to your network in six weeks, you could have a problem.

Finally, an administrator should maintain a map of the network, indicating the network addresses and routing protocols in use. This map should serve as the network design blueprint, assisting in spotting possible routing loops or configuration concerns.

Routing on and off a Wide Area Network

You must consider many factors when choosing a routing protocol for your enterprise. In this section, we discuss various network models and appropriate routing protocols.

Several Small Offices

If the network in question is relatively small—perhaps a dozen locations or less, where each has its own subnet plus an Internet connection—consider using no routing protocol. Whenever possible, the simplest solution is best. If a routing protocol is required, however, then RIP may be the simplest solution, as in the following circumstances:

- When connecting to a server that supports routing so the server can dynamically choose the best path

- When routers that do not support any other protocols are employed (common in the Internet Access Device [IAD] market for Small-Office/Home-Office [SOHO] firewall/NAT/broadband devices)

Hub and Spoke

Many corporations have a central office, with many satellites or branches. Usually, all branch offices connect directly to the hub where enterprise systems (such as ERP packages), a mainframe, and most servers reside. The distinguishing feature on this network is that the router in the hub needs to know how to get to many sites, but the routers at the branch offices only have a single connection out of the office (or perhaps only two, when a slow backup link is used to provide a failover option for a fast primary link).

If there is only one connection, or only one connection is used at any one time, what sense does it make to use precious bandwidth (not to mention router processor and memory resources) advertising all routes to each spoke? For routers on the ends of the spokes, all you need is a single default route that points to the hub. In this situation, an **On-Demand Routing (ODR)** protocol is a good choice.

If the hub-and-spoke environment uses frame relay, be wary of implementing any distance vector protocols. Frame relay and ATM use virtual circuits, so one physical interface can actually be logically partitioned into several logical interfaces. Commonly, all these terminate at a hub, so to get from Router A to Router C, you must go in and back out the same interface on Router B. So, when Router A advertises its networks to Router B, Router B receives and installs them in its routing table, but it won't send them back out the same interface, so Router C never receives the routing updates. Why? Split horizon means that it doesn't advertise to avoid what appears to be an apparent routing loop (but isn't).

Multiprotocol

Cisco's EIGRP protocol can support routing of both IPv4 and IPv6 traffic at the same time. This can conserve a lot of resources in some cases. Of course, it does require that you use only Cisco equipment.

Mobile Users

Some of the most difficult types of networks to implement and manage are those in which the users are always moving around. From laptop and PDA users to telecommuters and companies that frequently rearrange workspaces to accommodate changes in personnel, it is clear that trends are emerging in the new millennium that yesterday's TCP/IP wasn't built to handle.

Fortunately, the last few years witnessed a remarkable maturation of technologies to support a highly mobile workforce. This includes data-enabled cellular devices, 802.11 wireless technologies from a through g and beyond, broadband wireless technologies, and lots of dial-up and broadband for home-based connections. But how does IP work with this? Primarily, via DHCP. Unfortunately, there are many applications, such as voice and security, for which hosts need to maintain a stable IP address, regardless of where they are currently located or connected.

In turn, this raises an interesting question: How can you route packets if your host uses an IP address that isn't part of the local subnet? Although this is actually a workable scenario, it's by no means obvious. The following sections offer two possible solutions to the problem of "mismatched addresses."

Mobile IP

Mobile IP is defined by the IETF in RFCs 2003 through 2006 and RFC 3220 (which obsoletes RFC 2002). Mobile IP allows an IP host to travel anywhere there is a Mobile IP **agent** (a router configured with the protocol) and still maintain its home IP address. At a high level, it works like this: The host uses the ICMP Router Discovery protocol to determine whether it's on its home network or a foreign network. If it is on a foreign network, it registers with a Foreign Agent. The Foreign Agent then routes packets to the Home Agent. The Home Agent establishes a tunnel back to the Foreign Agent, which then delivers the packets to the host.

An application for this technology might be carrying an IP phone from one office to another on your company's network. This technology has many applications in the military because military units are highly mobile yet need to retain a static IP address for security reasons.

 Mobile IPv6 will be covered in Chapter 12.

Local Area Mobility

This technology is a Cisco proprietary feature that is similar to Mobile IP but operates by using the routing table. It is much simpler, with very little impact on the network. When a router is configured with Local Area Mobility (LAM), it watches for traffic on its LAN that does not match its own IP address. When it finds this traffic, it installs an ARP entry in its cache and a **host route** (a route entry with a 32-bit subnet mask) in its routing table. LAM is then redistributed into the primary routing protocol. Soon, all the other routers learn of the host route and forward the appropriate traffic. Hosts on the home subnet are still able to communicate with the estranged node because the router on the home subnet proxies ARP (RFC 826) for it and then routes the packets to the next hop listed in its routing table.

One of the keys to this technology's operation is the host route. This works because when routers look up an address in the routing table, they always take the longest match. For instance, if the routing table has an entry for 192.168.1.0/24 and the mobile host is 192.168.1.57, then a 192.168.1.57/32 route is propagated through the network, and each router has both routes in its table. If a router has a packet destined for 192.168.1.42, it doesn't match the 192.168.1.57/32 entry (obviously), but it does match the 192.168.1.0/24 entry. Conversely, when a packet arrives destined for 192.168.1.57, it matches both entries, but it prefers the longer one (/32) because it is more specific.

Routing to and from the Internet

As of this writing, BGPv4 is the exterior routing protocol in use on the Internet. Although BGP probably doesn't deserve its arcane reputation, it certainly requires a major hardware investment if it is to be deployed properly. Fortunately, only a few companies have networks complex enough to require BGP. As a general rule, only networks that connect to multiple Internet providers should use BGP. Even so, no discussion of routing would be complete without covering this essential networking protocol because it is part and parcel of the Internet backbone (as far as such an entity really exists; BGP actually enables numerous high-volume communications providers to act in concert to function like a single backbone, even though it's composed of numerous autonomous but cooperating systems).

Although BGP is a distance vector protocol, it tracks hops between pairs of autonomous systems instead of tracking hop counts for actual routers. As an example, let's say AS100 advertises a route to network 67.24.20.0/22 into AS200 and AS2000. When a route is advertised out of an AS, the BGP includes an AS number. So AS200 and AS2000 receive 67.24.20.0/22 100. AS200 then advertises it to AS300 and prepends its AS number so AS300 receives a route of 67.24.20.0/22 200 100. At the same time, AS2000 and AS300 advertise that route to AS3000 and prepend their AS numbers. So, AS3000 receives two routes:

- 67.24.20.0/22 2000 100
- 67.24.20.0/22 300 200 100

All other metrics being equal (and BGP has a lot of other metrics), AS3000 prefers the shorter AS path through AS2000 and AS100. It is important to note that even if the path through AS2000 has 20 router hops and the path through AS300 has three, AS3000 still prefers the shorter AS path because it has no way of knowing the actual distances involved. Remember that this protocol is largely administrative; in the real world, these decisions are often based on dollars and agreements between network service providers (NSPs) rather than the actual best physical path.

Even for corporate networks that use two or more ISPs, it is generally preferable to advertise only a default route from each ISP and configure the BGP and IGP redistribution to determine which default route it should take. It was common to redistribute an IGP into a BGP, but because many networks now use private RFC 1918 addresses, such as 10.0.0.0, and Network Address Translation, redistribution into BGP is pointless.

Securing Routers and Routing Behavior

The two aspects of routing services that must be secured are the routers and the routing protocols. Routers contain network addressing information and a doorway between networks. These doorways should be guarded closely to ensure no malicious packets cross them.

Securing routers is similar to securing most host systems. You should turn off unnecessary services, shut down unnecessary listening ports, configure strong access security to prevent tampering, and of course, secure physical access to the boxes. Assign strong passwords to routers and use an encrypted communications technology to access them. Too often in days of yore, network administrators used standard Telnet to access and configure their routers. Because Telnet sends unencrypted login names and passwords across the network, this makes such routers susceptible to eavesdropping by network analyzers. More modern techniques rely on establishing VPN connections for remote access, using SSL to establish a secure Web session, or SSH (Secure Telnet) to authenticate users and encrypt network traffic.

Securing routing protocols is somewhat more challenging. It's necessary to prevent prying eyes from seeing the information disclosed by the routing protocols because they contain information that makes internal systems much easier to attack. It's also important to prevent denial of service (DoS) attacks when unauthorized users forge fake routing packets and attempt to make your routers create loops or black holes, or worse, forward the traffic to the attacker, at which point it might be able to capture the transported data.

Unfortunately, securing routing protocols requires cooperation from the protocols themselves. For instance, OSPF, as seen in the packet headers, supports several forms of authentication, including MD5. Configuring this authentication means that a router will not form an adjacency with another router unless it knows the password. RIPv1, on the other hand, has no security, whereas RIPv2 has a password, but it is of little value because it is sent in plain text. Thus, it's important to consider where routing protocol traffic will be visible and select the routing protocol accordingly. Anything that will traverse the network or another public network (such as a cable company's local network segment) should use OSPF or another equally secure network routing protocol.

For more information on TCP/IP security issues and options, refer to Chapter 11 and Appendix B.

Troubleshooting IP Routing

Most IP routing problems deal with a lack of connectivity across routers. Numerous utilities and tools are available to test route connectivity. The following four tools are included with Windows Server 2008, Windows Vista, and Windows 7:

- *Traceroute/Tracert*—Used to trace an IP packet from a source computer to its destination
- *Ping*—Used to send ICMP Echo messages and test connectivity
- *Pathping*—Used to discover the path from a host to a destination

For more information on Traceroute/Tracert, Ping and Pathping, refer to Chapter 5. For command syntax, refer to Appendix C.

Chapter Summary

- Because they manage access to the networking medium, data link protocols also manage the transfer of datagrams across the network. Normally, this means negotiating a connection between two communications partners and transferring data between them. Such transfers are called point-to-point because they move from one interface to another on the same network segment or connection.

- When WAN protocols, such as PPP, come into play, it's possible to use the following to establish links that can carry IP and other datagrams from a sender to a receiver: analog phone lines; digital technologies, which include ISDN, DSL, or T-carrier connections; or switched technologies, such as X.25, frame relay, or ATM. At the Data Link layer, this means that protocols must deliver services, such as delimitation, bit-level integrity checks, addressing (for packet-switched connections), and protocol identification (for links that carry multiple types of protocols over a single connection).

- Ethernet II frames are the most common frame type on LANs, but a variety of other frame types exist that carry TCP/IP over Ethernet networks. Other Ethernet frame types that can carry TCP/IP include Ethernet 802.2 LLC frames.

- Understanding frame layouts is crucial for proper handling of their contents, regardless of the type of frame in use. Such frame types typically include start markers or delimiters (sometimes called preambles), destination and source MAC layer addresses, a Type field that identifies the protocol in the frame's payload, and the payload itself, which contains the actual data inside the frame. Most TCP/IP frames end with a trailer that stores a Frame Check Sequence field used to provide a bit-level integrity check for the frame's contents. By recalculating a special value called a cyclical redundancy check (CRC) and comparing it to the value stored in the FCS field, the NIC can accept the frame for further processing or silently discard it when a discrepancy occurs.

- At the lowest level of detail, it's important to understand the differences in field layouts and meanings when comparing various frame types for any particular network medium. You should understand the differences between the various types of Ethernet frames.

- Because hardware/MAC layer addresses are so important when identifying individual hosts on any TCP/IP network segment, it's imperative to understand how TCP/IP manages the translation between MAC layer addresses and numeric IP addresses. ForTCP/IP, the Address Resolution Protocol (ARP) provides this all-important role and helps create and manage the ARP cache. Because ARP can check the validity of the address assigned to any machine by performing an ARP request for a machine's own address, ARP also can detect IP address duplication when it occurs on a single network segment.

- Understanding ARP packet fields greatly helps to illuminate the address resolution process, particularly the use of the all-zeroes address in the Target Hardware Address field to indicate that a value is needed. ARP also includes information about hardware type, protocol type, length of hardware address (varies with the type of hardware), length of protocol address, and an Opcode field that identifies what kind of ARP or RARP packet is under scrutiny.

- A more advanced mechanism called proxy ARP permits a router to interconnect multiple network segments and make them behave like a single network segment. Because this means that hardware addresses are required from all segments that act like a single network segment, proxy ARP's job is to: forward ARP requests from one actual network segment to another, when required; enable hardware address resolution; and then deliver corresponding replies to their original senders. Also, when a router configured for proxy ARP receives an ARP broadcast, it responds with its own address. When it receives the subsequent data packet, it forwards this along, according to its routing tables.

- Network layer protocols make their way into the Data Link layer through a process known as data encapsulation. Building IP datagrams, therefore, depends on understanding how to map the contents of an IP packet into a datagram that carries an IP packet as its payload. This process requires obtaining a numeric IP address for the destination (and may involve initial access to name resolution services such as DNS) and then using ARP (or the ARP cache) to map the destination address to a hardware address. (It is possible to use the hardware address of a known router or a default gateway instead, which can then begin the routing process from the sending network to the receiving network.)

- When a frame must travel from one network segment to another, a process to resolve its route must occur. Local destinations can be reached with a single transfer at the Data Link layer, but remote destinations require forwarding and multiple hops to get from sender to receiver. Thus, it's important to understand the role of local routing tables that describe all known local routes on a network as well as the role of the default gateway that handles outbound traffic when exact routes are not known. Here, ICMP comes into play to help manage best routing behaviors and report when destinations may be unreachable.

- Other important characteristics of IP datagrams include: Time to Live (TTL) values, which prevent stale frames from persisting indefinitely on a network; fragmentation of incoming frames when the next link on a route uses a smaller MTU than the incoming link (reassembly of fragments always occurs when frames ultimately arrive at the destination host); and service delivery options to control packet and route priorities (seldom used, but worth understanding).

- IP traffic can be prioritized using Differentiated Services or Type of Service designations. Although Type of Service was defined in the original specification, current network prioritization implementations are based on Differentiated Services functions, which place a DSCP value in the IP header. This DSCP value is examined by routers along a path, and the traffic is forwarded according to the router configuration for that DSCP traffic type. In addition, Explicit Congestion Notification enables routers to notify each other of congested links before they must drop packets. These services streamline IP traffic to ensure minimal delay for high-priority traffic and a minimum of packet loss.

■ Routing protocols and routers provide a mechanism that can forward traffic from a sender's subnet to an intended receiver's subnet. Generally, routers depend on access to tables of information that describe known routes and default routers so traffic can be directed within an internetworked environment, or packets forwarded to other networks.

■ Routers depend on various routing protocols to manage the packet-forwarding process. Interior routing protocols are designed for use within autonomous routing domains, such as those that fall under the purview and control of a single company or organization. Exterior routing protocols provide a means whereby routers belonging to multiple companies or organizations can safely and securely forward data and manage routing information among the parties involved in a common connection.

■ Distance vector routing protocols such as RIP represent the oldest and simplest type of routing protocols, in which the number of router transitions (called hops) provides a crude metric of routing cost, and where no routing loops should occur as part of the routing topology. Link-state routing protocols, such as OSPF, provide more sophisticated routing metrics and controls, and they not only can deal with multiple routes between a sender and receiver but can use more powerful route metrics to balance loads across such links, or failover from less expensive to more expensive routes, as needed.

■ The OSPF protocol supports much more sophisticated routing structures that break up a network into routing areas to help optimize routing tables and behavior. In addition, OSPF recognizes special categories of routing areas, such as a backbone area (where all individual areas interconnect) and autonomous systems, which represent individual routing regions that fall under specific administrative and management control. In such cases, area border routers may connect separate routing areas to the backbone or to other routing areas.

■ Routing characteristics, which determine how long it takes route information (and changes) to stabilize within a group of routers that share information, help to determine what kinds of routing protocols to use in specific applications. One important characteristic is convergence (how long it takes routing protocols to calculate optimal routes following updates), including techniques such as split horizon, poison reverse, and Time to Live settings. Other important characteristics include information update mechanisms (whether broadcast or multicast), Router Advertisements, and how routing domains may be logically subdivided to help manage complexity and reduce router traffic.

■ Managing routing on a complex network means understanding how and when to use exterior and interior routing protocols as well as how to establish the right kinds of connections between multiple routing domains. Private WAN links, Internet connections, and Mobile IP users all require special handling where routing is concerned to make sure that systems and services behave as required. It's especially important to understand how and when interior routing protocols, such as OSPF, must interoperate with exterior routing protocols, such as BGP.

■ Because router tables define the topology and behavior of IP networks, it's essential to manage router security and updates as safely as possible. For those reasons, using strong passwords and secure links to access and update routers and their configurations is absolutely essential.

- IPv4 and IPv6 differ in a number of areas. IPv4 uses ARP to solicit link-layer addresses, whereas IPv6 uses NDP. IPv4 depends on routers to fragment packets to transfer links with different MTUs, but for IPv6, only the source node sets the size of packets using NDP Discovery. IPv6 uses multicasts rather than broadcasts to send a single message to multiple nodes. IPv6 nodes listen for only those multicasts that are sent to their group or device type.

- IPv6 Routing Mechanisms perform the same function as their IPv4 counterparts, to ensure that packets successfully traverse different routing domains to arrive at their destination. Mechanisms include how IPv6 routing decisions are made and Weak or Strong Host behavior. IPv6 routers determine which route in its routing table to use to make a forwarding decision by comparing bits in the prefix address for routing table entries to the same bits in the destination address. Network nodes can be set to Strong or Weak Host behavior, depending on traffic speed and security concerns.

- IPv6 Multicast Listener Discovery specifies multicast behaviors as well as MLD packets and message types. MLD is the original protocol designed for IPv6, and MLDv2 updates it for IGMPv3. MLD is used by routers to discover multicast listeners on directly connected links. Routers can both send queries and be multicast listeners. Members of a multicast group can be located anywhere, depending on the scope of their group. MLD uses three message types: Query messages, Report messages, and Done messages.

- IPv6 routing protocols are RIPng, OSPFv3, EIGRP for IPv6, IS-IS for IPv6, and MP-BGP. EIGRP and BGP implementations have changed little for IPv6. Multiprotocol EIGRP added protocol-dependent module support for IPv6 but continues to operate as it has done under IPv4. BGP added multiprotocol extensions to allow it to operate on IPv6 networks. Specific extensions are NEXT HOP, AGGREGATOR, and NLRI, but other than the extensions, BGP works the same way it did under IPv4. RIPng is based on RIP for IPv4, but RIPng now uses IPv6 for transport, uses IPv6 prefixes and an IPv6 next-hop address. It also uses a multicast group for all RIP updates sent using UDP. OSPFv3 for IPv6 differs from its IPv4 counterpart in that it has removed addressing semantics from its packets and LSAs. It also runs on a per-link basis rather than per-subnet, generalizes its flooding scope, and removes authentication form the protocol.

4

Key Terms

Address Resolution Protocol (ARP)   This Network layer protocol translates numeric IP addresses into the equivalent MAC layer addresses necessary to transfer frames from one machine to another on the same cable segment or subnet.

adjacencies database   A database of the local network segment and its attached routers. Designated routers share the adjacencies database view across link-state networks.

agent   In general, a piece of software that performs services on behalf of another process or user. In the case of Mobile IP, the agent in question is a special piece of router software that tunnels from a remote subnet to a user's home subnet to set up connections for a specific static IP address.

area border router (ABR) A router used to connect separate areas.

areas Groups of contiguous networks. Areas are used in link-state routing to provide route table summarization on larger networks.

ARP cache A temporary table in memory that consists of recent ARP entries. Entries in the ARP cache are discarded after two minutes on Windows 2000, Windows XP, and later systems.

autonomous system (AS) A group of routers that is under a single administrative authority.

autonomous system border router (ASBR) A router that connects an independent routing area, or AS, to another AS or the Internet.

backbone area A required area to which all other routers should be attached directly or through a tunnel.

backup designated router (BDR) The router with the second-highest priority on a broadcast segment of a link-state network. The BDR allows service to be restored quickly in the event of an outage affecting the DR. *See also* designated router.

bit-level integrity check A special mathematical calculation performed on the payload of a packet (a datagram at the Data Link layer) before the datagram is transmitted, whose value may be stored in a datagram's trailer. The calculation is performed again on the receiving end and compared to the transmitted value. If the two values agree, the reception is assumed to be error-free; if the two values disagree, the datagram is usually silently discarded (no error message).

black hole A point on the network where packets are silently discarded.

Border Gateway Protocol (BGP) An interdomain routing protocol that replaces the Exterior Gateway Protocol (EGP) and is defined in RFC 1163. BGP exchanges reachability information with other BGP routers. RFC 4760 defines the multiprotocol extensions that let BGP operate on IPv6 networks.

circuit switching A method of communications wherein a temporary or permanent connection between a sender and a receiver, called a circuit, is created within a communications carrier's switching systems. Because temporary circuits come and go constantly, circuits are switched around all the time—hence, the term.

converge The process of ensuring that all routers on a network have up-to-date information about available networks and their costs.

counting to infinity A network routing problem caused by a routing loop. Packets circulate continuously until they expire.

cyclical redundancy check (CRC) A special 16- or 32-bit equation performed on the contents of a packet. The result of the CRC equation is placed in the Frame Check Sequence field at the end of a frame. A CRC is performed by NICs on all outgoing and incoming packets.

data encapsulation The technique whereby higher-level protocol data is enclosed within the payload of a lower-layer protocol unit and labeled with a header (and possibly a trailer) so the protocol data unit may be safely transmitted from a sender to a receiver.

data link address The address of the local machine based on the hardware address. The data link address also is referred to as the MAC address.

default gateway The name given to the router IP address through which a machine attached to a local network must pass outbound traffic to reach beyond the local network, thereby making that address the "gateway" to the world of IP addresses outside the local subnet. Also, a gateway of last resort, where packets are sent when no host route entry or network entry exists in the local host's route table.

delimitation   The use of special marker bit strings or characters, called delimiters, that distinguish the payload of a PDU from its header and trailer and that also may mark the beginning (and possibly the end) of a PDU itself, as transmitted.

delimiter   A special bit string or character that marks some boundary in a PDU, be it at the beginning or end of a PDU, or at the boundary between the header and the payload, or the payload and the trailer.

designated router (DR)   The router with the highest priority on a segment of a link-state network. A DR advertises LSAs to all other routers on the segment.

diameter   The number of hops that a network routing protocol can span; RIP has a network diameter of 15; most other routing protocols (such as OSPF and BGP) have an unlimited network diameter.

Differentiated Services (Diffserv)   A method for providing different levels of service to network traffic based on a marker placed in the IP header.

Dijkstra algorithm   An algorithm used to compute the best route on a link-state network.

distance vector   The source point or location for determining distance to another network.

distance vector routing protocol   A routing protocol that uses information about the distances between networks rather than the amount of time it takes for traffic to make its way from the source network to the destination network. RIP is a distance vector routing protocol.

E1   A standard European digital communications service used to carry 30 64-Kbps digital voice or data channels, along with two 64-Kbps control channels, for a total bandwidth of 2.048 Mbps of service. E1 is widely used outside North America as a replacement for T1 service.

E3   A standard European digital communications service used to carry 16 E1 channels for a total bandwidth of 34.368 Mbps of service. E3 is widely used outside North America as a replacement for T3 service.

Ethernet II frame type   The de facto standard frame type for TCP/IP communications.

Explicit Congestion Notification (ECN)   A method for notifying next-hop devices that a link is experiencing congestion and packet loss is imminent at the current transmission rates.

exterior gateway protocols (EGPs)   Routing protocols used to exchange routing information between separate autonomous systems.

external route entry   A route entry received from a different area.

forwarding table   The actual table referenced to make forwarding decisions on a link-state network.

fragment   In the context of IP networking, a piece of a larger set of data that must be divided to cross a network that supports a smaller MTU than the original packet size.

Fragment Offset field   The field that defines where a fragment should be placed when the entire data set is reassembled.

Frame Check Sequence (FCS)   The type of bit-level integrity check used in the trailer of PPP datagrams; the specific algorithm for the FCS is documented in RFC 1661. The FCS field contains a CRC value. All Ethernet and token ring frames have an FCS field.

hardware address The address of the NIC. This address is typically used as the data link address.

Hello process A process that link-state routers use to discover neighbor routers.

High-Level Data Link Control (HDLC) A synchronous communication protocol.

host route A routing table entry with a 32-bit subnet mask designed to reach a specific network host.

host route entry A route table entry that matches all 4 bytes of the desired destination. Network route table entries only match the network bits of the desired address.

IEEE 802.3 The IEEE-defined standard for a carrier sense, multiple access method with collision detection.

informational/supervisory format A connection-oriented format that can be used by LLC packets.

inter-autonomous system routing A term used in BGP that refers to the ability to provide routing between autonomous systems.

interdomain routing protocols Routing protocols used to exchange information between separate autonomous systems.

interior gateway protocols (IGPs) Routing protocols used within an autonomous system.

internal route entry A route entry learned from within the same area as the computing device.

Internet Protocol Control Protocol (IPCP) A special TCP/IP Network Control Protocol used to establish and manage IP links at the Network layer.

intra-autonomous system routing A term used in BGP that refers to the ability to provide routing within an autonomous system.

intradomain routing protocol A routing protocol used to exchange routing information within an autonomous system.

Ipconfig A command-line utility used to identify the local host's data link address and IP address.

lifetime value The time that a packet can remain on the network. Routers discard packets when their lifetimes expire.

Link Control Protocol (LCP) A special connection negotiation protocol that PPP uses to establish point-to-point links between peers for ongoing communications.

link-state A type of routing protocol that uses and shares information only about adjacent neighbors and that uses transit time to assess link costs rather than hop counts or routing distances.

link-state advertisement (LSA) A packet that includes information about a router, its neighbors, and the attached network.

link-state routing protocol A routing protocol based on a common link-state picture of the network topology. Link-state routers can identify the best path based on bandwidth, delay, or other path characteristics associated with one or more links available to them. OSPF is a link-state routing protocol.

Logical Link Control (LLC) The data link specification for protocol identification as defined by the IEEE 802.2 specification. The LLC layer resides directly above the Media Access Control layer.

master router In link-state routing, a router that distributes its view of the link-state database to slave routers.

name resolution process The process of obtaining an IP address based on a symbolic name. DNS is a name resolution process.

neighbor routers On a link-state network, neighbor routers are connected to the same network segment.

Network Control Protocols (NCPs) A family of TCP/IP Network layer protocols used to establish and manage protocol links made at the Network layer (TCP/IP's Internet layer).

Network Layer Reachability Information (NLRI) The information about available networks and the routes whereby they may be reached, which routing protocols collect, manage, and distribute to the routers or other devices that use such routing protocols.

network route entry A route table entry that provides a next-hop router for a specific network.

next-hop router The local router that is used to route a packet to the next network along its path.

On-Demand Routing (ODR) A low-overhead feature that provides IP routing for sites on a hub-and-spoke network. Each router maintains and updates entries in its routing table only for hosts whose data passes through the router, thus reducing storage requirements and bandwidth.

Open Shortest Path First (OSPF) A sophisticated Layer 3 or TCP/IP Internet layer routing protocol that uses link-state information to construct routing topologies for local internetworks and provides load-balancing capabilities.

packet priority A TOS priority that defines the order in which packets should be processed through a router queue.

pad Bytes placed at the end of the Ethernet Data field to meet the minimum field length requirement of 46 bytes. These bytes have no meaning and are discarded by the incoming data link driver when the packet is processed.

pass-through autonomous system routing A term used in BGP routing, this routing technique is used to share BGP routing information across a non-BGP network.

plain text password A password that is transferred across the cable in plain ASCII text.

point-to-point A type of Data Link layer connection in which a link is established between exactly two communications partners, so the link extends from one partner (the sender) to the other (the receiver).

Point-to-Point Protocol over Ethernet (PPPoE) A protocol used by many Internet service providers (including telecommunications companies and cable TV operators) to authenticate and manage broadband subscribers.

poison reverse A process used to make a router undesirable for a specific routing path. This process is one of the methods used to eliminate routing loops.

preamble The initial sequence of values that precedes all Ethernet packets. Placed on the front of the frame by the outgoing NIC and removed by the incoming NIC, the preamble is used as a timing mechanism that enables receiving IP hosts to properly recognize and interpret bits as 1s or 0s.

protocol identification (PID) A datagram service necessitated when any single protocol carries multiple protocols across a single connection (as PPP can do at the Data Link layer);

PIDs permit individual datagram payloads to be identified by the type of protocol they contain.

protocol identification field   A field that is included in most headers to identify the upcoming protocol. The PID of Ethernet headers is the Type field. The PID of IP headers is the Protocol field.

proxy ARP   The process of replying to ARP requests for IP hosts on another network. A proxy ARP network configuration effectively hides subnetting from the individual IP hosts.

Registry setting   A configuration that controls the way in which Windows devices operate. There are numerous settings that define how Windows computers operate in a TCP/IP environment.

Reverse Address Resolution Protocol (RARP)   A Layer 2 or TCP/IP Network Access protocol that translates numeric IP addresses into MAC layer addresses (usually to verify that the identity claimed by a sender matches its real identity). This protocol was superseded by DHCP.

route priority   A TOS priority that defines the network to route packets. The router must support and track multiple network types to make the appropriate forwarding decision based on the TOS defined in the IP header.

route resolution process   The process that a host undergoes to determine whether a desired destination is local or remote and, if remote, which next-hop router to use.

Routing Information Protocol (RIP)   A simple, vector-based TCP/IP networking protocol used to determine a single pathway between a sender and a receiver on a local internetwork.

routing loops   A network configuration that enables packets to circle the network. Split horizon and poison reverse are used to resolve routing loops on distance vector networks. OSPF networks automatically resolve loops by defining best paths through an internetwork.

routing protocol   A Layer 3 protocol designed to permit routers to exchange information about networks that are reachable, the routes by which they may be reached, and the costs associated with such routes.

routing tables   Local host tables maintained in memory. The routing tables are referenced before forwarding packets to remote destinations in order to find the most appropriate next-hop router for the packet.

Service Access Point (SAP)   A protocol identification field that is defined in the 802.2 LLC header that follows the MAC header.

slave router   On an OSPF network, this type of router receives and acknowledges link-state database summary packets from a master router.

split horizon   A rule used to eliminate the counting-to-infinity problem. The split horizon rule states that information cannot be sent back the same direction from which it was received.

Synchronous Data Link Control (SDLC)   A synchronous communication protocol.

Synchronous Optical Network (SONET)   A family of fiber-optic digital transmission services that offers data rates from 51.84 Mbps (OC-1) to 38.88 Gbps (OC-768).

T1   A digital signaling link whose name stands for trunk level 1; it is used as a standard for digital signaling in North America. T1 links offer aggregate bandwidth of 1.544 Mbps and can support up to 24 voice-grade digital channels of 64 Kbps each, or they may be split between voice and data.

T3   A digital signaling link whose name stands for trunk level 3; it is used as a standard for digital signaling in North America. T3 links offer aggregate bandwidth of 28T1s or 44.736 Mbps. T3 runs on coax or fiber-optic cable, or via microwave transmission, and it is becoming a standard link for small- and mid-scale ISPs.

T-carrier   The generic telephony term for trunk carrier connections that offer digital services to communications customers directly from the communications carrier itself (usually a local or long-distance phone or communications company). It is possible, however, to run trunk lines all the way from one location to another, but such lines will always transit to the carrier's premises at one or more points in such a connection.

unnumbered format   A format of 802.2 LLC packet that is connectionless.

Review Questions

1. An IPv6 node uses NDP to discover the link-layer address of the next-hop router by sending a Router Solicitation message as what kind of network message?

   a. anycast

   b. broadcast

   c. multicast

   d. unicast

2. Where is routing information stored in most routers and other similar devices?

   a. routing database

   b. routing table

   c. routing directory

   d. route lookup cache

3. At the command prompt on a Windows 7 computer, what command is used to show the routing table for the IPv6 interface?

   a. `netsh interface ipv6 show all routes`

   b. `netsh interface ipv6 show route`

   c. `netsh interface ipv6 show routes`

   d. `netsh interface ipv6 show routing table`

4. If an IPv6 router has multiple routes that lead to the correct destination address for a packet, how does it choose a route for the packet?

   a. It chooses one of the correct routes in its routing table, using a round-robin algorithm.

   b. It chooses the route with the largest link-MTU value.

   c. It chooses the route with the largest prefix length.

   d. It chooses the route with the route that matches the least number of high-order bits in the destination address.

5. Configuring hosts to be weak or strong can be performed on both IPv4 and IPv6 network nodes. True or False?

6. Upon receiving a packet sent by a source node, what is the first task an IPv6 router performs?

   a. checking the router's destination cache

   b. checking the router's routing table

   c. reducing the value of the Hop Limit field by 1

   d. running error checks on the packet header fields

7. When an IPv6 host receives a packet that is addressed to it, if the packet does not use UDP or TCP as its upper-layer protocol, how does the host respond?

   a. The destination host will check the destination port for the packet, and if it does not match a protocol running on the node, it will drop the packet and send the ICMPv6 error message "Protocol Corrupted or Missing."

   b. The destination host will check the packet's Next Header field, and if no matching application is found, it will send the ICMPv6 error message "Parameter Problem - No Protocol Found" and then drop the packet.

   c. The destination host will drop the packet and send to the sender the ICMPv6 error message "Protocol Corrupted or Missing."

   d. The destination host will pass the data to the appropriate protocol running on the host.

8. Which of the following routing protocols is a link-state protocol?

   a. OSPF

   b. IGRP

   c. BGP

   d. RIP

9. Of the following, which routing table types can an IPv6 routing table store? (Choose all that apply.)

   a. default route

   b. directly attached routes

   c. next-hop route

   d. remote routes

10. Which of the following definitions best explains split horizon?

    a. All routes that originate elsewhere are set to infinite distance.

    b. It prevents a router from advertising a network to the interface that provides the original network information.

    c. It avoids routing loops.

    d. It creates routing loops.

11. Which of the following definitions best describes a network that is in a converged state?

    a. Routers are waiting for table updates to finish propagating.

    b. All routers know current available networks and their associated costs.

    c. All routers use static routing tables.

    d. All routers use link-state routing protocols.

12. Which version of RIP in an IPv4 implementation uses multicast packets for updates rather than broadcasts?

    a. RIPv1

    b. RIPv2

    c. RIPv3

    d. OSPF

13. What gives BGP the ability to run on IPv6 networks?

    a. the addition of IPv6 address support for the Next Hop attribute

    b. the addition of IPX

    c. the addition of MPLS

    d. the addition of multiprotocol extensions

14. Which phenomenon causes a black hole to occur?

    a. One or more routers become unavailable.

    b. Link states change without notification.

    c. ICMP is disabled on a router.

    d. ICMP is enabled on a router.

15. What allows the IS-IS routing protocol to operate on IPv6 networks?

    a. the addition of two new type-length-values (TLVs) as extensions

    b. the addition of the ability to route intradomain traffic for the connectionless network service

    c. the neighborship process extended from the original IPv4 implementation

    d. the use of LSP packets

16. Both the IPv4 and IPv6 implementations of the OSPF routing protocol can manage multiple addresses and instances per interface. True or False?

17. Which of the following router designations helps make OSPF more efficient than RIP when it comes to managing local routing behavior?

    a. default gateway setting

    b. designated router setting

    c. Router Links Advertisement

    d. Network Links Advertisement

18. What is an update for the IPv6 routing protocol RIPng that did not exist in the IPv4 RIP implementation?

   a. use of a 15 hop radius

   b. use of distance-vector

   c. use of multicast for sending updates

   d. use of poison reverse

19. Multicast Listener Discovery, which is used by IPv6 routers to discover multicast listeners, is embedded in what protocol?

   a. ICMPv6

   b. IGMPv6

   c. IPv6

   d. UDP

20. When used over an asynchronous connection like an analog telephone link, PPP supports which of the following WAN encapsulation services? (Choose all that apply.)

   a. addressing

   b. bit-level integrity check

   c. delimitation

   d. protocol identification

21. For which of the following link types must PPP provide addressing as part of its WAN encapsulation services? (Choose all that apply.)

   a. analog telephone link

   b. T-carrier link

   c. X.25 connection

   d. ATM connection

22. What is the first step that an IP host performs when it receives an Ethernet II frame?

   a. Check the hardware address to see if it should be read further.

   b. Check the validity of the FCS value.

   c. Strip off the FCS field and hand the packet to the Data Link layer.

   d. Examine the payload to determine the actual destination address.

23. Which of the following statements best describes the role of the ARP cache?

    a. a special area of memory on routers where already-resolved IP hardware address translations are stored

    b. a special area of memory on IP hosts where already-resolved IP hardware address translations are stored

    c. a special file where already-resolved IP hardware addresses are stored as a computer is powered down, then read as it is powered back up

    d. a special file where translations from symbolic names to IP addresses are stored

24. When looking for a destination address for a datagram ultimately bound for a remote network, an IP host must check which structure to obtain the necessary information?

    a. ARP cache

    b. routing tables

    c. a source route request

    d. proxy ARP to get the hardware address for the destination machine

25. What happens when an IP host sends a reply to an IP host that requested its hardware address?

    a. Nothing happens, other than sending the reply.

    b. The sending host responds with an ARP request to the original requesting host.

    c. The sending host uses the contents of its reply to the requesting host to add an entry for the requesting host to its ARP cache.

    d. The sending host uses the contents of its reply to update the entry for the requesting host in its ARP cache.

Hands-On Projects

The following Hands-On Projects assume that you are working in a Windows Vista or Windows 7 environment, that you have installed the Wireshark software, that you have obtained the trace (data) files necessary to work through many of the Hands-On Projects in this book, and that the trace (data) files have been copied to writable media, such as a hard disk, on the computer on which you are working. If you do not have the files you need, see the "Read This Before You Begin" section at the beginning of the book or consult with your instructor.

Hands-On Project 4-1: Manage Your Local ARP Cache

Time Required: 10 minutes

Objective: Learn how to manage ARP entries on your computer.

Description: This project shows you how to view your local ARP cache.

1. Click the **Start** button, type **cmd** in the Start menu search box, right-click **cmd.exe** in the resulting list, and then select **Run as administrator**. A command prompt window opens.

2. At the command prompt, type **arp -a** and press **Enter** to view your ARP cache. Write any entries that appear in your ARP cache.

3. Type **arp -d** at the prompt and press **Enter** to delete your computer's ARP cache.

4. Type **arp -a** and press **Enter** to view your ARP cache again. Write the new entry that appears in your ARP cache. The cache should be empty.

5. Type **ping** *ip_address* where *ip_address* is a host on your local network, and then press **Enter**.

6. After the ping command has executed, type **arp -a** and press **Enter** to view your ARP cache again and write down the new entries. The ARP cache should only include entries for the host you pinged after clearing your ARP cache, as shown in Figure 4-42.

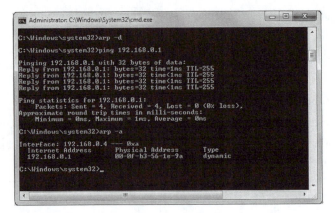

Figure 4-42 ARP cache on Windows 7
Source: Microsoft

Hands-On Project 4-2: Read Your Local IPv4 Route Table

Time Required: 10 minutes

Objective: Learn how to view the routing table for your computer's IPv4 interface.

Description: This project shows you how to use the netsh command to display the routing table for an IPv4 interface.

1. Click **Start,** type **cmd** in the Start menu search box, and then click **cmd.exe** in the resulting list. A command prompt window opens.

2. Type **netsh** and press **Enter**.

3. At the netsh prompt, type **interface ipv4** and press **Enter**.

4. At the prompt, type **show route** and press **Enter** to see the computer's IPv4 routing table, as shown in Figure 4-43.

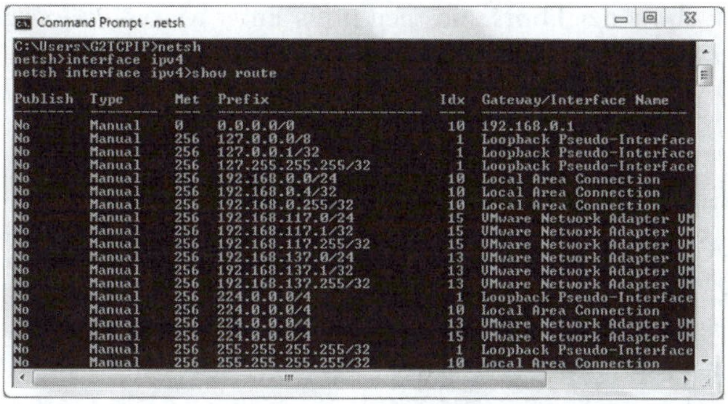

Figure 4-43 IPv4 routing table on Windows 7
Source: Microsoft

5. Type **exit** and press **Enter,** and then type **exit** and press **Enter** again to close the command prompt window.

Hands-On Project 4-3: Read Your Local IPv6 Route Table and Neighbors Cache

Time Required: 10 minutes

Objective: Learn how to view the routing table for your computer's IPv6 interface.

Description: The netsh command is used to display the routing table for the IPv6 interface on a Windows 7 computer.

1. Click **Start,** type **cmd** in the Start menu search box, and then click **cmd.exe** in the resulting list. A command prompt window opens.

2. Type **netsh interface ipv6 show route** and then press **Enter** to see the IPv6 routing table for your computer, as shown in Figure 4-44.

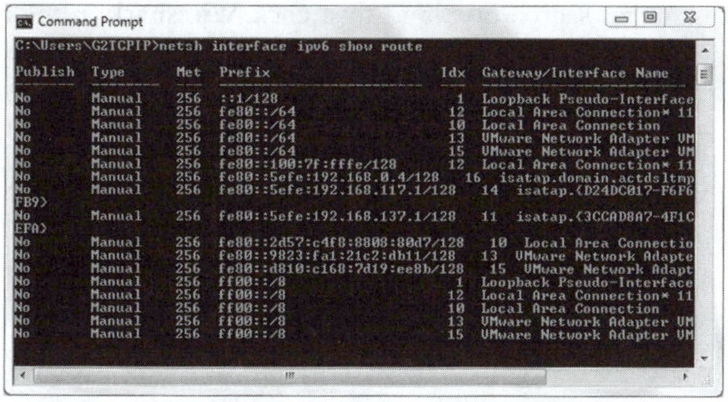

Figure 4-44 IPv6 routing table on Windows 7
Source: Microsoft

3. Type **netsh interface ipv6 show neighbors** and then press **Enter** to see IPv6 neighbor cache on the computer, as shown in Figure 4-45.

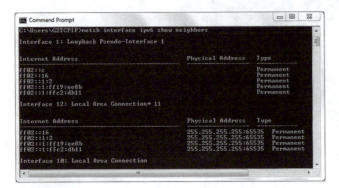

Figure 4-45 IPv6 neighbor cache on Windows 7
Source: Microsoft

4. Type **exit** and press **Enter** to close the command prompt.

Hands-On Project 4-4: Viewing IPv4 and IPv6 Routing Protocols in Wireshark

Time Required: 15 minutes

Objective: Learn how to recognize the differences among several different routing protocols and their packets as their data is displayed in Wireshark.

Description: In this project, you use Wireshark to view live captured or sample capture files of different routing protocols for both IPv4 and IPv6.

To view RIPv1 routing protocol data:

1. Click **Start**, point to **All Programs**, and then click **Wireshark**. Alternately, click **Start**, type **Wireshark** in the Start menu search box, and then click **Wireshark** in the resulting list.

2. In the main pane under Files, click **Sample Captures**.

3. Scroll down to Routing protocols and download the following files to a directory on your computer (alternately, these files may be in a local directory specified by your instructor):

   • eigrp-for-ipv6-auth.pcap

   • ospf.cap

   • RIP_v1

4. Navigate to the directory where you saved the capture files.

5. Double-click **RIP_v1**. (If the file does not open, you may have to change the file name to add the .cap extension.)

6. Click the first entry in the top pane to select it, which should be a RIPv1 request packet.

7. In the next pane below, select **Routing Information Protocol** and expand it and any subitems below, as shown in Figure 4-46.

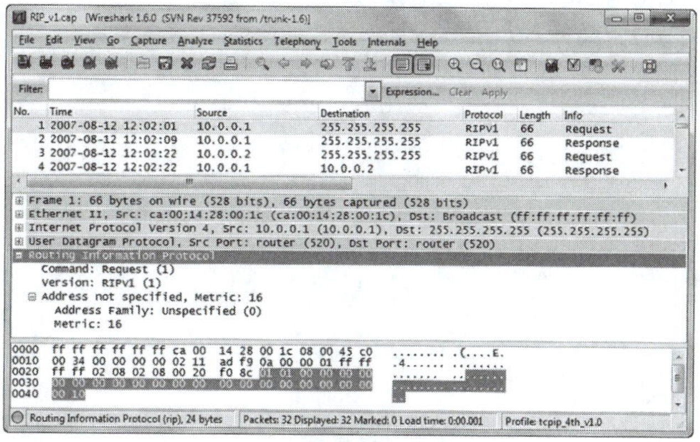

Figure 4-46 RIPv1 capture file output
Source: Wireshark

8. In the top pane, select a RIPv1 Response packet and view the change in the RIP output in the pane below.

9. Close Wireshark.

To view OSPF routing protocol hello packet data:

1. Navigate to the folder where you downloaded the routing capture files.

2. Double-click **ospf** to open it in Wireshark.

3. Select **Open Shortest Path First** and expand it.

4. Expand **OSPF Header, OSPF Hello Packet** and any subitems, as shown in Figure 4-47. (You may have to scroll down to view all the contents.)

5. Close Wireshark.

To view EIGRP routing protocol for IPv6 data:

1. Navigate to the folder where you downloaded the routing capture files.

2. Double-click **eigrp-for-ipv6-auth** to open it in Wireshark.

3. In the top pane, use the scroll bar to scroll to the bottom of the window, and then select an EIGRP Hello packet entry.

4. In the second pane, just below the top pane, select and expand **Cisco EIGRP**.

5. Expand all subitems, as shown in Figure 4-48. (You may have to scroll down to view all the contents.)

6. Close Wireshark.

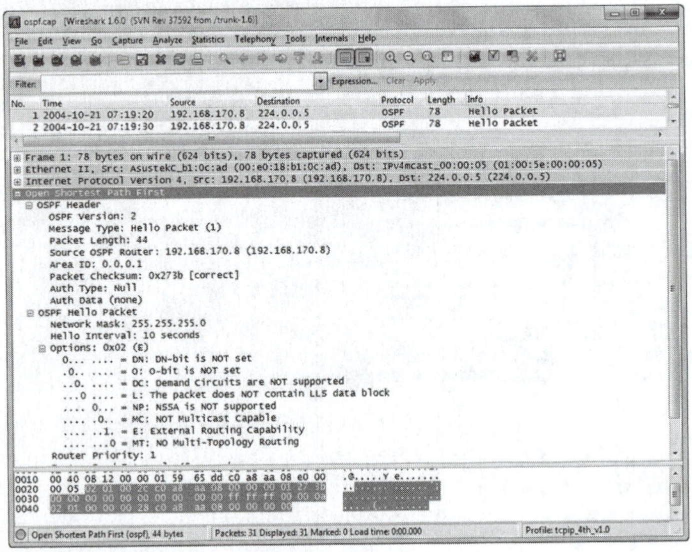

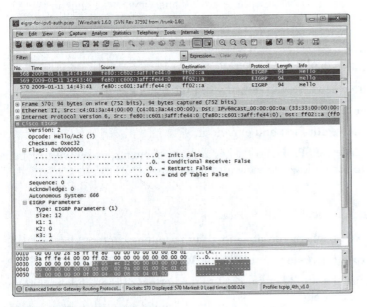

Figure 4-47 OSPF Hello Packet data
Source: Wireshark

Figure 4-48 EIGRP for IPv6 data
Source: Wireshark

Case Projects

Case Project 4-1: Examining a Trace File

You work in the headquarters of a large pharmaceutical company based in Atlanta, Georgia. A technician in your Portland, Oregon, office sent you a trace file for review. The technician states that she captured the communications from an IP host that cannot connect to anyone on the other side of the local router. The problematic IP host can communicate with all the local systems without any problems. What process might be problematic here? What should you look for in the trace file?

Case Project 4-2: Determining the Distance Traveled by an IPv6 Packet Based on the Hop Limit Value

You're interested in determining how far IPv6 packets traveled before reaching your company's gateway to the Internet. What field should you look at to determine the distance from the source? Can you make a definitive statement about the distance traveled based on this field?

Case Project 4-3: QoS on a TCP/IP Network

Explain the purpose of QoS on a TCP/IP network. Define the basic purpose of IP precedence, Type of Service, Diffserv, and Explicit Congestion Notification functionality. Give examples of how you might use QoS characteristics on your network.

Internet Control Message Protocol

After reading this chapter and completing the exercises, you will be able to:

- Explain the basics of the Internet Control Message Protocol (ICMP) and the roles it plays on networks
- Describe the specifications listed in RFC 792, which define the original ICMPv4 protocol, including its header format and the different types and formats of ICMPv4 messages
- Provide a basic overview of the ICMPv6 protocol, covering its header format and the different types and formats of ICMPv6 messages, including how error messages and informational message types are organized
- List the details of the different ICMPv6 error messages, including those that existed in ICMPv4 and have been upgraded as well as message types that were newly created for ICMPv6
- Describe the intricacies of all the different ICMPv6 informational messages, including those that existed under ICMPv4 and have been upgraded and those that have been newly created for use in ICMPv6
- Understand the general differences between ICMPv4 and ICMPv6
- Explain how Path MTU Discovery operates between IPv4 nodes, including the involvement of default packet MTUs, packet fragmentation, and the effect of a packet being marked for no fragmentation relative to ICMPv4 messaging
- Describe how Path MTU Discovery has been changed for IPv6 and the associated changes to ICMPv6 messages for this technology
- Describe the various processes for testing and troubleshooting with ICMP, including the use of network utilities such as Ping, Traceroute, and Pathping as well as routing sequences and security issues
- Explain network protocol analyzer data and use the data to decode ICMPv4 and ICMPv6 packets in order to understand their versions, types, sequencing, and other information

Although IP is certainly the best-known Network layer protocol in the TCP/IP family, it's by no means the only such protocol. This chapter covers **Internet Control Message Protocol (ICMP)**, an important error-handling and information-handling protocol that is an integral part of the TCP/IP suite of protocols, which also operates at the Network layer. This chapter starts with an overview of the various roles ICMP can play, next describes its capabilities, packet layouts, and field formats, and then explains how ICMP handles report errors, delivery errors, path discovery, Path Maximum Transmission Unit (MTU) Discovery, and other routing-related functions.

ICMP Basics

ICMP is an important Network layer protocol because it provides information about network connectivity and routing behavior that datagram-based, unreliable protocols, (such as IP or UDP) are unable to convey.

When it comes to diagnosing and repairing problems with TCP/IP connectivity, you must be able to obtain information about how packets move from their sources to their destinations on an IP internetwork. For any network node to communicate and exchange data with another network node, some way to forward packets from sender to receiver must exist. This concept is called **reachability**.

Normally, usable forwarding paths are discovered in the contents of local IP routing tables that reside on the various intermediary devices between sender and receiver.

Using specific kinds of messages, ICMP provides a way to return information to senders, about routes traveled (including reachability information) as packets get forwarded; it also provides a possible way to return error information to a sender when routing or reachability problems prevent delivery of an IP datagram. This capability nicely complements IP's datagram delivery services because ICMP provides what IP itself cannot: routing, reachability, and control information as well as delivery error reports.

ICMP's ability to report errors, congestion, or other network conditions does nothing to enhance IP's best-effort delivery approach. In fact, ICMP messages themselves are nothing more than specially formatted IP datagrams, with an 8-byte header, subject to the same conditions as other IP packets in the general network traffic. Although ICMP can report on errors or **network congestion** (which occurs when network traffic starts to exceed handling capacities), it's up to the IP host that receives incoming ICMP messages to act on the content of those messages. What ICMP has to say, and what hosts may choose to do about it, supplies the bulk of this chapter's content.

ICMP messages thus serve to keep hosts apprised of networking conditions and problems; they also equip hosts to use the best paths around the network. When a datagram cannot reach its intended recipient, an ICMP message alerts the sender. When a gateway (or router) can direct the host to a better (usually, this means shorter) network route, it sends a redirect message. As you work your way through this chapter, the types of ICMP messages will tell you more about how ICMP reports on network health and transmission problems.

Roles That ICMP Plays on IP Networks

As already mentioned, ICMP's job is to provide various information about IP routing behavior, reachability, routes between specific pairs of hosts, delivery errors, and so forth. ICMP provides information that is quite useful for network monitoring and troubleshooting. Table 5-1 lists ICMP message types, with a brief explanation of their uses and meanings.

Message Type	Use or Significance
Echo/Echo Reply	Supports functionality for reachability utilities like Ping and Tracert; essential when installing, configuring, and troubleshooting IP networks.
Destination Unreachable	Documents when routing or delivery errors prevent IP datagrams from reaching their destinations; code values are extremely important. Also used for Path MTU Discovery between pairs of hosts.
Source Quench	Permits a gateway to instruct a sending host to adjust (lower) its sending rate to ease congestion problems.
Redirect	Permits a gateway (router) on a nonoptimal route between sender and receiver to redirect traffic to a more optimal path.
Router Advertisement	Permits hosts to request information about local routers and permits routers to advertise their existence on an IP network.
Time Exceeded	Indicates that an IP datagram's TTL, or a fragmented IP datagram's reassembly timer, has expired; can indicate either a too-short TTL or the presence of a routing loop on a network (which must be removed).
Parameter Problem	Indicates that some error occurred while processing the IP header of an incoming datagram, causing that datagram to be discarded; a catchall for ambiguous or miscellaneous errors, it indicates that further investigation is required.

Table 5-1 **ICMP message types and their uses or significance**
© Cengage Learning 2013

The ICMP message types lay a foundation upon which serious TCP/IP network and router troubleshooting can rest. These ICMP message types and their applications are explored in greater depth throughout the rest of this chapter.

ICMPv4

ICMP is a core protocol in the IP suite, originally specified in April 1981 by RFC 777, which was obsoleted the following September by RFC 792. Computer operating systems use ICMPv4 primarily to send certain error messages to other networked nodes. Although ICMPv4 may not be known to average computer users, its most common manifestation—the `ping` command—is widely used to test the connection between one computer and another, even by those who may otherwise know very little about networking.

Although it can be considered a transport protocol, ICMPv4 differs from TCP and UDP in that it carries no payload and is not used by computer applications. Instead, ICMPv4 supports a series of network testing and error messages. In addition to the Ping utility, it supports Tracert/Traceroute, which traces an IP packet from a source computer to its destination, counting the number of hops made in transit and the time required for each hop. ICMP message types include: Echo Request, Echo Reply, Destination Unreachable, Router Advertisement, and many others.

Overview of RFC 792

Request For Comment (RFC) 792, titled "Internet Control Message Protocol," defines the basics for all valid ICMP messages and defines what kinds of information and services ICMP can deliver. This RFC also makes some key points about IP and ICMP. To help you better understand the relationship between these two Network layer TCP/IP protocols, we summarize them here:

- ICMP provides a mechanism for gateways (routers) or destination hosts to communicate with source hosts.

- ICMP messages take the form of specially formatted IP datagrams, with specific associated message types and codes. This chapter explains the types and codes associated with ICMP messages.

- ICMP is a required element in some implementations of TCP/IP, most notably those TCP/IP protocol stacks judged suitable for sale to the U.S. government, and ICMP is usually present to provide an essential part of IP's support fabric.

- ICMP reports errors only about processing of non-ICMP IP datagrams. To prevent an endless sequence of error messages, ICMP conveys no messages about itself and provides information only about the first fragment in any sequence of fragmented datagrams.

Although RFC 792 was published in 1981, it defines the primary functions of—and blueprints for—ICMP messages to this day. The many sections in this chapter that explain ICMP messages come directly from this document.

ICMPv4 Header

The value 1 in the IP header Protocol field denotes that an ICMP header follows the IP header (see Figure 5-1). The ICMP header consists of two portions—a constant portion and a variable one. In this section, we cover each portion of this header structure and the functions of the various ICMP packet types, with examples of ICMP query and error messages found on the network.

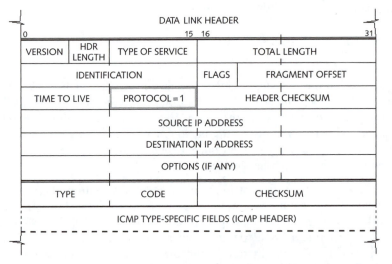

Figure 5-1 Protocol field value "1" indicating that the ICMP header follows the IP header
© Cengage Learning 2013

Constant ICMP Fields ICMP packets contain only three required fields after the IP header: Type, Code, and Checksum. In some ICMP packets, however, additional fields provide information or details about the message or message-specific information. For example, an ICMP Redirect packet must include the address of the gateway for the packet redirect. Upon receipt of this packet, a host should add a dynamic route entry to its routing tables and begin using the new routing information immediately. Figure 5-1 shows the constant fields of the ICMP header.

Refer to RFCs 792, 1191, and 1256 for further details on the ICMP frame structures listed in this section.

Type Field The Type field identifies types of ICMP messages that can be sent on the network. Table 5-2 lists the assigned ICMP type numbers that correspond to the various types of ICMP messages. The list is based on IANA documentation. For the most current version of this list, visit *http://www.iana.org/assignments/icmp-parameters/ icmp-parameters.xml.*

Type Number	Name	Reference
0	Echo Reply	RFC 792
1	Unassigned	
2	Unassigned	
3	Destination Unreachable	RFC 792
4	Source Quench	RFC 792
5	Redirect	RFC 792
6	Alternate Host Address	JBP
7	Unassigned	
8	Echo	RFC 792
9	Router Advertisement	RFC 1256
10	Router Solicitation	RFC 1256
11	Time Exceeded	RFC 792
12	Parameter Problem	RFC 792
13	Timestamp	RFC 792
14	Timestamp Reply	RFC 792
15	Information Request	RFC 792

Table 5-2 ICMPv4 types, names, and references (*continues*)

Type Number	Name	Reference
16	Information Reply	RFC 792
17	Address Mask Request	RFC 950
18	Address Mask Reply	RFC 950
19	Reserved (for Security)	Solo
20–29	Reserved (for Robustness Experiment)	ZSu
30	Traceroute	RFC 1393
31	Datagram Conversion Error	RFC 1475
32	Mobile Host Redirect	David Johnson
33	IPv6 Where-Are-You	Bill Simpson
34	IPv6 I-Am-Here	Bill Simpson
35	Mobile Registration Request	Bill Simpson
36	Mobile Registration Reply	Bill Simpson
37	Domain Name Request	Bill Simpson
38	Domain Name Reply	Bill Simpson
39	SKIP	Markson
40	Photuris	RFC 2521
41	ICMP messages utilized by experimental mobility protocol	RFC 4065
42–255	Reserved	JBP

Table 5-2 ICMPv4 types, names, and references (*continued*)
© Cengage Learning 2013

Not all these types are currently in use. Some are in development, and others are used only for experimental purposes.

 The initials "JBP" identify Jon B. Postel, who was a major player in the development of the Internet Protocol suite. With a long beard and an intensely brilliant mind, Postel helped shape the communications system of the Internet and millions of private networks until his untimely death in October 1998. You can learn more about this luminary at *www.postel.org/remembrances*.

Code Field Many of these ICMP packet types have a Code field. Table 5-3 lists the codes and definitions that can be used with ICMP Destination Unreachable packets.

Code	Definition
0	Net Unreachable
1	Host Unreachable
2	Protocol Unreachable
3	Unreachable
4	Needed and Don't Fragment was Set
5	Source Route Failed
6	Destination Network Unknown
7	Destination Host Unknown
8	Source Host Isolated
9	Communication with Destination Network Is Administratively Prohibited
10	Communication with Destination Host Is Administratively Prohibited
11	Destination Network Unreachable for Type of Service
12	Destination Host Unreachable for Type of Service
13	Communication Administratively Prohibited
14	Host Precedence Violation
15	Precedence Cutoff in Effect

Table 5-3 **Type 3: Destination Unreachable codes**
© Cengage Learning 2013

Table 5-4 lists the codes and definitions that can be used with ICMP Redirect packets.

Code	Definition
0	Redirect Datagram for the Network (or subnet)
1	Redirect Datagram for the Host
2	Redirect Datagram for the Type of Service and Network
3	Redirect Datagram for the Type of Service and Host

Table 5-4 **Type 5: Redirect codes**
© Cengage Learning 2013

Table 5-5 lists the codes and definitions that can be used with ICMP Alternate Host Address packets.

Code	Definition
0	Alternate Address for Host

Table 5-5 **Type 6: Alternate Host Address code**
© Cengage Learning 2013

Table 5-6 lists the codes and definitions that can be used with ICMP Time Exceeded packets.

Code	Definition
0	Time to Live Exceeded in Transit
1	Fragment Reassembly Time Exceeded

Table 5-6 **Type 11: Time Exceeded codes**
© Cengage Learning 2013

Table 5-7 lists the codes and definitions that can be used with ICMP Parameter Problem packets.

Code	Definition
0	Pointer Indicates the Error
1	Missing a Required Option
2	Bad Length

Table 5-7 **Type 12: Parameter Problem codes**
© Cengage Learning 2013

Table 5-8 lists the codes and definitions that can be used with ICMP Photuris packets.

Code	Definition
0	Bad SPI
1	Authentication Failed
2	Decompression Failed
3	Decryption Failed
4	Need Authentication
5	Need Authorization

Table 5-8 **Type 40: Photuris codes**
© Cengage Learning 2013

Checksum Field The Checksum field provides error detection for the ICMP header only. The fields that follow the Checksum field vary, depending on the particular ICMP message that is sent. In the next section, we examine the most common ICMP packet types, the interpretation of their codes, and their complete ICMP structures.

Types of ICMPv4 Messages

There are many ICMP message types, but they fall into two general categories: error messages and informational messages. All ICMPv4 messages use a common message format and are sent and received using a simple set of protocol rules. Otherwise, the details of ICMP messages differ depending on the specific message type.

ICMPv4 error messages are used by routers and network nodes to inform any source node that a datagram it transmitted has met with a problem on the network affecting its delivery status. These ICMPv4 message types usually require some sort of response from the sending node. Certainly, if a message is sent to a source node stating that its packets were undeliverable, the sender will want to discover what the problem is and seek a solution. What follows are brief descriptions of the individual message types.

Destination Unreachable The Destination Unreachable message is returned to the source node when a packet that was sent could not be delivered to the destination address. There are a few reasons why a packet might fail to be delivered. Some packets contain erroneous parameters, such as invalid IP addresses; sometimes, a router is unable to reach the network where the destination is located. Because IPv4 is an unreliable protocol, it does not guarantee that sent packets always reach their destinations, although a "best effort" will be made. If a packet doesn't arrive at its destination, the Destination Unreachable message is returned to the sending node along with a portion of the datagram that could not be delivered. The sender can then use this information to decide how to correct the problem.

Source Quench This message is used to tell the source node to reduce the rate of speed at which it sends packets to the destination node. Usually, network nodes can buffer packets "on the fly" when traffic is coming in too fast to be processed; but the size of a device's buffer is limited, and when the buffer is full and the receiving node cannot process traffic fast enough to reduce buffer volume, it sends a Source Quench message to the sending node. Usually, the source node responds by slowing down the transmission rate until it stops receiving Source Quench messages. Source Quench messages are limited because they only contain the information that the destination is congested; they don't tell the source node what it should do about the problem. Also, there is no message sent to the source telling it when the destination's buffer is no longer full and is, therefore, able to receive data at an increased rate. The type of response to the message is left entirely up to the source node.

The higher-level TCP protocol has a much more effective flow-control mechanism that is used to regulate the transmission of packets between two network devices.

Time Exceeded This message is sent in two circumstances. The first is when a packet's Time to Live (TTL) field is decremented to zero by routers on the network before the packet reaches its destination. The second is when some of the fragments of a message do not reach the destination node by the time the node's reassembly timer reaches zero.

The first situation occurs when a packet is caught in a routing loop where convergence has not occured between routers over which route to take to a destination. The packet goes between a group of routers repeatedly until the packet's TTL value drops to zero. Besides a routing loop, a packet's TTL can be decremented to zero if the TTL value is set too low to reach a destination. Thus, if the original TTL value is set to 7 when it actually takes 14 hops to reach the destination, this message will be sent. In this circumstance, a Time Exceeded message is sent to the source node by the router that receives the packet whose hop count reaches a zero value.

In addition, the destination node sends a Time Exceeded message when a source node's message has to be broken into fragments. If the first fragment arrives at the destination node, a timer is set alloting only a specific amount of time that the node will wait for all the remaining fragments to be received so it can reassemble that message. If one or more fragments are not yet received when the timer reaches zero, all fragments are discarded and the Time Exceeded message is sent to the source node by the destination node.

See Chapter 4 for more information about routing loops.

Redirect A first-hop router sends a **Redirect** message to a source network node when it receives a packet that could be managed more efficiently by another first-hop router. For instance, let's say you have two routers for a local network. Router A is the default gateway to the Internet. Router B is the gateway to another local network in the same company. If a computer has been configured to use Router A as its default first-hop router and it sends a packet to a computer on the company's other local network, Router A recognizes that Router B could handle the packet more efficiently. Router A forwards the packet to Router B and sends a Redirect message to the sending node telling it to use Router B as the first-hop router to the other local network. Technically, this isn't an error message, but for ICMPv4, it's classified as such. (For ICMPv6, it's reclassified as an informational message.) Redirect messages are used to provide a limited amount of routing information to a node; routers do not send Redirect messages to other routers.

Parameter Problem This is a "generic" error message that can be sent back to the source node by any device on the network when that device detects an error in any header field in an IP packet. This message type contains a special pointer field used to tell the source node the type of problem that occured in the packet's header. When a device on a network discovers a packet with a bad parameter in one of its header fields, the node will drop the packet and send the Parameter Problem message back to the source node.

Numerous ICMPv4 messages provide information that have nothing to do with error correction. Although there are nine current messages of this type, most occur in pairs. Thus, most of them, such as Echo Request and Echo Reply, are best presented two at a time.

The original ICMP standard included two more message types: Information Request and Information Reply. They are not part of the ICMPv4 implementation because their functions are currently managed by other protocols, such as BOOTP, DHCP, and RARP.

Echo Request and Echo Reply These message types are used for connectivity testing between network nodes. Network Node A sends an Echo Request message to Node B, which, upon receipt of the request, sends an Echo Reply message confirming receipt. The most common implementation of these messages is with the use of the Ping utility. In the event that an Echo Request is unable to reach the destination node, an error message is sent from the device that receives an Echo message but is unable to forward it. One such error message is the Destination Unreachable message mentioned earlier in this section.

Technically, an Echo Request message is referred to as "Echo (Request)" or just "Echo" for ICMPv4.

Timestamp Request and Timestamp Reply Routers use this pair of messages on a network to synchronize their system clocks for date and time. Each device on a network has a system clock by which it knows the date and time; however; no two devices have exactly matching times. This can sometimes cause problems when devices work together. Any device that wants to synchronize its system time with another device sends a Timestamp Request message to the second device, and that device responds with a Timestamp Reply. This method of time synchronization doesn't work very well on large networks, particularly the Internet, because of the time it takes for the ICMPv4 messages to travel back and forth. For larger networks and modern network infrastructures, devices use the Network Time Protocol (NTP) to establish the same exact time on their system clocks.

Technically, a Timestamp Request is referred to as "Timestamp (Request)."

Router Advertisement and Router Solicitation This pair of messages allows a network node not manually configured with the address of a first-hop router to ask for and receive information about routers on the local network. A network node, if it does not know of any routers on the network when it first powers up, sends an ICMPv4 Router Solicitation message using the multicast address for "all routers": 224.0.0.2. This allows only routers to receive the request and avoids needlessly contacting all devices on the network. Routers respond to the node with information about themselves. Periodically, routers send out Router Advertisement messages using the multicast "all devices" 224.0.0.1 address. Nodes that need router information or need their router information updated receive the advertisement and update their information about local routers. Even though a node can learn about local routers through advertisements, using solicitation messages avoids computers having to wait and listen after they've powered up to discover routers' addresses. Use of this router discovery method is considered optional. It is typical for computers to receive the IP address for the default router dynamically using DHCP. It is important to remember that Router Advertisement messages are not used between routers to exchange routing information, nor do they impart complex routing tables to network nodes. Nodes contain only the information they need to communicate with computers on the local network and to know how to contact routers to communicate with nodes on other networks. Routers use routing protocols such as RIP and OSPF to exchange routes with other routers.

See Chapter 4 for more information about routers, routing tables, and routing protocols.

Address Mask Request and Address Mask Reply This pair of messages is used to supply subnet mask information about other computers on the network to the node sending the Address Mask Request. Although a node may know the IP address of another node on the network, it will not know how to interpret the IP address unless it knows what subnet mask applies to the address. After all, an address of 192.168.0.3 is "subdivided" differently, depending on whether it uses a subnet mask of 255.255.255.0. or a subnet mask of 255.255.255.240. The node sending the message will usually send it to a router either via unicast or broadcast. The router responds to the node using a Reply message informing the node of the subnet mask used by the local network (the node's subnet mask that is also the same subnet mask of every computer on the local network). Unlike Router Advertisement and Router Solicitation messages, routers do not regularly advertise subnet information. They only transmit subnet data in response to a request from a network node. Using Address Mask Request and Address Mask Reply messages is considered optional. Most computers acquire information about what subnet mask they're supposed to use via DHCP.

Traceroute This message type is similar to Echo Request and Echo Reply messages except that instead of just testing for basic connectivity, this ICMPv4 message traces the exact sequence of routers used to send a packet from the source to the destination node on a hop-by-hop basis. On Windows computers, these messages are sent using the Tracert utility. On other operating systems, such as Linux, Traceroute is used. Although the utility names may be different, the underlying ICMPv4 messaging system is identical. A Traceroute message is sent as a single packet containing a special Traceroute IP option that is recognized by routers receiving the packet as a test message. The routers forward the packet along the route to the destination, and each router forwarding this message responds to the source node with a Traceroute message containing the IP address and or name of the router and the amount of time in milliseconds (ms) the hop required.

Sending a Traceroute message as a single packet is actually an experimental method defined by RFC 1393. The original method was to send a group of messages, one to each router along the path, with the TTL field containing a value for the number of hops to reach each successive router (1, and then 2, and then 3, and so on), making use of Time Exceeded error messages to "trace" the router hop. This takes an excessive amount of traffic and time, and the route between source and destination may change in the time it takes to run this implementation of Traceroute.

The Variable ICMP Structures and Functions

Several ICMP packets, such as an ICMP Redirect, must send specific information in the ICMP portion of the packet. These packets support additional fields, as defined in this section.

Types 0 and 8: Echo Reply and Echo Request Packets ICMP Type 0 is used for Echo Reply packets; ICMP Type 8 is used for Echo Request packets. The Code field is always set to 0 on these packets. Both ICMP packets use the same structure, as shown in Figure 5-2.

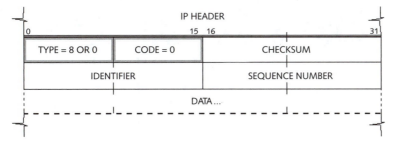

Figure 5-2 ICMP Echo Request and Echo Reply packet structure
© Cengage Learning 2013

RFC 792 states that the Identifier and Sequence fields aid matching Echo messages with Echo Replies. For example, RFC 792 states that an "identifier might be used like a port in TCP or UDP to identify a session, and the sequence number might be incremented on each Echo Request sent. The echoer returns these same values in the Echo Reply."

Windows Server 2008, Windows Vista, and Windows 7 ping packets display the following characteristics:

- The Identifier field is set to 512 decimal (or 0x200).

- On the first echo sent, the Sequence Number field value is set to a multiple of 512 decimal (0x200). In each subsequent echo, this field is incremented by 256 decimal (02100).

- The data field contains the value "abcdefghijklmnopqrstuvwabcdefghi."

Figure 5-3 shows the decode of an Echo Request packet from 10.2.10.2 to 10.2.99.99. Figure 5-4 shows the response.

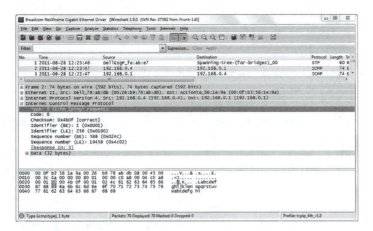

Figure 5-3 ICMP Echo Request packet
Source: Wireshark

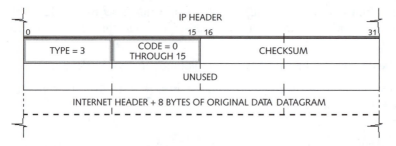

Figure 5-4 ICMP Echo Reply packet
Source: Wireshark

As you can see in Figures 5-3 and 5-4, the Identifier and Sequence Number fields match on the request and reply. The data contained in the ICMP packet also matches.

Type 3: Destination Unreachable Packets Network troubleshooters often closely track ICMP Destination Unreachable packets. As you learn in this section, some versions of these packets can indicate a configuration or service fault somewhere on the network. ICMP Destination Unreachable packets use the structure shown in Figure 5-5.

IP HEADER

TYPE = 3	CODE = 0 THROUGH 15	CHECKSUM
UNUSED		
INTERNET HEADER + 8 BYTES OF ORIGINAL DATA DATAGRAM		

0   15 16   31

Figure 5-5 ICMP Destination Unreachable packet structure
© Cengage Learning 2013

As shown in Figure 5-5, the host that sends the Destination Unreachable packet must return the IP header and 8 bytes of the original datagram that triggered this response. For example, Figure 5-6 shows that if an IP host sends a DNS query to a host that does not support DNS (Step 1 in Figure 5-6), the ICMP Destination Unreachable reply contains the IP header and the first 8 bytes of data in the UDP Header from the original DNS query (Step 2 in Figure 5-6). By looking at the ICMP packet alone, we can tell exactly what triggered the ICMP reply, who sent the original problem packet, and the source and destination port numbers contained in the original packet (because these numbers are contained within 8 bytes following the IP header).

The RFCs use the terms "Internet header" and "IP header" interchangeably, whereas many protocol analyzers, including Wireshark, simply use the term "IP header" or "header."

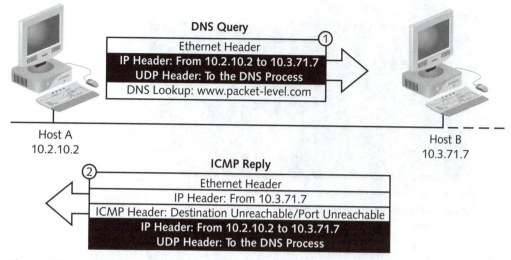

Figure 5-6 ICMP packets with content from triggering packet
© Cengage Learning 2013

It may be confusing to see two IP headers in a single packet when you examine these ICMP packets. Remember to read the packet from start to finish to identify the IP header that is being used to get the datagram through the network (the first IP header in the packet) and the IP header that is simply being sent to identify the problem (the second IP header).

Although RFC 792 only requires the 8 bytes that follow the IP header to be sent in an ICMP reply, it is acceptable and even desirable for as much data as possible to be returned.

As depicted in Figure 5-5, a total of 16 (0 through 15) possible codes are currently assigned to the ICMP Destination Unreachable type number. Not all codes are commonly used, but the RFC defines them in case they should ever be needed. Here are definitions of each code:

- *Code 0 Net Unreachable*—Code 0 packets may be sent by routers to indicate that the router knows about the network number used in the incoming packet but believes the route is not up at this time—or perhaps it is too far away to reach.

- *Code 1 Host Unreachable*—A router sends this reply to report that it could not locate the destination host. Currently, this reply also is sent when the destination network is unknown. Figure 5-7 shows an Echo Reply indicating that the destination of an Echo Request packet is unreachable. This can occur when a host is offline, when part of the network is down owing to a switch or router failure, or when the host IP address does not exist.

- *Code 2 Protocol Unreachable*—A host or router sends this error message to indicate that the protocol defined in the IP header cannot be processed. For example, if an **Internet Group Management Protocol (IGMP)** packet is sent to a host using a TCP/IP stack that does not support or understand IGMP, the host issues this Protocol Unreachable field. This reply is specifically associated with the values contained in the IP header's Protocol field.

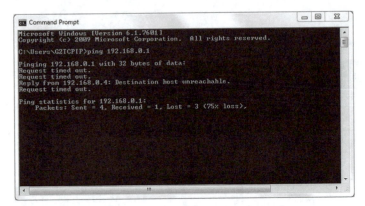

Figure 5-7 Destination Unreachable echo reply
Source: Microsoft

- *Code 3 Port Unreachable*—A host or router sends this reply to indicate that the sender does not support the process or application you are trying to reach. For example, if a host sends a NetBIOS Name Service packet (port 53) to a host that does not support NetBIOS Name Service, the ICMP reply would be structured like the packet shown in Figure 5-8.

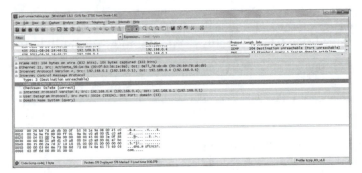

Figure 5-8 ICMP packet indicating that the destination port 53 is unreachable on the target
Source: Wireshark

- *Code 4 Fragmentation Needed and Don't Fragment Was Set*—There are two versions of this ICMP reply: the standard version, which simply states the packet had the Don't Fragment bit set when it reached a router that needed to fragment it, and the PMTU version, which includes information about the restricting link.

As shown in Figure 5-9, routers that support PMTU Discovery place the MTU of the restricting link into the 4-byte area previously marked "unused" by RFC 792.

- *Code 5 Source Route Failed*—A router sends this ICMP reply to indicate that it cannot use the strict or loose source routing path specified in the original packet. If the original packet defined strict source routing, perhaps the router does not have access to the next router indicated in the strict route path list. If the original packet defined loose source routing, perhaps the router knows there is no next-hop router that can forward the packet.

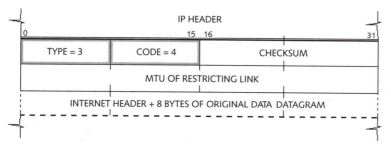

Figure 5-9 ICMP Destination Unreachable structure used for PMTU Discovery
© Cengage Learning 2013

- *Code 6 Destination Network Unknown*—This ICMP packet is obsolete. Routers send the Code 1: Host Unreachable message when they do not know about and cannot forward packets to the desired network.

- *Code 7 Destination Host Unknown*—A router sends this ICMP packet to indicate that it cannot reach a directly connected link, such as a point-to-point link.

- *Code 8 Source Host Isolated*—This ICMP packet is obsolete. Previously, routers sent this packet to indicate that a host was isolated and its packets could not be routed.

- *Code 9 Communication with Destination Network Is Administratively Prohibited*—A router sends this ICMP packet to indicate that the router was configured to block access to the desired destination network. Because these communications may be blocked for security reasons, most routers do not generate these ICMP messages.

- *Code 10 Communication with Destination Host Is Administratively Prohibited*—A router sends this ICMP message to indicate that the desired host cannot be reached because the router was configured to block access to the desired destination host. Again, for security reasons, many routers won't generate this message.

- *Code 11 Destination Network Unreachable for Type of Service*—A router sends this ICMP message to indicate that the Type of Service (TOS) requested in an incoming IP header, or the default TOS (0), is not available through this router for the desired network. Only routers that support TOS can send this type of ICMP message.

- *Code 12 Destination Host Unreachable for Type of Service*—A router sends this ICMP message to indicate that theTOS requested in an incoming IP header is not available through this router for that specific host. Only routers that support TOS can send this type of ICMP message.

- *Code 13 Communication Administratively Prohibited*—A router sends this ICMP message to indicate that the router cannot forward a packet because packet filtering prohibits such activity. Because packet filtering is usually applied for security reasons, many routers do not send this reply to maintain secrecy regarding their filtering configurations.

- *Code 14 Host Precedence Violation*—A router sends this ICMP message to indicate that the Precedence value defined in the sender's original IP header is not allowed for the source or destination host, network, or port. This also results in the discard of the offending packet.

- *Code 15 Precedence Cutoff in Effect*—A router sends this ICMP message to indicate that a network administrator imposed a minimum level of precedence to obtain service from a router, and a lower-precedence packet was received. Such packets are discarded and also may result in transmission of this ICMP message.

Type 4: Source Quench A router or host may use Source Quench as a way to indicate that it is becoming congested or overloaded. For example, if a router is overloaded and begins to drop packets, it may send a Source Quench message to hosts to request that they slow or stop sending data to that router. This reduces the amount of incoming traffic, thereby giving the router or the host time to recover from overload conditions.

When a Windows Server 2008, Windows Vista, or Windows 7 host receives a Source Quench message, it checks whether the ICMP Source Quench message indicates trouble with TCP communications. If so, the Windows Server 2008, Windows Vista, or Windows 7 host treats the Source Quench message as a lost TCP segment. By default, most current routers do not issue Source Quench messages because these can further congest a problematic link.

ICMP Source Quench packets use the structure shown in Figure 5-10.

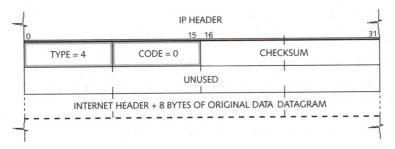

Figure 5-10 ICMP Source Quench packet structure
© Cengage Learning 2013

Type 5: Redirect Routers send ICMP Redirect messages to hosts to indicate that a preferable route exists. ICMP Redirect packets use the structure shown in Figure 5-11. The ICMP Redirect packet has a 4-byte field for the preferred gateway's address.

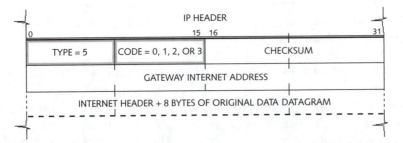

Figure 5-11 ICMP Redirect packet structure
© Cengage Learning 2013

Ideally, clients should update their routing tables to indicate the optimal path to be used for subsequent communications. There are four codes that define whether the ICMP Redirect packet contains a new route to a full host address or network address. In addition, some redirection information points to a path used for a specific Type of Service.

- *Code 0 Redirect Datagram for the Network (or Subnet)*—A router can send this ICMP message to indicate that there is a better way to get to the desired network. Because routers cannot determine which portion of a destination address is the network portion and which portion is the host portion, they use Code 1 in the ICMP Redirect replies.

- *Code 1 Redirect Datagram for the Host*—A router can send this ICMP message to indicate that there is a better way to get to the desired host. This is the most common ICMP Redirect message seen on networks.

- *Code 2 Redirect Datagram for the Type of Service and Network*—A router can send this ICMP message to indicate that there is a better way to get to the desired network using the desired TOS. Again, because routers cannot determine which portion of a destination address is the network portion and which portion is the host portion, they use Code 3 in ICMP Redirect replies for TOS issues.

- *Code 3 Redirect Datagram for the Type of Service and Host*—A router can send this ICMP message to indicate that there is a better way to get to the destination host using the TOS requested.

Types 9 and 10: Router Advertisement and Router Solicitation Hosts send Router Solicitation packets, and routers respond with Router Advertisement packets. ICMP Router Solicitation packets use the structure shown in Figure 5-12.

This Solicitation packet structure is very simple. It needs only to contain the ICMP Type and Code number. Such packets are addressed to the all-router multicast address 224.0.0.2 by default. In some cases, hosts may be configured to send these packets to the broadcast address (in case the local routers do not process multicast packets). An ICMP Router Advertisement packet structure is illustrated in Figure 5-13.

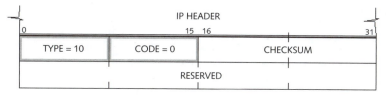

Figure 5-12 ICMP Router Solicitation packet structure
© Cengage Learning 2013

The ICMP Router Advertisement packets include the following fields after the ICMP Checksum field:

- *# of Addresses*—The number of router addresses advertised in this packet.

- *Address Size*—The number of 4-byte increments used to define each router address advertised. Because this version includes a 4-byte Precedence field as well as a 4-byte IP Address field, the Address Size value is 2 (2 + 2 + 4 bytes).

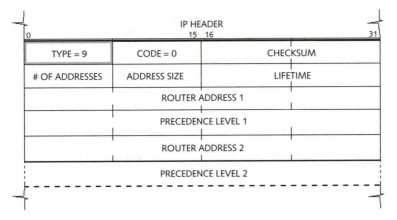

Figure 5-13 ICMP Router Advertisement packet structure
© Cengage Learning 2013

- *Lifetime*—The maximum number of seconds that this router information may be considered valid.
- *Router Address 1*—The sending router's local IP address.
- *Precedence Level 1*—Preference value of each router address advertised. Higher values indicate greater preferences. A higher precedence level may be configured at a router (if the router supports the option) to ensure that one router is more likely to become the default gateway for local hosts.
- *Router Address 2* and *Precedence Level 2*—If there are additional router values, they will follow with their precedence levels.

Type 11: Time Exceeded Routers (Time to Live Exceeded in Transit) or hosts (Fragmentation Reassembly Time Exceeded) can send these ICMP packets. ICMP Time Exceeded packets use the structure shown in Figure 5-14.

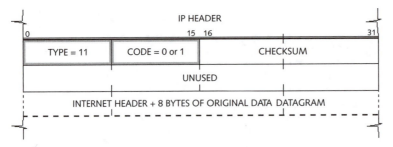

Figure 5-14 ICMP Time Exceeded packet structure
© Cengage Learning 2013

There are two codes that can be used in ICMP Time Exceeded packets—Code 0 and Code 1.

- *Code 0 Time to Live Exceeded in Transit*—A router sends this ICMP message to indicate that a packet arrived with a TTL value of 1. Routers cannot decrement the TTL value to 0 and forward it, so they must discard the packet and send this ICMP message.

- *Code 1 Fragment Reassembly Time Exceeded*—A host sends this ICMP message when it does not receive all fragment parts before the expiration (in seconds of holding time) of the TTL value of the first fragment received.

When a router is acting as a host and assembling packets, it may issue a Code 1: Fragment Reassembly Time Exceeded message.

When the first packet of a fragment set arrives at the destination, the TTL value is interpreted as "seconds of lifetime remaining." A timer begins counting down in seconds. If all fragments of the set do not arrive before the timer expires, the entire fragment set is considered invalid. The receiver sends this message back to the originator of the fragment set, causing the original packet to be resent.

Type 12: Parameter Problem This message type indicates problems not covered by the other ICMP error messages. ICMP Parameter Problem packets use the structure shown in Figure 5-15.

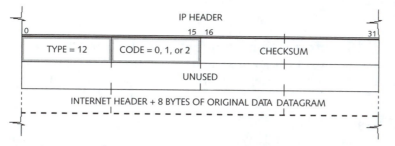

Figure 5-15 ICMP Parameter Problem packet structure
© Cengage Learning 2013

There are three codes that can be used in ICMP Parameter Problem messages.

- *Code 0 Pointer Indicates the Error*—This ICMP code includes a Pointer field that indicates where in the returned IP header and datagram the error occurred.

- *Code 1 Missing a Required Option*—This ICMP code indicates that the sender expected some additional information in the Option field of the original packet.

- *Code 2 Bad Length*—This ICMP code indicates that the original packet structure had an invalid length.

Types 13 and 14: Timestamp and Timestamp Reply The ICMP Timestamp message was defined as a method for one IP host to obtain the current time. The value returned is the number in milliseconds since midnight, **Universal Time (UT)**, formerly referred to as Greenwich Mean Time (GMT). ICMP Timestamp and ICMP Timestamp Reply packets both use the same structure, as shown in Figure 5-16.

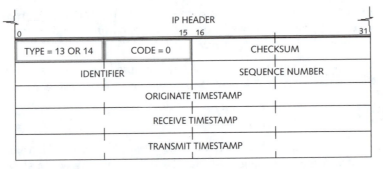

Figure 5-16 ICMP Timestamp and Timestamp Reply packet structure
© Cengage Learning 2013

The Timestamp requester enters the current send time in the Originate Timestamp field. The receiver enters its current time value in the Receive Timestamp field as the packet is processed. The receiver next places the current Timestamp in the Transmit Timestamp field at the moment it sends the packet back to the requester.

Other protocols, such as **Network Time Protocol (NTP)**, provide a more robust and functional **time synchronization** method.

Types 15 and 16: Information Request and Information Reply These ICMP messages provide a way for a host to find out what network it is on. ICMP Information Request and ICMP Information Reply packets both use the same structure, as shown in Figure 5-17.

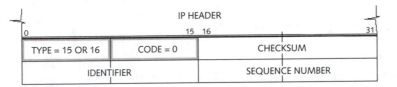

Figure 5-17 ICMP Information Request and Information Reply packet structure
© Cengage Learning 2013

To use this feature, a host sends an Information Request packet and leaves the source and destination IP address fields set to 0. The destination hardware address is broadcast. Routers reply using the Information Reply packet. The IP header in the replies contains the network address, thereby enabling hosts to learn their network addresses.

Types 17 and 18: Address Mask Request and Address Mask Reply The ICMP Address Mask Request and Address Mask Reply processes are intended to provide diskless hosts with a method to determine their network mask information. ICMP Address Mask Request and Address Mask Reply packets both use the same structure, as shown in Figure 5-18.

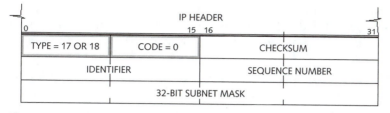

Figure 5-18 ICMP Address Mask Request and Address Mask Reply packet structure
© Cengage Learning 2013

Type 30: Traceroute This is an interesting ICMP packet type. It is documented in RFC 1393, but it is not currently in use because it requires added functionality in the IP routers it traverses. Adding functionality to routers is costly and requires numerous resources to build, implement, and test new code. Basically, the Traceroute process requires a host to send a single IP packet with the new Traceroute option (the IP Traceroute Option packet) to a destination. The destination sends an IP Traceroute Option Reply packet. When forwarding these packets, routers along the path are automatically triggered to send an ICMP Traceroute Return packet to the host that initiated the Traceroute process. This ICMP Traceroute packet contains information taken from the IP Traceroute Option Outbound and Return packets as they passed the local router.

The ICMP Traceroute packets use the structure shown in Figure 5-19.

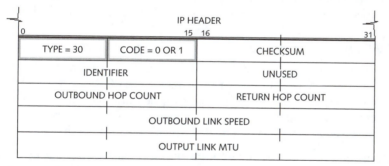

Figure 5-19 ICMP Traceroute packet structure
© Cengage Learning 2013

The Outbound Hop Count field indicates the hop count seen on the outbound IP Traceroute Option packet as it arrived at the router. The Return Hop Count field contains the hop count value seen in the return IP Traceroute Option packet when it arrived at the local router. The Output Link Speed indicates the speed of the link over which the IP Traceroute packet is next sent. This field is defined in bytes per second, not bits per second. The Output Link MTU indicates the MTU size of the link over which the IP Traceroute Option Outbound/Return packet is sent next.

By taking full advantage of ICMP's various capabilities, it's possible to examine how IP is working and how it gets from "here" to "there" on a network. But because it's also possible to put ICMP to work for nefarious ends, security measures may prevent its use for Ping or Tracert when entering some networks. You have to accept this as a consequence of network administrators' cautious approach to revealing information about their networks to outsiders. Nevertheless, you will find ICMP and its various services invaluable in managing your own networks, and in troubleshooting reachability problems when they occur.

ICMPv6

ICMPv6 provides the same basic mechanism for error reporting and information exchange between networked devices as ICMPv4. The specifications for ICMPv4 are over 30 years old, and a new version of ICMP is required for modern network messaging requirements. ICMPv6 message types still fall into two main groups: error messages and informational messages. However, the message types in these categories have changed, some of them significantly.

Overview of ICMPv6

ICMPv6 was originally specified by RFC 1885, which was then obsoleted by RFC 2463. The current specification is RFC 4443, "Internet Control Message Protocol (ICMPv6) for Internet Protocol Version 6 (IPv6) Specification." ICMPv6 is described as having message types and message type formats updated for use with the IPv6 protocol. Not all message types are defined by this one RFC. For instance, whereas RFC 4443 discusses Destination Unreachable and Packet Too Big messages, RFC 4861 defines Router Renumbering and Redirect Messages.

Message types that previously used other protocols now use ICMPv6, and new message types have been created that didn't exist in ICMPv4. For instance, Multicast Listener Discovery (MLD) is integrated as an ICMPv6 sub-protocol. ICMPv6 takes on a much larger role than ICMPv4.

Types of ICMPv6 Messages

To illustrate the number and type of ICMPv6 messages currently defined, Table 5-9 presents their types, names, and RFC document references. Type numbers 0–127 cover error messages. Type numbers 128–255 cover informational messages. Some message names are the same as their ICMPv4 counterparts, but many of them are completely new. You can see how many different RFCs are involved in describing different ICMPv6 messages in Table 5-9.

Although the information in this table is current as we write this, please visit *www.iana.org/assignments/icmpv6-parameters* for the latest updates.

Type	Name	Reference
0	Reserved	RFC 4443
1	Destination Unreachable	RFC 4443
2	Packet Too Big	RFC 4443
3	Time Exceeded	RFC 4443
4	Parameter Problem	RFC 4443
100	Private experimentation	RFC 4443
101	Private experimentation	RFC 4443

Table 5-9 ICMPv6 message types

Type	Name	Reference
102–126	Unassigned	none
127	Reserved for expansion of ICMPv6 error messages	RFC 4443
128	Echo Request	RFC 4443
129	Echo Reply	RFC 4443
130	Multicast Listener Query	RFC 2710
131	Multicast Listener Report	RFC 2710
132	Multicast Listener Done	RFC 2710
133	Router Solicitation	RFC 4861
134	Router Advertisement	RFC 4861
135	Neighbor Solicitation	RFC 4861
136	Neighbor Advertisement	RFC 4861
137	Redirect Message	RFC 4861
138	Router Renumbering	RFC 2894
139	ICMP Node Information Query	RFC 4620
140	ICMP Node Information Response	RFC 4620
141	Inverse Neighbor Discovery Solicitation Message	RFC 3122
142	Inverse Neighbor Discovery Advertisement Message	RFC 3122
143	Version 2 Multicast Listener Report	RFC 3810
144	Home Agent Address Discovery Request Message	RFC 6275
145	Home Agent Address Discovery Reply Message	RFC 6275
146	Mobile Prefix Solicitation	RFC 6275
147	Mobile Prefix Advertisement	RFC 6275
148	Certification Path Solicitation Message	RFC 3971
149	Certification Path Advertisement Message	RFC 3971
150	ICMP messages utilized by experimental mobility protocols such as Seamoby	RFC 4065
151	Multicast Router Advertisement	RFC 4286
152	Multicast Router Solicitation	RFC 4286
153	Multicast Router Termination	RFC 4286
154	FMIPv6 Messages	RFC 5568

Table 5-9 ICMPv6 message types (*continues*)

5

Type	Name	Reference
155	RPL Control Message	RFC-ietf-roll-rpl-19.txt
156–199	Unassigned	N/A
200	Private experimentation	RFC 4443
201	Private experimentation	RFC 4443
255	Reserved for expansion of ICMPv6 informational messages	RFC 4443

Table 5-9 **ICMPv6 message types** (*continued*)
© Cengage Learning 2013

All message types listed in Table 5-9 are registered for IETF RFC publication as standards, informational or experimental.

ICMPv6 Header

RFC 4443 describes the general format of ICMPv6 messages. Specific message types may have their own unique formatting beyond what is illustrated here. An IPv6 header and potentially one or more extension headers will come before the ICMPv6 message. The Next Header value for the ICMPv6 header is 58 in the immediately preceding header. Figure 5-20 shows the general format of the ICMPv6 message header.

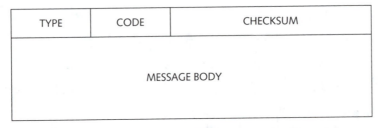

Figure 5-20 General format of the ICMPv6 message header
© Cengage Learning 2013

The Type field contains the type of message, and its value determines the format of the remaining data. The values for the Type field for the different message types appear in the Type column in Table 5-9. The Code field contains the value of the message type and is used to generate an additional level of message granularity. For example, for Echo Request, Echo Reply, and Neighbor Advertisement messages, the Code value is set to 0. The Checksum field performs the usual function of detecting data corruption in the ICMPv6 message, as well as in parts of the IPv6 header. The contents of the Message Body depend on the message type. As previously stated, ICMPv6 messages come in two general types: error messages and informational messages. The following sections will describe the more commonly used ICMPv6 error and information messages.

ICMPv6 Error Messages

As you saw in the text introducing Table 5-9, ICMPv6 error messages fall into a range from 0 to 127, and those Type values are all defined in RFC 4443. Error messages discussed in this section are Destination Unreachable, Packet Too Big, Time Exceeded, and Parameter Problem. Other error message types are either reserved, unassigned, or set aside for private experimentation. Except for Packet Too Big messages, each of these error types corresponds to an ICMPv4 equivalent, at least in terms of how they are named. However, version 6 of this protocol updates packet structure and other features of each of these messsages.

Destination Unreachable Messages

Like IPv4, IPv6 is an unreliable protocol, which means it does not guarantee delivery of IP packets but makes a "best effort" to deliver packets. It is expected that packets will be lost or undeliverable from time to time, which is where the Destination Unreachable message in ICMPv6 comes in. When a packet cannot be delivered to its destination for various reasons, such as the packet containing an invalid destination address, the router encountering this packet will send a Destination Unreachable message back to the source node. This message will include a code telling the basic reason for the inability to deliver the packet, including part or all of the packet that was not delivered.

Once the source node receives the Destination Unreachable message, the node is responsible for deciding a response. One possible problem in this circumstance is that, just as the source node's packet didn't reach its destination, the Destination Unreachable message may not reach the source node. In this case, the source node will not know a problem has occurred and will continue to try to send the packet to the destination node until it receives an error message. Figure 5-21 shows the format for the ICMPv6 Destination Unreachable message type. Table 5-10 describes the values of the fields for this message format.

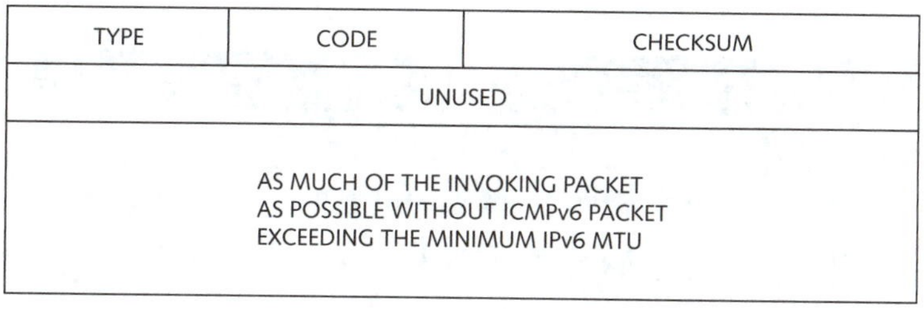

TYPE	CODE	CHECKSUM
UNUSED		
AS MUCH OF THE INVOKING PACKET AS POSSIBLE WITHOUT ICMPv6 PACKET EXCEEDING THE MINIMUM IPv6 MTU		

Figure 5-21 Destination Unreachable message format
© Cengage Learning 2013

Field Name	Description
Type	1
Code	0 – No route to destination 1 – Communication with destination administratively prohibited 2 – Beyond scope of source address 3 – Address unreachable 4 – Port unreachable 5 – Source address failed ingress/egress policy 6 – Reject route to destination
Unused	No code values use this field, and it must be set to 0 by the source node and ignored by the destination node.

Table 5-10 Destination Unreachable message format fields
© Cengage Learning 2013

Destination Unreachable messages typically are produced by routers or by the IPv6 layer in the source node in response to encountering a packet that cannot be delivered to the destination for any reason other than network congestion. The value in the Code field informs the sending node of the reason the packet was unable to be delivered. The destination node typically sends this type of message with a Code 4 when encountering a packet in which the node has no listener for the packet's upper-layer transport protocol, such as UDP, and if no alternative exists for the transport protocol to inform the source node.

Packet Too Big Messages

This new ICMPv6 error message type is required because of how IPv6 manages data fragmentation and reassembly. IPv6 routers do not fragment packets to accommodate the link MTU to the next hop. Source nodes are required to use Path MTU (PMTU) Discovery to determine the smallest MTU size for all links in the PMTU from source to destination. This works in theory, but routes can change after the computer completes initial discovery action and the packets are sent, and the source node's message may encounter a link MTU smaller than the packet MTU size. In that event, the router that receives a packet too large for the link to the next hop will drop the packet and send a Packet Too Big message back to the source node. The source node will then modify the MTU to fit the smaller link MTU and resend the message.

The format of the Packet Too Big message is identical to that of the Destination Unreachable message seen in Figure 5-21, except that the Unused field in the Destination Unreachable message is the MTU field in the Packet Too Big message. Table 5-11 describes the values of the fields for the Packet Too Big message format.

Field Name	Description
Type	2
Code	0 - Set to 0 by the source node and ignored by the destination node
MTU	The Maximum Transmission Unit value of the next-hop link

Table 5-11 **Packet Too Big message format fields**
© Cengage Learning 2013

Packet Too Big messages must be sent by routers that cannot forward a packet because it exceeds the MTU size limitation of the outgoing link. Part of the information being sent back to the source node is PMTU Discovery data that will allow the source node to "resize" its packets so that they will be able to traverse a smaller link MTU. The Packet Too Big message is an exception to one of the rules regarding when to send an ICMPv6 error message. Unlike all other error message types, Packet Too Big messages can be sent in response to messages with an IPv6 multicast destination address or a link-layer multicast or broadcast address. Usually, ICMPv6 messages are only sent in response to IPV6 unicast packets.

Time Exceeded Messages

This message type is substantially similar to its ICMPv4 counterpart. A Time Exceeded message can be sent back to the source node if the packet exceeds the value in its Hop Limit field prior to being delivered to the destination node. The router that receives the packet and decrements the Hop Limit field to zero will drop the packet and send the Time Exceeded message to the source node. Also, if the message has been fragmented by the IPv6 source node, when the destination node receives the first fragment, it sets a timer, basically so it doesn't have to wait forever in order to receive all fragments for reassembly. If the timer value gets to zero before all the fragments arrive, the packets are dropped and the Time Exceeded message is sent to the source node.

See the "Types of ICMPv4 Messages" section earlier in this chapter for more about Time Exceeded messages.

The format of the Time Exceeded message is identical to the Destination Unreachable message, including the presence of and reason for the Unused field. The value of the Type field is set to 3 for this message type, and the values for the Code field are:

- 0—Hop limit exceeded in transit
- 1—Fragment reassembly time exceeded

A common reason for routers to decrement a packet's Hop Limit field to 0 prior to delivery is the presence of a routing loop. Another possible reason is that the value of the Hop Limit field was set too low by the source node, such as when the number of hops from source to destination is 9 but the Hop Limit field is set to 7.

Parameter Problem Messages

Like their ICMPv4 counterparts, ICMPv6 Parameter Problem messages are considered "generic" messages as opposed to ones that respond to a specific error. This message type is sent to the source node when some kind of problem with a packet has been encountered in one of the packet's fields or parameters in the IPv6 header. The error has to be serious enough to cause the device sending the message to drop the packet.

The Parameter Problem message is considered generic because it is triggered by any serious error in a packet header field, but a special pointer field is used to indicate the specific field where the error was found. Because all or part of the original packet is included in the Parameter Problem message (up to the size of the ICMP message format), the source node is provided with information about the error. The Code value also communicates information about what sort of problem occurred.

The Problem Parameter message format is identical to that of the Destination Unreachable message format except that the Unused field in the Destination Unreachable message is the Pointer field in the Parameter Problem message. Table 5-12 describes the values of the fields for the Parameter Problem message format.

Field Name	Description
Type	4
Code	0 – Erroneous header field encountered 1 – Unrecognized Next Header type encountered 2 – Unrecognized IPv6 option encountered
Pointer	The pointer extends beyond the end of the ICMPv6 packet if the field with the error is beyond what can fit within the maximum size of an ICMPv6 error message.

Table 5-12 **Parameter Problem message format fields**

Codes 1 and 2 are more informative subsets of the 0 code. The pointer identifies the octet of the original IPv6 packet header where the error was found. Errors can be located and identified by the pointer in the IPv6 packet header and in extension headers.

ICMPv6 Informational Messages

Type codes for informational messages exist in the 128–255 range (see Table 5-9 for details) and include a long list of message types specified by multiple RFC documents. This section covers the most common ICMPv6 informational messages: Echo Request and Echo Reply, Router Advertisement and Router Solicitation, Neighbor Advertisement and Neighbor Solicitation, Redirect, and Router Renumbering. Although these represent eight message types, most occur in pairs, such as Echo Request and Echo Reply messages, so information about "paired" messages is presented in tandem.

As with ICMPv4 informational message types, ICMPv6 messages are not used to report errors but to provide information to the source node regarding some test, support, or diagnostic function being performed between nodes on the IPv6 network. Informational messages can contain mandatory, recommended, and optional parameters depending on the message type and the conditions under which the message was generated.

Echo Request and Echo Reply Messages

These message types are specified in RFC 4443 and perform a basic connectivity test between two network nodes, just as they do under ICMPv4. Each IPv6 network node is required to implement an ICMPv6 Echo responder function that accepts Echo Request messages and generates the corresponding Echo Reply messages. Nodes should also implement an application-layer interface that is used to generate and receive these diagnostic messages.

One ICMPv6 change that does not affect technical features or performance is a name change. In ICMPv4, the initial message was called Echo or Echo (Request). This name changes to Echo Request in ICMPv6.

Figure 5-22 illustrates the format for Echo Request and Echo Reply messages.

TYPE	CODE	CHECKSUM
IDENTIFIER		SEQUENCE NUMBER
DATA ...		

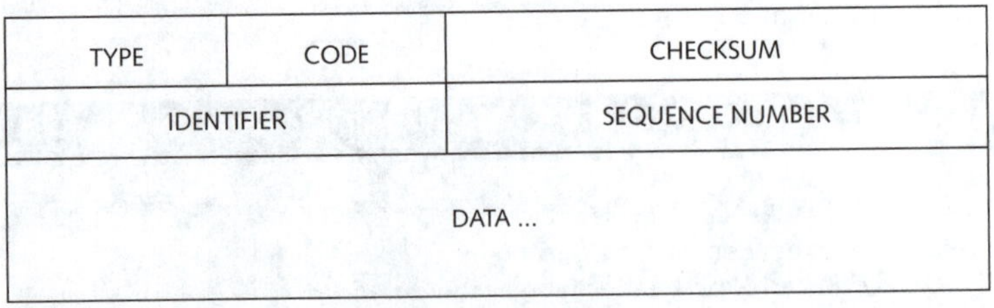

Figure 5-22 Format for Echo Request and Echo Reply messages
© Cengage Learning 2013

Table 5-13 describes the values of the fields for these message formats.

Field Name	Description
Type	128 – Echo Request messages 129 – Echo Reply messages
Code	0 – both message types
Identifier	For Echo Request messages, an identifier helps in matching Echo Replies to Echo Requests; it may be 0. For Echo Replies, it is the identifier from the invoking Echo Request message.
Sequence Number	For Echo Request messages, it is a number to aid in matching Echo Replies to this Echo Request; it may be 0. For Echo Reply messages, it is the number from the invoking Echo Request.

Table 5-13 Echo Request and Echo Reply message format fields
© Cengage Learning 2013

Data for Echo Request messages may consist of zero or more octets of arbitrary data. Data for Echo Reply messages is data from the invoking Echo Request messages. The source address of an Echo Reply message sent in response to a unicast Echo Request must be the same as the destination address of the Echo Request message. Echo Reply messages are also sent in response to an Echo Request sent to an IPv6 multicast and anycast address. In this case, the source address of the reply must contain the unicast address of the node responding to the Echo Request.

Router Advertisement and Router Solicitation Messages

ICMPv6 Router Solicitation and Router Advertisement messages are specified in RFC 4861, "Neighbor Discovery for IP version 6 (IPv6)." As you previously learned about these ICMPv4 message types, when a network node powers up, if it doesn't know the location of its default router, it sends a Router Solicitation message to elicit a router response. Routers periodically send out Router Advertisement messages to nodes on each local interface announcing their presence and how they can be located. ICMPv6 Router Solicitation and Router Advertisement messages function in the same way as the ICMPv4 versions of these messages.

Router discovery in IPv6 works similarly to router discovery in IPv4 except that the router discovery function has been integrated into the Neighbor Discovery (ND) protocol and has become part of a suite of discovery utilities that are used between network nodes and routers. The format for Router Solicitation and Router Advertisement messages are not alike; Figure 5-23 shows the Router Solicitation message format sent by IPv6 network nodes.

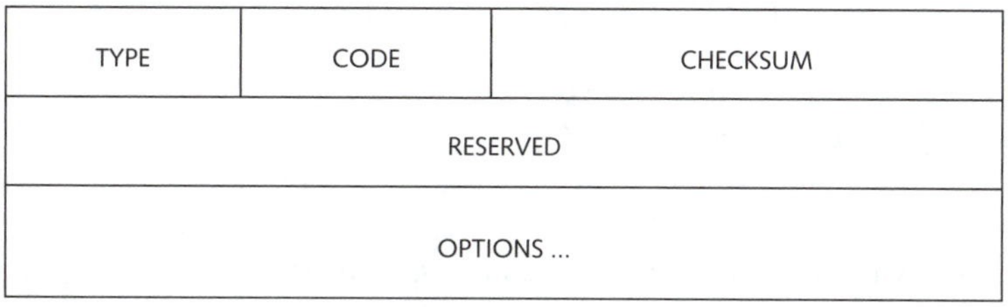

TYPE	CODE	CHECKSUM
RESERVED		
OPTIONS …		

Figure 5-23 ICMPv6 Router Solicitation message format
© Cengage Learning 2013

As you can see, this is a typical ICMPv6 message format. Table 5-14 describes the values of the fields for this message format.

Field Type	Description
Type	133
Code	0
Checksum	This is the checksum specified for ICMPv6 messages.
Reserved	This is an unused field that is set to 0 by the source node and ignored by the destination node.
Options	RFC 4861 specifies the source link-layer address as the only valid option for this message type if it is known. The address is not included if it is unspecified but otherwise should be included on link layers that have addresses. Future versions of this protocol may define new, valid options for use in this field, but any options destination nodes do not recognize should be ignored.

Table 5-14 Router Solicitation message format fields
© Cengage Learning 2013

Figure 5-24 shows you the format for Router Advertisement messages, which is quite different from router solicitation messages.

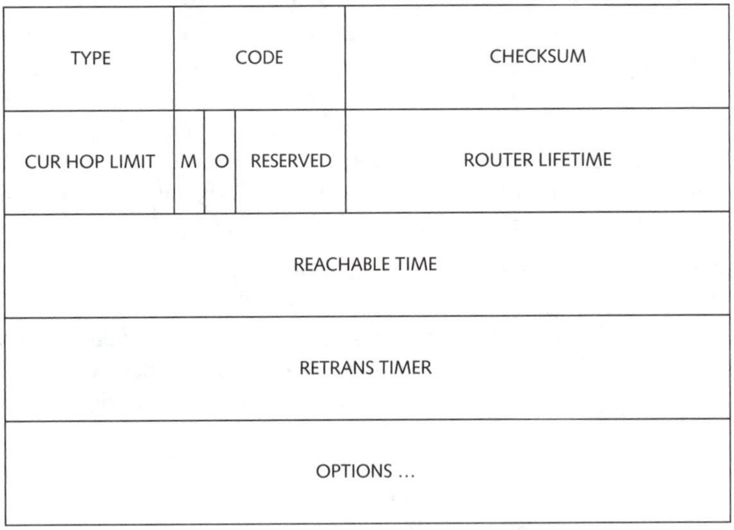

Figure 5-24 ICMPv6 Router Advertisement message format
© Cengage Learning 2013

Table 5-15 describes the values of the fields for this message format.

Field Name	Description
Type	134
Code	0
Checksum	This is the checksum specified for ICMPv6 messages.
Cur Hop Limit	This is an unsigned 8-bit integer, and the default value should be the value in the IPv6 packet's Hop Count field for all outgoing packets. The value should be set to 0 if it is unspecified by the router.
M Flag	This is a 1-bit "Managed address configuration" flag and is set to indicate that addresses are available through DHCPv6. If the M flag is set, the O flag becomes redundant and can be ignored because DHCPv6 will provide all available configuration information.
O Flag	This is a 1-bit "Other configuration" flag and, when set, indicates that other configuration information is available through DHCPv6, such as DNS or other server-related information.
Reserved	This is a 6-bit unused field that must be set to 0 by the sending router and must be ignored by any receiving node.
Router Lifetime	This is a 16-bit unsigned integer and indicates the lifetime of the default router in seconds. The field can contain a maximum value of 65535; however, sending rules limit this value to 9000. A value of 0 in this field indicates that the router is not a default router and should not appear on the default router list. The router lifetime value only applies to the router's availability as a default router and does not affect the validity of any information contained in the other fields of this messsage.
Reachable Time	This is a 32-bit unsigned integer and is the time, in milliseconds, that a node assumes a neighbor is reachable after having accepted a reachability confirmation. If this field has a value of 0, the reachable time is unspecified by the router.
Retrans Timer	This is a 32-bit unsigned integer and is the time, in milliseconds, between retransmitted Neighbor Solicitation messages. If this field has a value of 0, the retrans time is unspecified by the router.
Options	Available options include source link-layer address, MTU, and Prefix information. Source link-layer address is the address of the interface from which the advertisement was sent and is only used on link layers that possess addresses. A router may omit this option to enable inbound load sharing across multiple link-layer addresses. MTU should be sent on links with a variable MTU and may be sent on other links. Prefix Information are options specifying on-link prefixes and/or are used for stateless address autoconfiguration. This information should include all router on-link prefixes so multihomed hosts have complete prefix information.

Table 5-15 **Router Advertisement message format fields**
© Cengage Learning 2013

Router Solicitation messages are usually sent to the IPV6 multicast address for "all routers," which will be ignored by any other device type on the network. Router Advertisement messages are sent to the IPv6 multicast address for "all nodes" on the local link. A Router Advertisement message sent in response to a specific Router Solicitation message is sent as a unicast message to the soliciting network node.

Neighbor Solicitation and Neighbor Advertisement Messages

Neighbor Solicitation and Neighbor Advertisement messages are specified in RFC 4861 and are part of the IPv6 Neighbor Discovery protocol. IPv6 network nodes send Neighbor Solicitations in order to request the link-layer address of a target node and, at the same time, send the target node their own link-layer address. Neighbor Solicitation messages are sent multicast when a node needs to resolve a neighbor's address and sent unicast when a node needs to verify that it can reach a neighbor. Figure 5-25 illustrates the format of a Neighbor Solicitation message.

TYPE	CODE	CHECKSUM
RESERVED		
TARGET ADDRESS		
OPTIONS ...		

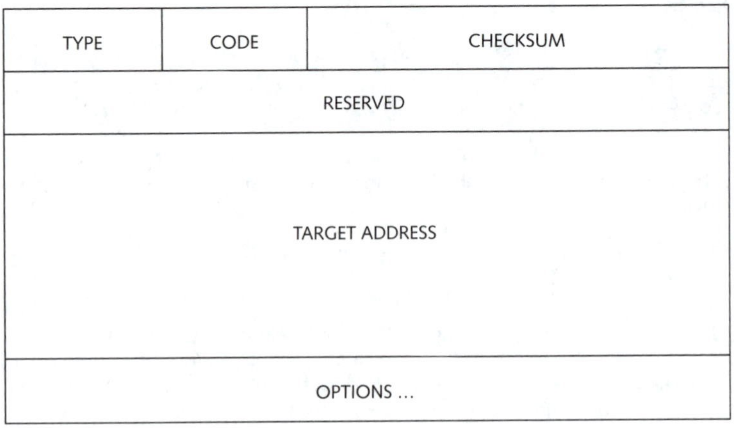

Figure 5-25 Neighbor Solicitation message format
© Cengage Learning 2013

The Type value for this message is 135, and the Code value is 0. The values of the Checksum and Reserved fields are as they've previously been described for ICMPv6 messages in this section. The Target Address is the IPv6 address of the target node of the solicitation message and cannot be a multicast address.

The only possible option for this message is the source link-layer address, which cannot be added when the source address is unspecified. Otherwise, the address must be included in all unicast and multicast solicitations.

IPv6 network nodes send Neighbor Advertisement messages in response to Neighbor Solicitations. They also send unsolicited Neighbor Advertisements to propagate new information more quickly. When sent in response to a specific Neighbor Solicitation message, the Neighbor Advertisement response is sent as a unicast to the soliciting node. When sent unsolicited, the Neighbor Advertisement is sent to the multicast "all nodes" address.

The Neighbor Advertisement message format is almost identical to the Neighbor Solicitation message format, except in the Reserved field there are three possible flags:

- *R Flag*—This is the Router flag; when set, it indicates that the sender is a router. This flag is typically used for Neighbor Unreachability Detection to identify a router that changes to a host.

- *S Flag*—This is the solicited flag; when set, it indicates that the advertisement was sent in response to a Neighbor Solicitation message from the Destination address. This flag is used for reachability confirmation and must not be set in multicast advertisements or in unsolicited unicast advertisements.

- *O Flag*—This is the override flag; when set, it indicates that the advertisement should override an existing cache entry and update the cached link-layer address. It should not be set in solicited advertisements for anycast addresses or in solicited proxy advertisements, but it should be set in any other solicited and unsolicited advertisements.

The value of the Type field is set to 136 for Neighbor Advertisements.

The only possible option in the current implementation of this message is target link-layer address, which is the source node's address. This address must be set on link layers that have addresses when responding to multicast solicitations.

Redirect Messages

Specified by RFC 4861 in its ICMPv6 implementation, Redirect messages were considered error messages under ICMPv4. These messages don't actually describe an error but rather provide the information to a network node that it needs to change which router it is using on the local link to send messages to a particular destination. This message type is used on a network that has more than one local router. Network nodes don't have information on which packets to send to which routers depending on their destination addresses, so nodes typically send all packets to one default router.

A classic scenario for this is a network that uses one router as the gateway to the Internet and another router to send traffic to other organization-internal networks that are on different local links. If a node sends a packet to the gateway router as its default when the destination address indicates an internal location on a different local link, the gateway router will forward the packet to the other router and, at the same time, send a Redirect message to the source node, saying, in essence: "For traffic to this network, use the other router as the default."

Figure 5-26 shows the formatting for ICMPv6 Redirect messages.

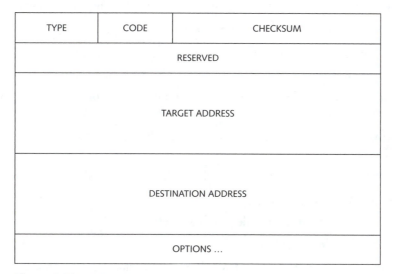

Figure 5-26 ICMPv6 Redirect message format
© Cengage Learning 2013

The Type value for this message type is 137, and the Code value is 0. The checksum is the typical ICMPv6 checksum function, and the Reserved field is unused and operates as described elsewhere in this section.

The Target Address is the IPv6 address of the default or "better" first-hop router the node is using to forward its traffic to the destination address. This field can contain the same address as the Destination Address field if the target is considered the endpoint of the network communication. If the target is a router, this field will contain the link-local address for the router interface that is directly connected to the local link on which the source node is located.

The Destination Address is the IPv6 address of the destination node. The only possible option for the current implementation of this message is the target link-layer address, and it should be included if it is known to the source node. As much as possible of the source node's original packet should be included in the Redirect message, up to the limit of the maximum size of the ICMPv6 message.

Router Renumbering Messages

Router Renumbering for IPv6 is specified in RFC 2894 and allows address prefixes on routers to be configured and reconfigured with the ease of Neighbor Discovery and Address Autoconfiguration for network nodes. This allows administrators to update the prefixes used and advertised by IPv6 routers throughout a site.

Router Renumbering takes advantage of the vast 128-bit IPv6 address space, which provides a great deal of flexibility, allowing network administrators to assign different "meanings" to different bits in the address structure. In practice, Router Renumbering is a straightforward process. A network administrator generates at least one Router Renumbering message that provides a list of router prefixes to be renumbered. When a router receives such a message, it checks to see if any of the addresses for any of its interfaces match the prefixes in the message. If so, then the router changes the matched prefixes to the new ones learned from the message. There is an option in the Router Renumbering message that can require routers to send a Router Renumbering Result message to provide a response to the sender verifying that the renumbering message was successful.

There are three types of Router Renumbering messages:

- *Commands*—These are sent to routers; they have a Code value of 0.
- *Results*—These are responses sent by routers; they have a Code value of 1.
- *Sequence Number Reset*—These are used to synchonize a reset of the sequence number and cancel the cryptographic keys; they have a Code value of 255.

Each of these message types has different values in the ICMPv6 header Code fields and in the contents of the Message Body field.

The Router Renumbering message format is fairly simple, being composed of only three fields:

- IPv6 Header and Extension Headers
- ICMPv6 and Router Renumbering Header (16 octets)
- Router Renumbering Message Body

Router Renumbering messages are carried in ICMPv6 packets that have a particular formatting. Figure 5-27 shows you the formatting of the Router Renumbering message header.

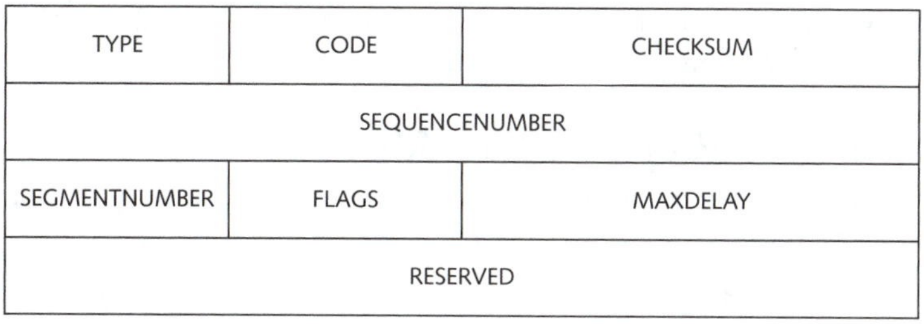

TYPE	CODE	CHECKSUM
SEQUENCENUMBER		
SEGMENTNUMBER	FLAGS	MAXDELAY
RESERVED		

Figure 5-27 ICMPv6 Router Renumbering message header format
© Cengage Learning 2013

Table 5-16 describes the values of the fields for this message format.

Field Name	Description
Type	138
Code	0 – Router Renumbering Command 1 – Router Renumbering Result 255 – Sequence Number Reset
Checksum	This is the checksum specified for ICMPv6 messages.
SequenceNumber	This is an unsigned 32-bit sequence number that must be non-decreasing between Sequence Number Resets.
SegmentNumber	This is an unsigned 8-bit field that contains values for different types of Router Renumbering messages having the same SequenceNumber.
Flags	T = Test command, with 0 meaning that the router configuration is to be modified and 1 meaning that it is a test message and only a simulation with no command to process configuration changes. R = Result requested, with 0 indicating that a Result must not be sent and 1 indicating that the router must send a result message after processing the command message. A = All interfaces, with 0 indicating that the command must not be applied to interfaces that are administratively shut down and 1 indicating that the command must apply to all interfaces regardless of their administrative status. S = Site specific, with 0 indicating that the command must be applied to interfaces regardless of site affiliation and 1 indicating that the command must be applied to only interfaces belonging to the same site. This flag will be ignored unless the router treats interfaces as belonging to different sites. P = Processed previously, with 0 indicating that the Result message contains a complete report of processing the command message and 1 indicating that the command message was previously processed and the router is not processing it again.
MaxDelay	This is an unsigned 16-bit field that specifies the maximum amount of time in milliseconds that a router must delay sending any reply to the command message. Some implementations may assign a random delay.
Reserved	This field must be set to 0 by the sender and ignored by all receivers.

Table 5-16 ICMPv6 Router Renumbering message header fields
© Cengage Learning 2013

As mentioned earlier in this section, there are a number of other ICMPv6 informational messages available, based on different RFC specifications. See Table 5-9 for the complete list.

A Short Comparison of ICMPv4 and ICMPv6 Messages

ICMPv4 and ICMPv6 perform the same basic functions; however, ICMPv6 provides added functionality. ICMPv4 and ICMPv6 share the following general message types:

- Connectivity-checking messages
- Error-checking messages
- Informational messages
- Fragmentation required messages

Only ICMPv6 offers the following general message types:

- Address Assignment messages
- Address Resolution messages
- Multicast Group Management messages
- Mobile IPv6 Support messages

The principal difference between these two versions of the ICMP protocol is the integration of different messaging types under the ICMPv6 protocol. Different message types in IPv4 used different transport types, but in IPv6 they all use ICMPv6 for transport. ICMPv4 doesn't offer any sort of relationship between a message's Type value and the actual message type. ICMPv6 organizes all error messages in the Type value range 0–127 and all informational messages in the Type value range 128–255; thus, message "typing" is better organized in ICMPv6.

Path MTU Discovery

Path MTU (PMTU) Discovery in IPv4 networks allows routers to notify nodes via ICMPv4 messages if they need to change the MTU size of the packets they are sending via ICMPv4 messages. Each PMTU is made up of a number of links between the source and destination node, and each link can have a different MTU size. The PMTU is the size of the smallest MTU for an individual link. Packet size is usually managed either through fragmentation or PMTU Discovery. It is common practice for IPv4 routers to fragment packets if the link connected to the outgoing interface has a smaller MTU than the packet size. Sometimes, packets are fragmented more than once, depending on the conditions on the various links between source and destination. Once all the fragments arrive at their destination, the destination node reassembles the fragments into the original message and then processes the message.

Ideally, network nodes want to send packets that are the largest size possible and that will still traverse the path without being fragmented in order to move messages with the greatest efficiency. Originally, all packets were set to an MTU of 576 bytes. Even today, a sending computer must ask the destination node for permission to send larger packets, but this permission is commonly given. Another way sending nodes can transmit packets more efficiently is by setting the Don't Fragment (DF) flag on packets. Nodes don't have a great deal of routing information and set the packet MTU for the size tolerated on the local subnet. If those packets go through without error, then the node will continue to send packets with that MTU through its default router.

If the packet MTU is too large, the node will receive the ICMPv4 message Destination Unreachable. A common reason for packets being undeliverable is that they have too large an MTU and the DF flag is set so routers can't fragment them. When the DF flag is set and the packet MTU is too large, a router that is unable to forward the packets drops them and then sends a Fragmentation Needed message to the source node. The node can set the packet MTU to a smaller size or remove the DF flag so that resent packets can be fragmented if necessary.

Changes to PMTU

IPv6 MTU sizing and fragmentation have been updated to improve the efficiency and quality of sending and receiving network traffic. One way this was achieved was by setting the default MTU for packets to 1280 bytes. Another method was to eliminate fragmentation of packets once they've been sent from the source node. IPv6 routers are unable to fragment packets in transit. If a packet needs to be fragmented in order to be delivered to the destination, the source node must perform this task.

Although PMTU Discovery was used on IPv4 networks, it has been vastly improved for IPv6. Source nodes are now able to use PMTU to become aware of the smallest link MTU on an arbitrary path and then set packet MTUs accordingly. This isn't a perfect system, because the route can change during transit and packets can be routed to links with smaller MTUs. Because the router cannot fragment these packets, it drops them and sends an ICMPv6 Packet Too Big message back to the source node. Once the source node receives the Packet Too Big message, it reduces the packet MTU size and retransmits. If the source node receives subsequent Packet Too Big messages, it will continue to reduce the packet MTU size until the error messages stop.

If the source node needs to fragment its packets, it does so in much the same way that nodes and routers fragmented IPv4 packets, except that the use of IPv6 extension headers complicates the process. That's because some extension headers, such as Destination and Hop-By-Hop options, cannot be fragmented. Any unfragmentable part of an IPv6 packet must be included in every fragment of the original packet. The fragmented packets are then sent and, upon successful delivery, reassembled by the destination node.

 IPv6 PMTU Discovery and packet MTU sizing and fragmentation are also discussed in Chapter 3. Also, in this chapter, see the "Path MTU Discovery with ICMP" section for additional details.

Testing and Troubleshooting Sequences for ICMP

ICMP's most common uses are for testing and troubleshooting. Two well-known IP utilities, Ping and Traceroute, rely on ICMP to perform **connectivity tests** and **path discovery**.

Connectivity Testing with Ping

Although many people may be familiar with the Ping utility, they may not be aware that Ping is actually a form of **ICMP Echo communication**. An **ICMP Echo Request packet** consists of an Ethernet header, IP header, ICMP header, and some undefined data. The Ping process is quite simple, actually. First, the client transmits this packet to the target network. Upon receipt, the target echoes back the data, as shown in Figure 5-28.

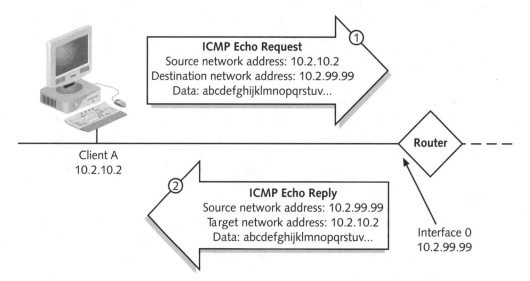

Figure 5-28 Ping utility uses ICMP Echo Requests and Echo Replies
© Cengage Learning 2013

The ICMP Echo Request is a connectionless process with no guarantee of delivery—it is truly a best-effort process.

Most Ping utilities send several Echo Requests to the target in order to obtain an **average response time**. These response times are displayed in **millisecond**s (thousandths of a second) following "time=," as shown in Figure 5-29, but they should not be considered evidence of the typical **round-trip time** between devices. These times should be considered a snapshot of the current round-trip time. The Microsoft Ping utility lists the IP address of the responding device, the bytes contained in the Ping response, the round-trip time, and the TTL value in the response packet.

Figure 5-29 Ping utility providing feedback on success and round-trip times
Source: Microsoft

The Ping utility included with Windows Server 2008, Windows Vista, and Windows 7 sends a series of four ICMP Echo Requests with a one-second ICMP Echo Reply Timeout value. The Echo Requests consist of 32 bytes of data (an alphabetical pattern as the data payload) in a **fragmentable** IP packet. The Ping utility supports IP addresses and names and uses traditional name resolution processes to resolve symbolic names to IP addresses, whenever possible. Figure 5-29 shows the results of a Ping operation.

Most TCP/IP stacks do not allow you to ping the broadcast address because all receiving hosts would respond to the sender and most likely overwhelm it. Most TCP/IP stacks typically do not respond to ICMP Echo Requests sent to a multicast or broadcast address either—another safeguard against overwhelming a host that has somehow managed to send an ICMP Echo Request to the broadcast or multicast address.

The **command-line parameter**s used with the `ping` command can affect the appearance and functionality of these ICMP Echo packets. Here are a few of the parameters available with the Ping utility:

- –l *size*, where *size* is the number of data bytes to send
- –f, which sets the Don't Fragment bit
- –i *TTL*, where *TTL* sets the value of the TTL field in the IP header
- –v *TOS*, where *TOS* sets the TOS (type of service) field value in the IP header
- –w *timeout*, where *timeout* sets the number of milliseconds to wait for a reply

Appendix C, "Command-Line IP Utilities," provides a complete list of supported `ping` command parameters.

Path Discovery with Traceroute

The **Traceroute** utility uses **route tracing** to identify a **path** from the sender to the target host. Using ICMP Echo Requests and some manipulation of the TTL value in the IP header, Traceroute results provide a list of routers along a path as well as the round-trip latency time to each router. Some implementations of Traceroute also attempt to resolve the names of the routers along a path.

Here are the steps that Traceroute uses to identify the path from the local host (Host A) to a remote host (Host B) across an internetwork, as shown in Figure 5-30.

1. Host A sends an ICMP Echo Request packet to Host B's IP address with a TTL value of 1. Router 1 cannot decrement the TTL value to 0 and forward the packet, so Router 1 discards the packet and sends an ICMP Time Exceeded-TTL Exceeded in Transit message back to Host A. Router 1 sets the TTL value of this ICMP Time Exceeded message to a default value, such as 128. Host A notes the IP address of the responding router (Router 1).

2. Host A sends an ICMP Echo Request packet to Host B's IP address with a TTL value of 2. Router 1 decrements the ICMP Echo Request packet's TTL value to 1 and forwards the packet to the next-hop router (Router 2). Router 2 cannot decrement the TTL value

to 0 and forward the packet, so Router 2 discards the packet and sends an ICMP Time Exceeded-TTL Exceeded in Transit message back to Host A. Router 2 sets the TTL value of this ICMP Time Exceeded message to a default value, such as 128. Host A notes the IP address of the second router (hop) along the path.

3. Host A sends an ICMP Echo Request packet to Host B's IP address with a TTL value of 3. Router 1 decrements the ICMP Echo Request packet's TTL value to 2 and forwards the packet to the next-hop router (Router 2). Router 2 decrements the ICMP Echo Request packet's TTL value to 1 and forwards the packet to the next-hop router (Router 3). Router 3 cannot decrement the TTL value to 0 and forward the packet, so Router 3 discards the packet and sends an ICMP Time Exceeded-TTL Exceeded in Transit message back to Host A. Router 3 sets the TTL value of this ICMP Time Exceeded message to a default value, such as 128. Host A notes the IP address of the third router (hop) along the path.

4. Host A sends an ICMP Echo Request packet to Host B's IP address with a TTL value of 4. Router 1 decrements the ICMP Echo Request packet's TTL value to 3 and forwards the packet to the next-hop router (Router 2). Router 2 decrements the ICMP Echo Request packet's TTL value to 2 and forwards the packet to the next-hop router (Router 3). Router 3 decrements the ICMP Echo Request packet's TTL value to 1 and forwards the packet to the final destination (Host B). Host B sends an ICMP Echo Reply packet. Host A notes the round-trip time for the ICMP Echo test to Host B.

The command-line parameters that **Tracert** (the Windows version of Traceroute) uses can affect the appearance and functionality of this process. The following list provides a few of the parameters available with the Tracert utility that is included with Windows Server 2008, Windows Vista, and Windows 7:

*   –d, which instructs Tracert to not perform a DNS reverse query on the routers
*   –h *max_hops*, where *max_hops* defines the maximum TTL value to use
*   –w *timeout*, where *timeout* indicates how long to wait for a reply before displaying an asterisk (*)

For a complete list of supported Tracert parameters, refer to Appendix C. Figure 5-30 illustrates how Traceroute, employing ICMPv4 Echo packets, uses the TTL value in IPv4 packets.

Path Discovery with Pathping

Available for all versions of Windows since Windows 2000, the **Pathping** utility is a command-line utility that uses ICMP Echo packets to test router and link latency as well as packet loss. For more information on Pathping, refer to Appendix C.

Path MTU Discovery with ICMP

RFC 1191, "Path MTU Discovery," defines a method for discovering a **Path MTU** (**PMTU**) using ICMP. In Chapter 3, we focused on how a router can fragment an IP packet destined for a network with a smaller MTU. We also indicated that fragmentation does not make optimal use of bandwidth owing to the high **overhead** from the multiple headers required to get one chunk of data across the network. PMTU Discovery

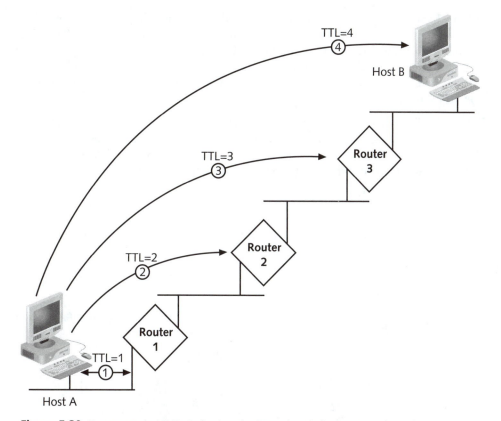

Figure 5-30 Traceroute in ICMPv4 altering the TTL value to find routers along the path
© Cengage Learning 2013

enables a source to learn the currently supported MTU across an entire path, without requiring fragmentation.

Using PMTU, a host always sets the Don't Fragment bit in the IP header to 1 (indicating that the packet cannot be fragmented by a router along the path). If a packet is too large to be routed on a network, the receiving router discards the packet and sends an ICMP Destination Unreachable: Fragmentation Needed and Don't Fragment Set message back to the source. PMTU-capable routers also include the MTU of the **restricting link** (a link that does not support forwarding based on the current packet format and configuration) in the ICMP reply.

Upon receipt of a "Fragmentation Needed and Don't Fragment was Set" ICMP reply that indicates the restricting link's MTU size, the PMTU host must either reduce the MTU size of the message accordingly and retransmit the data or remove the Don't Fragment flag in the IP header and retransmit the packet using the original size. Reducing the size based on the restricting link's MTU size ensures the packet crosses the router that previously discarded it.

During this process, a PMTU host may receive a "Fragmentation Needed and Don't Fragment Flag was Set" ICMP response from one router, decrease its MTU size, and retransmit only to have another "Fragmentation Needed and Don't Fragment Flag was Set" ICMP packet sent from another router farther along the path. The process of PMTU Discovery continues until the **end-to-end minimum MTU size** is discovered. Finally, the host should be able to send a packet with an MTU that enables it to travel through the entire path without being discarded by a router or fragmented for the purpose of network transmission efficiency.

The PMTU Discovery process continues to recheck itself after the PMTU is discovered in case another path becomes available. For example, consider the network depicted in Figure 5-31. Host A and Host B can both use the same MTU—18,000 bytes. Their communications use Path #1—packets greater than 1,500 bytes must be fragmented.

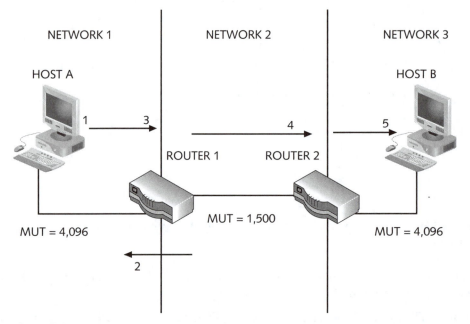

Figure 5-31 PMTU Discovery automatically determines the PMTU of a path to eliminate fragments
© Cengage Learning 2013

Let's examine, step by step, the PMTU process shown in Figure 5-31:

1. Host A, on Network 1 with an MTU of 4,096 bytes, sends a 4,096-byte packet to Host B. The packet is sent to Router 1 (Host A's default **gateway**).

2. Router 1 knows this 4,096-byte packet cannot be sent on Network 2 because its link MTU only tolerates packets of 1,500 bytes or less. Router 1 discards the packet and sends Host A a "Fragmentation Needed and Don't Fragment Flag was Set" ICMP packet that indicates that 1,500 is the MTU of the next link.

3. Host A resends the packet using a maximum MTU size of 1,500.

4. Router 1 forwards the packet across Network 2 to Router 2.

5. Router 2 receives the packet and forwards it to Network 3, where it arrives at Host B.

The PMTU specification defined in RFC 1191 requires that the PMTU host periodically try a larger MTU to see if the **allowable data size** has increased.

Looking at the same scenario using ICMPv6 and PMTU Discovery, Host A should use the discovery process to determine the smallest link-MTU for the entire PMTU between itself and Host B and then set the packet MTU at 1,500 bytes. Assuming the route doesn't change before Host A sends its packets, Host A's message should successfully transverse Router 1, be forwarded by Router 2, and safely arrive at Network 3 to be delivered to Host B.

If, after Host A sets the packet MTU to 1,500, the Network 2 link-MTU should become smaller—say 1,000 bytes—then, when Host A's packets arrive at Router 1, the router would determine that the MTU of the packets was too large, drop the packets, and send an ICMPv6 Packets Too Big message back to Host A. Host A would then reset the MTU of its packets to an MTU of 1,000 bytes and retransmit the message. If the Network 2 link-MTU remains at 1,000 bytes, then the packets will be forwarded from Router 1 to Router 2 and then be successfully delivered at Host B.

Returning to the original ICMPv4 example, if Router 1 uses a routing protocol that recognizes the **throughput difference** between Network 1 and Network 2, Router 1 should use a separate link that will accommodate the difference when forwarding packets. This path change is transparent to Host A, the PMTU client.

This is why the specification recommends that, following receipt of a "Fragmentation Needed and Don't Fragment was Set" ICMP packet, the PMTU host try sending a packet larger than the current PMTU no sooner than five minutes after it was decreased. The specification also dictates that **backward compatibility** be provided to routers that cannot include the MTU value in the "Fragmentation Needed and Don't Fragment was Set" ICMP packet, by gradually decreasing the PMTU size until no more "Fragmentation Needed and Don't Fragment was Set" ICMP packets are sent back by the router.

PMTU Discovery is enabled by default on all versions of Windows since Windows 2000, but you can set two optional PMTU parameters in Windows Server 2008, Windows Vista, and Windows 7—EnablePMTUDiscovery and EnablePMTUBHDetect—to disable PMTU Discovery, if necessary. Neither option is present by default; they must be manually added to the Registry. (A reboot is required for the changes to take effect.) The EnablePMTUDiscovery Registry setting enables or disables PMTU Discovery on the Windows host, as shown in Table 5-17.

Registry Information	Details
Location	HKEY_LOCAL_MACHINE\SYSTEM\ CurrentControlSet\Services\Tcpip\Parameters
Data type	REG_DWORD
Valid range	0 or 1
Default value	1
Present by default	No

Table 5-17 **EnablePMTUDiscovery Registry setting**
© Cengage Learning 2013

Setting the EnablePMTUDiscovery value to 0 disables this process.

The EnablePMTUBHDetect Registry setting defines if the Windows Server 2008, Windows Vista, or Windows 7 host should detect black hole routers. A black hole router **silently discards** packets without indicating any cause, thereby thwarting **auto-recovery** or **auto-reconfiguration** attempts. Many administrators disable ICMP responses for security reasons.

For example, if a router does not support PMTU and is configured so it will not send ICMP **Destination Unreachable packets**, the PMTU host may send a large packet that never gets routed. Without some feedback from the router, the host cannot determine that PMTU was the problem. The host would simply retransmit the packet until a timeout or **retry counter** expires, and the communication would be unsuccessful. If the EnablePMTUBHDetect setting is enabled, the PMTU host retries the large MTU a few times and, if no response is received, automatically sets the PMTU to 576 bytes.

See Table 5-18 for information about the EnablePMTUBHDetect Registry setting.

Registry Information	Details
Location	HKEY_LOCAL_MACHINE\SYSTEM\CurrentControlSet\Services\Tcpip\Parameters
Data type	REG_DWORD
Valid range	0 or 1
Default value	0
Present by default	No

Table 5-18 **EnablePMTUBHDetect Registry setting**
© Cengage Learning 2013

The EnablePMTUBHDetect setting is disabled by default.

Routing Sequences for ICMP

Whereas routing protocols, such as Routing Information Protocol (RIP) and Open Shortest Path First (OSPF), provide route information to routers on a network, ICMP can provide routing information to hosts. Routers can use ICMP to provide a default gateway to a host (if the host requests assistance). Routers can also send ICMP messages, called ICMP Redirect messages, to redirect a host to another router that offers a more **optimal route**. This is further discussed later in this chapter, in the section titled "Redirection to a Better Router."

Section 4.3 of RFC 1812, "Requirements for IP Version 4 Routers," describes how IP routers should handle **ICMP error messages** and **ICMP query messages**.

Router Discovery IP hosts typically learn about routes through manual configuration of the default gateway parameter and redirection messages. When a host boots up without a default gateway setting, that host may issue an **ICMP Router Solicitation** packet to locate a local router. Windows Server 2008, Windows Vista, and Windows 7 hosts automatically send ICMP Router Solicitation packets when they boot up without a default gateway setting. This behavior, as you learn later in this section, corresponds to a configurable parameter. This process is referred to as ICMP Router Solicitation and **ICMP Router Discovery**. IP hosts send ICMP Router Solicitations, and routers reply with ICMP Router Advertisements.

By default, the ICMP Router Solicitation packet is sent to the all-routers IP multicast address 224.0.0.2. Although RFC 1812 dictates that IP routers "must support the router part of the ICMP Router Discovery protocol on all connected networks on which the router supports either IP multicast or IP broadcast addressing," many do not. If a router does not support the router portion of ICMP Router Discovery, host Router Solicitation requests go unanswered.

For an IP host that resides on a network that supports multiple IP routers, the IP host may receive multiple replies—one reply from each locally connected IP router. Typically, the hosts accept and use the first reply received as the default gateway. Figure 5-32 depicts a network that consists of multiple routers and a host that is missing its default gateway setting. In this scenario, Host B, 10.2.10.2, sends an IP multicast to locate a local router to use as a default gateway. Because Router 1 supports the router portion of ICMP Router Discovery, it replies with its own IP address. Host A adds Router 1's IP address to its routing tables.

In Figure 5-32, only one router—the local router—replies. Router 2 is not on the same network as Host B, and the IP multicast is not forwarded by Router 1. Host A is already configured with a default gateway; it does not need to perform ICMP Router Solicitation.

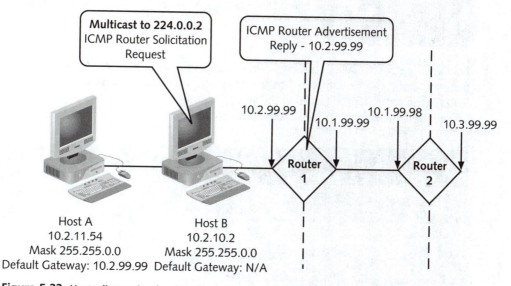

Figure 5-32 Hosts discovering local routers using the Router Discovery process
© Cengage Learning 2013

This process describes how Router Discovery operates under ICMPv4 but also adequately describes how these messages operate in ICMPv6. However, the specification for the process is from the more recent RFC 4861. IPv6 Neighbor Discovery specifications are also used to describe ICMPv6 Router Discovery messages.

Windows Server 2008, Windows Vista, and Windows 7 hosts can be reconfigured so that they will not use ICMP Router Solicitation. The reconfiguration is done by editing the PerformRouterDiscovery Registry setting, as shown in Table 5-19.

Registry Information	Details
Location	HKEY_LOCAL_MACHINE\SYSTEM\CurrentControlSet\Services\Tcpip\Parameters\Interfaces\<interface>
Data type	REG_DWORD
Valid range	0 or 1
Default value	1
Present by default	No

Table 5-19 **PerformRouterDiscovery Registry setting**
© Cengage Learning 2013

Changing the PerformRouterDiscovery value to 0 disables the ICMP Router Discovery process.

Windows Server 2008 has an additional valid range option: (2) enable only if DHCP sends the Perform Router Discovery option.

On Windows Server 2008, Windows Vista, and Windows 7 hosts, the SolicitationAddressBCast Registry setting can be configured to use a subnet broadcast (such as 10.2.255.255) during the Router Discovery process instead of the all-routers multicast address. See Table 5-20 for information about the SolicitationAddressBCast Registry setting.

Registry Information	Details
Location	HKEY_LOCAL_MACHINE\SYSTEM\CurrentControlSet\Services\Tcpip\Parameters\Interfaces\<interface>
Data type	REG_DWORD
Valid range	0 or 1
Default value	0
Present by default	No

Table 5-20 **SolicitationAddressBCast Registry setting**
© Cengage Learning 2013

Changing the SolicitationAddressBCast value to 1 enables the Windows Server 2008, Windows Vista, or Windows 7 host to use the IP subnet broadcast to perform ICMP Router Solicitation.

Router Advertising As mentioned, IP hosts typically learn about routes through the manually configured default gateway setting and the process of redirection (covered in the next section). Alternately, some routers can be configured to send periodic ICMP Router Advertisement packets. These periodic ICMP Router Advertisements do not mean that ICMP is a routing protocol. They simply allow hosts to passively learn about **available routes**.

Routers can periodically send these ICMP Router Advertisements in response to ICMP Router Solicitation packets. If configured to do so, routers periodically send **unsolicited** ICMP Router Advertisements to the all-hosts multicast address 224.0.0.1. These advertisements typically include the IP address of the router that sent the ICMP Router Advertisement packet. The router also includes a Lifetime value to indicate how long the receiving host should keep the route entry. The default Lifetime value for route entries is 30 minutes. After 30 minutes has passed, the **expired route entry** is removed from the route tables and the host may issue a new ICMP Router Solicitation packet or wait and passively listen for an ICMP Router Advertisement packet. The default **advertising rate** is between 7 and 10 minutes.

ICMP Router Advertising is covered in greater detail in RFC 1256, "ICMP Router Discovery Messages."

Redirection to a Better Router ICMP can be used to point a host to a better router, if required. For example, in a scenario working with ICMPv4, in Figure 5-33, 10.2.99.99 is the default gateway setting for Host A (10.2.10.2/16). This host wants to communicate with Host B at IP address 10.3.71.7.

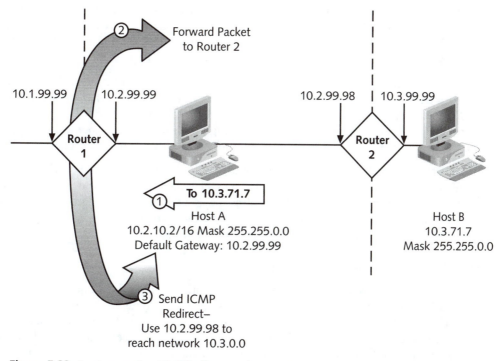

Figure 5-33 Routers sending ICMP Redirects to hosts indicating optimal path
© Cengage Learning 2013

Host A's route resolution process goes through the following steps:

1. Host A places its own network mask (255.255.0.0) on the destination address 10.3.71.7 to determine that Host B is on another network.

    Host A examines its routing tables to locate a route entry. Host A looks for a route entry with the longest match (that is, an entry that matches the destination host IP address with a network mask of 255.255.255.255 or a portion of the destination host IP address with a shorter subnet mask). No such entry exists.

    Host A examines its routing tables to locate a default gateway entry. Host A's default gateway setting is 10.2.99.99.

    Host A examines its ARP cache to locate an entry for 10.2.99.99's hardware address. Host A finds the hardware address 00:10:7B:81:43:E3 associated with 10.2.99.99's IP address.

    Host A builds a packet addressed to the IP address 10.3.71.7 and sends this packet to the default gateway's hardware address.

2. When Router 1 receives the packet, it performs the required error-checking tasks, strips off the datalink header, and ensures the packet TTL is greater than 1. Once this process is successfully completed, Router 1 checks its routing tables to determine how to forward the packet. Router 1 locates an entry in its routing tables saying that, to get to the destination network, it needs to forward the packet to Router 2, then notes that the next hop along the path is back onto the same subnet as Host A to Router 2. Router 1 forwards the packet to Router 2.

3. Router 1 then sends an ICMP Redirect packet to Host A. The ICMP Redirect packet indicates that 10.2.99.98 is the optimal router address to use when trying to reach network 10.3.0.0. Host A does not need to resend the packet. The next time Host A communicates with Host B, it will address packets to 10.2.99.98's hardware address.

The redirection process only serves IP hosts; it does not serve IP routers. In other words, if one router forwards a packet to another router that does not offer an optimal path, no ICMP Redirect packet is sent back to the first router to notify it of a better path. The packet is simply forwarded. We rely on robust routing protocols that use **metrics** to determine the best path. Chapter 4 provides additional information on IP routing protocols.

Redirect messages for ICMPv6 operate pretty much the same way they do under ICMPv4. However, for organizational purposes, they are classified not as error messages but as informational messages. Of course, IPv6 addressing is used instead, and the Redirect message contains as much of the original message sent by the source node up to the limit of the link MTU attaching the router's interface to the source node.

Security Issues for ICMPv4

Because ICMP provides information about network configurations and connectivity status, you can use it to learn how a network is designed and configured. Unfortunately, hackers also can use ICMP as part of a **reconnaissance process** to learn about active network addresses and active processes. These reconnaissance processes often precede a network break-in. Because ICMP can be used as an information-gathering tool, some companies limit the amount of ICMP traffic that flows through their networks.

When **hacker**s decide to infiltrate a network, they typically start with a list of the IP hosts on the network (unless the target is a single known system). An **IP address scanning** process is one method of obtaining a list of the active hosts on a network. The IP **host probe** is performed by sending a ping packet (ICMP Echo Request packet) to each host within a range and noting the responses. The devices that reply are considered valid targets to the hacker. Typically, the next step in the hack is a port scanning.

Once hackers know the addresses of the active devices on the network, they can target their next reconnaissance process, the port scan, to those devices. Because many systems do not reply to pings sent to the broadcast address, typical IP host scans are sent unicast to each possible address. Such a scan process is typically scripted rather than handled manually, one address at a time. That explains why so many online IP tool Web sites, such as *www.snapfiles.com/freeware/ network/fwscanner.html*, as well as hacker sites, offer tools that scan specific IP address ranges (usually, by supplying only starting and ending addresses).

Advanced ICMP attacks are certainly possible, mostly involving unintended usage of the ICMP protocol specification or clever ploys to trick a routing device into yielding topological information about the networks it identifies. Only a few methods are briefly described here.

ICMP Redirect Attack As described previously, ICMP can be used to manipulate traffic flow between hosts. An attacker can just as easily redirect traffic to his machine and perform any number of man-in-the-middle style attacks, which usually consist of trust-based service exploitation. At this point, the attacker is now able to perform many forms of network-based attacks on the target machine, such as connection hijacking and denial of service, and he can potentially obtain login credentials by sniffing.

ICMP Router Discovery This protocol specification is also susceptible to attack on the local network segment, providing a potential attacker with another man-in-the-middle possibility. During the discovery process, a Router Solicitation message finds its way to an attacker's machine. Timing is critical, as the attacker must cleanly intercept the solicitation, stifle the original response from the immediate router, or race back to the target host with a forged response before the router does. The attacker spoofs a response back to the target host, indicating that his machine is actually the immediate router in question and not the actual router on the network segment. No authentication is performed during this process, so the recipient has no way of knowing that this response is bogus.

Inverse Mapping Sometimes, it isn't what the hacker knows about the network layout so much as what the perimeter devices will tell him. One method of determining live targets on a network is by using **inverse mapping**, which works like this: When a filtering device is detected between an attacker and his potential target, he can interrogate the routing device in an unusual way—by intentionally sending packets to vacant network addresses. Upon receipt of a packet destined for a nonexistent host, the intermediary router will gladly pass it on anyway (ICMP being a stateless protocol, the router knows no better). Once that packet reaches an internal router, however, one that is more knowledgeable in the valid and available network addresses, it will promptly reply with a Host Unreachable message for every bogus entry requested. The attacker then may logically deduce which addresses correspond to a live target.

Firewalking   Firewalking is the process of walking a firewall ACL or ruleset to determine what it filters and how. This is a two-phase attack method, involving an initial Traceroute to discover hop count to a firewall appliance. Once this filtering device is identified by the Traceroute, a second wave of attack follows, and this one consists of sending a packet with a TTL of one greater than the final hop count (between attacker and firewall). The goal is to elicit a Time Exceeded response from beyond the firewall, indicating a live and responsive target.

Now that you understand some of the various uses and abuses that ICMP supports, it's time to dig deeper into the layout that ICMP messages follow and the various message types that ICMP supports. These topics provide the subject matter for the rest of this chapter.

Security Issues for ICMPv6

ICMPv6 has built-in security features that are designed to prevent attacks sent from another network segment. These features include the value in the Hop Limit field being set at 255. Also, the source address of ICMPv6 packets must be either link-local or unspecified (::/128) for all Router Advertisement and Neighbor Solicitation messages. However, no mechanism is currently specified that would prevent an attacker on the local network from exploiting ICMPv6 to compromise the network.

Authentication for ICMPv6 packet exchanges is managed using the IP Authentication Header (IPv6-AUTH) or the IP Encapsulating Security Payload Header (IPv6-ESP). IPv6-ESP also provides confidentiality for these exchanges.

ICMPv6 is protected by IPsec, but this presents a security bootstrap problem because IPsec is not available when a computer is at this state. When booting up, a network node sends a Router Solicitation message requesting Router Advertisements from all local routers. Unfortunately, Router Solicitation messages are completely insecure, much like ARP in IPv4 networks. Neighbor Discovery messages have the same problem in that they do not have any security during booting. Routing Advertisement messages are totally dependent on IPsec Authentication Header security.

In short, except for the items already mentioned, ICMPv6 security is similar to ICMPv4. It runs on top of the IPv6 protocol and utilizes security features much like IPv4 ARP does, which is insecure. Solutions for these ICMPv6 vulnerabilities have yet to be formally specified as standards, although individual vendors of internetworking devices may implement proprietary solutions.

Decoding ICMP Packets

The structure of ICMP and other network packets can seem theoretical when viewed as a diagram or discussed in a narrative, but tools such as Wireshark can capture and decode ICMP packets for examination. Although there is a wide variety of different message types carried by the ICMP protocol, as mentioned earlier in this chapter, the ICMP packet is made up of a basic format. Using Wireshark, that structure can be investigated and information about the packet's version number, header length, type, ID, and other information can be easily decoded and the specifics regarding the packet revealed.

ICMPv4

The basic ICMPv4 packet hasn't changed in 30 years, and the format is very well known. To examine the ICMPv4 packet format, just generate ICMPv4 traffic in the form of an Echo Request and Response using the Ping utility or Tracert tool in Windows (Traceroute in Linux), and then use Wireshark to capture that traffic. Once done, a specific ICMP packet can be selected in the Wireshark UI, and the details can be examined. For the purpose of this demonstration, a Tracert message was sent from a node to *www.cisco.com*, and the Echo Reply message will be decoded. Figure 5-34 provides the details.

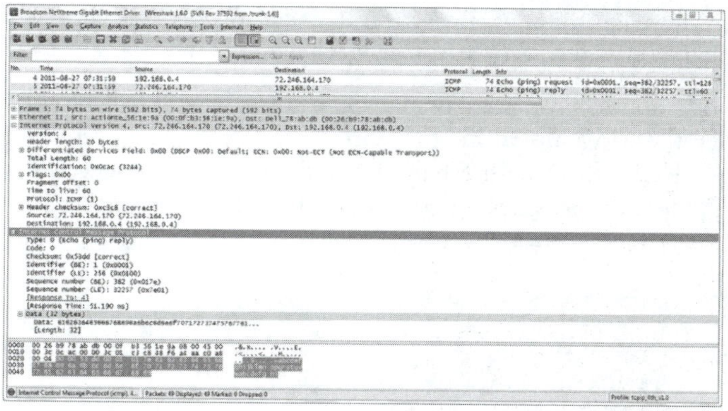

Figure 5-34 ICMPv4 Echo Reply packet format for decode
Source: Wireshark

The ICMPv4 Echo Reply is sent by a receiving network node, which can be a personal computer, server, router, or other network device, in response to an Echo (Request) message sent by the source node. Table 5-21 describes the details of each ICMPv4 packet field seen in Figure 5-34.

Field Type	Description
Type	0 (Echo (ping) Reply), indicating the type of ICMPv4 message.
Code	0, which is the code for both Echo (Request) and Echo Reply messages.
Checksum	0x53dd [correct], indicating no error was found in the ICMPv4 header.
Identifier	BE (big-endian) and LE (little-endian) each have a separate entry, and they both refer to which bytes are the most significant (BE) and least significant (LE) in multibyte data types and describe how the sequence of bytes is stored in the computer's memory.
Sequence number	BE (big-endian) and LE (little-endian) each have a separate entry, and they both refer to which bytes are the most significant (BE) and least significant (LE) in multibyte data types and describe how the sequence of bytes is stored in the computer's memory.
Response Time	51.190 ms, or the amount of time in milliseconds the responding host took to reply to the Echo (Request) message. (Note that just above this field is a notation indicating to which Echo (Request) packet this reply is responding.)
Data	The encapulated data payload for this Echo Reply message expressed, which is 32 bytes in length.

Table 5-21 ICMPv4 Echo Request and Echo Reply Message format fields
© Cengage Learning 2013

For more information on "endianness" and its use in Wireshark, visit *http://en.wikipedia.org/wiki/Endianness*.

ICMPv6

Comparisons between ICMPv4 and ICMPv6 are expected, particularly when attempting to describe the structural and functional differences between the two versions of the ICMP protocol and their packets. Wireshark can easily capture and decode ICMPv6 Echo Request and Echo Reply messages to illustrate the makeup of the ICMPv6 packet format and provide a visual reference for comparison with the ICMPv4 packet format.

Two Windows 7 network nodes have been used to exchange ICMPv6 Echo Request and Reply packets, generating the necessary traffic for Wireshark to capture. From there, a Message Reply packet was selected in the Wireshark UI and its output revealed. Figure 5-35 shows you the details. Table 5-22 provides a description of the ICMPv6 packet fields.

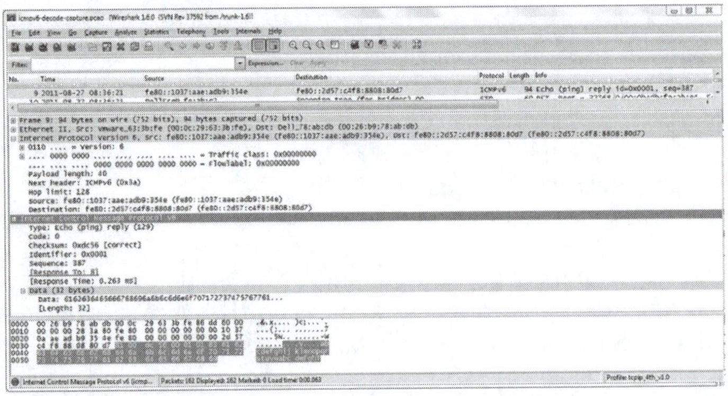

Figure 5-35 ICMPv6 Echo Reply packet format for decode
Source: Wireshark

Field Type	Description
Type	129 Echo (ping) Reply, indicating that this is an ICMPv6 Echo Reply message.
Code	0, which is the code for both Echo Request and Echo Reply messages.
Checksum	0xdc56 [correct], indicating no error was found in the ICMPv6 header.
Identifier	ICMPv6 Echo Request and Reply messages use a single, unique identifier, and Wireshark does not provide BE and LE entries.
Sequence number	387 is the number in sequence for this packet.
Response Time	0.263 ms, or the amount of time in milliseconds the responding host took to reply to the Echo Request message. (Note that just above this field is a notation indicating to which Echo Request packet this reply is responding.)
Data	The encapulated data payload for this Echo Reply message expressed, which is 32 bytes in length.

Table 5-22 ICMPv6 Echo Request and Echo Reply Message format fields

In terms of formatting, the ICMPv4 and ICMPv6 packets used for Echo Reply messages are almost the same. The most obvious difference is the use of the Type value for each packet. ICMPv6 associates the Type value with the actual function of the message, whereas ICMPv4 does not. Wireshark presents the Identifier and Sequence number for ICMPv4 packets with values for BE and LE where as it does not for ICMPv6 echo packets.

Chapter Summary

- ICMP provides vital feedback about IP routing and delivery problems. ICMP also provides important IP diagnostic and control capabilities that include reachability analysis, congestion management, route optimization, and timeout error reports.

- Although ICMP messages fall within various well-documented types and behave as a separate protocol at the TCP/IP Network layer, ICMP is really part of IP itself, and its support is required in any standards-compliant IP implementation. RFC 792 describes ICMP, but numerous other RFCs (such as 950, 1191, and 1812) describe additional details about how ICMP should behave, and how its messages should be generated and handled.

  Both ICMPv4 and ICMPv6 messages are organized into two general types: error messages and informational messages. Many of these messages are similar in both versions of the ICMP protocol, such as Echo Request and Echo Reply messages, PMTU Discovery, Router Solicitation and Router Advertisement, and Traceroute. Others, such as Packet Too Big and Router Renumbering, are completely new in ICMPv6.

- Two vital TCP/IP diagnostic utilities, known as Ping and Traceroute (invoked as Tracert in the Windows environment), use ICMP to measure round-trip times between a sending and receiving host, and to perform path discovery for a sending host and all intermediate hosts or routers between sender and receiver.

- ICMP also supports PMTU Discovery between a sender and a receiver, which optimizes performance of data delivery between pairs or hosts by avoiding fragmentation en route. This occurs by establishing the smallest MTU required for the path between sender and receiver, and then transmitting all datagrams of that size or smaller from the sending host.

  ICMPv6 introduces numerous changes into MTU management and PMTU discovery, such as the default IPv4 packet MTU being changed from 576 bytes to 1,280 bytes for IPv6. IPv6 routers do not fragment packets, so the sending host must use PMTU to establish the smallest link MTU in the PMTU and impart the correct packet MTU to messages before transmission. If an IPv6 packet is too large for a link MTU, a router will send an ICMPv6 Packet Too Big message to the source node, and that node will respond by reducing the MTU of its packets and resending the message.

- Route and routing error information from ICMP derives from numerous types of ICMP messages. These include the ICMP Router Solicitation messages (which hosts use to locate routers) and ICMP Router Advertisement messages (which routers use to advertise their presence and capabilities) as well as the various codes for the ICMP Destination Unreachable message, which documents many possible causes for delivery failures.

ICMPv6 error and information messages are organized by type, with error messages being in the 1–127 range and informational messages being in the 128–255 range. ICMPv4 messages do not associate the message function with the Type value.

- ICMP also supports route optimization through its ICMP Redirect message type, but this capability is normally restricted only to trusted sources of information because of potential security problems that uncontrolled acceptance of such messages can cause.

- Although ICMP has great positive value as a diagnostic and reporting tool, those same capabilities can be turned to nefarious purposes as well, which makes security issues for ICMP important. When hackers investigate networks, ICMP host probes often represent early stages of attack.

- Understanding the meaning and significance of the ICMP Type and Code fields is essential to recognizing individual ICMP messages and what they are trying to communicate. ICMP message structures and functions can vary, depending on the information that any such message seeks to convey.

- ICMPv4 and ICMPv6 Echo messages have a very similar formatting when decoded in the Wireshark network protocol analyzer, with only small differences being noticed, such as the Type value and how Identifiers and Sequence Numbers are expressed.

Key Terms

advertising rate   The rate at which a service (typically a routing service) is announced on a network. An example of an advertising rate is the 10-minute advertising rate for ICMP Router Advertisement packets.

allowable data size   The amount of data that can be transferred across a link; the MTU.

auto-reconfiguration   The process of automatically changing the configuration of a device.

auto-recovery   The process of automatically recovering from a fault.

available routes   The known functional routes on an internetwork. Available routes are not necessarily the optimal routes. On IP networks, routers periodically advertise available routes.

average response time   The median time required to reply to a query. The history of network average response times is used to provide a measurement for comparison of current network responses.

backward compatibility   A feature that enables a device, process, or protocol to operate with earlier versions of software or hardware that do not support all the latest, up-to-date, or advanced features. For example, a PMTU host can automatically and incrementally reduce the MTU size it uses until it learns the supported PMTU size.

command-line parameter   Options added to a command issued at a prompt (not in a windowed environment). For example, in the command arp -a, the -a is the parameter for the command arp.

connectivity tests   Tests to determine the reachability of a device. IP Ping and Traceroute are two utilities that can be used for connectivity testing.

Destination Unreachable message   An ICMP error message sent from a router to a network host notifying the host that its message could not be delivered to its destination.

Destination Unreachable packets ICMP packets that indicate a failure to reach a destination due to a fragmentation problem, parameter problem, or other problem. Implemented in ICMPv4 and ICMPv6.

end-to-end minimum MTU size The smallest data size that can be sent from one host to another host on an internetwork. Packets may be fragmented to reach the end-to-end minimum MTU size, or the PMTU process can be used to determine the minimum size.

expired route entry A route entry that is considered "too old" and won't be used to forward data through an internetwork. Expired route entries may be held in a routing table for a short time in anticipation that the route will become valid again as another device advertises it.

firewalking A two-staged reconnaissance method involving an initial perimeter device discovery phase and subsequent inverse mapping of filtered devices (by eliciting Time Exceeded responses).

fragmentable Able to be fragmented. A packet must have the May Fragment bit set in order to allow an IP packet to be fragmented, if necessary.

gateway In the TCP/IP environment, a term used to refer to a Network layer forwarding device typically known as a router. The default gateway is the router a host sends a packet to when the host has no specific route to a destination.

hacker A person who uses computer and communications knowledge to exploit information or functionality of a device.

host probe A reconnaissance process used to determine which hosts are active on an IP network. Typically, the Ping process is used to perform a host probe.

ICMP Echo communication An ICMP process whereby a host sends an Echo packet to another host on an internetwork. If the destination host is active and able, it echoes back the data that is contained in the ICMP Echo packet.

ICMP Echo Request packets Packets that are sent to a device to test connectivity. If the receiving device is functional and can reply, it should echo back the data that is contained in the data portions of the Echo Request packets. Implemented in ICMPv4 and ICMPv6.

ICMP error message An error message sent using the ICMP protocol. Destination Unreachable, Time Exceeded, and Parameter Problem are examples of ICMPv4 and ICMPv6 error messages.

ICMP query message An ICMP message that contains requests for configuration or other information. ICMP Echo Request and Router Solicitation are examples of ICMPv4 and ICMPv6 query messages.

ICMP Router Discovery A process in which hosts send ICMP Router Solicitation messages to the all-router multicast address. Local routers that support the ICMP Router Discovery process reply with an ICMP Router Advertisement unicast to the host. The advertisement contains the router's address and a Lifetime value for the router's information. Supported for ICMPv4 and ICMPv6.

ICMP Router Solicitation The process that a host can perform to learn of local routers. An ICMP Router Solicitation message is sent to the all-routers multicast address.

Internet Control Message Protocol (ICMP) A key protocol in the TCP/IP protocol suite that provides error messages and the ability to query other devices. IP Ping and Traceroute utilities use ICMPv4 and ICMPv6.

Internet Group Management Protocol (IGMP) A protocol that supports the formation of multicast groups. Hosts use IGMP to join and leave multicast groups. Routers track IGMP memberships and only forward multicasts on a link that has active members of that multicast group.

inverse mapping The process of identifying live network hosts (mapping internal network layout) positioned behind a filtering device by probing for addresses known not to be in use.

IP address scanning Commonly used by hackers, the process of sending ping packets (ICMP Echo Request packets) to each host within an IP address range to obtain a list of active hosts in that range. All devices that reply may be probed further to determine if they represent valid targets for attack.

metrics Measurements that may be based on distance (hop count), time (seconds), or other values.

millisecond One-thousandth of a second.

network congestion A condition that occurs when the delivery time for packets (also known as network latency) increases beyond normal limits. Congestion can result from several causes, including problems with network links, overloaded hosts or routers, or unusually heavy network usage levels. Packet loss is identified as a characteristic of network congestion.

Network Time Protocol (NTP) A time synchronization protocol defined in RFC 1305. NTP provides the mechanisms to synchronize and coordinate time distribution in a large, diverse Internet operating at varying speeds.

optimal route The best route possible. Typically, routing protocols are used to exchange routing metric information to determine the best route possible. The optimal route is defined as either the route that is quickest, most reliable, most secure, or considered best by some other measurement. When TOS is not used, the optimal route is either the closest (based on hop count) or the highest throughput route.

overhead The non-data bits or bytes required to move data from one location to another. The datalink header is the overhead required to move an IP packet from one device to another across a network. The IP header is additional overhead required to move a packet through an internetwork. Ideally, bandwidth, throughput, and processing power should be devoted to moving high amounts of data bytes—not high amounts of overhead bytes.

path The route that a packet can take through an internetwork.

path discovery The process of learning possible routes through a network.

Path MTU (PMTU) The MTU size that is supported through an entire path; the lowest common denominator MTU through a path. The Path MTU is learned through the PMTU Discovery process.

Pathping A Windows utility used to test router and path latency as well as connectivity.

reachability The ability to find at least one transmission path between a pair of hosts so they can exchange datagrams across an internetwork.

reconnaissance process The process of learning various characteristics about a network or host. Typically, reconnaissance probes precede network attacks.

redirect To point out another path. Using ICMP, a router can redirect a host to another, more optimal router.

restricting link A link that does not support forwarding based on the current packet format and configuration. PMTU is used to identify restricting links so hosts can resend packets using an acceptable MTU size.

retry counter A counter that tracks the number of retransmissions on the network. The most common retry counter found in TCP/IP networking is the TCP retry counter. If a communication cannot be completed successfully before the retry counter expires, the transmission is considered a failure.

round-trip time The amount of time required to get from one host to another host and back. The round-trip time includes the transmission time from the first point to the second point, the processing time at the second point, and the return transmission time to the first point.

route tracing A technique for documenting which hosts and routers a datagram traverses in its path from the sender to the receiver. (The `traceroute` and `tracert` commands use ping in a systematic way to provide this information.)

silent discard The process of discarding a packet without notification to any other device that such a discarding process occurred. For example, a black hole router silently discards packets that it cannot forward.

throughput difference The comparative difference in throughput between two paths. Throughput is measured in Kbps or Mbps.

time synchronization The process of obtaining the exact same time on multiple hosts. Network Time Protocol (NTP) is a time synchronization protocol.

Traceroute *See* Tracert.

Tracert The name of the Windows command that uses multiple `ping` commands to establish the identity and round-trip times for all hosts between a sender and a receiver.

Universal Time (UT) Sometimes called Universal Coordinate Time (UCT), Greenwich Mean Time (GMT), or Zulu Time. A time scale based on the Earth's rotation.

unsolicited Unrequested. Unsolicited replies are typically advertisements that occur on a periodic basis. For example, ICMP Router Advertisements typically occur on a 7–10 minute basis.

Review Questions

1. Path MTU Discovery is only available for IPv6. True or False?

2. What is the name of the concept that indicates that a path exists between two TCP/IP hosts on an internetwork?

    a. path discovery

    b. PMTU

    c. reachability

    d. route tracing

3. Which RFC describes the ICMPv6 error message type Packet Too Big?

    a. 2710

    b. 2894

    c. 4443

    d. 4861

4. It's up to the IP host that receives incoming ICMP messages to act on the content of those messages. True or False?

5. Which of the following RFCs describes ICMP?

   a. 792

   b. 950

   c. 1191

   d. 1812

6. ICMPv6 messages are organized by Type codes. Which range of codes is used for ICMPv6 informational messages?

   a. 0–127

   b. 64–128

   c. 128–255

   d. 256–512

7. ICMP reports errors only about IP datagrams. Errors about error messages are not reported. True or False?

8. Which of the following ICMP message types relates to reachability analysis?

   a. Destination Unreachable

   b. Echo/Echo Reply

   c. Redirect

   d. Source Quench

9. Which of the following ICMP message types reports delivery errors?

   a. Destination Unreachable

   b. Echo/Echo Reply

   c. Redirect

   d. Source Quench

10. Which of the following ICMP message types relates to congestion control?

    a. Destination Unreachable

    b. Echo/Echo Reply

    c. Redirect

    d. Source Quench

11. Which ICMPv6 informational message type was considered an Error message in ICMPv4?

    a. Echo Reply

    b. Redirect

    c. Router Advertisement

    d. Router Renumbering

12. Which of the following Windows command-line utilities performs connectivity or reachability tests?

    a. Ping

    b. Tracert

    c. Traceroute

    d. Ipconfig

13. Which of the following Windows command-line utilities performs path discovery tests?

    a. Ping

    b. Tracert

    c. Traceroute

    d. Ipconfig

14. Which of the following command-line parameters for the `ping` command governs the Time to Live value?

    a. –f

    b. –i

    c. –l

    d. –w

15. Which of the following command-line parameters for the `ping` command governs the Reply Timeout value?

    a. –f

    b. –i

    c. –l

    d. –w

16. Which of the following path discovery command-line parameters turns off reverse DNS lookups?

    a. –a

    b. –d

    c. –h

    d. –w

17. What additional functionality does the Pathping utility provide?

    a. reports on all visited hosts and routers between a sender and a receiver

    b. resolves all possible IP addresses into symbolic names for visited nodes

    c. uses the ICMP Traceroute message type

    d. tests router and link latency

18. Which of the following statements best defines the intent of the PMTU process?

    a. determines the largest possible MTU in the path between sender and receiver

    b. determines the smallest possible MTU in the path between sender and receiver

    c. instructs the sender on what MTU to use to avoid further fragmentation en route

    d. justifies the inclusion of the Don't Fragment flag in ICMP messages

19. Which of the following statements best describes a black hole router?

    a. a router that discards all incoming traffic

    b. a router that does not support PMTU but is configured to send Destination Unreachable messages

    c. a router that does not support PMTU and is configured not to send Destination Unreachable messages

    d. a router that does not support PMTU

20. Which value in bytes is the default MTU for IPv6 packets?

    a. 512

    b. 576

    c. 1024

    d. 1280

21. Which of the following accurately represents the default advertising rate for unsolicited ICMP Router Advertisements?

    a. every 30 seconds

    b. every 60 seconds

    c. two to five minutes

    d. 7 to 10 minutes

22. The ICMP redirection process serves only IP routers, not IP hosts. True or False?

23. What type of scan occurs when a series of ping requests for a range of IP addresses is performed?

    a. port scan

    b. protocol scan

    c. host probe (scan)

    d. network mapping

24. Which of the following ICMP Type numbers identify Echo and Echo Reply messages? (Choose all that apply.)

    a. 0

    b. 1

    c. 3

    d. 8

    e. 30

25. Which of the following ICMP Type numbers relate to Router Advertisement and Router Solicitation messages? (Choose all that apply.)

   a. 8

   b. 9

   c. 10

   d. 11

   e. 12

Hands-On Projects

Hands-On Projects 5-1 through 5-4 assume that you are working in a Windows Vista or Windows 7 Professional environment, that you have installed the Wireshark for Windows software, and that you have acquired the trace (data) files necessary to work through many of the Hands-On Projects in this book.

Hands-On Project 5-1: Ping Another Device on a Network Using ICMPv4 Echo Requests

Time Required: 10 minutes

Objective: Send Echo Request messages to a host on your network, receive Echo Reply messages, and capture the transaction in Wireshark.

Description: This project shows you how to use the Ping utility at a Windows command prompt to test connectivity with another local computer and capture the exchange of I CMPv4 packets using the Wireshark packet analyzer.

1. Click the **Start** button, type **cmd** in the Start menu search box, and then press **Enter**. A command prompt window opens.

2. At the command prompt, type **ping** and press **Enter** to view the available command-line parameters. Keep the command prompt window open while you follow the next steps to launch the Wireshark program.

3. Click the **Start** button, point to **All Programs**, and then click **Wireshark**.

4. Click **Capture** on the menu bar, and then click **Interfaces**.

5. Identify the active interface, and then click the **Start** button to the right. (There may be more than one interface, and this is okay.)

6. Switch to the command prompt window by clicking its icon on the Windows taskbar, or use **Alt+Tab** to make the command prompt window active. (If you have other applications or windows open, you may have to press **Alt+Tab** several times to select the command prompt window.)

7. Type **ping** *ip_address*, where *ip_address* is the address of another device on the network. You should have some packets in your Wireshark trace buffer.

8. Do not close the command prompt window. Click the **Wireshark** icon on the taskbar, or use **Alt+Tab** to make the Wireshark window active.

9. Click **Capture** on the menu bar, and then click the **Stop** button to stop Wireshark from capturing any more packets.

10. Scroll through the packets you captured in your trace buffer. You should see several ICMP Echo Request and ICMP Echo Reply packets. Because no filter was applied before running this capture, you may have other students' traffic in your buffer as well as your own.

11. Click **File** on the menu bar, and then click **Close**. In the Wireshark dialog box, click **Continue without Saving**. Leave the Wireshark and command prompt windows open and proceed immediately to the next project.

Hands-On Project 5-2: Build a Filter for Your Own Traffic

Time Required: 10 minutes

Objective: Use a temporary capture filter on Wireshark to observe only traffic involving a local host.

Description: This project assumes you are continuing from Hands-On Project 5-1 and are building a temporary filter for your own traffic.

1. In Wireshark, click **Capture Options** in the capture section of the screen. The Capture Options window appears. Underneath the Interface text box is an entry titled IP address. Note this IP address for the next step in this exercise.

2. Next to the Capture Filter button, type **host** *ip_address*, where *ip_address* is the IP address of your computer, which you noted in the previous step. See Figure 5-36.

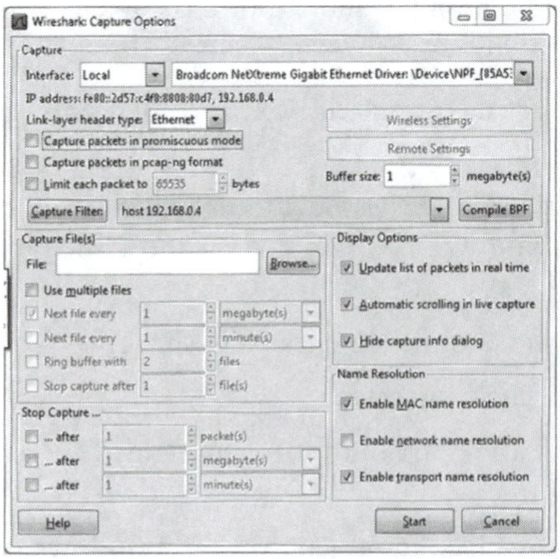

Figure 5-36 Creating a temporary filter in the Capture Options box
Source: Wireshark

3. Click the **Start** button in the lower-right of the box to start packet captures using the temporary filter.

4. Switch to the command prompt and ping another host on the local network.

5. Switch back to Wireshark and notice that only traffic sent to your computer's IP address, such as Echo Reply messages, appears in Wireshark.

6. Click **Capture,** and then click **Stop** to stop capturing packets.

7. Close Wireshark. Because the filter was temporary, it will not be available the next time you use Wireshark.

To learn more about correct Wireshark filter syntax, go to *http://wiki. wireshark.org/CaptureFilters*.

Hands-On Project 5-3: Capture ICMPv6 Echo Response and Echo Reply Packets

Time Required: 10 minutes

Objective: Capture ICMPv6 Echo Request and Echo Reply packets for analysis in Wireshark.

Description: In this project, you use the Ping utility to send ICMPv6 Echo Request packets to a IPv6-capable local host, receive ICMPv6 Echo Reply messages, and capture this traffic in Wireshark. (If your instructor previously had you create an IPv6 capture filter in Wireshark, you can optionally use this filter.)

1. Open Wireshark, and then open a command prompt.

2. If your instructor previously had you create an IPv6 capture filter in Wireshark, apply the filter by using the drop-down filter menu to select the proper filter, and then click **Apply**; otherwise, skip this step.

3. In Wireshark, click **Capture**, click **Interfaces**, and next to the desired interface, click **Start** to begin capturing traffic.

4. Ping the IPv6 address of a device of a fellow student on the local network by typing **ping -6 *ipv6-address%<interface-id>***, where *ipv6-address* is the local IPv6 address of the computer and *interface-id* is the unique identifier for the IPv6 network interface on the computer, such as fe80::d810:c168:7d19:ee8b%14. (The % sign is required to separate the IPv6 address from the interface ID. Your fellow student can discover the computer's IPv6 address and interface ID by typing **ipconfig/all** at the command prompt and then locating the link-local IPv6 address.)

5. In Wireshark, click **Capture** and then click **Stop** to stop capturing traffic.

6. Select an ICMPv6 Echo Request capture in the list. In the data that appears below, expand **Internet Protocol Version 6** and **Internet Control Message Protocol v6**, as shown in Figure 5-37.

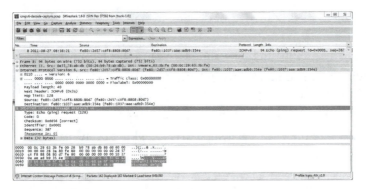

Figure 5-37 ICMPv6 Echo Request traffic

Source: Wireshark

7. Close Wireshark, but leave the command prompt open for Hands-On Project 5-4.

Hands-On Project 5-4: Capturing ICMPv6 Neighbor Solicitation and Neighbor Advertisement Messages

Time Required: 10 minutes

Objective: Observe IPv6 hosts sending ICMPv6 Neighbor Solicitation and Neighbor Advertisement messages.

Description: In this project, you use Wireshark to observe ICMPv6 Neighbor Solicitation and Neighbor Advertisement traffic when an IPv6 host first comes online. Ideally, you should have an IPv6 filter created in Wireshark. This will require your computer to be online and that you have a partner who has an IPv6-capable computer that is off. Your partner's computer will be booting during the exercise.

1. Start Wireshark and, if one is available, apply the IPv6 capture filter.

2. Your partner should boot his or her computer at this point.

3. In Wireshark, click **Capture**, click **Interfaces**, and then, next to the desired interface, click **Start**.

4. Observe the IPv6 traffic on the network until you see ICMPv6 Neighbor Solicitation and Neighbor Advertisement traffic. (If none occurs after your partner's computer boots, have your partner ping your IPv6 local-link address. Remember, you can find your computer's local-link address by typing **ipconfig/all** at the command prompt and then locating the link-local IPv6 address in the output. Have your partner use the instructions in step 4 of Hands-On Project 5-3 to correctly ping your computer.)

5. Once you have captured ICMPv6 Neighbor Discovery traffic, stop the capture process.

6. Select a Neighbor Solicitation packet and observe its structure. An example is shown in Figure 5-38.

7. Select a Neighbor Advertisement packet and observe its structure. An example is shown in Figure 5-39.

8. Close Wireshark and the command prompt.

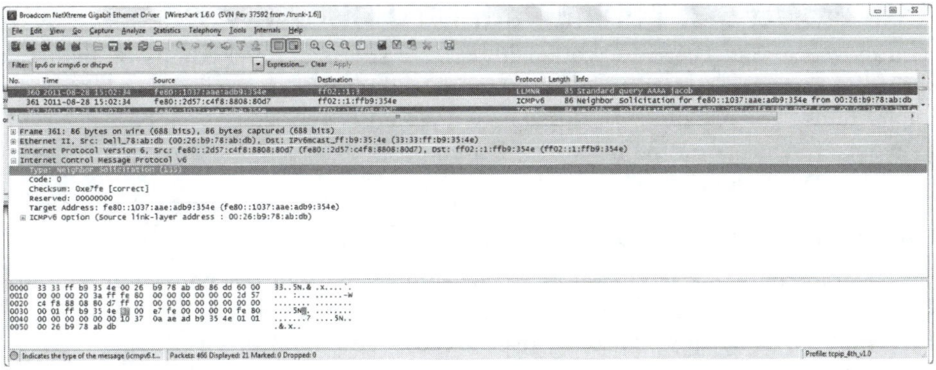

Figure 5-38 ICMPv6 Neighbor Solicitation packet structure
Source: Wireshark

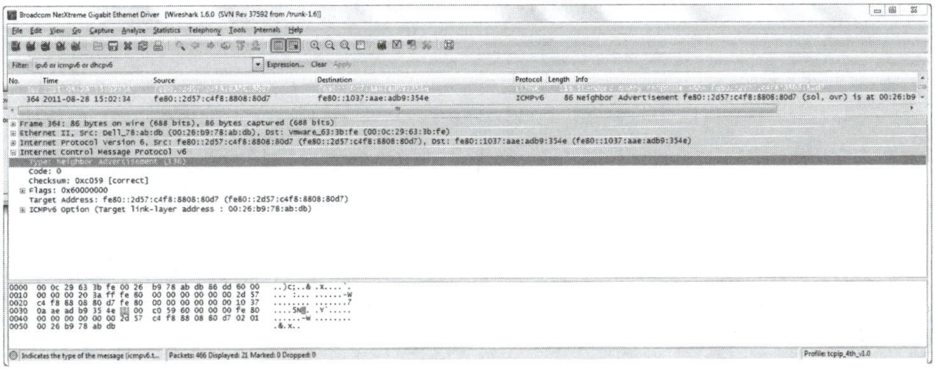

Figure 5-39 ICMPv6 Neighbor Advertisement packet structure
Source: Wireshark

Case Projects

Case Project 5-1: Determining Default Gateway Settings

Let's say you have reconfigured a network using brand-new routers. You are not certain if you configured the most appropriate default gateway settings for your hosts. How can you use an analyzer to determine if your default gateway settings are appropriate?

Case Project 5-2: ICMPv6 Security Issues

You are asked to check your company's configurations to determine if any filters should be built to stop certain ICMPv6 traffic. Your supervisor asks for a list of ICMPv6 traffic or issues that are of concern and the reasons why such concerns could be a problem. Build a list for your supervisor. Include packet types or specific circumstances in which ICMPv6 traffic could compromise network security.

Case Project 5-3: Testing Path MTU Discovery

You moved to San Diego to work with a large sports apparel company. Its network grew through various corporate acquisitions—it is truly a mix of media, speeds, computers, and applications. You are not sure if this network's hosts and routers support PMTU Discovery to reduce fragments on the network. Write a brief plan defining how you can test this network for PMTU support.

Case Project 5-4: Researching Jon Postel

Throughout the RFCs, you've noticed the initials JBP and the name Jon B. Postel. Access IANA's Web site (*www.iana.org*) and search for information on Jon Postel. Write a single paragraph defining Jon Postel's effect on the development of IP and related Internet protocols.

Neighbor Discovery in IPv6

After reading this chapter and completing the exercises, you will be able to:

- Describe Neighbor Discovery in IPv6 and how it compares to ARP in IPv4
- Explain Neighbor Discovery message interaction between hosts and routers
- Describe the process flow for how a node determines that its IPv6 address is unique and how it communicates on the IPv6 network
- Explain each of the main Neighbor Discovery messages and what information each of them provides to a node
- Identify the data components that a host stores in local memory to facilitate IPv6 communications with other nodes
- Describe how a host receives updates concerning better first-hops to access nodes not on-link
- Identify, when capturing and reviewing ICMPv6 data using a network protocol analyzer, the Neighbor Discovery messages and option fields in those packets using specific decode filters

ICMPv6 has similar operations to ICMPv4, many of which were described in Chapter 5. This chapter covers the details of Neighbor Discovery—ICMPv6 processes used specifically to initiate and maintain node-to-node communications on a network.

Neighbor Discovery has five functional processes that nodes execute in order to communicate with neighbor nodes on the network, whether on-link or off-link. (On-link means that the nodes are actively attached and interacting with the current network.) Those processes are: Router Solicitation, Router Advertisement, Neighbor Solicitation, Neighbor Advertisement, and Redirect.

This chapter describes the packet layouts and field formats of Neighbor Discovery messages and options as well as the operational details of the Neighbor Discovery processes, with packet capture examples.

Understanding Neighbor Discovery

The IPv6 **Neighbor Discovery (ND)** protocol, specified in RFC 4861 and RFC 5942 (with additional options contained in other RFCs), defines a variety of discovery mechanisms. These mechanisms permit nodes to find out what link they are located on, learn link address prefixes, learn where a link's working routers reside, discover link neighbors, and discover which neighbors are active. The ND protocol can even associate a link-layer address (such as an Ethernet MAC address) with an IPv6 address. Upon start-up, ND also provides information about how nodes should configure their IPv6 addresses to communicate on the network.

To accomplish these and related goals, ND uses five ICMPv6 message types:

- *Router Solicitation (RS) (ICMPv6 type 133)*—When an interface becomes active, a node may send a Router Solicitation message, asking any routers connected to the local link to identify themselves by sending their Router Advertisement messages immediately (rather than waiting for the next scheduled advertisement).

- *Router Advertisement (RA) (ICMPv6 type 134)*—Routers periodically or upon request send out messages that contain at least one and possibly more of their own link-layer addresses, the network prefix for the local subnet, the Maximum Transmission Unit (MTU) for the local link, suggested hop limit values, and other parameters useful for nodes on the local link. Router Advertisement messages can also contain flagged parameters to indicate what type of address autoconfiguration process new nodes should use to join the network.

- *Neighbor Solicitation (NS) (ICMPv6 type 135)*—A node can send a Neighbor Solicitation message to find (or verify) the link-layer address for a local node, to see if that node is still available, or to check that its own address is not in use by another node, which is known as **Duplicate Address Detection (DAD)**.

- *Neighbor Advertisement (NA) (ICMPv6 type 136)*—When requested, or when its own link-layer address changes, a node sends a Neighbor Advertisement message that includes its IPv6 address and its link-layer address. This helps to establish physical adjacency (which is often more important than logical adjacency by address) to neighboring nodes.

- *Redirect (ICMPv6 type 137)*—When a router knows a better first-hop for a particular destination address (which could be off-link), it sends a Redirect message to the sender indicating that the sender should contact a different router to send subsequent packets.

Another case would be when a node attempts to contact a node on the same segment by first sending the packet to a router. In its Redirect message, that router identifies that the destination exists on the same network segment as the sender. A router might also use Redirect messages to balance traffic loads across multiple interfaces.

IPv6 nodes are devices that implement the IPv6 protocol. There are two types of IPv6 nodes: routers and hosts. Routers forward IPv6 packets not addressed to themselves; hosts include any node that is not a router.

ND makes only sparing use of messages. Although a Neighbor Solicitation message is made to a special multicast address, the Neighbor Advertisement message sent in response is a unicast sent directly to the soliciting node. Also, nodes do not periodically advertise their existence, as routers do.

ND makes use of multicast addresses, such as the "all routers" address with link-local scope (FF02::2), the "all nodes" address with link-local scope (FF02::1), and a special address called the **solicited-node address**. The solicited-node address is a multicast address with link-local scope that helps reduce the number of multicast groups to which nodes must subscribe to make themselves available for solicitation by other nodes on their local links. A single node may have multiple unicast addresses and multiple anycast addresses. The higher-order bits (prefix) of these addresses may be different. A node may have addresses from more than one access provider, for example. To effectively mask these differences (which are irrelevant to Neighbor Solicitation), every node is required to compute and join the solicited-node address for each unicast and anycast address assigned to it. The solicited-node address is FF02::1:FF*xx.xxxx*, in which *xx.xxxx* relates to the lowest-order [rightmost] 24 bits of the unicast or anycast address associated with that interface.

Comparing IPv6 Neighbor Discovery Protocols to IPv4 Protocols

ND takes over the functions that ARP and Reverse ARP handled in IPv4. It also performs many of the functions that ICMP Router Discovery and ICMP Redirect handled in IPv4 as part of a more compact, efficient mechanism for managing local addresses and adjacency information. Table 6-1 compares IPv6 ND protocols to their counterpart IPv4 protocols.

IPv6	IPv4
Neighbor Solicitation	ARP Request
Neighbor Advertisement	ARP Reply
Router Solicitation	Router Solicitation
Router Advertisement	Router Advertisement
Redirect	Redirect
Duplicate Address Detection	Gratuitous ARP
Neighbor cache	ARP cache

Table 6-1 **Comparing IPv6 ND to IPv4 protocols**

Neighbor Discovery Message Formats

This section introduces the five primary message types for ND and describes their functions and capabilities. In addition, new options that have been added to original ND operations are included in this section along with relevant RFC reference information. Packet format diagrams and packet decode examples are included to provide clarity to the text. These message formats provide the foundation for IPv6 operational processes for node-to-node communications.

Router Solicitation

When a host's interface initializes, it may not wait for the next Router Advertisement message to be received; it may instead send a Router Solicitation message to determine if any IPv6 routers are on the network segment and, if so, learn the network prefix and other parameters relating to address autoconfiguration.

For an Ethernet interface, the Router Solicitation message is composed of the following:

- Ethernet header:
  - Source address is the MAC address of the host interface.
  - Destination address is 33:33:00:00:00:02.
- IPv6 header:
  - Source address is the IPv6 address of the interface or the so-called **unspecified address** (if an interface does not already have an IPv6 address).
  - Destination address is the link-local scope all-routers multicast address FF02::2.
- Hop Limit:
  - Set to 255 (an 8-bit integer value).

Table 6-2 describes the ICMPv6 Router Solicitation message format fields and their values.

ICMP Field	Description
Type	133
Code	0
Checksum	This is the checksum specified for ICMPv6 messages.
Reserved	This is an unused field that is set to 0 by the source node and ignored by the destination node.
Options	RFC 4861 specifies the source link-layer address as the only valid option for this message type, if it is known. The address is not included if it is unspecified but otherwise should be included on link layers that have addresses. Future versions of this protocol may define new, valid options for use in this field, but any options that destination nodes do not recognize should be ignored.

Table 6-2 ICMPv6 Router Solicitation message format fields

Figure 6-1 shows the ICMPv6 Router Solicitation packet structure.

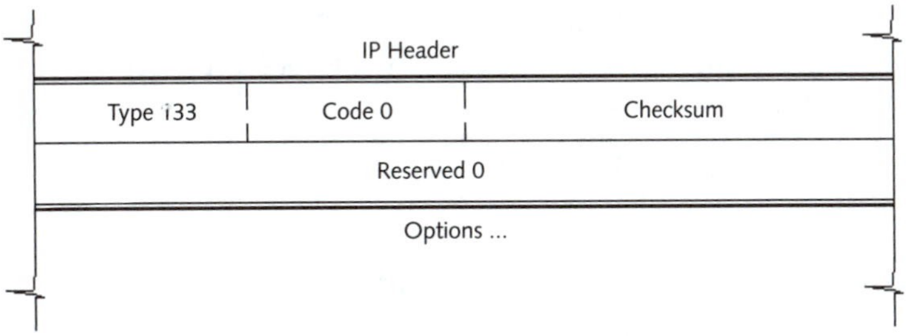

Figure 6-1 ICMPv6 Router Solicitation packet structure
© Cengage Learning 2013

Figure 6-2 shows an ICMPv6 Router Solicitation packet, in which the ICMPv6 fields are set to the following:

- Type set to 133.
- Code set to 0.
- Checksum is as computed.
- ICMPv6 option is the MAC address of the source.

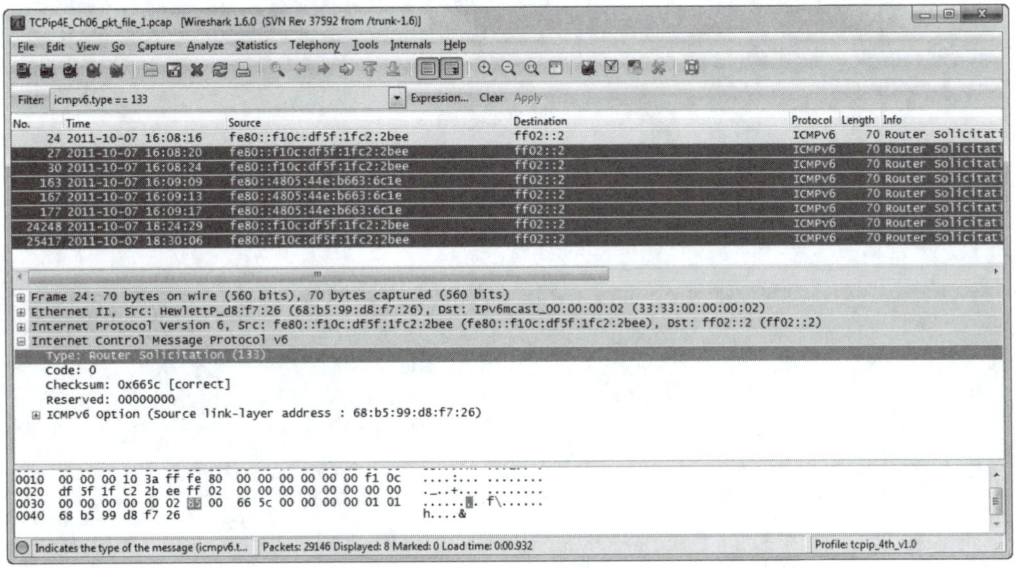

Figure 6-2 ICMPv6 Router Solicitation packet
Source: Wireshark

By default, IPv6 nodes will send a Router Solicitation multicast request for configuration parameters immediately upon start-up. This should provide hosts with the network-layer configuration information they need to join the local network.

Router Advertisement

Routers periodically send Router Advertisement messages to inform hosts of link prefixes (if address autoconfiguration is enabled), link MTU, valid and preferred lifetimes, and other possible options. Routers also reply to Router Solicitation messages received by a node using Router Advertisement messages.

For an Ethernet interface, the Router Advertisement message is composed of the following:

Ethernet header:

- Source address is the MAC address for the host interface.
- Destination address is 33:33:00:00:00:01.

IPv6 header:

- Source address is the link-local address for the interface.
- Destination address is the link-local scope all-nodes multicast address FF02::1 or the source address for the interface.

Hop Limit:

- Set to 255 (an 8-bit integer value).

Table 6-3 describes the ICMPv6 Router Advertisement message format fields and their values.

ICMP Field	Description
Type	134
Code	0
Checksum	This is the checksum specified for ICMPv6 messages.
Cur Hop Limit	This is an unsigned 8-bit integer, and the default value should be the value in the IPv6 packet's Hop Count field for all outgoing packets. The value should be set to 0 if it is unspecified by the router.
M Flag	This is a 1-bit Managed Address Configuration flag and is set to indicate that addresses are available through DHCPv6. If the M flag is set, the O flag becomes redundant and can be ignored because DHCPv6 will provide all available configuration information.
O Flag	This is a 1-bit Other Configuration flag; when set, it indicates that other configuration information is available through DHCPv6, such as DNS or other server-related information.
H Flag	This is a 1-bit Home Agent flag; when set, it indicates to the host that the router is also functioning as a Mobile IPv6 home agent. (RFC 6275)
Prf Flag	This is a 2-bit Default Router Preference flag; when set, it tells hosts to prefer this router over other routers. If the Router Lifetime is set to 0, then this flag must be set to 00. Valid values are 11 for low, 00 for medium (default), and 01 for high. 10 is reserved and, if received by a node, must act on the value as if it were 00. (RFC 4191)
P Flag	This is a 1-bit Proxy flag, an experimental definition that is not required to be used (as of this writing). (RFC 4389)

Table 6-3 ICMPv6 Router Advertisement message format fields

ICMP Field	Description
Reserved	This is a 2-bit unused field that must be set to 0 by the sending router and must be ignored by any receiving node.
Router Lifetime	This is a 16-bit unsigned integer that indicates the lifetime of the default router in seconds. The field can contain a maximum value of 65535; however, sending rules limit this value to 9000. A value of 0 in this field indicates that the router is not a default router and should not appear on the default router list. The router lifetime value only applies to the router's availability as a default router and does not affect the validity of any information contained in the other fields of this message.
Reachable Time	This is a 32-bit unsigned integer and is the time, in milliseconds, that a node assumes a neighbor is reachable after having accepted a reachability confirmation. If this field has a value of 0, the reachable time is unspecified by the router.
Retrans Timer	This is a 32-bit unsigned integer and is the time, in milliseconds, between retransmitted Neighbor Solicitation messages. If this field has a value of 0, the retrans time is unspecified by the router.
Options	Available options include source link-layer address, MTU, Prefix Information, Advertisement Interval, Home Agent Information, and Route Information.

Source link-layer address is the address of the interface from which the advertisement was sent and is only used on link layers that possess addresses. A router may omit this option to enable inbound load sharing across multiple link-layer addresses.

MTU should be sent on links with a variable MTU and may be sent on other links.

Prefix Information options specify on-link prefixes and/or are used for stateless address autoconfiguration. This information should include all router on-link prefixes so multihomed hosts have complete prefix information.

Advertisement Interval is the time, in milliseconds, between Router Advertisement messages sent by this router. (RFC 6275)

Home Agent Information provides two options for use by the node if this router is acting as a Home Agent and the router only sends this information if the Home Agent flag is set. (RFC 6275)

Route Information contains additional route prefixes (if available) to the node to be included in their routing table. (RFC 4191)

Future versions of this protocol may define new, valid options for use in this field, but any options that destination nodes do not recognize should be ignored. |

Table 6-3 **ICMPv6 Router Advertisement message format fields** (*continued*)
© Cengage Learning 2013

Figure 6-3 shows the ICMPv6 Router Advertisement packet structure.

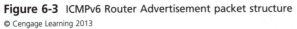

```
                        IP Header

   Type 134      |   Code 0    |        Checksum
 Cur  Hop  Limit  |M|O|H|Prf|P|Rsvd|      Router Lifetime
                     Reachable Time
                     Retrans Time
                       Options ...
```

Figure 6-3 ICMPv6 Router Advertisement packet structure
© Cengage Learning 2013

Figure 6-4 shows an ICMPv6 Router Advertisement packet, in which the ICMPv6 fields are set to the following:

- Type set to 134.
- Code set to 0.
- Checksum is as computed.
- Current Hop Limit is 64.
- Flags all set to 0.
- Router lifetime set to 1,800 seconds.
- Reachable time set to 0 seconds.
- Retransmission timer set to 0 milliseconds.
- ICMPv6 option: one is the MAC address of the source, another is the (network) prefix of 2001:db8:1ab:ba5e::/64.

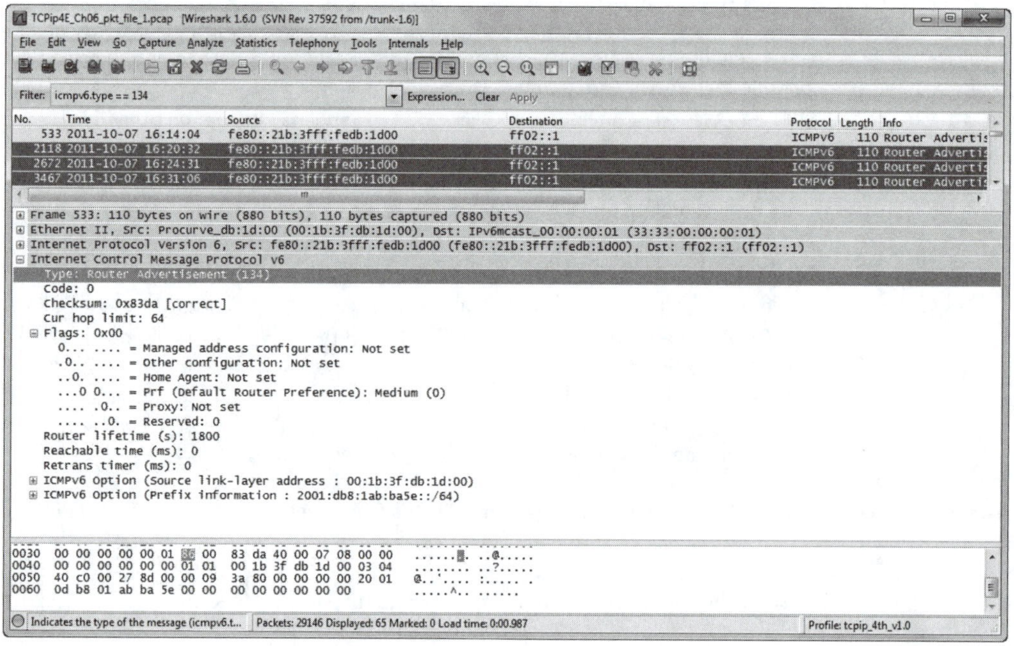

Figure 6-4 ICMPv6 Router Advertisement packet

Source: Wireshark

Routers will respond to a Router Solicitation request with a Router Advertisement packet, but they will also emit the same packet at regular intervals as configured to do so. Either way, network hosts can use this information to establish a working network configuration for themselves.

Neighbor Solicitation

A node can send a Neighbor Solicitation message to find (or verify) the link-layer address of a local node, to see if a node is still available, or to check that its own address is not already in use by another node (Duplicate Address Detection, or DAD). When a node is resolving an address, it sends a multicast message; when the node seeks to verify the reachability of a neighbor, it sends a unicast message.

For an Ethernet interface, the Neighbor Solicitation message is composed of the following:

Ethernet header:

- Source address is the MAC address of the host interface.
- Destination address is either the MAC address of the solicited-node address of the target (multicast NS) or the MAC address of the unicast address of the target (unicast NS).

IPv6 header:

- Source address is the IPv6 address of the interface or the unspecified address for DAD.
- Destination address is either the solicited-node address of the target (multicast NS) or the unicast address of the target (unicast NS).

Hop Limit:

- Set to 255 (an 8-bit integer value)

Table 6-4 describes the ICMPv6 Neighbor Solicitation message format fields and their values.

ICMP Field	Description
Type	135
Code	0
Checksum	This is the checksum specified for ICMPv6 messages.
Reserved	This is an unused field that is set to 0 by the source node and ignored by the destination node.
Target Address	This is the IPv6 address of the target. May not be a multicast address.
Options	RFC 4861 specifies the source link-layer address as the only valid option for this message type, if it is known. The address is not included if it is unspecified but otherwise should be included on link layers that have addresses. Future versions of this protocol may define new, valid options for use in this field, but any options that destination nodes do not recognize should be ignored.

Table 6-4 ICMPv6 Neighbor Solicitation message format fields
© Cengage Learning 2013

Figure 6-5 shows the ICMPv6 Neighbor Solicitation packet structure.

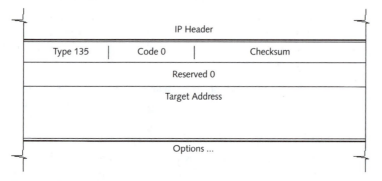

Figure 6-5 ICMPv6 Neighbor Solicitation packet structure
© Cengage Learning 2013

Figure 6-6 shows an ICMPv6 Neighbor Solicitation packet, in which the ICMPv6 fields are set to the following:

- Type set to 135.
- Code set to 0.
- Checksum is as computed.
- Reserved is set to 0.
- Target address set to the neighbor IPv6 address of fe80::21b:3fff:fedb:1d00.
- The ICMPv6 option is the MAC address of the source.

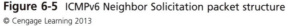

Figure 6-6 ICMPv6 Neighbor Solicitation packet
Source: Wireshark

Neighbor solicitation seeks to determine the link-layer address for a node's neighbors, which respond to Neighbor Solicitation packets with their own Neighbor Advertisement packets (see the next section). Also, network nodes send out Neighbor Solicitations for their own network addresses upon joining a link to make sure that their chosen addresses are not already taken.

Neighbor Advertisement

A node sends a solicited Neighbor Advertisement message when requested (responding to a Neighbor Solicitation message). If its own link-layer address changes or its role changes, the node will send an unsolicited Neighbor Advertisement message to more quickly propagate new address information.

For an Ethernet interface, the Neighbor Advertisement message is composed of the following:

Ethernet header:

- Source address is the MAC address of the host interface.
- Destination address is either the unicast MAC address of the NS or 33:33:00:00:00:01 for an unsolicited NA.

IPv6 header:

- Source address is the IPv6 address of the interface.
- Destination address is the source address of the Neighbor Solicitation or, if the source address of the Neighbor Solicitation is the unspecified address, the all-nodes multicast address FF02::1.

Hop Limit:

- Set to 255 (an 8-bit integer value)

Table 6-5 describes the ICMPv6 Neighbor Advertisement message format fields and their values.

ICMP Field Type	Description
Type	136
Code	0
Checksum	This is the checksum specified for ICMPv6 messages.
R Flag	This is a 1-bit Router flag; when set, it informs nodes that this message came from a router. If a router changes to a host, it also uses this flag in the Neighbor Unreachability Detection process.
S Flag	This is a 1-bit Solicited flag; when set, the message is a reply to a Neighbor Solicitation. This flag must not be set in unsolicited unicast or multicast advertisements.
O Flag	This is a 1-bit Override flag; when set, it informs the node to update a cached link-layer address or override an existing cache entry. If the node receives the message and does not have a cache entry for the link-layer address, the node will update its cache, even if the flag is not set. If the flag is set to 1, it is used for solicited and unsolicited messages except for anycast and solicited proxy advertisements.

Table 6-5 ICMPv6 Neighbor Advertisement message format fields (*continues*)

ICMP Field Type	Description
Reserved	This is an unused field that is set to 0 by the source node and ignored by the destination node.
Target Address	This is the IPv6 address of the node sending the Neighbor Solicitation message. If the message is an unsolicited Neighbor Advertisement, then the address is that of the link-layer address that has changed.
Options	RFC 4861 specifies the target link-layer address, which is the source node's address, as the only valid option for this message. This address must be set on link layers that have addresses when responding to multicast solicitations. Future versions of this protocol may define new, valid options for use in this field, but any options that destination nodes do not recognize should be ignored.

Table 6-5 ICMPv6 Neighbor Advertisement message format fields (*continued*)
© Cengage Learning 2013

Figure 6-7 shows the ICMPv6 Neighbor Advertisement packet structure.

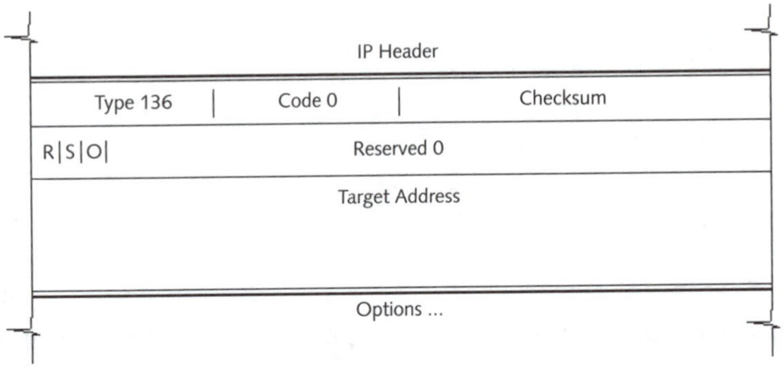

Figure 6-7 ICMPv6 Neighbor Advertisement packet structure
© Cengage Learning 2013

Figure 6-8 shows an ICMPv6 Neighbor Advertisement packet in which the ICMPv6 fields are set to the following:

- Type set to 136.
- Code set to 0.
- Checksum is as computed.
- Router flag is set, indicating that this packet came from a router.
- Solicited flag is set, indicating the packet is reply to an NS request.
- Override flag is set, indicating the receiver to update or override a cache entry in its table.
- Target address set to the neighbor IPv6 address of fe80::21b:3fff:fedb:1d00.
- The ICMPv6 option is the MAC address of the target.

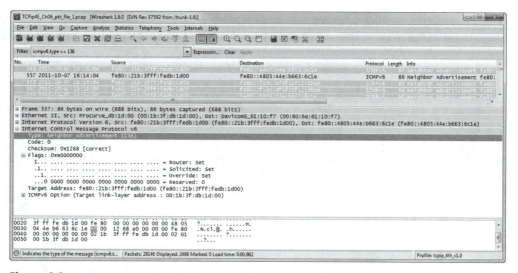

Figure 6-8 ICMPv6 Neighbor Advertisement packet

Source: Wireshark

The key role for Neighbor Advertisement is to declare link-layer addresses that are already in use, so that network nodes can learn the addresses of their neighbors, or check to make sure that any address they choose for themselves is not already taken.

Redirect

Routers send Redirect messages to inform a host of a better first-hop router for a destination. Routers also send Redirect messages to inform a host that a destination node is on-link (when this occurs, it is usually because prefixes are different between the sending host and the destination node).

For an Ethernet interface, the Redirect message is composed of the following:

Ethernet header:

- Source address is the MAC address of the host interface.
- Destination address is the unicast MAC.

IPv6 header:

- Source address is the link-local address of the interface.
- Destination address is the SA of the node that triggered the redirect.

Hop Limit:

- Set to 255 (an 8-bit integer value)

Table 6-6 describes the ICMPv6 Redirect message format fields and their values.

ICMP Field Type	Description
Type	137
Code	0
Checksum	This is the checksum specified for ICMPv6 messages.
Reserved	This is an unused field that is set to 0 by the source node and ignored by the destination node.
Target Address	The Target Address is the IPv6 address of the default or "better" first-hop router that the node is using to forward its traffic to the destination address. This field can contain the same address as the Destination Address field if the target is considered the endpoint of the network communication. If the target is a router, this field will contain the link-local address for the router interface that is directly connected to the local link on which the source node is located.
Destination Address	The destination address is the IPv6 address for the destination node.
Options	Available options include Target link-layer address and Redirect Header. The target link-layer address is the address of the target and should be included if known to the source node. The redirected header includes as much as possible of the original packet that triggered the redirect, not to exceed 1,280 bytes.

Table 6-6 ICMPv6 Redirect message format fields
© Cengage Learning 2013

Figure 6-9 shows the ICMPv6 Redirect packet structure.

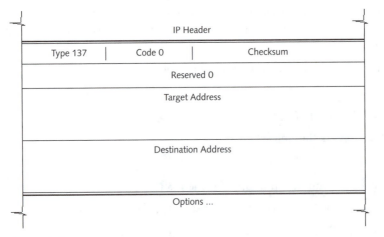

Figure 6-9 ICMPv6 Redirect packet structure
© Cengage Learning 2013

Figure 6-10 shows an ICMPv6 Redirect packet, in which the ICMPv6 fields are set to the following:

- Type set to 137.
- Code set to 0.

- Checksum is as computed.
- Reserved set to 0.
- Target address set to the IPv6 address of fe80::216:c7ff:fe5d:87c0, which is the link-local address of the "better" router for the node to communicate to the destination IPv6 address.
- Destination address of 2001:db8:1ab:2001::100.
- ICMPv6 options: one set to the Target MAC address of 00:16:c7:5d:87:c0 (the "better" router), another indicating that this is a Redirected message.

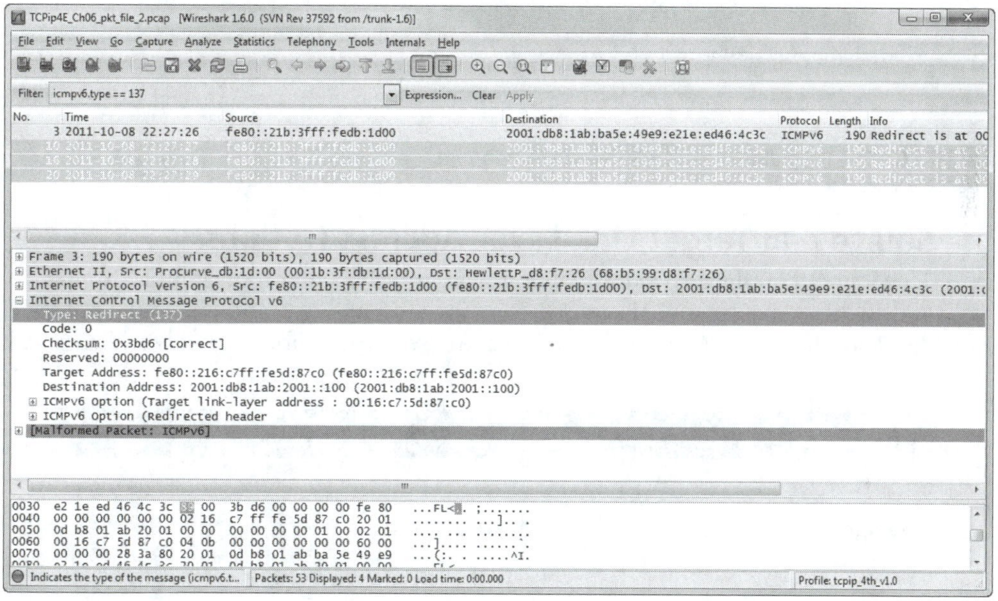

Figure 6-10 ICMPv6 Redirect packet
Source: Wireshark

A router will send a redirect message when it seeks to point a host to a more preferable router (one with a shorter hop count to the destination) or to inform the host that a destination is available on-link. Redirects help keep local routing optimized in the face of changing conditions and also reflect status as various destinations come on- and off-link.

Neighbor Discovery Option Formats

ND messages may, but are not required to, include one or more options, and a specific option may be repeated multiple times in a single message. The Type field is an 8-bit identifier for the type of option. Table 6-7 lists the ICMPv6 ND message option types and their associated reference RFCs. The Length field is an 8-bit unsigned integer field defined by the Type of option and/or the functions within the option. A value of 0 is invalid, and nodes that receive an ND with an option length set to 0 should discard the packet. Additional fields are defined by the individual options and should be padded, if necessary, to end on a 64-bit boundary.

Type	Option Name	Reference
1	Source Link-Layer Address	RFC 4861—Neighbor Discovery for IP version 6 (IPv6)
2	Target Link-Layer Address	RFC 4861
3	Prefix Information	RFC 4861
4	Redirected Header	RFC 4861
5	MTU	RFC 4861
7	Advertisement Interval	RFC 6275—Mobility Support in IPv6
8	Home Agent Information	RFC 6275
24	Route Information	RFC 4191—Default Router Preferences and More-Specific Routes

Table 6-7 ICMPv6 Neighbor Discovery message option types
© Cengage Learning 2013

Source and Target Link-Layer Address Options

The Source Link-Layer Address option is used in Neighbor Solicitation, Router Solicitation, and Redirect messages. This option contains the link-layer address of the sender. Table 6-8 describes the ICMPv6 Source Link-Layer Address option format fields and their values.

Field Type	Description
Type	1
Length	1 (if Ethernet)
Source Link-Layer Address	The link-layer address of the sender of the packet

Table 6-8 ICMPv6 Source Link-Layer Address option format fields
© Cengage Learning 2013

Figure 6-11 shows the ICMPv6 Source Link-Layer Address option packet structure.

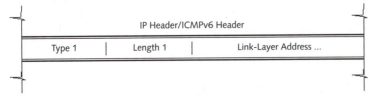

Figure 6-11 ICMPv6 Source Link-Layer Address option packet structure
© Cengage Learning 2013

Figure 6-12 shows an ICMPv6 Source Link-Layer Address option packet in which the ICMPv6 option fields are set to the following:

- Type set to 1, for source link-layer address.
- Length set to 1.
- Link-layer address is the MAC address of the source.

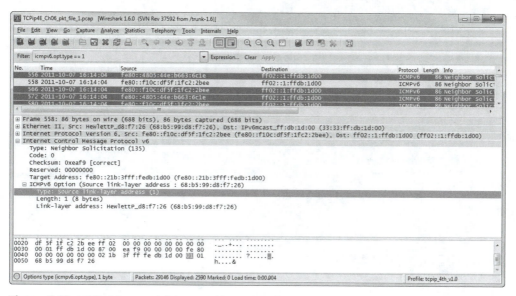

Figure 6-12 ICMPv6 Source Link-Layer Address option packet
Source: Wireshark

The Target Link-Layer Address option is used in Neighbor Advertisement and Router Advertisement messages. This option contains the link-layer address for the target. Table 6-9 describes the ICMPv6 Target Link-Layer Address option format fields and their values.

Field Type	Description
Type	2
Length	1 (if Ethernet)
Target Link-Layer Address	The link-layer address of the target

Table 6-9 ICMPv6 Target Link-Layer Address option format fields
© Cengage Learning 2013

Figure 6-13 shows the ICMPv6 Target Link-Layer Address option packet structure.

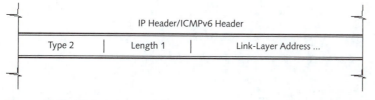

Figure 6-13 ICMPv6 Target Link-Layer Address option packet structure
© Cengage Learning 2013

Figure 6-14 shows an ICMPv6 Target Link-Layer Address option packet in which the ICMPv6 option fields are set to the following:

- Type set to 2, for target link-layer address.
- Length set to 1.
- Link-layer address is the MAC address of the target.

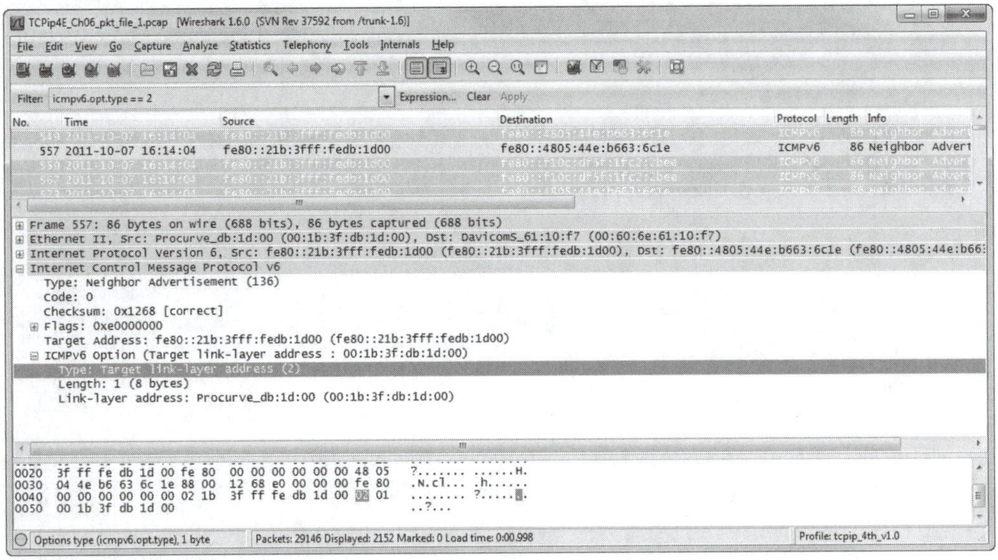

Figure 6-14 ICMPv6 Target Link-Layer Address option packet

Source: Wireshark

Prefix Information Option

The Prefix Information option is used in Router Advertisement messages. The option contains prefix information for on-link addresses and prefixes used for address autocon-figuration. Table 6-10 describes the ICMPv6 Prefix Information option format fields and their values.

Field Type	Description
Type	3
Length	4
Prefix Length	This is an 8-bit unsigned integer and indicates the number of leading bits that constitute the prefix address. The valid range for this field is 0 to 128 bits. When combined with the L flag, it provides the necessary prefix information for on-link determination.
L	This is a 1-bit On-Link flag; when set, it indicates that the prefix address(es) can be used for on-link determination. When the flag is not set, the advertisement does not imply that the prefix is either on-link or off-link.

Table 6-10 ICMPv6 Prefix Information option format fields

Field Type	Description
A	This is a 1-bit Autonomous Address-Configuration flag; when set, it indicates that the prefix address(es) can be used for stateless address autoconfiguration.
R	This is a 1-bit Router Address flag; when set, it indicates that the prefix address is a complete router address. This flag is used when the router is acting as a Home Agent router, as described in RFC 6275. (Also see the Router Advertisement message in the previous section of this chapter.) A node's interpretation of this flag is independent of the On-Link (L) and Autonomous Address-Configuration flags.
Reserved1	This is an unused field that is set to 0 by the source node and ignored by the destination node.
Valid Lifetime	This is a 32-bit unsigned integer and indicates the valid lifetime, in seconds, of the on-link prefix as well as for stateless address configuration. Setting the field to all 1 bits would be a Valid Lifetime of infinity.
Preferred Lifetime	This is a 32-bit unsigned integer and indicates the valid lifetime, in seconds, of the address generated by using the prefix and stateless address autoconfiguration remains as a preferred address. The value of this field must not exceed the value in the Valid Lifetime field in order to avoid preferring an address that is no longer valid. Setting the field to all 1 bits would be a Preferred Lifetime of infinity.
Reserved2	This is an unused field that is set to 0 by the source node and ignored by the destination node.
Prefix	The Prefix field contains the IPv6 address or IPv6 prefix address of the on-link segment used by nodes for stateless autoconfiguration, if needed. The bits in this field combined with the bit value of the Prefix Length field make the complete IPv6 prefix address. If the combined value of these two fields is less than 128 bits, then the remaining bits must be set to 0 and those bits are ignored by the node. A router must not send a local-link prefix, and a host should ignore that prefix, if received.

Table 6-10 ICMPv6 Prefix Information option format fields (*continued*)
© Cengage Learning 2013

Figure 6-15 shows the ICMPv6 Prefix Information Option packet structure.

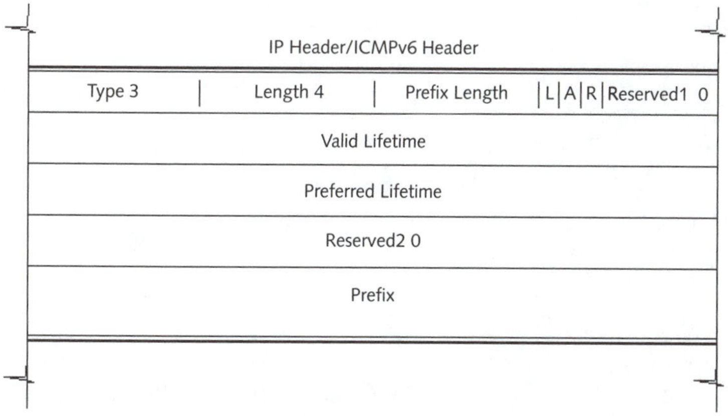

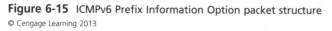

Figure 6-15 ICMPv6 Prefix Information Option packet structure
© Cengage Learning 2013

Figure 6-16 shows an ICMPv6 Prefix Information Option packet in which the ICMPv6 option fields are set to:

- Type is 3 for prefix information.
- Length is 4.
- Prefix length is 64.
- The L flag is set, indicating that the prefix can be used for on-link determination.
- The A flag is set, indicating that the prefix address can be used for stateless address autoconfiguration.
- The Reserved flag is set to 0.
- Valid lifetime is set to 2,592,000 seconds.
- Preferred lifetime is set to 604,800 seconds.
- Reserved is not set, indicating it is not used.
- Prefix is set to 2001:db8:1ab:ba5e::, which is the network prefix.

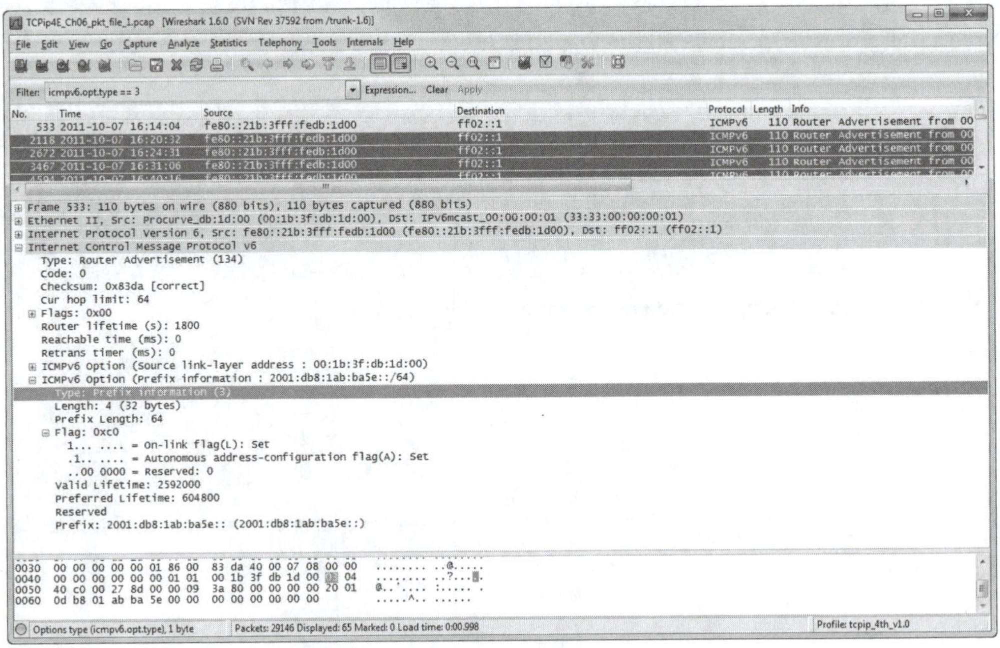

Figure 6-16 ICMPv6 Prefix Information Option packet
Source: Wireshark

Redirected Header Option

The Redirected Header option is sent in Redirect messages and contains all or part of the original IPv6 packet being redirected. Table 6-11 describes the ICMPv6 Redirected Header option format fields and their values.

Field Type	Description
Type	4
Length	This is the length of the entire option in 8-byte blocks.
Reserved	This is an unused field that is set to 0 by the source node and ignored by the destination node.
IP header + data	The redirected header includes as much as possible of the original packet that triggered the redirect, not to exceed 1,280 bytes.

Table 6-11 **ICMPv6 Redirected Header option format fields**
© Cengage Learning 2013

Figure 6-17 shows the ICMPv6 Redirected Header option packet structure.

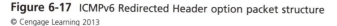

```
            IP Header/ICMPv6 Header
   Type 4    |   Length   |      Reserved 0
                      Reserved
                    IP header + data
```

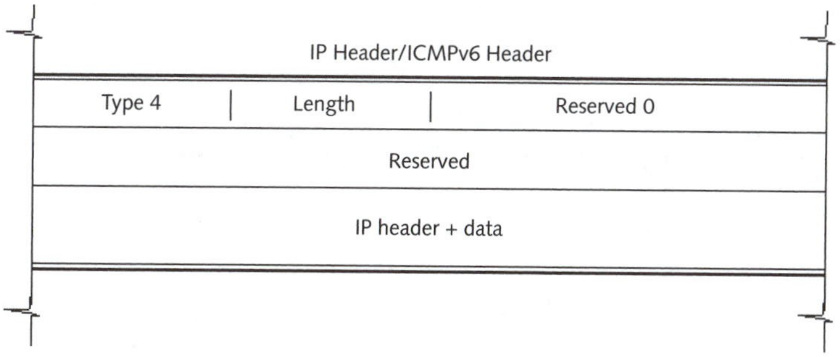

Figure 6-17 ICMPv6 Redirected Header option packet structure
© Cengage Learning 2013

Figure 6-18 shows an ICMPv6 Redirected Header option packet in which the ICMPv6 option fields are set to:

- Type is 4, for redirected header.
- Length is set to 11.
- Reserved is not set, indicating it is not used.
- IP header and data set to as much as can fit into 1,280 bytes.

MTU Option

The MTU option is sent in Router Advertisement messages to provide a common MTU value for nodes on the same network segment. Table 6-12 describes the ICMPv6 MTU option format fields and their values.

Figure 6-19 shows the ICMPv6 MTU option packet structure.

Figure 6-20 shows an ICMPv6 MTU option packet in which the ICMPv6 option fields are set to:

- Type set to 5, for the MTU option that is sent in this RA.
- Length set to 1.
- Reserved not set, indicating not used.
- MTU value is 1500.

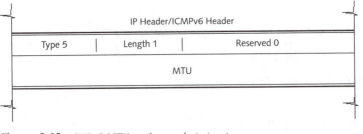

Figure 6-18 ICMPv6 Redirected Header option packet
Source: Wireshark

Field	Description
Type	5
Length	1
Reserved	This is an unused field that is set to 0 by the source node and ignored by the destination node.
MTU	This is a 32-bit unsigned integer and indicates the recommended MTU for the link.

Table 6-12 ICMPv6 MTU option format fields
© Cengage Learning 2013

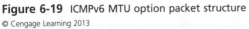

Figure 6-19 ICMPv6 MTU option packet structure
© Cengage Learning 2013

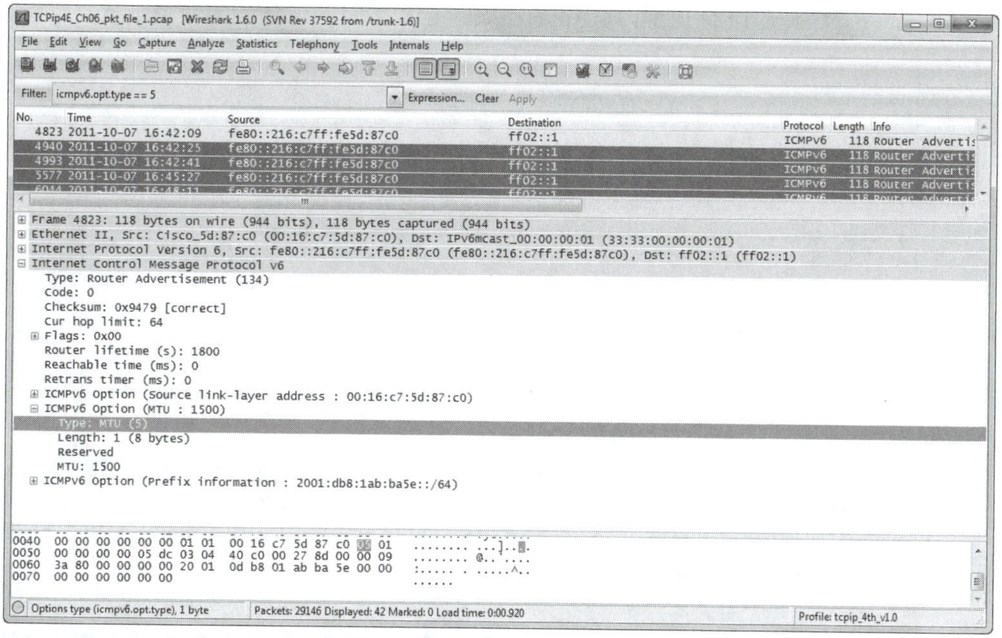

Figure 6-20 ICMPv6 MTU option packet
Source: Wireshark

Advertisement Interval Option

The Advertisement Interval option, if included, is used in Mobile IPv6 by mobile nodes receiving Router Advertisement messages for their movement detection algorithm, as described in RFC 6275. Table 6-13 describes the ICMPv6 Advertisement Interval option format fields and their values.

Field Type	Description
Type	7
Length	1
Reserved	This is an unused field that is set to 0 by the source node and ignored by the destination node.
Advertisement Interval	This is a 32-bit unsigned integer and is the time, in milliseconds, between unsolicited Router Advertisement messages sent by this router.

Table 6-13 ICMPv6 Advertisement Interval option format fields
© Cengage Learning 2013

Figure 6-21 shows the ICMPv6 Advertisement Interval option packet structure.

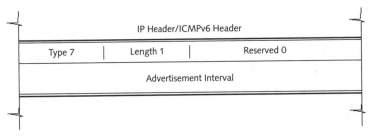

Figure 6-21 ICMPv6 Advertisement Interval option packet structure
© Cengage Learning 2013

Home Agent Information Option

Home Agents may include the Home Agent Information option in their Router Advertisement messages, but it should not be included if the Home Agent (H) bit is not set. Additional information can be obtained in RFC 6275. Table 6-14 describes the ICMPv6 Home Agent Information option format fields and their values.

Field Type	Description
Type	8
Length	1
Reserved	This is an unused field that is set to 0 by the source node and ignored by the destination node.
Home Agent Preference	This is a 16-bit unsigned integer and is used for determining the preference order of the available home agents.
Home Agent Lifetime	This is a 16-bit unsigned integer and indicates the valid lifetime, in seconds, of the home agent. The maximum value is 18.2 hours, and a value of 0 is not valid.

Table 6-14 ICMPv6 Home Agent Information option format fields
© Cengage Learning 2013

Figure 6-22 shows the ICMPv6 Home Agent Information option packet structure.

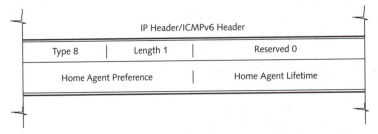

Figure 6-22 ICMPv6 Home Agent Information option packet structure
© Cengage Learning 2013

Route Information Option

The Route Information option is sent in Router Advertisement messages to specify individual routes for hosts to add to their Default Router List, as described in RFC 4191. Table 6-15 describes the ICMPv6 Route Information option format fields and their values.

Field Type	Description
Type	24
Length	1
Prefix Length	This is an 8-bit unsigned integer and indicates the number of leading bits that make up the prefix address. The valid range for this field is 0 to 128 bits.
Resvd	This is an unused field that is set to 0 by the source node and ignored by the destination node.
Prf	This is a two-bit flag and indicates to hosts to prefer this router over other routers. If the reserved value of 10 is received, a node must ignore the Router Information option.
Resvd	This is an unused field that is set to 0 by the source node and ignored by the destination node.
Route Lifetime	This is a 32-bit unsigned integer; it indicates the valid lifetime, in seconds, that the prefix is valid for route determination. Setting the field to all 1 bits would be a Router Lifetime of infinity.
Prefix	The Prefix field contains the IPv6 address or IPv6 prefix address of the on-link segment. If the value in this field is less than 128 bits, then the remaining bits must be set to 0, and those bits are ignored by the node.

Table 6-15 ICMPv6 Route Information option format fields
© Cengage Learning 2013

Figure 6-23 shows the ICMPv6 Route Information option packet structure.

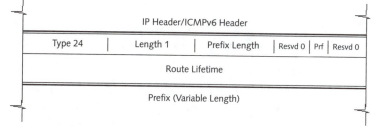

Figure 6-23 ICMPv6 Route Information option packet structure
© Cengage Learning 2013

Conceptual Host Model

RFC 4861 does not exactly mandate how the ND process is to operate on all nodes; rather, it defines what must occur for the ND process to be successful. The ND definition for this operation is known as the conceptual host model, which represents information that a host should maintain, in some form, in order to communicate effectively in an IPv6 network. Some manufacturers have chosen different methods in their IPv6 protocol stacks to implement some of the component processes within ND to allow for proper communications with other IPv6-capable nodes.

The conceptual host model is primarily concerned with operational behavior by hosts. Routers have many of the same operational requirements, but they have additional needs such as routing operations controlled by routing protocols (if implemented) and some of the other data components that may be obtained and stored differently.

We will discuss two main elements of how a node communicates with a neighbor node: node data (known as conceptual data structures in RFC 4861) and how the node obtains that data (known as the conceptual sending algorithm in RFC 4861).

Storing Neighbor Data on a Host

For a node to communicate with a neighbor node via IPv6, it needs to know the following: the neighbor's link-layer address, if the neighbor is a host or a router, has the node recently communicated with the neighbor, and if the node itself has a list of routers (i.e., default gateway). The node may also need to know the parameters for other protocols and/or systems, such as Mobile IPv6.

For each active network interface, a node needs to store all the following information:

- *Neighbor cache*—A table of information containing the on-link address for each neighbor. It may include the link-layer address, the neighbor's state of reachability, and whether the neighbor is a host or a router.

- *Destination cache*—A table of information containing data about destinations to which traffic has been sent, including both on-link and off-link nodes. The destination IPv6 address is mapped to the next-hop address of the neighbor. Data not related to ND may also be stored in the destination cache, such as the PMTU and round-trip timers. This list may also be updated from Redirect messages.

- *Prefix list*—A table of information containing data from Router Advertisement messages of the on-link prefix addresses. In addition, each entry has an invalidation timer so it can expire prefixes as they become invalid. Link-local prefixes have an infinite invalidation timer regardless of whether a Router Advertisement message is received for the link-local prefix or not.

- *Default router list*—This contains IP addresses of routers that have sent Router Advertisement messages. Each entry also includes its invalidation timer value.

Conceptual Sending Algorithm

For a node to communicate with a neighbor node, it needs to find out the IP address of the next-hop by examining its destination cache to learn the associated link-layer address by examining its neighbor cache. If the node does not have these addresses available, it invokes a process called "next-hop determination" to populate its caches and lists with its neighbor's addressing information. This process is known as the conceptual sending algorithm.

The conceptual sending algorithm follows this procedure:

1. Examine the destination cache for an entry that matches the destination address.

2. If there is such an entry in the destination cache, proceed to Step 5.

3. If there is no entry in the destination cache, then invoke the next-hop determination process:

   a. Examine the prefix list for a prefix that matches the destination address prefix.

   b. If the destination address prefix matches a prefix in the prefix list, set the next-hop address to the destination address, and then proceed to Step 4.

    c. If there is no matching prefix, then examine the router list for a default router.

    d. If the router list has a router entry to be used as a default router, set the next-hop address to the default router address, and then proceed to Step 4.

    e. If there are no router entries in the router list, then error out with ICMP destination unreachable.

4. Create a destination cache entry with the new value (from either 3b or 3d).

5. Obtain the next-hop address from the destination cache.

6. Examine the neighbor cache for the next-hop's link-layer address.

7. If there is a link-layer address for the next-hop address in the neighbor cache, proceed to Step 9.

8. If there is no link-layer entry in the neighbor cache for the next-hop address, then invoke the address resolution process to determine the link-layer address.

    a. If the link-layer address resolution is successful, update the neighbor cache with the link-layer address, and proceed to Step 9.

    b. If the link-layer address resolution is unsuccessful, then error out with ICMP destination unreachable.

9. Send the packet to the link-layer address from the neighbor cache.

Figure 6-24 shows a flow chart of the conceptual sending algorithm process.

Neighbor Discovery Process

As mentioned previously, ND involves a number of processes:

- *Address Resolution*—Discovering the on-link neighbors utilizing Neighbor Solicitation and Neighbor Advertisement messages

- *Neighbor Unreachability Detection*—Determining whether or not a neighbor that a node previously communicated with remains available

- *Duplicate Address Detection*—Determining if the assigned IPv6 address is in use by a node on the current network (on-link) and, if so, providing an error to the system in order to obtain a different IPv6 address

- *Router Discovery*—Nodes discovering their default gateways and their prefixes, if available

- *Redirect Function*—Routers informing hosts that there is a better first-hop in order to send packets to other nodes

All these processes help a node quickly and efficiently update its locally cached data, such as the link-layer addresses for neighbors and routers, network prefixes, and destination address paths. This is especially helpful when a router fails, because the host can quickly find an alternate router to forward its traffic. (This assumes more than one router is on the network segment, which may not always be the case.)

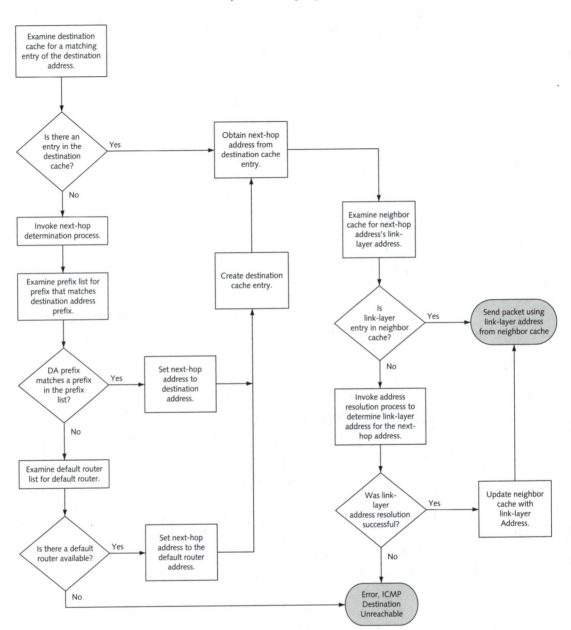

Figure 6-24 Conceptual sending algorithm process
© Cengage Learning 2013

Address Resolution

A node invokes the Address Resolution process when it wants to send a packet to an on-link neighbor but the sender does not know the link-layer address for the target node. A series of Neighbor Solicitation and Neighbor Advertisement messages may be used to resolve the link-layer address for the target node. Note that Address Resolution is not used for resolving multicast addresses, as they are not on-link.

The sending node sends a Neighbor Solicitation message to the solicited-node multicast address for its neighbor, which is derived from the target's IPv6 address and includes its own link-layer address in the Source Link-Layer Option field.

The IPv6 portion of the header comprises FF02::1:FF prepended to the last 24 bits of the target IPv6 address, which is the solicited-node multicast address. For the Ethernet header, 33:33: is prepended to the last 32 bits of the solicited-node multicast address. These are the destination addresses that the sending node uses for its Neighbor Solicitation message.

The target node, if on-link, sends a Neighbor Advertisement (reply) message back to the Neighbor Solicitation message sender that includes its link-layer address in the Target Link-Layer Option field.

When the sender receives the Neighbor Advertisement message from the target (reply), it updates its neighbor cache with the link-layer address of the target. The node can then send the packet to the neighbor.

If the sender does not receive a reply within the appropriate time parameters, then Address Resolution has failed and the sender provides an error ICMP destination unreachable.

Figure 6-25 shows the first step of the Address Resolution process, Neighbor Solicitation, based on the following hypothetical address data:

- Node A has a link-layer (Ethernet MAC) address of 00:11:22:33:44:55 and a link-local address of FE80::1:2:3:1.

- Node B has a link-layer address of 00:55:66:77:88:99 and a link-local address of FE80::5:6:7:2.

Node A sends a multicast Neighbor Solicitation message with the destination MAC address of 33:33:FF:07:00:02 and the destination IPv6 address of FF02::1:FF07:2.

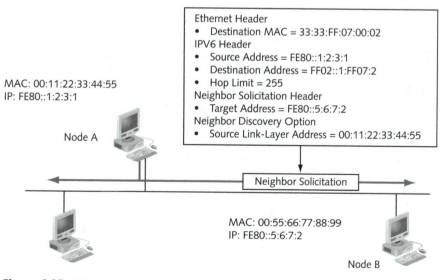

Figure 6-25 Address Resolution process: Step 1, Neighbor Solicitation
© Cengage Learning 2013

Figure 6-26 shows the second step of the Address Resolution process, Neighbor Advertisement, in which Node B sends a unicast Neighbor Advertisement message to Node A.

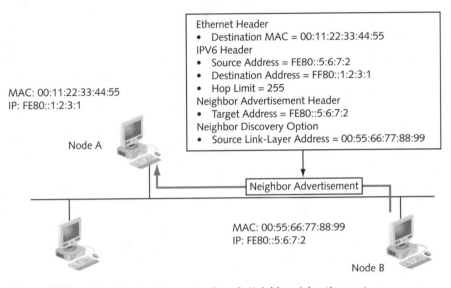

MAC: 00:11:22:33:44:55
IP: FE80::1:2:3:1

Node A

Ethernet Header
• Destination MAC = 00:11:22:33:44:55
IPV6 Header
• Source Address = FE80::5:6:7:2
• Destination Address = FF80::1:2:3:1
• Hop Limit = 255
Neighbor Advertisement Header
• Target Address = FE80::5:6:7:2
Neighbor Discovery Option
• Source Link-Layer Address = 00:55:66:77:88:99

Neighbor Advertisement

MAC: 00:55:66:77:88:99
IP: FE80::5:6:7:2

Node B

Figure 6-26 Address Resolution process: Step 2, Neighbor Advertisement
© Cengage Learning 2013

Neighbor Unreachability Detection

Neighbor Unreachability Detection (NUD) is used for node-to-neighbor-node verification of on-link communications capability, which includes host-to-host, host-to-router, and router-to-host reachability. Routers may use NUD to verify reachability between other routers, but generally there are routing protocols implemented on router-to-router links, so NUD is not strictly necessary for this purpose.

Nodes consider neighbors reachable if there have been recent communications by an upper-layer protocol such as TCP or if the node has recently sent a Neighbor Solicitation message and received the neighbor's Neighbor Advertisement message, which has the Solicited flag set to 1 and subsequently updates its neighbor cache.

The neighbor cache has a state assignment for each entry in the table that includes a timer value that determines the "reachable" capability for the neighbor. If a reachable timer has expired and the node needs to send a packet to the associated neighbor, the node will invoke the Address Resolution process to update its neighbor cache table accordingly.

If a node receives an unsolicited Neighbor Advertisement message or a Router Advertisement message in which the Solicited flag is set to 0, then the node does not consider those messages as confirmation that the neighbor is actually reachable. This only allows the receiver to know there is a sender, but the sender of the Router Advertisement message does not know of the receiver because a reply message is not required by a receiver.

RFC 4861 defines the following five states for a neighbor cache entry:

- *INCOMPLETE*—Address resolution is being performed on the entry. A Neighbor Solicitation message has been sent to the solicited-node multicast address of the target, but the corresponding Neighbor Advertisement message has not yet been received. If a Neighbor Advertisement message is not received after MAX_MULTICAST_SOLICIT (default value of three transmissions), then address resolution has failed and the neighbor entry is removed from the cache.

- *REACHABLE*—The neighbor is considered reachable when either a solicited Neighbor Advertisement message is received or an upper-layer protocol communication indicating forward progress is received within the REACHABLE_TIME variable that is refreshed each time a packet indicating forward progress is received.

- *STALE*—After the REACHABLE_TIME of 30,000 milliseconds has elapsed because of inactivity (no forward progress packets) in communications with the neighbor, the entry is changed to STALE. In addition, if an unsolicited Neighbor Discovery message that also advertises its link-layer is received, the entry is changed to the STALE state to ensure that a proper address resolution process is completed when the node needs to send a packet to the neighbor.

- *DELAY*—After the entry has been changed to STALE and the node sends the first packet to the neighbor, the state changes to DELAY and the DELAY_FIRST_PROBE_TIME variable is set to a default of five seconds. If a reachability message is received within the timer period, the state changes to REACHABLE; otherwise, the state is changed to PROBE. The DELAY state allows upper-layer protocols time to provide reachability confirmation.

- *PROBE*—When the entry changes to the PROBE state, the node sends unicast Neighbor Solicitation messages to the cached link-layer address of the neighbor based on the MAX_UNICAST_SOLICIT variable, which has a default value of three transmissions, and the RETANS_TIMER, which has a default value of 1,000 milliseconds. The neighbor entry is removed from the table if the maximum number of retransmissions and time is exceeded and no response has been received by the neighbor.

Duplicate Address Detection

As a node initially joins a link, it must first determine whether or not its unicast IPv6 address is already in use by another node. Whether the node's IPv6 address is configured via stateless, stateful, or manual configuration, DAD must be performed. Neighbor Solicitation and Neighbor Advertisement messages are used for the DAD process, which is detailed in RFCs 4861 and 4862.

To perform DAD, a node sends a multicast Neighbor Solicitation message configured with the destination MAC address and the destination IPv6 address consisting of its tentative IPv6 address, with the source address in the IPv6 header as the unspecified address "::" (it does not include its own link-layer address in the Source Link-Layer Address Option field).

Figure 6-27 shows the first step of the DAD, Neighbor Solicitation, which includes the following hypothetical address configuration:

- Node A has a tentative link-local address of FE80::1:2:3:1.

- Node B has a link-layer address of 00:55:66:77:88:99 and a link-local address of FE80:: 1:2:3:1.

Node A sends a multicast Neighbor Solicitation message with the destination MAC address of 33:33:FF:03:00:01, a destination IPv6 address of FF02::1:FF03:1, and a source IPv6 address of ::.

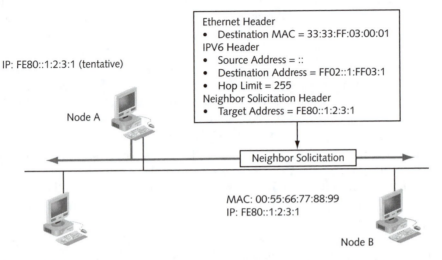

IP: FE80::1:2:3:1 (tentative)

Node A

Ethernet Header
- Destination MAC = 33:33:FF:03:00:01

IPV6 Header
- Source Address = ::
- Destination Address = FF02::1:FF03:1
- Hop Limit = 255

Neighbor Solicitation Header
- Target Address = FE80::1:2:3:1

Neighbor Solicitation

MAC: 00:55:66:77:88:99
IP: FE80::1:2:3:1

Node B

Figure 6-27 Duplicate Address Detection process: Step 1, Neighbor Solicitation
© Cengage Learning 2013

If a neighbor node has the same multicast MAC address that is in the multicast Neighbor Solicitation message, it will receive and process the message. The neighbor node will configure a multicast Neighbor Advertisement message with the destination MAC and IPv6 addresses of the link-local scope all-nodes multicast address. In addition, the Solicited flag field will be set to 0.

Figure 6-28 shows the second step of the DAD process, Neighbor Advertisement:

Node B sends a multicast Neighbor Advertisement message.

When the sending node detects a multicast Neighbor Advertisement message that has the Target address that is the same as its tentative IPv6 address, it cannot assign the desired IPv6 address to its interface and should create an error.

If the node does not receive a multicast Neighbor Advertisement message that indicates a neighbor is using the same IPv6 address, it assigns the desired IPv6 address to the interface.

Router Discovery

Router Discovery is used by nodes to discover neighbor routers on the local link, learn prefixes, configure their default gateway, and other possible configuration parameters relating to autoconfiguration (stateless or stateful) useful to the node.

Routers send unsolicited Router Advertisement messages advertising their availability and addresses. After sending three initial packets (by default), routers send Router Advertisement messages at random intervals, based on a timer variable. These advertisement messages supply configuration parameters that may include a default hop limit, network prefixes, routes

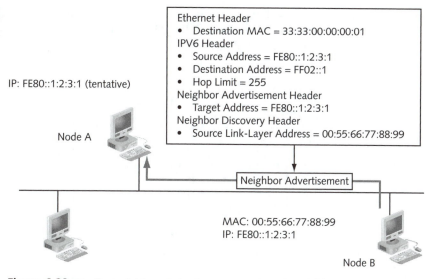

IP: FE80::1:2:3:1 (tentative)

Ethernet Header
- Destination MAC = 33:33:00:00:00:01

IPV6 Header
- Source Address = FE80::1:2:3:1
- Destination Address = FF02::1
- Hop Limit = 255

Neighbor Advertisement Header
- Target Address = FE80::1:2:3:1

Neighbor Discovery Header
- Source Link-Layer Address = 00:55:66:77:88:99

Node A

Neighbor Advertisement

MAC: 00:55:66:77:88:99
IP: FE80::1:2:3:1

Node B

Figure 6-28 Duplicate Address Detection process: Step 2, Neighbor Advertisement
© Cengage Learning 2013

available, MTU for the local link, and flags alerting the node to use an address protocol like DHCPv6 to obtain an IPv6 address and other network services devices (like DNS). In addition, the advertisement will contain a Router Lifetime field, which informs the node as to the length of time the router should be available as a default router.

Nodes send multicast Router Solicitation messages as soon as they start, not waiting for a router to send its Router Advertisement messages. Routers respond to these multicast Router Solicitation messages with a multicast Router Advertisement message indicating configuration parameters for nodes. This is how a node determines whether it should autoconfigure its IPv6 address with included prefix information (stateless), use DHCPv6 (stateful), or use a combination of both—for example, use prefix information for its IPv6 address and use a DHCPv6 server for other network services information like DNS addresses.

If a router becomes unavailable to a node, that node will invoke the NUD process, and either a new default router will be chosen from its router list or the node will send a Router Solicitation message as it attempts to discover a new default gateway.

A node starting up sends a multicast Router Solicitation message with the destination MAC and IPv6 addresses of the link-local scope all-nodes multicast address and the unspecified address as the source IPv6 address (unless it already has a unicast address, in which case it will use that as the source IPv6 address).

Figure 6-29 shows the first step of the Router Discovery process, Router Solicitation, which includes the following hypothetical address configuration:

- Node A has a link-layer (Ethernet MAC) address of 00:11:22:33:44:55 and no link-local address.

- Router has a link-layer address of 00:55:66:77:88:99 and a link-local address of FE80::5:6:7:2.

Node A sends a multicast Router Solicitation message with the destination MAC address of 33:33:00:00:00:02, the destination IPv6 address of FF02::2, and the unspecified source IPv6 address of ::. I does not include its own link-layer address in the Source Link-Layer Address Option field.

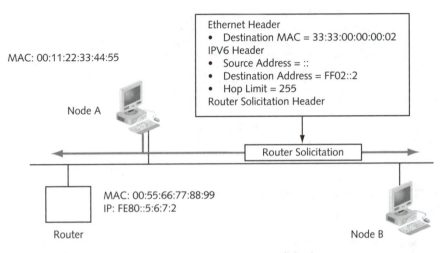

Figure 6-29 Router Discovery process: Step 1, Router Solicitation
© Cengage Learning 2013

Routers that receive a multicast Router Solicitation message on their local link will send a multicast Router Advertisement message to the all-nodes multicast address unless the Router Solicitation message was sent from a node that included its unicast address, at which point the router will send the Router Advertisement message to the node. In addition, the router will include prefix and other configuration parameters based on its configuration.

Figure 6-30 shows the second step of the Router Discovery process, Router Advertisement, which includes the following hypothetical address configuration: Router sends a multicast Router Advertisement message with the destination MAC address of 33:33:00:00:00:01, the destination IPv6 address of FF02::1, and FE80::5:6:7:2 as the source IPv6 address. In addition, it includes configuration parameters and prefix information.

Redirect Messages

Routers send Redirect messages to inform hosts that there is a better first-hop router to send packets to a specific destination. In addition, Redirect messages are used by routers to inform a host that a destination node is an on-link neighbor.

Nodes generally have a single entry in their default router lists, and all packets destined to nodes that are off-link are sent to their default gateway. If the network has multiple routers and a router receives packets from a node for which it determines that it is not the most optimal route to the destination node, that router will send a Redirect message to the originating node informing it about the closer router. The router will also forward that first packet from the originating node to the next-hop router.

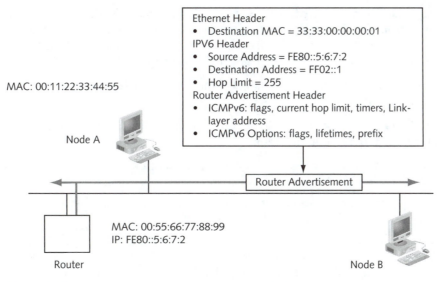

MAC: 00:11:22:33:44:55

Ethernet Header
- Destination MAC = 33:33:00:00:00:01

IPV6 Header
- Source Address = FE80::5:6:7:2
- Destination Address = FF02::1
- Hop Limit = 255

Router Advertisement Header
- ICMPv6: flags, current hop limit, timers, Link-layer address
- ICMPv6 Options: flags, lifetimes, prefix

Node A

Router Advertisement

MAC: 00:55:66:77:88:99
IP: FE80::5:6:7:2

Router

Node B

Figure 6-30 Router Discovery process: Step 2, Router Advertisement
© Cengage Learning 2013

Nodes may also send packets to their default gateway destined to a node that they believe to be off-link because of the destination node prefix not being in their prefix list. The router may determine that the destination node is actually on-link and will send a Redirect message to the originating node so that it can update its prefix list.

The following are the basic steps in the Redirect process:

1. A host sends a unicast packet to its default gateway.

2. The router receives the packet and determines that the source address of the originating host is a neighbor. In addition, the router determines that the destination address has a better first-hop on a different router and that the address of the next-hop is also a neighbor.

3. The router sends the originating host a Redirect message, which includes the following elements:

   a. The Target Address field is set to the address to which the host should send subsequent packets for the specific destination address:

      i. If the target is a next-hop router, then the target address is that router's link-local address.

      ii. If the target is a host, then the target address is set to the same address as in the Destination Address field of the received packet.

   b. This also requires the following options settings or values:

      i. The Target Link-Layer Address option is set to the link-layer address for the target if the router knows it.

      ii. The Redirected header field incorporates as much of the original packet that triggered the Redirect as it can (up to 1280 bytes).

4. When a host receives a Redirect message, it should update its destination cache with the address from the Target Address field so that subsequent packets are directed to the appropriate node. In addition, if the Redirect message includes the Target Link-layer Address option, it should create or update its neighbor cache entry.

Routers do not update their routing tables if they receive a Redirect message; nor do hosts send Redirect messages.

Figure 6-31 shows the first step of the Redirect process, Host Sending, based on the following hypothetical addressing information:

- Node A has a link-layer (Ethernet MAC) address of 00:11:22:33:44:55, a link-local address of FE80::1:2:3:1, and a global address of 2001:db8:0:1:1:2:3:1.

- Router 1 has a link-layer address of 00:55:66:77:88:99, a link-local address of FE80::5:6:7:2, and a global address of 2001:db8:0:1:5:6:7:2.

- Router 2 has a link-layer address of 00:55:66:22:88:34, a link-local address of FE80::5:6:2:4, and a global address of 2001:db8:0:1:5:6:2:4. On its second network interface, it has a link-layer address of 00:55:66:33:77:56, a link-local address of FE80::5:6:3:4, and a global address of 2001:db8:0:2:5:6:3:4.

- Node B has a link-layer address of 00:11:22:66:22:77, a link-local address of FE80::1:2:6:7, and a global address of 2001:db8:0:2:1:2:6:7.

Node A needs to send a packet to another node that is off-link; therefore, it sends a unicast packet to its default gateway with the destination MAC address of 00:55:66:77:88:99, the destination IPv6 address of 2001:db8:0:2:1:2:6:7, and the source IPv6 address of 2001:db8:0:1:1:2:3:1.

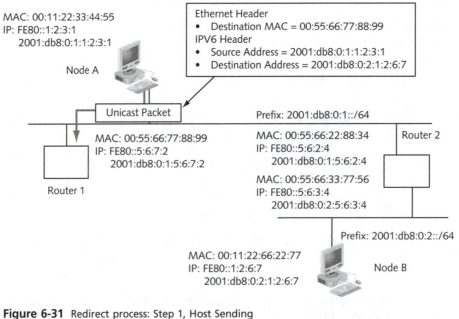

Figure 6-31 Redirect process: Step 1, Host Sending
© Cengage Learning 2013

Figure 6-32 shows the second step of the Redirect process, Redirect Message: Router 1 receives the packet from Node A and performs address resolution for the destination address 2001:db8:0:2:1:2:6:7. Router 2 informs Router 1 that it is the next-hop for the destination node. Router 1 sends a redirect message to Node A informing it that subsequent packets destined for node 2001:db8:0:2:1:2:6:7 should be sent to Router 2 at 2001: db8:0:1:5:6:2:4 instead.

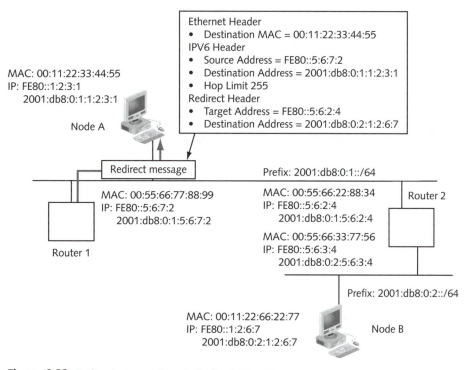

Figure 6-32 Redirect process: Step 2, Redirect message
© Cengage Learning 2013

Figure 6-33 shows the third step of the Redirect process, Router Forwarding Initial Packet:

Router 1 forwards the initial packet received from Node A and destined for node 2001: db8:0:2:1:2:6:7 to Router 2 at 2001:db8:0:1:5:6:2:4 because it is the next-hop for the destination node and will route the packet accordingly.

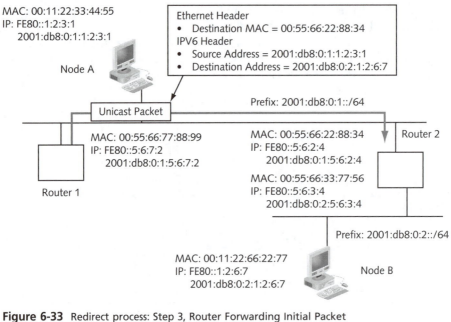

MAC: 00:11:22:33:44:55
IP: FE80::1:2:3:1
 2001:db8:0:1:1:2:3:1

Node A

Ethernet Header
- Destination MAC = 00:55:66:22:88:34
IPV6 Header
- Source Address = 2001:db8:0:1:1:2:3:1
- Destination Address = 2001:db8:0:2:1:2:6:7

Unicast Packet

Prefix: 2001:db8:0:1::/64

MAC: 00:55:66:77:88:99
IP: FE80::5:6:7:2
 2001:db8:0:1:5:6:7:2

Router 1

MAC: 00:55:66:22:88:34
IP: FE80::5:6:2:4
 2001:db8:0:1:5:6:2:4

MAC: 00:55:66:33:77:56
IP: FE80::5:6:3:4
 2001:db8:0:2:5:6:3:4

Router 2

Prefix: 2001:db8:0:2::/64

MAC: 00:11:22:66:22:77
IP: FE80::1:2:6:7
 2001:db8:0:2:1:2:6:7

Node B

Figure 6-33 Redirect process: Step 3, Router Forwarding Initial Packet
© Cengage Learning 2013

Chapter Summary

- IPv6 introduces a Neighbor Discovery protocol that helps support stateless autoconfiguration and provides improved support for mobile users.

- The conceptual host model represents information that a host should maintain, in some form, in order to communicate effectively in an IPv6 network.

- Router Solicitation and Router Advertisement messages help nodes learn network prefixes and other stateless and/or stateful address autoconfiguration capabilities. These allow nodes on the network to find better first-hop paths and find alternate routers, if required.

- Neighbor Solicitation and Neighbor Advertisement messages help nodes discover neighbor nodes that are on-link or off-link, perform Duplicate Address Detection, or verify that a node remains available for communications.

Key Terms

Duplicate Address Detection (DAD) A method for checking the IPv6 address that a node wishes to use by sending a Neighbor Advertisement message to see if it is already in use by some other node. If the message elicits no response, the address will be used; otherwise, a different address will be selected for checking using DAD.

Neighbor Advertisement (NA) Nodes send Neighbor Advertisement messages that include their IPv6 and link-layer addresses to maintain information about local addresses and on-link status.

Neighbor Discovery (ND) A protocol in IPv6 that permits nodes and routers on a local link to keep one another updated about any recent changes in their network connectivity or status.

Neighbor Solicitation (NS) Neighbor Solicitation messages are used to find (or verify) the link-layer address for a local node, to see if that node is still available, or check that an address is not in use by another node.

Redirect A message, or advertisement, sent out by a router to inform a sending node that there is a better first-hop router to access a destination node that is off-link or to inform the sending node that the destination node is on-link even though the network prefix is different.

Router Advertisement (RA) A message, or advertisement, sent out by a router, either periodically or on request, which contains its own link-layer address, the network prefix of the local subnet, the MTU for the local link, suggested hop limit values, and other parameters useful for nodes on the local link. RAs can also contain flagged parameters indicating the type of autoconfiguration that new nodes should use.

Router Solicitation (RS) Network nodes use RS messages to ask routers connected to a local link to identify themselves by immediately sending an RA message rather than waiting for the next scheduled advertisement to appear. An RS message acts like a RA request, in other words.

solicited-node address A multicast address with link-local scope, which helps reduce the number of multicast groups to which nodes must subscribe in order to make themselves available for solicitation by other nodes on their local links. The solicited-node address is FF02::1:FF*xx.xxxx*, in which "*xx.xxxx*" stands for the lowest-order (rightmost) 24 bits of the unicast or anycast address associated with that interface.

unspecified address A reserved address used as a source address if a node does not have an assigned IPv6 address. The unspecified address is "::".

Review Questions

1. Which of the following ICMPv6 type numbers relate to Router Solicitation and Router Advertisement messages? (Choose all that apply.)

    a. 133

    b. 135

    c. 137

    d. 134

    e. 136

2. How does a host interpret the Managed Address Configuration flag in a Router Advertisement message?

    a. When set to 0, hosts must use an address configuration protocol such as DHCPv6 to obtain non-address configuration information.

    b. When set to 1, hosts must not use an address configuration protocol such as DHCPv6 to obtain non-address configuration information.

    c. When set to 1, hosts must use an address configuration protocol such as DHCPv6 to obtain address configuration information.

    d. When set to 0, hosts must not use an address configuration protocol such as DHCPv6 to obtain address configuration information.

3. The link-local scope all-nodes multicast address is which of the following?

    a. FF02::1

    b. FF01::1

    c. FF02::2

    d. FF01::2

4. A host invoking the Duplicate Address Detection process sends what type of message?

    a. Router Advertisement

    b. Neighbor Solicitation

    c. Neighbor Advertisement

    d. Broadcast Query

5. When a node starts up and does not have an IPv6 address, it uses which address as its source address when sending a Router Solicitation message?

    a. solicited-node address

    b. MAC address

    c. specified address

    d. unspecified address

6. What type of packet is a node sending to another node that is on-link?

    a. unicast

    b. multicast

    c. broadcast

    d. anytimecast

7. What type of packet is a node sending when it sends a Neighbor Solicitation message for address resolution?

    a. unicast

    b. multicast

    c. broadcast

    d. allcast

8. When a router sends a Redirect message to a host, which of the following choices best represents the intent of such a message?

    a. To inform the host that a better first-hop router is available

    b. To inform the host that there are two routers that the host can use

   c. To inform the host that there is no router usable for those messages

   d. To inform the host that the host should send all packets to the core router

9. A node's prefix list uses an indefinite invalidation timer for which type of entry?

   a. neighbors on-link

   b. routers off-link

   c. link-layer

   d. link-local

10. According to the host sending algorithm, which two conditions must be met in order for a host to send a packet to a destination node's link-layer address? (Choose all that apply.)

   a. Destination address is in the destination cache.

   b. Destination address is in the prefix list.

   c. Link-layer entry is in the router cache.

   d. Link-layer entry is in the destination cache.

   e. Link-layer entry is in the neighbor cache.

11. Upon receipt of the Other Configuration flag in a Router Advertisement message, which of the following best represents how the host should respond?

   a. When set to 1, hosts may not use an address configuration protocol such as DHCPv6 to obtain non-address configuration information.

   b. When set to 1, hosts may use an address configuration protocol such as DHCPv6 to obtain non-address configuration information.

   c. When set to 1, hosts must use an address configuration protocol such as DHCPv6 to obtain address configuration information.

   d. When set to 1, hosts must not use an address configuration protocol such as DHCPv6 to obtain address configuration information.

12. What is one possible condition upon which a node will send an unsolicited Neighbor Advertisement message?

   a. when the link-layer address of its next-hop router changes

   b. when its own link-local address changes

   c. when the link-layer address of its nearest neighbor changes

   d. when its own link-layer address changes

13. Upon receipt of the L Flag in the Prefix Options of the Router Advertisement message, which choice best represents how the host should respond?

   a. When set to 1, the host should use the prefix received for on-link address determination.

   b. When set to 0, the host should use the prefix received for on-link address determination.

   c. When set to 1, the host should use the prefix received for off-link address determination.

   d. When set to 0, the host should use the prefix received for off-link address determination.

14. An ICMPv6 Duplicate Address Detection message is closely related to which ICMP message?

    a. Reverse ARP

    b. Forward ARP

    c. Gratuitous ARP

    d. Grateful ARP

15. Which RFC most completely defines Neighbor Discovery for IPv6?

    a. 4191

    b. 4361

    c. 4862

    d. 4861

16. If using Wireshark to analyze a large packet capture from the network, which filter would be configured to display only packets that are Neighbor Advertisement messages?

    a. icmpv6.type == 136

    b. icmpv6.type == 135

    c. icmpv6.type == 134

    d. icmpv6.type == 133

17. Which of the following represents the five states of a neighbor cache entry?

    a. INCOMPLETE, UNREACHABLE, STALE, DELAY, PROBE

    b. INCOMPLETE, REACHABLE, STALE, DELAY, PROBE

    c. INCOMPATIBLE, REACHABLE, STALE, DELAY, PROBE

    d. INCOMPLETE, REACHABLE, STRONG, ON-TIME, PROBE

18. How frequently do routers send unsolicited Router Advertisement messages?

    a. an initial sending of three packets, then every 60 seconds

    b. an initial sending of two packets, then at random intervals

    c. an initial sending of one packet, then every 60 seconds

    d. an initial sending of three packets, then at random intervals

19. Which of the following are basic rules of operations for nodes (routers and hosts) concerning Redirect messages?

    a. Routers update their routing tables if they receive Redirect messages. Hosts can send Redirect messages.

    b. Routers do not update their routing tables if they receive Redirect messages. Hosts can send Redirect messages.

    c. Routers do not update their routing tables if they receive Redirect messages. Hosts do not send Redirect messages.

    d. Routers update their routing tables if they receive Redirect messages. Hosts do not send Redirect messages.

20. Which of the following choices permit a node to consider a neighbor to be reachable? (Choose all that apply.)

    a. Unsolicited Router Solicitations are received within the REACHABLE_TIME variable.

    b. Upper-layer protocol indicates backward progress within the REACHABLE_TIME variable.

    c. Solicited Neighbor Advertisements are received within the REACHABLE_TIME variable.

    d. Upper-layer protocol indicates forward progress within the REACHABLE_TIME variable.

    e. Unsolicited Neighbor Advertisements are received within the REACHABLE_TIME variable.

21. Which of the following ICMPv6 type numbers relates to Neighbor Solicitation messages?

    a. 134

    b. 136

    c. 133

    d. 135

    e. 137

22. The link-local scope all-routers multicast address is which of the following?

    a. FF01::1

    b. FF02::1

    c. FF01::2

    d. FF02::2

23. In a Router Advertisement message, which two combined Prefix Information options comprise the IPv6 prefix address?

    a. Prefix Length and Preferred Lifetime

    b. Prefix and Length

    c. Prefix and Prefix Length

    d. Prefix Length and the L flag

24. Which Neighbor Discovery messages will include the source link-layer address of the sender in its options field? (Choose all that apply.)

    a. Neighbor Advertisement

    b. Redirect

    c. Router Advertisement

    d. Neighbor Solicitation

    e. Reply Solicitation

25. Which choice best represents how a host should behave upon receipt of the H flag in the Prefix Options of the Router Advertisement message?

    a. When set to 1, the router is functioning as a Mobile IPv6 home agent.

    b. When set to 0, the router is functioning as a Mobile IPv6 hello agent.

    c. When set to 1, the router is functioning as a Mobile IPv6 hello agent.

    d. When set to 0, the router is functioning as a Mobile IPv6 home agent.

Hands-On Projects

Hands-On Projects 6-1 through 6-5 assume that you are working in a Windows Vista or Windows 7 Professional environment, that you have installed the Wireshark for Windows software, and that you have acquired the trace (data) files necessary to work through many of the Hands-On Projects in this book.

Hands-On Project 6-1: View ICMPv6 Neighbor Discovery Messages

Time Required: 10 minutes

Objective: Use Wireshark to view a trace file and configure filters to view ICMPv6 Neighbor Discovery messages.

Description: This project shows you how to use Wireshark to configure specific filters using the supplied trace file and view individual Neighbor Discovery messages. The use of filters allows for easier and often quicker viewing of a specific component in large trace files and/or real-time capturing of data. You will find and view Router Solicitation, Router Advertisement, Neighbor Solicitation, and Neighbor Advertisement messages.

1. Click **Start**, point to **All Programs**, and then click **Wireshark**.

2. Click **File** on the menu bar, click **Open**, select the **ch6_trace file**, and click **Open**.

3. In the field to the right of the Filter button, type **icmpv6.type == 133** and select **Apply** in order to view a Router Solicitation message. An example of the Wireshark filter configuration and output is shown in Figure 6-34.

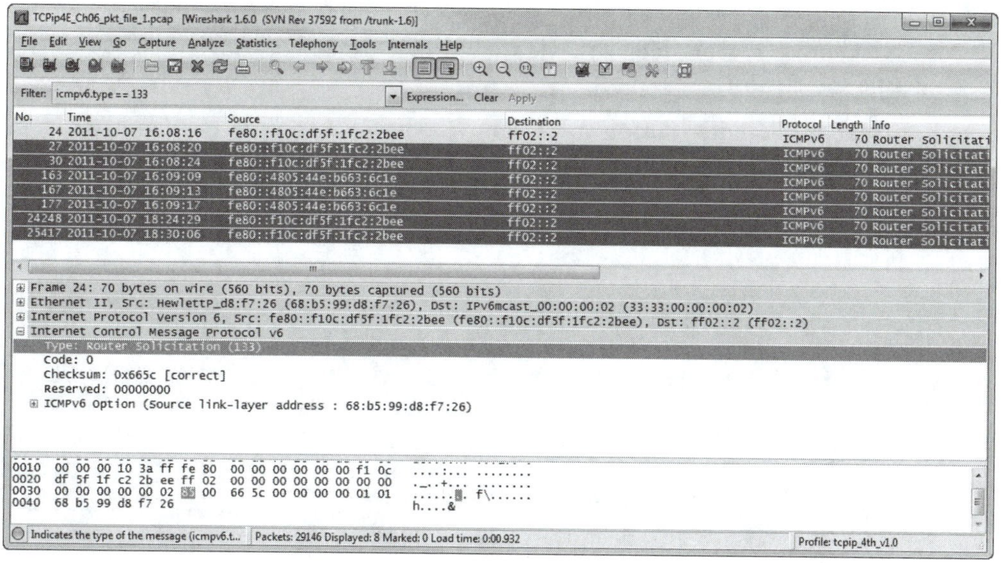

Figure 6-34 ICMPv6 Router Solicitation packet
Source: Wireshark

4. Select one of the packets and observe its structure. In the packet details pane, select the plus sign (+) next to Internet Control Message Protocol v6 and view the Type field.

5. Select **Clear**. In the field to the right of the Filter button, type **icmpv6.type == 134** and select **Apply** to view a Router Advertisement message.

6. Select one of the packets and observe its structure. In the packet details pane, select the plus sign (+) next to Internet Control Message Protocol v6 and view the Type field.

7. Select **Clear**. In the field to the right of the Filter button, type **icmpv6.type == 135** and select **Apply** to view a Neighbor Solicitation message.

8. Select one of the packets and observe its structure. In the packet details pane, select the plus sign (+) next to Internet Control Message Protocol v6 and view the Type field.

9. Select **Clear**. In the field to the right of the Filter button, type **icmpv6.type == 136** and select **Apply** view a Neighbor Advertisement message.

10. Select one of the packets and observe its structure. In the packet details pane, select the plus sign (+) next to Internet Control Message Protocol v6 and view the Type field.

11. Select **Clear** in order to remove these filters and prepare for the next lab.

Hands-On Project 6-2: Build a Filter to View a Neighbor Advertisement Message for a Specific Host

Time Required: 10 minutes

Objective: Use Wireshark to view a trace file and configure filters to view a Neighbor Advertisement message.

Description: This project assumes you are continuing from Hands-On Project 6-1. You will be configuring specific filters to view individual Neighbor Advertisement messages for a specific source host.

1. Next to the Filter button, type **icmpv6.type == 136 && ipv6.addr == fe80::4805:44e:b663:6c1e** and select **Apply** to view the specific Neighbor Advertisement messages. An example of the Wireshark filter configuration and output is shown in Figure 6-35.

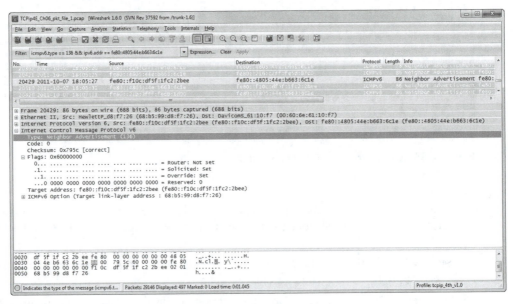

Figure 6-35 ICMPv6 Neighbor Advertisement packet

Source: Wireshark

2. Select one of the packets and observe its structure. In the packet details pane, select the plus sign (**+**) next to Internet Protocol Version 6 and the plus sign (**+**) next to the Internet Control Message Protocol v6 and view the Source and Type fields.

3. Select **Clear** in order to remove these filters and prepare for the next lab.

Hands-On Project 6-3: Build a Filter to View a Neighbor Advertisement Message That Is a Reply Message to an NS-DAD Message

Time Required: 10 minutes

Objective: Use Wireshark to view a trace file and configure filters to view Neighbor Advertisement messages that illustrate a reply to a Neighbor Solicitation DAD message.

Description: This project assumes you are continuing from Hands-On Project 6-2. You will be configuring specific filters to view individual Neighbor Advertisement messages that are Duplicate Address Detection reply messages.

1. Next to the Filter button, type **icmpv6.type == 136 && ipv6.addr == ff02::1** and select **Apply** in order to view the specific Neighbor Advertisement messages. An example of the Wireshark filter configuration and output is shown in Figure 6-36.

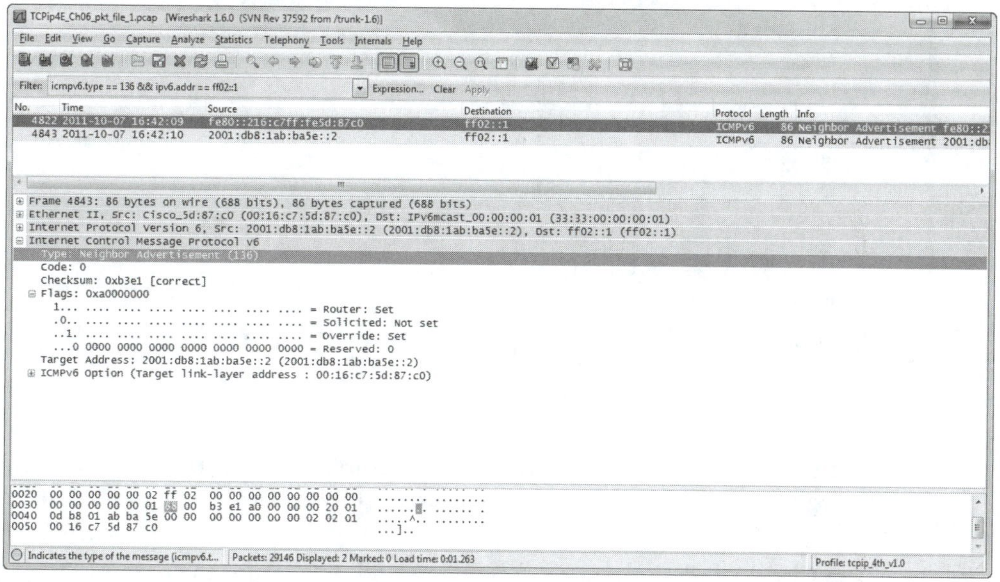

Figure 6-36 ICMPv6 Neighbor Advertisement packet
Source: Wireshark

2. Select one of the packets and observe its structure. In the packet details pane, select the plus sign (+) next to Internet Control Message Protocol v6.

3. Select **Clear** in order to remove these filters and prepare for the next lab.

Hands-On Project 6-4: Build a Filter to View a Router Advertisement Message that has the M and O Flags Set

Time Required: 10 minutes

Objective: Use Wireshark to view a trace file and configure filters to view Router Advertisement messages.

Description: This project assumes you are continuing from Hands-On Project 6-3. You will be configuring specific filters to view individual Router Advertisement messages that have the M and O flags set.

1. Next to the Filter button, type **icmpv6.nd.ra.flag.m == 1 && icmpv6.nd.ra.flag.o == 1** and select **Apply** to view the specific Router Advertisement messages. An example of the Wireshark filter configuration and output is shown in Figure 6-37.

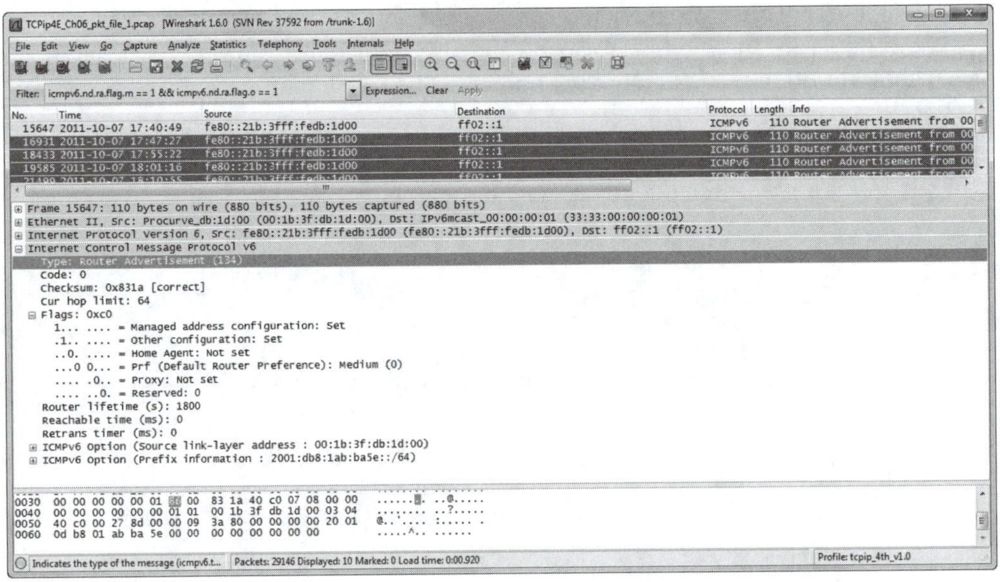

Figure 6-37 ICMPv6 Router Advertisement packet
Source: Wireshark

2. Select one of the packets and observe its structure. In the packet details pane, select the plus sign (+) next to Internet Control Message Protocol v6 and also select the plus sign (+) Flags.

3. Select **Clear** in order to remove these filters and prepare for the next lab.

Hands-On Project 6-5: Build a Filter to View a Router Advertisement Message that has Prefix Information

Time Required: 10 minutes

Objective: Use Wireshark to view a trace file and configure filters to view Router Advertisement messages.

Description: This project assumes you are continuing from Hands-On Project 6-4. You will be configuring specific filters to view individual Router Advertisement messages that have the Prefix option included and the On-link flag set.

1. Next to the Filter button, type **icmpv6.opt.type == 3** and select **Apply** in order to view the specific Router Advertisement messages. An example of the Wireshark filter configuration and output is shown in Figure 6-38.

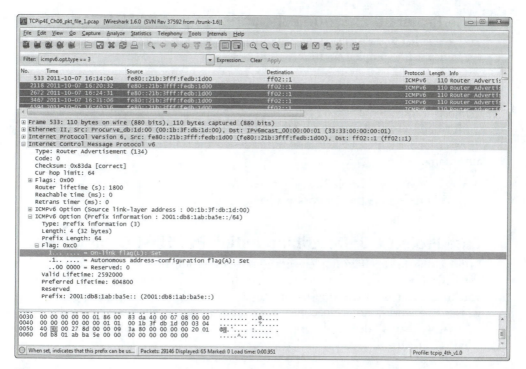

Figure 6-38 ICMPv6 Router Advertisement packet
Source: Wireshark

2. Select one of the packets and observe its structure. In the packet details pane, select the plus sign (**+**) next to Internet Control Message Protocol v6, select the plus sign (**+**) for the ICMPv6 Option (for Prefix), and select the plus sign (**+**) Flags.

3. Close Wireshark.

Case Projects

CASE PROJECTS

Case Project 6-1: Understanding Neighbor Solicitation and Neighbor Advertisement Messages

In preparing for an IPv6 implementation at your company, you are responsible for providing basic IPv6 operations information to the desktop support team. One of the topics in your document is to describe the overall functions of Neighbor Discovery operations, specifically Neighbor Solicitation and Neighbor Advertisement messages and what they provide an IPv6 node on the network.

Detail the components these two ND processes provide and also provide the specific Wireshark display filter required to quickly view these processes when capturing network traffic.

Case Project 6-2: Troubleshooting a Specific Network Problem

You are called to assist in troubleshooting a network problem that has occurred soon after a significant IPv6 implementation.

Some network hosts seem to have network access, but their browsers do not resolve URLs that are entered. The network technicians troubleshooting the problem have discovered that the hosts in question can ping other network hosts on a different network segment, but only via IPv6 addresses. Hosts on the other network segment can resolve URLs entered into their browsers. As a note, all network hosts derive their IPv6 addresses using stateful address autoconfig.

What could be the possible issue or issues? And what Wireshark display filter could you use to quickly determine the network problem?

Case Project 6-3: Describing Initial IPv6 Host Communications

In preparing for an IPv6 implementation at your company, you are responsible for providing basic IPv6 operations information to the desktop support team. One of the topics in your document is to describe the initial IPv6 communications process that a host invokes when its network interface becomes active and what information it retains locally as a result of what it "learns" during those processes. Create a corresponding description to document what is learned and retained in that process.

chapter 7

IP Address Autoconfiguration

After reading this chapter and completing the exercises, you will be able to:

- Explain the basic services that DHCP/DHCPv6 offers to its clients and explain its background
- Explain the specifics of IP/IPv6 address management using DHCP/DHCPv6
- Explain the DHCP Discovery, renewal, and release processes
- Explain the basic DHCP/DHCPv6 packet structure and types of DHCP/DHCPv6 messages in use
- Describe broadcast and unicast addressing for IPv4 as well as multicast addressing for IPv6
- Describe relay agent communications for both IPv4 and IPv6
- Discuss Microsoft DHCP scopes for IPv4 and differences in IPv6 scope configuration
- Use DHCP/DHCPv6 troubleshooting utilities

If there were any particular TCP/IP Application layer protocol and service that could vie for the designation "a TCP/IP network administrator's best friend," it would have to be IP Autoconfiguration, such as **Dynamic Host Configuration Protocol (DHCP)**. DHCP holds this position because it eliminates the tedious labor involved in managing IP addresses manually. Old-fashioned manual management requires administrators to configure each IP host machine or network interface by hand and to keep track of which machines (or interfaces on multihomed machines) use which IP addresses. With DHCP in the picture, inflexible administrators who want to continue managing addresses manually can still do so. Those who aren't so inflexible can use DHCP to hand out addresses to clients as needed while maintaining fixed or static address assignments for key hosts such as IP gateways, wireless access points, database or other application servers, and so forth.

Autoconfiguration allows a host to find the information it needs to set up its own IP networking parameters by querying other nodes. BOOTP was an early attempt at this kind of capability. DHCP is a common autoconfiguration tool deployed across many parts of the Internet today.

Three things combine to make autoconfiguration particularly important for the Internet. The first is the sheer number of nodes to be configured. Network administrators would be kept very busy indeed if they had to configure each node by hand. The second is the rate of change and the frequency of renumbering. Changing ISPs can mean renumbering many network hosts. Without renumbering to match actual network topology, routing performance suffers. The better the autoconfiguration tools, the easier it is for network administrators to renumber hosts efficiently. The third and perhaps most compelling reason for autoconfiguration is user mobility. Mobile nodes that may roam from one part of the network to another include not only laptops but also cellular phones, smartphones, and other personal devices. The potential advantages of a system that allows these devices to connect seamlessly to the Internet from any location are great.

This chapter covers DHCP and DHCPv6 in detail, including IP address management and mechanisms for address discovery, lease or allocation, renewal, and release. After explaining DHCP/DHCPv6 packet structure and fields, this chapter clarifies broadcast and unicast addressing for IPv4, clarifies multicast addressing for IPv6, describes relay agent communications, and discusses Microsoft DHCP scopes. Finally, you are introduced to some DHCP/DHCPv6 troubleshooting tips and utilities.

Understanding Autoaddressing

Although DHCP is considered the most common form of address autoconfiguration (especially for IPv4), it is not the only mechanism for clients to obtain an address automatically. A few years after DHCP became a basic "normal operations mode" for network clients to automatically receive their IP addresses, Microsoft introduced a mechanism for clients to "self-address" without other systems interacting—that is, no "addressing server." This method allowed network-connected clients to communicate if there was no DHCP server available, but it was limited in its capability. This "stateless autoconfiguration" addressing scheme could not be routed to other connected networks. It is formally known as Automatic Private IP Addressing (APIPA).

When the designers of IPng (IP Next Generation, which became known as IPv6) were formulating the new IP operations, they wanted a more robust and controllable system for address autoconfiguration. Even though IPv6 address autoconfiguration operates in a similar manner to IPv4 address autoconfiguration, there are some differences. There is still DHCP capability, known as stateful or DHCPv6, and there is also a stateless autoconfiguration method, with some of the same constraints as its IPv4 counterpart. In IPv6, the primary difference is that nodes can use either method or a combination of both methods. In all cases for IPv6 address autoconfiguration, the Router Advertisement is the control mechanism used by clients, informing them about which autoconfiguration method to use, including the capability for clients to change methods "midstream." This latter capability is the foundation for automatic network renumbering, in which little interaction may be required by personnel to accomplish such a goal.

We will discuss all of these capabilities and their details in this chapter. Initially, we will start with DHCP at a high level, then move into each protocol and its specifics.

Introducing Dynamic Host Configuration Protocol

Dynamic Host Configuration Protocol (DHCP) is a service that provides a way for a client computer that lacks an IP address assignment to request one from any listening DHCP server—without the help of an administrator. This is a great solution for client or desktop machines because their users normally have no pressing need to maintain the same IP address over time. However, DHCP also provides a mechanism for reserving certain IP addresses for specific hosts. Called static address allocation, it assigns an address to a device that can't change unless a DHCP administrator manually forces it do so. This is ideal for devices that require fixed IP addresses, such as gateways, wireless access points, and servers of many kinds (Web, database, storage, and so forth). Thus, DHCP works very well to manage IP addresses for just about any conceivable usage.

In addition to providing a usable IP address, DHCP can deliver the necessary configuration information to clients to tell them the addresses of their IP gateways, the addresses for one or more DNS servers for domain name resolution, and so forth. DHCP also manages address allocations over time so that a group of machines larger than some particular range of IP addresses can share that address range and still obtain access to the network and the Internet.

The whole point of DHCP is to make it possible to administer client IP address assignments and configuration data from a single, centralized server instead of requiring administrators to manually configure hosts one at a time. As organizations grow and the number of hosts that must be managed increases, DHCP quickly becomes a necessity rather than a luxury.

DHCP traces its origins to a protocol named BOOTP, which is short for "Bootstrap Protocol." BOOTP was developed in the 1970s as a way of providing sufficient network access for diskless workstations to access startup information across the network instead of having to read it from a local disk drive. Today, DHCP packets use message formats similar to what BOOTP used, but BOOTP itself is seldom used anymore. It is defined in RFC 951, and DHCP provides backward compatibility to BOOTP clients. Therefore, if any BOOTP requests occur on a network, chances are good that a DHCP server will handle such service requests, as specified in RFC 1534 (which defines interoperability between DHCP and BOOTP).

Microsoft always had a vested interest in DHCP, viewing it as a key ingredient in managing IP configuration data for numerous desktops. Representatives from Microsoft helped define RFCs 1534, 2131, 2132, and 2241, all of which are important to DHCP's definition and operation. Thus, it should come as no surprise that Microsoft's implementation of DHCP is highly regarded and supports all the RFCs just mentioned.

DHCP servers can manage one or more ranges of IP addresses, each of which may be called an **address pool** (if considered as a range of available addresses from which unused addresses may be allocated) or an **address scope** (if considered as a range of numeric IP addresses that fall under DHCP's control). Within any individual IP address scope (usually represented as a contiguous range of IP addresses), DHCP can exclude individual addresses or address ranges from dynamic allocation to client machines, often by dividing an address range into two disjointed pools: one dynamic, the other static. This approach permits DHCP to manage already assigned IP addresses for devices such as routers, gateways, or servers. DHCP can allocate all remaining unallocated addresses to clients on demand; each such allocation is called an address lease (or lease, for short).

How DHCP Works

Here's a brief rundown of how DHCP works from a client's perspective:

1. When TCP/IP is configured on a client computer, the *Obtain an IP address automatically* option is the only necessary setup element and is the default configuration for Windows Vista, Windows 7, and Windows Server 2008 (see Figure 7-1). The DHCP service is automatic, which explains the terrific appeal that DHCP holds for network administrators and users alike.

2. When the workstation attempts to access the network, it broadcasts a DHCP address request to the network because the network has no IP address. It can make this broadcast because it is configured as a **DHCP client.**

3. All **DHCP servers** present on the same broadcast domain receive the request and send back a message that indicates a willingness to grant an address lease, if an address is available.

 If no DHCP server is present in some broadcast domain, a special piece of software called a **DHCP relay agent** must be present in that broadcast domain. The DHCP relay agent forwards the address request to a DHCP server whose address it knows. Such relays may be installed on Windows Server 2008 machines or on routers attached to other subnets that are not part of a DHCP broadcast domain. After that, the relay acts as an intermediary between the DHCP server and the client.

4. The client accepts an address lease offer (usually the first one it receives) and sends a packet to the server that extended the offer.

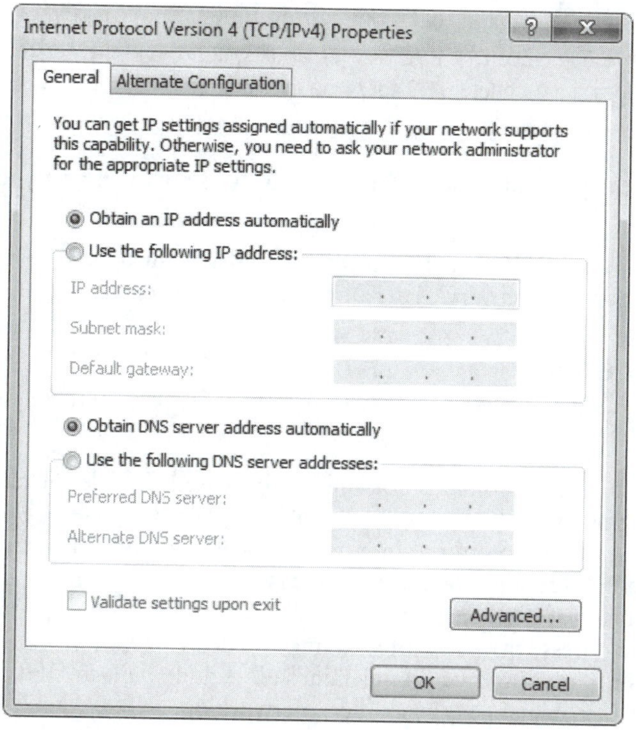

Figure 7-1 Enabling DHCP in the Internet Protocol (TCP/IP) Properties dialog box
Source: Microsoft

5. In reply, the server proffers an IP address for a specific period of time (hence the name *lease*) that the client uses thereafter.

6. When half the lease period expires, the client attempts to renew the lease. Usually, the DHCP server that granted the lease will renew it, but if it doesn't respond, the client tries to renew it again at other times during the lease period. Only if the client is unable to renew its lease before expiration must that client repeat the DHCP request process, as described in Step 2.

Role of Leases

Again, leases are "loans" of an address for a specific amount of time. They play an integral role in how you run your network. The lengths of leases vary, as described in the following list:

- Leases that range from one to three weeks in length are typical on networks in which machines seldom move and the workforce is stable. In this case, long leases do not cause "address starvation" when a user is unable to obtain an IP address because all available addresses are in use.

- Lease periods average between one and three days for networks on which lots of temps or roving workers come and go regularly.

- Lease periods of four to eight hours are common on ISP networks where clients come and go all the time.

By default, Windows Server 2008 sets DHCP leases at eight days. There are numerous DHCP servers for Linux systems, and the default DHCP leases are generally 12 to 24 hours.

You can use the numbers in the preceding list as guidelines for how you might set your leases on a Windows DHCP server.

You can view lease information in DHCP packets using an analyzer, such as Wireshark. See the section titled " DHCP Address Discovery" later in this chapter for details.

DHCP Software Elements

The following three pieces of software work together to define a complete DHCP networking environment:

- *DHCP client*—The DHCP client software (or similar software available for most other modern operating systems) is enabled at a client machine when you select the *Obtain an IP address automatically* option in the Internet Protocol (TCP/IP) Properties window, shown in Figure 7-1. This software broadcasts requests for service and lease renewal requests on behalf of its clients, and it handles address and configuration data for the client when an address lease is granted. Windows Server 2008, Windows Vista, Windows 7, Macintosh, Linux, and UNIX machines all include built-in DHCP client software. DHCP is, in fact, a mainstay of modern networking.

- *DHCP server*—DHCP server software listens and responds to client and relay requests for address services. The DHCP server also manages address pools and related configuration data. Most current DHCP servers (UNIX and Windows Server 2008) can manage multiple address pools.

- *DHCP relay agent*—DHCP clients broadcast address requests to their network segments. Because broadcasts are not forwarded through routers, the job of the DHCP relay agent software is to intercept address requests on a local cable segment and repackage those requests as a unicast to one or more DHCP servers. The DHCP relay agent software is configured with the IP address of the DHCP server so that the relay agent software can send DHCP requests directly to the DHCP server. A **DHCP Request** is a message from a client to a server, requesting some kind of service. In response to a client request, the server sends a **DHCP Reply** message to the relay agent, which then uses the requester's MAC layer address to forward the reply back to the client that requested an address. Note that most subsequent DHCP requests—such as lease renewals or surrenders—occur as unicast messages, because as soon as a machine obtains an IP address and a default IP gateway address, it is able to communicate directly with the DHCP server and no longer needs an intermediary.

DHCP Lease Types

A DHCP server recognizes two types of address leases:

- *Manual*—With a **manual address lease**, the administrator explicitly assigns an IP address manually by associating a client's hardware address with a specific IP address to be leased to that client. Use this type of address lease if you want DHCP to manage all

IP addresses but you also want to control some address assignments directly. On large networks, this is easier than assigning fixed IP addresses on individual machines. Because configuring manual address leases is labor intensive, however, this technique is used only when absolutely necessary—for example, for routers, gateways, wireless access points, and servers, all of which benefit from persistent, unchanging IP addresses. Manual address leases come from the static address pool on a DHCP server.

- *Dynamic*—The DHCP server assigns addresses for specific periods of time. Use a **dynamic address lease** to assign addresses to clients or other machines when fixed IP addresses are not required. Given the prevalence of clients on most networks, this is the most prevalent type of DHCP address lease. Dynamic address leases come from the dynamic address pool and represent those addresses not already reserved for static allocation.

A typical IP addressing scheme on a network might look like this:

- *Servers* have static IP addresses because their DNS entries must stay consistent. This applies to name servers for DNS, e-mail servers, login hosts, file and print servers, database servers, and any server with resources to which users regularly attach. If they're managed through DHCP, they will be granted addresses from the static address pool.

- *Routers* (or IP gateways, be they routers or other machines, as well as other devices that act as network resources, such as bridges, wireless access points, and so forth) have static IP addresses because their addresses are key parts of any subnet's IP configuration. Likewise, any boundary or border routers must be treated the same way because they represent points of entry (and exit) between internal and external networks.

- *Clients* use dynamic IP addresses because they initiate the connections to the servers, and the servers simply respond to the clients based on the clients' IP addresses. The server does not need to maintain a list of client names and IP addresses in a table. The clients can change their IP addresses many times and still receive responses from the server.

More about DHCP Leases

Even though clients usually keep their addresses indefinitely, they can cancel their address leases at any time, thereby returning their addresses to the pool of free IP addresses that the DHCP server manages. On Windows computers (Windows 9x and newer versions), the `ipconfig` command supports the `/release` and `/renew` switches to permit clients to release or renew their current DHCP leases at will. Clients ordinarily attempt to renew existing releases by default, but you can instruct a DHCP server to deny lease renewals or even cancel leases, when necessary.

Here's a brief explanation of how DHCP integrates with DNS:

- Server addresses (and sometimes their associated services) are advertised using DNS, which resolves domain names into IP addresses and vice versa.

- DNS is not a dynamic environment, so all address updates must be entered manually (either through a GUI interface, on Windows Server 2008, or by editing text files, on UNIX systems).

- Client addresses usually come into play only when e-mail addresses of the form *user@domain.name* must be resolved. E-mail servers can resolve this information from MX records associated with the client's domain name (not his or her IP address), so dynamic address resolution works perfectly well for clients and e-mail. Hence, client addresses typically have no impact on DNS, or vice versa, and can change as needed.

The inability of older DNS implementations to update their domain name-to-IP address (A) and IP address-to-domain name (PTR) records dynamically explains why DHCP has been used primarily for managing client addresses. As mentioned in Chapter 8 of this book, newer DNS versions (such as Dynamic DNS, or DDNS, which Microsoft includes with all Windows operating systems since Windows 2000) can create ways for DHCP to communicate name-to-address mapping changes to DNS servers. Even so, the problem of the delay inherent in waiting for changes to propagate through the entire global DNS database remains unaltered, so public IP addresses (and their mappings) tend to change as little as possible anyway. (It's not unusual for propagation delays for DNS to take 48 hours or more before an old address ages out completely and is replaced throughout by a new one.) At present, only clients are not adversely affected by using dynamic IP addresses, which explains why DHCP remains such an important client IP address management tool today.

IPv4 Autoconfiguration

There are two types of IPv4 address autoconfiguration mechanisms available on a host network interface: DHCP and Automatic Private IP Addressing (APIPA).

Most modern operating systems are configured to have their IP addresses automatically provided to them via DHCP from DHCP servers. If a DHCP server does not respond to the host's DHCP request, APIPA is generally configured on the host as a fallback operation to self-assign a link-local IP address.

Automatic Private IP Addressing (APIPA)

Dynamic configuration of IPv4 link-local addresses is also known as APIPA. Initially implemented by Microsoft starting in Windows 98, the idea was adopted by other manufacturers; subsequently, RFC 3927 was drafted to formally standardize the operation.

As specified in RFC 3927, address block 169.254.0.0/16 is reserved for this use. However, only 169.254.1.0 through 169.254.254.255 are allowed host addresses; the first 256 and last 256 addresses are reserved. The 169.254/16 addresses should not be configured for use in DHCP and DNS servers, nor manually configured on interfaces or routed to other networks. These addresses are used for link-local communications only.

APIPA is used by interfaces as a failover mechanism to self-assign an IPv4 address if the initial DHCP requests are not answered. However, a network interface will continue to send DHCP requests approximately every five minutes. If a DHCP server subsequently replies with an IP address assignment for the host, the APIPA address is released from the interface in favor of the DHCP-provided IP address, given that an interface is only allowed to have one IPv4 address assigned to it when in the autoconfiguration mode. APIPA operates only on interfaces that are configured for DHCP, which means that if a manual IP address is assigned to an interface, APIPA is disabled.

The APIPA address assignment uses a pseudo-random number generator (from the allowed address range previously described) to derive what should be a unique address. The process of validating the address for uniqueness on the network basically follows the same procedure used for a DHCP-assigned address.

 For more information on the duplicate IP address ARP broadcast, refer to the section titled "Hardware Addresses in the IP Environment" in Chapter 4.

The value of APIPA is to allow hosts to communicate on the local link of the network, although that address will not allow routed communications to hosts on other networks (as defined in RFC 3927) and, therefore, may not be as useful if servers and/or services are not locally available. This local link-only address was primarily designed for small networks in which all devices, servers, and/or services would most likely be available.

DHCPv4

When a DHCP client has no IP address (when booting for the first time or after a lease expires), it must broadcast a request for an IP address; this initial activity is called **DHCP Discovery**. DHCP servers that can hear this **discovery broadcast** offer an IP address to a client for a specific amount of time (the **lease time**). The default DHCP lease time varies according to which server is used. DHCP messages from a client to a server are sent to the DHCP server on port number 67. DHCP messages from a server to a client are sent to the DHCP client on port number 68.

DHCP Discovery relies on an initial DHCP broadcast. Naturally, routers do not forward these discovery broadcasts, so the entire DHCP Discovery is restricted to a local broadcast domain. Thus, there must be some process that listens for DHCP Discovery messages on any local network segment where such broadcasts are likely to occur. Because it is impractical to place a DHCP server on every network segment, the DHCP specification includes the **relay agent process** to help route DHCP Discovery broadcasts to another network segment. The details for the relay agent process are covered in detail in the section titled "Communications with a DHCP Relay Agent" later in this chapter.

Multiple DHCP servers may be placed on a network to share the responsibility of address assignment and provide some measure of fault tolerance. In this case, the address pool must be divided between the DHCP servers so that they do not hand out the same address to multiple devices. Microsoft recommends that one server be configured to distribute 70 to 80 percent of the addresses; the second server should be configured to distribute the remaining 20 to 30 percent of the addresses. If the address pools overlap, two clients may receive the same address (one client from the first DHCP server, the other client from the second DHCP server). Servers and clients use PING and ARP as error prevention methods to ensure clients have unique addresses.

DHCP servers typically PING an address before offering it to the client, and clients broadcast gratuitous ARP packets to determine if an address is already in use. If the address is in use, the client transmits a DHCP decline message to the DHCP server. The DHCP server must block that address from being assigned again and offer the client a new IP address.

Windows Server 2008 also offers **Windows clustering**, which allows two or more servers to be managed as a single system. Windows clustering provides failover detection of an application or server and automatically transfers the server role to an alternate server.

DHCP Address Discovery When a DHCP client boots up, DHCP performs a Standard Address Discovery to enable it to communicate on the network. After discovery completes successfully, the DHCP client tests its IP address using a duplicate IP address ARP broadcast or gratuitous ARP.

DHCP Discovery uses four packets, the first letters of which, in sequence, form the name "DORA," which makes them easy to remember:

- DHCP **D**iscover packet
- DHCP **O**ffer packet
- DHCP **R**equest packet
- DHCP **A**cknowledgment packet

Figure 7-2 shows summary packets from a DHCP Discovery. Packet #1 is the Discover packet from the DHCP client. Packet #5 is the Offer packet from the server. Packet #6 is the Request packet from the client. Packet #7 is the Acknowledgment packet that finishes the process.

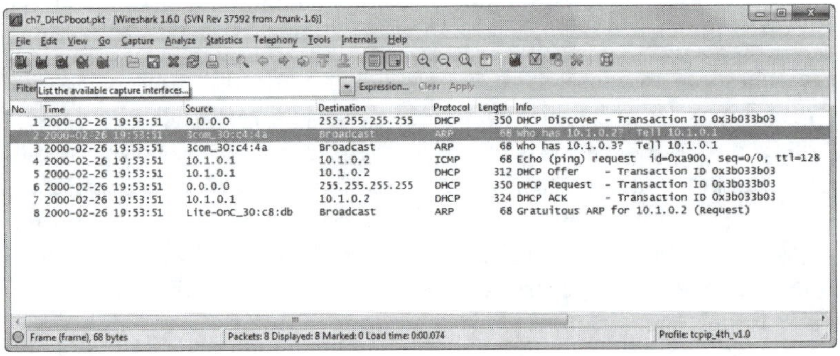

Figure 7-2 DHCP Discovery sequence
Source: Wireshark

During the DHCP Discovery sequence (also known as the boot sequence), the DHCP client receives an IP address and a lease time. The client determines the renewal and rebind time based on the value of the lease time.

In the next four sections, we examine each packet in the Discovery process—Discover, Offer, Request, and Acknowledgment—and learn how the DHCP client obtains an IP address and lease time.

Discover Packet During the DHCP Discovery process, the client broadcasts a Discover packet that identifies the client's hardware address. The Discover packet's IP header contains the source IP address 0.0.0.0 because the client does not yet know its address. The IP header contains the all-nets broadcast destination address 255.255.255.255, as shown in Figure 7-2.

If the DHCP client was on the network before, the client may also define a **preferred address**, which is typically the last address the client used (this is a modern refinement that applies primarily to Windows 2000 and newer versions).

In IPv6, which you'll soon learn more about, the term *preferred address* refers to an address, among the many that may be associated with the same interface, whose use by higher-layer protocols is unrestricted.

NOTE

Figure 7-3 shows a Discover packet that includes a preferred address, 10.0.99.2. In this packet, we compressed the Packet Info header, Ethernet header, IP header, and UDP header to focus on the BOOTP and DHCP packet content. The UDP header includes the source port 68 and the destination port 67.

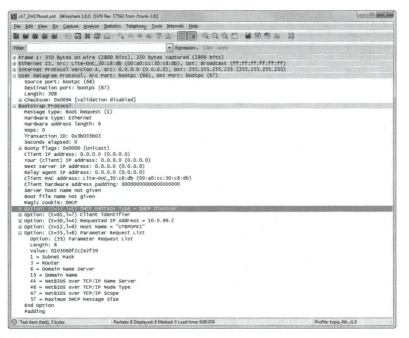

Figure 7-3 DHCP Discover packet

Source: Wireshark

Because DHCP is built upon the BOOTP foundation, many analyzer vendors still use the term *BOOTP* when defining the port numbers and the heading values. Wireshark uses the term *BOOTP* for the initial header definition inside its decodes.

NOTE

In the DHCP Discover packet shown in Figure 7-3, the **Message Type** value is 1; this indicates that this packet is a DHCP Discover packet.

The **Client Identifier** field value is based on the client's hardware address (00-A0-CC-30-C8-DB).

During the IP address request (and even separately, if desired), a DHCP client can ask for other configuration data. Note that in Figure 7-3 the client includes a series of requests at the end of the standard DHCP Discover request. These requests are **DHCP options** and are explained in RFC 2132, "DHCP Options and BOOTP Vendor Extensions." These options are listed online in their entirety at *www.iana.org*. Windows users will find the Knowledge Base article "How to Request Additional DHCP Options from a DHCP Server" (*support.microsoft.com/kb/312468*) equally illuminating.

The options listed in Figure 7-3 include the following:

- *Option 1*—Client's subnet mask
- *Option 3*—Routers on the client's subnet
- *Option 6*—Domain name servers
- *Option 15*—Domain name
- *Option 44*—NetBIOS over TCP/IP name servers (a.k.a. WINS in Microsoft terminology)
- *Option 46*—NetBIOS over TCP/IP node type
- *Option 47*—NetBIOS over TCP/IP scope
- *Option 57*—Maximum DHCP message size

The DHCP server may not answer any configuration option requests until the client accepts the IP address. These options are covered in the section entitled "DHCP Options Fields" later in this chapter.

Offer Packet The DHCP server sends the Offer packet to offer an IP address to the DHCP client. If the DHCP server can ARP the workstation's MAC address, it sends this packet by unicast to the DHCP client; otherwise, the entire DHCP Discovery sequence will use the broadcast method.

The Offer packet includes the IP address that is offered to the client and, sometimes, answers to the requested options in the DHCP Discover packet.

Figure 7-4 shows the DHCP Offer packet decoded by Wireshark. In this packet, we compressed the Packet Info header, Ethernet header, and IP header.

Note in the IP Address field that the DHCP server offers 10.1.0.2 to the client. Apparently, the server could not offer the preferred address. The DHCP Offer packet also includes the IP address of the DHCP server (10.1.0.1), the IP lease time (1,800 seconds, which appears as 30 minutes in the figures), and the subnet mask (255.255.0.0).

In the IP header, the DHCP server addresses this packet to the offered IP address, 10.1.0.2, even though at this point the DHCP client does not recognize that address. The data link header addresses this packet directly to the destination hardware address; that's all that is needed to get this packet to the destination. Assuming the DHCP server was able to ARP the target client, the IP header does not even need to be referenced to route this packet because it's sent from one device to another on the same subnet.

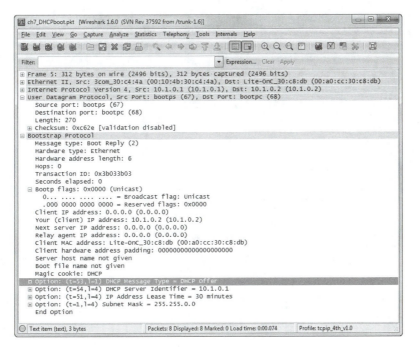

Figure 7-4 DHCP Offer packet
Source: Wireshark

Request Packet Once the Offer packet is received, the client can either accept the offer by issuing a DHCP Request packet or reject the offer by sending a DHCP Decline packet. Typically, a client sends a Decline only if it receives more than one Offer. For example, if there is more than one DHCP server on the subnet, the client may receive multiple replies. The client would respond with a Request to the first Offer received and send a Decline to the second and any subsequent Offers it receives.

Figure 7-5 shows a DHCP Request packet. In this Request, you can see the client now requests answers to the same parameters listed in the original Discover packet. The client now knows the DHCP server's address and places the Offered address in the Requested IP Address field.

In the IP header, this packet is sent to the IP broadcast address even though the client knows the IP address of the DHCP server. See the section titled "Broadcast and Unicast in DHCP" later in this chapter for more information about when a DHCP server uses broadcast or unicast.

Again, the client requests numerous parameters from the DHCP server. If possible, the server should respond with the answers to the client's parameter queries.

Acknowledgment Packet The Acknowledgment packet is sent from the server to the client to indicate the completion of the four-packet DHCP Discovery process. This response

Figure 7-5 DHCP Request packet
Source: Wireshark

contains answers to any configuration options requested by the client in the previous Request packet. Figure 7-6 shows the DHCP Acknowledgment (ACK) packet.

The Acknowledgment packet shown in Figure 7-6 includes the following answers to the client's request for information:

- The client subnet mask is 255.255.0.0.
- The client's router (default gateway) address is 10.0.0.1.
- The client's DNS server address is 10.0.0.1.

Successful completion of this four-packet process does not mean the client starts using the IP address immediately. Most IP hosts perform a duplicate IP address test immediately following the Acknowledgment packet receipt. For example, after the Discovery packet sequence completes successfully, the DHCP client sends an ARP packet that lists the IP address 10.1.0.2 as the target IP address and the source IP address.

Address Renewal Process When a DHCP client receives an address from a DHCP server, the client also receives a lease time and notes the time that the address was received.

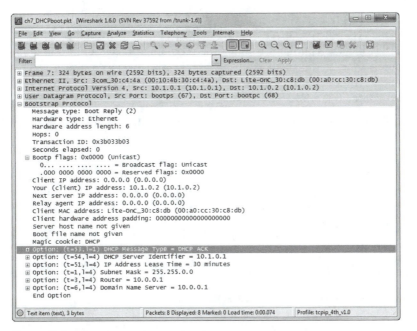

Figure 7-6 DHCP ACK packet

Source: Wireshark

The lease time defines how long the client can keep the address. The DHCP client then computes the renewal time (T1) and rebinding time (T2) based on the lease time. In the middle of the lease period, the client starts a **renewal process** to determine if it can keep the address after the lease time expires. If the client cannot renew the address from that DHCP server within the stipulated lease period, that client must begin the process of renewing the address from another DHCP server (assuming the original DHCP server is no longer available). This is called the **rebinding process**. If rebinding fails, a client must completely **release** its address.

Renewal Time (T1) T1 is defined as the time that the client tries to renew its network address by contacting the DHCP server that sent the original address to the client. The Renewal packet is unicast directly to the DHCP server.

The DHCP specification, RFC 2131, defines the default value for T1 as:

0.5 * duration_of_lease (i.e., lease time)

This is equal to one-half the lease time.

If the DHCP client does not receive a reply to the renewal request, it will divide the remaining time between the current time and the T2 time and then retry the renewal request.

Rebinding Time (T2) T2 is defined as the time that the client begins to broadcast a renewal request for an extended lease time from another DHCP server. The DHCP specification, RFC 2131, defines the default value for T2 as:

0.875 * duration_of_lease

If the DHCP client does not receive a reply to the rebind request, the DHCP client reduces the time remaining between the current rebinding time and the expiration of the lease time and retry. The DHCP client continues to retry the rebinding process until one minute before the **lease expiration time**. If the client is unsuccessful in renewing the lease, it must give up the address at the expiration of the lease time and **reinitialize** (i.e., start DHCP Discovery all over again, using source IP address 0.0.0.0).

Figure 7-7 shows the relationship between the lease time, T1, T2, and the eventual address expiration.

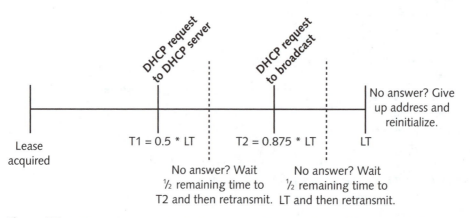

Figure 7-7 DHCP timeline includes the lease time (LT), renewal time (T1), and rebinding time (T2)
© Cengage Learning 2013

Figure 7-8 shows the summary of a client that performs the renewal and rebinding processes before finally giving up and reinitializing. As you see in the figure, repeated DHCP communications directly to the DHCP server are an indication that the DHCP client is in the renewal process. When we see the client start to send broadcasts from a valid IP address, we can assume the client is now in the rebinding process. Finally, the client changes its source IP address to 0.0.0.0 when the rebinding process fails, and it must rebroadcast a DHCP Discover packet.

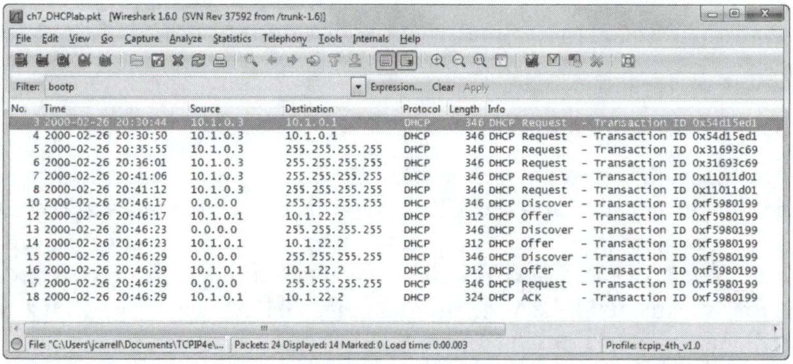

Figure 7-8 DHCP renewal, rebinding, and reinitializing process
Source: Wireshark

DHCP Address Release Process Though not required by the specification, the client should release its address by sending a DHCP Release packet to the server (called the release process). The DHCP Release packet is sent over UDP, and the DHCP server does not send any acknowledgment. If the client does not send the DHCP Release packet, the DHCP server automatically releases the address at the lease expiration time.

In the Windows environment, the `ipconfig` command includes both `/release` and `/renew` options, in which `/release` forces any Windows host that obtains its address using DHCP to release that address, and in which `/renew` issues a request to renew an existing address lease.

Whenever a DHCP client releases its IP address lease, this automatically causes DHCP Discovery to commence immediately. That's based on the assumption that any working network interface needs an IP address to perform its intended functions—an assumption that turns out to be completely warranted.

DHCP Packet Structures In this section, we cover the DHCP packet structures and define the field values and options. Figure 7-9 shows the standard DHCP packet structure.

UDP HEADER - DESTINATION PORT 67 (to server) OR 68 (to client)			
0	15	16	31
OPCODE	HARDWARE TYPE	HARDWARE LENGTH	HOPS
TRANSACTION ID NUMBER			
SECONDS SINCE BOOT		FLAGS	
CLIENT IP ADDRESS			
YOUR IP ADDRESS			
SERVER IP ADDRESS			
GATEWAY IP ADDRESS			
CLIENT HARDWARE ADDRESS (16 bytes)			
SERVER HOST NAME (64 bytes)			
BOOT FILE (128 bytes)			
OPTIONS (Message type option is required)			

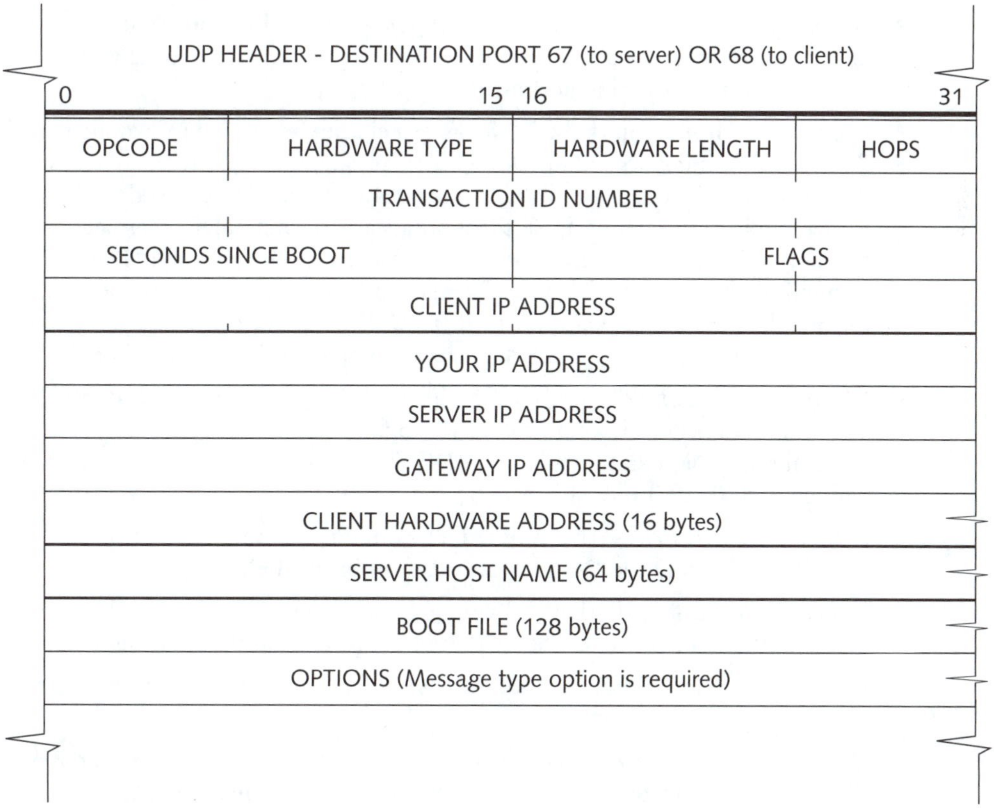

Figure 7-9 DHCP packet structure
© Cengage Learning 2013

DHCP Fields Here are the definitions for the DHCP fields:

- *Operation Code (OPCODE) or Message Type field*—This 1-byte field indicates whether this packet is a DHCP Request (0x01) or DHCP Reply (0x02). The detail on the type of request or reply is defined in the DHCP options section as a message type. See the section titled "DHCP Options Fields" later in this chapter for more details.

- *Hardware Type field*—This 1-byte field identifies the hardware address type and matches the values assigned for ARP hardware type definitions. The hardware type list is defined by IANA and maintained at *www.iana.org*. The value 1 denotes the hardware as 10-MB Ethernet.

- *Hardware Length field*—This 1-byte field indicates the length of the hardware address. For example, the value 6 is used for 10-MB Ethernet to indicate a 6-byte hardware address.

- *Hops field*—This field is set to 0 by the client and may be used by relay agents as they assist a client in obtaining an IP address and/or configuration information. See the section titled "Communications with a DHCP Relay Agent" later in this chapter for more information.

- *Transaction ID Number field*—This 4-byte field contains a random number selected by the client and is used to match requests and responses between the client and server.

- *Seconds Since Boot or Seconds Elapsed field*—This 2-byte field indicates the number of seconds that have elapsed since the client began requesting a new address, or since the renewal of an existing address.

- *Flags field*—The first bit of the 2-byte Flags field can be toggled to 1 to indicate that the DHCP client cannot accept unicast MAC layer datagrams before the IP software is completely configured. As explained in the section titled "DHCP Address Discovery" earlier in this chapter, the DHCP client broadcasts the initial Discover packet. The DHCP server can respond with either a unicast or broadcast Offer packet. In Figure 7-4, the server responds with a unicast packet. If a client cannot accept these unicast packets, it toggles the broadcast bit in the Flags field to 1. If a DHCP server or relay agent sends a unicast packet to the client, it may discard it. The remaining bits in this 2-byte field are set to 0.

- *Client IP Address field*—The DHCP client fills in this 4-byte field with its IP address after it is assigned and bound to the IP stack. This field also is filled in during the renewal and rebind states. When the DHCP client first boots up, however, this field is padded with 0.0.0.0.

- *Your IP Address field*—This 4-byte field contains the address being offered by the DHCP server. Only the DHCP server can fill in this field.

- *Server IP Address field*—This 4-byte field contains the IP address of the DHCP server to use in the boot process. The DHCP server puts its address in this field.

- *Gateway or Relay Agent IP Address field*—This 4-byte field contains the address of the DHCP relay agent, if one is used.

- *Client Hardware Address field*—This 16-byte field contains the MAC address of the client. Upon receipt by the DHCP server, this address is maintained and associated with the IP address assigned to the client. In case this field is deemed to be insufficient, the Client Identifier option (61) can be used to provide unique identification of a machine.

- *Server Host Name field*—This 64-byte field can contain the server host name, but such information is optional. This field can contain a null-terminated string (all 0s).

- *Boot File field*—This field contains an optional boot filename or null-terminated string.

- *DHCP Option field*—This field is used for optional parameters (described in detail in the following section).

DHCP Options Fields DHCP options are used to expand the data that is included in the DHCP packet. The DHCP options are listed in Table 7-1. As you review this table, you will begin to realize the power of DHCP.

Tag	Name	Length*	Meaning
0	Pad	0	None
1	Subnet Mask	4	Subnet mask value
2	Time Offset	4	Time offset in seconds from UTC
3	Router	N	N/4 router addresses
4	Time Server	N	N/4 time server addresses
5	Name Server	N	N/4 IEN-116 server addresses
6	Domain Server	N	N/4 DNS server addresses
7	Log Server	N	N/4 logging server addresses
8	Quotes Server	N	N/4 quotes server addresses
9	LPR Server	N	N/4 printer server addresses
10	Impress Server	N	N/4 Impress server addresses
11	RLP Server	N	N/4 RLP server addresses
12	Hostname	N	Hostname string
13	Boot File Size	2	Size of boot file in 512-byte chunks
14	Merit Dump File	N	Client to dump and name the file to dump it to
15	Domain Name	N	DNS domain name of the client
16	Swap Server	N	Swap server address
17	Root Path	N	Path name for root disk
18	Extension File	N	Path name for more BOOTP info
19	Forward On/Off	1	Enable/disable IP forwarding
20	SrcRte On/Off	1	Enable/disable source routing
21	Policy Filter	N	Routing policy filters

Table 7-1 DHCP options (*continues*)

Tag	Name	Length*	Meaning
22	Max DG Assembly	2	Max datagram reassembly size
23	Default IP TTL	1	Default IP Time to Live
24	MTU Timeout	4	Path MTU aging timeout
25	MTU Plateau	N	Path MTU plateau table
26	MTU Interface	2	Interface MTU size
27	MTU Subnet	1	All subnets are local
28	Broadcast Address	4	Broadcast address
29	Mask Discovery	1	Perform mask discovery
30	Mask Supplier	1	Provide mask to others
31	Router Discovery	1	Perform router discovery
32	Router Request	4	Router solicitation address
33	Static Route	N	Static routing table
34	Trailers	1	Trailer encapsulation
35	ARP Timeout	4	ARP cache timeout
36	Ethernet	1	Ethernet encapsulation
37	Default TCP TTL	1	Default TCP Time to Live
38	Keepalive Time	4	TCP keep-alive interval
39	Keepalive Data	1	TCP keep-alive garbage
40	NIS Domain	N	NIS domain name
41	NIS Servers	N	NIS server addresses
42	NTP Servers	N	NTP server addresses
43	Vendor Specific	N	Vendor-specific information
44	NETBIOS Name Srv	N	NETBIOS name servers
45	NETBIOS Dist Srv	N	NETBIOS datagram distribution
46	NETBIOS Node Type	1	NETBIOS node type
47	NETBIOS Scope	N	NETBIOS scope
48	X Window Font	N	X Window font server
49	X Window Manager	N	X Window display manager
50	Address Request	4	Requested IP address
51	Address Time	4	IP address lease time

Table 7-1 DHCP options (*continued*)

Tag	Name	Length*	Meaning
52	Overload	1	Overload "sname" or "file"
53	DHCP Msg Type	1	DHCP message type
54	DHCP Server Id	4	DHCP server identification
55	Parameter List	N	Parameter request list
56	DHCP Message	N	DHCP error message
57	DHCP Max Msg Size	2	DHCP maximum message size
58	Renewal Time	4	DHCP renewal time (T1)
59	Rebinding Time	4	DHCP rebinding time (T2)
60	Class ID	N	Class identifier
61	Client ID	N	Client identifier
62	NetWare/IP Domain	N	NetWare/IP domain name
63	NetWare/IP Option	N	NetWare/IP sub options
64	NIS-Domain-Name	N	NIS+ v3 client domain name
65	NIS-Server-Addr	N	NIS+ v3 server addresses
66	Server-Name	N	TFTP server name
67	Bootfile-Name	N	Boot filename
68	Home-Agent-Addrs	N	Home agent addresses
69	SMTP-Server	N	Simple Mail server addresses
70	POP3-Server	N	Post Office server addresses
71	NNTP-Server	N	Network News server addresses
72	WWW-Server	N	WWW server addresses
73	Finger-Server	N	Finger server addresses
74	IRC-Server	N	Chat server addresses
75	StreetTalk-Server	N	StreetTalk server addresses
76	STDA-Server	N	ST Directory Assistance addresses
77	User-Class	N	User class information
78	Directory Agent	N	Directory agent information
79	Service Scope	N	Service location agent scope
80	Naming Authority	N	Naming authority
81	Client FQDN	N	Fully qualified domain name

Table 7-1 DHCP options (*continues*)

Tag	Name	Length*	Meaning
82	Relay Agent Information	N	Relay agent information
83	Agent Remote ID	N	Agent remote ID
84	Agent Subnet Mask	N	Agent subnet mask
85	NDS Servers	N	Novell Directory Services
86	NDS Tree Name	N	Novell Directory Services
87	NDS Context	N	Novell Directory Services
88	IEEE 1003.1 POSIX	N	IEEE 1003.1 POSIX time zone
89	FQDN	N	Fully qualified domain name
90	Authentication	N	Authentication
91	Vines TCP/IP	N	Vines TCP/IP server option
92	Server Selection	N	Server selection option
93	Client System	N	Client system architecture
94	Client NDI	N	Client network device interface
95	LDAP	N	Lightweight Directory Access Protocol
96	IPv6 Transitions	N	IPv6 transitions
97	UUID/GUID	N	UUID/GUID-based Client Identifier
98	User-Auth	N	Open Group's user authentication

Table 7-1 DHCP options (*continued*)

*"N" in length column represents a variable number.

Source: www.iana.org

The complete list of DHCP options is found on the IANA Web site at *www.iana.org/ assignments/bootp-dhcp-parameters*.

DHCP Option 53: Message Type

Only one DHCP option is required in all DHCP packets: Option 53: DHCP Message Type. This required option indicates the general purpose of any DHCP message. The eight DHCP message types are listed in Table 7-2.

Number	Message Type	Description
0x01	DHCP Discover	Sent by the DHCP client to locate available servers
0x02	DHCP Offer	Sent by the DHCP server to the DHCP client in response to message type 0x01 (this packet includes the offered address)
0x03	DHCP Request	Sent by the DHCP client to the DHCP server requesting offered parameters from one server specifically—as defined in the packet

Table 7-2 DHCP message types

Number	Message Type	Description
0x04	DHCP Decline	Sent by the DHCP client to the DHCP server indicating invalid parameters
0x05	DHCP ACK	Sent by the DHCP server to the DHCP client with configuration parameters, including the assigned network address
0x06	DHCP NAK	Sent by the DHCP client to the DHCP server to refuse a request for configuration parameters
0x07	DHCP Release	Sent by the DHCP client to the DHCP server to relinquish a network address and cancel the remaining lease
0x08	DHCP Inform	Sent by a DHCP client to the DHCP server to ask for only configuration parameters (the client already has an IP address)

Table 7-2 DHCP message types (*continued*)

Source: www.iana.org

The list of DHCP message types is found on the IANA Web site at *http://www.iana.org/assignments/bootp-dhcp-parameters/bootp-dhcp-parameters.xml#message-type-53*.

As you may recall, the DHCP boot sequence uses the following message types:

- *DHCP Message Type 1*—Discover (client to server)
- *DHCP Message Type 2*—Offer (server to client)
- *DHCP Message Type 3*—Request (client to server)
- *DHCP Message Type 5*—ACK (server to client)

This sequence of messages represents the exchanges that occur when a client requests an address for the first time, or whenever it must negotiate a new lease.

Because the `ipconfig` parameters `/release`, `/renew`, `/showclassid`, and `/setclassid` all involve DHCP, each one is associated with one or more DHCP message types as well (primarily within the context of DHCP Message Type 3, with numerous other options).

Broadcast and Unicast in DHCP As you examine DHCP communications, you will note that they use a strange mix of broadcast and unicast addressing. DHCP clients must broadcast service requests until they obtain IP addresses following successful completion of the DHCP Discovery, Offer, Request, and Acknowledgment processes. DHCP clients use unicast addressing after they obtain an address for a local DHCP server or relay agent. This entire behavior is described in RFC 2131.

DHCP servers examine DHCP packets coming from clients to determine whether they should use broadcast or unicast packets for their responses.

Table 7-3 clarifies when a DHCP server uses broadcast and when it uses unicast.

Communications with A DHCP Relay Agent The DHCP boot process relies heavily on broadcasts, but most routers do not forward broadcasts. This forces the need for one DHCP server on each network segment or the use of a relay agent on network segments where no DHCP server is directly attached to send discover broadcasts to remote DHCP servers.

Gateway IP Address Setting	Client IP Address Setting	Address Used
non-zero	N/A	Unicast packets from DHCP server to the relay agent
0	non-zero	Unicast DHCP Offer and DHCP ACK messages to the client IP address
0	0	[Broadcast bit set] DHCP server broadcasts DHCP Offer and DHCP ACK messages to0xFF.FF.FF.FF
0	0	[Broadcast bit not set] DHCP server unicasts DHCP Offer and DHCP ACK messages to the client IP address and the value contained in the Your IP Address field

Table 7-3 DHCP broadcast and unicast rules
© Cengage Learning 2013

The relay agent function is typically loaded on a router connected to the segment containing DHCP clients. This relay agent device is configured with the address of the DHCP server and can communicate using unicast packets directly with that server.

Figure 7-10 shows the general design of a network that supports a DHCP relay agent.

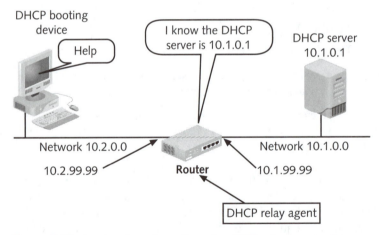

Figure 7-10 A network configuration using DHCP relay agent software on a router
© Cengage Learning 2013

In Figure 7-10, the DHCP client broadcasts a DHCP Discover message on network 10.2.0.0. The router is configured with DHCP relay agent software. This relay agent accepts the DHCP broadcast and sends a unicast packet to the DHCP server at 10.1.0.1 on behalf of the DHCP client. The relay agent includes the hardware address of the DHCP client inside the DHCP Discover packet. Note also that the relay agent sends this request from its IP address on the network of the DHCP client (10.2.99.99).

The DHCP server notes the source IP address and uses this information to determine the IP network upon which the true requester is located. The DHCP server responds directly to the DHCP relay agent, which, in turn, replies to the DHCP client.

Figure 7-11 shows the communication sequence on a network that supports a DHCP relay agent.

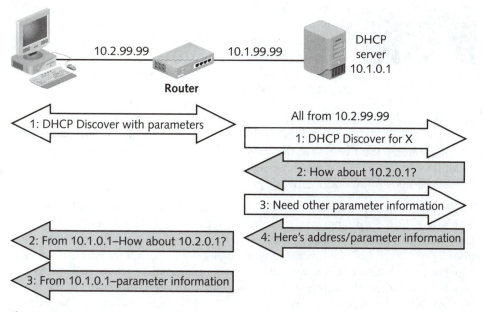

Figure 7-11 DHCP relay communications process
© Cengage Learning 2013

IPv6 Autoconfiguration

There are two basic approaches to IPv6 autoconfiguration: stateless and stateful. **Stateless autoconfiguration** simply presents required router configuration information to all comers. DHCP for IPv6 is known as DHCPv6 and is considered **stateful autoconfiguration** because the DHCPv6 server must maintain awareness of the status or state of its pool of available addresses, the presence or absence on the network of permitted clients, and a variety of other parameters. Each method has its advantages and disadvantages, as described in the following sections.

Although autoconfiguration is primarily for hosts rather than routers, all interfaces on a link, including all interfaces in any attached routers, must at least perform a duplicate address check upon initializing.

Types of IPv6 Autoconfiguration

This section describes stateless and stateful address autoconfiguration as well as a combination of the two.

Stateless Address Autoconfiguration For segments and nodes that support multi-casting, RFC 4862 proposes several tools to support stateless autoconfiguration of attached nodes. The ND protocol allows routers to be configured to present the minimum information a host needs when joining a network link. This information includes the network prefix of the segment and the router's own address, and it may include the segment MTU and preferred number of "maximum hops" for various routes.

The router does not supply any other information, such as the DNS server address. If such information is required, the router can direct a node using stateless autoconfiguration to a DHCP server to obtain the rest of the information it needs to complete its configuration. This is a combination of stateless and stateful autoconfiguration, covered in more detail below.

When an interface initializes on an IPv6 network segment or link (usually on node startup), it first configures its own link-local address. This means calculating its own 64-bit interface ID (using either the EUI-64 or the Privacy method, both of which are discussed in more detail later in this chapter) and forming a link-local address by appending that interface ID to the well-known link-local network prefix of FE80:: (defined in RFC 4291).

While performing the duplicate address check, the host (not a router) will also send a Router Solicitation (RS) to prompt any attached routers to send their Router Advertisement (RA). Even though routers periodically send RAs, the host will proactively send one or more RAs in order to "speed up" the process in determining if an IPv6 router is actually on the network segment and, therefore, be able to use address configuration parameters (flags) that may be present in the RAs. The router can provide a network prefix in order for the host to add its interface ID to the network prefix to create a "global" unicast address. IPv6 hosts know that there may be more than one response to such solicitations, and they are prepared to cache and update results from multiple attached routers. If no routers are present on a local link, the host should use a stateful autoconfiguration method, such as DHCPv6.

To forestall spoofing attacks, hosts use a default value of two hours for the valid lifetime when encountering any RA that attempts to set the valid lifetime to a value less than two hours. The one exception to this rule occurs when RAs use IPv6 Authentication headers. When an RA is authenticated, nodes update the valid lifetime of their addresses as directed.

For more about the functions of ND and specific flags available in RAs, see Chapter 6.

Figure 7-12 shows an ICMPv6 Router Advertisement packet, with the A and L flags set to "on" for stateless address autoconfiguration of nodes.

Stateful Address Autoconfiguration The router may instead be configured to not supply the network prefix in the RA but supply flags for the host to obtain its IPv6 address via DHCPv6. In its basic tasks and broad outlines, DHCPv6 is much like DHCPv4 under IPv4. Both are stateful methods for configuring hosts. Both rely on dedicated servers to hold databases of information about hosts and their IP and other configuration parameters.

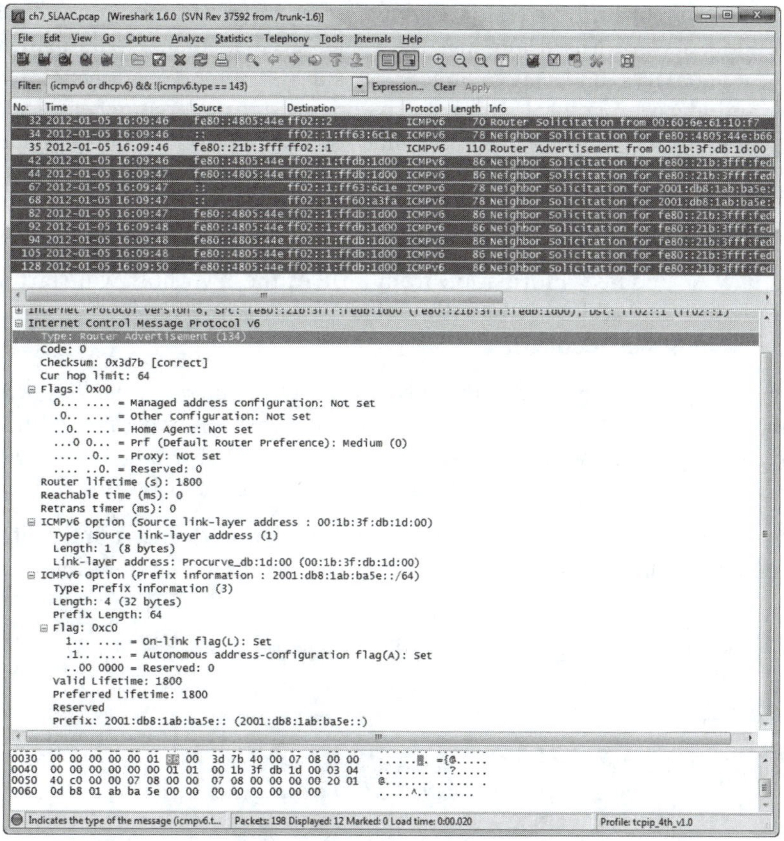

Figure 7-12 ICMPv6 Router Advertisement packet—SLAAC

Source: Wireshark

Hosts connect to the DHCP server as clients and download the information they need to set themselves up for IP.

Apart from obvious differences in the length and format of the addresses themselves, DHCPv6 has some significant differences from earlier versions. Perhaps the most far reaching is that nodes under IPv6 can gain at least a locally functioning address without any help from DHCPv6. In effect, this means that all DHCPv6 clients are fully functioning hosts and able to search actively for the server using multicast solicitations. DHCPv6 clients can, for example, discover whether their DHCPv6 servers are on the local link. In addition, they can use a relay server on the local segment to receive configuration information from an off-link server. Another significant difference from DHCPv4 is that a DHCPv6 server does not supply the default gateway address to a host. A host derives that information from the RA.

In this stateful autoconfiguration operation, the router is configured with its RA A flag set to "off" and the M and O flags set to "on," informing the host to obtain its IPv6 address from a DHCPv6 server. The host will then send DHCPv6 solicit messages in order to locate a DHCPv6 server and obtain its address as well as any other information the DHCPv6 server may supply, such as the DNS server address.

DHCPv6 also shares certain primary features with stateless autoconfiguration under IPv6. All autoconfigured addresses are leased and use the same "dual lifetimes" paradigm for name lease renewal. All interfaces under IPv6 inherently support multiple addresses (sometimes multiple global, and always one local address). To support dynamic renumbering, IPv6 hosts using autoconfiguration of either type must continue listening to RAs that may contain:

- New and/or updated information in timers
- Flags, which may direct the hosts to configure and start using a new address

Upon receiving new or updated information from an RA, the IPv6 host will start a process whereby it stops using old addresses based on timer information received or known, and starts using new addresses as required.

DHCPv6 can generally be set up to dynamically update DNS records. This is a key part of maintaining efficient routing. Networks can renumber, and that renumbering will be reflected quickly in DNS, thereby removing (or at least mitigating) one of the strongest objections to the whole idea of automatic renumbering—the threat of extended periods of traffic disruption.

Figure 7-13 shows an ICMPv6 Router Advertisement packet, with the A and L flags set to "off" and the M and O flags set to "on" for stateful address autoconfiguration of nodes.

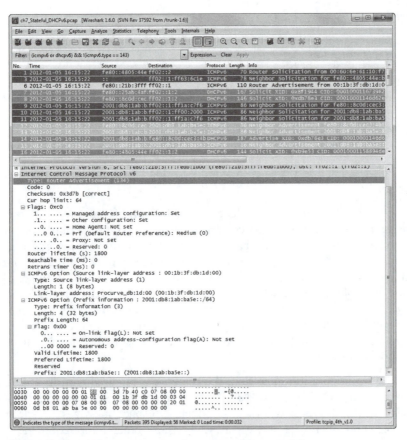

Figure 7-13 ICMPv6 Router Advertisement packet—stateful

Source: Wireshark

Combination of Stateful and Stateless Address Autoconfiguration Stateless autoconfiguration can be used alone or in conjunction with a stateful autoconfiguration method, such as DHCPv6, and then it may be referenced as DHCPv6 stateless. Routers on the local link can be configured to provide pointers to DHCPv6 servers that may provide only certain "other" types of network configuration information, such as DNS and time server addresses. The router in this case is configured with its RA A and L flags set to "on," the M flag set to "off," and the O flag set to "on." The router provides the network prefix, and the DHCPv6 server provides the DNS server information for hosts. This will most likely be a common deployment strategy, because at this time there is no provision for routers to provide DNS server information to hosts. RFC 6106, which will allow routers to provide a field for the DNS server address, has not been standardized as of this writing.

Figure 7-14 shows an ICMPv6 Router Advertisement packet, with the A, L, and O flags set to "on" and the M flag set to "off" for DHCPv6 stateless address autoconfiguration of nodes.

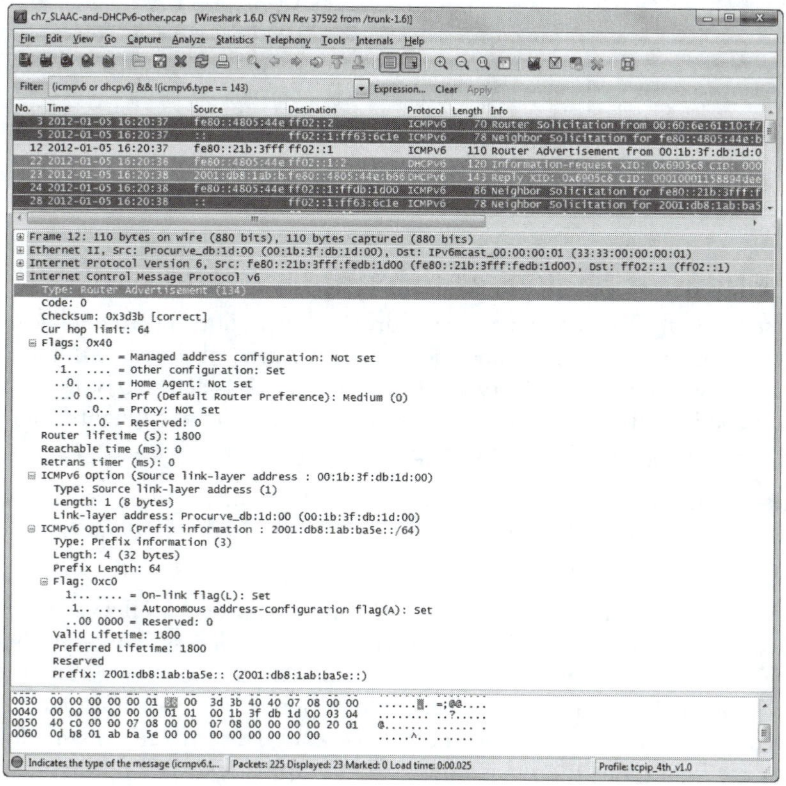

Figure 7-14 ICMPv6 Router Advertisement packet—combination DHCPv6 stateless
Source: Wireshark

Table 7-4 describes the IPv6 address autoconfiguration options, what flags are set in the RAs, where the network prefix is derived from, where the node interface ID is derived from, and where the "other" options, such as DNS server address, are derived from.

Address Autoconfiguration Method	RA – ICMP Field		RA – Prefix Information Option		Prefix Derived From	Interface ID Derived From	Other Configuration Options
	M Flag	O Flag	A Flag	L Flag			
SLAAC	0	0	1	1	RA	M-EUI-64 or Privacy	Manual
Stateful (aka DHCPv6)	1	1	0	1	DHCPv6	DHCPv6	DHCPv6
Combination of SLAAC and DHCPv6	0	1	1	1	RA	M-EUI-64 or Privacy	DHCPv6
Combination of stateless and DHCPv6 (will result in three IPv6 addresses)	1	1	1	1	RA and DHCPv6	M-EUI-64 or Privacy and DHCPv6	DHCPv6

Table 7-4 IPv6 Autoconfiguration address options
© Cengage Learning 2013

Functional States of an IPv6 Autoconfigured Address

The functional state of an IPv6 autoconfigured address is much different from what is found in IPv4. In IPv4, you must manually renumber hosts on a network (the time-consuming "touch" method) or get addresses from a DHCP server but wait hours to days before existing timers expire. IPv6 address autoconfiguration is so valuable because it enables you to configure lifetime timers in RAs, thereby automating "en masse" renumbering and significantly reducing the wait time.

Functional states are considered tentative, preferred, or deprecated. Addresses are considered valid or invalid, based on lifetime timer configurations. Here are descriptions of each in order of operation:

- Tentative addresses occur as a node initializes an interface on an IPv6 network segment or link in order to configure its own link-local address. To verify that this "tentative" address is actually unique on the local link, the node sends out an NS with this address as its destination. If another node responds, the node must stop trying to autoconfigure the link-local address and subsequently be configured manually. If no duplicates are found, the address is now a valid address and the node assigns the address to the interface as preferred. This verification process is known as Duplicate Address Detection (DAD), which was introduced in Chapter 6. If the node receives packets addressed to this address while it is in the tentative state, the node should discard those packets unless they are related to the DAD process.

- Valid addresses are usable based on the Valid Lifetime field in the Prefix Information option of an RA or the Valid Lifetime field in the DHCPv6 IA Address option, and they are in either the preferred or deprecated state of operation. The valid lifetime value must be equal to or greater than the preferred lifetime value. When the valid lifetime expires, the address becomes invalid.

- Preferred addresses are usable for all communications based on the Preferred Lifetime field in the Prefix Information option of an RA or the Preferred Lifetime field in the DHCPv6 IA Address option. When the preferred lifetime expires but the valid lifetime is still valid, the address moves to deprecated.

- Deprecated addresses allow nodes to continue to function while they renew the lease on their addresses. Deprecated addresses may be used normally but should not be used for anything other than the completion of sessions initiated before the address was deprecated. However, while in the deprecated state, if another node initiates a new session, the host will continue to receive/send traffic. When the valid lifetime expires, the address becomes invalid.

- Invalid addresses cannot be used as either the source or destination address when the valid lifetime expires.

Node Interface Identifiers

Node interface identifiers (IDs) for IPv6 addressing are used to ensure that the IPv6 address is unique among all other IPv6 addresses; they are generally 64 bits long. The node interface ID can be construed from different sources, the three most common being: the Modified EUI-64 format; a random number generator to create a 64-bit number; the Cryptographically Generated Addresses (CGA) process. After the interface ID has been computed, the process for creating the complete IPv6 address via the various autoconfiguration options will continue.

The Modified EUI-64 is defined in RFC 4291 and is based on the IEEE-defined 64-bit extended unique identifier (EUI-64) in which the MAC address is padded with an embedded 0xFF and 0xFE between the leftmost 3 bytes and the rightmost 3 bytes. In addition, the seventh bit of the first byte (known as the "u" or universal/local bit) is inverted, which allows the address to indicate universal scope. Although no specific use has been defined for this "universal scope" definition, it was put in place for future capabilities.

RFC 4291 also has provisions for creating interface IDs on interfaces that may not have a 48-bit MAC address, such as serial links and tunnel endpoints.

Another method for creating host interface IDs is discussed in RFC 4941, "Privacy Extensions for Stateless Address Autoconfiguration in IPv6," which defines the use of a random number generator to compute a unique 64-bit number. There is also discussion about having interface types that do not have a MAC address using this process as well as having them use this method as a form of security, because the Modified EUI-64 method uses the interface's MAC address as part of its IPv6 address and, therefore, could allow that node to be exploited.

Later Microsoft operating systems (Windows Vista, Windows 7, and Windows Server 2008/2008 R2) use the random number generator approach to creating the identifier ID as their default operations. This function can be disabled by a command line entry: `netsh interface ipv6 set global randomizeidentifiers=disabled`. At that point, the OS uses the Modified EUI-64 approach to all interface IDs in the host.

Figures 7-15, 7-16, and 7-17 show the default setting of the Randomize Identifier option on a Windows 7 client, how to change the default from enable to disable to support the Modified EUI-64 format, and the `ipconfig` output after the client interface has been enabled on the network configuring a new link-local address.

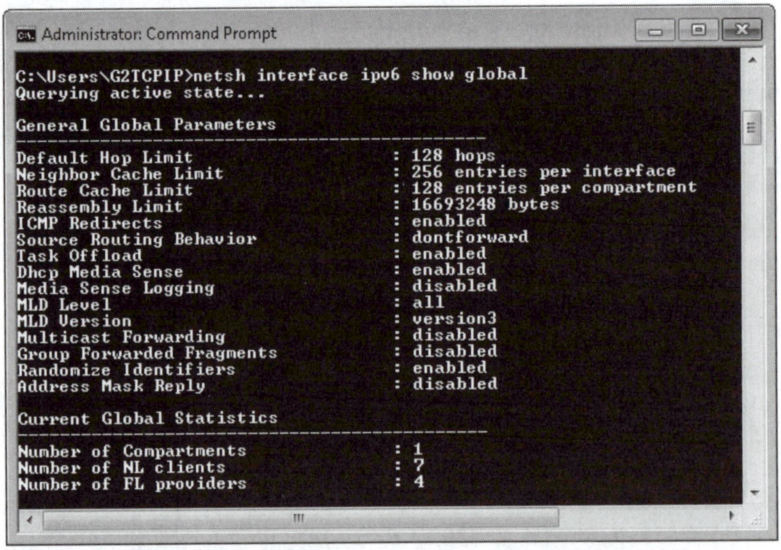

Figure 7-15 Default state in Windows 7 with Randomize Identifiers enabled
Source: Microsoft

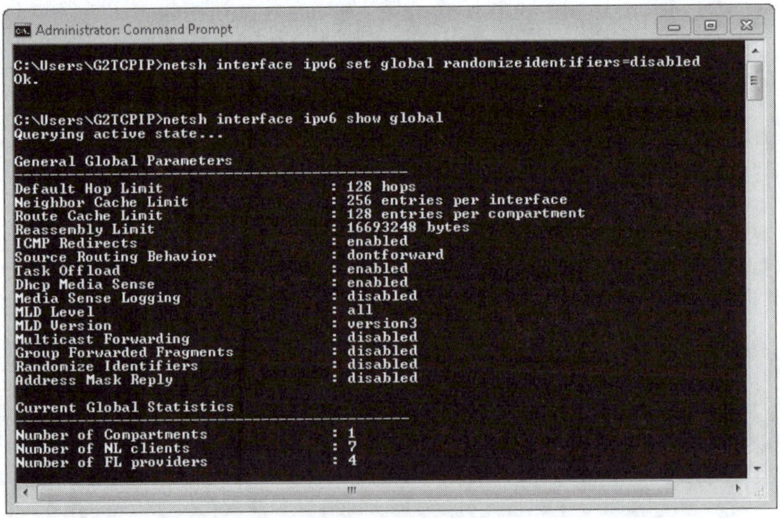

Figure 7-16 Disabled Randomize Identifiers to support Modified EUI-64
Source: Microsoft

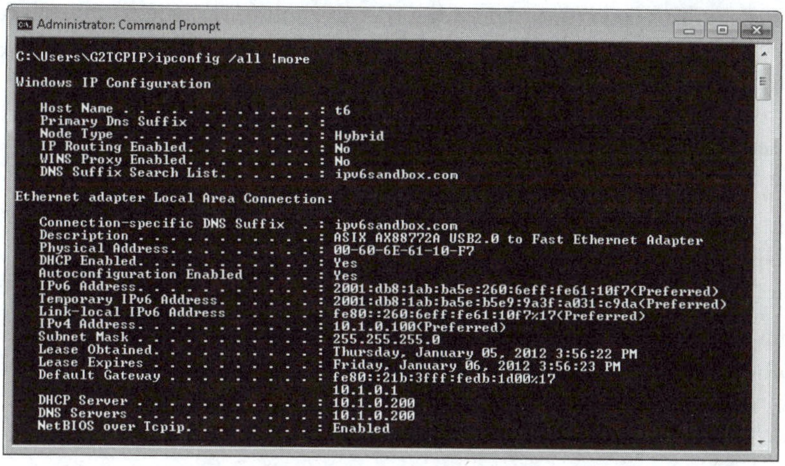

Figure 7-17 View with Modified EUI-64 IPv6 address on client
Source: Microsoft

RFC 4941 added the stipulation that a node using SLAAC as its autoconfiguration method will compute an additional IPv6 address known as the "temporary" address and the temporary address is assigned "preferred" status. This address is to be used for all outbound communications from the node. It will also be recomputed periodically as part of security provisions in the RFC. However, real-world deployments in which this process is used may experience significant troubleshooting hardships if the various hosts on a network continually change their IPv6 addresses. RFC 4941 does stipulate that node software should have the capability of disabling this temporary address creation process. Generally, this function is enabled by default. Figure 7-18 shows the output of `ipconfig`, in which the temporary IPv6 address is configured.

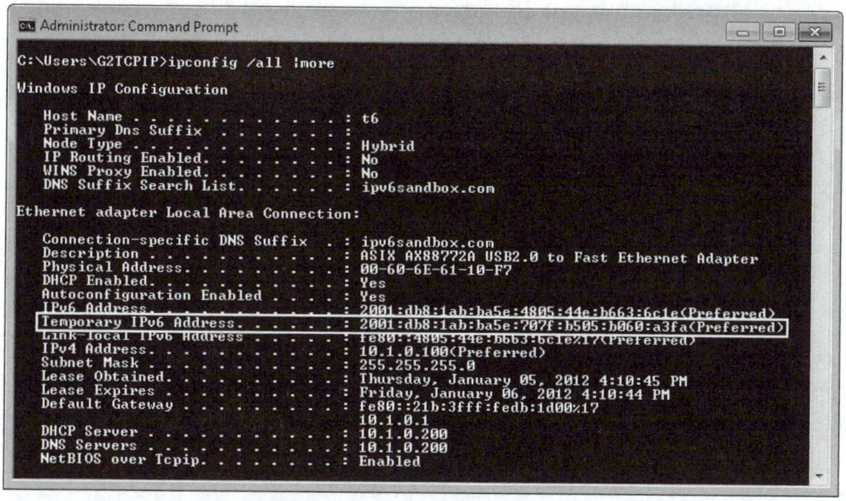

Figure 7-18 View with temporary IPv6 address
Source: Microsoft

For those who are security conscious, there's another method for creating an interface ID: the Cryptographically Generated Addresses (CGA) process defined in RFC 3972. This process works by generating a cryptographic hash of the node's public key (of a public/private key pair) along with the network prefix (as supplied by an RA). The private key is then used to sign messages sent from this node. In this environment, a public key infrastructure (PKI) is not required on the network.

In order for the CGA-computed address to function on the network, the Secure Neighbor Discovery (SEND) protocol must be running on the network defined by RFC 3971, which provides additional fields for ND to exchange keys.

However, at this time, very few operating systems support SEND, and therefore it is difficult to deploy CGA in a network. In addition, CGA is very processor intensive and can be attacked easily with a NS flood towards a SEND-enabled node, causing a slowdown of the system as it attempts to process all the public key operations.

DHCPv6

DHCPv6 is defined in RFC 3315. However, other RFCs—4861, 4862, and their associated updates—define components that are needed for the process to fully operate. As discussed earlier in this chapter, routers require certain configurations in order to support stateful and/ or a combination of stateless and stateful address autoconfiguration. Combining DHCPv6 services with the RA configurations provides the system required to support stateful address autoconfiguration. DHCPv6 servers are not required to be on-link to all hosts, given that DHCPv6 relay service that's configured on routers will forward client DHCPv6 requests to the DHCPv6 server and that the server will reply with the appropriate IPv6 address to be relayed to the client.

DHCPv6 uses different UDP ports than DHCP in IPv4. Clients listen for DHCPv6 messages on UDP port 546, whereas servers and relay agents listen for DHCPv6 messages on UDP port 547.

DHCPv6 uses two specific multicast addresses:

- *FF02::1:2*—A link-scope multicast address used by clients to commuicate with on-link servers and relay agents that are members of this group
- *FF05::1:3*—A site-scope multicast address used by a relay agent to communicate with a server, and on-site servers being members of this group

In DHCPv6, IPv6 addresses are not bound to MAC addresses, as they are in DHCPv4; they are bound to the DHCP Unique Identifier (DUID). The DUIDs must all be globally unique, each client and server must have one, and the DUID should not change after initial assignment, even if hardware changes.

Because IPv6 addresses are bound to a DUID, the DHCPv6 binding table or log file may not provide much assistance for troubleshooting because the DUID may not have any information within it that uniquely identifies a specific hardware interface or device.

DUIDs may be defined in one of three methods (additional DUID types may be defined in the future):

- *DUID-LLT*—Link-layer address plus time
- *DUID-EN*—Vendor-assigned unique ID based on Enterprise Number
- *DUID-LL*—Link-layer address

Another difference with IPv6 addressing is the object known as the Identity Association (IA). The IA is a mechanism for servers and clients to identify and manage a group of IPv6 addresses. It is composed of an identity association identifier (IAID) and associated configuration information. Each host must have a unique IAID for each interface it may have. The IAID for a specific IA must be maintained after restarts of the host.

When a host sends a Solicit request to a DHCPv6 server, the client also provides the specific IAID assigned to the interface in the request. The DHCPv6 server captures and stores the IAID in the lease table. Figure 7-19 shows a Windows Server 2008 R2 with IPv4 and IPv6 views of DHCP services of both the lease tables.

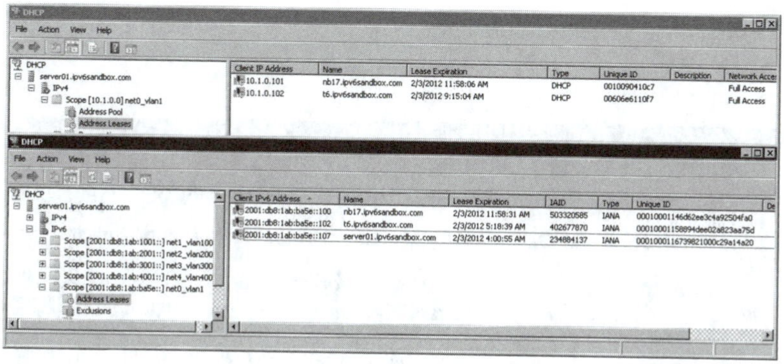

Figure 7-19 Windows Server 2008 R2 DHCP address lease tables
Source: Wireshark

The power of IPv6 address autoconfiguration is realized when a network has the requirement to be readdressed, with as much minimal impact to network operations as possible. By changing the timer values and network prefixes (if required) in the router RA configuration and creating new scopes in the DHCPv6 server, as each host with an autoconfigured address receives the RAs, it will update the timers and allow for the "older" addresses to start the process towards deprecation and allow the "new" addresses to start new communications.

DHCPv6 Messages There are numerous DHCPv6 message types that occur between nodes, servers, and relay agents. Table 7-5 describes the DHCPv6 message format fields and their values for messages between nodes and servers.

Figure 7-20 shows the DHCPv6 message packet structure for messages between nodes and servers.

Table 7-6 lists the DHCPv6 message types, the respective numeric values for the message types, which device sends and receives the message, and the message description.

Field	Description
Msg-type	This is a 1-byte field that defines the messages sent between nodes, servers, and relay agents. See Table 7-6 for additional details.
Transaction-id	This is a 3-byte field comprising the transaction ID for a specific message exchange.
Options	This is a variable-sized field sent by a node requesting an IPv6 address and possible other information, such as DNS address.

Table 7-5 DHCPv6 message format fields for messages between nodes and servers
© Cengage Learning 2013

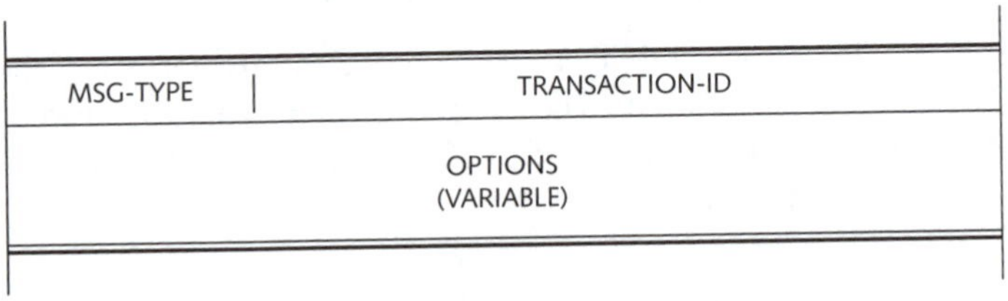

Figure 7-20 DHCPv6 message packet structure for messages between nodes and servers
© Cengage Learning 2013

Message	Value	From	To	Description
SOLICIT	1	Node	Server	Sent by nodes to locate DHCPv6 servers.
ADVERTISE	2	Server	Node	Sent by servers replying to a node Solicit message.
REQUEST	3	Node	Server	Sent by a node requesting an IPv6 address and possible other information, such as DNS address.
CONFIRM	4	Node	Server	Sent by a node to any server to verify that the address it has is still valid on the connected link.
RENEW	5	Node	Server	Sent by a node to the DHCPv6 server where it received its original information, to extend lifetime timers and other information, as required.
REBIND	6	Node	Server	Sent by a node to any server if it did not receive a reply to its Renew request.
REPLY	7	Server	Node	Sent by a server in reply to Solicit, Renew, Rebind, Release, Decline, and Information-Request messages, and containing appropriate information for the node.
RELEASE	8	Node	Server	Sent by a node informing the server it no longer will be using the assigned address.
DECLINE	9	Node	Server	Sent by a node to inform the server that the address it was assigned is already in use.
RECONFIGURE	10	Server	Node	Sent by a server to a node so the node can execute a Renew or Information-Request in order to receive new/updated information.

Table 7-6 IPv6 DHCPv6 message types

Message	Value	From	To	Description
INFORMATION-REQUEST	11	Node	Server	Sent by a node to request only information, but not an IPv6 address. This is the "other" information, and occurs when the O flag is set on "on" and the M flag is set on "off" in the RA.
RELAY-FORW	12	Relay Agent	Server	Sent by a relay agent on behalf of a node request or by another relay agent, when the server is not on-link.
RELAY-REPL	13	Server	Relay Agent	Sent by a server in reply to the message sent by a relay agent.
LEASEQUERY	14	Node	Server	Sent by a node to any available server to get information on its leases, defined in RFC 5007.
LEASEQUERY-REPLY	15	Server	Node	Sent by a server to inform a client of its lease information, defined in RFC 5007.
LEASEQUERY-DONE	16	Server	Node	Sent by the server indicating the end of a group of LEASEQUERY replies, defined in RFC 5460.
LEASEQUERY-DATA	17	Server	Node	Sent by a server if more than one client's data is to be sent for a LEASEQUERY, defined in RFC 5460.

Table 7-6　IPv6 DHCPv6 message types (*continued*)
© Cengage Learning 2013

Unless otherwise noted, messages are defined in RFC 3315. The latest updates to this list are available at *www.iana.org/assignments/dhcpv6-parameters/dhcpv6-parameters.xml*.

Table 7-7 describes the DHCPv6 options fields.

Field	Description
Option-code	This is a 2-byte field that contains the specific option. See Table 7-8 for additional details.
Option-len	This is a 2-byte field containing the option-data fields length.
Option-data	This is a variable-sized field containing the data for the option.

Table 7-7　DHCPv6 options fields
© Cengage Learning 2013

Figure 7-21 shows the DHCPv6 options packet structure.

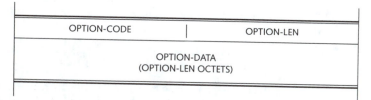

Figure 7-21　DHCPv6 options packet structure
© Cengage Learning 2013

Table 7-8 lists the DHCPv6 options, the respective numeric values for the message types, and the message descriptions.

Option	Value	Description
OPTION_CLIENTID	1	Used by the client to provide the server its DUID
OPTION_SERVERID	2	Used by the server to provide the client its DUID
OPTION_IA_NA	3	Used to carry the Identity Association for nontemporary addresses and parameters.
OPTION_IA_TA	4	Used to carry the Identity Association for temporary addresses and parameters
OPTION_IAADDR	5	Specifies an IPv6 address and other options for an IA_NA or IA_TA
OPTION_ORO	6	Used by a client to specifiy a list of options being requested from a server
OPTION_PREFERENCE	7	Used by a server to influence selection of a server for the client
OPTION_ELAPSED_TIME	8	Used by a client to indicate how long the client has been trying to complete the DHCPv6 transaction
OPTION_RELAY_MSG	9	Contains the DHCPv6 message in a Relay-Forward or Relay-Reply message
OPTION_AUTH	11	Contains information to authenticate the contents and identity of a DHCPv6 message
OPTIN_UNICAST	12	Used by a server to inform a client that it can communcate to the server via a unicast address
OPTION_STATUS_CODE	13	Returns a status code relating to a DHCPv6 message
OPTION_RAPID_COMMIT	14	Used by a client to inform the server that it can support the two-message exchange for an IPv6 address assignment
OPTION_USER_CLASS	15	Used by a client to inform the server of the type or category of user or application it is, so that the server can supply specific configuration information
OPTION_VENDOR_CLASS	16	Used by a client to identify the vendor of the hardware the client is operating
OPTION_VENDOR_OPTS	17	Used by servers and clients to exchange vendor-specific information.
OPTION_INTERFACE_ID	18	Used by a relay agent to send the interface information on which the client message was received
OPTION_RECONFIGURE_MSG	19	Used by a server when it sends a Reconfigure message to a client to inform the client whether it should reply with a Renew message or an Information-Request message

Table 7-8 DHCPv6 options fields

Option	Value	Description
OPTION_RECONF_ACCEPT	20	Used by a client to inform a server whether or not it will accept a Reconfigure message; a server uses this option to inform the client whether or not to accept a Reconfigure message
OPTION_SIP_SERVER_D	21	SIP server domain list; SIP outbound proxy server for clients to use, defined in RFC 3319
OPTION_SIP_SERVER_A	22	SIP server IPv6 address for clients to use, defined in RFC 3319
OPTIN_DNS_SERVER	23	IPv6 addresses of DNS recursive name server, defined in RFC 3646
OPTION_DOMAIN_LIST	24	Domain list, defined in RFC 3646
OPTION_IA_PD	25	Used to carry the prefix delegation identity association as well as the parameters and prefixes associated with it, defined in RFC 3633
OPTION_IAPREFIX	26	Specifies IPv6 address prefixes for IA_PDs, defined in RFC 3633
OPTION_NIS_SERVERS	27	NIS server list for nodes, defined in RFC 3898
OPTION_NISP_SERVERS	28	NIS+ server list for nodes, defined in RFC 3898
OPTION_NIS_DOMAIN_NAME	29	Used by NIS sevrers to inform the client of the NIS Domain Name, defined in RFC 3898.
OPTION_NISP_DOMAIN_NAME	30	Used by NIS+ servers to inform the client of the NIS+ Domain Name, defined in RFC 3898.
OPTION_SNTP_SERVERS	31	SNTP server available via IPv6 for nodes, defined in RFC 4075.
OPTION_INFORMATION_ REFRESH_TIME	32	Used by the server to inform the client to refresh its other configuration information because there are no timers to refresh DHCPv6 configuration information are supplied when the O flag is used, defined in RFC 4242
OPTION_BCMCS_SERVER_D	33	BCMCS Control Server Domain Name List, defined in RFC 4280
OPTION_BCMCS_SERVER_A	34	BCMCS Control Server IPv6 address, defined in RFC 4280
OPTION_GEOCONF_CIVIC	36	Defines the civic location of the client or the DHCPv6 server, defined in RFC 4776
OPTION_REMOTE_ID	37	May be added by DHCPv6 relay agents that terminate permanent or switched circuits to identify the remote client end of the circuit, defined in RFC 4649
OPTION_SUBSCRIBER_ID	38	Used by providers to separately identify subscriber systems, defined in RFC 4580
OPTION_CLIENT_FQDN	39	Allows a client to inform the DHCPv6 of its FQDN, defined in RFC 4704
OPTION_PANA_AGENT	40	Contains IPv6 addresses for PANA Authentication Agents available to a PANA client, defined in RFC 5192

7

Table 7-8 DHCPv6 options fields (*continues*)

Option	Value	Description
OPTION_NEW_POSIX_TIMEZONE	41	Contains POSIX TZ strings that express timezone information in a character-based string, defined in RFC 4833
OPTION_NEW_TZDB_TIMEZONE	42	References a name from the timezone entry of the TZ database, defined in RFC 4833
OPTION_ERO	43	Sent by a relay agent to a DHCPv6 server requesting a list of options from the server, defined in RFC 4994
OPTION_LQ_QUERY	44	Used to identify a query in a LEASEQUERY message, defined in RFC 5007
OPTION_CLIENT_DATA	45	Used by a client on a link to encapsulate data in a LEASEQUERY-REPLY message, defined in RFC 5007
OPTION_CLT_TIME	46	Identifies how long ago the server communicated with the client, defined in RFC 5007
OPTION_LQ_RELAY_DATA	47	Identifies how long ago the client communicated with the server, defined in RFC 5007
OPTION_LQ_CLIENT_LINK	48	Used by a client in a LEASEQUERY-REPLY message to identify the links the client has one or more bindings, defined in RFC 5007
OPTION_MIP6_HNINF	49	Allows a mobile node to exchange home network information with the DHCPv6 server, defined in "DHCP Options for Home Information Discovery in MIPv6" (*draft-ietf-mip6-hiopt-17.txt*)
OPTION_MIP6_RELAY	50	Allows the relay agent to send the home network information of a mobile node to the DHCPv6 server, defined in "DHCP Options for Home Information Discovery in MIPv6" (*draft-ietf-mip6-hiopt-17.txt*)
OPTION_V6_LOST	51	Allows a client to obtain a LoST server domain name, defined in RFC 5223
OPTION_CAPWAP_AC_V6	52	Contains one or more IPv6 addresses of CAPWAP ACs that are available to a WTP, defined in RFC 5417
OPTION_RELAY_ID	53	Contains the DUID from the relay agent, defined in RFC 5460
OPTION-IPv6_Address-MoS	54	MoS IPv6 address option for the DHCPv6 server, defined in RFC 5678
OPTION-IPv6_FQDN-MoS	55	MoS Domain List, defined in RFC 5678
OPTION_NTP_SERVER	56	Provides one address for either an NTP or a SNTP server, defined in RFC 5908
OPTION_V6_ACCESS_DOMAIN	57	Provides the domain name for an access network, defined in RFC 5986
OPTION_SIP_UA_CS_LIST	58	Provides a list of domain names for SIP User Agent Configuration Service Domains, defined in RFC 6011

Table 7-8 DHCPv6 options fields (*continued*)

Option	Value	Description
OPT_BOOTFILE_URL	59	Used by the DHCPv6 server to send a URL for a boot file for a client to use, defined in RFC 5970
OPT_BOOTFILE_PARAM	60	Used by the DHCPv6 server to specifiy parameters for a boot file for a client, defined in RFC 5970
OPTION_CLIENT_ARCH_TYPE	61	Allows a client to inform a DHCPv6 server of its supported architecture types, so the server can supply the most correct boot file, defined in RFC 5970
OPTION_NII	62	Allows a client to inform a DHCPv6 server that it supports a Universal Network Device Interface (UNDI), defined in RFC 5970
DHCPv6 GeoLoc Option	63	Used by a client to inform the DHCPv6 server of its coordinate-based geographic location, defined in RFC 6225
OPTION_AFTR_NAME	64	Used to provide the Address Family Transition Router's (AFTR's) FQDN to a B4 element, defined in RFC 6334
OPTION_ERP_LOCAL_DOMAIN_-NAME	65	Used by a client to request the ERP Local Domain Name from the DHCPv6 server, defined in RFC 6440
OPTION_RSOO	66	Used by a relay agent to send the RSOO in the Relay-Forward message to a DHCPv6 server, so that options the client is requesting will be sent by the DHCPv6 server and passed through the relay agent, defined in RFC 6422

Table 7-8 DHCPv6 options fields (*continued*)
© Cengage Learning 2013

Unless otherwise noted, options are defined in RFC 3315. The latest updates to this list are available at *www.iana.org/assignments/dhcpv6-parameters/dhcpv6-parameters.xml*.

Table 7-9 describes the DHCPv6 Relay-Forward message format fields and their values for messages between relay agents and servers.

Field	Description
Hop-count	This is a 1-byte field that indicates the number of relay agents that have relayed the message.
Link-address	This is a 16-byte field comprising the global address of the relay agent that is on the same segment as the requesting node, in order for the server to supply the correct scoped address in the reply message.
Peer-address	This is a 16-byte field comprising the node's address that the message came from.
Options	This is a variable-sized field that includes a Relay Message option and may include other options from the relay agent.

Table 7-9 DHCPv6 Relay-Forward message format fields
© Cengage Learning 2013

Table 7-10 describes the DHCPv6 Relay-Reply message format fields and their values for messages between relay agents and servers.

Field	Description
Hop-count	Duplicated from the original Relay-Forward message
Link-address	Duplicated from the original Relay-Forward message
Peer-address	Duplicated from the original Relay-Forward message
Options	This is a variable-sized field that includes a Relay Message option and may include other options from the relay agent.

Table 7-10 DHCPv6 Relay-Reply Message format fields
© Cengage Learning 2013

Figure 7-22 shows the DHCPv6 message packet structure for messages between relay agents and servers. The packet structure is the same for both Relay-Forward and Relay-Reply messages.

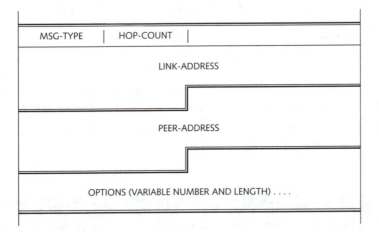

Figure 7-22 DHCPv6 message packet structure for messages between relay agents and servers
© Cengage Learning 2013

DHCPv6 Stateful Message Exchange In order for the stateful autoconfiguration process to be successful, the host tries to locate a router to inform it "what to do." Effectively, the RA tells the host to ask a DHCPv6 server for its IPv6 address and "other" information. The router should have its A flag set to "off" and the L, M, and O flags set to "on." If the host does not receive a reply to its RS, the host continues the process and queries for a DHCPv6 server on-link.

The basic DHCPv6 process follows these six steps:

1. The host sends a Router Solicitation.

2. The router replies to the host with a Router Advertisement, with its A flag set to "off" and the L, M, and O flags set to "on."

3. The host sends a Solicit message looking for any DHCPv6 servers at the link-scope multicast address FF02::1:2 for on-link servers.

4. The DHCPv6 server replies to the host with an Advertise message, informing the host that it can provide an IPv6 address and other configuration options that it may have.

5. The host sends a Request message, requesting an IPv6 address and other configuration options (such as DNS address and domain name).

6. The DHCPv6 server sends the host a Reply message with an IPv6 address, other configuration options it may have available (such as DNS address and domain name), and timers information.

Figure 7-23 shows the DHCPv6 stateful message exchange with the six messages referenced above and the specific information of the Reply packet the host received. Packets 1 and 6 are the router exchange, packets 16 and 19 are the initial DHCPv6 exchange, and packets 198 and 199 are the final DHCPv6 exchange between the host and the server.

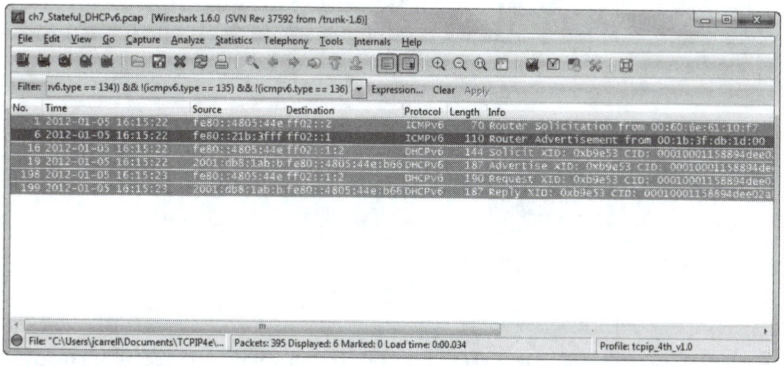

Figure 7-23 DHCPv6 stateful message exchange
Source: Wireshark

DHCPv6 Stateless Message Exchange

DHCPv6 Stateless Message Exchange In order for the DHCPv6 stateless auto-configuration process to be successful, the host tries to locate a router to inform it "what to do." Effectively, the RA tells the host that it has the network prefix information and to ask a DHCPv6 server for the "other" information. The router should have its A, L, and O flags set to "on" and the M flag set to "off." If the host does not receive a reply to its RS, the host continues the process and queries for a DHCPv6 server on-link. Ensuring the configuration of the on-link router or relay agent is important because, in this case, the result might be that the client receives "too much" information.

The basic DHCPv6 stateless process follows these four steps:

1. The host sends a Router Solicitation.

2. The router replies to the host with a Router Advertisement, with its A, L, and O flags set to "on" and the M flag set to "off."

3. The host sends an Information-Request message, requesting only other configuration options (such as DNS address and domain name), looking for any DHCPv6 servers at the link-scope multicast address FF02::1:2 for on-link servers. The host also uses the supplied prefix for its network prefix to prepend to the interface ID it has generated.

4. The DHCPv6 server sends the host a Reply message with the other configuration options it may have available (such as DNS address and domain name).

Figure 7-24 shows the DHCPv6 stateless message exchange with the four messages referenced previously and the specific information of the Reply packet the host received. Packets 3 and 12 are the router exchange, and packets 22 and 23 are the DHCPv6 exchange between the host and the server.

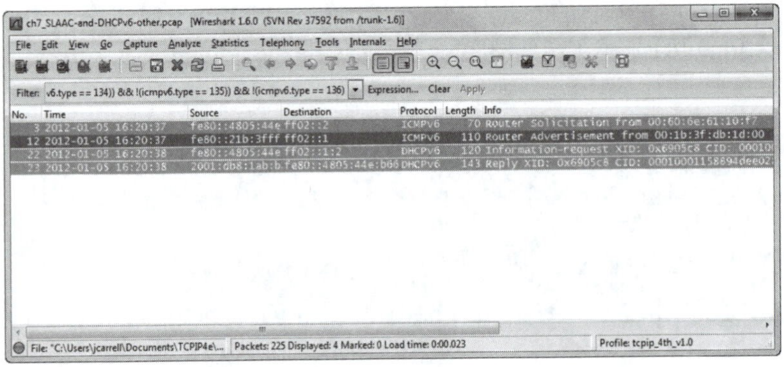

Figure 7-24 DHCPv6 stateless message exchange
Source: Wireshark

DHCPv6 Relay Message Exchange The DHCPv6 relay process is basically the same as DHCPv6 stateful. However, the location of the DHCPv6 server is not on-link; therefore a DHCPv6 relay agent must be on-link to the host. In this case, the router is configured with DHCPv6 relay (known as *helper address* in IPv4) on the segment where this host is located, and the router has IPv6 connectivity to the DHCPv6 server on a different segment.

The basic DHCPv6 relay process follows these 10 steps:

1. The host sends a Router Solicitation.

2. The router replies to the host with a Router Advertisement, with its A and L flags set to "off" and the M and O flags set to "on."

3. The host sends a Solicit message looking for any DHCPv6 servers at the link-scope multicast address FF02::1:2 for on-link servers.

4. The router relay-forwards the host Solicit message to the DHCPv6 server.

5. The DHCPv6 server relay-replies to the router with an Advertise message, informing the host that it can provide an IPv6 address and other configuration options that it may have.

6. The router replies with the Advertise message to the host.

7. The host sends a Request message, requesting an IPv6 address and other configuration options (such as DNS address and domain name).

8. The router relay-forwards the host Request message to the DHCPv6 server.

9. The DHCPv6 server relay-replies to the router with a Reply message with an IPv6 address, other configuration options it may have available (such as DNS address and domain name), and timers information.

10. The router replies with the Reply message to the host.

Figure 7-25 shows the DHCPv6 relay message exchange with the 10 messages referenced above and the specific information of the Reply packet the host received. Packets 1 and 2 are the router exchange, packets 3 through 6 are the initial relay/DHCPv6 exchange, and packets 7 through 10 are the final relay/DHCPv6 exchange between the host and the server.

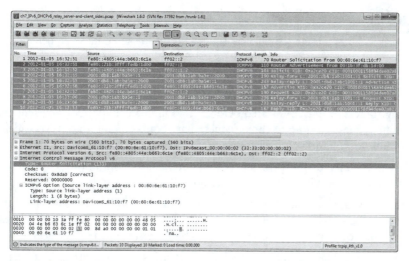

Figure 7-25 DHCPv6 Relay message exchange
Source: Wireshark

In all cases of IPv6 address autoconfiguration, the DAD process must be executed to verify uniqueness of any assigned IPv6 address. The three DHCPv6 processes outlined above are simplified to show just the DHCPv6 and related ICMPv6 messages (RAs) required for the DHCPv6 process to operate. There are additional message exchanges not noted, such as NS and NA messages.

IPv6 Autoconfiguration Process

The IPv6 autoconfiguration processes are basically defined in RFC 4862 (stateless) and RFC 3315 (stateful). The overall process generally operates using both of these, starting with stateless and moving into stateful, assuming of course that nodes are still in their default configuration.

The general IPv6 address autoconfiguration process follows these basic steps:

1. The node creates an interface ID using (generally) either the modified EUI-64 method or the random number generator.

2. The well-known link-local prefix of FE80:: is prepended to the newly created interface ID to form a complete link-local address. This address is in the tentative state while awaiting verification.

3. The node sends a NS message with its link-local address as the destination. (This is the DAD verification process.) Although this address on the interface is in this tentative state, it will only accept traffic that is in response to its NS.

4. If an NA is not received, then the address is considered unique and moves to the preferred state and is assigned to the interface. If an NA is received, then the address is a duplicate and the autoconfiguration process ends. At this point, the interface will require manual configuration.

According to RFC 4862, after a link-local address has been established on a node, the continuation of the IPv6 autoconfiguration process applies to hosts and not routers. Because routers supply RAs that contain information used in the autoconfiguration process by hosts, routers should be configured manually. Routers will generate their own link-local address following the above steps, but all other IPv6 addresses on a router should be configured.

5. The host sends an RS to the all-routers multicast address FF02::2 trying to ascertain if there are any routers on-link. As stated before, although routers periodically send RAs, the host sends one request (and up to three requests) as soon as its interface is considered fully up after the link-local address moves to the preferred state.

6. If an RA is not received, the host starts the stateful autoconfiguration process, which was described in the previous DHCPv6 section.

7. If an RA is received, the host examines the RA message looking for variables and flags to determine its settings and what to do next. Settings such as hop count, reachable timer, retransmission timer, and MTU (if available) are set on the interface.

8. If the L flag (on-link flag) is set to "on," the host adds the network prefix to its prefix cache and proceeds to the next step. If the L flag is set to "off," proceed to the next step.

9. If the A flag (autonomous address-configuration flag) is set to "on," then two IPv6 addressses are created (if the A flag is set to "off," proceed to Step 12):

   a. Generate a stateless address using the network prefix as discovered from the RA and prepend it to the interface ID created during Step 1. Also set the prefix length, valid lifetime and preferred lifetime timers, as provided in the RA.

   b. Generate a temporary stateless address by creating a new interface ID using a random number generator and prepending that with the network prefix in the RA.

10. The host sends an NS message with its global unicast address as the destination, as well as the tempoary global unicast address as the destination. (This is DAD.) Although each of these addresses on the interface are in this tentative state, each accepts only traffic that is in response to its NS.

11. If an NA is not received, the address is considered unique, moves to the preferred state, and is assigned to the interface. If an NA is received, the address is a duplicate and is not initialzed on the interface. If the temporary address is a duplicate, it can be regenerated and tested multiple times in order to find a unique address. In either case, proceed to the next step.

12. If the M flag (managed address configuration flag) is set to "on," start the stateful autoconfiguration process to receive an IPv6 address and other information the DHCPv6 server may offer. If not, proceed to the next step.

13. If the O flag (other configuration flag) is set to "on," start the stateful autoconfiguration process to receive other information (such as the DNS server address) the DHCPv6 server may offer. If not, this is the end of the IPv6 address autoconfiguration process.

Figure 7-26 shows a flow chart of the IPv6 address autoconfiguration process. This flow chart is a simplified process diagram, as other options and/or flags may be enabled and require a subprocess to be repeated.

Autoconfiguration in Microsoft Windows Operating Systems

Address autoconfiguration for Windows Server 2008 R2, Windows Vista, and Windows 7 is enabled so that a computer will self-assign an IPv4 and an IPv6 set of addresses, at a minimum, and be able to communicate on-link. In this mode, basic networking can occur without manual address configuration. Although those connected computers can communicate with one another, unless there is a router on-link, there is no communications off-link.

IPv4 autoconfiguration support for Windows Server 2008 R2, Windows Vista, and Windows 7 follows these basic guidelines:

- DHCP is the default configured mechanism for obtaining an IP address.
- APIPA is configured to be active by default and will autoconfigure an IPv4 address only if the client does not receive an IP address from a DHCP server.
- Manually configuring an IPv4 address disables both DHCP and APIPA.

IPv6 autoconfiguration support for Windows Server 2008 R2, Windows Vista, and Windows 7 follows these basic guidelines:

- The link-local address will be generated using a random number generator instead of the Modified EUI-64 format for the interface ID portion appended to FE80::. This behavior can be changed by executing the netsh command to disable the randomize identifiers global option.
- If the A flag is set to "on" in an RA, the global unicast address will be generated using the same interface ID as in the link-local address appended to the prefix as received in the RA.

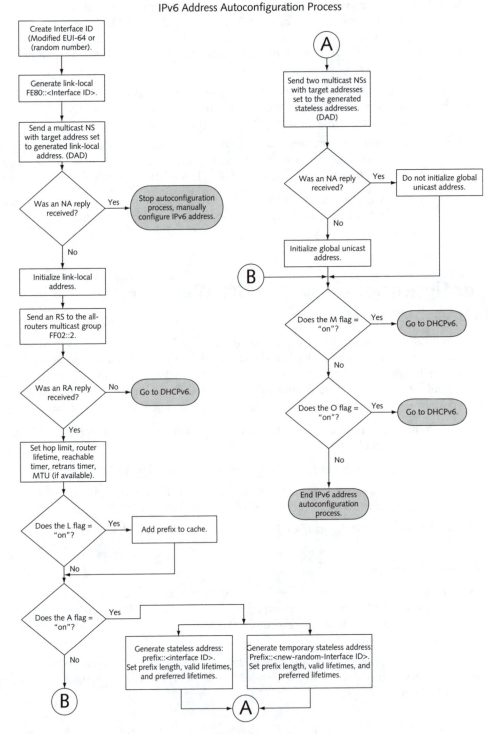

Figure 7-26 IPv6 address autoconfiguration process

- If the A flag is set to "on" in an RA, a temporary global unicast address will be generated using a random number generater (different from the initial interface ID) only on Windows Vista and Windows 7, not on Windows Server 2008 R2. This behavior can be changed by executing the `netsh` command to globally enable (or disable) the privacy state option.

- Because the chances of a duplicate address are considered small with a random number generated for the interface ID, these operating systems will not wait for the DAD process to complete before sending the RS to find any on-link routers. This operation is known as optimistic DAD.

- If no RAs are received, these operating systems will start the stateful address process—that is, send a DHCPv6 Solicit message looking for any DHCPv6 servers either on-link or via a DHCPv6 relay service.

- Manually configuring an IPv6 addess does not disable the IPv6 address autoconfiguration process on a host. This is the exact opposite of manually configured address operations in IPv4. Which is to say, if an IPv6 address is manually configured, link-local, SLAAC, and DHCPv6 addresses may also be configured depending on the router settings of the autoconfiguration option flags.

Microsoft Windows Server 2008 DHCP Scopes

Address **scopes** (often referred to simply as "scopes") define a set of addresses that a DHCP server can assign to clients.

Windows Server 2008 R2 supports the creation of a DHCP **superscope**. Superscopes are collections of scopes that contain sets of nonconsecutive IP addresses that can be assigned to a single network; they are also often used with contiguous public class C addresses in a supernetting scenario or when CIDR is in effect. For example, to assign 10.2.3.x and 10.4.3.x addresses to the same network, two scopes must be created (one scope assigning the 10.2.3.x addresses and the other scope assigning the 10.4.3.x addresses). These two scopes must be combined into one superscope to enable the DHCP server to allocate addresses in either network range to the DHCP clients on that network. Older versions of DHCP server software (before the release of Service Pack 4 for Windows NT 4.0 Server) could not build superscopes. Superscopes apply only to IPv4 because IPv6 does not have the CIDR capabilities.

For IPv6 scopes, there are a few differences in Windows Server 2008 R2 compared to IPv4 scopes. First, in IPv4 scopes, you can configure address pools, which are the valid from/to ranges of addresses that the DHCP server can provide to hosts. In IPv6 scopes, you can configure exclusions, which are addresses not to be provided to hosts. Another difference is that in IPv4 scopes one can configure the router option in the Scope Options field, which provides the default gateway address to a host. In the IPv6 scope, there is no option to provide the router address, as that is derived by a host via the RA that the host receives when it sends an RS (that is, if the host does receive an RA). Figure 7-27 shows Windows Server 2008 R2 with IPv4 address pools and IPv6 exclusions configured.

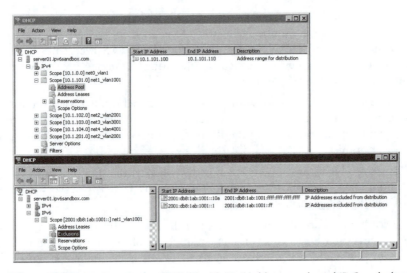

Figure 7-27 Windows Server 2008 R2 with IPv4 address pools and IPv6 exclusions
Source: Microsoft

Setting Up A Simple DHCP Server

More complex and full-featured DHCP servers (like the one built into Windows Server 2008) or software installed on a UNIX or Linux server include tools and capabilities beyond simple address pool definition and static or dynamic address allocations. Nevertheless, it's interesting to look at a simple DHCP server to get a sense of what's involved in using one to manage IP addresses. What's missing in the D-Link wireless access point we use as an example here are superscopes (discussed in the previous section), directory services tie-ins, and so forth. In the screenshots and discussions that follow, we use the D-Link Xtreme N Gigabit Router (model number DIR-655) as the source for the information we present; you can find more information about this device at *www.dlink.com/DIR-655*. We chose this wireless router because it supports IPv6 for WAN and LAN/WLAN. We configured an IPv6-in-IPv4 tunnel to an IPv6 tunnel broker in order to provide full IPv6 connectivity to the Internet. Note that the DIR-655 must be hardware version B1 or newer, as the older models do not have IPv6 and cannot be upgraded for IPv6 capability.

To begin using this utility, you must establish a Web session with the device. This is a two-step process that requires entering the URL for the device into the address field in a Web browser, and then supplying an administrator account name and password to gain access to the software. Next, you must click the SETUP tab and then click the NETWORK SETTINGS button in the left pane.

The screen shown in Figure 7-28 appears by default when NETWORK SETTINGS is opened for the first time. This particular screen includes settings for the local area network (ROUTER SETTINGS) on which it operates, DHCP SERVER SETTINGS, and ADD DHCP RESERVATIONS. We will discuss all three.

Figure 7-28 D-Link DHCP configuration
Source: D-Link

We begin with the ROUTER SETTINGS section, as shown in Figure 7-28, where you configure the device's base IPv4 address for the internal network:

- *Router IP Address*—The default LAN IP address for the router is 192.168.0.1. This will be the default gateway provided to all clients via the DHCP server. The Router IP address should not be one of the addresses in the DHCP IP address range that we will discuss in the next section.

- *Subnet Mask*—The default subnet mask is 255.255.255.0. The subnet mask that is configured is the same mask used by the DHCP server.

- *Device Name*—The device's default host name is "dlinkrouter." This is a logical name and not used in DHCP server functions.

- *Local Domain Name*—This is an optional field in which you can configure a domain name of choice. It will be used by the DHCP server when supplying the domain name option to clients.

- *Enable DNS Relay*—This option is checked by default. The DHCP server will supply a DNS address to clients and, in this case, will supply the router's IP address as the DNS server. The router will then relay DNS requests to the DNS server as configured in the Internet tab configuration context.

We will now examine the fields that show under DHCP SERVER SETTINGS on that screen and explain how they work and discuss their significance. Before we do that, however, it's important to note that this DHCP server software distinguishes between DHCP IP Address Range (addresses that the DHCP server itself can hand out as it sees fit, subject to normal lease periods, renewals, and releases) and DHCP Reservations (addresses that administrators hand out as they see fit, which are called static because, once assigned, they do not expire or require renewals until the administrator manually changes related settings). Here, then, are the field values in the DHCP SERVER SETTINGS section, as shown in Figure 7-28:

- *Enable DHCP Server*—By default, this is selected to enable the DHCP server; deselect this box to stop the DHCP server.

- *DHCP IP Address Range*—This option has two fields (the starting address and the ending address) for making dynamic IP address assignments. The default setting for a local subnet is a starting address of 192.168.0.100 and an ending address of 192.168.0.199 (the end of the local subnet).

- *DHCP Lease Time*—This specifies the duration of a dynamic address lease. Duration varies by usage characteristics, as explained earlier in the chapter. Here, the value is 1440 minutes, or 24 hours—a fairly common value on networks.

- *Always broadcast*—Check this box to broadcast the DHCP server to LAN/WLAN clients (checked by default).

- *NetBIOS announcement*—NetBIOS allows hosts to discover all the computers on the network; by enabling this feature, the DHCP server offers NetBIOS configuration settings.

- *Learn NetBIOS from WAN*—This option allows WINS information to be learned from the WAN side of the network.

- *NetBIOS Scope*—This allows configuration of a NetBIOS domain name for network hosts. If the preceding option is enabled, this function has no effect.

- *NetBIOS node type*—This is used to select the type of NetBIOS nodes on the network.

- *Primary WINS IP Address* and *Secondary WINS IP Address*—WINS is a special name service built for use on a Windows network. In fact, WINS (which stands for Windows Internet Name Service) was introduced with Windows NT, remains available in Windows 2008 servers, and manages the association between workstation names and IP addresses on the networks over which they have purview. WINS complements DHCP in that it manages the workstation name-to-IP address mapping automatically, in much the same way that DHCP manages MAC address-to-IP address mapping and related configuration data for its clients. There is no WINS server on the local network, so the default address 0.0.0.0 is left unaltered.

The ADD DHCP RESERVATION section is where static IP addresses can be assigned to specific client devices. As seen in Figure 7-28, we also clicked the Computer name field button to show the settings for an existing static address assignment. Otherwise, all the values are blank, which makes it less interesting to look at and less easy to explain in the list of fields that follows:

- *Enable*—Select this box to add a DHCP reservation.

- *Computer Name*—Enter a host computer host name or select one from the drop-down box.

- *IP Address*—This is the IP address to be associated with the network interface that has the MAC address specified in the next field. Notice that this kind of address assignment on a wireless access point is a great security technique, because it permits administrators to associate valid local IP addresses only with network interfaces for which the MAC address is already known. Any other network device that attempts to gain an address to access the network will be denied such access, as long as the dynamic pool is turned off. Many networks take this approach to lock outsiders out of their wireless networks.

- *MAC Address*—This is the MAC address burned into firmware on the network interface for which an IP address is supplied. On a Windows host, use the `ipconfig /all` command to get the MAC address for the interface for which you wish to enable access; it shows up as the value associated with the Physical Address field in that listing.

The final sections in the Network Settings collection of panes is a DHCP RESERVATION LIST and the NUMBER OF DYNAMIC DHCP CLIENTS list. Both of these sections provide a way to check current active assignments for the DHCP server and will come in handy for those seeking to inspect or investigate the IP address assignments currently under the DHCP server's management.

Next, we click the IPV6 button in the left pane. This section allows for different IPv6 configuration options, depending on your ISP offering, as well as different tunnel options for those IPSs that don't offer IPv6 connectivity at this time. As shown in Figure 7-29, we already have an IPv6-in-IPv4 tunnel to an IPv6 tunnel broker. This allows IPv6 connectivity on the LAN/WLAN side of the network and a way to move native IPv6 traffic, via the IPv4 tunnel, to the tunnel broker, where it is decapsulated onto a native IPv6 network. In addition, IPv6 connectivity allows for an IPv6 /64 network on the LAN/WLAN side of the DIR-655.

The first section we need to configure to support stateful autoconfiguration is the IPv6 DNS SETTINGS. By selecting the *Use the following DNS address* option, we can manually configure the IPv6 DNS addresses to be used for DHCPv6 to send hosts. As seen in Figure 7-29, we have configured a primary IPv6 DNS server address from the tunnel broker.

The LAN IPv6 ADDRESS SETTINGS section is where the LAN/WLAN-side IPv6 global unicast address is configured:

- *Enable DHCP-PD*—Select this box if the ISP's router supports the prefix delegation function. For our IPv6 tunnel, we will manually configure the LAN-side IPv6 address to be routed through to the tunnel.

- *LAN IPv6 Address*—Enter the LAN-side IPv6 address. Note that only a /64 IPv6 address is supported.

- *LAN IPv6 Link-Local Address*—This IPv6 is automatically generated using the Modified EUI-64 format.

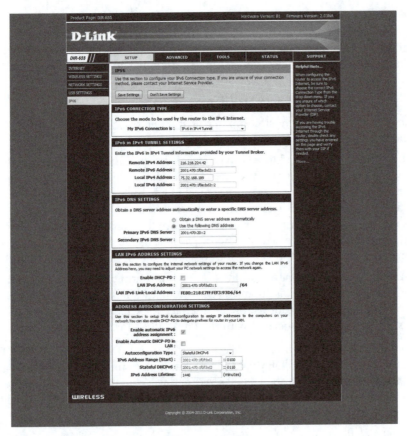

Figure 7-29 D-Link DHCPv6 configuration
Source: D-Link

The ADDRESS AUTOCONFIGURATION SETTINGS is the last section where the DHCPv6 configuration takes place. Stateless and stateful DHCPv6 can be configured in this section. One option that is different from the Microsoft DHCPv6 configuration is that here you define the start and end range of IPv6 addresses to provide clients. The following options are configured to support stateful DHCPv6:

- *Enable automatic IPv6 address assignment*—Select this box to enable the DHCPv6 server.

- *Enable Automatic DHCP-PD in LAN*—Select this option to provide prefix delegation to other routers that may be on-link.

- *Autoconfiguration Type*—Select this box and choose SLAAC+RDNSS, SLAAC+Stateless DHCPv6, or Stateful DHCPv6. Since we have a /64 IPv6 subnet on the LAN side, we chose Stateful DHCPv6.

- *IPv6 Address Range (Start)*—The prefix side of this option was prefilled when we configured the LAN IPv6 Address in the previous section. All that needs to be configured here is the starting address of host portion of the IPv6 address.

- *Stateful DHCPv6*—The prefix side of this option was prefilled when we configured the LAN IPv6 address in the previous section. All that needs to be configured here is the ending address of host portion of the IPv6 address. (The Stateful DHCPv6 field is actually for the ending host address, although the name may not exactly indicate this.)

- *IPv6 Address Lifetime*—This specifies the address lifetime as supplied in the RA. Duration will vary by usage characteristics, as explained earlier in the chapter. Here, the value is 1440 minutes, or 24 hours.

Figure 7-30 shows the `ipconfig` output of a client connected to the DIR-655, with both IPv4 and IPv6 configuration.

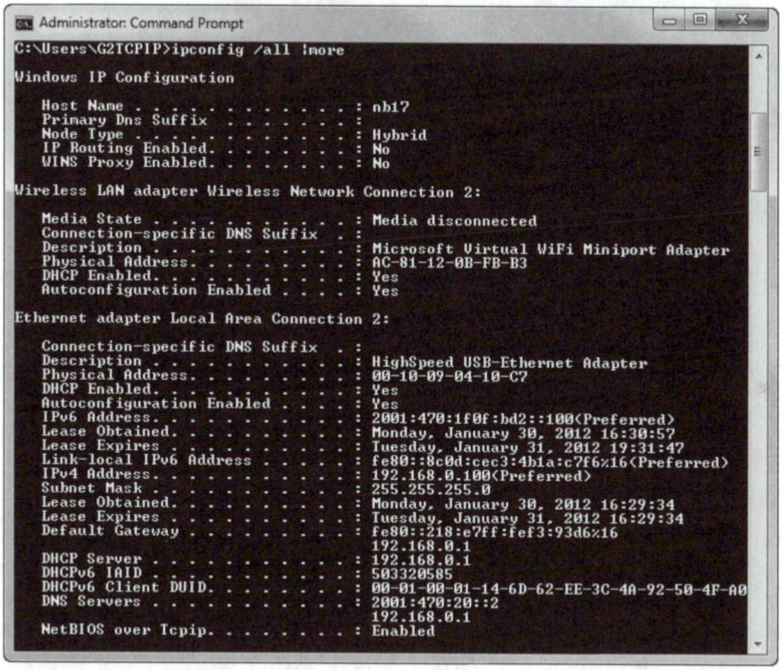

Figure 7-30 Windows 7 client connected to D-Link via IPv4 and IPv6
Source: Microsoft

Troubleshooting DHCP

One good way to troubleshoot DHCP and DHCPv6 is to use a protocol analyzer, such as Wireshark. With an analyzer, you can compare a problematic boot sequence with the standard four-packet boot sequence. The analyzer can display the sequence of messages that occurs on a network, which then may be compared to the usual, prescribed sequence.

To determine what address a Windows Server 2008, Windows Vista, or Windows 7 device was assigned, run the Ipconfig utility. This tool, shown in Figure 7-31, displays the current IP addresses.

Figure 7-31 Output of Ipconfig utility on Windows 7 client
Source: Microsoft

You can release and/or renew an IPv4 or IPv6 address using the following commands:

- *ipconfig /release*—Releases the IP address for the specified adapter
- *ipconfig /renew*—Renews the IP address for the specified adapter
- *ipconfig /release6*—Releases the IPv6 address for the specified adapter
- *ipconfig /renew6*—Renews the IPv6 address for the specified adapter

Another important troubleshooting technique is to inspect the server configuration and to check all the related settings. For Dynamic Address Pool settings, pay particular attention to the starting address(es) for the managed pool(s), pool range(s), subnet masks, and gateway address. For Static Address Pool settings, subnet masks and gateway addresses are likewise important, but you'll also want to double-check static IP assignments and related MAC addresses. Unless all of these are correct, DHCP won't work properly, if at all. Routine testing after initial setup should flush out most of these problems pretty quickly, however.

Finally, check your DHCP server documentation for information about log files. Many DHCP servers maintain voluminous log files that provide lots of useful detail about normal server operation as well as problems, errors, or unexpected events. If you check the DHCP log file documentation for Windows, you'll see that it includes information about where the log files reside (C:\Windows\System32\DHCP on DHCP servers) and what kinds of event IDs are collected therein. You should also see log files for both IPv4 and IPv6; the IPv6 log files include "V6" in the filename. DHCP log files for other DHCP servers, such as for UNIX or Linux varieties, vary somewhat but generally address the same issues and concerns. Table 7-11 shows the typical DHCP event IDs you're likely to encounter in a Windows DHCP log file.

Event ID	Explanation
00	The log was started.
01	The log was stopped.
02	The log was temporarily paused because of low disk space.
10	A new IP address was leased to a client.
11	A lease was renewed by a client.
12	A lease was released by a client.
13	An IP address was found to be in use on the network.
14	A lease request could not be satisfied because the scope's address pool was exhausted.
15	A lease was denied.
20	A BOOTP address was leased to a client.

Table 7-11   **Windows DHCP Log File Event IDs**
© Cengage Learning 2013

Individual events appear as records or lines of text in the log file, with fields in the following sequence:

- *ID*—Event ID number
- *Date*—Date event was recorded
- *Time*—Time event was recorded
- *Description*—Description of event type (e.g., ID 11 is described as "Renew")
- *IP Address*—Numeric IP address of DHCP client
- *Host Name*—Domain name for DHCP client
- *Mac Address*—MAC address for DHCP client

The "Analyze DHCP Server Log Files" TechNet article applies to Windows Server 2008 and lists additonal DHCP logging event information. The article is available at *technet.microsoft.com/en-us/library/dd183591%28WS.10%29.aspx*.

Here again, careful examination of the log file will often show when errors or problems occurred and can quickly pinpoint causes and suggest solutions. Consult your DHCP server documentation for such details, where applicable. The key is to obtain and compare as many sources of information as possible and to learn to recognize typical problems and errors as they occur.

Chapter Summary

- DHCP provides a way for computers to obtain usable, unique IP addresses and necessary TCP/IP configurations even when no IP addresses were assigned to those machines. As long as a DHCP server or relay is available on the cable segment where an initial DHCP Request message is broadcast, the DHCP service makes it easy and automatic to include computers on a TCP/IP network.

- From the administrative side, DHCP makes it easy to define and manage pools of IP addresses, which Microsoft calls a scope when referring to a set of IP addresses under DHCP's management and a superscope when referring to a collection of IP address scopes.

- DHCP's origins lie in an earlier TCP/IP Application layer protocol called BOOTP, which was used to enable diskless workstations to boot remotely across a network. Basic BOOTP and DHCP formats are entirely compatible, so by configuring a router to forward BOOTP, it also forwards DHCP packets.

- DHCP supports two types of address allocation: manual, in which administrators directly manage addresses, and dynamic, in which addresses are allocated with explicit expiration intervals called leases. Many of DHCP's functions and messages relate to obtaining, renewing, and releasing dynamic address leases, primarily for client machines.

- When a DHCP client starts, it begins the process of DHCP Discovery, during which the client receives an IP address and lease. In the middle of the lease interval, the client starts a lease renewal process to determine if it can keep the address past the lease time. If not, the client releases its IP address and starts the Discovery process over again.

- DHCP supports a wide variety of message types and options, but only Message Type 53 (DHCP Message) is mandatory for any given DHCP message.

- Because DHCP can ferry a surprisingly large range of configuration information (including all kinds of network services, such as e-mail and NetBIOS over TCP/IP), the protocol makes use of several message options.

- A protocol analyzer is especially effective when diagnosing DHCP and DHCPv6 difficulties, particularly those related to the DHCP/DHCPv6 boot sequence. Server status information and DHCP/DHCPv6 logs are likewise useful when troubleshooting DHCP services.

- Clients supporting IPv6 have new operations for address autoconfiguration, relaying on network routers and/or DHCPv6 servers to provide global unicast addresses, but an IPv6 node will always be able to communicate on-link with their link-local addresses.

- DHCPv6 operates much like DHCP for IPv4, but there are differences in message types, options available, and so forth.

- DHCPv6 can be used either as stand-alone address configuration to clients or in combination with SLAAC; note that at this time there is no provision for default gateway configuration in a DHCPv6 server, but that could change in the future.

- DHCPv6 operates with multicast messages, as there are no broadcast messages in IPv6.

- DHCPv6 is a completely new service, compared to DHCP's origins.

Key Terms

address pool   A contiguous range of numeric IP addresses, defined by a starting IP address and an ending IP address, to be managed by a DHCP server.

address scope   *See* scope.

DHCP client   The software component on a TCP/IP client, usually implemented as part of the protocol stack software, that issues address requests, lease renewals, and other DHCP messages to a DHCP server.

DHCP Discovery   The four-packet sequence used to obtain an IP address, lease time, and configuration parameters. The four-packet sequence includes the Discover, Offer, Request, and Acknowledgment packets.

DHCP options   Parameter and configuration information that defines what the DHCP client is looking for. Two special options—0:Pad and 255:End—are used for housekeeping. Pad simply ensures that the DHCP fields end on an acceptable boundary, and End denotes that there are no more options listed in the packet.

DHCP relay agent   A special-purpose piece of software built to recognize and redirect DHCP Discovery packets to known DHCP servers.

DHCP Reply   A DHCP message that contains a reply from a server to a client's DHCP Request message.

DHCP Request   A DHCP message from a client to a server requesting some kind of service; such messages occur only after a client receives an IP address and can use unicast packets (not broadcasts) to communicate with a specific DHCP server.

DHCP server   The software component that runs on a network server of some kind, responsible for managing TCP/IP address pools or scope and for interacting with clients to provide them with IP addresses and related TCP/IP configuration data on demand.

discovery broadcast   The process of discovering a DHCP server by broadcasting a DHCP Discover packet onto the local network segment. If a DHCP server does not exist on the local segment, a relay agent must forward the request directly to the remote DHCP server. If no local DHCP server or relay agent exists, the client cannot obtain an IP address using DHCP.

dynamic address lease   A type of DHCP address lease in which each address allocation comes with an expiration timeout so address leases must be renewed before expiration occurs or a new address will have to be allocated instead. Used primarily for client machines that do not require stable IP address assignments.

lease expiration time   The end of the lease time. If a DHCP client does not renew or rebind its address by the lease expiration time, it must release the address and reinitialize.

lease time   The amount of time that a DHCP client may use an assigned DHCP address.

manual address lease   A type of DHCP address lease wherein the administrator takes full responsibility for managing address assignments (using DHCP only as a repository for such assignment data).

Message Type   A required option that indicates the purpose of a DHCP packet; the eight message types are Discover, Offer, Request, Decline, Acknowledge, Negative Acknowledge (NAK), Release, and Inform.

preferred address   An address the DHCP client remembers from the previous network session. Most DHCP client implementations maintain a list of the last IP addresses they used and indicate a preference for the last-used address. This adds a somewhat static view of the network addressing system, but there is no guarantee the clients can continue to receive the same address each time they boot. In IPv6, the term *preferred address* refers to the one address among the many that may be associated with the same interface, whose use by higher-layer protocols is unrestricted.

rebinding process   The process of contacting any DHCP server through the use of a broadcast to obtain renewal of an address.

reinitialize   To begin the standard DHCP Discovery sequence anew after failure of the renewal and rebinding processes. During the reinitializing phase, the DHCP client has no IP address and uses 0.0.0.0 as its source address.

relay agent process   A process or execution thread that executes on a local host (which may be on a Windows workstation, server, or router) and forwards DHCP broadcasts as unicasts directed to a remote DHCP server for clients operating outside a DHCP broadcast domain.

release   To deactivatie an IP address on a client by formally sending a DHCP Release packet (MessageType 0x07) to the DHCP server. If a client shuts down without sending the Release packet, the DHCP server maintains the lease until expiration.

renewal process   The process of renewing the IP address for continued use. By default, a DHCP client begins the renewal process halfway between the lease grant and the lease expiration time.

scope   Defined by Microsoft as a group of addresses that can be assigned by a Microsoft DHCP server. Other vendors refer to this as an address pool or address range.

stateful autoconfiguration   A method for providing IPv6 address assignments by a DHCPv6-enabled server to requesting hosts on a network.

stateless autoconfiguration   A method allowing nodes to automatically configure an IPv6 address without manual configuration, minimal configuration of an on-link router, and no DHCPv6 server.

superscope   Defined by Microsoft as a collection of IP address scopes, as managed by any single DHCP server. Other vendors refer to this as a collection of address pools or address ranges.

Windows clustering   Windows Server technology that enables automatic restoration of services to an alternate server upon detection of a primary server failure.

Review Questions

1. DHCP manages only IP addresses. True or False?

2. When a node receives a Router Advertisement, what flag is required to be set to "on" in order for the node to perform SLAAC?

   a. A flag

   b. M flag

   c. R flag

   d. S flag

3. Which of the following terms describe a single group of IP addresses managed by DHCP? (Choose all that apply.)

   a. address pool

   b. address group

   c. address scope

   d. address superscope

4. An IPv6 address on a host moves from the preferred state to the deprecated state when which of the following events occurs?

   a. The preferred lifetime timer expires and the valid lifetime timer is valid.

   b. The preferred lifetime timer is valid and the valid lifetime timer is expired.

   c. The preferred lifetime timer expires and the valid lifetime timer is expired

   d. The preferred lifetime timer is valid and the valid lifetime timer is valid.

5. Which of the following represent a valid DHCP software component? (Choose all that apply.)

   a. DHCP client

   b. DHCP resolver

   c. DHCP server

   d. DHCP primary master

   e. DHCP secondary master

   f. DHCP relay

6. Which of the following represent a valid enhancement found in DHCPv6 or a valid related enhancement that is part of the basic IPv6 environment? (Choose all that apply.)

   a. IPv6 interfaces support multiple addresses in DHCPv6.

   b. IPv6 nodes must listen for address updates to support automatic renumbering.

   c. Nodes under IPv6 can obtain locally functioning addresses without any interaction with DHCP.

   d. DHCPv6 servers and routers can be configured to send advertisements in authenticated form.

   e. DHCPv6 can be set up to dynamically update DNS records.

7. When a DHCP server is not available on the same cable segment as a DHCP client, which techniques permit the DHCP client's initial DHCP broadcast requests to be serviced? (Choose all that apply.)

   a. None do. A DHCP server must be available on any cable segment or broadcast domain where a DHCP client resides.

   b. Installing a DHCP relay agent on any cable segment or broadcast domain where a DNS server is not directly attached.

   c. Installing a remote DHCP agent on any cable segment or broadcast domain where a DNS server is not directly attached.

   d. Configuring internal routers to forward BOOTP from cable segments or broadcast domains where DHCP clients reside to segments where DHCP servers reside.

   e. Configuring internal routers to forward BOOTP from cable segments or broadcast domains where DHCP servers reside to segments where DHCP clients reside.

8. How does a DHCP relay forward the DHCP server's reply to a client's initial address request?

   a. It uses a temporary IP address created for the requester.

   b. It uses the IP address offered to the requester.

   c. It uses the MAC layer address for the requester.

   d. It broadcasts a reply, for which the requester listens.

9. The Neighbor Discovery protocol in IPv6 supports stateless autoconfiguration of attached nodes. True or False?

10. When a node creates a link-local address, which of the following methods for creating an Interface ID can be appended to the well-known link-local prefix FE80::?

    a. a 64-bit randomly generated address

    b. the 64-bit MAC address

    c. the 64-bit modified EUI-64 address

    d. a 64-bit cryptographically generated address

11. Which issue explains why DHCP was not traditionally used to manage server and router addresses?

    a. Routers and servers require static IP address assignments.

    b. DHCP is a client-only solution.

    c. DHCP may only be updated manually, so it's not suitable for servers or routers.

    d. Servers and routers often depend on DNS, which must be manually updated when addresses change.

12. Which of the following types of machines is best suited for dynamic IP address assignment? (*Hint*: Some kinds of machines require persistent IP addresses to remain easy to find on the Internet; others do not.)

    a. servers

    b. routers

    c. clients

    d. none of the above

13. Which activities occur during the process of IPv6 autoconfiguration? (Choose all that apply.)

    a. The node checks its calculated link-local address with a Neighbor Solicitation to make sure that address is not already in use.

    b. The node makes a Router Solicitation to obtain Router Advertisements from attached routers.

    c. The node attempts to calculate a link-local address by prepending its EUI-64 interface ID with the well-known link-local prefix.

    d. Once a DHCP server is identified, it always provides all necessary information to complete the autoconfiguration process.

    e. all of the above

14. Which of the following UDP port numbers are associated with DHCP?

    a. 57 and 58

    b. 67 and 68

    c. 77 and 78

    d. 116 and 117

15. Which of the following best explain why a DHCP Discover packet is broadcast to the local network segment? (Choose all that apply.)

    a. because the address of a DHCP server is not known

    b. because the client has no IP address and cannot send a unicast

    c. because the client's network address is unknown

    d. because the client's host address is unknown

16. What type of packet does a DHCP server send to a DHCP client in reply to a Discover packet?

    a. Reply packet

    b. Offer packet

    c. Release packet

    d. Renewal packet

17. Which flag is required to be set to "on" in a Router Advertisement for a host to send a request to a DHCPv6 server?

    a. A flag

    b. L flag

    c. N flag

    d. M flag

18. How does a DHCP client accept an offer from a DHCP server?

    a. by issuing a DHCP Accept packet

    b. by issuing a DHCP Request packet

    c. by issuing a DHCP Decline packet

    d. by issuing a DHCP Renewal packet

19. When a node sends a Router Solicitation, what type of message is it?

    a. an anycast message

    b. a broadcast message

    c. a unicast message

    d. a multicast message

20. On a Windows 7 host, if the host does not receive a Router Advertisement in response to its Router Solicitation, what is its next step in the IPv6 address autoconfiguration process?

    a. Stop the IPv6 address autoconfiguration process.

    b. Continue sending RS messages until it receives an RA.

    c. Send a DHCPv6 Solicit message.

    d. Autoconfigure a global-unicast address using the link-local prefix.

21. What kind of DHCP packet does the server send to the client to denote completion of the DHCP Discovery process?

    a. DHCP Accept packet

    b. DHCP Request packet

    c. DHCP Acknowledgment (ACK) packet

    d. DHCP Renewal packet

22. Which of the following UDP port numbers are associated with DHCPv6?

    a. 117 and 118

    b. 67 and 68

    c. 546 and 547

    d. 47 and 48

23. A Windows Server 2008 R2 DHCPv6 server can supply which of the following to a node in response to a DHCPv6 request? (Choose all that apply.)

    a. an IPv6 address

    b. an IPv6 default gateway address

    c. a DNS server IPv6 address

    d. the domain name

24. In a DHCPv6 server, IPv6 addresses are bound to which of the following:

    a. MAC address of the host

    b. link-local address of the host

    c. DUID of the host

    d. IPv4 address of the host

Hands-On Projects

HANDS-ON PROJECTS

Hands-On Projects 7-1 through 7-4 assume that you are working in a Windows Vista or Windows 7 Professional environment. For Hands-On Projects 7-1 through 7-3, you must have Wireshark for Windows software installed, and you need to have acquired the trace (data) files necessary to work through many of the Hands-On Projects in this book.

Hands-On Project 7-1: Examine a DHCP Boot Sequence

Time Required: 10 minutes

Objective: Examine a DHCP boot sequence on a Windows client computer.

Description: This project shows you the different options that a client provides and requests when requesting an IP address from a DHCP server. In addition, you explore the different messages exchanged between a client and DHCP server.

1. Click **Start**, point to **All Programs**, and then click **Wireshark**.
2. Click **File** on the menu bar, click **Open**, select the **ch07_DHCPboot.pkt**, and click **Open**.
3. Click **Packet #1** to open the decode window. Answer the following questions:

    a. What value is contained in the Client Identifier field?

    b. How can you verify that the Client Identifier value is the same as the client's hardware address?

    c. What is the host name?

    d. Can this client accept unicast replies during the boot process?

    e. List the option codes (and their names) used in this DHCP packet.

4. Click through each packet trace in the summary window until you locate the DHCP Offer, Request, and ACK packets. Examine each DHCP packet. This is a normal DHCP boot sequence.

5. Close the ch07_DHCPboot.pkt file. Leave Wireshark open.

Hands-On Project 7-2: Examine DHCP Renewal, Rebind, and Reinitialize Sequences

Time Required: 15 minutes

Objective: Review the process of DHCP renewal, rebind, and reinitialize sequences on an exisiting network-connected client.

Description: In this project, you will review the process of DHCP renewal, rebind, and reinitialize sequences by examining a trace file in Wireshark.

1. In Wireshark, click **File**, click **Open**, select the **ch07_DHCPlab.pkt,** and click **Open.**

2. Click **Packet #3** to populate the decode window. Answer the following questions about this packet:

   a. Does this DHCP client already have an IP address?

   b. What message type is used in this packet?

   c. What is the purpose of this packet?

   d. Does the client receive a reply to this packet?

   e. What DHCP process is the client performing at this time?

3. Click through the packet capture summary window until you see Packet #5. Answer the following questions about this packet:

   a. Does this DHCP client still have an IP address?

   b. What is the message type used in this packet?

   c. What is the primary difference between this packet and Packet #3?

   d. Does the client receive a reply to this packet?

   e. What DHCP process is the client performing at this time?

4. Click through the packet capture summary window until you see Packet #10. Answer the following questions about this packet:

   a. Does this DHCP client still have an IP address?

   b. What is the message type used in this packet?

   c. Does the client receive a reply to this packet?

   d. What DHCP process is the client performing at this time?

5. Examine the remaining DHCP packets in the trace file. Did the client get the requested IP address?

6. Close the ch07_DHCPlab.pkt file. Leave Wireshark open.

Hands-On Project 7-3: Examine a DHCPv6 Boot Sequence

Time Required: 15 minutes

Objective: Examine a DHCPv6 boot sequence on a Windows client computer.

Description: This project shows you the different options that a client provides and requests when requesting an IPv6 address from a DHCPv6 server. In addition, you explore the different messages exchanged between a client and a DHCPv6 server.

1. In Wireshark, click **File**, click **Open**, select the **ch07_DHCPv6boot.pcap**, and click **Open**.
2. Click **Packet #4** to populate the decode window. Answer the following questions about this packet:

    a. Does this DHCPv6 client have an IPv6 global unicast address?

    b. What message type is used in this packet?

    c. What is the host name? (*Hint*: Look for domain.)

    d. Does the client receive a reply to this packet?

    e. What DHCPv6 process is the client performing at this time?

3. Click through each packet trace in the summary window until you locate the DHCPv6 Solicit, Advertise, Request, and Reply packets. Examine each DHCPv6 packet. This is a normal DHCPv6 boot sequence.

    a. What is the packet number where the DHCPv6 provides the final approval for an IPv6 address, and what is that IPv6 address assigned to the client?

4. Which packet is the DAD verification process for the client's global unicast address?
5. Close Wireshark.

Hands-On Project 7-4: View and Manage DHCP and DHCPv6 Lease Information

Time Required: 15 minutes

Objective: View and manage DHCP and DHCPv6 lease information on a Windows computer.

Description: In this project, you will view and manage DHCP and DHCPv6 lease information on a computer running the Windows Vista or Windows 7 operating system. This assumes that your computer is connected to a network that supports DHCP and DHCPv6 servers.

1. To open a command prompt window on the Windows desktop, click **Start**, type **cmd** in the Open text box, and then click **OK**.
2. To view current DHCP/DHCPv6 lease information for the machine, type **ipconfig /all** at the command prompt, and then press **Enter**. You will see a display similar to that in Figure 7-32; notice that the listed information indicates that DHCP and autoconfiguration are enabled, and it provides the address of the DHCP server. You will also see the DHCPv6 DUID number and the DHCPv6 Client DUID number.
3. To renew your current IPv4 address lease, type **ipconfig /renew** in the command window. Type **ipconfig /all** to observe how the lease information changes.

4. To force release of your current IPv4 address, type **ipconfig /release**. Type **ipconfig /all** to observe how lease information changes.

5. To renew your current IPv6 address lease, type **ipconfig /renew6** in the command window. Type **ipconfig /all** to observe how the lease information changes.

6. To force release of your current IPv6 address, type **ipconfig /release6**. Type **ipconfig /all** to observe how lease information changes.

7. Type **exit** at the command line to close the command prompt window and end this exercise.

Figure 7-32 Sample output of ipconfig utility on Windows 7 client
Source: Microsoft

Case Projects

Case Project 7-1: DHCP Design/Implementation

You are a network administrator for a large bagel manufacturer that has 32 bakeries located throughout the United States, United Kingdom, and Switzerland. Your company wants to move to a DHCP network design using private IP addresses. Each bakery consists of only three computers, but all the bakeries communicate with the corporate headquarters in Yonkers, New York. Design a DHCP solution for these locations.

Case Project 7-2: Static/Dynamic IPv4 Address Issues

You consult for various large networking companies. One of your clients reports that laptop users cannot connect to the network in the evening. They know the network is set up for DHCP addressing; they have, however, configured a static address for the laptop. The address is within the valid range of IP addresses defined for the network. Determine the cause of this problem.

Case Project 7-3: Troubleshooting DHCP Address Problems

Your design company installed two Microsoft DHCP servers—one on each of the two floors of your office building in Vienna, Austria. When your clients on the lower floors try to boot onto the network, they get a message that the IP address is in use. Determine the cause of the problem and recommend a solution for this network.

Case Project 7-4: DHCPv6 Design/Implementation

You are a network administrator for a large bagel manufacturer that has 32 bakeries located throughout the United States, United Kingdom, and Switzerland. It is one year after you designed and implemented DHCP for IPv4, and now you must design and implement a DHCPv6 solution for an IPv6 rollout. Because you have a DHCP services system in place, what are the key components that must be researched to verify whether the current infrastructure will support the IPv6 project?

chapter 8

Name Resolution on IP Networks

After reading this chapter and completing the exercises, you will be able to:

- Describe the characteristics of the various name resolution protocols, such as WINS, DNS, and LLMNR
- Explain how name resolution works in IPv4 networks, including the DNS database structure, the DNS namespace, DNS database records, the delegation of DNS authority, and the different types of DNS servers, and explain how name servers work
- Describe how name resolution works on IPv6 networks, including the use of AAAA records, how forward and reverse mapping works, the use of source and destination address selection, how rules are organized by the source and destination address algorithms, and the end-to-end address selection process
- Explain how name resolution is supported in Windows operating systems, including how host files are used, the function of the DNS server service and DNS dynamic updates, how Windows manages source and destination address selection, LLMNR support, working with ipv6-literal.net names, and the use of the peer name resolution protocol
- Describe the common sources for name resolution failure and use common name resolution troubleshooting tools such as NBTSTAT, NETSTAT, AND NSLOOKUP

If there is one TCP/IP Application layer service that provides the glue that ties together the entire Internet, it's the Domain Name System (DNS). That's because DNS provides the essential ability to convert symbolic domain names, such as *microsoft.com* and *course.com*, into corresponding numeric IP addresses, such as 207.46.130.108 and 69.32.148.124. Without that translation service, we human beings would have to remember numeric IP addresses for all our Internet destinations. DNS also supports other services, such as e-mail, by translating addresses of the form *etittel@edtittel.com* into the IP addresses for the proper server that can handle such traffic. Without DNS, you can safely speculate that the Internet would not be nearly as successful or as easy to use.

DNS is itself something of a technological tour de force. The combination of all DNS databases everywhere represents the entire mapping of all valid domain names to corresponding valid IP addresses, and these databases are located all over the Internet. Each individual database runs independently and, in some sense, is responsible for, as well as controls, the data it contains.

Despite its widely distributed and decentralized structure, DNS works very well and provides a robust, reliable, and stable foundation upon which Internet addressing depends. This is a profound validation of the "Internet model," where thousands of independent domains thrive and prosper by agreeing to a common set of rules and behaviors, where information sharing succeeds phenomenally without requiring firmly established, centralized controls or governance. By the time you finish reading this chapter, you should have a much keener appreciation of what a phenomenal accomplishment DNS represents.

Understanding Name Resolution Fundamentals

Name resolution is the process by which a computer maps the human-readable names people give to devices to the numeric addresses that computers use to identify those devices. In order for people to identify computers in a way that is understandable, human beings create a namespace or name architecture that is used in a networked system to describe how names are given to and utilized for machines. The process of assigning names to specific devices within a name architectured system is called name registration. The use of a namespace is for the convenience of human beings, but it requires a name resolution process so that when people identify a computer such as a Web server by a name (such as *www.google.com*), internetworking devices have a way of resolving that name into an IP address (such as 74.125.127.104), which they use to communicate with the device.

Before a network device can send an IP packet to its destination, name-to-address resolution must occur so that the source device can correctly address the packet. The source device initiates a process whereby it consults a resource in order to discover the address of the named device. There are three general methods used in the name resolution process.

One method is for a computer to consult a name-to-address file or table on its hard drive. Unless this file is continually and dynamically updated, it is very likely that the desired mapping will not be present. Static name tables that must be manually updated are only useful in very small local networks that experience little or no change in their namespaces.

A second method is for a computer to send a network broadcast stating that it is trying to send a packet to a specific computer name and requesting the computer's IP address. If the destination device receives this broadcast, it will send back its address to the sender so that name resolution can take place and the packet can be sent. This method is effective on local networks but does not help if the destination device is on another subnet of the same network or on a remote network, such as a computer trying to connect to a server located in a different part of the world.

The third method is for the source computer to contact a server that maintains a large and dynamically updated database of name-to-address entries that will provide the lookup service for the source device, send the correct address mapping, and allow the sending computer to transmit its packet. This method allows a computer to resolve names for virtually any networked device in the world, as long as that device is accessible.

Network Name Resolution Protocols

Name resolution has become a lot more sophisticated since the days when technicians and administrators manually added entries to an /etc/hosts file on a UNIX system. Back in the 1970s, ARPANET, the ancestor of the modern Internet, was small enough so that all the required name resolution data could be managed on each device in the hosts.txt file. However, as ARPANET grew, it became rather tiresome to add and remove information by hand for each computer, and so more automated methods were required. Name resolution on today's medium-to-enterprise-level networks and on the Internet would be impossible without modern name resolution protocols.

Name resolution protocols are procedures that govern the rules and conventions used in manually and dynamically providing for name resolution systems in a networked environment. These protocols provide the definitions and mechanisms involved in client and server applications that are used in name resolution. The communication behaviors of name resolution client and server programs are specified as well as where and how each protocol operates on the OSI model.

NetBIOS over TCP/IP

NetBIOS over TCP/IP (NetBT or NBT) was implemented to allow Windows 2000 and Windows XP computers to communicate with devices and share resources on the network running older Windows operating systems. In Windows 7, the default NetBIOS setting is to use the NetBIOS setting provided via DHCP. If a Windows 7 computer uses a static IPv4 address, it will automatically use NetBIOS over TCP/IP.

Broadly speaking, NetBIOS works by maintaining a list of unique names assigned to network resources; providing the services to establish, defend, and resolve these names; and carrying the necessary communications between applications that make use of these network resources. Named resources include files, services (processes), users, computers, and Windows workgroups and domains. NetBIOS ensures that names are accurate, current, and unique, and it provides the APIs with access to these resources. An application makes a call to the NetBIOS API to access a named resource or discover the names of available resources. Depending on the precise configuration of NetBIOS on the particular machine, NetBIOS may take a variety of steps to resolve the name to an address. It can then send messages to query the named resource, or it can open and maintain a session.

Traditionally, for most Windows clients, NetBIOS was the native method used to access network resources and share their own resources with others. A network with Windows 2000 or clients and servers didn't require NetBIOS. In practice, however, there are still some networks that require NetBIOS to share resources with clients.

NetBIOS has two serious drawbacks. The most serious is that it does not have a network component to its namespace. NetBIOS names are only names, not addresses. This differs from IP addresses, which have a host portion and a network portion. Because NetBIOS names only have a host portion, they are considered nonroutable. (Another way of saying this is that NetBIOS uses a flat namespace.) IP, by contrast, uses a hierarchical namespace, such as server.domain.com. NetBIOS requires TCP/IP or some other network-aware protocol to be useful across network boundaries.

The second drawback is less serious but seems even more intractable. NetBIOS is a chatty protocol, constantly sending short messages for a wide variety of purposes. This characteristic, which was trivial on the 20- to 40-machine networks of the 1980s, can be a significant weakness on networks with hundreds of clients, particularly when WAN connections are used for name resolution.

NBT is defined by RFC 1001, "Protocol Standard for a NetBIOS Service on a TCP/UDP Transport: Concepts and Methods," and RFC 1002, "Protocol Standard for NetBIOS Service on a TCP/UDP Transport: Detailed Specifications." NBT was implemented to correct the shortcomings of NetBIOS. NBT is typically used on networks that do not have access to a DNS server, are not operating in a domain, and are using older versions of Windows and Microsoft applications and services. Under these circumstances, NBT allows a computer to browse the network and locate other computers and services. It also allows file sharing across the network and provides name resolution services.

If the Windows computers on your network require NBT and if the device providing DHCP, such as a DSL modem, does not have a configuration setting that can provide NBT, you may have to manually enable NBT on your Windows computer. This task is performed in the Internet Protocol Version 4 (TCP/IPv4) Properties box. On the General tab, click the Advanced button. On the Advanced TCP/IP Settings box, click the WINS tab. And then, under NetBIOS setting, select the Enable NetBIOS over TCP/IP radio button.

On the vast majority of today's networks, it will be unnecessary to enable NBT, given that DNS use is ubiquitous, even in small office/home office (SOHO) environments. Also, the use of Windows 7 and modern Microsoft applications and services is rapidly rendering NBT unnecessary. NBT is not supported in IPv6, and there is no method of configuring the use of NBT in the properties of an IPv6 protocol for a network adapter.

WINS

Windows Internet Name Service (WINS) is a service that resolves NetBIOS names to IP addresses in routed networks. This requires the use of a WINS server on the network, such as Windows Server 2003. A Windows client computer must be configured to look for the IP address of one or more WINS servers on the network. WINS is ideally used in networks that require NBT for name resolution, which typically means a network using older versions of Windows or a mix of modern and older Windows computers.

The use of a WINS server on a network automates dynamic name resolution. For instance, when a DHCP server changes the IP address of a WINS-enabled network node, the WINS data for the computer is updated on the WINS server database. This reduces the need for nodes to issue IPv4 requests for NetBIOS name resolution.

If a Windows network node requires NetBIOS name resolution, it will first check its local NetBIOS computer name. It then looks at its local NetBIOS name cache for remote names. If the name-to-address mapping isn't found, the node forwards its NetBIOS query to the primary WINS server configured in the IPv4 properties of its network adapter. If the primary WINS server does not respond, it will query any other WINS servers it is configured for, if they exist. Only if no WINS server responds will the node send a broadcast NetBIOS query to the local subnet. Finally, if these attempts have been unsuccessful, the node will check its LMHOSTS file and then its HOST file for the mapping.

WINS servers rely on direct communications (unicasts) between themselves and the clients (end nodes) attempting to register and resolve NetBIOS names. WINS clients configured as p-nodes, m-nodes, or h-nodes may attempt to register or resolve NetBIOS names by contacting the WINS server(s) configured for their use. When interacting with the WINS server, all three node types behave the same way.

WINS-enabled clients can be configured to use more than one WINS server. Older WINS clients could only be configured to use one primary and one secondary WINS server. Windows 2000 and Windows XP clients can be configured to use 11 secondary WINS servers. The client attempts to use the primary WINS server first. (This is the first in the list, if you are configuring the client from the Advanced TCP/IP Settings dialog box.) If the primary WINS server does not respond, the client uses any secondary WINS server(s) configured for it, using them in the order listed in the Advanced TCP/IP Settings dialog box. You should avoid using more than one or two secondary WINS servers, because the WINS client will query each WINS server in its list, attempting name resolution until the list is exhausted. This can cause an unnecessary increase in network traffic.

When a node, user, or process with a NetBIOS name signs on to the network or starts up, it attempts to register its name. If it is configured to use WINS, it sends a Name Registration Request packet to the WINS server. If the name is in the proper form for NetBIOS names and no record for that name already exists in the WINS server's database, the WINS server sends a positive Name Registration Reply packet to the node and enters the name in its database. The WINS server's response includes the TTL (six days by default) for the name. The node attempts to renew this name at half the TTL value—three days' time if it received the default TTL. If a name is not renewed within the TTL, the name is released and made available for use by the next entity attempting to register it.

If the name already exists in the database, the WINS server sends a **Wait Acknowledgment (WACK)** to the node attempting to register. This message acknowledges the receipt of the Name Registration Request packet without either granting or denying it, but asks the node to wait. At the same time, the WINS server attempts to contact the registered owner of the name to see if the name is still in use. If the owner responds, then the WINS server sends a negative Name Registration Reply packet to the node attempting to register the name. If the registered owner does not respond, then the WINS server grants the name to the node attempting to register, sending it a positive Name Registration Reply packet. (In earlier versions of WINS, the server responded to an apparent name conflict by asking the registering node itself to send a challenge to the name holder.)

In some circumstances, the WINS server may issue either a Name Conflict Demand packet or a Name Release Demand packet to a name holder or a node, attempting to register a name in conflict. These so-called "demand" packets are requests that have no response associated with them. They are treated as imperatives, and a node must comply. The Name Conflict Demand packet tells a node that its name is in conflict. The node notifies the user of this situation, and the node eventually releases the name. The Name Release Demand packet tells the receiving node to remove the name immediately from its name table. Typically, these types of packets are only sent when, for example, you are reconfiguring your network and names and addresses are being assigned and reassigned in rapid succession.

WINS servers support a special name registration regime called *burst mode*. When a large network first comes to life at the start of the workday, for example, many hundreds or thousands of Name Registration Requests may pour in within a few seconds. To prevent the WINS server from being overwhelmed by a sudden spike in utilization, WINS servers can go into burst mode. In burst mode, the server responds to every Name Registration Request packet with a positive Name Registration Reply without attempting to resolve any conflicts. The trick is this: It includes in each positive response a small TTL, and it gives a slightly different TTL to each node. Because the nodes will attempt to renew their names in half the TTL, name conflict resolutions can be deferred until the spike passes. In this way, the server itself can fan out the queue, spreading the workload over a longer time period.

You can change the queue size that triggers burst mode handling (it's set to 500 registrations by default) in the WINS Server Console. WINS servers have a maximum capacity of 25,000 name resolution/refresh queries. For example, if the burst queue is set for 500 entries and more than 500 requests arrive, the next 100 WINS name registration requests will be responded to with a TTL of 5 minutes. Each additional 100 requests will add another 5 minutes to the TTL, up to a maximum of 50 minutes. If WINS client registration requests continue to arrive at burst levels, the next set of 100 queries is answered with the starting TTL of 5 minutes, repeating the entire process until the maximum intake level is reached.

Linux and UNIX machines can also access NetBIOS resources using the **Samba** suite of applications for those operating systems. Samba uses SMB and NetBT for resource sharing on IP networks. When properly configured, Samba hosts can access resources through any WINS server, and Windows clients can access resources through the Samba server, all using a core of NetBT. Samba, like Linux, is Open Source software (it can be altered and redistributed without fees or restrictions).

As with the use of NBT, WINS services are largely unnecessary in modern Windows network environments because of the widespread use of DNS servers for name resolution. The versions of Windows that once utilized NBT and WINS are no longer supported by Microsoft and are considered obsolete. WINS is not supported in IPv6, and there is no method for configuring the IPv6 protocol properties of the network adapter of a Windows 7 computer to point to a WINS server. DNS is the primary method of name resolution for IPv6-enabled computers.

DNS

Domain Name System (DNS) is described by RFC 1034, "Domain Names - Concepts and Facilities," and RFC 1035, "Domain Names - Implementation and Specification." Although DNS is thought of as both a database containing resource records (RR) and a client/server application for requesting and receiving name-to-address mappings, this section focuses on the protocol viewpoint. DNS is a system used for naming computers and network services and using a hierarchical structure for organizing those objects into domains. DNS is the commonly used naming system for TCP/IP networks, including the Internet, and is used to locate network objects by their human-readable names. When a name resolution query for a computer or service name is submitted by a network node to a DNS server, the server performs a lookup in its database and returns the IP address of the object to the requesting network node if the name-to-address mapping exists in its local database. The network node can then send its message to the computer or service using the correct IP address.

RFC 3596 describes the DNS extensions for IPv6. IPv6 extensions are required because applications using the current implementation of DNS expect address queries to return 32-bit addresses. IPv6 uses a 128-bit address space, which is completely out of scope for a network DNS client using IPv4. To support IPv6 addresses in DNS, the required extensions are:

- A resource record type that will map a domain or computer name to an IPv6 address
- Domains defined to support lookups based on addresses
- Queries under the current DNS system conducting additional processing for both IPv4 and IPv6 addresses

IPv6 extensions for DNS do not create a new DNS version and are designed to be compatible with existing applications, with continuing support for IPv4 addresses. DNS is a vast topic, and more complexity is added because of the implementations for both IPv4 and IPv6 environments. DNS and IPv6 extensions for DNS will be discussed in greater detail later in this chapter in the sections "Name Resolution in IPv4 Networks" and "Name Resolution in IPv6 Networks."

LLMNR

Link-Local Multicast Name Resolution (LLMNR), which is defined by RFC 4795, is a protocol based on the DNS packet format. LLMNR allows IPv4 and IPv6 network nodes to perform name resolution for other devices connected to the same local link. Windows Server 2008, Windows Vista, and Windows 7 all support LLMNR. Use of LLMNR is limited to a single network segment because this protocol is not designed to cross router boundaries. The goal of this protocol is to provide name resolution services in environments where DNS cannot be used.

LLMNR is ideal for smaller networks and other environments that don't or can't provide DNS name resolution and that require name resolution for both IPv4 and IPv6 nodes. The protocol uses a simple request/reply exchange to resolve computer names to IPv4 or IPv6 addresses. On IPv4-only networks, Windows computers can use NetBT to provide name resolution services on a local link, but this is ineffective with IPv6 nodes.

There is a typical exchange involved in using LLMNR:

1. The LLMNR sending node transmits an LLMNR query to the link-scope multicast address.
2. The responding node answers the query, but only if it is authoritative for the name in the query. It responds with a unicast UDP packet to the sending node.
3. When the sending node receives the response, it processes the information and completes the name-to-address resolution.

LLMNR messages can also be sent using TCP, but TCP LLMNR messaging is not supported by Windows Vista.

For IPv4 nodes, the link-scope multicast address is 224.0.0.252. Nodes listening for this address instruct their Ethernet adapters to listen for frames containing the 33-33-00-01-00-03 destination multicast address. For IPv6 nodes, the address is FF02:0:0:0:0:0:1:3 (FF02::1:3). Both IPv4 and IPv6 link-scope multicast addresses are scoped so that multicast-enabled routers do not forward query messages off the local subnet. Nodes listening for this address instruct their Ethernet adapters to listen for frames containing the 01-00-5E-00-00-FC destination multicast address.

DNS servers are authoritative for a portion of the DNS namespace assigned to them, starting with the assigned name. LLMNR hosts, by comparison, are authoritative for only the names specifically assigned to them. For example, an LLMNR node that has been assigned the name tcpip4e example.com is not authoritative for all the other names that start with tcpip4e.example.com.

The LLMNR packet format is based on the DNS packet format specified in RFC 1035 for both queries and responses. LLMNR should send UDP queries and responses that are large enough to be transmitted across the local link without requiring fragmentation. The default packet size of 512 octets is used when the link MTU is uncertain. LLMNR implementations are required to accept UDP queries and responses up to the size of the smallest link MTU or 9194 octets. This is calculated from the size of an Ethernet jumbo frame, which is 9216 octets, minus 22 octets for the header. The LLMNR header format is similar but not identical to the DNS header format. Figure 8-1 illustrates the specific structure.

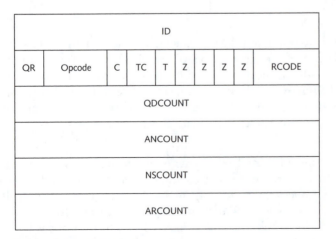

Figure 8-1 LLMNR header format
© Cengage Learning 2013

Name Resolution in IPv4 Networks

The impetus for DNS came early in the Internet's development. That's because early methods for resolving symbolic names (such as *microsoft.com* and *course.com*) to numeric IP addresses relied completely on static text files, called **HOSTS**. The files contained a list of every known host name, their possible aliases, and corresponding numeric IP addresses. This approach was simple to implement and worked on a small scale (under 500 hosts). By 1982, however, the ARPANET (the Internet's government-sponsored predecessor) had around 800 hosts, which made it increasingly difficult to maintain all the HOSTS files needed to translate any and all domain names to their corresponding IP addresses, and vice versa. (See RFC 2235 for a nice Internet timeline.)

When the number of known hosts (and domain names) exceeded 1000 in 1984, maintaining and distributing a current, static HOSTS file for the whole Internet turned into a time-consuming and difficult problem. System administrators began to balk at the requirement to perform daily downloads of increasingly large files, and the environment began growing and changing faster than static methods could handle gracefully.

Paul Mockapetris created the original RFCs for DNS—namely, RFCs 882 and 883—in response to this situation. He built the first reference implementation of DNS, which he named *JEEVES*. Kevin Dunlap wrote another implementation of DNS, called **BIND (Berkeley Internet Name Domain)**, for BSD UNIX version 4.3. Since then, BIND has become the most popular DNS implementation in use, and it's available for most versions of UNIX, as well as for Windows Server 2003 and Windows Server 2008.

From its very beginnings, DNS was designed as a distributed database of information about domain names and addresses. Individual portions of such databases are sometimes called **database segments,** meaning they include (or define) only a portion of the overall namespace that DNS can access for its clients.

DNS combines a number of virtues, such as allowing local control over domain name database segments. This lets servers maintain control over the domain names and related IP addresses that fall under their purview. DNS allows control over distinct portions of the global database for the Internet as a whole so that those individuals charged with managing specific domain names and addresses—a role called *administrative responsibility* in DNS-speak—can do their jobs without outside interference.

Data from all database segments is available everywhere. Because any host on the Internet can communicate with any other host on the Internet, name-to-address translations must be available for all hosts as well. DNS makes it possible to find valid domain names anywhere on the Internet and obtain the IP addresses to which those names correspond, among other services. This function is really what makes today's Internet possible.

Database information is robust and highly available. DNS is a key service on the Internet. Without name resolution, remote hosts can be difficult or impossible to access (as anyone who has encountered an occasional problem with DNS can attest). Thus, it is essential that DNS be both robust (resilient in the face of errors and failures) and highly available (quick to respond to requests for service). Support for replication permits multiple copies of the same data to be maintained on separate servers and thereby avoids the potential loss of access to data that a single-copy system would allow.

By incorporating this support, DNS is highly robust. By **caching** DNS data from one or more database segments on one or more DNS servers, DNS also provides a mechanism whereby it can attempt to satisfy name resolution requests locally before attempting them remotely, thereby greatly improving the speed of such name resolution. This does pose the interesting problem of update propagation, which becomes necessary when old name-to-address translations are replaced by new ones or as certain domain names are decommissioned and taken out of use. Basically, it takes time for such changes to propagate throughout the entire Internet's collection of DNS servers, where old references are likely to persist for some time after changes or deletions occur. That's why one should expect to wait 30 minutes up to 48 hours before changes made at an authoritative DNS server propagate into other DNS servers that may have cached copies of older information, and to reestablish consistency between an original DNS record and all its many copies elsewhere on the Internet.

Although DNS was designed nearly 20 years ago and has been subject to various enhancements and improvements, it still represents one of the most effective uses of **distributed database technology** in the world today. It may seem complex on first exposure, but its basic functions and capabilities are remarkably simple, especially considering the volume of data involved.

DNS Database Structure

The structure of the DNS database mirrors the structure of the domain namespace itself. This can best be understood as a **tree structure** (actually, it's an inverted tree because the **root** is usually drawn at the top of such a figure). In the domain namespace, all domains meet at the root, which is identified by a single period (.). Beneath the root, you find the top-level or primary domains. In the United States, these top-level domains usually take the form of the following three-letter codes:

- *.com*—Used primarily for commercial organizations
- *.edu*—Used for educational institutions, such as schools, colleges, and universities
- *.gov*—Used for the U.S. federal government
- *.mil*—Used for the U.S. military
- *.net*—Used primarily for service providers and online organizations
- *.org*—Used primarily for nonprofit organizations, associations, and professional societies

You also see domain names that end in two- or three-letter country codes, as specified in ISO Standard 3166. In this system, *.us* stands for United States, *.ca* for Canada, *.fr* for France, *.de* for Germany (Deutschland), and so forth. For a complete list of such codes, consult the listing at *www.iana.org/cctld/cctld-whois.htm*. Recently, this list of top-level domains has been greatly expanded to include new three-or-more-letter codes such as .biz, .info, .name, and so forth. (See the list at *www.internic.net/faqs/new-tlds.html* for more information.)

Organizational domain hierarchies sit beneath the top-level domain names. For small outfits, such as those in which your authors work—*edtittel.com* and the Protocol Analysis Institute, LLC—this might consist of single domain names, such as *edtittel.com* or *www.packet-level.com*.

For large organizations, such as IBM, you might see domain names with four or more components, each separated by a period, as in *houns54.clearlake.ibm.com* (please note that this domain name no longer resolves, but we kept the example because it works well and illustrates our point nicely). The components are described in the section titled "The DNS Namespace," which follows this section.

The tree diagram for *houns54.clearlake.ibm.com* is depicted in Figure 8-2. It's a bit of a misnomer to think of the leading entry in the domain name—for example, *www*, *ftp*, *nntp*, and so forth—as designating firmly and completely a specific server role (Web, FTP, newsfeed, and so forth). Although using such designations is common practice, it's by no means an explicit rule, as illustrated by many organizations that omit such designations from their Web server addresses (for example, *http://slashdot.org*).

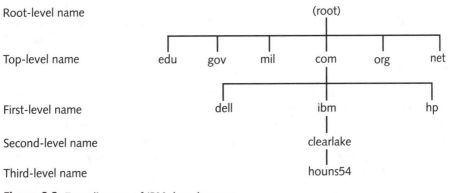

Figure 8-2 Tree diagram of IBM domain name
© Cengage Learning 2013

The entire domain space for the Internet fits beneath the root. Thirteen root name servers (named A.ROOT-SERVERS.NET., B.ROOT-SERVERS.NET., etc.) act as the top of the DNS hierarchy worldwide. They provide the ultimate source for all name lookups that can't be resolved through other means, as you'll learn later in this chapter.

Note that domain names start at the bottom of the tree and work their way up, and each name is followed by a period to delimit one part of the name from another. Thus, the tree in Figure 8-2 translates into *houns54.clearlake.ibm.com*. When you examine record data in DNS database files, you will see a final period at the end of each domain name, which refers to the root of the DNS hierarchy rather than the end of a statement of some kind. The final period is important when constructing **fully qualified domain names** (FQDNs). In fact, an FQDN consists of all elements of a domain name, in which each is followed by a period and the final period stands for the root of the DNS hierarchy itself.

One more essential ingredient is required for DNS to work—there must be at least one valid IP address to go along with each unique domain name. To this day, maintaining that name-to-address correspondence remains the most important function of DNS.

The DNS Namespace

Each location in the DNS namespace corresponds to some node in the graphical tree that depicts its structure, as shown in Figure 8-2. In fact, each node in that tree forms the root of a new subtree in the overall hierarchy, in which each such subtree represents a database segment (also known as a domain) in the overall domain namespace.

DNS gets its great power and flexibility from arbitrarily partitioning the tree and creating subtrees for database information, wherever needed. In fact, domains (such as *ibm.com*) can be broken into **subdomains** (such as *clearlake.ibm.com*), as needed. This permits local control over database segments; in essence, it's a form of **delegation of authority**. In addition, although a domain requires registration (for a fee) with a central authority, local administrators can create subdomains easily, at no charge.

By taking custodianship of database segments far enough down into the domain hierarchy, local administrative groups can take responsibility for all the names and addresses that they manage. The problem of managing a huge, complex namespace (the total Internet) becomes more controllable by breaking it up into many smaller subdomains, which basically function as containers for specific sets of DNS servers, addresses, users, and machines that are small enough for one or two network administrators to manage.

At a fundamental level, then, it also is important to recognize that any valid domain name ultimately resides within some specific DNS database. Although there can be multiple copies of such data, only one copy functions as a master and acts as the primary reference against which all changes must be applied. Only one specific server controls that entry. This concept is explained in greater detail in the next section, where you'll learn more about the kinds of records that can exist in a DNS database.

DNS Database Records

Data associated with domain names, address records, and other specific data of interest to the Domain Name System is stored on a DNS server in special database records called **resource records (RRs)**. Resource records are divided into four classes, of which only the Internet class is of interest to most users. (There are other classes that work only at MIT, and there's another special-purpose class that's no longer used.)

Within the Internet class, records are in a named taxonomy of record types, as documented in pages 13 through 21 of RFC 1035. The nine most commonly used RR types are listed in alphabetical order and explained below:

- **Address (A) record**—Stores domain name-to-IP address translation data.
- **Canonical name (CNAME) record**—Used to create aliases.
- **Host information (HINFO) record**—Stores descriptive information about a specific Internet host.
- **Mail exchange (MX) record**—Used to route SMTP-based e-mail on the Internet and identify the IP address for a domain's master e-mail server.
- **Name server (NS) record**—Used to identify all DNS servers in a domain.
- **Pointer (PTR) record**—Stores IP address-to-domain name translation data and supports the operation known as a **reverse DNS lookup**.

- **Start of Authority (SOA) record**—Identifies the name server that is authoritative for a specific **DNS database segment;** in other words, it identifies the master DNS server for a specific domain or subdomain.

- **Service location (SRV) record**—Sometimes simply called a Service record, this is designed to provide information about available services and used in the Windows Active Directory environment to map the name of a service to the name of a server that offers such service. Active Directory (AD) clients and domain controllers use SRV records to determine IP addresses for (other) domain controllers. This record type is described in RFC 2052.

- **Text (TXT) record**—Used to add arbitrary text information to a DNS database, usually for documentation.

- **Well-known services (WKS) record**—Lists the IP-based services (Telnet, FTP, HTTP, and so forth) that an Internet host can supply.

In the sections that follow, you'll learn more about these individual record types and how they are used, including snippets of data from some actual DNS database files. As is the case with so many other UNIX-derived data files, DNS database files consist entirely of text-only (ASCII) data and are, therefore, easy to inspect using the text editor of your choice.

Delegating DNS Authority

As a company the size of IBM or an organization the size of the U.S. Air Force might readily agree, some domains are simply too big and too complex to reside in a single database container. That's the primary reason DNS permits the database record for the **primary DNS server** for *ibm.com* to delegate authority for various subdomains to DNS servers lower in the domain namespace.

Such delegation of authority translates into assignment of authority for subdomains to different domain name servers, usually at various locations within an organization's overall scope and geographical layout. Once such authority is delegated, the database for the *ibm.com* name server includes NS records that point to name servers that are authoritative for specific subdomains. In addition, the *ibm.com* server's database might contain certain database records for addresses that do not fall into any specific subdomains. These could include certain addresses and other information at corporate headquarters or field staff information for those who lack a permanent site affiliation. This structure is quite flexible and can be adapted to nearly any kind of company organization or geographical layout.

The organization of the global DNS database is designed to make it quick and easy for name servers to point to other name servers when the first name servers are not authoritative for specific subdomains. Thus, much of what's involved in navigating the domain namespace that DNS servers manage collectively consists of following records that point to specific, authoritative name servers for specific subdomains. This is what permits name servers to forward proper DNS records when name resolution requests originate at the root of the DNS hierarchy.

Types of DNS Servers

There are three types of DNS servers that you may encounter in any given DNS subdomain. These are discussed in the next sections.

Primary DNS Server The primary master name DNS server (or primary or **master server**) is where the primary DNS database files for the domain(s) or subdomain(s) for which that server is authoritative reside. This file is an ASCII snapshot of the DNS database that the server loads into memory while it runs. This database segment is called a **zone**; therefore, this file is sometimes called a **zone file** or a **zone data file**. The **primary master** is distinguished from other name servers for a domain by its ability to always read its data from a zone file on disk when the DNS service starts up. The designation of primary master is also an important configuration item when setting up a DNS server of any kind. For any DNS zone, there can be only one primary master name server.

The nomenclature that some Windows clients use to designate preferred and alternate DNS servers in the Internet Protocol (TCP/IP) Properties window may call the first server primary—this has nothing to do with the DNS server's role per se, but rather with the order in which clients use DNS servers for name resolution. In fact, it's good practice to point clients at a caching-only server, where one is available; and by definition, such a server can never be a primary DNS server.

Secondary DNS Server A **secondary DNS server** (also called a secondary, a **secondary master**, or a **slave server**) gets its data for the zone from the master server for that zone. In most DNS implementations, a secondary can read its data from a local file, but it always checks to see if its on-disk version is as current as the version on the primary server. It does so by checking a specific field in its SOA record and comparing it to a corresponding value in the master server's database. Where differences are noted, the secondary can update its database from the primary domain name server. This is called a **zone transfer**. It's important to understand that the zone data on a secondary server always originates from a primary server. Most DNS implementations, however, include ways to limit updates only to data that has changed on the primary (which must then be copied to the secondary). This is called an **incremental zone transfer** as opposed to a full copy, or replication, of the zone file from primary DNS to one or more secondary DNS servers. Any DNS zone should have at least one secondary master name server (although multiple secondaries may exist) as well as the (mandatory) primary name server.

Secondary, or slave, DNS servers are important because they provide a backup copy of the domain database for a specific zone. Thus, secondary DNS servers can continue to handle name service requests for their zones even if the primary name server goes out of service. In addition, secondary servers can help distribute the load for DNS lookups when they are available. Often, DNS servers that are authoritative, or primary, for specific zones also function as slave, or secondary, DNS servers for other nearby zones. This permits hosts in one zone to gain easy access to DNS data from those other zones.

Caching Servers Caching servers store recently accessed DNS records from other domains to avoid incurring the performance overhead involved in making a remote query each time a resource outside the local domain is accessed. The best way to understand how caching works is to examine the distinction between your refrigerator and the grocery store. Just as your refrigerator determines what you can eat right now, what's in your cache defines what names outside the local domain can be resolved immediately. Likewise, the grocery store defines a big set of foods you might eat, and the global DNS database defines a big set of all the names and addresses you might try to resolve.

Although either primary or secondary DNS servers can provide caching functions, it's also possible to set up and configure separate **caching-only servers** within a specific domain. The goal of a caching-only server is to speed access to specific domain names by storing a copy of the lookup data locally, while providing neither primary nor secondary DNS server functions. Size and Internet access volume are the factors that determine if an organization implements separate caching-only servers. Only large organizations and service providers typically need to specialize their DNS services to this extent. For smaller organizations, primary or secondary responses for inbound lookups can occur alongside cache lookups for outbound traffic without significantly affecting performance.

In the Windows environment, servers that provide Active Directory (AD) services or other capabilities related to defining and applying group policy mechanisms, access controls, user and account information, and so forth are called domain controllers. Although many Windows Server 2003 or Windows Server 2008 domain controllers do in fact also operate as DNS servers, this combination is neither required nor always recommended. But when Windows Servers and AD are part of a network's infrastructure, important relationships between AD and DNS are typical and necessary.

8

How Domain Name Servers Work

A TCP/IP client is usually some application or service that encounters a domain name for which it needs an IP address. When a TCP/IP client uses a **resolver** to send a name query to a DNS server, that client obtains the address for the DNS server it queries from its TCP/IP configuration data. Servers are queried in the order in which they appear in TCP/IP configuration files (or related Registry entries, which is how this works in modern versions of Windows), starting from the top down. This explains why you want to vary the order in which DNS servers are listed when manually configuring clients to balance the load across multiple DNS servers.

Supplying one or more DNS server addresses is yet another service that DHCP performs automatically for its clients as part of the DHCP server "options."

The sequence of lookups that produces some kind of reply from whichever domain name server is queried works as follows:

1. DNS servers retrieve name data from the general domain namespace.

2. If a given DNS server is authoritative, it provides data about those zones for which it is authoritative.

3. When queried, any given DNS server will search its cached domain name data and answer queries for which that server is not authoritative, unless that query originates from a root server (which requires the authoritative DNS server for the zone in question to respond).

4. When a local server does not have the information available in its database or its name cache, it may turn to a caching-only server or to other known name servers in the "neighborhood." (Here, the term *neighborhood* refers to the collection of domains for which any given server may be either a primary or a secondary master name server, or for which the addresses of caching-only servers are known.)

5. If none of these searches produces a result, the name server sends a request for name resolution to a root server, which directs the query to the **authoritative server** for the database segment in question. The root server locates the authoritative server by contacting the root server for the domain and then following NS pointers to the right authoritative server. This process always produces some kind of answer. (Usually, it's the IP address that goes with the name that's to be resolved, but sometimes it can be an error message instead.)

This process is known as **domain name resolution**, or **name resolution**. It is interesting that while resolvers issue queries, DNS servers actually handle the real name resolution part of the activity that occurs to resolve such requests.

The saying among DNS aficionados is that "all name queries end at the root." That's because the root is the top of the DNS hierarchy, and it knows how to get to any subdomain in the entire hierarchy. This saying also recognizes that any name resolution requests that can't be handled locally or in the neighborhood must go up to a root server to obtain further resolution.

The real process is actually a bit more complex, so first we will explain some related terminology.

Recursive Query

Most DNS resolvers issue what is called a **recursive query** from the client side. This means they delegate to the first DNS server they contact the task of going out and finding the necessary address translation (or error message) on their behalf. In computer science terms, a recursive query is a query that keeps working until an answer of some kind is forthcoming. Thus, if the first DNS server contacted can't resolve a domain name, the server asks the "closest known" name servers in its neighborhood for assistance. When other name servers respond to the first name server's queries, they either provide an answer from their own databases or caches or they provide pointers to other name servers judged to be "closer" to the domain name being sought.

The first DNS server keeps asking for information until it is found because the query is recursive. It issues repeated iterative queries by following pointers to other name servers, which may be at higher levels within the **domain name hierarchy** or within different subtrees of the DNS name hierarchy altogether. (For example, if a referred server recently visited the domain namespace near where the requested name resides, that server can short-circuit the process of navigating the domain namespace up the requesting server's hierarchy, through the root, and down another part of the hierarchy.) This process repeats until a definitive answer is received, a root server is contacted, or the search terminates in an error condition of some kind. (More information about what happens when the search hits a root server is provided later in this section.) In the grand DNS server hierarchy, any DNS server can issue iterative queries, but only a DNS client or a root server can issue recursive queries.

Iterative or Nonrecursive Queries

When one DNS server receives a recursive request, that DNS server issues what are called **iterative queries,** or **nonrecursive queries,** to the name servers in its hierarchy, or to servers provided as pointers in reply to earlier iterative requests, until an answer is received. Iterative queries do not cause other queries to be issued, so the client (or root-level DNS server) that issues a recursive request can be thought of as driving the iterative query process. It navigates the name hierarchy heading for the DNS server that's authoritative for the domain in which the requested name resides, or until it gets to a server that can provide a nonauthoritative reply to its query.

In other words, if a DNS server receives a recursive query, it issues iterative queries until one of two events occurs: A server that it queries answers the query, or an error message, such as "unknown domain," "unknown domain name," or "invalid domain name," is returned.

From another viewpoint, the difference between a recursive query and an iterative query is that a name server that's presented with a recursive query must produce an answer of some kind, whereas a name server that's presented with an iterative query can simply reply with a pointer to another name server that may (or may not) be able to provide the information requested. You'd think that a name server handling a recursive query could issue its own recursive queries to pass responsibility for resolving the name request to another server. But in practice, only one server fields a recursive query and keeps issuing iterative queries until it gets a definitive answer of one kind (the IP address that matches the domain name) or another (an error message that explains why an IP address can't be supplied).

The reason some recursive name queries involve a root server is not because the root servers keep all names in the entire DNS namespace close at hand. Rather, it is because a root server always knows how to find whatever DNS server is authoritative for the domain (or subdomain) where the actual data resides. Thus, if all else fails, the root can definitely help get the query resolved.

In fact, whenever a name query arrives at a root server and that server cannot handle the request from its own cache, that root server launches its own recursive query for all domains under its purview. This query climbs down the domain namespace until it reaches the server that is authoritative for the domain requested—or until the root server receives a reply that indicates that the request cannot be resolved, for whatever reason. Notice that this kind of query cannot be satisfied with a nonauthoritative answer; it must make contact with the name server that's authoritative for the domain being queried. The root server then uses the reply to its recursive query to reply to the originating DNS server's iterative query (which, in turn, satisfies the resolver's original recursive query), and the name resolution process ends at long last.

Because the root has access to all elements in the namespace, it can get to an authoritative name server for any domain or domain segment. It does so by following the NS records in the zone databases that it traverses on its way to the DNS server that possesses the proper SOA record. In fact, that's the real explanation for the saying that all name queries end at the root.

Importance of DNS Caching

As mentioned, most DNS servers can store the results of previous name queries using a form of local data storage called caching. Only if the server needs to resolve a name or address that's not in the cache does it actually need to issue any further queries for name or address resolution.

Thus, the first DNS server to receive a recursive query for information outside the zones in its database first checks its cache to see if the information needed to resolve that request is already present. If it is, it grabs that data from the cache, and there's no need to launch any iterative queries to locate the requested information. Also, as iterative queries navigate the name hierarchy seeking resolution, the other name servers contacted check if they can answer the query from their caches in addition to their zone databases. This produces a **nonauthoritative response** to a name query but can significantly speed the resolution process. Root server requests, however, always go to the name server that's authoritative for the domain that contains the requested name or address in order to make completely sure that data is obtained directly from the source. That's why such a reply is called an **authoritative response**.

The value of data in a DNS cache is much like the freshness of food in your refrigerator in that such data goes stale over time. Note that all data in a DNS cache has an expiration value, after which it is automatically deleted. In fact, DNS data values include all kinds of timing information, which you'll see when we examine an SOA record later in this chapter. Many DNS server implementations perform regular database clean-ups wherein they systematically inspect each DNS database record and decide whether to keep, attempt to refresh, or delete records based on this information. On Windows DNS servers, the process of removing aged-out records is called scavenging and is performed once every seven days by default, if the Scavenging option is enabled in the DNS Manager MMC Console.

DNS servers cache name and address pairs for addresses they resolved, and they keep information about name requests that result in error messages. This kind of information is called **negative caching**, but it achieves the same result as positive caching. That is, a negative cache value allows an error message to be accessed locally instead of requiring that a query be issued, followed by waiting for an error message to come back on its own. Obtaining error messages from IP services often means waiting for numerous timeout intervals to expire, so this can save users lots of time!

In fact, you already know that there is a special kind of DNS server called a caching-only server. Although such special-purpose servers are not available for all DNS implementations, they are an option when configuring Windows servers for DNS. It's important to understand that the sole function of a caching-only server is to look up data outside the local zone and store those results in its cache. Over time, the value of this cache is increasingly evident because users don't have to wait for information from other servers outside the local zone to obtain results for many of their name queries.

DNS Configuration Files and Resource Record Formats

Thinking back to the origins of DNS, it's easy to describe the contents of the database files that organize DNS data as a way of representing HOSTS file data in the form of equivalent DNS resource records, along with other necessary information that DNS itself uses. This additional information includes marking sources of authority, handling mail exchange records, and providing information about well-known services.

The files that map host names to addresses are usually named *domain*.dns. In this case, *domain* is the local domain name, or subdomain name, for the zone that the DNS server covers. For example, the DNS server for edtittel.com is named *edtittel.com.dns*.

Files that map addresses to domain names for reverse lookups are usually called *addr.in-addr.arpa.dns*, in which *addr* is the network number for the domain in reverse order, without any trailing 0s(if any). For ipv6testlabs.com, whose network number is 75.32.168.188, that file is named *188.168.32.75.in-addr.arpa.dns*. Sometimes, such files are also called *in-addr.arpa* files after the label that appears at the end of each reversed address in the files' PTR records. Note that other implementations of DNS (primarily BIND) use a different naming convention for these files, but all DNS implementations require these files to operate properly no matter how they're named. Essentially, these files contain a snapshot of the DNS database in static form as stored when the database is copied to disk or before the DNS server is shut down.

Every DNS zone file must contain SOA and NS records plus records about host names or addresses in that zone. "A" (address) records provide name-to-address mapping data or a forward lookup mapping, whereas PTR records provide address-to-name mapping data or a reverse lookup mapping. The CNAME records allow you to define aliases for hosts in your zone, mostly as a convenience to make entering such data inside zone files more efficient. Thus, you could define *h54.clearlake.ibm.com* as an alias for *houns54.clearlake.ibm.com*, which means typing 21 keystrokes instead of 25.

Next, you'll take a look at the data you find in the most common DNS RR types.

Start of Authority Record

The first entry in any DNS file—which means both *domain.dns* and *addr.in-addr.arpa.dns* files—must be an SOA record. The SOA record identifies the current name server (or another name server in the same domain or subdomain) as the best source of information for data in its zone. It's important to understand that even though secondary name servers obtain their data from the primary name server in a domain, both secondary and primary name servers can designate themselves as authoritative in their own SOA records. This functionality is, in fact, what allows load balancing across a primary and one or more secondary DNS servers in a domain.

Here's a sample SOA record that shows its contents:

```
tree.com. IN SOA apple.tree.com. sue.pear.tree.com(
1 ; Serial
10800 ; Refresh after 3 hours
3600 ; Retry after 1 hour
604800 ; Expire after 1 week
86400 ) ; Minimum TTL of 1 day
```

Here's a line-by-line breakdown of this record (note that each semicolon character identifies an in-line comment, which is simply documentation to help explain code to human readers):

- *tree.com. IN SOA apple.tree.com. sue.pear.tree.com*—All DNS records follow the basic format of this line, in which *tree.com.* is the name of the domain to which the zone file applies, IN indicates that this record belongs to the Internet class of record types, SOA indicates that the type of record is a Start of Authority record, *apple.tree.com.* is the FQDN for the primary name server for the domain, and *sue.pear.tree.com* is a way of expressing the e-mail address *sue@pear.tree.com* for the administrator who's responsible for that server. Everything else that appears between the opening and closing parentheses supplies specific attributes for this particular SOA record.

- *Serial*—This is an unsigned 32-bit number for the original value. (This is what secondary name servers use to compare with the primary's value to see whether they need to update their records.) This number is incremented each time the value is updated on the primary name server (and will, therefore, be copied to the secondary name servers each time they check to see if their records need to be updated).

- *Refresh*—This specifies the number of seconds that can elapse until the zone database needs to be refreshed (10,800 seconds equals three hours, hence the comment field). This guarantees that no secondary servers will ever be more than three hours out of sync with the primary master. It also specifies the interval at which the secondary checks with the primary to learn if any changes have been made to zone definitions or information.

- *Retry*—This specifies the number of seconds that should be allowed to elapse before a failed refresh is attempted again (3,600 seconds equals one hour).

- *Expire*—This specifies the number of seconds that should be allowed to elapse before the zone database is no longer authoritative. This reflects the value of a counter that allows the DNS server to calculate how long it has been since the last update occurred. Secondary DNS servers will also discard zone data if a refresh cannot be accomplished within this interval. That's because it's better to have no old data on hand than to have stale and possibly incorrect or irrelevant data on hand.

- *MinimumTTL*—This specifies how long any resource record should be allowed to persist in another nonauthoritative DNS server's cache. In other words, this is the value that sets how long a cached entry can persist on DNS servers outside the zone from when the record originates (86,400 seconds equals 24 hours, or one day). Adjusting this number will affect how long it takes for DNS servers to update their caches, so it's important to understand that longer values mean a server has to handle fewer queries but that users will have to wait longer for information changes to become visible. Whereas shorter values may make changes available more quickly, they will also increase overall levels of server activity—a typical tradeoff.

Address and Canonical Name Records

In the example that follows, we show how Address (A) and Canonical Name (CNAME) records are used, typically in the domain.dns file (for example, *tree.com.dns* for *tree.com*). Then, as before, we explain examples of each record type in detail and show how to use comments to annotate a DNS configuration file:

```
; Host addresses
localhost.tree.com. IN A 127.0.0.1
pear.tree.com. IN A 172.16.1.2
apple.tree.com. IN A 172.16.1.3
peach.tree.com. IN A 172.16.1.4
; Multi-homed host
hedge.tree.com. IN A 172.16.1.1
hedge.tree.com. IN A 172.16.2.1
```

```
; Aliases
Pr tree.com IN CNAME pear.tree.com
h.tree.com IN CNAME hedge.tree.com
a.tree.com IN CNAME apple.tree.com
h1.tree.com IN CNAME 172.16.1.1
h2.tree.com IN CNAME 172.16.2.1
```

Given the foregoing text, consider the following:

```
localhost.tree.com. IN A 127.0.0.1
```

The preceding sets the address for the FQDN for the domain name *localhost*, which translates into *localhost.tree.com*, equal to the loopback address. This value is required to allow users to reference the name *localhost* or *loopback* in IP commands and queries. Because these names are commonly used when troubleshooting IP connectivity (especially with the `ping` command), it's important to provide definitions for these names.

Now, consider this line:

```
pear.tree.com. IN A 172.16.1.2
```

The preceding sets the address for the FQDN pear.tree.com, equal to the IP address 172.16.1.2.

Now, consider the following lines:

```
h1.tree.com IN CNAME 172.16.1.1
h2.tree.com IN CNAME 172.16.2.1
```

Defining names for individual interfaces is important because it allows them to be accessed by name on a router or any other IP host that's attached to multiple subnets through multiple network interfaces. (Such devices are called **multihomed** because they are attached to multiple subnetworks.) This is much more convenient than requiring their numeric IP addresses. Interface names are useful for querying SNMP statistics or when pinging individual interfaces. DNS, by default, accesses only the first IP address for a host when multiple entries for a single domain name are defined (as must be the case for multihomed devices). Associating a name with each interface lets you call those interfaces by name rather than having to remember each one's individual numeric IP address.

On the other hand, configuring how a DNS server responds to requests for name-to-address resolution where one domain name corresponds to multiple IP addresses lies at the heart of a technique called **DNS round robin** load balancing. Simply put, this permits a DNS server to keep track of which IP addresses it has provided most recently for a specific translation and to rotate the IP addresses within the pool or list of addresses available. The DNS server can distribute the processing load that resolving such requests leads to (for example, when a group of multiple Web servers might be available to handle incoming user connection requests) so no one server gets overloaded.

Although it's fairly easy to implement, DNS round robin is also subject to some important drawbacks. These are inherited from the DNS hierarchy itself and from DNS record TTL times, which makes undesired address caching difficult to manage. Moreover, its simplicity means that should any remote servers go down unpredictably, inconsistencies may be introduced into their DNS tables. That said, this technique, when used in concert with other DNS load-balancing and clustering methods, can produce good results in some situations, particularly those where DNS servers must handle large query volumes.

 The CNAME record lists the alias first and the true domain name second, and neither domain name ends in a period (and thus is not a true FQDN; those exist only in the A and PTR records).

Mapping Addresses to Names

The records in the db.addr file are provided to support **reverse DNS lookups** (in which you begin with an IP address and want to know the domain name that goes with it). For this reason, the order of the octets in the address portions for individual names in the record is reversed. In other words, just as you start with the name that's lowest in the domain name hierarchy when stipulating a domain name, you start at the "back" of the IP address (the fourth octet) and work your way up to the "front" of the address (the first octet). Thus, the hierarchical organization of domain names is matched by a corresponding hierarchical organization for IP addresses, starting from the host portion and working into the network portion, in reverse order.

Reverse address lookups are used primarily to determine if the IP address that a user presents matches the domain name from which the user claims to originate. (When those fail to match, this can be a sign of an impersonation attempt, sometimes called **IP spoofing**; the packet claims to originate on some network other than its true address.) This functionality is built into many UNIX applications, such as rlogin; and several OS vendors actually include a reverse lookup in their resolvers.

Here's a sample of a file named *16.172.in-addr.arpa.dns*:

```
1.1.16.172.in-addr-arpa.  IN PTR hedge.tree.com
2.1.16.172.in-addr-arpa.  IN PTR pear.tree.com
3.1.16.172.in-addr-arpa.  IN PTR apple.tree.com
4.1.16.172.in-addr-arpa.  IN PTR peach.tree.com
```

Notice how the addresses match the addresses from the earlier tree.com.dns file, in reverse order. Note also how each reversed address ends with the string *.in-addr-arpa.*, including a period on the end. That's because all these addresses are in the IP address space defined for the Internet, originally known as the ARPANET.

There's a direct correspondence between the addresses on the left side and the domain names on the right side. If you want to specify the other interface for *hedge* (the 172.17.1.1 address mentioned in the earlier file), you must do that in the file named *17.172. in-addr. arpa.dns*, not in the file named *16.172.in-addr.arpa.dns*. Each subnet gets its own such file.

There is one more caveat when dealing with reverse DNS lookups, and that is that the file structure of reverse DNS lookups is classful, which means that such files must follow the logical subdivisions of IP addresses into Classes A, B, and C. Thus, DNS can become quite confused if your network is not organized neatly in /8, /16, or /24 subnets (which correspond to Class A, B, and C addresses, respectively). If you need to configure reverse lookups for a classless network (which is one in which subnet divisions do not fall on Class A, B, or C boundaries, such as in CIDR-based implementations), read the "best practices" solution proposed in RFC 2317. Basically, as that document describes, the extra points of delegation can be introduced by extending the *in-addr.arpa* tree downwards, so the first address (or the first address and the network mask length) in the corresponding address space forms the first component in the name for each subsidiary zone. The example in Item 4 of RFC 2317 shows all the details necessary to establish and use this hierarchy.

Name Resolution in IPv6 Networks

The Domain Name System (DNS) continues to operate in IPv6 environments. By extension, that means DNS must also operate in hybrid IPv4–IPv6 environments, because side-by-side operation of IPv4 and IPv6 networks is likely for the foreseeable future. The basic mechanisms of DNS continue unaltered in IPv6-capable implementations, but the task of name resolution is made more complex by the multiple addresses that IPv6 hosts and interfaces can own. As with other forms of IPv6 address handling and management, this makes scope information important when resolving DNS in an IPv6 environment. Likewise, the vastly larger IPv6 address space makes hierarchy even more important when it comes to resolving IPv6 name lookups than it was with IPv4. Among other things, this change results in the introduction of a new, reverse hierarchy tree named *ip6.arpa* to replace the old *in-addr.arpa* tree used for reverse lookups and also in DNS PTR records.

 You will read about and hear people in the industry refer to "DNSv6" to describe IPv6 support in DNS. However, no RFCs as of this writing use the term "DNSv6." In addition, there is no single RFC that completely describes DNS running on IPv6. RFCs that address DNS and IPv6 include RFC 2874, "DNS Extensions to Support IPv6 Address Aggregation and Renumbering," RFC 3901, "DNS IPv6 Transport Operational Guidelines," and RFC 4339, "IPv6 Host Configuration of DNS Server Information Approaches."

Some experts claim with ample justification that DNS is the starting point for any IPv6 implementation, because IPv6 clients need name resolution services every bit as much as IPv4 clients do. Many implementations depend on creating a caching-only DNS server to handle IPv6-only sites and using IPv4 mechanisms to support DNS at hybrid sites. (It's worth pointing out in this connection that DNS data is independent of whichever IP version a DNS server uses itself.) In 2004, ICANN announced the addition of an IPv6 name server address to the root DNS zone, which currently supports IPv6 for top-level domains that include France (*.fr*), Japan (*.jp*), and Korea (*.kr*), among numerous others.

What IPv6 offers that IPv4 does not is a backup service that can stand in for DNS, should it not have been configured into a client, or if a DNS server isn't available to respond to service requests for some reason. The LLMNR protocol uses the same message format that conventional DNS uses but runs on different ports. For LLMNR, each node becomes authoritative for its own names, whereas a service request uses a local link multicast and the responder replies with a unicast packet. This permits local operations to proceed even in the absence of a DNS server (but of course this doesn't help with remote or nonlocal access). Microsoft began offering a DNS server implementation that supports IPv6 as part of Windows Server

2003, and IPv6 is supported in Windows Server 2008, Windows Vista, and Windows 7. DNS support for IPv6 is also supported in BIND (version 8.2.4 or later) and various UNIX distributions.

LLMNR was mentioned at the beginning of this chapter and will be covered in more detail in the section "Name Resolution Support in Windows Operating Systems."

The following sections discuss IPv6 support in DNS, source and destination address selection algorithms for IPv6, and end-to-end IPv6 address selection.

DNS in IPv6

When IPv4 address exhaustion was anticipated and IPv6 was first specified by the IETF, DNS was extended to support the longer IPv6 address space. This was accomplished primarily by adding new record types, because the DNS A record will not support 128-bit IPv6 addresses.

Originally, RFC 1886 defined the DNS extensions supporting IPv6, but RFC 3596 subsequently obsoleted the original specification. The **AAAA record** was developed to accommodate larger IPv6 addresses, and ip6.int was created to support IPv6 reverse-mapping domain; ipv6.int subsequently was deprecated, and ip6.arpa is the current special domain for reverse lookups.

The AAAA record is used specifically for the Internet, and each record can store a single IPv6 address. Figure 8-3 illustrates the format of an AAAA record.

ipv6-host   IN   AAAA   2001::2D57:C4F8:8808:80D7

Figure 8-3 AAAA resource record format
© Cengage Learning 2013

An AAAA query for a particular domain name on the Internet will return all the related AAAA records contained in the answer section of the response but will not trigger any additional section processing. As mentioned earlier, ip6.arpa is a special domain used for reverse-mapping of the IPv6 address namespace, with the domain rooted at ip6.arpa. Each level of subdomain under the ip6.arpa represents four bits out of the 128-bit IPv6 address, with the least-to-most significant (low-order to high-order) bits going from left to right.

IPv6 addresses in the ip6.arpa domain are represented by a sequence of "nibbles" separated by periods and having *ip6.arpa* as the name suffix. Each nibble is a hexadecimal character. According to the RFC 3596 specification, the IPv6 address 2001:db8:4321:12:34:567:89ab:ef is represented as the domain name f:e:0:0:b:a:9:8:7:6:5:0:4:3:0:0:2:1:0:0:1:2:3:4:8:b:d:0:1:0:0:2.ip6.arpa. Each domain name has a PTR record attached in the same manner as in-addr.arpa. For the previous example, the PTR record would be f:e:0:0:b:a:9:8:7:6:5:0:4:3:0:0:2:1:0:0:1:2:3:4:8:b:d:0:1:0:0:2.ip6.arpa IN PTR sample.ip6.domain.com.

A byte or octet is made up of 8 bits. A nibble is a part of a byte and is made up of 4 bits. In reverse mapping, as you'll see later in this section, each character in an IPv6 address string is made up of one nibble.

All A record query types, such as name server (NS), location of services (SRV), and mail exchange (MX), must be redefined in order to perform both A and AAAA additional processing. The name server must add any relevant IPv4 and IPv6 addresses that are available locally to the additional section of the response when processing and replying to a query. A and AAAA records can coexist in a forward-mapping zone, but some resolvers look up AAAA records before A records, even if the host cannot actually communicate with all IPv6 addresses. If a domain name has both an IPv4 and an IPv6 address, any computer with a resolver that must look up AAAA records first will have to wait until the IPv6 address connection times out (assuming the device cannot make a connection using IPv6) before connecting with IPv4. Until all resolvers are able to look up the address that will provide the quickest response, a workaround for this problem is to assign IPv4 and IPv6 addresses to different domain names, as shown in Figure 8-4.

```
domain-name      IN   A      72.246.164.170
domain-name.v6   IN   AAAA   2001::2D57:C4F8:8808:80D7
```

Figure 8-4 A and AAAA record for a domain name
© Cengage Learning 2013

Although forward mapping involves sending a request to a remote host with its domain name and requesting its IP address, reverse mapping is just the opposite. You send a query with an IP address and request a reply with the remote computer's host name. If you have a host with a domain name of *sample.domain.com* and an IPv6 address of 2001:db8:4321:12:34:567:89ab:ef, the reverse-mapping zone would be f:e:0:0:b:a:9:8:7:6:5:0:4:3:0:0:2:1:0:0:1:2:3:4:8:b:d:0:1:0:0:2.ip6.arpa.

IPv6 reverse-mapping zones on a DNS server contain numerous PTR records and must contain one SOA record and one or more NS records, just like IPv4 reverse-mapping zones. However, unlike IPv4, where reverse mapping is infrequently delegated to the server adminis-trator, IPv6 supports delegated reverse mapping. That means the administrator can create the reverse-mapping zone files using the ip6.arpa domain for the address range assigned to their machine. To add a large number of PTR records to an IPv6 reverse-mapping zone manually, use the $ORIGIN control statement, as shown in Figure 8-5. This figure only shows part of the reverse zone file, and the addresses and records are fictitious.

```
$ORIGIN f:e:0:0:b:a:9:8:7:6:5:0:4:3:0:0:2:1:0:0:1:2:3:4:8:b:d:0:1:0:0:2.ip6.arpa
1.a    PTR    sample.domain-v6.com
1.b    PTR    mail.domain-v6.com
```

Figure 8-5 Sample IPv6 reverse-mapping zone file using the $ORIGIN control statement
© Cengage Learning 2013

It is more common for hosts to register their AAAA and PTR records using dynamic updates so that manual entries will be infrequently required. For IPv6, any address that is forward-mapped using AAAA RR will also be reverse mapped using RR PTR because PTR records must point back to a valid AAAA record (or A record, in the case of IPv4 addresses). This sounds simple, but in IPv6 there are a couple of potential problems. If IPv6 addresses are configured using **Stateless Address Autoconfiguration (SLAAC)** or DHCPv6, those addresses may also provide Dynamic DNS (DDNS) updates to both forward- and reverse-mapped zones. This means a DNS administrator cannot actually verify that each PTR record is pointing to a valid AAAA record in the reverse zone. Also, by default, Windows Vista and later versions can generate a randomly assigned IPv6 address for each network connection session, which can then only be mapped using DDNS. Either condition would allow for inaccurately mapped PTR to AAAA records.

RFC 5855 discusses name servers for both IPv4 and IPv6 reverse-lookup zones and specifies the secure and stable set of name server names for both *in-addr.arpa* (IPv4) and *ip6.arpa* zones. The difference in naming schemes allows *in-addr.arpa* and *ip6.arpa* to be delegated to two different sets of name servers for the purpose of providing operational separation of the infrastructure used for each zone. For instance, if *in-addr.apra* name servers should fail, there would be no impact on ip6.arpa servers or IPv6 reverse lookup operations. For more information, go to *www.ietf.org* and search for RFC 5855.

Source and Destination Address Selection

IPv6 default address selection is a proposed standard specified by RFC 3484. The architecture for IPv6 addressing allows multiple unicast addresses to be assigned to a computer's network interface. These addresses can have different reachability scopes. These scopes are link-local, site-local, and global. The addresses can also be preferred or deprecated.

 Site-local was deprecated in RFC 3879, and although it may still be used, it should be ignored. The use of site-local may still be seen on older TCP/IP stacks for devices supporting IPv6.

For this reason, name resolution for IPv6 is a more complex process for computers than name resolution in IPv4. A computer using IPv4 networking typically has only one network interface with only one IPv4 address assigned. For instance, an IPv6 computer with a single physical network interface can have the following address scopes assigned to the interface:

- A link-local address scoped to the local subnet for the computer.
- A global address scoped to the Internet.

Although a network interface isn't required to possess all three address scopes, it is possible for the interface to be configured for all three. If the computer is multihomed, then each interface on the machine can be assigned up to three address scopes. If the computer must also communicate with IPv4 nodes, it can have one or more tunnel interfaces with link-local and global address scopes assigned. Different interfaces can also be designated for different uses. For security reasons, global address prefixes can have temporary addresses and public addresses assigned. A temporary address uses a randomly determined interface ID. If the computer is a mobile IPv6 node, it can also have both a home address and a care-of address.

For an IPv6 node with multiple addresses assigned to an interface, multiple IPv6 addresses are returned in the DNS Name Query Response message, making the selection of the source and destination IPv6 address complex. The source and destination address must be matched to each other for both the address scope and purpose. In other words, the IPv6 node should select the matching link-local source address and the link-local destination address and the matching global source address and global destination address. Destination addresses must also be sorted based on preference.

RFC 3484 specifies two algorithms for determining source and destination addresses:

- *Source address selection algorithm*—Selects the best source address match for the destination address

- *Destination address selection algorithm*—Sorts through the possible destination addresses and orders them by preference

Although application developers do not have to create applications that provide their own selection algorithms, if the applications do possess source and destination selection algorithms, they override the IPv6 selection algorithms. In other words, if an application has a source address selection algorithm, the application will select the source address and not the IPv6 default algorithm. However, the IPv6 default destination address algorithm is not discarded if the application specifies a destination address. If the application only provides a destination name, the IPv6 algorithm will still order destination addresses by preference. If the application provides the destination address, it can also override the default order of preference of the IPv6 default algorithm.

Computers keep a policy table for sorting destination addresses. The table organizes addresses by address prefix, precedence, and label. The address prefix with the highest precedence in the table is the most preferred destination address. The address label and its classification and label values are used to match source address preferences to destination addresses. A typical policy table on a Windows 7 computer is illustrated in Figure 8-6. Windows XP SP1 and later versions, Windows Vista, Windows 7, Windows Server 2003, and Windows Server 2008 all maintain default IPv6 interface policy tables.

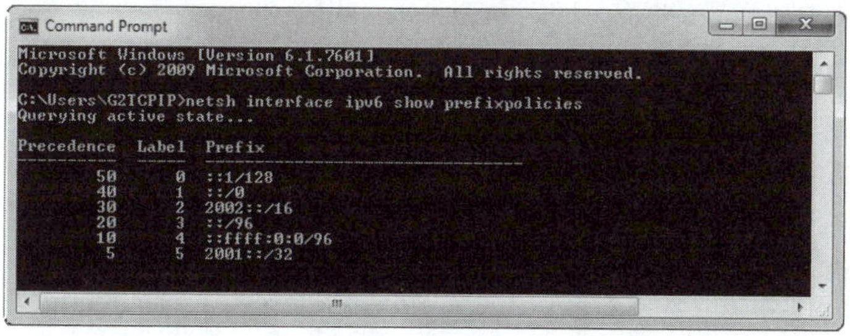

Figure 8-6 Default policy table on Windows 7 computer
Source: Microsoft

Source Address Selection Algorithm

This algorithm creates the output of a single source address that is to be used with a destination address. If more than one IPv6 source address is assigned to an interface, the algorithm provides the address with the highest preference for a given IPv6 destination address. For nodes, the algorithm selects the source address that matches one in a list of possible unicast destination addresses assigned to the interface of the next-hop device for the destination. For routers, this list of possible destination addresses can include those assigned to any forwarding interface on a router.

How addresses are ordered in a candidate set is defined by a list of eight pairwise comparison rules. Each rule places a greater than, less than, or equal to ordering on the two source addresses in relation to each other and to the rule. If the result is a tie, the remaining rules are applied in order to the two tying addresses until the tie is broken. Once an address is selected from the tie, the other address (or addresses, if there are multiple ties) is discarded and not considered by subsequent rules in the list. When comparing two addresses in a candidate set such as Source1 and Source2, if Source1 is greater than Source2 in relation to a destination address (D-Addr), it is referred to as *prefer Source1*.

Rules are processed in the algorithm sequentially, so when performing the calculations for source address selection, the algorithm begins with Rule 1, attempts to satisfy the requirements of the rule, and then proceeds to the next rule.

Rule 1: Prefer the source address that equals the destination address.

> If Source1 equals D-Addr, prefer Source1.
>
> If Source2 equals D-Addr, prefer Source2.

Rule 2: Prefer the source address that has the appropriate scope for D-Addr.

> In the case where Scope Source1 is less than Scope Source2: If Scope Source1 is less than Scope D-Addr, prefer Source2, otherwise prefer Source1.
>
> In the case where Scope Source2 is less than Scope Source1: If Scope Source2 is less than Scope D-Addr, prefer Source1, otherwise prefer Source2.

Rule 3: Prefer addresses that are not depreciated.

> If Source2 is depreciated and Source1 is not, prefer Source1.
>
> If Source1 is depreciated and Source2 is not, prefer Source2.
>
> If both source addresses are not depreciated, both addresses are at the same preference level.

Rule 4: Prefer a home address (for IPv6 mobile).

> If Source1 is both a home address and a care-of address and Source2 is not, prefer Source1.
>
> If Source1 is a home address and Source2 is a care-of address, prefer Source1.
>
> If Source2 is both a home address and a care-of address and Source1 is not, prefer Source2.
>
> If Source2 is a home address and Source1 is a care-of address, prefer Source2.
>
> If neither Source1 nor Source2 is a home address, Source1 and Source2 have the same preference level.

Rule 5: For routers, prefer the source address that is assigned to the next-hop interface pointing at D-Addr.

> If Source1 is assigned to the interface used to send packets to D-Addr, prefer Source1.
>
> If Source2 is assigned to the interface used to send packets to D-Addr, prefer Source2.

If neither Source1 nor Source2 is assigned to the outgoing interface for D-Addr or if both Source1 and Source2 are assigned to the outgoing interface for D-Addr, Source1 and Source2 have the same preference level.

Rule 6: Prefer the source address that has the same label in the prefix policy table as D-Addr.

If the label for Source1 matches the label for D-Addr and the label for Source2 does not match the label of D-Addr, prefer Source1.

If the label for Source2 matches the label of D-Addr and the label for Source1 does not match the label of D-Addr, prefer Source2.

If neither Source1 nor Source2 has the same label as D-Addr or if both Source1 and Source2 have the same label as D-Addr, Source1 and Source2 have the same preference level.

Rule 7: Prefer the source address that uses a public address over the source address that uses a temporary address.

If Source1 uses a public address and Source2 uses a temporary address, prefer Source1.

If Source2 uses a public address and Source1 uses a temporary address, prefer Source2.

If both Source1 and Source2 use public addresses or if both Source1 and Source2 use temporary addresses, Source1 and Source2 have the same preference level.

Rule 8: Prefer the source address that has the longest matching prefix with D-Addr.

If the matching prefix length of Source1 and D-Addr is greater than the matching prefix length of Source2 and D-Addr, prefer Source1.

If the matching prefix length of Source2 and D-Addr is greater than the matching prefix length of Source1 and D-Addr, prefer Source2.

If both Source1 and Source2 have the same longest matching prefix length, Source1 and Source2 have the same preference level.

Rule 2 must be implemented and given a high priority among the rules because of its effect on interoperability. For Rule 7, the specification states that there must be a mechanism in place to allow an application to prefer temporary addresses over public addresses, probably using an API extension. Rule 8 may be superseded if an implementation has another mechanism for choosing among source address pairs.

Destination Address Selection Algorithm

The purpose of the destination address selection algorithm is to sort through the list of possible IPv4 and IPv6 destination addresses and order them from highest to lowest preference. IPv4 destination addresses are expressed as IPv4 mapped addresses so that the algorithm can locate the attributes of the IPv4 address in the policy table. IPv4 mapped addresses are expressed in the format ::ffff:w.x.y.z and are scoped as follows:

- Public IPv4 addresses are scoped as global.
- Automatic Private IP Addressing (APIPA) addresses are scoped as link-local.

The algorithm takes the list of destination addresses, sorts them, and generates a new list expressed as a pairwise comparison wherein (for our purposes) address Dest1 appeared in the original list before Dest2. Source(D) indicates a chosen source address for a specific destination (D).

Source(D) is considered undefined if there is no source address that exists for a destination. For IPv6 addresses, this means that CandidateSource(D) is an empty set.

How addresses are ordered in a candidate set is defined by a list of 10 pairwise comparison rules that are applied in order. If one rule determines the selection, the remaining rules are ignored. If a precedence tie occurs, later rules are used to break the tie.

As with the Source Address Selection algorithm, these rules are processed, so when performing destination address selection, the algorithm begins with Rule 1, attempts to satisfy the requirements of the rule, and then proceeds to the next rule.

Rule 1: Prefer a destination that is reachable over one that is not.

> If Dest2 is known to be unreachable or if the source address for Dest2 is undefined, prefer Dest1.
>
> If Dest1 is known to be unreachable or if the source address for Dest1 is undefined, prefer Dest2.
>
> If both Dest1 and Dest2 are reachable or if they are both unreachable, Dest1 and Dest2 have the same preference level.

Rule 2: Prefer the destination that matches the scope of the source address.

> If the scope of Dest1 is the same as the source address scope and the scope of Dest2 is not the same as the source address scope, prefer Dest1.
>
> If the scope of Dest2 is the same as the source address scope and the scope of Dest1 is not the same as the source address scope, prefer Dest2.
>
> If both Dest1 and Dest2 have the same scope as the source address or if they both have a different scope than the source address, Dest1 and Dest2 have the same preference level.

Rule 3: Prefer a destination address with a source address that is not deprecated.

> If the source address for Dest1 is not deprecated and the source address for Dest2 is deprecated, prefer Dest1.
>
> If the source address for Dest2 is not deprecated and the source address for Dest1 is deprecated, prefer Dest2.
>
> If Dest1 and Dest2 are both deprecated or both not deprecated, Dest1 and Dest2 have the same preference level.

Rule 4: Prefer a destination with a source address that is a home address (for IPv6 mobile).

> If the source address for Dest1 is both a home address and a care-of address and the source address for Dest2 is not, prefer Dest1.

If the source address for Dest1 is a home address and the source address for Dest2 is a care-of address, prefer Dest1.

If the source address for Dest2 is both a home address and a care-of address and the source address for Dest1 is not, prefer Dest2.

If the source address for Dest2 is a home address and the source address for Dest1 is a care-of address, prefer Dest2.

If neither Dest1 nor Dest2 is a home address or care-of address, Dest1 and Dest2 have the same preference level.

Rule 5: Prefer a destination address that has the same label from the prefix policy table as its source address.

If the label of the source address for Dest1 matches the label for Dest1 and the label of the source address for Dest2 does not match the label for Dest2, prefer Dest1.

If the label of the source address for Dest2 matches the label for Dest2 and the label of the source address for Dest1 does not match the label for Dest1, prefer Dest2.

If both Dest1 and Dest2 match the labels of their respective source addresses or do not match their respective source addresses, Dest1 and Dest2 have the same preference level.

Rule 6: Prefer a destination address that has the highest precedence in the prefix policy table.

If the precedence for Dest1 is higher than the precedence for Dest2, prefer Dest1.

If the precedence for Dest2 is higher than the precedence for Dest1, prefer Dest2.

If Dest1 and Dest2 have the same precedence, Dest1 and Dest2 have the same preference level.

Rule 7: Prefer a native IPv6 destination over an IPv6 transition technology destination.

If an IPv6 transition technology destination is used for Dest2 and not for Dest1, prefer Dest1.

If an IPv6 transition technology destination is used for Dest1 and not for Dest2, prefer Dest2.

If both Dest1 and Dest2 use an IPv6 transition technology destination or both use a native IPv6 destination, Dest1 and Dest2 have the same preference level.

Rule 8: Prefer a destination address with the smallest scope.

If the scope for Dest1 is smaller than the scope for Dest2, prefer Dest1.

If the scope for Dest2 is smaller than the scope for Dest1, prefer Dest2.

If the scope for both Dest1 and Dest2 is the same, Dest1 and Dest2 have the same preference level.

<u>Rule 9</u>: Prefer a destination address possessing the longest matching prefix length with its source address.

> If the matching prefix length of Dest1 and its source address is larger than the matching preference length of Dest2 and its source address, prefer Dest1.

> If the matching prefix length of Dest2 and its source address is larger than the matching preference length of Dest1 and its source address, prefer Dest2.

> If Dest1 and Dest2 have the same longest matching preference length with their respective source addresses, Dest1 and Dest2 have the same preference level.

<u>Rule 10</u>: Otherwise, leave the order unchanged.

> If Dest1 came before Dest2 in the original list, prefer Dest1.

> If Dest2 came before Dest1 in the original list, prefer Dest2.

Rules 9 and 10 may be superseded if the implementation has another way to sort destination addresses.

Using Address Selection

There is a large number of possible examples for how source and destination address selection can be used, and presenting all of them, or even a sizable collection, is beyond the scope of this book. However, the following scenarios will provide a "flavor" of how address selection is used in actual network environments.

Address Selection from End to End Seeing how the process of source and destination selection works from beginning to end will help you understand how the rules in the algorithms previously outlined operate in a real network environment. Take the example of an IPv4/IPv6 network node called Node1. Node1 has multiple physical network interfaces, with each interface configured with multiple addresses. Here's a high-level description of the end-to-end process of Node1 communicating to a remote host:

1. The operator on Node1 uses an application to send a message to a remote Web server, querying the remote host for its configured addresses.

2. The remote host replies with multiple addresses, including one IPv4 address and several IPv6 addresses.

3. Node1 uses the source address selection algorithm to select the most preferred source address to use with each of the remote host's IPv6 destination addresses.

4. Node1 uses the destination address selection algorithm to sort the IPv4 and IPv6 destination addresses in order of preference.

5. The application used by Node1's operator is provided with the ordered destination addresses and their related source addresses.

6. The application attempts to use the source/destination address pairs until a set of addresses is successful in establishing communications with the remote host.

Let's take a closer look at the addresses involved, starting with the interfaces on Node1. Node1 has two network interfaces: a LAN interface and an ISATAP tunneling interface.

The LAN interface has five addresses:

- An IPv6 global address that is nondeprecated and for public use
- An IPv6 global address that is deprecated and for temporary use
- An IPv6 link-local address that is nondeprecated
- A public/global IPv4 address that is nondeprecated

The ISATAP tunneling interface has two addresses:

- A global address that is nondeprecated
- A link-local address that is nondeprecated

Now all of the source addresses are accounted for. Let's take a look at the destination addresses returned from the remote host:

- A public/global IPv4 address
- An IPv6 global address
- An IPv6 ISATAP global address

The source address algorithm performs the calculation that matches the remote host's IPv6 global address with Node1's IPv6 global address. This address must be nondeprecated and for public use because the source's scope matches the destination's and the source address is public. The algorithm also matches the destination's ISATAP global address with Node1's global address because of matching scopes.

When ordering the remote host's destination addresses, the destination address selection algorithm organizes them in the following order, highest to lowest preference:

1. IPv6 global address, because native IPv6 addresses are preferred over tunneling addresses like ISATAP
2. ISATAP address, because IPv6 tunneling addresses are preferred over IPv4 addresses
3. IPv4 public address

Therefore, when Node1 tries to communicate with the remote Web host, it will first try the IPv6 global pair, then the IPv6 ISATAP tunneling address pair, and finally the matching IPv4 source and destination addresses.

Changing the Destination Address Scope Preference Now that you've seen how address selection works in a start-to-finish example, we will drill down into a smaller and more specific task. You learned earlier in the chapter that computers keep a policy table for sorting destination addresses and that the table organizes addresses by prefix, precedence, and label. Usually, the destination address selection algorithm rule (Rule 8) gives preference to destination addresses with the smallest scope. As an administrator, you may want to change the policy table to reverse the default preference.

Figure 8-6 shows the policy table at the command prompt.

For instance, in an older TCP/IPv6 stack supporting site-local, a link-local destination is usually sorted before a site-local destination because the link-local destination has a smaller scope. The same is the case when a site-local destination is sorted before a global destination. Your company may have a business case that requires larger scope destinations to be sorted before smaller scope destinations. Using the Windows command *netsh interface ipv6 set prefixpolicy*, you can change the default order in which address scopes are sorted by assigning greater precedence to smaller address scopes.

Once this has been accomplished, when the destination address sorting algorithm runs, it will sort destination address scopes starting with the largest and then going to smaller scopes.

Possible source address candidates include 2001:db8::2 or fec0::2 or fe80::2. The unsorted list of destination addresses includes 2001:db8::1 or fec0::1 or fe80::1. With the policy table now configured to sort from largest scope to smallest, the selection result for destination addresses is sorted as 2001:db8::1 (src 2001:db8::2), then fec0::1 (src fec0::2), then fe80::1 (src fe80::2), based on preferred higher precedence.

Remember, site-local was depreciated in RFC 3879. It may still be used in some environments, such as the one described above, but it should be ignored in by nodes.

Name Resolution Support in Windows Operating Systems

Although there are numerous mechanisms used for network hosts to resolve names to IP addresses, there are specific methods used for Windows operating systems. Because Windows is the preeminent computer operating system in the home, small business, and enterprise spaces, it is important to understand how name-to-address resolution is managed by Windows client and server computers.

As mentioned earlier in this chapter, NetBIOS and WINS are the historical and native name resolution methods for Windows, but these technologies have been made obsolete by the ubiquitous presence of DNS. That being said, there are several technologies used in a Windows environment that are part of the name resolution process and are important to understand.

Hosts File

The hosts file on a Windows computer is one method of resolving a host name to an IP address. The file is stored locally on the Windows computer and must be updated manually, which makes this an impractical method for name resolution in a frequently changing network environment. On a Windows 7 computer, you can locate the hosts file at *C:\Windows \System32\drivers\etc*. To view and edit this file, open Notepad as an administrator, and then navigate to the etc directory. The file should look like what is illustrated in Figure 8-7:

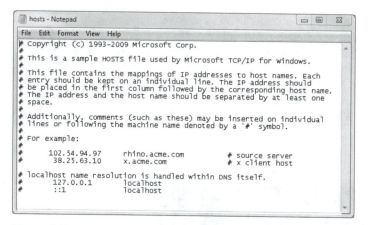

Figure 8-7 Hosts file on Windows 7 computer

Source: Microsoft

As you can see, all name-to-address mappings in the hosts file are commented out with hash-marks (#s), meaning that the computer will ignore any entries in this file. You can allow the computer to read any of the mappings listed in this file by removing the hashmark and saving the file or adding a name-to-address pair without commenting the line entry. Notice that the IPv4 (127.0.0.1) and IPv6 (::1) localhost name-to-address mappings are commented out because DNS manages that resolution.

A hosts file can still be used effectively with DNS. For instance, when you add a mapping to the file and save it, the contents of the hosts file are automatically loaded into the DNS client resolver cache, which Windows Sockets applications use for name resolution for both local and remote networks. The primary advantage of using a hosts file is that it is easily edited by the computer's user. The computer user can create easy-to-remember nicknames for hosts and map them to IP addresses in the hosts file. As explained previously, though, this method does not scale well for storing a large number of host names, and maintaining such a file requires a lot of administrative effort.

As you can see in Figure 8-7, a hosts file can map both IPv4 and IPv6 addresses to computer host names. IPv4 host file entries are unicast addresses using the traditional dotted decimal notation, such as 127.0.0.1, for the localhost. IPv4 entries can also map an IP address to the fully qualified domain name (FQDN), such as the entry 192.168.0.1 srv01.server.home.com s1. The IPv4 address is 192.168.0.1, the FQDN is srv01.server.home.com, and the nickname for the host is s1. Because server name-to-address mappings tend not to change over time, it is probably safe to add this entry, but if the server's address ever changes, then this computer will not be able to resolve the FQDN to the new IP address. It would be ineffective to use a static mapping in a hosts file for a client computer because a computer tends to receive dynamic address assignments from a DHCP server and its IP addresses can change frequently.

IPv6 entries in a hosts file are global or site-local addresses expressed in the traditional colon hexadecimal notation. IPv6 link-local addresses should not be placed in a hosts file because there is no method to specify the zone ID for those addresses. Because link-local addresses are not unique and can be reused on a network, it is possible (however unlikely) that two identical link-local addresses would exist within the same site or organization.

 An example of zone ID use is an IPv6 computer with two different network interfaces, each connected to a different subnet. Each interface can have identical IPv6 link-local addresses but use different zone IDs.

The format of a link-local address and zone ID is IPv6_address%zone ID. In Figure 8-8, the link-local address and zone ID is fe80::d810:c168:7d19:ee8b%15, making the zone ID for this address 15.

```
Command Prompt

     Connection-specific DNS Suffix  . :
     Description . . . . . . . . . . . : UMware Virtual Ethernet Adapter for UMnet
     Physical Address. . . . . . . . . : 00-50-56-C0-00-08
     DHCP Enabled. . . . . . . . . . . : No
     Autoconfiguration Enabled . . . . : Yes
     Link-local IPv6 Address . . . . . : fe80::d810:c168:7d19:ee8b%15(Preferred)
     IPv4 Address. . . . . . . . . . . : 192.168.112.1(Preferred)
     Subnet Mask . . . . . . . . . . . : 255.255.255.0
     Default Gateway . . . . . . . . . :
     DHCPv6 IAID . . . . . . . . . . . : 369119318
     DHCPv6 Client DUID. . . . . . . . : 00-01-00-01-12-C0-59-DA-00-26-B9-78-AB-DB
     DNS Servers . . . . . . . . . . . : fec0:0:0:ffff::1%1
                                         fec0:0:0:ffff::2%1
                                         fec0:0:0:ffff::3%1
     NetBIOS over Tcpip. . . . . . . . : Enabled

Tunnel adapter isatap.{3CCAD8A7-4F1C-43AD-8C3F-0205E1164EFA}:

     Media State . . . . . . . . . . . : Media disconnected
     Connection-specific DNS Suffix  . :
     Description . . . . . . . . . . . : Microsoft ISATAP Adapter
     Physical Address. . . . . . . . . : 00-00-00-00-00-00-00-E0
     DHCP Enabled. . . . . . . . . . . : No
     Autoconfiguration Enabled . . . . : Yes
```

Figure 8-8 Example of IPv6 link-local address and zone ID
Source: Microsoft

This is the reason you will find only global and site-local IPv6 addresses in a hosts file. Since site-local has been deprecated, you should not add this address type in a local hosts file.

DNS Resolver

DNS has two basic components: a server component and a client-side component. On the client computer, the DNS **name resolver** is responsible for initiating and sequencing DNS queries that result in name resolution for an application running on the computer. The resolver can issue two different types of queries:

- *Nonrecursive query to a DNS server*—This results in the server responding with a record for the domain for which the server is authoritative and where the server does not have to query other DNS servers in order to provide the response.

- *Recursive query to a DNS server*—This results in the server responding with a record by querying other DNS servers, if so required, in order to reply with a complete answer to the query.

In short, a DNS resolver is any computer that is capable of conducting a recursive search of the DNS server system in order to respond to computers sending DNS queries with the correct name resolution data.

Client Side of DNS As just mentioned, a name resolver (also called a resolver) is a piece of software on a Windows client computer that accesses DNS name servers. Resolvers issue requests for service, called **name queries** or **address requests,** to domain name servers. An address request seeks to resolve a domain name to a corresponding numeric IP address: It simply provides a symbolic domain name and expects a numeric IP address in return. This kind of activity is what enables end-users to type a URL into the address text box in a Web browser and ultimately connect to a server where that Web site is running (and translating the URL into an IP address is a key step in attempting such a connection). A name query, also known as an **inverse DNS query** or reverse DNS lookup, seeks to resolve an address to a domain name. Essentially, it seeks to obtain a symbolic domain name to match up with a numeric IP address for an incoming request packet of some kind. Usually, reverse lookups are used to make sure that the putative requester and the actual requester are part of the same domain by comparing the domain name reported in such packets to the actual sender's numeric IP address.

Resolvers also interpret responses from the name servers that they query, regardless of whether those responses contain resource record data or error messages. Such errors may stem from any of the following causes, among others:

- Invalid domain name
- Invalid IP address
- Inability to locate an IP address that corresponds to the requested domain name
- Inability to reach an authoritative name server for the requested domain

Each Windows computer maintains a DNS client resolver cache. This is a table that holds entries of both the hosts file and the host names the computer attempted to resolve using DNS. The table includes both successful and unsuccessful DNS name resolution attempts. Names in the cache that were unsuccessfully resolved are called negative cache entries. Entries in the cache made because of DNS queries are not permanent. They are maintained only for the value of the Time to Live (TTL), which was set by the DNS server that has the name resolution stored in its local database. Cache entries from the computer's hosts file do not have a TTL and are considered permanent unless the entry is removed from the hosts file. To view the DNS client resolver cache table on a Windows computer, type `ipconfig/displaydns` at the command prompt and press Enter. The result will look similar to what is shown in Figure 8-9, although it can be longer than that; the figure shows only a few of the table's entries.

Based on whether the response to a query is an IP address, a domain name, other resource record (RR) data, or an error message, a resolver sends the appropriate information to the application that requested access to a resource through a domain name. In most cases, the resolver is built right into the TCP/IP stack for whatever operating system is in use, as is the case with modern versions of Windows, including Windows Vista, Windows 7, Windows Server 2003, and Windows Server 2008.

DNS Server Service

Although older Windows servers such as Windows NT relied on NetBIOS and WINS for name resolution, modern Windows server implementations such as Windows Server 2003

Figure 8-9 Resolver cache output
Source: Microsoft

and Windows Server 2008 depend on DNS. For any Windows environment that wants to use AD, DNS is an absolute requirement.

A Windows Server 2008 machine configured for the DNS server role offers IPv6 support for:

- Longer address space
- Background loading of zone data to speed up response to client queries
- Read-only domain controllers (RODCs)
- GlobalNames zones that help when it is not practical to use single-label name resolution
- Global query block lists to reduce client computer vulnerability to malicious parties using DNS dynamic updates to register hosts that are posing as legitimate servers

Because DNS is an open protocol and its standards are defined by RFCs, Windows servers in the DNS server role must support and comply with all the DNS-specific standards. This allows Windows servers to interoperate with any other DNS server implementation, including BIND, which is the most commonly used DNS software on the Internet, typically run on UNIX-like operating systems.

As previously mentioned, the multitude of advantages offered by Active Directory (AD) would be completely unavailable without DNS. Windows Server 2003 and Windows Server 2008 naturally support DNS, and the first domain controller created for a domain can automatically install and configure the DNS Server service on that server. For Windows Server 2003,

DNS zone storage in AD enhancements was added. This allows DNS zones to be stored in the domain or in AD application directory partitions, which are data structures stored in AD and used for various replication purposes. Zones can be stored in specified partitions so you can control which set of domain controllers will replicate which zone's data. Windows DNS servers also integrate with other services, such as DHCP and WINS.

Windows servers also support stub zones, which are copies of a zone that contains only the resource records needed to identify authoritative DNS servers for that zone. This allows a Windows DNS server hosting a parent zone and a stub zone for a parent zone's delegated child zone to receive updates from the authoritative DNS servers for the child zone. The DNS server service on Windows supports DNS dynamic updates, as specified by RFC 2136; this allows DNS client computers to automatically register their DNS names and IP addresses with the DNS server. Administrators can also configure dynamic update zones that are integrated with AD for secure updates, so that only authorized computers can make changes to a server's resource records.

The DNS server service on Windows supports incremental zone transfers between servers so that only the portions of a zone that have changed are replicated, conserving network bandwidth. Recently created resource record types such as Asynchronous Transfer Mode Address (ATMA) and service location (SRV) resource records are now supported, which expands the DNS name database service.

Enabling DNS on a Windows network requires that all Windows client and server computers have DNS configured. DNS servers broadcast their names and IP addresses on the network so that they can be located. Windows Server 2008 supports DNS traffic for both IPv4 and IPv6. By default, IPv6 configures the site-local addresses of DNS servers as the well-known addresses fec0:0:0:ffff::1, fec0:0:0:ffff::2, and fec0:0:0:ffff::3. The dnscmd command-line utility also supports the use of both IPv4 and IPv6 addresses. Windows Server 2008 DNS servers also support sending recursive queries to IPv6-only DNS servers, as well as ip6.arpa domain namespace for reverse lookups. The server forwarder list supports both IPv4 and IPv6 addresses as well.

DNS Dynamic Update

As mentioned earlier, Dynamic DNS (DDNS) is the method used by Windows servers to allow automatic machine registration and record updating on DNS servers; it is described in RFC 2136. Any Windows computer—including Windows XP, Windows Vista, Windows 7, Windows Server 2003, and Windows Server 2008—can automatically register an A record for its host name and IPv4 address with the Windows DNS server that is authoritative for the zone associated with its connection's DNS suffix.

The process of dynamic updating is fairly straightforward from a high-level viewpoint:

1. A client computer sends a DNS query to locate an authoritative DNS server.

2. The local name server responds with the IP address, host name, and zone name of the authoritative DNS server for that zone.

3. The client computer attempts to dynamically update the authoritative DNS server.

4. The authoritative DNS server replies with a success or failure message.

For Step 3, the request sent by the client computer to the authoritative name server can include a list of prerequisites that must be fulfilled before the update can occur. These prerequisite conditions can include:

- The resource record set exists.
- The resource record set does not exist.
- The name is currently in use.
- The name is not currently in use.

The authoritative name server reviews the prerequisites and determines if they have been completed. Upon completion, the authoritative name server responds to the update request. If the prerequisites are not fulfilled, the update fails. In either case, a message of the success or failure status is sent to the requesting client computer, and if there is a failure, the client computer records the event in its system event log.

It is extremely common for a client computer to receive its IP address dynamically from a DHCP server. In this case, the client only registers its A resource record in the DNS server's forward lookup zone because, by default, the DHCP server is responsible for registering PTR resource records in the name server's reverse lookup zone. The update process occurs whenever a computer's host name or IP address changes. Dynamic registration can also occur whenever a computer is restarted, when a computer's DHCP lease is renewed, when an administrator runs `ipconfig /registerdns` on a computer from the command prompt, or after 24 hours have passed since the last DNS registration. If a computer is configured statically with an IP address, DNS registration will occur whenever the static address is changed. Automatic registration is also triggered when the Net Logon service is started on domain controllers or when a member server is promoted to a domain controller.

For client computers using IPv4, the DHCP client service sends the updates rather than the DNS client service. This is true regardless of whether the client computer has its IP address configured dynamically through DHCP or has a static IP address configuration because the DHCP client service is responsible for providing IP address information to the Internet Protocol (TCP/IP) component. For computers using IPv6 addressing, the IPv6 protocol sends the updates when the computer is started or when an IPv6 address on the computer is added or changed.

As mentioned earlier in this chapter, secure Dynamic DNS updates are available only for zones that are integrated into AD. Once a zone is integrated, users and groups can be added or removed from the ACL for the zone or resource record using the DNS snap-in on the Windows Server 2003 or Windows Server 2008 DNS server. Once a zone is integrated, only authorized computers are allowed to make Dynamic DNS updates to DNS servers. Also, administrators can change the zone to allow both secure and unsecure dynamic updates if desired. When a client computer attempts a dynamic update, it will first attempt an unsecure update; if the update is rejected, it will attempt a secure update.

To review the latest enhancements for the DNS server service on Windows Server 2008, go to *http://technet.microsoft.com/en-us/network/bb629410*.

Source and Destination Address Selection

Windows network nodes running IPv4 typically have a single network interface that is assigned one IPv4 address and uses DNS for name resolution. For this Windows computer, source and destination address selection is very straightforward. The source address is always the IPv4 address assigned to its network interface. The destination address is the address returned by a DNS Name Query Response message when the computer is attempting to make a connection and send a packet to the destination computer.

Windows Vista, Windows 7, and Windows Server 2008 use a different TCP/IP stack from previous versions of Windows. When a Windows computer has more than one IP address configured for a network interface, the new stack will choose one unicast address to use as the computer's source IP address in compliance with the standards set in RFC 3484. While this RFC was written for IPv6, the Windows TCP/IP stack will attempt to apply the specifications to IPv4 addresses as well, although some of the rules for the source address selection algorithm will not be followed.

For IPv4 addresses, the following source address selection algorithm rules apply only when the application hasn't specified a source address:

- If the destination address is the same as the one for the source address, prefer that address.
- If the source address is the same as the address assigned to the network interface sending the packet, prefer that address.
- If the source address has the longest matching prefix with the next hop IP address, prefer that address.
- If the source address has the longest matching prefix with the destination address, prefer that address.

You will most likely encounter problems using the source address algorithm on Web servers that have numerous IP addresses and when firewall rules are set to examine source IP addresses.

Destination address selection is how a computer determines which destination address to use for a remote host after querying a name server. For IPv4, the DNS server returns a list of addresses and the client computer selects the destination IP address that is at the top of the list. The server makes the list selection so it is always in control of which IPv4 destination address the client computer making the query will use.

In IPv4 networks, DNS round robin is used as a method of destination address selection. When a client queries a DNS server for a destination address, the server responds by providing a list of IP addresses of several servers, if available, that provide the same service on the network. The client always chooses the IP address at the top of the list, but the list results are randomized for each requesting computer so that different computers making the same request on the network will each receive a list with a different IP address at the top. This allows load balancing for redundant service hosts on a network, such as FTP servers and Web servers, so that no one server receives all or most of the service requests on the network.

Windows Vista and Windows 7 computers support IPv6 destination address selection, as defined by RFC 3484. This IPv6 destination addresses specification also affects IPv4 destination address selection. Although the destination address selection algorithm uses 10 rules, Rule 9, which states that the preferred destination address is the one with the longest matching prefix, contradicts DNS round robin, which requires that the client simply choose the first address in the list provided by the DNS server. When the destination address selection algorithm is applied, the Windows Vista or Windows 7 computer will choose the IPv4 destination address complying with the longest matching prefix requirement, and that address will not always be at the top of the list of provided addresses.

To understand how this works, let's take a look at an example. Let's say a particular computer's source IP address is 192.168.0.1. In dotted binary, it is 11000000.10101000. 00000000.00000001. This computer sends a query for the destination address of a server on the network and receives a list from the name server. Here is a sample list expressed both as IPv4 dotted notation and in dotted binary:

192.168.0.214 = 11000000.10101000.00000000.11010110

192.168.0.47 = 11000000.10101000.00000000.00101111

192.168.0.4   = 11000000.10101000.00000000.00000100

192.168.0.10 = 11000000.10101000.00000000.00001010

192.168.0.55 = 11000000.10101000.00000000.00110111

If the computer uses DNS round robin, it should select 192.168.0.214 as the destination address and attempt to make a connection; however, if the destination address selection algorithm is applied, Rule 9 will always choose 192.168.0.4 because that address has the longest matching prefix with the source address.

If the DNS round robin method is preferred, an administrator can override the default behavior dictated by RFC 3484, but this will require that a Registry key be added to each computer. The process is specified for Windows Vista and Windows Server 2008 at *http://support.microsoft.com/default.aspx?scid=kb;EN-US;968920.*

LLMNR Support

As mentioned earlier in this chapter, Link-Local Multicast Name Resolution (LLMNR) is a name resolution method used when DNS servers are not available on the network. LLMNR is specified by RFC 4795 and is supported and enabled by default on Windows Vista, Windows 7, and Windows Server 2008. This method performs name resolution for both IPv4 and IPv6 addresses on a local network segment.

In addition to performing name resolution, LLMNR on client computers will attempt to search for a domain controller (DC) on the domain, assuming the computers exist within an AD environment. This search requirement attempts to prevent a client computer from associating with a more distant domain controller or one located over a slow link by specifying the computer's local DC. The LLMNR feature is used primarily on a network in which DNS exists but has failed because of a network or server problem or when the computer exists in an AD domain but the local domain controller has failed.

As already stated, LLMNR has the specific advantage of working with IPv4 and IPv6. Although NetBIOS and WINS could work for name resolution for IPv4 networks, it has no option for IPv6 computers. In addition to being used when DNS fails on larger networks, LLMNR can be used for home, small office, and ad hoc networks in which DNS is not required or would have too high an administrative cost to deploy. However, LLMNR is only effective on local networks and will not replace DNS if communication is required with other subnets or the Internet. Windows Vista, Windows 7, and Windows Server 2008 will attempt name resolution using LLMNR only when all attempts at name resolution using DNS have failed.

In addition to sending name resolution requests using UDP multicasts, LLMNR can be used for reverse mapping by sending a unicast address to a specific IP address requesting its host name. The destination computer must be LLMNR-enabled to reply; if it is, the responding computer will send the requesting computer its host name. LLMNR computers must also verify that their host names are unique on the local subnet. This check is usually performed when the computer starts, when it reboots, or when its network interface settings are changed. If the computer cannot verify that it has a unique host name, it will indicate this when responding to LLMNR queries.

The typical request-response actions of LLMNR name resolution are as follows:

1. A host computer attempts to perform name resolution by sending a query to the primary DNS server.

2. If the host fails to receive a response from the primary DNS server, it attempts to query any alternative DNS servers for which it has a record.

3. If the host fails to connect to its primary and any alternative DNS server without errors, LLMNR becomes the host's failover name resolution method.

4. The host sends a multicast LLMNR query using UDP, transmitting the destination IP address and requesting a host name.

5. The LLMNR query is heard by every LLMNR-capable computer on the local subnet, but the query is not forwarded to other subnets by the gateway router.

6. All LLMNR-capable computers compare the IP address sent by the requesting host to their own, and if there is not a match, they disregard the query.

7. If an LLMNR-capable computer's IP address matches the address sent in the LLMNR query, the computer will respond with a unicast message to the requesting host with its host name.

Although LLMNR is enabled by default for Windows Vista, Windows 7, and Windows Server 2008, it can be disabled either using Group Policy in AD domains or using the Registry for individual computers. For an individual computer that is not in an AD domain, create and edit the Registry key HKEY_LOCAL_MACHINE\SOFTWARE\Policies\Microsoft\Windows NT\DNSClient\EnableMulticast = 0x0. By Group Policy, use Computer Configuration\ Administrative Templates\Network\DNS Client\Turn off Multicast Name Resolution = Enabled. The details are located at the Windows Vista Forums: *www.vistax64.com/vista-networking-sharing/152250-how-disable-llmnr.html.* You can also disable Network Discovery to disable LLMNR, as documented in this example for Windows 7: *http://windows.microsoft.com/en-US/windows7/Enable-or-disable-network-discovery.*

Working with ipv6-literal.net Names

Windows Vista, Windows 7, and Windows Server 2008 support the use of **ipv6-literal.net names,** which are specified by RFC 2732. These are names that can be used by applications and services that are unable to recognize the syntax of IPv6 addresses. An ipv6-literal.net name involves a minor conversion of the computer's IPv6 address by replacing the colons (:) with hyphens (-) and appending .ipv6-literal.net to the end of the name.

For instance, you can convert the global address 2001:db8::adc2:2131 to an ipv6-literal.net name this way: 2001:db8–adc2-2131.ipv6-literal.net. To use the same ipv6-literal.net name in a URL, you could write it as http://[2001:db8::adc2:2131]. Notice that when the address is within the square brackets, the colons are not converted to hyphens. The use of the square brackets is supported in Windows but not with legacy software, so if you want to ensure that all software types can read the address, you must use the literal name for the global address: http://2001:db8–adc2-2131.ipv6.literal.net.

If you need to specify a link-local address and its zone ID, you would replace the percentage sign (%) with an "s". Here's an example: The link-local address and zone ID fe80::d810:c168:7d19:ee8b%15, when converted to an ivp6-literal.net name, becomes fe80–d810-c168-7d19-ee8bs15.ipv6-literal.net. To use a more practical example, if you needed to use an ipv6-literal.net name to specify a **Universal Naming Convention (UNC) path** to a directory named "documents" on a computer with a link-local address, it would look like \\fe80–d810-c168-7d19-ee8bs15.ipv6-literal.net\documents. A somewhat more involved path for the same address would look like \\fe80--d810-c168-7d19-ee8bs15.ipv6-literal.net\windows\system32\drivers\etc. The same address, using the square bracket method, looks like \\[fe80::d810:c168:7d19:ee8b%15]\windows\system32\drivers\etc.

RFC 2732 has been obsoleted by RFC 3986, which provides generic syntax for **Uniform Resource Identifiers (URIs)** and addresses—not only ipv6-literal.net names but, more generally, URLs and URNs (Uniform Resource Names). This means that RFC 3986 obsoleted a number of other RFCs and that only part of RFC 3986 addresses IPv6 literal-names. Windows also supports RFC 3986's implementation of IPv6-literal addresses in URI syntax. However, it does not specify a way to include a scope ID, and a URI is considered nonuniform when the scope ID is present. Windows applications such as WinINet support the older use of IPv6 literals. This includes using http://[2001:db8::adc2:2131] for global addresses; \\[fe80::d810:c168:7d19:ee8b%15]\ or http://[fe80::d810:c168:7d19:ee8b%15]/ are used where a zone or scope ID needs to be supported.

For more information about RFC 3986 and IPv6 literals, go to *http:// ietf.org*, search for RFC 3986, and then search the document for "IPv6."

Peer Name Resolution Protocol

Peer Name Resolution Protocol (PNRP) is a Microsoft Windows IPv6 proprietary peer-to-peer name resolution system that was first developed for Windows XP SP2 and then updated for Windows Vista. In Windows 7, Windows Remote Assistance uses PNRP when making an Easy Connect connection. PNRP is also supported on Windows Server 2008 but not on any edition of Windows Server 2003. PNRP provides secure dynamic name registration in an all but serverless environment, requiring a server only for bootstrap. The system scales extremely well up to billions of names, has fault-tolerant qualities, and boasts of having no performance bottlenecks. Name registration occurs in real time with no administrative effort and is capable of resolving addresses, ports, and sometimes extended payloads, allowing PNRP to resolve names for both devices and services on the network. PNRP uses public key cryptography to allow for secured name publication but also permits unsecured name publication.

For more information about PNRP and Windows 7, go to *http:// blogs.msdn.com/b/p2p/archive/2008/11/19/peer-to-peer-based-features-in-win-7.aspx.*

PNRP allows a host to publish its peer name and IPv6 address in a PNRP cloud. Other PNRP-capable hosts can resolve the peer name, retrieve the peer's IPv6 address and any other published information, and then establish a peer-to-peer connection. Peer names are published in PNRP clouds, which fall into specific groups, depending on scope:

- *Global cloud*—Maps to the IPv6 global address scope; peer names of PNRP-capable computers can be published to the Internet using this cloud. There can be only one global cloud.

- *Link-local cloud*—Maps to the IPv6 link-local address scope; peer names of PNRP-capable computers can be published within the subnet to which the host is attached. There can be as many link-local clouds as there are subnets.

- *Site-specific cloud*—Maps to the IPv6 site-local address scope, but this cloud type has been deprecated, although it remains supported in PNRP.

A PNRP name is the end point for network communication and can be almost anything you want to resolve to an IPv6 address, such as a computer, group, service, or user. Peer names can include IPv6 addresses and potentially other information about the peers. When resolved by other hosts, they can retrieve not only the peer's address but whatever other information was included about the peer. Peer names can be registered as either secured or unsecured. Unsecured peer names are published in plain text, which means they are vulnerable to spoofing, and they can be published by anyone with no verification. More than one network entity can publish the same peer name, such as when members of a group publish a peer name that is associated with that group.

PNRP peer names are made up of an authority and a qualifier. The authority uses a Secure Hash Algorithm 1 (SHA1) hash of an associated public key expressed in hexadecimal characters for secure publication. For an unsecure peer name, the secure hash is replaced by the value 0. The qualifier is a unicode string containing up to 150 characters, which allows different peer names to be published for different services.

Peer names are required to create PNRP IDs, which are 128 bits long and made up of the following:

- The peer-to-peer (P2P) ID, which is 128 high-order bits and a has the peer name that is assigned as the network end point

- The peer name of the end point, published in the format authority.classifier

- The service location, which is 128 low-order bits and is a generated numeric value that identifies different instances of the same P2P ID within the cloud

Figure 8-10 shows the structure of a PNRP ID.

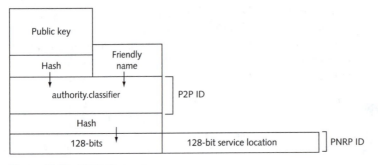

Figure 8-10 PNRP ID structure
© Cengage Learning 2013

This combination of P2P IDs and service locations allows multiple PNRP IDs to be registered by the same computer. Every host that exists within a PNRP cloud maintains a cache table of PNRP IDs, including its own registered ID and those that have been published to the cloud. All PNRP IDs stored on all hosts in the cloud make up a distributed hash table. Each entry on a given host in its cache contains a peer's PNRP ID, its certified peer address (CPA), and its IPv6 address. The CPA is a self-signed certificate that provides authentication for the PNRP ID and contains the IP address, protocol number, and port number data.

There are two parts to the PNRP name resolution process: end point determination and PNRP ID resolution. To determine the existence and availability of an end point in the cloud, the requesting peer performs one of two actions. Either it attempts to determine the IPv6 address of the destination peer to make a connection or it attempts to determine the IPv6 address of the peer that published a service, group, or other desired element. During this phase, PNRP uses an iterative process for locating the peer node that published the PNRP ID and, with each iteration, contacts peer nodes in the cloud that are progressively closer to the target peer.

Once the target end point is determined, PNRP name resolution is attempted. To do this, the requesting peer examines its peer cache for the cloud to see if there is a match between the PNRP ID it acquired for the end point in its cache. If a match is found, the requesting peer sends a PNRP Request message to the target peer's PNRP ID requesting its name and any other available information and then waits for a reply. If a match is not found, the requesting peer will send a PNRP Request message to the PNRP ID that is the closest match to the target found in its cache. The peer receiving this message examines its own cache to see if there is an exact match for the PNRP ID that is being sought by the requesting peer. If a match is found, that data is sent in a reply to the requesting peer. If it is not found, the closest match is sent to the requesting peer. The requesting peer continues the process through whatever number of iterations are necessary to locate the target peer that registered the PRNP ID. Once the target peer is found, it returns its name and whatever information that is available about it.

Troubleshooting Name Resolution Problems and Failures

Despite the robust capabilities and many advantages of DNS, it does suffer from some shortcomings. Chief among these is that DNS database updates usually require that a qualified administrator—one with the proper knowledge and necessary access rights to the zone files—operate directly on the DNS database files or use special-purpose tools (such as Nsupdate in the UNIX environment) to make changes. The requirement that DNS databases be edited makes it a chore to manage updates. All Windows operating systems since Windows 2000 support Dynamic DNS (DDNS), but in order to maximize its benefits, the Windows DNS implementation must be linked to an AD database to work (with DHCP also communicating with AD).

In essence, the Windows linkage between DNS and AD requires no changes to DNS itself, beyond establishing such a link. AD actually tracks domain name-to-address relationships as they change over time, with the help of DHCP, and submits necessary update requests to the DNS server when such changes occur. Therefore, AD is automating what a DNS administrator would otherwise have to do manually. This implementation works best with AD-aware Microsoft operating systems. Standard DDNS implementations use a dynamic update facility described in RFC 2136 and are interoperable with the Microsoft DNS implementation in Windows Server 2003 and Windows Server 2008, provided that such servers manage AD-integrated DNS zones. Even with these improvements to DNS, direct interaction with DNS zone files is still sometimes required, whether it be through editing zone files in an ASCII editor, using a command-line tool such as Nsupdate, or by using a GUI interface, as in the Windows implementation.

Another problem to which DNS falls prey might be called "propagation delay," which relates to the amount of time it takes for cached values to catch up with changes to authoritative databases after changes are made to those "master copies" of DNS records. This explains why service providers routinely warn their customers that it might take as long as three days for a name-to-address translation to become completely effective on the Internet, as when transferring a domain name from one provider to another (which invariably means changing the underlying IP address associated with that domain name).

This delay results from the effect of the TTL value associated with a database entry, which may persist beyond its actual valid life when changes occur. Assume that the prior version of the changed record was read from the database one second before the update occurred. If the standard default TTL remains unchanged at 24 hours, this means the TTL persists for 23 hours, 59 minutes, and 59 seconds past the time when that value changes. Additional copies of that value from another cache can add as much as another 24 hours to that value. Also, some servers set TTL values for longer periods and thereby extend the window when an incorrect value appears current following a change. The upshot is that it might conceivably take as long as three days for old values to disappear from caches on the Internet, thereby allowing the new value to operate free of outdated competition, as it were. Two days is a more typical upper boundary for this phenomenon, however.

Common Sources of Failure

There are generally two common sources of name resolution failure. A negative response to a query (such as "name not found") may be returned or a positive response to a query may be returned with an incorrect name.

One common cause of a negative result is an incorrect domain suffix appended to a queried name. The solution to this is to use a fully qualified domain name (FQDN), which specifies the exact location in the tree hierarchy in DNS, including the top-level and root domains. For instance, an incorrect suffix may have been appended to the local host name samplehost. An example of the FQDN is samplehost.domain.com.

Other causes of a "name not found" error include incorrect IP configuration on a client or server, querying a name server that is not authoritative for the name being looked up, or inability to connect to the correct name server, because of either a server or network issue.

Problems with not being able to connect to a name server can also be caused by a broken delegation or other recursion problem. This happens when one or more DNS servers in a path of a recursive query cannot respond to and forward the correct information. Recursion problems can be caused by queries timing out before they are finished, a server failing to respond during a query, or a server providing incorrect information during a query.

Causes for positive but incorrect name server responses can include incorrect data stored in the name server's resolver cache, which requires the cache be flushed. If that doesn't correct the problem, then there is likely an issue with authoritative data. This can be caused by incorrect data being stored in the primary zone if the name server is a primary server. It is sometimes caused by operator error when entering zone information, a problem with AD replication, or a problem with dynamic update. If the server is hosting a secondary copy of the zone, then it may be pulling incorrect data from the master server.

If the secondary server cannot pull a zone transfer from the master server, resulting in an incorrect data response, the master server may be refusing to send zone transfers to the secondary server. The master server may be limiting zone transfers to a specific group of servers but the necessary secondary server is not on that list. Also verify that the DNS resolver service is started and that the name server is running and is connected to the network.

Tools for Troubleshooting NetBIOS and WINS Problems

When the network itself is in good shape, the failure of NetBIOS services is most often the result of misconfiguration of end nodes or server failure. Poor performance, on the other hand, is more likely to be the cumulative result of minor configuration errors in the server, or in some significant number of end nodes. Server topology also has a large impact on overall performance. Setting up WINS services for a network with many subnets requires not only considerations of security and availability but of load optimizing across WAN links. Push-type replication partners, in true NetBIOS fashion, can be very chatty. You have to weigh the frequency of WINS server updates against the frequency of incorrect positive Name Query responses. Incorrect name resolutions can also generate significant traffic and generally degrade performance.

The tools that are useful for diagnosing and troubleshooting TCP/IP networks in general are also useful in maintaining NetBIOS and WINS services. Ping is an excellent way to test connectivity, for example. Traceroute and Netstat are also useful diagnostic tools. The following sections look more closely at several tools that are useful in troubleshooting name resolution problems.

Tools for Troubleshooting DNS Problems

The process of troubleshooting DNS for IPv4 and IPv6 is essentially the same. The main differences are knowing how to specify an IPv6 name server and how to format forward and reverse mappings for each IP version. One important thing to keep in mind when using DNS troubleshooting utilities is that they point to IPv4 addressing by default. When you use, for example, the `nslookup` command and query *www.example.com*, the information that is returned is for A records. You need to specify IPv6 lookups explicitly in order to see AAAA record data. To do so with `nslookup`, you need to know the domain name of the Web server and name server accessible via IPv6 and then use the following command:

`nslookup -type=AAAA ipv6.domain.com ns1.domain.com`

The output will be:

```
Name:        ipv6.domain.com
Address:     ipv6 formatted address
```

Nbtstat

Nbtstat is a command-line program that returns statistics on NetBIOS, using NetBT if TCP/IP is installed on the machine from which it is run. Nbtstat is available on all Windows XP, Windows Vista, and Windows 7 client computers and on Windows Server 2003 and Windows Server 2008 servers. This is a simple tool that can give you instant feedback on the state of particular NetBIOS clients and on NetBIOS name resolution in general. The -n argument returns a list of all the local NetBIOS names in a tabular form similar to what is shown in Table 8-1. The -r argument returns a list of names resolved by broadcast and by WINS, and includes a summary count of name resolutions and registrations by each method. The -s argument returns the NetBIOS sessions table, showing open sessions with

8

NetBIOS Suffix (Hex)	Meaning	Used with This Name	Used with This Name Type
00	Workstation service	*Computername*	Unique name
01	Messenger service	*Computername*	Unique name
03	Messenger service	*Computername*	Unique name
06	Remote Access Server (RAS)	*Computername*	Unique name
1F	NetDDE service	*Computername*	Unique name
20	Server service	*Computername*	Unique name
21	RAS Client service	*Computername*	Unique name
BE	Network Monitor Agent service	*Computername*	Unique name
BF	Network Monitor Application service	*Computername*	Unique name
00	Registers the computer as a member of the Windows or workgroup	*Domainname*	Group name
1B	Registers the computer as the domain	*Domainname*	Group name
1C	Domain controllers	*Domainname*	Group name
1E	Used to facilitate browser elections	*Domainname*	Group name
03	Messenger service	*Username*	Unique name

Table 8-1 NetBIOS suffixes and meanings

their destination IP address. The -S (uppercase "S") argument shows the same thing, but it attempts to resolve the remote host name using the HOSTS file. The NetBIOS suffixes in Table 8-1 are from Windows networking, but applications such as Microsoft Exchange can also use NetBIOS names.

 For a full list of the arguments and their syntaxes, type `nbtstat` with no argument at a command prompt.

Nbtstat is a fast way to check the status of a particular NetBIOS host or get a quick snapshot of NetBIOS name resolution activity on the local network segment. If, for example, a node appears to have trouble communicating with the WINS server, issuing the **nbtstat** command may show it is actually attempting to use broadcast name resolution.

Netstat

The Netstat command prompt utility shows active TCP connections, listening ports, Ethernet statistics, IPv4 statistics, and IPv6 statistics. Data for IPv4 includes statistics for IP, ICMP, TCP, and UDP protocols. Data for IPv6 includes IPv6, ICMPv6, TCP over IPv6, and UDP over IPv6 protocols. When you type `netstat` at the command prompt without any parameters and press Enter, all the active TCP connections on the computer are returned. Netstat is available on Windows, UNIX, and UNIX-like computers, but the Windows version is less robust than the *nix version and offers fewer options.

Table 8-2 shows the common parameters used with the netstat command.

Parameter	Description
-a	Lists all current connections and open, listening ports on the local system
-e	Displays Data Link layer statistics (also can be used with the -s parameter)
-n	Displays addresses and port numbers in numerical form
-p	Shows the connections for the specified protocol. The protocol defined may be UDP or TCP. When used with the -s parameter, the protocol definition IP also may be used.
-r	Displays the routing table (also see the ROUTE command)
-s	Displays, by default, statistics organized based on the protocols, such as IP, UDP, and TCP (also can be used with the -p parameter to define a subset of the default)
interval_seconds	Redisplays the statistics on a regular basis using the interval_seconds value between displays. Press Ctrl+C to stop displaying the statistics. If this parameter is not included, the statistics appear only once.

Table 8-2 Common `netstat` command parameters
© Cengage Learning 2013

Nslookup

Windows and UNIX, among other operating systems, include support for this versatile utility, which offers general name server lookup capabilities. (The "Ns" in Nslookup comes from the abbreviation for name server information in any NS record in a DNS database.) By default, **Nslookup** queries the default name server specified in the current machine's TCP/IP configuration.

The `nslookup` command provides access to all kinds of DNS information, either from the current default server or from a server whose name or IP address you provide as an argument to this command. It is an essential tool for testing, when configuring or troubleshooting a DNS server.

The syntax for the `nslookup` command takes the following form, in which *domain-name* is the domain name to be looked up and [*name-server*] is the name server on which to look it up:

nslookup *domain-name* [*name-server*]

Here, the use of square brackets indicates that the *name-server* argument is optional because Nslookup uses the default name server if no alternate server is specified. Two examples appear in Figure 8-11; the first uses the default, and the second uses an authoritative name server for the domain specified. (Note the differences in output.)

Figure 8-11 Examples of the `nslookup` command
Source: Microsoft

Note that the default name server in the first command is identified as aus-dns-cac-01-dmfe0. austin.rr.com, and provides a "Non-authoritative answer" label before showing a name and address for ns1.io.com. In the second command, another name server, ns2.io.com at the io.com domain, is referenced and shows the name and address without the "Non-authoritative answer" label.

This slight difference is the only way you can tell when a name server is authoritative for a particular domain name (and it depends on what it *doesn't* tell you). Note also that in each response, the name and IP address of the name server where the lookup occurred appear first, and the results of the lookup appear second.

Nslookup Details To display the help screen for Nslookup, type `nslookup` at the command line. On Windows machines, this means typing `nslookup` inside a command window with no arguments. (To open such a window, click Start and, in the search box, type cmd, then press Enter.) This puts the Nslookup utility in charge of the command line, as signaled by the > prompt that appears instead of the more usual C:\> prompt on the preceding line in the figure. At this point, you can enter the string help, and the screen shown in Figure 8-12 appears. Linux users can go straight to the command shell and skip these Windows preliminaries.

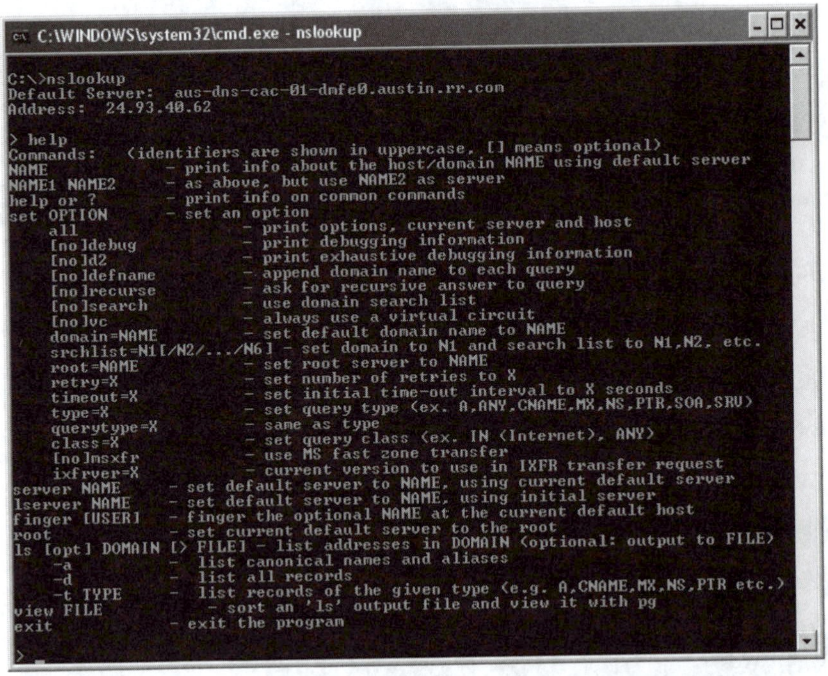

```
C:\WINDOWS\system32\cmd.exe - nslookup

C:\>nslookup
Default Server:  aus-dns-cac-01-dmfe0.austin.rr.com
Address:  24.93.40.62

> help
Commands:   (identifiers are shown in uppercase, [] means optional)
NAME            - print info about the host/domain NAME using default server
NAME1 NAME2     - as above, but use NAME2 as server
help or ?       - print info on common commands
set OPTION      - set an option
    all             - print options, current server and host
    [no]debug       - print debugging information
    [no]d2          - print exhaustive debugging information
    [no]defname     - append domain name to each query
    [no]recurse     - ask for recursive answer to query
    [no]search      - use domain search list
    [no]vc          - always use a virtual circuit
    domain=NAME     - set default domain name to NAME
    srchlist=N1[/N2/.../N6] - set domain to N1 and search list to N1,N2, etc.
    root=NAME       - set root server to NAME
    retry=X         - set number of retries to X
    timeout=X       - set initial time-out interval to X seconds
    type=X          - set query type (ex. A,ANY,CNAME,MX,NS,PTR,SOA,SRV)
    querytype=X     - same as type
    class=X         - set query class (ex. IN (Internet), ANY)
    [no]msxfr       - use MS fast zone transfer
    ixfrver=X       - current version to use in IXFR transfer request
server NAME     - set default server to NAME, using current default server
lserver NAME    - set default server to NAME, using initial server
finger [USER]   - finger the optional NAME at the current default host
root            - set current default server to the root
ls [opt] DOMAIN [> FILE] - list addresses in DOMAIN (optional: output to FILE)
    -a              - list canonical names and aliases
    -d              - list all records
    -t TYPE         - list records of the given type (e.g. A,CNAME,MX,NS,PTR etc.)
view FILE       - sort an 'ls' output file and view it with pg
exit            - exit the program
>
```

Figure 8-12 ICMP Nslookup **help screen**
Source: Microsoft

As you can see, there is a lot of information you can obtain with the nslookup command. In the section that follows, we explore a few of the more common uses for the nslookup command.

Using Nslookup You already know how to identify your default domain name server. (Simply enter the nslookup command with no arguments, as indicated at the top of the command prompt window shown in Figure 8-12.) After you enter Nslookup's command mode (symbolized by the > prompt), you can use the set option command to examine specific types of resource records. In Figure 8-13, we show what happens when you set the type of record reported to NS (name server), which is that it shows all NS records in the DNS database for that domain; *set type=ns* is the syntax for that action.

Notice that the lookup still uses the default name server (aus-dns-cac-01-dmfe0.austin.rr.com) to look up this information. That's because we didn't specify a different name server as a second argument on the io.com command line. To learn how to fully use Nslookup, try the various record types and perform lookups yourself.

Figure 8-13 Examining io.com's NS records
Source: Microsoft

You might be tempted to extract information from certain well-known name servers. In particular, you might try running the ls -a (list canonical names and aliases) or ls -d (list all records) commands. Although you may get the occasional name server to cooperate, in most cases you should see output that looks like the information shown in Figure 8-14.

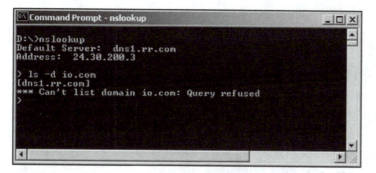

Figure 8-14 Nslookup error message
Source: Microsoft

If you think about the notion of managing IP security as partly protecting your addresses and resources, you should understand that there's a very good reason why most name servers don't provide this kind of information to anyone except a privileged few administrators. That's because showing this kind of data to random outsiders gives them a perfect map of the IP addresses and domain names used within the DNS zone, for which the server contains the database segment. That's just what hackers need to mount an informed attack on a network, and that's why you shouldn't be able to access that information on any DNS servers except those you administer yourself. In fact, by default, most sites refuse such requests and refuse any DNS update records from all requesters, except for a select group of IP addresses for "trusted hosts" or "trusted users" (allow by exception). Those sites that neglect to block such requests can fall prey to man-in-the-middle or other attacks based on deliberately false or misleading address translations.

Should you ever be required to manage a DNS server, make sure you thoroughly explore the nslookup command. Properly used, Nslookup can be an invaluable troubleshooting tool. In the next sections of this chapter, we'll examine typical packet traces for DNS traffic on the network. This gives you the chance to see how some of the mechanisms we explained in this chapter actually work.

Nslookup and IPv6 When you type `nslookup` at the command prompt and enter interactive mode, receiving the `Nslookup` prompt, you can enter either the type in the domain name or IP address of the host and receive the name and address of the default server, if available. For IPv6 hosts, you must specify either the global IPv6 address or the domain name used specifically for IPv6. For instance, typing `www.cisco.com` at the `Nslookup` prompt will return the name, address, and aliases used by the cisco.com domain. Performing the same task using the domain name www.ipv6.cisco.com will yield results for the cisco.com server being used for IPv6.

If your ISP and primary DNS server do not support IPv6 and you type `www.ipv6.cisco.com` at the `Nslookup` interactive prompt, the DNS request may time out without returning the desired data.

If the command `nslookup www.ipv6.cisco.com` doesn't work for you, try using the noninteractive mode; at the prompt, enter `nslookup -type=aaaa www.ipv6.cisco.com`. The results should look like what you see in Figure 8-15 (the command prompt was run as administrator).

Figure 8-15 Output of `Nslookup` for IPv6 host name
Source: Microsoft

If you want the `Nslookup` command to display AAAA record data only, at the `Nslookup` interactive prompt, type `set q=aaaa` and then enter the domain name of the server. To use `Nslookup` to display PTR records, at the interactive prompt, type `set q=PTR` and press Enter. Then, enter the reverse mapping zone, such as f:e:0:0:b:a:9:8:7:6:5:0:4:3:0:0:2:1:0:0:1:2:3:4:8:b:d:0:1:0:0:2.ip6.arpa.

Chapter Summary

- Because it provides the essential way to get from a symbolic, human-readable domain name for an Internet location to a corresponding numeric, machine-readable IP address, the Domain Name System provides the key address resolution service that makes today's Internet possible. It's almost impossible to overstate the importance of this service to the proper functioning of any large-scale TCP/IP-based internetwork.

- The impetus for DNS arose from the difficulty of maintaining static HOSTS files for computers on the ARPANET after the number of hosts climbed into the thousands. DNS was designed to create a flexible, reliable, and robust name and address resolution service that could scale to handle very large address spaces. Its designers succeeded better than they ever could have imagined.

- DNS name servers come in multiple varieties. For each zone, a primary name server is mandatory; it contains the master copy of the database for its zone. For each zone, one or more secondary name servers may be created. (At least one secondary name server is recommended for every zone to ensure improved reliability.) For large or heavily trafficked networks, caching-only name servers offload the task of resolving names and addresses outside the local zones for users, thereby freeing up the primary and secondary name servers for the zone to handle external incoming name resolution requests.

- DNS maintains its data on a large collection of name servers around the Internet by carving the domain namespace into a disjointed collection of domain or subdomain databases, also known as database segments, or database zones, each of which belongs to a single authoritative name server for that zone. This permits database segments to be controlled locally, yet available globally. The DNS design also includes provisions for a primary master name server and one or more secondary master name servers for each database zone to help improve reliability (if one DNS server fails, the others continue to function) and availability (proper configuration will balance query loads against all name servers for a zone, not just the primary).

- DNS databases consist of a collection of resource records (RRs), in which such databases consist of a collection of zone files that represents a static snapshot of those databases. Every zone file must include a Start of Authority (SOA) record to identify the name server that's primarily responsible for the database segments it manages. Other records in each zone file correspond to its function and may contain address-to-name mappings for normal domain name resolution, or name-to-address mappings for inverse or reverse DNS lookups.

- DNS clients rely on a software component called a resolver to interact with an available DNS server for name resolution services. Resolvers issue recursive queries that go to a designated DNS server, which either answers that query itself or queries other name servers until an answer is forthcoming. Ordinary DNS servers will accept either authoritative or nonauthoritative replies to their queries, but root DNS servers accept only authoritative replies to ensure the validity of the data they supply to DNS servers lower in the domain name hierarchy.

- DNS packet structures incorporate type information that identifies the kind of RR being carried and otherwise describes the record's contents and validity. Understanding DNS Application layer packet structures makes it much easier to appreciate DNS' simplicity and elegance.

- IPv6 networks use DNS extensions but must be able to work in hybrid IPv4–IPv6 environments. DNS servers in an IPv6 environment store name resolution data in AAAA records rather than in A records, which means that DNS servers and resolvers must maintain both types of records. This can also cause problems because some DNS resolvers default to looking up A records first and may time out before looking up AAAA records.

- IPv6 source and destination address selection is managed by algorithms that use a set of rules to determine how the selection process is managed. Because a device can have a network interface that is assigned multiple IPv6 address types (such as link-local, site-local, and global), the address selection process is more complicated than in IPv4 networks. Also, although these algorithms are written to work in the IPv6 address space, they also affect how IPv4 address selection operates, sometimes causing unanticipated or undesired selection outcomes.

- The Windows operating system supports a variety of name resolution technologies, such as hosts files, NetBIOS, WINS, and DNS. Windows client computers use DNS resolvers to issue service requests to DNS servers for name resolution. Windows DNS servers use the DNS server service to manage name resolution, which interoperates with Active Directory services. DNS dynamic update is a service that allows automatic machine registration and record updating on DNS servers. Windows supports Link-Local Multicast Name Resolution (LLMNR), which allows for name resolution on a subnet without the use of DNS. Windows also supports the use of ipv6-literal.net names and Peer Name Resolution Protocol (PNRP).

- There are a number of common causes of name resolution problems and failures, such as hardware or network problems as well as misconfiguration of fully qualified domain name suffixes. The two most common errors are a name-not-found error and a positive error with incorrect information. The most common tools for diagnosing name resolution errors are Nbtstat, Netstat, and Nslookup.

Key Terms

AAAA record   A DNS resource record that maps IPv6 addresses to hosts within a domain.

address (A) record   A DNS resource record that maps IPv4 addresses to hosts within a domain.

address request   A DNS service request for an IP address that matches a domain name.

authoritative response   A reply to a query from the name server that's authoritative for the zone in which the requested name or address resides.

authoritative server   The DNS server that's responsible for one or more particular zones in the DNS database environment.

BIND (Berkeley Internet Name Domain)   The most popular implementation of DNS server software on the Internet today (originally introduced as part of BSD UNIX 4.3). Today, there are BIND implementations available for nearly every computing platform, including Windows Server 2003 and Windows Server 2008.

caching   Storing remote information locally, once obtained, so that if it is needed again, it may be accessed much more quickly. Both DNS resolvers (clients) and DNS servers cache DNS data to lower the odds that a remote query will have to be resolved.

caching server   A DNS server that stores valid name and address pairs already looked up, along with invalid names and addresses already detected. Any DNS server can cache data, including primary, secondary, and caching-only DNS servers.

caching-only server   A DNS server that does not have primary or secondary zone database responsibilities; this type of server is used only to cache already resolved domain names and addresses, as well as related error information.

canonical name (CNAME) record   The DNS RR used to define database aliases, primarily to make it quicker and easier to edit and manage DNS zone files.

database segment   *See* DNS database segment.

delegation of authority   The principle whereby one name server designates another name server to handle some or all of the zone files for the domain or subdomains under its purview. The DNS NS resource record provides the pointer mechanism that name servers use to delegate authority.

distributed database technology   A database that's managed by multiple database servers, each of which has responsibility for some distinct portion of a global database. As such, DNS is nonpareil in its effective use of distributed database technology.

DNS database segment   A distinct and autonomous subset of data from the DNS name and address hierarchy. A DNS database segment usually corresponds to a DNS database zone and is stored in a collection of interrelated zone files. *See also* zone and zone file.

DNS round robin   A method of managing server congestion in which a DNS server keeps track of which IP addresses it has provided most recently for a specific translation and rotates them within the pool or list of addresses available. The DNS server can distribute the processing load, thus avoiding server congestion.

domain name hierarchy   The entire global namespace for the domain names that DNS manages on the Internet. This space includes all registered and active (and therefore, valid and usable) domain names.

domain name resolution   The process whereby DNS translates a domain name into a corresponding numeric IP address.

fully qualified domain name (FQDN)   A special form of a domain name that ends with a period to indicate the root of the domain name hierarchy. You must use FQDNs in DNS A and PTR resource records.

host information (HINFO) record   A DNS resource record that provides information about some specific host, as specified by its domain name.

HOSTS   A special text file that lists known domain names and corresponding IP addresses, thereby defining a static method for domain name resolution. Until DNS was implemented, HOSTS files provided the sole means for name resolution on the precursor to the Internet, the ARPANET.

incremental zone transfer   A type of DNS query that limits updates from a primary DNS server to one or more secondary DNS servers only to data that has changed on the primary server.

inverse DNS query   A DNS query that supplies an IP address for conversion to a corresponding domain name. Inverse DNS queries are often used to double-check user identities to make sure that the domain names they present match the IP addresses in their packet headers. *See also* IP spoofing.

IP spoofing   A technique whereby a programmer constructs an IP packet that presents domain name credentials that differ from the IP address in the packet header. IP spoofing is often used in illicit network break-in attempts or to impersonate users or packet origination.

ipv6-literal.net name   A name for an IPv6 address used for services on computers that do not recognize IPv6 address syntax. Also referred to as an ipv6 literal.

8

iterative query A DNS query that targets one specific DNS server and terminates with whatever response may be forthcoming, whether that response is a definite answer, an error message, a null (no information) reply, or a pointer to another name server.

Link-Local Multicast Name Resolution (LLMNR) A protocol that provides name resolution services on local networks for IPv4 and IPv6 Windows computers.

mail exchange (MX) record A DNS resource record that's used to identify the domain name for the e-mail server that handles any particular domain or subdomain, or that's used to route e-mail traffic from one e-mail server to another while e-mail is in transit from sender to receiver.

master server *See* primary DNS server.

multihomed Containing multiple network interfaces capable of attaching to multiple subnets.

name query An inverse DNS query that seeks to obtain a domain name for a corresponding numeric IP address.

name resolution *See* domain name resolution.

name resolution protocols Procedures that govern the rules and conventions used in manually and dynamically providing for name resolution systems in a networked environment.

name resolver A client-side software component, usually part of a TCP/IP stack implementation, that's responsible for issuing DNS queries for applications and relaying whatever responses come back to those applications.

name server (NS) record The DNS resource record that identifies name servers that are authoritative for some particular domain or subdomain. Often used as a mechanism to delegate authority for DNS subdomains downward in the domain name hierarchy.

Nbtstat A command-line program that returns statistics on NetBIOS, using NetBT if TCP/IP is installed on the machine from which it is run. Nbtstat is a simple tool that displays the state of particular NetBIOS clients and NetBIOS name resolution in general.

negative caching A technique for storing error messages in a local cache so that repeating a query that previously produced an error message can be satisfied more quickly than if that query was forwarded to some other DNS name server.

nonauthoritative response Name, address, or RR information from a DNS server that's not authoritative for the DNS zone being queried (such responses originate from caches on such servers).

nonrecursive query *See* iterative query.

Nslookup A widely implemented command-line program that supports DNS lookup and reporting capabilities. The "Ns" in this command name stands for "name server," so it's reasonable to think of this as a general-purpose name server lookup tool.

Peer Name Resolution Protocol (PNRP) A name resolution protocol used for peer-to-peer network environments and that provides secure and scalable resolution services.

pointer (PTR) record The DNS resource record that's used for inverse lookups to map numeric IP addresses to domain names.

primary DNS server The name server that's authoritative for some particular domain or subdomain and has primary custody over the DNS database segment (and related zone files) for that domain or subdomain.

primary master *See* primary DNS server.

recursive query A type of DNS query that continues until a definitive answer is forthcoming, be it a name-address translation, contents of the requested resource record(s), or an error message of some kind. Clients issue recursive queries to their designated name servers, which issue iterative queries to other name servers until the initial recursive request is resolved.

resolver *See* name resolver.

resource record (RR) One of a series of predefined record types in a DNS database or a DNS zone file.

reverse DNS lookups *See* inverse DNS query.

root The highest level in the domain name hierarchy, symbolized by a final period in a fully qualified domain name. Root DNS servers provide the glue that ties together all the disparate parts of the domain name hierarchy. They also provide name resolution for queries that might otherwise go unresolved.

Samba A free software service that provides file and print sharing for Windows and that can interoperate with other operating systems such as Linux.

secondary DNS server A DNS server that contains a copy of a domain or subdomain database, along with copies of the related zone files, but which must synchronize its database and related files with whatever server is primary for that domain or subdomain.

secondary master *See* secondary DNS server.

Service location (SRV) record Designed to provide information about available services, and used in the Windows Active Directory (AD) environment to map the name of a service to the name of a server that offers such service. AD clients and domain controllers use SRV records to determine IP addresses for (other) domain controllers.

slave server *See* secondary DNS server.

Start of Authority (SOA) record The DNS resource record that's mandatory in every DNS zone file; identifies the server or servers that are authoritative for the domain or subdomain to which the zone files or database correspond.

Stateless Address Autoconfiguration (SLAAC) A mechanism where an IPv6 host creates its own addresses using a combination of locally available address data and information advertised by routers.

subdomain A named element within a specific domain name, denoted by adding an additional name and period before the parent domain name. Thus, clearlake.ibm.com is a subdomain of the ibm.com domain.

text (TXT) record A DNS resource record that can accommodate arbitrary ASCII text data, often used to describe a DNS database segment, the hosts it contains, and so forth.

tree structure A type of data structure that's organized, such as a taxonomy or a disk drive listing, in which the entire container acts as the root, and in which subcontainers may include either other lower-level subcontainers or instances of whatever kinds of objects may occur within a container. The domain name hierarchy adheres to an inverted tree structure because the root usually appears at the top of diagrams drawn to represent it.

Universal Naming Convention (UNC) path Also referred to as a Uniform Naming Convention path or an UNC path, this is a naming format that points to the location of devices and resources on a network.

Uniform Resource Identifier (URI) A character string that is used to identify a resource on the Internet and includes URLs and URNs.

Wait Acknowledgment (WACK) A message sent by a network device such as a WINS server to acknowledge the receipt of a message from a sending node and directing the sending node to wait rather than sending more packets or expecting more data.

well-known services (WKS) record A DNS resource record that describes the well-known IP services available from a host, such as Telnet, FTP, and so forth. WKS records are less available to outsiders than they once were because they identify hosts that could become points of potential attack.

zone A portion of the domain name hierarchy that corresponds to the database segment managed by some particular name server or collection of name servers.

zone data file Any of several specific files used to capture DNS database information for static storage when a DNS server is shut down or when a secondary DNS server requests synchronization with its primary DNS server's database.

zone file *See* zone data file.

zone transfer The DNS mechanism in which a secondary DNS server gets its data for the zone from the master server for that zone. The secondary server checks a specific field in its SOA record and compares it to a corresponding value in the master server's database. Where differences are noted, the secondary updates its database from the primary domain name server.

Review Questions

1. What method of name resolution was used on the Internet prior to the introduction of DNS?

   a. Dynamic name resolution

   b. Static name resolution

   c. Active name resolution

   d. Passive name resolution

2. Link-Local Multicast Name Resolution (LLMNR) is a name resolution protocol that works in what kind of environment?

   a. IPv4 exclusively

   b. IPv6 exclusively

   c. In a single subnet

   d. In site-local and global networks

3. What is the name of the reverse hierarchy tree for DNS extensions in an IPv6 environment?

   a. in-addr.arpa

   b. ip6.arpa

   c. ipv6.arpa

   d. ipv6-addr.arpa

4. Which of the following characterize valid aspects of DNS? (Choose three all that apply.)

   a. Local control over domain name database segments

   b. Designation of optional primary name servers and mandatory secondary name servers

   c. Data from all database segments, available everywhere

   d. Highly robust and available database information

5. In Windows 7, the default NetBIOS setting is to use whatever NetBIOS setting is provided dynamically by DHCP or, if the computer uses a static IPv6 address, automatically use NetBIOS over TCP/IP. True or False?

6. Top-level domain names include two- and three-letter country codes as well as organizational codes, such as .com, .edu, and .org. True or False?

7. What is the process whereby a DNS server higher in the domain name hierarchy confers responsibility for portions of the global DNS database on DNS servers lower in its hierarchy?

   a. Subordination of authority

   b. Database consolidation

   c. Delegation of authority

   d. Database segmentation

8. IPv6 uses what means to provide source and destination address selection?

   a. A single source and destination address selection algorithm is used.

   b. A source address selection algorithm and a destination address selection algorithm are used.

   c. For source address selection, a set of eight algorithms is used; for destination address selection, a set of 10 algorithms is used.

   d. IPv6 uses the same process for source and destination address selection that IPv4 uses.

9. Which DNS resource record is used for IPv6 host addresses?

   a. A

   b. AAAA

   c. PTR

   d. MX

10. Which of the following ipv6-literal.net names can be read by Windows and any legacy software?

   a. http://2001:db8–adc2-2131.ipv6.literal.net

   b. http://[2001:db8::adc2:2131]

   c. http://[2001:db8--adc2-2131]

   d. http://2001:db8--adc2-2131-ipv6-literal-net

11. IPv6 destination address selection may interfere with what IPv4 DNS destination address process for Windows computers?

    a. LLMNR

    b. Nbtstat

    c. PNRP

    d. Round robin

12. Which DNS resource record maps domain names to IPv4 host addresses?

    a. A

    b. SOA

    c. PTR

    d. MX

13. Any type of DNS server also can be a caching-only server. True or False?

14. The primary benefit of caching DNS data is:

    a. Faster lookups

    b. Reduced remote network traffic

    c. Balanced DNS server load

    d. Increased server reliability

15. A DNS server that's primary for one DNS database zone can also be secondary for one or more other DNS database zones. True or False?

16. What is the maximum number of primary database servers allowed in any single DNS database zone?

    a. 1

    b. 2

    c. 4

    d. 8

    e. 16

17. It is mandatory to have one or more secondary DNS servers for any DNS database zone. True or False?

18. What size or type of organization is most likely to benefit from a caching-only DNS server? (Choose all that apply.)

    a. Small

    b. Medium

    c. Large

    d. Service provider

19. What kinds of data are most likely to show up in a response to a DNS query of any kind? (Choose all that apply.)

    a. Address forwarding instructions

    b. DNS resource records

    c. Address impersonation alerts

    d. Error messages

20. Which of the following query sequences represents a typical DNS lookup?

    a. Iterative, then recursive

    b. Recursive, then iterative

    c. Static, then dynamic

    d. Dynamic, then static

21. Why do "all DNS queries end at the root?"

    a. The root maintains a copy of the global DNS database.

    b. The root can access any and all authoritative name servers for any database segment.

    c. Any DNS server can access the root at any time.

    d. Multiple root servers prevent the root of the domain name hierarchy from becoming bogged down with requests.

22. When using the `nslookup` command, an authoritative response is _____:

    a. explicitly labeled as such

    b. available only if the authoritative name server is explicitly targeted for lookup

    c. available only by request, using the -a option

    d. implied by the absence of "non-authoritative response" in the reply

23. It is necessary to add resource records for the DNS root servers to the cache of any DNS server during initial configuration and setup. True or False?

24. Peer Name Resolution Protocol (PNRP) is supported on which of the following Windows operating systems? (Choose all that apply.)

    a. Windows XP SP2

    b. Windows Vista

    c. Windows Server 2003

    d. Windows Server 2008

25. On a computer running Windows 7, the correct command for discovering the name and address of www.ipv6testlabs.com is **nslookup -aaaa www.ipv6testlabs.com**. True or False?

Hands-On Projects

Hands-On Project 8-1: Working with the DNS Resolver Cache

Time Required: 10 minutes

Objective: Discover how to view and manipulate a computer's DNS resolver cache.

Description: In this project, you will learn to use basic ipconfig commands at the Windows command prompt to view, flush, and reset the DNS resolver cache on a PC.

1. Click the **Start** button and type **cmd** in the Start menu search box.

2. Right-click **cmd.exe** and click **Run as administrator**.

3. When prompted, click **Yes**.

4. To view your DNS resolver cache, at the prompt, type **ipconfig /displaydns** and press **Enter**. The output will be similar to what is displayed in Figure 8-16.

```
Command Prompt
docs.google.com

    Record Name . . . . . : docs.google.com
    Record Type . . . . . : 1
    Time To Live . . . . : 21133
    Data Length . . . . . : 4
    Section . . . . . . . : Answer
    A (Host) Record . . . : 173.194.33.38

    Record Name . . . . . : docs.google.com
    Record Type . . . . . : 1
    Time To Live . . . . : 21133
    Data Length . . . . . : 4
    Section . . . . . . . : Answer
    A (Host) Record . . . : 173.194.33.39

    Record Name . . . . . : docs.google.com
    Record Type . . . . . : 1
    Time To Live . . . . : 21133
    Data Length . . . . . : 4
    Section . . . . . . . : Answer
    A (Host) Record . . . : 173.194.33.40

    Record Name . . . . . : docs.google.com
    Record Type . . . . . : 1
    Time To Live . . . . : 21133
```

Figure 8-16 DNS resolver cache
Source: Microsoft

5. At the prompt, type **ipconfig /flushdns** and press **Enter**.

6. Once you receive the success message and your cache has been purged, at the prompt, type **ipconfig /displaydns** and press **Enter**.

7. After you receive the message stating that your resolver cache could not be displayed, open a Web browser and visit several Web sites, such as *www.google.com* and *www.microsoft.com*.

8. Close the Web browser and, at the command prompt, type **ipconfig /displaydns**, press **Enter**, then notice how there are entries in your resolver cache similar to those in Figure 8-17.

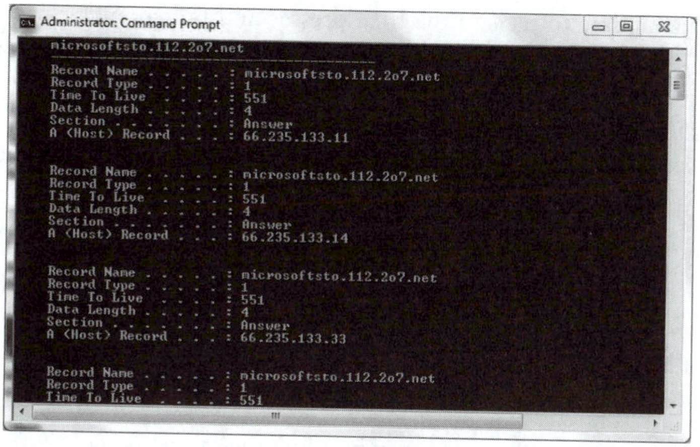

Figure 8-17 New entries in DNS resolver cache
Source: Microsoft

9. At the prompt, type **ipconfig /registerdns** and press **Enter** to refresh the computer's DHCP lease and re-register its DNS names. You will receive a message stating that the process has been initiated and that any errors will be reported in the Event Viewer in 15 minutes.

10. To view the computer's IPv6 prefix policies, at the command prompt, type **netsh interface ipv6 show prefixpolicies** and then press **Enter**.

11. At the prompt, type **exit** and press **Enter** to close the command prompt.

Hands-On Project 8-2: Setting Windows 7 to use DNS Dynamic Updates

Time Required: 10 minutes

Objective: Find out how to configure a Windows 7 computer to use DNS dynamic updates.

Description: In this project, you will learn how to use the utilities in a Windows 7 computer's Ethernet properties for IPv4 to configure how the computer registers its IP address, host name, and domain name with a DNS server dynamically.

1. Click the **Start** button, and then click **Control Panel**.

2. When the Control Panel opens, if necessary, select **View by Large icons**.

3. Click **Network and Sharing Center**.

4. Click **Change adapter settings**.

5. Right-click the **Local Area Connection** applet and then click **Properties**.

6. In the Local Area Connections Properties box, select **Internet Protocol Version 4 (TCP/IPv4)** and then click **Properties**.

7. On the General tab, click the **Advanced** button.

8. In the Advanced TCP/IP Settings box, click the **DNS** tab.

9. To use DNS dynamic update to register the IP addresses and full computer name of your computer for this connection, select the **Register this connection's addresses in DNS** check box (it should be selected by default).

10. If you want to use DNS dynamic update to register the IP addresses and domain name for this connection, select the **Use this connection's DNS suffix in DNS registration** check box.

11. Click **Cancel** so that you don't save your changes.

12. Close the rest of the dialog boxes and the Control Panel.

Hands-On Project 8-3: Convert an IPv6 Address into an ipv6-literal.net Name

Time Required: 10 minutes

Objective: Discover how to convert IPv6 addresses into ipv6-literal.net names.

Description: In this project, you will use a Web application to convert one or more IPv6 addresses into ipv6-literal.net names, including literal Windows, URL literals, UNC literals, ip6.arpa, and more.

1. Open a Web browser, type or paste the URL **http://ipv6-literal.com/** into the address bar, and then press **Enter**.

2. Open a command prompt, type **ipconfig /all**, and then press **Enter**.

3. In the output in the command prompt, find your computer's link-local IPv6 address.

4. Click the **Start** button, type **notepad** in the Search box, and then click **Notepad**.

5. Right-click in the command prompt window and then click **Select All**.

6. Press **Enter** to copy.

7. In Notepad, right-click in a blank area and then click **Paste**.

8. Locate the link-local IPv6 address, highlight it, and press **Ctrl+C** to copy it to the Clipboard.

9. At the ipv6-literal.com site, paste the IPv6 address into the Enter IPv6 address field using the **Ctrl+V** key combination, and then click **Convert**.

10. In the Result area of the page, review the information presented, which should look like the output shown in Figure 8-18.

Figure 8-18 Output at ipv6-literal.com
Source: ipv6-literal.com

11. You may enter other IPv6 addresses and see the output; when you're done, close the command prompt, the Web browser, and Notepad without saving the file.

Hands-On Project 8-4: Capture and Examine Your Own DNS Traffic

Time Required: 10 minutes

Objective: See how to examine the DNS traffic on your computer.

Description: In this project, you will capture DNS traffic on your own network and examine the resulting packet. This project assumes that you are working in a Windows 7 environment and that you installed the Wireshark program.

1. Click the **Start** button, type **wireshark** in the Search box, and then press **Enter**.

2. Open a Web browser.

3. In the Wireshark toolbar, click **Capture** and then click **Interfaces**.

4. Next to the Ethernet interface for your computer, click **Start**.

5. Use the Web browser to visit several Web sites, such as *www.microsoft.com*, *www.cisco.com*, and *www.juniper.net*, and then close the Web browser.

6. In the Wireshark toolbar, click **Capture** and then click **Stop** to stop capturing packets.

7. In the Wireshark main pane, scroll down until you see the first DNS entry in the Protocol column and Standard query in the Info column. Select the first entry.

8. In the pane immediately beneath, select and expand **Domain Name System (query)**.

9. Expand **Flags**, expand **Queries**, and then expand the domain name under Queries, as shown in Figure 8-19.

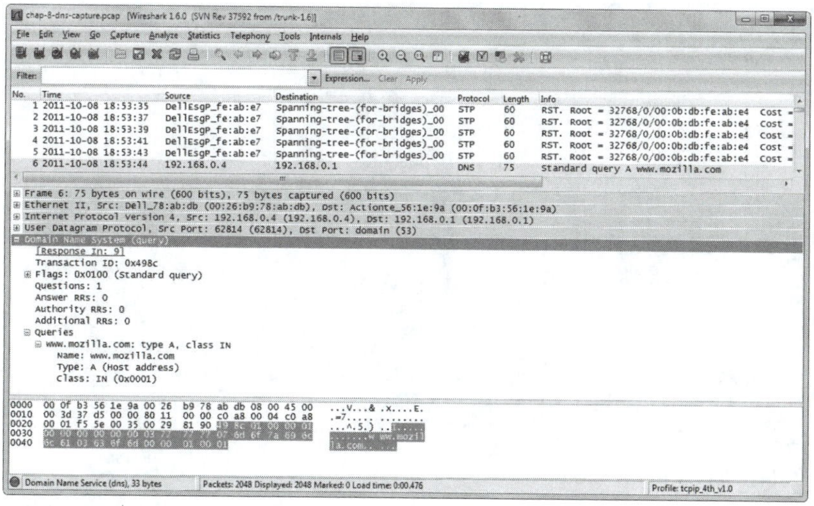

Figure 8-19 DNS Queries data in Wireshark

Source: Wireshark

10. In the Wireshark main pane, in the Info column, select an entry saying Standard query response.

11. In the pane just beneath, expand **Domain Name System (response)**, expand **Answers**, and then expand one of the domain names under Answers.

12. After you have finished examining the information, close Wireshark.

Hands-On Project 8-5: Install DNS Server Software and Configure Lookup Zones

Time Required: 30 minutes

Objective: Install and configure a DNS server.

Description: In this project, you will learn the basic steps involved in installing the DNS server software that's included as part of all server versions of Windows Server 2008. You also create forward and reverse lookup zones. These steps were created using Windows Server 2008 R2. If you use a different server version, or if your server is configured for several roles, your steps may vary.

1. Click the **Start** button, point to **Administrative Tools**, and then click **Server Manager**.

2. In the menu list on the left, right-click **Roles** and then click **Add Roles**.

3. In the Add Roles Wizard screen, click **Server Roles**.

4. In the Select Server Roles screen shown in Figure 8-20, click **DNS server**, and then click **Next**.

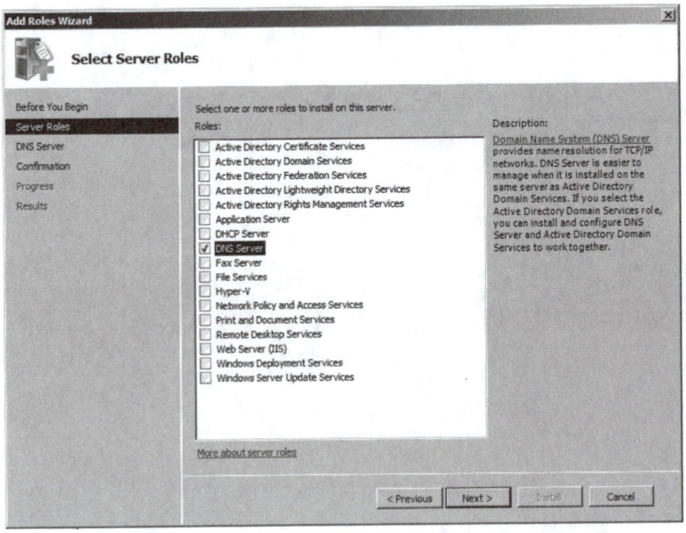

Figure 8-20 Select Server Roles screen
Source: Microsoft

5. On the DNS Server screen, read the introduction and then click **Next**.

6. On the Confirm Installation Selections screen, click **Install**.

7. Once the DNS Server role is successfully installed, note the message on the screen stating that you can configure DNS using the DNS Server Wizard in DNS Manager. Click **Close.**

8. In Server Manager, expand **Roles,** if necessary, expand **DNS Server, DNS,** and expand the server name.

9. Right-click **Forward Lookup Zones** and click **Add New Zone.**

10. When the Welcome to the New Zone Wizard launches, click **Next.**

11. On the Zone Type screen, verify that **Primary zone** is selected, as shown in Figure 8-21, and then click **Next.**

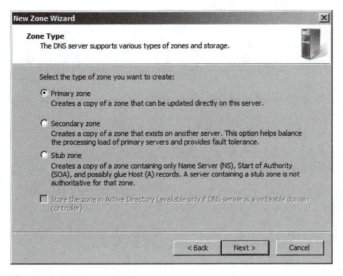

Figure 8-21 Zone Type screen
Source: Microsoft

12. On the Zone Name screen, provide a name for the zone over which this server will have authority (such as mydomain1.com), and then click **Next.**

13. On the Zone File screen shown in Figure 8-22, use the filename provided by default or provide your own, and then click **Next.**

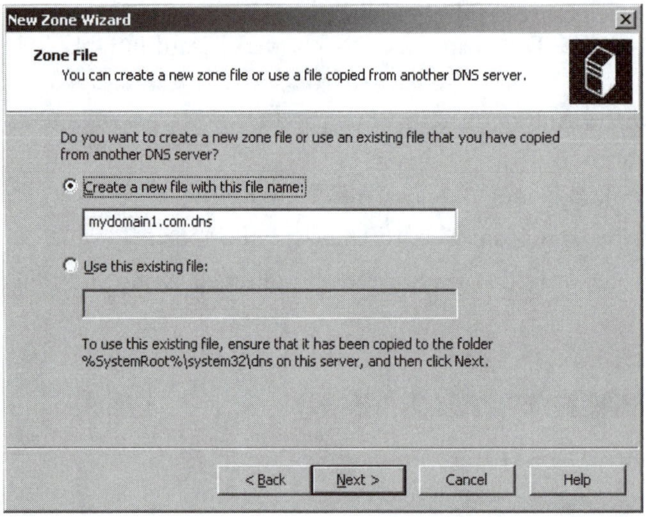

Figure 8-22 Zone File screen
Source: Microsoft

14. On the Dynamic Update screen, click **Do not allow dynamic updates** option, if necessary, and then click **Next**.

15. On the Completing the New Zone Wizard screen, verify that the information presented is correct and then click **Finish**.

Hands-On Project 8-6: Create Additional Zones

Time Required: 10 minutes

Objective: Configure additional zones on a DNS server.

Description: In this project, you will learn how to create an additional DNS forward lookup zone.

1. Click the **Start** button, point to **Administrative Tools**, and then click **DNS**.

2. Double-click the DNS server name in the left pane to expand the entry, select the **Forward Lookup Zones** folder, and then select **New Zone** from the Action menu. The New Zone Wizard starts.

3. On the Welcome to the New Zone Wizard screen, click **Next**.

4. On the Zone Type screen, select the **Primary zone** option, if necessary, and then click **Next**.

5. On the Zone Name screen, provide a name for the zone over which this server will have authority (such as mydomain2.com), and then click **Next**.

6. On the Zone File screen, use the filename provided by default or provide your own, and then click **Next**.

7. On the Dynamic Update screen, click the **Do not allow dynamic updates** option, if necessary, and then click **Next**.

8. The Completing the New Zone Wizard screen displays the settings to be implemented. Click **Finish**.

9. Close any open windows.

Case Projects

Case Project 8-1: Gathering IPv6 Address Data to Configure a Name Server

You are an administrator for the local DNS server for your company, and you have been tasked with manually adding the IPv6 reverse mapping zones for your company's domain to the server's config file. The IPv4 domain name for your company's Web site is abcxyz.com, and the IPv6 domain name is abcxyz-v6.com. You must know the IPv4 and IPv6 addresses for your company's domain and any subdomains, such as marketing.abcxyz.com and marketing.abcxyz-v6.com or sales.abcxyz.com and sales.abcxyz-v6.com, so you can configure the corresponding A and AAAA records as well as the ip6.arpa reverse mapping zone names for each IPv6 address. Determine where you would find this data, and then, once you have gathered that information, construct the beginning of an IPv6 reverse mapping zone based on that information. Use the $ORIGIN control statement and the following format:

$ORIGIN ip6.arpa name

PTR record

PTR record

See the section "Name Resolution in IPv6 networks" in this chapter for examples.

Case Project 8-2: Explaining the Use of Caching-Only DNS Servers

Explain what it is about the communications architecture and flow of TCP/IP traffic that makes caching-only servers useful for ISPs. Please consider the way that IP clients connect to most ISPs and how their TCP/IP stacks are configured when you formulate your answer.

Case Project 8-3: Understanding the Minimum Number of DNS Servers in a Network Infrastructure

Explain why two name servers is the minimum number you would ever want to run in an organization's networked IP environment. Consider the following factors, which can influence the total number of name servers present on a typical organization's internetwork:

- If a name server is available directly on each network or subnet in a local internetwork, routers need not become potential points of failure. Consider also that multihomed hosts make ideal locations for DNS because they can directly service all the subnets to which they're connected.

- In an environment in which diskless nodes or network computers depend on a server for network and file access, installing a name server on that particular server at a minimum makes DNS directly available to all such machines.

- Where large time-sharing machines—such as mainframes, terminal servers, or clustered computers—operate, a nearby DNS server can offload name services from the big machine, yet still provide reasonable response time and service.

- Running an additional name server at an off-site location—logically, at the site of the ISP from which your organization obtains an Internet connection—keeps DNS data available even if your Internet link goes down or local name servers are unavailable. A remote secondary name server provides the ultimate form of backup and helps to ensure DNS reliability.

Given the foregoing information and the fact that the organization operates three subnets at each of its Indiana locations along with a large clustered terminal server at each location, explain how XYZ might want to operate as many as nine name servers for its network environment.

chapter 9

TCP/IP Transport Layer Protocols

After reading this chapter and completing the exercises, you will be able to:

- Explain the key features and functions of the User Datagram Protocol and the Transmission Control Protocol
- Explain, in detail, the header fields and functions of the UDP packet, as well as port numbers, processes, and how UDP behaves when used as a transport protocol by IPv6
- Explain in detail, the mechanisms that drive segmentation, reassembly, and retransmission for TCP as well as how TCP behaves when used as a transport protocol by IPv6
- Describe how UDP and TCP pseudo-headers are organized with the IPv6 header and extension headers
- Explain the differences between connectionless and connection-oriented transport mechanisms
- Choose between using User Datagram Protocol and Transmission Control Protocol

Whereas TCP/IP's Network layer protocols provide network address, routing, and delivery functions, TCP/IP's Transport layer protocols provide the mechanisms necessary to move messages of arbitrary size from sender to receiver across a network. Although the Transmission Control Protocol (TCP), which helps give the overall protocol stack its name, is arguably more important than the only other TCP/IP Transport layer protocol—the User Datagram Protocol (UDP)—both of these protocols perform vital roles in enabling the transfer of arbitrary data across a network. As you make your way through this chapter, you will come to understand the vital concepts involved in connectionless transport mechanisms versus **connection-oriented transport mechanisms** and the impact these mechanisms have on complexity, robustness, reliability, and overhead.

We begin the chapter with a comparison of these two protocol types.

Understanding UDP and TCP

UDP and TCP actually function as peers, and both are very important to the transport function in networking, but they fulfill highly different roles. To understand how UDP and TCP work, we need to briefly cover what the Internet Protocol (IP) does, because both UDP and TCP help provide transport for IP.

IP operates at the Network layer of the OSI model and is responsible for providing the means to transfer variable length data sequences from a source host to a destination host on both a single network and across multiple networks. There are a number of services that IP does not provide. IP is considered connectionless, unacknowledged, and unreliable. This means that although network traffic usually gets where it's supposed to go, there are no guarantees. Your message may or may not get to its destination, but based on IP, you will never know for sure.

If all applications required a guarantee of acknowledged delivery, then the only protocol that would be needed is TCP; however, TCP comes at the cost of both time and bandwidth because it provides connection-oriented, reliable Transport layer addressing and it manages acknowledgments, which all consume time. UDP also provides Transport layer addressing for IP, but it is used for applications that do not need verified delivery. Information may be lost, but there's a gain in speed and a reduced use of network bandwidth. The decision to use UDP or TCP is based on the requirements of the application sending data across the network.

UDP with IPv4 and IPv6

Connectionless protocols provide the simplest kind of transport services because they simply package messages that are taken, as is, from the TCP/IP Application layer into datagrams. A datagram adds a header to the higher-layer data and passes it to the Internet Protocol (IP) layer, where that datagram is fitted with an IP header and packaged, after which it may be transmitted across the network. This method is called **best-effort delivery** because it offers no built-in error-checking or retransmission capability to improve reliability.

UDP is a simple protocol that is used by applications that contain their own connection-oriented timeout values and retry counters, similar to those provided by TCP. This turns out to be a smart design decision on most modern networks because the overhead of providing the various delivery guarantees and reliability mechanisms that TCP delivers comes at a cost. More capability means more overhead because of the information that must be gathered, exchanged, and managed to provide such capability.

UDP runs up to 40 percent faster than TCP, under some conditions, because it does next to nothing. In practice, datagrams in a UDP sequence usually match the size of the maximum transmission unit (MTU) for the medium at the transmitting machine. The exception is the last datagram, which needs to be only as long as the final leftover payload and header information require. The Application layer protocol requires only simple services from UDP because the Application layer protocol handles its own reassembly and error management for the data.

It is typical for connectionless protocols to handle the following kinds of tasks:

- *Message checksum*—Although connectionless protocols don't track transmission behavior or completeness of delivery (that's what best-effort delivery means), they can optionally include a checksum for each datagram. This makes it easy for the Transport layer protocol to report to a higher-layer protocol whether the packet made it to the destination in the same form as when it left the sender, without having to handle the potentially complicated details involved.

- *Higher-layer protocol identification*—Generally speaking, all TCP/IP Transport layer protocols use source and destination port address fields in their headers to identify specific Application layer protocols on the sending and receiving hosts so they can exchange messages at that higher layer. This protocol identification mechanism identifies an Application layer protocol through the well-known port addresses associated with most higher-layer TCP/IP protocols and services. This mechanism also permits application processes that use those protocols or services to exchange data to identify each other uniquely while individual or multiple streams of communications between a sender and a receiver are underway. Thus, even though a connectionless protocol has no internal methods for creating, managing, and terminating connections, it does provide a mechanism for such activities to occur at the Application layer. You'll learn considerably more about port addresses and their various uses throughout this chapter.

 As a protocol running over IPv4, UDP is little or no different than UDP running over IPv6. The UDP protocol has not been updated independently in the new version of the IP protocol; however, UDP can function differently, depending on what IPv6 requires. For instance, when a jumbogram is used in IPv6, requiring a longer than standard payload, both UDP and TCP need to be adapted to meet this requirement. This is described in RFC 2675. See Chapter 3 for the details about IPv6 jumbograms.

Although other protocols have been updated for IPv6, such as ICMPv4 being updated to ICMPv6, it's more accurate to say "UDP over IPv6" instead of "UDPv6." You can see this by using the `netstat` command at the Windows command prompt. Typing `netstat -sp udp` will return the netstat connection statistics for UDP for IPv4, as shown in Figure 9-1.

Figure 9-1 Netstat UDP statistics for IPv4
Source: Microsoft

Typing `netstat -sp udpv6` provides the same information, but for UDP over IPv6, as shown in Figure 9-2.

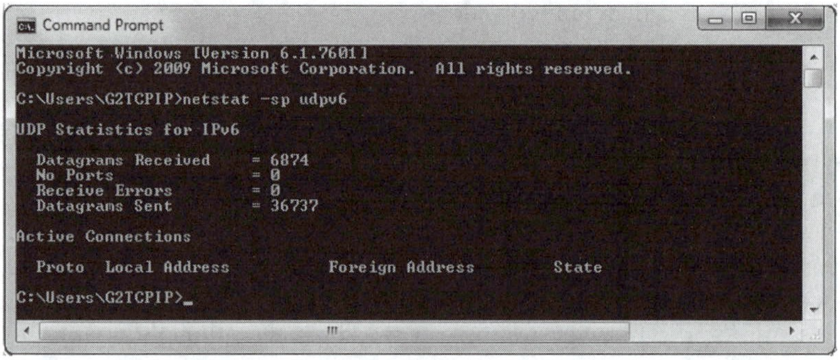

Figure 9-2 Netstat UDP statistics for IPv6
Source: Microsoft

RFC 2460, which specifies IPv6, describes how UDP operates differently over IPv4 than over IPv6. One difference is that, unlike UDP running over IPv4, when an IPv6 network node sends data using UDP, the UDP checksum is required rather than optional. The IPv6 computer must calculate a UDP checksum for the packet and the pseudo-header. However, much of how UDP operates under IPv6 is the same as under IPv4. How UDP runs as an upper layer protocol under IPv4 and IPv6 is discussed in more detail later in this chapter.

TCP with IPv4 and IPv6

TCP is a connection-oriented protocol. Applications that rely on data reaching its destination use TCP instead of UDP.

Note that connection-oriented protocols do the following:

- Create a **logical connection** directly between two peers on an internetwork.
- Track the transfer of data and ensure that it arrives successfully through **acknowledgments** and **sequence number tracking**. An acknowledgment is a **positive response** to indicate explicitly that a specific set of data arrived intact.
- Use sequence number tracking to identify the amount of data transferred and any **out-of-order packets**.
- Have a **timeout mechanism** that indicates when a host waits too long to receive a communication and that such communication should be assumed lost.
- Have a **retry mechanism** that enables them to recover lost data by retransmitting it some specified number of times.

TCP offers connection-oriented services with sequencing, **error recovery**, and a **sliding window** mechanism. Because of TCP's **end-to-end reliability** and flexibility, it is the preferred transport method for applications that transfer large quantities of data and require reliable delivery services.

TCP hosts create a **virtual connection** with each other using a **handshake process**. During the handshake process, hosts exchange a sequence number that is used to track data as it transfers from one host to another.

TCP transfers data as a continuous stream of bytes, with no knowledge of the underlying **messages** or message boundaries that might be contained in that **byte stream**. Upon receipt, the upper-layer application interprets the byte stream to read the messages contained therein.

The maximum TCP segment size is 65,495 bytes. This number is reached by subtracting 20 bytes for an IP header and another 20 bytes for the TCP header from the Total Length Size field value. Figure 9-3 depicts how data is segmented and prefaced by a series of headers, including a TCP header, an IP header, and the Ethernet header.

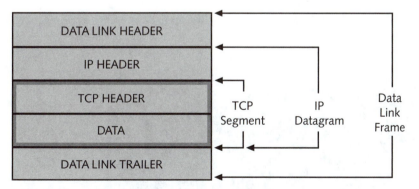

Figure 9-3 Packet headers and different protocol layers
© Cengage Learning 2013

As previously mentioned, UDP and TCP do not have v6 versions to match IPv6. Both protocols are essentially unchanged in terms of providing transport for IPv6. However, IPv6 may make different use of TCP depending on its requirements, such as IPv6 jumbograms. It's more accurate to say that "TCP runs over IPv6" rather than refer to "TCPv6." As with UDP, this can be demonstrated using the `netstat` command at the Windows command prompt. Type `netstat -sp tcp` to see the network statistics for TCP running over IPv4, as shown in Figure 9-4.

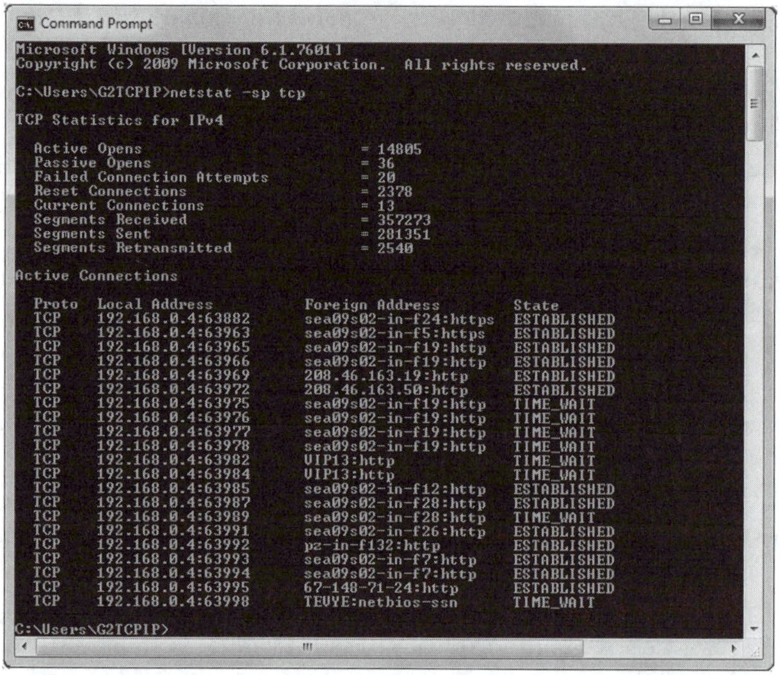

Figure 9-4 Netstat TCP statistics for IPv4
Source: Microsoft

Type `netstat -sp tcpv6` to view the network statistics of TCP running over IPv6, as shown in Figure 9-5.

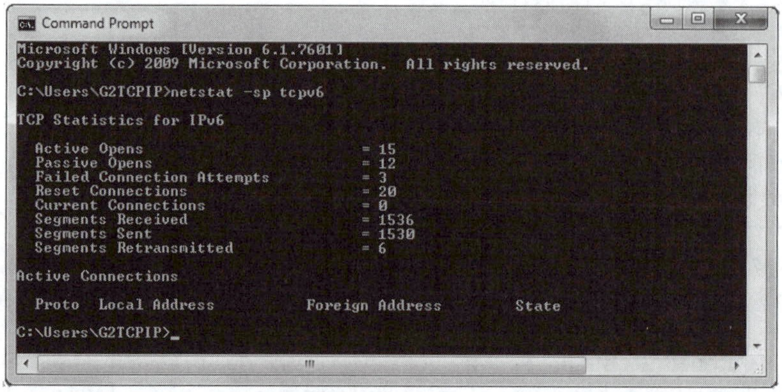

Figure 9-5 Netstat TCP statistics for IPv6
Source: Microsoft

Although TCP itself hasn't changed, how it operates may be modified based on characteristics of IPv6 vs. IPv4. For instance, when calculating the maximum payload size, TCP must adjust to the larger size of the IPv6 header. When performing this function for the IPv4 header, TCP's **maximum segment size (MSS)** option is calculated as the maximum packet size minus 40 octets, which is 20 octets for the minimum-length IPv4 header and 20 octets for the TCP header. When an IPv6 node is using TCP, the MSS must be calculated as the maximum packet size minus 60 octets, which is 20 octets for the TCP header and 40 octets for the minimum-length IPv6 header, assuming an IPv6 header with no extension headers. How TCP runs as an upper layer protocol under IPv4 and IPv6 is discussed in more detail later in this chapter.

User Datagram Protocol

UDP was originally specified by RFC 768 in 1980. Because UDP is the only connectionless TCP/IP protocol at the Transport layer, it should come as no surprise that all the characteristics ascribed to connectionless TCP/IP protocols apply directly and completely to UDP itself. Consider the following characteristics and limitations of UDP:

- *No reliability mechanisms*—Datagrams are not sequenced and are not acknowledged. Most applications or services that use UDP supply their own reliability mechanisms or track timeout values for datagrams and retransmit when a datagram's timeout counter expires.

- *No delivery guarantees*—Datagrams are sent without any promise of delivery, so, again, the Application layer must provide tracking and retransmission mechanisms.

- *No connection handling*—Each datagram is an independent message that the sender transmits without UDP providing any way to establish, manage, or close a connection between sender and receiver.

- *Identifies the Application layer protocol*—As noted previously, the UDP header includes fields that identify port addresses, also known as port numbers, for sending and receiving Application layer services or processes.

- *Checksum for entire message carried in UDP header*—As packaged, each UDP header may optionally include a checksum value that can be recalculated upon delivery and compared to the value as sent. It's up to the Application layer service or protocol to act on this information; UDP does nothing more than provide this data and does not require that a checksum be calculated per se.

- *No buffering services*—UDP doesn't manage where incoming data resides in memory before delivery or where outgoing data resides before transmission. All memory management for data in motion must be handled at the Application layer for services that use UDP; it sees strictly one datagram at a time.

- *No segmentation*—UDP provides no services to break up arbitrarily large messages into discrete, labeled chunks for transmission, or to reassemble sequences of labeled chunks upon reception. UDP only sends and receives datagrams; the Application layer protocol or service must handle segmentation and reassembly, as required.

9

Notice that UDP is as much defined by what it does not provide (all the characteristics it is missing are typical for TCP) as by what it does provide, which is a checksum mechanism and identification of port addresses for sender and receiver for higher-layer uses.

UDP Header Fields and Functions

When the Protocol field of an IP header contains the value 17 (0x11), the UDP header follows the IP header. The UDP header is short and simple—only 8 bytes long. The UDP header's main function is to define the process or application that is using the IP and UDP Network and Transport layers. Figure 9-6 shows the layout of the UDP header.

Anything preceded by "0x" is a hexadecimal number. That's why "0x11" is the hexadecimal equivalent of the decimal number 17.

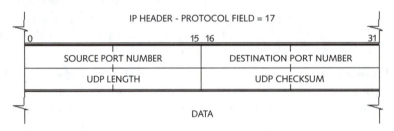

Figure 9-6 UDP header format
© Cengage Learning 2013

UDP is defined in RFC 768. In fact, the UDP header contains only four fields:

- Source Port Number field
- Destination Port Number field
- Length field
- Checksum field

In the next sections, we examine the field values and functions of the UDP header.

Source Port Number Field The Source Port Number field defines the application or process that sends the packet using the UDP header.

Port numbers are defined in three ranges: well-known port numbers, registered port numbers, and dynamic port numbers.

Well-Known Port Numbers (0 through 1023) Well-known port numbers are assigned to the key or **core services** that systems offer. Well-known port numbers are between 0 and 1023. Until 1992, the well-known port number range was between 1 and 255. Some common and well-known port numbers are listed in Table 9-1.

Registered Port Numbers (1024 through 49151) Registered port numbers are assigned to industry applications and processes; for example, 1433 is assigned to the Micro-soft SQL Server process. Some TCP/IP systems use values between 1024 and 5000 for tempo-rary port numbers, even though IANA recommends the very top of the port number space for use with dynamic ports, as described next.

Dynamic Port Numbers (49152 through 65535) **Dynamic ports** (also referred to as ephemeral ports) are used as **temporary ports** for specific communications while they're underway. When communications that use dynamic ports end, they become available for re-use four minutes thereafter. IANA defines this range of numbers—the **dynamic port numbers** range—to identify dynamic ports.

UDP	Port Number Application or Process
67	Bootstrap Protocol Server (also DHCP Server)
68	Bootstrap Protocol Client (also DHCP Client)
161	Simple Network Management Protocol (SNMP)
162	Simple Network Management Protocol (SNMP) Trap
520	Routing Information Protocol (RIP)

Table 9-1 Common well-known UDP port numbers
© Cengage Learning 2013

In most cases, the same UDP and TCP port number is assigned to an application or process. In some rare cases, however, assigned UDP and TCP port numbers do not support the same application or process—UDP port 520, for example. The UDP port number 520 is assigned to the Router Information Protocol (RIP). The TCP port number 520 is assigned to the Extended File Name Server (EFS) process. Please refer to *www.iana.org/assignments/port-numbers/* (hyphen included) for a complete list of assigned port numbers.

Table 9-1 lists some of the most commonly used UDP port numbers. UDP comes into play when reliability is not an issue, either because the sending host may not have sufficient "intelligence" to provide or understand reliability mechanisms (as is the case with DHCP) or because regular management, or routing, polling, or advertisement is not required. UDP is used when the constant communications required for verification functions diminishes the speed of delivery. In other circumstances, either the data carried or the services provided are sufficiently important—or one-time transmission is highly desirable—and increased needs for reliability or delivery guarantees come into play. That's when connection-oriented trans-port (discussed later in this chapter) is needed.

Destination Port Number Field This field value defines the destination application or process that uses the IP and UDP headers. In some instances, the source and destination port numbers are the same for client and server processes. In other instances, you may find a separate and unique number for the client and server process (as in the case of DHCP). The most common variation is to allow the client to use dynamic port numbers for its side of the communications and well-known port numbers, or registered port numbers, for the server side of the communications.

Length Field The Length field defines the length of the packet from the UDP header to the end of **valid data** (not including any data link padding, if padding is required). This field provides a redundant measurement because this information can be determined using the IP header value.

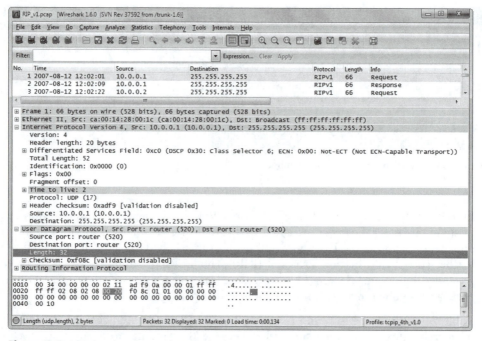

Figure 9-7 UDP header capture in Wireshark
Source: Wireshark

The following explains the Length fields shown in Figure 9-7:

- IP Header Length = 20 bytes.

- IP Total Length = 52. The data after the IP header is 32 bytes (subtract the 20-byte IP header).

- UDP Length = 32. The data after the IP header (including the UDP header) is 32 bytes, which we just learned from the Total Length field in the IP header. Subtract the 8-byte UDP header, and you know that there must be 4 bytes of data following the UDP header itself.

Checksum Field The UDP Checksum field is optional—in the case of Figure 9-7, the sender generated a checksum. If a checksum is used, the checksum calculation is performed on the contents of the entire datagram—namely, the UDP header (except the UDP Checksum field itself), the datagram payload, and a **pseudo-header**, which is derived from the IP header. The UDP pseudo-header is not actually contained in the packet; the UDP pseudo-header is used only to calculate the UDP header checksum and associate the UDP header with the IP header. This pseudo-header consists of the IP header Source Address field, the Destination Address field, an unused field (set to 0), the Protocol field, and the UDP Length field. Figure 9-8 shows the UDP pseudo-header.

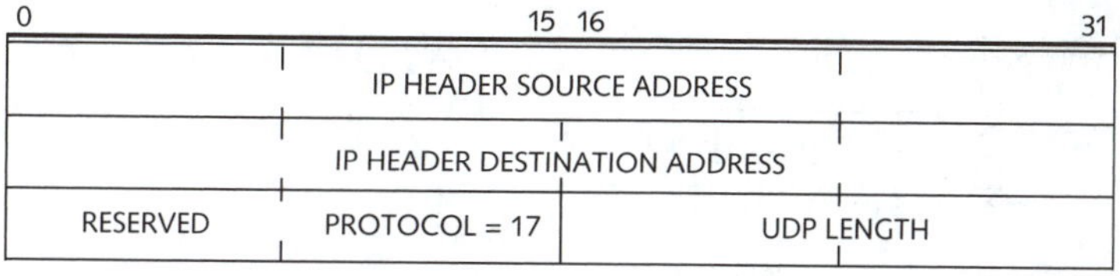

0	15 16	31
IP HEADER SOURCE ADDRESS		
IP HEADER DESTINATION ADDRESS		
RESERVED	PROTOCOL = 17	UDP LENGTH

Figure 9-8 IPv4 pseudo-header for UDP
© Cengage Learning 2013

UDP Port Numbers and Processes

Both UDP and TCP use port numbers to define the source and destination processes or applications. As mentioned in the "Destination Port Number Field" section earlier in this chapter, the source and destination port numbers are not necessarily the same within a conversation between two hosts. The first host may open a dynamic source port number to send a DNS query to standard port 53 (in fact, UDP is the preferred format for DNS queries, in which such messages are limited to 512 bytes in length). Upon receipt of the DNS query packet, the second host examines the IP header to identify the Transport layer protocol in use. Next, the second (receiving) host examines the Destination Port Number field to determine how to handle the incoming packet (where well-known port 53 indicates it's a DNS query).

Figure 9-9 shows how packets are demultiplexed based on the type number, protocol number, and port number.

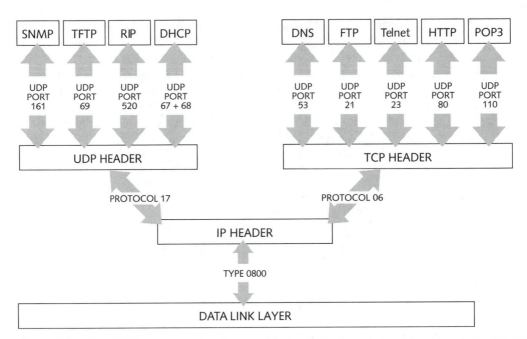

Figure 9-9 TCP and UDP communications forwarded to Application layer protocols based on destination port
© Cengage Learning 2013

By default, Windows Vista, Windows 7, and Windows Server 2008 support a port range of 49152 to 65535. Previous versions of Windows supported a port range of 1025 to 5000 by default.

You can increase the supported maximum user port numbers by adding the MaxUserPort Registry setting, as shown in Table 9-2.

Registry Information	Details
Location	HKEY_LOCAL_MACHINE\SYSTEM\ CurrentControlSet\Services\Tcpip\Parameters
Data type	REG_DWORD
Valid range	5000–65534
Default value	5000
Present by default	No

Table 9-2 MaxUserPort Registry setting
© Cengage Learning 2013

UDP's fundamental simplicity is clearly reflected in the relatively small number of UDP-related Registry values and settings for Windows 2003, Windows Server 2008, Windows Vista, and Windows 7.

UDP and IPv6

The UDP header format wasn't specifically updated for a newer version to coincide with IPv6. IPv6 treats UDP as an upper-layer transport protocol and manages UDP in accordance with its requirements. UDP hasn't changed, but IPv6 and IPv4 treat UDP a bit differently. All the information for UDP headers, port numbers, and processes that are valid under IPv4 remain valid under IPv6.

To demonstrate how UDP operates under IPv6, if the UDP protocol includes addresses from the IPv6 header in its checksum computation, the protocol must be modified for use over IPv6 to include 128-bit IPv6 addresses rather than 32-bit IPv4 addresses. This is also true for the TCP protocol. When computing the checksum, an IPv6 pseudo-header is used that mirrors or imitates the actual IPv6 header.

For more information about IPv6 pseudo-headers, see the Chapter 3 section titled "Upper-Layer Checksums in IPv6."

Figure 9-10 illustrates the structure of the IPv6 pseudo-header for UDP.

Source Address		
Destination Address		
UDP Length		
Zeros		Next Header
Source Port		Destination Port
Length		Checksum
Data		

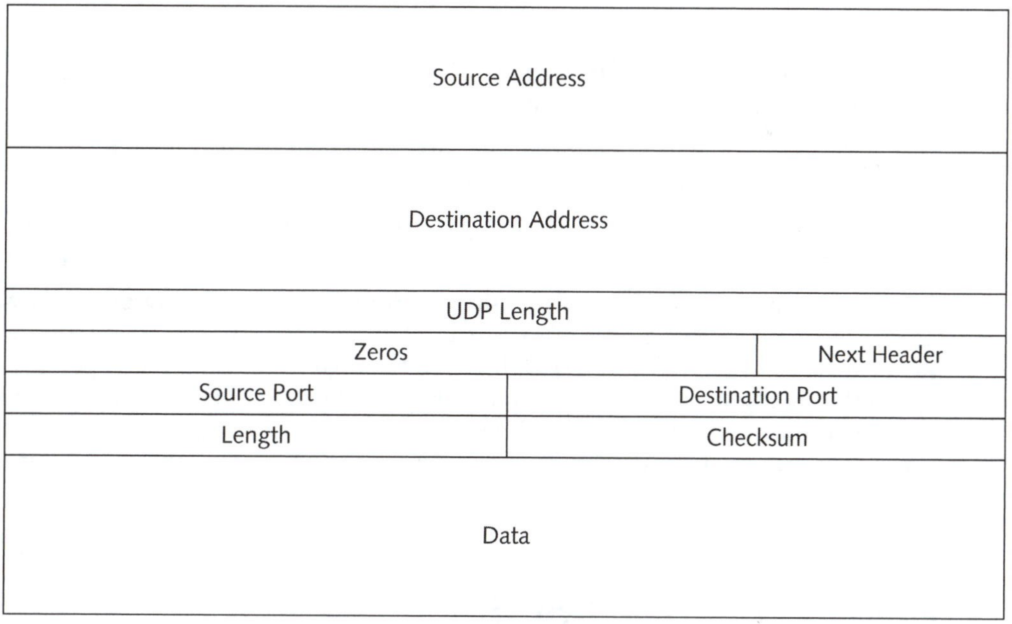

Figure 9-10 IPv6 pseudo-header for UDP
© Cengage Learning 2013

The UDP header provides the source port, destination port, length, and checksum; it also contains the data; and it is appended to the header so that it becomes part of the IPv6 pseudo-header. The specifics of each field in the pseudo-header are:

- Source Address is the address of the source node taken from the IPv6 header.

- Destination Address is the final destination of the packet. If the IPv6 packet does not have a routing header, that is the destination address in the IPv6 header. If the routing header is present, then the address will be the last element in the routing header at the originating node. At the receiving node, the address is in the Destination Address field of the IPv6 header.

- UDP Length is the length of the UDP header plus the data the UDP packet contains. Because UDP carries its own length information, that is the value populating the UDP length field.

- Next Header is the value of the upper-layer protocol, which in this case is UDP and has a value of 17.

- Source Port is the port number used by the sending node to transmit the packet; it is useful if a reply from the receiving node is required. The value should be 0 if no reply is needed.

- Destination Port is the port to be used by the receiving node to accept the packet as long as a valid port number is present.

- Length is the length of the UDP header and data in bytes and is also the value used in the pseudo-header's UDP Length field.

- Checksum is the field used for error-checking the header and data; though optional for IPv4, it is mandatory under IPv6.

- The Data field contains whatever data is being sent from the source to the destination node.

The Next Header field in the pseudo-header contains identifying information about the UDP header. The Next Header field in the IPv6 header contains information about the next extension header, if it's present, between the IPv6 header and the upper-layer header. When the checksum is calculated, if the resulting value is 0, it must be changed to the hex value FFFF and placed in the UDP header. If the value is not changed from 0, when the packet arrives at the destination node, the node will discard the UDP packet and log an error.

Transmission Control Protocol

TCP is one of the core protocols that allow Transport layer services for large networks, including the Internet. It is one of the original protocols at this layer that works with IP, and it provides reliable transportation of network traffic from source to destination. TCP is responsible for providing ordered delivery of a stream of bytes from an application on one network node to an application on another network node. Communications between two computers that are being established through TCP use a **three-way handshake** procedure.

TCP and IPv4

In this section, we cover these primary functions and features of TCP communications:

- Start-up connection process (TCP handshake)
- Keep-alive process
- Connection termination
- Sequence and acknowledgment process
- Error-detection and error-recovery processes
- Congestion control
- Sliding window
- Header fields and functions

TCP Startup Connection Process The TCP start-up connection process (TCP hand-shake) begins with a handshake between two hosts. One host initiates the handshake to another host to (a) ensure that the destination host is available, (b) ensure that the destination host is listening on the destination port number, and (c) inform the destination host of the initiator's sequence number so the two sides can track data as it is transferred.

The TCP handshake uses a three-step process between two hosts, as depicted in Figure 9-11.

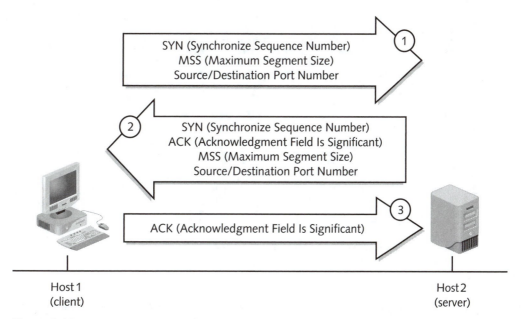

SYN (Synchronize Sequence Number)
MSS (Maximum Segment Size)
Source/Destination Port Number   ①

② SYN (Synchronize Sequence Number)
ACK (Acknowledgment Field Is Significant)
MSS (Maximum Segment Size)
Source/Destination Port Number

ACK (Acknowledgment Field Is Significant)   ③

Host 1
(client)

Host 2
(server)

Figure 9-11 TCP three-packet handshake

1. Host 1 sends a TCP packet to Host 2. This packet does not contain any data; it contains only Host 1's starting sequence number (indicated by the SYN bit setting of 1), the source and destination port numbers, and an indication of the MSS that can fit in each TCP packet.

2. Host 2 responds with its starting sequence number (indicated by the SYN bit setting of 1 in the packet) and an indication of the MSS. The Acknowledgment bit is set to 1 in this reply and acknowledges receipt of the first packet of the handshake. Host 2 also uses the source and destination port numbers that correspond to the ones defined in Step 1.

3. Host 1 acknowledges receipt of Host 2's sequence number and segment size information. This third packet completes the handshake process.

For details on the sequence numbers and how they increment, refer to the section titled "TCP Sequence and Acknowledgment Process" later in this chapter. Next, we look inside the packets to get a feel for what a TCP header contains during the connection establishment phase.

Handshake Packet #1 Figure 9-12 shows the capture of the TCP header of Packet #1 of the handshake.

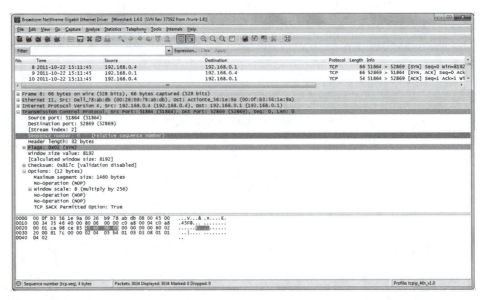

Figure 9-12 TCP capture of first packet in handshake
Source: Wireshark

Wireshark displays sequence numbers relative to their orientation within the stream under examination.

In Packet #1, the sender, Host 1, inserts a relative self-assigned initial sequence number in the TCP header Sequence Number field (0). This packet has one flag set—SYN (for Synchronize sequence number)—to indicate that this packet is used to synchronize the sequence numbers between hosts.

The Header Length field defines the length of the TCP header, counted in 32-bit words in the first two parts of the data exchange and 20 bytes for the last part, which is typical for regular data exchanges.

In this packet, Host 1 defined an MSS of 1,460 bytes. This value is appropriate for an Ethernet packet, the size of which can be calculated as follows:

```
1,460      Data after TCP header
   20      Typical TCP header size
   20      Typical IP header size
   18      Typical Ethernet header size (including 4-byte CRC)
1,518      Maximum Ethernet packet size
```

MSS and MTU are often confused. MSS is the amount of data that can fit in a packet after the TCP header. MTU is the amount of data that can fit inside a MAC header. For example, an Ethernet frame typically has an MTU of 1,518 bytes. The MSS value is 1,460.

The TCP header also defines the desired process or application for this connection—port 52869, which is a dynamic/private port number established for a private connection between two hosts on a LAN.

Handshake Packet #2 Figure 9-13 shows the TCP header of Packet #2 of the handshake process.

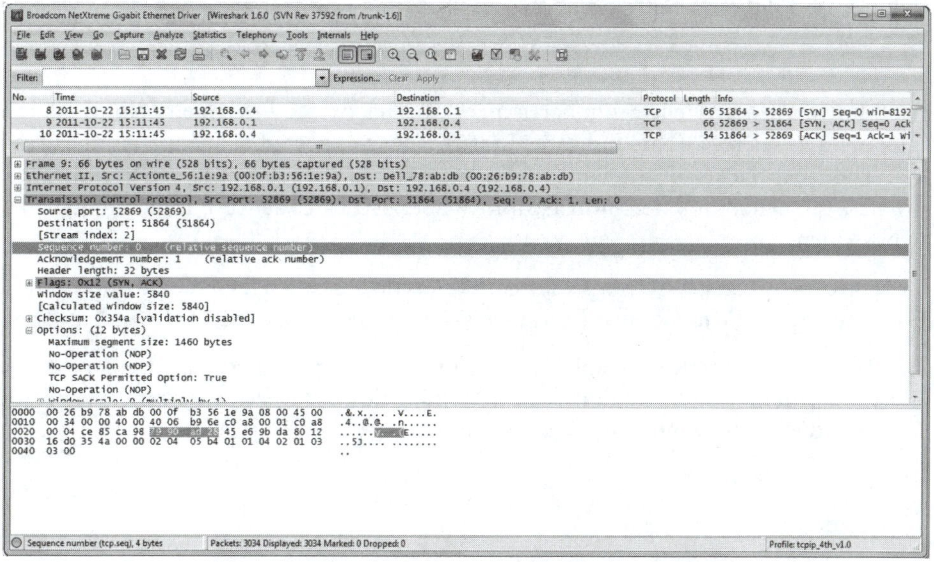

Figure 9-13 TCP capture of second packet in handshake

Source: Wireshark

Host 2 defined its relative starting sequence number as 0. The Acknowledgment Number field relative value is 1, which is the next sequence number that Host 2 expects to receive from Host 1. This packet has two flags set: SYN and ACK (synchronizing and acknowledging receipt of Host 1's first packet). This packet also indicates that the MSS is 1,460 bytes from this host.

Handshake Packet #3 Figure 9-14 shows the TCP header of Packet #3 of the handshake.

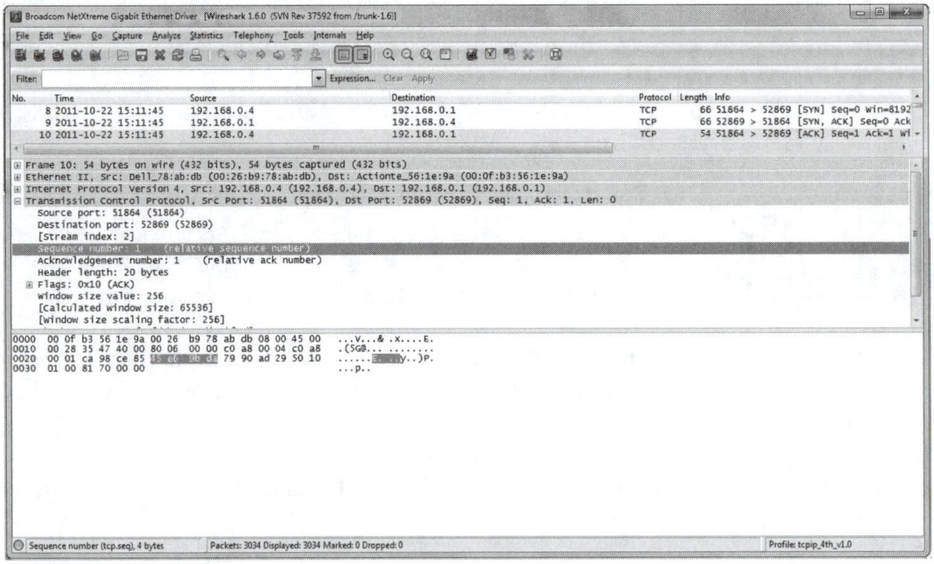

Figure 9-14 Third packet in TCP handshake
Source: Wireshark

Host 1's relative sequence number is now 1. The Acknowledgment Number field relative value is now set to 1. This indicates that the next expected sequence number from Host 2 is 1. The final packet in the handshake process has the ACK flag set to indicate receipt of Host 2's sequence number information, where ACK sequence numbers equal the original SYN sequence numbers incremented by one (SYN# = ACK# + 1).

There are two Registry settings that can be used to control TCP connection establishment. The first, the TcpMaxConnectRetransmissions Registry setting, is defined in Table 9-3.

The TcpMaxConnectRetransmissions Registry setting defines the number of SYN **retries** sent when attempting to establish a TCP connection. The second setting, the TcpNumConnections Registry setting, is defined in Table 9-4.

Registry Information	Details
Location	HKEY_LOCAL_MACHINE\SYSTEM\CurrentControlSet\Services\Tcpip\Parameters
Data type	REG_DWORD
Valid range	0–0xFFFFFFFF
Default value	2
Present by default	No

Table 9-3 **TcpMaxConnectRetransmissions Registry setting**
© Cengage Learning 2013

Registry Information	Details
Location	HKEY_LOCAL_MACHINE\SYSTEM\CurrentControlSet\Services\Tcpip\Parameters
Data type	REG_DWORD
Valid range	0–0xFFFFFE
Default value	0xFFFFFE (16,777,214) connections
Present by default	No

Table 9-4 **TcpNumConnections Registry setting**
© Cengage Learning 2013

The TcpNumConnections setting defines the number of TCP connections that can be open at one time. Because the maximum number of connections possible also is the default value, there is seldom any valid reason to change this setting. Thus, you won't find this value in most Windows registries you inspect.

TCP Half-Open Connections TCP half-open connections occur when the handshake process does not end successfully with a final ACK. The **half-open connection** communication sequence occurs in the following order:

```
SYN  >>>>>
<<<<<  ACK SYN
<<<<<  ACK SYN
<<<<<  ACK SYN
```

In this case, Host 1 sends the first handshake packet, the SYN packet, to Host 2. Host 2 replies with an ACK SYN packet. Host 1 should finish the handshake by sending the third packet, the ACK packet, but it does not. Perhaps Host 1 lost network connectivity or locked up. Host 2 resends the ACK SYN packet in an attempt to complete the handshake process. This connection is considered half open. It is taking up resources on Host 2; we do not know the status of Host 1. This failed communications process is known as a **two-way handshake**.

One **denial of service (DoS)** attack—the SYN attack—uses this two-way handshake with the incrementing source port to overload the destination. If you see excessive connection establishment routines back to back, you should be suspicious about their cause.

TCP Keep-Alive Process Once the TCP connection is established, a **keep-alive process** can maintain the connection when there is no data sent across the wire. Maintaining the connection eliminates the need to repeat the handshake process for each bit of data sent across the wire. The Application layer may perform keep-alive processes, such as the NetWare **watchdog process**, that maintain a connection between a NetWare host and server. If the application cannot maintain a connection, the keep-alive process may become the responsibility of TCP. If implemented, only the server process initiates TCP keep-alives.

TCP keep-alives are disabled by default on Windows XP, Windows Vista, Windows 7, Windows Server 2003, and Windows Server 2008, although any application may enable TCP keep-alives, if desired by its programmer. The aforementioned Windows operating systems have two keep-alive Registry settings. The KeepAliveTime setting defines how long to wait before sending the first TCP keep-alive packet. By default, KeepAliveTime is set at a fairly long two hours, which is an extremely long interval for any computer application (and might therefore justify using whatever maximum value the other side of a connection expects or assumes). This outsized interval also explains why many experts describe keep-alive behavior in Windows as "disabled by default"—it's not actually disabled, just so long as to be practically so. To establish a shorter interval, you'd instantiate this key in the Windows Registry (it's described in Table 9-6) and give it a more typical setting, such as 30,000 for half a minute or 60,000 for a minute. The KeepAliveInterval setting defines the delay between keep-alive retransmissions when no acknowledgments are received. By default, it's set at 1 second (1,000 milliseconds), which is fairly typical for most TCP/IP implementations. Normally, keep-alive settings don't need to be altered, except when working with applications that have explicit keep-alive requirements.

You can change the setting of the KeepAliveTime Registry entry, as shown in Table 9-5.

Registry Information	Details
Location	HKEY_LOCAL_MACHINE\SYSTEM\CurrentControlSet\Services\Tcpip\Parameters
Data type	REG_DWORD
Valid range	0–0xFFFFFFFF
Default value	0x6DDD00 (7,200,000) milliseconds (two hours)
Present by default	No

Table 9-5 KeepAliveTime Registry setting

You can alter the KeepAliveInterval time by setting its Registry entry, as shown in Table 9-6.

Registry Information	Details
Location	HKEY_LOCAL_MACHINE\SYSTEM\CurrentControlSet\Services\Tcpip\Parameters
Data type	REG_DWORD
Valid range	0–0xFFFFFFFF
Default value	0x3E8 (1000) milliseconds (1 second)
Present by default	No

Table 9-6 **KeepAliveInterval Registry setting**
© Cengage Learning 2013

The number of retries is defined by theTcpMaxDataRetransmissions Registry setting (covered in the section titled "TCP Error-Detection and Error-Recovery Process" later in this chapter).

TCP Connection Termination
The TCP connection termination process requires four packets. As shown in Figure 9-15, Host 1 sends a TCP packet with the FIN and ACK flags set. The second peer, Host 2, sends an ACK in response. Host 2 now sends a TCP packet with FIN and ACK flags set. Finally, Host 1 returns an ACK response.

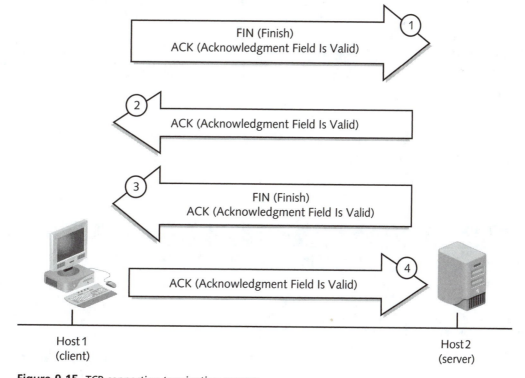

Figure 9-15 TCP connection termination process
© Cengage Learning 2013

TCP Connection States TCP communications go through a series of connection states, as listed in Table 9-7.

Connection State	Description
CLOSED	There is no TCP connection.
LISTEN	The host is listening and ready to accept a connection on a port.
SYN SENT	The host sent a SYN packet.
SYN RECD	The host received a SYN packet and sent a SYN-ACK response.
ESTABLISHED	The three-way handshake completed successfully (regardless of which host initiated it). Data can be transferred (providing there is an acceptable window size available).
FIN-WAIT-1	The first FIN-ACK packet to close a connection was sent.
FIN-WAIT-2	The host sent a FIN-ACK packet and received an ACK response.
CLOSE WAIT	The host received a FIN-ACK and sent a FIN-ACK. This might also indicate a passive close, when a server receives only the first FIN from a client (we show the process in its entirety here to be as explicit as possible).
LAST ACK	The host sent an ACK in response to the FIN-ACK that it received.
CLOSING (Closed)	A FIN-ACK packet was received, but the ACK value does not match the FIN-ACK sent. This indicates that both sides are attempting to close the connection at the same time.
TIME WAIT	Both sides sent FIN-ACKs and ACKs. The connection is closed, but the hosts must wait before reusing any of the connection parameters.

Table 9-7 TCP connection states
© Cengage Learning 2013

You can control the **Time Wait delay**, which is the amount of time that a TCP host waits before reusing parameters.

To control the Time Wait delay, set the TcpTimedWaitDelay Registry value, as shown in Table 9-8.

Registry Information	Details
Location	HKEY_LOCAL_MACHINE\SYSTEM\CurrentControlSet\Services\Tcpip\Parameters
Data type	REG_DWORD
Valid range	30–300
Default value	0xF0 (240 seconds)
Present by default	No

Table 9-8 TcpTimedWaitDelay Registry setting
© Cengage Learning 2013

In the next section, we examine how data is tracked to ensure reliable delivery.

TCP Sequence and Acknowledgment Process

The sequence and acknowledgment process guarantees that packets are ordered properly and protects against missing segments. During the handshake process, each side of the connection selects its own starting sequence number. Each side increments its sequence number value by the amount of data included in the outbound packet.

For example, Figure 9-16 shows the summary of the transfer process. The arrows link the acknowledgments with the data set they are acknowledging. Packets #1 and #5 are acknowledgments for data received earlier but not caught in the trace.

Packet	Source	Destination	Summary					Seq#+data=Next Seq#
1	IP-10.3.71.7	IP-10.3.30.1	Src= 1046,Dst= 1050,.A....,S=	9363103,L=	0,A=	8406691,W= 8760		
2	IP-10.3.30.1	IP-10.3.71.7	Src= 1050,Dst= 1046,.A....,S=	8411071,L= 1460,A=	9363103,W= 8760			S 8411071+1460=8412531
3	IP-10.3.30.1	IP-10.3.71.7	Src= 1050,Dst= 1046,.A....,S=	8412531,L= 1460,A=	9363103,W= 8760			S 8412531+1460=8413991
4	IP-10.3.30.1	IP-10.3.71.7	Src= 1050,Dst= 1046,.A....,S=	8413991,L= 1460,A=	9363103,W= 8760			S 8413991+1460=8415451
5	IP-10.3.71.7	IP-10.3.30.1	Src= 1046,Dst= 1050,.A....,S=	9363103,L=	0,A=	8409611,W= 8760		
6	IP-10.3.30.1	IP-10.3.71.7	Src= 1050,Dst= 1046,.A....,S=	8415451,L= 1460,A=	9363103,W= 8760			S 8415451+1460=8416911
7	IP-10.3.30.1	IP-10.3.71.7	Src= 1050,Dst= 1046,.A....,S=	8416911,L= 1460,A=	9363103,W= 8760			S 8416911+1460=8418371
8	IP-10.3.71.7	IP-10.3.30.1	Src= 1046,Dst= 1050,.A....,S=	9363103,L=	0,A=	8412531,W= 8760		
9	IP-10.3.30.1	IP-10.3.71.7	Src= 1050,Dst= 1046,.A....,S=	8418371,L= 1460,A=	9363103,W= 8760			S 8418371+1460=8419831
10	IP-10.3.30.1	IP-10.3.71.7	Src= 1050,Dst= 1046,.A....,S=	8419831,L= 1460,A=	9363103,W= 8760			S 8419831+1460=8411291
11	IP-10.3.71.7	IP-10.3.30.1	Src= 1046,Dst= 1050,.A....,S=	9363103,L=	0,A=	8415451,W= 5840		
12	IP-10.3.71.7	IP-10.3.30.1	Src= 1046,Dst= 1050,.A....,S=	9363103,L=	0,A=	8418371,W= 2920		
13	IP-10.3.71.7	IP-10.3.30.1	Src= 1046,Dst= 1050,.A....,S=	9363103,L=	0,A=	8421291,W= 0		Set Window to 0
14	IP-10.3.71.7	IP-10.3.30.1	Src= 1046,Dst= 1050,.A....,S=	9363103,L=	0,A=	8421291,W= 8760		Set Window back to 8760

These are ACKs for earlier data.

Figure 9-16 Acknowledgment sequence numbers

Source: Ethereal

Packets #2, #3, and #4 contain data (1,460 bytes in each packet). Packet #8's Acknowledgment Number field value indicates that it is acknowledging all data received up to Packet #2 (up to byte 8412531). Packet #11 acknowledges data up to byte 8415451 (Packet #4).

It is interesting that in this trace file, we see the host send an ACK noting that the window size (the receiver's available buffer space) is now set to 0. It almost immediately transmits another ACK, setting the window size back to 8,760 for this file transfer.

When you analyze the sequence and acknowledgment process, keep this equation in mind:

Sequence Number In + Bytes of Data Received = Acknowledgment Number Out

Figure 9-17 depicts a simple sequenced communication. (Remember, the Acknowledgment Number field contains the value of the next sequence number expected from the other side.)

Except during the TCP start-up and **teardown sequences**, the Acknowledgment Number field increments only when data is received. Because the data flow can change directions (Host 1 sends data to Host 2, and then Host 2 sends data back to Host 1), the Sequence Number field on one side may be incremented for a while, and then stop being incremented as the Sequence Number field on the other side of the communication begins to be incremented.

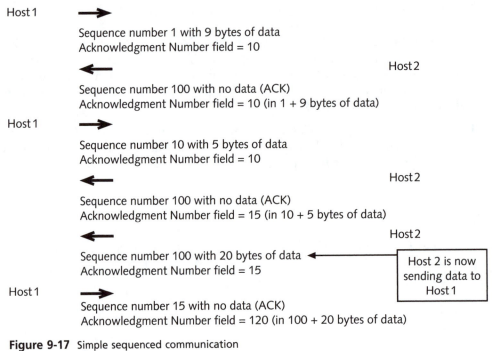

Figure 9-17 Simple sequenced communication
© Cengage Learning 2013

Figure 9-17 starts with Host 1 sending data and then reverses when Host 2 has data to send (see the fifth communication sequence listed in the figure). This is typical of two-way communications.

TCP Error-Detection and Error-Recovery Process There are many reasons why communication sequences fail. For instance, a sender's data packet may be involved in a collision, or the acknowledgment may never make it back because there are problems with the routers along the path. Whatever the reason for communication errors, TCP was designed with an error-recovery process to detect and recover from such errors.

The first error-detection and error-recovery mechanism is the **retransmission timer**. The value specified by this timer is referred to as the **retransmission timeout (RTO)**. Every time data is sent, the retransmission timer starts. When replies are received, the retransmission timer stops. The host measures the round-trip time (RTT). This RTT and an average deviance from the RTT are used to determine the RTO setting.

When the retransmission timer expires, because no ACK reply for data sent is received, the sender retransmits the first unacknowledged TCP data segment first. The sender then doubles its RTO value. The RTO value doubles each time the sender retransmits the TCP data segment. This process continues until the sender reaches its retransmission limit.

In Windows XP, Windows Vista, Windows 7, Windows Server 2003, and Windows Server 2008, the maximum retransmission count is set in the TcpMaxDataRetransmissions Registry setting, as shown in Table 9-9.

Registry Information	Details
Location	HKEY_LOCAL_MACHINE\SYSTEM\CurrentControlSet\Services\Tcpip\Parameters
Data type	REG_DWORD
Valid range	0–0xFFFFFFFF
Default value	5
Present by default	No

Table 9-9 TcpMaxDataRetransmissions Registry setting
© Cengage Learning 2013

Based on the TCP retransmit process, the retransmission operation occurs in the following increments:

- 1st retransmit: RTO seconds
- 2nd retransmit: 2 x RTO seconds
- 3rd retransmit: 4 x RTO seconds
- 4th retransmit: 8 x RTO seconds
- 5th retransmit: 16 x RTO seconds

Figure 9-18 provides an example of the retransmit timer in action. Here, the host, 10.3.30.1, sends Packet #2 but never receives an Acknowledgment packet. The Acknowledgment packet would contain the Acknowledgment Number field value 5405497. This trace shows the retransmission process getting exponentially longer between retransmissions.

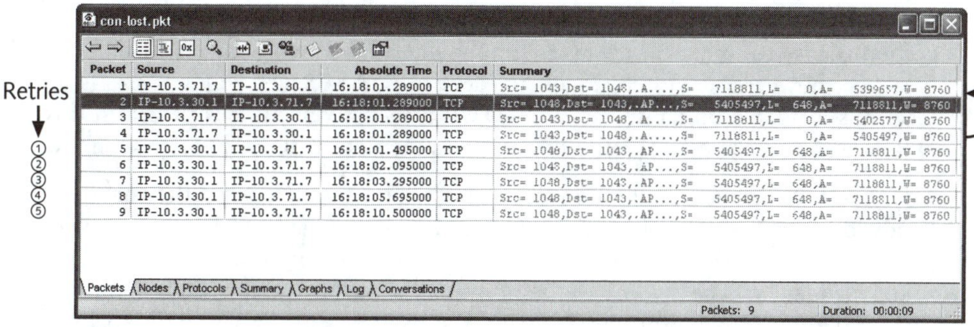

Figure 9-18 Server sends TCP packets at exponentially longer interval times
Source: Ethereal

Note that the retransmissions do not fall on exact exponential boundaries; this is not unusual. Sometimes the process does not occur on an exact boundary; other times the analyzer processing time affects the timestamps.

In Windows XP, Windows Vista, Windows 7, Windows Server 2003, and Windows Server 2008, the TcpInitialRTT Registry setting defines the initial RTO at 3 seconds, as shown in Table 9-10.

This TcpInitialRTT value is used for the timeout of the handshake packets and the initial data segments sent over a new connection. As successive segments are sent, the RTO value is adjusted from this TcpInitialRTT value to a value represented by the current RTT.

Registry Information	Details
Location	HKEY_LOCAL_MACHINE\SYSTEM\CurrentControlSet\Services\Tcpip\Parameters
Data type	REG_DWORD
Valid range	0–0xFFFF (seconds)
Default value	3 (seconds)
Present by default	No

Table 9-10 **TcpInitialRTT Registry setting**
© Cengage Learning 2013

TCP Congestion Control Congestion is the overloading of the network or a receiver. Overloading of the network occurs when there is too much data on the network medium. Adding more data ensures overloading and causes packet loss. Overloading a receiver occurs when the number of data bytes is greater than the **advertised window** (defined in the Window field in the receiver's TCP header). The **current window** is always the lesser of what the network and receiver can handle.

Figure 9-19 depicts the elements of the network and receiver congestion. The network congestion is easy to understand; this is simply what the network can handle. The receiver window size, however, is more difficult to identify. The receiver window size is defined by the receiver's available buffer space. When TCP data is received, it is placed in this **TCP buffer area**. The Application layer protocol retrieves the data from the buffer at its own rate.

TCP has four defined congestion control mechanisms to ensure the most efficient use of **bandwidth** along with quick error and congestion recovery. TCP supports **windowing**—the process of sending numerous data packets in sequence without waiting for an intervening acknowledgment. The size of the window is based on the amount of traffic the network can handle (the congestion window) and the receiver's available buffer space (the receiver's advertised window). The two mechanisms, defined in detail in RFC 5681, are:

- Slow Start/Congestion Avoidance
- Fast Retransmit/Fast Recovery

In the next sections, we examine each of these mechanisms in detail.

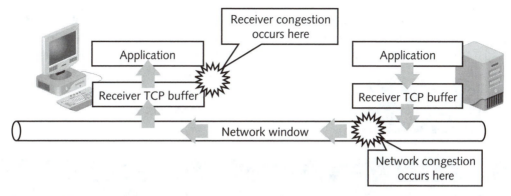

Figure 9-19 Network window and receiver window determine current congestion window size
© Cengage Learning 2013

Slow Start/Congestion Avoidance When a TCP host starts, the size of the congestion window is not known. The initial value of the window being used is twice the sender's MSS setting. For example, if a host's MSS value is 1460, the initial window the host uses is 2,920 bytes. The MSS increases this window for every ACK received that acknowledges new data.

Once the window size has increased using the **Slow Start algorithm**, if an error occurs (a timeout), the window size is divided in half. Next, the **Congestion Avoidance algorithm** is used to increase the window size in a linear manner. Congestion is detected whenever three or more duplicate ACK packets (known as a triple-ACK) or timeout events occur, and timeout events are considered more serious than duplicate acknowledgments. The most common algorithms halve the congestion window when triple-ACKs occur (this is called the Reno algorithm), whereas others reduce the congestion window to equal current MSS size (this is called the Tahoe algorithm).

Fast Retransmit/Fast Recovery When an out-of-order data segment is received, the Fast Retransmit process requires the receiver to immediately send **duplicate ACKs**. These duplicate ACKs both indicate which sequence number was expected. The Fast Recovery process dictates that when a host receives three duplicate ACKs, it must immediately start retransmitting the **lost segments** without waiting for the retransmission timer to expire.

The window size gradually increases, as defined in RFC 2581. The maximum receive window size can be set using the GlobalMaxTcpWindowSize Registry setting, as shown in Table 9-11.

Registry Information	Details
Location	HKEY_LOCAL_MACHINE\SYSTEM\CurrentControlSet\Services\Tcpip\Parameters
Data type	REG_DWORD
Valid range	0–0x3FFFFFFF (bytes)
Default value	0x4000 (16,384 bytes)
Present by default	No

Table 9-11 GlobalMaxTcpWindowSize Registry setting
© Cengage Learning 2013

The maximum receive window size for an interface can be set using the TcpWindowSize Registry setting, as shown in Table 9-12. This setting, if it exists, overrides the GlobalMax-TcpWindowSize Registry setting for the interface on which it is configured.

NOTE For more information about the Windows Registry, go to *http://support. microsoft.com/kb/256986* or use a search engine to search for the string "Windows registry information for advanced users."

Registry Information	Details
Location	HKEY_LOCAL_MACHINE\SYSTEM\CurrentControlSet\Services\Tcpip\Parameters \Interface\Interfacename
Data type	REG_DWORD
Valid range	0–0xFFFF (bytes)
Default value	0xFFFF (or the larger of four times the maximum TCP MSS size on the network or 8,192 bytes)
Present by default	No

Table 9-12 TcpWindowSize Registry setting
© Cengage Learning 2013

TCP Sliding Window TCP supports a sliding window mechanism, which is a management method for data transmission used to determine the amount of unacknowledged data that can go out on the wire from any sender. This should not be confused with an advertised window—the amount of data for which a receiver has buffer space available. To understand the sliding window mechanism better, consider a stream of data divided conceptually into the pieces shown in Figure 9-20. If you look at the data that is sent and you move from left to right over it, the left side of the window is the data that was acknowledged. The right side defines the boundary of data that can be sent, based on the receiver's advertised window.

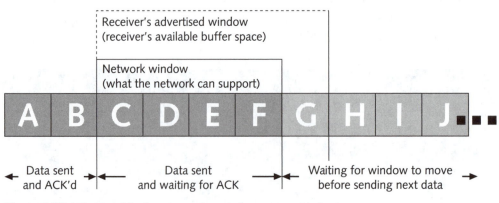

Figure 9-20 Window slides based on acknowledgments received
© Cengage Learning 2013

The data set A+B was sent and acknowledged. The current data set is C+D+E+F, and the sender is waiting for an acknowledgment. The amount of unacknowledged data on the network can increase as data transmissions are successful. The window now moves to the right, and the next data set—G+H+I+J in this example—is sent. The window continues to slide to the right as acknowledgments are received.

There are some interesting exceptions to the standard windowing operation. For example, the **Nagle algorithm** (named after John Nagle, author of RFC 896) specifies that when small data segments are being sent but not acknowledged, no other small segments can be sent. The existence of small data is seen in interactive applications such as Telnet.

Another interesting aspect of TCP windowing is the **Silly Window Syndrome (SWS)**. SWS is caused when enough data is sent to a TCP host to fill its receiver buffer, thereby putting the receiver in a **zero-window state**. The receiver advertises a window size of 0 until the Application layer protocol retrieves data from the receiver buffer. In an SWS situation, the Application layer protocol retrieves only 1 byte from the buffer. This causes the host to advertise a window size of 1. Upon receipt of this window information, the sender transmits a single byte of information. The new window size is certainly the most inefficient method of data transfer. Receivers can avoid SWS by not advertising a new window size until they have at least as much buffer space as the MSS value. Senders can avoid this problem by not sending data until the advertised window is at least the size of the MSS value.

TCP Header Fields and Functions Now we examine the TCP header structure shown in Figure 9-21. You should recognize some characteristics of the TCP header, such as the Source and Destination Port Number fields. Let's examine the TCP header structure.

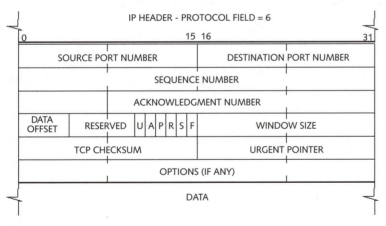

Figure 9-21 20-byte TCP header
© Cengage Learning 2013

Source Port Number Field See the Source Port Number field definition in the "UDP Header Fields and Functions" section earlier in this chapter.

Destination Port Number Field See the Destination Port Number field definition in the "UDP Header Fields and Functions" section earlier in this chapter.

Sequence Number Field This field contains a number that uniquely identifies the TCP segment. This sequence number provides an identifier that enables TCP receivers to identify when parts of a communication stream are missing. The sequence number increments by the number of data bytes contained in the packet. For example, in Figure 9-22, the current TCP sequence number is 69151887, and the packet contains 265 bytes of data (subtract the 20-byte IP header length and the 20-byte TCP header length from the Total Length field value of 305, as seen in the IP header).

This example uses actual rather than relative number sequencing in Wireshark. To disable relative number sequencing for Wireshark, in the menu bar, click **Edit** and then click **Preferences**. In the left pane of the Preferences window, expand **Protocols**, scroll down and then select **TCP**. In the right pane, remove the selection from the Relative sequence numbers check box, click **Apply**, and then click **OK**.

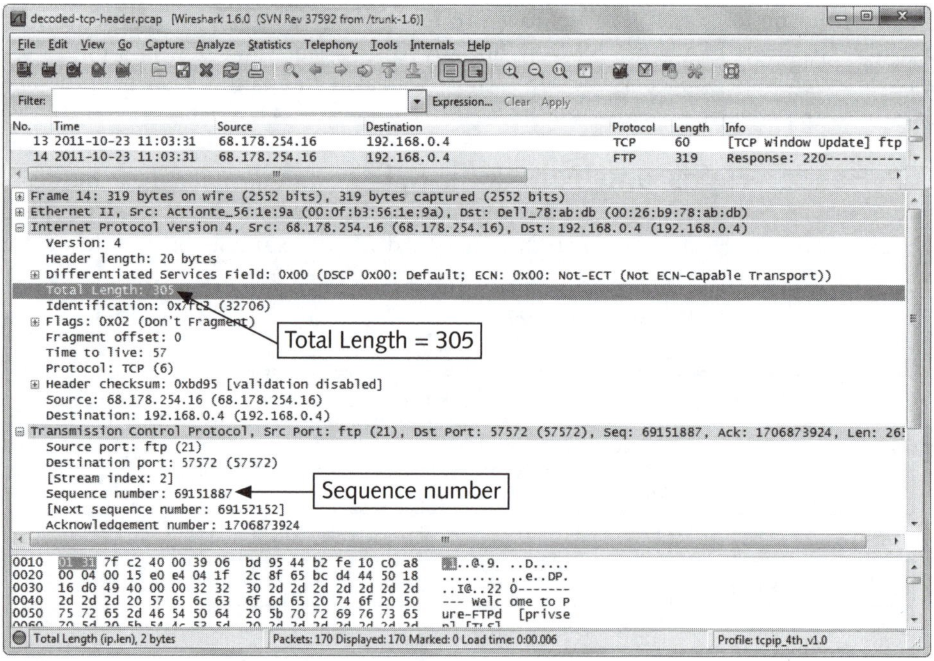

Figure 9-22 Decoded TCP header
Source: Wireshark

Each TCP host self-assigns its own sequence number. The process of incrementing this sequence number is covered in detail in the "TCP Sequence and Acknowledgment Process" section earlier in this chapter.

The initial sequence number used in a TCP connection is defined by the host and, for security purposes, should be randomly assigned. Sequence number prediction is a method used to hijack a TCP connection by guessing the initial sequence number used by a host. The majority of TCP stack implementations today use randomizing algorithms to make the initial sequence number difficult, if not impossible, to guess. Insecure TCP stack implementations may increment the initial sequence number used for new connections by a static, predictable count.

Acknowledgment Number Field The Acknowledgment Number field indicates the next expected sequence number from the other side of the communication. For example, in Figure 9-22 the sender states that the next TCP expected sequence number from the other host is 1706873924.

Header Length Field This field defines the length of the TCP header in 4-byte increments. (Some protocol analyzers indicate this field as the Offset field.) We need this field because the TCP header length can vary, depending on the TCP header options used. Although the UDP Option field is rarely used, the TCP Option field is almost always used during the TCP connection setup to establish the maximum amount of data that can be placed after a TCP header.

Flags Field Table 9-13 describes the flag settings used in the TCP header.

Flag	Setting Description
URG (Urgent)	Indicates the Urgent Pointer field should be examined. If this flag is set, the Urgent Pointer field tells the receiver where it should start reading bytes contained in the data portion of the packet.
ACK (Acknowledgment)	The acknowledgment number indicates the next expected sequence number from the other TCP peer.
PSH (Push)	Data travels through outbound buffers (on the sending host) and inbound buffers (on the receiving host) immediately. This is used for time-critical or single-stroke applications. Upon receipt of a packet with the Push flag set, the receiver must not buffer the data. The data must pass directly up to the Application layer protocol. That explains why this treatment is normally reserved for the final TCP segment in a sequence of segments: this forces the now complete collection up to the application for immediate servicing.
(Reset)	Closes the connection. This is used to shut down the connection entirely. This flag also is used to refuse a connection (for whatever reason).
SYN (Synchronize)	Synchronizes sequence numbers—handshake process. This flag is used during the handshake process to indicate that the sender is notifying the TCP peer of its Sequence Number field value.
FIN (Finish)	The transaction is finished. This flag is used to indicate that the host completed a transaction. The FIN flag itself does not explicitly close the connection. If both peers send TCP FIN packets and respond with appropriate ACKs, however, the connection will be closed.

Table 9-13 TCP flag settings

9

Window Size Field This field indicates the size of the TCP receiver buffer in bytes. For example, in Figure 9-22, the sender indicates that it can receive a stream of data up to 5,840 bytes in length. A window size of 0 indicates that a sender should stop transmitting—the receiver's TCP buffer is full.

TCP Checksum Field This TCP checksum is a bit strange, just like the UDP checksum. The checksum is performed on the contents of the TCP header and data (not including data link padding) as well as on the pseudo-header derived from the IP header. The TCP pseudo-header is similar to the UDP header—it is only used for the checksum calculation; it is not an actual header itself. The TCP pseudo-header consists of three fields taken from the IP header: the IP Source Address field value, the IP Destination Address field value, and the Protocol field value. The TCP pseudo-header also includes the value of the TCP Length field.
You can get more information about the TCP pseudo-header from RFC 793.

Urgent Pointer Field This field is relevant only if the URG pointer is set. If the URG pointer is set, the receiver must examine this field to see where to look/read first in the packet. RFC 1122 interprets the Urgent Pointer field value differently than does RFC 793. Windows 2000, Windows XP, Windows Vista, Windows 7, Windows Server 2003, and Windows Server 2008 can be configured to interpret the Urgent Pointer field according to RFC 1122, if desired. See Table 9-14 for TcpUseRFC1122UrgentPointer Registry setting information.

By default, the aforementioned Windows operating system hosts are configured to use the Urgent Pointer field interpretation defined in RFC 793, also known as the BSD mode (because it was first implemented on Berkeley System Distribution versions of UNIX).

Registry Information	Details
Location	HKEY_LOCAL_MACHINE\SYSTEM\CurrentControlSet\Services\Tcpip\Parameters
Data type	REG_DWORD
Valid range	0–1
Default value	0
Present by default	No

Table 9-14 **TcpUseRFC1122UrgentPointer Registry setting**
© Cengage Learning 2013

TCP Options Field() This Options field is used to contain data considered optional in the TCP header. One option you may see in use is the MSS option; it is used in the first two packets of the three-way handshake process. The purpose of this option is to define what segment size the hosts support. The hosts use the lowest common denominator between the two MSS values.

Some of the TCP options are listed in Table 9-15.

Option	Definition	Reference
2	Maximum Segment Size—Defines the maximum amount of data that the sender can place after the TCP header	RFC 1323
3	Window Scale—Expands the TCP window size value to a 32-bit value while using the 16-bit field	RFC 2018
4	Selective ACK (SACK) Permitted—States that the sender can use **Selective Acknowledgments** to ACK-specific packets within a set of data segments	
5	SACK—Used within the SACK packet	RFC 2018
8	Timestamps—Specifically sets the RTO value and overrides any calculated RTO defined.	RFC 1323

Table 9-15 TCP options
© Cengage Learning 2013

The complete "TCP Option Numbers" list can be found online at *www.iana.org/assignments/tcp-parameters*. Here again, the complexity and broad capability of TCP mean that this list of options is neither short nor terribly straightforward. Fortunately, it is only occasionally necessary to venture into TCP options beyond those documented in this section.

TCP and IPv6

As mentioned in the section "UDP and IPv6," there is no new version of TCP that maps to IPv6. TCP remains unchanged as a transport protocol. The only difference is in the way IPv6 and IPv4 treat TCP. This is what results in changed behavior for this upper-layer protocol. As with UDP, if TCP must include the 128-bit addresses from the IPv6 header, it must be modified to do so. Because checksum calculations for UDP and TCP are mandatory under IPv6, TCP uses an IPv6 pseudo-header for the purpose. The pseudo-header is constructed of the source address, destination address, TCP length, zeros, and Next Header fields plus the fields found in the TCP header, as shown in Figure 9-23.

9

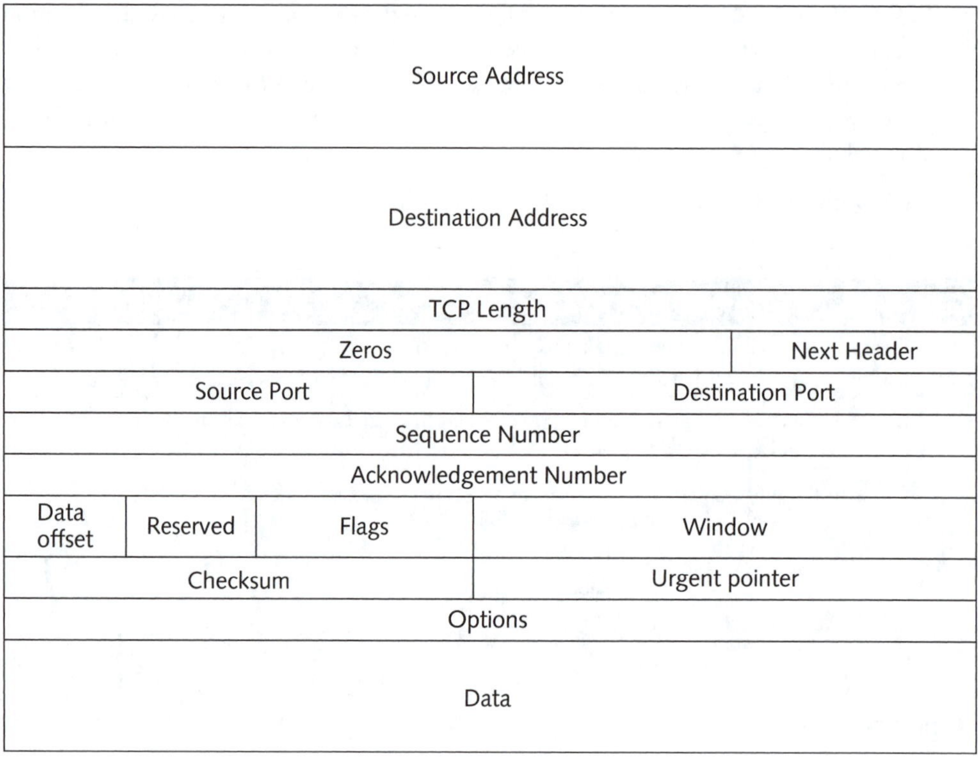

Source Address		
Destination Address		
TCP Length		
Zeros		Next Header
Source Port		Destination Port
Sequence Number		
Acknowledgement Number		
Data offset	Reserved	Flags	Window
Checksum		Urgent pointer
Options		
Data		

Figure 9-23 IPv6 pseudo-header for TCP
© Cengage Learning 2013

In the TCP Length field (otherwise known as the Upper-Layer Packet Length field) in the pseudo-header, because TCP doesn't provide its own length information, the value from the Payload Length field in the IPv6 header is used, minus the length of any extension headers that exist, if any, between the IPv6 header and the upper-layer header. The value populating the Next Header field is 6, which indicates that the upper-layer protocol is TCP. Besides this, the other fields in the IPv6 pseudo-header for TCP are the same as they are for the IPv6 pseudo-header for UDP. Also, the TCP header under IPv6 is identical to that used with IPv4.

As explained earlier in this chapter, upper-layer protocols such as TCP, when calculating the maximum payload size, must include the larger IPv6 header size compared to IPv4 headers. For the MSS option, the IPv4 header size is calculated at 20 octets for the minimum-length header plus 20 octets for the minimum-length TCP header, whereas the IPv6 header size is 40 octets rather than 20. The minimum-length TCP header size remains the same.

UDP, TCP, and IPv6 Extension Headers

As you learned in Chapter 3, IPv6 headers put all optional data in extension headers. An extension header contains optional Internet-layer data that is stored in separate headers between the IPv6 header and the upper-layer transport pseudo-header. While Chapter 3 presented extension headers in detail, here they are presented only to clarify the structural relationship between the IPv6 header and the UDP or TCP pseudo-header.

The IPv6 header and each extension header, if present, contain a Next Header field. In the IPv6 Next Header field, if no extension headers are present, the Next Header field will contain the value of the upper-layer protocol used with IPv6, such as UDP or TCP. Figure 9-24 shows you a high-level illustration of a IPv6 header with no extension headers and using TCP as the transport protocol, including how the Next Header field points to the TCP pseudo-header.

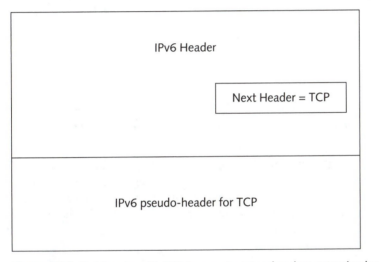

Figure 9-24 IPv6 header with TCP transport protocol and no extension headers
© Cengage Learning 2013

The IPv6 packet can include one or more extension headers, and if they are present, the structure of the packet will look like what is shown in Figure 9-25. For this example, a packet will be presented with three extension headers and using UDP as the transport protocol.

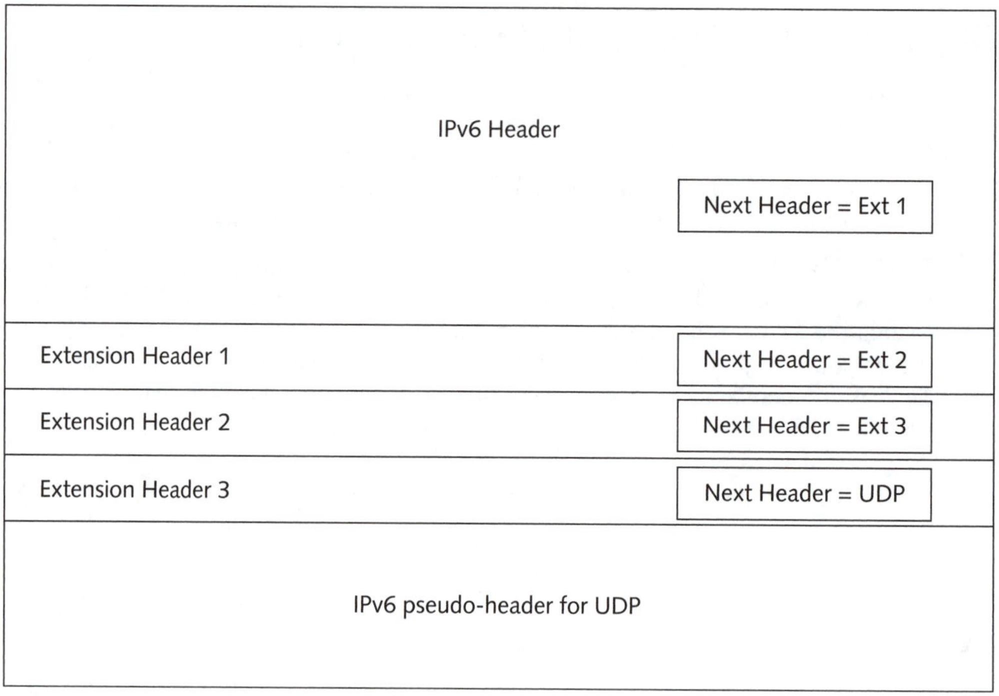

Figure 9-25 IPv6 header with UDP transport protocol and three extension headers
© Cengage Learning 2013

The Next Header field in the IPv6 header will identify the first extension header. The Next Header field in the first extension header will identify the second extension header, the Next Header field in the second extension header will identify the third extension header, and the Next Header field in the third extension header will identify the transport protocol, which in this case is the value 17 for UDP.

Choosing between TCP and UDP

Given that TCP is robust and reliable and that UDP is not, why would any Application layer protocol or service choose UDP for transport when TCP is readily available? The short answer is overhead. Because TCP is robust and reliable, it carries a lot of baggage, including additional header fields, and explicit meta-messages in the form of TCP messages that convey information about the connection rather than data to be passed across that connection.

For some lightweight services, such as Microsoft Messenger Service (which you can run from the command line using the net send command and which pops up a message on the target screen or screens), TCP is overkill, and UDP is used instead. For other applications that may be invoked during boot up, or when a computer has only limited network capability (perhaps it can only broadcast), UDP provides an obvious vehicle to transport boot requests for BOOTP and address requests for DHCP.

Likewise, for applications, such as RIP, that rely on regular updates of routing tables and track timeout values as part of ordinary behavior, the extra reliability of TCP isn't necessary, and UDP is used instead. Finally, some application developers decided to create their own specific reliability and delivery mechanisms, such as those used in NFS, to guarantee delivery of files across a network, rather than relying on the general-purpose mechanisms in TCP. In most of these cases, avoiding unneeded complexity, or improving overall performance, drives the selection of UDP.

On the other hand, TCP was designed in an era when 300-bps communication was considered fast, and when noisy lines or intermittent communications problems made long-haul, reliable transmission of data inherently risky without access to a robust, reliable transport service. For purely local area network use, TCP is probably overkill in all cases. But as soon as the Internet comes into play, where anything goes and often does (both wrong and right), TCP's reliability and robustness still have great value. That explains why most information delivery services designed for use on the Internet tend to use TCP transports rather than UDP, simply because they allow application developers to concentrate on providing a service rather than handling reliability and delivery issues. For example, NFS was originally designed (and is still primarily used) as a local area file access method. That design decision favored UDP because it offered faster performance; FTP, which offers similar file access mechanisms over the Internet, defers to TCP to ensure reliable delivery between any two points on the globe.

Historically, TCP is a more important transport than UDP, and is still used for the majority of TCP/IP Application layer protocols and services. It is not as important, however, as it once was because long-haul and local area networks have significantly increased speed, capacity, and reliability since TCP/IP first appeared on the scene. Although TCP remains popular as a transport, it's important to remember that it's always faster (but not necessarily easier) to manage robustness and reliability at the hardware level rather than at the software level. With the availability of cell-oriented transmission technologies, such as ATM and SONET, there are those who might argue that TCP's days are numbered because these lower-layer transmission technologies could make TCP's capabilities unnecessary. As long as the Internet infrastructure remains the hodgepodge of transmission technologies that it is today, however, TCP will continue to play a vital role in ensuring correct and complete delivery of important data.

Chapter Summary

- Transport layer protocols come in two types: connectionless, which are lightweight, unreliable, and provide only best-effort delivery service, and connection-oriented, which provide robust, reliable end-to-end delivery services, including explicit acknowledgment, segmentation, and reassembly of arbitrary-sized messages, connection negotiation and management mechanisms, and retransmission of missing or erroneous segments. Because connectionless protocols are lightweight, they outperform connection-oriented protocols due to lower internal message overhead and the fact that they have no need for control and management of message traffic (acknowledgments, retransmissions, congestion control, and so on).

- The User Datagram Protocol (UDP) is the connectionless protocol associated with the TCP/IP protocol suite. It is commonly associated with Application layer protocols and services, such as BOOTP, DHCP, SNMP, NFS, and RIP, that either provide their own reliability mechanisms or do without such mechanisms.

- In keeping with its simple capabilities, the UDP header is short and simple, consisting primarily of a protocol identifier in the IP header, an optional checksum value, and source and destination port addresses for the Application layer protocols or processes on the sending and receiving ends of a transmission.

- The Transmission Control Protocol (TCP) is the heavyweight, connection-oriented protocol that helps name the TCP/IP protocol suite. It remains associated with the majority of TCP/IP Application layer protocols, especially those such as Telnet, FTP, and SMTP, in which reliable data delivery is desirable.

- In keeping with its more diverse, more robust capabilities, the TCP header is longer and more complex, including a variety of flags, values, and message types used to deliver acknowledgments, manage traffic flow, request retransmissions, and negotiate connections between hosts.

- Appropriate (and historical) uses for UDP concentrate on Application layer services that manage their own reliability and connections, such as NFS, and on chatty protocols and services, such as DHCP, SNMP, or RIP. The chatty protocols and services rely on simple controls and fail-safes and on broadcast of periodic transmissions to handle potential reliability, deliverability, or reachability problems.

- Appropriate (and historical) uses for TCP concentrate on providing reliable delivery of user services, such as terminal emulation (Telnet and remote utilities), file transfer (FTP), e-mail (SMTP), and news (NNTP), where potentially important data must be delivered whole and intact or not at all (and flagged with an error message).

- Although there are no updated versions for TCP and UDP that correspond to IPv6, the functions of these transport protocols are treated differently when used by IPv4 or IPv6. TCP and UDP are incorporated as pseudo-headers with the IPv6 header for calculating checksums, and they must be modified to accommodate the larger IPv6 address space. TCP and UDP pseudo-headers are incorporated structurally, between the IPv6 header and any IPv6 extension headers that may be present.

Key Terms

acknowledgment Notification of successful receipt of data. The ACK flag is set in acknowledgment packets.

advertised window The amount of data that a receiver states it can handle in its TCP buffer space.

bandwidth A measurement of the amount of information that can cross a network. For example, Ethernet has 10-Mbps bandwidth available.

best-effort delivery A simple network transport mechanism that relies on the underlying Network, Data Link, and Physical layer facilities available to handle delivery of PDUs from sender to receiver without adding additional robustness or reliability features; UDP uses best-effort delivery.

byte stream A continuous stream of data that contains no boundaries.

congestion A condition of overload on a network or at a receiver. When the network is congested, senders cannot continue to send TCP packets. To avoid congesting a receiver, the receiver advertises a window size of 0.

Congestion Avoidance algorithm   A defined method for avoiding overloading a network. This mechanism is used to slowly and incrementally increase the window size of communications.

connectionless protocol   A protocol that simply sends datagrams without establishing, managing, or otherwise handling a connection between sender and receiver; UDP is a connectionless Transport layer protocol.

connection-oriented transport mechanisms   A Transport layer protocol that establishes a session between two computers, provides error checking, and guarantees delivery.

core services   Primary and key services used in TCP/IP networking. FTP, DNS, and DHCP are considered core services. These services are assigned the well-known port numbers between 0 and 1023.

current window   The actual window size being used at the time. A sender determines the current window size by using the receiver's advertised window and the network congestion window (what the network can handle).

Denial of service (DoS)   An attack that causes a system to refuse services because it is busy handling attack requests. For example, repeated two-way handshakes may be caused by a TCP SYN attack.

duplicate ACKs   A set of identical acknowledgments that is sent back to back to a TCP sender to indicate that out-of-order packets were received. Upon receipt of these duplicate ACKs, the sender retransmits the data without waiting for the retransmission timer to expire.

Dynamic ports   *See* temporary port.

dynamic port number   A temporary port number used just for one communication process. These port numbers are cleared after the connection is closed and a four-minute wait time.

end-to-end reliability   A characteristic offered by connection-oriented services to guarantee that data arrives successfully at the desired destination.

error recovery   The procedure for retransmitting missing or damaged data. Two examples of error recovery are the immediate drop in the current window size and the immediate retransmission of data before the retransmission timer expires.

half-open connection   A TCP connection that is not completed with a final acknowledgment. These half-open connections may be an indication of a TCP SYN attack.

handshake process   The process of setting up a virtual connection between TCP peers. The handshake process consists of three packets used to set up the starting sequence number that each TCP peer will use for communications. The TCP peers also exchange the receiver window size and an MSS value during this process.

keep-alive process   The procedure of maintaining an idle connection. TCP connections can be kept alive through TCP keep-alive packets if configured to do so. If the Application layer protocol offers a keep-alive process, the TCP layer should not perform the keep-alive process.

logical connection   A virtual connection between hosts, sometimes referred to as a circuit. The TCP handshake is used to set up a logical connection between TCP peers.

lost segment   A section of TCP data that does not arrive at the destination. Upon detection of a lost segment, a TCP sender must decrease the congestion window to one-half of the previous window size. Lost segments are assumed to be caused by network congestion.

9

Maximum Segment Size (MSS) The maximum amount of data that can fit in a TCP packet after the TCP header. Each TCP peer shares the MSS during the handshake process.

messages Data that has distinct boundaries and command information within the packet.

Nagle algorithm A method stating that when small packets are sent but not acknowledged, no further packets shall be sent. The Nagle algorithm is relevant on a network that supports numerous small packets because of its support of interactive applications, such as Telnet.

out-of-order packets Packets that do not arrive in the order defined by the sequence number. When a TCP host receives out-of-order packets, that host sends duplicate ACKs that indicate the packets arrived out of order.

positive response An affirmative acknowledgment that data was received. TCP headers with the ACK flag set indicate that the Acknowledgment Number field is valid and provide the next-expected sequence number from the TCP peer.

pseudo-header A false header structure used to calculate a checksum. The UDP and TCP checksums are based on the pseudo-header values.

retransmission timeout (RTO) The time value that determines when a TCP host retransmits a packet after it was lost. The RTO value is exponentially increased after an apparent connection loss.

retransmission timer The timer that maintains the RTO value.

retries The number of times a TCP peer resends data when no acknowledgment is received.

retry mechanism A method for detecting communication problems and resending data across the network.

Selective Acknowledgment Also referred to as SACK, this method defines how a TCP peer can identify specific segments that were successfully received. This functionality is defined in RFC 2018.

sequence number tracking The process of following the current sequence number sent by a TCP peer and sending an acknowledgment value to indicate the next-expected sequence number.

Silly Window Syndrome (SWS) A TCP windowing problem caused by an application removing only small amounts of data from a full TCP receiver buffer, thereby causing a TCP peer to advertise a very small window. To address this problem, TCP hosts wait until the window size reaches the MSS value.

sliding window A set of data that is sent along a sliding timeline. As transmitted data is acknowledged, the window moves over to send more data to the TCP peer.

Slow Start algorithm A method for sending data in exponentially increasing increments, starting typically at twice the MSS value. The Slow Start algorithm is used to learn the network's maximum window size.

TCP buffer area A queuing area used to hold incoming and outgoing TCP packets. If a TCP packet has the Push flag set, the packet should not be held in either the incoming or outgoing TCP buffer area.

teardown sequence The process of closing a TCP connection.

temporary port A port that is used for the duration of the connection. The port numbers assigned to temporary ports are also called dynamic port numbers or ephemeral port numbers.

three-way handshake A TCP negotiation process between two computers attempting to establish a network session.

Time Wait delay An amount of time that a TCP host must not use connection parameters after closing down that connection.

timeout mechanism A method for determining when to stop resending data across packets. The timeout mechanism consists of a retry timer and a maximum number of retries.

two-way handshake A two-packet handshake that is not fully completed. This process is indicative of the TCP SYN attack.

valid data Data that follows the headers but does not consist of any padding or extraneous data.

virtual connection A logical connection between two TCP peers. The virtual connection requires end-to-end connectivity.

watchdog process A process used by NetWare servers to determine whether the NetWare clients are still active and maintaining the connection between the two devices.

windowing The process of acknowledging multiple packets with a single acknowledgment.

zero-window state A situation in which a TCP peer advertises a window value of 0. A TCP host cannot continue sending to a TCP peer that advertises a window of zero.

Review Questions

1. Which of the following TCP/IP protocols are Transport layer protocols? (Choose all that apply.)

   a. IP

   b. TCP

   c. UDP

   d. FTP

2. Which of the following services are characteristic of a connection-oriented protocol? (Choose all that apply.)

   a. connection handling

   b. delivery guarantees

   c. segmentation and reassembly

   d. message-level checksum in header

   e. explicit transmission acknowledgment

3. Which of the following services does UDP provide?

   a. segmentation

   b. optional header checksum

   c. identification of source and destination port addresses

   d. explicit transmission acknowledgment

   e. reassembly

4. In an IPv6 header with five extension headers and a UDP pseudo-header, which Next Header field points to the UDP pseudo-header?

   a. the Next Header field in the IPv6 header

   b. the Next Header field in the first extension header

   c. the Next Header field in the last extension header

   d. the Next Header field in the UDP pseudo-header

5. What range of addresses traditionally defines a well-known port address?

   a. 0–1023

   b. 1–512

   c. 10–4097

   d. 0–65535

6. What range of addresses corresponds to the registered port numbers?

   a. 0–1023

   b. 1024–65535

   c. 1024–47999

   d. 1024–49151

7. What range of addresses corresponds to the dynamic port numbers?

   a. 0–1023

   b. 1024–49151

   c. 49152–65535

   d. 49152–64000

8. Identical UDP and TCP port numbers always map to the same TCP/IP protocol or service. True or False?

9. When the UDP checksum is calculated for IPv6, what is the result if the checksum value is 0?

   a. The 0 is changed to the FFFF hex value and placed in the UDP header.

   b. The 0 is placed in the Zeros field in the IPv6 header.

   c. The 0 indicates that an error occurred in the checksum calculation, and the packet is discarded at the source node.

   d. The 0 is always the correct result of the checksum calculation, and the packet is then successfully sent to its destination.

10. What does TCP use to track the transfer of data and its successful delivery? (Choose all that apply.)

    a. logical connection between peers

    b. acknowledgments

    c. sequence numbers

    d. retry mechanism

11. What makes TCP preferable for reliable delivery requirements?

    a. sequencing

    b. error recovery

    c. end-to-end reliability

    d. use of the handshake process

12. The TCP process used to maintain an active connection between peers is called _____ .

    a. TCP start-up connection

    b. TCP connection termination

    c. keep-alive

    d. congestion control

13. How many steps occur in the TCP handshake process?

    a. three

    b. four

    c. five

    d. None of the above.

14. Which of the following statements best defines a half-open connection?

    a. The handshake process does not end with a final SYN.

    b. The handshake process does not end with a final ACK.

    c. The handshake process does not end with a final FIN.

    d. The handshake process does not end with a final RST.

15. From where does the IPv6 pseudo-header acquire the information for the Upper-Layer Packet Length field when using TCP as the transport protocol?

    a. the value in the Length field in the TCP header

    b. the value in the Payload Length field in the IPv6 header

    c. the value resulting from the checksum calculation

    d. the value in the Next Header field in the IPv6 header

16. What is the proper response to a TCP connection termination?

    a. Host 1 sends a TCP packet with no data, with FIN and ACK flags set.

    b. Host 2 sends a TCP packet with no data, with FIN and ACK flags set.

    c. Host 2 sends an ACK to respond followed by a TCP packet with no data and FIN and ACK flags set.

    d. Host 1 returns an ACK response.

17. What makes up the value in the UDP Length field of the IPv6 pseudo-header when using UDP for the transport protocol?

    a. the length of the UDP header

    b. the length of the UDP header plus the data

    c. the length of the UDP header plus the checksum value

    d. the length of the UDP header minus the length of the IPv6 header

18. Which of the following mechanisms is part of TCP's error-detection and error-recovery capabilities?

    a. sequencing and reassembly

    b. retransmission timer

    c. explicit acknowledgment

    d. congestion control

19. The current TCP window size is always the greater of what the network and the receiver can handle at any given moment. True or False?

20. Where is TCP data stored when it is received?

    a. on the receiver's network interface controller

    b. inside the TCP window

    c. in the TCP buffer area

    d. inside the network window

21. What is the initial size of the TCP congestion window?

    a. twice the maximum receiver buffer size

    b. twice the maximum transfer unit size

    c. twice the sender's MSS

    d. twice the receiver's MSS

22. What sequence of events signals the TCP Fast Recovery process?

    a. duplicate ACKs

    b. three sets of duplicate ACKs

    c. duplicate FINs

    d. three duplicate FINs

23. Which statements define the edges of the TCP sliding window mechanism? (Choose all that apply.)

    a. acknowledged data plus the receiver's window size

    b. all data that was received

    c. all data pending transmission

    d. all data that was acknowledged

24. Which of the following values are valid TCP Flag settings? (Choose all that apply.)

    a. SYN

    b. ACK

    c. NUL

    d. FIN

    e. PSH

25. When calculating the maximum segment size (MSS) for TCP, what is the difference between the IPv4 header size and the IPv6 header size?

    a. The IPv6 header size is 10 octets larger than the IPv4 header size.

    b. The IPv6 header size is 20 octets larger than the IPv4 header size.

    c. The IPv6 header size is 30 octets larger than the IPv4 header size.

    d. There is no difference in size.

Hands-On Projects

The following Hands-On Projects assume that you are working in a Windows 7 environment, that you installed the Wireshark software, and that you have acquired the trace (data) files for this book as provided by your instructor.

Hands-On Project 9-1: Examine the UDP Header Structure

Time Required: 10 minutes

Objective: Examine the structure of a UDP packet in Wireshark.

Description: This project lets you capture data on the network relevant to making an FTP connection, locate an upper layer protocol such as DNS that uses UDP for transport, and examine the UDP header. Alternately, your instructor may provide a sample capture file for this exercise. For the former, you will need to use an FTP client to connect to an FTP server, either on the local network or on the Internet. (An FTP client such as Filezilla is appropriate, and your instructor will have to provide you with the IP address or domain name and the login instructions for the appropriate server.) You can also use the command line to make an FTP connection, if so directed by your instructor.

1. Click **Start**, point to **All Programs**, and then click **Wireshark**.

2. In Wireshark, click **Capture**, and then click **Interfaces**. In the Capture Interfaces window, click **Start** next to the name of your Ethernet adapter. (If using a capture file provided by your instructor, click **File**, click **Open**, and then navigate to the location of the desired capture file and open it.)

3. Open an FTP client on your computer and use the instructions provided by your instructor to connect to an FTP server. (This step is not necessary if you are to examine a capture file provided by your instructor.)

4. In your FTP client, navigate in the FTP server's directory structure, visiting several locations. When you are done, close the FTP client to end the connection.

5. In Wireshark, click **Capture**, click **Interfaces**, and in the Capture Interfaces window, click **Stop** to stop the capture process. Close the Capture Interfaces window.

6. In the Wireshark top pane, scroll through the list of packets and select one that indicates DNS in the Protocol column as shown in Figure 9-26.

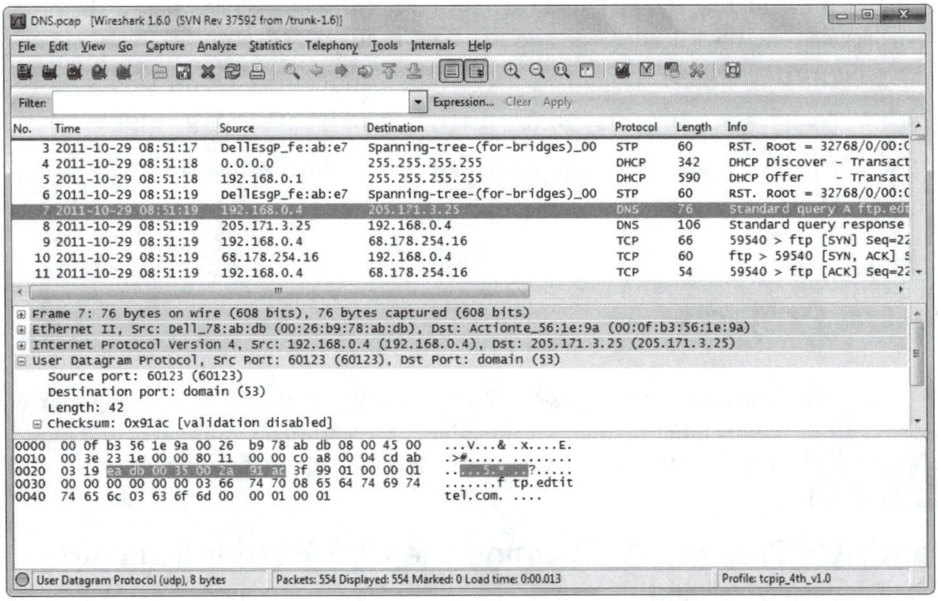

Figure 9-26 DNS packet capture in Wireshark

Source: Wireshark

7. In the primary pane, just beneath the top pane, expand **User Datagram Protocol** and answer the following questions:

   a. What type of source port is used in this communication?

   b. What is the destination port used for this communication?

   c. What is the length of the UDP header?

   d. How can you determine the upper-layer protocol being used by the destination port information?

8. Close the FTP client if you used it for the packet capture and close Wireshark, first saving the capture if you are told to do so by your instructor.

Hands-On Project 9-2: Examine the TCP Header in IPv4 and IPv6

Time Required: 15 minutes

Objective: Examine the structure of a TCP packet using Wireshark.

Description: In this project, you will examine the structure of a TCP packet that was captured on a network using 6to4, which is a mechanism used to allow IPv6 packets to be sent and received on an IPv4 network. This will allow you to view how both IPv4 and IPv6 access and utilize TCP as an upper-layer transfer protocol. You will need access to the 6to4.pcap capture file provided by your instructor. This project requires that relative number sequencing in Wireshark is disabled. To do this, review the instructions in this chapter under "Sequence Number Field."

1. Open Wireshark by clicking **Start,** point to **All Programs,** and then click **Wireshark.**

2. In Wireshark, click **File,** click **Open,** navigate to the location of the 6to4.pcap file provided by your instructor, and then open the file.

3. In the top pane in Wireshark, in the Protocol column, locate the first instance of TCP and select it.

4. In the primary pane, just below the top pane, expand **Internet Protocol Version 4.**

5. Scroll down in this pane and expand **Transmission Control Protocol,** as shown in Figure 9-27.

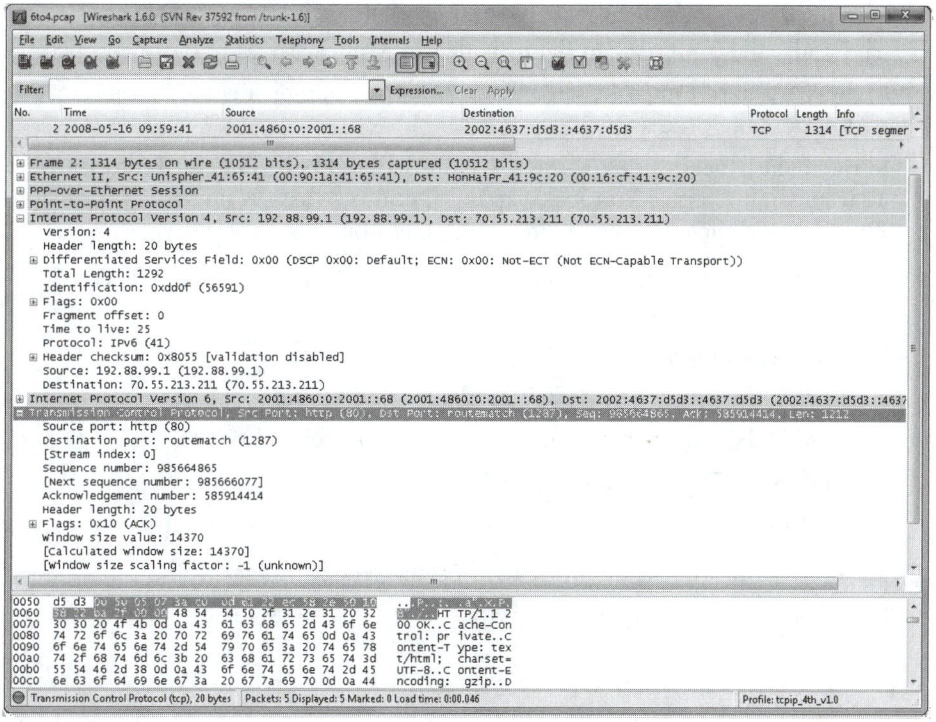

Figure 9-27 TCP packet capture under IPv4
Source: Wireshark

6. Answer the following questions for the TCP header:

   a. What is the source port for TCP, and what protocol type is using TCP for transport?

   b. What is the destination port, and what does the port number indicate?

   c. What is the acknowledgment number that is expected from the destination by the source?

   d. What is the header length?

7. To examine TCP under IPv6, close **Internet Protocol Version 4** and expand **Internet Protocol Version 6**.

8. With IPv6 selected and expanded, has the data under TCP that you previously examined changed? If so, how has it changed? And if not, why has it not changed?

9. When you are finished, close the **6to4.pcap** file but leave Wireshark open so you can perform Hands-On Project 9-3.

Hands-On Project 9-3: Examine the TCP Handshake Process

Time Required: 15 minutes

Objective: Examine the TCP handshake between two nodes.

Description: In this project, you will use a sample capture file to examine the packet exchange involved between two nodes on a network involved in the TCP handshake process. You will need to know the location of the tcp-handshake-capture.pcap file, which will be provided by your instructor. For this activity, Wireshark should already be open.

1. In Wireshark, click **File**, click **Open**, navigate to the location of the tcp-handshake-capture.pcap file provided by your instructor, and then open the file.

2. In the Wireshark top pane, select Packet number **8**, which is the first packet in the three-part handshake process.

3. In the main pane, just below the top pane, expand both **Internet Protocol Version 4** and **Transmission Control Protocol**, expand **Options**, which is under Transmission Control Protocol, and then answer the following questions for Packet 8:

   a. What field under Internet Protocol Version 4 indicates that this is a TCP-based communication?

   b. What type of source port is used in this communication?

   c. What is the length of the TCP header?

   d. What is the sequence number used by the source?

   e. What is the Window size value?

4. In the Wireshark top pane, select Packet **9** and then answer the following questions:

   a. What is the sequence number used by the sender of Packet 9?

   b. Do both sides of this communication use the same MSS?

5. Select Packet **10** in the Wireshark top pane and then answer the following questions:

    a. Did this handshake complete properly?

    b. What is the length of this TCP header?

    c. Are any TCP options defined in this packet?

    d. What is the calculated window size?

6. Close the capture file and then close Wireshark.

Case Projects

CASE PROJECTS

Case Project 9-1: Network Inventory Using Wireshark

A company hires you to inventory its network. You must document all the network devices, their addresses (hardware and network), and the applications that run on the network. Describe how you can use Wireshark to obtain a listing of the network applications.

Case Project 9-2: Discovering Dynamic Port Numbers

One of your work tasks is to inventory all the software running on the network. You've been running Wireshark on your network for several weeks now. You've built a long list of all the source and destination port numbers seen on your network. As you examine this list, you find that there are more than 100 port numbers that are not listed on the IANA port list. There are also about 20 port numbers that belong to applications you know are not running on your network. What happened? Why are your research results so far off base?

Case Project 9-3: TCP Windows Size Problem

You work for a large banking firm headquartered in New York. Your internetwork consists of more than 100 primary servers and about 3,000 clients scattered along the east coast of the United States. Over the past month, you have been looking at the performance statistics of the network and the critical devices. Today, you are examining the file transfer traffic to and from one of your main servers. You notice that the window size is very small in all the file transfers to and from this device. What could be the reason? How can you investigate further?

Case Project 9-4: Understanding Duplicate ACKs

An Internet-based wholesaler of pharmaceutical supplies hires you as a network technician. The network consists of 20 Web servers that host your company's e-commerce system. Several of your e-commerce servers are suddenly receiving duplicate ACKs from the server that maintains your worldwide shipping rates. Is this a problem worth investigating? If so, what will you look for?

chapter 10

Transitioning from IPv4 to IPv6: Interoperation

After reading this chapter and completing the exercises, you will be able to:

- Describe the various methods that allow IPv4 and IPv6 networks to interact, including dual stack and tunneling through the IPv4 cloud
- Explain hybrid IPv4/IPv6 network and node types, such as basic hybrid, nested hybrid, and true hybrid
- Explain how an IPv6 transition address works
- Describe the various IPv4/IPv6 transition mechanisms, such as dual stacks and IPv6-over-IPv4 tunneling
- Describe the different tunneling configuration types and their device interactions
- Explain the ISATAP tunneling mechanism, including its components, addressing, and routing and router configuration
- Explain the 6to4 tunneling mechanism, including its components, addressing and routing, and communication procedures
- Explain the Teredo tunneling system, including its components, addressing and routing, and processes

The implementation of IPv6 is long overdue, yet it is barely present as a networking technology on today's Internet, corporate, and private networks. Unfortunately, the transition from IPv4 to IPv6 isn't as simple as installing some new internetworking hardware, adding the appropriate software updates, and then flipping a switch. The worldwide networking infrastructure that consists of the Internet, as well as all the public and private business and home networks, is unimaginably vast. It will take years to make all the necessary changes to implement and roll out a fully functioning IPv6 Internet.

In the meantime, all the IPv4 networks must continue to function. No commercial enterprise can afford to be offline for any appreciable length of time or it will lose business. Universities require continual network access. So do nonprofit organizations, grade schools, libraries, and individual homes. Networks cannot be taken down a piece at a time and have the IPv4 components replaced by IPv6 devices and software. The two IP versions have to coexist.

As IPv6 network infrastructure components are introduced, they will have to "live" in a mostly IPv4 world, but they will also have to be able to communicate with other IPv6 devices over IPv4. As more and more IPv6 devices and networks are created, there will be an impressively large and confusing mix of IPv4 and IPv6 traffic crossing each other's domains, allowing everyone who is connected to talk to each other using one or the other protocol version. Eventually, the transition will be complete and IPv6 will be the dominant version of IP around the world. Until then, interaction methods for IPv4 and IPv6 must be developed and maintained.

How Can IPv4 and IPv6 Interact?

IPv6 and IPv4 will probably exist side by side for many years. There will be no moment of throwing the switch to light up the new Internet and shut down the old one—the transition will be gradual. On June 8, 2011, the Internet Society hosted World IPv6 Day. Almost 400 major corporations—including Google, Yahoo!, and Facebook—published both IPv4 and IPv6 versions of their Web sites online to assess the general readiness of business network infrastructures and the Internet as a whole to support IPv6 traffic. Results were encouraging, but we still have a long way to go before IPv6 is used as the primary Internet Protocol (IP).

The designers of IPv6 anticipated a slow cutover and created a set of techniques to allow IPv6 to function adequately in a world dominated by IPv4. The designers also built in tools to allow IPv6 to support the legacy installations of IPv4 as the transition progresses to its desired conclusion.

Dual-Stack Approach

The obvious solution to an Internet running two versions of IP is to have it populated by hosts and routers that also run two versions of IP. With trivial exceptions, the wires, airwaves, and glass fibers don't care which protocol they're carrying. The same network will support both versions, if only the hosts and, more importantly, the routers can support both sets of protocols.

Almost from the beginning, IPv6 has enjoyed wide support among leading manufacturers, who continue to support it and are bringing products to market, implementing different parts of the full IPv6 suite in a phased manner. Experimental or production versions of the IPv6 stack are available for nearly all host platforms, with variations in terms of what parts of the full suite of protocols they implement, as well as how they implement them.

Dual-stack implementations for individuals or small offices may work as experiments, but they are limited, for the near term, by the lack of dual-stack routers at ISPs located at the edge of the Internet. The most important dual-stack machines will be the routers themselves. A dual-stack router can provide a connection between the IPv4 Internet and an office (or set of ISP customers) that already has made the switch to IPv6. As discussed in the next section, these early adopters will communicate with one another via tunneling through the IPv4 cloud.

Tunneling through the IPv4 Cloud

The Internet will probably move to IPv6 "from the edges in." That is, IPv6 will be adopted first by smaller organizations that have greater flexibility and a higher tolerance for the difficulties of pioneering. From the points of view of route aggregation and bandwidth usage, these smaller organizations are at the edges, whereas high-capacity networks are at the center. How are these islands of IPv6 that are adrift in a vast ocean of IPv4 routers and hosts supposed to communicate with one another? Through tunnels.

To send a packet to a distant IPv6 network through intervening IPv4 routers, the IPv6 packet is formed normally and sent to a router capable of encapsulating it in an IPv4 packet. The routers on both ends of the tunnels must be dual-stack routers, capable of understanding both IPv4 and IPv6. When the interim IPv4 packet reaches the distant IPv6 dual-stack router, that router strips off the IPv4 packet and routes the packet on its local IPv6 network normally. IPv4-compatible IPv6 addresses were designed expressly for this kind of situation, where IPv6 routers need to understand IPv4.

An alternate scheme is the 6to4 tunneling method, as specified in RFC 3056. For IPv4 nodes or networks with public IPv4 addresses, a legitimate IPv6 address is formed by adding the 32 bits of the IPv4 address to the network prefix 2002::/16. This creates an address of the following form: 2002::IPv4address:SLA:Interface_ID. The interface ID is the normal 48 bits, plus the added 16 bits 0xFFFE, and the seventh bit of the first byte inverted, to create a 64-bit EUI-64 formatted IPv6 address (see RFC 4291). The site-level address is the normal 16 bits, and the combination of the 2002::/16 prefix and the 32 bits of the IPv4 address makes up the first 48 bits of the new address.

In the longer term, this scheme will inflict many of the problems of IPv4 routing onto IPv6 routers. In the short term, however, when IPv6 addresses are few and far between, it provides a way to connect widely dispersed IPv6 islands without any need for configured tunnels.

IPv6 Rate of Adoption

The address crunch is not going away, but neither are the addresses already granted under IPv4. The biggest push for the adoption of IPv6 is coming from those who were not a part of the initial Internet "land rush" of the 1990s—countries outside Europe and North America, particularly those in East Asia. Switching to IPv6 means that whole classes of technology not even considered by the designers of the Internet must be developed.

The makers of technologies, such as cellular phones and smartphones, have two reasons to embrace IPv6. First, mobile network providers require access to the address space provided by IPv6 (covered in Lesson 2), because communications technologies need vast numbers of connected users to achieve network effects. Network effects are a kind of "critical mass" for information access and exchange that occurs when most members in some identifiable population participate in a communications or information system. For example, consider the relative usefulness of possessing one of the 35 million telephones in New York City in 2006 versus possessing one of the three telephones in Dodge City, Kansas in 1902. Sometimes, a lot more users make a technology much more useful, simply because the large numbers constitute a powerful interest group and a virtual economy in which service providers and retailers will want to participate.

The second reason these new technologies may embrace IPv6 is because communications technologies need the improved functionality of the IPv6 protocol suite, particularly to keep mobile users connected to the services and information they want to access while they're in motion.

Transitioning to IPV6: The Reality

We may not fully realize how much Internet congestion is the result of the headaches of routing and sharing scarce IPv4 addresses until IPv6 begins to come into its own. However, IPv6 has not been deployed at nearly the rate predicted in the early stages of its development. Deploying it in an enterprise or service provider network is challenging and risky because of the technical obstacles inherent in the protocol and because of the interoperability with IPv4. These challenges severely affect the adoption of IPv6.

As discussed in Chapter 2, IPv6 was developed to provide a solution for the ever-dwindling IPv4 address space. Industry participants reacted in a number of ways to the potential of IPv6. Initially, the service-provider segment of the market pushed for the protocol because it was seen as a mechanism for streamlining the global routing table and ultimately eliminating private address space altogether. The router and switch vendors saw the protocol as a marketing opportunity and quickly began supporting IPv6. The engineers in the service-provider segment saw IPv6 as a solution to solve a specific problem.

The following sections identify some of the difficulties that still limit widespread deployment of IPv6, despite the enthusiasm of these various industry groups.

Interoperability

Interoperability means that one technology can work with another technology. This is a concern for any technology because vendors sometimes develop technologies that are based on standards but don't work with other vendors' technologies based on the same standards. This concern applies to IPv4 and IPv6, where successful communication at the IP layer might require all devices to run either IPv4 or IPv6, or where some kind of address translation might be needed to permit the two protocols to work together.

Network address translation (NAT) is used throughout the industry today to provide translation between private IP addresses and public IP addresses. Using NAT is certainly a possibility for IPv4/IPv6 translations; however, certain technologies, such as voice over IP (VoIP) and real-time audio/video, do not work with NAT, further exacerbating the problem of creating an effective translation that is both workable and universal.

Within an individual organization, the transition to IPv6 requires a substantial investment of both time and resources. In addition, the transition strategy varies according to the type of organization. In fact, companies must learn about the various options for transitioning to IPv6 before developing a migration plan. A structured, organization-wide approach is recommended, with the first step being to set up a lab environment to test network services and applications. From a high-level point of view, when creating the IPv6 lab environment, first develop network management procedures for your IPv6 network, and then connect your lab to another IPv6 network to test interoperability.

All transition plans involve interim solutions that provide the framework for an IPv6 environment to some extent. However, these miss the big picture, given that they deal with the network infrastructure, not the services the network provides.

For example, let's say an enterprise environment has decided to migrate to IPv6. The transition is relatively complex, but it results in there being IPv6-addressed hosts on the network. The question is whether it helped the enterprise meet its business goals just because all the routers, switches, and network infrastructure devices can route and transport IPv6 packets. What if IPv6 is positioned as an alternative to IPv4 but is not an extension of the address space? This would be a major obstacle to IPv6 deployment. IP addresses represent end points that deliver a service, whether within an operating system, in routing tables, or embedded in the application code. Therein lies the problem. If the end points that provide services are not compatible with IPv6, there is no value to deploying IPv6.

Network Elements

When transitioning to IPv6, the following network elements and software tools, which are required to support the network infrastructure and services, must be considered:

- Clients
- Servers
- Routers
- Gateways
- VoIP networks
- Network management nodes
- Transition nodes
- Firewalls

Software

On the software side, there are a number of utilities designed to monitor, report on, and manage the network infrastructure, including:

- Network management utilities
- Network Internet infrastructure applications
- Network systems applications
- Network end-user applications
- Network high-availability software
- Network security software

Without a conversion from IPv4 to IPv6, application services such as DNS, DHCP, and FTP are incompatible with the IPv6 address space. In addition, IPv6 hosts cannot reach Internet Web servers within the IPv4 address space. So, to efficiently and effectively transition to IPv6, all hosts, servers, and applications must be transitioned to IPv6.

The IETF has developed transition plans that focus on the parallel deployment of the IPv4 and IPv6 address spaces. However, these plans do not solve the interoperability problem. They define recommendations for deploying IPv6 on elements such as Mail servers, for example, but for IPv6 to interoperate, all elements must communicate via IPv6. Proposing NAT as a long-term solution defies logic, given that NAT is currently deployed for IPv4.

Transitioning to IPv6 from the Windows Perspective

Today, Windows Server 2008, Windows Vista, and Windows 7 support a TCP/IP implementation that integrates IPv4 and IPv6 in a dual-stack configuration that Microsoft calls its Next Generation TCP/IP stack. That said, Microsoft also indicates that it has no plans to support IPv6 on versions of Windows prior to Windows Server 2003 and Windows XP SP1.

Microsoft also offers a large collection of learning materials and information on transitioning from IPv4 to IPv6 on its Web site at *http://technet.microsoft.com/en-us/network/bb530961*. In its "IPv6 Transition Technologies" white paper, the company puts particular emphasis on how it supports tunneling from both sides (from IPv6 through IPv4 back to IPv6, and from IPv4 through IPv6 back to IPv4).

Microsoft further indicates its support for what is sometimes called "6over4" addresses. Here, a valid 64-bit unicast prefix is prepended to an interface identifier that takes the form ::WWXX:YYZZ, which maps to a unicast IPv4 address of the form w.x.y.z in colon hexadecimal notation (e.g., the IPv4 address 131.107.4.92 maps to FE80::836B:45C). This supports automatic tunneling as defined in RFC 2529. Microsoft also supports "6to4" addresses that take the prefix 2002:WWXX:YYZZ::/48, in which this notation converts from a public IP address of the form w.x.y.z, as in the preceding example. This supports automatic tunneling as defined in RFC 3056.

In addition, Microsoft supports **Intra-Site Automatic Tunnel Addressing Protocol (ISATAP)**, specified in RFC 5214 in which addresses are composed of a valid 64-bit unicast address prefix and an IPv4 interface identifier, so that ::0:5EFE:w.x.y.z maps to a standard IPv4 interface address of the form w.x.y.z. Finally, Microsoft supports the tunneling technology known as Teredo, documented in RFC 4380, which permits IPv6 and IPv4 traffic to traverse one or more IPv4 NATs. The solution neatly bypasses the problem of protocol translation in NATs by encapsulating such traffic in an IPv4 UDP message rather than labeling the protocol field in the IPv4 header as 41 (which normally indicates ICMP messages used for experimental mobility protocols and won't be translated or forwarded by most NAT servers). This provides what Microsoft calls a "last resort transition technology for IPv6 connectivity" in that, if native IPv6, 6to4, or ISATAP connectivity is available, Teredo won't be used.

Overall, this shows that Microsoft is strongly committed to supporting ongoing interoperability between IPv4 and IPv6 networking domains, as well as to providing or supporting technologies to help ease the transition. The same thing is true for most other major platform vendors, and for the open source community that stands behind the widely available Linux distributions.

Availability

IPv6 address availability and component support are other obstacles that have traditionally inhibited deploying an IPv6 solution. Although most service providers are beginning to upgrade their infrastructures to support IPv6, the assignment and distribution of addresses has not been widely implemented. This is because of the immaturity of the consumer market for IPv6 deployment. So, we have a Catch-22 scenario: Consumers will deploy IPv6 only when they are forced to, and providers are unwilling to sink significant funds into supporting IPv6 if there is no market for it.

Consequently, there has not been a huge push to develop IPv6 solutions until recently, and a number of the network elements and software solutions required for complete interoperability have not been developed. Most of the IPv6 deployments are in Asia and Europe, in areas that were behind in the deployment of IPv4 infrastructures. These environments are ahead of the curve for two reasons. One, the market is forcing IPv6 onto the consumers, which creates demand for provider support. Two, a lot of the solutions are deployed initially with IPv6. The interoperability issues still exist, but the deployment timelines are much more aggressive. Availability is changing rapidly in the United States, with Comcast aggressively rolling out IPv6 using dual-stack solutions. AT&T and other providers are offering consumer IPv6 in some form, usually as tunneling technology.

What's Next?

Convincing executive managers that deploying an IPv6 solution is a robust and necessary strategy is an obstacle in itself because the benefits, such as return on investment, may not be readily visible. However, this does not mean that the IPv6 transition can be ignored. A major event that may accelerate the deployment of IPv6 is the announcement that the Department of Defense (DoD) will be IPv6 ready by 2012. Both IPv4 and IPv6 have been DoD mandatory standards since 2005. The original projected year for full IPv6 readiness was 2010, but delays in IPv6 implementation have been caused by commercial vendors' perception of the DoD as a minor participant in the overall communications industry market. If the DoD achieves its goal, this will accelerate the development of new technologies and solutions as vendors realize they must compete to provide services to the DoD.

An historical overview of DoD's adoption of IPv6 can be found at *http://ipv6.com/articles/military/Military-and-IPv6.htm.*

There are tremendous obstacles to an all-IPv6 world; however, these obstacles must be overcome eventually. Understanding these obstacles can help provide a roadmap to the day when IPv6 is a necessity.

Hybrid IPv4/IPv6 Networks and Node Types

As previously stated, network administrators will not be able to simply "flip a switch" and transition their networks from IPv4 to IPv6. There will be a significant transition period where both versions of IP will coexist in the same environment. As software and hardware components are upgraded, IPv6 devices will need to be able to talk to each other over an IPv4 infrastructure. IPv4 and IPv6 nodes will also need to communicate with each other, either over an IPv4 core network or over an IPv6 core network, or over different subnets, some of which will be IPv4 and some IPv6. In general, these "mixed" environments are called hybrid networks.

Although all the possible configurations of IPv4/IPv6 hybrid networks and nodes may appear confusing at first, the evolution of networks from IPv4 to IPv6 must proceed in a orderly fashion so that organizations can continue to function and serve their customers during the transition process. An exhaustive representation of all the possible transitional network designs is beyond the scope of this textbook, but the following sections discuss some examples of IPv4/IPv6 hybrid network models.

Basic Hybrid Network Model

The **basic hybrid network model** is an example of how IPv6-capable sites communicate with each other over the IPv4 Internet backbone. Each site is presumed to contain IPv6 individual nodes, and each site possesses a gateway that manages IPv6-to-IPv4 transition traffic. IPv6 nodes encapsulate their IPv6 packets in IPv4 data packets and then transmit them to the default local site gateway. The gateway forwards these packets from the IPv6 network through the IPv4 Internet using tunneling technology. At the receiving site, also presumed to use an IPv6 gateway and presumed to be IPv6 capable, the packets are received, removed from the IPv4 encapsulation, and routed to their specific destinations.

On the IPv6 site, individual nodes register their IPv6 site local addresses with the gateway router. When all IPv6 nodes are published, their addresses are mapped to a single IPv6 static address so that IPv4 networks in other sites on the Web can address traffic to the nodes at the IPv6 site. The gateway maintains an IPv4-to-IPv6 address mapping table so that the IPv6 nodes can receive information sent to them using IPv4 addresses. Figure 10-1 shows a high-level view of the basic hybrid model.

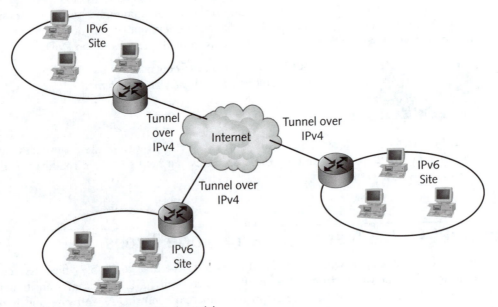

Figure 10-1 Basic hybrid network model
© Cengage Learning 2013

This model's components can reverse to show how individual IPv4 sites can communicate with each other over an IPv6 Internet backbone; however, it is more feasible to implement IPv4-to-IPv6 transition efforts at the organizational level. It is likely that the last network to become fully IPv6 capable will be the Internet itself.

Nested Hybrid Network Model

The **nested hybrid network model** can be considered an adaptation of the basic hybrid model. The core IPv4 Internet remains the same, but sites can be IPv4 or IPv6 or a nested combination of the two. In the nested model, the most likely design would be a small IPv6 "island" existing within a larger IPv4 network. As in the basic hybrid network model, the IPv6 nodes would register their addresses, but this time with a local gateway that exists between the IPv6 subnet and the larger IPv4 site. IPv6 nodes would encapsulate their packets in IPv4 data packets and send them to their local gateways; the gateways would then read the routing information and forward the packets to either an IPv4 node on a different subnet within the IPv4 site or the default gateway to the Internet. Figure 10-2 shows how an IPv4/IPv6 site nested within the larger context of other sites and the Internet looks.

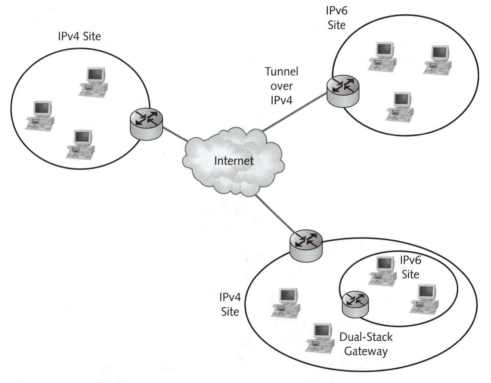

Figure 10-2 Nested hybrid network model
© Cengage Learning 2013

The nested model could also be used for an IPv6 site that requires one or more "islands" of IPv4 subnets. This sort of model would most likely be deployed to make use of legacy applications or operating systems that are difficult or expensive to transition to IPv6 platforms. IPv4 nodes would send their packet to a dual-stack gateway capable of mapping IPv4-to-IPv6 addresses and then forward that data to IPv6 nodes on a native IPv6 network.

True Hybrid Network Model

The **true hybrid network model** can represent a number of hybrid configurations, but it assumes that a site has a variety of different subnets, based on IP version implementation. Some subnets within the site contain IPv4-only nodes; some contain IPv6-only nodes; and some contain dual-capable IPv4/IPv6 nodes. Each subnet must use a dual-stack gateway capable of managing both IPv4 and IPv6 traffic. For convenience and organizational simplicity, this model assumes that each subnet contains nodes that are like each other. That is, there are no IPv4-only or IPv6-only nodes on the same subnet, given that communication would not be possible between them without some type of translation mechanism.

This model also assumes that the backbone is IPv4. The site gateway needs to have the same dual-stack abilities as each subnet gateway because it will also be managing both IPv4 and IPv6 traffic exiting the site. Traffic coming in from the Internet will be either native IPv4 packets or IPv6 packets encapsulated in IPv4 packets. Once packets are received from outside the site, the gateway will need to examine them, remove any encapsulation (if present) if the traffic is destined for an IPv6 subnet, and then forward the packet. Of course, IPv4 traffic addressed to nodes on an IPv4 subnet would be handled without any encapsulation or translation services. Figure 10-3 provides a picture of such a "mixed" site that's connected to the Internet.

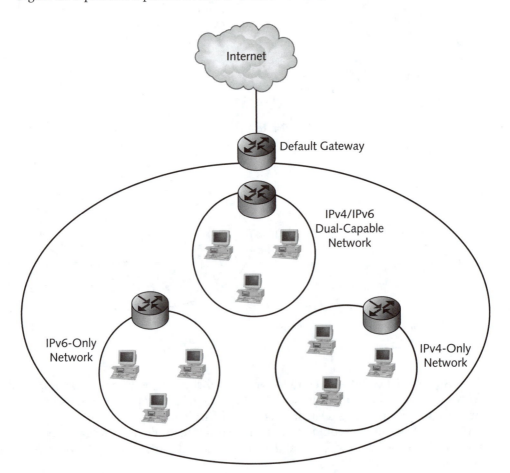

Figure 10-3 Site with mixed IPv4 and IPv6 subnets
© Cengage Learning 2013

This is a true hybrid environment in that there is no version of IP that is dominant at the core. All internetworking devices within the site's network infrastructure must be capable of managing both IPv4 and IPv6 traffic. The IPv4/IPv6 dual-capable subnet does not contain separate IPv4 nodes and IPv6 nodes; rather, each node in the subnet is IPv4/IPv6 capable. Just as in the other subnets within the site, each node's use of an IP version is the same as the other nodes'. Because the Internet is presumed to be IPv4, all traffic should be sent to the site's default gateway as either native IPv4 packets or IPv6 encapsulated in IPv4 packets.

This mixed environment could accommodate a core infrastructure dedicated to a specific IP version. In that scenario, the primary network infrastructure's hardware and software would use either IPv4 or IPv6, and the site would contain the mix of subnets shown in Figure 10-3. If, for example, the core was IPv4, then IPv6 subnets would have to encapsulate their data to communicate with the core and to send traffic through the default gateway to the Internet. IPv4/IPv6-capable subnets would send traffic (as IPv4 packets) off the subnet to their local gateways.

IPv6 Transition Addresses

One of the challenges in IPv4/IPv6 communication is the issue of addresses. IPv4 addressing and IPv6 addressing are radically different in terms of format, size, and memory requirements. As you learned in Chapter 2, IPv4 uses a 32-bit address space and IPv6 uses a 128-bit address. IPv4 uses a dot-notation, such as 192.168.0.4, and IPv6 uses a colon notation, such as FE80::2D57:C4F8:8808:80D7. Another complication is that some IPv4 addresses include a colon when they need to describe both an IP address and port number—for example, 192.168.0.1:80. This results in problems for an **IP address parser** that attempts to translate an IPv4 address into its IPv6 equivalent. An address format is required whereby an IP parser is able to distinguish between IPv4 and IPv6 address formats for management across mixed network types.

In this context, an IP address parser is a component of an internetworking device such as a router that analyzes the headers of an incoming IP packet to determine its source, destination and possibly the version of IP used in the packet header.

One transition address method is using literal IPv6 addresses in URLs. As described in the section "Working with ipv6-literal.net Names" in Chapter 8, IPv6 addresses can be expressed in a literal format in either a URL or FQDN so that they can be used in Web browsers, for instance, without the requirement to completely translate the IPv6 address into its IPv4 equivalent. "Literals" also allow information such as port numbers, prefixes, and lengths to be incorporated in the address without introducing any ambiguity that would result in the address not being understood. For the specific details regarding IPv6 literal addresses, see Chapter 8.

Another address transition method is **Stateless IP/ICMP translation algorithm (SIIT)**, which is specified in RFC 6145. SIIT was created as a replacement for NAT-PT, which was originally specified in RFC 2766 and subsequently documented in RFC 4966. The SIIT specification describes two domains, an IPv4 domain and an IPv6 domain, joined by one or more IP/ICMP translators called XLATs. SIIT defines a type of IPv6 address called IPv4 translated addresses that can be formatted as ::ffff:0:0:0/96 or ::ffff:0:a.b.c.d, in which a.b.c.d is the IPv4 address notation. This address translation method allows IPv6 nodes to communicate with IPv4-only nodes without the IPv6 node possessing a permanent IPv4 address on its network adapter. The translation method works in both directions, allowing IPv4-only nodes to send traffic to IPv6 computers through the XLAT translator. See RFC 6144 and RFC 6145 for full details about the framework for IPv4-to-IPv6 translation and the IP/ICMP translation algorithm.

Transition Mechanisms

IPv4/IPv6 transition mechanisms are technologies designed to allow the protocols and network infrastructure elements to be used in the transition from one version of the Internet Protocol to the next. More specifically, they are methods and address types that provide for communication between network nodes that use only IPv4 or only IPv6 to interact with each other or with network resources. Ideally, rolling out a new protocol on a network involves installing and configuring the protocol on all network nodes and internetworking devices within a specific infrastructure. This would mean transitioning the entire network en masse from the older protocol to the new one. Although this might be a reasonable solution in a small to mid-range company, it would be totally unworkable for enterprise-level organizations and impossible for WAN environments, especially the Internet.

For this reason, the transition from IPv4 to IPv6 requires that multiple stages occur in the move from a pure IPv4 environment to one that exclusively uses IPv6. During the transition stages, the organization will be using both IPv4 and IPv6 devices, and they must be able to talk to each other in order to maintain network use and organizational productivity during the change, which could last for months or, more likely, years. There are several mechanisms available to assist in the IPv4/IPv6 transition, each with its advantages and challenges.

Dual Protocol Stacks for IPv4 and IPv6

A dual-stack protocol for a host or router is implemented at the level of the device's operating system, allowing the device to support both IPv4 and IPv6, either as independent protocols or in a hybrid form. Windows 7 is a dual-stack operating system because it allows the computer to communicate on the network using either IPv4 or IPv6. Some dual-stack devices are able to communicate with both IPv4-only devices and IPv6-only devices on the same network. Dual-stack implementations use special addressing—such as SIIT, which was previously mentioned—to allow a dual-stack device to communicate with a machine using only a single IP version.

Most modern operating systems have IPv6 enabled by default, including Windows 7, Windows Vista, Windows Server 2008/2008 R2, and Mac OS X 10.4 and later, as well as current Linux distributions. However, many network infrastructure devices, such as routers, do not enable IPv6 but may have a feature option that allows them to have IPv6 enabled or can be purchased with a feature that enables IPv6. Also, many network devices still do not support IPv6.

RFC 4213 describes a number of basic transition mechanisms for IPv6 hosts and routers, including the dual-IP-layer operation. Network nodes that are considered dual stack have the ability to send and receive network traffic using other IPv4 and IPv6 packets. However, that a node is dual-stack-capable does not automatically mean that both protocols are enabled. Such devices may have both stacks enabled, only IPv4 enabled with IPv6 disabled, or only IPv6 enabled with IPv4 disabled. Obviously, if a dual-stack device has only one protocol enabled (say, IPv4), it will behave just like a single protocol device.

Until this point, we've been using the terms *dual stack* and *dual layer* interchangeably, but they are actually different types of architecture. To understand the difference, keep in mind that, during an infrastructure's transition from only IPv4 to only IPv6, network traffic on a mixed IPv4/IPv6 network must be routable across devices using either or both protocol versions. This is also true for devices attempting to access applications and services that are available using either only IPv4 or only IPv6. To allow a node to connect to devices and applications under these circumstances, the node must have either a dual-IP-layer architecture or a dual-stack architecture.

Dual-IP-Layer Architecture

A network node possessing a **dual-IP-layer architecture** has both IPv4 and IPv6 protocols operating in a single Transport layer implementation. Another way of looking at it is to imagine a single, vertical chimney or stack in the OSI model connecting the Network layer and the Transport layer. The Network layer contains the IP protocol, which includes both IPv4 and IPv6, and the Transport layer contains the various transport protocols, including TCP and UDP. In the dual-IP-layer architecture, TCP and UDP in the Transport layer can simultaneously access either IPv4 or IPv6 in the Network layer. Figure 10-4 shows how this is constructed.

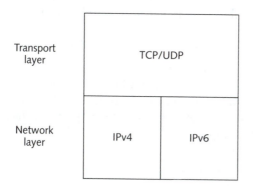

Figure 10-4 Dual-IP-layer architecture
© Cengage Learning 2013

Notice that the Transport layer is a single stack, whereas the Network layer represents a dual layer, with IPv4 and IPv6. Each IP version can access a single Transport layer rather than having dual transport stacks for each IP protocol. The dual-IP-layer architecture allows a network node to create the following types of IP packets:

- IPv4 packets
- IPv6 packets
- IPv6-over-IPv4 packets

To do this under a single Transport layer stack, an upper-layer transport protocol accesses IPv4, IPv6, or both IP versions, as shown in Figure 10-5.

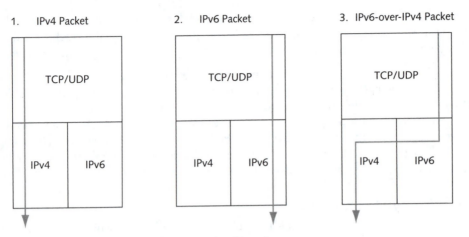

Figure 10-5 Single Transport layer accessing IP versions
© Cengage Learning 2013

If a native IPv4 or IPv6 application on the source device needs to contact its equivalent on the destination device, the Transport layer protocol uses the obvious version of IP at the Network layer to create the necessary packets, which are then transmitted. If an IPv6 application on the source needs to communicate with an IPv4 receiver, the Transport layer accesses IPv6 at the Network layer and then encapsulates the IPv6 packet in an IPv4 header before transmission. This is described in more detail in the upcoming section, "IPv6-over-IPv4 Tunneling."

Dual-stack Architecture

In contrast to the dual-IP-layer architecture, a computer possessing a **dual-stack architecture** maintains separate stacks at both the Network and Transport layers. In other words, each version of the IP protocol at the Network layer has its own upper-layer protocol stack at the Transport layer. Figure 10-6 shows how this appears.

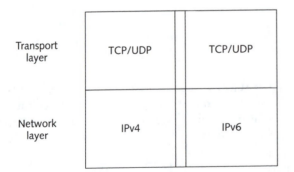

Figure 10-6 Dual-stack architecture
© Cengage Learning 2013

This computer is still capable of generating the same types of IP packets, but depending on the requirements of the Application layer protocols, a different stack is accessed at the Transport layer as well as at the Network layer. The dual-stack architecture allows a network node to create the following types of IP packets:

- IPv4 packets
- IPv6 packets
- IPv6-over-IPv4 packets

Figure 10-7 illustrates how the Application layer accesses the dual stacks at the Transport layer to generate different IP version packets depending on the requirements of applications on the source and destination network nodes.

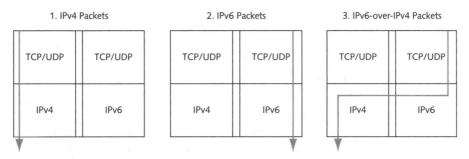

Figure 10-7 Dual Transport layer accessing IP versions
© Cengage Learning 2013

Although the process is different than a dual-IP-layer architecture, the result is identical. The network node is allowed to communicate with the same destination nodes and applications on a mixed IPv4/IPv6 network infrastructure, regardless of which dual architecture is being used by the node at the operating system level. Notice that even though the Transport and Network layers maintain separate stacks, once the Application layer has accessed the Transport layer stack for the IPv6 network stack and the IPv6 packet has been created, the IPv6 network stack can still access the IPv4 network stack and encapsulate the IPv6 packet in an IPv4 header prior to transmission onto the network. However, machines capable of dual-stack architecture are commonly attached to both IPv4 and IPv6 networks and create packet types compatible for each of these networks.

Dual Architecture and Tunneling

Neither dual-IP-layer nor dual-stack architecture requires IPv6-over-IPv6 tunneling to be effective as a transition mechanism. Dual-architecture nodes can produce either IPv4 or IPv6 packets and forward them to a gateway router. If, for instance, the node is constructing a message for an IPv6 destination node on a different subnet, it can create an IPv6 packet and forward it to a dual-stack-capable gateway router. The router notes that it is an IPv6 packet and that the destination is an IPv6 node on a remote network. The router encapsulates the IPv6 packet in an IPv4 header so it can be sent across the IPv4 network infrastructure. The packet is decapsulated by the gateway router at the destination network and delivered to the IPv6 node in its native IP protocol version.

The dual-architecture-capable sending node, if sending to an IPv4 destination, can construct an IPv4 packet and send it to the gateway. The gateway transmits the IPv4 packet, without any form of encapsulation, across the IPv4 network infrastructure. The destination IPv4 network receives and delivers the packet in the same manner as if the packet originated from an IPv4-only node.

Another implementation of dual architecture works as a transition mechanism but requires no tunneling at all. The dual-architecture-capable node would need two network interfaces, one for IPv4 and the other for IPv6. The IPv4 interface would use a default route to an IPv4 gateway for "normal" network communications across the IPv4 network architecture to IPv4 destination nodes. The IPv6 interface would send traffic only on its own subnet so that the sending node could create and transmit IPv6 packets for those IPv6-only destination nodes on its own subnet. If an IPv6 gateway router was present (or a dual-IPv4/IPv6-capable gateway with separate IPv4 and IPv6 interfaces off the subnet) and its IPv6 interface pointed across an IPv6 network infrastructure, then the dual-architecture-capable sending node could transmit IPv6 packets to IPv6 destination nodes on remote subnets without any form of tunneling.

IPv6-over-IPv4 Tunneling

Dual-architecture-capable nodes allow a single computer to communicate to both IPv4-only and IPv6-only destination nodes without any tunneling mechanism in most cases, but often some form of tunneling must be deployed. **IPv6-over-IPv4 tunneling** is used to allow IPv6 network nodes to send packets over an IPv4 network infrastructure. The situation requiring this tunneling mechanism is on a network in which network nodes are IPv4 only, IPv6 only, or dual enabled. However, the core internetworking routers are primarily IPv4-only enabled while these devices are slowly transitioning to IPv6. Although some routers may be IPv6 capable, until the entire infrastructure is transitioned to IPv6, tunneling will be required to ensure that IPv6 packets are able to traverse those portions of the network that only support IPv4.

After the IPv6 packet is created by the source network node, it must be encapsulated in an IPv4 header. When the IPv4 header is created, the protocol field value is set at 41 to indicate that it is an encapsulated IPv6 packet. The IPv4 header's Source and Destination fields are set to the IPv4 addresses of the end points of the IPv6-over-IPv4 tunnel so that the packet can safely be transmitted across the IPv4 infrastructure. Figure 10-8 provides a high-level example of the relevant fields in the IPv6 packet being encapsulated in an IPv4 header. For further details about IPv4 and IPv6 header construction, see Chapter 3.

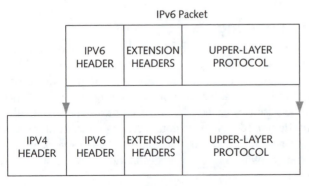

Figure 10-8 IPv6-over-IPv4 encapsulation

IPv6-over-IPv4 tunneling presents a challenge for IPv6 header construction. The IPv6 path MTU for the destination is configured at a value of 20 less than the path MTU of an IPv4 destination. Although an IPv6 node sets the path MTU for a packet to ensure its arrival at the destination node without fragmentation, the path MTU for IPv4 may not be stored for the tunnel, requiring that the packet be fragmented by an IPv4 router along the path. To accommodate this eventuality, the source node must set the value of the Don't Fragment flag in the IPv4 header to 0 so that fragmentation will be allowed.

The source node determines which packets must be encapsulated based on the routing information the node maintains in its own routing table. The encapsulating node consults the destination address, then refers to the routing table, then determines which packets must be tunneled, using the prefix mask and match techniques. The encapsulating node also determines the end-point addresses from the configuration data contained for the tunnel. Only packets with a value of 41 in the Protocol field and with IPv4 source addresses are allowed to traverse the matching tunnel. Once the packet arrives at the receiving end point of the tunnel, which is usually the receiving node, the packet is reassembled if it has been fragmented in transit, the IPv4 encapsulation is removed, and the node processes the IPv6 packet up the stack to the receiving application.

DNS Infrastructure

A critical transition mechanism in an IPv4/IPv6 network environment is the DNS infrastructure. As you saw in Chapter 8, DNS records and DNS name resolution management are handled differently for IPv4 and IPv6. Network devices and applications are accessed by name by other devices and applications. In a network infrastructure containing both IPv4 and IPv6 nodes, if the DNS service does not have the ability to resolve names to both IPv4 and IPv6 addresses, network communication will be severely inhibited or will fail completely.

To transition name resolution services from IPv4 to IPv6 on a mixed network, DNS servers must be configured for dual stack and support both A records for IPv4 nodes and AAAA records for IPv6 nodes to allow names to be resolved into addresses. To allow addresses to be resolved into domain names for reverse queries, DNS servers must contain PTR records in the IN-ADDR.ARPA domain for IPv4 domains and may optionally contain PTR records in the IP6.ARPA domain for IPv6 nodes. These resource records can be added manually or by using DNS dynamic updates.

In mixed IPv4/IPv6 environments, the DNS resolver libraries on network nodes must have the ability to manage both A and AAAA records. This is required regardless of whether the DNS packets are carried by IPv4 or by IPv6 packets. DNS servers provide name resolution services without knowing if network nodes are IPv4 and/or IPv6 capable. Once a node receives name resolution data containing A and AAAA records, it may still choose to order the information that is sent up the stack to the application based on a specific preference, such as IPv6 first and then IPv4 or IPv4 first and then IPv6. This assumes the application has not made a request for a preference. An application can select which address type the resolver provides, or it can request both versions of IP; however, the resolver cannot make the decision to serve only one version of IP or another. Once an order of preference has been served to the application, the application will attempt to make a connection using the first IP version offered. If a connection cannot be made, it will attempt the next option presented. See the section "Name Resolution in IPv6 Networks" in Chapter 8 for more information about source and destination address selection.

Tunneling Configurations for Mingling IPv4 and IPv6

The tunneling mechanism configurations are defined by RFC 4213 and are used to describe the various device connections requiring IPv4-to-IPv6 tunneling. Because it will take time to create and deploy an IPv6 routing infrastructure on a network, the IPv4 infrastructure will need to continue to be functional and carry both IPv4 and IPv6 traffic. As previously mentioned, tunneling allows IPv6 traffic to be carried on IPv4 networks encapsulated in IPv4 headers. The foundational mechanisms for tunneling require two devices, one at each end of the tunnel.

The **encapsulator** is the node at the sending end of the tunnel, and it is responsible for encapsulating the IPv6 packet in an IPv4 header, then transmitting the packet in the tunnel. The **decapsulator** is the receiving node at the other end of the tunnel, and it is responsible for reassembling any fragmented packets, removing the IPv4 header encapsulation, and processing the IPv6 packet. The encapsulator may be required to maintain information about the tunnel, such as the tunnel MTU. The tunneling process allows IPv6 traffic to be transmitted over an IPv4 routing infrastructure. IPv4/IPv6 nodes and routers tunnel IPv6 datagrams over areas of IPv4 routing topology by encapsulating the datagrams in IPv4 packets. Although the description of encapsulator and decapsulator could easily identify the sending node to the receiving node, there are several device types upon which tunneling configurations can be applied:

- Router-to-router
- Host-to-router and router-to-host
- Host-to-host

Each configuration is capable of tunneling IPv6 packets over areas of an IPv4 routing topology, but they are used in different ways.

Router-to-Router

IPv4/IPv6-capable routers that are linked in an IPv4 routing infrastructure can tunnel IPv6 packets between each other by creating an end-to-end path. The created tunnel extends the length of one segment of the path used by the IPv6 packet to travel from source to destination.

Router-to-router paths are most likely to use configured tunneling because they require specifically configured end points to the tunnel. Configured tunneling requires that an administrator configure the end points of a tunnel; otherwise, the configuration is performed automatically by the configuration mechanisms of the operating system. The other tunneling device combinations can also use configured tunneling, if necessary. The types of tunneling configurations include 6to4 routers tunneling over an IPv4 WAN, two IPv6-only routing domains tunneling over an IPv4 WAN, and an IPv6 test lab tunneling over an IPv4 LAN infrastructure. Different types of tunnels will be discussed later in this section.

The link between the two **router-to-router** tunnel end points is a logical segment that makes up part of the overall path between the source and the destination, and this segment represents a single hop in the overall path. The routes within the infrastructure point to the IPv4/IPv6 edge router. Each router using tunneling has an interface representing the IPv6-over-IPv4 tunnel. Figure 10-9 shows a logical view of a router-to-router tunneled segment.

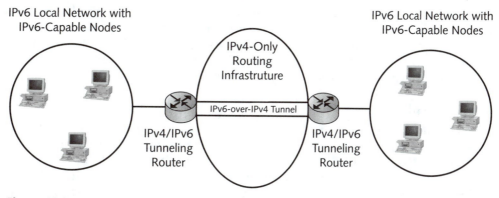

Figure 10-9 Router-to-router tunnel
© Cengage Learning 2013

In this simple example, two IPv6 "islands" are able to communicate with each other using router-to-router tunneling over an infrastructure that is otherwise uniformly IPv4.

Host-to-Router and Router-to-Host

This tunneling topology represents the first and last legs of a packet's trip from source to destination. For host-to-router, IPv4/IPv6 nodes tunnel their IPv6 packets to an intermediary IPv4/IPv6 router that can be reached over an IPv4 infrastructure. This tunnel spans the first segment of the packet's end-to-end path, eventually leading to the destination node. Router-to-host tunnels are the last segment in the path and are created by the IPv4/IPv6 router that is the last hop of the IPv6 packet.

For the first segment in this path, the sending node creates a tunnel interface that is one end point of the IPv6-over-IPv4 tunnel, then a route is added using this interface. The route added to the interface is usually the **default route**. The IPv6 packet is tunneled using the data for the matching route, the tunnel interface, and the destination address of the IPv4/IPv6 node. For the last segment, the IPv4/IPv6 router creates a tunnel and adds a route, which is usually a subnet route, between itself and the destination node over the IPv4 infrastructure. The data used to create the tunnel is the matching subnet route, the tunnel interface, and the destination address of the IPv4/IPv6 node. Figure 10-10 shows how this tunneling mechanism works.

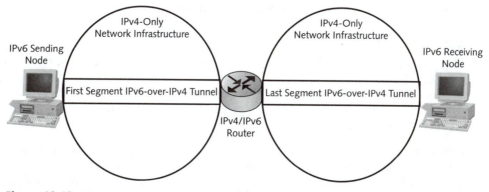

Figure 10-10 Host-to-router and router-to-host tunnels
© Cengage Learning 2013

Examples of **host-to-router and router-to-host** tunnels include IPv4/IPv6 hosts tunneling over an IPv4 network to reach the Internet, an Intra-site Automatic Tunnel Addressing Protocol (ISATAP) node tunneling over an IPv4 network to an ISATAP router to reach the Internet, and an ISATAP router tunneling over an IPv4 network to reach an ISATAP node. ISATAP will be covered in more detail later in this chapter.

Host-to-Host

For a **host-to-host** tunnel, two IPv6 nodes are linked directly using a tunnel over an IPv4 network infrastructure. The tunnel describes the entire end-to-end path rather than just one segment. With both IPv6 nodes connected over the IPv4 network, the link between them represents a single hop. Each of the two nodes creates an tunnel interface for IPv6 over IPv4. The route used usually indicates that both nodes are on the same IPv4 logical subnet. The tunnel is created using sending interface, optional route data, and the destination address. Figure 10-11 shows a host-to-host tunnel.

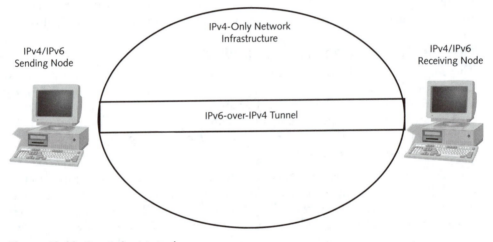

Figure 10-11 Host-to-host tunnel
© Cengage Learning 2013

Examples of host-to-host tunnels are an IPv4/IPv6 node using ISATAP addresses to tunnel across an IPv4 network to another IPv4/IPv6 node and an IPv4/IPv6 node using IPv4-compatible addresses to tunnel across an IPv4 network to another IPv4/IPv6 node.

Types of Tunnels

RFC 2893 originally specified two different tunneling types, configured and automatic, but RFC 4213, which made RFC 2893 obsolete, removed references to automatic tunneling and the use of IPv4-compatible addresses. It also removed the default configured tunnel using the IPv4 "anycast address." However, automatic tunneling technologies are specified under separate RFCs and will discussed later in this chapter.

As mentioned previously in this chapter, configured tunnels require that end point addresses be determined in the encapsulator device from configuration data stored for each tunnel. Configured tunnels can be manually set up by an administrator at the command prompt on routers and network nodes. The tunnel interface must be selected using static routes for the tunnel interface.

On a Windows 7 node, you can use the `netsh interface` command to create a configured tunnel. The command syntax is `netsh interface ipv6 add v6v4tunnel` `[interface=]<string>` `[localaddress=]<IPv4 address>` `[remoteaddress=]` `<IPv4 address>`. Here, `[interface=]<string>` is the "human friendly" name of the interface and is enclosed in double quotation marks; `[localaddress=]<IPv4 address>` is the IPv4 address of the **tunneling interface** of the sending node; and `[remoteaddress=]` `<IPv4 address>` is the IPv4 address of the tunneling interface of the receiving node. An example of this command is `netsh interface ipv6 add v6v4tunnel "Sample"` `192.168.0.1 10.9.8.7`.

Although RFC 4213 does not specify automatic tunneling, each tunneling technology is specified individually. The most recent specification for ISATAP is RFC 5214, whereas the information for the 6to4 tunneling definition can be found in RFC 3056 and Teredo tunneling information can be found in RFC 4380. Each of these tunneling solutions is supported in the IPv6 protocol for Windows Vista, Windows 7, and Windows Server 2008. By definition, automatic tunneling technologies do not require manual configuration, and the tunnel end points are determined by the use of routes, next-hop addresses based on the IPv6 destination addresses, and logical tunnel interfaces. Each of these Windows-supported IPv6-over-IPv4 tunneling technologies will be discussed in the following sections of this chapter.

ISATAP

The Intra-Site Automatic Tunnel Addressing Protocol (ISATAP) is used to connect dual-stack IPv4/IPv6 devices across IPv4 network infrastructures. From the perspective of the ISATAP protocol, an IPv4 network appears as an IPv6 link layer. ISATAP enables automatic tunneling for both global and private IPv4 addresses and offers a Non-Broadcast Multiple Access (NBMA) abstraction similar to what is specified in RFC 2491, RFC 2492, and RFC 3056. ISATAP interfaces use the same basic tunneling mechanisms originally specified in RFC 4213, Section 3.

RFC 5214 is an informational document that made obsolete the previous experimental-category version documented in RFC 4214. A new architecture called **Routing and Addressing in Networks with Global Enterprise Recursion (RANGER)** has been developed that builds on ISATAP to include IPv6 autoconfiguration; it is documented in RFC 5720, which is informational and not a standard at the time of this writing.

Overview

ISATAP automatic tunneling, which can be applied to dual-stack devices, implements router-to-host, host-to-router, and host-to-host address assignments so that any two IPv6 nodes can communicate with each other over an IPv4 network infrastructure. ISATAP is supported on Windows Vista, Windows 7, Windows Server 2003, and Windows Server 2008. Additionally, Windows XP SP 1 (and updated in SP 2) has the ability to automatically assign link-local ISATAP addresses to each IPv4 network interface as an ISATAP tunneling interface. These addresses are fixed as FE80::5EFE:w.x.y.z for private addresses or FE80::200:5EFE:w.x.y.z for public addresses.

In April 2008, ISATAP became supported in the Linux operating system kernel starting with linux-2.6.25 but is not supported in Mac OS as of this writing.

ISATAP IPv6 automatic tunneling can be used in domains that adhere to security specifications found in RFC 5214, which considers both IPv6-specific and IPv4-specific attacks. However, IP-level protection such as IPv6 encryption and authentication security should be avoided, given that they add little (since ISATAP is already encrypted) and reduce efficiency. Also, IPv4 security measures will not protect IPv6 traffic once it exits the ISATAP domain. Primary security risks include spurious ip-protocol-41 spoofing attacks, which can be defended against by restricting access to the site and maintaining a current **Potential Router List (PRL)** that contains a list of IPv4 addresses used to advertise the ISATAP interfaces of the routers used by nodes for filtering decisions.

ISATAP nodes must observe functionality requirements for IPv6 computers found in RFC 4294 as well as requirements for dual-IP-layer operations documented in RFC 4213. ISATAP interface identifiers must conform to the specifications found in RFC 4291 for interface identifiers in IPv6 unicast addresses. This means that they must be unique addresses within a subnet prefix and that an address will preferably not be assigned to more than one node over a broader scope.

For more about IPv6 unicast addressing, see Chapter 2.

ISATAP encapsulation for nodes uses addresses mapped to a link-layer address using a static computation such as the last four octets of an IPv4 address.

ISATAP Components

A high-level overview of ISATAP components describes the basic, logical infrastructure involving two ISATAP-capable IPv6 nodes communicating over an IPv4 network infrastructure. The ISATAP deployment requires two or more logical ISATAP subnets. These subnets are IPv4-only networks that are assigned a 64-bit IPv6 subnet prefix. The ISATAP configuration requires ISATAP-capable nodes and routers. ISATAP nodes use an ISATAP tunneling interface to encapsulate IPv6 traffic within IPv4 headers that are then sent to other ISATAP nodes on the same ISATAP subnet. If an ISATAP node needs to send traffic to another node on a different subnet, an ISATAP router is required. A simple network containing all the required ISATAP components is shown in Figure 10-12.

ISATAP nodes can operate in IPv4-only and IPv6-capable networks. Nodes on the IPv4-only networks communicate with each other using link-local ISATAP addresses using their ISATAP tunneling interfaces; however, this does not allow them to communicate with other IPv6 nodes on other IPv6 subnets. To communicate off the local network using ISATAP global addresses, an ISATAP node must tunnel to an ISATAP router.

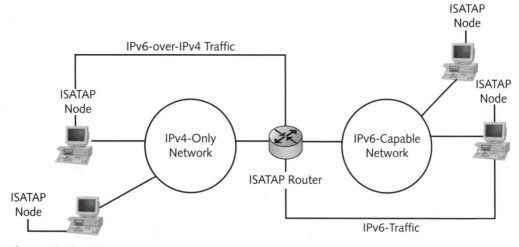

Figure 10-12 ISATAP components
© Cengage Learning 2013

ISATAP nodes locate an ISATAP router by using address prefixes advertised by the ISATAP router that identifies the logical ISATAP subnet for the nodes. Once the nodes receive these advertisements, they use the address prefixes to configure unique link-local and global ISATAP addresses. When an ISATAP router receives a packet, depending on how it is addressed, it forwards the packet either to another host on the logical ISATAP subnet or to an IPv6 host on another subnet. The router can forward these packets to IPv4 networks or to IPv6 routing domains. The ISATAP router must be the default router for all ISATAP hosts that need to route network traffic.

ISATAP nodes use the default route of ::/0 and set that address on their tunneling interface as the next-hop address for the link-local address of the router. When an ISATAP node sends a packet addressed to another node on a different subnet, the packet is tunneled to the IPv4 address on the tunneling interface of the ISATAP router that connects to the IPv4-only network. Once the router receives the IPv6 packet, it forwards it out the interface connected to the IPv4-only network. Although traffic can also be addressed to nodes on an IPv6-capable network, the existence of such a network is not required for ISATAP to perform its tunneling functions. If an IPv6-capable network exists, the ISATAP router is perceived by the IPv6 nodes on that network as an advertising router.

Router Discovery for ISATAP Nodes

ISATAP interfaces use the neighbor discovery mechanisms described in RFC 4861 to detect the presence of other nodes, determine their link-layer addresses, and maintain their own reachability data regarding paths to active neighbors. In addition, ISATAP nodes maintain a PRL that contains entries for the IPv4 addresses of available ISATAP routers as well as a timer representing the advertising ISATAP interface of the routers. Router and prefix discovery for both ISATAP hosts and routers is described in RFC 4861.

Because ISATAP sees IPv4 as incapable of multicast and broadcast transmissions, link-layer nodes are unable to perform ICMPv6 router discovery in the usual prescribed way. The link-layer address associated with any IPv6 address is contained in the lower-order bits of the IPv6 address, so neighbor discovery is not really required. Because of the lack of multicast support, automatic router discovery cannot be used. This is the reason ISATAP hosts use PRLs to maintain current information about ISATAP routers. ISATAP nodes send infrequent ICMPv6 router discovery messages out of their tunneling interfaces to determine if the routers on the PRL are currently in operation and reachable.

When an ISATAP router sends a solicited Router Advertisement, the advertisement is sent directly to the soliciting node that is attempting to update its PRL. Because this is a unicast message, other ISATAP nodes on the network will not receive the information in the advertisement. By default, ISATAP nodes attempt to update their PRLs every 3,600 seconds (i.e., once an hour).

An ISATAP node can initialize an interface's PRL with IPv4 addresses that have been manually configured on the interface by an administrator, using DNS FQDNs or via DHCPv4. Domain names can also be received either manually or using DHCPv4. FQDNs can be resolved into IPv4 addresses by using static host file lookup, by querying the DNS service, or by querying the site-specific name service.

Once the PRL for an ISATAP interface is initialized, the node sets a timer for the interface to refresh the PRL in "3600 seconds." Once the timer value expires, the PRL is reinitialized using the methods previously described.

ISATAP Addressing and Routing

Because ISATAP nodes support both IPv4 and IPv6, they can be configured with both addresses either manually or dynamically. ISATAP addresses use the locally administered interface identifier, with the format *::0:5EFE:w.x.y.z*. In this address, *w.x.y.z* is the IPv4 private unicast address of the machine. IISATAP nodes can also use an address formatted *::200:5EFE:w.x.y.z*, in which *w.x.y.z* is the IPv4 public unicast address. An ISATAP interface identifier can also be combined with a 64-bit prefix that is valid for IPv6 unicast addresses and can include link-local, unique local, and global prefixes. The interface identifier part of the ISATAP address is embedded with an IPv4 address, and this address is used to determine the destination address for the IPv4 header so that an ISATAP IPv6 packet with an IPv6 destination address can be tunneled across an IPv4 network infrastructure.

When computers running Windows 7 or Windows Server 2008 are assigned both IPv4 and IPv6 addresses, they are also automatically assigned ISATAP addresses. For instance, a Windows 7 node with an IPv4 address of 192.168.0.1 will have a link-local ISATAP address of FE80::5EFE:192.168.0.1 To test connectivity from an ISATAP node to another ISATAP node, you can use the ping utility at the command prompt. For instance, if you were on the same IPv4 local network as 192.168.0.4, you could ping the IPv4 address of the node at the command prompt by typing `ping 192.168.0.4`, or you could ping its ISATAP address by typing `FE80::5EFE:192.168.0.4`. If pinging the ISATAP address, as previously shown, does not work, you may have to add the zone ID at the end of the address. This is because the ISATAP address is a link-local address. For instance, to indicate a zone ID of 7, type `ping FE80::5EFE:192.168.0.4%7`.

Using the ISATAP addresses shown in the previous paragraph to ping another node will work even when there is no active ISATAP router available. With a router present, the

ISATAP prefix will be advertised to nodes on the local subnet and the prefix will become part of the address for each ISATAP node. Figure 10-13 shows an example of how ISATAP prefix addressing is used.

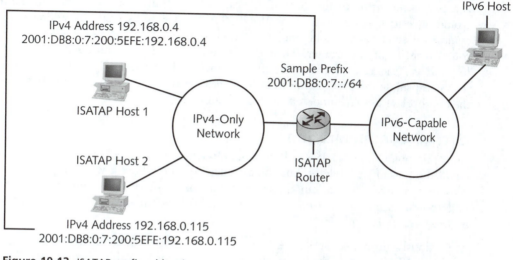

Figure 10-13 ISATAP prefix addressing
© Cengage Learning 2013

For the ISATAP configuration in Figure 10-13, the ISATAP router is advertising a global 64-bit unicast prefix of 2001:DB8:0:7::/64 on the local network, and when each host receives its update from the router, it incorporates the prefix into its ISATAP address on its tunneling interface. This addressing is important for ISATAP routing because the prefix identifies the subnet on which the ISATAP nodes are located and allows routes from other subnets to be calculated to these nodes, enabling computers, such as the one in the IPv6-capable network, to send packets to ISATAP host 1 and ISATAP host 2 via the ISATAP router.

Each device involved in communicating on or off an ISATAP network uses different routes to direct traffic from source to destination nodes. An ISATAP network node has the option of using two different route types. If an ISATAP node wants to communicate with another ISATAP node on the same logical network, it can create a node-to-node tunnel without directing traffic to the router. The on-link route uses the logical ISATAP subnet prefix acquired through Router Advertisement on the ISATAP interface for the sending end point of the tunnel. To send a packet off the logical subnet, the sending ISATAP node must use the default route on the ISATAP interface that leads to the next-hop address of the ISATAP router. This utilizes node-to-router tunneling and allows the ISATAP node to communicate with computers on other subnets across one or more IPv4 network domains.

To direct traffic, ISATAP routers can choose from two routes. The router uses the **on-link route** for the ISATAP subnet on its ISATAP interface to perform router-to-host tunneling and connect to other ISATAP nodes on the logical ISATAP subnet, using the prefix it advertised to that subnet. This routing information is the same as is used by an ISATAP node when it wants to communicate with another ISATAP node on the logical subnet. An

ISATAP router also uses a default route on its LAN or ISATAP tunneling interface with a next-hop address of a router for an IPv6-capable network. This allows the router to forward traffic from the ISATAP logical subnet addressed to computers on IPv6 networks.

Besides ISATAP nodes and ISATAP routers, devices and routers from other subnets need routes to send traffic to the ISATAP logical subnet. Routers serving IPv6-capable networks would have to maintain a route to the ISATAP router as its next-hop address. IPv6 nodes could then send packets with the destination address of an ISATAP node on their default route to their gateway router. Their IPv6 gateway could then consult its routing table and forward the packet to the IPv6 interface of the ISATAP router. The ISATAP router would then encapsulate the IPv6 packet in an IPv4 header and tunnel it across the IPv4 network to the appropriate ISATAP node on the logical subnet.

ISATAP Communications

Until this point, how an ISATAP network node communicates with other nodes has been handled on a fairly high level, but you also need to know how it works in specific examples. This section covers two common scenarios: how an ISATAP node contacts another ISATAP node on the same logical subnet and how an ISATAP node communicates with an IPv6 node on a different subnet.

As previously mentioned, an ISATAP node uses host-to-host tunneling to create a connection to another ISATAP node on the logical subnet. The subnet is logical in the sense that the nodes do not actually operate within a physical subnet, such as IPv4 nodes all communicating on a LAN and sharing a common IPv4 address and subnet mask scheme. These computers may exist on different IPv4 subnets, but because they are ISATAP capable and operate within the same site or organization, they can communicate "virtually" as if they were on a subnet. In terms of organizing host-to-host and host-to-router communication, all ISATAP nodes can be considered as existing on the same "logical" ISATAP subnet.

In this example, ISATAP node 1 wants to send a packet to ISATAP node 2. Node 1 resolves the address of node 2 using a DNS name query and performs an IPv6 route determination to discover the closest matching route to the destination address. Because both nodes are on the same logical ISATAP subnet, the route is defined by the prefix that both nodes acquired from the ISATAP router during the latest Router Advertisement. Node 1 selects the on-link route and sets the next-hop address to the destination address of node 2.

Node 1's IPv6 packet is encapsulated in an IPv4 header at the ISATAP tunneling interface for node 1. The destination address for the IPv4 header is set using the last 32 bits of the next-hop or destination address, which is the IPv4 address of node 2. Node 1 uses source address determination to select the best source address to use in the IPv4 packet, which in this case is the IPv4 address of node 1. It then transmits the packet out its ISATAP tunneling interface across the IPv4 network. Even though the virtual link between node 1 and node 2 is end-to-end and viewed as a single hop, both computers may actually exist on different IPv4 subnets. The IPv4 header is still routed across one or more IPv4 routers until it reaches the IPv4 subnet for the destination node. Once node 2 receives the encapsulated packet, it strips off the IPv4 header and processes the IPv6 packet information up the OSI stack to the Application layer.

The process of an ISATAP host communicating with an IPv6 node on an IPv6-capable subnet involves two different connections: a host-to-router tunnel from the ISATAP node to the ISATAP router and a connection between the ISATAP router and the IPv6-capable subnet. In this example, ISATAP node 1 wants to send a packet to IPv6 node A. Node 1 performs name resolution, as before, and makes a route determination, discovering that it must send the packet to the default route, leading to the ISATAP router as its next-hop address. Because the packet must cross an IPv4 network to reach the router, node 1 sends the data to its ISATAP tunneling interface for encapsulation in an IPv4 header. The header's next-hop address is set to the IPv4 address of the ISATAP router, with the destination address for node A expressed as an IPv6 address in the encapsulated IPv6 packet. Node 1 again determines the best source address and then transmits the packet.

The packet is sent from node 1 to the ISATAP router via the host-to-router IPv6-over-IPv4 tunnel. The IPv4 interface of the ISATAP router receives the packet, reads the routing instructions and destination data, and determines that the Protocol field has a value of 41. This tells the router that this is an IPv6 packet. It performs a route determination, locates the closest matching route, and sends the packet to the interface with the IPv6 network as its next-hop address, which is the default route ::/0. The interface strips off the IPv4 header and forwards the packet to the IPv6 gateway router for the IPv6 subnet where node A is located. The IPv6 router receives the packet, notes that the destination address matches IPv6 node A, which is located off its IPv6 LAN interface, and then forwards the packet out that interface to node A. Node A receives the packet and processes it up the OSI stack to the Application layer.

Keep in mind that both these end-to-end scenarios are very simple and that in a production environment the routing process would be more complex. However, all the essential steps in communicating both ISATAP node to ISATAP node and ISATAP node to IPv6 node are present.

Configuring an ISATAP Router

Computers running Windows Vista, Windows 7, or Windows Server 2008 can be configured as ISATAP routers as long as they have already been set up to forward IPv6 traffic across their LAN interfaces. The device will also have to be configured to use a default route that it will publish on the network. ISATAP routing is not enabled on these Windows operating systems by default, and ISATAP routers configured on these Windows OSs can only perform advertising or advertising and forwarding functions.

ISATAP configuration is performed at the command prompt, and many of the commands require that you are running the command prompt as an administrator. You will need to determine the ISATAP interface on the computer you want to configure as an ISATAP router using the `ipconfig /all` command. The output will show you one or more interfaces labeled Tunnel adapter isatap, as shown in Figure 10-14.

Notice that Figure 10-14 shows three separate ISATAP adapters (with the names Microsoft ISATAP Adapter, Microsoft ISATAP Adapter #2, and Microsoft ISATAP Adapter #3) in the Description fields. None of the adapters has an address configured, and only adapter #3 is associated with a DNS Suffix, which in this case is the device providing gateway services from the LAN to the Internet.

Once you have located the name or index of the desired ISATAP interface, you can enable advertising on that interface by using the command syntax `netsh interface ipv6 set interface` *ISATAPInterfaceNameOrIndex* `advertise=enabled`, in

Figure 10-14 Output of `ipconfig /all` command
Source: Microsoft

which *ISATAPInterfaceNameOrIndex* is the name or index of the interface. Figure 10-15 shows an example of this command run on a Windows 7 computer.

Figure 10-15 Set advertising on ISATAP interface
Source: Microsoft

You can disable advertising on the interface by running the same command but replacing the word "enabled" with "disabled."

Although the `ipconfig /all` command will show you the name of the ISATAP interface(s) on your computer, you will need to use the command `netsh interface ipv6 show interface` to see the ISATAP index. All the IPv6 interfaces, regardless of their connection state, are listed. The index is found in the Idx column. For instance, if the desired ISATAP interface has an index of 11, you can substitute that value for the interface name when enabling advertising, as in `netsh interface ipv6 set interface 11 advertise=enabled`. You must be running the command prompt as an administrator for this command to execute. If you are not, you will receive a notice informing you to elevate your privileges.

Once you have set the ISATAP interface to advertise, your next step is to add routes for the prefix of the logical ISATAP subnet to the same ISATAP interface. Previously in this chapter, the sample prefix 2001:DB8:0:7::/64 was used, and we can include it in the current example commands. The command syntax to add a route to an ISATAP interface is `netsh interface ipv6 add route` *IPv6AddressPrefix/PrefixLength ISATAPInterface NameOrIndex* `publish=yes`, in which *IPv6AddressPrefix/PrefixLength* is the prefix length and *ISATAPInterfaceNameOrIndex* is the name or index number of the desired interface. Keeping all the sample values we have used before, an example of the command to add a route would be `netsh interface ipv6 add route 2001:DB8:0:7::/64 11 publish=yes`. This command must also be run with administrative permission at the command prompt.

In order for ISATAP nodes to find the ISATAP router, it is desirable that the router's IPv4 address resolve to a name that includes "isatap." The Windows client computer does a DNS query so it can configure its ISATAP address. However, when the Windows computer or server was first named and configured, it may not have been set up with the idea that it would later become an ISATAP router; thus, the computer name may have nothing to do with "isatap." To set the name of the router's ISATAP interface to be recognized as an ISATAP interface, run the command `netsh interface isatap set router` *AddressOrName*, in which *AddressOrName* is either the IPv4 address or the name associated with the interface. Do not use an FQDN in place of either the interface name or the IPv4 address of the interface.

To enable advertising and forwarding on the ISATAP interface of the router, you must execute a number of commands. So far, we have enabled advertisements, published a route using a 64-bit prefix, and set the ISATAP interface IPv4 address to resolve to "isatap."

To enable forwarding on the LAN interface to an IPv6-capable network, use the command syntax `netsh interface ipv6 set interface` *LANInterfaceNameOrIndex* `forwarding=enabled`, in which *LANInterfaceNameOrIndex* is the name or index associated with the IP address of the LAN interface. To enable advertising from the router to the IPv6-capable network, execute the command syntax `netsh interface ipv6 set interface` *ISATAPInterfaceNameOrIndex* `forwarding=enabled advertise=enabled`, in which *ISATAPInterfaceNameOrIndex* is the name or index number associated with the ISATAP interface. To add a default route to the interface on the router facing the IPv6-capable network, use the command syntax `netsh interface ipv6 add route ::/0` *LANInterfaceNameOrIndex* `nexthop=`*IPv6RouterAddress* `publish=yes`, in which *LANInterfaceNameOrIndex* is the name or index number associated with the IPv6 facing interface and `nexthop=`*IPv6RouterAddress* is the IPv6 address of the next-hop router you want to receive your advertisements.

10

6to4

6to4 is another IPv4-to-IPv6 transition technology that allows IPv6 packets to be sent across IPv4 network infrastructures, including the IPv4 Internet, without explicitly configuring IPv6-over-IPv4 tunnels. The current specification for 6to4 is documented in RFC 3056, which defines a method for assigning an interim and unique IPv6 address prefix to any site that already possesses one or more globally unique IPv4 addresses and can specify an encapsulation method for sending IPv6 packets over IPv4 using the unique prefix address. The RFC 3056 specifications apply to sites rather than to individual network nodes and scale indefinitely by limiting the number of sites that are served by special relay routers.

Overview

6to4 avoids the need to configure the distinct tunnels required by ISATAP through the use of special relay servers. ISATAP relay servers allow communication of 6to4 sites to travel over IPv4 networks and to communicate with IPv6-capable networks. 6to4 technology is designed to be especially useful in the initial phases of the IPv4-to-IPv6 transition because it does not require that any IPv6 nodes be available between a sending and a receiving node.

6to4 may be applied to a specific network node or to a local network. Hosts must possess a global IPv4 address, and the host must have the ability to encapsulate IPv6 packets in IPv4 headers and to decapsulate incoming encapsulated IPv6 traffic. Any node that can forward such packets is considered a router.

6to4 addressing on an IPv6 network employs autoconfiguration, which uses the last 64 bits as the host address and the first 64 bits as the IPv6 prefix. The first 16 bits of the prefix always use the identifier 2002: (as defined in RFC 3056). The next 32 bits are the IPv4 address, and the last 16 bits are chosen randomly by the router. IPv6 hosts using 6to4 acquire the first 64 bits of the prefix by Router Advertisement, as occurs in ISATAP prefix addressing. Figure 10-16 shows a graphic example of the prefix addressing scheme, including how an IPv4 address is integrated into the prefix.

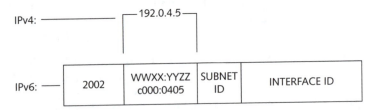

Figure 10-16 6to4 prefix addressing scheme
© Cengage Learning 2013

When a 6to4 router receives an encapsulated packet with the reserved prefix of 2002::/16, the router recognizes the packet as a 6to4 packet and routes it accordingly. 6to4 is only meant to be used to allow IPv6 nodes to communicate with other IPv6 nodes across an IPv4 network. It does not allow IPv6 nodes to communicate with IPv4-only devices.

6to4 technology has not been without its problems, such as large numbers of misconfigured nodes and poor network performance. To address these issues, IETF issued an advisory in RFC 6343 that specified deployment methods that will hopefully avoid connectivity failures and retry delays. Additionally, users and local network administrators may not be aware that the connection problems are caused by 6to4 or even that 6to4 is being used as a connectivity mechanism. This makes accurate troubleshooting impossible and inhibits IPv4-to-IPv6 transition implementation because the workaround for these connection problems is often to disable IPv6.

6to4 Components

6to4 infrastructure configurations are made up of essential components. As with the ISATAP component example previously presented in this chapter, the 6to4 component setup represents the minimal expression of a 6to4 network. In production, the relationship of the various 6to4 components can be much more involved.

A 6to4 network configuration is made up of four basic components. The first is the 6to4 node, which is a PC with one or more IPv6 addresses. The node must at least have a global IPv6 address with the 2002::/16 prefix to qualify as a 6to4 node. The outstanding quality of a 6to4 node is that it isn't required to perform any IPv6-over-IPv4 tunneling and does not need any manual configuration to create a 6to4 address using address autoconfiguration methods.

The main characteristic of a **6to4 router** is that it uses a 6to4 tunneling interface to forward 6to4 addressed packets between a 6to4 node in a site and other 6to4 devices. This includes 6to4 routers, 6to4 relays, and 6to4 node/routers. A 6to4 router is the device most likely to require manual configuration. 6to4 router commands are presented later in this section. Within any given 6to4 site, the 6to4 router is responsible for advertising the prefix address so that 6to4 nodes on the site can autoconfigure their 6to4 addresses.

A **6to4 relay** is a specialized device that acts as an IPv6/IPv4 router. It is able to forward 6to4-addressed packets to other 6to4 devices across an IPv4 network and to IPv6 devices in IPv6-capable networks.

A **6to4 node/router** (also called a 6to4 host/router) is an IPv4/IPv6 device that uses a 6to4 tunneling interface to send and receive 6to4-addressed packets. What makes it different from a standard 6to4 router is that it doesn't forward 6to4 traffic to other 6to4 nodes, only to IPv6 nodes. The typical configuration of such a device is a Windows 7 computer that has an IPv4 address on one network interface that is directly connected to the Internet. Figure 10-17 shows a simple 6to4 infrastructure containing all the 6to4 components.

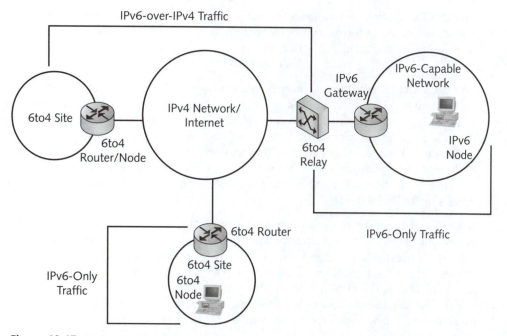

Figure 10-17 6to4 network infrastructure

6to4 Addressing and Routing

In the overview for this section, you saw the basic format of 6to4 prefix addressing, including a diagram presented in Figure 10-16. Any 6to4 site must possess at least one valid globally unique 32-bit IPv4 address in order for 6to4 addressing to occur. The address must be allocated to the site by a formal address registry, such as a service provider, and it cannot be a private IPv4 address. Although the first 16 bits of the prefix are always 2002:, 13 bits are permanently assigned by IANA as the Top Level Aggregator (TLA) identifier, with a numeric value of 0x0002 combined with IPv6 format prefix 001 that, when expressed as an IPv6 address prefix, is 2002::/16. The format of the 6to4 address prefix matches the format of a normal /48 IPv6 prefix, and it, like any other valid IPv6 prefix, can be used, to generate automated address assignment and discovery. If the IPv4 address is assigned to the site dynamically, the 6to4 prefix will be dynamic as well, changing every time the IPv4 address assignment changes.

Applying this to a 6to4 network example, a 6to4 gateway router directly attached to the Internet receives an IPv4 address assignment from a service provider, and this address represents the site address. The 6to4 gateway creates a 48-bit prefix, such as 2002: DB8:0::/48, for which DB8:0 is the hexadecimal expression of the IPv4 address the router acquired from the service provider. The 6to4 router has the option of manually or automatically configuring the Subnet ID part of the 64-bit prefix. In our example, the sub-net ID is created by the router and then a fully capable network prefix is created. Once the prefix is created, the 6to4 router advertises the prefix 2002:DB8:0:7::/64 on the LAN interface attached to the private 6to4 network. The IPv6 nodes in the 6to4 site receive the 6to4 router's advertisement containing the prefix, and each node automatically configures its IPv6 address based on the prefix.

Like ISATAP devices, 6to4 network devices use on-link and default routes. A 6to4 node will use an on-link route for the private subnet prefix used by the LAN interface of the 6to4 gate-way router to communicate within the subnet, and it will use the next-hop address of the router's LAN interface as its default route when it wants to communicate off the subnet.

The 6to4 router will use an on-link route to forward traffic to and from nodes on the private subnet. A separate on-link route is used by the router on its 6to4 tunneling interface to perform router-to-router tunneling to other 6to4 routers and 6to4 relays. When using this route type to connect to 6to4 relays, it is not for the purpose of forwarding IPv6 traffic to IPv6-capable sites or across an IPv6 network. It is for router-to-host tunneling to 6to4 node/routers. The router uses a default route on its 6to4 tunneling interface with the next-hop address of the 6to4 relay when it is forwarding IPv6 traffic to IPv6-capable networks traversing an IPv6 Internet.

A 6to4 relay uses an on-link route on its tunneling interface to perform router-to-router communication with 6to4 routers and router-to-host communication with 6to4 node/routers. It uses a default route on its LAN or tunneling interface, which has a next-hop address of the next router or the gateway router for an IPv6 network, including an IPv6 Internet. The 6to4 relay uses this route to forward IPv6 traffic to IPv6 networks and nodes. IPv6-capable routers in an IPv6 Internet route to the 6to4 prefix address 2002::/16 to communicate with a 6to4 relay and to forward traffic from IPv6 networks to 6to4 sites and nodes.

6to4 Communication

There are a number of communication models in a 6to4 infrastructure, including node-to-node/ router and node-to-node. For instance, let's say 6to4 node 1 wants to send traffic to 6to4 node/router A. The first step in this process is for node 1 to resolve node/router A's address using a DNS query. Node 1 then performs route determination and locates the closest matching route to the destination address, which, in this case, is the default route to the next-hop address of the local interface on the 6to4 router. Node 1 constructs an IPv6 packet and sends it to its IPv6 interface, using the default route to the 6to4 gateway router.

Once the 6to4 router receives the packet, it performs route determination and locates the closest matching route to the destination address. Because the destination address is an IPv6 address that must traverse an IPv4 network, the router sends the packet to its 6to4 tunneling interface for processing. The 6to4 interface configures an IPv4 destination address in the IPv4 header that will encapsulate the IPv6 packet. The IPv4 destination address uses the corresponding 32 bits in the second and third groups of the next-hop address, which is the 6to4 node/router's IPv4 public address. The 6to4 router determines that its public IPv4 address is the best source address to use, and it transmits the packet out of its tunneling interface. Once the encapsulated packet reaches 6to4 node/router A, it enters the tunneling interface configured with a public IPv4 address. The node/router reads the value of the protocol field as 41, strips the IPv4 encapsulation, and passes the IPv6 packet to the IPv6 protocol to be processed up the OSI stack.

In communication between a 6to4 node and a IPv6 host, the route between sender and receiver must go from sending node to router, from router to relay, and then from relay to receiving node. The first part of the process requires the sending node to perform name resolution and routing determination processes as usual. The 6to4 node sends its IPv6 packet across the default route to the next-hop address, which is the internal facing interface of the 6to4 gateway router for the network.

When the router receives the packet, it performs route determination and locates the closest matching route, which, in this case, is the default route to the next-hop IPv6 address of the 6to4 relay. The packet is sent to its 6to4 tunneling interface to be processed. Because the packet must cross an IPv4 network to reach the relay, it is encapsulated in an IPv4 header. The IPv4 header's IPv4 destination address is made up of the 32 bits corresponding to the second and third groups of the 6to4 destination address, which is the 6to4 relay's public IPv4 address. The router determines the best source address to use, which is its public IPv4 address, and transmits the encapsulated packet out its tunneling interface.

The packet is received by the tunneling interface on the 6to4 relay. The relay reads the value of 41 in the Protocol field, strips the IPv4 encapsulation, and sends the IPv6 packet to the IPv6 protocol for further processing. The relay performs route determination and selects its default route to the next-hop IPv6 gateway router of the IPv6-capable network where the destination node is located. This process assumes that the relay will use a native IPv6 interface to forward the IPv6 packet and that the packet will cross an IPv6 Internet to reach the IPv6 gateway router.

Once the IPv6 gateway for the IPv6-capable network receives the IPv6 packet, because no tunneling is involved, it reads the destination address for the packet, determines that the route to the destination is on its local LAN interface, and forwards the packet to the IPv6 destination node. The node receives the IPv6 packet and processes it up the OSI stack.

Using ISATAP and 6to4 Together

It is possible to use ISATAP and 6to4 technologies together for network communication that would otherwise be difficult to achieve. An ISATAP node may be able to communicate with other nodes within its logical subnet but unable to connect to computers on other networks. Normally, an ISATAP host could not receive advertisements from a 6to4 router and, without those advertisements, could never create an address that would let it use the 6to4 router as a gateway off its subnet. However, the 6to4 router could also be manually configured as an ISATAP router for the ISATAP network containing the relevant ISATAP node. An A record must be added to the site's DNS server that points to the 6to4 router's ISATAP name and resolves to an IPv4 address.

Once this is accomplished, the ISATAP node will be able to perform name-to-address resolution for the 6to4 router's ISATAP name, receive a Router Advertisement in response to a Router Solicitation message, and configure its link-local ISATAP address. The ISATAP node then configures a default route to the 6to4 router in order to send traffic off the ISATAP subnet using the 6to4 router as its gateway.

Teredo

Teredo is another IPv4-to-IPv6 transition technology that allows IPv6 connections between two IPv6 network nodes across an IPv4 network infrastructure. What makes Teredo different from ISATAP and 6to4 is that it is able to operate from behind home routers and broadband devices using network address translation (NAT). It accomplishes this by using a platform-independent tunneling protocol. This protocol can allow an IPv6 packet to cross an IPv4 network by encapsulating the IPV6 packet within an IPv4 UDP datagram. Once encapsulated, the datagram is routed across the IPv4 infrastructure like any other IPv4 packet and even can be routed across NAT devices. Once the datagram arrives at its destination, it is decapsulated and delivered to the receiving IPv6 node. Another characteristic of this transition mechanism is that it was developed by Microsoft and formally standardized by RFC 4380.

Overview

In order for Teredo traffic to be able to cross IPv4 NAT and make IPv6 connections, the Teredo service tunnels IPv6 packets over IPv4 UDP, using Teredo servers and Teredo relays. Teredo servers are stateless and are responsible for managing only small amounts of traffic between Teredo client computers. Teredo relays perform IPv6 routing between the Teredo service and IPv6-capable networks. Teredo relays also can interoperate with network nodes using other transition technologies, such as 6to4.

However, Teredo does not depend on edge routers the way 6to4 does; instead, it provides tunneling from node to node. Even if 6to4 could be enabled to tunnel across NAT at the edge device, it would still not provide full connectivity if there were multiple NAT devices between the source and destination addresses. NAT can only translate the TCP and UDP upper-layer protocols, which is why Teredo works across NAT; but NAT cannot, in most cases, be configured to translate other protocols, including protocol 41, which is used by both ISATAP and 6to4 for tunneling.

Like ISATAP and 6to4, Teredo is designed to be a transition service and is not meant to be a permanent IPv6 technology. As IPv6 achieves dominance and IPv4 continues to approach retirement, transition mechanisms for IPv6 communication across IPv4 networks should be removed.

Teredo Components

The essential components of a Teredo system are a Teredo client, **Teredo server, Teredo relay,** and **Teredo host-specific relay.** The Teredo client is an IPv4/IPv6 network node that possesses a Teredo tunneling interface that allows network traffic between Teredo clients, using host-to-host tunneling, or between a node and a Teredo relay by using host-to-router tunneling.

A Teredo server is an IPv4/IPv6 node that is connected to both an IPv4 Internet and an IPv6 Internet using different interfaces. As a stateless server, it uses the same amount of memory regardless of how many clients it must support. It provides the data and services for the initial configuration of all clients it supports and acts as a facilitator for communication between different Teredo clients and between Teredo clients and IPv6-only network nodes. This server does not forward packets for Teredo clients. A Teredo server does not have to be on the same physical subnet as the Teredo clients it serves, and can be located across an IPv4 Internet.

The Teredo relay is an IPv4/IPv6 router that uses host-to-router and router-to-router tunneling to forward packets from Teredo clients on IPv4 networks to IPv6 nodes on an IPv6-capable network and from those IPv6 nodes to Teredo clients. It does not forward packets between two Teredo clients. The relay represents the component of the Teredo system that is the furthest end of the Teredo tunnel. Because the relay consumes a great deal of bandwidth, it is limited as far as the number of simultaneous client connections it can support. Each relay supports a specific group of Teredo clients, such as a company or business group, an ISP, or some other sizable network infrastructure.

A Teredo host-specific relay is an IPv4/IPv6 node directly connected to both an IPv4 Internet and an IPv6 Internet and that communicates with Teredo client nodes over its IPv4 connection without going through a Teredo relay. The IPv4 connection can be either through a public or private IP4 address and through an intermediate NAT device. The IPv6 connection can be either through a direct connection or through another IPv6 transition mechanism, such as 6to4. The host-specific relay has a range of service for only the node on which the relay service runs.

Though not an "official" Teredo component, the Teredo system is designed to allow Teredo nodes to communicate across an IPv4 Internet—specifically, to IPv6 nodes on IPv6-capable networks—so the presence of an IPv6 device can be considered a "required component."

Teredo Addressing and Routing

Teredo addresses are made up of five components:

- *Prefix*—the 32-bit Teredo service prefix
- *Server IPv4*—the 32-bit IPv4 address of the Teredo server
- *Flags*—a set of 16 bits that documents the type of address and NAT being used
- *Port*—the obfuscated mapped UDP port used by the Teredo service running in the client
- *Client IPv4*—the obfuscated mapped IPv4 address used by the client

Figure 10-18 provides a graphic view of the address structure.

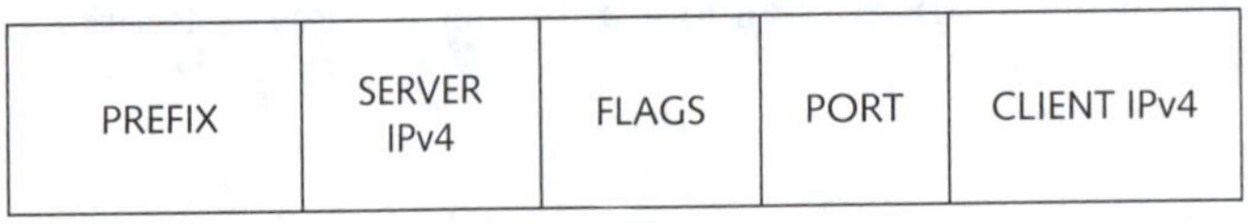

PREFIX	SERVER IPv4	FLAGS	PORT	CLIENT IPv4

Figure 10-18 Teredo address structure
© Cengage Learning 2013

The 32-bit Teredo prefix uses the address space 2001::/32, which is reserved for Teredo by IANA. Teredo uses a global IPv4 address and UDP port in its address structure, and the translation of the address/port allows Teredo-addressed traffic to pass through NAT devices.

The Teredo address Flags field contains the following bit types:

  C—the cone flag

  R—reserved for future use

  U—the universal/local flag, with a value set to 0

  G—the individual/group flag, with a value set to 0

  A—a randomly set 12-bit flag

In the Teredo address Flags field, the A flag offers some protection from address scans initiated by malicious parties on the Internet. The bits in the A flag are set to a 12-bit randomly generated value, and when a malicious user performs an address scan and is able to determine the rest of the Teredo address, the A bits require the scan to attempt up to 4,096 different addresses to find the correct one being used.

In the Teredo address Port and Client IPv4 fields, the port and address data for the Teredo client is obfuscated or hidden. This is accomplished by reversing each port and address number. Packets transmitted by a Teredo client map the source UDP port to the different UDP port by the NAT service, and that external port is used for all Teredo traffic by the Teredo node. When the Teredo node sends a packet, the obfuscated IPv4 address of the node is mapped by the NAT service to a different external IPv4 address that is used for all Teredo traffic.

For a Teredo client to acquire its Teredo address, it must discover the IPv4 address of the Teredo server that is providing services to the client. The C bits in the address's Flags field must be set to 1 if the node is located behind a NAT device, with the U and G bits set to 0 and the A bits set randomly. The address is then constructed, starting with the Teredo prefix of 2001::/32, then with the colon hexadecimal notation of the Teredo server's IPv4 address, then with the Flag bits properly set, and finally with the port and client IPv4 data added and obfuscated.

Like other IPv4/IPv6 transition mechanisms, Teredo uses online and default routes; however, Teredo client nodes use routes somewhat differently than other Teredo devices. A Teredo node uses a default route that sees all IPv6 destination addresses as on-link and using Teredo tunneling interfaces. The next-hop address for the default route is the IPv6 destination address of the desired IPv6 node and set to its Teredo interface.

All other Teredo devices use either on-link or default routes. An on-link route is set to the Teredo prefix and uses the Teredo tunneling interface, allowing communication with other Teredo devices. A default route is one that uses a LAN or tunnel interface attached to an IPv6 Internet so that traffic from these Teredo devices can reach IPv6-capable networks.

Teredo Processes

In an end-to-end Teredo communication model, the first action that occurs is that the Teredo client node connects to the Teredo server to perform a qualification procedure. This is when the client determines if it is located behind a **cone NAT, restricted NAT,** or **symmetric NAT.** If the node is located behind a symmetric NAT, it will fail to qualify with the Teredo server because symmetric NAT requires that the same IPv4 address and port of the node be mapped to the external IPv4 address and port of the NAT device. The Teredo addressing process requires that both the nodes IPv4 address and port mappings be changed on the public-facing interface of the NAT device. When located behind a symmetric NAT, more entries must be added to the NAT translation table before the node can send unicast packets.

If the Teredo client node is located behind a cone NAT, it incorporates its obfuscated port and IPv4 address in the Teredo Port and IPv4 Client fields, and the mapping to the port and IPV4 address of NAT occurs. If the Teredo node isn't located behind NAT, when the Teredo node sends an IPv6 packet, it must first engage in an exchange of **Teredo bubble packets** through the Teredo server that will allow communication along a path that does not include a NAT device.

To manage communication between two Teredo nodes if each node is on a different site and both nodes are behind restricted NAT, a particular set of actions needs to occur.

1. Teredo node A creates a bubble packet that contains no data and that is used to create and maintain NAT translation mappings between node A and Teredo node B.

2. Teredo node A then sends a bubble packet directly to Teredo node B.

3. When the restricted NAT for node A forwards the bubble packet, it creates a source-specific NAT translation table entry that will allow future packets from node A to be accepted by node B's restricted NAT and forwarded to node B.

4. The restricted NAT for node B receives the bubble packet, but because it is (most likely) not configured to receive traffic with an arbitrary UDP port number and IPv4 address, it discards the initial packet (any subsequent packets will be accepted and forwarded, as stated in the previous step).

5. Teredo node A sends a second bubble packet to node B through the Teredo server that services node B with the IPv4 destination address set to the address of the Teredo server.

6. The Teredo server for node B forwards the bubble packet to node B, which is received by node B's restricted NAT and forwarded to node B.

7. Teredo node B replies by sending a bubble packet directly to node A, which, when received by node A's restricted NAT, is accepted and forwarded, because of the source-specific NAT translation table entry created when node A sent its first bubble packet to node B.

8. Source-specific mappings are present for both restricted NATs after node A receives node B's bubble packet, and both node A and node B are able to send traffic directly to each other with no further negotiation necessary.

10

When a Teredo node wants to communicate with another Teredo node behind two different cone NATs, the NAT translation table entries for each node are set to allow communication between any source UDP port and IPv4 address. Teredo nodes on two different sites can communicate directly without having to use an intermediary Teredo device. The connection between the two devices represents a virtual end-to-end link, as if both devices were located on the same subnet.

When a Teredo node wants to communicate with an IPv6 node on an IPv6-capable site, the Teredo node relies heavily on the Teredo relay that is aware of the IPv6 site. Teredo relays advertise their availability to IPv6-capable sites, letting them know the relay can forward traffic to Teredo client nodes. Any given Teredo relay services only a particular portion of the IPv6 Internet, such as customers of an ISP. The Teredo node that wants to communicate with a specific IPv6 node must first discover which Teredo relay is servicing the IPv6 node's IPv6 network. Teredo nodes perform discovery through a rather roundabout procedure:

1. The Teredo node encapsulates an ICMPv6 echo request packet addressed to the desired IPv6 node in a UDP datagram and then sends the datagram to the Teredo server that provides services for the Teredo node.

2. The Teredo server receives the datagram, decapsulates it, and forwards it to the IPv6 destination address.

3. The Teredo relay servicing the IPv6-capable network containing the IPv6 destination node receives the ICMPv6 echo request packet and forwards it to the IPv6 destination address.

4. Through the echo response packet, the Teredo node discovers the port and IPv4 address of the Teredo relay.

5. The Teredo node sends all future IPv6 traffic to the desired IPv6 node encapsulated in UDP datagrams, and the datagrams are addressed to the UDP port and IPv4 address of the Teredo relay.

Figure 10-19 shows the Teredo components and logical network connections across IPv4 and IPv6 Internets.

To avoid spoofing, the initial ICMPv6 echo request packet contains a large random number in its payload. When the initial echo response packet is sent, it contains the same large random number, which the Teredo node verifies before proceeding with further communication. The Teredo server is only involved in the qualification procedure and in exchanging bubble packets and ICMPv6 packets; it drops out of the communication loop when actual data is being sent and received. This reduces the load on the Teredo server to enable scaling and enhances security because data never goes through the server and cannot be stored on that device.

Although the Teredo service is available on Windows 7, the Teredo interface is enabled by default, but it is inactive. Although the `ipconfig /all` command will show that there is a Teredo Tunneling Pseudo-Interface present, it will also indicate that the interface is disconnected. Unlike ISATAP, the `show interface ipv6 interface` command isn't specific to Teredo interfaces. To see the status of the Teredo interface, you can use the `netsh interface teredo show status` command to reveal the interface status, which will show as offline, by default.

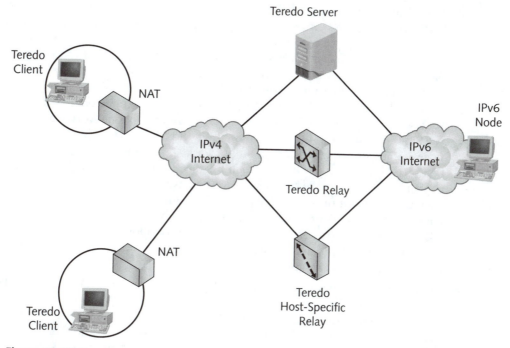

Figure 10-19 Teredo components and network communications
© Cengage Learning 2013

You can enable the Teredo interface on a Windows 7 computer by using the command `netsh interface teredo set state [type][servername][refreshinterval][clientport]`, in which *type* is the type of state, such as `disabled`, `client`, `enterpriseclient`, or `server`; in which *servername* is the name of the Teredo server, such as `teredo.ipv6.microsoft.com`; in which *refreshinterval* is the amount of time, in seconds, after which the client will refresh its settings, and in which *clientport* is the client's UDP port, which can also be set automatically by the system. Running `netsh interface teredo show state` may indicate that the computer's Teredo interface is still offline. If the error indicates "client is in a managed network," the client state will need to be set to `enterpriseclient`, not `client`. Other problems can include port setting misconfiguration, Teredo being blocked by a third-party firewall, or that the Teredo server configured for the client is misconfigured or unavailable.

Chapter Summary

- During the transition from IPv4 to IPv6, there will be a lengthy period of time when both protocols exist side by side. IPv4 and IPv6 devices and networks will need to be able to communicate with each other, and IPv6 packets will need to find a way to cross IPv4-only network domains. Obstacles to this transition include IPv4/IPv6 interoperability, the complexity of planning and implementing migration mechanisms, the availability of IPv6 addresses from service providers, and the enormous investment of time and resources required by private and public organizations worldwide.

- Several different IPv4/IPv6 hybrid networks and nodes can be used to facilitate the transition, depending on an organization's need and the transition stage it's moving into. The basic hybrid model allows IPv6 networks to communicate with each other over an IPv4 backbone network. This involves a straightforward process in which packets from an IPv6 node are encapsulated into IPv4 headers by IPv6 gateway routers and then transmitted over the IPv4 Internet to the receiving IPv6 network and node. Although the IPv4 header would be routed across potentially multiple IPv4 routers between the source and destination, from the IPv6 network's point of view, it is as if an end-to-end tunnel was constructed directly between the IPv6 source and the IPv6 destination. A nested hybrid model works on a similar principle, but here the IPv6 network more likely exists within a larger IPv4 LAN. A true hybrid network consists of a mixed set of IPv4 and IPv6 subnets, all interacting on an IPv4 LAN and communicating off of the LAN across an IPv4 Internet. Regardless of the model, addressing during the transition process must allow devices to perform IPv6-to-IPv4 address translation or offer another mechanism for allowing an IPv6 packet to use IPv4 source and destination addresses, so it can be carried across the IPv4 Internet and arrive at an IPv6 destination.

- Transition mechanisms can use a dual-IP-layer architecture or a dual-stack architecture. A dual-IP-architecture allows a device using both IPv4 and IPv6 to create packets by using a common source for upper-layer TCP and UDP protocols. For a device using a dual-stack architecture, each network layer protocol uses a separate Transport layer stack. In other words, on a computer capable of using IPv4 and IPv6, IPv4 would access its own dedicated stack for TCP and UDP, and IPv6 would access a separate and dedicated Transport layer stack. Regardless of which stack architecture is being used, IPv6-over-IPv4 tunneling is the common transmission mechanism to send IPv6 packets over an IPv4 network domain. The DNS infrastructure in a transition network must be able to manage for A and AAAA records in order to resolve domain names to both IPv4 and IPv6 addresses. This is required not only of network name servers but also of name resolvers running on individual network nodes.

- IPv6-over-IPv4 tunneling involves different device configurations, depending on the tunneling mechanism being employed. Router-to-router components typically involve routing devices that are both IPv6 and IPv4 capable. They are most commonly used in creating the end points of the tunnel across a large IPv4 domain. Host-to-router and router-to-host configurations represent the first and last legs of a network packet's journey. The IPv6 sending host creates the IPv6 packet and sends it to its gateway router. The router encapsulates the packet in an IPv4 header and sends it out its public IPv4 interface. At the opposite end of the tunnel, the receiving router accepts the packet, strips off the header, and forwards the IPv6 packet out its interior IPv6-facing interface to the receiving IPv6 node. Host-to-host configurations allow the sending IPv6 host to create a virtual end-to-end connection to the receiving host without relying on a gateway to perform encapsulation and tunneling. The three tunneling mechanisms are ISATAP, 6to4, and Teredo.

- ISATAP is an automatic tunneling mechanism that allows IPv6 ISATAP network nodes to communicate across an IPv4 network through an ISATAP router to an IPv6-capable network. ISATAP nodes use specially formatted addresses based on an ISATAP identifier combined with the IPv4 address of the device's private unicast address. Both ISATAP nodes and routers have the option of using an on-link route or a default route. For nodes, the on-link route lets them send traffic directly to other ISATAP nodes, and its default route is to the ISATAP router when traffic is addressed to an IPv6 node. ISATAP routers use their on-link routes for traffic to the ISATAP subnet and for their default route to the next-hop router on the IPv6 capable network.

- 6to4 is an IPv4-to-IPv6 transition technology characterized by its ability to allow IPv6 packets to be sent across IPv4 networks and the use of relay servers. 6to4 special relay servers facilitate communication between 6to4 sites over IPv4 networks. This does away with the requirement of configuring tunnels across the IPv4 infrastructure. 6to4 components include 6to4 nodes, 6to4 routers, 6to4 relays, and 6to4 node/routers. A 6to4 node is a PC possessing one or more IPv6 addresses. A 6to4 router uses 6to4 tunneling interfaces to relay communications between a 6to4 node and other 6to4 devices, including routers, relays, and nodes. A 6to4 relay is a specialized device that acts as an IPv4/IPv6 router and can forward 6to4 addressed packets across IPv4 networks. A 6to4 node/router is an IPv4/IPv6 device that uses 6to4 tunneling interfaces to send and receive 6to4 addressed packets. 6to4 and ISATAP can be used together for network communications when a 6to4 router is manually configured as an ISATAP router, allowing an isolated ISATAP node to locate the 6to4 router and receive Router Advertisements.

- Teredo is another IPv4-to-IPv6 transition technology. It is characterized by its unique ability to operate behind routers and broadband devices with NAT enabled. Teredo nodes can communicate across IPv4 networks by encapsulating IPv6 packets inside IPv4 UDP datagrams. Teredo components include Teredo servers, which are IPv4/IPv6 nodes that pass traffic between IPv6 sites and IPv4 networks, Teredo relays, which are IPv4/IPv6 routers that use host-to-router and router-to-host tunneling to forward packets from Teredo clients on IPv6 capable networks across IPv4 networks, and Teredo host-specific relays, which are IPv4/IPv6 nodes directly attached to both an IPv4 Internet and an IPv6 Internet and communicate with Teredo nodes without going through a relay.

10

Key Terms

6to4 node/router   Also called a 6to4 host/router, this device sends and receives 6to4-addressed traffic but does not forward traffic to other 6to4 nodes, only to IPv6 nodes.

6to4 relay   A specialized device that routes network traffic sent from 6to4 nodes to IPv6-capable networks.

6to4 router   A device that forwards 6to4 traffic to other nodes across IPv4 networks, including 6to4 and IPv6 nodes.

basic hybrid model   A virtual network infrastructure model describing IPv6 nodes existing in a IPv4 core backbone, such as the Internet, and communicating with each other using a tunneling technology.

cone NAT   A NAT solution that provides a permanent port and IP address mapping between an internal and public network.

decapsulator   The receiving node at the other end of the tunnel, which is responsible for reassembling any fragmented packets, removing the IPv4 header encapsulation, and processing the IPv6 packet.

default route Generally, the route used by a network device to communicate to other devices on a different physical or virtual subnet, leading to the next-hop device, which is typically a router.

dual-IP-layer architecture An IPv4/IPv6-capable computer in which both versions of IP access a single Transport layer stack.

dual-stack architecture An IPv4/IPv6-capable computer in which each version of IP accesses a separate Transport layer stack.

dual-stack implementation A basic IPv4-to-IPv6 transition technology that allows both versions of the IP protocol to run side by side in an operating system.

encapsulator The node at the sending end of the tunnel, which is responsible for encapsulating the IPv6 packet in an IPv4 header, then transmitting the packet in the tunnel.

host-to-host An IPv6-over-IPv4 tunneling configuration representing a virtual end-to-end link between IPV6 capable nodes across an IPv4 network.

host-to-router and router-to-host An IPv6-over-IPv4 tunneling configuration that represents the first and last hops of IPv6 traffic from the IPv6 starting node, through routing over an IPv4 network, to the IPv6 destination node.

interoperability The ability of two diverse technologies to interact with each other.

Intra-Site Automatic Tunnel Addressing Protocol (ISATAP) An IP4-to-IPv6 mechanism that allows dual-stack network nodes to send IPv6 packets across IPv6 networks using tunneling.

IP address parser A method of verifying that a string is an IP address and, if so, determining if the address is IPv4 or IPv6.

IPv6-over-IPv4 tunneling A mechanism in which a network device generates an IPv6 packet and encapsulates the packet in an IPv4 header for transmission across an IPv4 network.

nested hybrid network model A virtual network infrastructure model describing IPv6-capable networks embedded within a larger core IPv4 LAN and communicating with other IPv6 networks, within and outside the IPv4 LAN, using a tunneling technology.

network address translation (NAT) A technology that translates an IP address used in one network, such as a private LAN, to a different IP address used in a different network, such as the public Internet.

on-link route Generally, a route used by a network node to communicate with another network node on the same physical or virtual subnet.

Potential Router List (PRL) A method used by ISATAP nodes to maintain a current list of routes and routers, since ISATAP prevents the use of automatic router discovery.

restricted NAT A NAT technology that maps the internal IP address and port of a computer only to specific IP addresses and port numbers, restricting access to others.

Routing and Addressing in Networks with Global Enterprise Recursion (RANGER) An architectural networking framework providing scalable routing and addressing in networks with global enterprise recursion. RANGER is built on ISATAP technology.

router-to-router An IPv6-over-IPv4 tunneling configuration in which two IPv4/IPv6-capable routers are linked to transmit IPv6 traffic across an IPv4 network infrastructure.

stateless IP/ICMP translation algorithm (SIIT) An IPv4/IPv6 address translation model designed to replace NAT-PT and characterized by two domains, an IPv4 domain and an IPv6 domain, that communicate over an IP/ICMP translator.

symmetric NAT   A NAT solution that requires the same IP address and port number to be mapped from the internal network to the external network.

Teredo   Also known as Teredo tunneling, this IPv6-over-IPv6 transition technology allows Teredo nodes to communicate with IPv6 nodes over an IPv4 network infrastructure, even when the Teredo nodes are located on LAN behind a NAT.

Teredo bubble packets   Specialized packets sent by a Teredo node when it is not behind a NAT in order to initiate communication with an IPv6 network node.

Teredo host-specific relay   An IPv4/IPv6 node directly connected to both an IPv4 Internet and an IPv6 Internet and that communicates with Teredo client nodes over its IPv4 connection without going through a Teredo relay.

Teredo relay   An IPv4/IPv6 router that uses host-to-router and router-to-router tunneling to forward packets from Teredo clients on IPv4 networks to IPv6 nodes on an IPv6-capable network and from those IPv6 nodes to Teredo clients.

Teredo server   An IPv4/IPv6 stateless server device that connects to both IPv4 and IPv6 networks and facilitates communication between different Teredo nodes and between Teredo and IPv6 nodes.

true hybrid network model   A virtual network infrastructure model describing a varied environment of mixed IPv4, IPv6, and dual-IPv4/IPv6- capable networks embedded in a larger network infrastructure, with no one version of IP being dominant in the core.

tunneling interface   The network interface used by a device that performs encapsulation of IPv6 packets in IPv4 headers and is linked to the next-hop device over an IPv4 network infrastructure.

Review Questions

1. The dual-IP-layer approach allows a computer to run IPv4 and IPv6 side by side at the Network layer, and each IP stack must access a separate TCP/UDP stack at the Transport layer. True or False?

2. Which of the following are network elements that support a network infrastructure? (Choose all that apply.)

   a. clients

   b. network management and utilities

   c. routers

   d. VoIP networks

3. Of the following versions of Windows, which support an IPv4/IPv6 dual-stack configuration? (Choose all that apply.)

   a. Windows XP

   b. Windows Server 2003

   c. Windows Server 2008

   d. Windows Vista SP1

4. In 6to4 addressing, what does the w.x.y.z colon hexadecimal notation represent?

   a. a unicast IPv4 address

   b. a multicast IPv4 address

   c. a local-link IPv6 address

   d. a global IPv6 address

5. Which IPv6-over-IPv4 tunneling method supports address translation through NAT?

   a. 6to4

   b. ISATAP

   c. Teredo

   d. RANGER

6. Which hybrid IPv4/IPv6 network model contains a complete mix of IPv4, IPv6, and IPv4/IPv6 networks, with no specific version of IP being favored at the core?

   a. basic hybrid network model

   b. nested hybrid network model

   c. symmetric hybrid network model

   d. true hybrid network model

7. Which technology allows address translation between an IPv4 network domain and an IPv6 network domain through an XLAT translator?

   a. NAT-PT

   b. RANGER

   c. SIIT

   d. Teredo tunneling

8. Which dual-stack architecture allows IPv4 and IPv6 at the Network layer to access a single TCP/UDP stack at the Transport layer?

   a. dual-IP-layer architecture

   b. dual-network architecture

   c. dual-stack architecture

   d. dual-transport architecture

9. Of the following, which packet type or types is a computer using dual-stack architecture capable of generating?

   a. IPv4 packets only

   b. IPv6 packets only

   c. IPv4 and IPv6 packets simultaneously

   d. IPv6 or IPv4 packets

10. To support the transition from IPv4 to IPv6, DNS name servers must contain PTR records in the IN-ADDR.ARPA domain for IPv4 domains and may optionally contain PTR records in the IP6.ARPA domain for IPv6 nodes. True or False?

11. In mixed IPv4/IPv6 environments, the DNS resolver libraries on network nodes must have the ability to manage both A and AAAA records regardless of whether the DNS packets are carried by IPv4 or IPv6 packets. True or False?

12. Of the following tunnel configurations, which one is most likely to use configured tunneling because it requires specifically configured end points to the tunnel?

    a. host-to-host

    b. host-to-router

    c. router-to-host

    d. router-to-router

13. Of the following tunnel configurations, which one represents the very last segment of the end-to-end tunneling path?

    a. host-to-host

    b. relay-to-router

    c. router-to-host

    d. router-to-relay

14. Which architecture has been developed on top of ISATAP?

    a. 6to4

    b. RANGER

    c. SIIT

    d. Teredo

15. Which transition method supports the use of Potential Router Lists (PRLs) because it does not consider IPv4 routers capable of broadcasts?

    a. 6to4

    b. ISATAP

    c. Teredo

    d. RANGER

16. From which device does an ISATAP node receive the required address prefix?

    a. an ISATAP node/router

    b. an ISATAP relay

    c. an ISATAP router

    d. an ISATAP server

10

17. On Windows 7, the Teredo service is enabled and active by default. True or False?

18. Which command must you use at the command prompt to determine the names of the network interfaces (including the ISATAP interfaces) on a Windows 7 computer?

    a. `netsh interface show interface ipv6`

    b. `netsh interface isatap show interface`

    c. `netsh interface show interface isatap`

    d. `ipconfig /all`

19. For a 6to4 address prefix, how are the first 16 bits always expressed?

    a. FE80::/16

    b. 2001::/16

    c. 2002::/16

    d. ::/16

20. For the 6to4 transition technology, which device is capable of forwarding 6to4 packets to both 6to4 nodes and IPv6 nodes across an IPv4 network infrastructure?

    a. 6to4 node

    b. 6to4 node/router

    c. 6to4 relay

    d. 6to4 router

21. What must any 6to4 site possess in order for 6to4 addressing to occur?

    a. at least one valid globally unique 32-bit IPv4 address

    b. at least one valid globally unique 64-bit IPv4 address

    c. at least one valid globally unique 32-bit IPv6 address

    d. at least one valid globally unique 64-bit IPv6 address

22. What is the first step a 6to4 network node must take when it wants to send a packet to a 6to4 node/router?

    a. The node must construct an IPv6 packet and send it to the interface using the default route.

    b. The node must determine the closest matching source address.

    c. The node must perform route determination.

    d. The node must resolve the 6to4 node/router's address.

23. When will a Teredo node fail Teredo server qualification?

    a. when it is behind cone NAT

    b. when it is behind restricted NAT

    c. when it is behind symmetric NAT

    d. when it is not behind NAT

24. When must a Teredo node send a bubble packet?

    a. when it is behind cone NAT

    b. when it is behind restricted NAT

    c. when it is behind symmetric NAT

    d. when it is not behind NAT

25. What are the first steps in a Teredo node performing discovery?

    a. The Teredo node encapsulates an ICMPv6 echo request packet addressed to the desired IPv6 node in a UDP datagram and then sends the datagram to the Teredo server.

    b. The Teredo node encapsulates an ICMPv6 echo request packet addressed to the desired IPv6 node in a UDP datagram and then sends the datagram to the Teredo router.

    c. The Teredo node encapsulates an ICMPv6 echo request packet addressed to the desired IPv6 node in a UDP datagram and then sends the datagram to the Teredo relay.

    d. The Teredo node encapsulates an ICMPv6 echo request packet addressed to the desired IPv6 node in a UDP datagram and then sends the datagram to the destination IPv6 node.

Hands-On Projects

Hands-On Project 10-1: Examining Traffic on an ISATAP Network

Time Required: 15 minutes

Objective: In this project, you will examine network traffic between a host and an ISATAP router using ISATAP interfaces.

Description: Windows 7 and Windows Server 2008 R2 support ISATAP router functions. The following Hands-On Project shows you Router Solicitation and Router Response transactions between a host and an ISATAP using ISATAP interfaces. You will also examine a DNS query and response for the domain isatap.ipv6sandbox.com. For this project, you need the Wireshark capture file **isatap.pcap**, which contains the related network packet traffic. You also need to refer to the network lab configuration shown in Figure 10-20. This exercise assumes that Wireshark is installed on your computer.

1. Start Wireshark. (Click **Start**, point to **All Programs**, and then click **Wireshark**.)

2. In Wireshark, click **File**, click **Open**, navigate to the **isatap.pcap** capture file your instructor provided or that you downloaded from this book's companion Web site, and double-click the file.

3. Expand the Wireshark window and each of the columns in the main pane, so you can see all the listed data clearly, including the Protocol, Length, and Info columns.

4. Scroll down the list of packets (top pane) and select packet **#75**, which is labeled "Router Solicitation" in the Info column.

ISATAP Routing Lab

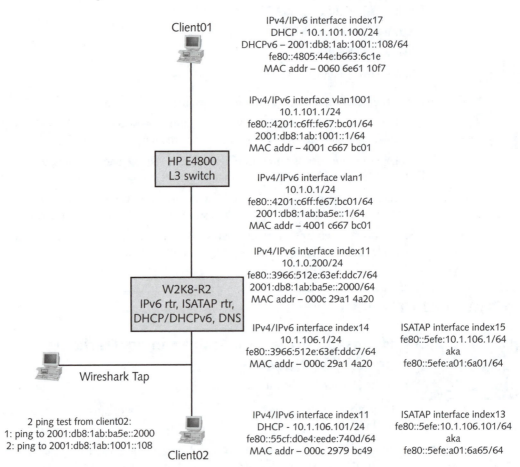

Figure 10-20 ISATAP network lab diagram
© Cengage Learning 2013

5. In the middle pane of the Wireshark window, expand **Internet Protocol Version 4** and then expand **Internet Protocol Version 6** and **Internet Control Message Protocol v6**.

6. Under Internet Protocol Version 6, locate the **Source** fields for both the IPv6 and IPv4 ISATAP addresses of the host sending the solicitation and then locate those IP addresses in the diagram in Figure 10-20.

7. Locate the **Destination** fields for both the IPv6 and IPv4 ISATAP addresses and locate those addresses in the diagram in Figure 10-20.

8. Make a note as to which network device is the sending source and which device is the destination by both host name and interface index name and number.

9. Under Internet Control Message Protocol v6, locate the **Type** field and verify that this is a router solicitation.

10. In the packet list (top pane), select packet **#76**, which is labeled "Router Advertisement" in the Info column.

11. Under Internet Protocol Version 6, locate the **Source** fields for the IPv6 and ISATAP IPv4 addresses of the source node and then locate those addresses in the diagram in Figure 10-20.

12. Under Internet Protocol Version 6, locate the **Destination** fields for the IPv6 and ISATAP IPv4 addresses of the source node and then locate those addresses in the diagram in Figure 10-20.

13. Make a note as to which network device is the sending source and which device is the destination by both host name and interface index name and number.

14. If necessary, expand **Internet Control Message Protocol v6** and, in the Type field, verify that this is a Router Advertisement.

15. Expand **ICMPv6 Option (Prefix information)** and then locate the **Prefix** field and make a note of the prefix.

16. Collapse all the fields you opened.

17. In the packet list, scroll down and select packet **#80**, which is labeled "Standard query A isatap.ipv6sandbox.com" in the Info column and listed as "DNS" in the Protocol column.

18. Expand **Domain Name System (query)**, expand **Queries**, and then expand **isatap.ipv6sandbox.com** to examine the A record DNS query.

19. In the packet list, select packet **#81**, which is labeled "Standard query response A 10.1.106.1" in the Info column and listed as "DNS" in the Protocol column.

20. Under Domain Name System (response), expand **Queries** and then expand **isatap.ipv6sandbox.com**, if necessary, to examine the information contained there.

21. Expand **Answers** and then expand **isatap.ipv6sandbox.com** to examine the information contained there, as shown in Figure 10-21.

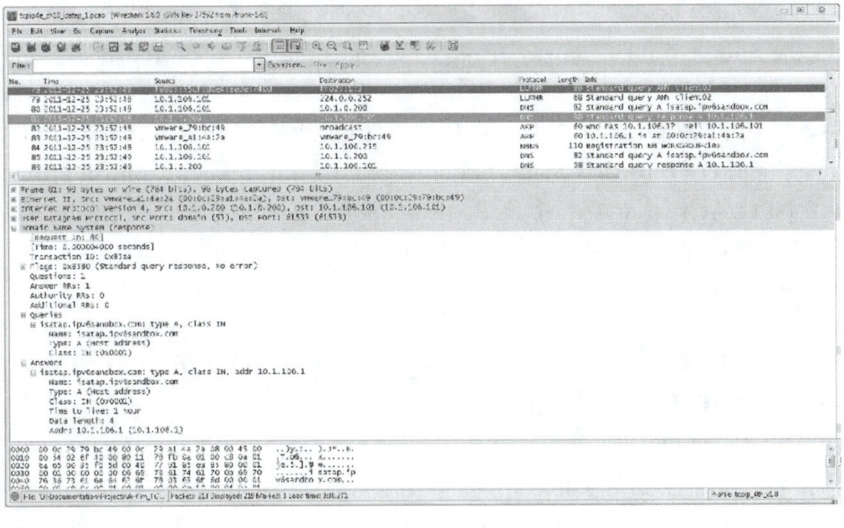

Figure 10-21 DNS query answer for isatap.ipv6sandbox.com
Source: Wireshark

22. Make notes about all the information you have gathered.

23. When you are finished, close Wireshark.

Hands-On Project 10-2: Examining a 6to4 Capture File

Time Required: 10 minutes

Objective: In this project, you will examine a 6to4 capture file illustrating the negotiation of communication between a source and destination node.

Description: This project provides a sample 6to4 packet capture for you to examine in order to view and understand the mechanics of node-to-node communication negotiations for the 6to4 transition technology. The location of the 6to4 sample packet will either be provided by your instructor or found at the Web address shown in the steps of this project.

1. Start Wireshark. (Click **Start**, point to **All Programs**, and then click **Wireshark**.)

2. In Wireshark, click **File**, click **Open**, and navigate to the location of the **6to4.pcap** file provided by your instructor. (Alternatively, go to *http://wiki.wireshark.org/SampleCaptures#IPv6_.28and_ tunneling_mechanism.29* and select **6to4.pcap**, then download the file to the desired directory on your computer.) Double-click the file to open it in Wireshark.

3. If necessary, expand the Wireshark window so that you can see all the columns in the upper pane of Wireshark.

4. Select packet number 5.

5. In the middle pane, expand **Internet Protocol Version 4** to see information about the IPv4 header encapsulating the IPv6 packet.

6. Locate the **Source** and **Destination** fields, and note the IPv4 addresses assigned to each field.

7. Collapse **Internet Protocol Version 4**, and expand **Internet Protocol Version 6** to see information about the IPv6 packet that has been encapsulated.

8. Locate the **Source** field and note the IPv6 address assigned to the 6to4 source node.

9. Locate the **Source 6to4 Gateway IPv4** field, and note the IPv4 address assigned to the 6to4 gateway router servicing the 6to4 source node.

10. Locate the **Destination** field, and note the IPv6 address assigned to the destination node.

11. Collapse **Internet Protocol Version 6**, and expand **Transmission Control Protocol**.

12. Expand **[SEQ/ACK analysis]** to see that the node is acknowledging receipt of the packet sent by the other node in the previous frame.

13. Close Wireshark.

Hands-On Project 10-3: Examining a Teredo Capture File and Router Solicitation Packet

Time Required: 10 minutes

Objective: In this project, you will examine a Teredo capture file and explore the details of a Router Solicitation sent by a Teredo network node.

Description: This project provides a sample Teredo packet capture for you to use in order to examine and understand Teredo. The location of the Teredo sample packet will either be provided by your instructor or found at the Web address shown in the steps of this project.

1. Click **Start**, type **Wireshark** in the Search box, and then press **Enter**.

2. In Wireshark, click **File**, click **Open**, and navigate to the location of the **Teredo.pcap** file provided by your instructor. (Alternatively, go to *http://wiki.wireshark.org/Sample Captures#IPv6_.28and_tunneling_mechanism.29* and select **Teredo.pcap**, then download the file to the desired directory on your computer.) Double-click the file to open it in Wireshark.

3. If necessary, expand the Wireshark window so that you can see all the columns in the upper pane of Wireshark.

4. Select packet number **6**, which is identified as "Router Solicitation" in the Info column of the upper pane.

5. In the middle pane, expand **Internet Protocol Version 4**.

6. Locate the **Protocol** field, and verify that UDP is the protocol being used.

7. Locate the **Source** and **Destination** fields, and note the IPv4 addresses being used.

8. Collapse **Internet Protocol Version 4**, and expand **User Datagram Protocol**.

9. Locate the **Source port** field, and note the port number being used by the UDP packet.

10. Locate the **Destination port** field, and note that a Teredo-identified port is being used.

11. Collapse **User Datagram Protocol**, and expand **Teredo IPv6 over UDP tunneling**.

12. Expand **Teredo Authentication header**, and note the information there.

13. Collapse **Teredo IPv6 over UDP tunneling**, and expand **Internet Protocol Version 6**.

14. Locate the **Next header** field, and note that it is ICMPv6.

15. Locate the **Source** field and note that it is an IPv6 local-link address.

16. Locate the **Destination** field and note the address type.

17. Collapse **Internet Protocol Version 6**, and expand **Internet Control Message Protocol v6**.

18. Expand **ICMPv6 Option (Source link-layer address)**, and note the information fields available.

19. Close Wireshark.

Case Projects

CASE PROJECTS

Case Project 10-1: Preparing a Network for IPv4-to-IPv6 Transition Technology Deployment

Your company is preparing to migrate from IPv4 to IPv6, and you are responsible for determining the steps that take the company up to deploying a transition technology. Your company uses Windows Vista and Windows 7 with the latest service packs for client computers as well as Windows Server 2003 and Windows

Server 2008 for your server infrastructure. You have determined that there are three critical steps that must occur before deploying a transition technology:

1. Adopt applications that are independent of IP version.

2. Upgrade name resolution services.

3. Upgrade client computers.

Briefly define the activities involved in each of these steps.

Case Project 10-2: Configuring Windows 7 Clients to Use Teredo

You run a computer network support business servicing home/office and small business clients, and one of your SMB clients wants to experiment with IPv4-to-IPv6 migration on the Windows 7 computers in her office. She has done some research and has heard that Windows 7 already supports IPv4/IPv6 dual stack as well as Teredo and ISATAP interfaces. Your client has also learned that Teredo client computers can even communicate through the NAT service running on her company's gateway. She wants to implement Teredo as a transition technology and asks you what some of the problems are in getting her Windows 7 computers to use Teredo to send IPv6 packets through her company's gateway router.

Case Project 10-3: Diagramming an ISATAP Encapsulated Header

As an IPv4-to-IPv6 transition technology, ISATAP allows an ISATAP network node to send an IPv6 packet over an IPv4 network by encapsulating the packet in an IPv4 header without the need for a preestablished tunnel across the IPv4 domain. Once the sending node determines the end point of the ISATAP tunnel, the IPv6 packet is sent to the node's ISATAP tunneling interface for encapsulation in the IPv4 header, setting the value in the Protocol field to 41, which indicates the IPv4 header contains an IPv6 packet. When the device at the end point of the tunnel receives the packet, it reads the value of the Protocol field and knows to decapsulate the IPv6 packet from the IPv4 header prior to accessing the Transport layer protocol (TCP or UDP) and sending the application data up the OSI stack. Given this information, create a diagram of the ISATAP packet as it is sent across the tunnel from the source to destination nodes. Include individual cells in the diagram for the application data, the transport header, the IPv6 header, and the IPv4 header. Within the IPv6 and IPv4 headers, include information regarding the Next Header field, Source and Destination address fields, and the Protocol field. The illustration can be a high-level diagram, but it must show each of the fields at its correct location within each header.

chapter 11

Deploying IPv6

After reading this chapter and completing the exercises, you will be able to:

- Explain IPv6 deployment requirements and considerations
- Plan an IPv6 deployment, including success criteria, architectural decisions, migration techniques, and the many tasks that must be completed
- Deploy IPv6 by establishing an IPv6 test/pilot network, migrate applications, upgrade IPv4-only hosts to IPv4/IPv6, and create a tunneled IPv6 environment using 6to4, Teredo, or ISATAP

In this chapter, we explore IPv6 deployments. More specifically, we discuss both the planning process and the deployment itself. As you read the chapter, you need to consider two important dimensions of the discussion: service provider versus enterprise and green-field versus legacy migration.

Internet and network **service providers** have a host of things to consider before they deploy IPv6 in their networks: addressing plans, the use of the address space they have been granted, multi-tenancy, and the need to support a much wider field of technologies across all their customers. With that in mind, we approach this chapter from an **enterprise** viewpoint, which means we'll discuss the challenges you are likely to face as you roll out IPv6 in a medium-sized company. Therefore, nuances having to do with the Internet and Multiprotocol Label Switching (MPLS) backbones are outside the scope of this chapter. Instead, we focus on what a typical enterprise needs to know about connecting to these networks.

The vast majority of IT projects involve upgrading or adding to an existing infrastructure. This is most often true for IPv6 deployment projects as well because almost all enterprises already have an IPv4 network in place. However, starting from a clean slate or "green field" is always simpler and, therefore, easier to understand. For this reason, our discussion assumes there is no legacy network. We also discuss several of the technologies used to migrate from IPv4 to IPv6, given that this is more likely what you'll be doing. We note, in each instance, whether we are assuming a **green-field migration** or a **legacy migration**, so as to avoid confusion.

Understanding IPv6 Deployment

The key point with IPv6 deployments is that they use a new "network layer" or "routed" protocol. To humans, the IPv6 protocol may appear to be just an upgrade or new version of TCP/IP v4; to the applications themselves, it is quite different.

Part of the reason for this is the way software accesses the network. When applications are written, they usually call functions in standard libraries that implement network tasks, such as starting a new TCP session with a peer or transmitting data. These canned libraries allow developers to enable their software to communicate over the network without having to understand much about how TCP/IP works. However, in most cases, the functions and libraries that developers use are specific to IPv4, which means that the developers have to update their applications to call an IPv6 function before their applications are "IPv6 native." The task of updating applications can take a long time and cost a lot of money, depending on the application. However, all applications would have to be converted to IPv6 before IPv4 could be retired.

As you explore IPv6 planning and deployment in this chapter, keep in mind that the Network layer protocol functionality on hosts is mostly deployed as software in the form of drivers and occasionally deployed as firmware or application-specific integrated circuits (ASICs) in the network interface controllers (NICs). New versions of all that software had to be written to support IPv6. They're not just upgrades to the old code. This became evident when you learned about the dual-stack technique for IPv4-to-IPv6 migrations (in Chapter 10), in which each node runs both protocols at the same time. That is not the same thing as binding one IP **driver** that supports both version 4 and version 6.

The difference in these software architectures is worth considering because of several important implications. A particularly notable implication is that the IPv4 software you are about to replace has an unprecedented maturity. Most IPv4 drivers are old, which means that most of the bugs have been worked out. In fact, IPv4 is so mature that the art of protocol analysis has languished of late, because it is almost unheard of to encounter network problems in which the root cause is either the protocol itself or the implementation of the protocol in a driver.

In contrast, although IPv6 has been around for many years, organizations have been slow to adopt it. Therefore, the network team can expect to do more troubleshooting in the future, and the troubleshooting is likely to be more difficult and involve more components, such as drivers and software. Remedial actions, such as upgrading the protocol drivers to newer versions, will need to be taken. Also, as more bugs are discovered in the early part of the life cycle, you can expect more frequent patch cycles.

IPv4 is also very mature from a security vulnerability standpoint, whereas IPv6 is relatively new. Expect security updates to come at a much faster pace as IPv6 becomes more widely adopted.

Another thing to consider when deploying IPv6 is the nature of networks and how that affects deployment planning. In the world of IT infrastructure, you have servers, storage, and networking domains. You can upgrade one server without upgrading another. You can change the type of storage for a server or application to another type without affecting the rest of the storage in your environment. This is not as true for networking. The nature of networking makes upgrades more complicated because networking touches all devices, which means you have to touch all the systems that use the network to perform an upgrade.

One last thing to consider is that, for most practical purposes, users in IPv4 assume they have a single IPv4 address per interface. This is slightly complicated by things like network address translation (NAT), in which you can have "inside" and "outside" addresses and the loopback address is always 127.0.0.1. However, most users don't realize this. In IPv6, each interface has several addresses. This was covered in Chapter 7; in this chapter, we briefly discuss the implications of having multiple addresses available.

Planning an IPv6 Deployment

IT projects start with a definition of the project in terms of what you hope to accomplish and what result would be considered successful, often in a **success criteria** format. (Success criteria are a list of conditions used to define whether an activity has completed successfully or not.) Next, you must create a list of tasks required to accomplish the goal, along with who will perform each task and the duration and effort of the task. Also, you must hold discussions about project funding and leadership, stakeholders, communication, timelines, and so on.

Although project management is outside the scope of this book, we begin this section with a discussion about goals. Then, we mention several **architectural decisions** (concerning protocols, hardware, tools, and so on) you'll have to make and list many of the things you'll need to think about. This list is not exhaustive, because each organizations' environment has different technical and political challenges, but it should get you started.

Success Criteria

Why are you deploying IPv6? The answer to this question usually has a significant impact on how and what you deploy. The reason for deploying IPv6 may determine your due dates and project funding, too. However, the answer is often either "because we're out of IPv4 addresses" or "because we need new features."

If a lack of addresses is what's driving the deployment, your goal is to simply make the transition as transparent as possible to your users. To be successful, you just need to give your users the same features they have today, with minimal disruption. You may add new features, assuming that doesn't change your budget or deadline. This also allows you the luxury of having a phased approach. For example, you can first roll out IPv6 in a particular region to cope with address scarcity and then do the remaining regions when it's convenient.

If the reason you're rolling out IPv6 is because your enterprise requires new features, such as mobility, that changes the definition of success for you. It also implies you will need to modify your test procedures to include the new functionality. More importantly, you can't simply use a transparent translation in the network between IPv4 and IPv6 and declare success, because you will have to expose the new IPv6 features to the users and applications directly to benefit your users.

Architectural Decisions

There are usually many ways to accomplish a task, and some are better than others. Whichever options you choose, you need to document, communicate, and deploy them consistently. As you progress through the architecture, you may find that making one decision will force you to change a previous decision, so tracking is important as you iterate through the list.

You will have to make architectural decisions regarding these items, which are discussed in the following sections:

- Interior routing protocol
- Exterior Gateway Protocol (EGP)
- External connections
- Router hardware and software selection
- Addressing schemes
- Stateful versus stateless autoconfiguration
- Quality of service (QoS)
- Security
- Tools
- Other network hardware (firewalls, load balancers, and so on)

Interior Routing Protocol You will need to convey reachability information about all those IPv6 addresses between routers in your network. There are many standard and **proprietary** (non-standards-based, geared toward a particular company or product line) options for routing IPv6, such as Open Shortest Path First version 3 (OSPFv3) or Enhanced Interior Gateway Routing Protocol (EIGRP) for IPv6, as discussed in Chapter 4. The options available to you will depend on what hardware and software vendors you choose and what models and licenses you buy. Generally, it's a good idea to decide which protocol is most appropriate and then pick a vendor that implements it well. Alternatively, you might have a set of hardware you must work with. If so, pick the best protocol supported by that hardware.

"Architecture" is the step in this process in which you determine which of the feasible options are best in context. For example, although it is technically possible to deploy IPv6 with static routes or Routing Information Protocol next generation (RIPng), these are usually feasible on only the smallest networks.

Consider the following while determining which routing protocol to use:

- *Size of the environment*—The number of sites, users, servers, and so on is a good overall indicator of complexity. Will you be able to make future updates to the environment in a weekend? Will the routing protocol allow you to segment the environment so that you can make changes in small phases? Will the protocol be manageable at the scale you anticipate?

- *Distance between sites*—In terms of latency and hops, some routing protocols handle higher values more gracefully than others.

- *Anticipated size of routing table*—Some protocols take more central processing unit (CPU) and memory to run than others, so consider how these might constrain your environment or affect your hardware costs.

- *Anticipated rate of change in routing table*—This was an issue only in the largest IPv4 environments, but with mobility, you need to consider an efficient routing protocol. Also consider what will happen if you use the "renumbering" feature.

- *Convergence times*—Is the routing protocol that's being considered capable of reconverging fast enough to meet your service level agreements (SLAs)? Will it converge fast enough to avoid dropping sessions?

- *Tweakability*—Will you need to customize or fine-tune the protocol? If so, will this protocol support what you need?

- *Skillset of the engineers and support technicians*—Before you make things too complex, ask yourself if you'd want to help a global resource troubleshoot this protocol when your pager rings at 4 a.m. or if you'll wish you'd done something simpler.

- *Potential for merger and acquisition activity*—A **merger and acquisition (M&A)** occurs when an organization buys another organization and combines assets, such as its IT environments. If there's any chance your organization will merge its infrastructure with another organization's, plan for it now. Before you finalize the architecture, consider how you would implement a merger using the routing protocol you chose. Assume the other network looks nothing like yours. Also assume it is a mix of IPv4 and IPv6 and is using a different transition plan.

- *Legacy compatibility*—If you're migrating from an existing IPv4 network, will the legacy IPv4 routing protocol impose constraints or facilitate the transition?

- *Future developments*—Will this routing protocol be around in 5 to 10 years? Will the vendor still support it? Is development on this protocol a priority for this vendor? Will the standards body add new features?

- *Support from multiple vendors*—If you're going to lock yourself into a single vendor by using a proprietary protocol, you'd better negotiate a great deal from the start because it may be a long time before you get to change vendors. Choosing a standards-based protocol supported by many vendors will offer more options in the long run.

Exterior Gateway Protocol (EGP) The most commonly used EGP is Border Gateway Protocol (BGP). What you need to consider is whether to implement it inside your network between sites. BGP has reserved a range of Autonomous System Numbers (ASNs) for private use that work much like so-called "private IP addresses" described in RFC 1918. These private and semi-private ASNs are only unique inside your network. Assigning each site a private ASN and using BGP on your wide area network (WAN) is a common practice that limits your Interior Gateway Protocol (IGP) to the LAN at each individual site, which usually has two advantages:

- It allows you to limit the **failure domain** by controlling the redistribution and injection of routes between IGP and EGP. That is, if something "breaks," everything in the failure domain experiences the outage. If your IGP spans your entire organization worldwide and an outage occurs, it may disrupt all sites until you fix it. If you break the IGP up so that an IGP exists in each site and the IGPs are separated by another protocol, perhaps only the users in the site where the failure occurred are disrupted.

- It tends to optimize your convergence times because IGPs are very fast but don't scale well; BGP scales much better but converges slower. If you set up your addressing correctly, changes or failures in a site won't cause BGP to change any routes, whereas a single, global IGP may communicate that change to every router in your enterprise.

Also consider using BGP at the borders of your network, including the Internet. The alternative is static default routing, which is preferable if your connection is single-homed. (In the generic sense, a **single-homed** connection has uplinks to a single switch, service provider, or other system. A multihomed connection has uplinks to two or more switches, service providers, or other systems.)

These EGP considerations aren't unique to IPv6, but the potential routing requirements of IPv6 may exceed a threshold and cause you to make a different decision than you made for IPv4 in the past.

External Connections External connections are substantially similar to IPv4 from a connectivity and security perspective, which means you still don't trust users and devices outside your network as much as you trust users inside and you still don't want to share administrative domains. Therefore, the familiar concepts of the Internet, intranets, extranets, and demilitarized zones (DMZs) still apply.

What has changed is you don't need to use NAT. A related change is the potential size of the **global Internet routing table**, also referred to as the BGP table, the Internet routing table, or the global BGP table. The global routing table holds all Internet address prefixes for the **default-free zone**, which is the set of all Internet networks that are operated without a default route. The global Internet routing table comprises the public Internet. Today, a high percentage of the Internet population uses private addresses behind NAT, so many large groups of users are reflected by only a single address in the global Internet routing table as part of an ISP's network. Assuming the efficiencies achieved by summarization remain constant, the global routing table should have about the same number of entries after the world converts to IPv6, but each entry will aggregate more addresses, which is fine. (This assumes no growth, which we know won't be the case, because new businesses and organizations will inevitably start up.)

The challenge comes when organizations want to multihome their networks. Multihoming, in this context, means connecting to two or more separate ISPs. The motivation is redundancy. When you multihome, you may need to apply for your own address space directly from the regional authority instead of receiving a portion of your ISP's address space. This is because multihoming involves at least two ISPs, and ISPs don't like advertising subnets that belong to other ISPs. The address space you receive will likely be a /48. A potential negative consequence is if everyone decides to multihome and receives a "small" /48 allocation (support for 65,000 /64 subnets per /48), the global address space will become highly fractured and result in a very large number of entries in the global Internet routing table.

 Recall that summarization allows you to reduce the size of the routing table by having one large prefix entry point the way to many smaller ones that share the same next hop. An analogy might be to say that from Colorado, to get to California, you go west. To get to Florida, you go east. Once you get to California, you will need to know more specific information, such as: To get to Los Angeles, take Highway 40 to Highway 15. Once in Los Angeles, you would need yet more details, such as which street and, finally, which driveway. The point is that, from Colorado, you don't want to have to sort through a list of every driveway in America; you just want a short list of the major geographical regions, and network backbone routers don't want to have separate entries for all 2^{128} IPv6 addresses or even all 2^{64} subnets. That would take an enormous amount of memory and processing power. Ideally, they would just have a short list of the ranges given to each ISP. Multihoming would be like adding two additional routes for the Greater Los Angeles Metro Area that says you can get there via Nevada but that if Nevada is unavailable, go through Arizona.

Another consideration is how you will handle mobility. In this context, mobility is the ability to move geographically, untethered by power or network cables. In IPv6, mobility is the ability to move from one network to another while retaining an IP address and ongoing sessions.

Again, the nuances of the Internet backbone are mostly the service provider's problem and beyond the scope of this book. However, it is helpful for you to understand how your decisions ultimately affect the Internet backbone, because if we all make responsible "good Internet citizen" choices and don't squander CPU and memory resources or make the backbone overly difficult to manage, the performance and cost will be better for everyone.

Router Hardware and Software Selection Selecting a router vendor for an IPv6 network is a substantially similar process to selecting a router vendor for an IPv4 network, and almost all router vendors claim to support IPv6. However, you want to pay particular attention to what that really means, because many of them have not yet implemented more than basic, mandatory functions. For protocols such as Ethernet or TCP/IP, mandatory functions are parts of the protocol that must be implemented by a vendor for its product to be considered compatible. There are typically also many optional functions that may or may not be implemented, depending on the nature of the product. This means there's a good chance that a given vendor won't support the transition mechanism you are planning to use—for example, many don't support Teredo.

You'll also want to thoroughly test your plans in a lab with the exact version of software you plan to use, because you may run into bugs or interoperability issues.

Addressing Schemes Unlike IPv4 addressing schemes, you don't have to perform IP subnetting in IPv6 because each subnet can support an extremely large number of hosts. Interestingly, this is likely to resurrect the old debate about large flat subnets with thousands of hosts. The argument against that was the number of broadcasts each host would have to process, effectively creating a "storm" and using up the host CPU and bandwidth. IPv6 doesn't have broadcasts, so you should consider virtual LAN (VLAN) topology, which is likely tied to current IPv4 subnets. For some of you, the answer may lie in a multistep approach in which each VLAN gets an IPv6 subnet now and then you combine them and use IPv6 renumbering later for a more efficient use of space.

Instead of worrying about sizing your subnets, most of the thought put into addressing schemes will be directed toward creating a hierarchy in the network portion of the address that is useful in identifying ownership, location, etc. Otherwise, you want to take into account these additional factors:

- Ability to easily summarize subnets
- Ability to easily construct firewall rules and access lists
- Ability to easily identify by function or location

Be sure to read RFC 5375, "IPv6 Unicast Address Assignment Considerations," which you can find at *tools.ietf.org/html/rfc5375*.

Stateful versus Stateless Autoconfiguration One challenge in networking is configuring clients. Specifically, the challenge is telling a diverse group, from servers to mobile phones to kiosks, what their network address is and how to get off the local subnet to the Internet—that is, the address of their default gateway. Assigning parameters such as their domain name is also a challenge.

As discussed in Chapter 7, IPv6 offers two dynamic options—stateful and stateless address autoconfiguration—in addition to the manual, static option. Stateful address autoconfiguration is accomplished via a new version of DHCP known as DHCPv6. Stateless address autoconfiguration is defined in the aptly named RFC 4862, "IPv6 Stateless Address Autoconfiguration."

Stateless autoconfiguration enables you to perform minimal configuration on the router so that it advertises the network prefix on the local link and the hosts generate their own unique IP addresses from that information. You don't need a DHCPv6 server. You also don't have to worry about leases or scopes, which are common in IPv4.

So, when should you use DHCPv6? When you need control over the environment, such as if you want to require authentication to access the network, or when you want to share more information than just the minimum needed for routing. For example, stateless autoconfiguration doesn't tell the client its domain name, and it won't update a Dynamic DNS (DDNS) system. You can read more details about DHCPv6 in RFC 3315.

You can also use a combination of the two. For example, it's fairly simple to have the clients assign their own addresses statelessly and retrieve other options from a DHCPv6 server.

One more consideration is privacy. Depending on which client you use, when you use stateless address autoconfiguration, the client may assign itself an address based on its hardware NIC (MAC address), known as an EUI-64 address. This is a globally unique address that can be tracked quite easily by any Web site, because the last 64 bits of the IPv6 address are always the same for a given client, no matter which network the client is on. Furthermore, because the first half of the interface ID is called the organizationally unique identifier, anyone you communicate with can easily look up the manufacturer of your client hardware and may be able to guess the model. Use of DHCPv6 for address assignment will result in a locally unique host identifier that changes when you move to a different network. Fortunately, Windows Vista, Windows 7, and Windows Server 2008 servers default to the Privacy format (see RFC 4941), so this may not be an issue if your organization has a homogenous environment with the latest Windows operating system.

Quality of Service (QoS) QoS in IPv6 is basically the same as diffserv in IPv4 as far as decisions about marking and scheduling of packets are concerned; however, there are two important differences:

- Packets in IPv6 can be very large, such as jumbograms, and fragmentation is done by the hosts, not intermediate systems like routers. Therefore, the potential exists for much greater jitter.

- IPv6 includes a **flow label**, which is a portion of the IPv6 header used for QoS.

In networking jargon, a **flow** is a conversation between two end points in which all the packets in the flow have the same source and destination addresses and the same Transport layer headers, such as the same TCP or UDP source and destination ports. More specifically, flows are unidirectional, so two flows make up a conversation. Examples of networking technologies that implement this concept are Cisco's NetFlow switching and MPLS labels.

In theory, you can assign per-hop behaviors based on individual flows. (Recall from Chapter 3 that per-hop behavior is a policy that is set independently on each router in the path that allows different decisions to be made regarding the handling of a packet, including prioritization and path, among others.) RFC 3697 requires that applications be able to assign values to the flow label. So, for example, the library of IPv6 network functions discussed at the beginning of this chapter may one day include an option for application developers to assign a number to the Flow Label field. This allows you to provide differentiated services to any packets in that flow based on a label instead of keeping track of or assuming applications are using the standard TCP or UDP ports. In addition to addressing old challenges, such as identifying the data session of an FTP transfer or running applications such as IP telephony that can use a range of hundreds of UDP ports, the flow label opens a new world of potential ways users can dynamically communicate with the network about how they want their traffic prioritized.

The architectural decisions around this are fairly limited until the application-level tools for manipulating flow label are widely implemented.

Security There are many aspects to security, and many of the design points in IPv6 reflect IPv4's long, painful history of inadequate security. That said, many of the security components native to IPv6 were duct-taped onto IPv4 years after its release. Internet Protocol Security

(IPSec) is a good example. Most IPv6 security features are described elsewhere in this book; here are security-related decisions you will need to make to deploy IPv6:

- *Securing network protocols*—Most of the routing protocols and protocols used for things such as Neighbor Discovery and Internet Control Message Protocol (ICMP) have options to use relatively robust authentication mechanisms. The advantage to using them is that it requires more skill on behalf of malicious users, therefore malicious activity will be less successful. The disadvantage is that security often complicates things, requiring more skill to configure and troubleshoot problems. Project changes will also be less successful.

- *Encrypting everything*—The idea that all traffic on a network can be encrypted is interesting but not without a few drawbacks. Namely, encryption remains CPU intensive unless it is offloaded to hardware accelerators, and encryption reduces the usability or effectiveness of many tools, such as sniffers.

- *No perimeter*—Your devices have a globally unique address. If your important traffic is encrypted from host to host, do you need a firewall to block the Internet and create a perimeter? It's hard to argue the pro-perimeter case if your organization allows people to use their laptops to work from home or the local coffee shop. One could make the case that the perimeter instead belongs in front of the data center.

Tools Tools in IPv6 are going to be interesting. At the time of this writing, the tools available are fairly minimal, so this section represents some speculation on the part of the authors, but consider how many tools in use on IPv4 networks today use techniques like Ping sweeps to detect or autodiscover hosts on the network. That is, you give the tool a subnet, such as 10.1.1.0/24, and it pings all 255 addresses (or sends a ping to the subnet broadcast address) and listens for responses. Ponder for a moment the futility of sweeping a typical IPv6 subnet, which contains 2^{64} possible addresses. In perspective, the entire IPv4 address space is only 2^{32}.

Some tools that support IPv6 are the latest versions of putty, Tera Term, tftpd32, and SNMP-based tools such as WhatsUpGold. In addition, Nmap and similar scanners support IPv6.

The point is that the techniques for managing devices in an IPv6 network are likely to change substantially, and so must the tooling. Gone will be the days of the network administrator keeping a spreadsheet that maps all the addresses in a subnet and shows which server, printer, router, or other device is assigned to each. Although the tools will mature, you will want to include in your plan some means of accomplishing the tasks you perform in IPv4, or at least be prepared to communicate why the old processes are no longer necessary.

Other Network Hardware It is likely that by the time you start your IPv6 deployment, many of the network devices in your environment will still not support IPv6. These network devices may include:

- Firewalls
- Load balancers
- Virtual private network (VPN) concentrators

- Secure Sockets Layer offload servers
- Traffic-metering devices
- SLA management tools that measure latency, jitter, and availability
- Route servers
- Wireless access points and bridges
- Fax machines and printers
- Key card readers
- Content delivery systems
- Proxy servers and caches
- Audio and video conference bridges
- IP telephony systems
- Protocol gateways, such as SNA TN3270 terminals
- WAN acceleration appliances

Given the impending migration, you must decide what to do about them, and many of the choices may be difficult and expensive. There are many potential strategies:

- *Changing to a similar product from another vendor that supports IPv6*—This may be a viable option if the price of the devices is low or if they are near the ends of their lives anyway. It may not be a viable option if the product implementation involves a great deal of customization.

- *Leaving the network device on IPv4 and translating or tunneling to the rest of your network*—This may be a viable option if the vendor claims IPv6 support is on their product roadmap and will be available in the near future.

- *Continuing to run a dual-protocol IPv4 and IPv6 network until all legacy devices have been upgraded or replaced*—This is only viable for devices that support dual-stack, which won't include many of the above.

Other factors that may affect your decision for each component are its location in the network and the way traffic passes through the system. For example, is it a transparent or passive bump-in-the-wire, or does it act as a host or router?

Migration and Transitioning Techniques

Chapter 10 described in detail the standardized techniques for transitioning from IPv4 to IPv6, as envisioned by the Internet Engineering Task Force (IETF). This section broadly groups the techniques into three categories—tunneling, translation, and dual stack—and discusses when you should use a given technique and why.

Tunneling There are many tunneling techniques, each of which involves embedding or encapsulating one protocol inside another for transport. You can put an IPv6 packet inside a Generic Routing Encapsulating (GRE) tunnel, MPLS, IPSec Encapsulating Security Payload (ESP), UDP, or Protocol 41 in order to let one IPv6 host communicate with another IPv6 host across an IPv4 backbone. Conversely, you can put IPv4 packets inside IPv6 packets to allow two IPv4 hosts to communicate over an IPv6 backbone. The primary types of IPv6 tunnels covered in this book (and discussed in detail in Chapter 10) are:

- 6to4

- ISATAP

- Teredo

The example in Figure 11-1 shows two native IPv6 speakers, Host A and Host B, separated by an IPv4 network. This is a common scenario early in migrations, when small pockets of devices are upgraded before the backbone, which could be the enterprise WAN or the IPv4 Internet itself. The illustration shows a tunnel configured between two routers, Router 1 and Router 2, at the border where the IPv4 network and IPv6 networks meet. (This is one of many examples, as the tunnel could have been drawn from host to host or from one host to one router or any combination thereof.) Routers inside the IPv4 network are oblivious to the presence of IPv6 inside the tunnel, but the tunnel end points must speak both IPv4 and IPv6.

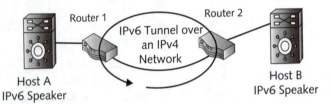

Figure 11-1 Example of a tunnel configured between two routers
© Cengage Learning 2013

Furthermore, you can administratively configure static tunnels on the routers, which are often called **configured tunnels,** or you can have the nodes automatically configure tunnels, which are called **automatic tunnels.**

As you can see, there are quite a few ways to set up tunneling, but take a step back and consider the concept of tunneling itself. Reasons you might consider this method as part of your deployment are:

- IPv4 network devices don't support IPv6.

- You're not permitted to modify the hosts to configure IPv6 for any number of reasons, such as lack of downtime window, regulatory restrictions, or the fact that you do not own or control the devices.

- You need to enable connectivity quickly between two or more isolated groups of hosts.

Reasons you wouldn't want to deploy tunnels are:

- Tunnels complicate the topology.

- You will have to pay very close attention to and carefully test the MTU on your links. As you learned earlier in this chapter, there is a big difference between the maximum packet sizes in IPv4 and IPv6, and intermediate nodes can't do fragmentation in IPv6.

Consider what might happen if a link failure caused your IPv4 network to reconverge and move your IPv6 tunnel to a backup link with a smaller MTU. If the result is that small packets are delivered and large packets are dropped, troubleshooting will be difficult because some applications will work and others won't. Users will be able to ping (assuming they don't change the ping data size), so they'll think the network is operating normally.

- Allowing tunnels in the environment is a major security risk for two reasons. First, traffic inside the tunnel can't be inspected by intrusion prevention systems (IPSs), filtered by firewalls, or captured by a sniffer for troubleshooting. Second, a nefarious insider could configure a tunnel across your firewall perimeter to allow unrestricted access to your internal network from the outside.

As for configured tunnels, it's fairly simple to set one up, but it's not very scalable if you need to configure dozens or hundreds because they're difficult to document and manage. The automatic tunnel alternative is more scalable because it doesn't turn your labor hours into a constraint; the downside is that you lose control and the migration can become less than deterministic, particularly when clients are mobile.

After you decide you need a tunnel and then decide to use a configured or automated tunnel, you'll need to decide which technology to use. Each technology has its niche uses. For example, if you need to tunnel through NAT, using UDP is a good choice, which could mean using Teredo. Otherwise, Teredo is a poor choice because of performance issues. If security is a concern, using IPSec might be the answer, but IPSec might be a poor choice if performance is your primary concern. If you don't have IPv4 multicast enabled across your environment, ISATAP is a better choice than 6over4, because 6over4 requires multicast to be enabled, but ISATAP does not. Conversely, ISATAP requires all hosts to be dual stack; thus, it is not recommended if you have substantial obstacles to enabling IPv6 drivers on your network devices.

As you can see, the optimal choice depends on the situation; you may need one or a combination of different migration techniques.

Translation   Generally, the translation group includes techniques that involve a middleman or intermediary that speaks both IPv4 and IPv6 and converts them or translates between them. Historically, protocol translation has been used with limited success, although it has never been architecturally elegant or free of drama. An example is SNA-to-TCP/IP translation used to connect mainframes to the IP networks in the 1980s and 1990s.

As with tunneling, there are many translation technologies specified in various RFCs and operating at various layers in the OSI model. Also like tunneling, translation is rife with issues. Because of the disadvantages associated with translation, it is widely considered a last resort. Unfortunately, administrators often need the last resort, so we will discuss a few of these techniques.

Figure 11-2 shows a network that has been converted to IPv6 but in which device Host B is only able to speak IPv4, for some reason. This is a common scenario late in migrations,

11

although we could have drawn the reverse as well, in which the network is still IPv4 but there is an IPv6-only host on it. (The second scenario is unlikely to be based on technology limitations of the host, because any host capable of speaking IPv6 is probably also capable of speaking IPv4. However, it is theoretically possible for an administrator to decide to configure only one protocol, because of a lack of IP addresses.) Figure 11-2 illustrates the basic translation technique in which Router 2 speaks both IPv4 and IPv6 and is configured to translate between them so that Host A and Host B can communicate successfully even though they do not speak the same protocol.

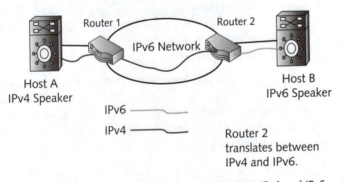

Figure 11-2 Example of basic translation between IPv4 and IPv6
© Cengage Learning 2013

NAT-PT and NAPT-PT are similar to IPv4's "NAT" and "PAT" (also known as "NAT Overload") in that the former translates IP addresses and the latter translates TCP and UDP ports. The IETF recommended this technique in RFC 2766 and revised its opinion in RFC 4966, which explains all the implementation issues associated with the technique. RFC 4966 is recommended reading, even more so than RFCs describing techniques you will actually use, because it offers good insight into the sorts of problems that can cause a transition project to go wrong. Learning from others' mistakes isn't always possible, so take advantage of it when you can.

RFC 6145 describes stateless IP/ICMP translation, or SIIT. As the name implies, this protocol translates the IP headers and also the ICMP support protocol. Like NAT-PT, SIIT requires the IPv6 node to have a temporary IPv4 address, which the IPv4 device needs in order to communicate.

There are other translation mechanisms, including a SOCKS-based protocol gateway, available for you to consider. However, all the translation mechanisms fundamentally fail to solve several of the major transition goals, which makes them unsuitable as a primary mechanism and relegates them to solving small, specific issues.

Dual Stack The current clear front-runner for most IPv4-to-IPv6 transitions is the dual-stack method. Figure 11-3 illustrates this concept. A dual-stack Host A is communicating to both Host B, which is an IPv6-only speaker, and Host C, which is an IPv4-only speaker. The network itself, meaning the routers and switches in the path, must speak both protocols.

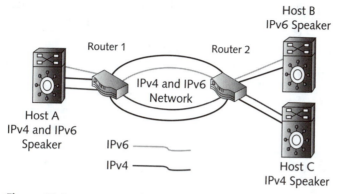

Figure 11-3 Dual-stack example
© Cengage Learning 2013

The dual-stack approach, as discussed in Chapter 10, requires each node to run both protocols independently and concurrently. This has several implications:

- It doesn't save any IPv4 addresses until the transition is over because each node still needs an IPv4 address.
- You have to support both protocols on all hosts until the transition is over.
- Your network infrastructure (routers, etc.) has to remain dual stack as well.
- It requires applications to make a choice between protocols. This can become quite complicated, as described in RFC 3484, "Default Address Selection for Internet Protocol 6." RFC 3484 starts out tackling the problem of which IPv6 address an application should select as a source address, given a choice of link-local, site-local, and globally unique addresses. In IPv4, you simply have the IP address and the loopback address (127.0.0.1). However, RFC 3484 also discusses the problem of address selection for a dual-stack host. Simply put, if you have two dual-stack hosts that want to communicate, how do they decide whether to talk IPv4 or IPv6 to each other? RFC 3484 presents a detailed set of rules that takes into account the scope (link, site, or global), whether the address is preferred or depreciated, and the preference for native addresses to 6to4. The RFC then proposes a policy table that allows administrators to manage and change the preferences.

More specifically, the rules in RFC 3484, in order, for selecting a source address are:

1. Prefer the same address.
2. Prefer the appropriate scope.
3. Avoid depreciated addresses.
4. Prefer home addresses.
5. Prefer outgoing interfaces.
6. Prefer a matching label.
7. Prefer public addresses.
8. Use the longest matching prefix.

Given multiple choices, the application will move down the list, in order, until the criteria distinguishes between the multiple choices, making a single choice preferred.

Similarly, there is a set of rules for choosing the destination address:

1. Avoid unusable destinations.

2. Prefer matching scope.

3. Avoid depreciated addresses.

4. Prefer home addresses.

5. Prefer matching label.

6. Prefer higher precedence.

You set precedence administratively in the policy table. See the default policy table in Figure 11-4.

7. Prefer native transport.

8. Prefer smaller scope.

9. Use longest matching prefix.

10. Otherwise, leave the order unchanged.

The default policy table is defined in RFC 3484 and shown in Figure 11-4.

Prefix	Precedence	Label
::1/128	50	0
::/0	40	1
2002 ::/16	30	2
::/96	20	3
::ffff:0:0/96	10	4

Figure 11-4 Default policy table defined in RFC 3484
© Cengage Learning 2013

One more consideration for dual-stack destination address selection is that it is possible to use DNS to make many applications prefer IPv6. Recall from Chapter 8 that IPv4 uses A records and IPv6 uses AAAA records. When applications are configured to query both A and AAAA records, the order of the records in the DNS server can determine which address is returned in the query. In other words, you can cause hosts that are configured to use both IPv4 and IPv6, running applications that are native IPv4 and IPv6 to automatically use IPv6 by ordering the records in DNS.

This can be a powerful tool because you can make a quick change in DNS and have it change all your hosts from preferring IPv4 to preferring IPv6. Also, if something goes wrong, it's easy to reverse that change. In other words, your backout plan is quick and easy, which is always a good thing.

Combining Techniques and a Phased Migration In the real world, it is rare that a single mechanism is used during an IPv4-to-IPv6 transition. As you can see, the various techniques are quite diverse, and each is appropriate for specific circumstances. Today's enterprises aren't homogenous environments that fit cleanly into a single, simple technique. Instead, they reflect a combination of many different applications and devices. It is likely that you will break your migration up in two different ways:

- *By device*—Some won't support dual stack, which is our primary, go-to choice. That means you may migrate most of the environment (for example, most of the servers and all the laptops) using dual stack but, at the same time, use a NAT-PT translator in front of some devices you can't change or that don't support dual stack.

- *By phase*—At the beginning of your migration, the devices are IPv4. At the end of your migration, the devices are IPv6. For most of the migration, however, they will be a mix that gradually changes. You may start by making some devices dual stack and gradually add IPv6 to them until all devices are dual stack. You then will start removing IPv4 from some devices and keep doing that until you've removed it from all the devices. The point is, it's not an abrupt transition, with only two or three discrete steps, but a long, slow transition (over weeks, months, or even years) in which you change the environment little by little.

This is important because the technique you choose for migration in a network that is predominantly IPv4 may not be the right choice for a network that is predominantly IPv6. You can approach the transition in phases and change transition methods between phases, as needed. In fact, having a finite state in the transition in which every device is running dual stack could be overwhelmingly inefficient in a large network. Again, depending on your actual environment, you might perform the migration as described, but only for one region at a time using a combination of dual stack and configured tunnels between regions.

Despite the fact that most of the RFCs mentioned in this chapter are between 5 and 12 years old, the techniques are not well honed and there is considerable work in progress to come up with a better "framework" for executing transitions. You can read the draft for replacing NAT-PT, which was depreciated in RFC 4966, at *http://tools.ietf.org/html/draft-ietf-behave-v6v4-framework-10*. This draft's goal is to allow IPv4 and IPv6 to "coexist in a somewhat rational manner" during migrations. There are two other drafts for stateful and stateless translation. There is hope that future migrations will be less painful.

Tasks

As you plan the project, you will need to organize a list of all the activities you need to do to accomplish your goals. The purpose of this section is to ensure that there are no gaps in your planning. However, many of the tasks will be nontechnical or only peripherally related to IPv6 itself and, therefore, well outside the scope of this book. In this section, we discuss only the tasks that involve IPv6.

Inventory Computers and Network Infrastructure Elements As you saw in the "Other Network Hardware" list, there are a lot of things connected to the network these days. Some organizations, particularly those with mature security and IT processes and those that follow an IT services management framework like the **Information Technology Infrastructure Library (ITIL)**, may already have an up-to-date inventory of all the devices attached to the network. Many other organizations, unfortunately, do not maintain current inventory records. Even if you have a complete inventory, it might not contain the specific information you need about a given device to make sure you don't disrupt its connectivity when you deploy IPv6.

Whether you're starting the inventory from scratch or already have the devices listed, you'll want to collect the following information about each one:

- Device identifiers (product name, serial number, location, etc.)
- The owner of the device and their contact information
- Any information about whether the device is considered mission critical or if an outage associated with the device would be classified according to a severity level, such as "severity 1" or "severity 2"
- Availability of the device—for example, it is only used during business hours, 8 to 5, or it has a weekly maintenance window on Saturday nights at midnight
- What switch, slot, and port the device is connected to

 A lot of preexisting inventories do not always accurately track switches, slots, and ports. Many servers have four to eight network adaptors or more, and routers and firewalls have many interfaces as well, but many inventories only reflect a single port and IP address. Therefore, be certain to validate this information, especially in cases in which devices are configured in mirrored pairs to support failover.

- The device's current IPv4 address and VLAN and whether it received the IP address statically, via DHCP, or via another method
- If the device requires anything unusual, like multicast
- Whether the device's model supports IPv6 and specific issues like interoperability or constraints on the number of addresses it supports, etc.
- What version of software or firmware the device is running and whether it will need to be upgraded
- Whether the device is under a maintenance contract from the manufacturer and, if so, how to get support for it
- What network management devices monitor it that might need to be updated

Going forward, you won't have to worry about sizing your IPv6 subnets to accommodate all these devices, but you will spend a good bit of time planning the coordination of change windows, remediating and upgrading the devices, and keeping track of what you've done.

Enterprise environments aren't static! You may not even make it through the list before someone has added or modified a device. It is practically impossible to keep current by continuing to go over the same ground doing one survey after another. A better method is to create a process for adding devices to the network that includes updating your inventory. And although it's not perfect, a good way to enforce that policy is through network-based authentication. This may influence your decision regarding stateful and stateless autoconfiguration.

Inventory Applications Application remediation is perhaps the most critical and difficult task, given that applications are notoriously difficult to inventory and the impact of missing an application could be a significant outage—and the cost of upgrading applications to support IPv6 can be enormous.

One challenge in inventorying applications is simply identifying what constitutes an application. On one extreme, an operating system like Windows is made of hundreds of components running as services, and many of them may require attention. On the other extreme, a single "application" may be scaled across many physical servers. In any event, a great deal of thought should precede this activity.

Acquire IPv6 Addresses After you make the decision about whether to multihome or not, you will have to acquire some IPv6 addresses. You usually receive addresses as a block from your service provider. If you choose to multihome, you may need to go to your Regional Internet Registry (RIR) to get a block assigned to you. You must first demonstrate that your organization meets the qualifications; blocks of IPv6 addresses are not issued to anyone who simply requests them.

To determine who your RIR is, go to *www.iana.org/numbers*. In North America, this will be ARIN, which you can contact at *www.arin.net*.

Work with Providers Assuming you have a legacy WAN network and that you're satisfied with your current service provider's pricing and service, the easiest and least expensive course of action would be to run IPv6 over the same circuits.

It would generally be a bad idea to attempt to tie a migration from one service provider to another to the migration from IPv4 to IPv6. The reason is that when you migrate from one service provider to another, you go through a period during which you have circuits from both vendors connected to your sites, so the cost of your network is doubled. This is usually covered in the migration plan, but the plan will assume a brief period, such as a few months, of double-paying. If you attempt to coordinate with another project, such as an IPv6 deployment, you have a substantial risk that any delays in the IPv6 deployment (which are likely) will affect the schedule of your service provider transition and could force you to double-pay for the circuits for an extended period of time.

In any event, make sure you understand what the capabilities of your service provider are for IPv6. Discuss the way they do QoS, and their pricing structure for different classes of service and service levels. Ask if they offer any support or services for the transition, such as managing translation servers or tunnel brokers.

Finally, be sure to review your plans with them and coordinate the schedules with them, given that they will have tasks to perform in the migration as well, like enabling IPv6 on their routers (even though they may support it, it may be disabled until you request it for security reasons).

Remediate Software and Servers Although this task is critical, it's not one the network team usually performs. The server and application development teams normally update the software for IPv6. However, the network team needs to provide some information and education about the new IPv6 network. Part of this information will be to convince them why it's necessary to spend the time and money to upgrade. Part of this information will be to explain how and when to upgrade.

For IPv4, you might provide network information for configuring servers and applications upon request. For example, when someone wants to install a new server, you give them the IP address for a server, its subnet mask, default gateway, and DNS name. In the future, you will need to supply similar kinds of information for IPv6. It would be a good idea to prepare a presentation explaining how things have changed. For example, if the server team believes it should always use static addresses on servers for reliability, you may have to educate it on how each interface on a server will have several addresses and how they configure themselves in IPv6.

The actual task of remediating software is going to be the critical path for most projects and will determine how long you have to maintain dual stack, tunnels, or translation services.

Create a Test Lab A test lab is a good idea for most projects, but it is critical for IPv6 for several reasons:

- You need a **sandbox** (an IT environment isolated from the production environment) to test the network devices to ensure functionality and interoperability and identify any bugs. You don't want to do this on the production network because an unexpected bug might cause a significant outage.

- The application developers and other administrators will need a place to test their applications and various models of hosts as they remediate and upgrade them to be IPv6 native.

When you build the lab, consider that you will likely want to use it to test different techniques across multiple phases of the migration. Those techniques are likely to continue to evolve over the next several years as the Internet community figures out better ways to effect transitions. So the lab should be semi-permanent, given that you will need to continue testing over the years, and it should contain the same equipment that you plan to use in production.

Figure 11-5 shows an example of what a lab might look like. Note that this example takes advantage of virtualization technology to keep costs low and flexibility high.

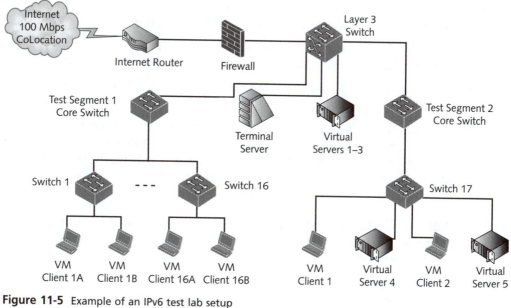

Figure 11-5 Example of an IPv6 test lab setup
© Cengage Learning 2013

Update Routers Obviously, this task will be one of the core components of the transition. You will probably update each router multiple times as you initially enable IPv6 routing and later add and remove various tunnels. Before each step, take care to not exceed the CPU's capacity, memory, or throughput on the box. Remember that some processes that may be handled in hardware ASICs for IPv4, such as processing access lists, might be handled in software for IPv6, which could substantially increase the load on the CPU and, in turn, dramatically reduce performance. In addition to the load created from simply handling twice as many protocols and twice as many routes, the way the new protocol is processed might change.

In many ways, this will be an advantage because several of the key design points in IPv6 were included to improve performance, such as the way the IPv6 headers are constructed and the fact that routers no longer do fragmentation. Just because it's supposed to improve performance doesn't mean it will. Test it.

Update Virtual Network Devices In today's highly virtualized environments, "the network" actually extends well into the server. In most server-based hypervisors, there are one or more virtual switches or bridges that act much like a real switch in that they participate in Spanning Tree and have virtual ports that connect in software to the virtual NICs on virtual machines. Although these virtual network entities are usually Layer 2 only, that is not always the case. Regardless, you need to test them to ensure that they can handle the IPv6 features, from multicast to Jumbo Frames.

Update DNS Updating DNS should be relatively straightforward. You will likely accomplish this by upgrading your DNS server software to a version that supports IPv6 and then adding the AAAA records and PTR records for reverse lookups. You won't need to do a great deal of complicated coordination, but this task is a predecessor to most other tasks because it won't do much good to convert hosts to IPv6 if they can't resolve names.

If you use DDNS, or if you choose to perform the migration via the order of A and AAAA records in DNS, this task will become considerably more complex and the coordination more critical.

Either way, you should research the alternatives for commercial and free DNS servers and consider the location of the server and the physical computer it's running on.

Because clients still discover their DNS servers' IP addresses through DHCPv6 options or static configuration, you can easily install new DNS servers without affecting the current ones and test them as much as you like. Then, move clients to them by changing the DNS server parameter in DHCPv6. Or, when you visit each client or server to install and configure the IPv6 driver, you can change any static DNS settings at that time.

Update to DHCPv6 Updating DHCP is optional, since devices can autoconfigure, but if you're going to implement DHCPv6 to get around the limitations of autoconfiguration, then the planning will be similar to DNS. You'll want to research and evaluate DHCPv6 servers and what features they support.

Going live with a new DHCPv6 server takes more finesse, as the new DHCPv6 server won't know what IP addresses have already been leased out, so you can get IP address conflicts. Usually, this is done by reducing the DHCPv6 lease time before the migration to an hour or so instead of the usual 3-day to 7-day lease times. That way, when you do the cutover in a 2-to-3-hour change window, all the clients will ask for new leases sometime during the window. Afterwards, you can set the lease time back to normal.

Update Tools Sorting out your management tools is always a challenge, especially when dealing with a new protocol that so few people have experience in managing. Your legacy IPv4 tools are a good place to start, but keep in mind that although IPv6 solves some problems, which means you may no longer need particular old tools, it will create some new problems for which no tools currently exist. Some tools to consider are:

- *Protocol analyzers*—This includes the sniffer that you use to capture packets and the analyzer software you use to decode them. Most protocol analyzers can decode IPv6 packets, but don't be surprised if the analysis is weak or if implementation issues appear. For example, will the analyzer be able to handle large packets, such as 2 gigabytes or more?

- *Monitors*—This includes tools that periodically verify the status of some device or application to make sure it is still functioning. Usually, this was done with ICMP PINGs.

- *SLA managers*—These devices usually perform synthetic transactions that mimic real production application traffic and gather response time or performance statistics. The statistics give you an apples-to-apples comparison of performance over time as conditions in the network change.

- *Configuration management databases (CMDBs) and managers*—Configuration management databases and associated tools keep track of the configuration of your network devices and let you know if something changes or allow you to easily copy the configuration onto a new box if you have to replace something because of hardware failure.

- *Terminal servers and out-of-band (OOB) gateways*—These devices let you hop onto an out-of-band management network or access the serial console port on a router or switch.

- *IP Address Management (IPAM)*—These tools are quite popular in legacy IPv4 networks because they solve several issues regarding tracking and assignment of scarce resources and they facilitate DDNS. The challenges in IPv6 won't be about scarcity but about tracking, because manually recording 128-bit addresses in a spreadsheet isn't efficient, especially when each NIC could have three or more addresses. Although it is possible to disable the link-local address in some clients, this would not meet RFC guidelines.

Deploying and Using IPv6

In this section, we take a detailed look at a few of the common tasks involved in deploying IPv6. For most of the tasks, we will focus on how to accomplish the task technically, using one or more popular commercial or freeware products.

Establish an IPv6 Test/Pilot Network

Establishing a test network is one of the first tasks you'll do. There may be somewhat of a Catch-22 involved, though, as you select products for the lab. A best practice is to use the same make and model of routers and switches in the lab that you will use in production; however, part of the purpose of a test lab is to evaluate and test devices, so which devices do you initially use in the lab environment? If you don't have the budget to procure several models of routers and switches from several different vendors, you can often get demo or loaner gear temporarily from several vendors for evaluation purposes.

There are several fundamental functions you'll need to provide in the lab in addition to the network gear you intend to test. These include:

- *A way to get to the lab*—Your lab needs to be a sandbox. That means, it needs to be isolated from the production network so that no matter what happens in the lab, it doesn't affect your normal network services to your users. A common solution for this is a **jump box**—a proxy server or terminal server that has one interface on the production network for you to access a terminal via Secure Shell (SSH) or access a virtual desktop. It also has an interface in the lab. From a security standpoint, this is sometimes referred to as a **bastion host**. In any event, the other alternative is to have the lab completely disconnected and accessed only by physically entering the location and plugging your laptop into the device consoles. This is usually more secure than necessary for mundane network testing, and it prevents remote workers from accessing the lab. Remote access to the lab is often handy, given that network teams are usually geographically dispersed.

- *Method of injecting routes*—In order to test scalability and performance and just to make sure things look "normal," it's a good idea to pump a large number of routes into the lab routers. This can be a little challenging because you just isolated your lab, so it's not connected to your production network or the Internet, and you probably don't have more than a handful of routes inside the lab. Usually, the way this task is accomplished is to take a spare router of some sort and designate it as your external border and have it advertise the routes. Virtual router software running on Linux can be used for this if you don't have an old box handy. You can usually create dozens or hundreds of loopback interfaces or static routes pointing to the null0 interface and then redistribute those into the lab. (In routing, null interfaces are typically used for preventing routing loops.) If you want to test thousands or tens of thousands of routes, you could connect this border router to the Internet or your production network, but you would have to apply controls to make sure prefixes were only announced into your lab and nothing is announced back out.

- *WAN simulator*—These devices slow traffic down to mimic latency and bandwidth of typical WAN links. They are useful in testing convergence over the WAN. That is, your network will probably converge quickly over a few directly connected Ethernet cables. When you separate the routers by hundreds or thousands of miles, the latency will slow the convergence down considerably. A WAN simulator is handy but not always necessary.

- *Traffic simulator*—This device sends various IPv6 traffic to test for functionality and load. For example, you may want to send a few hundred concurrent DHCPv6 requests to the servers when you are evaluating DHCPv6 products to see which ones respond fastest. You should plan to stress-test your network by sending a large amount of typical user traffic (HTTP browsing, file transfers of office documents, etc.) through any IPv4-to-IPv6 tunneling or translation devices to make sure they can handle the expected peak load. This is especially true if you are encrypting the traffic.

- *Sniffer and protocol analyzer*—Use this extensively to inspect the traffic produced by the simulator as it passes each component in the infrastructure to see if it was altered. You'll also want to watch the actual protocol interactions for Neighbor Discovery, Router Advertisement messages, DHCPv6, and so on.

- *Instances of each server type and client type*—This is important because the IPv6 drivers you want to test have to interface with the adapters, which vary by device. You can't assume that what works with one adapter will work with all others. For the servers, you should test the virtualization software and hypervisors extensively—and keep in mind the compatibility issues. Each vendor often interprets the standard in subtly different ways that often cause problems. If you want to make sure your implementation goes well, test every piece of hardware and software and driver.

- *Configuration repository*—This allows you to keep a copy of the config on each of the devices and add some comments about it, such as the results of testing, problems or bugs encountered, etc. This is a handy thing to keep over time as well, and it is a requirement for many of the industry certifications, particularly if your enterprise is involved in healthcare or credit card processing.

The testing you'll do in this lab involves three main phases. Here's what you'll do in each phase:

1. Evaluate the many brands and models of network devices. Your procurement organization may have some say in the process you follow to ensure a fair comparison that doesn't favor any particular vendor. Generally, it's a bad idea to focus your evaluation criteria on performance at this stage. Rather, you should focus on interoperability with your legacy and other equipment.

2. Reconfigure the lab using the exact models you selected to create an exact physical replica of as much of your network as you can afford. Hopefully, this is at least two entire sites.

You will then test the configurations of the devices to make sure they work exactly as anticipated. This testing should pay particular attention to making sure that failover works and that, after the artificially induced "failure" is over, the devices restore themselves to exactly the way they were prior to the failure. You'll also want to test the filtering you do. For example, if you create access lists to filter packets or routes, you'll want to verify with a sniffer that the behavior is as anticipated. After all your tests are completed and your configurations are set, you'll **promote** (move) these configurations to their peer devices in production.

3. Use the lab to test servers and applications as you attempt to update them to be IPv6 native.

After these three main phases are complete, keep the lab up to date, so you can use it in future phases of the migration or in post-migration, as you progress through the life cycle of your architecture and network devices.

Start Migrating Applications

Once your lab is up and running, with an IPv6-enabled network and servers, your application people can start bringing in their software to test. Although the actual coding is beyond the scope of this book, there are a few things that need to be done during this activity:

- Make sure the application people track any changes they make to the infrastructure. This includes driver updates, operating system updates, and so on.

- Track any changes to requirements—for example, DNS records. An application may take advantage of IPv6 features, like multicasting or anycasting, or security features. If it does, your designs will have to meet those requirements, so make sure you enable them in the network before they update their applications in production. Sometimes, applications also use IP addresses as part of their registration or copy-protection schemes. These usually require static addresses, so you may need to modify your addressing plans to accommodate this.

Upgrade IPv4-Only Hosts to IPv4/IPv6

At some point in the deployment plan, you will be ready to start upgrading hosts, likely to a dual-stack configuration. Although there are hundreds of brands and types of hosts that you may need to upgrade, this section covers one popular example, a Windows PC. Because the individual commands, syntax, and interfaces vary greatly by operating system and function, it isn't practical to memorize them. Instead, focus on understanding what the commands are accomplishing to achieve functionality.

You should also consider how you will make the change consistently on dozens, hundreds, or thousands of similar devices. The type of interface, such as a command-line interface (CLI) versus a graphical user interface (GUI), can make a big difference. Some larger organizations have automated systems that allow you to make changes without touching the devices themselves.

Automating networking-related changes can result in loss of connectivity to the automation systems, which may suddenly require you to touch hundreds or thousands of devices manually to restore service. Therefore, a great deal of care is warranted, and thoroughly testing the changes in a lab environment is strongly recommended.

If your PC is running Windows XP Service Pack 2 (SP2) or earlier, or if it is running Windows Server 2003 or earlier, you need to install IPv6. To do this, open a command prompt window and type the `netsh interface ipv6 install` command. Your host will likely process for a minute or two, display "OK" and then return you to the command prompt. IPv6 installation is not necessary for Windows Vista, Windows 7, Windows Server 2008, or Windows Server 2008 R2 because the IPv6 protocol is already installed and enabled by default.

Look at the interface and addresses by typing `netsh interface ipv6 show address`. The results are shown in Figure 11-6. Your computer may have many interfaces. Most will have a wireless Ethernet interface and a FastEthernet or Gigabit Ethernet copper interface that shows up as a "Local Area Connection" interface. If you have VPN software for connecting to your enterprise network, that will also show up as an interface. If you have virtualization products like VMware installed, those will cause several virtual interfaces to show up in this list. You should also see a loopback interface.

```
C:\windows\system32\cmd.exe

C:\Users\G2TCPIP>netsh interface ipv6 show address

Interface 1: Loopback Pseudo-Interface 1

Addr Type  DAD State    Valid Life  Pref. Life Address
---------  -----------  ----------  ---------- -------------------------
Other      Preferred    infinite    infinite   ::1

Interface 15: Wireless Network Connection

Addr Type  DAD State    Valid Life  Pref. Life Address
---------  -----------  ----------  ---------- -------------------------
Other      Preferred    infinite    infinite   fe80::691f:45c7:9059:a34b%15

Interface 24: isatap.gateway.2wire.net

Addr Type  DAD State    Valid Life  Pref. Life Address
---------  -----------  ----------  ---------- -------------------------
Other      Deprecated   infinite    infinite   fe80::5efe:192.168.1.76%24

Interface 16: Wireless Network Connection 2

Addr Type  DAD State    Valid Life  Pref. Life Address
---------  -----------  ----------  ---------- -------------------------
Other      Deprecated   infinite    infinite   fe80::c023:c456:10c2:1a7c%16

Interface 13: Local Area Connection

Addr Type  DAD State    Valid Life  Pref. Life Address
---------  -----------  ----------  ---------- -------------------------
Other      Deprecated   infinite    infinite   fe80::c011:52a0:edd1:5ace%13

Interface 22: isatap.{B2E038DA-2C83-4D59-A175-2680C3BB42A6}

Addr Type  DAD State    Valid Life  Pref. Life Address
---------  -----------  ----------  ---------- -------------------------
Other      Deprecated   infinite    infinite   fe80::5efe:192.168.47.1%22
```

Figure 11-6 Results of the `netsh interface ipv6 show address` command
Source: Microsoft

NOTE By default, you will have ISATAP and Teredo interfaces for the Ethernet NIC in Windows Vista and Windows 7 and an ISATAP interface for each of the other interfaces, such as wireless LANs, virtual machines, and so on.

Each interface receives an IPv6 link-local address and possibly others, depending on whether the interfaces are active and find a router advertising their subnets.

For more information on the interfaces themselves, execute the `netsh interface ipv6 show interface` command. As shown in Figure 11-7, the results display a list of all the interfaces configured on the computer, their names, MTUs, and whether they're connected or disconnected.

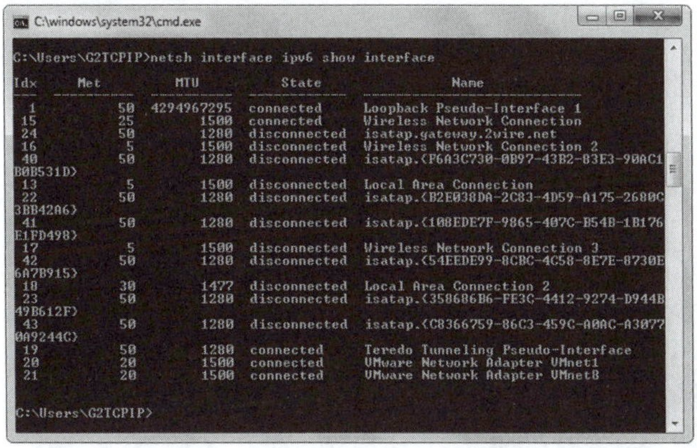

Figure 11-7 Results of the `netsh interface ipv6 show interface` command
Source: Microsoft

You should also look at the default settings, including privacy. Issue two commands: `netsh interface ipv6 show global` and `netsh interface ipv6 show privacy`. Examples of these commands are shown in Figures 11-8 and 11-9.

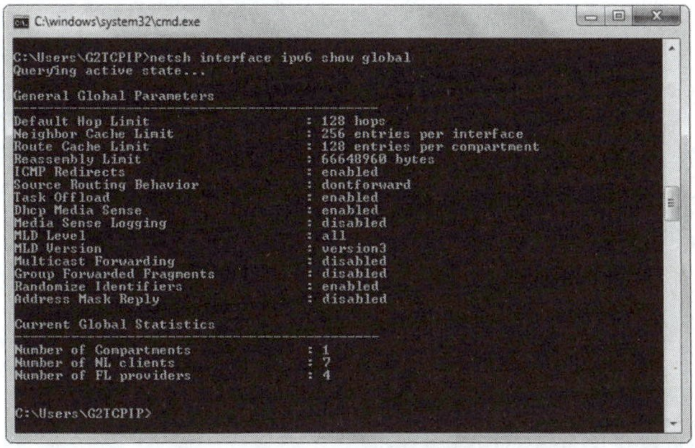

Figure 11-8 Results of the `netsh interface ipv6 show global` command
Source: Microsoft

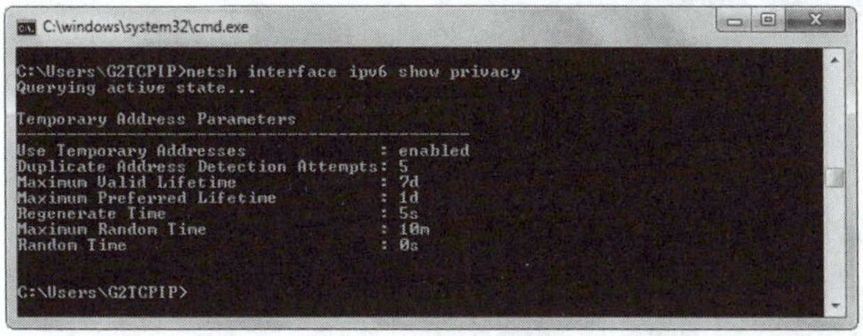

Figure 11-9 Results of the `netsh interface ipv6 show privacy` command
Source: Microsoft

These commands show important information for diagnostics and troubleshooting and can help you ensure that the environment is set up like you designed it. Although you can change most of these settings, it's unlikely you'll need to.

One set of parameters you might want to change during your migration, as discussed previously, is the policy table that controls the order of selection. You can see this in Windows using the `netsh interface ipv6 show prefixpolicies` command. The default is shown in Figure 11-10.

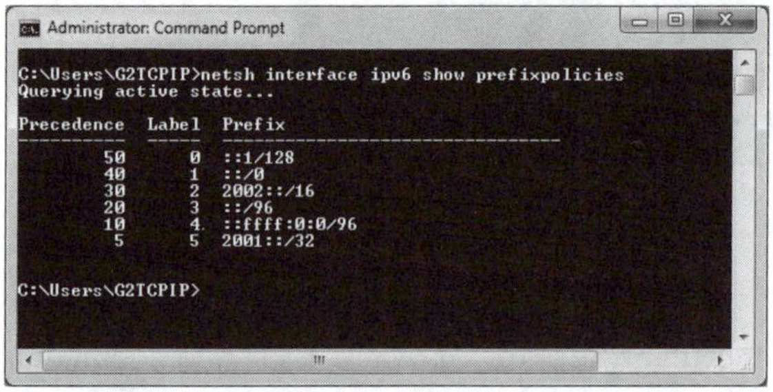

Figure 11-10 Results of the `netsh interface ipv6 show prefixpolicies` command
Source: Microsoft

As you are considering how you want your hosts configured, you may want to look at the `netsh interface ipv6 dump` command (shown in Figure 11-11), the output of which can be used to create a handy configuration file. For example, from the command prompt, type `netsh interface ipv6 dump > cheese.txt`. If you then type `dir` and press Enter, you should find a file called cheese.txt in the directory, which contains the output of the `dump` command. You can edit this text file with any common editor, such as Microsoft Word or edit.exe, or you can simply view the contents by entering the command `more cheese.txt`. As you can see when viewing the text file, there are few commands required for a simple configuration.

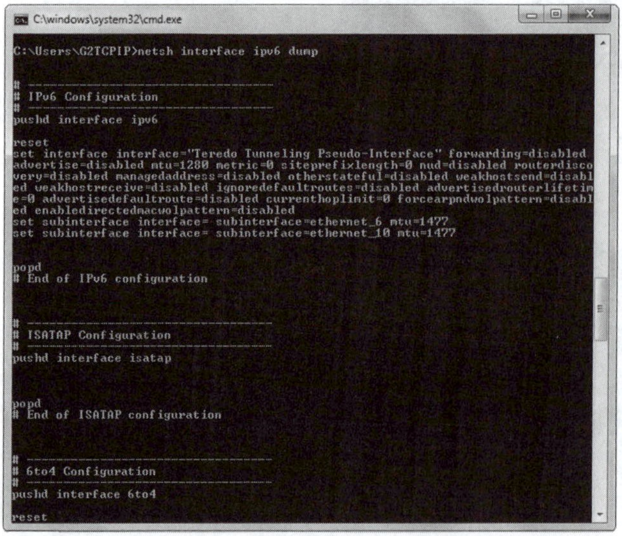

Figure 11-11 Results of the `netsh interface ipv6 dump` command
Source: Microsoft

After you configure all your tunnels, policies, and so on, you can use this file to make a script that you can run on all the Windows hosts in your environment to install and configure IPv6 consistently.

Create a Tunneled IPv6 Environment Using 6to4

At this point, you have an operational client capable of communicating locally and, if it's on an IPv6 network with an adjacent IPv6-speaking router, capable of communicating globally. Let's assume, however, that the client you just configured is deep in an IPv4 network, with no IPv6 neighbors around, yet it still needs to communicate with IPv6 servers and applications in a remote data center. This scenario is quite likely because users are so mobile. For example, you might migrate one office to IPv6/IPv4, but before you can schedule the changes for another office, some of the employees at the first office travel to a meeting in the second office. They need to be able to reach their IPv6 servers at their home office from the remote office that is IPv4 only.

This challenge can be solved with a few different tunneling technologies. In this case, you can implement a simple solution, which is a 6to4 tunnel. In the next section, we will solve the same problem with ISATAP. ISATAP is much more appropriate, of course, because it is more dynamic.

The 6to4 tunnel is configured with the `netsh interface ipv6 add v6v4tunnel` command. Although it can be a router-to-router tunnel, in this case the tunnel will be from the Windows PC to a IPv6/IPv4 router. Conceptually, this is quite simple: a dual-stack machine has one interface on the IPv4 network that you are on and another interface on the IPv6 network that you want to get to, and it acts as a gateway between the two networks. So you create a tunnel from a virtual interface on the PC (also dual stack) to this gateway and stuff your IPv6 traffic through the tunnel.

There are three basic parameters for configuring the tunnel. The first is a simple name, and the next two are the IPv4 addresses of the local and remote ends of the tunnel. An example of the configuration command is `netsh interface ipv6 add v6v4tunnel "mytunnel" 10.1.2.3 10.100.1.1`.

NOTE You can use any names you want, but it's generally a good idea to go with more useful names than "mytunnel." For example, if you are configuring one tunnel to the IPv6 Internet and two more tunnels to your two datacenters, you might name them "Internet," "EastDC," and "WestDC," respectively. Using descriptive labels will make it easier for you and others to troubleshoot later.

Create a Tunneled Environment Using ISATAP

As discussed previously, ISATAP is a much better choice for connecting dual-stack clients to their IPv6 resources when they are in an IPv4-only network. An ISATAP tunneled environment is shown in Figure 11-12. The configuration is pretty simple and involves only a few steps, which are listed here briefly and then covered in more depth:

1. Configure an ISATAP router.

2. Add a name record for ISATAP to DNS pointing toward the IPv4 address of the ISATAP router you configured in Step 1.

3. Configure ISATAP on the clients.

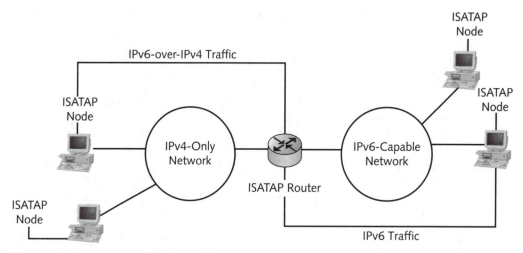

Figure 11-12 ISATAP tunneled environment
© Cengage Learning 2013

Configuring an ISATAP Router

Configuring an ISATAP Router For Step 1, you need a dual-stack box capable of forwarding traffic. Ideally, this is a dedicated, hardware-based router. However, in this chapter, for ease of understanding, we will describe the configuration required to convert a Windows server to an ISATAP router. This is a good way to learn, but carefully consider the performance ramifications of trying to use a Windows server as a gateway between your IPv4 and IPv6 networks.

Enable ISATAP by entering the command `netsh interface ipv6 isatap set router <x.x.x.x>`, in which x.x.x.x is the IPv4 interface on the box.

Next, tell the server you actually want it to be a router and forward traffic with the command `netsh interface ipv6 set interface <y> forwarding=enabled advertise=enabled`, in which y is the IPv6 tunnel interface's number or name.

To find an interface's number, use the command `netsh interface ipv6 show interface` and look in the Idx column. The name is something you assigned when you created the interface. For example, we used "mytunnel" in the previous section. You can use either a number or the interface name.

 Sometimes, it's easier to use names because when you're scripting you never know if the user has created other interfaces on their own. In such a case, when your script creates an interface on their PC, it will have a different number than everyone else's. However, if you name the interface when you create it and then refer to the name, you can avoid this problem. You could perform some error checking in your script to ensure that additional interfaces don't already exist. If they do exist, do not automatically delete them, because doing so could cause an application to crash.

Finally, add the routes you want the router to advertise. You will need to repeat this command for each prefix you wish to advertise. The `add route` command is flexible and has many arguments and parameters because there are many different ways you might want to add routes, including changing the metric, the age, the next-hop, and so on. The command you use is `netsh Interface Ipv6 add route <prefix/<length <y> publish=yes`, in which y is the interface number or name again.

Configuring DNS Once you have the router set up, it's time to configure DNS. You must ensure that the host can resolve the name "ISATAP." This step can be accomplished in several different ways:

- Add an entry in the \etc\hosts file for ISATAP and skip the DNS configuration step.
- For Windows hosts still using NetBIOS, put the entry into WINS.
- If you use DNS (which is recommended), add the A record (not AAAA) for a hostname of ISATAP in your domain that points to the IPv4 address of the router configured in Step 1. Run `dnscmd /config /globalqueryblocklist` wpad in order for the DNS to respond to isatap queries.

Configuring ISATAP on the Clients If the client already has IPv6 installed, you don't have to configure the client, but make sure that it can resolve the name "ISATAP." This can be done in any of the ways mentioned in the previous bulleted list, or you can manually tell the client the ISATAP router address using the command `netsh interface ipv6 isatap set router <x.x.x.x>`, in which x.x.x.x is the IPv4 address of the ISATAP router configured in Step 1.

Manual client configuration is acceptable for a learning environment, but you should not configure clients in an enterprise environment manually. If you ever need to change your ISATAP router, it's far easier to change one DNS entry than manually delete and reenter the updated `set router` command on hundreds of client devices.

Once the client resolves the ISATAP name, it sends an IPv6 solicitation message to the ISATAP router, which responds with advertisements. The configuration is pretty dynamic.

Exploring Some Network Administration Tasks

There are several other commands that you will use during the course of various daily network administration tasks. One important thing to understand is the IPv6 routing tables. Note that all IP devices have routing tables, not just routers. Routes get into the table via several mechanisms. The most common way is from the configurations of directly connected interfaces. Of course, you can also statically define routes or use a routing protocol to dynamically receive routes, and the act of configuring a "default gateway" installs a default route.

Even more than in legacy IPv4 networks, understanding the routing tables of relatively simple devices like laptops will be important as you start to add numerous tunnels, many of which will dynamically create themselves. You will want to understand which prefixes are being sent over which interfaces and which tunnels. To do this in Windows, use the `netsh interface ipv6 show route` command, as shown in Figure 11-13.

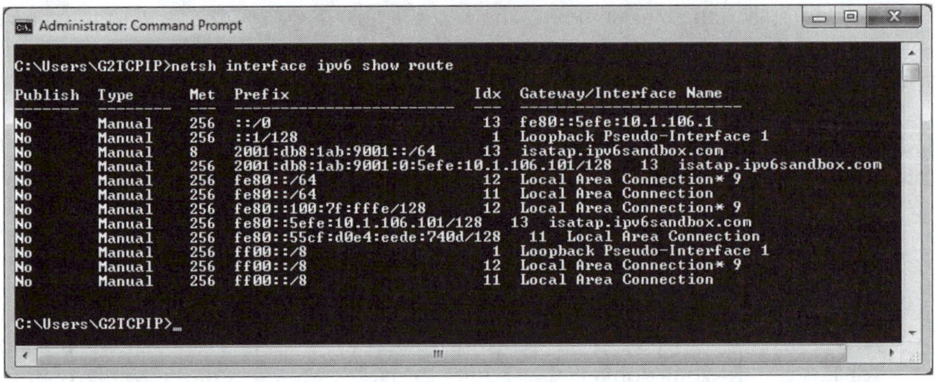

Figure 11-13 Results of the `netsh interface ipv6 show route` command
Source: Microsoft

Although we haven't focused on multicast in this chapter, if it is implemented, you will definitely want visibility into the multicast goings-on in your network. One of the most critical pieces of diagnostic information for multicast is understanding what multicast addresses are in use. You can find this on your Windows system using the command `netsh interface ipv6 show joins`, as shown in Figure 11-14.

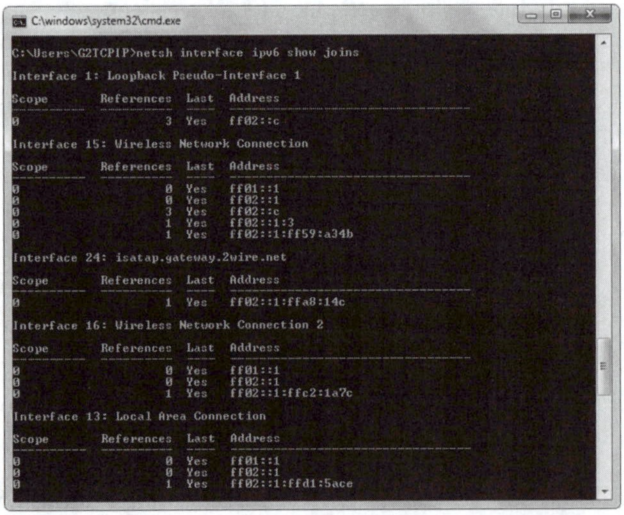

Figure 11-14 Results of the `netsh interface ipv6 show joins` command
Source: Microsoft

The most often used diagnostic command for IPv4 is the `ping` command. In Windows, you can use the same command to test IPv6 connectivity by pinging IPv6 addresses. To do so, simply execute the `ping` command followed by the IPv6 address you want to ping. An example is shown in Figure 11-15.

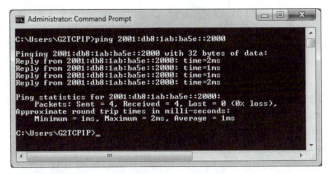

Figure 11-15 Results of a `ping` command
Source: Microsoft

The DHCP protocol hasn't worked flawlessly over the years—computers frequently become confused about their addresses. Thus, administrators often have to give the system a little kick to get rid of an old address and acquire a new one. The related IPv4 commands in Windows are `ipconfig /release` followed by `ipconfig /renew`. The equivalent commands for IPv6 in Windows are `ipconfig /release6` and `ipconfig /renew6`.

Chapter Summary

- IPv6 deployments use a Network layer or routed protocol differently than IPv4 deployments do. The IPv6 protocol may seem like an upgrade or new version of TCP/IP v4 to most people, but to the applications themselves, it is quite different.

- The Network layer protocol functionality on hosts is mostly deployed as software, in the form of drivers, and occasionally deployed as firmware or application-specific integrated circuits (ASICs) in the network interface controllers (NICs). New versions of all that software had to be written to support IPv6.

- IPv4 software is mature, and most IPv4 drivers are relatively defect free. IPv6 is just coming into popular use and, therefore, may require more troubleshooting and patch cycles.

- IPv6 deployment planning includes the creation of success criteria, which are the results that signal a successful deployment. You must also make architectural decisions, determine which migration technique(s) you will use, and create a checklist of tasks that must be completed.

- Architectural decisions may include the following: interior routing protocol, Exterior Gateway Protocol (EGP), external connections, router hardware and software selection, addressing schemes, stateful versus stateless address autoconfiguration, quality of service (QoS), security, tools, and other network hardware (firewalls, load balancers, and so on).

- Migration techniques include tunneling, translation, dual stack, or a combination of these techniques and a phased migration.

- You should create a checklist of tasks to accomplish during an IPv6 deployment. The checklist should include the following tasks (at a minimum): inventory computers and network infrastructure elements, inventory applications, acquire IPv6 addresses, work with providers, remediate software and servers, create a test lab, update routers, update virtual network devices, update DNS, update DHCP, and update tools.

- In many cases, especially in larger environments, it's important to establish an IPv6 test lab or pilot network before deploying IPv6. A test lab enables you to evaluate different brands and models of network devices, reconfigure the lab using the exact models you selected to create an physical replica of your network, and use the lab to test servers and applications as you attempt to update them to be IPv6 native.

Key Terms

architectural decisions In formal architecture methodologies, a list that documents decisions that are made, along with the rationale, alternatives, impact, and derived requirements.

automatic tunnel An IPv6 tunnel created and destroyed by the protocol when needed, without having an administrator manually involved.

bastion host A security concept that uses a host to separate two networks or security zones. The host does not forward packets, like a router or firewall. Instead, security-oriented applications running on the host are used for interaction between the two zones.

configured tunnel An IPv6 tunnel that an administrator creates manually.

default-free zone (DFZ) In Internet routing, a set of all the Internet networks that are operated without a default route. Also, a set of all the autonomous systems (ASs) that do not require a default route to send a destination packet. DFZ routers, collectively, have complete BGP tables.

driver Software used by the operating system to interface with specific hardware components.

enterprise In the context of this chapter, the IT environment of an end-user organization, which is usually a business.

failure domain The collection of IT components in the environment that are disrupted by a single component failure.

flow In networking, a conversation between two end points in which all the packets in the flow have the same source and destination addresses and the same Transport layer headers.

flow label A portion of the IPv6 header used for QoS.

global Internet routing table The set of all Internet address prefixes in the default-free zone, which comprise the public Internet.

green-field environment A new empty environment, unencumbered by older systems or a need for backward compatibility.

Information Technology Infrastructure Library (ITIL) A standard for performing IT service management, organized by domains, including event, incident, problem, change, and so on.

jump box A type of bastion host that is usually a terminal server or proxy server that allows administrators to access systems in another network without actually having direct network connectivity, meaning neither network has a route to the other network.

legacy environment An environment that has existing production systems that must be accommodated, usually temporarily, while it is upgraded.

merger and acquisition (M&A) Activity undertaken by companies as a result of purchasing one another or otherwise combining their assets, which often includes combining all their IT environments, as a cost-saving measure.

promote The act of moving an IT component from one life cycle stage or environment to the next, such as moving an application from "development" to "test" to "QA" to "Staging" to "Production."

proprietary An IT component that is not standards based and useable by anyone without license; instead, it is the property of a particular entity that may or may not charge for use but nevertheless controls its features and development.

sandbox An IT environment that is isolated from the production network for the purpose of testing or containing things that could disrupt service on the production network—for example, testing failover scenarios or virus or botnet removal features.

service provider In contrast with "enterprise," the IT environment of an organization that provides service to multiple customers—for example, an Internet service provider.

single-homed The act or state of having uplinks to a single system. For example, an enterprise network with redundant connections to a single ISP would be considered single-homed, whereas having connections to two different ISPs would be multihomed.

success criteria In project management, a list of conditions used to define whether an activity has completed successfully or not.

11

Review Questions

1. Which of the following are reasons for upgrading to IPv6? (Choose all that apply.)

   a. You can have as many public addresses as you want.

   b. You are out of IPv4 addresses.

   c. You need features provided by IPv6.

   d. It is less complex and easier to understand.

2. "Dual stack" refers to _____ .

   a. having stacks of routers in adjacent datacenter racks, for redundancy

   b. a system that is running either IPv4 or IPv6

   c. a system that is running both IPv4 and IPv6

   d. a system that is running two instances of IPv6

3. Which of the following are reasons to implement tunnels as part of an IPv6 migration? (Choose all that apply.)

   a. You have an IPv4 host that cannot be upgraded but needs to talk to the rest of the IPv6 network.

   b. You have a dual-stack host connected to an IPv4 network, and it needs to talk to the rest of the IPv6 network.

   c. You have two islands of IPv6 hosts separated by an IPv4 network.

   d. You have two islands of IPv4 hosts separated by an IPv6 network.

4. Which of the following steps is not involved in enabling ISATAP on an IPv6 network?

   a. configuring an ISATAP router

   b. adding an A record for ISATAP in DNS

   c. adding an AAAA record for ISATAP in DNS

   d. configuring the clients

5. Which of the following is a valid reason to use stateful autoconfiguration?

   a. Clients need a unique IP address.

   b. Clients need to know their default gateway.

   c. Clients need to know their DNS server and domain suffix.

   d. There is no valid reason.

6. Where can you get a block of IPv6 addresses if you are in the United States and plan to single-home your network?

   a. an electronics store

   b. IANA

   c. your ISP

   d. ARIN

7. Where can you get a block of IPv6 addresses if you are in the United States and plan to multihome your network?

   a. an electronics store

   b. IANA

   c. your ISP

   d. ARIN

8. What does the Windows command `netsh interface ipv6 dump` do?

   a. outputs a list of commands that can be used to rebuild the current IPv6 configuration

   b. outputs diagnostic information about IPv6 that you can send to Microsoft for analysis

   c. nothing

   d. resets the configuration to factory defaults and wipes the buffers and counters

9. Why should you create and use a test lab?

   a. to evaluate products

   b. to test applications as they are migrated to IPv6

   c. to test designs and create standardized configurations

   d. all of the above

10. Which tools should you include in a test lab? (Choose all that apply.)

    a. traffic simulator

    b. protocol analyzer

    c. AED box

    d. jump box

11. What is the preferred method for migrating networks from IPv4 to IPv6?

    a. tunnels

    b. dual stack

    c. translation

    d. Convert everything at once.

12. You need to tunnel through NAT. Which of the following is the best choice?

    a. Teredo

    b. 6to4

    c. ISATAP

    d. none of the above

13. A host is running IPv6. You connect the host to an IPv4 network with no IPv6 routers. What happens by default to the host?

    a. It will not be able to talk to any IPv6 hosts.

    b. It will be able to talk to the IPv6 Internet.

    c. It will only be able to talk to your IPv6 intranet.

    d. It will only be able to talk to IPv6 nodes on its local link.

14. How many link-local IPv6 addresses does a node have?

    a. one

    b. one per interface

    c. as many as you configure

    d. none, because only routers have link-local addresses

15. Your decision to multihome your enterprise network will increase the number of prefixes in the default-free zone. How will this affect routers in the IPv6 Internet? (Choose all that apply.)

    a. increases memory required to store the routing table

    b. increases time to look up entries in the routing table

    c. increases the size of packets in the routers

    d. increases the number of prefix announcements between routers

16. Which of the following would not affect your choice of interior routing protocol for IPv6?

    a. your legacy IPv4 protocol

    b. your hardware vendor

    c. the size of your circuits

    d. the size and complexity of your network

17. Which of the following have IPv6 routes?

    a. all IPv6 nodes

    b. only IPv6 routers

    c. IPv6 routers and servers but not laptops

    d. only devices running an IPv6 routing protocol

18. What kinds of activities are appropriate to perform in a sandbox?

    a. test routing protocol changes

    b. test tunneling schemes

    c. test security products

    d. all of the above

19. What will happen to a legacy IPv4 application that is not IPv6 native after you have upgraded your clients to be IPv6-only?

    a. The server will automatically translate from IPv4 to IPv6 to talk to the clients.

    b. The clients will automatically translate from IPv6 to IPv4 to talk to the application.

    c. The application will automatically translate from IPv4 to IPv6 to talk to the clients.

    d. Clients will be unable to communicate with the application.

20. How many host addresses are there in a Class A IPv6 network?

    a. 2^{128}

    b. 2^{64}

    c. $2^{64} - 2$

    d. none, because IPv6 doesn't use classes

Hands-On Projects

Hands-On Project 11-1 assumes that you are working in a Windows Vista or 7 Professional environment. Hands-On Project 11-2 requires a computer with an operating system that does not have IPv6 installed.

Hands-On Project 11-1: Explore Route Servers

Time Required: 30 minutes

Objective: Find detailed information about the global IPv4 and IPv6 routing tables.

Description: In this project, you log into a live route server hosted by a tier 1 service provider. You will run several show commands to get current information about the Internet routing.

Most ISPs offer public route servers. These are used by network engineers at customer sites and ISPs for troubleshooting and generic information. Most route servers for internal use are Linux-based servers, so the route information exists in text files and can be easily manipulated with scripts to create reports or track changes in various routes over time. External route servers like the one you will use are usually router-based. You can find a list of publicly accessible route servers at *www.netdigix.com/servers.html* and another at *www.traceroute.org/#Route%20Servers*. If, for any reason, the specific route server used in Project 11-1 is unavailable, choose another route server from one of these Web sites.

1. Open a command prompt window in Windows (click **Start**, type **cmd**, and press **Enter**) or start a Telnet client and telnet to route-server.ip.att.net. From the Windows command prompt, do this by typing `telnet route-server.ip.att.net`.

If you're running Windows Vista or Windows 7 and need to enable the Telnet client, click **Start > Control Panel**. Click **Programs** and then click **Programs and Features**. In the left pane, click the **Turn Windows features on or off** link. Scroll down and check the **Telnet Client** checkbox. Click **OK**. You can also install the Telnet client from a command prompt in Windows Vista, Windows 7, and Windows Server 2008 by issuing the following command: `pkgmgr /iu:"TelnetClient"`.

2. Follow the on-screen instructions for logging in. At the time of this writing, the username is rviews and no password is required. The route-server> prompt appears, as shown in Figure 11-16.

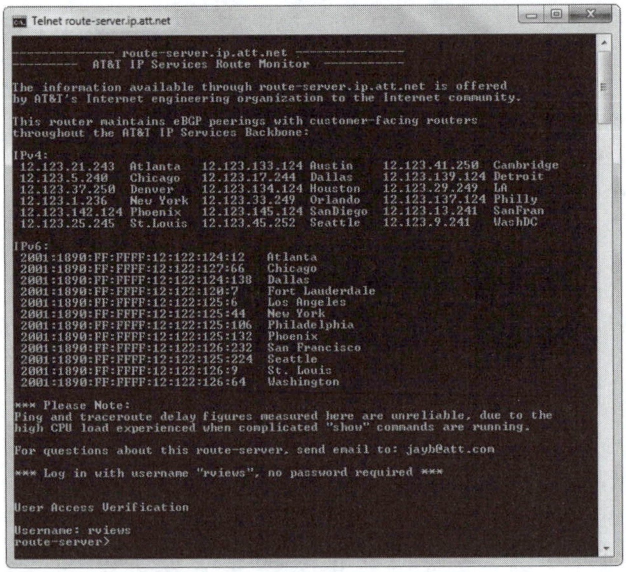

Figure 11-16 Logging in to the route server
Source: Microsoft

3. Type **show ip route summary** and press **Enter**. Study the output (shown in Figure 11-17), paying particular attention to the total number of IPv4 subnets in the global Internet routing table (which may be labeled "bgp") and the memory used.

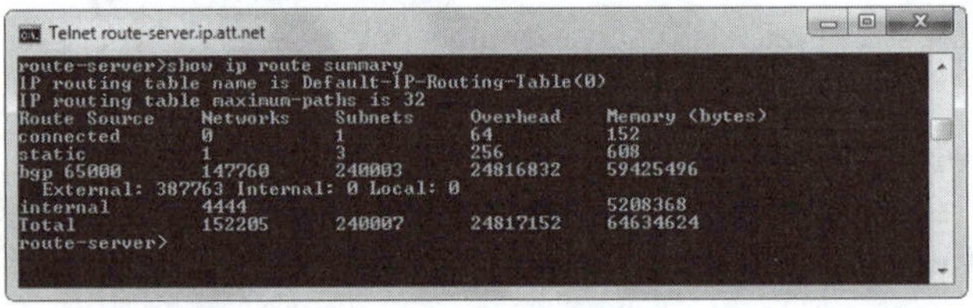

Figure 11-17 Results of the show ip route summary command run against the route server
Source: Microsoft

4. Type **show ipv6 route summary** and press **Enter**. Press **Enter** several more times to display all the entries. Study the output (shown in Figure 11-18), paying particular attention to the total number of IPv6 subnets in the routing table and the memory used.

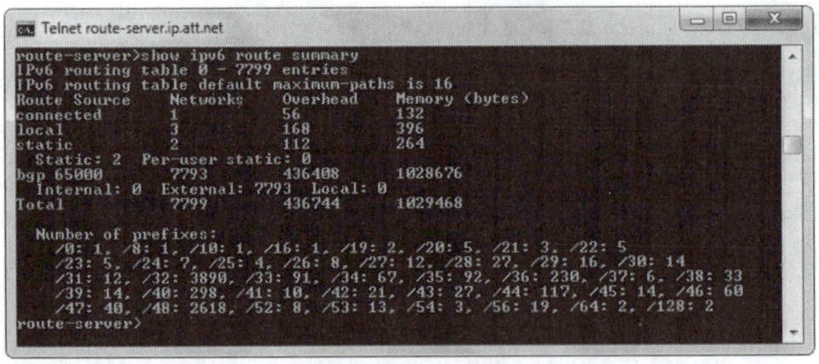

Figure 11-18 Results of the show ipv6 route summary command run against the route server
Source: Microsoft

5. Type **show bgp ipv4 unicast summary** and press **Enter**. Press **Enter** several more times to display all the entries. Study the output (shown in Figure 11-19), and make a note of the table version. Also note the memory used by the BGP protocol.

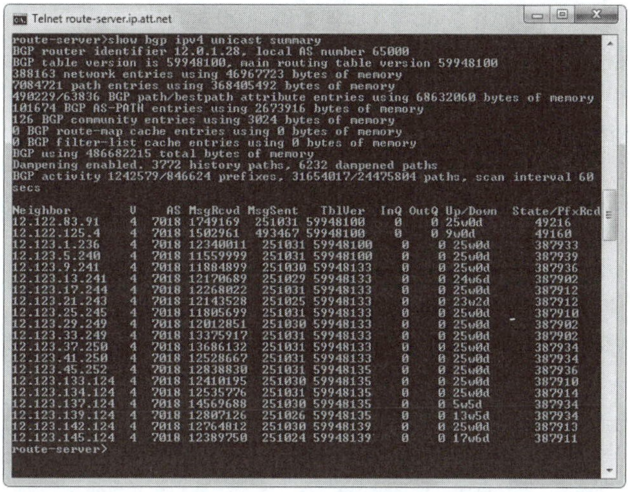

Figure 11-19 Results of the `show bgp ipv4 unicast summary` command run against the route server
Source: Microsoft

6. Type **show bgp ipv6 unicast summary** and press **Enter**. Study the output (shown in Figure 11-20), and make a note of the table version. Compare the total memory used by the BGP protocol for IPv6 to that of IPv4. Compare the memory per route. Press **q** to stop scrolling.

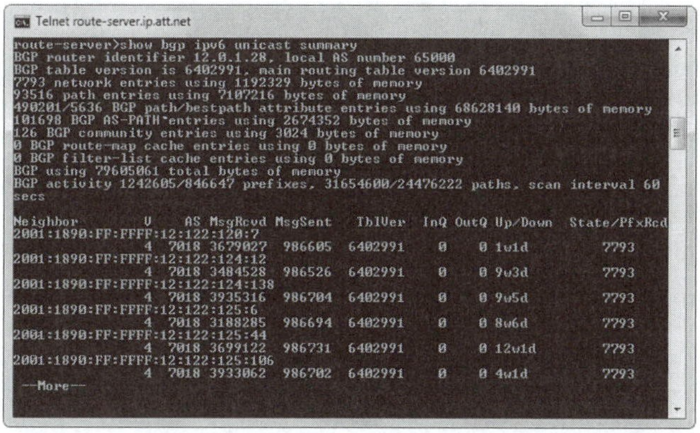

Figure 11-20 Results of the `show bgp ipv6 unicast summary` command run against the route server
Source: Microsoft

7. Wait about one minute and then repeat Steps 5 and 6. Compare the rate of change in the table versions. Is the IPv4 or IPv6 table changing more often? Which do you think will be changing faster five years from now? Ten years from now?

8. Type **show ipv6 route** and press **Enter**. The IPv6 routing table appears. Type **show bgp ipv6 unicast** and press **Enter**. The detailed BGP entries appear. Note the "Path" on the right is a list of Autonomous System Numbers that the route traveled through to reach this server. Also note the output from both commands is hundreds of pages long and displays thousands of routes. Press **q** to stop scrolling.

9. Type **show ipv6 ?** to see a list of other IPv6 commands you are allowed to execute on this route server. Feel free to explore.

10. When you're finished, exit the Telnet session and command prompt.

Hands-On Project 11-2: Explore an IPv6 Configuration

Time Required: 15 minutes

Objective: Learn about system behavior as IPv6 is installed.

Description: In this project, you run several different show commands to explore an IPv6 configuration.

1. Open a Windows command prompt window. (Click **Start**, type **cmd** in the Start menu search box, and then click **cmd.exe** in the resulting list.)

2. At the command prompt, type **netsh interface ipv6 show interface** and press **Enter**. Study the output. How many tunneling "pseudo" interfaces did Windows automatically create for you?

3. Type **netsh interface ipv6 show address** and press **Enter**. Study the output. Are your IPv6 addresses built using your hardware MAC address? Note which addresses are built by embedding your IPv4 address, and note how Windows switches from hex to dotted decimal notation partway through the addresses to make them easier to read.

4. Type **netsh interface ipv6 show prefixpolicies** and press **Enter**. Study the output.

5. Type **netsh interface ipv6 show route** and press **Enter**. Study the output. Where is your default route going? Why do you have a route pointing towards the tunnel?

6. Type **netsh interface ipv6 show** to view a list of other IPv6 commands you can execute. Feel free to explore.

7. Close the command prompt window.

Case Projects

Case Project 11-1: Creating a Test Lab

You are a network engineer for a midsized government contractor working on a project for a national government lab. Your network consulting company has been hired to convert several of the lab offices from IPv4 to IPv6. You have convinced your manager that you need a test lab for your IPv6 migration.

He says the sales team didn't include any money for a lab in its proposal to the customer. To get the capital for the lab from the CIO, you need to write a justification and create a Bill of Materials for the infrastructure and tools for the lab. Include any hardware and software you think you will need.

Case Project 11-2: Create a Migration Plan

You are the lead network engineer for a large manufacturing company that has 16 datacenters, over 300 offices around the world, and over 180,000 employees. Your company has grown over the past 30 years through dozens of acquisitions, and each acquisition used different products and made very inefficient use of the RFC 1918 private IP ranges, so that you have actually exhausted all the private IP ranges. Your manager is panicking. She asks you to put together a high-level transition plan that will accommodate the next merger and eventually replace IPv4 with IPv6 across the whole company. In the plan, include a list of the technologies you intend to use and how and when.

chapter 12

Securing TCP/IP Environments

After reading this chapter and completing the exercises, you will be able to:

- Explain basic concepts and principles for maintaining computer and network security
- Explain the anatomy of an IP attack
- Recognize common points of attacks inherent in TCP/IP architecture
- Maintain IP security problems
- Discuss the importance of honeypots and honeynets for network security

TCP/IP was designed in an age when networking was a marvel of technology and when network access was available only to a privileged few. The basic protocols that supported the environment were generally devoid of security features or functions. In fact, it's possible to describe TCP/IP's inherent security model as "optimistic" in the sense that even obvious exposure of potentially valuable information—such as accounts and passwords—was not considered unsafe or unsound until the Internet had been around for quite some time.

Much of what you will learn in this chapter involves addressing potential holes or points of exposure left open in the original implementations of many IP-based protocols and services. Securing TCP/IP, therefore, requires that you recognize and understand such potential exposures, comprehend how they may be addressed, learn how to assess potential security threats or vulnerabilities, and act accordingly. Thus, TCP/IP security is a matter of routine observance, regular assessment, and keeping up with potential sources of attack, threat, and vulnerability.

Understanding Network Security Basics

When people think of computer or network security, attackers are always on their minds. An **attacker** is the source of an attack sequence, and a **victim** is the target of an attack. A **hacker** is someone who uses computer and communications knowledge to exploit information or the functionality of a device; some hackers have no intention of doing any damage to a system or network, but others do. A **cracker** is a person who attempts to break into a system for malicious purposes, using techniques that do not necessarily involve deep system skills or knowledge. Protecting a system or network does mean closing the door against outside attack, but it also means protecting your systems, data, and applications from any other sources of damage or harm (inadvertent or intentional), whether they originate inside or outside your organization's boundaries. Thus, planning for disaster recovery, making regular backups, using antivirus software, and maintaining physical security over computing resources can be every bit as important to security as thwarting external intrusions.

All forms of network security focus on three major areas: physical security, personnel security, and system/network security. We like to think of these areas as a tripod that rests equally on each of its metaphorical legs.

- *Physical security*—You must take steps to prevent unauthorized users from taking physical possession of your servers, routers, firewalls, and other network gear. **Physical security** is synonymous with "controlling physical access"; therefore, you should carefully monitor any equipment that is important to your computer's or network's security or that could compromise that security. This means locking up such gear in equipment rooms or wiring closets and being sure that ventilation and power supplies are adequate. It might also mean checking visitors, using ID badges, or even using special card-key locks to permit only authorized users to access the equipment.

- *Personnel security*—The best passwords and access controls in the world are worthless unless your staff knows how to maintain **personnel security**, which is the aspect of security that concentrates on informing users about security matters and training them on proper application of security policies, procedures, and practices. When passwords are too hard to remember and there is no security policy to forbid such behavior, it's typical for people to tack notes on their monitors, with their passwords for all to see (and use). It's important that your organization formulate a **security policy**, which is a document that represents the concrete manifestation of an organization's requirements for security practices, rules, and procedures. Make sure employees follow that policy and avoid forms of laziness and "cheating" that can undo the best physical and software security measures.

- *System and network security*—Also known as **software security**, this includes analyzing the current software environment, identifying and eliminating potential points of exposure, closing well-known back doors, and preventing documented exploits. Although the other two legs of the tripod are equally important, we concentrate on system and network security in this chapter, because this is a book on TCP/IP.

The following sections discuss a variety of security topics, such as the principles of IP security; typical IP attacks, exploits, and break-ins; and common types of IP-related attacks. In addition, you will learn which IP services are most vulnerable and how to recognize illicit points of entry, such as holes and back doors.

Principles of IP Security

Given the many potential points of attack and the many ways in which the unscrupulous can try to take advantage of those uninformed about IP security, here are some things we strongly suggest you apply to your system:

- *Avoid unnecessary exposure*—Install no unused or unneeded IP-based protocols or services on your servers. Each point of entry is also a point of potential attack. Why expose something that you don't need or use?

- *Block all unused ports*—A relatively simple software program called a **port scanner** can attempt to communicate with any IP-based system while cycling through all the valid TCP and UDP port addresses. Use a port scanner on your firewalls and servers, because hackers will do so whenever they can. Close all unused ports; each open port can invite attack.

- *Prevent internal address "spoofing"*—When someone wants to break into a network, he or she often sends packets from outside the network that masquerade as internal communications from an internal subnet. This technique relies on formulating packets that appear to be legitimate on casual inspection but that could never legally take the form in which they appear (hence the term "IP spoofing"). There's no way that a packet that claims to originate inside your network should ever show up at a router or firewall interface where external traffic enters your network. Make sure you check for, and specifically block, spoofing attempts.

- *Filter out unwanted addresses*—By subscribing to Internet and e-mail monitoring services, such as mail.com, and obtaining lists of undesirable or questionable Internet addresses, you can preempt potential points of attack (or spam) by rejecting packets from certain domain names and IP addresses. Obviously, whenever actual attacks occur, you might also want to block the addresses from which they originate.

- *Exclude access by default, include access by exception*—This is what we call a **pessimistic security model**; it excludes users from access to resources by default and then adds whatever resources users need access to as exceptions to the general exclusionary rule. This keeps permissive defaults (like those that the Windows NTFS file system uses) from allowing users access to resources you don't want them to see.

- *Restrict outside access to "compromisable" hosts*—Any time you expose information, resources, or services to the public, you should expect attacks and be able to recover from compromises without undue loss of services or data. That's why only hosts that can be compromised without causing harm to your organization should be exposed, and why maintaining safe, private copies of public data also is important.

- *Protect all clients and servers from obvious attack*—Today, conventional wisdom calls for adding security software to any client or server that interacts with the network. At a minimum, this means installing, using, and keeping the following components up to date: antivirus software, anti-spyware, anti-spam, pop-up blockers, and both applications and operating system security patches. You can get a sense of current best practices for home users in this area by visiting the Microsoft Safety & Security Center Web page at *www.microsoft.com/protect*. The security technologies mentioned in this paragraph also represent a minimum standard for the workplace, and many organizations typically exceed the minimum to protect their desktops and servers.

- *Do unto yourself before others do unto you*—Perform regular attacks on your own systems and networks to be sure you've closed all obvious points of attack, addressed all existing exploits, and covered all security bases. Make this kind of activity part of your regular maintenance routine and monitor security-related mailing lists and newsgroups for late-breaking news and information. Consider hiring an outside security firm to attack your systems and networks if you really want to be sure your security is sufficiently tight.

In general, if you've taken reasonable precautions, you may not be break-in proof, but you will be better off than most organizations. Remember that you don't have to create a system or network that's impossible to compromise, just one that's hard enough to compromise that a run-of-the-mill hacker or cracker realizes you know what you're doing and therefore looks for other, more vulnerable, locations to attack.

Typical TCP/IP Attacks, Exploits, and Break-Ins

Fundamental protocols—including IP and TCP or UDP—offer no built-in security controls. In many cases, successful attacks against TCP/IP networks and services rely on two powerful weapons: profiling or footprinting tools and a working knowledge of the weaknesses or implementation problems (a.k.a. bugs) that permit unauthorized access, if probed. Profiling IP networks permits would-be malefactors to identify potential targets for attacks; knowledge of bugs and weaknesses suggests what kinds of attacks to attempt. You must learn how to recognize the bugs and how to counter, mitigate, or patch weaknesses.

The following sections discuss key network and computer security terminology, key weaknesses in TCP/IP, and how the flexibility of TCP/IP can contribute to security breaches.

Key Terminology

Here are descriptions of some key terms involving network and computer security:

- An **attack** is an attempt to obtain access to information, to damage or destroy such information, or to otherwise compromise system security or usability, preferably without detection until the deed has been done. The most extreme case, of course, is when outsiders obtain administrative access to a system, at which point they can do whatever they want with it.

- An **exploit** reveals a system vulnerability and is often documented, either by the manufacturer or by an attacker. Fortunately, when exploits are published by attackers, the software manufacturers and anti-malware software engineers find out about them as quickly as the bad guys and can start working out ways to prevent them from being repeated. That is why it's so important to keep up with new exploits (and related patches and fixes) as they are reported. You can do so by subscribing to security-focused mailing lists such as *www.windowsitpro.com/home.aspx*, *www.cert.org*, and *http://technet.microsoft.com/en-us/security/bb291012*.

- A **break-in** is a successful attempt to compromise a system's security. This can be something as innocuous as gaining unauthorized access to directories, or it can be taking over complete control of a system. Most security experts acknowledge that the bulk of system break-ins are not reported publicly because organizations do not wish to advertise their security problems.

Key Weaknesses in TCP/IP

As you already learned, each IP-based service can be associated with one or more well-known port addresses on which it listens for service requests. These addresses represent TCP or UDP ports and are designed to begin the process of responding to legitimate requests for service. Unfortunately, the same ports that handle perfectly valid requests for service can become well-advertised points of attack. Also, TCP/IP was designed using what's called an **optimistic security model**, meaning that the designers didn't consider whether the mechanisms they were creating to handle service requests could expose servers to hijacking attempts or compromise of their data and services.

There are many ways in which attackers can exploit TCP/IP to launch an attack:

- They can impersonate valid users of well-known accounts (such as the root account on a UNIX host or the Administrator account on Windows 2000 and later) and repeatedly try to guess the associated passwords. Successfully stealing a valid user name and password permits **user impersonation,** a system or network attack technique whereby an unauthorized user presents valid credentials that rightfully belong to an authorized user and then exploits whatever rights and privileges the impersonated user's identity allows. Trying every possible password for an account is called a **brute force password attack**.

- They can take over existing communications sessions by inserting IP packets that shift control to them and their machines. This is called **session hijacking**.

- They can snoop inside packets moving across the Internet to look for unprotected account and password information (which could lead to user impersonation) or other sensitive information. This is called **packet sniffing** or **packet snooping**.

12

- They can use a technique known as **IP spoofing,** whereby the attacker sends packets to a target host but substitutes the IP address of another host on the LAN or the Internet. This makes the traffic appear to come from this host. This is typically done to bypass access control lists on a router or on the host itself.

- They can create so much traffic aimed at a particular protocol or service that the underlying server is overwhelmed, or they can create pathologically incomplete or incorrect packets that cause a server to wait forever for data that never arrives. Because this results in blocking legitimate users from accessing a service, it's called a denial of service, or DoS, attack.

Flexibility versus Security

Designers of TCP/IP and most other protocols try to make their protocols as flexible as possible. A great deal of this flexibility comes from peripheral protocols, such as Internet Control Message Protocol (ICMP), Internet Control Message Protocol version 6 (ICMPv6), Address Resolution Protocol (ARP), Simple Network Management Protocol (SNMP), and various routing protocols.

Ironically, the interaction between these protocols and IP is what is compromised most often. Therefore, much of modern security practice is nothing more than disabling the features these protocols provide. For example, on a normal network, the proxy ARP function can be very useful because it allows hosts to communicate across a routed network without having their default gateways manually configured—that is, it adds flexibility. However, an attacker could either deny service to a host or redirect traffic from a host to its own machine by sending illegitimate proxy ARPs. You can prevent this by disabling proxy ARP or by manually configuring MAC addresses and disabling ARP altogether.

IP also features a great deal of flexibility, such as the ability to broadcast to all hosts without manually specifying each address and the ability to support multiple Layer 2 topologies by fragmenting large frames into smaller ones. Unfortunately, disabling these core features would render the entire protocol useless, so alternate solutions must be found to prevent these features from being used for wrongdoing. These solutions typically involve products that are external to the protocol, such as proxy servers and firewalls, rather than a reconfiguration of the protocol itself.

The question becomes whether the security of your data—let's say you're responsible for a network of 1,000 PCs—is worth the effort to prevent the attack. Answering this question is one reason corporations expend so much effort on security assessments, because in most cases that answer is "Yes!"

Common Types of IP-Related Attacks

Although attacks on IP protocols and services vary considerably, they fall into five categories:

- *DoS attacks*—In a DoS attack, a service is inundated with requests, or malformed service requests, which cause a server to hang or freeze, preventing it from responding to input. In either case, legitimate users are denied access to a server's services because it is kept completely busy or becomes unavailable. Although DoS attacks don't involve any destruction of data or any outright compromises of system or network security, they do deny users access to services that might otherwise be available on the server under attack. Unfortunately, DoS attacks are easy to mount and difficult to stop, and certain IP services are unusually vulnerable to such attacks. Although DoS attacks pose more of a nuisance than a security threat, they are no less vexing when they occur.

- *Man-in-the-middle (MITM) attacks*—In a **man-in-the-middle (MITM) attack**, the attacker is able to intercept traffic from both parties to a communication and either pass the traffic unaltered to the other end of the communication link or forge a reply from either side. This type of attack, if properly executed, is especially dangerous because it results in eavesdropping on private conversations without the knowledge of the parties involved in the communication.

- *IP service attacks*—Numerous IP services are subject to attacks that are, therefore, called **IP service attacks**. Often, these occur through the IP service's well-known ports, but sometimes they occur through other ports. Either way, they can expose the underlying systems to inspection or manipulation, particularly when the underlying file system is accessible. For example, services that permit anonymous logins, such as FTP and HTTP (Web), are notoriously prone to file system penetration when access roots for anonymous users coincide with file system roots for drives or logical disk volumes.

- *IP service implementation vulnerabilities*—Sometimes, hackers discover bugs in specific implementations of IP services on particular platforms that can be exploited to permit normally illegal operations to occur on machines where those services are available. Windows NT, for instance, was subject to several debugger-based attacks when developers left debugging switches active in code and the switches were exploited through a TCP/IP-based network session to assert system-level access for anonymous or null user sessions (which normally can't do much of anything on a well-secured system).

- *Insecure IP protocols and services*—Some protocols, such as FTP and Telnet, can require user account names and passwords to permit access to their services. But these protocols do not encrypt that data; if malefactors sniff IP packets between senders and receivers while this information is visible, they can obtain valid account name and password pairs with which to break into a system. There isn't much you can do about this, except to restrict public access to those systems for which compromise won't be a problem. Otherwise, you must require users to switch to more secure implementations of such services, when they're available—as is the case with Secure Telnet (Stelnet), Secure Shell (SSH), and Secure FTP (SFTP), for instance. Alternatively, you can force users to use virtual private network (VPN) connections (which encrypt all traffic between senders and receivers) when insecure protocols or services are employed.

Which IP Services are Most Vulnerable?

One kind of IP service that's vulnerable to attack is a so-called remote logon service. A **remote logon service** is any type of network service that permits users elsewhere on a network to use the network to log on to a system as if they were attached locally while operating remotely.

This includes the well-known Telnet remote terminal emulation service as well as the so-called Berkeley Remote Utilities, also known as **r-utils**. This set of utilities includes **rexec** for executing remote commands, **rsh** for launching a remote UNIX shell, and **rpr** for printing remotely, among others. The inclusion of these r-utils in the Berkeley Software Distribution (BSD) version of UNIX, back in the 1980s, is what gave this set of utilities its name. It is the utilities' weak authentication mechanisms, however, that open the door for an attacker to execute remote commands or sessions on machines elsewhere on the network, thereby making them a security threat.

Along the same lines, remote control programs, such as RDP, LogMeIn, and GoToMyPC are security threats. For instance, older versions of the Symantec program pcAnywhere were open to other pcAnywhere clients elsewhere on a network, by default, and required no password for access.

Other services that can be vulnerable to attack are those that permit **anonymous access**, which is a type of IP service access wherein users need not provide explicit account and password information. FTP and Web services, among others, sometimes allow anonymous access, making the services conspicuous targets. That's one reason we strongly recommend that any such services and data you offer to the Internet should be mirrored elsewhere, preferably somewhere safe that's not publicly accessible. It's also why many organizations choose to situate their public Web servers at an ISP or use commercial Web-hosting services. In that situation, an attack on a publicly accessible system cannot simultaneously turn into an attack on an in-house network. Most organizations maintain one or two backup copies of any public server on other private networks that are not publicly accessible. They can use a private copy to re-create a public one on short notice, should the public one become compromised or damaged by a successful attack.

Backup media, emergency repair discs, Registry copies, and so on can contain hashed versions of passwords. Well-known password-hashing algorithms offer the safest method for protecting password information. By using a brute force password attack, hackers can try hashing all possible combinations of letters, numbers, and symbols until they find a hash that equals the hash in the password file. If the passwords are long enough and contain an appropriate mix of letters, numbers, and symbols, this attack can take a very long time to run and is less likely to succeed.

However, hackers can launch a dictionary attack, which consists of creating hashed values for all words in a specialized dictionary of terms, then comparing those values to the hashed values in password files. Because uninformed users often choose passwords that appear in an English dictionary, they inadvertently reduce the time required to crack a password from weeks to seconds. For those in the know, this grim possibility also explains why strong passwords are a must for most Windows and UNIX systems.

Sadly, almost any IP service can become a potential point of attack. The more sensitive the information that a service is known to carry, or the greater the range of access a service is granted (such as SNMP, which sets and collects system configuration and management data on servers, routers, hubs, switches, and other network devices), the more likely the service is to provide a potential point of illicit entry into a system or network. Ultimately, nothing in the broad world of IP services is entirely exempt from compromise!

Holes, Back Doors, and Other Illicit Points of Entry

The following terms apply to both operating systems and the IP services that run on them, because either may become points of attack:

- *Hole*—A **hole** is a weak spot or known place of attack on any common operating system, application, or service. In the UNIX world, outsiders employ numerous techniques to hijack the superuser account and gain root-level access to a machine. Likewise, Windows 2000 and Windows XP are subject to some well-crafted exploits that can crack the Administrator account and give outsiders unlimited access to a system.

- *Back door*—A **back door** is an undocumented and illicit point of entry into an operating system or application added by a system's programmers to bypass normal security. Although neither UNIX nor Windows 2000 (or later) offers such things, there are plenty of ways in which obtaining physical access to a machine delivers the same results, or in which access to encrypted password files can occur through guile or ignorance. Thus, for example, Windows NT 4.0 was prone to an attack called GetAdmin, wherein the presence of a debugging flag that was inadvertently left turned on in the operating system kernel made it possible for any user account except Guest to be added to the local Administrators group. Although this is not, strictly speaking, a back door, it gave any user Administrator-level access, which means it had to be taken seriously and quickly repaired. (For more information, see Microsoft Knowledge Base article Q146965.)

- *Vulnerability*—According to the National Institute of Standards and Technology publication *Risk Management Guide for Information Technology Systems*, a **vulnerability** is a weakness that can be accidentally triggered or intentionally exploited.

Any knowledgeable systems professional with the right toolkit can break into just about any system in 15 minutes or less if allowed unsupervised and unrestricted access to the computer on which such a system resides. Thus, no matter how well you secure your IP environment, if you don't think holistically and include all aspects of your systems in your security plan, your IP security efforts may be for naught.

Phases of IP Attacks

IP attacks typically follow a pattern that begins with a reconnaissance or **discovery process**, in which the attacker learns about active systems or processes on the network. Next, the attacker launches the actual attack, such as planting malicious software on a **compromised host** (a host on which unauthorized access was gained) or disrupting host operations through a DoS attack. Finally, the attacker tries to remove evidence of the attack. A **stealthy attacker** is one who hides his tracks and may cover his tracks by deleting log files or terminating any active direct connections.

Reconnaissance and Discovery Phases

There are several types of reconnaissance probes and discovery processes that can be used to identify active hosts or processes. For example, a simple PING sweep can be used to identify the active hosts on an IP network. A **PING sweep** is an operation that sends ICMP Echo Request packets to a range of IP addresses to determine which hosts are active.

A port probe is another reconnaissance process used to detect the UDP-based and TCP-based services running on a host. Figures 12-1 and 12-2 show the traces of a TCP port probe process. As you can see in these figures, the host 10.1.0.2 sends TCP handshake packets (SYN) to 10.1.0.1, incrementing the destination port number in each subsequent packet.

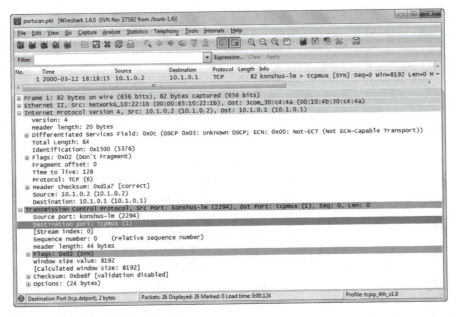

Figure 12-1 Initial TCP port probe
Source: Wireshark

Figures 12-1 and 12-2 show a simplistic TCP port probe. To escape detection from network protection schemes, an attacker typically varies the destination port number and interpacket time. The original location can also be disguised for the attacker by proxying attack probes through unwitting intermediary hosts, such as publicly available SOCKS and SQUID proxies, overly permissive FTP servers (FTP bounce attack), or zombie hosts. SOCKS is a client-server protocol, used in many companies and organizations, that enables a server to step between clients and external resources in order to screen and protect inside communications from the outside world. SQUID is an open-source program that caches Web and other Internet content on a UNIX-based proxy server closer to the user than the original content site (and thereby speeds repeat access times by eliminating longer Internet access paths). Because both of these services obscure actual points of origin for Internet communications, they can be used to disguise their real points of origin while performing their normal tasks and services. A zombie host is a computer that's been compromised, usually by malware that includes a Trojan

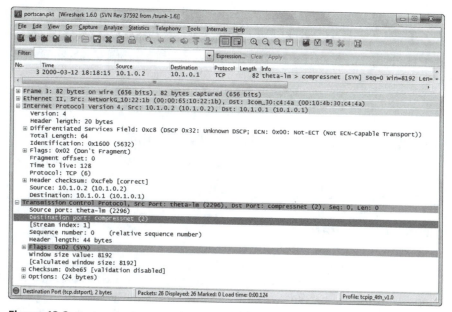

Figure 12-2 Port probe incrementing the destination port number by one in each attempt
Source: Wireshark

horse and remote control software so that it acts at the direction of a cracker, often without the knowledge (and invariably without the consent) of its owner.

The purpose of reconnaissance is to find out what you have and what is vulnerable. Tools such as **nmap,** a type of port scanner, are very effective in discretely identifying hosts, including their IP addresses, operating system types, and versions.

If you plan to use reconnaissance tools such as port scanners, vulnerability assessment tools, or similar software on your network, make sure you provide notification and request permission in advance. Unwitting network or security staff may otherwise respond to your efforts as they would to an actual attack.

Attack

Once the attacker determines vulnerabilities, he or she can attempt to exploit them. The attack may be a **brute force attack** that overwhelms the victim, or it may be a simple, elegant, minimal-packet process that confuses and disrupts operations on the victim. SYN Flood and Smurf are examples of brute force attacks.

Cover-Up

In an effort to escape detection, many attackers delete log files that could indicate an attack occurred. Therefore, **computer forensics,** an examination of any traces left behind by an attack, may be necessary. The integrity of such log files is of utmost importance because they are easily manipulated and might misreport or omit informative events or activities.

Common Attacks and Entry Points in More Detail

As you've learned, TCP/IP is by its very nature a trusting protocol stack. Over the years, designers, implementers, and product developers have tried to secure the protocol and plug holes or vulnerabilities whenever possible. The following sections provide more details about common attacks, about which all knowledgeable IP professionals must be concerned.

Viruses, Worms, and Trojan Horse Programs

There are several types of **malicious code**, which is also known as **malware**. This code can disrupt operations or corrupt data. **Viruses**, worms (often referred to as mobile code), and Trojan horses are three such types of malicious code.

Adware and Spyware

Adware is a type of software that opens the door for a compromised machine to display all kinds of unsolicited and unwanted advertising, often of an unsavory nature. **Spyware** is unsolicited and unwanted software that stealthily takes up unauthorized and uninvited residence on a computer. It then gathers information about its user(s), including account names, passwords, and other sensitive data it can glean during normal system operation, information that it ultimately exports to some malicious third party for misuse.

Denial of Service Attacks

Denial of service (DoS) attacks are a type of attack designed to interrupt or completely disrupt operations of a network device or network communications. By overloading a network device or confusing it in some way, an attacker can cause the device or network to deny service to other users or hosts on a network. The name "denial of service" originates from recognizing that an overloaded victim cannot provide services to its valid clients.

DoS-related attacks include SYN Flood, broadcast amplification attacks, and buffer overflow. All these attacks exist because protocols do not enforce rules for "operational exploitation"; rather, software implementations are required to enforce rules regulating usage of the protocol itself. These attacks are less complicated than other attacks, such as session hijacking, because their only goal is to break off communications rather than to divert stolen data or gain unauthorized access to a computer.

For example, older exploits against the BIND daemon, as well as exploits against the Sun Microsystem snmpXdmid service, could result in terminating those services, thereby creating a denial of service. Buffer overflows are discussed later in this chapter.

Distributed Denial of Service Attacks

Distributed denial of service (DDoS) attacks are DoS attacks that are launched from numerous devices. In August 2003, a DDoS attack brought down the Microsoft corporate Web site.

DDoS attacks consist of four main elements:

- Attacker
- Handler

- Agent
- Victim

The attacker comes from a host that sets up an attack sequence, as shown in Figure 12-3. Often, the attacker is nowhere to be found when an attack is actually launched. It sets up the attack to transpire minutes, hours, days, or even months after it has left the scene and covered its tracks. The attacker first locates a host that it can compromise. This compromised host becomes the **handler**, or manager, for the DDoS.

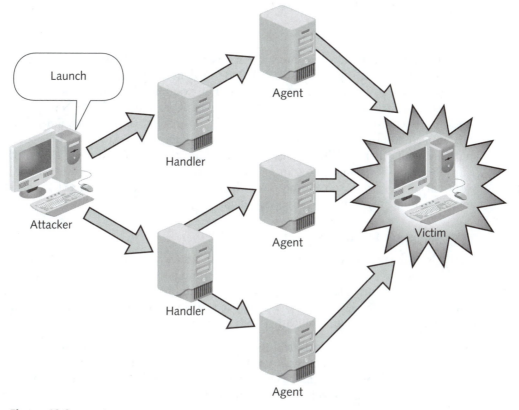

Figure 12-3 Attack sequence
© Cengage Learning 2013

The handler locates and recruits other insecure hosts to act as **agents**, or subordinate devices. It is interesting to note that there can be more than one handler in a sophisticated DDoS attack. There also can be more than one agent per handler. Some communications must occur between the handler and agent to manage their relationship. Often, a file on the handler lists the IP addresses or names of known agents. Likewise, the agents may keep information about their handlers.

Agents actually launch the attack on the victim. At a time determined by the attacker, a handler sends the agents a "go-ahead" message to begin the attack. The attacker is actually long gone by that point.

Buffer Overflows/Overruns

Buffer overflows are common attacks that, strictly speaking, are not related to TCP/IP. Instead, they exploit a weakness in programs that expect to receive a fixed amount of input. By sending more data than is expected, or planned for, an attacker can "overrun" a program's input buffer. In some cases, that extra data can be used to execute commands on the computer with the same privileges as the program it overruns. This is why you should avoid running processes such as IIS under the System, Administrator, or Domain Administrator accounts and instead set up separately named accounts, which don't need all-encompassing rights and privileges. Otherwise, compromise of the service might allow the compromiser to take over an entire system or domain.

Spoofing

Spoofing is borrowing identity information, such as an IP address, domain name, NetBIOS name, or TCP or UDP port numbers, to hide or deflect interest in attack activities. Several attacks are based on this spoofing technique. For example, there are some NetBIOS attacks in which an attacker sends spoofed NetBIOS Name Release or NetBIOS Name Conflict messages to a victim machine. This can force a victim to remove its own valid name from its name table and not respond to other valid NetBIOS requests. Now, the victim cannot communicate with other NetBIOS hosts, which may affect its ability to resolve NetBIOS names with WINS, block its ability to transfer files or communicate with other hosts on a local network, or even stymie some aspects of Windows DNS that link NetBIOS names to IP addresses, domains, and other important data.

TCP Session Hijacking

TCP session hijacking is a complex and difficult attack to mount. The purpose of such an attack is not to deny service but to masquerade as an authorized user to gain access to a system. An attacker must successfully communicate with both parties to an active TCP session—that is, with both the server and client involved. At the same time, the attacker must prevent these two parties from communicating with each other.

In theory, session hijacking is difficult because the attacker must sniff the connection between the victim and server and then wait until a TCP session is established, such as a Telnet session. Once established, the attacker must predict the next TCP sequence number and spoof the source address on packets to the client and server so it appears to the client that the attacker is actually the server.

Recall that the TCP protocol uses the sequence number to acknowledge data received from its session partner and to let the partner know how much data it is sending.

Once a session is hijacked, the attacker can send packets to the server to execute commands, change passwords, or worse. For a detailed description of a variant of this attack, visit *www.insecure.org/stf/iphijack.txt*.

Network Sniffing

One method of passive network attack is based on network "sniffing," or eavesdropping, on network communications using a protocol analyzer or other sniffing software. The same tool that you use in this course to observe and understand the contents and order of packets on an IP network can be deliberately misused in the wrong hands.

What can a network analyzer see? Plenty. Figure 12-4 and Figure 12-5 show how an analyzer can display unencrypted login names and passwords, respectively, from a standard FTP session.

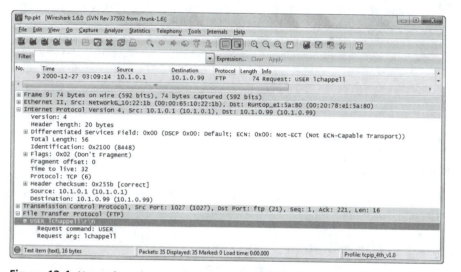

Figure 12-4 Network analyzer displaying unencrypted login name
Source: Wireshark

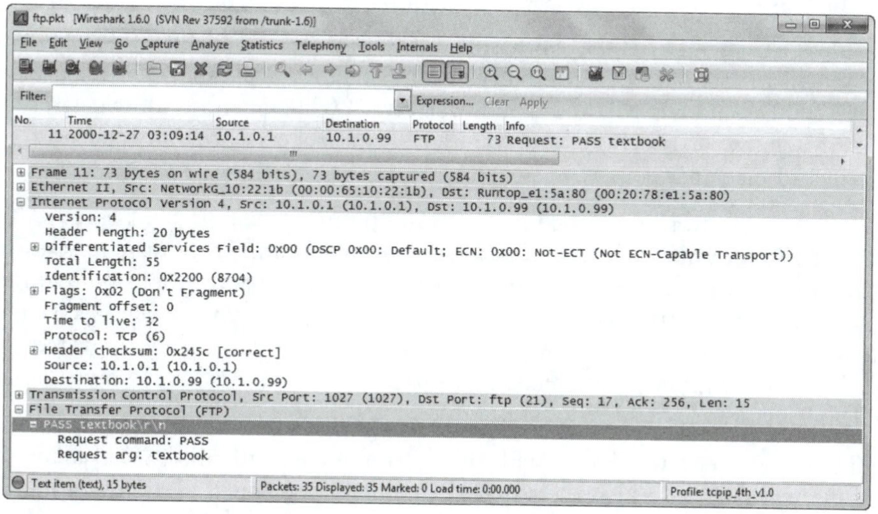

Figure 12-5 Network analyzer displaying unencrypted password
Source: Wireshark

12

Numerous network analyzers are available to eavesdrop on networks, including tcpdump (UNIX), OmniPeek (Windows), Network Monitor (Windows), and Wireshark.

There are also anti-sniff software packages available to detect and alert you to packet sniffers on your network. AntiSniff by SecuriTeam (formerly the L0pht group) is one example. Such packages are something of a hack themselves in that they bend the rules of networking by detecting NICs operating in promiscuous mode.

Anti-sniff software can't detect network analyzers on "mirrored" or "span" ports, nor can it detect analyzers using passive taps, because such ports can only receive incoming transmissions. They cannot transmit data, including ICMP Echo Reply packets, onto the network. This is important because most intrusion detection systems (IDSs) operate in promiscuous mode as well. This also makes it feasible for a sophisticated attacker to use an anti-sniff package to detect an IDS. Recognizing that an IDS is active permits an attacker to take extra precautions to avoid detection. You'll learn about IDSs later in this chapter.

Maintaining IP Security

The following sections cover some of the elements that must be included as part of routine security maintenance.

Applying Security Patches and Fixes

Many attacks take advantage of known operating system faults and security holes for which patches and fixes are freely available. It is, therefore, a lapse in security to allow such attacks to succeed because such success clearly demonstrates that administrators are delinquent in keeping their systems current with security updates.

For example, on July 16, 2003, Microsoft released Security Bulletin MS03-026. It warned system administrators that a vulnerability in the RPC implementation for Windows NT 4.0, Windows 2000, Windows XP, and Windows Server 2003—in short, all widely used modern versions of Windows except Windows Me—enabled attackers to run any code of their choosing on affected machines.

For good reason, Microsoft assigned its "Critical" severity rating (the highest possible) to this vulnerability. In an unprecedented outreach to customers, this dire warning was repeated a week later in a special mass e-mailing to all registered recipients of Microsoft's security bulletins and technical updates. Despite repeated warnings and copious news coverage, press reports indicated that perhaps over a million systems were infected by the Blaster worm or the Nachi (which exploited the vulnerability reported in MS03-026) within four weeks of the bulletin's initial release.

How did this happen? Interviews with victims reveal that administrators either missed or ignored the warnings or added the patch to the list they planned to apply during their next regularly scheduled maintenance interval. They were caught unprotected even though they were forewarned about potential attack.

Knowledge Base article 823980 is the best source on the RPC vulnerability (see *support.microsoft.com/?kbid=823980*). For Security Bulletin MS03-026, see *www.microsoft.com/technet/security/bulletin/MS03-026. mspx*.

In general, Microsoft security bulletins may be accessed or searched at the Microsoft Tech-Center Web site at *http://technet.microsoft.com/en-us/security/bulletin*. In fact, we urge all readers responsible for Windows systems to sign up for e-mail notification; you can do so on the Microsoft Technical Security Notifications page at *http://technet.microsoft.com/en-us/ security/dd252948*. Likewise, other system and software vendors typically maintain their own lists of security issues and concerns. They also make such information available through mailing lists, so you needn't miss any important notifications that may occur. You should make regular visits to their sites or sign up for their mailing lists, as your needs and preferences dictate.

It is, however, absolutely essential not just to know about security patches and fixes, as the debacle following the release of MS03-026 illustrates, but to install them (which can be a big headache in large production environments) before the unpatched systems can be exploited. Chronic failure to do so is what makes this issue such a huge security problem.

Security Update Process As with any product, a continual cycle of maintenance is required to ensure proper operation. Whether the operating system is Windows Server 2008, Windows 7, Linux, or even Cisco's IOS, it's necessary to look at long lists of bugs and vulnerabilities. The security update process takes into account the need to patch and maintain systems on an as-needed basis. Typically, this process involves four steps:

1. *Evaluate the vulnerability*—A vulnerability is critical if it affects software that is installed and used on a system. If a particular software package is not installed, the patch for that package is not relevant. If the software *is* installed but is not used, however, the patch is every bit as relevant as if the software were running. That's because if the software is simply installed, its vulnerabilities create potential points of attack (and entry).

2. *Retrieve the patch or update*—If a vulnerability is critical, download relevant software patches or updates.

3. *Test the patch or update*—It's important to test updates and patches prior to full-scale deployment. That's because any patch or update should be treated as unknown or unreliable code until it's tested. In some cases, when patches or updates are applied, unwanted results can occur. These include performance degradation, situations where newer patches or updates break older patches, and outright system or application failures. That's why you must test new patches and updates thoroughly and expeditiously. As the deployment of a patch is delayed because of insufficient testing or confidence in testing, the window of opportunity for an attacker to exploit related vulnerabilities widens.

4. *Deploy the patch or update*—After patches and updates are sufficiently tested and their impact on system performance and behavior is deemed negligible or nonexistent, they may be deployed on production systems. If patches or updates do cause problems, it may be necessary to devise workarounds or failsafe strategies. These should be designed

to prevent exploits from causing large-scale service interruptions or data losses when problems with patches stymie their deployment and vulnerabilities can't be remedied.

Knowing Which Ports to Block

Many exploits and attacks are based on common vulnerabilities. Table 12-1 indicates ports that should be blocked, if possible, to minimize chances of attack. If you implement our recommended pessimistic security approach, you'll block all such ports as a matter of course and allow only specific exceptions—for example, an upstream DNS server at a trusted ISP or service provider, from which you obtain DNS updates and with which you share your DNS zone files to improve external access to name-and-address mapping data.

Port	Service
TCP 21	FTP
TCP 22	SSH remote login
TCP 23	Telnet
TCP 25	SMTP
TCP 53	DNS
UDP 53	DNS
TCP 110	POP3
TCP 111	RPC
TCP 143	IMAP
UDP 161	SNMP

Table 12-1 Recommended ports to block
© Cengage Learning 2013

Using IP Security (IPSec)

The IP Security Protocol Working Group (IPSEC) defined **IP Security (IPSec)** as an optional add-in security layer to IPv4-based networks that want or need more security than the original implementation can provide. That explains why IPSec includes numerous components, all of which use cryptographic security services to support explicit and strong authentication, provide integrity and access controls for data shipped across a network, and mechanisms to ensure the confidentiality of IP datagrams.

IPSec is optional in IPv4 but is a required part of IPv6.

IPSec specifies an integrated set of security tools and the relationships among them. It also provides various kinds of security at the IP layer (and at higher layers). Specifically, RFC 2401 says the goals of IPSec are to provide the following kinds of security:

- *Access control*—**Access control** means restricting who may view or use certain resources, including access to bandwidth or a computer as well as access to information. Authentication is critical for access control. IPSec provides various forms of authentication. In addition, the standards mandate particular forms of access control for particular parts of the security system itself.

- *Connectionless integrity*—**Connectionless integrity** is defined in two parts. *Integrity* means a communication is not changed. *Connectionless* means that this integrity check does not extend to the connection itself (by detecting packets arriving out of sequence, for example). Instead, a function that provides connectionless integrity checks the integrity of each packet individually. IPSec's authentication capabilities support this goal.

- *Data origin authentication*—**Data origin authentication** is the ability to verify that the data received did in fact come from the named source. IPSec's authentication capabilities support this goal.

- *Protection against replays*—Replay attacks capture legitimate traffic, such as a sequence of packets from a user logon, and send the traffic again, masquerading as a trusted communications partner. Countermeasures against replays (**protection against replays**) include placing a unique and frequently changing token in each communication, so that seeing a previously used token in an supposedly new communication would prove it a replay and thereby invalidate it. IPSec provides a form of partial sequence integrity.

- *Confidentiality*—**Confidentiality** prevents unauthorized people from viewing communications. IPSec supports the use of a variety of encryption tools to provide confidentiality.

- *Limited traffic flow confidentiality*—By supporting certain types of tunneling, IPSec can, to some extent, hide the true path between two communications partners; this is referred to as **limited traffic flow confidentiality**. It prevents an adversary from knowing who is talking to whom, or when.

To achieve the security goals in the preceding list, IPSec relies on a whole suite of applications and security protocols. The most important of these are the **Authentication Header (AH)** and the **Encapsulating Security Payload (ESP)** header. AH specifies the true origin of a packet, thereby preventing address spoofing and connection theft; it provides integrity checking and a limited defense against replay attacks. ESP provides encryption services under IPSec. (IPSec, AH, and ESP were discussed in Chapter 3.)

In addition, IPSec relies on a variety of protocols to handle the generation and distribution of keys as well as the exchange of other security data required to coordinate secure communications among partners. These include the Internet Key Exchange (IKE) protocol, the Internet Security Association and Key Management Protocol (ISAKMP), the IP security Domain of Interpretation (DOI) for ISAKMP, and tools specified in other drafts and RFCs. Individual algorithms, such as Triple-DES encryption (3DES), are covered in their own RFCs or drafts. Compression, though not strictly a part of IPSec, must be used in a way that is compatible with encryption and authentication. RFC 2393 specifies the IP Compression (IPComp) standards. Various parts of IPSec support negotiation of compression techniques.

Protecting the Perimeter of the Network

The following are some important devices and services that you can use to help protect the perimeter of your networks:

- *Bastion host*—In medieval times, a bastion was a fort designed to repel the attacks of enemies and prevent their advances into the inner keep of a castle. In network security terms, a **bastion host** is a hardened computer specifically designed to resist and oppose illicit or unwanted attempts at entry and whose job is to guard the boundary between internal and external networks. Thus, firewall services, proxy servers, and IDSs are usually situated on some type of bastion host. Normally, bastion hosts run only software related to their boundary management functions. It's not a good idea to use them for more routine network services (such as database, file and print, e-mail, and so forth), not only because that exposes them to direct attack but because you want bastion hosts to concentrate entirely on their primary functions of protecting your network boundaries.

- *Boundary (or border) router*—A **boundary router,** also known as a **border router,** sits on the boundary between networks (usually between private networks under the purview of some organization and public networks where "anything goes"). Because such routers often block access on the basis of IP addresses, domain names, or socket addresses, these devices sometimes are called screening routers. On the best-protected networks, outside attackers must penetrate a screening router before they can even begin to attack a firewall. Often on such networks, a kind of demilitarized zone is defined between the screening router and the firewall, where externally accessible resources (those "compromisable hosts" we talked about earlier) also might reside.

- *Demilitarized zone (DMZ)*—A **demilitarized zone (DMZ)** is a sort of virtual "no-man's land" or buffer area that sits between an internal network and the outside world (usually the Internet) and that's accessible to both outsiders and insiders. Many organizations that host their own Internet servers or services situate them in a DMZ (with private copies of the same information safely ensconced somewhere on the inside network) as a way of making them public without completely exposing them to the outside world. It's common for a screening router, or a screening router and a firewall, to be installed between the DMZ and the outside world. Likewise, it's common for a firewall, or a firewall and a screening router, to be installed between the DMZ and the inside world.

- *Firewall*—A **firewall** is a specially "hardened" software service or software/ hardware product that erects a barrier in order to inspect and control traffic flow between networks (usually between networks that are inside and outside a boundary). Firewalls operate at the Internet (Layer 3), Transport (Layer 4), and Application (Layers 5 through 7) layers of the TCP/IP network model. Thus, firewalls can inspect the payloads of IP packets and follow sequences of such packets to determine if higher-level attacks are underway as well as to inspect domain names, IP and port addresses, and other Layer 3 information. Firewalls often include proxy server software and IDSs as part of their overall configurations so that all boundary-checking facilities are on a single hardened device.

- *Network address translation*—Network address translation (NAT) software permits internal network addresses to be "translated" into public network addresses when packets leave inside networks so that only public IP addresses are exposed on the public Internet. This prevents would-be hackers from learning much about the addressing scheme inside a private network, which goes a long way toward foiling break-in attempts. NAT often is used in tandem with private IP addresses, as defined in RFC 1918, as an extra security mechanism. (There's nothing inherently security related about using NAT, but because private IP addresses can't be routed on the public Internet, that makes it nearly impossible to spoof such addresses in an external attack.)

- *Proxy server*—This is a special set of software services that interposes itself between users and servers so that users connect with a proxy service that then connects to a target service rather than having users connect directly with services. This gives proxy software a chance to block unwanted types of access or connections and inspect user behavior for suspicious activities. Proxy server software often runs on firewalls because firewalls define the boundary between "inside" and "outside" on most networks.

- *Screening host*—When users from outside the network attach to a service inside the network, they actually attach to the firewall, which establishes a proxy session into the private side of the network from there. Thus, the firewall appears to be the **screening host** upon which all externally accessible services reside, even though this is not usually the case.

- *Screening router*—Also known as a border router; the term **screening router** refers to the ways in which such devices can be used to filter inbound and/or outbound traffic on the basis of IP and port addresses, domain names, and requested protocols or services.

Major Firewall Elements Should you find yourself considering a firewall, be aware that firewalls usually incorporate four major elements:

- *Screening router functions* permit the firewall to block or filter traffic according to numerous values or criteria (including domain name, IP address, port address, and message type).

- *Proxy service functions* permit the firewall to interpose itself in all communications between networks to protect address privacy, perform NAT services, and monitor for suspicious activities.

- *"Stateful inspection" of packet sequences and services* means that the firewall makes decisions to permit or deny a packet based on other packets. Compared to a **screening firewall**, in which all traffic to a given port is blocked regardless of any other packet, a stateful firewall is more sophisticated. For instance, it does not allow a TCP packet with the SYN-ACK flag to pass unless it previously saw a TCP packet between the same source and destination with the SYN flag set. Likewise, it does not allow an ICMP Echo Reply to pass unless it previously saw an ICMP Echo Request. This allows it to prevent the kinds of attacks that only reveal themselves over time, based on ongoing patterns of behavior. (For example, DoS attacks and dictionary password attacks both involve highly repetitive network traffic patterns.) By watching for such patterns and blocking them as they're noticed, stateful inspection permits a firewall to keep operating even when attacks are underway. This also is a function associated with IDSs.

- *Virtual private network services* deal with systems and services that do not themselves encrypt any traffic. Earlier, we mentioned that one way to accommodate inherently insecure services that send account names and passwords in the clear (unencrypted) is to embed them within VPN connections, which normally encrypt all traffic. (Strictly speaking, VPNs use tunneling protocols and need not encrypt tunneled traffic; practically speaking, virtually all such traffic is encrypted to provide an extra layer of privacy and protection.) Thus, it should come as no surprise that this kind of functionality is becoming increasingly important on firewalls.

We hope it's clear that any firewall is like a router in that it must have at least two network interfaces (and IP addresses) to do its job: one for the outer side of the connection and the other for the inner side of the connection, where the firewall forms the boundary between the two. It is also not unusual for firewalls to offer what are called reverse proxy services, which makes it possible for the firewall to act as a screening host and present the external appearance that all internal services are situated on the firewall itself.

Basics of Proxy Servers Proxy servers act as the dispatcher or intermediary between clients on an internal network and servers on external networks, such as the Internet. The proxy server accepts requests from clients, such as for files or Web pages, masks the client's IP address, and forwards them to external servers. When the external server returns the requested resource, the proxy server passes it along to the client. A few benefits of a proxy server are filtering, security, and caching.

A proxy server can also perform "reverse proxying," in which external clients request resources from certain internal servers. The proxy sends requests to the internal server and then delivers the resources to the client. Reverse proxying explains how a proxy server can screen addresses on the public Internet as well as prevent external users from achieving direct access to internal resources. This is how many companies block employees from accessing sites with questionable content, based on domain name or IP address filters. In fact, a proxy server can operate at the Application layer and block specific newsgroups in a newsreader as well.

Another important proxy behavior is called caching. When users request remote resources (such as particular Web pages), a proxy server can store those pages locally for some time after the requests. If those pages are requested again before they time out of the cache, the request can be satisfied locally rather than requiring another HTTP "get" operation to re-read those same pages from the original server. On sites where users are active and multiple users access identical materials, caching can improve performance for users as well as lower bandwidth consumption on the public Internet. That's what we call a "win-win" situation!

However, a cache is also a valuable location for a system attack because it makes pages previously viewed accessible to other users. For this reason, network administrators should be on the lookout for cache-related exploits and apply all relevant patches and fixes to cache collection and management software.

Implementing Firewalls

When implementing boundary controls, you often link your network and its users to the Internet. Although it's possible to just link an internal network to the Internet without managing the boundary between them, it's blatantly irresponsible to do so. Even a network with no information assets worth protecting should avoid taking such a chance (what amounts to no security policy) because it could be used as a launching point for a DoS attack, which could lead to significant liability issues. On the other hand, it's worth noting that the most secure networks allow no connections to the Internet at all and usually operate a separate unclassified network if their users require such access. They even go to extreme lengths to make sure that users can't transfer files from the secure network to the unsecured network (including disabling or removing floppy drives and other removable media from the secured network's computers).

Step-by-Step Firewall Planning and Implementing Because most security policies operate somewhere between the two extremes of "anything goes" (totally optimistic) and "no connection" (totally pessimistic), you will find the following set of steps useful when planning and implementing firewalls and proxy servers on your networks:

1. *Plan*—Before you actually acquire a firewall, you should research firewalls in general and assess your needs in particular. The planning phase consists of reviewing what's available, selecting the most likely candidates, obtaining information, and analyzing what you learn.

   You should become familiar with security-related mailing lists or newsgroups to look for late-breaking reports on attacks, exploits, or known software problems or deficiencies. Although vendors are a good source for such information, they're not always that willing to share bad news with you. Therefore, it's important to check user information sources, security advisory groups, and other more neutral sources of information to make sure you're getting the whole story.

   If a vendor offers training or consulting services to help you through these phases, investigate those offerings. You might also want to ask the vendor, (as well as the broader community) for a consulting referral to ensure access to expert help if and when you need it.

2. *Establish requirements*—Before you can use a firewall, you must know what you want it to do and how you will use it. To establish requirements, you must document the characteristics of your network environment, decide what traffic you want to permit and what traffic you want to disallow, and apply your security policy to your decisions to make sure all the pieces fit together properly.

3. *Install*—Having obtained a firewall (and proxy server and/or IDS, where relevant), you must install the related hardware and software to put it to work. Start out by placing it off the beaten track; in other words, when you bring up the firewall for the first time, it shouldn't be in the production role of managing the boundary right away. Run it in a controlled environment, out of public view, until it's ready to go into place during the implementation phase discussed later.

4. *Configure*—Once the physical elements and the software that goes with them are installed, the real fun begins. You must research and analyze the firewall's default configuration and learn how to alter it to meet your specific requirements. Try to make as few assumptions as possible, and verify the settings you chose against the firewall's documentation. If you're questioning a specific setting, check the manufacturer's Web site for a support forum and then search for the setting name. It's likely that others have had the same concern. Also, contact the vendor and make sure you have the most

current version of software and the most up-to-date patches and fixes. Products sometimes sit on shelves for months before passing into buyers' hands, and this kind of technology sits still for no one. Doing this will protect you from potential exploits when you implement your firewall.

5. *Test*—Inspect the configuration settings you made for the firewall and related software. Compare them to your requirements to ensure your requirements are being met. Being human, you will find the occasional mistake that needs cleaning up, and you may discover unexpected side effects from factory defaults, which require change or correction.

6. *Attack*—During this phase, you should run a port scanner, a security monitor or analyzer, and other tools an attacker might use against your network. Wireless networks often are obvious points of outside attack, so using scanning or probing tools such as Kismet (*www.insecure.org/tools.html*) or NetStumbler (*www.netstumbler.com*) to inspect your wireless networks is every bit as important as doing it for your wired networks. The idea is to bang on your configuration to see how it looks and behaves from the outside. Obviously, you want to exercise as much of your firewall's capabilities as you can to see how it behaves when under attack.

7. *Tune*—In response to what you learn in the test and attack phases, refine your configuration and do your best to meet your security policy's requirements to the extent that the hardware and software allow. Repeat the **test-attack-tune cycle** (Steps 5 through 7) as many times as necessary until no changes are needed from one iteration to the next.

8. *Implement*—Now that you've fixed the defaults, rooted out faulty assumptions, and closed the door on potential points of attack, you're ready to put the firewall (and related software) into production. At this point, you've checked everything that you can to make sure you've created as secure an implementation as possible, so you should be able to proceed with confidence.

9. *Monitor and maintain*—Post-implementation is when the real work begins. You must monitor event logs, traffic statistics, and error messages from the firewall, but you also should monitor security newsgroups and mailing lists for new exploits (particularly those that might involve your environment). That way, you'll be ready to make the necessary adjustments.

Our last word on this subject: Don't ever work straight out of the box with a firewall or proxy server without checking for additional changes, updates, patches, fixes, and workarounds. The state of the art has probably advanced since that product went into the box, so it's your job to catch up!

Remember that 90 percent of the costs of running a system are related to maintenance (not acquisition and training), so maintenance and upkeep are the most important parts of managing a firewall. In fact, maintenance and upkeep are key ingredients in keeping any network safe, sound, and secure, because the security landscape is always changing, and there are new attacks, exploits, and vulnerabilities to contend with daily.

Roles of IDS and IPS in IP Security

An **intrusion detection system (IDS)** is a special-purpose software system that inspects ongoing patterns of network traffic for signs of impending or active attack. IDSs make it easier to automate recognition of and response to potential attacks and other suspicious forms of network traffic. Unlike systems that require human monitoring and pattern recognition skills to be applied to network traffic and usage patterns (including firewalls that lack built-in IDS capability), IDSs continuously scan network traffic, seeking to recognize intrusion attempts in real time and respond to them as they occur. Most IDSs disconnect a user who exhibits suspicious behavior and run a reverse DNS lookup to identify that user's real IP address and location (as much as is possible). Some IDSs can even send e-mails to intermediate ISPs to inform them that their sites are being used to stage or relay attacks. Most IDSs automatically gather records of suspicious behavior to create a "paper trail" should prosecution occur.

The problem with old-fashioned manual systems is that any hope of catching an attacker requires network administrators to notice immediately whenever an attack is underway. Also, IDSs can perform ongoing, continuous statistical analyses of traffic and individual account characteristics. Thus, they can detect "slow break-in attempts" (where repeated password guesses may be deliberately spaced over time to escape detection) and unusual usage patterns in user accounts. IDSs also can stifle DoS attacks and deal with lots of other problems that humans might not notice until it's too late.

Increasingly, firewalls include hooks to allow them to interact with IDSs, or they include their own built-in IDS capabilities. We believe that automating this function will become increasingly prevalent and affordable as Internet access and related security concerns become even more prevalent.

In fact, there's already a new class of software that deals with intrusions. Instead of an intrusion detection system (IDS), this is called an intrusion prevention system, or IPS. Whereas IDSs are more or less passive and concern themselves primarily with monitoring and logging possible intrusion attempts, IPSs are active (even proactive) and concern themselves with recognizing and foiling recognizable attacks or typical pre-attack behaviors such as footprinting. In fact, IPSs provide another form of access control and work something like an Application-layer firewall.

IPSs make access control decisions on the basis of application content rather than by looking at IP addresses or port numbers, as most traditional firewalls do. IPSs sometimes also act on a host to deny potentially malicious activity. Thus, rather than being competitive, IPS and IDS are complementary and are often used together. In fact, an IPS must be able to work as a good IDS to prevent false positives (patterns of activity that look like intrusion attempts but that do not represent actual intrusions). What makes IPSs attractive is that by also focusing on unwanted access or behavior (such as applications accessing or altering Windows Registry keys without permission, altering or replacing system files, and so forth), they can prevent attacks for which detailed signatures may not yet be available.

Honeypots and Honeynets

Given their importance for network security—specifically, for diverting attackers from other more serious goals—we'd be remiss if we failed to mention honeypots and honeynets. A **honeypot** is a computer system deliberately set up to entice and trap attackers. Although a honeypot may appear to be part of a network, it is actually isolated and protected, and it is stocked with information or resources designed to look attractive to attackers. Honeypots are useful for surveillance and also provide early warning of potential attacks.

A **honeynet** takes the honeypot concept and broadens it from a single system to what looks like a network of such systems. That explains why some experts define a honeynet as a collection of two or more honeypots on the same network. Honeynets are more common on large, dispersed, or heterogeneous networks where a single honeypot may not be enough to permit administrators to use them for surveillance or early warning of attack at multiple sites.

For more information on honeypots or honeynets, visit The Honeynet Project at *www.honeynet.org*.

Chapter Summary

- In security terms, an attack represents an attempt to break into or otherwise compromise the privacy and integrity of an organization's information assets. An exploit reveals a vulnerability, whereas a break-in is usually the result of a successful attack.

- In its original form, TCP/IP implemented an optimistic security model, given that little or no protection was built into its protocols and services. Recent improvements, enhancements, and updates to TCP/IP have converted the protocol suite to a more pessimistic security model. Unfortunately, TCP/IP remains prey to many kinds of attacks and vulnerabilities, including denials of service (which may be from a single source or distributed across numerous sources), service attacks, service and implementation vulnerabilities, man-in-the-middle attacks, and more.

- Basic principles of IP security include avoiding unnecessary exposure by blocking all unused ports and installing only necessary services. They also include judicious use of address filtering to block known malefactors and stymie address spoofing. We advocate adoption of a pessimistic security policy wherein access is denied, by default, and allowed only with strict exceptions. Finally, it's a good idea to monitor the Internet for security-related news and events—especially news of exploits—and regularly attack your own systems and networks to learn how to block or defeat documented attacks.

- It's necessary to protect systems and networks from malicious code such as viruses, worms, and Trojan horses. Such protection means using modern antivirus software, which should be part of any well-built security policy.

- Would-be attackers usually engage in a well-understood sequence of activities, called reconnaissance and discovery, as they attempt to footprint systems and networks, looking for points of attack. Judicious monitoring of network activity, especially through an IDS, can help block such attacks (and may even be able to identify their sources, if not their perpetrators).

- Maintaining a secure network boundary remains a key ingredient for good system and network security. This usually involves the use of screening routers, firewalls, and proxy servers, which may be on separate devices or may be integrated into a single device that straddles the network boundary. Some network architectures also make use of a DMZ between the internal and external networks, where services can more safely be exposed to the outside world and where inside users can access proxy, caching, and other key services for external network access.

- Keeping operating systems secure in the face of new vulnerabilities is a necessary and ongoing process. This process includes evaluation of the vulnerability, retrieval of the update, testing of the update, and deployment of the patch or update.

- A honeypot is a computer system deliberately set up to entice and trap attackers. A honeynet takes the honeypot concept and broadens it from a single system to what looks like a network of such systems.

Key Terms

access control   The act of restricting who may view or use certain resources, including access to bandwidth or a computer as well as access to information.

adware   A type of software that displays all kinds of unsolicited and unwanted advertising on a compromised computer; the advertising is often of an unsavory nature.

agent   The device that inflicts the attack on the victim in a DDoS attack.

anonymous access   A type of IP service access wherein users need not provide explicit account and password information; this applies to FTP and Web services, among others.

attack   An attempt to break into or compromise a system or network, or to deny access to that system or network.

attacker   The actual source of an attack sequence. Clever attackers in a DDoS attack often hide behind a handler and an agent.

Authentication Header (AH)   A header in an IP packet and/or the security protocol that uses that extension header. AH specifies the true origin of a packet by preventing address spoofing and connection theft, and it provides integrity checking and a limited defense against replay attacks.

back door   An undocumented and illicit point of entry into a system or a network, often built into software or a system by its original engineers.

bastion host   A specially hardened computer designed to straddle the boundary between internal and external networks, where firewalls, proxy servers, IDSs, and border routing functions normally operate.

border router   A network device that straddles the boundary between internal and external networks and manages both the inbound traffic permitted to reach the inside networks and the outbound traffic allowed to proceed beyond the boundary.

boundary router   *See* border router.

break-in   An attempt to impersonate a valid user on a system or otherwise gain entry to a system or network in order to obtain illicit access to the resources and information it contains.

12

brute force attack An attack that typically consists of numerous requests for service. This type of attack focuses on overloading the resources of the victim, including the CPU, disk access, or other local resources.

brute force password attack A systematic attempt to guess all possible password strings as a way of trying to break into a system.

compromised host A host on which unauthorized access was gained. A compromised host can no longer be considered a trusted system and should be handled according to the site's incident response and recovery procedure.

computer forensics The process of examining the "footprints" that an attacker leaves behind. Some areas of interest include the temp files—deleted files that remain in the Recycle Bin or in a recoverable state—and local system memory.

confidentiality The ability to restrict access to some resource by any but authorized users. The typical approach is encryption, rendering the data unusable without the keys and algorithm needed to decrypt it.

connectionless integrity In IPSec or similar security regimes, the ability to provide integrity, but without the ability to ensure the connection itself.

cracker A person who attempts to break into a system by impersonating valid users or by using other methods of penetration that do not necessarily involve deep system skills or knowledge.

data origin authentication In IPSec or similar security regimes, the ability to verify the source of received information or to check that the source possesses some trusted token.

demilitarized zone (DMZ) An intermediate network that sits between the boundary of an organization's internal networks and one or more external networks, such as the Internet. A DMZ is usually separated from external networks by a screening router, and from internal networks by a screening router and a firewall.

denial of service (DoS) attack A type of network attack that involves overwhelming a server with invalid, malformed, or illegitimate requests for service.

discovery process The process of learning which computers or processes are running on a network.

distributed denial of service (DDoS) attack A special, coordinated attack in which multiple hosts wage denial of service attacks at the same time. The result is a massive overflow of pending service requests that can overwhelm a server or even a server farm.

Encapsulating Security Payload (ESP) A header in an IP packet and/or the security protocol that uses that extension header. ESP provides encryption under IPSec.

exploit A documented system break-in technique that's published for potential reuse by others.

firewall A special type of bastion host that performs traffic inspection and screening to prevent unauthorized external access to internal networks and manage internal access to external networks.

hacker A person who uses computer and communications knowledge to exploit information or functionality of a device.

handler A manager system in a DDoS attack. The handler is a compromised host on which an attacker has placed DDoS code; it locates agents to perform the actual attack on a victim system.

hole A system or software vulnerability that defeats, bypasses, or ignores system or software security settings and restrictions.

honeynet A network that contains two or more honeypots, which are computers set up to deliberately attract, entice, and entrap would-be attackers.

honeypot A computer system deliberately set up to attract, entice, and entrap would-be attackers, often by being made to appear part of a larger network (when it is actually isolated and protected) and by exposing apparently valuable or interesting information and resources.

intrusion detection system (IDS) A special-purpose software system that inspects ongoing patterns of network traffic for signs of impending or active attack. Most IDSs can foil break-in attempts and also attempt to establish the identity of the attacker or attackers. Best of all, IDSs work automatically and require no immediate human attention to handle most attacks.

IP Security (IPSec) A security specification supporting various forms of encryption and authentication, along with key management and related supporting functions.

IP service attack A system attack that concentrates on known characteristics and vulnerabilities of one or more specific IP services or that uses well-known port addresses associated with such services for its own nefarious ends.

IP spoofing An attack in which the attacker sends packets to a target host but substitutes the IP address of another host on the LAN or the Internet. This makes the traffic appear to come from this host. This is typically done to bypass access control lists on a router or on the host itself

limited traffic flow confidentiality In IPSec, the ability to defeat traffic analysis by hiding the path, frequency, source, destination, and volume of traffic between correspondents.

malicious code A program that is written with the intent of harming, compromising, or disrupting host operations.

malware A synonym for malicious code that identifies a broad class of programs written with the intent of harming, compromising, or disrupting host operations.

man-in-the-middle (MITM) attack A type of system or network attack whereby an attacking system interposes itself between the target network and the next normal link on that network's usual routing chain.

nmap A port scanner that is primarily UNIX or Linux based, nmap should be part of any IP administrator's attack toolkit.

optimistic security model The original basis for TCP/IP security, this model assumes that it is safe to enforce little or no security on normal network communications.

packet sniffing A technique that involves using a protocol analyzer to decode and examine the contents of IP packets to attempt to identify sensitive information, including accounts and passwords, for subsequent break-in attempts or other nefarious purposes.

packet snooping *See* packet sniffing.

personnel security The aspect of security that concentrates on informing users about security matters and training them on proper application of security policies, procedures, and practices.

pessimistic security model A model of system and network security that assumes it is always necessary to enforce strong security measures and so calls for access to all resources to be denied to all users by default, then allowed only to those with a legitimate need to access such resources on a case-by-case basis.

physical security That aspect of security that concerns itself with limiting physical access to system and network components to prevent unauthorized users from attempting direct attacks on such components. Because lax physical security can easily lead to compromise, strong physical security is always a good idea.

PING sweep An ICMP Echo-based operation used to locate active devices on a network. The term "sweep" refers to the process of testing an entire range of IP addresses for active devices.

port scanner A special-purpose software tool that cycles through either well-known TCP and UDP ports with easy vulnerabilities or all possible TCP and UDP port addresses, looking for open ports that then can be probed for access or exploited for vulnerabilities.

protection against replays The ability to distinguish between "live" traffic from a trusted source and copies of such traffic masquerading as authentic communications. Protection against replays is typically based on packet sequence numbering and checking.

remote logon service Any type of network service that permits users elsewhere on a network to use the network to log on to a system as if they were attached locally while operating remotely. Such services are favorite attack points because they're designed to give outsiders access to systems and service.

rexec An abbreviation for *remote execution*, this is a BSD UNIX remote utility that permits network users to execute single commands on a remote host.

rpr An abbreviation for *remote print*, this is a BSD UNIX remote utility that permits network users to print a file on a remote host.

rsh An abbreviation for *remote shell*, this is a BSD UNIX remote utility that permits network users to launch and operate a session on a remote host.

r-utils An abbreviation for *Remote Utilities*, this is a collection of software programs, originally included as part of BSD UNIX v4.2, designed to provide remote access and login services for users. Hence, they are a common point of attack.

screening firewall A firewall model whereby all traffic to a given port is blocked, regardless of any other packet. All traffic traversing the firewall must be explicitly defined.

screening host The role that a firewall or proxy server plays when presenting an internal network service for external consumption.

screening router A boundary router that's been configured to monitor and filter inbound traffic on the basis of IP or port addresses, domain names, or spoofing attempts.

security policy A document that represents the concrete manifestation of an organization's requirements for security practices, rules, and procedures, and which identifies all assets worth protecting and lays out disaster or business recovery processes should system loss or compromise occur.

session hijacking An IP attack technique whereby an imposter takes over an ongoing communications session between a client and server, thereby assuming whatever rights and permissions the hijacked session may enjoy. This is a difficult technique to pull off, and recent changes to TCP sequence numbers make this harder to accomplish today than it was prior to their implementation.

software security The aspect of security that focuses on monitoring and maintaining systems and software to prevent and oppose as many potential sources of attack as possible. From this perspective, software security is both a mindset and a regular routine rather than a "set it and forget it" kind of activity.

spoofing Spoofing occurs when incoming IP traffic exhibits addressing mismatches. Address spoofing occurs when an external interface ferries traffic that purports to originate inside a network, or when a user presents an IP address that doesn't match a domain name. Domain name spoofing occurs when a reverse lookup of an IP address does not match the domain from where the traffic claims to originate.

spyware   Unsolicited and unwanted software that takes up stealthy, unauthorized, and uninvited residence on a computer and gathers information about its user(s), including account names, passwords, and other sensitive data it can glean during normal system operation, which it will ultimately export for misuse to some malicious third party.

stealthy attacker   An attacker that hides its tracks. Stealthy attackers may ensure that no log entries implicate their actions and that no live connections remain after they launch their attacks.

test-attack-tune cycle   The most important part of deploying security systems or components, this set of activities should be repeated until test and attack operations produce no further changes to system or component configuration or tuning.

user impersonation   A system or network attack technique whereby an unauthorized user, to gain entry, presents valid credentials that rightfully belong to an authorized user and then exploits whatever rights and privileges the impersonated user's identity allows.

victim   The focus of an attack.

virus   A code that can spread through a machine to alter or destroy files.

vulnerability   Any aspect of a system that is open to attack, especially any well-known protocol, service, subsystem, or hole that is documented and relatively easy to exploit.

Review Questions

1. More than 70 percent of all network or system break-ins originate outside an organization's network boundary. True or false?

2. Which of the following does *not* account for the vast majority of losses of data or services from systems and networks?

    a. viruses

    b. power outages

    c. internal security breaches

    d. external security breaches

3. Which of the following statements best explains why physical security for network and system components and devices is so important?

    a. Physical access to components and devices is necessary for successful penetration of hardened systems.

    b. Any good security policy must address physical security concerns.

    c. Physical access to components and devices makes it possible for a knowledgeable intruder to break into such systems.

    d. None of the above; physical security is not an important concern.

4. Which of the following correctly lists the three legs of network security?

    a. network, boundary, software

    b. physical, personnel, system and network security

    c. physical, personnel, component

    d. physical, network, software

12

5. Which of the following document types is an attacker most likely to use when attempting to break into a system or network?

   a. attack profile

   b. exploit

   c. security policy

   d. password hash

6. TCP/IP implements a pessimistic security policy. True or false?

7. When an attacker systematically tries all conceivable passwords for an account, what is this attack called?

   a. brute force attack

   b. session hijacking

   c. packet sniffing

   d. brute force password attack

8. Which of the following types of attack is the least likely to result in damage or loss of data?

   a. IP service attack

   b. man-in-the-middle attack

   c. DoS or DDoS attack

   d. virus

   e. buffer overflow

9. By default, which of the following IP services send(s) accounts and passwords in clear text when authenticating users? (Choose all that apply.)

   a. FTP

   b. Telnet

   c. Stelnet

   d. Web access using SSL

10. Which one of the following common characteristics makes both FTP and HTTP (Web) vulnerable IP services?

   a. TCP transport

   b. long timeout variables

   c. anonymous login

   d. protocols that encrypt data

11. Which of the following definitions best describes a back door?

   a. a weak spot or known point of attack on any common operating system

   b. an undocumented and illicit point of entry into a system or application

   c. any protocol, service, or system facility known to be susceptible to attack

   d. an alternate, but legitimate, means of entry into a system or application

12. Which of the following best describes a vulnerability?
   a. a weak spot or known point of attack on any common operating system
   b. an undocumented and illicit point of entry into a system or application
   c. any protocol, service, or system facility known to be susceptible to attack
   d. an alternate, but legitimate, means of entry into a system or application

13. Which of the following is *not* a recognized principle of IP security?
   a. Avoid unnecessary exposure.
   b. Block all unused ports.
   c. Prevent address spoofing.
   d. Enable access by default, deny access by exception.
   e. Do unto yourself before others do unto you.

14. Which of the following are examples of malicious code? (Choose all that apply.)
   a. virus
   b. worm
   c. Trojan horse
   d. Windows 7

15. Which of the following could be examples of the desired affect of a DoS attack? (Choose all that apply.)
   a. interrupting operations
   b. powering down operations
   c. completely disrupting operations
   d. upgrading operations

16. Which of the four main elements in a DDoS attack is least likely to be actively engaged when an attack occurs?
   a. attacker
   b. handler
   c. agent
   d. victim

17. Which two of the four main elements in a DDoS attack coordinate and execute the actual attack? (Choose two.)
   a. attacker
   b. handler
   c. agent
   d. victim

12

18. What technique might an attacker use to hide or deflect interest in attack behaviors or activities?

    a. user impersonation

    b. spoofing

    c. man-in-the-middle attack

    d. reconnaissance

19. What technique might an attacker use to forge replies to senders and receivers?

    a. IP service attack

    b. back door attack

    c. DDos and DoS attack

    d. man-in-the-middle attack

20. What is the most common step that attackers take to attempt to escape detection after a successful break-in?

    a. Reconfigure the system to give themselves administrative privileges.

    b. Delete log files to remove all traces of the attack.

    c. Reformat all hard drives to destroy any potential evidence.

    d. Copy all password files for other systems.

21. Which of the following statements best explains the importance of applying system and application patches and fixes?

    a. As vulnerabilities or exploits are exposed, system and application vendors provide patches and fixes to repair, defeat, or mitigate potential attacks. Thus, it's usually a good idea to apply them.

    b. Applying patches and fixes is an important part of general system and application maintenance.

    c. It's necessary to apply only patches and fixes that are relevant to actual, ongoing security problems.

    d. It's a good idea to wait until a patch or fix has been around for a while to see if it works appropriately.

22. DNS functions on which UDP and/or TCP ports? (Choose all that apply.)

    a. TCP 53

    b. TCP 21

    c. UDP 21

    d. UDP 53

23. IPSec provides enhanced security features at which layer?

    a. IP layer

    b. ground layer

    c. data link layer

    d. physical layer

24. What type of computer should be used to house firewall and/or proxy server software?

    a. secure host

    b. bastion host

    c. screening host

    d. screening router

25. Which of the following tools are candidates for an attack toolkit? (Choose all that apply.)

    a. Wireshark

    b. nmap

    c. tcpdump

    d. footprinting tools

Hands-On Projects

The following Hands-On Projects assume that you are working in a Windows 7 or Windows Vista environment, that you installed the Wireshark for Windows software, and that you have acquired the trace (data) files for this book as provided by your instructor.

Hands-On Project 12-1

Time Required: 10 minutes

Objective: Examine a local scan in Wireshark.

Description: This project lets you examine a trace file of an ARP-based reconnaissance probe. As you scroll through the ARP broadcasts, you should notice that this scan has some redundancy built in—for example, it repeats a broadcast for 10.0.0.55 and a few other IP addresses.

To examine a local scan:

1. Start the **Wireshark for Windows** program.

2. Click **File**, click **Open**, select the trace file **arpscan.pkt** included with your data files, and then click the **Open** button. The packet summary window appears. This file contains a reconnaissance probe using ARP broadcasts to find active hosts.

3. Select **Packet #1** in the trace file (if not already highlighted). The packet decode window displays the content of this frame. You see the Ethernet header addressed to broadcast (0xFF-FF-FF-FF-FF-FF).

4. Expand the **Ethernet II** and **Address Resolution Protocol** subtrees in the middle capture window to scroll through the packet and answer the following questions:

   a. What is the IP address of the device sending out the ARP broadcasts?

   b. What hosts were discovered?

   c. How could this type of scan be used on a small routed network?

5. Close the **arpscan.pkt** trace file and proceed immediately to Hands-On Project 12-2.

Hands-On Project 12-2

Time Required: 15 minutes

Objective: Examine a port scan in Wireshark.

Description: This project lets you examine a TCP-based port scan. TCP and UDP port scans are effective methods of reconnaissance, so you should learn to spot them as they take place.

1. Click **File**, click **Open**, select the trace file **portscan.pkt** included with your data files, and then click the **Open** button. The packet summary window appears. This file contains a TCP reconnaissance probe process.

2. Click **Packet #1** and expand the **Internet Protocol Version 4** and **Transmission Control Protocol** subtrees to view the full details of the packet. The first packet was sent to destination port number 1. What TCP flag is set in this packet?

3. Select the **Packet #2** entry in the upper capture window. Examine the flags in the response packet. What flags are set in this packet?

4. Click through the remaining packets in the trace file and answer these questions:

   a. How obvious is this port probe?

   b. If this probe continues through all the ports, will it detect the DHCP service process?

   c. Based on this set of probes, what ports are active on the destination device?

5. Close the **Wireshark for Windows** program.

Hands-On Project 12-3

Time Required: 15 minutes

Objective: Create a filter in Wireshark to catch port scans to blocked ports.

Description: Your firewall is configured to block all TCP handshake packets sent to the Echo port. This project helps you learn how to build a filter in Wireshark to check for any packets sent to the Echo port and test this filter on the portscan.pkt trace file to ensure it works properly.

1. Start the **Wireshark for Windows** program.

2. Click **Analyze,** and then click **Display Filters** to open the Display Filter window.

3. Click **New,** and enter the name **Echo-port filter** in the Filter name text box.

4. In the Filter string text box, enter **tcp.port == 7** (the Echo port number). This filter will locate packets from and to port 7.

5. Click **Apply,** and then click **OK** to close the Display Filter window.

6. Close any currently open packet captures. Next, test the filter to see if it can catch the Echo packets in the portscan.pkt file.

7. Click **File,** click **Open,** select **portscan.pkt,** and then click the **Open** button. The packet summary window appears.

8. Click **Analyze,** and then click **Display Filters** to open the Display Filter window.

9. In the Display Filter section, scroll down and select **Echo-port filter** and then click the **Apply** button. The filter is applied to the packets. Click **OK.**

   Note that the upper capture window now shows the packets that match the selection criteria. Did your filter work? Do you see packets to and from the Echo port? This filter can be used to catch packets addressed to or from the Echo port. For example, if you set up a firewall to block all traffic to and from the Echo port, you can test the firewall by setting up this filter inside the firewall.

10. Close the **Wireshark for Windows** program.

Hands-On Project 12-4

Time Required: 10 minutes

Objective: Set up a Boolean filter in Wireshark to locate all traffic to and from suspect port numbers.

Description: This project helps you learn how to create a complex filter to look for traffic that uses the standard Back Orifice and Trinoo port numbers (31337, 31335, and 27444). This project illustrates how filters can be built to capture specific attack traffic crossing the network.

The suspect port numbers you use in this project are:

- 31337 Back Orifice
- 31335 Trinoo agent to handler communications
- 27444 Trinoo handler to agent communications

To set up a filter to catch traffic associated with Back Orifice and Trinoo communications:

1. Start the **Wireshark for Windows** program.

2. Click **Capture,** and then click **Capture Filters** to open the Capture Filter window. Click the **New** button.

3. Enter the name **BO-Trinoo** in the Filter name text box.

4. Because you are interested in packets that match 31337, 31335, or 27444, use the OR operand between sequence points of the capture filter string. Enter the following in the Filter string text box: **port 31337 or port 31335 or port 27444.**

5. Click **OK** to close the Capture Filter window.

6. Close the **Wireshark for Windows** program.

By running this filter on a network, you can capture traffic that is on the way to or coming from these suspect ports.

Case Projects

CASE PROJECTS

Case Project 12-1: Firewall Filters

You are the network security technician for a large shoe manufacturer based in Detroit, MI. Your internetwork connects six buildings through fiber links. You have experienced numerous attacks on your corporate Web server. The company CEO decides to pay for a firewall. Describe the filters you will implement in your firewall, and note how you will test your firewall.

Case Project 12-2: Firewall Research, Planning, and Implementation

Your network currently has an old basic technology firewall that needs a software upgrade in order to support the newer security features and capabilities that are available. However, your manager would rather invest in a newer technology firewall solution that is more capable and can provide protection for the network. In addition, it has been decided that perhaps a single firewall protecting the external side of the network may not be sufficient for overall network and systems protection. Your manager has tasked you with the "firewall replacement" project. Your goals are to design a new firewall protection strategy that offers a multi-layered approach using firewalls for network protection. You must also produce a report that lists firewall vendors who will meet your needs and the overall plan for selection and deployment of the new firewall solution.

Student and Instructor Online Resources

Student and instructor resources for this book are available at *www.cengage.com*. To locate the resources, search for **Guide to TCP/IP** in the Higher Education catalog.

The resources include the trace (data) files and software that are required to complete the Hands-On Projects in the book. The Web site also includes documents that contain descriptions and links to additional networking software and utilities recommended by the authors for TCP/IP analysis and understanding, along with information on IPv4 address classes A through E, binary arithmetic, supernets, IPv4 and IPv6 RFCs, and more.

Tools

The following tools required for the Hands-On Projects in this book are available for download by students and instructors:

- Bitcricket IP Calculator (WildPackets, Inc.)
- Wireshark for Windows (Wireshark Foundation/Riverbed Technologies)

These tools are listed and defined in the following sections.

Bitcricket IP Calculator

IP Subnet Calculator is a Windows-based calculator used to determine IP address configurations using class-based and classless IP network addresses. Originally developed by Scott Haugdahl, this tool is distributed by WildPackets, Inc.

Wireshark for Windows

Wireshark for Windows is the open-source protocol analyzer used throughout this book. Versions of Wireshark exist for Windows, UNIX/Linux, and Apple OS X systems, all of which include standard analyzer features: packet capture and analysis, visual representation of network traffic, and more.

Trace (Data) Files

The publisher's online resources Web site for this book provides a link to a downloadable self-extracting file that contains all the trace files used in the Hands-On Projects in *Guide to TCP/IP*, 4th edition. These trace files are in .cap, .pkt, or .pcap format and can be opened in Wireshark. Table A-1 lists the trace files for this book.

File	Chapter	Description
6to4.pcap	9, 10	Contains packets captured on a network using 6to4 for encapsulation.
arpscan.pkt	12	Shows an ARP-based reconnaissance probe process. This ARP scan is probably generated by a program—the ARP queries are not generated manually.
ch06_trace.pcap	6	Contains Router Solicitation, Router Advertisement, Neighbor Solicitation, and Neighbor Advertisement messages.
ch07_DHCPboot.pkt	7	Shows the basic DHCP boot sequence, including the DHCP Discover, Offer, Request, and Acknowledgment. Notice that ARP is used to test two addresses before assigning one and that the DHCP client uses ARP to test the assigned address before using it.
ch07_DHCPlab.pkt	7	Contains some DHCP reconnect sequences. Note the ICMP Echo packets used to test addresses.
ch07_DHCPv6boot.pcap	7	Contains messages exchanged between a client and a DHCPv6 server during the DHCPv6 boot sequence.
eigrp-for-ipv6-auth.pcap	4	Contains EIGRP routing protocol for IPv6 data.
IPv4Fields.pcap	3	Contains IPv4 traffic that allows you to explore IPv4 headers.
IPv6Fields.pcap	3	Contains IPv6 traffic that allows you to explore IPv6 headers and DHCPv6 traffic.
isatap.pcap	10	Contains Router Solicitation and Router Response transactions between a host and an ISATAP router using ISATAP interfaces.
ospf.cap	4	Contains OSPF routing protocol hello packet data.
portscan.pkt	12	Contains TCP reconnaissance probe process.
RIP_v1	4	Contains RIPv1 Request and RIPv1 Response packets.
tcp-handshake-capture.pcap	9	Contains the packet exchange involved between two nodes on a network involved in the TCP handshake process.
Teredo.pcap	10	Contains packets captured on a network using Teredo for encapsulation.

Table A-1 Trace files
© Cengage Learning 2013

Glossary

:: In IPv6 addresses, a pair of colon characters stands for several contiguous 16-bit groups, each of which is all zeroes. This notation can be used only once in any address.

4.2BSD The version of the Berkeley Software Distribution (BSD) of UNIX that was the first to include a TCP/IP implementation.

6to4 A method of allowing IPv6 network nodes to communicate with each other over an IPv4 network by special encapsulation of IPv6 packets.

6to4 node/router Also called a 6to4 host/router, this device sends and receives 6to4-addressed traffic but does not forward traffic to other 6to4 nodes, only to IPv6 nodes.

6to4 relay A specialized device that routes network traffic sent from 6to4 nodes to IPv6-capable networks.

6to4 router A device that forwards 6to4 traffic to other nodes across IPv4 networks, including 6to4 and IPv6 nodes.

AAAA record A DNS resource record that maps domain names to IPv6 addresses.

Acceptable Use Policy (AUP) A formal policy document that dictates what kinds of online behavior or system use are acceptable to the overall user community.

access control The act of restricting who may view or use certain resources, including access to bandwidth or a computer as well as access to information.

acknowledgment Notification of successful receipt of data. The ACK flag is set in acknowledgment packets.

address (A) record A DNS resource record that maps domain names to IPv4 addresses.

address masquerading A method of mapping many internal (i.e., private), nonroutable addresses to a single external (i.e., public) IP address for the purpose of sharing a single Internet connection—also referred to as "address hiding."

address pool A contiguous range of numeric IP addresses, defined by a starting IP address and an ending IP address, to be managed by a DHCP server.

address request A DNS service request for an IP address that matches a domain name.

Address Resolution Protocol (ARP) This Network layer protocol translates numeric IP addresses into the equivalent MAC layer addresses necessary to transfer frames from one machine to another on the same cable segment or subnet.

address scope *See* scope.

addressing A method of assigning a unique symbolic name or numerical identifier to an individual network interface on a network segment to make every such interface uniquely identifiable (and addressable).

adjacencies database A database of the local network segment and its attached routers. Designated routers share the adjacencies database view across link-state networks.

Advanced Research Projects Agency (ARPA) An agency within the U.S. Department of Defense that funded forward-thinking research in computing technology.

advertised window The amount of data that a receiver states it can handle in its TCP buffer space.

advertising rate The rate at which a service (typically a routing service) is announced on a network. An example of an advertising rate is the 10-minute advertising rate for ICMP Router Advertisement packets.

adware A type of software that opens the door for a compromised machine to display all kinds of unsolicited and unwanted advertising, often of an unsavory nature.

agent 1. In general, a piece of software that performs services on behalf of another process or user. In the case of Mobile IP, the agent in question is a special piece of router software that tunnels from a remote subnet to a user's home subnet to set up connections for a specific static IP address. 2. The device that inflicts the attack on the victim in a DDoS attack.

aggregatable global unicast address The layout of these IPv6 addresses breaks the leftmost 64 bits of the address into explicit fields to allow for easier routing. Specifically, it allows routes to these addresses to be "aggregated"—that is, combined into a single entry in the router table.

alarm Notification of events or errors on the network.

allowable data size The amount of data that can be transferred across a link; the MTU.

anonymous access A type of IP service access wherein users need not provide explicit account and password information; this applies to FTP and Web services, among others.

anycast address A type of ordinary address in IPv6 that can be assigned to more than one host or interface. Packets pointed to an anycast address are delivered to the holder of that address nearest to the sender in terms of routing distance. An anycast address does not apply to IPv4.

anycast packet An IPv6 multicast method that permits multiple recipients to be designated for a single message, usually for a single cable segment or broadcast domain.

Application layer The uppermost layer of the ISO/OSI network reference model (and the TCP/IP model) where the interface between the protocol suite and actual applications resides.

application process A system process that represents a specific type of network application or service.

Application Specific Integrated Circuit (ASIC) A special-purpose form of integrated circuit that provides a way to implement specific programming logic directly into chip form, thereby providing the fastest possible execution of such programming logic when processing data. ASICs are what make it possible for high-speed, high-volume routers to perform complex address recognition and management functions that can keep up with data volumes and time-sensitive processing needs.

architectural decisions In formal architecture methodologies, a list that documents decisions that are made, along with the rationale, alternatives, impact, and derived requirements.

area border router (ABR) A router used to connect separate areas.

areas Groups of contiguous networks. Areas are used in link-state routing to provide route table summarization on larger networks.

ARP cache A temporary table in memory that consists of recent ARP entries. Entries in the ARP cache are discarded after 2 minutes on Windows 2000, Windows XP, and later systems.

ARPANET An experimental network, funded by ARPA, designed to test the feasibility of a platform-neutral, long-distance, robust, and reliable internetwork that provided the foundation for what we know today as the Internet.

attack An attempt to break into or compromise a system or network, or deny access to that system or network.

attacker The actual source of an attack sequence. Clever attackers in a DDoS attack often hide behind a handler and an agent.

Authentication Header (AH) A header in an IP packet and/or the security protocol that uses that extension header. AH specifies the true origin of a packet by preventing address spoofing and connection theft, and it provides integrity checking and a limited defense against replay attacks.

authoritative response A reply to a query from the name server that's authoritative for the zone in which the requested name or address resides.

authoritative server The DNS server that's responsible for one or more particular zones in the DNS database environment.

automatic tunnel An IPv6 tunnel created and destroyed by the protocol when needed, without having an administrator manually involved.

autonomous system (AS) A group of routers that is under a single administrative authority.

autonomous system border router (ASBR) A router that connects an independent routing area, or AS, to another AS or the Internet.

auto-reconfiguration The process of automatically changing the configuration of a device.

auto-recovery The process of automatically recovering from a fault.

available routes The known functional routes on an internetwork. Available routes are not necessarily the optimal routes. On IP networks, routers periodically advertise available routes.

average response time The median time required to reply to a query. The history of network average response times is used to provide a measurement for comparison of current network responses.

backbone area A required area to which all other routers should be attached directly or through a tunnel.

back door An undocumented and illicit point of entry into a system or a network, often built into software or a system by its original engineers.

backup designated router (BDR) The router with the second-highest priority on a broadcast segment of a link-state network. The BDR allows service to be restored quickly in the event of an outage affecting the DR. *See also* designated router.

backward compatibility A feature that enables a device, process, or protocol to operate with earlier versions of software or hardware that do not support all the latest, up-to-date, or advanced features. For example, a PMTU host can automatically and incrementally reduce the MTU size it uses until it learns the supported PMTU size.

bandwidth A measurement of the amount of information that can cross a network. For example, Ethernet has 10-Mbps bandwidth available.

basic hybrid model A virtual network infrastructure model describing IPv6 nodes existing in a IPv4 core backbone, such as the Internet, and communicating with each other using a tunneling technology.

bastion host A specially hardened computer designed to straddle the boundary between internal and external networks, where firewalls, proxy servers, IDSs, and border routing functions normally operate.

Best Current Practice (BCP) A specific type of Internet RFC document that outlines the best ways to design, implement, and maintain TCP/IP-based networks.

best-effort delivery A simple network transport mechanism that relies on the underlying Network, Data Link, and Physical layer facilities available to handle delivery of PDUs from sender to receiver without adding additional robustness or reliability features; UDP uses best-effort delivery.

BIND (Berkeley Internet Name Domain) The most popular implementation of DNS server software on the Internet today (originally introduced as part of BSD UNIX 4.3). Today, there are BIND implementations available for nearly every computing platform, including Windows Server 2003 and Windows Server 2008.

Bitcricket IP Calculator A downloadable subnet mask calculator produced by WildPackets that provides both IPv4 and IPv6 support.

bit-level integrity check A special mathematical calculation performed on the payload of a packet (a datagram at the Data Link layer) before the datagram is transmitted, whose value may be stored in a datagram's trailer. The calculation is performed again on the receiving end and compared to the transmitted value. If the two values agree, the reception is assumed to be error-free; if the two values disagree, the datagram is usually silently discarded (no error message).

black hole A point on the network where packets are silently discarded.

Border Gateway Protocol (BGP) An interdomain routing protocol that replaces Exterior Gateway Protocol (EGP) and is defined in RFC 1163. BGP exchanges reachability information with other BGP routers. RFC 4760 defines the multiprotocol extensions that let BGP operate on IPv6 networks.

border router A network device that straddles the boundary between internal and external networks and manages both the inbound traffic permitted to reach the inside networks and the outbound traffic allowed to proceed beyond the boundary.

boundary router *See* border router.

break-in An attempt to impersonate a valid user on a system or otherwise gain entry to a system or network in order to obtain illicit access to the resources and information it contains.

broadcast A specific type of network transmission (and address) meant to be noticed and read by all recipients on any cable segment where that transmission appears; a way of reaching all addresses on any network.

broadcast address The all-1s address for a network or subnet, which provides a way to send the same information to all interfaces on a network.

broadcast packet A type of network transmission intended for delivery to all devices on the network. The Ethernet broadcast address is 0xFF-FF-FF-FF-FF-FF for IPv6 and 255.255.255.255 for IPv4.

brute force attack An attack that typically consists of numerous requests for service. This type of attack focuses on overloading the resources of the victim, including the CPU, disk access, or other local resources.

brute force password attack A systematic attempt to guess all possible password strings as a way of trying to break into a system. Such an attack literally attempts all conceivable character combinations that might represent a valid password.

byte stream A continuous stream of data that contains no boundaries.

cable segment Any single collection of network media and attached devices that fits on a single piece of network cable or within a single network device, such as a hub or, in a virtual equivalent, a local area network emulation environment on a switch.

caching Storing remote information locally, once obtained, so that if it is needed again, it may be accessed much more quickly. Both DNS resolvers (clients) and DNS servers cache DNS data to lower the odds that a remote query will have to be resolved.

caching-only server A DNS server that does not have primary or secondary zone database responsibilities; this type of server is used only to cache already resolved domain names and addresses as well as related error information.

caching server A DNS server that stores valid name and address pairs already looked up, along with invalid names and addresses already detected. Any DNS server can cache data, including primary, secondary, and caching-only DNS servers.

canonical name (CNAME) record The DNS RR used to define database aliases, primarily to make it quicker and easier to edit and manage DNS zone files.

capture filter A method used to identify specific packets that should be captured into a trace buffer based on some packet characteristic, such as source or destination address.

Carrier Sense Multiple Access with Collision Detection (CSMA/CD) A formal name for Ethernet's contention management approach. CSMA means "listen before attempting to send" (to make sure no later message tramples on an earlier one) and "listen while sending" (to make sure messages sent at roughly the same time don't collide with one another).

Centre Europeen de Researche Nucleaire (CERN) The European Organization for Nuclear Research, where Tim Berners-Lee invented protocols and services for the World Wide Web between 1989 and 1991.

checkpoint A point in time at which all system state and information is captured and saved so that, after a subsequent failure in systems or communications, operations can resume at that point in time, with no further loss of data or information.

checksum A special mathematical value that represents the contents of a message so precisely that any change in the contents will cause a change in the checksum—calculated before and after network transmission of data and then compared. If transmitted and calculated checksums agree, the assumption is that the data arrived unaltered.

circuit switching A method of communications wherein a temporary or permanent connection between a sender and a receiver, called a circuit, is created within a communications carrier's switching systems. Because temporary circuits come and go constantly, circuits are switched around all the time—hence, the term.

Classless Inter-Domain Routing (CIDR) A form of subnet masking that does away with placing network and host address portions precisely on octet boundaries and instead uses the /n prefix notation, in which n indicates the number of bits in the network portion of whatever address is presented.

command-line parameter Options added to a command issued at a prompt (not in a windowed environment). For example, in the command arp -a, the -a is the parameter for the command arp.

Commercial Internet Exchange (CIX) An early consortium of commercial Internet users that pioneered the extension of Internet use to e-commerce and business communications.

compromised host A host on which unauthorized access was gained. A compromised host can no longer be considered a trusted system and should be handled according to the site's incident response and recovery procedure.

computer forensics The process of examining the "footprints" that an attacker leaves behind. Some areas of interest include the temp files—deleted files that remain in the Recycle Bin or in a recoverable state—and local system memory.

cone NAT A NAT solution that provides a permanent port and IP address mapping between an internal and public network.

confidentiality The ability to restrict access to some resource by any but authorized users. The typical approach is encryption, rendering the data unusable without the keys and algorithm needed to decrypt it.

configured tunnel An IPv6 tunnel that an administrator manually creates.

congestion A condition of overload on a network or at a receiver. When the network is congested, senders cannot continue to send TCP packets. To avoid congesting a receiver, the receiver advertises a window size of 0.

Congestion Avoidance algorithm A defined method to avoid overloading a network. This mechanism is used to slowly and incrementally increase the window size of communications.

congestion control A TCP mechanism, also available from other protocols, that permits network hosts to exchange information about their ability to handle traffic volumes and

thereby causes senders to decrease or increase the frequency and size of their upcoming communications.

connectionless A networking protocol that does not require network senders and receivers to exchange information about their availability or ability to communicate; also known as "best-effort delivery."

connectionless integrity In IPSec or similar security regimes, the ability to provide integrity, but without the ability to ensure the connection itself.

connectionless protocol A protocol that simply sends datagrams without establishing, managing, or otherwise handling a connection between sender and receiver; UDP is a connectionless Transport layer protocol.

connection-oriented protocol A type of networking protocol that relies on explicit communications and negotiations between sender and receiver to manage delivery of data between the two parties.

connection-oriented transport mechanisms A Transport layer protocol that establishes a session between two computers, provides error checking, and guarantees delivery.

connectivity tests Tests to determine the reachability of a device. IP Ping and Traceroute are two utilities that can be used for connectivity testing.

constant-length subnet masking (CLSM) An IP subnetting scheme in which all subnets use the same size subnet mask, which therefore divides the subnetted address space into a fixed number of equal-size subnets.

converge The process of ensuring that all routers on a network have up-to-date information about available networks and their costs.

core services Primary and key services used in TCP/IP networking. FTP, DNS, and DHCP are considered core services. These services are assigned the well-known port numbers between 0 and 1023.

counting to infinity A network routing problem caused by a routing loop. Packets circulate continuously until they expire.

cracker A person who attempts to break into a system by impersonating valid users or by using other methods of penetration that do not necessarily involve deep system skills or knowledge.

current window The actual window size being used at the time. A sender determines the current window size by using the receiver's advertised window and the network congestion window (what the network can handle).

cyclical redundancy check (CRC) A special 16-bit or 32-bit equation performed on the contents of a packet. The result of the CRC equation is placed in the Frame Check Sequence field at the end of a frame. A CRC is performed by NICs on all outgoing and incoming packets.

daemon Taken from James Clerk Maxwell's famous physics idea, a daemon is a computer process whose job is to "listen" in connection attempts for one or more specific network services and hand off all valid attempts to temporary connections known as sockets attempts.

data encapsulation The technique whereby higher-level protocol data is enclosed within the payload of a lower-layer protocol unit and labeled with a header (and possibly a trailer) so the protocol data unit may be safely transmitted from a sender to a receiver.

data frame The basic PDU at the Data Link layer, which represents what is transmitted or received as a pattern of bits on a network interface.

data link address The address of the local machine based on the hardware address. The data link address is also referred to as the MAC address.

Data Link layer Layer 2 of the ISO/OSI network reference model. The Data Link layer is responsible for enabling reliable transmission of data through the Physical layer at the sending end and for checking such reliability upon reception at the receiving end.

data origin authentication In IPSec or similar security areas, the ability to verify the source of received information or to check that the source possesses some trusted token.

database segment *See* DNS database segment.

data segment The basic PDU for TCP at the Transport layer. *See also* segment.

datagram The basic protocol data unit at the TCP/IP Network Access layer. Used by connectionless protocols at the Transport layer, a datagram simply adds a header to the PDU, supplied from whichever Application layer protocol or service uses a connectionless protocol, such as UDP; hence, UDP is also known as a datagram service.

decapsulator The receiving node at the other end of the tunnel, which is responsible for reassembling any fragmented packets, removing the IPv4 header encapsulation, and processing the IPv6 packet.

decode The interpreted value of a PDU, or a field within a PDU, performed by a protocol analyzer or similar software package.

decoding The process of interpreting the fields and contents of a packet and presenting the packet in a readable format.

default gateway The name given to the router IP address through which a machine attached to a local network must pass outbound traffic to reach beyond the local network, thereby making that address the "gateway" to the world of IP addresses outside the local subnet. Also, a gateway of last resort, where packets are sent when no host route entry or network entry exists in the local host's route table.

default-free zone (DFZ) In Internet routing, a set of all the Internet networks that are operated without a default route. Also, a set of all the autonomous systems (ASs) that do not require a default route to send a destination packet. DFZ routers, collectively, have complete BGP tables.

default route Generally, the route used by a network device to communicate to other devices on a different physical or virtual subnet, leading to the next-hop device, which is typically a router.

Defense Information Systems Agency (DISA) The DoD agency that took over operation of the Internet when ARPA surrendered its control in 1983.

delegation of authority The principle whereby one name server designates another name server to handle some or all of the zone files for the domain or subdomains under its purview. The DNS NS resource record provides the pointer mechanism that name servers use to delegate authority.

delimitation The use of special marker bit strings or characters, called delimiters, that distinguish the payload of a PDU from its header and trailer and that also may mark the beginning (and possibly the end) of a PDU itself, as transmitted.

delimiter A special bit string or character that marks some boundary in a PDU, be it at the beginning or end of a PDU, or at the boundary between the header and the payload, or the payload and the trailer.

demilitarized zone (DMZ) An intermediate network that sits between the boundary of an organization's internal networks and one or more external networks, such as the Internet. A DMZ is usually separated from external networks by a screening router, and from internal networks by a screening router and a firewall.

demultiplexing The process of breaking up a single stream of incoming packets on a computer and directing its components to the various active TCP/IP processes based on socket addresses in the TCP or UDP headers.

denial of service (DoS) attack An attack that causes a system to refuse services because it is busy handling attack requests. For example, repeated two-way handshakes may be caused by a TCP SYN attack.

designated router (DR) The router with the highest priority on a segment of a link-state network. A DR advertises LSAs to all other routers on the segment.

destination port number A port address for incoming TCP/IP communication that identifies a target application or service process.

Destination Unreachable message An ICMP error message sent from a router to a network host notifying the host that its message could not be delivered to its destination.

Destination Unreachable packets ICMP packets that indicate a failure to reach a destination due to a fragmentation problem, parameter problem, or other problem. Implemented in ICMPv4 and ICMPv6.

DHCP client The software component on a TCP/IP client, usually implemented as part of the protocol stack software, that issues address requests, lease renewals, and other DHCP messages to a DHCP server.

DHCP Discovery The four-packet sequence used to obtain an IP address, lease time, and configuration parameters. The four-packet sequence includes the Discover, Offer, Request, and Acknowledgment packets.

DHCP options Parameter and configuration information that defines what the DHCP client is looking for. Two special options—0:Pad and 255:End—are used for housekeeping. Pad simply ensures that the DHCP fields end on an acceptable boundary, and End denotes that there are no more options listed in the packet.

DHCP relay agent A special-purpose piece of software built to recognize and redirect DHCP Discovery packets to known DHCP servers.

DHCP Reply A DHCP message that contains a reply from a server to a client's DHCP Request message.

DHCP Request A DHCP message from a client to a server requesting some kind of service; such messages occur only after a client receives an IP address, and they can use unicast packets (not broadcasts) to communicate with a specific DHCP server.

DHCP server The software component that runs on a network server of some kind, responsible for managing TCP/IP address pools or scope and for interacting with clients to provide them with IP addresses and related TCP/IP configuration data on demand.

diameter The number of hops that a network routing protocol can span; RIP has a network diameter of 15; most other routing protocols (such as OSPF and BGP) have an unlimited network diameter.

Differentiated Services (Diffserv) A method for providing different levels of service to network traffic based on a marker placed in the IP header.

Dijkstra algorithm An algorithm used to compute the best route on a link-state network.

discovery broadcast The process of discovering a DHCP server by broadcasting a DHCP Discover packet onto the local network segment. If a DHCP server does not exist on the local segment, a relay agent must forward the request directly to the remote DHCP server. If no local DHCP server or relay agent exists, the client cannot obtain an IP address using DHCP.

discovery process The process of learning which computers or processes are running on a network.

display filters Filters that are applied to the packets that reside in a trace buffer for the purpose of viewing only the packets of interest.

distance vector The source point or location for determining distance to another network.

distance vector routing protocol A routing protocol that uses information about the distances between networks rather than the amount of time it takes for traffic to make its way from the source network to the destination network. RIP is a distance vector routing protocol.

distributed database technology A database that's managed by multiple database servers, each of which has responsibility for some distinct portion of a global database. As such, DNS is nonpareil in its effective use of distributed database technology.

distributed denial of service (DDoS) attack A special, coordinated type of denial of service attack in which multiple hosts (which may number into the thousands) wage denial of service attacks at the same time.

divide and conquer A computer design approach that consists of decomposing a big, complex problem into a series of smaller, less complex, and interrelated problems, each of which can be solved more or less independently of the others.

DNS database segment A distinct and autonomous subset of data from the DNS name and address hierarchy. A DNS database segment usually corresponds to a DNS database zone and is stored in a collection of interrelated zone files. *See also* zone and zone file.

DNS round robin A method of managing server congestion in which a DNS server keeps track of which IP addresses it has provided most recently for a specific translation and rotates them within the pool or list of addresses available. The DNS server can distribute the processing load, thus avoiding server congestion.

domain name A symbolic name for a TCP/IP network resource; the Domain Name System (DNS) translates such names into numeric IP addresses so outbound traffic may be addressed properly.

domain name hierarchy The entire global namespace for the domain names that DNS manages on the Internet. This space includes all registered and active (and therefore, valid and usable) domain names.

domain name resolution The process whereby DNS translates a domain name into a corresponding numeric IP address.

Domain Name System (DNS) The TCP/IP Application layer protocol and service that manages an Internet-wide distributed database of symbolic domain names and numeric

IP addresses so that users can ask for resources by name and get those names translated into the correct numeric IP addresses.

domain The name of a first-level entry in the domain name hierarchy, such as *cengage.com* or *whitehouse.gov*.

dot quad *See* dotted decimal notation.

dotted decimal notation The name for the format used to denote numeric IP addresses, such as 172.16.1.7, wherein four numbers are separated by periods (dots).

Draft Standard A Standard RFC that has gone through the draft process, been approved, and for which two reference implementations must be shown to work together before it can move on to Internet Standard status.

driver Software used by the operating system to interface with specific hardware components.

dual IP layer architecture An IPv4/IPv6-capable computer in which both versions of IP access a single Transport layer stack.

dual-stack architecture An IPv4/IPv6-capable computer in which each version of IP accesses a separate Transport layer stack.

dual-stack implementation A basic IPv4-to-IPv6 transition technology that allows both versions of the IP protocol to run side by side in an operating system.

duplicate ACKs A set of identical acknowledgments that is sent back to back to a TCP sender to indicate that out-of-order packets were received. Upon receipt of these duplicate ACKs, the sender retransmits the data without waiting for the retransmission timer to expire.

Duplicate Address Detection (DAD) A method for checking the IPv6 address that a node wishes to use by sending a Neighbor Advertisement message to see if it is already in use by some other node. If the message elicits no response, the address will be used; otherwise, a different address will be selected and likewise checked using DAD.

dynamic address lease A type of DHCP address lease in which each address allocation comes with an expiration timeout so address leases must be renewed before expiration occurs or a new address will have to be allocated instead. Used primarily for client machines that do not require stable IP address assignments.

Dynamic Host Configuration Protocol (DHCP) A TCP/IP-based network service and Application layer protocol that supports leasing and delivery of TCP/IP addresses and related configuration information to clients that would otherwise require static assignment of such information. For that reason, DHCP is a profound convenience for both network users and administrators.

Dynamic Host Configuration Protocol version 6 (DHCPv6) The version of DHCP updated for IPv6. DHCPv6 defines the behavior of servers and clients in the stateful assignment of parameters for configuration of the clients' network (and other) settings; it can interoperate with stateless autoconfiguration.

dynamic port number A temporary port number used just for one communication process. These port numbers are cleared after the connection is closed and a 4-minute wait time.

dynamic port *See* temporary port.

dynamically assigned port address A temporary TCP or UDP port number allocated to permit a client and server to exchange data with each other only as long as their connection remains active.

E1 A standard European digital communications service used to carry 30 64-Kbps digital voice or data channels, along with two 64-Kbps control channels, for a total bandwidth of 2.048 Mbps of service. E1 is widely used outside North America as a replacement for T1 service.

E3 A standard European digital communications service used to carry 16 E1 channels, for a total bandwidth of 34.368 Mbps of service. E3 is widely used outside North America as a replacement for T3 service.

Encapsulating Security Payload (ESP) A header in an IP packet and/or the security protocol that uses that extension header. ESP provides encryption under IPSec.

encapsulation Enclosure of data from an upper-layer protocol between a header and a trailer (the trailer is optional) for the current layer to identify sender and receiver and, possibly, include data integrity check information.

encapsulator The node at the sending end of the tunnel, which is responsible for encapsulating the IPv6 packet in an IPv4 header, then transmitting the packet in the tunnel.

encryption The process of rendering data unintelligible in a way that is reversible by applying a secret key.

end-to-end connection A network connection in which the original sending and receiving IP addresses may not be altered and in which a communications connection extends all the way from sender to receiver while that connection remains active.

end-to-end minimum MTU size The smallest data size that can be sent from one host to another host on an internetwork. Packets may be fragmented to reach the end-to-end minimum MTU size, or the PMTU process can be used to determine the minimum size.

end-to-end reliability A characteristic offered by connection-oriented services to guarantee that data arrives successfully at the desired destination.

enterprise The IT environment of an end-user organization; usually it is a business.

error recovery The procedure for retransmitting missing or damaged data. Two examples of error recovery are the immediate drop in the current window size and the immediate retransmission of data (before the retransmission timer expires).

error-detection mechanism A method for detecting corrupted packets. The CRC process is an example of an error-detection mechanism.

Ethernet A network access protocol based on carrier sense, multiple access, and collision detection.

Ethernet collision fragments The garbled traffic on a network produced when two packets transmitted at about the same time collide, resulting in a hodgepodge of signals.

Ethernet II frame type The de facto standard frame type for TCP/IP communications.

EUI-64 format An IEEE transformation permitting the burned-in MAC addresses of NICs to be padded in particular ways to create globally unique 64-bit interface identifiers for each interface.

expired route entry A route entry that is considered "too old" and won't be used to forward data through an internetwork. Expired route entries may be held in a routing table for a short time in anticipation that the route will become valid again as another device advertises it.

Explicit Congestion Notification (ECN) A method for notifying next-hop devices that a link is experiencing congestion and packet loss is imminent at the current transmission rates.

exploit A documented system break-in technique that's published for potential reuse by others.

extended network prefix The portion of an IP address that represents the sum of the network portion of the address plus the number of bits used for subnetting that network address; a Class B address with a three-bit subnetting scheme would have an extended network prefix of /19—16 bits for the default network portion, plus 3 bits for the subnetting portion of that address, with a corresponding subnet mask of 255.255.224.0.

extension headers For IPv6 packets, these are optional headers or containers, placed between the IPv6 header and the upper-layer header, that allow more features to be added to the packet as required.

exterior gateway protocols (EGPs) Routing protocols used to exchange routing information between separate autonomous systems.

external route entry A route entry received from a different area.

failure domain The collection of IT components in the environment that are disrupted by a single component failure.

firewalking A two-staged reconnaissance method involving an initial perimeter device discovery phase and subsequent inverse mapping of filtered devices (by eliciting Time Exceeded responses).

firewall A network boundary device that sits between the public and private sides of a network and provides a variety of screening and inspection services to ensure that only safe, authorized traffic flows from outside to inside.

flow 1. A set of packets for which a source requires special handling by intervening routers. 2. A conversation between two end points in which all the packets in the flow have the same source and destination addresses and the same Transport layer headers.

flow label A portion of the IPv6 header used for QoS.

forwarding table The actual table referenced to make forwarding decisions on a link-state network.

fragment A piece of a larger set of data that must be divided to cross a network that supports a smaller MTU than the original packet size.

Fragment Offset field The field that defines where a fragment should be placed when the entire data set is reassembled.

fragmentable Able to be fragmented. A packet must have the May Fragment bit set in order to allow an IP packet to be fragmented, if necessary.

fragmentation The process of dividing a packet into multiple smaller packets to cross a link that supports a smaller MTU than the link where the packet originated.

frame The basic Data Link layer PDU for the ISO/OSI reference model.

Frame Check Sequence (FCS) The type of bit-level integrity check used in the trailer of PPP datagrams; the specific algorithm for the FCS is documented in RFC 1661. The FCS field contains a CRC value. All Ethernet and token ring frames have an FCS field.

fully qualified domain name (FQDN) A special form of a domain name that ends with a period to indicate the root of the domain name hierarchy. You must use FQDNs in DNS A and PTR resource records.

gateway In the TCP/IP environment, a term used to refer to a Network layer forwarding device typically known as a router. The default gateway is the router a host sends a packet to when the host has no specific route to a destination.

global Internet routing table The set of all Internet address prefixes in the default-free zone, which comprise the public Internet.

hacker A person who uses computer and communications knowledge to exploit information or functionality of a device.

half-open connection A TCP connection that is not completed with a final acknowledgment. These half-open connections may be an indication of a TCP SYN attack.

handler A manager system in a DDoS attack. The handler is a compromised host on which an attacker has placed DDoS code. The handlers locate agents to perform the actual attack on a victim system.

handshake process The process of setting up a virtual connection between TCP peers. The handshake process consists of three packets used to set up the starting sequence number that each TCP peer will use for communications. The TCP peers also exchange the receiver window size and an MSS value during this process.

hardware address The address of the NIC. This address is typically used as the data link address.

header That portion of a PDU that precedes the actual content for the PDU and usually identifies sender and receiver, protocols in use, and other information necessary to establish context for senders and receivers.

Hello process A process that link-state routers use to discover neighbor routers.

High-Level Data Link Control (HDLC) A synchronous communication protocol.

Historic Standard An Internet RFC that was superseded by a newer, more current version.

hole A system or software vulnerability that defeats, bypasses, or ignores system or software security settings and restrictions.

honeynet A network that contains two or more honeypots, which are computers set up to deliberately attract, entice, and entrap would-be attackers.

honeypot A computer system deliberately set up to attract, entice, and entrap would-be attackers, often by being made to appear part of a larger network (when it is actually isolated and protected) and by exposing apparently valuable or interesting information and resources.

hop A single transfer of data from one network to another through some kind of networking device. Router-to-router transfers are often called hops. The number of hops often provides a rough measure of the distance between a sender's network and a receiver's network.

host information (HINFO) record A DNS resource record that provides information about some specific host, as specified by its domain name.

host portion The rightmost bits in an IP address, allocated to identify hosts on a supernetwork, network, or subnetwork.

host probe A reconnaissance process used to determine which hosts are active on an IP network. Typically, the Ping process is used to perform a host probe.

host route A routing table entry with a 32-bit subnet mask designed to reach a specific network host.

host route entry A route table entry that matches all 4 bytes of the desired destination. Network route table entries only match the network bits of the desired address.

host TCP/IP terminology for any computer with one or more valid TCP/IP addresses (hence, reachable on a TCP/IP-based network). A host also can be a computer that offers TCP/IP services to clients.

HOSTS A special text file that lists known domain names and corresponding IP addresses, thereby defining a static method for domain name resolution. Until DNS was implemented, HOSTS files provided the sole means for name resolution on the precursor to the Internet, the ARPANET.

host-to-host An IPv6-over-IPv4 tunneling configuration representing a virtual end-to-end link between IPV6-capable nodes across an IPv4 network.

host-to-router and router-to-host An IPv6-over-IPv4 tunneling configuration that represents the first and last hops of IPv6 traffic from the IPv6 starting node, through routing over an IPv4 network, to the IPv6 destination node.

Hypertext Transfer Protocol (HTTP) The TCP/IP Application layer protocol and service that supports access to the World Wide Web.

ICMP Echo communication An ICMP process whereby a host sends an Echo packet to another host on an internetwork. If the destination host is active and able, it echoes back the data that is contained in the ICMP Echo packet.

ICMP Echo Request and Reply packets Packets that are sent to a device to test connectivity. If the receiving device is functional and can reply, it should echo back the data that is contained in the data portions of the Echo Request packets. Implemented in ICMPv4 and ICMPv6.

ICMP error message An error message sent using the ICMP protocol. Destination Unreachable, Time Exceeded, and Parameter Problem are examples of ICMPv4 and ICMPv6 error messages.

ICMP query message An ICMP message that contains requests for configuration or other information. ICMP Echo Request and Router Solicitation are examples of ICMPv4 and ICMPv6 query messages.

ICMP Router Discovery A process in which hosts send ICMP Router Solicitation messages to the all-router multicast address. Local routers that support the ICMP Router Discovery process reply with an ICMP Router Advertisement unicast to the host. The advertisement contains the router's address and a lifetime value for the router's information. Supported for ICMPv4 and ICMPv6.

ICMP Router Solicitation The process that a host can perform to learn of local routers. An ICMP Router Solicitation message is sent to the all-routers multicast address.

IEEE 802 A project undertaken by the IEEE in 1980 that covers Physical and Data Link layers for networking technologies in general (802.1 and 802.2), plus specific networking technologies, such as Ethernet (802.3).

IEEE 802.3 The IEEE-defined standard for a carrier-sense, multiple-access method with collision detection.

incremental zone transfer A type of DNS query that limits updates from a primary DNS server to one or more secondary DNS servers to only data that has changed on the primary server.

Information Technology Infrastructure Library (ITIL) A standard for performing IT service management, organized by domains, including event, incident, problem, change, and so on.

informational/supervisory format A connection-oriented format that can be used by LLC packets.

Institute of Electrical and Electronic Engineers (IEEE) An international organization that sets standards for electrical and electronic equipment, including network interfaces and communications technologies.

inter-autonomous system routing A term used in BGP that refers to the ability to provide routing between autonomous systems.

interdomain routing protocols Routing protocols used to exchange information between separate autonomous systems.

interface identifier In IPv6 addressing, unicast and anycast addresses have the lower-order bits of their addresses reserved for this bit string that uniquely identifies a particular interface, either globally or (at a minimum) locally.

interior gateway protocols (IGPs) Routing protocols used to exchange information within an autonomous system.

internal route entry A route entry learned from within the same area as the computing device.

International Organization for Standardization (ISO) An international standards organization based in Geneva, Switzerland, that sets standards for information technology and networking equipment, protocols, and communications technologies.

International Organization for Standardization Open Systems Interconnection *See* International Organization for Standardization, and Open Systems Interconnection.

Internet Architecture Board (IAB) The organization within the Internet Society that governs the actions of both the IETF and the IRTF and has final approval authority for Internet standards.

Internet Assigned Numbers Authority (IANA) The arm of the ISOC originally responsible for registering domain names and allocating public IP addresses. This job is now the responsibility of ICANN.

Internet Control Message Protocol (ICMP) A key protocol in the TCP/IP protocol suite that provides error messages and the ability to query other devices. IP Ping and Traceroute utilities use ICMPv4 and ICMPv6.

Internet Corporation for Assigned Names and Numbers (ICANN) The organization within the Internet Society responsible for proper assignment of all domain names and numeric IP addresses for the global Internet. ICANN works with private companies called name registrars to manage domain names, and with ISPs to manage assignment of numeric IP addresses.

Internet Engineering Task Force (IETF) The organization within the Internet Society that's responsible for all currently used Internet Standards, protocols, and services as well as for managing the development and maintenance of Internet Requests for Comments (RFCs).

Internet Group Management Protocol (IGMP) A protocol that supports the formation of multicast groups. Hosts use IGMP to join and leave multicast groups. Routers track IGMP memberships and only forward multicasts on a link that has active members of that multicast group.

Internet Network Information Center (InterNIC) A quasi-governmental agency that was responsible for assigned names and numbers on the Internet (this responsibility now falls on ICANN).

Internet Protocol (IP) The primary Network layer protocol in the TCP/IP suite. IP manages routing and delivery for traffic on TCP/IP-based networks.

Internet Protocol Control Protocol (IPCP) A special TCP/IP Network Control Protocol used to establish and manage IP links at the Network layer.

Internet Protocol version 4 (IPv4) The original version of IP that's still in widespread public use, although IPv6 is currently fully specified and moving into global deployment and use.

Internet Protocol version 6 (IPv6) The latest version of IP, which is moving into global deployment and use (IPv4 remains the predominant TCP/IP version in use but will slowly be supplanted by IPv6).

Internet Research Task Force (IRTF) The forward-looking research and development arm of the Internet Society. The IRTF reports to the IAB for direction and governance.

Internet service provider (ISP) An organization that, as a primary line of business, provides Internet access to individuals or organizations. Currently, ISPs are the source of public IP addresses for most organizations seeking Internet access.

Internet Society (ISOC) The parent organization under which the rest of the Internet governing bodies fall. ISOC is a user-oriented, public-access organization that solicits end-user participation and input to help set future Internet policy and direction.

Internet Standard An RFC document that specifies the rules, structure, and behavior of a current Internet protocol or service. Also called a Standard RFC.

internetwork Literally, a "network of networks," an internetwork is better understood as a collection of multiple interconnected physical networks that together behave as a single logical network (of which the Internet is the prime example).

interoperability The ability of two diverse technologies to interact with each other.

intra-autonomous system routing A term used in BGP that refers to the ability to provide routing within an autonomous system.

intradomain routing protocols Routing protocols used to exchange routing information within an autonomous system.

Intra-Site Automatic Tunnel Addressing Protocol (ISATAP) An IP4-to-IPv6 mechanism that allows dual stack network nodes to send IPv6 packets across IPv6 networks using tunneling.

intrusion detection system (IDS) A special-purpose software system that inspects ongoing patterns of network traffic, looking for signs of impending or active attack. Most IDSs can foil break-in attempts and also attempt to establish the identity of the attacker or attackers.

inverse DNS query A DNS query that supplies an IP address for conversion to a corresponding domain name. Inverse DNS queries are often used to double-check user identities to make sure that the domain names they present match the IP addresses in their packet headers. *See also* IP spoofing.

inverse mapping The process of identifying live network hosts (mapping internal network layout) positioned behind a filtering device by probing for addresses known not to be in use.

IP address parser A method of verifying that a string is an IP address and, if so, determining if the address is IPv4 or IPv6.

IP address scanning Commonly used by hackers, the process of sending ping packets (ICMP Echo Request packets) to each host within an IP address range to obtain a list of active hosts in that range. All devices that reply may be probed further to determine if they represent valid targets for attack.

IP gateway TCP/IP terminology for a router that provides access to resources outside the local subnet network address. (A default gateway is the name given to the TCP/IP configuration entry for clients that identify the router they must use to send data outside their local subnet areas.)

IP renumbering The process of replacing one set of numeric IP addresses with another set of numeric IP addresses either because of a change in ISPs or an address reassignment.

IP Security (IPSec) A security specification supporting various forms of encryption and authentication, along with key management and related supporting functions.

IP service attack A system attack that concentrates on known characteristics and vulnerabilities of one or more specific IP services or that uses well-known port addresses associated with such services for its own nefarious ends.

IP spoofing A technique whereby a programmer constructs an IP packet that presents domain name credentials that differ from the IP address in the packet header. IP spoofing is often used in illicit network break-in attempts or to impersonate users or packet origination.

IPCONFIG A command-line utility used to identify the local host's data link address and IP address.

ipv6-literal.net name A name for an IPv6 address used for services on computers that do not recognize IPv6 address syntax. Also referred to as an ipv6 literal.

IPv6-over-IPv4 tunneling A mechanism in which a network device generates an IPv6 packet and encapsulates the packet in an IPv4 header for transmission across an IPv4 network.

ISO/OSI network reference model The official name for the seven-layer network reference model used to describe how networks operate and behave.

iterative query A DNS query that targets one specific DNS server and terminates with whatever response may be forthcoming, whether that response is a definite answer, an error message, a null (no information) reply, or a pointer to another name server.

jumbogram A specification for allowing very large (beyond 4-gigabyte) packets to be transported using IPv6. Used only in special circumstances, such as on large backbone routes.

jump box A type of bastion host that is usually a terminal server or proxy server that allows administrators to access systems in another network without actually having direct network connectivity, meaning neither network has a route to the other network.

keep-alive process The procedure of maintaining an idle connection. TCP connections can be kept alive through TCP keep-alive packets if configured to do so. If the Application layer protocol offers a keep-alive process, the TCP layer should not perform the keep-alive process.

Layer 3 switch A type of networking device that combines hub, router, and network management functions within a single box. Layer 3 switches make it possible to create and manage multiple virtual subnets in a single device while offering extremely high bandwidth to individual connections between pairs of devices attached to that device.

layer A single component or facet in a networking model that handles one particular aspect of network access or communications.

lease expiration time The end of the lease time. If a DHCP client does not renew or rebind its address by the lease expiration time, it must release the address and reinitialize.

lease time The amount of time that a DHCP client may use an assigned DHCP address.

lifetime value The time that a packet can remain on the network. Routers discard packets when their lifetimes expire.

limited traffic flow confidentiality In IPSec, the ability to defeat traffic analysis by hiding the path, frequency, source, destination, and volume of traffic between correspondents.

Link Control Protocol (LCP) A special connection negotiation protocol that PPP uses to establish point-to-point links between peers for ongoing communications.

link MTU This is the MTU capacity of a specific link within a Path MTU. The smallest-link MTU determines the MTU size of IPv6 packets for the path.

link-local address The addressing scheme that is designed to be used only on a single segment of a local network.

Link-Local Multicast Name Resolution (LLMNR) A protocol that provides name resolution services on local networks for IPv4 and IPv6 Windows computers.

link-state protocol *See* link-state routing protocol.

link-state advertisement (LSA) A packet that includes information about a router, its neighbors, and the attached network.

link-state routing protocol A routing protocol based on a common link-state picture of the network topology. Link-state routers can identify the best path based on bandwidth, delay, or other path characteristics associated with one or more links available to them and shares information only about their adjacent neighbors. OSPF is a link-state routing protocol.

local area network (LAN) A single network cable segment, subnet, or logical network community that represents a collection of machines that can communicate with one another more or less directly (using MAC addresses).

logical connection A virtual connection between hosts, sometimes referred to as a circuit. The TCP handshake is used to set up a logical connection between TCP peers.

Logical Link Control (LLC) The data link specification for protocol identification as defined by the IEEE 802.2 specification. The LLC layer resides directly above the Media Access Control layer.

loopback address An address that points directly back to the sender. In IPv4, the Class A domain 127.0.0.0 (or 127.0.0.1 for a specific machine address) is reserved for loopback. In IPv6, there is a single loopback address, written "::1" (all 0s, except for that last bit, which is 1). By passing traffic down through the TCP/IP stack, then back up again, the loopback address can be used to test a computer's TCP/IP software.

lost segment A section of TCP data that does not arrive at the destination. Upon detection of a lost segment, a TCP sender must decrease the congestion window to one-half the previous window size. Lost segments are assumed to be caused by network congestion.

mail exchange (MX) record A DNS resource record that's used to identify the domain name for the e-mail server that handles any particular domain or subdomain, or that's used to route e-mail traffic from one e-mail server to another while e-mail is in transit from sender to receiver.

malicious code A program that is written with the intent of harming, compromising, or disrupting host operations.

malware A synonym for malicious code that identifies a broad class of programs written with the intent of harming, compromising, or disrupting host operations.

man-in-the-middle (MITM) attack A type of system or network attack in which an attacking system interposes itself between the target network and the next normal link on that network's usual routing chain.

manual address lease A type of DHCP address lease wherein the administrator takes full responsibility for managing address assignments (using DHCP only as a repository for such assignment data).

master router In link-state routing, a router that distributes its view of the link-state database to slave routers.

master server *See* primary DNS server.

Maximum Segment Size (MSS) The maximum amount of data that can fit in a TCP packet after the TCP header. Each TCP peer shares the MSS during the handshake process.

maximum transmission unit (MTU) The biggest single chunk of data that can be transferred across any particular type of network medium—for example, 1,518 bytes is the MTU for conventional Ethernet.

Media Access Control (MAC) address A special type of network address, handled by a sublayer of the Data Link layer, normally preassigned on a per-interface basis to uniquely identify each such interface on any network cable segment (or virtual facsimile).

Media Access Control (MAC) layer A sublayer of the Data Link layer. This layer is part of the Media Access Control definition, in which network access methods, such as Ethernet and token ring, apply.

media flow control The management of data transmission rates between two devices across a local network medium that guarantees the receiver can accept and process input before it arrives from the sender.

merger and acquisition (M&A) Activity undertaken by companies as a result of purchasing one another or otherwise combining their assets, which often includes combining all their IT environments as a cost-saving measure.

messages Data that has distinct boundaries and command information within the packet.

Message Type A required option that indicates the purpose of a DHCP packet; the eight message types are Discover, Offer, Request, Decline, Acknowledge, Negative Acknowledge (NAK), Release, and Inform.

metrics Measurements that may be based on distance (hop count), time (seconds), or other values.

millisecond One-thousandth of a second.

multicast address One of a block of addresses reserved for use in sending the same message to multiple interfaces or nodes. Members of a community of interest subscribe to a multicast address in order to receive router updates, streaming data (video, audio, teleconferencing), and so on. In IPv4, the Class D block of addresses is reserved for multicast. In IPv6, all multicast addresses begin with 0xFF. ICANN, with the help of IANA, manages all such address adjustments.

multicast packet A packet sent to a group of devices, often multiple routers.

multihomed Containing multiple network interfaces capable of attaching to multiple subnets.

multiplexing The process whereby multiple individual data streams from Application layer processes are joined together for transmission by a specific TCP/IP transport protocol through the IP protocol.

Nagle algorithm A method stating that when small packets are sent but not acknowledged, no further packets shall be sent. The Nagle algorithm is relevant on a network that supports numerous small packets through support of interactive applications, such as Telnet.

name query An inverse DNS query that seeks to obtain a domain name for a corresponding numeric IP address.

name resolution process The process of obtaining an IP address based on a symbolic name. DNS is a name resolution process.

name resolution *See* domain name resolution.

name resolution protocols Procedures that govern the rules and conventions used in manually and dynamically providing for name resolution systems in a networked environment.

name resolver A client-side software component, usually part of a TCP/IP stack implementation, that's responsible for issuing DNS queries for applications and relaying whatever responses come back to those applications.

name server (NS) record The DNS resource record that identifies name servers that are authoritative for some particular domain or subdomain. Often used as a mechanism to delegate authority for DNS subdomains downward in the domain name hierarchy.

National Center for Supercomputing Applications (NCSA) An arm of the University of Illinois at Urbana-Champaign, where supercomputer research is undertaken and where the first graphical Web browser, Mosaic, was developed and released in 1993.

National Science Foundation (NSF) A U.S. government agency charged with oversight and support for government-funded scientific research and development. *See also* NSFNET.

negative caching A technique for storing error messages in a local cache so that repeating a query that previously produced an error message can be satisfied more quickly than if that query was forwarded to some other DNS name server.

Neighbor Advertisement (NA) Nodes send Neighbor Advertisement messages that include their IPv6 and link-layer addresses to maintain information about local addresses and on-link status.

Neighbor Discovery (ND) A protocol in IPv6 that permits nodes and routers on a local link to keep one another updated about any recent changes in their network connectivity or status.

neighbor routers On a link-state network, neighbor routers are connected to the same network segment.

Neighbor Solicitation (NS) These are used to find (or verify) the link-layer address for a local node, to see if that node is still available, or check that an address is not in use by another node.

nested hybrid model A virtual network infrastructure model describing IPv6-capable networks embedded within a larger core IPv4 LAN and communicating with other IPv6 networks, within and outside the IPv4 LAN, using a tunneling technology.

network address That portion of an IP address that consists of the network prefix for that address; an extended network prefix also includes any subnetting bits. All bits that belong to the extended network prefix show up as 1s in the corresponding subnet mask for that network.

Network Address Translation (NAT) A technology that modifies IP address information in a router, changing the public address used on the Internet to private addresses used on internal networks.

network analysis Another term for protocol analysis.

network congestion A condition that occurs when the delivery time for packets (also known as network latency) increases beyond normal limits. Congestion can result from several causes, including problems with network links, overloaded hosts or routers, or unusually heavy network usage levels. Packet loss is identified as a characteristic of network congestion.

Network Control Protocol (NCP) Any of a family of TCP/IP Network layer protocols used to establish and manage protocol links made at the Network layer (TCP/IP's Internet layer).

Network File System (NFS) A TCP/IP-based, network-distributed file system that permits users to treat files and directories on machines elsewhere on a network as an extension of their local desktop file systems.

network interface controller (NIC) A hardware device used to permit a computer to attach to and communicate with a local area network.

Network layer Layer 3 of the ISO/OSI network reference model. The Network layer handles logical addresses associated with individual machines on a network by correlating human-readable names for such machines with unique, machine-readable numeric addresses. It uses addressing information to route a PDU from a sender to a receiver when the source and destination do not reside on the same physical network segment.

Network Layer Reachability Information (NLRI) The information about available networks and the routes whereby they may be reached, which routing protocols collect, manage, and distribute to the routers or other devices that use such routing protocols.

network portion The leftmost octets or bits in a numeric IP address, which identify the network and subnet portions of that address. The value assigned to the prefix number identifies the number of bits in the network portion of a IP address. (For example, 10.0.0.0/8 indicates that the first 8 bits of the address are the network portion for the public Class A IP address.)

network prefix That portion of an IP address that corresponds to the network portion of the address; for example, the network prefix for a Class B address is /16, meaning that the first 16 bits represent the network portion of the

address and 255.255.0.0 is the corresponding default subnet mask.

network reference model *See* ISO/OSI network reference model.

network route entry A route table entry that provides a next-hop router for a specific network.

Network Service Access Point (NSAP) This is a type of heirarchical address scheme that is used to implement Open System Interconnection (OSI) network layer addressing and is a logical point between the network and transport layers in the OSI model.

network services A TCP/IP term for a protocol/service combination that operates at the Application layer in the TCP/IP network model.

Network Time Protocol (NTP) A time synchronization protocol defined in RFC 1305. NTP provides the mechanisms to synchronize and coordinate time distribution in a large, diverse Internet operating at varying speeds.

next-hop router The local router that is used to route a packet to the next network along its path.

nmap A port scanner that is primarily UNIX or Linux based, nmap should be part of any IP administrator's attack toolkit.

nonauthoritative response Name, address, or RR information from a DNS server that's not authoritative for the DNS zone being queried (such responses originate from caches on such servers).

nonrecursive query *See* iterative query.

NSFNET A public network operated by the National Science Foundation in the 1980s to support the Internet backbone.

Nslookup A widely implemented command-line program that supports DNS lookup and reporting capabilities. The "Ns" in this command name stands for "name server," so it's reasonable to think of this as a general-purpose name server lookup tool.

numeric address See numeric IP address.

numeric IP address An IP address expressed in dotted decimal or binary notation.

octet TCP/IP terminology for an 8-bit number; numeric IPv4 addresses consist of four octets.

On-Demand Routing (ODR) A low-overhead feature that provides IP routing for sites on a hub-and-spoke network. Each router maintains and updates entries in its routing table only for hosts whose data passes through the router, thus reducing storage requirements and bandwidth.

on-link route Generally, a route used by a network node to communicate with another network node on the same physical or virtual subnet.

Open Shortest Path First (OSPF) A sophisticated Layer 3 or TCP/IP Internet layer routing protocol that uses link-state information to construct routing topologies for local internetworks and provides load-balancing capabilities.

Open Systems Interconnection (OSI) The name of an open-standard internetworking initiative undertaken in the 1980s, primarily in Europe, and originally intended to supersede TCP/IP. Technical and political problems prevented this anticipated outcome from materializing, but the ISO/OSI reference model is a legacy of this effort.

optimal route The best route possible. Typically, routing protocols are used to exchange routing metric information to determine the best route possible. The optimal route is defined as either the route that is quickest, most reliable, most secure, or considered best by some other measurement. When TOS is not used, the optimal route is either the closest (based on hop count) or the highest throughput route.

optimistic security model The original basis for TCP/IP security, this model assumes that it is safe to enforce little or no security on normal network communications.

organizationally unique identifier (OUI) A unique identifier assigned by IANA or ICANN that's used as the first 3 bytes of a NIC's MAC layer address to identify its maker or manufacturer.

out-of-order packets Packets that do not arrive in the order defined by the sequence number. When a TCP host receives out-of-order packets, that host sends duplicate ACKs that indicate the packets arrived out of order.

overhead The non-data bits or bytes required to move data from one location to another. The datalink header is the overhead required to move an IP packet from one device to another across a network. The IP header is additional overhead required to move a packet through an internetwork. Ideally, bandwidth, throughput, and processing power should be devoted to moving high amounts of data bytes—not high amounts of overhead bytes.

oversized packets Packets that exceed the MTU for the network and usually point to a problem with a NIC or its driver software.

packet A generic term for a PDU at any layer in a networking model. The term is properly applied to PDUs at Layer 3, or the TCP/IP Internet layer.

packet filter A specific collection of inclusion or exclusion rules that are applied to a stream of network packets and determine what is captured (and what is ignored) from the original input stream.

packet header *See* header.

packet priority A TOS priority that defines the order in which packets should be processed through a router queue.

packet sniffing A technique that involves using a protocol analyzer to decode and examine the contents of IP packets to attempt to identify sensitive information, including accounts and passwords for subsequent break-in attempts or other nefarious purposes.

packet snooping *See* packet sniffing.

packet trailer *See* trailer.

packet-switched network A network in which data packets may take any usable path between sender and receiver, where sender and receiver are identified by unique network addresses and there's no requirement that all packets follow the same path in transit (although they often do).

pad Bytes placed at the end of the Ethernet Data field to meet the minimum field length requirement of 46 bytes. These bytes have no meaning and are discarded by the incoming data link driver when the packet is processed.

pass-through autonomous system routing Used in BGP routing, this routing technique shares BGP routing information across a non-BGP network.

path The route that a packet can take through an internetwork.

path discovery The process of learning possible routes through a network.

Path MTU (PMTU) The MTU size that is supported through an entire path; the lowest common denominator MTU through a path.

Path MTU (PMTU) Discovery A technique used by IPv6 nodes to determine the size of packets that can be transmitted along a proposed network path from a source to a network address.

Pathping A Windows utility used to test router and path latency as well as connectivity.

payload That portion of a PDU that contains information intended for delivery to an application or to a higher-layer protocol (depending on where in the stack the PDU is situated).

pcap A generic term (short for "protocol capture") for a special network interface driver designed to permit capture of all network traffic in promiscuous mode while running. Although originally associated with the tcpdump open source command-line protocol analyzer, pcap is widely used in protocol analyzers today, including the Wireshark protocol analyzer.

peer layer Analogous layers in the protocol stacks on a sender and a receiver; the receiving layer usually reverses whatever operations the sending layer performs (which is what makes those layers peers).

Peer Name Resolution Protocol (PNRP) A name resolution protocol used for peer-to-peer network environments and that provides secure and scalable resolution services.

per-domain behavior (PDB) In differentiated service, this is a class of descriptors of available service levels or a way of describing the entities offering such differentiated service levels—in this case, a "domain." Services are provided as specified throughout the domain and change at the edge of the domain. PDBs are available across all hops within a given domain.

per-hop behavior (PHB) In differentiated service, this is a class of descriptors of available service levels, or a way of describing protocols and priorities applied to a packet on traversing a router "hop."

personnel security The aspect of security that concentrates on informing users about security matters and training them on proper application of security policies, procedures, and practices.

pessimistic security model A model of system and network security that assumes it is always necessary to enforce strong security measures and so calls for access to all resources to be denied to all users by default, then allowed only to those with a legitimate need to access such resources on a case-by-case basis.

Physical layer Layer 1 in the ISO/OSI network reference model. The Physical layer is where connections, communications, and interfaces—hardware and signaling requirements—are handled.

physical numeric address Another term for MAC layer address (or MAC address).

physical security That aspect of security that concerns itself with limiting physical access to system and network components to prevent unauthorized users from attempting direct attacks on such components. Because lax physical security can easily lead to compromise, strong physical security is always a good idea.

PING sweep An ICMP Echo-based operation used to locate active devices on a network. The term "sweep" refers to the process of testing an entire range of IP addresses for active devices.

plain text password A password that is transferred across the cable in plain ASCII text.

pointer (PTR) record The DNS resource record that's used for inverse lookups to map numeric IP addresses to domain names.

point-to-point A type of Data Link layer connection in which a link is established between exactly two communications partners, so the link extends from one partner (the sender) to the other (the receiver).

Point-to-Point Protocol (PPP) A Layer 2 or TCP/IP Network Interface layer protocol that permits a client and a server to

establish a communications link that can accommodate a variety of higher-layer protocols, including IP, AppleTalk, SNA, IPX/SPX, and NetBEUI. It is today's most widely used serial line protocol for making Internet connections.

Point-to-Point Protocol over Ethernet (PPPoE) A protocol used by many Internet service providers (including telecommunications companies and cable TV operators) to authenticate and manage broadband subscribers.

point-to-point transmission A type of network communication in which pairs of devices establish a communications link to exchange data with one another; the most common type of connection used when communicating with an Internet service provider.

Point-to-Point Tunneling Protocol (PPTP) A Layer 2 or TCP/IP Network Interface layer protocol that allows a client and a server to establish a secure, encrypted communications link for just about any kind of PPP traffic.

poison reverse A process used to make a router undesirable for a specific routing path. This process is one of the methods used to eliminate routing loops.

port number A 16-bit number that identifies either a well-known application service or a dynamically assigned port number for a transitory sender-receiver exchange of data through TCP or UDP. Also referred to as a port address.

port scanner A special-purpose software tool that cycles through either well-known TCP and UDP ports with easy vulnerabilities or all possible TCP and UDP port addresses, looking for open ports that then can be probed for access or exploited for vulnerabilities.

positive response An affirmative acknowledgment that data was received. TCP headers with the ACK flag set indicate that the Acknowledgment Number field is valid and provide the next-expected sequence number from the TCP peer.

Potential Router List (PRL) A method used by ISATAP nodes to maintain a current list of routes and routers, since ISATAP prevents the use of automatic Router Discovery.

preamble The initial sequence of values that precedes all Ethernet packets. Placed on the front of the frame by the outgoing NIC and removed by the incoming NIC, the preamble is used as a timing mechanism that enables receiving IP hosts to properly recognize and interpret bits as 1s or 0s.

precedence A definition of priority for an IP packet. Routers may process higher-priority packets before lower-priority packets when a router queue is congested.

preferred address An address the DHCP client remembers from the previous network session. Most DHCP client implementations maintain a list of the last IP addresses they used and indicate a preference for the last-used address. In IPv6, the term "preferred address" refers to the one address, among the many that may be associated with the same interface, whose use by higher-layer protocols is unrestricted.

pre-filter A type of data filter applied to a raw input stream in a protocol analyzer that selects only packets that meet its criteria for capture and retention. Because it is applied before data is captured, it's called a pre-filter.

Presentation layer Layer 6 of the ISO/OSI reference model. The Presentation layer is where generic network data formats are translated into platform-specific data formats for incoming data and vice versa for outgoing data. This is also the layer where optional encryption or compression services may be applied (or reversed).

primary DNS server The name server that's authoritative for some particular domain or subdomain and has primary custody over the DNS database segment (and related zone files) for that domain or subdomain.

primary master *See* primary DNS server.

private IP address Any of a series of Class A, B, and C IP addresses reserved by IANA for private use (documented in RFC 1918) and intended for uncontrolled private use in organizations. Private IP addresses may not be routed across the Internet because there is no guarantee that any such address is unique.

Process layer A synonym for the TCP/IP Application layer, where high-level protocols and services, such as FTP and Telnet, operate.

promiscuous mode operation Network interface card and driver operation used to capture broadcast packets, multicast packets, packets sent to other devices, and error packets.

promote To move an IT component from one life-cycle stage or environment to the next, such as moving an application from "development" to "test" to "QA" to "Staging" to "Production."

Proposed Standard An intermediate step for standards-level RFCs in which a Draft Standard goes through initial review, with two or more reference implementations to demonstrate interoperability between those implementations.

proprietary Describes an IT component that is not standards based and usable by anyone without license; instead, it is the property of a particular entity that may or may not charge for use but nevertheless controls its features and development.

protection against replays The ability to distinguish between "live" traffic from a trusted source and copies of such traffic masquerading as authentic communications. Protection against replays are typically based on packet sequence numbering and checking.

protocol A precise set of standards that governs communications between computers on a network. Many protocols function in one or more layers of the OSI reference model.

protocol analysis The process of capturing packets off the network for the purpose of gathering communication statistics, observing trends, and examining communication sequences.

protocol data unit (PDU) At any layer in a networking model, a PDU represents the package for data at that layer, including a header, a payload, and in some cases, a trailer.

protocol identification (PID) A datagram service necessitated when any single protocol carries multiple protocols across a single connection (as PPP can do at the Data Link layer); PIDs permit individual datagram payloads to be identified by the type of protocol they contain.

protocol identification field A field that is included in most headers to identify the upcoming protocol. The PID of Ethernet headers is the Type field. The PID of IP headers is the Protocol field.

protocol number An 8-bit numeric identifier associated with some specific TCP/IP protocol.

protocol stack A specific implementation of a protocol suite on a computer, including a network interface, necessary drivers, and whatever protocol and service implementations are necessary to enable the computer to use a specific protocol suite to communicate across the network.

protocol suite A named family of networking protocols, such as TCP/IP, IPX/SPX, or NetBEUI, in which each such family enables computers to communicate across a network.

proxy ARP The process of replying to ARP requests for IP hosts on another network. A proxy ARP network configuration effectively hides subnetting from the individual IP hosts.

proxy server A special type of network boundary service that interposes itself between internal network addresses and external network addresses. For internal clients, a proxy server makes a connection to external resources on the client's behalf and provides address masquerading. For external clients, a proxy server presents internal resources to the public Internet as if they are present on the proxy server itself.

pseudo-header A false header structure used to calculate a checksum. The UDP and TCP checksums are based on the pseudo-header values.

public IP address Any TCP/IP address allocated by IANA or ICANN (or by an ISP to one of its clients) for the exclusive use of some particular organization.

quality of service (QoS) A specific level of service guarantee associated with Application layer protocols in which time-sensitivity requirements for data (such as voice or video) require that delays be controlled within definite guidelines to deliver viewable or audible data streams.

reachability The ability to find at least one transmission path between a pair of hosts so they can exchange datagrams across an internetwork.

reassembly The process applied at the Transport layer in which messages segmented into multiple chunks for transmission across the network are put back together in the proper order for delivery to an application on the receiving end. The IP Fragment Offset field is used to identify the order of the fragments for reassembly.

rebinding process The process of contacting any DHCP server through the use of a broadcast to obtain renewal of an address.

reconnaissance process The process of learning various characteristics about a network or host. Typically, reconnaissance probes precede network attacks.

recursive query A type of DNS query that continues until a definitive answer is forthcoming, be it a name-address translation, contents of the requested resource record(s), or an error message of some kind. Clients issue recursive queries to their designated name servers, which issue iterative queries to other name servers until the initial recursive request is resolved.

redirect To point out another path. Using ICMP, a router can redirect a host to another, more optimal router.

Redirect A message, or advertisement, sent out by a router to inform a sending node that there is a better first-hop router to access a destination node that is off-link or to inform the sending node that the destination node is on-link even though the network prefix is different.

registered port A TCP or UDP port number in the range from 1024 to 65535 and associated with a specific Application layer protocol or service. IANA maintains a registered port number list at *www.iana.org*.

Registry setting A configuration that controls the way in which Windows devices operate. There are numerous settings that define how Windows computers operate in a TCP/IP environment.

reinitialize To begin the standard DHCP Discovery sequence anew after failure of the renewal and rebinding processes. During the reinitializing phase, the DHCP client has no IP address and uses 0.0.0.0 as its source address.

relay agent process A process or execution thread that executes on a local host (which may be on a Windows workstation, server, or router) and forwards DHCP broadcasts as unicasts directed to a remote DHCP server for clients operating outside a DHCP broadcast domain.

release To deactivate an IP address on a client by formally sending a DHCP Release packet (MessageType 0x07) to the DHCP server. If a client shuts down without sending the Release packet, the DHCP server maintains the lease until expiration.

remote logon service Any type of network service that permits users elsewhere on a network to use the network to log on to a system as if they were attached locally while operating remotely. Such services are favorite attack points because they're designed to give outsiders access to systems and services.

Remote Monitoring (RMON) A TCP/IP Application layer protocol designed to support remote monitoring and management of networking devices, such as hubs, servers, and routers.

renewal process The process of renewing the IP address for continued use. By default, a DHCP client begins the renewal process halfway between the lease grant and the lease expiration time.

Request for Comments (RFCs) IETF standards documents that specify or describe best practices, provide information about the Internet, or specify an Internet protocol or service.

resolver *See* name resolver.

resource record (RR) One of a series of predefined record types in a DNS database or a DNS zone file.

Resource Reservation Protocol (RSVP) A protocol aimed at regularizing and formalizing the practice of securing particular levels of service for traffic flows over the Internet.

restricted NAT A NAT technology that maps the internal IP address and port of a computer only to specific IP addresses and port numbers, restricting access to others.

restricting link A link that does not support forwarding based on the current packet format and configuration. PMTU is used to identify restricting links so that hosts can resend packets using an acceptable MTU size.

retransmission timeout (RTO) The time value that determines when a TCP host retransmits a packet after it is lost. The RTO value is exponentially increased after an apparent connection loss.

retransmission timer The timer that maintains the RTO value.

retries The number of times a TCP peer resends data when no acknowledgment is received.

retry counter A counter that tracks the number of retransmissions on the network. The most common retry counter found in TCP/IP networking is the TCP retry counter. If a communication cannot be completed successfully before the retry counter expires, the transmission is considered a failure.

retry mechanism A method for detecting communication problems and resending data across the network.

Reverse Address Resolution Protocol (RARP) A Layer 2 or TCP/IP Network Access protocol that translates numeric IP addresses into MAC layer addresses (usually to verify that the identity claimed by a sender matches its real identity). This protocol was superseded by DHCP.

reverse DNS lookups *See* inverse DNS query.

reverse proxying The technique whereby a proxy server presents an internal network resource (e.g., a Web, e-mail, or FTP server) as if it were present on the proxy server itself so that external clients can access internal network resources without seeing internal network IP address structures.

rexec An abbreviation for *remote execution*, this is a BSD UNIX remote utility that permits network users to execute single commands on a remote host.

root The highest level in the domain name hierarchy, symbolized by a final period in a fully qualified domain name. Root DNS servers provide the glue that ties together all the disparate parts of the domain name hierarchy. Root DNS servers provide name resolution for queries that might otherwise go unresolved.

round-trip time The amount of time required to get from one host to another host and back. The round-trip time includes the transmission time from the first point to the second point, the processing time at the second point, and the return transmission time to the first point.

route aggregation A form of IP address analysis that permits routers to indicate general interest in a particular network prefix that represents the "common portion"of a series of IP network addresses as a way of reducing the number of individual routing table entries that routers must manage.

route priority A TOS priority that defines the network to route packets. The router must support and track multiple network types to make the appropriate forwarding decision based on the TOS defined in the IP header.

route resolution process The process that a host undergoes to determine whether a desired destination is local or remote and, if remote, which next-hop router to use.

Router Advertisement (RA) A message, or advertisement, sent out by a router, either periodically or on request, which contains its own link-layer address, the network prefix of the local subnet, the MTU for the local link, suggested hop limit values, and other parameters useful for nodes on the local link. RAs can also contain flagged parameters indicating the type of autoconfiguration that new nodes should use.

router queue A router buffering system used to hold packets when the router is congested.

Router Solicitation (RS) Network nodes use RS messages to ask routers connected to a local link to identify themselves by immediately sending an RA message, rather than waiting for

the next scheduled advertisement to appear. An RS message acts like a RA request, in other words.

router-to-router An IPv6-over-IPv4 tunneling configuration in which two IPv4/IPv6-capable routers are linked to transmit IPv6 traffic across an IPv4 network infrastructure.

route tracing A technique for documenting which hosts and routers a datagram traverses in its path from the sender to the receiver. (The `traceroute` and `tracert` commands use ping in a systematic way to provide this information.)

Routing and Addressing in Networks with Global Enterprise Recursion (RANGER) An architectural networking framework providing scalable routing and addressing in networks with global enterprise recursion. RANGER is built on ISATAP technology.

Routing Information Protocol (RIP) A simple, vector-based TCP/IP networking protocol used to determine a single pathway between a sender and a receiver on a local internetwork.

routing The process whereby a packet makes its way from a sender to a receiver based on known paths (or routes) from the sending network to the receiving network.

routing loops A network configuration that enables packets to circle the network. Split horizon and poison reverse are used to resolve routing loops on distance vector networks. OSPF networks automatically resolve loops by defining best paths through an internetwork.

routing protocol A Layer 3 protocol designed to permit routers to exchange information about networks that are reachable, the routes by which they may be reached, and the costs associated with such routes.

routing tables Local host tables maintained in memory. The routing tables are referenced before forwarding packets to remote destinations in order to find the most appropriate next-hop router for the packet.

rpr An abbreviation for *remote print*, this is a BSD UNIX remote utility that permits network users to print a file on a remote host.

rsh An abbreviation for *remote shell*, this is a BSD UNIX remote utility that permits network users to launch and operate a login session on a remote host.

runts *See* undersized packets.

r-utils An abbreviation for *remote utilities*, this is a collection of software programs, originally included as part of BSD UNIX v4.2, designed to provide remote access and login services for users. Hence, they are a common point of attack.

Samba A free software service that provides file and print sharing for Windows and that can interoperate with other operating systems, such as Linux.

sandbox An IT environment that is isolated from the production network for the purpose of testing or containing things that could disrupt service on the production network—for example, testing failover scenarios or virus or botnet removal features.

scope Defined by Microsoft as a group of addresses that can be assigned by a Microsoft DHCP server. Other vendors refer to this as an address pool or address range.

scope identifier In IPv6, a 4-bit field limiting the valid range for a multicast address. In IPv6 multicast addresses, not all values are defined, but among those defined are the site-local and the link-local scope. Multicast addresses are not valid outside their configured scope and will not be forwarded beyond it.

screening firewall A firewall model whereby all traffic to a given port is blocked, regardless of any other packet. All traffic traversing the firewall must be explicitly defined.

screening host The role that a firewall or proxy server plays when presenting an internal network service for external consumption.

screening router A boundary router that's been configured to monitor and filter inbound traffic on the basis of IP or port addresses, domain names, or spoofing attempts.

secondary DNS server A DNS server that contains a copy of a domain or subdomain database, along with copies of the related zone files, but that must synchronize its database and related files with whatever server is primary for that domain or subdomain.

secondary master *See* secondary DNS server.

security policy A document that represents the concrete manifestation of an organization's requirements for security practices, rules, and procedures, and that identifies all assets worth protecting and lays out disaster or business recovery processes should system loss or compromise occur.

segment The name of the PDU for the TCP protocol in a TCP/IP environment.

segmentation The process whereby TCP takes a message larger than an underlying network medium's MTU and breaks it up into a numbered sequence of chunks less than or equal to the MTU in size.

selective acknowledgment Also referred to as SACK, this method defines how a TCP peer can identify specific segments that were successfully received. This functionality is defined in RFC 2018.

sequence number tracking The process of following the current sequence number sent by a TCP peer and sending an acknowledgment value to indicate the next-expected sequence number.

Service Access Point (SAP) A protocol identification field that is defined in the 802.2 LLC header that follows the MAC header.

Service location (SRV) record A record designed to provide information about available services, and used in the Windows Active Directory (AD) environment to map the name of a service to the name of a server that offers such service. AD clients and domain controllers use SRV records to determine IP addresses for (other) domain controllers.

service provider In contrast with "enterprise," the IT environment of an organization that provides service to multiple customers—for example, an Internet service provider.

session A temporary, but ongoing, exchange of messages between a sender and a receiver on a network.

session hijacking An IP attack technique whereby an imposter takes over an ongoing communications session between a client and server, thereby assuming whatever rights and permissions the hijacked session may enjoy. This is a difficult technique to pull off, and recent changes to TCP sequence numbers make this harder to accomplish today than it was prior to their implementation.

Session layer Layer 5 in the ISO/OSI reference model. The Session layer handles setup, maintenance, and tear-down of ongoing exchanges of messages between pairs of hosts on a network.

silent discard The process of discarding a packet without notification to any other device that such a discarding process occurred. For example, a black hole router silently discards packets that it cannot forward.

Silly Window Syndrome (SWS) A TCP windowing problem caused by an application removing only small amounts of data from a full TCP receiver buffer, thereby causing a TCP peer to advertise a very small window. To address this problem, TCP hosts wait until the window size reaches the MSS value.

single-homed The act or state of having uplinks to a single system. For example, an enterprise network with redundant connections to a single ISP would be considered single-homed, whereas having connections to two different ISPs would be multihomed.

site-local address This addressing scheme is limited to use in private networks within a specific site.

slave router On an OSPF network, this type of router receives and acknowledges link-state database summary packets from a master router.

slave server *See* secondary DNS server.

sliding window A set of data that is sent along a sliding timeline. As transmitted data is acknowledged, the window moves over to send more data to the TCP peer.

Slow Start algorithm A method for sending data in exponentially increasing increments, starting typically at twice the MSS value. The Slow Start algorithm is used to learn the network's maximum window size.

socket address A numeric TCP/IP address that concatenates a network host's numeric IP address (first 4 bytes) with the port address for some specific process or service on that host (last 2 bytes) to uniquely identify that process across the entire Internet.

socket *See* socket address.

software security The aspect of security that focuses on monitoring and maintaining systems and software to prevent and oppose as many potential sources of attack as possible. From this perspective, software security is both a mindset and a regular routine rather than a "set it and forget it" kind of activity.

solicited-node address A multicast address with link-local scope, which helps reduce the number of multicast groups to which nodes must subscribe in order to make themselves available for solicitation by other nodes on their local links. The solicited-node address is FF02::1:FF*xx.xxxx*, in which *xx.xxxx* stands for the lowest-order (rightmost) 24 bits of the unicast or anycast address associated with that interface.

source port number The sender's port address for a TCP or UDP PDU.

split horizon rule A rule used to eliminate the counting-to-infinity problem. The split horizon rule states that information cannot be sent back the same direction from which it was received.

spoofing Occurs when incoming IP traffic exhibits addressing mismatches. Address spoofing occurs when an external interface ferries traffic that purports to originate inside a network, or when a user presents an IP address that doesn't match a domain name. Domain name spoofing occurs when a reverse lookup of an IP address does not match the domain from where the traffic claims to originate.

spyware Unsolicited and unwanted software that takes up stealthy unauthorized and uninvited residence on a computer and gathers information about its user(s), including account names, passwords, and other sensitive data it can glean during normal system operation, which it will ultimately export for misuse to some malicious third party.

Start of Authority (SOA) record The DNS resource record that's mandatory in every DNS zone file; it identifies the server or servers that are authoritative for the domain or subdomain to which the zone files or database correspond.

stateful autoconfiguration A method for providing IPv6 address assignments by a DHCPv6-enabled server to requesting hosts on a network.

stateless address autoconfiguration (SLAAC) A mechanism by which an IPv6 host creates its own addresses using a combination of locally available address data and information advertised by routers.

stateless autoconfiguration A method allowing nodes to automatically configure an IPv6 address. Stateless autoconfiguration involves minimal configuration of an on-link router and does not require a DHCPv6 server.

stateless IP/ICMP translation algorithm (SIIT) An IPv4/IPv6 address translation model designed to replace NAT-PT and characterized by two domains, an IPv4 domain and an IPv6 domain, that communicate over an IP/ICMP translator.

statistics Short-term or long-term historical information regarding network communications and performance, captured by a protocol analyzer or other similar software.

stealthy attacker An attacker that hides its tracks. Stealthy attackers may ensure no log entries implicate their actions and no live connections remain after they launch their attacks.

subdomain A named element within a specific domain name, denoted by adding an additional name and period before the parent domain name. Thus, clearlake.ibm.com is a subdomain of the ibm.com domain.

subnet mask A special bit pattern that masks off the network portion of an IP address with all 1s.

subnetting The operation of using bits borrowed from the host portion of an IP address to extend and subdivide the address space that falls beneath the network portion of a range of IP addresses.

success criteria In project management, a list of conditions used to define whether an activity has completed successfully or not.

summary address A form of specialized IP network address that identifies the "common portion" of a series of IP network addresses used when route aggregation is in effect. This approach speeds routing behavior and decreases the number of entries necessary for routing tables.

supernetting The technique of borrowing bits from the network portion of an IP address and lending those bits to the host part, creating a larger address space for host addresses.

superscope Defined by Microsoft as a collection of IP address scopes, as managed by any single DHCP server. Other vendors refer to this as a collection of address pools or address ranges.

symbolic name A human-readable name for an Internet resource, such as *www.course.com* or *www.microsoft.com*; also a name used to represent a device instead of an address.

symmetric NAT A NAT solution that requires the same IP address and port number to be mapped from the internal network to the external network.

Synchronous Data Link Control (SDLC) A synchronous communication protocol.

Synchronous Optical Network (SONET) A family of fiber-optic digital transmission services that offers data rates from 51.84 Mbps (OC-1) to 38.88 Gbps (OC-768).

Systems Network Architecture (SNA) The name of a protocol suite developed by IBM for use in its proprietary mainframe-based and minicomputer-based networking environments.

T1 A digital signaling link whose name stands for trunk level 1; it is used as a standard for digital signaling in North America. T1 links offer aggregate bandwidth of 1.544 Mbps and can support up to 24 voice-grade digital channels of 64 Kbps each, or they may be split between voice and data.

T3 A digital signaling link whose name stands for trunk level 3; it is used as a standard for digital signaling in North America. T3 links offer aggregate bandwidth of 28T1s or 44.736 Mbps. T3 runs on coax or fiber-optic cable, or via microwave transmission, and it is becoming a standard link for small-scale and mid-scale ISPs.

T-carrier The generic telephony term for trunk carrier connections that offer digital services to communications customers directly from the communications carrier itself (usually a local or long-distance phone or communications company).

TCP buffer area A queuing area used to hold incoming and outgoing TCP packets. If a TCP packet has the Push flag set, the packet should not be held in either the incoming or outgoing TCP buffer area.

TCP/IP *See* Transmission Control Protocol/Internet Protocol.

teardown sequence The process of closing a TCP connection.

temporary port A port that is used for the duration of the connection. The port numbers assigned to temporary ports are also called dynamic port numbers or ephemeral port numbers.

Teredo Also known as Teredo tunneling, this IPv4-over-IPv6 transition technology allows Teredo nodes to communicate with IPv6 nodes over an IPv4 network infrastructure, even when the Teredo nodes are located on LAN behind a NAT.

Teredo bubble packets Specialized packets sent by a Teredo node when it is not behind a NAT, in order to initiate communication with an IPv6 network node.

Teredo host-specific relay An IPv4/IPv6 node directly connected to both an IPv4 Internet and an IPv6 Internet and that communicates with Teredo client nodes over its IPv4 connection without going through a Teredo relay.

Teredo relay An IPv4/IPv6 router that uses host-to-router and router-to-router tunneling to forward packets from Teredo clients on IPv4 networks to IPv6 nodes on an IPv6-capable network and from those IPv6 nodes to Teredo clients.

Teredo server An IPv4/IPv6 stateless server device that connects to both IPv4 and IPv6 networks and facilitates communication between different Teredo nodes and between Teredo and IPv6 nodes.

test-attack-tune cycle The most important part of deploying security systems or components, this set of activities should be repeated until test and attack operations produce no further changes to system or component configuration or tuning.

text (TXT) record A DNS resource record that can accommodate arbitrary ASCII text data, often used to describe a DNS database segment, the hosts it contains, and so forth.

three-way handshake A TCP negotiation process between two computers attempting to establish a network session.

throughput difference The comparative difference in throughput between two paths. Throughput is measured in Kbps or Mbps.

time synchronization The process of obtaining the exact same time on multiple hosts. Network Time Protocol (NTP) is a time synchronization protocol.

time to live (TTL) An indication of the remaining distance that a packet can travel. Though defined in terms of seconds, the TTL value is implemented as a number of hops that a packet can travel before being discarded by a router. The Time to Live field is often abbreviated as TTL.

time wait delay An amount of time that a TCP host must not use connection parameters after closing down that connection.

timeout mechanism A method for determining when to stop resending data across packets. The timeout mechanism consists of a retry timer and a maximum number of retries.

trace buffer An area of memory or hard disk space set aside for the storage of packets captured off the network by a protocol analyzer.

Traceroute See Tracert.

Tracert The name of the Windows command that uses multiple ping commands to establish the identity and round-trip times for all hosts between a sender and a receiver.

trailer An optional, concluding portion of a PDU that usually contains data integrity check information for the preceding content in that PDU.

Transmission Control Protocol (TCP) A robust, reliable, connection-oriented protocol that operates at the Transport layer in both the TCP/IP and ISO/OSI reference models and that gives TCP/IP part of its name.

Transmission Control Protocol/Internet Protocol (TCP/IP) The name of the standard protocols and services in use on the Internet, denoted by the names of the two key constituent protocols: the Transmission Control Protocol, or TCP, and the Internet Protocol, or IP.

Transport layer Layer 4 of the ISO/OSI network reference model and the third layer of the TCP/IP network model. The Transport layer handles delivery of data from sender to receiver.

Transport Relay Translator (TRT) This is a method that allows an IPv6 network node to send upper-layer protocol data such as TCP or UDP to an IPv4 network node.

tree structure A type of organized data structure, such as a taxonomy or a disk drive listing, in which the entire container acts as the root, and in which subcontainers may include either other lower-level subcontainers or instances of whatever kinds of objects may occur within a container. The domain name hierarchy adheres to an inverted tree structure because the root usually appears at the top of diagrams drawn to represent it.

true hybrid model A virtual network infrastructure model describing an environment of mixed IPv4, IPv6, and dual IPv4/IPv-capable networks embedded in a larger network infrastructure, with no one version of IP being dominant in the core.

tunneling interface The network interface used by a device that performs encapsulation of IPv6 packets in IPv4 headers and is linked to the next-hop device over an IPv4 network infrastructure.

two-way handshake A two-packet handshake that is not fully completed. This process is indicative of the TCP SYN attack.

Type of Service (TOS) A process used to define a type of path that a packet should take through the network. TOS options include the greatest throughput, lowest delay, and most reliability.

undersized packets Packets that are below minimum packet size requirements and point to potential hardware or driver problems.

unicast packet A packet sent to a single device on the network.

Uniform Resource Locator (URL) Web terminology for an address that specifies the protocol (http://), location (domain name), directory (/directory-name/), and filename (example.html) so that a browser can access a resource.

Universal Naming Convention (UNC) path Also referred to as a Uniform Naming Convention path or an UNC path, this is a naming format that points to the location of devices and resources on a network.

Universal Time (UT) Sometimes called Universal Coordinate Time (UCT), Greenwich Mean Time (GMT), or Zulu Time. this is a time scale based on the Earth's rotation.

unnumbered format A format of 802.2 LLC packet that is connectionless.

unsolicited Unrequested. Unsolicited replies are typically advertisements that occur on a periodic basis. For example, ICMP Router Advertisements typically occur on a 7–10 minute basis.

unspecified address In IPv6, the unspecified address is all 0s and can be represented as "::" in normal notation. This is essentially the address that is no address. It cannot be used as a destination address.

user impersonation A system or network attack technique whereby an unauthorized user, to gain entry, presents valid credentials that rightfully belong to an authorized user and then exploits whatever rights and privileges that the impersonated user's identity allows.

valid data Data that follows the headers but does not consist of any padding or extraneous data.

variable-length subnet masking (VLSM) A subnetting scheme for IP addresses that permits containers of various sizes to be defined for a network prefix. The largest subnet defines the maximum container size, and any individual container in that address space may be further subdivided into multiple, smaller subcontainers (sometimes called sub-subnets).

victim The focus of an attack.

virtual connection A logical connection between two TCP peers. The virtual connection requires end-to-end connectivity.

virtual private network (VPN) A network connection (containing one or more packaged protocols) between a specific sender and receiver in which information sent is often encrypted. A VPN uses public networks—like the Internet—to deliver secure, private information from sender to receiver.

virus A code that can spread through a machine to alter or destroy files.

Voice over IP (VoIP) A communications technology that allows voice and multimedia communication sessions over IP networks (for example, the Internet or an intranet).

vulnerability Any aspect of a system that is open to attack, especially any well-known protocol, service, subsystem, or hole that is documented and relatively easy to exploit.

Wait Acknowledgment (WACK) A message sent by a network device such as a WINS server to acknowledge the receipt of a message from a sending node and directing the sending node to wait rather than sending more packets or expecting more data.

watchdog process A process used by NetWare servers to determine whether the NetWare clients are still active and maintaining the connection between the two devices.

well-known port number A 16-bit number that identifies a pre-assigned value associated with some well-known Internet protocol or service that operates at the TCP/IP Application layer. Most well-known port numbers fall in the range from 0 to 1024. Also called a well-known port address.

well-known protocol An 8-bit number in the header of an IP packet that identifies the protocol in use, as per IANA.

well-known service A synonym for a recognizable TCP/IP protocol or service; these assignments are documented at the IANA site.

well-known services (WKS) record A DNS resource record that describes the well-known IP services available from a host, such as Telnet, FTP, and so forth. WKS records are less available to outsiders than they once were because they identify hosts that could become points of potential attack.

windowing The process of acknowledging multiple packets with a single acknowledgment.

Windows clustering Windows Server technology that enables automatic restoration of services to an alternate server upon detection of a primary server failure.

words Blocks of four 16-bit values in an IPv6 address; each word is separated by a colon, and there are eight words in every IPv6 address. If a word is made up of contiguous 0s, it can be compressed so that the 0s do not appear in the address but the colon separators remain.

X.25 A popular standard for packet-switched data networks, originally defined by the International Telephony Union (ITU), that's widely used for data communications networks outside North America.

zero-window state A situation when a TCP peer advertises a window value of 0. A TCP host cannot continue sending to a TCP peer that advertises a window of 0.

zone A portion of the domain name hierarchy that corresponds to the database segment managed by some particular name server or collection of name servers.

zone data file Any of several specific files used to capture DNS database information for static storage when a DNS server is shut down or when a secondary DNS server requests synchronization with its primary DNS server's database.

zone file *See* zone data file.

zone transfer The DNS mechanism in which a secondary DNS server gets its data for the zone from the master server for that zone. The secondary server checks a specific field in its SOA record and compares it to a corresponding value in the master server's database. Where differences are noted, the secondary server updates its database from the primary domain name server.

Index

A

ABRs (area border routers), 196

Acceptable Use Policies (AUPs), 4

access control, 677

Acknowledgment packet, DHCP, 383–385

Active Directory (AD) services, 455

address embedding, 90

addressing. *See also* IP address autoconfiguration; IP addressing

aggregatable global unicast, 85–86, 198

anycast, 84–85, 88

in DHCPv4, 384–387, 393

DNS queries in, 477

hardware, 161

IPv6, 622, 633

in ISATAP (Intra-Site Automatic Tunnel Addressing Protocol), 586–588

mapping to names, in DNS files, 462–463

in Network layer, 12

socket, 23

solicited-node, 323

source and destination address selection, 466–472, 481–482

spoofing, 132, 661, 664

at TCPIP Internet layer, 18

Address Mask Request and Address Mask Reply message, 264, 274–275

address masquerading, 70, 72

address name records, in DNS files, 460–462

address resolution, in Neighbor Discovery process, 348–350

Address Resolution Protocol (ARP). *See* ARP (Address Resolution Protocol)

adjacencies database, 192

adoption rates, IPv6, 565–566

Advanced Research Projects Agency (ARPA), U.S. Department of Defense (DoD), 2

advertised window, in congestion control, 538

Advertisement Interval option in NDP, 343–344

adware, 670

AF (Assured Forwarding) classes, 113

agent, Mobile IP, 229

aggregatable global unicast addresses, 85–86, 198

Akamai, 90

alarms, in protocol analysis, 27

All-New Switch Book: The Complete Guide to LAN Switching Technology, The (Seifert and Edwards), 29

allowable data size, 297

analog phone lines, 157

anti-sniff software, 674

anycast IPv6 addresses, 84–85, 88

anycast packets, 26

APIPA (automatic private IP addressing), 372, 378–379

AppleTalk, 17

AppleTalk Update-based Routing Protocol (AURP), 193

Application layer, 15, 20–21

applications, migrating, 639

application-specific integrated circuits (ASICs), 74, 616, 620

architectural decisions, in IPv6 deployment, 618–625

area border routers (ABRs), 196

Ariston Digital, 81

arithmetic, binary, 65

ARP (Address Resolution Protocol), 164–172

cache, 164, 169–171

fields and functions, 166–169

flexibility from, 664

MAC layer addresses and, 59

overview, 164–166

proxy, 171

reverse, 171–172

at TCP/IP Internet layer, 18

ARPA (Advanced Research Projects Agency), U.S. Department of Defense (DoD), 2

ARPANET, 2–4

ASICs (application-specific integrated circuits), 74, 616, 620

ASN (Autonomous System Numbers), 219, 620

ASs (autonomous systems), 197

Assured Forwarding (AF) classes, 113

ATM (Asynchronous Transfer Mode), 17, 157

attacks. *See* security, TCP/IP

AURP (AppleTalk Update-based Routing Protocol), 193

authentication, 130–132, 677

Authentication Header (AH), 677

autoconfiguration, IP address. *See* IP address autoconfiguration

automatic private IP addressing (APIPA), 372, 378–379

Autonomous System Numbers (ASN), 219, 620

autonomous systems (ASs), 197

available routes, router advertisements for, 301

average response time, Ping for, 292

Axis Communications, 81

B

backbone area, 196

back doors, as security threats, 667

backup designated router (BDR), 214

backward compatibility, 297

basic hybrid network model, 570

bastion host, to protect network, 678

BCP (Best Current Practice), 8

BDR (backup designated router), 214

Berkeley Remote Utilities, 666

Berkeley Software Distribution, 4

Best Current Practice (BCP), 8

"best-effort delivery," 19

BGP (Border Gateway Protocol)

as distance vector routing protocol, 189

for IPv4 routing, 218–219

in IPv6 deployment, 620

multiple services supported by, 184

at TCP/IP Internet layer, 19

binary arithmetic, 65

binary boundaries, 75

Bitcricket IP Calculator, 68

black hole router, 298

black holes, 196

BOOTP (Bootstrap Protocol), 19, 171–172, 373

Border Gateway Protocol (BGP). *See* BGP (Border Gateway Protocol)

boundary router, to protect network, 678

break-ins, 663

broadband cable infrastructures, 157

broadcast addressing

in DHCPv4, 393

in IPv4, 61–65

IPv6 elimination of, 84

broadcast packets, 26

broadcast routing, 195

buffer overflows/overruns, 672

bytes, in numeric addresses, 58

C

cable modems, 157

cable segments, 12

caching DNS server, 454–455, 457–458

canonical name records, in DNS files, 460–462

Carrier Sense Multiple Access with Collision Detection (CSMA/CD), 17

Centre European de Researche Nucleaire (CERN), 4

CGA (Cryptographically Generated Addresses), 404

chat, 115

checkpoints, in Session layer, 14

checksums

in fragmentation, 182

in ICMP, 260

in IP packet structure header field, 119

in Transport layer PDUs, 13

upper-layer, 137–138

CIDR (classless inter-domain routing), 68–70, 75, 198

circuit switching, 12, 157

Cisco Systems, 218, 228, 675

Client Identifier field, 382

client side, of DNS, 477

cloud, 485–486, 565

CLSM (constant-length subnet masking), 67–68

Code field, in ICMP, 258–260

Code Red worm, 5

command line parameters, for, Ping, 293

Commercial Internet Exchange (CIX), 4

community storage solutions, 115

compression, 677

conceptual host model, 345–346

conceptual sending algorithm, 346–348

cone NAT (network address translation), 599

confidentiality, 677

configuration files, DNS, 458–463

Congestion Avoidance algorithm, 539

congestion control, 115–116, 254, 538–540

connectionless integrity, 677

connectionless protocols, 19, 514

connection-management protocols, 16

connection-oriented protocols, 19, 516

connection states, TCP/IP, 534–535

connection termination, TCP/IP, 533

connectivity testing, 291–293

constant ICMP fields, 257

constant-length subnet masking (CLSM), 67–68

convergence, of routing tables, 189, 193

counting to infinity, 191

crackers, 660

CRC (cyclical redundancy check) procedure, 159

Cryptographically Generated Addresses (CGA), 404

CSMA/CD (Carrier Sense Multiple Access with Collision Detection), 17

current window, in congestion control, 538

D

DAD (Duplicate Address Detection), 329, 351–352, 400

daemons ("listener process"), 20

DARPA (Defense Advanced Research Projects Agency), U.S. Department of Defense (DoD), 3

database, DNS (Domain Name System), 450–453

data encapsulation, 23–24, 156

data frames, PDUs as, 12

data link address, 161

Data Link and Network layer protocols, 155–251

ARP (Address Resolution Protocol)

    cache, 169–171

    overview, 163–166

    packet fields and functions, 166–169

    proxy, 171

    reverse, 171–172

Ethernet frames, 159–163

fragmentation and reassembly, 181–183

in-house internetworks, 227

to and from Internet, 230

Internet Protocol, 175–180

IP datagram lifetime, 180–181

IP routing, 186–193

IPv4 routing, 210–219

    BGP (Border Gateway Protocol), 218–219

    EIGRP (Enhanced Interior Gateway Routing Protocol), 218

    OSPF (Open Shortest Path First), 214–218

    RIP (Routing Information Protocol), 210–214

IPv6 routing, 197–210, 219–226

    EIGRP for IPv6, 223

    IS-IS for IPv6, 223–225

    mechanisms for, 198–204

    MP-BGP for IPv6, 225–226

    multicast listener discovery, 204–210

OSPFv3 for IPv6, 221–223

RIPng for IPv6, 219–221

NDP Protocol, 172–174

overview, 156–157

PPP (Point-to-Point Protocol), 158–159

precedence, 184

routers

characteristics, 193–197

securing, 231

troubleshooting, 231–232

service delivery options, 183–184

TOS (type of service), 184–186

for wide-area networks (WANs), 228–230

Data Link layer

NBMA (nonbroadcast multiple-access network), 90

overview, 12

physical numeric address at, 59

data origin authentication, 677

data segments, 14

data size, allowable, 297

DB PHB (Delay Bound per-hop-behavior), 114

DDNS (Dynamic DNS updates), 466, 479–480

DDoS (distributed denial of service) attacks, 670–671

decodes, in protocol analysis, 24, 27

default gateway, 156, 164, 177

Default TTL Registry setting, 181

Defense Advanced Research Projects Agency (DARPA), U.S. Department of Defense (DoD), 3

Defense Communications Agency (DCA), 3

Defense Information Systems Agency (DISA), 3

Delay Bound per-hop-behavior (DB PHB), 114

demilitarized zone (DMZ), to protect network, 678

demultiplexing, 21

denial of service (DoS) attacks. See DoS (denial of service) attacks

deploying IPv6. See IPv6 deployment

designated router (DR), 214

destination address field, in IP packet structures, 120

destination address field, in IPv6 header, 125

destination options, in IPv6 extension headers, 127–128

destination port number, 23

Destination Unreachable packets, 261, 266–270, 298

DHCP (Dynamic Host Configuration Protocol)

BOOTP and, 19

broadcast addresses and, 61

in IP address autoconfiguration, 373–378

IP addresses and, 120

Microsoft Windows Server 2008 scopes, 419–420

server setup, 420–425

DHCP Unique Identifier (DUID), 404

DHCPv4

address release process, 387

address renewal process, 384–386

APIPA (automatic private IP addressing), 378–379

broadcast and unicast addressing, 393

DHCP Discovery, 379–384

DHCP relay agent, 374, 393–395

packet structures, 387–393

DHCPv6

messages, 405–412

overview, 404–405

relay message exchange, 414–415

stateless message exchange, 413–414

updating to, 636

diagnostic tool, loopback as, 82

Differentiated Services (Diffserv), 113–115, 184

Digital subscriber Line (DSL) connections, 157, 159

Dijkstra algorithm, 191, 215

"direct to disk" save option, in protocol analysis, 27

Discover packet, DHCP, 380–382

display filters, in protocol analysis, 26

distance vector routing protocols, 189–190, 210

distributed denial of service (DDoS) attacks, 670–671

divide and conquer approach, 8

DNS (Domain Name System)

caching, 457–458

configuration files and resource records, 458–463

configuring for ISATAP, 645

database records, 452–453

database structure, 450–451

delegating authority, 453

dynamic update, 479–480

in IPv6 networks, 464–466

namespace, 452

in Network layer, 12

as network protocol, 447

overview, 449–450

resolver, 476–477

server operations, 453–455, 455–457

server service, 477–479

in transitioning to IPv6, 579

troubleshooting, 488

updating, 635–636

domain controllers, 455

domain names, 58

Domain of Interpretation (DOI), 677

DoS (denial of service) attacks, 115, 231, 532, 664–665, 670

dotted decimal notation, 60

DR (designated router), 214

drop probability classification, 113

DSCP (differentiated services code point) identifier, 113

DSL (Digital Subscriber Line) connections, 157, 159

dual-IP-layer architecture, for transitioning to IPv6, 575–576

dual protocol stacks, for transitioning to IPv6, 574–575

dual stack, in IPv6 deployment, 628–631

dual-stack architecture, for transitioning to IPv6, 576–577

DUID (DHCP Unique Identifier), 404

duplicate ACKs, 539

Duplicate Address Detection (DAD), 329, 351–352, 400

dynamically assigned port address, 23

Dynamic DNS updates (DDNS), 466, 479–480

Dynamic Host Configuration Protocol (DHCP). See DHCP (Dynamic Host Configuration Protocol)

E

Echo Reply and Echo Request messages, 137, 262, 264–266, 282–283

ECN (Explicit Congestion Notification), 115–116, 184

e-commerce transactions, 115

Edwards, James, 29

EF (Expedited Forwarding) per-hop behavior (PHB), 114

EGP (Exterior Gateway Protocol), 189, 197, 620

EIGRP (Enhanced Interior Gateway Routing Protocol), 218, 223, 228

e-mail, protocols for, 21

Encapsulating Security Payload (ESP) header, 131–132, 677

encapsulation, data, 23–24

encryption, 70–71, 132

"end of data" flags, 11

end-to-end connection, secure, 70–71

end-to-end error-detection and error-recovery data, 13

end-to-end minimum MTU size, 296

Enhanced Interior Gateway Routing Protocol (EIGRP), 218, 223, 228

envelope information, in PDUs, 11

error detection

checksum as, 119

ICMPv6, 278–282

in protocol analysis, 26

in TCP/IP transport layer protocols, 536–538

in trailers, 11

in Transport layer, 13

Ethernet

collision fragments in, 26

Gigabit, 16, 159

local area networks (LANs) using, 3

NIC and, 11

PPP over (PPPoE), 17, 157

in TCP/IP Network Access layer, 16

Ethernet frames, 159–163

EUI-64 format, for interface identifiers, 80

Expedited Forwarding (EF) per-hop behavior (PHB), 114–115

Explicit Congestion Notification (ECN), 115–116, 184

exploits, 663

extended network prefix, 66

extendible intradomain routing protocol, 223

extension headers, 547–548

Exterior Gateway Protocol (EGP), 620

external conditions, in IPv6 deployment, 620

external route entry, 214

F

Facebook, 90, 564

Fast Retransmit process, 539

FCS (Frame Check Sequence), 158, 161

File Transfer Protocol (FTP), 20–21

filters, in protocol analysis, 26

firewalking, 304

firewalls, 75, 678, 680–682

flags, "end of data," 11

flags field, in IP packet structures, 117–118

flow label field, in IPv6 header, 123, 623

forwarding table, 192

FQDN (fully qualified domain name), 487

fragmentation

fragment IPv6 extension headers, 129–130

fragment offset field, in IP packet structures, 118

at IP layer, 13–14

in IP structures, 117

MTU, 18

reassembly and, 181–183

Frame Check Sequence (FCS), 158, 161

Frame relay service, 17

frames, PDUs as, 12

FTP (File Transfer Protocol), 20–21

full-duplex communication, 29

fully qualified domain name (FQDN), 487

G

gaming, online, 115

Gigabit Ethernet, 16, 159

globally unique identifiers, 81

Google, 90, 564

Greenwich Mean Time (GMT), 273

H

hackers, 81, 303, 660

half-open connections, TCP/IP, 531–532

handshake process, for virtual connections, 517, 527–530

hardware addresses. *See* Data Link and Network layer protocols

HDLC (High-level Data Link Control) protocol, 17, 158

header checksum field, in IP packet structures, 119

header length field, in IP packet structures, 111

headers. *See also* IP packet structures

authentication, 677

Encapsulating Security Payload (ESP), 677

envelope information in, 11

extension, for UDP, TCP, and IPv6, 547–548

ICMPv4, 256–260

ICMPv6, 278

PDU, 23–24

in TCP/IP transport layer protocols, 541–545

UDP (User Datagram Protocol), 520–523

Hello process, for neighbor routers, 192

Hitachi, 81

holes, as security threats, 667

Home Agent Information option in NDP, 344

honeypots and honeynets, for security, 684

hop-by-hop IPv6 extension headers, 127, 132

hop-by-hop options, 134–135

hop limit field, in IPv6 header, 125

hosts

in IP addressing, 74–75, 79–80

IPv6 deployment upgrading, 639–643

in Local Area Mobility, 229

in name resolution, 449, 474–476

host-to-host tunneling configuration, 582

host-to-router tunneling configuration, 581–582

HTTP (Hypertext Transfer Protocol), 4

hub and spoke routing, 228

hubbing out, in protocol analysis, 29

Hypertext Transfer Protocol (HTTP), 4

hypervisors, 635

I

IAB (Internet Architecture Board), 6

IANA (Internet Assigned Numbers Authority), 63, 73

IBM, Inc., 17, 158, 453

ICANN (Internet Corporation for Assigned Names and Numbers), 6, 63, 73

ICMCP (Internet Control Message Control Protocol), 126

ICMP (Internet Control Message Protocol), 253–320

decoding packets, 304–307

flexibility from, 664

ICMPv4 header, 256–260

ICMPv4 messages, 260–264, 290

ICMPv4 variable structures and functions, 264–276

Address Mask Request and Address Mask Reply message, 274–275

Destination Unreachable packets, 261, 266–270

Echo Reply and Echo Request packets, 264–266

Information Request and Information Reply message, 274

Parameter Problem message, 273

Redirect messages, 270–271

Router Advertisement and Router Solicitation, 271–272

Source Quench, 261

Time Exceeded packets, 261, 272–273

Timestamp and Timestamp Reply message, 273–274

Traceroute packet, 275–276

ICMPv6 error messages, 278–282

ICMPv6 headers, 278

ICMPv6 informational messages, 282–290

Echo Request and Echo Reply, 282–283

Neighbor Solicitation and Neighbor Advertisement, 286–287

Redirect, 287–288

Router Advertisement and Router Solicitation, 283–285

Router Renumbering, 288–290

ICMPv6 messages, 276–278, 290

IP network roles of, 254–255

overview, 254

PMTU (Path MTU) Discovery, 290–291

RFCs on, 255–256

SIIT (Stateless IP/ICMP translation algorithm), 573

at TCP/IP Internet layer, 18

troubleshooting, 291–304

Pathping for path discovery, 294

Ping for connectivity testing, 291–293

PMTU Discovery with ICMP, 294–298

routing sequences, 298–302

security issues, 302–304

Traceroute for path discovery, 293–294

ICMP Echo communication, 291

ICMP redirect attack, 303

ICMP Router Advertisements, 195–196

ICMP Router Discovery, 229, 298–300

ICMP Router Solicitation packets, 298

identification field, in IP packet structures, 117

IDS (intrusion detection system), 683

IEEE (Institute of Electrical and Electronic Engineers) networking standards, 16–17

IETF (Internet Engineering Task Force), 6, 78, 133, 568

IGMP (Internet Group Management Protocol), 62, 204, 267

IGPs (interior gateway protocols), 189

IHL (Internet Header Length), 111

IKE (Internet Key Exchange) protocol, 677

illegal boundaries of packets, 26

IMAP (Internet Message Access Protocol), 21

INETINFO.EXE process, in Windows Server 2008, 20

Information Request and Information Reply message, 274

Information Technology and Infrastructure Library (ITIL), 632

in-house internetwork, 227

instant messaging (IM), 115

Institute of Electrical and Electronic Engineers (IEEE) networking standards, 16–17

Integrated Services Digital Network (ISDN), 159

inter-autonomous system routing, 219

interdomain routing protocols, 218

interface identifiers, in IPv6 addressing, 80–81

interior routing protocol, in IPv6 deployment, 618–620

Intermediate System-to-Intermediate System (IS-IS), 223–225

internal route entry, 214

International Organization for Standardization Open Systems Interconnection network reference model (ISO/OSI network reference model), 8

Internet Architecture Board (IAB), 6

Internet Assigned Numbers Authority (IANA), 63, 73

Internet Control Message Protocol (ICMP). *See* ICMP (Internet Control Message Protocol)

Internet Corporation for Assigned Names and Numbers (ICANN), 6, 63, 73

Internet Engineering Task Force (IETF), 6, 78, 133, 568

Internet Explorer browser (Microsoft), 5

Internet Group Management Protocol (IGMP), 62, 204, 267

Internet Header Length (IHL), 111

Internet Key Exchange (IKE) protocol, 677

Internet layer, TCP/IP, 18–19

Internet Message Access Protocol (IMAP). *See* IMAP (Internet Message Access Protocol)

Internet Network Information Center (InterNIC), 5

Internet Official Protocol Standards, 7

Internet Protocol (IP), 175–180. *See also* TCP/IP (Transmission Control Protocol/Internet Protocol)

   fragmentation and reassembly, 181–183

   IP datagrams, 175–176, 180–181

   in IPv4 *versus* IPv6, 179–180

   route resolution, 176–179

   at TCP/IP Internet layer, 18

Internet Protocol Control Protocol (IPCP), 158

Internet Research Task Force (IRTF), 6

Internet routing protocols, 230

Internet Security Association and Key Management Protocol (ISAKMP), 677

Internet service providers (ISPs), 7, 69

Internet Society (ISOC), 4–6, 90, 564

internetwork, 3

Internetwork Packet Exchange/Sequenced Packet Exchange (IPX/SPX), 17

interoperability, IPv4 and IPv6, 566–567

intra-autonomous system routing, 219

Intra-Site Automatic Tunnel Addressing Protocol (ISATAP). *See* ISATAP (Intra-Site Automatic Tunnel Addressing Protocol)

intrusion detection system (IDS), 683

intrusion prevention system (IPS), 683

inventorying, in IPv6 deployment, 632–633

inverse DNS queries, 477

inverse mapping, 303

IP address autoconfiguration, 371–439

  DHCP (Dynamic Host Configuration Protocol), 373–378

  DHCP server setup, 420–425

  in IPv4, 378–395

    address renewal process, 384–386

    APIPA (automatic private IP addressing), 378–379

    DHCP address release process, 387–393

    DHCP broadcast and unicast, 393

    DHCP Discovery, 379–384

    DHCP relay agent, 393–395

  in IPv6, 395–417

    combination of stateful and stateless, 399–400

    DHCPv6 messages, 405–412

DHCPv6 overview, 404–405

DHCPv6 relay message exchange, 414–415

DHCPv6 stateless message exchange, 413–414

functional states of, 400–401

node interface identifiers, 401–404

process of, 415–417

stateful, 396–398

stateless, 396

  in Microsoft Windows operating systems, 417–419

  Microsoft Windows Server 2008 DHCP scopes, 419–420

  overview, 372–373

  troubleshooting, 425–427

IP addressing, 57–108

  in IPv4, 60–72

    access to, 72

    classes in, 60–61

    classless inter-domain routing in, 68–70

    end of, 76–77

    network, broadcast, and multicast, 61–65

    networks and subnet masks in, 65–66

    public *versus* private addresses in, 70–72

    schemes for, 73–75

    subnets and supernets in, 66–68

  IPv4 to IPv6 transition, 89–91

  in IPv6, 77–89

    aggregatable global unicast, 85–86

    allocations, 87–88

    anycast, 84–85

    format and notation, 79

    interface identifiers, 80–81

    introduction to, 77–78

    link-local and site-local, 86–87

    muliticast, 83–84

    network and host portions, 79–80

    scope identifier, 80

    special, 82

    subnetting considerations, 88–89

    unicast, 85

    in URLs, 82

  Network layer and, 12–13

  overview, 58–60

  public, 72–73

IP address scanning, 303

Ipconfig utility, 169–170

IP datagrams, 22, 175–176, 180–181

IP gateway, 62

IP network, 254–255

IP packet structures, 109–154

  IPv4 header fields and functions, 110–121

    destination address field, 120

    flags field, 117–118

    fragment offset field, 118

header checksum field, 119

header length field, 111

identification field, 117

options field, 120–121

padding in, 121

protocol field, 118–119

source address field, 120

time to live field, 118

total length field, 117

type of serice field, 111–116

version field, 111

IPv6

    MTU and packet handling in, 135–137

    upper-layer checksums in, 137–138

IPv6 extension headers, 125–135

    authentication, 130–131

    destination options, 127–128

    encapsulating security payload, 131–132

    fragment, 129–130

    hop-by-hop, 127

    IPv4 *versus*, 139-141

    jumbograms, 132–133

    ordering of, 126

    QoS (quality of service), 133–134

    router alerts and hop-by-hop options, 134–135

    routing, 128–129

IPv6 header fields and functions, 121–125

IP renumbering, 73

IP routing, 186–193

    characteristics of, 193–197

    overview, 186–187

    routing protocols and routed protocols, 188–193

    routing table entries, 188

    troubleshooting, 231–232

IPS (intrusion prevention system), 683

IPSec (IP Security), 71, 132, 676–678

IP Security Protocol Working Group, 676

IP service attacks, 665

IP spoofing, 664

IPv4. *See also* IP address autoconfiguration; IP addressing; IP packet structures; transitioning to IPv6

    BGP (Border Gateway Protocol) for, 218–219

    EIGRP (Enhanced Interior Gateway Routing Protocol) for, 218

    IPv6 *versus*, 179–180

    name resolution in, 449–455

        delgating DNS authority, 453

        DNS database records, 452–453

        DNS database structure, 450–451

        DNS namespace, 452

        DNS servers, 453–455

        overview, 449–450

NDP (Neighbor Discovery Protocol) *versus*, 323

OSPF (Open Shortest Path First) for, 214–218

overview, 6–7

RIP (Routing Information Protocol) for, 210–214

TCP/IP transport layer protocols

    congestion control, 538–540

    connection states, 534–535

    connection termination, 533

    error-detection and error-recovery process, 536–538

    half-open connections, 531–532

    header fields and functions, 541–545

    keep-alive process, 532–533

    sequence and acknowledgement process, 535–536

    sliding window mechanism, 540–541

    startup connection process, 527–531

UDP (User Datagram Protocol), 514–519

IPv6. *See also* IP address autoconfiguration; IP addressing; IP packet structures; transitioning to IPv6

adoption rates for, 565–566

EIGRP for, 223

IPv4 *versus*, 179–180

IS-IS (Intermediate System-to-Intermediate System) for, 223–225

MP-BGP for, 225–226

name resolution in, 463–474

   address selection examples, 472–474

   DNS (Domain Name System), 464–466

   source and destination address selection, 466–472

nslookup and, 494

OSPFv3 for, 221–223

overview, 6–7

RIPng for, 219–221

routing in, 197–210

   mechanisms of, 198–204

   multicast listener discovery in, 204–210

TCP/IP transport layer protocols and, 545–547

UDP (User Datagram Protocol) and, 514–519, 525–526

IPv6 deployment, 615–657

ISATAP for tunneled environment, 643–645

migrating applications, 639

network admnistration, 645–647

overview, 616–617

planning, 617–637

   architectural decisions, 618–625

migration and transitioning techniques, 625–631

   success criteria for, 618

   tasks, 631–637

6to4 for tunneled environment, 643

test/pilot network, 637–639

upgrading hosts, 639–643

ipv6-literal.net names, 484

IPX/SPX (Internetwork Packet Exchange/Sequenced Packet Exchange), 17

IRTF (Internet Research Task Force), 6

ISAKMP (Internet Security Association and Key Management Protocol), 677

ISATAP (Intra-Site Automatic Tunnel Addressing Protocol), 90, 583–591

addressing and routing, 586–588

communications, 588–589

components, 584–585

in IPv6 deployment, 643–645

Microsfot support of, 568

overview, 583–584

router configuration, 589–591

router discovery, 585–586

6to4 technology with, 596

ISDN (Integrated Services Digital Network), 159

IS-IS (Intermediate System-to-Intermediate System) for IPv6, 193, 223–225

ISOC (Internet Society), 564

ISO HDLC (High-level Data Link Control) protocol, 158

ISO/OSI network reference model (International Organization for Standardization Open Systems Interconnection network reference model), 8

ISPs (Internet service providers), 7, 69

iterative queries, in DNS resolvers, 457

ITIL (Information Technology and Infrastructure Library), 632

J

Jumbo Frames, 159

jumbograms, 132–133, 518

K

keep-alive process, TCP/IP, 532–533

L

LAM (Local Area Mobility), 229–230

LANs (local area networks), 3, 16

Lantronix, 81

latency, 115

Layer 3 switch, 74

LCP (Link Control Protocol), 158

leases, in DHCP, 375–378

libpcap application programming interface, 26

limited traffic flow confidentiality, 677

Link Control Protocol (LCP), 158

link-local and site-local IPv6 addresses, 86–87

Link-Local Multicast Name Resolution (LLMNR). *See* LLMNR (Link-Local Multicast Name Resolution)

link MTU, 136

Link-State Advertisements (LSAs), 192, 221–223

link-state routing protocols, 191–193

Linux, 446

LLC (Logical Link Control) sublayer, 59, 156, 162

LLMNR (Link-Local Multicast Name Resolution), 447–448, 463–464, 482–483

load-balancing, 200

Local Area Mobility (LAM), 229–230

local area networks (LANs), 3, 16

Logical Link Control (LLC) sublayer, 59, 156, 162

long-haul networks, 2–3

loop-avoidance schemes, 191

loopback special IP address, 82

loops, routing, 190–191

Love Letter worm, 5

LSAs (Link-State Advertisements), 192, 221–223

M

MAC (Media Access Control), 59, 156

malware, 670

man-in-the-middle (MITM) attacks, 665

mapping addresses to names, in DNS files, 462–463

master router, 216

Matsushita, 81

maximum segment size (MSS), in TCP, 519

maximum transmission unit (MTU). *See* MTU (maximum transmission unit)

Media Access Control (MAC) layer address, 59, 156

media flow control, 12

Microsoft Corp., 5, 372, 374, 401, 568, 674. *See also* Windows operating systems

migrating applications, 639

MILNET, 4

MITM (man-in-the-middle) attacks, 665

Mobile IP, 229

mobile users, routing for, 229

Mosaic browser, 5

most significant bits (MSBs), 111

MP-BGP for IPv6, 225–226

MPLS (Multiprotocol Label Switching) backbones, 616

MSBs (most significant bits), 111

MSS (maximum segment size), in TCP, 519

MTU (maximum transmission unit)

fragmentation of, 18, 117

in IP packet structures, 135–137

as option in NDP, 341–343

overview, 13

in UDP datagrams, 515

multicast addressing

allocation for, 88

broadcast update behavior *versus*, 195

in IPv4, 61–65

in IPv6, 83–84

in protocol analysis, 26

multicast listener discovery, 204–210

multihoming networks, 621

multiplexing, 21

Multiprotocol Label Switching (MPLS) backbones, 616

Multiprotocol Reachable NLRI attribute, 226

multiprotocol routing, 228

N

Nagle, John, 541

Nagle algorithm, 541

name queries, in DNS, 477

Name resolution, 441–512

DNS caching, 457–458

DNS configuration files and resource records, 458–463

Domain Name server operations, 455–457

in IPv4 networks, 449–455

delegating DNS authority, 453

DNS database records, 452–453

DNS database structure, 450–451

DNS namespace, 452

DNS servers, 453–455

overview, 449–450

in IPv6 networks, 463–474

address selection examples, 472–474

DNS (Domain Name System), 464–466

source and destination address selection, 466–472

network protocols for, 443–448

DNS (Domain Name System), 447

LLMNR (Link-Local Multicast Name Resolution), 447–448

NetBIOS over TCP/IP, 443–444

WINS (Windows Internet Name Service), 444–446

overview, 442–443

troubleshooting, 486–494

DNS problems, 488

failure sources, 487–488

Nbtstat, 489–490

NetBIOS and WINS problems, 488

Netstat, 490

Nslookup, 491–494

in Windows operating systems, 474–486

DNS dynamic update, 479–480

DNS resolver, 476–477

DNS server service, 477–479

hosts file, 474–476

ipv6-literal.net names, 484

LLMNR support, 482–483

peer name resolution protocol, 484–486

source and destination address selection, 481–482

name resolution process, 175

name server technology, 4

NAT (network address translation)

address substitution by, 72

IPv4 address constraints and, 76

in for IPv4 to IPv6 translations, 566

to protect network, 679

in Teredo technology, 596, 599

National Center for Supercomputing Applications (NCSA), 5

National Institute of Standards and Technology, 667

National Science Foundation (NSF), 4

NAT-PT (Network Address Translation-Protocol Translation), 91

NBMA (nonbroadcast multiple-access network) Data Link layer, 90

Nbtstat, 489–490

NCPs (Network Control Protocols), 158

NCSA (National Center for Supercomputing Applications), 5

NDP (Neighbor Discovery Protocol), 321–370

characteristics of, 172–174

conceptual host model, 345–347

for hardware addresses, 164

IPv4 protocols *versus*, 323

message formats in, 324–335

Neighbor Advertisement, 286–287, 331–333

Neighbor Solicitation, 286–287, 329–331

Redirect, 333–335

Router Advertisement, 326–328

Router Solicitation, 324–325

Neighbor Discovery process, 347–358

address resolution, 348–350

conceptual sending algorithm, 348

duplicate address detection, 351–352

Neighbor Unreachability Detection (NUD), 350–351

Redirect messages, 354–358

Router Discovery, 352–354

Secure Neighbor Discovery (SEND) protocol, 404

option formats in, 335–345

Advertisement Interval, 343–344

Home Agent Information, 344

MTU, 341–343

overview, 335–336

Prefix Information, 338–340

Redirected Header, 340–341

Route Information, 344–345

Source and Target Link-Layer Address, 336–338

overview, 322–323

neighborhood, 60, 66

neighbor routers, 192

Neighbor Solicitation (NS) multicast address, 83

Neighbor Unreachability Detection (NUD), 350–351

nested hybrid network model, 571

NetBIOS, 488

NetBIOS Enhanced User Interface (NETBEUI), 17

NetBIOS over TCP/IP, 443–444

Netscape Navigator browser, 5

netsh interface ipv6 show route command, 198

Netstat, 490

Network Access layer, TCP/IP, 16–18

network addressing

description of, 58

in IPv4, 61–65

in IPv6, 79–80

subnet masks in, 65–66

Network Address Translation (NAT). *See* NAT (network address translation)

network analysis. *See* protocol analysis

Network Control Protocols (NCPs), 158

Network File System (NFS), 20

networking model, TCP/IP, 15–20

network interface controllers (NICs), 11, 159, 616

Network Interface layer, 16

Network layer. *See also* Data Link and Network layer protocols

error-detection mechanism in, 119

IP addresses at, 59

in network reference model, 12–13

Network Layer Reachability Information (NLRI), 188

network perimeter security, 678–680

network prefix, 66

Network Service Access Point (NSAP) addressing, 88

network shell, 14

network sniffing, 673–674

network space, in IP addressing, 73–74

Network Time Protocol (NTP), 85, 274

Next Generation TCP/IP stack (Microsoft Corp.), 568

next header field, in IPv6 header, 123–125

NFS (Network File System), 20

NICs (network interface controllers), 11, 159, 616

NLRI (Network Layer Reachability Information), 188

node interface identifiers, 401–404

nonbroadcast multiple-access network (NBMA) Data Link layer, 90

Non-Querier routes, 205

nonrecursive queries, in DNS resolvers, 457, 476

Nortel bankruptcy asset sale, 75

NSAP allocation, in IPv6, 88

NSF (National Science Foundation), 4

NSFNET, 4

Nslookup, 491–494

NTP (Network Time Protocol), 85, 274

NUD (Neighbor Unreachability Detection), 350–351

numeric IP addresses, 58

O

octets, in numeric addresses, 58

Offer packet, DHCP, 382–383

On-Demand Routing (ODR) protocol, 228

Open Shortest Path First (OSPF) protocol. *See* OSPF (Open Shortest Path First) protocol

Optical Carrier (OC), 157

option formats in NDP, 335–345

   Advertisement Interval, 343–344

   Home Agent Information, 344

   MTU, 341–343

   overview, 335–336

   Prefix Information, 338–340

   Redirected Header, 340–341

   Route Information, 344–345

   Source and Target Link-Layer Address, 336–338

options field, in IP packet structures, 120–121

organizationally unique identifier (OUI), 59

OSI network reference model, 8–15

   layer behavior in, 10–15

   layer organization of, 8–10

OSPF (Open Shortest Path First) protocol

   in IPv4, 214–218

   multicast, 63

   multiple services supported by, 184

   at TCP/IP Internet layer, 19

OSPFv3 for IPv6, 221–223

OUI (organizationally unique identifier), 59

oversized packets, in protocol analysis, 26

P

Packet Internetwork Groper (PING), 18, 291–293

packets, 2, 13

packet sniffing and snooping, 663

packet-switched networks, 2–3

Packet Too Big message, 136, 179, 280

padding, in IP packet structures, 121

Parameter Problem message, 262, 273

pass-through autonomous system routing, 219

passwords, 666

patches and fixes, security, 674–676

path discovery, 293–294

Path MTU (PMTU) Discovery. *See* PMTU (Path MTU) Discovery

Pathping for path discovery, 294

payload length field, in IPv6 header, 123

payloads, 24

pcap (packet capture), 26

PDBs (per-domain behaviors), 133

PDUs (protocol data units)

   at Data link layer, 12

   headers of, 23–24

   at Network layer, 13

   overview, 11

   at Transport layer, 13–14

Peer Name Resolution Protocol (PNRP), 484–486

per-domain behaviors (PDBs), 133

performance, network, 24

per-hop behavior (PHB), 114, 133

pessimistic security model, 662

phased migration, in IPv6 deployment, 631

PHB (per-hop behavior), 114, 133

Physical layer, in network reference model, 11–12

physical numeric address, 59

PING (Packet Internetwork Groper), 18, 291–293

PIR (Public Interest Registry), 5

platform-independent tunneling protocol, 596

PMTU (Path MTU) Discovery, 118, 135–136, 179, 290–291, 294–298

PNRP (Peer Name Resolution Protocol), 484–486

Point-to-Point Protocol (PPP), 16–17, 157–159

point-to-point transmission, 12

Point-to-Point Tunneling Protocol (PPTP), 17

poison reverse scheme, 191, 194

POP3 (Post Office Protocol, version 3), 21

port addresses, 20

port numbers, 23, 523–524

port redirection, in protocol analysis, 29

ports, blocking, 661, 676

PPP (Point-to-Point Protocol), 16–17, 158–159

PPPoE (Point-to-Point Protocol over Ethernet), 157

PPTP (Point-to-Point Tunneling Protocol), 17

preamble, in Ethernet frames, 160–161

precedence

in Data Link and Network layer protocols, 184

in IPv6 header, 123

in Type of Service field, 111

preferred address, IPv6, 381

Prefix Information option in NDP, 338–340

Presentation layer, in network reference model, 14–15

primary DNS server, 454

privacy, 623

privacy extensions, 80–81

private addresses, public addresses *versus*, 70–72

Process layer, 20

promiscuous mode operation, 26–27

proprietary networks, 3

protocol analysis, 24–29, 425

protocol data units (PDUs). *See* PDUs (protocol data units)

protocol field, in IP packet structures, 118–119

protocol identification field, 159

protocol numbers, 21–23

protocol stack, 11

proxy servers

address masquerading and, 70

to protect network, 679–680

reverse proxying by, 72

public addresses, 70–73

Public Interest Registry (PIR), 5

Q

QoS (quality of service)

classifying traffic for, 75

in IPv6, 623

IPv6 extension headers for, 133–134

PHB (per-hop behavior) and, 114

Querier routes, 205

R

RARP (Reverse Address Resolution Protocol), 18, 59

reachability, 67, 223, 254

Real-time applications (RTAs), 115

reassembly, fragmentation and, 181–183

reconnaissance process, 302

recursive queries, in DNS resolvers, 456, 476

Redirected Header option in NDP, 340–341

Redirect messages

ICMPv4, 262, 270–271

ICMPv6, 287–288

NDP, 333–335, 354–358

redirector driver, 14

relay agent, DHCP, 393–395, 3974

relay message exchange, DHCPv6, 414–415

remote monitoring (RMON), 29

Renumbering, Router, 288–290

replay attacks, 677

Request packet, DHCP, 383

resource records, DNS, 452, 458–463

Resource Reservation Protocol (RSVP), 133

restricted NAT (network address translation), 599

retransmission timeout (RTO), in error detection, 536

Reverse Address Resolution Protocol (RARP), 18, 59

reverse proxying, 72

RFCs (Request for Comments)

IAB (Internet Architecture Board) and, 6

on ICMP (Internet Control Message Protocol), 255–256

on IPv6, 78

standards from, 7–8

RIP (Routing Information Protocol)

as distance vector routing protocol, 189

for IPv4, 210–214

at TCP/IP Internet layer, 19

RIPng for IPv6, 219–221

Risk Management Guide for Information Technology Systems (National Institute of Standards and Technology), 667

RMON (remote monitoring), in protocol analysis, 29

"rough consensus" for Internet standards, 6

round-trip time (RTT), in error detection, 536

route aggregation, 74

Route Information option in NDP, 344–345

Router Advertisement and Router Solicitation message, 263, 271–272, 283–285

Router Advertisement NDP message, 326–328

router alerts, 134–135

router discovery

in ISATAP (Intra-Site Automatic Tunnel Addressing Protocol), 585–586

in Neighbor Discovery process, 352–354

route resolution process, 164, 176–179

router queue, 111

Router Renumbering, 288–290

Router Solicitation NDP message, 324–325

router-to-host tunneling configuration, 581–582

router-to-router tunneling configuration, 580–581

routing. *See also* Data Link and Network layer protocols

CIDR (classless inter-domain routing), 68–70

classless inter-domain, 68–70

ICMP (Internet Control Message Protocol), 298–302

Internet Protocol (IP) for, 2

IPv6 extension headers for, 128–129

in ISATAP (Intra-Site Automatic Tunnel Addressing Protocol), 586–588

at TCP/IP Internet layer, 18

updating routers, 635

Routing Information Protocol (RIP). *See* RIP (Routing Information Protocol)

routing protocols, 210–226

BGP (Border Gateway Protocol), 218–219

EIGRP (Enhanced Interior Gateway Routing Protocol), 218

EIGRP for IPv6, 223

on in-house internetwork, 227

Internet, 230

IS-IS (Intermediate System-to-Intermediate System) for IPv6, 223–225

MP-BGP for IPv6, 225–226

OSPF (Open Shortest Path First) in IPv4, 214–218

OSPFv3 for IPv6, 221–223

RIP (Routing Information Protocol) in IPv4, 210–214

RIPng for IPv6, 219–221

in WANs (wide area networks), 228–230

routing tables

entries to, 188

IP host referring to, 164

reachability information on, 67

RSVP (Resource Reservation Protocol), 133

RTAs (real-time applications), 115

RTO (retransmission timeout), in error detection, 536

RTT (round-trip time), in error detection, 536

runts (undersized packets), 26

S

Samba suite, 446

scope identifier, in IPv6 addressing, 80

screening host, to protect network, 679

screening router, to protect network, 679

SDLC (SNA Data Link Control) protocol, 17, 158

secondary DNS server, 454

secure end-to-end connection, 70–71

Secure Neighbor Discovery (SEND) protocol, 404

securing routers, 231

security

Cryptographically Generated Addresses (CGA), 404

ICMP (Internet Control Message Protocol), 302–304

IPSec (IP Security), 132
in IPv6, 77–78, 623–624
of routers, 231

security, TCP/IP, 659–696
attack details, 670–674
attack phases, 667–669
blocking ports, 676
firewalls, 680–682
honeypots and honeynets, 684
IDS (intrusion detection system) and IPS (intrusion prevention system) in, 683
IP-related attacks, 664–665
IPSec (IP Security) for, 676–678
for network perimeter, 678–680
overview, 660–661
patches and fixes for, 674–676
principles of, 661–662
typical attacks, 662–664

Security Parameters Index (SPI) field, 131

segments, as PDUs at Transport layer, 14

Seifert, Rich, 29

Semeria, Chuck, 68

sequence and acknowledgment process, TCP/IP, 535–536

service delivery options, 183–184

service level agreements (SLAs), 114

Session layer, in network reference model, 14

sessions, socket addresses for, 23

SIIT (Stateless IP/ICMP translation algorithm), 573

Silly Window Syndrome (SWS), 541

Simple Mail Transfer Protocol (SMTP), 21

Simple Network Management Protocol (SNMP), 29

Sircam virus, 5

6to4 technology
in IPv6 deployment, 643
for transitioning, 565, 591–596
for tunneling, 90–91, 141

SLAs (service level agreements), 114

slave routers, 216

sliding window mechanism, in TCP/IP transport layer protocols, 540–541

Slow Start algorithm, in congestion control, 539

small offices, wide area network for, 228

SMTP (Simple Mail Transfer Protocol), 21

SNA (Systems Network Architecture), 17, 158

SNMP (Simple Network Management Protocol), 29

SOA (start of authority) record, in DNS files, 459–460

sockets, 23

software, DHCP, 376

SolarWinds IP Subnet Calculator, 68

solicited-node address, 323

SONET (Synchronous Optical Network) links, 157, 159

Sony, 81

source address field, 120, 125

Source and Target Link-Layer Address option in NDP, 336–338

source port number, 23

Source Quench, 261, 270

Source-Specific Multicast, 204

special IPv6 addresses, 82

SPI (Security Parameters Index) field, 131

split horizon scheme, 191, 194–195

spoofing, address, 132, 661, 664, 672

Spurgeon, Charles, 160

spyware, 670

Standard Address Discovery, 380

standards, 6, 7–8, 16–17

Stanford Research Institute (SRI), 3

start of authority (SOA) record, in DNS files, 459–460

startup connection process, TCP/IP, 527–531

stateful IP address autoconfiguration, 396–400, 622

Stateless Address Autoconfiguration (SLAAC), 396, 399–400, 466, 622

Stateless IP/ICMP translation algorithm (SIIT), 573

stateless message exchange, 413–414

statistics, in protocol analysis, 27

"stealing bits," in subnetting, 66

streaming media, 115

strong hosts, weak hosts *versus*, 199–201

subnetting

in IPv4 addressing, 65–68

in IPv6 addressing, 88–89

proxy ARP for, 171

subscription-based multicast addresses, 83

summary addresses, 74

supernetting, 66–68

switching technology, 29

SWS (Silly Window Syndrome), 541

symbolic names, 58

symmetric NAT (network address translation), 599

SYN DoS (denial of service) attack, 532

Systems Network Architecture (SNA), 17, 158

T

taps, in protocol analysis, 29

Target Link-Layer Address option in NDP, 336–338

T-carriers, 157, 159

TCP (Transmission Control Protocol), 19, 126

TCP/IP (Transmission Control Protocol/Internet Protocol), 1–55. *See also* security, TCP/IP

data encapsulation in, 23–24

history of, 2–7

networking model of, 15–20

OSI network reference model of, 8–15

layer behavior in, 10–15

layer organization of, 8–10

port numbers of, 23

protocol analysis of, 24–29

protocol numbers of, 21–23

RFCs (Request of Comments) and standards of, 7–8

sockets of, 23

TCP/IP transport layer protocols

IPv4 and, 527–545

congestion control, 538–540

connection states, 534–535

connection termination, 533

error-detection and error-recovery process, 536–538

half-open connections, 531–532

header fields and functions, 541–545

keep-alive process, 532–533

sequence and acknowledgment process, 535–536

sliding window mechanism, 540–541

startup connection process, 527–531

IPv6 and, 545–546, 545–547

UDP (User Datagram Protocol) and, 514–526, 547–549

description, 519–520

header fields and functions, 520–523

IPv4 and, 514–519

IPv6 and, 514–519, 525–526

port numbers and processes, 523–524

TCP session hijacking, 672

telephone systems, 12

Telnet, 20–21

tentative addresses, 400

Teredo technology

client, 597

host-specific relay, 597

for IPv6 transition, 596–601

relay, 597

server, 597

tunneling, 90

terminal emulation (Telnet), 20–21

test/pilot network, for IPv6 deployment, 637–639

throughput difference, between networks, 297

Time Exceeded packets, 261, 272–273

Timestamp and Timestamp Reply message, 273–274

time synchronization, 274

Time to Live (TTL)

ICMPv4, 261

IP packet lifetime and, 180

in IP packet structures, 118

in IPv4 routing, 194–195

TLVs (type-length values), 223

token ring, 16

tools, in IPv6, 624

TOS (type of service), 184–186

total length field, in IP packet structures, 117

trace buffer, in protocol analysis, 27

Traceroute for path discovery, 264, 275–276, 293–294

Tracert, 294

traffic class, in IPv6 header, 122–123

trailers, 11, 24

transitioning to IPv6

hybrid IPv4/IPv6 networks, 569–573

IPv4 and IPv6 interaction, 564–569

IPv6 transition addresses, 573–574

ISATAP (Intra-Site Automatic Tunnel Addressing Protocol), 583–591

addressing and routing, 586–588

communications, 588–589

components, 584–585

overview, 583–584

router configuration, 589–591

router discovery, 585–586

6to4 transition technology, 591–596

Teredo transition technology, 596–601

transition mechanisms, 574–579

DNS infrastructure, 579

dual architecture and tunneling, 577–578

dual-IP-layer architecture, 575–576

dual protocol stacks, 574–575

dual-stack architecture, 576–577

IPv6-over-IPv4 tunneling, 578–579

tunneling configurations, 580–583

translation, in IPv6 deployment, 627–628

Transmission Control Protocol (TCP). *See* TCP (Transmission Control Protocol)

Transmission Control Protocol/Internet Protocol (TCP/IP). *See* TCP/IP (Transmission Control Protocol/Internet Protocol)

Transport layer, 13–14, 19

Transport Relay Translator (TRT), 141

Triple-DES (3-DES) encryption, 677

Trojan horse programs, 670

troubleshooting

ICMP (Internet Control Message Protocol)

Pathping for path discovery, 294

Ping for connectivity testing, 291–293

PMTU Discovery with ICMP, 294–298

routing sequences, 298–302

security issues, 302–304

Traceroute for path discovery, 293–294

IP address autoconfiguration, 425–427

IP routing, 231–232

name resolution

DNS problems, 488

failure sources, 487–488

Nbtstat, 489–490

NetBIOS and WINS problems, 488

Netstat, 490

Nslookup, 491–494

TRT (Transport Relay Translator), 141

true hybrid network model, 572–573

TTL (time to live). *See* time to live (TTL)

tunneling

configurations for, 580–583

for IPv6 devices, 90–91

IPv6-over-IPv4, 578–579

6to4, 141

through IPv cloud, 565

as transition technique, 625–627

Windows PPP implementation and, 17

Type field, 257–258

type-length values (TLVs), 223

type of service field, in IP packet structures, 111–116

U

UDP (User Datagram Protocol)

extension headers of, 547–548

at TCP/IP Transport layer, 19

TCP/IP transport layer protocols, 514–526

description, 519–520

header fields and functions, 520–523

IPv4 and, 514–519

IPv6 and, 514–519, 525–526

port numbers and processes, 523–524

TCP *versus*, 548–549

as upper-layer header, 126

undersized packets, 26

Understanding IP Addressing: Everything You Ever Wanted to Know (Semeria), 68

unicast addressing, 85, 88, 393

unicast packets, 26

unicast point-to-point links, 141

Uniform Resource Identifiers (URIs), 484

Uniform Resource Locators (URLs), 20, 82

Universal Time (UT), 273

University of California at Los Angeles, 3

University of California at Santa Barbara, 3

University of Utah, 3

University of Wisconsin, 4

UNIX

daemons in, 20

holes, as security threats, 667

libpcap application programming interface (API) of, 26

Samba suite for, 446

TCP/IP support in, 4, 21

unsolicited ICMP Router Advertisements, 301

unspecified address, 82

upper-layer checksums, 137–138

URIs (Uniform Resource Identifiers), 484

URLs (Uniform Resource Locators), 20, 82

U.S. Air Force, 453

U.S. Department of Defense (DoD), 2, 569

User Datagram Protocol (UDP). *See* UDP (User Datagram Protocol)

user impersonation, 663

V

Van Jacobsen TCP compression protocol, 158

variable-length subnet masking (VLSM), 67–68

version field, 111, 122

videoconferencing, 115

virtual connections, 517

virtual network devices, 635

Virtual Private Networks (VPNs), 17, 231

viruses, 670

VLANs, 89

VLSM (variable-length subnet masking), 67–68

VoIP (Voice over IP), 20, 115, 566

VPNs (Virtual Private Networks), 17, 231

W

WANs (wide area networks)

point-to-point technique for, 157–158

routing protocols in, 228–230

in TCP/IP Network Access layer, 16

as unicast point-to-point links, 141

WCET (worst-case execution time), 115

weak hosts, strong hosts *versus*, 199–201

well-known port numbers, 20, 520

well-known protocols, 21

Wi-Fi, standards for, 17

Windows operating systems

IP address autoconfiguration in, 417–419

IPv6 transition in, 568

name resolution in

DNS dynamic update, 479–480

DNS resolver, 476–477

DNS server service, 477–479

hosts file, 474–476

ipv6-literal.net names, 484

LLMNR support, 482–483

peer name resolution protocol, 484–486

source and destination address selection, 481–482

NetBIOS for, 443

network interface controller in, 11

PPP implementation by, 17

routing table on, 199

Tracert in, 294

Windows Server

DHCP scopes, 419–420

domain controllers, 455

INETINFO.EXE process, 20

Ipconfig utility on, 169–170

WinPcap packet capture driver (pcap), 26

WINS (Windows Internet Name Service), 444–446, 488

wireless media, 16

Wireshark protocol analyzer, 25–28

"words," in numeric addresses, 58

World IPv6 Day (June 8, 2011), 90, 175, 564

World Wide Web, 4

worms, 670

worst-case execution time (WCET), 115

X

X.25 protocol, 16

Y

Yahoo!, 90, 564

Z

zero-window state, 541

zone data file, in primary DNS server, 454